# *Rick Steves'*

# FRANCE

Rick Steves & Steve Smith

## 2009

## KEY

- ▬▬▬■ Pedestrian-Friendly Area
- ▬▬▬■ Popular Shopping Area
- ═ ═ ═ ═ Tunnel
- Ⓜ Ⓡ Metro Station, RER Station
- ❶ Taxi Stand
- Ⓑ Batobus Boat Stops
- ▪ ▪ ▪ ▪ Paris Plage (mid-July–mid-Aug)
- 2ᴱ Arrondissement
- ■ Landmark or Point of Interest
- 𝒊 Tourist Information

| 0 km | 0.5 km |
| 0 mi | 0.25 mi |

## CENTRAL PARIS

- ❶ Carnavalet Museum
- ❷ To Champs-Elysées & Arc de Triomphe
- ❸ Cluny Museum
- ❹ Conciergerie
- ❺ Deportation Memorial
- ❻ Flower Market
- ❼ Ile St. Louis
- ❽ Jardin des Plantes
- ❾ Louvre Museum
- ❿ Luxembourg Garden
- ⓫ Museum of Jewish Art & History
- ⓬ Notre-Dame Cathedral
- ⓭ Obelisk, Place de la Concorde
- ⓮ Opéra Bastille
- ⓯ Opéra Garnier (Old Opera)
- ⓰ Orangerie Museum
- ⓱ Orsay Museum
- ⓲ Paris Story Film
- ⓳ Picasso Museum
- ⓴ Pompidou Center
- ㉑ Promenade Plantée Park Entry
- ㉒ Sainte-Chapelle
- ㉓ Seine River Boat Rides
- ㉔ St. Severin Church
- ㉕ St. Sulpice Church
- ㉖ Tuileries Garden

D Orry-la-Ville–Coye

13 Saint-Denis–Université

1 Gare de Saint-Denis

Théâtre Gérard Philipe
Marché de St-Denis
Basilique de St-Denis

Saint-Denis Porte de Paris

Cimetière de St-Denis
Hôpital Delafontaine
Cosmonautes
La Courneuve 6 Routes

Hôtel de Ville de La Courneuve

A B C D Aéroport Charles de Gaulle B

La Courneuve Aubervilliers

Stade Géo André
Danton
Le Bourget

Mitry-Claye B

Stade de France Saint-Denis

La Plaine Stade de France

La Courneuve 8 Mai 1945  7

La Courneuve–8 Mai 1945
Maurice Lachâtre
Drancy-Avenir
Hôpital Avicenne
Gaston Roulaud
Escadrille Normandie–Niémen
La Ferme
Libération

5 Bobigny Pablo Picasso

Jean Rostand
Auguste Delaune

Porte de Clignancourt

4

Simplon

Jules Joffrin

Marcadet Poissonniers

Château Rouge

Barbès Rochechouart

Funiculaire de Montmartre

Anvers

Fort d'Aubervilliers

12 Porte de la Chapelle

Marx Dormoy

La Chapelle

Gare du Nord

Aubervilliers–Pantin Quatre Chemins

Porte de la Villette

Corentin Cariou

Crimée

Riquet

Pantin

Hôtel de Ville de Bobigny

Pont de Bondy
Petit Noisy

Chelles Gournay E

Bobigny–Pantin Raymond Queneau

Église de Pantin

Noisy-le-Sec T 1

Tournan E

7bis

Stalingrad

Magenta

Louis Blanc

Château Landon

Gare de l'Est

Ourcq

Laumière

Jaurès

Bolivar

Porte de Pantin

Hoche

Danube

Botzaris

Pré St-Gervais

7bis

11 Mairie des Lilas

Cadet

Poissonnière

Château d'Eau

Strasbourg Saint-Denis

Colonel Fabien

Buttes Chaumont

Belleville

Pyrénées

Jourdain

Place des Fêtes

Télégraphe

3bis Porte des Lilas

Saint-Fargeau

Jacques Bonsergent

Goncourt

Couronnes

Ménilmontant

Pelleport

Grands Boulevards

Bonne Nouvelle

Réaumur Sébastopol

Sentier

Temple

Arts et Métiers

République

Oberkampf

Parmentier

Filles du Calvaire

Père Lachaise

Porte de Bagnolet

3 Gallieni

Étienne Marcel

Les Halles

Châtelet

Cité

Château Les Halles

11

Rambuteau

Hôtel de Ville

St-Sébastien Froissart

Chemin Vert

St-Paul

Richard Lenoir

Bréguet Sabin

Bastille

Rue Saint-Maur

Saint-Ambroise

Voltaire

Charonne

3bis Gambetta

Philippe Auguste

Alexandre Dumas

Avron

9 Mairie de Montreuil

Croix de Chavaux

Robespierre

Porte de Montreuil

Maraîchers

Pont Marie

St-Michel Notre-Dame

Cluny La Sorbonne

Maubert Mutualité

Cardinal Lemoine

Sully Morland

Ledru-Rollin

Faidherbe Chaligny

Rue des Boulets

2

6 Nation

Buzenval

Marne-la-Vallée Parcs Disneyland A

Vincennes

Saint-Mandé

Bérault

Boissy-Saint-Léger A

1 Château de Vincennes

Luxembourg

Jussieu

Gare de Lyon

Reuilly–Diderot

Montgallet

Porte de Vincennes

Picpus

Port-Royal

Place Monge

Quai de la Rapée

Bel-Air

Daumesnil

Michel Bizot

Denfert Rochereau

Censier Daubenton

Les Gobelins

Gare d'Austerlitz

10

Gare d'Austerlitz

Saint Marcel

Bercy

Dugommier

Porte Dorée

Porte de Charenton

Saint-Jacques

Campo Formio

Corvisart

Glacière

Place d'Italie

Chevaleret

Quai de la Gare

Parc de Bercy

Bibliothèque Fr. Mitterrand

Cour St-Émilion

Liberté

Charenton–Écoles

Cité Universitaire

5 Nationale

Olympiades 14

Bibliothèque Fr. Mitterrand

Ivry Pont Mandela

École Vétérinaire de Maisons-Alfort

Tolbiac

Maison Blanche

Porte d'Italie

Porte de Choisy

T 3 Porte d'Ivry

Ivry sur-Seine

École Vétérinaire de Maisons-Alfort

Maisons-Alfort–Stade

Stade Charléty
Poterne des Peupliers

Le Kremlin Bicêtre

Pierre et Marie Curie

Maisons-Alfort Alfortville

Maisons-Alfort Les Juilliottes

Gentilly

Villejuif Léo Lagrange

Mairie d'Ivry 7

Vitry sur-Seine

Créteil–L'Échat

Laplace

Villejuif Paul Vaillant-Couturier

Créteil–Université

Arcueil–Cachan

7 Villejuif–Louis Aragon

Le Vert de Maisons

8 Créteil–Préfecture

Les Ardoines

Orly Ouest
Orly Sud

Massy–Palaiseau
Versailles-Chantiers C

Dourdan
Saint-Martin-d'Étampes C

Malesherbes D

D Melun

# CONTENTS

**Introduction** . . . . . . . . . . . 1
  Planning . . . . . . . . . . . . . 3
  Practicalities. . . . . . . . . . . 7
  Money . . . . . . . . . . . . . . 10
  Sightseeing. . . . . . . . . . . . 14
  Sleeping . . . . . . . . . . . . . 15
  Eating. . . . . . . . . . . . . . 25
  Traveling as a
    Temporary Local . . . . . . . . 36
  Back Door Travel
    Philosophy. . . . . . . . . . . 37
▸ **Paris** . . . . . . . . . . . . . . 38
  Orientation . . . . . . . . . . . 39
  Tours . . . . . . . . . . . . . . 52
  Self-Guided Walk . . . . . . . . 56
  Sights . . . . . . . . . . . . . . 68
  Shopping. . . . . . . . . . . . . 103
  Nightlife . . . . . . . . . . . . . 105
  Sleeping. . . . . . . . . . . . . . 109
  Eating . . . . . . . . . . . . . . 134
  Transportation
    Connections . . . . . . . . . . 152
▸ **Near Paris** . . . . . . . . . . 166
  Versailles. . . . . . . . . . . . . 166
  Chartres Cathedral . . . . . . . . 180
  Giverny . . . . . . . . . . . . . 184
  Disneyland Paris . . . . . . . . . 186
▸ **Normandy** . . . . . . . . . . 189
  Rouen. . . . . . . . . . . . . . . 192
  Honfleur . . . . . . . . . . . . . 207
  Bayeux. . . . . . . . . . . . . . 220
  D-Day Beaches . . . . . . . . . . 229
  Mont St. Michel . . . . . . . . . 247

▸ **Brittany** . . . . . . . . . . . . 261
  Dinan . . . . . . . . . . . . . . 262
▸ **The Loire** . . . . . . . . . . . 278
  East of Tours: Amboise
    and Nearby . . . . . . . . . . 286
  West of Tours: Chinon
    and Nearby . . . . . . . . . . 315
▸ **Dordogne and Nearby** . . . 329
  Sarlat . . . . . . . . . . . . . . 335
  The Best of the
    Dordogne River Valley . . . . 348
  Cro-Magnon Caves. . . . . . . . 362
  Oradour-sur-Glane
    and Nearby . . . . . . . . . . 374
  St. Emilion and
    Bordeaux Wine Country . . 376
  Rocamadour. . . . . . . . . . . 380
  Lot River Valley . . . . . . . . . 389
▸ **Basque Country**. . . . . . . . 393
  French Basque Country. . . 398
  St. Jean-de-Luz. . . . . . . . . . 399
  Bayonne . . . . . . . . . . . . . 408
  Biarritz. . . . . . . . . . . . . . 412
  Villages in the French Basque
    Country . . . . . . . . . . . . 414
  Spanish Basque Country. . 419
  San Sebastián . . . . . . . . . . 420
  Hondarribia. . . . . . . . . . . 439
  The Bay of Biscay . . . . . . . . 440
  Guernica . . . . . . . . . . . . . 442
  Bilbao. . . . . . . . . . . . . . . 446

▶ **Languedoc** . . . . . . . . . . . . . . . 456
 Albi . . . . . . . . . . . . . . . . . . . . 458
 Carcassonne . . . . . . . . . . . . . . 472
 Collioure . . . . . . . . . . . . . . . . 489
▶ **Provence** . . . . . . . . . . . . . . . . 499
 Arles . . . . . . . . . . . . . . . . . . . 504
 Avignon . . . . . . . . . . . . . . . . . 524
 Pont du Gard, Les Baux,
  and Orange . . . . . . . . . . . . . 544
 Villages of the
  Côtes du Rhône . . . . . . . . . . 558
 Hill Towns of the Luberon . . . 571
 Isle-sur-la-Sorgue . . . . . . . . . 572
▶ **The French Riviera** . . . . . . . 585
 Nice . . . . . . . . . . . . . . . . . . . . 589
 Villefranche-sur-Mer . . . . . . . . 620
 The Three Corniches:
  Villefranche to Monaco . . . . 628
 Monaco . . . . . . . . . . . . . . . . . 632
 Antibes . . . . . . . . . . . . . . . . . 642
 Inland Riviera . . . . . . . . . . . . . 652
▶ **The French Alps** . . . . . . . . . 658
 Annecy . . . . . . . . . . . . . . . . . 660
 Chamonix . . . . . . . . . . . . . . . 668
▶ **Burgundy** . . . . . . . . . . . . . . . 691
 Beaune . . . . . . . . . . . . . . . . . 694
 Between Beaune and Paris . . 718
 Between Burgundy
  and the Loire . . . . . . . . . . . . 726
 Between Burgundy
  and Lyon . . . . . . . . . . . . . . . 732

▶ **Lyon and the
 Rhône Valley** . . . . . . . . . . . . 739
 Lyon . . . . . . . . . . . . . . . . . . . 740
▶ **Alsace** . . . . . . . . . . . . . . . . . 763
 Colmar . . . . . . . . . . . . . . . . . 766
 Route du Vin . . . . . . . . . . . . . 782
 Strasbourg . . . . . . . . . . . . . . . 793
▶ **Reims and Verdun** . . . . . . . 802
 Reims . . . . . . . . . . . . . . . . . . 803
 Verdun . . . . . . . . . . . . . . . . . 814

**France:
Past and Present** . . . . . . . **822**

**Appendix** . . . . . . . . . . . . . . . **831**
 Resources . . . . . . . . . . . . . . . 831
 Telephones, Email,
  and Mail . . . . . . . . . . . . . . . 838
 Transportation . . . . . . . . . . . . 848
 Recommended Itinerary
  by Train/Bus . . . . . . . . . . . . 850
 Recommended Itinerary
  by Car . . . . . . . . . . . . . . . . . 858
 Holidays and Festivals . . . . . . 867
 Conversions and Climate . . 869
 Essential Packing Checklist . 872
 Hotel Reservation Form . . . . 873
 Pronunciation Guide
  for Place Names . . . . . . . . . 874
 French Survival Phrases . . . . 879

**Index** . . . . . . . . . . . . . . . . . **881**

# France

*Bienvenue!* You've chosen well. France is Europe's most diverse, tasty, and, in many ways, most exciting country to explore. It's a multifaceted cultural bouillabaisse.

France is a place of gentle beauty, where the play of light transforms the routine into the exceptional. Here, travelers are treated to a blend of man-made and natural beauty like nowhere else in Europe. With luxuriant forests, forever coastlines, truly grand canyons, and Europe's highest mountain ranges, France has a cover-girl beauty from top to bottom. You'll also discover a dizzying array of artistic and architectural wonders—soaring cathedrals, chandeliered châteaux, and museums filled with the cultural icons of the Western world.

In many ways, France is a yardstick of human achievement. Here travelers can easily trace the whole of European history, from the earliest prehistoric cave paintings to Roman ruins that rival Italy's. In medieval times, France cultivated Romanesque and Gothic architecture, erecting the great cathedrals and basilicas of Notre-Dame, Chartres, Vézelay, and a dozen others. With their innovations, French architects set the trends for cities throughout Europe. French philosophers refined modern thought and politics. The châteaux of the Loire Valley and the grand palace of Versailles announced France's emergence as the first European superpower and first modern government. It was France that gave birth to

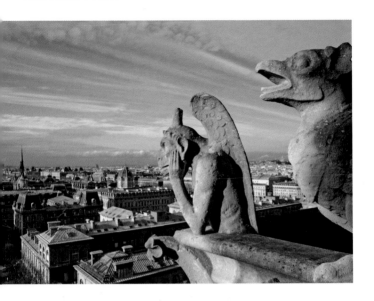

Impressionism and the foundations of modern art. Today's travelers can gaze dreamy-eyed at water lilies in Claude Monet's Giverny, rejoice amid the sunflowers of Provence that so moved a troubled Vincent van Gogh, and roam the sunny beaches that inspired Picasso and Matisse. And after all these centuries, France still remains at the forefront of technology, fashion, and—of course—cuisine.

There are two Frances: Paris…and the rest of the country. No other country in Europe is so dominated by its capital city. France's top-down government and cultural energy have always been centered in Paris, resulting in an overwhelming concentration of world-class museums, cutting-edge architecture, and historic monuments. Travelers can spend weeks in France and never leave Paris. Many do.

The other France venerates land, tradition, and a slower pace of life. After Paris, most travelers will be drawn to romantic hill towns and castles, meandering rivers and canals, and seas of vineyards that carpet this country's landscape. Village life has survived in France better than in most other European countries because France was slow to urbanize.

It was an agricultural country right up until World War II (when a smaller proportion of French citizens lived in cities than Italians did 500 years earlier). And today, even as young people are chasing jobs in the cities, France remains farm country. Everyone values the soil *(le terroir)* that brings the flavor to their foods and wines and nourishes a rural life that French people dream about. So while the country's brain resides in Paris, its soul lives in its villages—and that's where you'll feel the real pulse of France.

France offers arguably more regional diversity than any other country in Europe. Paris and the region around it (called Ile de France) is the "island" in the middle of it all. To the north are the dramatic D-Day beaches and English-style, thatched-roofed homes of Normandy. To the south, the river valleys of Loire and Dordogne regions feature luxurious châteaux, medieval castles, and hillside villages. Explore under-the-radar France to the far south and west, in the Spanish-tinged Languedoc and Basque regions. Closer to

Italy, sun-baked and windswept Provence offers Roman ruins and rustic charm, while the Riviera has sunny beaches and yacht-filled harbors. And in the north and east, travelers encounter snow-capped Alps, the venerable vineyards of Burgundy, and Germanic villages and cities in Alsace. Going between these regions feels like traveling in different countries. You can stay in France and feel like you've sampled much of Europe.

The forte of French cuisine is the astonishing variety of regional dishes. You'll enjoy Swiss-like fondue in the Alps, Italian-style pasta and pesto on the Riviera, Spanish paella in Languedoc, and German sauerkraut mixed with fine wine sauces in the Alsace. Each region also produces a wine that complements its cuisine—such as rich Burgundy wines that go perfectly with *coq au vin,* meaty wines from Languedoc to counter heavy cuisine (such as cassoulet), fruity Côtes du Rhône wines that work well with herb-infused Provençal dishes, and dry whites in Alsace that meld perfectly with the Germanic cuisine. And in Normandy and Brittany, you'll enjoy apple ciders with crêpes.

As if that weren't enough, France is also famous for its many pâtés, foie gras, hundreds of different cheeses, sizzling escargots, fresh oysters, crêpes, *herbes de Provence,* raw meats, fine wine sauces, French fries, duck and lamb dishes, pastries, bonbons, crème brûlée, and sorbets.

*L'art de vivre*—the art of living—is not just a pleasing French expression, it's a building block for a sound life. With five weeks of paid vacation, plus every Catholic holiday ever invented, the French have learned to enjoy life. It's no accident that France is home to café lounging, fine cuisine, Club Med vacations, barge cruising, and ballooning. You'll run headlong into that mindful approach to life at mealtime. The French insist on the best-quality croissants, mustard, and sparkling water; they linger over lunches; and an evening's entertainment can be nothing more than a multi-course meal with interesting friends. France demands that the traveler slow down and savor the finer things, or they'll miss the *what-matters-in-life* barge and blame the French for being lazy. One of your co-authors learned this lesson the hard way while restoring a farm house in Burgundy—and found that it's counterproductive to hurry a project past its "normal pace."

In spite of lavish attention to relaxation, the French are a productive people. French inventors gave us the metric system, pasteurization, high-speed trains, and Concorde airplanes. More importantly, this country recovered from the ashes of two debilitating world wars to generate the world's seventh-largest economy (larger than California's). This is thanks in part to determined government intervention that continues today (government spending is 53 percent of GDP). Wine, tourism, telecommunications, pharmaceuticals, cars, and Airbus planes are big moneymakers. France is also the European Union's leading agricultural producer and a chief competitor of the US. You'll pass endless wheat farms in the north, dairy farms in the west, vegetable farms and fruit orchards in the south...and vineyards everywhere.

With no domestic oil production, France has focused on nuclear power generation, which now accounts for more than 75 percent of the country's electricity production. Electricity is expensive, so the French are careful to turn out lights and conserve—something to remember when you leave your hotel room for the day or evening.

While France's economy may be one of the world's largest, the French remain skeptical about the virtues of capitalism and the work ethic. Business conversation is generally avoided, as it implies a fascination with money that the French find vulgar (it's considered gauche even to ask what someone does for a living). In France, CEOs are not glorified as celebrities—chefs are.

The French believe that the economy should support social good, not vice versa. This has produced a cradle-to-grave social security system of which the French are proud. France's poverty rate is half of that in the US, proof to the French that they are on the right track. On the other hand, if you're considering starting a business in France, think again—taxes are brutal (figure a total small-business tax rate of around 66 percent). France is routinely plagued with strikes, demonstrations, and slow-downs as workers try to preserve their hard-earned rights in the face of a competitive global economy.

As you travel, you'll find that the most "French" thing

# France Almanac

**Official Name:** It's officially the *République Française,* but locals just call it France.

**Population:** France has 61 million people (nearly twice the population of California). They're a mix of Celtic, Latin, and Teutonic DNA, plus many recent immigrants from around the globe—especially North Africa. Four of five French are (at least nominally) Roman Catholic. Every French citizen is expected to speak French.

**Area:** At 215,000 square miles, it's Western Europe's largest nation. (But Texas is still 20 percent bigger.)

**Latitude and Longitude:** 46°N and 2°E (similar latitude to the states of Washington, North Dakota, and Maine).

**Geography:** The terrain consists of rolling plains in the north and mountains in the southwest (Pyrénées), southeast (Alps), and south-central (Massif Central). Capping the country on both ends are 1,400 miles of coastline (Mediterranean and Atlantic). The Seine River flows east–west through Paris, the Rhône rumbles north–south 500 miles from the Alps to the Mediterranean, and the Loire travels east–west, roughly dividing the country into north and south. Mont Blanc (15,771 feet) is Western Europe's highest point.

**Major Cities:** Nearly one in five lives in greater Paris (12 million in the metropolitan area, 2.2 million in the city). Marseille on the Mediterranean coast has 820,000, and Lyon has 470,000.

**Economy:** France's gross domestic product is $2.56 trillion (bigger than California's $1.7 trillion); the GDP per capita is $33,200 (America's is $45,800). Though the French produce nearly a quarter of the world's wine, they drink much of it themselves. France's free-market economy is tempered by the government: high taxes (one of Europe's highest rates at 44 percent of GDP—compared to 33 percent in the US), government investment in industry, and social spending (to narrow the income gap between rich and poor). Hoping to jumpstart its economy, which is suffering from slow growth and 7 percent unemployment, France has recently upped its trademark 35-hour work week to 39 hours for many workers. Despite the three-hour lunch stereotypes, the French work as much as their EU neighbors—that is, 20 percent less than Americans (but with greater per-hour productivity).

**Government:** President Nicolas Sarkozy, elected by popular vote in 2007, heads a conservative government (but by conservative Americans' standards, it's leftist) along with the president-appointed Prime Minister, François Fillon. The upper-house Senate (331 seats) is elected by an electoral college; the National Assembly (577 seats) is chosen by popular vote. While France is a cornerstone of the European Union, many French are Euro-skeptics.

**Flag:** The Revolution produced the well-known *tricolore,* whose three colors are vertical bands of blue, white, and red.

**The Average Jean:** The average French person is 39 years old and will live a little longer than 80 years. This person eats lunch in 38 minutes (twice as fast as 25 years ago), and consumes a glass and a half of wine and a pound of fat a day. The average French citizen pops a bottle of champagne about every four months. The typical French woman is 5' 4", weighs 140 pounds, and wears a size 8–10 dress. The average worker enjoys five weeks of holiday and vacation a year. A dog is a part of one in three French households; cats are animals *non grata.*

about France is the French themselves. Be prepared to embrace (or at least understand) the cultural differences between yourself and your French hosts. You'll find the French to be reserved in the north and comparatively carefree in the sunny south. Throughout the country, they're more formal than we North Americans. When you enter a store, you'll be greeted not simply with a *"Bonjour,"* but with *"Bonjour, Monsieur/ Madame."* The proper response to the shopkeeper is *"Bonjour, Monsieur/Madame."* If there are others present, you'd say, *"Bonjour, Messieurs/Dames"*—just to make sure you don't leave anyone out. (For more on the French attitude toward language, see page 846.)

The French are overwhelmingly Catholic but not very devout, and are quick to separate church from state. They are less active churchgoers than Americans, whom they find *très* evangelical. And in France, you don't go to church to socialize or to help in charitable deeds (that's what taxes are for). France is also Europe's largest Muslim nation, with well over five million followers (there are twice as many Muslims in France as Protestants). The rapid influx of Muslim immigrants has led to considerable problems of assimilation and remains one of France's thorniest issues to resolve.

The French don't seem particularly athletic—unless you consider tossing little silver balls in the dirt *(pétanque,* a.k.a. *boules)* a sport. A few jog and exercise regularly, and fewer play on recreational teams—though you will find country lanes busy with bike riders hunched over handlebars on weekends. The French are avid sports-watchers. Soccer is king (even if legend Zinédine Zidane no longer plays), bike racing is big (they still think Lance used performance-enhancing drugs), and rugby is surprisingly popular for such a refined place. *Le basket* (basketball) is making a move, with a French league and several French NBA stars, including Tony ("Mr. Eva Longoria") Parker.

Another passion the French share with Americans is their love of movies. They admire Hollywood blockbusters, but they've also carved out their own niche of small-budget romantic comedies and thought-provoking thrillers.

Today's France will challenge many of your preconceptions. The French have a Michelin Guide certainty in their judgments and are often frank in how they convey their opinions. (Just ask about the best wine to serve with any given course.)

The French simply see the world differently than we do. The right to bear arms, the death penalty, miniscule paid vacations, and health care as a privilege rather than a basic

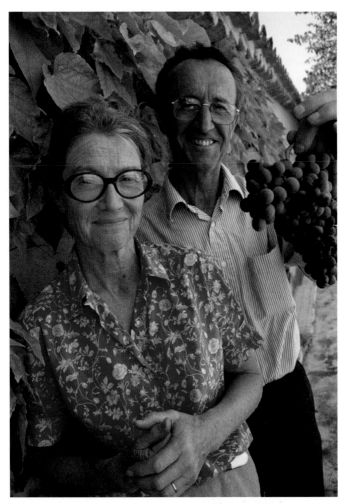

human right—these common American concepts confound the average Jean. Most of all, they don't understand the American need for everyone to be agreeable all of the time. Whether it's Iraq, Vietnam, or globalization, the French think it's important to question authority and not blindly submit to it. Blame this aversion to authority on their Revolution hangover.

The French can be a complicated people to understand for hurried travelers. (After all, these are the same people who invented existential malaise.) But remember where they've come from: In just a few generations, they've seen two world wars destroy villages, landscapes, and their self-respect. They've watched as America replaced them as the world's political and cultural superpower. In recent years, they've seen their country once again become a global force, with nuclear weapons (and nuclear energy), a space program, an international spy network, a strong currency, and their own ideas about geopolitics. Like Americans, they're trying to find their place in an increasingly global, multicultural world. Today, they just don't want to be taken for granted. And while the French may not love your country's politics, that has no bearing on how they will treat you as an individual—besides, they probably dislike their own politicians even more.

As you travel through this splendid country, come with an appetite to understand and a willingness to experience. Welcome new ideas and give the locals the benefit of your doubt. Accept France on its own terms and don't judge. Above all, slo-o-o-ow down. Spend hours in cafés lingering over *un bon café,* make a habit of making unplanned stops, hop on the *l'art de vivre* barge, and surrender to the play of light as the Impressionists did.

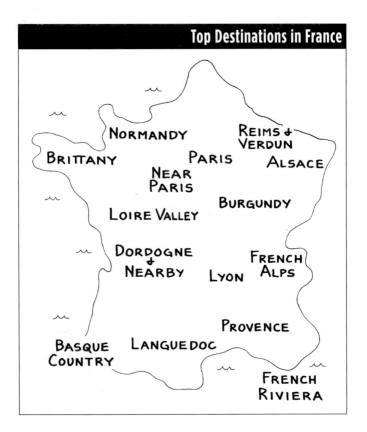

**Top Destinations in France**

NORMANDY
REIMS & VERDUN
BRITTANY
PARIS
ALSACE
NEAR PARIS
BURGUNDY
LOIRE VALLEY
DORDOGNE & NEARBY
FRENCH ALPS
LYON
PROVENCE
BASQUE COUNTRY
LANGUEDOC
FRENCH RIVIERA

# INTRODUCTION

France is nearly as big as Texas, with 61 million people and more than 400 different cheeses. *Diversité* is a French forte. This country features three impressive mountain ranges (the Alps, the Pyrénées, and the Massif Central), two coastlines that are as different as night and day (Atlantic and Mediterranean), cosmopolitan cities (such as Paris, Lyon, Strasbourg, and Nice—all featured in this book), and countless sleepy villages. From the Swiss-like Alps to the *molto* Italian Riviera, and from the Spanish Pyrénées to *das* German Alsace, you can stay in France and feel like you've sampled much of Europe—and never be more than a short stroll from a *bon vin rouge*.

We've covered the predictable must-sees while mixing in a healthy dose of Back Door intimacy. Along with seeing the Eiffel Tower, Mont St. Michel, and the French Riviera, you'll take a minivan tour of the D-Day beaches with our favorite guides, pedal your way from village to vineyard in the Alsace, marvel at 15,000-year-old cave paintings, and paddle a canoe down the lazy Dordogne River. You'll find a *magnifique* hill-town perch to catch a Provençal sunset, ride Europe's highest mountain lift over the Alps, and touch the quiet Romanesque soul of Burgundian abbeys and villages. You'll learn about each region's key monuments and cities with our walking tours and thoughtfully presented background information. Just as important, you'll meet the intriguing people who run your hotel, bed-and-breakfast, or restaurant. We've also listed our favorite local guides, all well worth the time and money, to help you gain a better understanding of this marvelous country's past and present.

The destinations covered in this book are balanced to include the most interesting cities and intimate villages, from jet-setting beach resorts to the traditional heartland. We've been selective, including only the most exciting sights and romantic villages. For example, there are hundreds of beautiful châteaux in the Loire region—but we cover just the best. And while there are dozens of Loire towns you could use for a home base, we recommend only the top two: Amboise and Chinon.

The best is, of course, only our opinion. But after spending half of our adult lives travel writing, lecturing, guiding tours, and gaining an appreciation for all things French, we've developed a sixth sense for what touches the traveler's imagination.

## About This Book

*Rick Steves' France 2009* is a personal tour guide in your pocket. Better yet, it's actually two tour guides in your pocket: The co-author of this book is Steve Smith. Steve has been traveling to France—as a guide, researcher, home owner, and devout Francophile—every year since 1985. He has restored an old farmhouse in Burgundy and today keeps one foot on each side of the Atlantic. Together, Steve and I keep this book up-to-date and accurate (though for simplicity, from this point "we" will shed our respective egos and become "I").

This book is organized by destination. Each of these destinations is a mini-vacation on its own, filled with exciting sights, strollable towns, homey affordable places to stay, and memorable places to eat. In the following chapters, you'll find these sections:

**Planning Your Time** suggests a schedule with thoughts on how best to use your limited time.

**Orientation** includes tourist information, specifics on public transportation, and easy-to-read maps designed to make the text clear and your arrival smooth.

**Sights,** described in detail, are rated:

▲▲▲—Don't miss.

▲▲—Try hard to see.

▲—Worthwhile if you can make it.

No rating—Worth knowing about.

**Self-Guided Walks** take you through interesting neighborhoods, with a personal tour guide in hand.

**Sleeping** describes my favorite hotels, from budget deals to cushy splurges.

**Eating** serves up a range of options, from inexpensive eateries to romantic bistros.

**Transportation Connections** outlines your options for traveling to destinations by train and bus. In car-friendly regions, I've included route tips for drivers.

**French History and Contemporary Politics** gives you a quick overview of France from the past to the present.

The **appendix** is a traveler's tool kit, with a handy packing checklist, recommended books and films, instructions on how to use the telephone, and useful French phone numbers. The detailed information on trains and driving includes a day-by-day description of my favorite three-week trip by car (page 858) or by train and bus (page 850). You'll also find a climate chart, festival list, hotel reservation form, pronunciation guide for French place names, and French survival phrases.

Browse through this book and select your favorite sights. Then have a *bon voyage*! Traveling like a temporary local, you'll get the absolute most out of every mile, minute, and euro. As you visit places I know and love, I'm happy you'll be meeting my favorite French people.

# PLANNING

## Trip Costs

Five components make up your total trip cost: airfare, surface transportation, room and board, sightseeing and entertainment, and shopping and miscellany.

**Airfare:** A basic round-trip flight from the US to Paris costs $800 to $1,600, depending on where you fly from and when (cheaper in winter). You can find cheaper round-trip flights from the US to London or Amsterdam, but the cost of train tickets (to get you back to London or Amsterdam for your flight home) eliminate most of your savings. Smaller budget airlines provide bargain service from several European capitals to many French cities (see "Cheap Flights" on page 866 for details). Within France, these inexpensive flights can get you between Paris and other major cities (such as Nice, Marseille, Strasbourg, Toulouse, Lyon, and Bordeaux), often at less cost than by train.

Always consider saving time and money in Europe by flying "open jaw"—into one city and out of another—for example, into Nice and out of Paris. Many find the easygoing Mediterranean city of Nice far easier than Paris as a starting point for their trip.

**Surface Transportation:** For a three-week whirlwind trip of my recommended destinations, allow $750 per person for public transportation (trains and buses) or $900 per person (based on two people sharing) for a three-week car rental, parking, tolls, gas, and insurance (figure about $250 total per week for gas and tolls). Leasing is worth considering for trips of two and a half weeks or more. Car rentals and leases are cheapest if arranged from the US. Train passes are normally available only outside of Europe. You may save money by simply buying tickets as you go (see "Transportation," page 848, for more details on car rentals, rail trips, and bus travel).

**Room and Board:** You can thrive in France on $135 a day

per person for room and board (allow $155 a day for Paris). A $135-a-day budget allows an average of $12 for breakfast, $18 for lunch, $40 for dinner with drinks, and $65 for lodging (based on two people splitting the cost of a $130 double room). That's doable. Students and tightwads do it on $50 a day ($25 per bed, $25 for meals and snacks).

**Sightseeing and Entertainment:** In cities, figure about $8–18 per major sight (Louvre $14, Abbey of Mont St. Michel $13), $6 for minor ones (climbing church towers), $25 for guided walks, and $40–50 for bus tours and splurge experiences (concerts in Paris' Sainte-Chapelle or a ride on the Chamonix gondola).

An overall average of $20–25 a day for sightseeing and entertainment works for most. Don't skimp here. After all, this category is the driving force behind your trip—you came to sightsee, enjoy, and experience France.

**Shopping and Miscellany:** Figure $5 per ice cream cone, coffee, or soft drink. Shopping can vary in cost from nearly nothing to a small fortune. Good budget travelers find that this category has little to do with assembling a trip full of lifelong and wonderful memories.

## Sightseeing Priorities

Depending on the length of your trip, here are my recommended priorities:

| | |
|---|---|
| 3 days: | Paris and maybe Versailles |
| 5 days, add: | Normandy |
| 7 days, add: | Loire |
| 10 days, add: | Dordogne, Carcassonne |
| 15 days, add: | Provence, the Riviera |
| 18 days, add: | Burgundy, Chamonix |
| 21 days, add: | Alsace, northern France |
| 23 days, add: | Basque Country |

For a day-by-day itinerary of a three-week trip, see the plans for drivers (page 858 in appendix) and for people using trains and buses (page 850).

For a more focused 10- to 14-day trip that highlights Paris, Provence, and the Riviera, fly into Paris and out of Nice, visit Paris, then take the TGV train from Paris to Avignon, rent a car there and drop it in Nice (or use trains, buses, and minivan tours to get around). This trip also works in reverse.

For travelers with a little more time, Burgundy and the Alps are about halfway between Paris and Provence and are easy to explore by car or train. If all you have is a week and it's your first trip to France, do Paris, Normandy, and the Loire.

## Major Holidays and Weekends

Popular places are even busier on weekends...and inundated on three-day weekends. Holiday weekends can make towns, trains, roads, and hotels more crowded than summer. The French are masters at the long weekend, and you're no match for them when it comes to driving and finding hotels during these peak periods. Book your accommodations well in advance for these times.

In 2009, be ready for unusually big crowds during these holiday periods: Easter weekend and the two weeks following it (April 10-24, busiest April 10-14), Labor Day (May 1-3), Ascension weekend (May 21-24), Pentecost weekend (May 29-June 1), Bastille Day (July 14) and the week during which it falls, Assumption weekend (Aug 14-16), and the winter holidays (Dec 20-Jan 4—note that Christmas week is quieter than the week of New Year's). These two holidays are usually quiet, but holidays nonetheless: All Saints' Day (Nov 1), and Armistice Day weekend (Nov 11). For information on festivals, see page 867 in the appendix.

## When to Go

Late spring and fall are best, with generally good weather and lighter crowds, though summer brings festivals, reliable weather, and long opening hours at sights. Book ahead for the holidays that occur throughout the year (see "Major Holidays and Weekends," above).

Europeans vacation in July and August, jamming the Riviera, the Dordogne, and the Alps (worst July 15–Aug 20), but leaving the rest of the country just lively enough. And while many French businesses close in August, the traveler hardly notices. Winter travel is fine for Paris, Nice, and Lyon, but you'll find smaller cities and villages buttoned up tight. Winter weather is gray, noticeably milder in the south (unless the wind is blowing), and colder and wetter in the north. Sights and tourist information offices keep shorter hours, and some tourist activities (such as English-language castle tours) vanish altogether. On the other hand, winter travel allows you to see cities though the lens of a local, as hotels, restaurants, and sights are wonderfully tourist-free. To get the latest weather forecast in English, dial 08 99 70 11 11, then press 1. Also see the climate chart in the appendix on page 870.

Thanks to France's relatively mild climate, fields of flowers greet the traveler much of the year:

**April–May:** Crops of brilliant yellow colza bloom, mostly in the north (best in Burgundy). Wild red poppies *(coquelicots)* begin sprouting in the south.

**INTRODUCTION**

## Know Before You Go

Your trip is more likely to go smoothly if you plan ahead. Check this list of things to arrange while you're still at home.

Be sure that your **passport** is valid at least six months after your ticketed date of return to the US. If you need to get or renew a passport, it can take up to two months (for more on passports, see www.travel.state.gov).

Book your rooms well in advance if you'll be traveling during any major **holidays** (see "Major Holidays and Weekends," previous page).

Call your **debit- and credit-card companies** to let them know the countries you'll be visiting, so that they'll accept (and not deny) your international charges. Confirm what your daily withdrawal limit is; consider asking to have it raised so you can take out more cash at each ATM stop. Ask about international transaction fees.

If you'll be **traveling with children,** read the list of suggestions on page 20.

All **high-speed trains** in France require a seat reservation—book as early as possible, because these trains fill fast. If you're taking an overnight train (especially to international destinations such as Rome), and you need a *couchette* (overnight bunk) or sleeper—and you *must* leave on a certain day—consider booking it in advance, even though it may cost more. For more on train travel, see page 848 and www.ricksteves.com/rail.

If you're planning on **renting a car** in France, you'll need your driver's license. It's recommended—but not required—that you also carry an International Driving Permit (IDP), available at your local AAA office ($15 plus the cost of two passport-type photos, www.aaa.com).

Since **airline carry-on restrictions** are always changing, visit the Transportation Security Administration's website (www.tsa.gov/travelers) for an up-to-date list of what you can bring on the plane with you...and what you have to check. Remember to arrive with plenty of time to get through security.

**June:** Red poppies pop up throughout the country. Late in June, lavender blooms begin covering the hills of Provence.

**July:** Lavender is in full swing in Provence, and sunflowers are awakening. Cities, towns, and villages everywhere overflow with carefully tended flowers.

**August–September:** Sunflowers flourish north and south.

**October:** In the latter half of the month, the countryside glistens with fall colors, as most trees are deciduous. Vineyards go for the gold.

## Travel Smart

Your trip to France is like a complex play—easier to follow and really appreciate on a second viewing. While no one does the same trip twice to gain that advantage, reading this book in its entirety before your trip accomplishes much the same thing.

Design an itinerary that enables you to visit museums and festivals on the right days. Note the days when sights are closed. Sundays have the same pros and cons as they do for travelers in the US: Special events and weekly markets pop up, sightseeing attractions are generally open, banks and most shops are closed, public transportation options are fewer, and there's no rush hour. Saturdays are virtually weekdays (without the rush hour).

If you're using public transportation, read up on the tips for trains and buses (see page 848). If you're driving, peruse my driving tips and study the examples of road signs (see page 863).

Be sure to mix intense and relaxed periods in your itinerary. To maximize rootedness, minimize one-night stands. Every trip (and every traveler) needs at least a few slack days. Pace yourself. Assume you will return.

Reread this book as you travel, and visit local tourist information offices. Upon arrival in a new town, lay the groundwork for a smooth departure; write down the schedule for the train or bus you'll take when you depart.

Plan ahead for laundry and picnics. Get online at Internet cafés or your hotel to research transportation connections, confirm events, check the weather, and get directions to your next hotel. Buy a phone card and use it for reservations, reconfirmations, and double-checking hours.

Connect with the culture. Set up your own quest for the best café, cathedral, crêpe, or whatever. Enjoy the friendliness of your French hosts. Slow down and be open to unexpected experiences. Ask questions—most locals are eager to point you in their idea of the right direction. Keep a notepad in your pocket for organizing your thoughts. Wear your money belt, and learn the local currency and how to estimate prices in dollars. Those who expect to travel smart, do.

# PRACTICALITIES

**Red Tape:** You need a passport—but no visa or shots—to travel in France. Your passport must be valid for at least six months beyond the time you leave France. Pack a photocopy of your passport in your luggage in case the original is lost or stolen. You are required to have proof of identity on you at all times in France.

**Time:** In France—and in this book—you'll use the 24-hour clock. It's the same through 12:00 noon, then keep going: 13:00,

# Just the FAQs, Please

**Whom do I call in case of emergency?**
Dial 17 for police help. In a medical emergency, call 15.

**What if my credit card is stolen?**
Act immediately. See "Damage Control for Lost Cards," page 11, for instructions.

**How do I make a phone call to, within, and from Europe?**
For detailed dialing instructions, refer to page 838.

**How can I get tourist information about my destination?**
France has a network of local tourist information offices (listed in each chapter of this book), as well as a national office in the US (see page 831). Note that Tourist Information is abbreviated **TI** in this book.

**What's the best way to pack?**
Light. For a recommended packing list, see page 873.

**Does Rick have other materials that will help me?**
For more info on Rick's guidebooks, public television series, free audiotours, public radio show, guided tours, travel bags, accessories, and railpasses, see page 832.

**Are there any updates to this guidebook?**
Check www.ricksteves.com/update for changes to the most recent edition of this book.

**Can you recommend any good books or movies for my trip?**
For suggestions, see page 835.

**Do I need to speak some French?**
Make an effort to at least learn the polite words: *bonjour, merci, s'il vous plaît, pardon,* and *au revoir.* Though many French people—especially those in the tourist trade, and in big cities—

14:00, and so on. For anything later than 12, subtract 12 and add p.m. (14:00 is 2:00 p.m.).

France, like most of continental Europe, is generally six/nine hours ahead of the East/West Coasts of the US. The exceptions are the beginning and end of Daylight Saving Time: Europe "springs forward" the last Sunday in March (two weeks after most of North America), and "falls back" the last Sunday in October (one week before North America). For a handy online time converter, try www.timeanddate.com/worldclock.

**Business Hours:** In France, most shops are open Monday through Saturday (10:00–12:00 & 14:00–19:00) and closed Sunday, though many small markets, *boulangeries* (bakeries), and street markets are open Sunday mornings until noon. On Mondays, some businesses are closed until 14:00, and possibly all day. Saturdays are like weekdays (but most banks are closed).

**Shopping:** For details on clothing-size conversions, see page speak English, you'll get better treatment if you learn and use the French pleasantries. For background information on the language barrier, see page 846. For a list of survival phrases, see page 879.

**Do you have information on driving, train travel, and flights?**
See "Transportation" on page 848.

**How much do I tip?**
Relatively little. For tips on tipping, see page 12.

**How do travelers handle strikes?**
Strikes are common in France, but are usually short-lived. See "Coping with Strikes" on page 849 for details.

**Will I get a student or senior discount?**
While discounts aren't listed in this book, seniors (age 60 and over), students with International Student Identification Cards, teachers with proper identification, and youths under 18 or even 26 can get discounts—but you have to ask. To inquire about a senior discount, ask, *"Réduction troisième âge?"* (ray-dook-see-ohn twah-zee-ehm ahzh). To get a teacher or student ID card, visit www.statravel.com or www.isic.org.

**How can I get a VAT refund on major purchases?**
See the details on page 12.

**How do I calculate metric amounts?**
Europe uses the metric system. A liter is about a quart, four to a gallon. A kilometer is six-tenths of a mile. I figure kilometers to miles by cutting them in half and adding back 10 percent of the original (120 km: 60 + 12 = 72 miles, 300 km: 150 + 30 = 180 miles). For more metric conversions, see page 869.

870 in the appendix. For customs regulations and VAT refunds (the tax refunded on large purchases made by non-EU residents), see page 12.

**Watt's Up?** Europe's electrical system is different from North America's in two different ways: the shape of the plug (two round prongs) and the voltage of the current (220 volts instead of 110 volts). For your North American plug to work in Europe, you'll need an adapter, sold inexpensively at travel stores in the US. As for the voltage, newer electronics or travel appliances (such as hair dryers, laptops, and battery chargers) automatically convert the voltage—if you see a range of voltages printed on the item or its plug (such as "110–220"), it'll work in Europe. Otherwise, you can buy a converter separately in the US (about $20).

**News:** Americans keep in touch via the *International Herald Tribune* (published almost throughout Europe). Every Tuesday, the European editions of *Time* and *Newsweek* hit the stands with articles of particular interest to European travelers. Sports addicts can get their daily fix online or from *USA Today*. Good websites include www.iht.com, http://news.bbc.co.uk, and www.european times.com.

# MONEY

## Cash from ATMS

Throughout Europe, cash machines (ATMs) are the standard way for travelers to get local currency.

Bring plastic—credit and/or debit cards. It's smart to bring two cards, in case one gets demagnetized or eaten by a temperamental machine.

As an emergency backup, bring several hundred dollars in hard cash. Avoid using currency exchange booths (lousy rates and/ or outrageous fees); if you have foreign currency to exchange, take it to a bank. Also avoid using traveler's checks, which are a waste of time (long waits at banks) and a waste of money (in fees).

To use an ATM to withdraw money from your account, you'll need a debit card (ideally with a Visa or MasterCard logo for maximum usability), plus a PIN code. Know your PIN code in numbers; there are only numbers—no letters—on European keypads.

Before you go, verify with your bank that your card will work overseas, and alert them that you'll be making withdrawals in Europe; otherwise, the bank may not approve transactions if it perceives unusual spending patterns. Also ask about international transaction fees; see "Credit and Debit Cards," below.

French cash machines are labeled *point d'argent* or *distributeur des billets* (the French call them *D.A.B.*—day-ah-bay). You'll find these cash machines all over France—they're always open and provide quick transactions.

Try to take out large sums of money to reduce your per-transaction bank fees. If the machine refuses your request, try again and select a smaller amount; some cash machines won't let you take out more than about €150 (don't take it personally). If that doesn't work, try a different machine.

To keep your cash safe, use a money belt—a pouch with a strap that you buckle around your waist like a belt and wear under your clothes. Thieves target tourists. A money belt provides peace of mind, allowing you to carry lots of cash safely. Don't waste time every few days tracking down a cash machine—withdraw a week's worth of money, stuff it in your money belt, and travel!

## Credit and Debit Cards

For purchases, Visa and MasterCard are more commonly accepted than American Express. Just like at home, credit or debit cards

---

# Exchange Rate

## 1 euro (€) = about $1.50

To convert prices in euros to dollars, add about 50 percent: €20 = about $30, €50 = about $75. (To get the latest rate and print a cheat sheet, see www.oanda.com.) Just like the dollar, the euro is broken down into 100 cents. You'll find coins ranging from 1 cent to 2 euros, and bills from 5 euros to 500 euros.

---

work easily at larger hotels, restaurants, and shops, but smaller businesses prefer payment in local currency (in small bills—break large bills at a bank or larger store). Your US credit and debit cards will not work in train- or Métro-ticket machines, at self-service gas pumps, or at freeway tollbooths.

**Fees:** Some credit- and debit-card transactions—whether purchases or ATM withdrawals—come with tacked-on "international transaction" fees of up to 3 percent plus $5 per transaction. To avoid unpleasant surprises, call your bank or credit-card company before your trip to ask about these fees. You may want to get a card that has low to no international transaction fees, such as Capital One (www.capitalone.com).

## Damage Control for Lost Cards

If you lose your credit, debit, or ATM card, you can stop people from using it by reporting the loss immediately to the respective global customer-assistance centers. Call these 24-hour US numbers collect: Visa (410/581-9994), MasterCard (636/722-7111), and American Express (623/492-8427). For another option (with the same results), you can call these toll-free numbers in France: Visa (08 00 90 11 79) and MasterCard (08 00 90 13 87). American Express has a Paris office, but the call isn't free (01 47 77 70 00, English spoken). Diners Club has offices in the US (702/797-5532, call collect) and Britain (from France, dial 00-44-1695-53760).

At a minimum, you'll need to know the name of the financial institution that issued you the card, along with the type of card (classic, platinum, or whatever). Providing the following information will allow for a quicker cancellation of your missing card: full card number, whether you are the primary or secondary cardholder, the cardholder's name exactly as printed on the card, billing address, home phone number, circumstances of the loss or theft, and identification verification (your birth date, your mother's maiden name, or your Social Security number—memorize this, don't carry a copy). If you are the secondary cardholder, you'll also need to provide the primary cardholder's identification-verification details. You can generally receive a temporary card within two or three business days in Europe.

If you promptly report your card lost or stolen, you typically won't be responsible for any unauthorized transactions on your account, although many banks charge a liability fee of $50.

## Tipping

Tipping *(donner un pourboire)* in France isn't as automatic and generous as it is in the US, but for special service, tips are appreciated, if not expected. As in the US, the proper amount depends on your resources, tipping philosophy, and the circumstances, but some general guidelines apply.

**Restaurants:** At cafés and restaurants, a 15 percent service charge *(service compris)* is generally included in the bill, though it's good form to tip 5 percent extra for good service. When you hand your payment plus a tip to your waiter, you can say, *"C'est bon"* (say bohn), meaning, "It's good" (and you don't want any change back). If you order a meal at a counter, don't tip.

**Taxis:** To tip the cabbie, round up. For a typical ride, round up to the next euro on the fare (to pay a €13 fare, give €14); for a long ride, round to the nearest €10 (for a €75 fare, give €80). If the cabbie hauls your bags and zips you to the airport to help you catch your flight, you might want to toss in a little more. But if you feel like you're being driven in circles or otherwise ripped off, skip the tip.

**Special Services:** It's thoughtful to tip a couple of euros to someone who shows you a special sight and who is paid in no other way. Tour guides at public sites sometimes hold out their hands for tips (€1–2) after they give their spiel; if I've already paid for the tour, I don't tip extra, unless they really impressed me. I don't tip at hotels, but if you do, give the porter a euro for carrying bags and leave a couple of euros in your room at the end of your stay for the maid if the room was kept clean. In general, if someone in the service industry does a super job for you, a tip of a couple of euros is appropriate...but not required.

**When in doubt, ask.** If you're not sure whether (or how much) to tip for a service, ask your hotelier or the tourist information office; they'll fill you in on how it's done on their turf.

## Getting a VAT Refund

Wrapped into the purchase price of your French souvenirs is a Value Added Tax (VAT) of about 19.6 percent. If you purchase more than €175 (about $265) worth of goods at a store that participates in the VAT-refund scheme, you're entitled to get most of that tax back. Getting your refund is usually straightforward and, if you buy a substantial amount of souvenirs, well worth the hassle. If you're lucky, the merchant will subtract the tax when you make your purchase. (This is more likely to occur if the store ships the goods to your home.) Otherwise, you'll need to:

**Get the paperwork.** Have the merchant completely fill out the necessary refund document, *Bordereau de Vente à l'Exportation*, also called a "cheque." You'll have to present your passport at the store.

**Get your stamp at the border or airport.** Process your cheque(s) at your last stop in the EU (e.g., at the airport) with the customs agent who deals with VAT refunds. It's best to keep your purchases in your carry-on for viewing, but if they're too large or dangerous (such as knives) to carry on, track down the proper customs agent to inspect them before you check your bag. You're not supposed to use your purchased goods before you leave. If you show up at customs wearing your chic new French ensemble, officials might look the other way—or deny you a refund.

**Collect your refund.** You'll need to return your stamped document to the retailer or its representative. Many merchants work with a service, such as Global Refund (www.globalrefund .com) or Premier Tax Free (www.premiertaxfree.com), which have offices at major airports, ports, or border crossings. These services, which extract a 4 percent fee, can refund your money immediately in your currency of choice or credit your card (within two billing cycles). If the retailer handles VAT refunds directly, it's up to you to contact the merchant for your refund. You can mail the documents from home, or quicker, from your point of departure (using a stamped, addressed envelope you've prepared or one that's been provided by the merchant)—and then wait. It could take months.

## Customs for American Shoppers

You are allowed to take home $800 worth of items per person duty-free, once every 30 days. The next $1,000 is taxed at a flat 3 percent. After that, you pay the individual item's duty rate. You can also bring in duty-free a liter of alcohol (slightly more than a standard-size bottle of wine; you must be at least 21), 200 cigarettes, and up to 100 non-Cuban cigars. You may take home vacuum-packed cheeses; dried herbs, spices, or mushrooms; canned fruits or vegetables including jams and vegetable spreads; and olive oil (many producers pack their oil in stainless steel canisters for easier transport). Red meats (even vacuum-packed or canned), and fresh fruits or vegetables are not permitted (but canned pâtés are allowed if goose, duck, or pork). Note that you'll need to carefully pack any bottles of wine and other liquid-containing items (jars of olives, etc.) in your checked luggage, due to the three-ounce limit on liquids in carry-on baggage. To check customs rules and duty rates before you go, visit www.cbp.gov, and click on "Travel," then "Know Before You Go."

# SIGHTSEEING

Sightseeing can be hard work. Use these tips to make your visits to France's finest sights meaningful, fun, fast, and painless.

## Plan Ahead

Set up an itinerary that allows you to fit in all your must-see sights. For a one-stop look at opening hours in the bigger cities, see the "At a Glance" sidebars. Most sights keep stable hours, but you can easily confirm the latest by calling the local TI.

Don't put off visiting a must-see sight—you never know when a place will close unexpectedly for a holiday, strike, or restoration. If you'll be visiting during a holiday, find out if a particular sight will be open by phoning ahead or visiting its website.

When possible, visit major sights first thing (when your energy is best) and save other activities for the afternoon. Hit the highlights first, then go back to other things if you have the stamina and time.

Going at the right time can also help you avoid crowds. This book offers tips on specific sights. For example, Paris' Louvre, Orsay, and Orangerie museums are open selected evenings, while the Pompidou Center is always open late. Evening visits are usually peaceful with fewer crowds. At Mont St. Michel or Carcassonne, it's best to arrive at about 17:00, spend the night, and explore in the morning before the crowds descend. Finally, do your best to visit these sights first thing or late: Château de Chenonceau, Les Baux, and the Pont du Gard.

Read ahead. To get the most out of the self-guided tours and sight descriptions in this book, read them before you visit. Several cities offer sightseeing passes that are worthwhile values for serious sightseers; plan ahead.

## At the Sights

All sights have rules, and if you know about these in advance, they're no big deal.

Some important sights have metal detectors or conduct bag searches that will slow your entry.

At churches—which often offer interesting art (usually free) and a cool, welcome seat—a modest dress code (no bare shoulders or shorts) is encouraged.

Major museums and sights require you to check daypacks and coats. They'll be kept safely. If you have something you can't bear to part with, stash it in a pocket or purse. If you don't want to check a small backpack, carry it (at least as you enter) under your arm like a purse. From a guard's point of view, a backpack is generally a problem, while a purse is not.

If you check a bag, the attendant may ask you (in French) if it contains anything of value—camera, phone, money, passport—since these cannot be checked.

Photography is sometimes banned at major sights. Look for signs or ask. If cameras are allowed, flashes or tripods are usually not. Flashes damage oil paintings and distract others in the room. Even without a flash, a handheld camera will take a decent picture (or buy postcards or posters at the museum bookstore). Video cameras are generally allowed.

Some museums have special exhibits in addition to their permanent collection. Some exhibits are included in the entry price; others come at an extra cost (which you may have to pay even if you don't want to see the exhibit).

Many sights rent audioguides, which offer dry-but-useful recorded descriptions in English (about €5). I've produced free audiotours for the major sites in Paris (see page 834). If you bring along your own pair of headphones and a Y-jack, two people can sometimes share one audioguide and save. Guided tours in English are most likely to occur during peak season (some are free, while others can cost up to €8 and range widely in quality).

Expect changes—paintings can be on tour, on loan, out sick, or shifted at the whim of the curator. To adapt, pick up any available free floor plans as you enter, and ask museum staff if you can't find a particular painting. Say the title or artist's name, or point to the photograph in this book, and ask for its location by saying, "*Où est?*" (oo ay).

Most important sights have an on-site café or cafeteria (usually a good place to rest and have a snack or light meal). The WCs at many sights are free and clean.

Key sights and museums have bookstores selling postcards and souvenirs. Before you leave, scan the postcards and thumb through the biggest guidebook (or skim its index) to be sure you haven't overlooked something that you'd like to see.

Most sights stop admitting people 30–60 minutes before closing time, and some rooms close early (generally about 45 minutes before the actual closing time). Guards usher people out, so don't save the best for last.

Every sight or museum offers more than what is covered in this book. Use this information as an introduction—not the final word.

## SLEEPING

Good-value accommodations in France are generally easy to find. Choose from one- to three-star hotels (two stars is my mainstay), bed-and-breakfasts *(chambres d'hôte, usually cheaper than hotels)*, hostels, campgrounds, and even homes *(gîtes, rented by the week)*.

I like hotels and B&Bs that are clean, small, central, traditional, friendly, and a good value. Most places I list have at least four of these six virtues. For tips on making reservations, see page 23.

## Types of Accommodations

### Hotels

In this book, the price for a double room ranges from €40 (very simple, toilet and shower down the hall) to €300-plus (maximum plumbing and more), with most clustering at about €80–110.

The French have a simple hotel-rating system based on amenities (zero through four stars, indicated in this book by * through ****). One star is modest, two has most of the comforts, and three is generally a two-star with a fan-cier lobby and more elaborately designed rooms. Four stars offer more luxury than you usually have time to appreciate. Two- and three-star hotels are required to have an English-speaking staff, though virtually all hotels I recommend have someone who speaks English (unless I note oth-erwise in the listing).

The number of stars usually does not reflect room size or guar-antee quality. Some two-star hotels are better than many three-star hotels. One- and two-star hotels are inexpensive, but some three-star (and even a few four-star) hotels offer good value, justi-fying the extra cost. Unclassified hotels (no stars) can be bargains or depressing dumps.

Most hotels have lots of doubles and a few singles, triples, and quads. Traveling alone can be expensive, as singles (except for the rare closet-type rooms that fit only one twin bed) are simply doubles used by one person—so they cost about the same as a double. Room prices vary within each hotel depending on size, and whether the room has a bath or shower, and twin beds or a double bed (tubs and twins cost more than showers and double beds). A triple and a double are often the same room, with a double or queen-size bed plus a sliver-size single. Quad rooms usually have two double beds. Hotels cannot legally allow more in the room than what's shown on their price list. Modern hotels generally have a few family-friendly rooms that open to each other (*chambres communiquantes*).

Hotels in France must charge a daily tax (*taxe du séjour*) of about €1 per person per day. While some hotels include it in the price list, most add it to your bill.

You can save as much as €20–25 by finding the rare room without a private shower or toilet. A room with a bathtub costs

# Sleep Code

**(€1 = about $1.50, country code: 33)**
To help you easily sort through these listings, I've divided the rooms into three categories based on the price for a standard double room with bath:

$$$ **Higher Priced**
$$ **Moderately Priced**
$ **Lower Priced**

To give maximum information in a minimum of space, I use the following code to describe the accommodations. Prices listed are per room, not per person. When a price range is given for a type of room (such as double rooms listing for €140–180), it means the price fluctuates with the season, size of room, or length of stay.

- **S** = Single room (or price for one person in a double).
- **D** = Double or Twin.
- **T** = Triple (generally a double bed with a single).
- **Q** = Quad (usually two double beds).
- **b** = Private bathroom with toilet and shower or tub.
- **s** = Private shower or tub only (the toilet is down the hall).
- **\*** = French hotel rating system, ranging from zero to four stars.

According to this code, a couple staying at a "Db-€140" hotel would pay a total of €140 (about $210) for a double room with a private bathroom. You can assume a hotel takes credit cards unless you see "cash only" in the listing. Unless otherwise noted, hotel staff speak basic English and breakfast is not included (but is usually optional).

about €10–15 more than a room with a shower and is generally larger. Hotels often have more rooms with tubs than showers, and are inclined to give you a room with a tub (which the French prefer).

A double bed is usually €5–10 cheaper than twins, though rooms with twin beds tend to be larger, and French double beds are smaller than American double beds. Many hotels have queen-size beds (a bed that's 63 inches wide—most doubles are 55 inches). To find out if a hotel has queen-size beds, ask, *"Avez-vous des lits de cent-soixante?"* (ah-vay-voo day lee duh sahn-swah-sahnt).

If you prefer a double bed (instead of twins) and a shower (instead of a tub), you need to ask for it—and you can save €10–20. If you'll take either twins or a double, ask generically for *une chambre pour deux* (room for two) to avoid being needlessly turned away.

## Types of Rooms

Study the price list on the hotel's website or posted at the desk, so you know your options. Receptionists often don't mention the cheaper rooms (they assume you want a private bathroom or a bigger room). Here are the types of rooms and beds:

| | |
|---|---|
| une chambre sans douche et WC | room without a private shower or toilet (uncommon these days) |
| une chambre avec cabinet de toilette | room with a toilet but no shower (some hotels charge for down-the-hall showers) |
| une chambre avec bain et WC | room with private bathtub and toilet |
| une chambre avec douche et WC | room with private shower and toilet |
| chambres communiquantes | connecting rooms (ideal for families) |
| un grand lit | double bed (55 inches wide) |
| deux petits lits | twin beds (30–36 inches wide) |
| un lit single | true single room |
| un lit de cent-soixante | queen-size bed (literally, 160 centimeters, or 63 inches, wide) |
| le king size | king-size bed (usually two twins pushed together) |
| un lit pliant | folding bed |
| un berceau | baby crib |
| un lit d'enfant | child's bed |

Hotels lobbies, halls, and breakfast rooms are now off-limits to smokers, though smokers can light up in their rooms. Still, I rarely smell any smoke in my rooms. Some hotels have non-smoking rooms or floors.

Most hotels offer some kind of breakfast, but it's rarely included in the room rates. The price of breakfast usually correlates with the price of the room: The more expensive the room, the more expensive the breakfast. This per-person charge can add up, particularly for families—so beware. While hotels hope you'll buy their breakfast, it's optional unless otherwise noted (for more on breakfast, see "Eating" on page 25).

Some hotels, especially in coastal resort towns, strongly encourage their peak-season guests to take *demi-pension* (half-pension)—that is, breakfast and either lunch or dinner. By law, they can't require you to take half-pension unless you are staying three or more nights, but, in practice, many do during summer.

## Keep Cool

If you're planning to visit France in the summer, the extra expense of an air-conditioned room can be money well spent, particularly in the south. Most hotel rooms with air-conditioners come with a control stick (like a TV remote) that generally has the same symbols and features: fan icon (click to toggle through wind power, from light to gale); louver icon (choose steady airflow or waves); snowflake and sunshine icons (cold air or heat, depending on season); clock ("O" setting: run X hours before turning off; "I" setting: wait X hours to start); and the temperature control (20 or 21 degrees Celsius is comfortable; also see the thermometer diagram on page 871).

While the food is usually good, it limits your ability to shop around. I've indicated where I think *demi-pension* is a good value.

Rooms are safe. Still, keep cameras and money out of sight. Towels aren't always replaced every day; drip-dry and conserve. If that French Lincoln Log pillow isn't your idea of comfort, American-style pillows (and extra blankets) are sometimes in the closet or available on request. To get a pillow, ask for *"Un oreiller, s'il vous plaît"* (uhn oar-ray-yay, see voo play).

If I mention "Internet Access" in a hotel listing, that means the hotel has at least one public terminal for guests to use. If I say "Wi-Fi," the hotel has wireless Internet for laptop users.

Your hotelier, a good source of advice, can direct you to the nearest launderette and Internet café. Some hoteliers will ask you to sign their *Livre d'Or* ("Golden Book," for client comments). They take this seriously and enjoy reading your remarks. To avoid the time-wasting line at the reception desk in the morning, ask if you can settle up your bill the evening before you leave.

**Modern Hotel Chains:** France is littered with sterile, ultra-modern hotels, usually located on cheap land just outside of town, providing drivers with low-stress accommodations. The antiseptically clean and cheap Formule 1 and ETAP chains (about €40–50 per room for up to three people), the more attractive Ibis hotels (€80–100 for a double), and the cushier Mercure and Novotels hotels (€110–170 for a double) are all run by the same company, Accor (www.accorhotels.com). While far from quaint, these can be a good value (particularly if you find deals on their website) and some are centrally located. A smaller chain, Kyriad, offers good prices and quality (Kyriad Prestige offers a bit more comfort; France tel. 08 25 00 30 03, from overseas tel. 33 1 64 62 46 46—push 1 to make a reservation, www.kyriad.com; these telephone numbers also work for eight affiliated chains, including

# Traveling with Kids

France is kid-friendly for young children, partly because so much of it is rural. (Teenagers, on the other hand, tend to prefer cities.) Both of this book's authors have kids (from 7 to 21 years old), and we've used our substantial experience traveling with children to improve this book. Our kids have greatly enriched our travels, and we hope the same will be true for you.

My kids' favorite places have been Mont St. Michel, the Alps, the Loire châteaux, Carcassonne, and Paris (especially the Eiffel Tower and Seine River boat ride)—and any hotel with a pool. To make your trip fun for everyone in the family, mix heavy-duty sights with kids' activities (playing miniature golf, renting bikes, and riding the little tourist trains popular in many towns). While Disneyland Paris is the predictable draw, my kids had more fun for half the expense simply by enjoying the rides in the Tuileries Garden in downtown Paris. If you're in France near Bastille Day, remember that firecracker stands pop up everywhere on the days leading up to July 14. Putting on their own fireworks show can be a highlight for teenagers.

Minimize hotel changes by planning three-day stops. Aim for hotels with restaurants, so the kids can go back to the room and play while you finish a quiet dinner.

I've listed public pools in many places (especially the south), but be warned: Public pools in France commonly require a small, Speedo-like bathing suit for boys and men (American-style swim trunks won't do)—though they usually have these little suits to loan. At hotel pools, either kind of suit will do.

For breakfast, croissants are a hit. For lunch and dinner, it's not hard to find *crêperies* with plenty of kid-friendly stuffings for both savory crêpes and sweet dessert crêpes. It's easy to find fast-food places and restaurants with kids' menus, but for food emergencies, I travel with a plastic container of peanut butter brought from home and smuggle small jars of jam from breakfast.

Swap babysitting duties with your partner if one of you wants to take in an extra sight. Kids homesick for friends can

Clarine, Climat de France, and Campanile). For a long listing of various hotels throughout France, see www.france.com, and for more personality, check www.charming-french-hotels.com.

## Bed-and-Breakfasts

B&Bs (*Chambres d'hôte*, abbreviated CH in this book)—a great deal—are generally found in smaller towns and rural areas. They offer double the cultural intimacy for a good deal less than most hotel rooms—and help compensate for the low value of the dollar. While you may lose some hotel conveniences—such as lounges, in-room phones, daily bed-sheet changes, and credit-card payments—I happily make the trade-off for the extra charm and lower keep in easy touch with cheap international phone cards and through Internet cafés.

For memories that will last long after the trip, keep a family journal. Pack a small diary and a glue stick. While relaxing at a café over a *citron pressé* (lemonade, needs sugar), take turns writing down the day's events, and include mementos such as ticket stubs from museums, postcards, or stalks of lavender.

**What to Bring:** Children's books are scarce and expensive in France. My children read more when traveling in Europe than while at home in the US, so don't skimp here. Bring peanut butter (hard to find in France)...or help your kids acquire a taste for Nutella, the tasty hazelnut-chocolate spread available everywhere. Choose items that are small and convenient for use on planes, trains, and in your hotel room: compact travel games, a deck of cards, a handheld video game, and drawing and coloring supplies. Bring your own drawing paper (it's expensive in Europe). For younger kids, Legos are easily packed and practical (it's also fun to purchase kits overseas, as Legos are sometimes different in Europe from those in the US). Budding fashionistas might enjoy traveling with—and buying new outfits for—a Corelle doll or another 16-inch doll. The French have wonderful doll clothes, with a much wider selection than what's typically found in the US.

Benadryl works miracles in keeping ears and noses open during flights—with the added benefit of sleepiness for most children. I give my kids Benadryl before bed for the first two nights in Europe, and they rarely have serious jet-lag issues. For traveling with infants, car-rental agencies usually have car seats for a small price, though you must reserve one ahead of time. And while most hotels have some sort of crib, I brought a portable crib and did not regret it. Cameras (even disposable ones) are a great investment to get your kids involved. For longer drives, books on tape or CD can be fun for the whole family (if carefully chosen). I recommend Peter Mayle's *A Year in Provence,* available on both cassette tape and CD (or put it on your MP3 player).

rates. This book and local tourist offices list B&Bs, often by the owner's family name. It's always OK to ask to see the room before you commit. While some CHs post small *Chambres* or *Chambres d'hôte* signs in their front windows, many are found only through the local tourist office.

I recommend reliable CHs that offer a good value and/or unique experience (such as CHs in renovated mills, châteaux, and wine *domaines*). While *chambres d'hôte* have their own star-rating system, it doesn't quite correspond to the hotels' rating system. So, to avoid confusion, I haven't listed these stars for CHs. But most of my recommended CHs have private bathrooms in rooms and some have common rooms with refrigerators. Doubles with breakfast generally cost €50–70 (breakfast may or may not be included—ask). *Tables d'hôte* are CHs that offer an optional, reasonably priced, home-cooked dinner (usually a fine value, must be requested in advance). While your hosts may not speak English, they will almost always be enthusiastic and pleasant.

## Hostels

You'll pay about €20 per bed to stay at a hostel *(auberge de jeunesse)*. Travelers of any age are welcome if they don't mind dorm-style accommodations (usually in rooms of four to eight beds) or meeting other travelers. Cheap meals are sometimes available, and kitchen facilities are usually provided for do-it-yourselfers. Expect youth groups in spring, crowds in the summer, snoring, and variability in quality from one hostel to the next. Family and private rooms are sometimes available on request, but it's basically boys' dorms and girls' dorms. You usually can't check in before 17:00 and must be out by 10:00. There is often a 23:00 curfew. Official hostels are marked with a triangular sign that shows a house and a tree. Some hostels accept reservations only by email. If you'll be staying for several days in an official hostel, consider buying a membership card before you go (www.hihostels.com).

## Camping

In Europe, camping is more of a social than an environmental experience. It's a great way for American travelers to make European friends. Camping costs about €15–20 per campsite per night, and almost every destination recommended in this book has a campground within a reasonable walk or bus ride from the town center and train station. A tent and sleeping bag are all you need. Many campgrounds have small grocery stores and washing machines, and some even come with discos and miniature golf. Hot showers are better at campgrounds than at many hotels. Local TIs have camping information. You'll find more detailed information in the annually updated *Michelin Camping France*, available in the US and at most French bookstores.

## Gîtes and Apartments

Throughout France, you can find reasonably priced rental homes that are ideal for families and small groups wanting to explore a region more closely.

*Gîtes* (zheet) are country homes (usually urbanites' second homes) that the government rents out to visitors who want a week in the countryside (homes are rented for at least a week at a time, from Saturday to Saturday). The objective of the *gîte* program was to save characteristic rural homes from abandonment and to make it easy and affordable for families to enjoy the French countryside.

The government offers subsidies to renovate such homes, then coordinates rentals to make it financially feasible for the owner. Today, France has more than 9,000 *gîtes*. One of your authors restored a farmhouse a few hours north of Provence, and even though he and his wife are American, they received the same assistance that French owners get.

*Gîtes* are best for drivers (they're usually rural, with little public-transport access) and ideal for families and small groups (since they can sleep many for the same price). Homes range in comfort from simple cottages and farmhouses to restored châteaux. Most have at least two bedrooms, a kitchen, a living room, a bathroom or two, and no sheets or linens (though you can usually rent them for extra). Like hotels, all *gîtes* are rated for comfort from one to four (using ears of corn—*épis*—rather than stars). Two or three *épis* are generally sufficient quality, but I'd lean toward three for more comfort. Prices generally range from €350–1,200 per week, depending on house size and amenities such as pools. For more information on *gîtes*, visit www.gites-de-france.fr/eng or www.gite .com. My readers also report finding long lists of non-*gîte* homes for rent through TIs and on the Internet, though these are usually more expensive than staying in a *gîte* (try www.villeetvillage.com).

While less common than *gîtes*, **apartments** can be rented in cities (also for a one-week minimum). Tourist offices have lists or recommended websites.

## Phoning

To make an international call to France, you'll need to know its country code: 33. To call France from the US or Canada, dial 011-33-local number (drop the initial 0 of the local number). If calling France from another European country, dial 00-33-local number (without the initial 0). For more information on telephoning, see page 838.

## Making Reservations

Given the quality of the places I've found for this book, I'd recommend that you reserve your rooms in advance, particularly during peak season and for Paris any time of year. Book several weeks ahead, or as soon as you've pinned down your travel dates. Note that some national holidays and major events jam things up and merit your making reservations far in advance (see "Major Holidays and Weekends," page 5). To make a reservation, contact hotels directly by email, phone, or fax.

Email is the clearest and most economical way to make a reservation. In addition, many hotel websites now have online reservation forms. If phoning from the US, be mindful of time zones (see page 8). Most hotels listed are accustomed to English-only travelers. To ensure you have all the information you need for your reservation, use the form in this book's appendix (also at www .ricksteves.com/reservation).

For more spontaneity, you can make reservations as you travel, calling hotels a few days to a week before your visit. If you prefer the flexibility of traveling without any reservations, you'll have greater success snaring rooms if you arrive at your destination early in the day. When you anticipate crowds, call hotels at about 9:00 on the day you plan to arrive, when the hotel clerk knows who'll be checking out and just which rooms will be available. If you encounter a language barrier, ask the fluent receptionist at your current hotel to call for you.

When you request a room for a certain time period, use the European style for writing dates: day/month/year. Hoteliers need to know your arrival and departure dates. For example, a two-night stay in July would be "2 nights, 16/07/09 to 18/07/09." Consider carefully how long you'll stay; don't assume you can extend your reservation for extra days once you arrive.

If you don't get a response within a few days, call to follow up. If the response from the hotel gives its room availability and rates, it's not a confirmation. You must tell them that you want that room at the given rate.

The hotelier will sometimes request your credit-card number for a one-night deposit. While you can email your credit-card information (I do), it's safer to share that personal info via phone call, fax, or secure online reservation form (if the hotel has one on its website).

If you must cancel your reservation, it's courteous to do so with as much advance notice as possible (a minimum of three days is standard in France; simply make a quick phone call or send an email). Family-run hotels and B&Bs lose money if they turn away customers while holding a room for someone who doesn't show up. Understandably, some hotels bill no-shows for one night.

Hotels in larger cities sometimes have strict cancellation policies: For example, you might lose a deposit if you cancel within one week of your reserved stay, or you might be billed for the entire visit if you leave early. Ask about cancellation policies before you book.

Always reconfirm your room reservation a few days in advance from the road. If you'll be arriving after 17:00, let them know. Don't have the tourist office reconfirm rooms for you; they'll take a commission.

On the small chance that a hotel loses track of your reservation, bring along a hard copy of their emailed or faxed confirmation.

# EATING

The French eat long and well. Relaxed lunches, three-hour dinners, and endless hours sitting in outdoor cafés are the norm. Here, chefs are as famous as great athletes, and mamas hope their babies grow up to be great cooks. Local cafés, cuisine, and wines should become a highlight of any French adventure. It's sightseeing for your palate. Even if the rest of you is sleeping in cheap hotels, let your taste buds travel first class in France. (They can go coach in England.)

You can eat well without going broke—but choose carefully: You're just as likely to blow a small fortune on a mediocre meal as you are to dine wonderfully for €20. Carefully read the information below, consider my restaurant suggestions in this book, and you'll do fine.

Waiters probably won't overwhelm you with friendliness. Notice how hard they work. They almost never stop. Cozying up to clients (French or foreign) is probably the last thing on their minds. To get a waiter's attention, say, "*S'il vous plaît*" (see voo play)—"please." For advice on tipping, see page 12.

Eating out improved dramatically for non-smokers in 2008 as, by law, all café and restaurant interiors must be smoke-free. Sidewalk tables are still open season for smokers, so expect your neighbors to smoke if you sit outside.

## Breakfast

*Petit déjeuner* (puh-tee day-zhu-nay) is traditionally *café au lait,* hot chocolate, or tea; a roll with butter and marmalade; and a croissant—though many hotels now provide breakfast buffets with fruit, cereal, yogurt, and cheese (usually for a few extra euros and well worth it). Breakfast, which costs about €6–15 at your hotel, is cheaper at corner cafés, but you won't get coffee refills (see also "Café Culture," on page 28). It's fine to buy a croissant or roll at a bakery and eat it with your cup of coffee at a café. Better still, some bakeries offer worthwhile breakfast deals with juice, croissant, and coffee or tea for about €4–5. If you crave eggs for breakfast, drop into a café and order *une omelette* or *œufs sur le plat* (fried eggs). You could also buy (or bring from home) plastic bowls and spoons, buy a box of cereal and a small box of milk, and eat in your room before heading out for coffee.

## Picnics

For many lunches—*déjeuner* (day-zhuh-nay)—I picnic, munch a take-away sandwich from a *boulangerie* (bakery), or get a crêpe from a *crêperie.*

Picnics can be first-class affairs and adventures in high cuisine. Be daring. Try the smelly cheeses, ugly pâtés, sissy quiches, and minuscule (usually drinkable) yogurts. Local shopkeepers are

# Market Day (Jour du Marché)

Try to buy some of your picnics at an open-air market. Market days are a big deal throughout France. They have been a central feature of life in rural areas since the Middle Ages. No single event better symbolizes the French preoccupation with fresh products and their strong ties to the small farmer than the weekly market. It's said that locals mark their calendars with the arrival of fresh produce. Notice the signs as you enter towns indicating the *jours du marché* (essential information to any civilized soul, and a reminder to non-locals not to park on the streets the night before).

Most *marchés* take place once a week in the town's main square and, if large enough, spill into nearby streets. Markets combine fresh produce; samples of wine and other locally produced beverages (such as brandies and ciders); and a smattering of nonperishable items, such as knives, berets, kitchen goods, and cheap clothing. The bigger the market, the greater the overall selection—particularly for nonperishable goods. Bigger towns (such as Beaune and Arles) may have two weekly markets. The biggest market days are usually on weekends, so that everyone can go.

Providing far more than fresh produce, market day is a weekly chance to resume friendships and get current on gossip. Friends catch up on Henri's barn renovation, see photos of Jacqueline's new grandchild, and relax over *un café*. Dogs are tethered to café tables while friends exchange kisses. Tether yourself to a café table, and observe: generally three cheek-kisses for good friends (left–right–left; but only two kisses in Paris) plus an extra kiss for friends you haven't seen in a while. You should never be in a hurry on market day. Allow the crowd to set your pace. Watch the interaction between vendor and client.

All perishable items are sold directly from the producers—no middlemen, no Visa cards, just really fresh produce. Most vendors follow a weekly circuit of markets they feel work best for them, and most show up every market day, year in and year out. Notice how much fun they have chatting up their customers and each other. Many speak enough English to allow you to learn about their product. Space rental is cheap (about €5–10, depending on the size). Markets end by 13:00—in time for lunch, allowing the town to reclaim its streets and squares.

accustomed to selling small quantities of produce. Try the tasty salads-to-go and ask for a plastic fork *(une fourchette en plastique)*. A small container is *une barquette*.

Gather supplies early for a picnic lunch; you'll probably visit several small stores to assemble a complete meal, and many close at noon for their lunch break. Look for a *boulangerie* (bakery), a *crémerie* or *fromagerie* (cheeses), a charcuterie (deli items, meats, salads, and pâtés), an *épicerie* or *magasin d'alimentation* (small grocery with veggies, drinks, and so on), and a *pâtisserie* (delicious pastries). While wine is taboo in public places in the US, it's *pas de problème* in France.

Open-air markets *(marchés)* are fun and photogenic and close at about 13:00 (many are listed in this book; local TIs have complete lists). Local *supermarchés* offer less color and cost, more efficiency, and adequate quality. Department stores often have supermarkets in the basement. On the outskirts of cities, you'll find the monster *hypermarchés*. Drop in for a glimpse of hyper-France in action.

In stores, unrefrigerated soft drinks, bottled water, and beer are one-third the price of cold drinks. Milk, bottled water, and boxed fruit juice are the cheapest drinks. Avoid buying drinks to-go at streetside stands; you'll find them far cheaper in a shop. Try to keep a water bottle with you. Water quenches your thirst better and cheaper than anything you'll find in a store or café. I drink tap water throughout France, filling my bottle in hotel rooms as I go.

## Sandwiches, Quiche, and Pizza

Throughout France, you'll find bakeries and small stands selling baguette sandwiches, quiche, and pizza-like items to go for €3–5. Usually filling and tasty, they also streamline the picnic process. (If you don't want your sandwich drenched in mayonnaise, ask for it *sans mayonnaise;* sahn my-oh-nehz). Here are some sandwiches you'll see:

*Jambon beurre* (zhahn-bohn bur): Ham and butter (boring for most).

*Fromage beurre* (froh-mahzh bur): Cheese and butter (white on white on beige).

*Poulet crudités* (poo-lay krew-dee-tay): Chicken with tomatoes, lettuce, carrots, and cucumbers.

*Thon crudités* (tohn krew-dee-tay): Tuna with tomatoes, lettuce, carrots, and cucumbers.

*Jambon crudités* (zhahn-bohn krew-dee-tay): Ham with tomatoes, lettuce, carrots, and cucumbers.

*Jambon* or *poulet à la provençal* (zhahn-bohn/poo-lay ah lah proh-vehn-sahl): Ham or chicken, usually with marinated peppers, tomatoes, and eggplant. I love these.

Look also for grilled *panini* sandwiches *à la italienne*.

# Coffee and Tea Lingo

By law, the waiter must give you a glass of tap water with your coffee or tea if you request it; ask for *"Un verre d'eau, s'il vous plaît"* (uhn vayr doh, see voo play).

## Coffee

| French | Pronounced | English |
|---|---|---|
| *un express* | uh nex-press | shot of espresso |
| *une noisette* | oon nwah-zeht | espresso with a shot of milk |
| *café au lait* | kah-fay oh lay | coffee with lots of steamed milk (closest to an American latte) |
| *un grand crème* | uhn grahn krehm | big café au lait |
| *un petit crème* | uhn puh-tee krehm | small café au lait |
| *un café allongé* (also called *café longue* or *café noir*) | uhn kah-fay ah-lohn-zhay (kah-fay lohn/ kah-fay nwar) | closest to an American cup of coffee |
| *un décaffiné* | uhn day-kah-fee-nay | decaf—available for any of the above drinks |

## Tea

| French | Pronounced | English |
|---|---|---|
| *un thé nature* | uhn tay nah-tour | plain tea |
| *un thé au lait* | uhn tay oh lay | tea with milk |
| *un thé citron* | uhn tay see-trohn | tea with lemon |
| *une infusion* | oon an-few-see-yohn | herbal tea |

## Café Culture

French cafés (and brasseries) provide budget-friendly meals and a refuge from museum and church overload. At a café, you can feel free to order only a bowl of soup or a salad or *plat* (main course) for lunch or dinner.

Cafés generally open by 7:00, but closing hours vary. Unlike restaurants, which open only for lunch and dinner and close in between, most cafés in bigger cities serve food throughout the day, making them the best option for a late lunch or early dinner. Note, though, that many cafés in smaller towns close their kitchens from about 14:00 until 18:00. Also, cafés generally have a more limited menu than restaurants.

If you're a novice, it's easier to sit and feel comfortable when you know the system. Check the price list first, which by law must be posted prominently. You'll see two sets of prices: you'll pay more for the same drink if you're seated at a table *(salle)* than if you're seated at the bar or counter *(comptoir)*.

**Standard Menu Items:** *Croque monsieur* (grilled ham-and-cheese sandwich) and *croque madame* (*monsieur* with a fried egg on top) are generally served day and night. Sandwiches are least expensive but plain—and much better at the *boulangerie* (bakery.) To get more than a piece of ham *(jambon)* on a baguette, order a sandwich *jambon crudité*, which means garnished with veggies. Omelets come lonely on a plate with a basket of bread. The daily special—*plat du jour* (plah dew zhoor), or just *plat*—is your fast, hearty, and garnished hot plate for €10–18. At most cafés, feel free to order only entrées (which in French means the starter course); many find these lighter and more interesting than a main course. A vegetarian can enjoy a tasty, filling meal by ordering two entrées. Regardless of what you order, bread is free; to get more, just hold up your bread basket and ask, *"Encore, s'il vous plaît."*

**Salads:** They're typically large—one is perfect for lunch or a light dinner, or split between two people as a first course. Among the classics are:

*Salade niçoise* (nee-swahz), a specialty from Nice, usually includes green salad topped with green beans, boiled potatoes, tomatoes, anchovies, olives, hard-boiled eggs, and lots of tuna.

*Salade au chèvre chaud* is a mixed green salad topped with warm goat cheese and toasted bread croutons.

*Salade composée* is "composed" of any number of ingredients, such as *lardons* (bacon), *comté* (a Swiss-style cheese), Roquefort (bleu cheese), *œuf* (egg), *noix* (walnuts), and *jambon* (ham, generally thinly sliced).

*Salade paysanne*, usually comes with potatoes *(pommes de terre)*, walnuts *(noix)*, tomatoes, ham, and egg.

*Salade aux gesiers* has chicken livers.

To get salad dressing on the side, order *la sauce à part* (lah sohs ah par).

For tips on beverages, see page 32.

## Restaurants

Choose restaurants filled with locals. Consider my suggestions and your hotelier's opinion, but trust your instinct. If a restaurant doesn't post its prices outside, move along. Refer to my restaurant recommendations to get a sense of what a reasonable meal should cost.

French restaurants usually open for dinner at 19:00 and are typically most crowded about 20:30 (the early bird gets the table). Last seating is usually about 21:00 or 22:00 in cities (even later in

# French Wine-Tasting 101

France is peppered with opportunities to taste wines. Look for vineyards posted with *Dégustation Gratuite* signs, which mean you're welcome to stop in for a free tasting. Some towns have *cave coopératives,* providing an excellent opportunity to taste wines from a number of local vintners in a single, less-intimidating setting (sometimes for a nominal price).

The American wine-tasting experience (I'm thinking Napa Valley) is generally informal, chatty, and entrepreneurial (baseball caps and golf shirts with logos). Throughout France, wine-tasting is a more serious, wine-focused experience.

Vintners are happy to work with you—if they can figure out what you want. When you enter a winery, it helps to know what you like (drier or sweeter, lighter or full-bodied, fruity or more tannic, and so on). The people serving you may know those words in English, but you're better off knowing and using the key words in French (see facing page).

For reds, you might be asked if you want to taste younger wines that still need maturing, or older wines, ready to drink now. (Whites and rosés are always ready to drink.) The French like to sample younger wines and determine how they will taste in a few years, which allows them to buy at cheaper prices and stash the bottles in their cellars. Americans want it now—for today's picnic. While many Americans like a big, full-bodied wine, most French tend to prefer more subtle flavors. They judge a wine by virtue of what food it would go well with—and a big, oaky wine would overwhelm most French cuisine (yes, even cheese courses).

Remember that the vintner is hoping that you'll buy at least a bottle or two. If you don't buy, you may be asked to pay a minimal fee for the tasting. They know that Americans can't take much wine with them, and they don't expect to make a big sale, but they do hope you'll look for their wines in the US. Some of the places I list will ship your purchase home—ask.

Paris and on the Riviera), and earlier in small villages during the off-season.

If a restaurant serves lunch, it generally begins at 11:30 and goes until 14:00, with last orders taken at about 13:30. In contrast, most cafés serve at least a limited menu all day. Go to a café if you're hungry when restaurants are closed (late afternoon), or anytime you want just a soup or salad.

If you ask for the *menu* (muh-noo) at a restaurant, you won't get a list of dishes; you'll get a fixed-price meal. *Menus,* which include three or four courses, are generally a good value if you're

## French Wine Lingo

Here are the steps you should follow when entering any wine-tasting:

1. Greetings, Sir/Madam: *Bonjour, Monsieur/Madame.*
2. We would like to taste a few wines.
   *Nous voudrions déguster quelques vins*
   (noo voo-dree-ohn day-goo-stay kehl-kuh van).
3. We want a wine that is _____ and _____.
   *Nous voudrions un vin _____ et _____*
   (noo voo-dree-ohn uhn van _____ ay _____).

Fill in the blanks with your favorites from this list:

| English | French | Pronounced |
|---|---|---|
| wine | *vin* | van |
| red | *rouge* | roozh |
| white | *blanc* | blahn |
| rosé | *rosé* | roh-zay |
| light | *léger* | lay-zhay |
| full-bodied, heavy | *robuste* | roh-boost |
| fruity | *fruité* | frwee-tay |
| sweet | *doux* | doo |
| tannic | *tannique* | tah-neek |
| jammy | *confituré* | koh-fee-tuh-ray |
| fine | *fin, avec finesse* | fahn, ah-vehk fee-nehs |
| ready to drink (mature) | *prêt à boire* | preh ah bwar |
| not ready to drink | *fermé* | fair-may |
| oaky | *goût de la chêne* | goo duh lah sheh-nuh |
| from old vines | *de vieille vignes* | duh vee-yay-ee veen-yah |
| sparkling | *pétillant* | pay-tee-yahn |

hungry: You'll get your choice of soup, appetizer, or salad; your choice of three or four main courses with vegetables; plus a cheese course and/or a choice of desserts. Service is included (*service compris* or *prix net*), but wine and other drinks are generally extra.

Many restaurants offer cheaper versions of their *menu*, with a choice of two rather than three or four courses. These pared-down *menus* are commonly called *formules* and feature an *entrée et plat* (first course and main dish), or *plat et dessert* (main dish and dessert). Most restaurants offer a *menu-enfant* (kids' menu).

Ask for *la carte* (lah kart) if you want to see a menu and order à la carte, like the locals do. Request the waiter's help in deciphering the French. Consider his or her recommendations and anything *de la maison* (of the house), as long as it's not an organ meat *(tripes, rognons,* and *andouillette).* Galloping gourmets should bring a menu translator; the *Marling Menu-Master* is good. The *Rick Steves' French Phrase Book,* with a menu decoder, works well for most travelers. Wines are often listed on a separate *carte des vins.*

Remember that in France an entrée is the first course, and *le plat* or *le plat du jour* is the main course with vegetables. At restaurants, it's common to order *une entrée* and *un plat,* or *un plat* and *un dessert,* or just *un plat* from *la carte.* Because small-size dinner salads are rare, I often split a big salad (of which several are usually available) with my companion, and get my own *plat principal* (this also works well for other starter courses). At better restaurants, it's considered inappropriate for two diners to share one main course.

At the end of your meal, your server is likely to ask if you're finished: *"Vous-avez terminé?"* (voo-zah-vay tehr-meen-nay). And then ask if you'd like anything else: *"Desirez-vous autre chose?"* (day-zee-ray-voo oh-truh shohz).

Restaurants are almost always a better value in the country-side than in Paris. If you're driving, look for red-and-blue *Relais Routier* decals on main roads outside cities, indicating that the place is recommended by the truckers' union. These truck-stop cafés offer inexpensive and hearty fare.

The local beer, which costs about €4 at a restaurant, is cheaper on tap *(une pression;* oon pres-yohn) than in the bottle *(bouteille;* boo-teh-ee). France's best beer is Alsatian; try Kronenbourg or the heavier Pelfort. *Une panaché* (oon pah-nah-shay) is a refreshing French shandy (beer and lemon soda).

**Regional Specialty Drinks:** For a refreshing before-dinner drink, order a *kir* (pronounced keer): a thumb's level of *crème de cassis* (black currant liqueur) topped with white wine. If you like brandy, try a *marc* (regional brandy, e.g., *marc de Bourgogne)* or an Armagnac, cognac's cheaper twin brother. *Pastis,* the standard southern France aperitif, is a sweet anise (licorice) drink that comes on the rocks with a glass of water. Cut it to taste with lots of water.

## Beverages at Cafés and Restaurants

**Water:** The French are willing to pay for bottled water with their meal *(eau minérale;* oh mee-nay-rahl) because they prefer the taste over tap water. Badoit is my favorite carbonated water *(l'eau gazeuse;* loh gah-zuhz). If you prefer a free pitcher of tap water, ask for *une carafe d'eau* (oon kah-rahf doh). Otherwise, you may unwittingly buy bottled water.

**Coffee and Tea:** See "Coffee and Tea Lingo" on page 28.

**Wine and Beer:** House wine at the bar is generally cheap and good (about €3 per glass at modestly priced places). At a restaurant, a bottle or carafe of house wine costs €8–18. To get inexpensive wine, order regional table wine (*un vin du pays;* uhn van duh pay) in a pitcher (*un pichet;* uhn pee-shay), rather than a bottle. Note though, that finer restaurants usually offer only bottles of wine.

If all you want is a glass of wine, ask for *un verre de vin rouge* for red wine or *blanc* for white wine (uhn vehr duh van roozh/blahn). A half-carafe of wine is *un demi-pichet* (uhn duh-mee pee-shay); a quarter-carafe (ideal for one) is *un quart* (uhn kar).

**Soft Drinks:** These cost about €4 in restaurants. Kids love the local lemonade; ask for *citron pressé* (see-trohn preh-say) and add sugar. If you order a *lemonade,* you'll get 7-Up or Sprite. The flavored syrups mixed with bottled water (*sirops à l'eau;* see-roh ah loh) are kid- and adult-friendly. Be adventurous and try *un diablo menthe* (uhn dee-ah-bloh mahnt; 7-Up with mint syrup) or *un diablo pêche* (pehsh; 7-Up with peach syrup). The ice cubes have melted since the last Yankee tour group left.

## French Cuisine

The following listing of items found commonly throughout France should help you navigate a typical French menu. For dishes specific to each region, see the "Cuisine Scene" section in every chapter but Paris (which borrows cuisines from all regions).

### First Course (Entrée)

*Salades:* With the exception of a *salade mixte* (simple green salad, often difficult to find), the French get creative with their *salades.* (See page 29, in "Café Culture", for good salad suggestions.)

*Crudités:* Made of raw and lightly cooked fresh vegetables, this mix usually includes grated carrots, celery root, tomatoes, and beets, often with a hefty dose of vinaigrette dressing. Remember that you can get the dressing on the side by requesting *la sauce à part* (lah sohs ah par).

*Escargots:* The snails of this famous French dish are usually cooked in parsley-garlic butter. You don't even have to like the snail itself. Just dipping your bread in garlic butter is more than satisfying. Prepared a variety of ways, the classic is *à la bourguignonne* (served in their shells).

*Huîtres:* Oysters, served raw any month, are particularly popular at Christmas and on New Year's Eve.

*Pâtés* and *Terrines:* Slowly cooked, ground meat (usually pork, though chicken and rabbit are also common) is highly seasoned and served in slices with mustard and *cornichons* (little pickles). Pâtés are smoother than the similarly prepared but chunkier *terrines.*

**Foie Gras:** Rich, buttery in consistency, and pricey, foie gras is made from the swollen livers of force-fed geese *(foie gras d'oie)* or ducks *(foie gras de canard)*. Spread it on toast with your knife, and never add mustard. For a real French experience, try this dish with some sweet white wine (often offered by the glass for an additional cost). For more on foie gras, see the sidebar on page 356.

## Main Course (Plat Principal)

Duck, lamb, and rabbit are popular in France, and each is prepared in a variety of ways. You'll also encounter various stew-like dishes that vary by region. The most common regional specialties are available almost everywhere and are described below.

**Coq au vin:** Native to Burgundy, this dish consists of rooster marinated ever so slowly in red wine, then cooked until it melts in your mouth. It's served (often family-style) with vegetables.

**Bœuf bourguignon:** Another Burgundian specialty, this classy beef stew is cooked slowly in red wine, with onions, potatoes, and mushrooms.

**Gigot d'agneau:** A specialty of Provence, a leg of lamb often grilled and served with white beans.

**Confit de canard:** A Southwest favorite from the Dordogne region is duck that has been preserved and cooked, and often served, in the same fat with potatoes (which have also been cooked in the fat). Not for dieters.

**Steak:** Referred to as *pavé*, *bavette*, or *entrecôte*, French steak is usually thinner than American steak and is always served with sauces (*au poivre* is a pepper sauce; *une sauce roquefort* is a bleu-cheese sauce). You will also see *steak haché*, which is a lean, gourmet hamburger patty served *sans* bun. By American standards, the French undercook meats: rare, or *saignant* (seh-nyahn), is close to raw; medium, or *à point* (ah pwan), is rare; and well-done, or *bien cuit* (bee-yehn kwee), is medium.

**Steak tartare:** This wonderfully French dish is for adventurous types only. It's very lean, raw hamburger served with spices (usually Tabasco, onions, salt, and pepper on the side) and topped with a raw egg.

**Saumon and truite:** You'll see salmon dishes served in various styles. Like steak, salmon always comes with sauce, most commonly a sorrel *(oiselle)* sauce. Trout *(truite)* is also fairly routine on menus.

**Daube:** Generally made with beef but sometimes lamb, this is a long and slowly simmered dish, typically paired with noodles or other pasta.

## Cheese Course (Le Fromage)

In France, the cheese course is served just before (or instead of) dessert. It not only helps with digestion, it gives you a great opportunity

> ## How Was Your Trip?
>
> Were your travels fun, smooth, and meaningful? If you'd like to share your tips, concerns, and discoveries, please fill out the survey at www.ricksteves.com/feedback. I value your feedback. Thanks in advance—it helps a lot.

to sample the tasty regional cheeses. Many restaurants will offer a cheese platter from which you select a few different cheeses. A good cheese plate has four cheeses: a hard cheese (such as Emmentaler—a.k.a., "Swiss cheese"), a flowery cheese (like Brie or Camembert), a bleu or Roquefort cheese, and a goat cheese. Those most commonly served are *brie de Meaux* (mild and creamy, from just outside Paris), Camembert (semi-creamy and pungent, from Normandy), *chèvre* (goat cheese with a sharp taste, usually from the Loire), and Roquefort (strong and blue-veined, from south-central France). If you'd like a little of several types of cheese from the cheese plate, say: *"Un assortiment, s'il vous plaît"* (uhn ah-sor-tee-mahn, see voo play). If you serve yourself from the cheese plate, observe French etiquette and keep the shape of the cheese. It's best to politely shave off a slice from the side or cut small wedges.

## Dessert (Le Dessert)

Here are typical desserts you'll find on many menus:

*Crème brûlée:* A rich, creamy, dense, and caramelized custard.

*Tarte tatin:* This is apple pie like grandma never made, with caramelized apples cooked upside down, but served upright.

*Mousse au chocolat:* Chocolate mousse.

*Ile flottante:* This lighter dessert consists of islands of meringue floating on a pond of custard sauce.

*Profiteroles:* Cream puffs filled with vanilla ice cream, smothered in warm chocolate sauce.

*Tartes:* Narrow strips of fresh fruit, baked in a crust and served in thin slices (without ice cream).

*Sorbets:* Known to us as sherbets, these light, flavorful, and fruity ices are sometimes laced with brandy. *Citron* (lemon) and *citron-vert* (lime) are particularly popular and refreshing.

*Glaces:* Ice cream, typically vanilla, chocolate, or strawberry *(fraise)*.

## Coffee (Café)

If you order espresso at a restaurant, it will always come after dessert. To have coffee with dessert, ask for *"café avec le dessert"* (kah-fay ah-vehk luh day-sayr). For more on tea and coffee, see page 28.

## TRAVELING AS A TEMPORARY LOCAL

We travel all the way to Europe to enjoy differences—to become temporary locals. You'll experience frustrations. Certain truths that we find "God-given" or "self-evident," such as cold beer, ice in drinks, bottomless cups of coffee, hot showers, and bigger being better, are suddenly not so true. One of the benefits of travel is the eye-opening realization that there are logical, civil, and even better alternatives.

With a history rich in human achievement, France is an understandably proud country. To enjoy its people, you need to celebrate the differences. A willingness to go local ensures that you'll enjoy a full dose of French hospitality.

If there is a negative aspect to the image the French have of Americans (apart from our foreign policy), it's that we are big, loud, aggressive, impolite, rich, superficially friendly, and a bit naive.

The French place a high value on speaking quietly in restaurants and on trains. Listen while on the bus or in a restaurant—the place can be packed, but the decibel level is low. Try to adjust your volume accordingly to show respect for their culture.

While the French look bemusedly at some of our Yankee excesses—and worriedly at others—they nearly always afford us individual travelers all the warmth we deserve. Judging from all the happy feedback I receive from travelers who have used this book, it's safe to assume you'll enjoy a great, affordable vacation—with the finesse of an independent, experienced traveler.

Thanks, and *bon voyage!*

# BACK DOOR TRAVEL PHILOSOPHY
### From *Rick Steves' Europe Through the Back Door*

Travel is intensified living—maximum thrills per minute and one of the last great sources of legal adventure. Travel is freedom. It's recess, and we need it.

Experiencing the real Europe requires catching it by surprise, going casual..."Through the Back Door."

Affording travel is a matter of priorities. (Make do with the old car.) You can travel—simply, safely, and comfortably—nearly anywhere in Europe for $120 a day plus transportation costs (allow more for bigger cities). In many ways, spending more money only builds a thicker wall between you and what you came to see. Europe is a cultural carnival, and, time after time, you'll find that its best acts are free and the best seats are the cheap ones.

A tight budget forces you to travel close to the ground, meeting and communicating with the people, not relying on service with a purchased smile. Never sacrifice sleep, nutrition, safety, or cleanliness in the name of budget. Simply enjoy the local-style alternatives to expensive hotels and restaurants.

Extroverts have more fun. If your trip is low on magic moments, kick yourself and make things happen. If you don't enjoy a place, maybe you don't know enough about it. Seek the truth. Recognize tourist traps. Give a culture the benefit of your open mind. See things as different but not better or worse. Any culture has much to share.

Of course, travel, like the world, is a series of hills and valleys. Be fanatically positive and militantly optimistic. If something's not to your liking, change your liking. Travel is addictive. It can make you a happier American as well as a citizen of the world. Our Earth is home to six and a half billion equally important people. It's humbling to travel and find that people don't envy Americans. Europeans like us, but, with all due respect, they wouldn't trade passports.

Globe-trotting destroys ethnocentricity. It helps you understand and appreciate different cultures. Regrettably, there are forces in our society that want you dumbed down for their convenience. Don't let it happen. Thoughtful travel engages you with the world—more important than ever these days. Travel changes people. It broadens perspectives and teaches new ways to measure quality of life. Rather than fear the diversity on this planet, travelers celebrate it. Many travelers toss aside their hometown blinders. Their prized souvenirs are the strands of different cultures they decide to knit into their own character. The world is a cultural yarn shop, and Back Door travelers are weaving the ultimate tapestry. Join in!

# PARIS

Paris—the City of Light—has been a beacon of culture for centuries. As a world capital of art, fashion, food, literature, and ideas, it stands as a symbol of all the fine things human civilization can offer. Come prepared to celebrate, rather than judge, the cultural differences, and you'll capture the romance and joie de vivre that Paris exudes.

Paris offers sweeping boulevards, chatty crêpe stands, chic boutiques, and world-class art galleries. Sip decaf with deconstructionists at a sidewalk café, then step into an Impressionist painting in a tree-lined park. Climb Notre-Dame and rub shoulders with the gargoyles. Cruise the Seine, zip up the Eiffel Tower, and saunter down avenue des Champs-Elysées. Master the Louvre and Orsay museums. Save some after-dark energy for one of the world's most romantic cities.

## Planning Your Time

For three very busy but doable days in Paris, I've listed sights in descending order of importance in the planning sections below. Therefore, if you have only one day, just do Day 1; for two days, add Day 2; and so on. When planning where to plug in Versailles (see next chapter), remember that the Château is closed on Mondays and especially crowded on Sundays and Tuesdays—try to avoid these days. For other itinerary considerations on a day-by-day basis, check the "Daily Reminder" on page 43.

### Day 1
**Morning:** Follow this book's Historic Paris Walk, featuring Ile de la Cité, Notre-Dame, the Latin Quarter, and Sainte-Chapelle.

**Afternoon:** Tour the Louvre.

**Evening:** Enjoy the Trocadéro scene and a twilight ride up the Eiffel Tower.

### Day 2

**Morning:** Wander the Champs-Elysées from the Arc de Triomphe down the grand avenue des Champs-Elysées to Tuileries Garden.

**Midday:** Cross the pedestrian bridge from the Tuileries Garden, then tour the Orsay Museum.

**Afternoon:** Tour the Rodin Museum, or the Army Museum and Napoleon's Tomb.

**Evening:** Cruise the Seine River, take Paris Vision's nighttime Illumination bus tour, or consider taking in a jazz club, cabaret, concert, or opera (see the Nightlife section later in this chapter).

### Day 3

**Morning:** Ride the RER suburban train out to Versailles.

**Afternoon:** Stroll the Marais neighborhood.

**Evening:** Visit Montmartre and the Sacré-Cœur basilica.

## ORIENTATION

Paris (population of city center: 2,170,000) is split in half by the Seine River, divided into 20 arrondissements (proud and independent governmental jurisdictions), circled by a ring-road freeway (the *périphérique*), and speckled with Métro stations. You'll find Paris easier to navigate if you know which side of the river you're on, which arrondissement you're in, and which Métro stop you're closest to. If you're north of the river (the top half of any city map), you're on the Right Bank (Rive Droite). If you're south of it, you're on the Left Bank (Rive Gauche). The bull's-eye of your Paris map is Notre-Dame, which sits on an island in the middle of the Seine. Most of your sightseeing will take place within five blocks of the river.

Arrondissements are numbered, starting at the Louvre and moving in a clockwise spiral out to the ring road. The last two digits in a Parisian zip

## Paris Neighborhoods

code are the arrondissement number. The abbreviation for "Métro stop" is "Mo." In Parisian jargon, the Eiffel Tower is on *la Rive Gauche* (the Left Bank) in the *7ème* (7th arrondissement), zip code 75007, Mo: Trocadéro.

Paris Métro stops are used as a standard aid in giving directions, even for those not using the Métro. As you're tracking down addresses, these words and pronunciations will help: Métro (may-troh), *place* (plahs—square), *rue* (roo—road), *avenue* (ah-vuh-noo), *boulevard* (boo-luh-var), and *pont* (pohn—bridge).

## Tourist Information

Paris tourist offices (abbreviated as **TI** in this book) have long lines, offer little information, and may charge for maps. But all you really need are this book and one of the freebie maps available at any hotel (or in the front of this book). Paris' TIs share a single phone number: 08 92 68 30 00 (from the US, dial 011 33 8 92 68 30 00).

If you must visit a TI, you can do so at several locations, including **Pyramides** (daily 9:00–19:00, at Pyramides Métro stop between the Louvre and Opéra), **Gares de Lyon and Nord** (both Mon–Sat 8:00–18:00, closed Sun), and **Montmartre** (daily 10:00–19:00, place du Tertre). The official website for Paris' TIs is www.parisinfo.com. Both **airports** have handy information offices (called ADP) with long hours and short lines (see "Airports," page 159).

*Pariscope:* The weekly €0.40 *Pariscope* magazine (or one of its clones, available at any newsstand) lists museum hours, art exhibits, concerts, festivals, plays, movies, and nightclubs. Smart sightseers rely on this for the latest listings.

**Other Publications:** Look for the *Paris Times,* which provides helpful English information and fresh insights into living in Paris (available at English-language bookstores, French-American establishments, the American Church, and online at www.the paristimes.com). The *Paris Voice,* with snappy reviews of concerts, plays, and current events, is available only online at www.paris voice.com. For a schedule of museum hours and English museum tours, pick up the free *Musées, Monuments Historiques, et Expositions* booklet at any museum.

**American Church and Franco-American Center:** This interdenominational church—in the rue Cler neighborhood, facing the river between the Eiffel Tower and Orsay Museum—is a nerve center for the American émigré community. Worship services are at 9:00 and 11:00 on Sunday; the coffee hour after church and the free Sunday concerts (generally Sept–June at 17:00—but not every week) are a good way get a taste of émigré life in Paris (reception open Mon–Sat 9:00–12:00 & 13:00–22:00, Sun 14:30–19:00, 65 quai d'Orsay, Mo: Invalides, tel. 01 40 62 05 00, www.acparis.org). It's also a handy place to pick up free copies of *Paris Times* (above) and *France-USA Contacts* (an advertisement paper with info on housing and employment for the 30,000 Americans living in Paris, www.fusac.fr).

## Arrival in Paris

For a comprehensive rundown of Paris' train stations and airports, see "Transportation Connections," page 152.

## Helpful Hints

**Heightened Security** *(Plan Vigipirate):* You may notice an abundance of police at monuments, on streets, and on the Métro, as well as security cameras at key sights. You'll go through quick and reassuring airport-like security checks at many major attractions. This is all part of Paris' anti-terror plan. The police are helpful, the security lines move quickly, and there are now fewer pickpocket problems on the Métro.

**Theft Alert:** Although the greater police presence has scared off some, troublesome thieves still thrive near famous monuments and on Métro and RER lines that serve high-profile tourist sights. Wear a money belt, put your wallet in your front pocket, loop your day bag over your shoulders, and keep a tight grip on your purse or shopping bag. Muggings are rare, but do occur. If you're out late, avoid the dark riverfront embankments and any place where the lighting is dim and pedestrian activity is minimal.

**Tourist Scams:** Be aware of the latest scams, including these current favorites. The "found ring" scam involves an innocent-looking person who picks up a ring on the ground, and asks if you dropped it. When you say no, the person examines the ring more closely, then shows you a mark "proving" that it's pure gold. He offers to sell it to you for a good price—several times more than he paid for it before dropping it on the sidewalk.

In the "friendship bracelet" scam, a vendor approaches you and asks if you'll help him with a demonstration. He proceeds to make a friendship bracelet right on your arm. When finished, he asks you to pay for the bracelet he created just for you. And since you can't easily take it off on the spot, he counts on you feeling obliged to pay up.

Distractions by "salesmen" can also function as a smoke-screen for theft—an accomplice picks your pocket as you try to wriggle away from a pushy vendor.

In popular tourist spots (such as in front of Notre-Dame) young ladies politely ask if you speak English, then pretend to beg for money while actually angling to pick your pocket.

**Street Safety:** Parisian drivers are notorious for ignoring pedestrians. Look both ways (many streets are one-way) and be careful of seemingly quiet bus/taxi lanes. Don't assume you have the right of way, even in a crosswalk. When crossing a street, keep your pace constant and don't stop suddenly. By law, drivers can miss pedestrians by up to just one meter—a little more than three feet (1.5 meters in the countryside). Drivers carefully calculate your speed and won't hit you, provided you don't alter your route or pace.

Paris' new "Vélib'" bike program, which offers short-term rentals to locals, means that more bikes than ever are on the roads (see "Bike Freedom for Parisians" on page 51). When crossing streets, beware of this silent transportation.

**Paris Museum Pass:** This worthwhile pass, covering most sights in Paris, is sold at TIs and museums. For detailed information, see page 68.

**Museum Strategy:** When possible, visit key museums first thing (when your energy is best) and save other activities for the afternoon. Remember, most museums require you to check daypacks and coats, and important museums have metal detectors that will slow your entry. The Louvre, Orsay, and Pompidou are open on selected nights (see "Paris at a Glance," page 66), making for peaceful visits with fewer crowds.

**Bookstores:** There are many English-language bookstores in Paris, where you can pick up guidebooks (at nearly double

# Daily Reminder

**Monday:** These sights are closed today: Orsay, Rodin, Marmottan, Carnavalet, Catacombs, Petit Palais, Victor Hugo's House, Montmartre Museum, Quai Branly, and Paris Archaeological Crypt. Giverny and the Château at Versailles are also closed (see next chapter); the Louvre and Eiffel Tower are more crowded because of these closings. The Army Museum (and Napoleon's Tomb) is closed the first Monday of each month in winter (Oct–May). Some small stores don't open until 14:00. Street markets such as rue Cler and rue Mouffetard are dead today. Some banks are closed. It's discount night at most cinemas.

**Tuesday:** Many museums are closed today, including the Louvre, Orangerie, Cluny, Pompidou, Picasso, and National Maritime, as well as the Grand Palais. The Eiffel Tower, Orsay, Versailles, and Giverny are particularly busy today.

**Wednesday:** All sights are open (Louvre until 21:45). The weekly *Pariscope* magazine comes out today. Most schools are closed, so many kids' sights are busy. Some cinemas offer discounts.

**Thursday:** All sights are open except the Sewer Tour. The Orsay is open until 21:45. Some department stores are open late.

**Friday:** All sights are open (Louvre until 21:45 and Orangerie until 21:00) except the Sewer Tour. Afternoon trains and roads leaving Paris are crowded; TGV train reservation fees are higher.

**Saturday:** All sights are open except the Jewish Art and History Museum and the Holocaust Memorial. The fountains run at Versailles (April–Sept). Department stores are jammed. The Jewish Quarter is quiet.

**Sunday:** Many sights are free the first Sunday of the month, including the Louvre, Orsay, Rodin, Cluny, and Picasso museums, the Arc de Triomphe (Oct–March only), and Pompidou Center. These free days at popular museums attract hordes of visitors.

Versailles is more crowded than usual on Sunday—but on the upside, the garden's fountains are running (April–Sept). Most of Paris' stores are closed on Sunday, but shoppers will find relief in the Marais neighborhood's lively Jewish Quarter, where many stores are open. Look for organ concerts at St. Sulpice and possibly other churches. The American Church often hosts a free evening concert (generally Sept–June at 17:00—but not every week). Many recommended restaurants in the rue Cler neighborhood are closed for dinner.

their American prices). Most carry this book. My favorite is the friendly **Red Wheelbarrow Bookstore** in the Marais neighborhood, run by mellow Penelope (Mon–Sat 10:00–19:00, Sun 14:00–18:00, 22 rue St. Paul, Mo: St. Paul, tel. 01 48 04 75 08). Others include **Shakespeare and Company** (some used travel books, daily 12:00–24:00, 37 rue de la Bûcherie, across the river from Notre-Dame, Mo: St. Michel, tel. 01 43 26 96 50), **W. H. Smith** (Mon–Sat 10:00–19:00, closed Sun, 248 rue de Rivoli, Mo: Concorde, tel. 01 44 77 88 99), **Brentanos** (Mon–Sat 10:00–19:00, closed Sun, 37 avenue de l'Opéra, Mo: Opéra, tel. 01 42 61 52 50), and **Village Voice** (Mon 14:00–19:00, Tue–Sat 10:00–19:00, Sun 12:00–18:00, near St. Sulpice Church at 6 rue Princesse, tel. 01 46 33 36 47).

**Public WCs:** Public toilets are free (though it's polite to leave a small tip if there's an attendant). Modern, sanitary street-booth toilets provide both relief and a memory (don't leave small children inside unattended). The restrooms in museums are free and the best you'll find. Or walk into any sidewalk café like you own the place, and find the toilet in the back. Keep toilet paper or tissues with you, as some toilets are poorly supplied.

**Parking:** Most of the time, drivers must pay to park curbside (buy parking card at *tabac* shops—see below), but not at night (19:00–9:00), all day Sunday, or anytime in August, when many Parisians are on vacation. There are parking garages under Ecole Militaire, St. Sulpice Church, Les Invalides, the Bastille, and the Panthéon; all charge about €20–27 per day (it's cheaper per hour the longer you stay). Some hotels offer parking for less—ask.

**Tobacco Stands** *(Tabacs):* These little kiosks—usually just a counter inside a café—sell cards for parking meters, public-transit tickets (usually), postage stamps, and...oh yeah, cigarettes. To find one anywhere in Paris, just look for a *Tabac* sign and the red, cylinder-shaped symbol above some (but not all) cafés.

## Getting Around Paris

Paris is easy to navigate. Your basic choices are Métro (in-city subway), RER (suburban rail tied into the Métro system), public bus, and taxi. (Also consider the hop-on, hop-off bus and boat tours, described under "Tours" on page 52.) You can buy tickets and passes at most *tabacs* (tobacco stands) and at Métro stations. While most Métro stations have staffed ticket windows, some smaller stations have only ticket-vending machines, for which you'll need coins (some take bills).

**Public-Transit Tickets:** The Métro, RER, and buses all work on the same tickets. (You can transfer between the Métro and RER on a single ticket, but combining a Métro or RER trip with a bus ride takes two tickets.) A **single ticket** costs €1.50. To save 25 percent, buy a *carnet* (kar-nay) of 10 tickets for €11.10 (that's €1.11 per ticket—€0.39 cheaper than a single ticket). It's less expensive for kids (ages 4–10 pay €5.50 for a *carnet*). *Carnets* can be shared between travelers.

**Passes:** The transit system has introduced a new chip-card, called the **Passe Navigo Découverte,** but for most tourists, *carnets* are still the better deal. The new Passe costs €21.50, runs Monday–Sunday (expires on Sun, even if you buy it on Fri), and requires a photo, which means it's not shareable. In contrast, two 10-packs of *carnets*—enough for most travelers staying a week—cost €22.50, are shareable, and don't expire until they're used.

If you do want the pass, ask for the *"Passe Navigo Découverte hebdomadaire"* (pahs nah-vee-go day-koo-vairt ehb-doh-mah-dair) and supply a small postage-stamp-size photo of yourself (bring your own, or use the €4 photo booths in major Métro stations). You buy a chip-embedded card (€5 one-time cost), then "load" a weekly value onto it (€16.50); this gives you free run of the bus and Métro system. At the Métro/bus turnstile, you scan your Passe to enter, and you're on your way.

A month-long version costs about €54—request a Passe Navigo *mensuelle* (mahn-soo-ehl, good from the first day of the month to the last, also requires photo). The pass covers only central Paris. You can pay more for passes covering regional destinations (such as Versailles), but for most visitors, this is a bad value. Instead, buy individual tickets for longer-distance destinations.

The overpriced **Paris Visite** passes were designed for tourists and offer minor reductions at minor sights (1 day/€9, 2 days/€14, 3 days/€19, 5 days/€28), but you'll get a better value with a cheaper *carnet* of 10 tickets or a Passe Navigo Découverte.

## By Métro

In Paris, you're never more than a 10-minute walk from a Métro station. Europe's best subway allows you to hop from sight to sight quickly and cheaply (runs daily 5:30–24:30 in the morning). Learn to use it. Color Métro maps are free at Métro stations, and included on freebie Paris maps at your hotel.

**Beware of Pickpockets:** Thieves dig the Métro. Be on guard. For example, if your pocket is picked as you pass through a turnstile, you end up stuck on the wrong side (after the turnstile bar has closed behind you) while the thief gets away. Stand away from Métro doors to avoid being a target for a theft-and-run just before the doors close. Any jostling or commotion—especially when boarding or leaving

## Métro Basics

- The same tickets are good on the Métro, RER (within the city), and city buses (but not to transfer between Métro/RER and bus).
- Save money by buying a *carnet* of tickets.
- Find your train by its end-of-the-line stops.
- Insert your ticket into the turnstile (brown stripe down), retrieve it, and keep it until the end of your journey.
- Beware of pickpockets, and don't buy tickets from men roaming the stations.
- Transfers *(correspondances)* within the Métro or RER system are free.
- At the end of your trip, choose the right exit *(sortie)* to avoid extra walking.
- Dispose of used tickets after your ride is completed (not before), to avoid confusing them with fresh ones.
- On some trains you must activate the door by pushing a button (but most open automatically).

### Key Words for the Métro and RER

| French | Pronounced | English |
| --- | --- | --- |
| *direction* | dee-rek-see-ohn | direction |
| *ligne* | leen-yuh | line |
| *correspondance* | kor-res-pohn-dahns | transfer |
| *sortie* | sor-tee | exit |

trains—is likely the sign of a thief or a team of thieves in action. Make any fare inspector show proof of identity (ask locals for help if you're not certain). Never show anyone your wallet.

**How the Métro Works:** To get to your destination, determine the closest "Mo" stop and which line or lines will get you there. The lines have numbers, but they're best known by their end-of-the-line stops. (For example, the La Défense/Château de Vincennes line, also known as line 1, runs between La Défense in the west and Vincennes in the east.) Once in the Métro station, you'll see blue-and-white signs directing you to the train going in your direction (e.g., *direction: La Défense*). Insert your ticket in the automatic turnstile, pass through, reclaim your ticket, and keep it until you exit the system (some stations require you to pass your ticket through a turnstile to exit). *Fare inspectors regularly check for cheaters and accept absolutely no excuses, so keep that ticket!*

Transfers are free and can be made wherever lines cross, providing you do so within 90 minutes. When you transfer, look for the orange *correspondance* (connection) signs when you exit your first train, then follow the proper direction sign.

| French | Pronounced | English |
|--------|-----------|---------|
| *carnet* | kar-nay | cheap set of 10 tickets |
| *Pardon, madame/monsieur.* | par-dohn, mah-dahm/ mes-yur | Excuse me, ma'am/ sir. |
| *Je descends.* | juh day-sahn | I'm getting off. |
| *Donnez-moi mon porte-monnaie!* | duh-nay-mwah mohn port-moh-nay | Give me back my wallet! |

**PARIS**

### Etiquette

- When waiting at the platform, get out of the way of those exiting the train. Board only once everyone is off.
- Avoid using the hinged seats near the doors of some trains when the car is jammed; they take up valuable standing space.
- In a crowded train, try not to block the exit. If you're blocking the door when the train stops, step out of the car and to the side, let others off, then get back on.
- Talk softly in the cars. Listen to how quietly Parisians communicate and follow their lead.
- On escalators, stand on the right and pass on the left.
- When leaving a station, hold the door for the person behind you.

Even though the Métro whisks you quickly from one point to another, be prepared to walk significant distances within stations to

reach your platform (most noticeable when you transfer). Escalators are common, but they're often out of order. To limit excessive walking, avoid transferring at these sprawling stations: Montparnasse-Bienvenüe, Châtelet–Les Halles, Charles de Gaulle–Etoile, Gare du Nord, and Bastille.

Before taking the *sortie* (exit) to leave the Métro, check the helpful *plan du quartier* (map of the neighborhood) to get your bearings, locate your destination, and decide which *sortie* you want. At stops with several *sorties*, you can save lots of walking by choosing the best exit.

After you exit the system, toss or tear your used ticket so you don't confuse it with your unused ticket—they look virtually identical.

## By RER

The RER (Réseau Express Régionale; air-ay-air) is the suburban arm of the Métro, serving outlying destinations (such as Versailles, Disneyland Paris, and the airports). These routes are indicated by thick lines on your subway map and identified by the letters A, B, C, and so on. Some routes are operated by France's railroad (SNCF) and are called Transilien; they function the same way and use the same tickets as the RER. For all of these trains, you need to insert your ticket in a turnstile to exit the system.

Within the city center, the RER works like the Métro, but can be speedier (if it serves your destination directly) because it makes fewer stops. Métro tickets and the Passe Navigo card are good on the RER when traveling in the city center. (You can transfer between the Métro and RER systems with the same ticket.) But to travel outside the city (to Versailles or the airport, for example), you'll need to buy a separate, more expensive ticket at the station window (or, to save time, at a ticket-vending machine) before boarding. Also, unlike the Métro, not every train stops at every station along the way; check the sign over the platform to see if your destination is listed as a stop (*"toutes les gares"* means it makes all stops along the way), or confirm with a local before you board.

## By City Bus

Paris' excellent bus system is worth figuring out. Remember, even though buses use the same tickets as the Métro and RER, you can't use a single ticket to transfer between the systems—though you can transfer from one bus to another (within 90 minutes, though doesn't work with tickets bought on board). One ticket buys you a bus ride anywhere in central Paris—but if you leave the city center (shown as zone 1 on the diagram aboard the bus), you must validate a second ticket.

Buses don't seem as romantic as the famous Métro and are subject to traffic jams, but savvy travelers know that buses can have you swinging through the city like Tarzan in an urban jungle. Anywhere you are, you can generally see a bus stop, and every stop comes complete with all the information you need: a good city bus map, route maps showing exactly where each bus that uses this stop goes, a frequency chart and schedule, a *plan du quartier* map of the immediate neighborhood, and a *soirées* map explaining night service, if available. While the Métro shuts down about 24:30 in the morning, some buses continue much later (called *Noctilien* lines, www.noctilien.fr).

Enter buses through the front door. Punch your ticket in the machine behind the driver, scan your Passe Navigo, or pay the higher cash fare to get your ticket from the driver.

**PARIS**

## Key Buses for Tourists

Of Paris' many bus routes, these are some of the most scenic. They provide a great, cheap, and convenient introduction to the city.

**Bus #69** runs east-west between the Eiffel Tower and Père Lachaise Cemetery by way of rue Cler (recommended hotels), quai d'Orsay, the Louvre, and the Marais (recommended hotels). For a self-guided tour, see "Bus #69 Sightseeing Tour" on page 53.

**Bus #87** also links the Marais and rue Cler areas, but stays mostly on the Left Bank, connecting the Eiffel Tower, St. Sulpice, Luxembourg Garden (more recommended hotels and restaurants), St. Germain-des-Prés, the Latin Quarter, the Bastille, and Gare de Lyon.

**Bus #24** runs east-west along the Seine riverbank from Gare St. Lazare to Madeleine, Place de la Concorde, Orsay Museum, the Louvre, St. Michel, Notre-Dame, and Jardin des Plantes, all the way to Bercy Village (cafés and shops).

**Bus #63** is another good east-west route, connecting the Marmottan Museum, Trocadéro (Eiffel Tower), pont de l'Alma, Orsay Museum, St. Sulpice, Luxembourg Garden, Latin Quarter/Panthéon, and Gare de Lyon.

(Remember: Tickets purchased from drivers do not allow transfers between buses). When you reach your destination, push the red button to signal you want a stop, then exit through the rear door. Even if you're not certain you've figured out the system, do some joy-riding (outside of rush hour: Mon–Fri 8:00–9:30 & 17:30–19:30). Be warned: Not all city buses are air-conditioned, so they can become rolling greenhouses on summer days. For information on some of Paris' most scenic and convenient routes, see "Key Buses for Tourists" above. Handy bus-system maps *(plan des autobus)* are available in any Métro station (and in the €6 *Paris Pratique* map book sold at newsstands). Major stops are displayed on the side of each bus. I've also listed the handiest bus routes for each recommended hotel neighborhood (see "Sleeping," page 109).

### By Taxi

Parisian taxis are reasonable, especially for couples and families. The meters are tamper-proof. Fares and supplements (described in English on the rear windows) are straightforward and tightly regulated.

A taxi can fit three people comfortably, and cabbies are legally required to accept four passengers at a time (you'll be charged €3 extra for the fourth person). Groups of up to five can use a *grand taxi*, which must be booked in advance—ask your hotelier to call.

Key Bus Routes

LEGEND

#24 - - -     #69 —
#63 - - -     #87 ····

PARIS

**Rates:** All Parisian taxis charge a €5.20 minimum. A 10-minute ride (e.g., Bastille to Eiffel Tower) costs about €12 (versus €1.11 per person to get anywhere in town using a *carnet* ticket on the Métro or bus). Higher rates are charged at rush hour and at night (17:00–10:00), all day Sunday, and to any of the airports. Your first bag is free; additional pieces of luggage are €1 each. To tip, round up to the next euro (at least €0.50).

**How to Catch *un Taxi:*** You can try waving down a taxi, but it's often easier to ask someone for the nearest taxi stand (*"Où est une station de taxi?"*; oo ay ewn stah-see-ohn duh taxi). Taxi stands are indicated by a circled "T" on good city maps, and on many maps in this book. When you summon a taxi by phone, the meter starts running as soon as the call is received, often adding €5 or more to the bill.

Taxis are tough to find during rush hour, when it's raining, and on Friday and Saturday nights, especially after the Métro closes (around 24:30 in the morning). If you need to catch a train or flight early in the morning, book a taxi the day before. Your hotelier can help.

## By Bike

Paris is surprisingly good by bicycle. Riders enjoy plenty of bike lanes, and the extensive parks have bike-friendly paths that enable anyone on two wheels to get around easily. I biked along the river from Notre-Dame to the Eiffel Tower in 15 minutes. The tourist board has a fine "Paris à Vélo" map showing all the dedicated bike paths.

**Fat Tire Bike Tours** (listed under "Tours," page 55) rents bikes *sans* tour for independent types (€2.50/hr, €15/24 hrs, includes helmets and locks, credit-card imprint required for deposit, €4 discount with book for daily rental, daily 9:00–18:00, ask for their map of suggested routes, 24 rue Edgar Faure, Mo: Dupleix, tel. 01 56 58 10 54, www.fattirebiketoursparis.com).

**Bike Freedom for Parisians:** Those high-tech bike racks you see all over town are part of the city's innovative **Vélib'** program (from *vélo* + *liberté* or *libre* = "bike freedom" or "free bike"), which gives locals with a Vélib' card access to 20,000 bikes around the city. Parisians pay €30 per year for the card, which they swipe to unlock the nearest Vélib' bike. (Tourists can pay to ride one, but US credit cards are unlikely to work in the machine.) The first half-hour of each ride is free; after that, riders are billed the longer they have the bike checked out. The system is well-designed—racks show not only the location of other nearby racks, but how many bikes are available there. At night, bikes are redistributed by truck so that busy locations always have enough bikes. The program is also comprehensive, involving aggressive citywide development of bike paths. Copenhagen tried a similar program, providing intentionally ugly and clumsy bikes to lower the risk of theft. Vélib's bikes, however, are great.

# TOURS

## By Bus

**Bus Tours**—**Paris Vision** offers bus tours of Paris, day and night (advertised in hotel lobbies). I'd consider a Paris Vision tour only for their night-time Illumination tour (see page 108). During the day, the hop-on, hop-off bus tours (listed immediately below) and the Batobus (see "By Boat," later in this section)—which both provide transportation between sights as well as commentary—are a better value.

**Hop-on, Hop-off Bus Tours**—Double-decker buses connect Paris' main sights while providing a basic running commentary, allowing you to hop on and hop off along the way. You get a disposable set of earplugs (dial English and listen to the so-so narration). You can get off at any stop, tour a sight, then catch a later bus. These are best in good weather, when you can sit up top. There are two companies: L'Open Tours and Les Cars Rouges; pick up their brochures showing routes and stops from any TI or on their buses. You can start either tour at just about any of the major sights, such as the Eiffel Tower, where both companies stop on avenue Joseph Bouvard.

**L'Open Tours** uses bright yellow buses and provides more extensive coverage (and slightly better commentary) on four different routes, rolling by most of the important sights in Paris. Their Paris Grand Tour (the green route) offers the best introduction. The same ticket gets you on any of their routes within the validity period. Buy your tickets from the driver (1 day-€29, 2 days-€32, kids 4–11 pay €15 for 1 or 2 days, allow 2 hours per tour). Two to four buses depart hourly from about 10:00 to 18:00; expect to wait 10–15 minutes at each stop (stops can be tricky to find—look for yellow signs; tel. 01 42 66 56 56, www.paris-opentour.com). A combo-ticket covers both the Batobus boats (described in "By Boat," page 54) and L'Open Tours buses (€44, kids under 12 pay €20, valid 3 days).

**Les Cars Rouges'** bright red buses offer largely the same service, with only one route and just nine stops, for less (recorded narration, adult-€24, kids 4–12 pay €12, good for 2 days, tel. 01 53 95 39 53, www.carsrouges.com).

## By Boat

**Seine Cruises**—Several companies run one-hour boat cruises on the Seine (by far best at night).

Two companies are convenient to the rue Cler hotels: **Bateaux-Mouches** departs from pont de l'Alma's right bank and has the

## Bus #69 Sightseeing Tour

Why pay €25 for a tour company to give you an overview of Paris, when city bus #69 can do it for €1.50? Get on the bus and settle in for a ride through some of the city's most interesting neighborhoods and past nonstop views. Or hop on and off using this bus as a fun way to connect many of Paris' most important sights (your ticket gives you 90 minutes if purchased at a Métro station). This scenic route crosses the city east-west, running between the Eiffel Tower and Père Lachaise Cemetery, and passes these great monuments and neighborhoods en route: Ecole Militaire, rue Cler, Les Invalides (Army Museum and Napoleon's Tomb), Louvre Museum, Ile de la Cité, Ile St. Louis, Hôtel de Ville, Pompidou Center, and the Marais. You don't have to do the whole enchilada; get on and off wherever you like. You'll learn how great the city's bus system is—and you'll wonder why you've been tunneling by Métro under this gorgeous city. And if you're staying in the Marais or rue Cler neighborhoods, line #69 is a useful route for just getting around town (except on Sun, when it doesn't run).

You can hop on Monday through Saturday, but avoid weekday rush hours (8:00-9:30 & 17:30-19:30), and hot days (no air-conditioning). Evening bus rides are magical in months when it gets dark enough to see the floodlit monuments before the bus finishes running (last trip at 21:15). In the rue Cler area, catch bus #69 eastbound at the Eiffel Tower on avenue Joseph Bouvard (the first stop is at the southwestern end of the avenue, across from the Eiffel Tower) or along rue St. Dominique. In the Marais, catch the bus westbound on rues St. Antoine and Rivoli.

biggest open-top, double-decker boats. But this company often has too many tour groups, causing these boats to get packed (€10, kids 4–12 pay €5, tel. 01 40 76 99 99, www.bateaux-mouches.com).

**Bateaux Parisiens** has smaller covered boats with handheld audioguides, fewer crowds, and only one deck (€11, kids 4–11 pay €5, discounted half-price if you have a valid France or France–Switzerland railpass—does not use up a day of a flexipass, leaves from right in front of the Eiffel Tower, tel. 08 25 01 01 01, www .bateauxparisiens.com). Both companies run daily year-round (April–Oct 10:00–22:30, 2–3/hr; Nov–March shorter hours, runs hourly).

**Vedettes du Pont Neuf** offers essentially the same one-hour tour as Bateaux Parisiens, but starts and ends at Pont Neuf, closer to recommended hotels in the Marais and Luxembourg Garden neighborhoods. The boats feature a live guide whose delivery (in English and French) is as stiff as a recorded narration—and as hard to understand, given the quality of their sound system (€11, kids 4–12 pay €6, tip requested, nearly 2/hr, daily 10:30–22:30, tel. 01 46 33 98 38).

**Hop-on, Hop-Off Boat Tour**—**Batobus** allows you to get on and off as often as you like at any of eight popular stops along the Seine: Eiffel Tower, Champs-Elysées, Orsay/place de la Concorde, the Louvre, Notre-Dame, St. Germain-des-Prés, Hôtel de Ville, and Jardin des Plantes. Safety-conscious glass enclosures turn the boats into virtual ovens on hot days (1 day-€12, 2 days-€14, boats run June–Aug 10:00–21:30, mid-March–May and Sept–Oct 10:00–19:00, Nov–early-Jan and Feb–mid-March 10:30–16:30, no service last three weeks in Jan, every 15–20 minutes, 45 min one-way, 90 min round-trip, worthless narration). If you use this for getting around—sort of a scenic, floating alternative to the Métro—this can be worthwhile. But if you just want a guided boat tour, Batobus is not as good a value as the regular tour boats described above. A special combo-ticket covers L'Open Tours buses (described above) and Batobus boats (€40, kids under 12 pay €17, valid 3 days, www.batobus.com).

**Low-Key Cruise on a Tranquil Canal**—**Canauxrama** runs a lazy 2.5-hour cruise on a peaceful canal without the Seine in sight. Tours start from place de la Bastille and end at Bassin de la Villette (near Mo: Stalingrad). During the first segment of your trip, you'll pass through a long tunnel (built at the order of Napoleon in the early 19th century, when canal boats were vital for industrial transport). Once outside, you glide—not much faster than you can walk—through sleepy Parisian neighborhoods and slowly climb through four double locks as a guide narrates the trip in French and English (€15, departs at 9:45 and 14:30 across from Opéra Bastille, just below boulevard de la Bastille, opposite #50—where the canal meets place de la Bastille, tel. 01 42 39 15 00). The same tour also goes in the opposite direction (from Bassin de la Villette to place de la Bastille). It's OK to bring a picnic on board.

## By Foot

**Paris Walks**—This company offers a variety of two-hour walks, led by British or American guides. Tours are thoughtfully prepared, and humorous. Don't hesitate to stand close to the guide to hear (€10–15, generally 2/day, private tours available, recorded English schedule tel. 01 48 09 21 40, www.paris-walks.com). Tours focus on the Marais (4/week), Montmartre (3/week), medieval Latin Quarter (Mon), Ile de la Cité/Notre-Dame (Mon), the "Two Islands" (Ile de la Cité and Ile St. Louis, Wed), *Da Vinci Code* sights (Wed), and Hemingway's Paris (Fri). Ask about their family-friendly tours. Call a day or two ahead to learn their schedule and starting point. Most tours don't require reservations, but specialty tours (such as the *Da Vinci Code* tour) require advance reservations and prepayment with credit card (not refundable if you cancel less than two days in advance).

**Context Paris**—These "intellectual by design" walking tours are led by docents (historians, architects, and academics) and cover both museums and neighborhoods, often with a fascinating theme (explained on their website). Try to book in advance, since groups are small and can fill up (limited to 6 participants, generally 3 hours long and €35–55 per person plus admissions, tel. 06 13 09 67 11, US tel. 888-467-1986, www.contextparis.com). They also offer private tours.

**Classic Walks**—If you'd prefer a more relaxed, low-brow walking tour, consider this outfit, run by Fat Tire Bike Tours (see "By Bike," below). Their 3.5-hour "Classic Walk" covers most major sights (€20, daily at 10:00, meet at office—see below). They also do two-hour walks on various themes and neighborhoods: Montmartre, French Revolution, World War II, *Da Vinci Code*, and Latin Quarter (€12, leave several times a week—see website for details, all walks get €2 discount with this book, 24 rue Edgar Faure, Mo: Dupleix, tel. 01 56 58 10 54, www.classicwalksparis.com).

**Private Guides**—For many, Paris merits hiring a Parisian as a personal guide. **Arnaud Servignat** is an excellent licensed local guide (€155/half-day, €260/day, also does car tours of the countryside around Paris for a little more, tel. 06 68 80 29 05, www.arnaud-servignat.com, arnotour@mac.com).

**Elizabeth Van Hest** is another highly likeable and capable guide (€175/half-day, €260/day, tel. 01 43 41 47 31, e.van.hest@erenis.fr). **Sylvie Moreau** is also good, and charges the same as Elizabeth (mobile 06 87 02 80 67, silvmor@gmail.com).

## By Bike

**Fat Tire Bike Tours**—A hardworking gang of young American expats runs an extensive program of bike tours, Segway tours, and walking tours, and rents bikes as well.

Their high-energy guides run four-hour bike tours of Paris, by day and by night. Reservations aren't necessary—just show up. On the day tour, you'll pedal with a pack of 10–20 riders, mostly in parks and along bike lanes, with a lunch stop in the Tuileries Gardens (€26, show this book for a €4 per-person discount, maximum 2 discounts per book, English only, tours leave daily rain or shine at 11:00, April–Oct at 15:00 as well). Nighttime tours are more lively and include a boat cruise on the Seine (€28, €4 discount with this book, April–Oct daily at 19:00, March daily at 18:00, end of Feb and all of Nov Tue, Thu, and Sat–Sun at 18:00, no night tours Dec–mid-Feb). Both tours meet at the south pillar of the Eiffel Tower, where you'll get a short history lesson, then walk six minutes to the Fat Tire office to pick up bikes (helmets available upon request at no extra charge, office open daily 9:00–19:00, 24 rue Edgar Faure, Mo: Dupleix, tel. 01 56 58 10 54, toll-free from North America 866-614-6218, www.fattirebiketoursparis.com). They also run bike tours to Versailles and Giverny (reservations required, see website for details). Their office has Internet access with English keyboards.

Fat Tire's pricey four-hour **City Segway Tours**—on futuristic stand-up motorized scooters—are novel in that you learn to ride a Segway while exploring Paris (you'll get the hang of it after about half an hour). These tours take no more than eight people at a time, so reservations are required (€75, daily at 9:30, March–Nov also at 14:00, April–Oct also at 18:30, www.citysegwaytours.com).

## Excursions from Paris

Many companies offer bus tours to regional sights, including all of the day trips described in this book. **Paris Vision** runs mass-produced, full-size bus and minivan tours to several popular regional destinations, including the Loire Valley, Champagne region, D-Day beaches, and Mont St. Michel. Minivan tours are more expensive, but more personal and given in English, and most offer convenient pickup at your hotel (€90–190/person). Their full-size bus tours are multilingual and cheaper than the minivan tours—worthwhile for some travelers simply for the ease of transportation to the sights (about €70, destinations include Versailles and Giverny). Paris Vision's full-size buses depart from 214 rue de Rivoli (Mo: Tuileries, tel. 01 42 60 30 01, www.parisvision.com).

# SELF-GUIDED WALK

## Historic Core of Paris Walk

(This information is distilled from the Historic Paris Walk chapter in *Rick Steves' Paris*, by Rick Steves, Steve Smith, and Gene Openshaw. A free audiotour version of this walk is available for people with iPods or other MP3 players at www.ricksteves.com and on iTunes.)

Allow four hours to do justice to this three-mile walk. Start where the city did—on the Ile de la Cité. Face Notre-Dame and follow the gray line on the "Historic Core of Paris" map (see page 58).

• *To get to Notre-Dame, ride the Métro to Cité, Hôtel de Ville, or St. Michel and walk to the big square facing the cathedral. View it from the bronze plaque on the ground (30 yards from the central doorway) marked "Point Zero." You're standing at the center of France, the point from which all distances are measured...*

### ▲▲▲Notre-Dame Cathedral

This 700-year-old cathedral is packed with history and tourists. Study its sculpture and windows, take in a Mass, eavesdrop on guides, and walk all around the outside.

The **cathedral facade** is worth a close look. The church is dedicated to "Our Lady" (Notre-Dame). Mary is center stage—cradling Jesus, surrounded by the halo of the rose window. Adam is on the left and Eve is on the right.

Below Mary and above the arches is a row of 28 statues known as the Kings of Judah. During the French Revolution, these biblical kings were mistaken for the hated French kings. The citizens stormed the church, crying, "Off with their heads!" All were decapitated, but have since been recapitated.

Speaking of decapitation, look at the carving above the doorway on the left. The man with his head in his hands is St. Denis. Back when there was a Roman temple on this spot, Christianity began making converts. The fourth-century bishop of Roman Paris, Denis, was beheaded. But these early Christians were hard to keep down. The man who would become St. Denis got up, tucked his head under his arm, headed north, paused at a fountain to wash it off, and continued until he found just the right place to meet his maker: Montmartre. (Although the name "Montmartre" comes from the Roman "Mount of Mars," later generations—thinking of their beheaded patron, St. Denis—preferred a less pagan version, "Mount of Martyrs.") The Parisians were convinced of this miracle, Christianity gained ground, and a church soon replaced the pagan temple.

Medieval art was OK if it embellished the house of God and told biblical stories. For a fine example, move to the base of the central column (at the foot of Mary, about where the head of St. Denis could spit if he were really good). Working around from the left, find God telling a barely created Eve, "Have fun, but no apples." Next, the sexiest serpent I've ever seen makes apples à la mode. Finally, Adam and Eve, now ashamed of their nakedness, are expelled by an angel. This is a tiny example in a church covered with meaning.

Now move to the right and study the carving above the **central portal.** It's the end of the world, and Christ sits on the throne of Judgment (just under the arches, holding both hands up). Below him an angel and a demon weigh souls in the balance; the demon cheats by pressing down. The "good" stand to the left, gazing up to heaven. The "bad" ones to the right are chained up and led off to a six-hour tour of the Louvre on a hot day. The

PARIS

# Historic Core of Paris

R I G H T　B A N K

TO LES HALLES

TO LOUVRE

QUAI DU LOUVRE　PONT NEUF

CHATELET (+R)

BLVD. SEBAST.

TOUR ST. JACQUES

TO POMPIDOU

RENARD

RUE　DE

RIVOLI

TO PLACE BASTILLE

FINISH

BOATS

PONT NEUF

S E I N E

QUAI DE L'HORLOGE

CHANGE

HOTEL DE VILLE

QUAI DE L'HOTEL DE VILLE

TO ORSAY + PONT DES ARTS

PALAIS DE JUSTICE

CITÉ

NOTRE DAME

MKT.

HÔTEL DIEU HOSPITAL

SAINTE-CHAPELLE

WC

RUE DE LUTECE

BLVD. DU PALAIS

START

NOTRE-DAME

CRYPT

PLACE PARVIS

PLACE ST. MICHEL

RUE ST. ANDRE-DES-ARTS

HUCHETTE

SHAKESPEARE + CO. BOOKS

PLACE ST. ANDRE DES-ARTS

ODEON

BLVD.

R. ST. SEVERIN

ST. MICHEL

RUE DE LA

RUE ST. JACQUES

LA GRANGE

QUAI TOURNELLE

TO ST. SULPICE

CLUNY

CLUNY MUSEUM

BLVD. ST.

ST.

MAUBERT MUTUALITE

GERMAIN

R. MONGE

L E F T　　B A N K

TO SORBONNE + LUXEMBOURG GARDEN

TO RUE MOUFFETARD

200 YARDS
200 METERS

➡ WALKING TOUR ROUTE

Ⓜ METRO STATION　　Ⓑ BATOBUS BOAT STOP

Ⓡ RER STOP　　⚐ VIEW

DCH

❶ Point Zero & Notre-Dame
❷ Deportation Memorial
❸ Ile St. Louis
❹ Latin Quarter
❺ Sainte-Chapelle
❻ Palais de Justice

❼ Cité Metro Stop & Flower Market
❽ Conciergerie
❾ Pont Neuf
❿ Center of Paris Plage (Beach)

"ugly" ones must be the crazy, sculpted demons to the right, at the base of the arch.

Wander through the interior. You'll be routed around the ambulatory, much as medieval pilgrims would have been. Don't miss the rose windows filling each of the transepts. Back outside, walk around the church through the park on the riverside for a close look at the flying buttresses.

The Neo-Gothic, 300-foot **spire** is a product of the 1860 reconstruction. Around its base are apostles and evangelists (the green men) as well as Eugène-Emmanuel Viollet-le-Duc, the architect in charge of the work. Notice how the apostles look outward, blessing the city, while the architect (at top, seen from behind the church) looks up the spire, marveling at his fine work.

The **archaeological crypt** is a worthwhile 15-minute stop if you have a Paris Museum Pass (€3.50, covered by Museum Pass, Tue–Sun 10:00–18:00, closed Mon, enter 100 yards in front of cathedral). You'll see Roman ruins, trace the street plan of the medieval village, and see diagrams of how the earliest Paris grew and grew, all thoughtfully explained in English.

**Cost, Hours, Location:** Free, cathedral open daily 7:45–19:00; Treasury-€3, not covered by Museum Pass, Treasury open daily 9:30–17:30; audioguide-€5, ask about free English tours, normally Wed and Thu at 12:00, Sat at 14:30; Mo: Cité, Hôtel de Ville, or St. Michel; tel. 01 42 34 56 10, www.cathedraledeparis.com. On Good Friday and on the first Friday of the month at 15:00, the (physically underwhelming) relic known as Jesus' Crown of Thorns is on display.

**Tower:** You can climb to the top of the facade between the towers, and then to the top of the south tower, 400 steps total, for a grand view (€7.50, covered by Museum Pass but no bypass line for passholders, daily April–Sept 10:00–18:30—also June–Aug Sat–Sun until 23:00, Oct–March 10:00–17:30, last entry 45 min before closing; to avoid crowds in peak season, arrive before 10:00 or after 17:00).

• *Behind Notre-Dame, cross the street, and enter through the iron gate into the park at the tip of the island. Look for the stairs and head down to reach the...*

## ▲Deportation Memorial (Mémorial de la Déportation)

This memorial to the 200,000 French victims of the Nazi concentration camps draws you into their experience. As you descend the steps, the city around you disappears. Surrounded by walls, you have become a prisoner. Your only freedom is your view of the sky and the tiny glimpse of the river below.

Enter the single-file chamber ahead. Inside, the circular plaque in the floor reads, "They went to the end of the earth and did not return." A hallway stretches in front of you, lined with 200,000 lighted crystals, one for each French citizen who died. Flickering at the far end is the eternal flame of hope. The tomb of the unknown deportee lies at your feet. Above, the inscription reads, "Dedicated to the living memory of the 200,000 French deportees sleeping in the night and the fog, exterminated in the Nazi concentration camps."

Above the exit as you leave is the message you'll find at other Holocaust sites: "Forgive, but never forget" (free, daily April–Sept 10:00–12:00 & 14:00–19:00, Oct–March 10:00–12:00 & 14:00–17:00, at the east tip of the island named Ile de la Cité, behind Notre-Dame and near Ile St. Louis, Mo: Cité, tel. 01 49 74 34 00).

• *Back on street level, look across the river (north) to the island called...*

## Ile St. Louis

If the Ile de la Cité is a tug laden with the history of Paris, it's towing this classy little residential dinghy laden only with boutiques, famous sorbet shops, and restaurants (see "Eating," page 146). This island wasn't developed until much later than the Ile de la Cité (17th century). What was a swampy mess is now harmonious Parisian architecture. The pedestrian bridge, pont St. Louis, connects the two islands, leading right to rue St. Louis-en-l'Ile. This spine of the island is lined with interesting shops. A short stroll takes you to the famous Berthillon ice cream parlor (#31). Loop back to the pedestrian bridge along the parklike quays (walk north to the river and turn left). This walk is about as peaceful and romantic as Paris gets.

Before walking to the opposite end of the Ile de la Cité, loop through the Latin Quarter (as indicated on the map on page 58).

• *From the Deportation Memorial, cross the bridge onto the Left Bank and enjoy the riverside view of Notre-Dame, window-shopping among the green book stalls and browsing through used books, vintage posters, and souvenirs. At the little park and church (over the bridge from the front of Notre-Dame), venture inland a few blocks, basically arcing through the Latin Quarter and returning to the island two bridges down at place St. Michel.*

## ▲Latin Quarter

The touristic fame of this neighborhood relates to its intriguing artsy, bohemian character. This was perhaps Europe's leading university district in the Middle Ages—home, since the 13th century, to the prestigious Sorbonne University. Back then, Latin was the language of higher education. And, since students here came from

# Eiffel Tower and Nearby

PARIS

The top level, called *le sommet* (900 feet), is tiny. (It can close temporarily without warning when it reaches capacity.) All you'll find here are wind and grand, sweeping views. The city lies before you, with a panoramic guide. On a good day, you can see for 40 miles.

The second level (400 feet) has the best views (up the short stairway, on the platform without the wire-cage barriers), souvenir shops, public telephones to call home, and a small stand-up café. While you'll save no money, consider taking the elevator up and the stairs down (five minutes from second level to first, five minutes more to ground) for good exercise and views.

The first level (200 feet) has exhibits, a post office (daily 10:00–19:00, cancellation stamp will read Eiffel Tower), a snack bar, WCs, and souvenirs. Read the informative signs (in English) describing the major monuments, see the entertaining free movie on the history of the tower, and don't miss a century of fireworks—including the entire millennium blast—on video. Then consider a drink or a sandwich overlooking all of Paris at the snack café (outdoor tables in summer) or at the city's best view bar/restaurant, **Altitude 95** (see page 138).

**Seeing It All:** If you don't want to miss a single level, here's a plan for getting the most out of your visit. Ride the lift to second level, then immediately line up and catch the next lift to the top. Enjoy the views on top, then ride back down to the second level. Frolic there for a while and take in some more views. When you're ready, head to the first level by taking the stairs (no line) or lining up for the elevator. Explore the shops and exhibits on this level, have a snack, then take the stairs (best) or lift back to earth.

**Cost, Hours, Location:** €4.80 to go to the first level, €7.80 to the second, and €12 to go to the top, not covered by Museum Pass. You can skip the elevator line and climb the stairs to the first or second level for €4.50, or €3 if you're under 25. The elevators and stairs are both free going down. Daily mid-June–Aug 9:00–24:45 in the morning, Sept–mid-June 9:30–23:45, last ascent to top at 22:30 and to lower levels via elevator at 23:00 or by stairs at 18:00. Mo: Bir-Hakeim and Trocadéro or Champ de Mars–Tour Eiffel RER stop (each about a 10-min walk away). Tel. 01 44 11 23 23, www.tour-eiffel.fr.

If you climb the stairs, or buy a ticket only to one of the lower levels, you can buy your way up once you're in the tower—ticket booths and machines on the first and second levels sell supplements to go higher (with no penalty).

**Tips:** To avoid most crowds, go early (get in line by 8:45, before it opens) or late in the day (after 20:00 May–Aug, after 18:00 in off-season—see above for last ascent times). Weekends and holidays are worst. Weekdays off-season are not as crowded. A new online reservation system may debut in 2009 allowing you to book a half-hour time slot for your visit—check their website (www.tour-eiffel.fr). Ideally, you should arrive with some light and stay as it gets dark.

To pass the time in line, pick up whatever free reading material is available at the ground-level tourist stands.

Before or after your tower visit, you can catch the Bateaux Parisiens boat for a Seine cruise (near the base of Eiffel Tower, see page 53 for details).

**Best Views:** The best place to view the tower is from Trocadéro Square to the north. It's a 10-minute walk across the river, a happening scene at night, and especially fun for kids. Consider arriving at the Trocadéro Métro stop for the view, then walking toward the tower. Another delightful viewpoint is the long, grassy field called Champ de Mars, to the south (great for dinner picnics). However impressive it may be by day, the tower is an awesome thing to see at twilight, when it becomes engorged with light, and virile Paris lies back and lets night be on top. When darkness fully envelops the city, the tower seems to climax—with a spectacular light show—at the top of each hour...for five minutes.

**Quai Branly Museum (Museé du Quai Branly)**—This is the best collection I've seen anywhere of so-called Primitive Art from Africa, Polynesia, Asia, and America. It's presented in a wild, organic, and strikingly modern building that's a sightseeing thrill in itself. This museum, opened in 2006, is still big news with locals. Masks, statuettes, musical instruments, clothes, voodoo dolls, and a variety of temporary exhibits and activities are artfully presented and exquisitely lit. It's not, however, accompanied by much printed English information—to really appreciate the exhibit, use the €5 audioguide. It's a 10-minute walk east (upriver) of the Eiffel Tower, along the river (€8.50, covered by Museum Pass, Tue–Sun 11:00–19:00, Thu–Sat until 21:00, closed Mon, 37 quai Branly, RER: Champ de Mars–Tour Eiffel or Pont de l'Alma, tel. 01 56 61 70 00, www.quaibranly.fr).

**National Maritime Museum (Musée National de la Marine)**—This extensive museum houses an amazing collection of ship models, submarines, torpedoes, cannonballs, *beaucoup* bowsprits, and naval you-name-it—including a small boat made for Napoleon. You'll find limited English information on the walls, but kids like the museum anyway (adults-€6.50, kids-€4.50, more during special exhibits, covered by Museum Pass, Wed–Mon 10:00–18:00, closed Tue, on left side of Trocadéro Square with your back to Eiffel Tower, tel. 01 53 65 69 53, www.musee-marine.fr).

▲**Paris Sewer Tour (Les Egouts de Paris)**—This quick, fascinating, and slightly stinky visit (a perfumed hanky helps) takes you along a few hundred yards of underground water tunnels in the world's first underground sewer system. Pick up the helpful English self-guided tour, then drop down into Jean Valjean's world of tunnels, rats, and manhole covers. (Victor Hugo was friends with the sewer inspector when he wrote *Les Misérables*.) You'll pass well-organized displays with helpful English information detailing the evolution of this amazing network. Over 1,500 miles of tunnels carry 317 million gallons of water daily through this underworld. It's the world's longest sewer system—so long, they say, that if it were laid out straight, it would stretch from Paris all the way to Istanbul. Don't miss the slide show, fine WCs just beyond the gift shop, and occasional tours in English.

Cost, Hours, Location: €4, covered by Museum Pass, May–Sept Sat–Wed 11:00–17:00, Oct–April Sat–Wed 11:00–16:00, closed Thu–Fri, located where pont de l'Alma greets the Left Bank, Mo: Alma-Marceau, RER: Pont de l'Alma, tel. 01 53 68 27 81.

**▲▲Army Museum and Napoleon's Tomb (Musée de l'Armée)**—The emperor lies majestically dead inside several coffins under a grand dome glittering with 26 pounds of gold—a goose-bumping pilgrimage for historians. Napoleon is surrounded by the tombs of other French war heroes and fine military museums in the Hôtel des Invalides. Follow signs to the "crypt" to find Roman Empire–style reliefs that list the accomplishments of Napoleon's administration. The Army Museum's WWI exhibit is well presented in English and complements its interesting and worthwhile WWII rooms. The section on French military history ("Louis XIV to Napoleon III") is slated to reopen in the spring of 2009...in *théorie*.

**Cost, Hours, Location:** €8, ticket covers Napoleon's Tomb and all museums within Les Invalides complex, includes audioguide for tomb, covered by Museum Pass, price drops to €6 an hour before closing time, always free for all military personnel with ID. Open daily April–Sept 10:00–18:00, mid-June–mid-Sept tomb stays open until 19:00, museum may be open Tue until 21:00, Oct–March until 17:00; last entry 30 min before closing, Oct–May closed first Mon of every month. The Hôtel des Invalides is at 129 rue de Grenelle; Mo: La Tour Maubourg, Varenne, or Invalides; tel. 01 44 42 38 77, www.invalides.org.

**▲▲Rodin Museum (Musée Rodin)**—This user-friendly museum is filled with passionate works by the greatest sculptor since

Michelangelo. The entire museum is being gradually renovated over the next few years; pick up the essential museum map to guide you. Auguste Rodin (1840–1917) sculpted human figures on an epic scale, revealing through the body their deepest thoughts and feelings. Rodin's statues rise from the raw stone around them, driven by the life force. With missing limbs and scarred skin, these are prefab classics, making ugliness noble. Rodin's people are always moving restlessly. Even the famous *Thinker* is moving. Rodin worked with many materials—he chiseled marble (though not often), modeled clay, cast bronze, worked plaster, painted, and sketched. He often created different versions of the same subject in different media.

Rodin lived and worked in this mansion, renting rooms alongside Henri Matisse, the poet Rainer Maria Rilke (Rodin's secretary), and the dancer Isadora Duncan. Well-displayed in the mansion where the sculptor lived and worked, exhibits trace Rodin's artistic development, explain how his bronze statues were cast, and show some of the studies he created to work up to his masterpiece (the unfinished *Gates of Hell*). Learn about Rodin's tumultuous relationship with his apprentice and lover, Camille Claudel. Mull over what makes his sculptures some of the most evocative since the Renaissance. For many, the gardens are the highlight of this museum. Here you'll find several of his greatest works, such as the *Thinker, Balzac,* the *Burghers of Calais,* and the *Gates of Hell.* The gardens are ideal for artistic reflection.

**Cost, Hours, Location:** €6, free on first Sun of the month, covered by Museum Pass. You'll pay €1 to get into the gardens only—which may be Paris' best deal, as many works are on display there (also covered by Museum Pass). Audioguides are €4, and baggage check is mandatory. Open April–Sept Tue–Sun 9:30–17:45, gardens close 18:45; Oct–March Tue–Sun 9:30–16:45, gardens close 17:00, last entry 30 min before closing, closed Mon. It's near the Army Museum and Napoleon's Tomb, 79 rue de Varenne, Mo: Varenne, tel. 01 44 18 61 10, www.musee-rodin.fr.

▲▲**Marmottan Museum (Musée Marmottan Monet)**—In this private, intimate, untouristy museum, you'll find the best collection anywhere of works by Impressionist headliner Claude Monet. Follow Monet's life through more than a hundred works, from simple sketches to the *Impression: Sunrise* painting that gave his artistic movement its start—and a name. You'll also enjoy large-scale canvases featuring the water lilies from his garden at Giverny (see next chapter).

**Cost, Hours, Location:** €8, not covered by Museum Pass, Tue 11:00–21:00, Wed–Sun 10:00–18:00, last entry 30 min before closing, closed Mon, 2 rue Louis Boilly, Mo: La Muette, tel. 01 44 96 50 33, www.marmottan.com. To get to the museum from the Métro stop, follow the brown museum signs six blocks down chaussée de la Muette through the park; pause to watch kids play on the old-time, crank-powered carousel.

## Left Bank

Just opposite Notre-Dame, on the left bank of the Seine, is the Latin Quarter. (For more information and a walking tour, see the "Historic Core of Paris Walk," page 56.)

▲▲**Cluny Museum (Musée National du Moyen Age)**—This treasure trove of Middle Ages (Moyen Age) art fills old Roman baths, offering close-up looks at stained glass, Notre-Dame carvings, fine goldsmithing and jewelry, and rooms of tapestries. The star here is the exquisite *Lady and the Unicorn* tapestry series: In five panels, a delicate, as-medieval-as-can-be noble lady introduces a delighted unicorn to the senses of taste, hearing, sight, smell, and touch.

**Cost, Hours, Location:** €6.50, free on first Sun of month, covered by Museum Pass, Wed–Mon 9:15–17:45, closed Tue, near corner of boulevards St. Michel and St. Germain at 6 place Paul Painlevé; Mo: Cluny–La Sorbonne, St. Michel, or Odéon; tel. 01 53 73 78 16, www.musee-moyenage.fr.

**St. Germain-des-Prés**—A church was first built on this site in A.D. 452. The church you see today was constructed in 1163 and is all that's left of a once sprawling and influential monastery. The colorful interior reminds us that medieval churches were originally painted in bright colors. The surrounding area hops at night with venerable cafés, fire-eaters, mimes, and scads of artists (free, daily 8:00–20:00, Mo: St. Germain-des-Prés).

**▲St. Sulpice Church and Organ Concert**—Since it was featured in *The Da Vinci Code,* this grand church has become a trendy stop for the book's many fans. But the real reason to visit is to see and hear its intimately accessible organ. For pipe-organ enthusiasts, this is one of Europe's great musical treats. The Grand Orgue at St. Sulpice Church has a rich history, with a succession of 12 world-class organists—including Charles-Marie Widor and Marcel Dupré—that goes back 300 years.

Widor started the tradition of opening the loft to visitors after the 10:30 service on Sundays. Daniel Roth (or his understudy) continues to welcome guests in three languages while playing five keyboards. (See www.danielrothsaintsulpice.org for his exact dates and concert plans.)

The 10:30–11:30 Sunday Mass (come appropriately dressed) is followed by a high-powered 25-minute recital. Then, just after noon, the small, unmarked door is opened (left of entry as you face the rear). Visitors scamper like sixteenth notes up spiral stairs, past the 19th-century Stairmasters that five men once pumped to fill the bellows, into a world of 7,000 pipes. You can see the organ and visit with Daniel (or his substitute, who might not speak English). Space is tight; only a few can gather around him at a time, and you need to be quick to allow others a chance to meet him. You'll generally have 20–30 minutes to kill (church views are great and there's a small lounge) before watching the master play during the next Mass; you can leave at any time. If you're late or rushed, show

TO ORSAY MUSEUM

TO LOUVRE VIA PONT DES ARTS

ST. GERMAIN-DES-PRES

SAINTE-CHAPELLE

ILE DE LA CITE

NOTRE DAME.

SEINE

BLVD.

CAFES DEUX MAGOTS + LA FLORE

DELACROIX MUSEUM

PLACE ST. MICHEL

RUE DU FOUR

ODEON

MABILLON

BLVD.

RUE ST. SEVERIN

RUE DES

CLUNY

BON MARCHE

SEVRES

VIEUX COLOMBIER

ST. SULPICE

CLUNY MUSEUM

GERMAIN

SEVRES-BAB.

ST. SULPICE

RUE

RUE

ECOLES

MAUBERT MUTUALITE

RUE DE

RASTAIL

RENNES

SHOPPING AREA

THEATRE ODEON

SORBONNE

CARD. LEMOINE

RENNES

VAUGIRARD

ST.

ST. ETIENNE DU MONT

RUE

BLVD.

LUXEMBOURG

POND

SOUFFLOT

RUE

MONGE

RUE DE

N.D. DES CHAMPS

GARDEN

PANTHEON

PLACE MONGE

MONTPARNASSE TOWER

KIDS' PLAY AREA

BLVD.

ST. JACQUES

RUE MOUFFETARD

BLVD.

LE SELECT CAFE

VAVIN

LA COUPOLE + LE DOME CAFES

MONTPARNASSE

PORT ROYAL

LATIN QUARTER

1/4 MILE

400 METERS

TO CATACOMBS

DCH

METRO STATION

RER STOP

up around 12:30 and wait at the little door. As someone leaves, you can slip in, climb up, and catch the rest of the performance (church open daily 7:30–19:30, Mo: St. Sulpice or Mabillon).

Tempting boutiques surround the church (see "Shopping," page 103), and nearby is the...

▲**Luxembourg Garden (Jardin du Luxembourg)**—Paris' most beautiful, interesting, and enjoyable garden/park/recreational area is a great place to watch Parisians at rest and play. It's ideal for families. These private gardens are property of the French Senate (housed in the château) and have special rules governing their use (e.g., where cards can be played, where dogs can be walked, where joggers can run, when and where music can be played). The brilliant flower beds are completely changed three times a year, and the boxed trees are brought out of the orangery in May. Challenge the card and chess players to a game (near the tennis courts), rent a toy sailboat, take your kids to the terrific play area in the southwest corner (small fee), or find a free chair near the main pond and take a breather (park open daily until dusk, Mo: Odéon, RER: Luxembourg).

The grand, Neoclassical-domed Panthéon, now a mausoleum housing the tombs of several great French figures, is just a block away.

PARIS

If you enjoy the Luxembourg Garden and want to see more green spaces, you could visit the more elegant **Parc Monceau** (Mo: Monceau), the colorful **Jardin des Plantes** (Mo: Jussieu or Gare d'Austerlitz, RER: Gare d'Austerlitz), or the hilly and bigger **Parc des Buttes-Chaumont** (Mo: Buttes-Chaumont).

▲**Panthéon**—This dramatic Neoclassical monument celebrates France's illustrious history and people, balances Foucault's pen-

dulum, and is the final home to many French VIPs. Step inside the vast building (360' by 280' by 270'). You'll trace the celebrated struggles of the French people (working clockwise around the church-like space): a martyred St. Denis picking up his head, St. Genevieve saving Paris from the Franks, St. Louis as king and cru-sader, Joan of Arc and her exploits, and so on.

**Foucault's pendulum** swings gracefully at the end of a 220-foot cable suspended from the towering dome. It was here in 1851 that the scientist Léon Foucault first demonstrated the rotation of the Earth. Watch as the pendulum's arc (appears to) shift as you and the earth rotate beneath it.

Stairs in the back lead down to the **crypt** where a pantheon of greats are buried, including famous French writers Victor Hugo *(Les Misérables, The Hunchback of Notre-Dame),* and Alexandre Dumas *(The Three Musketeers, The Count of Monte Cristo).* You'll also find the discoverers of radium, Polish-born Marie Curie and her French husband, Pierre, along with many others. An **exhibit** explores the building's fascinating history (good English descrip-tions). You can climb 206 steps to the **dome gallery** for fine views of the interior as well as the city (accessible only with an escort who leaves about every hour until 17:15—see schedule as you enter).

**Cost, Hours, Location:** €7.50, covered by Museum Pass, daily 10:00–18:30 in summer, until 18:00 in winter, last entry 45 minutes before closing (Mo: Cardinal Lemoine). Ask about occasional English tours or call ahead for schedule (tel. 01 44 32 18 00).

**Montparnasse Tower (La Tour Montparnasse)**—This 59-story superscraper—cheaper and easier to ascend than the Eiffel Tower—treats you to one of Paris' best views. (Some say the very best, as you can see the Eiffel Tower...and you can't see the Montparnasse Tower.) While there are plenty of dioramas identifying highlights of the star-studded vista, consider buying the €3 photo-guide, which makes a fun souvenir. As you zip up 56 floors in 38 seconds, watch the altimeter above the door. From the 56th floor, climb to the open

terrace at the 59th floor to enjoy
the surreal scene of a lonely man in
a box, and a helipad surrounded by
the window-cleaner track. Here,
690 feet above Paris, you can scan
the city with the wind in your hair,
noticing the lush courtyards hiding
behind grand street fronts. Back
inside and downstairs, you'll find a
small, overpriced café, fascinating
historic black-and-white photos,

and a plush little theater playing a worthwhile video that celebrates
the big views of this grand city (free, 12 min, shows continuously).

**Cost, Hours, Location:** €10, not covered by Museum Pass,
daily April–Sept 9:30–23:30, Oct–March 9:30–22:30, disappointing after dark, entrance on rue de l'Arrivée, Mo: Montparnasse-
Bienvenüe—from the Métro stay inside the station and simply
follow the signs for "La Tour," (tel. 01 45 38 52 56, www.tourmont
parnasse56.com). The tower is an efficient stop when combined
with a day trip to Chartres (see next chapter), which begins at the
Montparnasse train station.

▲**Catacombs**—These underground tunnels contain the anonymous bones of six million permanent Parisians. In 1786, the
Revolutionary government of Paris decided to relieve congestion
and improve sanitary conditions by emptying the city cemeteries
(which traditionally surrounded churches) into an official ossuary.
They found the perfect locale in the many miles of underground
tunnels from limestone quarries, which were, at that time, just
outside the city. For decades, priests led ceremonial processions of
black-veiled, bone-laden carts into the quarries, where the bones
were stacked into piles five feet high and as much as 80 feet deep
behind neat walls of skull-studded tibiae. Each transfer was complete when a plaque was placed, indicating the church and district
where the bones came from and the date that they arrived. Note
to wannabe Hamlets: An attendant checks your bag at the exit for
stolen souvenirs. A flashlight is handy. Being under 6'2" is helpful.

**Cost, Hours, Location:** €7, not covered by Museum Pass,
Tue–Sun 10:00–17:00, ticket booth closes at 16:00, closed Mon,
1 place Denfert-Rochereau, tel. 01 43 22 47 63. Take the Métro to
Denfert-Rochereau, then find the lion in the big traffic circle; if he
looked left rather than right, he'd stare right at the green entrance
to the Catacombs. You'll exit at 36 rue Remy Dumoncel, far from
where you started. If you walk to the right, to avenue du Général
Leclerc, you'll be equidistant from Métro stops Alésia (walk left)
and Mouton Duvernet (walk right).

## Champs-Elysées and Nearby

▲▲**Champs-Elysées**—This famous boulevard is Paris' backbone, and has the greatest concentration of traffic. All of France seems to converge on the place de la Concorde, the city's largest square. The Tour de France bicycle race ends here (on July 26 in 2009), as do all parades (French or foe) of any significance. While the Champs-Elysées has become as international as it is local, a walk here is still a must.

In 1667, Louis XIV opened the first section of the street as a short extension of the Tuileries Garden. This year is considered the birth of Paris as a grand city. The Champs-Elysées soon became *the* place to cruise in your carriage. (It still is today—traffic can be jammed up even at midnight.) One hundred years later, the café scene arrived. It was on place de la Concorde that the guillotine took the lives of about 1,200 people—including King Louis XVI and Marie-Antoinette. Back then it was called the place de la Révolution.

From the 1920s until the 1960s, this boulevard was pure elegance. Parisians actually dressed up to come here. It was mainly residences, rich hotels, and cafés. Then, in 1963, the government pumped up the neighborhood's commercial metabolism by bringing in the RER (commuter underground). Suburbanites had easy access, and *pfft*—there went the neighborhood.

The *nouveau* Champs-Elysées, revitalized in 1994, has new benches and lamps, broader sidewalks, all-underground parking, and a fleet of green-suited workers who drive motorized street cleaners. Blink away the modern elements and it's not hard to imagine the boulevard pre-1963, with only the finest structures lining both sides all the way to the palace gardens.

To saunter down the Champs-Elysées, take the Métro to the Arc de Triomphe, described below (Mo: Charles de Gaulle–Etoile; Métro stops every few blocks: Franklin D. Roosevelt, George V, and Charles de Gaulle–Etoile).

Inspect the fancy car dealerships—**Peugeot** at #136 (showing off its futuristic concept cars next to the classic models) and **Mercedes-Benz**, a block down at #118. In the 19th century, this was an area for horse stables; today, it's the district of garages, limo companies, and car dealerships. If you're serious about selling cars in France, you must have a showroom on the Champs-Elysées.

Next to Mercedes is the famous **Lido**, Paris' largest cabaret (and a multiplex cinema). You can walk all the way inside until 18:00 without a ticket. Check out the perky photos in the entryway, the R-rated videos, and the shocking prices. Paris still offers the kind of burlesque-type spectacles combining music, comedy, and scantily clad women that have been performed here since the 19th century. Movie-going on the Champs-Elysées provides another kind of fun, with theaters showing the very latest releases. Check to see if there are films you recognize, then look for the showings *(séances)*. A "v.o." *(version originale)* next to the time indicates the film will be shown in its original language.

The flagship store of leather-bag makers **Louis Vuitton** may be the largest single-brand luxury store in the world. Step inside. The store insists on providing enough salespeople to treat each customer royally—if there's a line, it means shoppers have overwhelmed the place.

**Fouquet's** café-restaurant (#99), under the red awning, is a popular spot among French celebrities and charges accordingly (€6 for espresso—the most expensive shot of espresso I've found in downtown Paris). Opened in 1899 as a coachman's bistro, Fouquet's gained fame as the hangout of France's WWI biplane fighter pilots—those who weren't shot down by Germany's infamous "Red Baron." It also served as James Joyce's dining room. Since the early 1900s, Fouquet's has been a favorite of French actors and actresses. The golden plaques by the entrance honor winners of France's Oscar-like film awards, the Césars—see plaques for Gérard Depardieu, Catherine Deneuve, Roman Polanski, Juliette Binoche, and many famous Americans (but not Jerry Lewis). Fouquet's was recently saved from foreign purchase and eventual destruction when the government declared it a historic monument. For his election-night victory party in 2007, the flamboyant

President Sarkozy, and France's glitterati, celebrated here.

**Ladurée** (two blocks downhill at #75, with green-and-purple awning) is a classic 19th-century tea salon/restaurant/*pâtisserie*. Its interior is right out of the 1860s. Non-patrons can discreetly wander in through the door farthest downhill and peek into the cozy rooms upstairs. A coffee here is *très élégant* (only €3.50). The bakery sells traditional macaroons, cute little cakes, and gift-wrapped finger sandwiches to go (your choice of four mini-macaroons for €7.20).

▲▲▲**Arc de Triomphe**—Napoleon had the magnificent Arc de Triomphe commissioned to commemorate his victory at the battle of Austerlitz. There's no triumphal

arch bigger (165 feet high, 130 feet wide). And, with 12 converging boulevards, there's no traffic circle more thrilling to experience—either from behind the wheel or on foot (take the underpass).

The foot of the arch is a stage on which the last two centuries of Parisian history have played out—from the funeral of Napoleon to the goose-stepping arrival of the Nazis, to the triumphant return of Charles de Gaulle after the Allied liberation. Examine the carvings on the pillars, featuring a mighty Napoleon and excitable Lady Liberty. Pay your respects at the Tomb of the Unknown Soldier (from World War I, at base of arch), where the flame is rekindled daily at 18:30.

The 284 steps lead to a cute museum about the arch, sweeping skyline panoramas, and a mesmerizing view down onto the traffic that swirls around the arch.

**Cost, Hours, Location:** Outside—free, always open. Interior—€9, free on first Sun of month Oct–March, free for kids under 18, covered by Museum Pass, daily April–Sept 10:00–23:00, Oct–March 10:00–22:30, last entry 30 min before closing, place Charles de Gaulle, use underpass to reach arch, Mo: Charles de Gaulle–Etoile, tel. 01 55 37 73 77, www.monum.fr.

▲**Opéra Garnier**—This gleaming grand theater of the belle époque was built for Napoleon III and finished in 1875. While the building is huge, the actual auditorium seats only 2,000. The real show was before and after the performance, when the elite of Paris—out to see and be seen—strutted their elegant stuff in the extravagant lobbies. Think of the grand marble stairway as a theater itself. As you wander the halls and gawk at the decor, imagine the place filled with the beautiful people of its day. The massive foundations straddle an underground lake (inspiring the mysterious world of the *Phantom of the Opera*). Visitors can peek from two boxes into the actual red-velvet performance hall to view Marc Chagall's colorful ceiling

(1964) playfully dancing around the eight-ton chandelier (guided tours take you into the performance hall). Note the box seats next to the stage—the most expensive in the house, with an obstructed view of the stage...but just right if you're here only to be seen.

The elitism of this place prompted a people's opera house built in the 1980s, symbolically on place de la Bastille, where the French Revolution started in 1789. This left the Opéra Garnier home only to ballet and occasional concerts. While the library/museum is of interest to opera buffs, anyone will enjoy the second-floor grand foyer and Salon du Glacier, iced with decor typical of 1900.

**Cost, Hours, Location:** €8, not covered by Museum Pass, daily 10:00–16:30, July–Aug until 18:00, closed during performances, 8 rue Scribe, Mo: Opéra, RER: Auber. To find out how get tickets to performances, see page 107.

**Tours:** English tours of the building run during summer and off-season weekends, usually at 11:30 and 14:00; call to confirm schedule (€12, includes entry, 90 min, tel. 01 40 01 17 89).

**Nearby:** The *Paris Story* film and Fragonard Perfume Museum (see below) are on the left side of the Opéra, and the venerable Galeries Lafayette department store (top-floor café with marvelous views, see page 103) is just behind. Across the street, the illustrious Café de la Paix has been a meeting spot for the local glitterati for generations. If you can afford the coffee, this spot offers a delightful break.

***Paris Story* Film**—Simultaneously cheesy, entertaining, and pricey, this film offers a painless overview of the city's turbulent and brilliant past, covering 2,000 years in 45 fast-moving minutes. The theater's wide-screen projection and cushy chairs provide a break from bad weather and sore feet, and the movie usually works for kids, but don't go out of your way to get here.

**Cost, Hours, Location:** €10, kids-€6, family of four-€26, not covered by Museum Pass. Individuals get a 20 percent discount with this book in 2009 (no discount on family rate). The film shows on the hour daily 10:00–18:00. Next to Opéra Garnier at 11 rue Scribe, Mo: Opéra, tel. 01 42 66 62 06.

**Fragonard Perfume Museum**—Near Opéra Garnier, two perfume shops masquerade as museums. Either location will teach you a little about how perfume is made (ask for the English handout), but the one on rue Scribe smells even sweeter—and it's in a beautiful 19th-century mansion (both free, daily 9:00–18:00, at 9 rue Scribe and 30 rue des Capucines, tel. 01 47 42 04 56, www.fragonard.com).

**▲▲Jacquemart-André Museum (Musée Jacquemart-André)**—This thoroughly enjoyable museum (with an elegant café) showcases the lavish home of a wealthy, art-loving, 19th-century

Parisian couple. After wandering the grand boulevards, get inside for an intimate look at the lifestyles of the Parisian rich and fabulous. Edouard André and his wife Nélie Jacquemart—who had no children—spent their lives and fortunes designing, building, and then decorating this sumptuous mansion. What makes the visit so rewarding is the excellent audioguide tour (in English, free with admission, plan on spending an hour with the audioguide). The place is strewn with paintings by Rembrandt, Botticelli, Uccello, Mantegna, Bellini, Boucher, and Fragonard—enough to make a painting gallery famous.

**PARIS**

**Cost, Hours, Location:** €10, not covered by Museum Pass, daily 10:00–18:00, at 158 boulevard Haussmann, Mo: Miromesnil or Saint-Philippe de Roule, bus #80 makes a convenient connection to Ecole Militaire, tel. 01 45 62 11 59, www.musee-jacquemart-andre.com.

**After Your Visit:** Consider a break in the sumptuous museum tearoom, with delicious cakes and tea (daily 11:45–17:45). From here, walk north on rue de Courcelles to see Paris' most beautiful park, **Parc Monceau.**

**Petit Palais (and its Musée des Beaux-Arts)**—In this free museum, you'll find a broad collection of paintings and sculpture from the 1600s to the 1900s. It's a museum of second-choice art, but the building itself is impressive, and there are a few 19th-century diamonds in the rough, including pieces by Courbet and Monet. The Palais also has a pleasant garden courtyard and café (Wed–Sun 10:00–18:00, Tue 10:00–20:00 for temporary exhibits, closed Mon, across from Grand Palais on avenue Winston Churchill, just west of place de la Concorde, tel. 01 53 43 40 00, www.petitpalais.paris.fr).

**Grand Palais**—This grand exhibition hall, built for the 1900 World's Fair, is used for temporary exhibits. The building's Industrial Age, erector-set, iron-and-glass exterior is grand, but the steep entry price is worthwhile only if the exhibit interests you. Get details on the current schedule from the TIs, in *Pariscope* (see page 40), or from www.rmn.fr (usually €10, not covered by Museum Pass, Thu–Mon 10:00–20:00, Wed 10:00–22:00, last entry 45 min before closing, closed Tue and between exhibitions, avenue Winston Churchill, Mo: Rond Point or Champs-Elysées, tel. 01 44 13 17 17).

**▲▲La Défense and La Grande Arche**—While Paris keeps its historic center classic and skyscraper-free, this district, nicknamed "le petit Manhattan," offers an impressive excursion into modern-day economic superpower France. La Défense was conceived more than 60 years ago as a US-style forest of skyscrapers that would accommodate the business needs of the modern world. Today, La Défense is a thriving business and shopping center, home to 150,000 employees and 55,000 residents.

Take the Métro to the La Défense stop and start with **La Grande Arche de la Fraternité,** the centerpiece of this ambitious complex (inaugurated in 1989 on the 200th anniversary of the French Revolution). The place is big—Notre-Dame Cathedral could fit under its arch. The "cloud"—a huge canvas canopy under the arch—is an attempt to cut down on the wind-tunnel effect this gigantic building creates. Glass capsule elevators whisk you up to a grand open-air view, a thrilling 20-minute movie (with English subtitles) on the mammoth construction project, and models of the arch. Take advantage of its free Internet access (in the computer exhibit) and don't skip the fascinating set of digital portraits by French artist Dimitri, illustrating *remanence*—"after imagery."

**Cost, Hours, Location:** La Grande Arche elevator-€9, kids-€7.50, family deals, not covered by Museum Pass, daily April–Sept 10:00–20:00, Oct–March until 19:00, RER or Mo: La Défense, follow signs to *La Grande Arche*, tel. 01 49 07 27 57, www .grandearche.com.

**The Esplanade:** La Défense is more than its eye-catching arch. Wander from the arch toward the city center along the Esplanade (a.k.a. "le Parvis") which is a virtual open-air modern art gallery, sporting pieces by Joan Miró (blue), Alexander Calder (red), and Yaacov Agam (the fountain with its colorful stripes and rhythmically dancing spouts), among others. *La Défense de Paris,* the statue that gave the area its name, recalls the 1871 Franco-Prussian war. Walking toward the Nexity Tower, you'll come to the Esplanade de la Défense Métro station, which zips you out of all this modernity and directly back into town.

## Marais Neighborhood and Nearby

The Marais neighborhood extends along the Right Bank of the Seine from the Pompidou Center to the Bastille. It contains more pre-revolutionary lanes and buildings than anywhere else in town and is more atmospheric than touristy. It's medieval Paris, and the haunt of the old nobility. This is how much of the city looked until, in the mid-1800s, Napoleon III had Baron Georges-Eugène Haussmann blast out the narrow streets to construct broad boulevards (wide enough for the guns and ranks of the army, too wide for revolutionary barricades), thus creating modern Paris. Originally a swamp *(marais)* during the reign of Henry IV, this area became the hometown of the French aristocracy. In the 17th century, big

PARIS

**Marais Neighborhood and Nearby**

shots built their private mansions *(hôtels)* close to Henry IV's stylish place des Vosges. When strolling the Marais, stick to the west–east axis formed by rue Sainte-Croix de la Bretonnerie, rue des Rosiers (heart of Paris' Jewish community), and rue St. Antoine. On Sunday afternoons, this trendy area pulses with shoppers and café crowds.

▲**Place des Vosges**—Study the architecture in this grand square: nine pavilions (houses) per side. Some of the brickwork is real, some is fake. Walk to the center, where Louis XIII sits on a horse surrounded by locals enjoying their community park. Children frolic in the sandbox, lovers warm benches, and pigeons guard their fountains while trees shade this retreat from the glare of the big city. Henry IV built this centerpiece of the Marais in 1605. As he'd hoped, this turned the Marais into Paris' most exclusive neighborhood. Just like Versailles 80 years later, this was a magnet for the rich and powerful of France. With the Revolution, the aristocratic splendor of this quarter passed. The area became working-class, filled with gritty shops, artisans, immigrants, and a Jewish community. **Victor Hugo** lived at #6, and you can visit his house (free, Tue–Sun 10:00–18:00, last entry at 17:40, closed Mon, 6 place des Vosges, tel. 01 42 72 10 16). Leave the place des Vosges through the doorway at the southwest corner of the square (near the three-star Michelin restaurant l'Ambrosie) and pass through the elegant **Hôtel de Sully** (great example of a Marais mansion, grand courtyard open until 19:00, fine bookstore inside) to rue St. Antoine.

▲▲**Pompidou Center (Centre Pompidou)**—Europe's greatest collection of far-out modern art is housed in the Musée National d'Art Moderne, on the fourth and fifth floors of this colorful exhibition hall. The building itself is "exoskeletal" (like Notre-Dame or a crab), with its functional parts—the pipes, heating ducts, and escalator—on the outside, and the meaty art inside. It's the epitome of modern architecture, where "form follows function." Once ahead of its time, the 20th-century art displayed in this museum has been waiting for the world to catch up with it.

Enter on the fifth floor, show your ticket, and ask for a floor plan *(plan du musée)*. The 20th century—accelerated by technology and fragmented by war—was exciting and chaotic, and this art reflects the turbulence of that century of change. In this free-flowing and airy museum (with great views over Paris), you'll come face to face with works by Henri Matisse, Pablo Picasso, Marc Chagall, Salvador Dalí, Andy Warhol, Wassily Kandinsky, Max Ernst, Jackson Pollock, and many more. And after so many Madonnas-and-Children, a piano smashed to bits and glued to the wall is refreshing.

The Pompidou Center and the square that fronts it are lively, with lots of people, street theater, and activity inside and out—a perpetual street fair. Kids of any age enjoy the fun, colorful fountain (called *Homage to Stravinsky*) next to the Pompidou Center. Ride the escalator for a great city view from the top (ticket or Museum Pass required). If you need a light meal or snack, try the places lining the Stravinsky fountain: Dame Tartine and Crêperie Beaubourg (to the right as you face the museum entrance; both have reasonable prices).

**Cost, Hours, Location:** €10, permanent collection covered by Museum Pass (but not special exhibitions), free on first Sun of month, Wed–Mon 11:00–21:00, ticket counters close at 20:00, closed Tue, Mo: Rambuteau or farther-away Hôtel de Ville, tel. 01 44 78 12 33, www.centrepompidou.fr.

▲▲**Jewish Art and History Museum (Musée d'Art et Histoire du Judaïsme)**—This fine museum, located in a beautifully restored Marais mansion, tells the story of Judaism throughout Europe, from the Roman destruction of Jerusalem to the theft of famous artworks during World War II. Displays illustrate the cultural unity maintained by this continually dispersed population.

You'll learn about the history of Jewish traditions from bar mitz-vahs to menorahs, and see the exquisite traditional costumes and objects central to daily life. Don't miss the explanation of "the Dreyfus affair," a major event in early 1900s French politics. You'll also see photographs of and paintings by famous Jewish art-ists, including Marc Chagall, Amedeo Modigliani, and Chaim Soutine. A small but moving section is devoted to the deportation of Jews from Paris during World War II.

Helpful audioguides and many English explanations make this an enjoyable history lesson (red numbers on small signs indi-cate the number you should press on your audioguide). Move along at your own speed.

**Cost, Hours, Location:** €7, more during special exhibits, includes audioguide, covered by Museum Pass, Mon–Fri 11:00–18:00, Sun 10:00–18:00, last entry one hour before closing, closed Sat, 71 rue du Temple, Mo: Rambuteau or Hôtel de Ville a few blocks farther away, tel. 01 53 01 86 60, www.mahj.org.

**Jewish Quarter**—Located along rue des Rosiers, the tiny yet colorful Jewish district of the Marais was once considered the largest in Western Europe. Today, while rue des Rosiers is lined with colorful Jewish shops and kosher eateries, the district is being squeezed by the trendy boutiques of modern Paris (visit any day but Saturday, when most businesses are closed—best on Sunday). If you're visiting at lunchtime, you'll be tempted by kosher pizza and plenty of cheap fast-food joints selling falafel "to go" (*emporter* means "to go"). The best falafel is at L'As du Falafel, with a bus-tling New York–deli atmosphere (at #34, sit-down or to go). The Sacha Finkelsztajn Yiddish bakery (at #27) is also good. The Jewish Quarter is also home to the Holocaust Memorial (see below).

**Holocaust Memorial (Mémorial de la Shoah)**—Commemorating the lives of the more than 76,000 Jews deported from France in World War II, this memorial's focal point is underground, where victims' ashes are buried. Displaying original deportation records, the museum takes you through the history of Jews in Europe and France, from medieval pogroms to the Nazi era (free, Sun–Fri 10:00–18:00, Thu until 22:00, closed Sat and certain Jewish holidays, 17 rue Geoffroy l'Asnier, tel. 01 42 77 44 72, www.memorialdelashoah.org).

**▲▲Picasso Museum (Musée Picasso)**—Tucked into a cor-ner of the Marais and worth ▲▲▲ if you're a Picasso fan, this museum contains the world's largest collection of Picasso's paint-ings, sculptures, sketches, and ceramics, and includes his small collection of Impressionist art. The art is well-displayed in a fine old mansion with a peaceful garden café. The room-by-room English introductions help make sense of Picasso's work—from the Toulouse-Lautrec-like portraits at the beginning of his career

## Marais Neighborhood

1. Place des Vosges & Victor Hugo's House
2. Hôtel de Sully
3. Pompidou Center
4. Jewish Art & History Museum
5. Jewish Quarter
6. Holocaust Memorial
7. Picasso Museum
8. Carnavalet Museum

**M** METRO STATION
**M** BATOBUS BOAT STOP
**T** TAXI STAND
**P** PARKING
**B** BUS STOP

200 YARDS
200 METERS

to his gray-brown Cubist period to his return-to-childhood, Salvador Dalí–like finish. The well-done English guidebook helps Picassophiles appreciate the context of his art and learn more about his interesting life. Most will be happy reading the posted English explanations while moving at a steady pace through the museum—the ground and first floors satisfied my curiosity.

**Cost, Hours, Location:** €6.50, covered by Museum Pass, additional fees for temporary exhibits, free on first Sun of month and for kids under 18 with ID, April–Sept Wed–Mon 9:30–18:00, Oct–March Wed–Mon 9:30–17:30, last entry 45 min before closing, closed Tue, 5 rue de Thorigny, Mo: St. Paul or Chemin Vert, tel. 01 42 71 25 21, www .musee-picasso.fr.

▲▲**Carnavalet Museum (Musée Carnavalet)**—The tumultuous history of Paris is well-portrayed in this hard-to-navigate museum, offering a good overview of everything from Louis XIV period rooms to Napoleon to the belle époque. The Carnavalet is housed in two Marais mansions connected by a corridor. The first half of the museum (pre-Revolution) dates from a period when people generally accepted the notion that some were born to rule, and most were born to be ruled. This section is difficult to follow (rooms numbered out of order, no English descriptions, and sections closed due to understaffing) so see it quickly, then concentrate your energy on the Revolution and beyond.

The Revolution is the museum's highlight. Fascinating exhibits cover this bloody period of French history, when atrocious acts were committed in the name of government "by, for, and of the people." The exhibits take you from events that led up to the Revolution to the storming of the 100-foot-high walls of the Bastille to the royal beheadings, and through the reigns of terror that followed. They then trace the rise and fall of Napoleon and end with the Paris Commune uprisings. While explanations are in French only, many displays are fairly self-explanatory.

**Cost, Hours, Location:** Free, Tue–Sun 10:00–18:00, closed Mon; avoid lunchtime (12:00–14:00), when many rooms close; 23 rue de Sévigné, Mo: St. Paul, tel. 01 44 59 58 58, www.carnavalet .paris.fr.

▲**Promenade Plantée Park**—This two-mile-long, narrow garden walk on a viaduct was once used for train tracks and is now a joy on foot. Part of the park is elevated. At times, you'll walk along the street until you pick up the next segment. The shops below the viaduct's arches (a creative use of once-wasted urban space) make for entertaining window-shopping.

**Cost, Hours, Location:** Free, opens Mon–Fri at 8:00, Sat–Sun at 9:00, closes at sunset. It runs from place de la Bastille (Mo: Bastille) along avenue Daumesnil to Saint-Mandé (Mo: Michel Bizot). From place de la Bastille (follow signs for *Sortie Opéra* or *Sortie rue de Lyon* from Bastille Métro station), walk down rue de Lyon with the Opéra immediately on your left. Find the steps up the red brick wall a block after the Opéra.

▲**Père Lachaise Cemetery (Cimetière du Père Lachaise)**—Littered with the tombstones of many of the city's most illustrious dead, this is your best one-stop look at Paris' fascinating, romantic past residents. The tree-lined cemetery is enclosed by a massive wall with peaceful, car-free lanes that encourage parklike meandering. Named for Father *(Père)* La Chaise, whose job was listening to Louis XIV's sins, the cemetery is relatively new, having opened in 1804 to accommodate Paris' expansion. Today, this city of the dead (pop. 70,000) still accepts new residents, but real estate prices are very high.

The 100-acre cemetery is big and confusing, with thousands of graves and tombs crammed every which way, and only a few pathways to navigate by. The helpful €2 map (sold at the flower stores located near either entry) will direct you to the graves of Frédéric Chopin, Molière, Edith Piaf, Oscar Wilde, Gertrude Stein, Jim Morrison, Héloïse and Abélard, and many more.

**Cost, Hours, Location:** Free, Mon–Sat 8:00–18:00, Sun 9:00–18:00, or until dusk if it falls before 18:00. It's down avenue du Père Lachaise from Mo: Gambetta (also across the street from the less-convenient Père Lachaise Métro stop and reachable via bus #69). Tel. 01 55 25 82 10.

## Montmartre

▲▲**Sacré-Cœur and Montmartre**—Stroll along Paris' highest hilltop (420 feet) for a different perspective on the City of Light. Walk in the footsteps of the people who've lived here—monks stomping grapes (1200s), farmers grinding grain in windmills (1600s), dust-coated gypsum miners (1700s), Parisian liberals (1800s), modernist painters (1900s), and all the struggling artists, poets, dreamers, and drunkards who came here for cheap rent, untaxed booze, rustic landscapes, and cabaret nightlife. With vineyards, wheat fields, windmills, animals, and a village tempo of life, it was the perfect escape from grimy Paris.

The five-domed, Roman-Byzantine–looking basilica of **Sacré-Cœur** took 44 years to build (1875–1919). It stands on a foundation of 83 pillars sunk 130 feet deep, necessary because the ground beneath was honeycombed with gypsum mines. The exterior is laced with gypsum, which whitens with age.

For an unobstructed panoramic view of Paris, climb 260 feet up the tight and claustrophobic spiral stairs to the top of the dome (church free, daily 7:00–23:00; €5 to climb dome, not covered by Museum Pass, daily June–Sept 9:00–19:00, Oct–May 10:00–18:00).

One block from the church, the **place du Tertre** was the haunt of Henri de Toulouse-Lautrec and the original bohemians. Today, it's mobbed with tourists and unoriginal bohemians, but it's still fun (to beat the crowds, go early in the morning). From here, follow rue des Saules (a block west), turn right, and find Paris' lone vineyard, and the Montmartre Museum (listed below).

To get to Montmartre, take the Métro to the Anvers stop (one more Métro ticket buys your way up the funicular and avoids the stairs, but the funicular may be closed for repairs) or the closer but less scenic Abbesses stop. A taxi to the top of the hill saves time and avoids sweat (costs about €10, €20 at night). For restaurant recommendations, see "Eating," page 151.

**Dalí Museum (L'Espace Dalí)**—This beautifully lit black gallery (well-described in English) offers a walk through statues, etchings, and paintings by the master of surrealism. Don't miss the printed interview on the exit stairs (€10, not covered by Museum Pass, daily 10:00–18:30, 11 rue Poulbot, tel. 01 42 64 40 10, www.daliparis.com).

**Montmartre Museum (Musée de Montmartre)**—This 17th-century home re-creates the traditional cancan and cabaret Montmartre scene, with paintings, posters, photos, music, and memorabilia (€7, includes audioguide, not covered by Museum Pass, Tue–Sun 11:00–18:00, closed Mon, 12 rue Cortot, tel. 01 49 25 89 39, www.museedemontmartre.fr).

**Pigalle**—Paris' redlight district, the infamous "Pig Alley," is at the foot of Butte Montmartre. *Ooh la la*. It's more racy than dangerous. Walk from place Pigalle to place Blanche, teasing desperate barkers and fast-talking temptresses. In bars, a €150 bottle of cheap champagne comes with a friend. Stick to the bigger streets, hang onto your wallet, and exercise good judgment. Cancan can cost a fortune, as can con artists in topless bars. After dark, countless tour buses line the streets, reminding us that tour guides make big bucks by bringing their groups to touristy nightclubs like the famous Moulin Rouge (Mo: Pigalle or Abbesses).

**Museum of Erotic Art (Musée de l'Erotisme)**—Paris' sexy museum has five floors of risqué displays—mostly paintings and drawings—ranging from artistic to erotic to disgusting, with a few circa-1920 porn videos and a fascinating history of local brothels tossed in. It's in the center of the Pigalle red light district (€8, no... it's not covered by Museum Pass, daily 10:00–2:00 in the morning,

72 boulevard de Clichy, Mo: Blanche, tel. 01 42 58 28 73, www .musee-erotisme.com).

# SHOPPING

Even staunch anti-shoppers may be tempted to partake in chic Paris. Wandering among the elegant and outrageous boutiques provides a break from the heavy halls of the Louvre, and, if you approach it right, a little cultural enlightenment.

Here are some tips for avoiding *faux pas* and making the most of the experience.

**French Etiquette:** Before you enter a Parisian store, remember the following points:

- In small stores, always say, *"Bonjour, Madame/Mademoiselle/Monsieur"* when entering and *"Au revoir, Madame/Mademoiselle/Monsieur"* when leaving.
- The customer is not always right. In fact, figure the clerk is doing you a favor by waiting on you.
- Except in department stores, it's not normal for the customer to handle clothing. Ask first before you pick up an item.
- For clothing size comparisons between the US and France, see page 870 in the appendix.
- Forget returns (and don't count on exchanges).
- Saturday afternoons are busiest.
- Observe French shoppers. Then imitate.
- Stores are generally closed on Sunday, except at the Carrousel du Louvre (underground shopping mall at the Louvre), and some shops near Sèvres-Babylone, along the Champs-Elysées, and in the Marais.
- Don't feel obliged to buy. The expression for "window-shopping" in French is *faire du lèche-vitrines* ("window-licking").

**Department Stores** (*Les Grands Magasins*)*:* Like cafés, department stores were invented here (surprisingly, not in America). Parisian department stores, monuments to a more relaxed and elegant era, begin with their showy perfume sections. Helpful information desks are usually nearby (pick up the handy store floor plan in English). Most stores have a good selection of souvenirs and toys at fair prices, plus reasonable restaurants; some have great view terraces. Choose from these great Parisian department stores: Galeries Lafayette (behind old Opéra Garnier, Mo: Opéra), Printemps (next-door to Galeries Lafayette), and Bon Marché (Mo: Sèvres-Babylone). Department stores are generally open Monday through Saturday from 10:00 to 19:00, some are open later on Thursdays, and all are jammed on Saturdays and closed on Sundays.

**Boutiques:** Allow yourself a vacation from your sightseeing-focused vacation by sifting through window displays, pausing at cafés, and observing the rhythm of neighborhood life. While the shops are more intimate, sales clerks are more formal—mind your manners.

Here are three very different areas to lick some windows:

• A stroll **from Sèvres-Babylone to St. Sulpice** allows you to sample smart, classic clothing boutiques while enjoying one of Paris' prettier neighborhoods—for sustenance along the way, there's La Maison du Chocolat at 19 rue de Sèvres, selling hand-made chocolates in exquisitely wrapped boxes.

• The ritzy streets connecting **place de la Madeleine and place Vendôme** form a miracle mile of gourmet food shops, jewelry stores, four-star hotels, exclusive clothing boutiques, and people who are better dressed than you. Fauchon, on place de la Madeleine, is a bastion of over-the-top food products, hawking €4,000 bottles of Cognac (who buys this stuff?). Hédiard, across the square at #21, is an older, more appealing, and more accessible gourmet food shop. Next door at #19, La Maison des Truffes sells black mushrooms for up to €1,000 a pound, and white truffles from Italy for €2,500 a pound.

• For more eclectic, avant-garde stores, peruse the artsy shops between the Pompidou Center and place des Vosges in the **Marais** (along rue Ste. Croix de la Bretonnerie and rue des Rosiers).

**Flea Markets:** Paris' sprawling weekend flea markets (*marché aux puces,* mar-shay oh poos; *puce* is French for "flea") are oversized garage sales. They started in the Middle Ages, when middlemen would sell old, flea-infested clothes and discarded possessions of the wealthy at bargain prices to eager peasants.

Today **Puces St. Ouen** (poos sahn-wahn), at Porte de Clignancourt, carries on that tradition. This is the mother of all flea markets, with more than 2,000 vendors selling everything from flamingos to faucets, but mostly antiques. This market shows off Paris' gritty, seamy underbelly and can be intimidating (Sat 9:00–18:00, Sun 10:00–18:00, Mon 11:00–17:00, closed Tue–Fri, pretty dead the first 2 weeks of Aug, tel. 01 58 61 22 90, www.st-ouen-tourisme.com and www.parispuces.com).

**Puces de Vanves** is comparatively tiny and civilized, and preferred by many flea-market connoisseurs who find better deals at less famous markets (Sat–Sun 7:00–17:00, closed Mon–Fri, Mo: Porte de Vanves). The mega **Puces de Montreuil** is the least organized and most traditional of them all, with chatty sellers and competitive buyers (Sat–Mon 8:00–18:00, closed Tue–Fri, Mo: Porte de Montreuil).

Some travelers find these markets claustrophobic, crowded, monster versions of those back home, though others find their French *diamants*-in-the-rough and return happy. Wear your money belt; pickpockets and scam artists thrive in these wall-to-wall-shopper events. Don't use ATM machines here if you can help it, as many are tampered with by con artists.

**Street Markets:** Several traffic-free street markets overflow with flowers, produce, fish vendors, and butchers, illustrating how most Parisians shopped before there were supermarkets and department stores. Good market streets include the rue Cler (Mo: Ecole Militaire), rue Montorgueil (Mo: Etienne Marcel), rue Mouffetard (Mo: Censier-Daubenton), Rue des Martyrs (Mo: Notre-Dame-de-Lorette), and rue Daguerre (Mo: Denfert-Rochereau). Browse these markets to collect a classy picnic (open daily except Sun afternoons and Mon, also closed for lunch 13:00–15:00).

**Souvenir Shops:** Avoid souvenir carts in front of famous monuments. Prices and selection are better in shops and department stores. The riverfront stalls near Notre-Dame sell a variety of used books, magazines, and tourist paraphernalia in the most romantic setting.

Whether you indulge in a new wardrobe, an artsy poster, or just one luscious pastry, you'll find that a shopping excursion provides a priceless slice of Parisian life.

# NIGHTLIFE

Paris is brilliant after dark. Save energy from your day's sightseeing and experience the City of Light lit. Whether it's a concert at the Sainte-Chapelle, a boat ride on the Seine, a walk in Montmartre, a hike up the Arc de Triomphe, or a late-night café, you'll see Paris come alive. Night walks in Paris are wonderful (and free). For a floodlit Seine river cruise, check out "Tours," on page 52.

The *Pariscope* magazine (€0.40 at any newsstand, in French) offers a complete weekly listing of music, cinema, theater, opera, and other special events. The *Paris Voice* website, in English, has a helpful monthly review of Paris entertainment (www.parisvoice.com).

## Music

**Jazz Clubs**— With a lively mix of American, French, and international musicians, Paris has been an internationally acclaimed jazz capital since World War II. You'll pay €12–25 to enter a jazz club (may include one drink; if not, expect to pay €5–10 per drink; beer is cheapest). See *Pariscope* magazine under "Musique" for listings, or, even better, the American Church's *Paris Voice* website for a good monthly review, or drop by the clubs to check out the calendars posted on their front doors. Music starts after 21:00 in most clubs. Some offer dinner concerts from about 20:30 on. Here are several good bets:

**Caveau de la Huchette,** a characteristic, old, jazz/dance club, fills an ancient Latin Quarter cellar with live jazz and frenzied dancing every night (admission about €11 on weekdays, €13 on weekends, €6 drinks, Tue–Sun 21:30–2:30 in the morning or later, closed Mon, 5 rue de la Huchette, Mo: St. Michel, recorded info tel. 01 43 26 65 05, www.caveaudelahuchette.fr).

For a spot teeming with late-night activity and jazz, go to the two-block-long rue des Lombards, at boulevard Sébastopol, midway between the river and the Pompidou Center (Mo: Châtelet). **Au Duc des Lombards** is one of the most popular and respected jazz clubs in Paris, with concerts nightly in a great, plush, 110-seat theater-like setting (admission about €20, cheap drinks, shows at 20:00 and 22:00, 42 rue des Lombards, tel. 01 42 33 22 88, www.ducdeslombards.fr). **Le Sunside,** run for 15 years by Stephane Portet, is just a block away. The club offers two little stages (ground floor and downstairs); one stage is devoted to contemporary world jazz, while the other features more traditional jazz—Dixieland and big band (concerts generally at 21:00, 60 rue des Lombards, tel. 01 40 26 21 25, www.sunset-sunside.com).

**Old-Time Parisian Cabaret on Montmartre: Au Lapin Agile**—This historic cabaret maintains the atmosphere of the heady days when bohemians would gather here to enjoy wine, song, and sexy jokes. For €24, you gather with about 25 French people in a dark room for a drink and as many as 10 different performers—mostly singers with a piano. Performers range from sweet and innocent Amélie types to naughty Maurice Chevalier types. While tourists are welcome, it's exclusively French, with no accommodation for English-speakers (and non-French-speakers will be lost). You sit at carved wooden tables in a dimly lit room, taste the traditional drink (brandy with cherries), and are immersed in a true Parisian ambience. The soirée covers traditional French standards, love ballads, sea chanteys, and more. The crowd sings along, as it has here for a century (Tue–Sun 21:00–2:00 in the morning, closed Mon, best to reserve ahead, 22 rue des Saules, tel. 01 46 06 85 87, www.au-lapin-agile.com).

**A Modern Cabaret near Canal St. Martin: Chez Raymonde**—This club proves that the art of dinner cabaret is still alive in Paris. Your evening begins with a good three-course dinner (including apéritif, wine, a half-bottle of champagne, and coffee) in an intimate dining room, where you get to know your neighbors. Around 22:00, the maître d'hôtel and the chef himself kick off the performance with a waltz together. Then it's feather boas, song, and dance—audience participation is encouraged (€85–100/person, Fri–Sun evenings only, dinner starts at 20:00 and performance usually finishes about 23:00, reservations necessary, 119 avenue Parmentier, Mo: Goncourt, Parmentier, or République, tel. 01 43 55 26 27, www.chez-raymonde.com). On Sunday afternoons, you can also attend a performance over lunch (€70–85, starts at 12:30).

**Classical Concerts**—For classical music on any night, consult *Pariscope* magazine (check "Concerts Classiques" under "Musique" for listings of fee and free events) and look for posters at tourist-oriented churches.

From March through November, these churches regularly host concerts: St. Sulpice, St. Germain-des-Prés, Ste. Madeleine, St. Eustache, St. Julien-le-Pauvre, and Sainte-Chapelle. It's well worth the €25 entry for the pleasure of hearing Mozart or Vivaldi while surrounded by the stained glass of the tiny Sainte-Chapelle (unheated—bring a sweater). Pick up concert schedules and tickets during the day at the small ticket booth to the left of the chapel entrance. Or call 01 42 77 65 65 to reserve ahead; you can leave your message in English (just speak clearly and spell your name). Seats are unassigned, so arrive 30 minutes early to snare a good view. There are often two concerts per evening at 19:00 and 20:30; specify which one you want when you buy or reserve your ticket.

Look also for daytime concerts in parks, such as the Luxembourg Garden. Even the Galeries Lafayette department store offers concerts. Many concerts are free *(entrée libre)*, such as the Sunday atelier concert sponsored by the American Church (generally Sept–June at 17:00 but not every week, 65 quai d'Orsay, Mo: Invalides, RER: Pont de l'Alma, tel. 01 40 62 05 00).

**Opera**—Paris is home to two well-respected opera venues. The **Opéra Bastille** is the massive modern opera house that dominates place de la Bastille. Come here for state-of-the-art special effects and modern interpretations of classic ballets and operas. In the spirit of this everyman's opera, unsold seats are available at a big discount to seniors and students 15 minutes before the show. Standing-room-only tickets for €15 are also sold for some performances (Mo: Bastille, tel. 01 43 43 96 96). The **Opéra Garnier,** Paris' first opera house, hosts opera and ballet performances. Come here for less expensive tickets and grand belle époque decor (Mo: Opéra).

Performance schedules are listed in *Pariscope* magazine, online (see below), and at the box offices. To get tickets for either opera house, call 08 92 89 90 90 (toll call, office closed Sun), or easier, reserve online at www.opera-de-paris.fr. You can also go direct to each opera's ticket office (open daily 11:00–18:00).

## Night Walks

Go for an evening walk to best appreciate the City of Light. Break for ice cream, pause at a café, and enjoy the sidewalk entertainers as you join the post-dinner Parisian parade. Consider these suggestions:

▲▲▲Trocadéro and Eiffel Tower—This is one of Paris' most spectacular views at night. Take the Métro to the Trocadéro stop and join the party on place du Trocadéro for a magnificent view of the glowing Eiffel Tower. It's a festival of gawkers, drummers, street acrobats, and entertainers. Pass the fountains and cross the river to the base of the tower, worth the effort even if you don't go up (daily June–Aug until 24:45, Sept–mid-June until 23:45). See "Eiffel Tower," page 80.

From the Eiffel Tower, you can stroll through Champ de Mars park past Frisbees, soccer balls, and romantic couples, and take the Métro home (Ecole Militaire stop, across avenue de la Motte-Picquet from far southeast corner of park). Or there's a handy RER stop (Champ de Mars–Tour Eiffel) two blocks west of the Eiffel Tower.

▲▲Champs-Elysées and the Arc de Triomphe—The avenue des Champs-Elysées glows after dark. Start at the Arc de Triomphe (observation deck open daily, April–Sept until 23:00, Oct–March until 22:30), then stroll down Paris' lively grand promenade. A right turn on avenue George V leads to the Bateaux-Mouches river cruises.

▲Ile St. Louis and Notre-Dame—This stroll features floodlit views of Notre-Dame and a taste of the Latin Quarter. Take the Métro (line 7) to the Pont Marie stop, then cross to Ile St. Louis. Turn right up rue St. Louis-en-l'Ile, stopping for dinner (or at least a Berthillon ice cream at #31 or Amorino Gelati at #47). Then cross pont St. Louis to Ile de la Cité, with a great view of Notre-Dame. Wander to the Left Bank on quai de l'Archevêché, and drop down to the river to the right for the best floodlit views. From May through September, you'll find fun bar-barges (daily until 2:00 in the morning, closed Oct–April, live music often Thu–Sun from 21:00). End your walk on place du Parvis Notre-Dame in front of Notre-Dame (on Sat–Sun in July–Aug, tower open until 23:00), or continue across the river to the Latin Quarter.

## After-Dark Bus Tour

Several companies offer evening tours of Paris. I've described the company offering the most tours below. These trips are sold through your hotel (brochures in lobby) or directly at the offices listed below. You save no money by buying direct.

Paris Illumination Tours, run by Paris Vision, connect all the great illuminated sights of Paris with a 100-minute bus tour in 12 languages. The double-decker buses have huge windows, but the most desirable front seats are sometimes reserved for customers who've bought tickets for the overrated Moulin Rouge. Left-side seats are better. Visibility is fine in the rain.

Warning: These tours are not for everyone. You'll stampede on with a United Nations of tourists, get a set of headphones, dial up your language, and listen to a tape-recorded spiel (which is interesting, but includes an annoyingly bright TV screen and a pitch for the other, more expensive excursions). Uninspired as it is, the ride provides an entertaining, first-night overview of the city at its floodlit and scenic best. Bring your city map to stay oriented as you go. You're always on the bus, but the driver slows for photos at viewpoints (€26/person, kids under 12 ride free, 1.5 hours, departures 19:00–22:00 depending on time of year, usually April–Oct only, reserve 1 day in advance, arrive 30 min early to wait in line for best seats, departs from Paris Vision office at 214 rue de Rivoli, across the street from Mo: Tuileries, tel. 01 42 60 30 01, fax 01 42 86 95 36, www.parisvision.com). Skip their pricier minivan night tours.

## SLEEPING

I've focused most of my recommendations in three safe, handy, and colorful neighborhoods: the village-like rue Cler (near the Eiffel Tower), the artsy and trendy Marais (near place de la Bastille), and the lively and Latin yet classy Luxembourg (on the Left Bank). Before reserving, read the descriptions of the neighborhoods. Each offers different pros and cons, and your neighborhood is as important as your hotel for the success of your trip.

Reserve ahead for Paris—the sooner, the better. Conventions clog Paris in September (worst), October, May, and June (very tough). There are unusually large crowds during holiday periods (see "Holidays and Festivals" on page 867), so book your accommodations well in advance. In August, when Paris is quiet, some hotels offer lower rates to fill their rooms (if you're planning to visit Paris in the summer, consider spending extra for an air-conditioned room). For advice on booking rooms, see "Making Reservations" on page 23.

Old, characteristic, budget Parisian hotels have always been cramped. Retrofitted with toilets, private showers, and elevators (as most are today), they are even more cramped. Some hotels include the hotel tax (*taxe du séjour*, about €1 per person per day), though most will add this to your bill.

Recommended hotels have an elevator unless otherwise noted. Quad rooms usually have two double beds. Because rooms with double beds and showers are cheaper than rooms with twin beds and baths, room prices vary within each hotel.

# Sleep Code

**(€1 = about $1.50, country code: 33)**
**S** = Single, **D** = Double/Twin, **T** = Triple, **Q** = Quad, **b** = bathroom,
**s** = shower only, * = French hotel rating system (0-4 stars).
Unless otherwise noted, hotel staff speak basic English and
breakfast is not included (but is usually optional).

To help you easily sort through these listings, I've divided
the rooms into three categories based on the price for a
standard double room with bath:

**$$$   Higher Priced:** Most rooms €150 or more.
**$$   Moderately Priced:** Most rooms between €100-150.
**$   Lower Priced:** Most rooms €100 or less.

Get advice from your hotel for safe parking. Consider long-term parking at either airport—Orly is closer and much easier for drivers to navigate than Charles de Gaulle. Garages are plentiful (€20–30/day, with special rates through some hotels). Curb parking is free at night (19:00–9:00), all day Sunday, and throughout the month of August. Self-serve launderettes are common; ask your hotelier for the nearest one (*"Où est un laverie automatique?"* ooh ay uh lah-vay-ree auto-mah-teek).

## Rue Cler

Lined with open-air produce stands six days a week, rue Cler is a safe, tidy, village-like pedestrian street. It's so French that when I step out of my hotel in the morning, I feel like I must have been a poodle in a previous life. How such coziness lodged itself between the high-powered government district and the wealthy Eiffel Tower and Les Invalides areas, I'll never know. This is a neighborhood of wide, tree-lined boulevards, stately apartment buildings, and lots of Americans. The American Church, American Library, American University, and many of my readers call this area home. Hotels here are relatively spacious and a good value, considering the elegance of the neighborhood and the higher prices of the more cramped hotels in other central areas. And for sightseeing, you're within walking distance of the Eiffel Tower, Army Museum, Seine River, and Orsay and Rodin museums.

Become a local at a rue Cler café for breakfast, or join the afternoon crowd for *une bière pression* (a draft beer). On rue Cler, you can eat and browse your way through a street full of pastry shops, delis, cheese shops, and colorful outdoor produce stalls. Afternoon *boules* (outdoor bowling) on the esplanade des Invalides is a relaxing spectator sport (look for the dirt area to the upper right as you face the front of Les Invalides; see sidebar on page 837). The manicured gardens behind the golden dome of the Army Museum are free, peaceful, and filled with flowers (at southwest corner of grounds, closes at about 19:00).

While hardly a happening night-life spot, rue Cler offers many low-impact after-dark activities. Take an evening stroll above the river through the parkway between pont de l'Alma and pont des Invalides. For an after-dinner cruise on the Seine, it's a 15-minute walk to the river and the Bateaux-Mouches (see page 53). For a post-dinner cruise on foot, saunter into Champ de Mars park to admire the glowing Eiffel Tower. For more ideas on Paris after hours, see "Nightlife" on page 105.

The American Church and Franco-American Center is the community center for Americans living in Paris. They host inter-denominational worship services (every Sun at 9:00 and 11:00) and occasional concerts (most Sun at 17:00 Sept–June—but not every week), and distribute the useful *France-USA Contacts* and *Paris Times* (reception open Mon–Sat 9:00–12:00 & 13:00–22:00, Sun 14:30–19:00, 65 quai d'Orsay, Mo: Invalides, tel. 01 40 62 05 00, www.acparis.org).

**Services:** There's a large **post office** at the end of rue Cler on avenue de la Motte-Picquet, and a handy **SNCF train office** at 78 rue St. Dominique (Mon–Sat 8:30–19:30, closed Sun, get there when it opens to avoid a long wait). At both of these offices, take a number and wait your turn. A smaller post office is closer to the Eiffel Tower on avenue Rapp, one block past rue St. Dominique toward the river.

**Markets:** Cross Champ de Mars park to mix it up with bargain-hunters at the twice-weekly open-air market, **Marché Boulevard de Grenelle,** under the Métro, a few blocks southwest of Champ de Mars park (Wed and Sun until 12:30, between Mo: Dupleix and Mo: La Motte-Picquet-Grenelle). Two grocery stores, both on rue de Grenelle, are open until midnight: **Epicerie de la Tour** (at #197) and **Alimentation** (at corner with rue Cler). **Rue St. Dominique** is the area's boutique-browsing street.

**Internet Access:** Two Internet cafés compete in this neigh-borhood: **Com Avenue** is best (about €5/hr, shareable and multi-use accounts, Mon–Sat 10:00–20:00, closed Sun, 24 rue du Champ de Mars, tel. 01 45 55 00 07); **Cyber World Café** is more expensive but open later (about €7/hr, Mon–Sat 12:00–22:00, Sun 12:00–20:00, 20 rue de l'Exposition, tel. 01 53 59 96 54).

**Laundry:** Launderettes are omnipresent; ask your hotel for the nearest. Here are three handy locations: on rue Auguer (between rue St. Dominique and rue de Grenelle), on rue Amélie (between rue St. Dominique and rue de Grenelle), and at the southeast corner of rue Valadon and rue de Grenelle.

**Métro Connections:** Key Métro stops are Ecole Militaire, La Tour Maubourg, and Invalides. The RER-C line runs from the pont de l'Alma and Invalides stations, serving Versailles to the west; Auvers-sur-Oise to the north; and the Orsay Museum, Latin Quarter (St. Michel stop), and Austerlitz train station to the east.

**Bus Routes:** Smart travelers take advantage of these helpful bus routes (see map on page 113 for stop locations): Line #69 runs east–west along rue St. Dominique and serves Les Invalides, Orsay, Louvre, Marais, and Père Lachaise Cemetery (Mon–Sat only—no Sun service; see sidebar, page 53). Line #63 runs along the river (the quai d'Orsay), serving the Latin Quarter along boulevard St. Germain to the east (ending at Gare de Lyon), and Trocadéro and the Marmottan Museum to the west. Line #92 runs along avenue Bosquet, north to the Champs-Elysées and Arc de Triomphe (far better than the Métro) and south to the Montparnasse Tower and Gare Montparnasse. Line #87 runs on avenue de la Bourdonnais and serves St. Sulpice, Luxembourg Garden, the Sèvres-Babylone shopping area, the Bastille, and Gare de Lyon (also more convenient than Métro for these destinations). Line #28 runs on boulevard de la Tour Maubourg and serves Gare St. Lazare.

## Sleeping in the Rue Cler Neighborhood
**(7th arrondissement, Mo: Ecole Militaire, La Tour–Maubourg, or Invalides)**
Rue Cler is the glue that holds this handsome neighborhood together.

### In the Heart of Rue Cler
Many of my readers stay in the rue Cler neighborhood. If you want to disappear into Paris, choose a hotel elsewhere. The first six hotels listed below are within Camembert-smelling distance of rue Cler; the others are within a 5- to 10-minute stroll. All hotels listed in the rue Cler area have elevators, air-conditioning, public Internet access terminals and Wi-Fi unless noted ("Wi-Fi only" means there's no computer available, but they do have Wi-Fi).

**$$$ Hôtel Relais Bosquet**\*** is a professional place with generous public spaces and comfortable rooms that feature effective darkness blinds. The staff are politely formal and offer free breakfast (good buffet, including eggs and sausage) to anyone booking direct with this book in 2009 (standard Db-€170, bigger Db-€190, check website for special discounts, extra bed-€25, 19 rue du Champ de Mars, tel. 01 47 05 25 45, fax 01 45 55 08 24, www.relaisbosquet.com, hotel@relaisbosquet.com).

# Rue Cler Hotels

1. Hôtel Relais Bosquet
2. Hôtel Beaugency
3. Grand Hôtel Lévêque
4. Hôtel du Champ de Mars
5. Hôtel de la Motte Picquet
6. Hôtels le Tourville & de Turenne
7. Hôtel Duquesne Eiffel
8. Hôtel La Bourdonnais
9. Hôtel de Londres Eiffel
10. Hôtel Eber Mars
11. Hôtel de la Tulipe
12. Hôtel Royal Phare
13. Hôtel Les Jardins d'Eiffel
14. Hôtel Muguet
15. Hôtel de l'Empereur
16. Hôtel du Cadran
17. Best Western Eiffel Park
18. Hôtel Kensington
19. Hôtel Prince
20. Hôtel St. Dominique
21. Hôtel de la Tour Eiffel
22. SNCF Office
23. Com Avenue Internet Café
24. Cyber World Internet Café
25. Late-Night Groceries (2)
26. Launderettes (3)

**$$$ Hôtel du Cadran\*\*\***, perfectly located a *boule* toss from rue Cler, welcomes you with a smart lobby, efficient staff, and stylish rooms featuring cool colors, mood lighting, and every comfort (Db-€205–230, 10 percent discount and free breakfast by entering the code "RickSteves" when you book by email or via their website, discount not valid for promotional rates on website; 10 rue du Champ de Mars, tel. 01 40 62 67 00, fax 01 40 62 67 13, www.hotelducadran.com, info@cadranhotel.com).

**$$$ Hôtel de la Motte Picquet\*\*\***, at the corner of rue Cler and avenue de la Motte-Picquet, is an intimate little place with plush rooms at fair prices (Sb-€150, standard Db-€160, bigger Db-€200, 30 avenue de la Motte-Picquet, tel. 01 47 05 09 57, fax 01 47 05 74 36, www.hotelmottepicquetparis.com, book@hotelmottepicquetparis.com).

**$$ Hôtel Beaugency\*\*\***, a solid value on a quieter street a short block off rue Cler, has 30 small rooms with standard furnishings and a lobby you can stretch out in (Sb-€105–115, Db-€115–155, Christelle and Amel offer a 20 percent discount with this book in 2009 if you reserve through the website and enter code word "RICK," discount valid only on a limited number of rooms, 21 rue Duvivier, tel. 01 47 05 01 63, fax 01 45 51 04 96, www.hotel-beaugency.com, infos@hotel-beaugency.com).

*Warning:* The next two hotels are super values, but very busy with my readers (reserve long in advance).

**$$ Grand Hôtel Lévêque\*\*** faces rue Cler with red and gray tones, a singing maid, and a sliver-sized slow-dance elevator. This busy hotel has a convivial breakfast/hangout room and four floors. Half the rooms have been renovated and cost more (S-€62–74, Db-€95–132, Tb-€132–144, 29 rue Cler, tel. 01 47 05 49 15, fax 01 45 50 49 36, www.hotel-leveque.com, info@hotel-leveque.com, helpful Christophe and Lidwine).

**$ Hôtel du Champ de Mars\*\***, with adorable pastel rooms and serious owners Françoise and Stephane, is a cozy rue Cler option. This plush little hotel has a small-town feel from top to bottom. The rooms are snug but lovingly kept, and single rooms can work as tiny doubles. It's an excellent value despite the lack of air-conditioning. This popular hotel receives an overwhelming number of reservations, so please be patient with them (Sb-€89, Db-€95, Tb-€119, 30 yards off rue Cler at 7 rue du Champ de Mars, tel. 01 45 51 52 30, fax 01 45 51 64 36, www.hotelduchampdemars.com, reservation@hotelduchampdemars.com).

## Near Rue Cler, Close to Ecole Militaire Métro Stop

The following listings are a five-minute walk from rue Cler, near Métro stop Ecole Militaire or RER: Pont de l'Alma.

$$$ **Hôtel le Tourville****, despite its four official stars, is really a top-notch three-star place. It's intimate and classy, from its living-room lobby and vaulted breakfast area to its pretty pastel rooms (small standard Db-€190, superior Db-€250, Db with private terrace-€290, junior suite for 3–4 people-€450, 16 avenue de Tourville, tel. 01 47 05 62 62, fax 01 47 05 43 90, www.hoteltourville .com, hotel@tourville.com).

$$$ **Hôtel Duquesne Eiffel***, a few blocks farther from the action, is hospitable. It offers handsome rooms, a welcoming lobby, and a big, hot breakfast (Db-€170–210, price grows with room size, Tb-€230, breakfast-€13, 23 avenue Duquesne, tel. 01 44 42 09 09, fax 01 44 42 09 08, www.hde.fr, Julie@hde.fr).

$$$ **Hôtel La Bourdonnais*** is _très_ Parisian, mixing an Old World feel with creaky, comfortable rooms and generous public spaces. Its mostly spacious rooms are traditionally decorated (Sb-€140, Db-€175, Tb-€195, Qb-€220, Sophie promises a 10 percent discount with this book through 2009, 111 avenue de la Bourdonnais, tel. 01 47 05 45 42, fax 01 45 55 75 54, www.hotel labourdonnais.fr, hlb@hotellabourdonnais.fr).

$$ **Hôtel Prince**, across from the Ecole Militaire Métro stop, has a spartan lobby, ugly halls, and plain-but-acceptable rooms for the price (Sb-€83, Db with shower-€105, Db with tub-€120, Tb-€130, no Internet access, 66 avenue Bosquet, tel. 01 47 05 40 90, fax 01 47 53 06 62, www.hotelparisprince.com, paris @hotel-prince.com).

$$ **Hôtel Eber Mars** has larger-than-most rooms with weathered furnishings, oak-paneled public spaces, and a beam-me-up-Jacques, coffin-sized elevator. Air-conditioning is planned for 2009 (Sb-€100, Db-€118–138, Tb-€170, Qb-€190, 20 percent cheaper Nov–March and July–Aug, first breakfast free with this book in 2009, 117 avenue de la Bourdonnais, tel. 01 47 05 42 30, fax 01 47 05 45 91, www.hotelebermars.com, reservation@hotelebermars.com, manager Mr. Eber is a wealth of information for travelers).

$ **Hôtel de Turenne** is modest, with the cheapest air-conditioned rooms I've found and a colorful, open lobby. While the halls are frumpy and the rooms are _très_ simple, the price is right. There are five true singles and several connecting rooms good for families (Sb-€69, Db-€79–92, Tb-€112, extra bed-€10, Wi-Fi only, 20 avenue de Tourville, tel. 01 47 05 99 92, fax 01 45 56 06 04, hotel.turenne.paris7@wanadoo.fr).

## Near Rue Cler, Closer to Rue St. Dominique (and the Seine)

$$$ **Hôtel de Londres Eiffel*** is my closest listing to the Eiffel Tower and Champ de Mars park. A good value, it offers immaculate, warmly decorated rooms, cozy public spaces, and a

service-oriented staff. Show them this book in 2009 for a free Seine cruise (inquire upon arrival). It's less convenient to the Métro (10-min walk) but handy to bus #69 and RER-C: Pont de l'Alma (Sb-€165, Db-€185, Db with Eiffel Tower view-€195–215, Tb-€245, check website for special rates, 1 rue Augerau, tel. 01 45 51 63 02, fax 01 47 05 28 96, www.londres-eiffel.com, info @londres-eiffel.com). The owners also have a good two-star hotel (Hôtel Apollon Montparnasse) in the Montparnasse area, with much lower rates—see www.londres-eiffel.com for details.

**$$$ Hôtel de la Tulipe\*\*\***, three blocks from rue Cler toward the river, is pricey but unique. The 20 small but artistically decorated rooms—each one different—come with stylish little bathrooms and surround a seductive, wood-beamed lounge and a peaceful, leafy courtyard (Db-€160, Tb-€180, two-room suite for up to five people-€280, friendly staff, no air-con, no elevator, 33 rue Malar, tel. 01 45 51 67 21, fax 01 47 53 96 37, www.paris-hotel -tulipe.com, hoteldelatulipe@wanadoo.fr).

**$$ Hôtel St. Dominique\*\***  has fair rates, an inviting lobby, a small courtyard, and traditionally decorated rooms—most with minibars and floral wallpaper (Db-€140–160, extra bed-€20, no air-con, no elevator, Wi-Fi only, 62 rue St. Dominique, tel. 01 47 05 51 44, fax 01 47 05 81 28, www.hotelstdominique.com, saint -dominique.reservations@wanadoo.fr).

**$ Hôtel de la Tour Eiffel\*\***  is a terrific two-star value on a quiet street near several of my favorite restaurants. The rooms are well-designed, spotless, and comfortable (snug Db-€79, bigger Db-€105–115, no air-con, elevator, Wi-Fi only, 17 rue de l'Exposition, tel. 01 47 05 14 75, fax 01 47 53 99 46, www.hotel -toureiffel.com, hte7@wanadoo.fr).

**$ Hôtel Kensington\*\***  is a fine budget value close to the Eiffel Tower and run by elegant Daniele. It's an unpretentious place with mostly small, simple, but well-kept rooms (Sb-€62, Db-€79, big Db on back side-€94, Eiffel Tower views for those who ask, no air-con, no Internet access, 79 avenue de la Bourdonnais, tel. 01 47 05 74 00, fax 01 47 05 25 81, www.hotel-kensington.com, hk@hotel-kensington.com).

### Near La Tour-Maubourg Métro Stop

The next three listings are within two blocks of the intersection of avenue de la Motte-Picquet and boulevard de la Tour Maubourg.

**$$$ Hôtel Les Jardins d'Eiffel\*\*\***, on a quiet street, feels like the modern motel it is, with professional service, its own parking garage (€24/day), and a spacious lobby. The 81 rooms are all designed for double occupancy (Sb/Db-€170–230; 15 percent Rick Steves discount when you book direct through 2009, or check website for special discounts; 8 rue Amélie, tel. 01 47 05 46 21, fax 01 45 55 28 08, www.hoteljardinseiffel.com, paris@hoteljardinseiffel.com).

**$$ Hôtel Muguet****, a peaceful, stylish, immaculate refuge, gives you three-star comfort for a two-star price. This delightful spot offers 43 tasteful rooms, a greenhouse lounge, and a small garden courtyard. The hands-on owner, Catherine, gives her guests a restful and secure home in Paris (Sb-€105, Db with one big bed-€135, twin Db-€135, small Db with view-€160, big Db with view and balcony-€190, Tb-€190, 11 rue Chevert, tel. 01 47 05 05 93, fax 01 45 50 25 37, www.hotelmuguet.com, muguet @wanadoo.fr, gentle Jacqueline runs reception).

**$$ Hôtel de l'Empereur**** lacks intimacy, but it's spacious and a fair value. Its 38 pleasant rooms come with real wood furniture and views but some noise; fifth-floor rooms have small balconies and Napoleonic views (Db-€108, Tb-€135, Qb-€155, 2 rue Chevert, tel. 01 45 55 88 02, fax 01 45 51 88 54, www.hotel empereur.com, contact@hotelempereur.com).

## Lesser Values in the Rue Cler Area

Given how fine this area is, these are acceptable last choices.

**$$$ Best Western Eiffel Park**** is a dead-quiet concrete business hotel with all the comforts, a relaxing lobby, 36 pleasant if unexceptional rooms, and a rooftop terrace (Db-€240, bigger "luxe" Db-€260, check online for promotional rates, 17 bis rue Amélie, tel. 01 45 55 10 01, fax 01 47 05 28 68, www.eiffelpark.com, reservation@eiffelpark.com).

**$ Hôtel Royal Phare**** , facing the busy Ecole Militaire Métro stop, is humble and ideal for backpackers. The 34 basic, pink-pastel rooms are unimaginative but sleepable. Rooms on the courtyard are quietest, with peek-a-boo views of the Eiffel Tower from the fifth floor up (Sb-€76, Db with shower-€80–95, Db with tub-€100, Tb-€105, fridges in rooms, 40 avenue de la Motte-Picquet, tel. 01 47 05 57 30, fax 01 45 51 64 41, www.hotel-royalphare-paris.com, hotel-royalphare@wanadoo.fr, friendly manager Hocin).

## Marais

Those interested in a more SoHo/Greenwich Village locale should

make the Marais their Parisian home. Once a forgotten Parisian backwater, the Marais now is one of Paris' most popular residential, tourist, and shopping areas. This is jumbled, medieval Paris at its finest, where classy stone mansions sit alongside trendy bars, antiques shops, and fashion-conscious boutiques. The streets are a fascinating parade of artists, students, tourists, immigrants, and baguette-munching babies in strollers. The Marais is also known as a hub of the Parisian gay and lesbian scene. This area is *sans doute* livelier (and louder) than the rue Cler area.

In the Marais, you have these major sights close at hand: Picasso Museum, Carnavalet Museum, Victor Hugo's House, the Jewish Art and History Museum, and the Pompidou Center. You're also a manageable walk from Paris' two islands (Ile St. Louis and Ile de la Cité), home to Notre-Dame and Sainte-Chapelle. The Opéra Bastille, Promenade Plantée park, place des Vosges (Paris' oldest square), Jewish Quarter (rue des Rosiers), and nightlife-packed rue de Lappe are also walkable. (For Marais sight descriptions, see page 95; for the Opéra, see page 107.)

Most of my recommended hotels are located a few blocks north of the Marais' main east–west drag, rue St. Antoine/rue de Rivoli.

**Tourist Information:** The nearest TI is in Gare de Lyon (Mon–Sat 8:00–18:00, closed Sun, all-Paris TI tel. 08 92 68 30 00).

**Services:** Most banks and other services are on the main street, rue de Rivoli, which becomes rue St. Antoine. Marais **post offices** are on rue Castex and at the corner of rue Pavée and rue des Francs Bourgeois. There's a busy **SNCF Boutique** where you can take care of all train needs on rue St. Antoine at rue de Turenne (Mon–Sat 8:30–20:30, closed Sun). A quieter SNCF Boutique is nearer Gare de Lyon at 5 rue de Lyon (Mon–Sat 8:30–18:00, closed Sun).

**Markets:** The Marais has two good open-air markets: the sprawling **Marché de la Bastille,** around place de la Bastille (Thu and Sun until 12:30); and the more intimate, untouristy **Marché de la place d'Aligre** (Tue–Sun 9:00–12:00, closed Mon, cross place de la Bastille and walk about 10 blocks down rue du Faubourg St. Antoine, turn right at rue de Cotte to place d'Aligre; or, easier, take Métro line 8 from Bastille in the direction of Créteil-Préfecture, get off at the Ledru-Rollin stop, and walk a few blocks southeast). A small **grocery shop** is open until 23:00 on rue St. Antoine (near intersection with rue Castex). To shop at a Parisian Sears, find the **BHV** next to Hôtel de Ville.

**Bookstore:** The Marais is home to the friendliest English-language bookstore in Paris, **Red Wheelbarrow.** Penelope sells most of my guidebooks at good prices, and carries a great collection of other books about Paris and France for both adults and children (Mon–Fri 10:00–19:00, Sat 10:00–12:00 & 14:00–19:00, Sun 14:00–18:00, 22 rue St. Paul, Mo: St. Paul, tel. 01 48 04 75 08).

**Internet Access:** Try **Paris CY** (Mon–Sat 8:00–20:00, Sun 13:00–20:00, 8 rue de Jouy, Mo: St. Paul, tel. 01 42 71 37 37), or **Cyber Cube** (daily 10:00–22:00, 12 rue Daval, Mo: Bastille, tel. 01 49 29 67 67).

**Laundry:** There are many launderettes; ask your hotelier for the nearest. Here are four you can count on: on impasse Guéménée (north of rue St. Antoine), on rue du Plâtre (just west of rue du Temple), on rue du Petit Musc (south of rue St. Antoine), and on rue Daval (near Cyber Cube).

**Métro Connections:** Key Métro stops in the Marais are, from east to west: Bastille, St. Paul, and Hôtel de Ville (Sully-Morland, Pont Marie, and Rambuteau stops are also handy). Métro service to the Marais neighborhood is excellent, with direct service to the Louvre, Champs-Elysées, Arc de Triomphe, and La Défense (all on line 1); the rue Cler area and Opéra Garnier (line 8 from Bastille stop); and four major train stations: Gare de Lyon, Gare du Nord, Gare de l'Est, and Gare d'Austerlitz (all accessible from Bastille stop).

**Bus Routes:** Line #69 on rue St. Antoine takes you eastbound to Père Lachaise Cemetery and westbound to the Louvre, Orsay, and Rodin museums, plus the Army Museum, ending at the Eiffel Tower (Mon–Sat only—no Sun service). Line #86 runs down boulevard Henri IV, crossing Ile St. Louis and serving the Latin Quarter along boulevard St. Germain. Line #87 follows a similar route, but also serves Gare de Lyon to the east and the Eiffel Tower and rue Cler neighborhood to the west. Line #96 runs on rues Turenne and François Miron and serves the Louvre and boulevard St. Germain (near Luxembourg Garden), ending at Gare Montparnasse. Line #65 runs from Gare de Lyon up rue de Lyon, around place de la Bastille, and then up boulevard Beaumarchais to Gare de l'Est and Gare du Nord.

**Taxis:** You'll find taxi stands on place de la Bastille (where boulevard Richard Lenoir meets the square), on the south side of rue St. Antoine (in front of St. Paul Church), and a quieter one on the north side of rue St. Antoine (where it meets rue Castex).

## Sleeping in the Marais Neighborhood

**(4th arrondissement, Mo: Bastille, St. Paul, and Hôtel de Ville)**
The Marais runs from the Pompidou Center to the Bastille (a 15-min walk), with most hotels located a few blocks north of the main east–west drag, the rue de Rivoli/rue St. Antoine. It's about 15 minutes on foot from any hotel in this area to Notre-Dame, Ile St. Louis, and the Latin Quarter. Strolling home (day or night) from Notre-Dame along the Ile St. Louis is marvelous.

All hotels listed in the Marais neighborhood have elevators, air-conditioning, public Internet access terminals, and Wi-Fi unless otherwise noted.

### Near Place des Vosges

**$$$ Hôtel Castex***,** a well-managed place with tiled floors and dark wood accents, is well-situated on a quiet street near place de

PARIS

# Marais Hotels

1. Hôtel Castex
2. Hôtel Bastille Spéria
3. Hôtel Daval
4. Hôtel Saint-Louis Marais
5. Grand Hôtel Jeanne d'Arc
6. Hôtel Lyon-Mulhouse
7. Hôtel Sévigné
8. Hôtel du 7ème Art
9. Hôtel du Sully
10. MIJE Hostels (3)
11. Hôtel de la Bretonnerie
12. Hôtel Caron de Beaumarchais
13. Hôtel du Vieux Marais
14. Hôtel Beaubourg
15. Hôtel de Nice
16. Hôtel du Loiret
17. BHV Department Store
18. Red Wheelbarrow Books
19. SNCF Boutique (Train Tickets)
20. Late-Night Grocery
21. Cyber Cube Internet Café & Launderette
22. Paris CY Internet Café
23. Launderettes (3)

**M** Metro Station
**T** Taxi Stand
**P** Parking
**B** Bus Stop w/ Route #

POMPIDOU CENTER
JEWISH MUSEUM
PICASSO MUSEUM
CARNAVALET MUSEUM
PLACE DES VOSGES
OPÉRA BASTILLE
PLACE DE LA BASTILLE
HOTEL DE VILLE
SEINE RIVER

200 YARDS
200 METERS

la Bastille. A clever system of connecting rooms allows families total privacy between two rooms, each with its own bathroom. The 30 rooms are narrow but tasteful; it's a good value year-round. Your fourth night is free in August and from November through February, except around New Year's (Sb-€120, Db-€150, Tb-€220, 5 percent discount and free buffet breakfast with this book through 2009, just off place de la Bastille and rue St. Antoine at 5 rue Castex, Mo: Bastille, tel. 01 42 72 31 52, fax 01 42 72 57 91, www .castexhotel.com, info@castexhotel.com).

**$$ Hôtel Bastille Spéria\*\*\***, a short block off place de la Bastille, offers business-type service. The walls are thin, but the 42 well-configured rooms are modern and comfortable, with big beds (Sb-115, Db-€140–178, child's bed-€20, good buffet breakfast-€13, 1 rue de la Bastille, Mo: Bastille, tel. 01 42 72 04 01, fax 01 42 72 56 38, www.hotel-bastille-speria.com, info@hotel -bastille-speria.com).

**$$ Hôtel Saint-Louis Marais\*\*** is a little hotel on a quiet residential street between the river and rue St. Antoine. The lobby is inviting and the 19 rooms have character (a few are at street level), but there's no air-conditioning, no elevator, and no Internet access (small Db-€115, standard Db-€140, Tb-€160, parking-€20, 1 rue Charles V, Mo: Sully Morland, tel. 01 48 87 87 04, fax 01 48 87 33 26, www.saintlouismarais.com, slmarais@noos.fr).

**$$ Hôtel du 7ème Art\*\***, two blocks south of rue St. Antoine toward the river, is a young, carefree, Hollywood-nostalgia place with a full-service café-bar and Charlie Chaplin murals (but no elevator and pay Wi-Fi). Its 23 good-value rooms have brown 1970s decor, but are comfortable enough. The large rooms are American-spacious (small Db-€93, standard Db-€105, large Db-€120–150, Tb-€140–170, extra bed-€20, 20 rue St. Paul, Mo: St. Paul, tel. 01 44 54 85 00, fax 01 42 77 69 10, www.paris-hotel-7art.com, hotel 7art@wanadoo.fr).

**$ Grand Hôtel Jeanne d'Arc\*\***, a lovely little hotel with thoughtfully appointed rooms, is ideally located for (and very popular with) connoisseurs of the Marais. It's a fine value and worth booking way ahead (three months in advance, if possible). Sixth-floor rooms have views, and corner rooms are wonderfully bright in the City of Light—though no rooms have air-conditioning and there's no Internet access. Rooms on the street can be noisy until the bars close (Sb-€62–89, Db-€89, larger twin Db-€116, Tb-€146, good Qb-€160, 3 rue de Jarente, Mo: St. Paul, tel. 01 48 87 62 11, fax 01 48 87 37 31, information@hoteljeannedarc.com).

**$ Hôtel Lyon-Mulhouse\*\***, well-managed by gregarious Nathalia, is located on a busy street barely off place de la Bastille. While less intimate than some, it is a solid deal, with pleasant, relatively large rooms—five are true singles with partial Eiffel

Tower views (Sb-€70, Db-€100, Tb-€130, Qb-€150, pay Wi-Fi, 8 boulevard Beaumarchais, Mo: Bastille, tel. 01 47 00 91 50, fax 01 47 00 06 31, www.1-hotel-paris.com, hotelyonmulhouse @wanadoo.fr).

**$ Hôtel Daval\*\***, an unassuming place with good rates on the lively side of place de la Bastille, is ideal for night owls. Ask for a quieter room on the courtyard side (Sb-€72, Db-€85, Tb-110, Qb-€125, 21 rue Daval, Mo: Bastille, tel. 01 47 00 51 23, fax 01 40 21 80 26, www.hoteldaval.com, hoteldaval@wanadoo.fr, Didier).

**$ Hôtel Sévigné\*\***, run by straight-faced owner Monsieur Mercier, is a snappy little hotel with lavender halls and 30 tidy, comfortable rooms at good prices (Sb-€68, Db-€81–92, Tb-€104; one-night, no-refund policy for any cancellation; no Internet access, 2 rue Malher, Mo: St. Paul, tel. 01 42 72 76 17, fax 01 42 78 68 26, www.le-sevigne.com, contact@le-sevigne.com).

**$ Hôtel du Sully,** sitting right on rue St. Antoine, is nothing fancy, but it is cheap. The entry is long and narrow, and the rooms are dimly lit but sleepable (Db-€65, Tb-€80, no elevator, no air-con, no Internet access, 48 rue St. Antoine, Mo: St. Paul, tel. 01 42 78 49 32, fax 01 44 61 76 50, www.sullyhotelparis.com, sullyhotel @orange.fr, run by friendly Monsieur Zeroual).

**$ MIJE Youth Hostels:** The Maison Internationale de la Jeunesse et des Etudiants (MIJE) runs three classy old residences that make a budget traveler's dream come true. Each is well-maintained, with simple, clean, single-sex (unless your group takes a whole room), one- to four-bed rooms for travelers of any age. The hostels are **MIJE Fourcy** (biggest and loudest, €11 dinners available with a membership card, 6 rue de Fourcy, just south of rue de Rivoli), **MIJE Fauconnier** (no elevator, 11 rue du Fauconnier), and **MIJE Maubisson** (smallest and quietest, no outdoor terrace, 12 rue des Barres). None has double beds or air-conditioning; all have private showers in every room (all prices per person: Sb-€49, Db-€36, Tb-€32, Qb-€30, credit cards accepted, includes breakfast but not towels, required membership card-€2.50 extra/person, 7-day maximum stay, rooms locked 12:00–15:00, curfew at 1:00 in the morning). They all share the same contact information (tel. 01 42 74 23 45, fax 01 40 27 81 64, www.mije.com, info @mije.com) and Métro stop (St. Paul). Reservations are accepted (six weeks ahead online, ten days ahead by phone)—though you must show up by noon, or call the morning of arrival to confirm a later arrival time.

## Near the Pompidou Center

These hotels are farther west, closer to the Pompidou Center than to place de la Bastille. The Hôtel de Ville Métro stop works well for all of these hotels, unless a closer stop is noted.

**$$$ Hôtel Caron de Beaumarchais\*\*\*** feels like a fluffy folk museum with 20 sweet little rooms and a lobby cluttered with bits from an elegant 18th-century Marais house. Short antique collectors should sleep here (small Db in back-€152, larger Db facing the front-€170, Wi-Fi only, 12 rue Vieille du Temple, tel. 01 42 72 34 12, fax 01 42 72 34 63, www.carondebeaumarchais.com, hotel @carondebeaumarchais.com).

**$$ Hôtel de la Bretonnerie\*\*\***, three blocks from the Hôtel de Ville, makes a fine Marais home. It has a warm, welcoming lobby, chic decor, and 29 tastefully appointed rooms with an antique, open-beam warmth (perfectly good standard "classic" Db-€130, bigger "charming" Db-€160, Db suite-€190, Tb/Qb-€190, Tb/Qb suite-€210, no air-con, between rue Vieille du Temple and rue des Archives at 22 rue Ste. Croix de la Bretonnerie, tel. 01 48 87 77 63, fax 01 42 77 26 78, www.bretonnerie.com, hotel@bretonnerie.com).

**$$ Hôtel du Vieux Marais\*\***, with a quirky owner and modern rooms that should all be renovated by the time you get there, is tucked away on a quiet street two blocks east of the Pompidou Center. Say *bonjour* to friendly bulldog Leelou, who runs the small lobby (Sb-€100–115, Db-€120–155, extra bed-€23, Wi-Fi only, just off rue des Archives at 8 rue du Plâtre, Mo: Rambuteau or Hôtel de Ville, tel. 01 42 78 47 22, fax 01 42 78 34 32, www.vieuxmarais .com, hotel@vieuxmarais.com).

**$$ Hôtel Beaubourg\*\*\*** is a good three-star value on a quiet street in the shadow of the Pompidou Center. The lounge is inviting, and the 28 rooms are wood-beam comfy (standard Db-€140, bigger twin Db-€160, rates vary wildly by season, 11 rue Simon Le Franc, Mo: Rambuteau, tel. 01 42 74 34 24, fax 01 42 78 68 11, www.hotelbeaubourg.com, htlbeaubourg@hotellerie.net).

**$$ Hôtel de Nice\*\***, on the Marais' busy main drag, is a turquoise-and-fuchsia "Marie-Antoinette-does-tie-dye" spot. Its narrow halls are littered with paintings and layered with carpets, and its 23 Old World rooms have thoughtful touches and tight bathrooms. Twin rooms, which cost the same as doubles, are larger and on the street side—but have effective double-paned windows (Sb-€85, Db-€115, Tb-€140, extra bed-€20, no Internet access, reception on second floor, 42 bis rue de Rivoli, tel. 01 42 78 55 29, fax 01 42 78 36 07, www.hoteldenice.com, contact@hoteldenice .com, laissez-faire management).

**$ Hôtel du Loiret\*** is a centrally located (some noise) and rare Marais budget hotel. If you can get past the lobby, you'll be surprised at how much better the rooms are (S with WC across hall-€50, Db-€70–90, Tb-€100, no air-con, 8 rue des Mauvais Garçons, tel. 01 48 87 77 00, fax 01 48 04 96 56, www.hotel-loiret .fr, hotelduloiret@hotmail.com).

## In the Historic Core, on Ile St. Louis

The peaceful, residential character of this river-wrapped island, its brilliant location, and its homemade ice cream have drawn Americans for decades, allowing hotels to charge dearly. There are no budget values here, but the island's coziness and proximity to the Marais, Notre-Dame, and the Latin Quarter help compensate for higher rates. All of the following hotels are on the island's main drag, rue St. Louis-en-l'Ile, where I list several restaurants (see "Eating," page 146). Use Mo: Pont Marie or Sully-Morland.

**$$$ Hôtel du Jeu de Paume****\*\*\*\***, occupying a 17th-century tennis center, is the most expensive hotel I list in Paris. When you enter its magnificent lobby, you'll understand why. Greet Scoop, *le chien*, then take a spin in the glass elevator for a half-timbered-tree-house experience. The 30 quite comfortable rooms are carefully designed and *très* tasteful, though small for the price (you're paying for the location and public spaces—check for deals on their website). Most rooms face a small garden; all are pin-drop peaceful (standard Db-€285, larger Db-€370, deluxe Db-€450, 54 rue St. Louis-en-l'Ile, tel. 01 43 26 14 18, fax 01 40 46 02 76, www.jeudepaumehotel.com, info@jeudepaumehotel.com).

**$$$ Hôtel de Lutèce***\*\*\*** charges top euro for its island address but comes with a sit-a-while wood-paneled lobby, a fireplace, and warmly designed rooms. Twin rooms are larger and the same price as double rooms (Db-€195, Tb-€235, 65 rue St. Louis-en-l'Ile, tel. 01 43 26 23 52, fax 01 43 29 60 25, www.hoteldelutece.com, info@hoteldelutece.com).

**$$$ Hôtel des Deux-Iles***\*\*\*** is bright and colorful, with marginally smaller rooms (Db-€180, Wi-Fi only, 59 rue St. Louis-en-l'Ile, tel. 01 43 26 13 35, fax 01 43 29 60 25, www.2iles.com, hotel.2iles@free.fr).

**$$$ Hôtel Saint-Louis***\*\*\*** has less personality but good rooms with parquet floors and comparatively good rates (Db-€145–160, extra bed-€50, Wi-Fi only, 75 rue St. Louis-en-l'Ile, tel. 01 46 34 04 80, fax 01 46 34 02 13, www.hotelsaintlouis.com, slouis@noos.fr).

## In the Historic Core, on Ile de la Cité

**$$ Hôtel Dieu Hospitel Paris** is the only Paris hotel with an Ile de la Cité address. It's located in the oldest city hospital of Paris, on the square in front of Notre-Dame (find the hospital on the map on page 58). Originally intended to receive families of patients, it now offers rooms for tourists, too. To get a spot in this prime location in front of Notre-Dame, with only 14 rooms, you'll need to book well in advance. You'll be surprised by the modern, comfortable decor and may even forget you're in a hospital (Sb-€104, Db-€115, some rooms have peek-a-boo views of Notre-Dame, 1 place du Parvis, tel. 01 44 32 01 00, www.hotel

## Hotels and Restaurants on Ile St. Louis

**VIEW**

**M** METRO STATION

**B** BATOBUS BOAT STOP

**1** Hôtel du Jeu de Paume
**2** Hôtel de Lutèce & Grocery
**3** Hôtel des Deux-Iles
**4** Hôtel Saint-Louis
**5** Le Tastevin Rest.
**6** Café Med
**7** La Brasserie de l'Île St. Louis

**8** Rests. Nos Ancêtres les Gaulois & La Taverne du Sergeant Recruteur
**9** Berthillon Ice Cream (3)
**10** Amorino Gelati
**11** Good Picnic Spot

-hospitel.com, hospitelhoteldieu@wanadoo.fr). Enter the hotel's main entrance, turn right, follow signs to wing B2, and take the elevator to the sixth floor.

## Luxembourg Garden

This neighborhood revolves around Paris' loveliest park and offers quick access to the city's best shopping streets and grandest café-hopping. Sleeping in the Luxembourg area offers a true Left Bank experience without a hint of the low-end commotion of the nearby Latin Quarter tourist ghetto. The Luxembourg Garden, boulevard St. Germain, Cluny Museum, and Latin Quarter are all at your doorstep. Here you get the best of both worlds: youthful Left Bank energy and the classic trappings that surround the monumental Panthéon and St. Sulpice Church. Hotels in this central area are more expensive than in other neighborhoods I list.

Having the Luxembourg Garden at your back door allows strolls through meticulously cared-for flowers, a great kids' play area, and a purifying escape from city traffic. Place St. Sulpice offers an elegant, pedestrian-friendly square and quick access to some of

Paris' best boutiques (see "Shopping," page 103). Sleeping in the Luxembourg area also puts several movie theaters at your fingertips (at Métro stop: Odéon), as well as lively cafés on boulevard St. Germain, rue de Buci, rue des Canettes, place de la Sorbonne, and place de la Contrescarpe, all of which buzz with action until late.

**Services:** The nearest **TI** is across the river in Gare de Lyon (Mon–Sat 8:00–18:00, closed Sun, all-Paris TI tel. 08 92 68 30 00). There are two useful **SNCF boutiques** for easy train reservations and ticket purchase: at 79 rue de Rennes and at 54 boulevard Saint-Michel (Mon–Sat 8:30–18:00, closed Sun).

**Markets:** The colorful street market at the south end of rue Mouffetard is a worthwhile 10- to 15-minute walk from these hotels (Tue–Sat 8:00–12:00 & 15:30–19:00, Sun 8:00–12:00, closed Mon, five blocks south of place de la Contrescarpe, Mo: Place Monge).

**Bookstore:** The **Village Voice** bookstore carries a full selection of English-language books (including mine), and is near St. Sulpice (Mon 14:00–19:00, Tue–Sat 10:00–19:00, Sun 12:00–18:00, 6 rue Princesse, tel. 01 46 33 36 47, www.villagevoicebookshop.com).

**Internet Access:** You'll find it at **Le Milk** (always open, between the Luxembourg Garden and Panthéon at 17 rue Soufflot).

**Métro Connections:** Métro lines 10 and 4 serve this area (10 connects to the Austerlitz train station, and 4 runs to the Montparnasse, Est, and Nord train stations). Neighborhood stops are Cluny–La Sorbonne, Mabillon, Odéon, and St. Sulpice. RER-B (Luxembourg station is handiest) provides direct service to Charles de Gaulle airport and Gare du Nord trains, and access to Orly airport via the Orlybus (transfer at Denfert-Rochereau).

**Bus Routes:** Buses #63, #86, and #87 run eastbound through this area on boulevard St. Germain, and westbound along rue des Ecoles, stopping on place St. Sulpice. Lines #63 and #87 provide direct connections west to the rue Cler area. Line #63 also serves the Orsay, Army, Rodin, and Marmottan museums to the west and Gare de Lyon to the east. Lines #86 and #87 run east to the Marais, and #87 continues to Gare de Lyon.

## Sleeping in the Luxembourg Garden Area
**(5th and 6th arrondissements, Mo: St. Sulpice, Mabillon, Odéon, and Cluny–La Sorbonne; RER: Luxembourg)**

While it takes only 15 minutes to walk from one end of this neighborhood to the other, I've located the hotels by the key monument they are close to (St. Sulpice Church, the Odéon Theater, and the Panthéon). Most hotels are within a five-minute walk of the Luxembourg Garden (and none is more than 15 minutes away).

All hotels listed in the Luxembourg Garden area have elevators, air-conditioning, public Internet access terminals, and Wi-Fi unless otherwise noted.

## Hotels near St. Sulpice Church

These hotels are all within a block of St. Sulpice Church and two blocks from famous boulevard St. Germain. This is nirvana for boutique-minded shoppers—and you'll pay extra for the location. Métro stops St. Sulpice and Mabillon are equally close.

**$$$ Hôtel de l'Abbaye\*\*\*\*** is a lovely refuge just west of Luxembourg Garden; it's a find for well-heeled connoisseurs of this area. The hotel's four-star luxury includes refined lounges inside and out, with 44 sumptuous rooms and every amenity at surprisingly reasonable rates (Db-€220, bigger Db-€335, suites and apartments available for €390–425, includes breakfast, 10 rue Cassette, tel. 01 45 44 38 11, fax 01 45 48 07 86, www.hotel-abbaye .com, hotel.abbaye@wanadoo.fr).

**$$$ Hôtel Relais St. Sulpice\*\*\*,** on the small street just behind St. Sulpice Church, is a dark little boutique hotel with a cozy lounge and 26 pricey and stylish rooms, most surrounding a leafy glass atrium. Top-floor rooms get more light and are worth requesting (Db-€180–215 depending on size, sauna free for guests, Wi-Fi only, 3 rue Garancière, tel. 01 46 33 99 00, fax 01 46 33 00 10, www.relais-saint-sulpice.com, relaisstsulpice@wanadoo.fr).

**$$$ Hôtel la Perle\*\*\*** is a spendy pearl in the thick of the lively rue des Canettes, a block off place St. Sulpice. At this snappy, modern, business-class hotel, sliding glass doors open onto the traffic-free street, and you're greeted by a fun lobby built around a central bar and atrium (standard Db-€185, bigger Db-€205, luxury Db-€235, check website or call for last-minute deals within five days of your stay, 14 rue des Canettes, tel. 01 43 29 10 10, fax 01 46 34 51 04, www.hotellaperle.com, booking @hotellaperle.com).

**$$ Hôtel Bonaparte\*\*,** an unpretentious place wedged between boutiques, is a few steps from place St. Sulpice. While the 29 Old World rooms don't live up to the handsome entry, they're adequately comfortable and generally spacious, with big bathrooms and molded ceilings (Sb-€100–120, Db-€133–155, big Db-€165, Tb-€175, includes breakfast, 61 rue Bonaparte, tel. 01 43 26 97 37, fax 01 46 33 57 67, www.hotelbonaparte.fr, reservation @hotelbonaparte.fr, helpful Fréderic and Eric at reception).

**$$ Hôtel le Récamier\*\*,** romantically tucked in the corner of place St. Sulpice, feels like grandma's house—but it has a new owner with big plans. For now, it has flowery wallpaper, dark halls, and clean, simple rooms, but all this should change in 2009. Regardless, the location is ideal (pre-renovation rates: S-€100, Sb-€120, D-€100, Db-€125, bigger Db-€140–150, Tb-€165, Qb-€190, no air-con, no Internet access, 3 bis place St. Sulpice, tel. 01 43 26 04 89, fax 01 46 33 27 73, hotelrecamier @wanadoo.fr).

PARIS

# Hotels and Restaurants near St. Sulpice and the Odéon Theater

200 YARDS
200 METERS

TO PONT DES ARTS

TO PONT NEUF & SEINE RIVER

TO LATIN QUARTER

ST. GERMAIN-DES-PRES

1. Hôtel de l'Abbaye
2. Hôtel Relais St. Sulpice
3. Hôtel la Perle
4. Hôtel Bonaparte
5. Hôtel le Récamier
6. Hôtel le Relais Médicis
7. Hôtel Michelet Odéon
8. La Crêpe Rit du Clown
9. Le Bistrot Henri IV
10. Lou Pescadou-Chez Julien Rest.
11. Chez Georges
12. Village Voice Books
13. To Internet Café & Panthéon

Ⓑ Bus Stop
Ⓜ Metro Station

## Near the Odéon Theater

These two hotels are between the Odéon Métro stop and Luxembourg Garden (five blocks east of St. Sulpice), and may have rooms when others don't. In addition to the Odéon Métro stop, the RER-B Luxembourg stop is a short walk away.

**$$$ Hôtel Relais Médicis*** is perfect in every way—if you've always wanted to live in a Monet painting and can afford it. Its 16 rooms surround a fragrant little garden courtyard and fountain, giving you a countryside break fit for a Medici in the heart of Paris. This delightful refuge is tastefully decorated with floral Old World charm, and is permeated with thoughtfulness (Sb-€172, Db-€208–228, deluxe Db-€258, Tb-€298, €30 cheaper mid-July–Aug and Nov–March, includes extravagant continental breakfast, faces the Odéon Theater at 23 rue Racine, tel. 01 43 26 00 60, fax 01 40 46 83 39, www.relaismedicis.com, reservation @relaismedicis.com, eager-to-help Isabelle runs reception).

**$$ Hôtel Michelet Odéon*** sits shyly in a corner of place de l'Odéon with big windows on the world. It's a decent value in this pricey area, with 24 spacious-but-simple rooms with modern decor and views of the square (Db-€105–130, Tb-€165, Qb-€185, no air-con, pay Wi-Fi, 6 place de l'Odéon, tel. 01 53 10 05 60, fax 01 46 34 55 35, www.hotelmicheletodeon.com, hotel@micheletodeon.com).

## Near the Panthéon and Rue Mouffetard

The last two listings are cheap dives, but in a great area.

**$$ Hôtel des Grandes Écoles*** is idyllic. A private cobbled lane leads to three buildings that protect a flower-filled garden courtyard, preserving a sense of tranquility rare in this city. Its 51 rooms are French-countryside-pretty, spotless, and reasonably spacious, but have no air-conditioning. This romantic spot is deservedly popular, so call well in advance (Db-€115–140 depending on size, extra bed-€20, parking garage-€30, Wi-Fi only, 75 rue du Cardinal Lemoine, Mo: Cardinal Lemoine, tel. 01 43 26 79 23, fax 01 43 25 28 15, www.hotel-grandes-ecoles.com, hotel.grandes.ecoles@wanadoo.fr, mellow Marie speaks English, Mama does not).

**$$ Hôtel des 3 Collèges*** greets clients with a sterile lobby, claustrophobic hallways, and unimaginative rooms with low ceilings...but decent rates (small Sb-€80, small Db-€110, bigger Db-€130–150, Tb-€132–165, pay Wi-Fi only, 16 rue Cujas, tel. 01 43 54 67 30, fax 01 46 34 02 99, www.3colleges.com, hotel@3colleges.com).

**$ Hôtel Cluny Sorbonne*** is welcoming and a good deal. It's located in the thick of things across from the famous university and below the Panthéon. Rooms are clean and comfortable, with wood furnishings (standard Db-€95, really big Db-€160, no

# Hotels and Restaurants near the Panthéon

**M** Metro Station
**R** R.E.R. Stop

1. Hôtel Cluny Sorbonne
2. Hôtel des 3 Collèges
3. Hôtel des Grandes Ecoles
4. Port-Royal-Hôtel
5. Hôtel de L'Espérance
6. Hôtel de France
7. Hôtel Central
8. Young & Happy Hostel
9. Hotel des Mines
10. Restaurant Perraudin
11. Le Soufflot Café
12. Place de la Sorbonne Eateries
13. Restaurant Polidor
14. Brasserie Bouillon Racine
15. Café Delmas
16. Le Mouffetard Café
17. Les Papillons Restaurant
18. Cave de Bourgogne
19. Internet Café
20. SNCF Boutique

air-con, 8 rue Victor Cousin, tel. 01 43 54 66 66, fax 01 43 29 68 07, www.hotel-cluny.fr, cluny@club-internet.fr).

**$ Hôtel Central\***, wedged between two cafés, has a smoky, dingy reception, a steep, slippery stairway, dumpy beds, and mildewed rooms. Bottom line: It's youth-hostel cheap, but with a charm only romantic hobos will appreciate. All rooms have showers, but toilets are down the hall (Ss-€33–38, Ds-€46–51, cash only, no elevator, no air-con, no Internet access, 6 rue Descartes, Mo: Cardinal Lemoine, tel. 01 46 33 57 93). Do your best to get a smile out of Madame Pilar, who doesn't speak English.

**$ Young & Happy Hostel** is easygoing, well-run, and English-speaking, with Internet access, kitchen facilities, and acceptable hostel conditions. It sits dead-center in the rue Mouffetard bar, café, and people action...which can be good or bad (all rates per person: bunk in 4- to 10-bed dorms-€24, 3- to 5-bed dorms-€26, double rooms-€28, includes breakfast, sheets-€2.50, credit cards accepted, no air-con, no lockers but safety box at reception, rooms closed 11:00–16:00 but reception stays open, no curfew, 80 rue Mouffetard, Mo: Place Monge, tel. 01 47 07 47 07, fax 01 47 07 22 24, www.youngandhappy.fr, smile@youngand happy.fr).

### Farther Away from the Seine, at the Bottom of Rue Mouffetard

These hotels, away from the Seine and other tourists in an appealing workaday area, offer more room for your euro. They require a longer walk or Métro ride to sights, but often have rooms when other accommodations are booked up. Rue Mouffetard is the bohemian soul of this area, running south from its heart—place de la Contrescarpe—to rue de Bazeilles. Two thousand years ago, it was the principal Roman road south to Italy. Today, this small, meandering street has a split personality. The lower half thrives in the daytime as a pedestrian shopping street. The upper half sleeps during the day but comes alive after dark, teeming with bars, restaurants, and nightlife. Use Métro stops Censier-Daubenton or Les Gobelins.

**$$ Hôtel de France\*\***, on a busy street, offers modest but comfortable rooms. It's scheduled for a complete makeover in late 2008 that will add air-conditioning, so the information below may change. Currently, the best and quietest rooms are *sur la cour* (on the courtyard), though streetside rooms are acceptable (Sb-€95, Db-€100–115, Tb-€140, 108 rue Monge, Mo: Censier-Daubenton, tel. 01 47 07 19 04, fax 01 43 36 62 34, www.hotelfrancequartier latin.com, hotel.de.fce@wanadoo.fr).

**$ Port-Royal-Hôtel*** has only one star, but don't let that fool you. Its 46 rooms are polished top to bottom and have been well-run by the same proud family for 68 years. You could eat off the floors of its spotless, comfy rooms...but you won't find air-conditioning, Internet access, or Wi-Fi. Ask for a room away from the street (S-€41–55, D-€55, Db-€79–89 depending on size, big shower down the hall-€3, cash only, nonrefundable cash deposit required, on busy boulevard de Port-Royal at #8, Mo: Les Gobelins, tel. 01 43 31 70 06, fax 01 43 31 33 67, www.hotelportroyal.fr, portroyal hotel@wanadoo.fr).

**$ Hôtel de L'Espérance**** is a terrific two-star value. It's quiet, pink, and cushy, with feminine rooms and canopy beds (Sb-€75–80, Db-€80–90, Tb-€107, no Internet access, 15 rue Pascal, Mo: Censier-Daubenton, tel. 01 47 07 10 99, fax 01 43 37 56 19, www.hoteldelesperance.fr, hotel.esperance@wanadoo.fr).

### On the South Side of Luxembourg Garden

**$ Hôtel des Mines**** is less central but worth the walk. Its 50 well-maintained rooms are a good value and come with updated bathrooms and a welcoming lobby (standard Db-€100, bigger Db-€100–120, Tb-€144, Qb-€170, check for Web deals, between Luxembourg and Port-Royal stations on the RER-B line, a 10-min walk from Panthéon, one block past Luxembourg Garden at 125 boulevard St. Michel, tel. 01 43 54 32 78, fax 01 46 33 72 52, www .hoteldesminesparis.com, hotel@hoteldesminesparis.com).

# Near Place de la République
**(10th and 11th arrondissements, Mo: République, Oberkampf)**

The three budget accommodations below are in the neighborhood north of the Marais, between place de la République and Canal St. Martin. This area is untouristy, young, and *très* international (read "melting pot"). It's definitely unpolished (and edgy to some) and more remote—but if you can put up with some rough edges and don't mind using the Métro and buses for all your sightseeing, you'll find some good deals here.

**$ Hôtel de Nevers*** is a cheap one-star hotel with a historic elevator and pretty good rooms for the price, despite the dim lighting (D-€44–50 with free shower down the hall, Ds-€55, Db-€65, Tb-€75, Qb-€84, 53 rue de Malte, tel. 01 47 00 56 18, fax 01 43 57 77 39, www.hoteldenevers.com, reservation@hoteldenevers.com).

**$ Auberge de Jeunesse Jules Ferry** is a relaxed youth hostel right on the parkway that runs above Canal St. Martin. Arrive before 10:00 or book online to be assured a room (€22 per bunk in pleasant, sink-equipped 2-, 4-, or 6-bed rooms, higher rates for non-members; small lockers available, rooms closed 10:30–14:00, 8 boulevard Jules Ferry, tel. 01 43 57 55 60, fax 01 43 14 82 09, www.hihostels.com).

# Hotels near Place de la République

Ⓜ –METRO STATION

**200 YARDS**

**200 METERS**

ST. LOUIS HOSPITAL

TO GARE DU NORD & GARE DE L'EST

CANAL ST. MARTIN

Ⓜ Jacques Bonsergent

Goncourt Ⓜ

❹ Post

ST. MARTIN

Ⓜ PLACE DE LA RÉPUBLIQUE

Ⓜ

Ⓜ République

RUE DE LA FONTAINE DU ROI

❸

❷

TURBIGO

Post

✚ Ⓜ Temple

TO PÈRE LACHAISE CEMETERY

❶

R. TIMBAUD

Oberkampf Ⓜ

Filles du Calvaire Ⓜ

RUE OBERKAMPF

PASSAGE

AMELOT

TO PLACE BASTILLE

10 MIN. WALK TO MARAIS

DCH

❶ Hôtel de Nevers

❷ Auberge de Jeunesse Jules Ferry (Hostel)

❸ Hostel Absolute Paris

❹ La Marine Restaurant

**$ Hostel Absolute Paris** is part two-star hotel, part four-beds-per-room hostel. It faces the canal and is filled with backpackers. The rooms are industrial-strength clean and adequate—but worth considering only if you want dorm-style accommodations (€24 each in 4-bed room with private bathroom, Db-€85, Tb-€100, includes breakfast, Internet access, 1 rue de la Fontaine du Roi, tel. 01 47 00 47 00, fax 01 47 00 47 02, www.absolute-paris.com, bonjour@absolute-paris.com).

# EATING

The Parisian eating scene is kept at a rolling boil. Entire books (and lives) are dedicated to the subject. Paris is France's wine-and-cuisine melting pot. While it lacks a style of its own (only French onion soup is truly Parisian), it draws from the best of France. Paris could hold a gourmets' Olympics and import nothing.

Cafés are happy to serve a *plat du jour* (garnished plate of the day, about €12–18) or a chef-like salad (about €10–12) day or night, while restaurants expect you to enjoy a full dinner. Restaurants open for dinner at about 19:00, and small local favorites get crowded after 21:00. Most of the restaurants listed below accept credit cards. Smokers dominate outside tables.

To save money, review the budget eating tips in this book's Introduction. Go to bakeries for quick take-out lunches, or stop at a café for a lunch salad or *plat du jour*, but linger longer over dinner. To save even more, consider picnics (tasty take-out dishes available at *charcuteries*).

**Good Picnic Spots:** The Palais Royal (across place du Palais Royal from the Louvre) is a good spot for a peaceful, royal picnic, as is the little triangular Henry IV park on the west tip of Ile de la Cité. The pedestrian pont des Arts bridge, across from the Louvre, has great views and plentiful benches, as does the Champ de Mars park below the Eiffel Tower. For great people-watching, try the Pompidou Center (by the *Homage to Stravinsky* fountains), the elegant place des Vosges (closes at dusk), the gardens behind Les Invalides, and the Tuileries and Luxembourg gardens (parks close at dusk).

## Restaurants

My recommendations are centered around the same great neighborhoods for which I list accommodations (above); you can come home exhausted after a busy day of sightseeing and have a good

---

# Restaurant Price Code

To help you choose among these listings, I've divided the restaurants into three categories, based on the price for a typical meal without wine.

**$$$ Higher Priced**—Most meals €35 or more.
**$$ Moderately Priced**—Most meals between €20–35.
**$ Lower Priced**—Most meals less than €20.

---

selection of restaurants right around the corner. And evening is a fine time to explore any of these delightful neighborhoods, even if you're sleeping elsewhere. Most restaurants I've listed in these areas have set-price *menus* between €15 and €30. In most cases, the few extra euros you pay are well-spent, and open up a variety of better choices. You decide.

If you are traveling outside of Paris, save your splurges for the countryside, where you'll enjoy regional cooking for less money. Many Parisian department stores have huge supermarkets hiding in the basement and top-floor cafeterias that offer affordable, low-risk, low-stress, what-you-see-is-what-you-get meals.

## Rue Cler Neighborhood

The rue Cler neighborhood caters to its residents. Its eateries, while not destination places, have an intimate charm. I've provided a full range of choices from cozy ma-and-pa diners to small and trendy boutique restaurants to classic, big bistros. You'll generally find great dinner *menus* for €20–30, *plats du jour* for about €14–18, and meal-sized salads for €10–12. Eat early with tourists or late with locals. For all restaurants listed in this area, use the Ecole Militaire Métro stop (unless another station is listed).

### Close to Ecole Militaire, Between Rue de la Motte-Picquet and Rue de Grenelle

**$$$ Le Florimond** is good for a special occasion. The setting, while spacious and quiet, is also intimate and welcoming. Locals come for classic French cuisine with elegant indoor or breezy streetside seating. Friendly English-speaking Laurent—with his playful ties changing daily—serves one small room of tables gracefully and loves to help with suggestions. Try the explosively tasty stuffed cabbage (€36 *menu*, closed Sun, reservations smart, good house wine by the carafe, affordable wine selection, 19 avenue de la Motte-Picquet, tel. 01 45 55 40 38).

**$$ Restaurant Pasco,** perched elegantly overlooking Les Invalides, is semi-dressy, with a special enthusiasm for fish. The

PARIS

# Rue Cler Restaurants

↑ 5 MIN. WALK
TO SEINE RIVER
& AMERICAN CHURCH

RUE DE L'UNIVERSITE

RUE MALAR

RUE NICOT

ST. PIERRE

AVENUE

RUE ST.

ST. DOMINIQUE

RUE CLER

RUE AMELIE

RUE NICOT

COMTE

MAUBOURG

RUE BOSQUET

R. DE L'EXPO

RUE

GRENELLE

RUE

DE VALADON

RUE PSICHARI

RUE

DE LA MOTTE PICQUET

TOUR MAUBOURG

La Tour-Maubourg

M

AUGEREAU

DE MARS

ST. JEAN

RUE DUVIVIER

RUE DU CHAMP

RUE DE MARS

CHEVET

BOURDONNAIS

ARMY MUSEUM & NAPOLEON'S TOMB

POST

← TO EIFFEL TOWER &

Ecole Militaire

M

M

M METRO STATION

CHAMP DE MARS

AVENUE DUQUESNE

AVE DE TOURVILLE

DCH

← KIDS' PLAY AREA

AVENUE

200 YARDS
200 METERS

1 Le Florimond

2 Restaurant Pasco

3 La Terrasse du 7ème

4 Café le Bosquet

5 Café du Marché & Tribeca Italian Rest.

6 Crêperie Ulysée en Gaule

7 Petite Brasserie PTT

8 To Altitude 95 Rest. & Jules Verne Restaurant

9 Au Petit Tonneau

10 La Fontaine de Mars

11 Le P'tit Troquet

12 Billebaude Bistro

13 Chez Agnès

14 L'Ami Jean

15 Chez Pierrot

16 Café Constant

17 La Varangue

18 La Gourmandise Pizzeria

19 Real McCoy

20 Late-Night Groceries (2)

21 Julien's Bakery

22 Café la Roussillon

23 O'Brien's Pub

owner, Pasco Vignes, attracts a local clientele with his modern Mediterranean cuisine, generously endowed with olive oil. While there's some outdoor seating, I'd come here for the red-brick-cozy interior (€20 *plats*, €20–34 *menus,* daily, reservations smart, 74 boulevard de la Tour Maubourg, Mo: La Tour Maubourg, tel. 01 44 18 33 26).

**$$ La Terrasse du 7ème** is a sprawling, happening café with grand outdoor seating and a living room–like interior with comfy love seats. Located on a corner, it overlooks a busy intersection with a constant parade of people. Chairs are set up facing the street, as a meal here is like dinner theater—and the show is slice-of-life Paris. Consider their Spring Plate for an adventurous gourmet starter (€16 daily *plats*, no fixed-price *menu*, good €13 *salade niçoise,* daily until at least 24:00 and sometimes until 2:00 in the morning, at École Militaire Métro stop, tel. 01 45 55 00 02).

**$$ Café le Bosquet** is a modern, chic Parisian brasserie with dressy waiters and your choice of the mod-elegant interior or sidewalk tables on a busy street. Come here for a bowl of French onion soup, or a full three-course *menu* with good fish and meat choices. Say *bonsoir* to owner Jean-François, who likes to be called Jeff. Escargots are great here; the house red wine is plenty good, too (€15 *plats,* closed Sun, reservations smart Fri–Sat, fun menu includes vegetarian options, corner of rue du Champ de Mars and avenue Bosquet, 46 avenue Bosquet, tel. 01 45 51 38 13).

**$ Café du Marché** boasts the best seats, coffee, and prices on rue Cler. The owner's philosophy: Brasserie on speed—crank out good food at great prices to trendy locals and savvy tourists. It's high-energy, with waiters who barely have time to smile... *très* Parisian. This place is ideal if you want to eat an inexpensive, one-course meal among a commotion of people and are willing to go with the small, fresh menu. The chalkboard lists your choices: good, hearty €10 salads or more filling €10 *plats du jour* (Mon–Sat 11:00–23:00, Sun 11:00–17:00, arrive before 19:30 for dinner—it's packed at 21:00, and service can be slow; free water served without a grimace, at the corner of rue Cler and rue du Champ de Mars, at 38 rue Cler, tel. 01 47 05 51 27).

**$ Tribeca Italian Restaurant,** next door to Café du Marché, is run by the same people with essentially the same formula. They offer similar (if not even better) value and more space, a calmer ambience, and more patient service. This family-friendly eatery offers €12 pizzas and €12 Italian *plats.*

**$ Crêperie Ulysée en Gaule** offers the best cheap seats on rue Cler. Their crêpes are €3–10 to go, with no extra charge to sit for readers of this book if you buy a drink. The Ulysée family— Stephanos, Chrysa, Marcos, and English-speaking Vassilis—seem to make friends with all who drop by for a bite. The family loves to serve Greek dishes, and their excellent crêpes are your least expensive rue Cler hot meal (open daily, 28 rue Cler, tel. 01 47 05 61 82).

## Between Rue de Grenelle and the River

**$$$ Altitude 95** is in the Eiffel Tower, 95 meters (about 300 feet) above the ground. Reserve a month in advance for a view table (€36 lunches, €65 dinners, daily 12:00–21:45, dinner seatings nightly at about 19:00 and 21:00, bar open until 23:00; before you ascend to dine, drop by the booth between the north/*nord* and east/*est* pillars to buy your Eiffel Tower ticket and pick up a pass that enables you to skip the line; Mo: Bir-Hakeim or Trocadéro, RER: Champ de Mars-Tour Eiffel, tel. 01 45 55 20 04, fax 01 47 05 94 40). Also in the Eiffel Tower is the even more expensive **Jules Verne Restaurant,** described on page 80.

**$$$ Au Petit Tonneau** is a souvenir of old Paris. Fun-loving owner-chef Madame Boyer prepares everything herself, wearing her tall chef's hat like a crown as she rules from her family-style kitchen. The small, plain dining room doesn't look like it's changed in the 26 years she's been in charge. Her steaks and lamb are excellent (€8–10 starters, €18 *plats,* open daily, 20 rue Surcouf, Mo: La Tour Maubourg, tel. 01 47 05 09 01).

**$$$ La Fontaine de Mars** is a longtime favorite for locals, charmingly situated on a classic, tiny Parisian street and jumbled square. It's a happening scene, with tables jammed together for the serious business of good eating. Reserve in advance for a table on the ground floor (or in summer on the square), or eat upstairs without the fun street-level ambience (€20 *plats du jour,* superb foie gras, open nightly, where rue de l'Exposition and rue St. Dominique meet, 129 rue St. Dominique, tel. 01 47 05 46 44).

**$$ Le P'tit Troquet,** a petite eatery taking you back to the Paris of the 1920s, is gracefully and earnestly run by Dominique. The fragile elegance here makes you want to hug a flapper. Dominique is particularly proud of her foie gras and lamb, and of her daughter's breads and pastries. The delicious, three-course €32 *menu* comes with traditional choices. Its delicate charm and gourmet flair make this restaurant a favorite of connoisseurs (opens at 18:00, closed Sun, reservations smart, 28 rue de l'Exposition, tel. 01 47 05 80 39).

**$$ Billebaude,** run by patient Pascal, is an authentic Parisian bistro where the focus is on what's fresh and meats from the hunt (€29 *menu,* closed Sun–Mon, 29 rue de l'Exposition, tel. 01 45 55 20 96).

**$$ Chez Agnès,** the smallest of my recommended Paris restaurants, is not for everyone. It's tiny, flowery, family-style, and filled with kisses on the cheek. Eccentric but sincere Agnès (a French-Tahitian Rosie O'Donnell) does it all—cooking in her minuscule kitchen and serving, too. Agnès, who cooks "French with an exotic twist" and clearly loves her work, makes children feel right at home. Don't come for a quick dinner (€23 *menu,* closed Mon, 1 rue Augereau, tel. 01 45 51 06 04).

**$$ L'Ami Jean** offers excellent Basque specialties at fair prices. The chef has made his reputation on the quality of his cuisine. Arrive by 19:30 or call ahead (€33 *menu,* closed Sun–Mon, 27 rue Malar, Mo: La Tour Maubourg, tel. 01 47 05 86 89).

**$$ Chez Pierrot** is a warm, welcoming bistro with 12 tables served by smiling Linda. On a quiet street, it offers large portions of traditional fare—try the beef stew (€18 *plats,* €12 big salads, daily, 9 rue Amélie, tel. 01 45 51 50 08).

**$ Café Constant** is a tiny, cool, two-level place that feels more like a small bistro–wine bar than a café. They serve delicious and affordably priced dishes in a fun setting to a well-established clientele (€14 *plats,* closed Sun–Mon, corner of rue Augereau and rue St. Dominique, next to recommended Hôtel Londres Eiffel).

**$ La Varangue** is an entertaining one-man show featuring English-speaking Philippe, who ran a French catering shop in Pennsylvania for three years. He lives upstairs, and has found his niche serving a mostly American clientele who are all on a first-name basis. The food is cheap and basic (don't come here for high cuisine), the tables are few, and he opens early (at 17:30). Norman Rockwell would dig his tiny dining room—with the traditional kitchen sizzling just over the counter. Philippe is so fun and accessible that you are welcome to join him in the kitchen and help cook your meal. Try his snails and chocolate cake...but not together (€12 *plats,* €17.50 *menu,* always a vegetarian option, closed Sun, 27 rue Augereau, tel. 01 47 05 51 22).

**$ La Gourmandise** is a tiny, friendly pizzeria across the street from La Varangue. Its good, cheap pizza is ideal for kids (closed Sun, eat in or take out, 28 rue Augereau, tel. 01 45 55 45 16).

### Picnicking in Rue Cler

Rue Cler is a moveable feast that gives "fast food" a good name. The entire street is clogged with connoisseurs of good eating. Only the health-food store goes unnoticed. A festival of food, the street is lined with people whose lives seem to be devoted to their specialty: polished produce, rotisserie chicken, crêpes, or cheese.

For a magical picnic dinner at the Eiffel Tower, assemble it in no fewer than five shops on rue Cler. Then lounge on the best grass in Paris, with the dogs, Frisbees, a floodlit tower, and a cool breeze in the parc du Champ de Mars.

**Asian delis** (generically called *Traiteur Asie*) provide tasty, low-stress, low-price take-out treats (€6 dinner plates, the one on rue Cler near rue du Champ de Mars has tables). **Crêperie Ulysée en**

Gaule (described earlier), the Greek restaurant on rue Cler across from Grand Hôtel Lévêque, sells take-away crêpes. **Real McCoy** is a little shop selling American food and sandwiches (closed Sun, 194 rue de Grenelle). There's a small **late-night grocery** at 197 rue de Grenelle (open daily until midnight), and another where rues Cler and Grenelle cross. For excellent baguettes and sandwiches, try **Julien's** bakery at 85 rue St. Dominique.

### Breakfast in Rue Cler

Hotel breakfasts, while convenient, are generally not a good value. For a great rue Cler start to your day, drop by the **Petite Brasserie PTT**, where Jerome and Alexi promise Rick Steves readers a *deux pour douze* breakfast special (2 "American" breakfasts—juice, a big coffee, croissant, bread, ham, and eggs—for €12; closed Sun, a two-minute walk from most area hotels, opposite 53 rue Cler).

### Nightlife in Rue Cler

This sleepy neighborhood is not ideal for night owls, but there are a few notable exceptions. **Café du Marché** and **La Terrasse du 7ème** (both listed earlier) are busy with a Franco-American crowd until at least midnight, as is the younger **Café la Roussillon** (occasional happy hours 18:00–20:00—but every hour seems happy, €10 salads, €13 *plats*, fine for a French pub atmosphere, corner of rue de Grenelle and rue Cler). **O'Brien's Pub** is a relaxed Parisian rendition of an Irish pub, full of Anglophones (77 avenue St. Dominique, Mo: La Tour Maubourg).

## In the Marais Neighborhood

The trendy Marais is filled with locals enjoying good food in colorful and atmospheric eateries. The scene is competitive and changes all the time. I've listed an assortment of eateries—all handy to recommended hotels—that offer good food at reasonable prices, plus a memorable experience.

### Dining on Romantic Place des Vosges

On this square, which offers Old World Marais elegance, you'll find several different eateries (use Bastille or St. Paul Métro stop). Enjoy a square stroll around the entire arcade—fun art galleries alternate with enticing restaurants. Choose the restaurant that best fits your mood and budget; all have arcade seating and provide big space-heaters to make outdoor dining during colder months an option. Also consider a drink or dessert on the square at Café Hugo or Nectarine after eating elsewhere.

$$$ **Ma Bourgogne** is a classic old eatery where you'll sit under warm arcades in a whirlpool of Frenchness, as bow-tied and black-aproned waiters serve you traditional French specialties:

# Marais Restaurants

1. Ma Bourgogne
2. Nectarine & Café Hugo
3. Brasserie Bofinger
4. Chez Janou
5. Les Bonnes Soeurs
6. La Bastoche
7. Vins des Pyrénées
8. Au Temps des Cerises
9. Au Bourguignon du Marais
10. L'Ebouillanté
11. Restaurante Sant Antonio
12. BHV Cafeteria
13. Place du Marché Ste. Catherine Eateries
14. L'Enoteca Wine Bar
15. Camille Brasserie
16. Le Rouge Gorge
17. Chez Marianne
18. L'As du Falafel
19. Bistrot les Sans Culottes
20. Au Petit Fer à Cheval & La Belle Hortense
21. La Perla Bar
22. Le Pick-Clops Bar Rest.

Ⓜ METRO STATION
Ⓣ TAXI STAND
Ⓟ PARKING

blood-red steak, lots of French fries, escargot, and great red wine. While service comes with few smiles, the staff of this venerable Marais fixture enjoy their work and care about your experience. Monsieur Cougourou (koo-gah-roo), who's run this place since de Gaulle was sniveling at Americans, offers anyone with this book a free *amuse-bouche* ("amusement for your mouth") of steak tartare. This is your ideal chance to try this "raw spiced hamburger" delicacy without dedicating an entire meal to it...and the quality here is famous (€35 *menu,* daily, dinner reservations smart, cash only, at northwest corner at #19, tel. 01 42 78 44 64).

**$$ At Les Bonnes Soeurs,** barely off the square, Cecile and Alexandra cater to a somewhat younger and more local clientele by mixing modern and traditional fare with fun ambience (*plats* from €16, no *menu,* daily, 8 rue du pas de la Mule, tel. 01 42 74 55 80).

**$ Nectarine** is small and demure—with a wicker, pastel, and feminine atmosphere. This peaceful teahouse serves healthy €10 salads, quiches, and €12–14 *plats du jour* day and night. Its menu lets you mix and match omelets and crêpes, and the huge desserts are splittable (daily, at #16, tel. 01 42 77 23 78).

**$ Café Hugo,** named for the square's most famous resident, is best for drinks only, as the cuisine does not live up to its setting (daily, at #22).

### Near the Bastille

To reach these restaurants, use the Bastille Métro stop.

**$$ Brasserie Bofinger,** an institution for over a century, is famous for fish and traditional cuisine with Alsatian flair. You're surrounded by brisk, black-and-white-attired waiters. The sprawling interior features elaborately decorated rooms reminiscent of the Roaring Twenties. Eating under the grand 1919 *coupole* is a memorable treat (as is using the "historic" 1919 WC downstairs). Check out the boys shucking and stacking seafood platters out front before you enter. Their €32 three-course *menu,* while not top cuisine, is a good value. If you've always wanted one of those picturesque seafood platters, this is a good place—you can take the standard platter or create one à la carte (open daily and nightly, fun kids' menu, 5 rue de la Bastille, don't be confused by the lesser "Petite" Bofinger across the street, tel. 01 42 72 87 82).

**$$ Chez Janou,** a Provençal bistro, tumbles out of its corner building and fills its broad sidewalk with happy eaters. At first glance, you know this is a find. Don't let the trendy and youthful crowd intimidate you—it's relaxed and charming, with helpful and patient service. While the curbside tables are inviting, I'd sit inside (with very tight seating) to immerse myself in the happy commotion. The style is French Mediterranean, with an emphasis on vegetables (€15–18 *plats du jour* that change with the season, daily from 19:45, 2 blocks beyond place des Vosges at 2 rue Roger Verlomme, tel. 01 42 72 28 41). They're proud of their 81 different varieties of *pastis* (licorice-flavored liqueur, €3.50 each, browse the list above the bar).

**$$ La Bastoche** (Parisian slang for "the Bastille") is cozy and welcoming. Step down into an 18th-century building with exposed timbers and a great mural of the storming of the old prison, and choose from a nice selection of traditional French fare at good prices. Caring owners Sylvie and Lise work hard to please (€23 3-course *menu*, daily, 7 rue St. Antoine, one block away from the Bastille, tel. 01 48 04 84 34).

**$$ Vins des Pyrénées** ("Wines of the Pyrenees") is a fun bistro that attracts a young, lively crowd with its convivial setting, varying *menus* with lots of choices, reasonable wine list, and hardworking, English-speaking owner, Olivier. Don't come here for a romantic dinner (€15–20 *plats*, daily, 25 rue Beautreillis, tel. 01 42 72 64 94).

**$ Au Temps des Cerises** is a *très* local wine bar, with a woody 1950s atmosphere, tight seating, and wads of character. While they serve three-course, €15 lunch *menus*, I'd come here for wine and heavy munchies pre- or post-dinner—or even for dinner. "Dinner" is limited to bread, dry sausage, cheese, and wine served by goateed Yves and his wife, Michele. While full plates of cold cuts run around €13, a small mixed plate of cheese (€5), meat (€5), and a carafe of good wine (€4–8) surrounded by the intimate Old World ambience can make a good light meal (Mon–Sat until about 22:00, closed Sun, at rue du Petit-Musc and rue de la Cerisaie).

### Closer to Hôtel de Ville

These eateries, near the Pompidou Center, appear on the map on page 141. To reach them, use the Hôtel de Ville Métro stop.

**$$$ Au Bourguignon du Marais** is an attractive wine bar-bistro for Burgundy-lovers, where excellent wines (available by the glass) blend with a good selection of well-designed dishes and efficient service (Philippe is clearly in charge). The *œufs en meurette* were the best I've ever had, and the *bœuf bourguignon* could feed two (€10–14 starters, €18–22 *plats*, closed Sun–Mon, indoor and outdoor seating, 52 rue Francois Miron, tel. 01 48 87 15 40).

**$ L'Ebouillanté** is a breezy crêperie-café, romantically situated near the river on a broad, cobbled lane behind a church. With great outdoor seating and an artsy, cozy interior, it's ideal for an inexpensive and relaxing tea, snack, or lunch—or for dinner on a warm evening. Try a *brick*, the light-hearted chef's specialty (think beefy crêpe). The salads and desserts are also good (€13 *plats*, €15 2-course *menu*, Tue–Sun 12:00–22:00, closed Mon, 6 rue des Barres, tel. 01 42 71 09 69).

**$ Restaurante Sant Antonio** is bustling and cheap, serving up €10 pizzas and salads on a fun Marais square (daily, barely off rue de Rivoli on place du Bourg Tibourg).

**$ BHV Department Store**'s fifth-floor cafeteria provides nice views, an escape from the busy streets below, and no-brainer, point-and-shoot cafeteria cuisine (Mon–Sat 11:30–18:00, closed Sun, at intersection of rue du Temple and rue de la Verrerie, one block from Hôtel de Ville).

## In the Heart of the Marais

These are closest to the St. Paul Métro stop.

**$$ *On place du Marché Ste. Catherine:*** This small, romantic square, just off rue St. Antoine, is an international food festival cloaked in extremely Parisian, leafy-square ambience. On a balmy evening, this is clearly a neighborhood favorite, with a handful of restaurants offering €20–30 meals. Study the square, and you'll find two popular French bistros (**Le Marché** and **Au Bistrot de la Place,** each with €23 3-course *menus,* tight seating indoors and out, both open daily) and other inviting eateries serving a variety of international food—Russian, Korean, Italian, and so on. You'll eat under the trees, surrounded by a futuristic-in-1800 planned residential quarter.

**$$ L'Enoteca** is a high-spirited, half-timbered spot serving affordable Italian cuisine (no pizza) with a tempting *antipasti* bar. It's a relaxed, open setting with busy, blue-aproned waiters serving two floors of local eaters (€15 pastas, €20 *plats,* €30 3-course *menu,* open daily, across from L'Excuse at rue St. Paul and rue Charles V, 25 rue Charles V, tel. 01 42 78 91 44).

**$ Camille,** a traditional corner brasserie, is a neighborhood favorite with great indoor and sidewalk seating. Its waiters serve €13 salads and very French *plats du jour* (€20) from the chalkboard list to a down-to-earth but sophisticated clientele (daily, 24 rue des Francs Bourgeois at corner of rue Elzévir, tel. 01 42 72 20 50).

**$ Le Rouge Gorge**'s relaxed wine bar and bistro is 10-table cozy. Come for a meal (€16–20 dinner *plats* based on monthly themes), a coffee, or a glass of wine. Friendly François, the owner, will send you downstairs to the *cave* (cellar) to choose your wine; there are different prices for take-out wine purchases (closed Sun, 8 rue St. Paul, tel. 01 48 04 75 89).

**$ Several** hardworking **Asian fast-food eateries,** great for a €6 meal, line rue St. Antoine.

## On Rue des Rosiers in the Jewish Quarter

To reach the Jewish Quarter, use the St. Paul Métro stop.

**$ Chez Marianne,** a neighborhood fixture, offers classic Jewish meals and Parisian atmosphere. Choose from several indoor zones with a cluttered wine shop/deli ambience, or sit outside. You'll select from two dozen "Zakouski" elements to assemble your €15 plate (great vegetarian options, eat cheap with a €6 falafel sandwich, or even cheaper with takeout, long hours daily, corner of rue des Rosiers and rue des Hospitalieres St. Gervais, tel. 01 42 72 18 86). For takeout, pay inside first and get a ticket before you order outside.

$ **L'As du Falafel** rules the falafel scene in the Jewish quarter. Monsieur Isaac, the "Ace of Falafel" here since 1979, brags he's got "the biggest pita on the street...and he fills it up." Apparently, it's Lenny Kravitz's favorite, too. Your inexpensive Jewish cuisine comes on plastic plates, in a bustling setting that seems to prove he's earned his success. While the €6.50 "special falafel" is the big hit, many Americans enjoy his lighter chicken version *(poulet grillé)* or the tasty and filling *assiette de falafel*. Their take-out service draws a constant crowd; the interior is air-conditioned (day and night until late, closed Sat, 34 rue des Rosiers).

## Picnicking in the Marais

Picnic at peaceful place des Vosges (closes at dusk) or on the Ile St. Louis *quais* (see next page). Stretch your euros at the basement supermarket of the **Monoprix** department store (closed Sun, near place des Vosges on rue St. Antoine). You'll find a small **grocery** open until 23:00 near 48 rue St. Antoine.

## Nightlife in the Marais

The best scene for hard-core night owls is the dizzying array of wacky eateries, bars, and dance halls on **rue de Lappe.** This street is what the Latin Quarter aspires to be. Just east of the stately place de la Bastille, it's one of the wildest nightspots in Paris and not for everyone. Sitting amid the chaos like a Van Gogh painting is the popular, old-time **Bistrot les Sans Culottes.**

Trendy cafés and bars—popular with gay men—also cluster on rue Vieille du Temple, rue des Archives, and rue Ste. Croix de la Bretonnerie (closing at about 2:00 in the morning). You'll find a line of bars and cafés providing front-row seats for the buff parade on rue Vieille du Temple, a block north of rue de Rivoli (the horseshoe-shaped **Au Petit Fer à Cheval** bar-restaurant and the atmospheric **La Belle Hortense** bookstore/wine bar are the focal points of the action). Nearby, rue des Rosiers bustles with youthful energy, but there are no cafés to observe from. **Vins des Pyrénées** (described earlier) is young and fun—find the small bar in the back. **La Perla** is full of Parisian yuppies in search of the perfect margarita (26 rue François Miron).

$ **Le Pick-Clops** bar-restaurant is a happy peanuts-and-lots-of-cocktails diner with bright neon, loud colors, and a garish local crowd. It's perfect for immersing yourself in today's Marais world—a little boisterous, a little edgy, a little gay, fun-loving, easygoing...and no tourists. Sit inside, on old-fashioned diner stools, or streetside to watch the constant Marais parade. The name means "Steal the Cigarettes"—but you'll pay €10 for your big salad (daily 7:00–24:00, 16 rue Vieille du Temple, tel. 01 40 29 02 18).

The most enjoyable peaceful evening may be simply donning your floppy "three musketeers" hat and slowly strolling around place des Vosges, window-shopping the art galleries.

## Ile St. Louis

The Ile St. Louis is a romantic and peaceful neighborhood where you can amble around for plenty of promising dinner possibilities. Cruise the island's main street for a variety of options, from cozy *crêperies* to Italian eateries (intimate pizzerias and upscale) to typical brasseries (a few with fine outdoor seating facing the bridge to Ile de la Cité). After dinner, sample Paris' best sorbet and stroll across to the Ile de la Cité to see Notre-Dame illuminated, or enjoy a scenic drink on the deck of a floating café moored under Notre-Dame's right transept. All these listings line the island's main drag, rue St. Louis-en-l'Ile (see map on page 125; to get here, use the Pont Marie Métro stop). Consider skipping dessert to enjoy a stroll licking the best ice cream in Paris (described under "Ice-Cream Dessert," next page).

$$$ **Le Tastevin** is an intimate mother-and-son-run restaurant serving top-notch traditional French cuisine with white-tablecloth, candlelit, gourmet elegance under heavy wooden beams. The romantic setting (and the elegantly romantic local couples enjoying the place) makes you naturally whisper. The three-course *menus* start at about €38 and offer plenty of classic choices that change with the season to ensure freshness (daily, reserve for late-evening dining, good wine list, 46 rue St. Louis-en-l'Ile, tel. 01 43 54 17 31; owner Madame Puisieux and her gentle son speak just enough English).

$$$ *Medieval Theme Restaurants:* **La Taverne du Sergeant Recruteur,** famous for its rowdy, medieval-cellar atmosphere, is ideal for hungry warriors and their wenches who like to swill hearty wine. For as long as anyone can remember, they've served up a rustic all-you-can-eat buffet with straw baskets of raw veggies and bundles of sausage (cut whatever you like with your dagger), massive plates of pâté, a meat course, and all the wine you can stomach for €41. The food is just food; burping is encouraged. If you want to eat a lot, drink a lot of wine, be surrounded by tourists, and holler at your friends while receiving smart-aleck buccaneer service, this food fest can be fun. And it comes with a historic

twist: The "Sergeant Recruiter" used to get young Parisians drunk and stuffed here, then sign them into the army (daily from 19:00, #37 rue St. Louis-en-l'Ile, tel. 01 43 54 75 42). Next door, **Nos Ancêtres les Gaulois** is a bit goofier and grittier, and serves the same basic formula. As the name implies ("Our Ancestors the Gauls"), this place makes barbarians feel right at home (tel. 01 46 33 66 07). You might swing by both and choose the..."ambience" is not quite the right word...that fits your mood.

$$ **La Brasserie de l'Ile St. Louis** is situated at the prow of the island's ship as it faces Ile de la Cité, offering purely Alsatian cuisine (try the *choucroute garni* for €18), served in a Franco-Germanic setting with no-nonsense brasserie service. This is a good balmy-evening perch for watching the Ile St. Louis promenade—or, if it's chilly, the interior is plenty characteristic for a memorable night out (closed Wed, no reservations, 55 quai de Bourbon, tel. 01 43 54 02 59).

$ **Café Med,** near the pedestrian bridge to Notre-Dame at #77, has inexpensive salads, crêpes, and a €13–20 *menu* served in a tight but cheery setting (open daily, limited wine list, tel. 01 43 29 73 17). Two similar *crêperies* are just across the street.

### Riverside Picnic

On sunny lunchtimes and balmy evenings, the *quai* on the Left Bank side of Ile St. Louis is lined with locals who have more class than money, spreading out tablecloths and even lighting candles for elegant picnics. And tourists can enjoy the same budget meal. There's a handy grocery store at #67 on the main drag (Wed–Mon until 22:00, closed Tue) that has tabouli and other simple, cheap, take-away dishes for your picnicking pleasure.

### Ice-Cream Dessert

Half the people strolling Ile St. Louis are licking an ice-cream cone, because this is the home of *les glaces Berthillon*. The original **Berthillon** shop, at 31 rue St. Louis-en-l'Ile, is marked by the line of salivating customers (closed Mon–Tue). Another Berthillon shop is across the street, and there's one more around the corner on rue Bellay (all are located on map on page 125). The three shops are so popular that the wealthy people who can afford to live on this fancy island complain about the congestion they cause. For a less famous but at least as tasty treat, the home-made Italian gelato a block away at **Amorino Gelati** is giving Berthillon competition (no line, bigger portions, easier to see what you want, and they offer little tastes—Berthillon doesn't need to, 47 rue St. Louis-en-l'Ile, tel. 01 44 07 48 08). Having some of each is not a bad thing.

## Luxembourg Neighborhood

Sleeping in the Luxembourg neighborhood puts you near many appealing dining and after-hours options. Because my hotels in this area cluster around the Panthéon and St. Sulpice Church (see page 126), I've organized restaurant listings the same way. Restaurants near the Panthéon tend to be calm, those around St. Sulpice more boisterous; it's a short walk from one area to the other. Anyone sleeping in this area is close to the inexpensive eateries that line the always-bustling rue Mouffetard.

### Near the Panthéon

For locations, see the map on page 130. These eateries are served by the Cluny–La Sorbonne Métro stop and the RER-B Luxembourg station.

**$$ Restaurant Perraudin** is a welcoming, family-run, red-checkered-tablecloth eatery understandably popular with tourists. Friendly Monsieur Correy serves classic *cuisine bourgeoise* with an emphasis on Burgundian dishes in air-conditioned comfort. The decor is vintage turn-of-the-20th-century, with big mirrors and old wood paneling (€19 lunch *menus*, €30 dinner *menus, bœuf bourguignon* is a specialty here, between the Panthéon and Luxembourg Garden at 157 rue St. Jacques, tel. 01 46 33 15 75).

**$ Le Soufflot Café,** between the Panthéon and Luxembourg Garden, is well-positioned for afternoon sun. It has a nifty library-like interior, lots of outdoor tables, point-blank views of the Panthéon, and friendly service (Frédéric and Serge are owners). The cuisine is café-classic: good €10 salads, omelets, and *plats du jour* (daily, a block below the Panthéon on the right side of rue Soufflot as you walk toward Luxembourg Garden, tel. 01 43 26 57 56).

**$ *Place de la Sorbonne:*** This cobbled and green square, with a small fountain facing the Sorbonne University just a block from the Cluny Museum, offers several opportunities for a quick outdoor lunch or light dinner. At the tiny **Baker's Dozen,** you'll pay take-away prices for salads and sandwiches you can sit down to eat (€5 salad and quiche special, Mon–Sat until 17:00, closed Sun). **Café de l'Ecritoire** is a typical, lively brasserie with happy diners enjoying €11 salads, €13 *plats,* and fine square seating (daily, tel. 01 43 54 60 02). **Patios,** with appealing decor inside and out, seems more popular. It serves inexpensive Italian fare, including pizza (daily until late).

### Near the Odéon Theater

To reach these, use the Odéon Métro stop.

**$$ Brasserie Bouillon Racine** takes you back to 1906 with an Art Nouveau carnival of carved wood, stained glass, and old-time lights reflected in beveled mirrors. The over-the-top decor, energetic waiters, and affordable menu combine to give it an inviting conviviality. Check upstairs before choosing a table. Their roast suckling pig (€18) is a house favorite. There's good beer on tap and a fascinating history on the menu (€18 *plats*, €29 *menu*, traditional French with lots of fish and meat, daily 12:00–14:00 & 19:00–23:00, 3 rue Racine, tel. 01 44 32 15 60, Phillipe).

**$$ La Méditerranée** is all about fish in a pastel and dressy setting...with similar clientele. The scene and the menu are sophisticated while accessible, and the view of the Odéon is *formidable*. The sky-blue tablecloths and the lovingly presented dishes add to the romance (€18–27 *plats*, €32 3-courses *menus*, open daily, smart to book ahead, facing the Odéon at 2 place de l'Odéon, tel. 01 43 26 02 30).

**$ Restaurant Polidor,** a bare-bones neighborhood fixture since the 19th century, is much-loved for its unpretentious quality cooking, fun old-Paris atmosphere, and fair value. Stepping inside, you know this is a winner—noisy, happy diners sit tightly at shared tables as waiters chop and serve fresh bread. The selection features classic bourgeois *plats* from every corner of France; their *menu fraîcheur* is designed for lighter summer eating (€12–15 *plats*, €20–30 3-course *menus*, daily 12:00–14:30 & 19:00–23:00, cash only, no reservations, 41 rue Monsieur-Le-Prince, tel. 01 43 26 95 34, Amelia).

## On Rue Mouffetard

Lying several blocks behind the Panthéon, rue Mouffetard is a conveyer belt of comparison-shopping eaters with wall-to-wall budget options (fondue, crêpes, Italian, falafel, and Greek). Come here to sift through the crowds and eat a less expensive meal (you get what you pay for). This street stays up late and likes to party (particularly around place de la Contrescarpe). The gauntlet begins on top, at thriving place de la Contrescarpe, and ends below where rue Mouffetard stops at St. Médard Church. Both ends offer fun cafés where you can eat, drink, and watch the action. The upper stretch is pedestrian and touristic; the bottom stretch is purely Parisian. Anywhere between is no-man's land for consistent quality. Still, strolling with so many fun-seekers is enjoyable, whether you eat or not. To get here, use the Censier-Daubenton Métro stop.

**$ Café Delmas,** at the top of rue Mouffetard on picturesque place de la Contrescarpe, is *the* place to see and be seen. Come here for a before- or after-dinner drink on the broad outdoor terrace, or for typical but pricey café cuisine (€15 salads, €20 *plats*, great chocolate ice cream, open daily).

**$ Le Mouffetard,** a traditional café with a lively location in the heart of rue Mouffetard, is good for an inexpensive lunch or dinner (€13 lunches, €16 2-course *menus*, closed Sun evening and all day Mon, 116 rue Mouffetard, tel. 01 43 31 42 50).

**PARIS**

**$** Bar-restaurant **Les Papillons** is a down-and-dirty local diner where a few outdoor tables tangle with pedestrians and no one seems to care (€12 *plats*, closed Sun–Mon, 129 rue Mouffetard, tel. 01 43 31 66 50).

**$ Cave de Bourgogne** is *très* local and serves reasonably priced café fare at the bottom of rue Mouffetard. Outside has picture-perfect tables on a raised terrace; inside is warm and cozy (€13–16 *plats*, specials listed on chalkboards, daily, 144 rue Mouffetard).

## Near St. Sulpice Church

*Rue des Canettes and Rue Guisarde:* For an entirely different experience, roam the streets between the St. Sulpice Church and boulevard St. Germain, abounding with restaurants, *crêperies*, wine bars, and jazz haunts (use Mo: St. Sulpice). Find rue des Canettes and rue Guisarde, and window-shop the many French and Italian eateries—most with similar prices, but each with a slightly different feel. For tasty crêpes, try **$ La Crêpe Rit du Clown** (Mon–Sat 12:00–23:00, closed Sun, 6 rue des Canettes, tel. 01 46 34 01 02). For good ambience and above-average bistro fare in a zone where every restaurant looks the same, consider **$$ Le Bistrot Henri IV** (daily, only indoor seating, 6 rue Princesse, tel. 01 46 33 51 12) or **$$ Lou Pescadou–Chez Julien** (daily, some outdoor seating, 16 rue Mabillon, tel. 01 43 54 56 08).

And for a bohemian pub lined with black-and-white photos of the artsy and revolutionary French '60s, have a drink at **Chez Georges.** Sit in a cool little streetside table nook, or venture downstairs to find a hazy, drippy-candle, traditionally French world in the Edith Piaf–style dance cellar (cheap drinks from old-fashioned menu, Tue–Sat 14:00–2:00 in the morning, closed Sun–Mon and in Aug, 11 rue des Canettes).

# Eating Elsewhere in Paris

## Along Canal St. Martin, North of République

Escape the crowded tourist areas and enjoy a breezy canalside experience. Take the Métro to place de la République and walk down rue Beaurepaire to Canal St. Martin. There you'll find a few worthwhile cafés with similarly reasonable prices. **$ La Marine** is a good choice (daily, 55 bis quai de Valmy, tel. 01 42 39 69 81). In the summertime, most bars and cafés offer beer and wine to go *(à emporter)*, so you can take it to the canal's edge and picnic there with the young locals.

## In the Galerie Vivienne, behind the Palais Royal

**$$ Le Grand Colbert,** appropriately located in the elegant Galerie Vivienne (see page 76), gives its clients the feel of a luxury restaurant at moderate prices. It's a stylish, grand brasserie with hurried waiters, leather booths, and brass lamps, serving all the classic dishes from steak *frites* to escargots (*menus* from €41, daily, 4 rue Vivienne, Mo: Palais Royal/Musée du Louvre or Pyramides, tel. 01 42 86 82 38).

## Near the Louvre

**$ Café le Nemours,** a staunchly Parisian fixture serving pricey but good light lunches, is tucked into the corner of the Palais Royal adjacent to the Comédie Française. With elegant brass and Art Deco style, and outdoor tables under an arcade two minutes from the pyramid, it's a great post-Louvre retreat (fun and filling €11 salads, open daily; leaving the Louvre, cross rue de Rivoli and veer left to 2 place Colette—see Louvre map on page 75; Mo: Palais Royal, tel. 01 42 61 34 14).

## Near Opéra Garnier

**$ Bouillon Chartier** is a noisy, old, classic eatery. It's named for the bouillon it served the neighborhood's poor workers back in 1896, when its calling was to provide an affordable warm meal for those folks. Workers used to eat *à la gamelle* (from a tin lunchbox). That same spirit—complete with surly waiters and a cheap menu—survives today. Among more than 300 simple seats and 15 frantic waiters, you can still see the restaurant's napkin drawers for its early regulars (€18 *menus*, daily 11:30–15:00 & 18:00–22:00, east of the Opéra Garnier near boulevard Poissonniere, 7 rue de Faubourg-Montmartre, Mo: Grands Boulevards, tel. 01 47 70 86 29).

## Montmartre

Montmartre is extremely touristy, with many mindless mobs following guides to cancan shows. But the ambience is undeniably fun, and an evening up here overlooking Paris is a quintessential experience in the City of Light. The steps in front of Sacré-Cœur are perfect for a picnic with a view. Along the touristy main drag (near place du Tertre and just off it), several fun piano bars serve crêpes with great people-watching. To reach this area, use the Anvers Métro stop.

**$$ Restaurant Chez Plumeau,** just off jam-packed place du Tertre, is touristy yet moderately priced, with formal service but great seating on a tiny, characteristic square (elaborate €16 salads, €16–20 *plats*, closed Wed, place du Calvaire, tel. 01 46 06 26 29).

**$ L'Eté en Pente Douce** hides under generous branches below the crowds on a classic neighborhood corner. It features fine indoor and outdoor seating, €10 *plats du jour* and salads, vegetarian options, and good wines (daily, 23 rue Muller, many steps below Sacré-Cœur to the left as you leave, down the stairs below the WC, tel. 01 42 64 02 67).

## Dinner Cruises

The following companies all offer dinner cruises (reservations required). Bateaux Mouches and Bateaux Parisiens have the best reputations and the highest prices. They offer multicourse meals and music in aircraft carrier–size dining rooms with glass tops and good views. For both, proper dress is required—no denim, shorts, or sport shoes; Bateaux Mouches requires a jacket and tie for men. The main difference between these companies is the ambience: Bateaux Mouches offers violin and piano to entertain your romantic evening, while Bateaux Parisiens boasts a lively atmosphere with a singer, band, and dance floor.

**Bateaux Mouches,** started in 1949, is hands-down the most famous. You can't miss its sparkling port on the north side of the river at pont de l'Alma. The boats usually board 19:30–20:15, depart at 20:30, and return at 22:45 (€130/person, RER: Pont de l'Alma tel. 01 42 25 96 10, www.bateauxmouches.com).

**Bateaux Parisiens** leaves from Port de la Bourdonnais, just east of the bridge under the Eiffel Tower. Begin boarding at 19:45, leave at 20:30, and return at 23:00 (€100–145/person, 3 price tiers, depends on seating, tel. 08 25 62 75 13, www.bateauxparisiens .com). The middle level is best. Pay the few extra euros to get seats next to the windows—it's more romantic and private, with sensational views.

**Le Capitaine Fracasse** offers the budget option (€50/person, €70 with wine; tables are first-come, first-serve, so get there early; boarding times vary by season and day of week, closed Mon, walk down stairs in the middle of Bir Hakeim bridge near the Eiffel Tower to Iles aux Cygne, Mo: Champs de Mars-Tour Eiffel, tel. 01 46 21 48 15, www.croisiere-paris.com).

# TRANSPORTATION CONNECTIONS

## Trains

Paris is Europe's rail hub, with six major train stations and one minor one, each serving different regions: Gare de l'Est (eastbound trains), Gare du Nord (northern France and Europe), Gare St. Lazare (northwestern France), Gare d'Austerlitz (southwestern France and Europe), Gare de Lyon (southeastern France and Italy), Gare Montparnasse (northwestern France and TGV service to France's southwest), and a smaller station, Gare de Bercy, the departure point for most night trains to Italy. Any train station has schedule information, can make reservations, and sells tickets for any destination. Unless you happen to pass a station in your sightseeing, buying tickets is handier from an SNCF neighborhood office; see the list on page 155. It's worth the small fee.

All six main train stations have banks or change offices,

# Paris Train Stations

## Paris Train Stations & Destinations

**①** Gare Nord: To London, Brussels, Amsterdam & N. France (also Chantilly & Auvers-sur-Oise)

**②** Gare Montparnasse: To SW France (Languedoc & Dordogne), Loire Valley, Brittany (also Chartres) & Mont St. Michel

**③** Gare de Lyon: To Italy & SE France (Burgundy, Alps, Provence & Riviera; also Fontainebleau & Melun/Vaux-le-Vicomte)

**④** Gare de Bercy: Night trains to Italy

**⑤** Gare de l'Est: To NE France (Reims, Champagne & Alsace), S. Germany, Switzerland & Austria

**⑥** Gare St. Lazare: To Normandy (also Vernon/Giverny)

**⑦** Gare d'Austerlitz: To SW France, Loire Valley & Spain

ATMs, train information desks, telephones, cafés, newsstands, and clever pickpockets. Because of security concerns, not all have baggage checks.

Each station offers two types of rail service: long distance to other cities, called *Grandes Lignes* (major lines); and suburban service to outlying areas, called *banlieue* or RER. Both *banlieue* and RER trains serve outlying areas and the airports; the only difference is that *banlieue* lines are operated by SNCF (France's train system, called Transilien) and RER lines are operated by RATP (Paris' Métro and bus system). You may also see ticket windows identified as *Ile de France*. This is for Transilien (SNCF) trains serving destinations outside Paris in the Ile de France region (usually no more than an hour from Paris).

Paris train stations can be intimidating, but if you slow down, avoid peak times, take a deep breath, and ask for help, you'll find them manageable and efficient. Bring a pad of paper for clear communication at ticket/info windows. All stations have helpful *accueil* (information) booths; the bigger stations have roving helpers, usually in red vests. They're capable of answering rail questions more quickly than the information or ticket windows.

To make your trip go more smoothly, be sure to review the many train tips in "Transportation," on page 848 in the appendix.

## Station Overview

Here's an overview of Paris' major train stations. Métro and RER trains, as well as buses and taxis, are well-marked at every station. When arriving by Métro, follow signs for *Grandes Lignes–SNCF* to find the main tracks.

### Gare du Nord

This vast station serves cities in northern France and international destinations north of Paris, including Copenhagen, Amsterdam, and the Eurostar to London (see "To London by Eurostar Train," page 158). Arrive early to allow time to navigate this station. Monet-esque views over the trains and peaceful, air-conditioned cafés hide on the upper level, past the Eurostar ticket windows (find the cool view WCs down the steps in the café).

**Key Destinations Served by Gare du Nord** *Grandes Lignes:* **Brussels** (about 2/hr, 1.5 hrs), **Bruges** (about 2/hr, 2.5 hrs, change in Brussels), **Amsterdam** (nearly hourly, 4–5 hrs, change in Brussels), **Copenhagen** (7/day, 14–18 hrs, two night trains), **Koblenz** (9/day, 5 hrs, most change in Köln), and **London** via Eurostar Chunnel train (12–15/day, 2.5 hrs, tel. 08 36 35 35 39).

**By** *Banlieue*/**RER Lines: Charles de Gaulle Airport** (4/hr, 30 min, runs 5:00–24:00, track 4).

### Gare Montparnasse

This big and modern station covers three floors, serves lower Normandy and Brittany, and offers TGV service to the Loire Valley and southwestern France, as well as suburban service to Chartres. Air France buses to Orly and Charles de Gaulle airports stop in front of the station, down the escalators and outside. City buses are outside to the left (#28 connects conveniently to the rue Cler area).

# SNCF Boutiques

You can save time and stress by buying train tickets or making train reservations at an SNCF boutique. These small branch offices of the French National Rail Company are conveniently located throughout Paris, with offices near most of my recommended hotels and museums and at Orly and Charles de Gaulle Airports. Arrive when they open to avoid lines (generally open Mon–Sat 8:30–19:00 or 20:00, closed Sun).

**Historic Core**
- 18 rue du Pont Neuf, Mo: Pont Neuf

**Marais**
- 2 rue de Turenne, Mo: St. Paul
- 5 rue de Lyon, Mo: Gare de Lyon

**Near Major Museums**
- Musée d'Orsay RER station, below Orsay Museum
- Forum des Halles Shopping Mall, 4th floor, returns office *(Salle d'Echanges)*, Mo: Châtelet–Les Halles

**Champs Elysées**
- 229 rue du Faubourg Saint-Honoré, Mo: St Philippe du Roule

**Farther North on the Right Bank**
- 53 rue Chaussée d'Antin, Mo: Chaussée d'Antin (near Opéra Garnier and Galeries Lafayette)
- 32/34 rue Joubert, Mo: Haussman–St Lazare (near Gare St. Lazare)
- 71/73 boulevard Magenta, Mo: Gare du Nord (Gare du Nord)
- 82 avenue de la Grande Armée, Mo: Porte Maillot (near Hôtel Concorde–Lafayette and Beauvais Airport bus stop)

**Montmartre**
- 27 rue Lepic, Mo: Blanche

**Eiffel Tower/Rue Cler**
- 80 rue Saint Dominique, Mo: La Tour Maubourg
- 19 rue de Passy, Mo: Passy (near Marmottan Museum)
- Invalides Métro/RER station

**Latin Quarter/Luxembourg Garden**
- 54 boulevard Saint-Michel, Mo: Cluny-Sorbonne
- 79 rue de Rennes, Mo: St. Sulpice

**Farther South on the Left Bank**
- 17 rue Littré, Mo: Montparnasse-Bienvenüe (near Luxembourg Garden)
- 68 avenue du Maine: Mo. Montparnasse-Bienvenüe
- 30 avenue d'Italie, in Centre Commerciale Galaxie, Mo: Place d'Italie

**Key Destinations Served by Gare Montparnasse:**
**Chartres** (10/day, 1 hr, *banlieue* lines), **Amboise** (12/day, 1.5 hrs, transfer in St. Pierre-des-Corps, requires TGV reservation; non-TGV trains leave from Gare d'Austerlitz), **Pontorson/Mont St. Michel** (7/day, 4–5.5 hrs, via Rennes or Lison, some with bus from Rennes), **Dinan** (6/day, 4 hrs, change in Rennes and Dol), **Bordeaux** (20/day, 3.5 hrs), **Sarlat** (7/day, allow 6 hrs; 3/day with change in Bordeaux–St. Jean or Libourne, then TGV; 4/day to Souillac, then bus), **Toulouse** (13/day, 5–7 hrs, most require change, usually in Bordeaux or Montpellier), **Albi** (6/day, 6–7.5 hrs, change in Toulouse, also night train), **Carcassonne** (14/day, 6.5 hrs, most require changes in Toulouse or Montpellier, direct trains take 8 hrs, night train also available), **Tours** (18/day, 1 hr), **Madrid** (3/day, 13.5 hrs, one overnight via Irun, more night trains from Gare d'Austerlitz), and **Lisbon** (1/day, 21.5 hrs via Irun or Madrid).

## Gare de Lyon

This huge and bewildering station offers TGV and regular service to southeastern France, Italy, and other international destinations (for more trains to Italy, see "Gare de Bercy," facing page). Don't leave this station without relaxing in Le Train Bleu Restaurant lounge, up the stairs opposite track G.

*Grande Ligne* trains arrive and depart from street level, but are divided into two areas (tracks A–N in the blue area, and 5–23 in the yellow area). They are connected by the long platform along tracks A and 5, and by the hallway adjacent to track A and opposite track 9.

**Air France buses** to Montparnasse (easy transfer to Orly Airport) and direct to Charles de Gaulle Airport stop outside the station's main entrance (opposite tracks A–L, walk across the parking lot—the stop is opposite the Café Européen on the right; €13, 2/hr, normally at :15 and :45 after the hour).

**Key Destinations Served by Gare de Lyon: Disneyland** (RER line A-4 to Marne-la-Vallée-Chessy, at least 3/hr, 45 min), **Beaune** (nearly hourly, 2.5 hrs, most require change in Dijon), **Dijon** (nearly hourly, 1.5 hrs), **Chamonix** (8/day, daily July–Aug and Dec–April, Fri–Sun only May–June and Sept–Nov, may be more frequent in May, 6–8 hrs, night train possible), **Annecy** 6–8 hrs, night train possible), **Annecy** (13/day, 4–5 hrs, many with change in Lyon), **Lyon** (at least hourly, 2 hrs), **Avignon** (9/day in 2.5 hrs to Avignon TGV station, 5/day in 3.5 hrs to Avignon Centre-Ville station, more connections with change—3–4 hrs), **Arles** (17/day, 2 direct TGVs in 4 hrs, 15 with change in Avignon in 5 hrs), **Nice** (10/day, 6 hrs, may require change, 11-hr night train possible out of Gare d'Austerlitz), **Venice** (3/day, 4/night, 10–13 hrs with change in Milan; 1 direct overnight, 13 hrs, important to reserve ahead), **Rome** (3/day, 13–16 hrs, plus several overnight options, important to reserve ahead), **Bern** (11/day, 5–5.5 hrs, 1 direct train in morning and 1 in evening, otherwise 1–2 changes), **Interlaken** (nearly hourly, 6.5 hrs, night train possible via Basel from Gare de l'Est), and **Barcelona** (3/day, 9 hrs, 1–2 changes; night train possible from Gare d'Austerlitz).

PARIS

### Gare de Bercy

This smaller station handles some night train service to Italy (Mo: Bercy, one stop east of Gare de Lyon on line 14).

### Gare de l'Est

This two-floor station (with underground Métro) serves eastern France and international destinations east of Paris. It is relatively easy to navigate. All trains depart at street level from tracks 1–30. Ticket sales are in the hall opposite track 12. All other services are down the escalator through the hall opposite track 16 (baggage check, car rental, WC, small grocery store and Métro access).

**Key Destinations Served by Gare de l'Est: Colmar** (12/day with TGV, 3.5 hrs, change in Strasbourg), **Strasbourg** (hourly with TGV, 2.5 hrs), **Reims** (12/day with TGV, 45 min), **Verdun** (2/day, 1.75 hrs with TGV and shuttle bus; non-TGV 6/day, 3–3.5 hrs, change in Metz or Chalon), **Munich** (4/day, 6–7 hrs, some require changes), **Interlaken** (night train possible via Basel with changes at 5:00 and 8:00), **Vienna** (7/day, 12–17 hrs, 1–3 changes, night train), **Zürich** (2/day direct, 4 hrs; 7/day with changes, 5–6.5 hrs; night train), **Berlin** (6/day, 8–9 hrs, 1–2 changes, many via Belgium; 1 direct night train, 11.25 hrs) and **Prague** (5/day, 12–18 hrs, night train possible via Berlin).

### Gare St. Lazare

This relatively small station serves upper Normandy, including Rouen and Giverny. The station is undergoing renovation, so be prepared for the temporary displacement of shops and services. There is no baggage check.

**Key Destinations Served by Gare St. Lazare: Giverny** (train to Vernon, 6/day, more on Sat, get there in time to visit the gardens, 45 min—see schedule in "Giverny" on page 184—then bus or taxi 15 min to Giverny), **Rouen** (hourly, 1–1.5 hrs), **Honfleur** (13/day, 2–3.5 hrs, via Lisieux, then bus), **Bayeux** (11/day, 2.5 hrs, 3 require change in Caen), **Caen** (14/day, 2 hrs), and **Pontorson/ Mont St. Michel** (2/day, 4–5.5 hrs, via Caen; more trains from Gare Montparnasse).

### Gare d'Austerlitz

This small station provides non-TGV service to the Loire Valley, southwestern France, and Spain. To get to the Métro, you must walk outside and along either side of the station.

**Key Destinations Served by Gare d'Austerlitz: Versailles** (via RER line C, 4/hr, 30–40 min), **Amboise** (10/day direct in 2 hrs; faster TGV connection from Gare Montparnasse), **Cahors** (5/day, 5 hrs, also 1 direct night train; other slower trains from Gare Montparnasse), **Barcelona** (1/night, 12 hrs; day trains from Gare de Lyon), and **Madrid** (2/night, 13 hrs direct, 16 hrs via Irun; day trains from Gare Montparnasse).

## To Brussels and Amsterdam by Thalys Train

The pricey Thalys train has the monopoly on the rail route between Paris and Brussels (for a cheaper option, try the Eurolines bus; see next page). Without a railpass, you'll pay about €80–100 second class for the Paris–Amsterdam train (compared to €45 by bus) or about €60–80 second class for the Paris–Brussels train (compared to €25 by bus). Even with a railpass, you need to pay for train reservations (second class-€14.50; first class-€27, includes a meal). Book at least a day ahead, as seats are limited (www.thalys.com). Or hop on the bus, Gus.

## To London by Eurostar Train

The fastest and most convenient way to get from the Eiffel Tower to Big Ben is by rail. Eurostar is the speedy passenger train that zips you from downtown Paris to downtown London (at least 15/day, 2.5 hrs) faster and more easily than flying.

Channel fares are reasonable but complicated. Prices vary depending on how early you reserve, whether you can live with restrictions, and whether you're eligible for any discounts (children, youth, seniors, round-trip travelers, and railpass-holders all qualify). For specifics, visit www.ricksteves.com/rail/eurostar.htm.

Refund and exchange restrictions are serious, so don't reserve until you're sure of your plans (only the most expensive are fully refundable). You can check and book fares by phone or online in the US (order online at www.ricksteves.com/rail/eurostar.htm, prices listed in dollars; order by phone at US tel. 800-EUROSTAR) or in France (French tel. 08 92 35 35 39, www.eurostar.com, prices listed in euros).

If you buy from a US company, you'll pay for ticket delivery in the US; if you book with the European company, you'll pick up your ticket at the train station. In Europe, you can buy your Eurostar ticket at any major train station in any country, at neighborhood SNCF offices, or at any travel agency that handles train tickets (expect a booking fee). Passholder discount tickets can be

**Eurostar Routes**

ENGLAND

LONDON

EBBS-FLEET

ASHFORD

CALAIS FRÉTHUN

AMSTERDAM

NETH.

BELG.

LILLE

BRUSSELS

FRANCE

PARIS

50 MI
100 KM

—— EUROSTAR
--- CHANNEL TUNNEL
····· OTHER RAIL

purchased at Eurostar departure stations, online, or by phone, but may be harder to get at other train stations and travel agencies.

As with airfares, the most expensive and flexible option is a full-fare one-way ticket with no restrictions on refundability (figure about $425 in first class, $310 second class). Cheaper tickets (for second-class, one-way tickets, figure $90–200) come with more restrictions and are limited in number and sell out quickly. Those traveling with a railpass that covers France or Britain should look first at the passholder fare (about $90–160 for second-class), a good value for one-way Eurostar trips.

*Taking the Eurostar:* Check in at Gare du Nord (see page 154) at least 30 minutes in advance for your Eurostar trip. It's very similar to an airport check-in: You pass through airport-like security, fill out a customs form, show your passport to customs officials, and find a TV monitor to locate your departure gate. The currency-exchange booth here has rates about the same as you'll find on the other end.

## Buses

The main bus station is the Gare Routière du Paris-Gallieni (28 avenue du Général de Gaulle, in suburb of Bagnolet, Mo: Gallieni, tel. 01 49 72 51 51). Buses provide cheaper—if less comfortable and more time-consuming—transportation to major European cities. The bus is also the cheapest way of crossing the English Channel; book at least two days in advance for the best fares. Eurolines' buses depart from here (tel. 08 36 69 52 52, www.eurolines.com). Look on their website for offices in central Paris.

## Airports
### Charles de Gaulle Airport

Paris' primary airport has three terminals: T-1, T-2, and T-3. Most flights from the US use T-1 or T-2. To see which terminal serves your airline, check your ticket, or contact the airport (toll tel. 3950, www.adp.fr). The RER (Paris suburban train, connecting to Métro) stops at T-2 and near T-1 and T-3, and the TGV (tay-zhay-vay, stands for *train à grande vitesse*—high-speed, long-distance train) station is at T-2. The new CDGVAL automated shuttle train connects the terminals with the TGV and RER stations and parking garages (free, every 10 min, 24/7). Pickpockets prey on jet-lagged tourists on shuttles between terminals, and on RER trains. Don't take an unauthorized taxi from the men greeting you on arrival; official taxi stands are well-signed.

**Terminal 1 (T-1):** This circular terminal has one main entry and covers three floors—arrival (*arrivées,* top floor), departure (*départs,* one floor down) and shops/boutiques (basement level). For information on getting to Paris, see "Transportation Between Charles de Gaulle Airport and Paris," below.

*Arrival Level:* You'll find a variety of services at the gates listed below. Expect changes during construction.

- Gate 36: Called "Meeting Point" (Point de Rencontre), this gate has an information counter with English-speaking staff, a café, and an ATM.
- Gate 34: Outside are Air France buses to Paris (see "Transportation Between Charles de Gaulle Airport and Paris") and Orly Airport (see "Connecting Paris' Airports," both later in this section).
- Gate 30: Outside are Roissy-Buses to Paris (buy tickets from driver) and hotel shuttle buses *(navettes hôtels).*
- Gates 24–30: Car-rental desks.
- Gate 18: Taxis outside.
- Gates 12–14: Baggage storage (open daily, drop-off 10:00–16:00, pickup 8:30–19:30, tel. 01 48 16 34 90).

*Departure Level (niveau 3):* Flight check-in, restaurants, a PTT (post office), a pharmacy, boutiques, and a handy grocery store one floor below the ticketing desks (*niveau* 2 on the elevator).

**Terminal 2 (T-2):** This long, horseshoe-shaped terminal is dominated by Air France and is divided into six subterminals (or halls), each identified by a letter (A through F). Baggage storage in T-2 is at both 2A (door 3, daily 8:00–20:00, tel. 01 48 16 20 16) and 2F (arrival level, door 4, daily 7:00–19:00, tel. 01 48 16 20 64). Free shuttle buses constantly circle, connecting the halls with the RER and the TGV station every seven minutes. The RER and TGV stations are below the Sheraton Hotel (and are within walking distance of some of the halls). Stops for shuttle buses, Air France buses, and Roissy-Buses are all well-marked, near each hall, and described below. ADP's orange information desks are located near Gate 6 in each hall. Car-rental offices, post offices, pharmacies, and ATMs *(point d'argent)* are also well-signed.

**Transportation Between Charles de Gaulle Airport and Paris:** Three efficient public-transportation routes, taxis, and

**Charles de Gaulle Airport**

TERMINAL 1

UNDERGROUND WALKWAYS

TERMINAL 3

CONTROL TOWER

**R** RER STOP
**P** PARKING

TO LILLE & BRUSSELS

TERMINAL 2

TO ROISSY-EN-FRANCE, **3**, A-1 FREEWAY & PARIS

2 B    2 D    2 F

2 A    2 C    2 E

CONTROL TOWER

TRAIN STATION (TGV & **R**) & SHERATON HOTEL

**N**

**1** Hôtel Ibis
**2** Novotel
**3** To Hôtel Campanile, Hôtel Kyriad Prestige & B&B Hôtel

DCH

TO DISNEYLAND PARIS, DIJON, LYON & AVIGNON

airport shuttle vans link the airport's terminals with central Paris. All are well-marked, and stops are centrally located at all terminals. If you're carrying lots of baggage—or are just plain tired—taxis are well worth the extra cost (avoid the airport shuttle vans going in the airport-to-Paris direction).

To get to the rue Cler area, the Roissy-Bus to Opéra and transferring to Métro line 8 is the most convenient public-transport route; get off the Métro at the La Tour Maubourg or Ecole Militaire stop. To reach the Marais, your best public-transport option is the Air France bus to the Gare de Lyon, with a quick trip on Métro line 1 to the Bastille, St. Paul, or Hôtel de Ville stop. Both the Roissy-Bus and Air France bus options are described below. For the Luxembourg Garden area, take RER-B to the Luxembourg stop. All your options into Paris are well-marked, but if you have trouble, ask any airport employee.

**RER line B (RER-B) trains** stop at T-2 and near T-1, then stop in central Paris at Gare du Nord, Châtelet–Les Halles, St. Michel, and Luxembourg (€8.50, 4/hr, runs 5:00–24:00, 30 min to Gare du Nord). Buy tickets from the machines (requires €8.50 in coins, some machines take bills) or at the often-crowded ticket windows. To get out to the airport from the city, take RER line B, and make sure the sign over the platform shows *Roissy–Charles de*

*Gaulle* as a stop served (the line splits, not every line B train serves the airport). If you're not clear, ask another rider *(air-o-por sharl duh Gaul?)*. Beware of pickpockets on these trains; wear your money belt. The other transportation options described below have far fewer theft problems.

**Roissy-Buses** run every 15–20 minutes to the Opéra Métro stop (€8.50, runs 6:30–21:00, 50 min, buy ticket on bus). You'll arrive at a bus stop on rue Scribe on the left side of the Opéra building. To get to the Métro entrance, turn left out of the bus and walk counterclockwise around the Opéra to the front. The Métro station entrance is on the island in the middle of the square. For rue Cler hotels, take Métro line 8 (direction: Balard) to La Tour Maubourg or Ecole Militaire. For hotels in the Marais neighborhood, take line 8 (direction: Créteil Préfecture) to the Bastille stop. You can also take a taxi (about €12) to any of my listed hotels from behind the Opéra (the stand is in front of Galeries Lafayette department store).

**Air France buses** serve central Paris and continue to Orly Airport (at least 2/hr, 5:45–23:00). Allow 45 minutes to the Arc de Triomphe and Porte Maillot; 45 minutes to the Gare de Lyon train station; and 60 minutes to Montparnasse Tower/train station. To reach Marais hotels from the Gare de Lyon, take Métro line 1 (direction: La Défense) to the Bastille, St. Paul, or Hôtel de Ville stops; or walk 10 minutes up rue de Lyon to place de la Bastille. A ticket costs €14 one-way, €20 round-trip (pay driver).

**Taxis** run about €50 for up to three people (more if traffic is bad). Your hotel can call for a taxi to the airport. Specify that you want a real taxi *(un taxi normal)*, and not a limo service that costs €20 more (and gives your hotel a kickback).

**Airport vans** also go straight to and from your hotel, but are not a good option to take from the airport to Paris; you have to book them in advance even though you don't know exactly when you'll arrive (getting baggage, going through customs). However, they are a good budget option *to* the airport (particularly for single travelers or families of four or more, as that's too many for a taxi). If your hotel does not work with a van service, reserve directly (book at least a day in advance—most hoteliers will make the call for you). Airport vans cost about €35 for one person, €45 for two, and €55 for three. **Golden Air** is reliable (from Paris to Charles de Gaulle: €27 for one person, €17 per person for two; from Charles de Gaulle to Paris: €35 for one person, €20 per person for two; these special prices promised with this book in 2009, tel. 01 34 10 12 92, fax 01 34 10 93 89, www.paris-airport-shuttle-limousine .com, goldenair@wanadoo.fr).

A **Disneyland shuttle** is at each terminal (€17, every 45 min, daily 8:30–19:45).

## Sleeping at or near Charles de Gaulle Airport

**Hôtel Ibis**\*\*, outside the Charles de Gaulle-1 RER stop, is huge and offers standard and predictable accommodations (Db-€95–120, near *navette* stop, free and fast shuttle bus to all terminals, tel. 01 49 19 19 19, fax 01 49 19 19 21, www.ibishotel.com, h1404 @accor.com).

**Novotel**\*\*\* is next door and the next step up. Book early for the best rates (Db-€120–170, can rise to €260 for last-minute rooms, tel. 01 49 19 27 27, fax 01 49 19 27 99, www.novotel.com, h1014@accor.com). Both have simple restaurants.

## Orly Airport

This airport feels small. It's good for rental-car pickup and drop-off, as it's closer to Paris and far easier to navigate than Charles de Gaulle Airport.

Orly has two terminals: Ouest (west) and Sud (south). Air France flights arrive at Ouest, and all others use Sud. At the Sud terminal, you'll exit the baggage claim (near Gate H) and see signs directing you to city transportation, car rental, and so on. Turn left to enter the main terminal area, where you'll find exchange offices with bad rates, an American Express office, an ATM, the ADP counter (*Espace Tourisme*, a quasi-tourist office that offers free city maps and basic sightseeing information, open until 24:00), and an SNCF rail desk (next to ADP, daily 7:45–12:00 & 13:00–20:00, sells train tickets and even Eurailpasses). Downstairs is a sandwich bar, WCs, a bank (same bad rates), a newsstand (buy a phone card), and a post office. Car-rental offices are located in the parking lot in front of the terminal opposite Gate C. For flight info on any airline serving Orly, call 3950. For information on either of Paris' major airports, visit www.adp.fr.

**Transportation Between Orly Airport and Paris:** Several efficient public-transportation routes, taxis, and a couple of airport vans link Orly with central Paris. The gate locations listed below apply to Orly Sud, but the same transportation services are available from both terminals.

**Air France buses** (outside Gate K) run to Montparnasse train station (with many Métro lines) and to the Invalides Métro stop (€9 one-way, €14 round-trip, 4/hr, 40 min to Invalides). These buses are handy for those staying in or near the rue Cler neighborhood (from Invalides bus stop, take the Métro to La Tour Maubourg or Ecole Militaire to reach recommended hotels; see also "RER trains," next page). Remember that to continue on the Métro, you'll need to buy a separate ticket (for ticket types and prices, see "Getting Around Paris" on page 44).

**Jetbus** (outside Gate H, €5.70, 4/hr) is the quickest way to the Paris Métro and a good way to the Marais and Luxembourg

Garden neighborhoods. Take the Jetbus to the Villejuif–Louis Aragon Métro stop. To reach the Marais neighborhood, take the Métro to the Sully-Morland stop. For the Luxembourg area, take the same train to the Censier-Daubenton or Place Monge stop. If taking the Jetbus from the Marais to the airport, make sure before you board the Métro that your train is going to Villejuif–Louis Aragon (not Mairie d'Ivry), as the route splits at the end of the line.

The **Orlybus** (outside Gate H, €6.20, 3/hr) takes you to the Denfert-Rochereau RER-B line and the Métro, offering Métro access to central Paris, including the Luxembourg Area and Notre-Dame Cathedral, as well as the Gare du Nord train station.

**Shuttle Buses to Disneyland** also depart from Gate H (€17, daily 8:30–19:45, confirm gate and schedule at ADP *Espace Tourisme* office—described earlier).

These two routes provide access to Paris via **RER trains:** an ADP shuttle **(Orly Rail bus)** takes you to RER-C (Pont d'Orly stop), with connections to Gare d'Austerlitz, St. Michel/Notre-Dame, Musée d'Orsay, Invalides, and Pont de l'Alma stations and is handy for some rue Cler hotels (outside Gate G, 4/hr, €6). **Orlyval trains** take you to the Antony stop on RER-B (serving Luxembourg, Châtelet–Les Halles, St. Michel, and Gare du Nord stations in central Paris, €9.50, includes RER ticket).

**Taxis** are to the far right as you leave the terminal, at Gate M. Allow €28–38 with bags for a taxi into central Paris.

**Airport vans** are good for single travelers or families of four or more (too many for a taxi) if going from Paris to the airport (see page 162 for a company to contact; from Orly, figure about €23/1 person, €30/2 people, less per person for larger groups and kids).

## Beauvais Airport

Budget airlines such as Ryanair use this airport, offering dirt-cheap airfares, but leaving you 50 miles north of Paris. Still, this small airport has direct buses to Paris (see below). It's ideal for drivers who want to rent a car here and head to Normandy or north to Belgium. The airport is basic (the terminal for departing passengers and baggage claim is under a tent, and waiting areas are crowded and have few services), but it's being improved as it deals with an increasing number of passengers (airport tel. 08 92 68 20 66, www.aeroportbeauvais.com; Ryanair tel. 08 92 68 20 73, www.ryanair.com).

**Transportation Between Beauvais Airport and Paris: Buses** depart from the airport about 20 minutes after flights arrive and take 90 minutes to reach Paris. Buy your ticket at the little kiosk to the right as you exit the airport (€14). Buses wait nearby and depart once they are full (baggage goes underneath), and arrive at Porte Maillot on the west edge of Paris, which has a Métro and RER stop. The closest taxi stand is across the street at Hôtel Concorde LaFayette.

Buses depart Paris for Beauvais Airport three hours and 15 minutes before scheduled flight departures. Catch the bus at Porte Maillot in the parking lot on boulevard Pershing next to Hôtel Concorde LaFayette. Arrive with enough time to purchase your bus ticket before boarding (Beauvais Airport tel. 08 92 68 20 66, www.aeroportbeauvais.com).

**Trains** connect Beauvais' city center and Paris' Gare du Nord (20/day, 80 min).

**Taxis** run from Beauvais Airport to Paris: €130 to central Paris, €12 to Beauvais' train station or city center.

## Connecting Paris' Airports

**Air France buses** directly and conveniently link Charles de Gaulle and Orly airports (roughly 2/hr, 5:45–23:00, 80 min, €17).

**RER line B** also connects Charles de Gaulle and Orly but requires a transfer to the Orlyval train and isn't as easy as the Air France bus (5/hr, 90 min, €18). This line splits at both ends: Heading to Orly, take trains that serve the Antony stop (then tranfer to Orlyval train); heading to Charles de Gaulle, take trains that end at the airport ("Roissy-CDG"), not Mitry-Claye.

Connect to and from the Beauvais Airport train at Gare du Nord (see "Beauvais Airport," previous page).

**Taxis** are easiest, but pricey (€80 between Charles de Gaulle and Orly, €115 between Charles de Gaulle and Beauvais, €135 between Orly and Beauvais).

# NEAR PARIS

*Versailles • Giverny • Chartres Cathedral •*
*Disneyland Paris*

Efficient trains bring dozens of day trips within the grasp of temporary Parisians. Europe's best palace at Versailles, the flowery gardens at Giverny that inspired Monet, the awesome cathedral of Chartres, and a mouse-run amusement park await the traveler looking for a refreshing change from urban Paris.

# Versailles

Every king's dream, Versailles was the residence of the French king and the cultural heartbeat of Europe for about 100 years—until the Revolution of 1789 ended the notion that God deputized some people to rule for him on Earth. Louis XIV spent half a year's income of Europe's richest country turning his dad's hunting lodge into a palace fit for a divine monarch. Louis XV and Louis XVI spent much of the 18th century gilding Louis XIV's lily. In 1837, about 50 years after the royal family was evicted, King Louis Philippe opened the palace as a museum. Europe's next-best palaces are Versailles wannabes.

Visiting Versailles can seem daunting because of its size and hordes of visitors. But it's easy. Arm yourself with a pass to skip ticket-buying lines and arrive early to avoid the crowds. I've provided all the details in "Orientation," next page. First-timers can simply follow my recommended strategy in "Planning Your Time at Versailles" on page 169.

Note that the entire complex is undergoing extensive renovation in 2009, so expect some closures and changes. Restoration projects may close the Opera House through June 2009. The renovated Petit Trianon is now open.

# ORIENTATION

**Cost:** I recommend buying either a Paris Museum Pass or Versailles' "Le Passeport" Pass, both of which give you access to the most important parts of the complex (see "Passes," later in this section).

You can also buy individual tickets to each of the three different sections:

**1.** The **Château,** the main palace, costs €13.50 (€10 after 15:00, under 18 always free, includes audioguide). Your Château ticket includes the King's and Queen's State Apartments (with the famous Hall of Mirrors), the Royal Chapel, the Opera House (closed through June 2009), and several lesser rooms.

**2.** The **Domaine de Marie-Antoinette,** the estate of the queen, costs €9 April–Oct; €5 after 16:00 and Nov–March; under 18 always free. This ticket gives you access to the far part of the Gardens and entry into several small palaces: the queen's Hamlet, the Grand and Petit Trianons, and a smattering of nearby buildings.

**3.** The **Gardens** are free, except on weekends April–Sept, when the fountains blast and the price is €8 (see "Fountain Spectacles," page 173).

**Passes:** Smart travelers arrive at Versailles with one of these two passes in hand. Either pass can save you money—and both allow you to skip the long ticket-buyer lines (though everyone must endure the security check before entering the palace).

The **Paris Museum Pass** covers the Château and the Domaine de Marie Antoinette (a €22.50 value). The Paris Museum Pass does not include audioguides and does not cover the Gardens on Fountain Spectacle weekends. For Paris Museum Pass pricing and details, see page 68 in the Paris chapter.

The **Le Passeport** one-day pass is a good deal if you don't have a Paris Museum Pass and you want to see the whole shebang. Le Passeport covers your entrance to the Château, Domaine de Marie-Antoinette, and Gardens. It also covers several things not covered by the Paris Museum Pass: audioguides, weekend Fountain Spectacles, and even the round-trip train from Paris (if you buy it in Paris at one of the RER stations that serves Versailles). You can also buy a Le Passeport at the Versailles TI or Château box office.

**Near Paris**

TO BEAUVAIS AIRPORT,
LILLE, LONDON,
BRUSSELS &
AMSTERDAM

20 MILES
30 KM

N

TO ROUEN

PONTOISE

AUVERS

CHANTILLY
• SENLIS

GIVERNY
• VERNON

DE GAULLE AIRPORT

C-1

D-1

B-3

TO BAYEUX & MONT ST. MICHEL

TO REIMS & EPERNAY

PARIS

A-4

DISNEYLAND PARIS

VERSAILLES

C-5

VERSAILLES CHANTIERS

TO DIJON + LYON

B-2

RER U

D-2

ANTONY

ORLY AIRPORT

VAUX-LE-VICOMTE
• MELUN

CHARTRES

FONTAINEBLEAU

TO RENNES + MONT ST. MICHEL

TO LOIRE

DCH

—|—|— SNCF (LONG DIST.) TRAINS

--- BUS

—A-4— RER COMMUTER TRAINS W/ LINE INDICATED

..... OTHER TRANSPORT (BIKE, TAXI, CAR...)

### One-Way Travel Times From Appropriate Train Station in Paris

| | |
|---|---|
| Chartres – 60 min | Vernon (Giverny) – 60 min |
| Versailles – 40 min | Auvers-sur-Oise – 90 min |
| Vaux-le-Vicomte – 45 min | Orly Airport – 30 min |
| Fontainebleau – 60 min | Charles de Gaulle Airport – 30 min |
| Chantilly – 45 min | Disneyland Paris – 45 min |
| Reims – 45 min | |

From April–Oct, Le Passeport costs €20 Mon–Fri, €25 Sat–Sun; from Nov–March it's €16 Tue–Sun. This pass is a poor value on Mon, when only the Domaine de Marie-Antoinette and Gardens are open.

**Hours:** The **Château** is open Tue–Sun April–Oct 9:00–18:30, Nov–March 9:00–17:30, closed Mon year-round. The **Domaine de Marie-Antoinette** is open daily April–Oct 12:00–18:30, Nov–

**Chartres**

TO PARIS
GARE MONTPARNASSE

VIEW

200 YARDS
200 METERS

TRAIN
STATION

MUSÉE
DES
BEAUX
ARTS

FOOT
BRIDGE

INT'L.
STAINED
GLASS
CENTER

PL.
SEMARD

CATHEDRAL

PONT
BOUJOU

PLACE
CHATELET

POST

PLACE
POISSON-
ERIE

MONOPRIX

COVERED
MKT.

CURE
RIVER

PLACE
DES
EPARS

❶ Hôtel Châtelet
❷ Hôtel Jehan de Beauce
❸ Hôtel le Boeuf Couronné
❹ Le Pichet Restaurant
❺ Le Café des Arts
❻ Les Picholines Restaurant

❼ Le Bistrot de la Cathédrale
❽ Trois Lys Crêperie
❾ Access to Crypt (Through "La Crypte" Bookstore)
❿ To Internet Café & Launderette
⓫ Launderettes (2)

**NEAR PARIS**

down times when the train returns to Paris (last train generally departs Chartres around 21:00). Exiting the Chartres station, you'll see the spires of the cathedral dominating the town, a five-minute walk uphill. On your way to the cathedral, stop at the TI (see "Information," later in this section).

**Combining with Versailles:** TER trains link Versailles and Chartres frequently (up to 30/day), on the route from Paris to Le Mans. In Versailles, this train stops at the Chantiers station (that's "Versailles C.H.")—not the Versailles R.G., or Rive Gauche, station listed in this book's Versailles visit (see page 171). The Versailles C.H. station is a 25-minute walk to the palace (just ask locals, "Château?").

**Bring:** Binoculars, if you got 'em. You can rent binoculars at a souvenir shop near the south porch of the church (€1.50/hr, €20 deposit, at 10 cloître Notre-Dame).

**Information:** At the **TI,** pick up the good free map with basic information on the town and cathedral. The TI has specifics on cathedral tours with Malcolm Miller, and also rents audioguides for the old town—both are described below (open April–Sept Mon–Sat 9:00–19:00, Sun 9:30–17:30; Oct–March Mon–Sat 9:00–18:00, Sun 9:30–17:00; located 100 yards in front of church, tel. 02 37 18 26 26, www.chartres-tourisme.com).

The church has two **bookstores.** One is inside near the entrance; the other—called La Crypte—is outside near the south porch (church tel. 02 37 21 59 08, www.diocese-chartres.com).

**Cathedral Tours by Malcolm Miller:** This fascinating English scholar, who moved here nearly 50 years ago, has dedicated his life to studying this cathedral—and sharing its wonder through his 75-minute guided lecture tours. No reservation is needed—just show up (€10, offered Mon–Sat at 12:00 and 14:45, no tours last half of Aug and Jan–Feb). Some take both of his tours, as every tour is different. Tours begin inside the church at the orange-and-purple *Cathedral Tours* sign by the bookstore. Consult this sign for changes or cancellations. He also offers private tours (private tour info tel. 02 37 28 15 58, fax 02 37 28 33 03, millerchartres@aol.com). For a detailed look at Chartres' windows, sculpture, and history, pick up Malcolm Miller's two guidebooks (sold at cathedral).

**Audioguides:** You can rent audioguides from the bookstore inside the cathedral near the entrance. Routes include the cathedral (€4.20, 45 min), the choir only (€3.20, 25 min), or both (€6.20, 70 min). The TI offers an audioguide for the often-missed old town (€5.50, €8.50/double set, about 2 hours, available only at the TI, leave passport as a deposit).

**Crypt Tours:** The crypt (which means "hidden") is the foundation of the previous, ninth-century church. Today, these foundations can be visited only as part of a very boring guided tour in French (with an English handout). You'll see remnants of the earlier churches, a modern copy of the old wooden Mary-and-baby statue, and hints of the old well and Roman wall (€2.70; April–Oct at 11:00, 14:15, 15:15, and 16:30; June–July also at 17:15, 2/day Nov–March, 30-min tours start in La Crypte bookstore, located outside church near south porch, tel. 02 37 21 75 02).

# SLEEPING

**(€1 = $1.50, country code: 33)**

Chartres, a good getaway from Paris, can also be a first or last overnight stop for those flying to or from Orly Airport.

The first two hotels face each other (200 yards straight out of train station, 300 yards below cathedral).

got a taste of his own medicine, Maximilien de Robespierre (€6.50, €10 combo-ticket with Sainte-Chapelle, both covered by Museum Pass, daily April–Sept 9:30–18:00, Oct–March 10:00–17:00, last entry 30 min before closing, 4 boulevard du Palais, Mo: Cité, tel. 01 53 40 60 80, www.monum.fr).

• *Back outside, turn left on boulevard du Palais and head toward the river (north). On the corner is the city's oldest public clock. The mechanism of the present clock is from 1334, and even though the case is Baroque, it keeps on ticking.*

*Turn left onto quai de l'Horloge and walk west along the river, past the round medieval tower called "The Babbler." The bridge up ahead is the pont Neuf, where we'll end this walk. At the first corner, veer left into a sleepy triangular square called place Dauphine. Marvel at how such coziness could be lodged in the midst of such greatness as you walk through the park to the end of the island (the departure point for Seine river cruises offered by Vedettes du Pont Neuf; see page 53). At the equestrian statue of Henry IV, turn right onto the bridge and take refuge in one of the nooks on the Eiffel Tower side.*

## Pont Neuf

This "new bridge" is now Paris' oldest. Built during Henry IV's reign (about 1600), its 12 arches span the widest part of the river. The fine view includes the park on the tip of the island (note Seine tour boats), the Orsay Museum, and the Louvre. These turrets were originally for vendors and street entertainers. In the days of Henry IV, who originated the promise of "a chicken in every pot," this would have been a lively scene.

• *As for now, you can tour the Seine by boat, continue to the Louvre, or head to the...*

## Paris Plage (Beach)

The Riviera it's not, but this fanciful faux beach—assembled in summer along a two-mile stretch of the Seine on the Right Bank—is a fun place to stroll, play, and people-watch on a sunny day. Each summer since 2002, the Paris city government has shut down the embankment's highway and trucked in potted palm trees, hammocks, lounge chairs, and 2,000 tons of sand to create a colorful urban beach. You'll also find "beach cafés," climbing walls, prefab pools, trampolines, *boules,* a library, beach volleyball, badminton, and Frisbee areas in three zones: sandy, grassy, and wood-tiled. As you take in the playful atmosphere, imagine how much has changed here since the Middle Ages when this was a grimy fishing community (free, mid-July–mid-Aug daily 7:00–24:00, no beach off-season; on the Right Bank of the Seine, just north of the Ile de la Cité, between pont des Arts and pont de Sully).

# Paris at a Glance

▲▲▲**Notre-Dame Cathedral** Paris' most beloved church, with towers and gargoyles. **Hours:** Cathedral daily 7:45–19:00; tower daily April–Sept 10:00–18:30—also June–Aug Sat–Sun until 23:00, daily Oct–March 10:00–17:30; Treasury daily 9:30–17:30. See page 57.

---

▲▲▲**Louvre** Europe's oldest and greatest museum, starring *Mona Lisa* and *Venus de Milo*. **Hours:** Wed–Mon 9:00–18:00, closed Tue. Most wings open Wed and Fri until 21:45. See page 70.

---

▲▲▲**Orsay Museum** Nineteenth-century art, including Europe's greatest Impressionist collection. **Hours:** Tue–Sun 9:30–18:00, Thu until 21:45, closed Mon. See page 77.

---

▲▲▲**Sainte-Chapelle** Gothic cathedral with peerless stained glass. **Hours:** Daily March–Oct 9:30–18:00, Nov–Feb 9:00–17:00. See page 62.

---

▲▲▲**Eiffel Tower** Paris' soaring exclamation point. **Hours:** Daily mid-June–Aug 9:00–24:45 in the morning, Sept–mid-June 9:30–23:45. See page 80.

---

▲▲▲**Arc de Triomphe** Triumphal arch with viewpoint, marking start of Champs-Elysées. **Hours:** Always viewable; inside daily April–Sept 10:00–23:00, Oct–March 10:00–22:30. See page 92.

---

▲▲▲**Versailles** The ultimate royal palace (Château), with a Hall of Mirrors, vast gardens, a grand canal, plus a queen's playground (Domaine de Marie-Antoinette). **Hours:** Château—April–Oct Tue–Sun 9:00–18:30, Nov–March Tue–Sun 9:00–17:30, closed Mon. Domaine—daily April–Oct 12:00–18:30, Nov–March 9:00–17:30. Gardens generally open daily 9:00 until sunset. See page 166.

---

▲▲**Orangerie Museum** Monet's water lilies, plus works by Utrillo, Cézanne, Renoir, Matisse, and Picasso, in a lovely setting. **Hours:** Wed–Mon 12:30–19:00, Fri until 21:00, closed Tue. See page 77.

---

▲▲**Army Museum and Napoleon's Tomb** The emperor's imposing tomb, flanked by army museums. **Hours:** Daily April–Sept 10:00–18:00—mid-June–mid-Sept tomb stays open until 19:00, museum open until 21:00, Oct–March 10:00–17:00, Oct–May closed first Mon of every month. See page 84.

---

▲▲**Rodin Museum** Works by the greatest sculptor since Michelangelo, with many sculptures in a peaceful garden. **Hours:** April–Sept Tue–Sun 9:30–17:45, Oct–March Tue–Sun 9:30–16:45, closed Mon. See page 84.

**▲▲Marmottan Museum** Untouristy art museum focusing on Monet. **Hours:** Tue 11:00–21:00, Wed–Sun 10:00–18:00, closed Mon. See page 85.

**▲▲Cluny Museum** Medieval art with unicorn tapestries. **Hours:** Wed–Mon 9:15–17:45, closed Tue. See page 85.

**▲▲Champs-Elysées** Paris' grand boulevard. **Hours:** Always open. See page 90.

**▲▲Jacquemart-André Museum** Art-strewn mansion. **Hours:** Daily 10:00–18:00. See page 93.

**▲▲La Défense and La Grande Arche** The city's own "little Manhattan" business district and its colossal modern arch. **Hours:** Daily April–Sept 10:00–20:00, Oct–March until 19:00. See page 94.

**▲▲Pompidou Center** Modern art in colorful building with city views. **Hours:** Wed–Mon 11:00–21:00, closed Tue. See page 97.

**▲▲Jewish Art and History Museum** Displays history of Judaism in Europe. **Hours:** Mon–Fri 11:00–18:00, Sun 10:00–18:00, closed Sat. See page 97.

**▲▲Picasso Museum** World's largest collection of Picasso's works. **Hours:** April–Sept Wed–Mon 9:30–18:00, Oct–March Wed–Mon 9:30–17:30, closed Tue. See page 98.

**▲▲Carnavalet Museum** Paris' history wrapped up in a 16th-century mansion. **Hours:** Tue–Sun 10:00–18:00, closed Mon. See page 100.

**▲▲Sacré-Cœur** White basilica atop Montmartre with spectacular views. **Hours:** Daily 7:00–23:00. See page 101.

**▲Panthéon** Neoclassical monument to French notables. **Hours:** Daily 10:00–18:30 in summer, until 18:00 in winter. See page 88.

**▲Opéra Garnier** Grand belle époque theater with a modern ceiling by Chagall. **Hours:** Daily 10:00–16:30, July–Aug until 18:00. See page 92.

**▲Père Lachaise Cemetery** Final resting place for Paris' illustrious dead. **Hours:** Mon–Sat 8:00–18:00, Sun 9:00–18:00. See page 101.

# SIGHTS

## Paris Museum Pass

In Paris, there are two classes of sightseers
—those with a Paris Museum Pass, and
those who stand in line. Serious sightseers
save time and money by getting this pass.

### Buying the Pass

The pass pays for itself with four admissions
in two days, and lets you skip the ticket
line at most sights (2 days/€30, 4 days/€45,
6 days/€60, no youth or senior discount).
It's sold at the participating museums,
monuments, and TIs (even at airports). Try

to avoid buying the pass at a major museum (such as the Louvre),
where the supply can be spotty and lines long. For more info, call
01 44 61 96 60 or visit www.parismuseumpass.com.

Tally up what you want to see from the list on opposite
page—and remember, an advantage of the pass is that you skip
to the front of most lines, which can save hours of waiting, especially in summer. Note that at a few sights (including the Louvre,
Sainte-Chapelle, and Notre-Dame's tower), everyone has to shuffle
through the slow-moving baggage-check lines for security—but
you still save time by avoiding the ticket line.

The pass isn't worth buying for children and teens, as most
museums are free or discounted for those under 18 (teenagers may
need to show ID as proof of age). Of the few museums that charge
for children, some allow kids in free if their parent has a Museum
Pass, while others charge admission, depending on age (the cutoff
age varies from 5 to 18). The free directory that comes with your pass
lists the current hours of sights, phone numbers, and the price that
kids pay. If a sight is free for kids, they can skip the line with their
passholder parents. (Paris' museums don't offer senior discounts.)

Think ahead to make the most of your pass. Validate it only
when you're ready to tackle the covered sights on consecutive days.
Make sure the sights you want to visit will be open (Mondays and
Tuesdays are big days for museums to be closed). The Paris Museum
Pass even covers most of Versailles (your other option for Versailles
is the Le Passeport pass, which also covers the RER train ride to
Versailles; see page 169). On days that you don't have pass coverage,
visit free sights as well as sights that aren't covered by passes.

Keep in mind that sights such as the Arc de Triomphe and
Pompidou Center are open later in the evening, and that the
Louvre, Orsay, and Orangerie are open later on selected evenings,
allowing you to stretch the day for your Paris Museum Pass.

**$$ Hôtel Châtelet***,** run by friendly Chantal, Marilou, Franck, and Nathalie, is comfortable, from its welcoming lobby to its spotless, spacious, well-furnished rooms. Choose between plush, modern, recently renovated "privilege" rooms with air-conditioning, or the cheaper "standing" rooms with Old World charm (Sb-€88–118, Db-€102–130, extra bed-€22, parking-€7.50, 6 avenue Jehan de Beauce, tel. 02 37 21 78 00, fax 02 37 36 23 01, www.hotelchatelet.com, reservation@hotelchatelet.com).

**$ Hôtel Jehan de Beauce**** is basic, clean (despite the shabby hallways), and quiet. Some of its rooms have tiny bathrooms (S-€38, Ss-€52–58, Sb-€60, D-€49, Ds-€57–63, Db-€68, Tb-€72, 19 avenue Jehan de Beauce, tel. 02 37 21 01 41, fax 02 37 21 59 10, jehandebeauce@club-internet.fr).

**$ Hôtel le Boeuf Couronné**** is warmly run by Madame Vinsot, with 21 clean but slightly worn rooms and a handy location (S-€32, Sb-€50, D-€37, Db-€60–70, elevator, 15 place Châtelet, tel. 02 37 18 06 06, fax 02 37 21 72 13).

# EATING

**Le Pichet,** run by friendly Marie-Sylvie and Xavier, is reasonable and homey, with good daily specials (€12–18 *plats*, €12–15 daily *menu*, closed Tue and Sun evenings and all day Wed, 19 rue du Cheval Blanc, near TI, tel. 02 37 21 08 35).

**Le Café des Arts** is a sleek, modern place just a block from the cathedral. It's perfect for a quick, reasonably priced three-egg omelet or salad. Yvon, the owner, prides himself on the delicious €6–14 *tartines*—warm, open-faced sandwiches served with a small salad (€16–18.50 *menus*, 45–47 rue des Changes, tel. 02 37 21 07 05).

**Les Picholines** is a favorite for Mediterranean-inspired cuisine. Come here to get your fix of tapas and olives, or to feast on €11–14 pastas and salads (€14–19 lunch *menu*, €23–28 dinner *menu*, open daily, rue du Cheval Blanc, tel. 02 37 36 85 84).

**Le Bistrot de la Cathédrale** is fine for salads and traditional bistro fare, but you'll pay for the view (*menus* from €20, open daily, south side of cathedral at 1 cloître Notre-Dame, tel. 02 37 36 59 60).

**Trois Lys Crêperie** makes good, cheap crêpes just across the river on pont Boujou (closed Sun–Mon, 3 rue de la Porte Guillaume, tel. 02 37 28 42 02).

# Giverny

Claude Monet spent 43 of his most creative years here (1883–1926). His gardens and home, a ▲ sight, are unfortunately split by a busy road and packed with tour-ists. Arrive early or late (see "Avoiding Crowds," below), explore the gardens, then take the pedestrian tunnel into Monet's famous lily-pad land. The path leads over the Japanese Bridge, under weeping willows, and past countless scenes that leave artists aching for an easel. Back on the other side, continue your visit with a wander through his mildly interesting home. The jammed gift shop at the exit is the actual skylighted studio where Monet painted his water-lily masterpieces.

**Cost and Hours:** €5.50, €4 for gardens only, April–Oct Tue–Sun 9:30–18:00, last entry 17:30, closed Mon and Nov–March, open some Mon holidays—check website, tel. 02 32 51 28 21, www.fondation-monet.com.

**Nearby Sights:** The Museum of American Art (Musée d'Art Américain, turn left when leaving Monet's place and walk 100 yards) is devoted to American artists who followed Claude to Giverny (same price and hours as Monet's home). Monet and his garden had a great influence on American artists of his day.

If you miss your train back to Paris, spend an hour in pleasant little Vernon while you wait for the next train.

**Avoiding Crowds:** While lines may be long and tour groups may trample the flowers, true fans still find magic in the gardens. Minimize crowds by arriving by 9:15 (get in line, it opens at 9:30), during lunchtime, or after 16:00. If you're traveling by train, take the first departure from Paris.

**Getting There by Tour:** Big tour companies do a Giverny day trip from Paris for around €70; ask at your hotel.

**By Car:** From Paris's Périphérique ring road, follow A-13 toward Rouen, get off at Vernon, follow *Centre-Ville* signs, then signs to Giverny.

**By Train:** Take the Rouen-bound train from Paris' Gare St. Lazare station to Vernon (6/day, more on Sat, about €23 round-trip, 45 min one-way, 4 miles from Giverny, no baggage check). From the Vernon train station to Monet's garden (4 miles one-way), you have four good options: by bus, taxi, bike, or on foot.

The Vernon–Giverny **bus** meets arriving trains for the 15-minute run to Giverny (no buses on Mon) and takes you back to

# Giverny

NOT TO SCALE

RUE CLAUDE

PARKING LOT

ENTRANCE

EXIT

WATER LILY STUDIO
GIFT SHOP & EXIT

TO MUSEUM OF AMERICAN ART & ⑥

HOUSE

WALLED GARDEN
(CLOS NORMAND)

MONET

④

TO VERNON
(4 MILES)
& BIKE PATH

D-5 ROAD

PATH

①

② ③

WATER GARDEN

DCH

① Pedestrian Tunnel
② Japanese Bridge
③ Water Lily Pond
④ Hôtel la Musardière
⑤ Café & Sandwich Stand
⑥ To Café at Museum of American Art & Hôtel Baudy

**NEAR PARIS**

meet the return train to Paris. If you miss the last bus, find others to share a taxi (see below). The stop to Giverny is in front of Vernon's train station, facing Café du Chemin de Fer (don't dally, the bus leaves soon after your train arrives). The ticket office at Monet's home in Giverny has bus schedules for the return trip. The bus stop for the return trip is in the bus parking lot on the opposite side of the main road, by the roundabout. The stop is the first one on your right. Look for the white #18 bus marked *Vernon–Giverny Car.*

If you take a **taxi,** allow €12 for up to three people, €13 for four (tel. 06 77 49 32 90, 06 76 08 50 78, or 02 32 21 31 31). With buses meeting every train, taxis are unnecessary (unless you miss the bus). Taxis wait in front of the station in Vernon.

You can rent a **bike** at Café du Chemin de Fer opposite the train station (€12, tel. 02 32 21 16 01), and follow a paved bike path *(piste cyclable)* that runs from near Vernon along an abandoned railroad right-of-way (figure about 30 min to Giverny). Get the easy-to-follow map to Giverny with your bike and leave the train

station paralleling tracks to your right. Take the first left and follow that to the river, cross the river, turn right, and meet the bike
trail. There's a lovely riverside park on the left side of the bridge
after crossing the Seine (where you turn right for the bike path).

Hikers can go on **foot** to Giverny, following the bike
instructions above, and take a bus or taxi back.

## SLEEPING AND EATING

(€1 = $1.50, country code: 33)

**$$ Hôtel la Musardière**\*\* is nestled in the village of Giverny two
blocks from Monet's home (exit home and go right). It's cute and
welcoming, with a reasonable and homey *crêperie*-restaurant (Db-
€72–82, 123 rue Claude Monet, tel. 02 32 21 03 18, fax 02 32 21 60
00, www.lamusardiere.fr, hotelmusardieregiverny@wanadoo.fr).

You'll find a **café and sandwich stand** near the entrance
to Monet's home and a peaceful **garden café** at the Museum of
American Art (surrounded by gardens Monet would appreciate,
but a little pricey).

The rose-colored **Hôtel Baudy** was the American artists'
hangout and offers an appropriately pretty setting for lunch or din-
ner (*menus* from €23, popular with tour groups, closed Sun eve and
Mon, 5-min walk past Museum of American Art at 81 rue Claude
Monet, tel. 02 32 21 10 03).

# Disneyland Paris

Europe's Disneyland is a remake of California's, with most of the
same rides and smiles. The main difference is that Mickey Mouse
speaks French, and you can buy wine with your lunch. My kids
went ducky.

Disneyland is easy to get to, and worth a day, if Paris is handier
than Florida or California.
Saturday, Sunday, Wednesday,
public holidays, and any day in
July and August are the most
crowded. After dinner, crowds
are gone. Food is fun and not
outrageously priced. (Still, many
smuggle in a picnic.) The free
FASTPASS system is a worth-
while timesaver (get FASTPASS
card at entry, good for five most

popular rides, insert card in machine at ride to get a window of time to enter—often within about 45 minutes). You'll also save time by buying your tickets ahead (at airport TIs, some Métro stations, or along the Champs-Elysées at the TI, Disney Store, or Virgin Megastore). Disney brochures are in every Paris hotel. For Disneyland information and reservations, call 08 25 30 60 30 (€0.15/min) or try www.disneylandparis.com or www.mickey -mouse.com.

**Walt Disney Studios:** This zone, which opened in 2002 next to the original 10-year-old amusement park, has a Hollywood focus geared for an older crowd, with animation, special effects, and movie-magic "rides." The Aerosmith Rock 'n' Roller Coaster is nothing special. The highlight is the Stunt Show Spectacular, filling a huge back-lot stadium five times a day for 45 minutes of car chases and thriller filming tips. An actual movie sequence is filmed with stunt drivers, audience bit players, and brash MTV-style hosts.

**Cost:** Disneyland Paris and Walt Disney Studios charge the same. You can pay separately for each or buy a combined ticket for both, called a "Hopper" ticket. A one-day pass to either park is about €60 for adults and €50 for kids aged 3–11 (check their web-site for special offers). There's no charge for kids under 3. In the summer, save 25 percent by going after 17:00.

For entry to both parks, adults pay about €80 for one day, €120 for two days, and €138 for three days (less for kids). Regular prices are discounted about 25 percent Nov–March and promotions are offered occasionally (check www.disneylandparis.com).

**Hours:** Disneyland is open daily mid-July–Aug 10:00–23:00, Sept–mid-July 10:00–19:00, some weekends have longer hours—check website or at ticket office. Walt Disney Studios is open summer daily 9:00–18:00; winter Mon–Fri 10:00–18:00, Sat–Sun 9:00–18:00.

**Getting There:** By **car,** Disneyland is about 40 minutes (20 miles) east of Paris on the A-4 autoroute (direction: Nancy/Metz, exit #14). Parking is about €10 per day at the park.

**By RER:** The slick 45-minute RER trip is the best way to Disneyland from downtown Paris. Take RER line A-4 to Marne-la-Vallée-Chessy; check the signs over the platform to be sure Marne-la-Vallée-Chessy is served, because the line splits near the end (catch RER line A-4 from Paris' Charles de Gaulle–Etoile, Auber, Châtelet–Les Halles, or Gare de Lyon stations, about €8 each way, 3/hr, drops you 45 min later right in the park). The last train back to Paris leaves shortly after midnight. When returning, remember to use your same RER ticket for your Métro connection in Paris.

**By Train:** Pricey **TGV** trains connect Disneyland directly with **Charles de Gaulle Airport** (10 min), the **Loire Valley** (1.5 hrs, Tours–St. Pierre-des-Corps station, 15 min from Amboise), **Avignon** (3 hrs, TGV station), **Lyon** (2 hrs, Part Dieu station), and **Nice** (6 hrs, main station).

**By Bus:** Both of Paris' major airports have direct **shuttle buses** to Disneyland Paris (about €17, daily 8:30–19:45, every 45 min).

## SLEEPING

**(€1 = $1.50, country code: 33)**

Most are better off sleeping in reality (Paris), though with direct buses and freeways to both airports, Disneyland makes a convenient first- or last-night stop. Seven different Disney-owned hotels offer accommodations at or near the park in all price ranges. Prices are impossible to pin down, as they vary by season and by the "package deal" you choose (deals that include park entry are usually a better value). The cheapest is **Davy Crockett's Ranch,** but you'll need a car. **Hôtel Santa Fe\*\*** offers the best midrange value, with frequent shuttle service to the park. The most expensive is **Disneyland Hotel\*\*\*\***, right at the park entry, about twice the price of the Santa Fe. To reserve any Disneyland hotel, call 01 60 30 60 30, fax 01 60 30 60 65, or check www.disneylandparis.com. The prices you'll be quoted include entry to the park.

# NORMANDY

Sweeping coastlines, half-timbered towns, and thatched roofs punctuate the green, rolling hills of Normandy. Parisians call Normandy "the 21st arrondissement." It's their escape—the nearest beach. The Brits also consider this area close enough for a weekend away (the BBC came through loud and clear on my car radio).

Despite the peacefulness you feel in today's Normandy, the region's history is filled with war. It was founded by Viking Norsemen who invaded from the north, settled here in the ninth century, and gave Normandy its name. A couple hundred years later, William the Conqueror invaded England from Normandy. His victory is commemorated in a remarkable tapestry at Bayeux. A few hundred years after that, France's greatest cheerleader, Joan of Arc (Jeanne d'Arc), was convicted of heresy in Rouen, and burned at the stake by the English, against whom she rallied France during the Hundred Years' War. And in 1944, Normandy hosted a World War II battle that changed the course of history.

The rugged, rainy coast of Normandy harbors wartime bunkers and enchanting fishing villages such as little Honfleur. And, on the border of Brittany, the almost surreal island abbey of Mont St. Michel rises serene and majestic, oblivious to the tides of tourists.

## Planning Your Time

Honfleur, the D-Day beaches, and Mont St. Michel each merit overnight visits. At a minimum, you'll want a full day for the D-Day beaches and a half-day each in Honfleur and on Mont St. Michel. In 2009, Normandy celebrates the 65th anniversary of the D-Day landings—so prepare for big crowds from June 1–10.

If you're driving between Paris and Honfleur, Giverny (see

previous chapter) or Rouen (covered in this chapter) are worthwhile stops; by train, they're best as day trips from Paris. The WWII memorial museum in Caen works well as a stop between Honfleur and Bayeux (and the D-Day beaches). Mont St. Michel must be seen early or late to avoid the masses of midday tourists.

Dinan, just 45 minutes by car from Mont St. Michel, offers a fine introduction to Brittany (see next chapter). Drivers can enjoy Mont St. Michel as a day trip from Dinan.

For practical information in English about Normandy, see http://normandy.angloinfo.com.

## Getting Around Normandy

This region is ideal with a car. If you're driving into Honfleur from the north, take the impressive but pricey Normandy Bridge (pont de Normandie, €5 toll). If you're driving between Mont St. Michel and Dinan, follow my recommended scenic route (see page 260).

Trains from Paris serve Rouen, Caen, Bayeux, Mont St. Michel (via Pontorson or Rennes), and Dinan, though service between these sights can be frustrating. Plan ahead: For bus information in English, check with the local TI. Buses make Giverny, Honfleur, Arromanches, and Mont St. Michel accessible to train stations in nearby towns, though Sundays have little—if any—bus service. Mont St. Michel is a challenge by train, except from Paris. Enterprising hotel owners in Bayeux operate a minivan service between Bayeux and Mont St. Michel for €55 round-trip per person, filling a critical need for those without cars (see page 229).

## Cuisine Scene in Normandy

Normandy is known as the land of the four Cs: Calvados, Camembert, cider, and *crème*. The region specializes in cream sauces, organ meats (sweetbreads, tripe, and kidneys—the "gizzard salads" are great), and seafood *(fruits de mer)*. Dairy products are big here. Local cheeses are Camembert (mild to very strong; see sidebar), Brillat-Savarin (buttery), Livarot (spicy and pungent), Pavé d'Auge (spicy and tangy), and Pont l'Evêque (earthy flavor). Normandy is famous for its powerful Calvados apple brandy, Benedictine brandy (made by local monks), and three kinds of alcoholic apple ciders (*cidre* can be *doux*—sweet; *brut*—dry; or *bouché*—sparkling, and the strongest). Try a *kir normand* (crème de cassis and cider), and look also for *poiret,* a tasty pear cider.

## Camembert Cheese

This cheap, soft, white, Brie-like cheese is sold all over France (and America) in distinctive, round, wooden containers. Camembert has been known for its cheese for 500 years, but local legend has it that today's cheese got its start in the French Revolution, when a priest on the run was taken in by Marie Harel, a Camembert farmer. He repaid the favor by giving her the secret formula from his own hometown—Brie.

From cow to customer, Camembert takes about three weeks to make. High-fat milk from Norman cows is curdled with rennet, ladled into round, five-inch molds, sprinkled with *Penicillium camemberti* bacteria, and left to dry. In the first three days, the cheese goes from the cow's body temperature to room temperature to refrigerator cool (50 degrees).

Two weeks later, the ripened and aged cheese is wrapped in wooden bands and labeled for market. Like wines, Camembert cheese is controlled by government regulations and must bear the "A.O.C." *(Appellation d'Origine Contrôlée)* stamp of approval.

Remember, restaurants serve only during lunch (11:30–14:00) and dinner (19:00–21:00, later in bigger cities); cafés serve food throughout the day.

# Rouen

This 2,000-year-old city mixes Gothic architecture, half-timbered houses, and contemporary bustle like no other place in France.

Busy Rouen (roo-ohn) is France's fifth-largest port and Europe's biggest food exporter (mostly wheat and grain). While its cobbled old town is a delight to wander, the city feels less welcoming at night. Rouen works best for me as a day trip.

Rouen is nothing new. It was a regional capital during Roman times, and France's second-largest city in medieval times (with 40,000 residents—only Paris had more). In the ninth century, the Normans made the town their capital. William the Conqueror called it home before moving to England. Rouen walked a political tightrope between England and France for centuries. An English base during the Hundred

Years' War, it was here where Joan of Arc was burned (in 1431).

Rouen's historic wealth was based on its wool industry and trade—for centuries, it was the last bridge across the Seine River before the Atlantic. In April 1944, as America and Britain weakened German control of Normandy before the D-Day landings, Allied bombers destroyed 50 percent of Rouen. While the industrial suburbs were devastated, most of the historic core survived, keeping Rouen a pedestrian haven. And on summer evenings, a sound-and-light show transforms the facade of its Notre-Dame Cathedral into the changing colors of Monet's Impressionist canvas (mid-June–mid-Sept).

## Planning Your Time

Rouen, with convenient connections to Paris (hourly, 1–1.5-hour trains from Gare St. Lazare), makes an easy day trip if you want a dose of a much smaller—yet lively—French city. Considering the easy Paris connection and Rouen's handy location in Normandy, drivers can save money and headaches by seeing Paris, then taking the train to Rouen to pick up a rental. Store your bags in the car—leaving it in the secure rental lot—and visit Rouen before heading out (for car-rental companies, see "Helpful Hints," page 196).

# ORIENTATION

While Paris embraces the Seine, Rouen ignores it. The area we're most interested in is bounded by the river to the south, the Museum of Fine Arts (esplanade Marcel Duchamp) to the north, rue de la République to the east, and place du Vieux Marché to the west. It's a 20-minute walk from the train station to the river. Everything of interest is within a 10-minute walk from the Notre-Dame Cathedral.

## Tourist Information

The TI faces the cathedral. Pick up the map with information on Rouen's museums. The TI also has audioguide tours covering the cathedral and Rouen's historic center for €5 per person, though my walking tour (page 196) is enough for most (May–Sept Mon–Sat 9:00–19:00, Sun 9:30–12:30 & 14:00–18:00; Oct–April Mon–Sat 9:00–18:00, Sun 10:00–13:00; 25 place de la Cathédrale, tel. 02 32 08 32 40, www.rouentourisme.com). A small office in the TI changes money (closed during lunch year-round).

## Arrival in Rouen

**By Train:** Rue Jeanne d'Arc cuts down from Rouen's train station (no baggage storage) through the town center to the Seine River. Day-trippers should **walk** from the station down rue Jeanne d'Arc to rue du Gros Horloge—a busy pedestrian mall in the medieval center. This cobblestone street connects place du Vieux Marché and Joan of Arc Church (to your right, the starting point of my self-guided "Welcome to Rouen" walk) with Notre-Dame Cathedral (to your left).

Rouen's **subway** (Métrobus) whisks travelers from under the train station to the Palais de la Justice in one stop (€1.50, descend and buy tickets from machines one level underground, then validate ticket on subway two levels down). From the station, take a train headed to Technopole or Georges Braque. Returning to the station, take the direction Boulingrin and get off at Gare-Rue Verte.

**Taxis** (to the right as you exit station) will take you to any of my recommended hotels for about €7.

**By Bus:** Rouen's bus station is just off rue Jeanne d'Arc, near the river. As you exit the station, turn left and walk up rue Jeanne d'Arc, then turn right on pedestrian-friendly rue du Gros Horloge to reach most hotels and the cathedral. (To find the start of my waking tour, turn left on rue du Gros Horloge.)

**By Car:** Assume you'll get lost—then found. Follow signs for *Centre-Ville* and *Rive Droite* (right bank). Park near place du Vieux Marché or near the cathedral (parking structures available at both). You can park free overnight along the river (metered until 19:00), or pay to park more securely in one of many well-signed underground lots. La Haute Vieille Tour parking garage, between the cathedral and the river, is handy (€10/day). If you get turned around (likely because of the narrow, one-way streets), aim for the highest cathedral spires you spot.

If leaving Rouen for Honfleur, the fastest way is to follow blue autoroute signs to *Le Havre*, then *Caen*.

## Helpful Hints

**Closed Days:** Rouen's museums are closed on Tuesday, and many sights also close midday (12:00–14:00). The cathedral is closed Monday morning and during Mass (Tue–Sat at 10:00, Sun and holidays at 8:30, 10:30, and 12:00). The Joan of Arc Church is closed Fri and Sun mornings, and during Mass.

**Market Days:** The best open-air market is on place St. Marc, a few blocks east of St. Maclou Church. It's filled with antiques and other good stuff (all day Tue, Fri, and Sat; on Sun until 13:30). There's also a smaller market on place du Vieux Marché, by the Joan of Arc Church (Tue–Sun until 13:30, closed Mon).

**Supermarket:** It's inside the **Monoprix,** at the back of the store (Mon–Sat 8:30–21:00, closed Sun, on rue du Gros Horloge).

**Internet Access: Place Net** is just behind the cathedral (Mon–Sat 12:00–23:00, Sun 14:00–23:00, 37 rue de la République, tel. 02 32 78 02 22). Or surf with a view of the Joan of Arc Church

# Rouen

200 YARDS
200 METERS

Ⓜ METRO STATION
Ⓟ PARKING

TRAIN STATION

BLVD. l'YSER

BLVD. MARNE

JOAN OF ARC TOWER MUSEUM

PLACE DU VIEUX MARCHE & COVERED MARKET

Museum of CERAMICS

MUSEUM OF FINE ARTS

JOAN OF ARC CHURCH

SQUARE VERDREL

R. THIERS

MUSEUM OF IRONWORKS

Post

R. GANTERIE

PALACE OF JUSTICE

RUE DE GROS

JOAN OF ARC MUSEUM

BIG CLOCK

OLD

R. JUIFS

HORLOGE

ST. NIC

CITY

RUE OURS

Post

ST. ROMAIN

ST. OUEN

RUE FAULX

EAU DU ROBEC

AMIENS

PLAGUE CEMETERY

MARTAIN-VILLE

BUS STN.

CHARETTES QUAI

HAVRE

R. GEN. LECLERC

THEATRE DES ARTS

QUAI BOURSE

NOTRE-DAME

R. ALSACE

ST. MACLOU

QUAI P. CORNEILLE

SEINE R.

TO A-5 FREEWAY & PARIS

DCH

**NORMANDY**

❶ Hôtel Mercure
❷ Hôtel de la Cathédrale
❸ Hôtel Cardinal
❹ Chez Nous Restaurant
❺ Crêperie le St. Romain, Fayencerie Augy China Shop & Dame Cakes
❻ Le Maupassant & Le Terre-Neuvas Rests.

❼ Flunch Cafeteria
❽ Internet Cafés (2)
❾ ABC Books
❿ SNCF Boutique (Train Tickets)
⓫ Hertz
⓬ Monoprix Dept. Store/ Groceries

at **Cybernet** (Mon–Sat 10:00–21:00, Sun 14:00–19:00, has English keyboards and Wi-Fi, 47 place du Vieux Marché, tel. 02 35 07 73 02).

**English Bookstore: ABC Books** has nothing but English-language books—some American but mostly British (Tue–Sat 10:00–18:00, closed Sun–Mon, south of Eglise St. Ouen at 11 rue des Faulx, tel. 02 35 71 08 67).

**Taxi:** Call **Les Taxi Blancs** (tel. 02 35 61 20 50 or 02 35 88 50 50).

**Car Rental: Hertz** is across from the train station (Mon–Fri 8:00–12:00 & 14:00–19:00, Sat 8:00–12:00 & 14:00–18:00, closed Sun, 130 rue Jeanne d'Arc, tel. 02 35 70 70 71). **Europcar** has an office inside the station (Mon–Fri 8:00–12:30 & 13:30–19:00, Sat 8:30–12:00 & 14:00–18:00, closed Sun, tel. 02 35 88 21 20), as does **Avis** (tel. 02 35 88 60 94).

**SNCF Boutique:** Visit their office in town at the corner of rue aux Juifs and rue Eugène Boudin (Mon–Sat 10:00–19:00, closed Sun).

# SELF-GUIDED WALK

## Welcome to Rouen

On this 90-minute walk, you'll see the essential historical Rouen sights. Remember that many sights are closed midday (12:00–14:00). This walk is designed for day-trippers coming by train (it begins a 10-minute downhill walk from the station). Drivers should park at or near place du Vieux Marché (parking garage available).

You'll start at place du Vieux Marché, then walk the length of rue du Gros Horloge to Notre-Dame Cathedral. From there, walk four blocks west to the plague cemetery, loop up to the church of St. Ouen, and return along rues de l'Hôpital and Ganterie, ending at the Museum of Fine Arts (a five-minute walk to the train station). The map on page 199 highlights our route.

• *If arriving by train, walk down rue Jeanne d'Arc, and turn right on rue du Guillaume le Conquérant. This takes you to our starting point...*

### Place du Vieux Marché

Surrounded by half-timbered buildings, this old market square has a covered produce market, a park commemorating Joan of Arc's burning, and a modern church named after her. The market leads to the garden, where a tall aluminum cross marks the spot where Rouen publicly punished and executed people. The pillories stood here, and during the Revolution, the town's guillotine made 800 people "a foot shorter at the top." In 1431, Joan of Arc—only 19 years old—was burned at this site. As the flames engulfed her, an English soldier said, "Oh my God, we've killed a saint." (Nearly 500 years later, Joan was canonized, and the soldier was proved right.)

# Joan of Arc
## (1412–1431)

The cross-dressing teenager who rallied French soldiers to drive out English invaders was born the illiterate daughter of a humble farmer. One summer day, in her dad's garden, 13-year-old Joan heard a heavenly voice accompanied by bright light. It was the first of several saints (including Michael, Margaret, and Catherine) to talk to her during her short life.

In 1429, the young girl was instructed by the voices to save France from the English. Dressed in men's clothing, she traveled to see the king and predicted that the French armies would be defeated near Orléans—as they were. King Charles VII equipped her with an ancient sword and a banner saying "Jesus, Maria," and sent her to rally the troops.

Soon, "the Maid" *(la Pucelle)* was bivouacking amid rough soldiers, riding with them into battle, and suffering an arrow wound to the chest—all while liberating the town of Orléans. On July 17, 1429, she held her banner high in the cathedral of Reims as Charles was officially proclaimed king of a resurgent France.

Joan and company next tried to retake Paris (1429), but the English held out. She suffered a crossbow wound through the thigh, and her reputation of invincibility was tarnished. During a battle at Compiègne (1430), she was captured and turned over to the English for £10,000. In Rouen, they chained her by the neck inside an iron cage, while the local French authorities (allied with the English) plotted against her. The Inquisition—insisting that Joan's voices were "false and diabolical"—tried and sentenced her to death for being a witch and heretic.

On May 30, 1431, Joan of Arc was tied to a stake on Rouen's old market square (place du Vieux Marché). She yelled, "Rouen! Rouen! Must I die here?" Then they lit the fire; she fixed her eyes on a crucifix and died chanting, "Jesus, Jesus, Jesus."

After her death, Joan's place in history was slowly rehabilitated. French authorities proclaimed her trial illegal (1455), prominent writers and artists were inspired by her, and the Catholic Church finally beatified (1909) and canonized her (1920) as St. Joan of Arc.

A waxy **Joan of Arc Museum,** facing the square, tells the story of this inspirational teenager of supreme faith who, after hearing voices for several years, won the confidence of her countrymen, was given an army, and rallied the French against their English invaders. Those touched by her story will enjoy this little museum with excellent English information and nifty models throughout (€4, daily mid-April–Sept 9:30–19:00, Oct–mid-April

10:00–12:00 & 14:00–18:30, enter through a souvenir shop across from the church, tel. 02 35 88 02 70, www.jeanne-darc.com).

Between the museum and the church are the **ruins** of a 15th-century church that once stood on this spot (destroyed during the French Revolution).

The modern **Joan of Arc Church** (Eglise Jeanne d'Arc)—worth ▲▲—is a tribute to the young woman who was canonized in 1920 and later became the patron saint of France. The church, completed in 1979, feels Scandinavian inside and out—another reminder of Normandy's Nordic roots. Sumptuous 16th-century windows, salvaged from a church lost in World War II, were worked into the soft architectural lines. With a ship's-hull vaulting, the church is a delightful place, similar to churches designed by the architect Le Corbusier (free entry, €0.50 English pamphlet, Mon–Thu and Sat 10:00–12:15 & 14:00–18:00, Fri and Sun 14:00–18:00, closed Fri and Sun mornings and during Mass). There's a public WC 30 yards from the church doors.

• *Leave the square with Joan's church on your left and walk on the pedestrian pathway toward rue Jeanne d'Arc.*

Fifty yards before the medieval McDonald's is a chocolate shop, **Les Larmes de Jeanne d'Arc de Rouen** (at #163), which would love to tempt you with its chocolate-covered almond "tears *(larmes)* of Joan of Arc." While you must resist touching the chocolate fountain, you are welcome to taste a tear. The first one is free; a small bag costs about €7.

• *Your route continues across busy rue Jeanne d'Arc and up pedestrian-happy rue du Gros Horloge—the town's main shopping street since Roman times—to the...*

## Big Clock (Gros Horloge)

This impressive, circa 1528 Renaissance clock, le Gros Horloge (groh oar-lohzh), decorates the former city hall. Is something missing? Not really. In the 16th century, an hour hand offered ample precision; minute hands became necessary only in a later, faster-paced age. The lamb at the end of the hour hand is a reminder that wool rules—it was the source of Rouen's wealth. The town medallion features a sacrificial lamb, which has both religious and commercial significance. The black-and-silver orb above the clock makes one revolution in 29 days. The clock's artistic highlight fills the underside of the arch (walk underneath and stretch your back), with the "Good Shepherd" and lots of sheep.

To see the inner workings and an extraordinary panorama over Rouen (including a memorable view of the cathedral), climb the clock tower's 100 steps. You'll tour several rooms with the help of an audioguide that suffers from a Goldilocks-and-the-Three-Bears narration. The big bells ring on the hour—a deafening

# Welcome to Rouen Self-Guided Walk

200 YARDS
200 METERS

1. Place du Vieux Marché
2. Joan of Arc Museum
3. Joan of Arc Church
4. Big Clock
5. Palace of Justice
6. Notre-Dame Cathedral
7. Rue St. Romain
8. Fayencerie Augy
9. St. Maclou Church
10. Half-Timbered Buildings
11. Plague Cemetery
12. Museum of Fine Arts

**P** PARKING
**M** METRO STATION

NORMANDY

experience if you're in the tower (€6, includes audioguide, Tue–Sun 10:00–12:00 & 14:00–18:00, closed Mon).

• *Walk under le Gros Horloge and take a one-block detour left on rue Thouret to see the...*

## Palace of Justice (Palais de Justice)

This flamboyantly Gothic building, once the home of Normandy's *parlement,* had been covered with grime, but years of cleaning are near an end. The result is striking; you'll see pockmarks on the side of the building that faces rue Jeanne d'Arc—leftovers from bombings during the Normandy invasion. Look for the English-language plaque on the iron fence.

• *Double back to rue du Gros Horloge, then turn left until you reach...*

## ▲▲Notre-Dame Cathedral (Cathédrale Notre-Dame)

This cathedral is a landmark of art history. You're seeing essentially what Claude Monet saw as he painted 30 different studies of this frilly Gothic facade at various times of the day. Using the physical building only as a rack upon which to hang light, mist, dusk, and shadows, Monet was capturing "impressions." One of the results is in Rouen's Museum of Fine Arts, and four others are at the Orsay Museum in Paris. Find the plaque showing two of these paintings (in the corner of the square, about 30 paces to your right as you exit the TI).

Enter the cathedral (Tue–Sun 8:00– 19:00, Mon 14:00–19:00; closed during Mass Tue–Sat at 8:00 and 10:00, Sun at 8:30, 10:30, and 12:00).

• *Stand at the back and look down the **nave.***

This is a classic Gothic nave—four stories of pointed-arch arcades, the top one filled with windows to help light the interior. Today, the interior is lighter than intended, because the original colored glass (destroyed mostly in World War II) was replaced by clear glass. Why such a big cathedral in a small town? Until the 1700s, Rouen was the second largest city of France—rich from its wool trade and its booming port.

• *Circle counterclockwise three-quarters of the way around the church along the side aisle.*

The side chapels and windows have descriptions in English. These chapels display an assortment of styles through the centuries—for example, windows with bold blues and reds are generally from the 13th century. Look for photos halfway down on the right that show devastating WWII bomb damage to the cathedral.

# The Hundred Years' War
## (1336–1453)

It would take a hundred years to explain all the causes, battles, and political maneuverings of this century-plus of warfare between France and England, but here goes:

In 1300, before the era of the modern nation-state, the borders between France and England were fuzzy. French-speaking kings had ruled England, English kings owned the south of France, and English merchants dominated trade in the north. Dukes and lords in both countries were aligned more along family lines than by national identity. When the French king died without a male heir (1328), both France and England claimed the crown, and the battle was on.

England invaded the more populous country (1345) and—thanks to skilled archers using armor-penetrating long-bows—won big battles at Crécy (1346) and Poitiers (1356). Despite a truce, roving bands of English mercenaries stayed behind and supported themselves by looting French villages. The French responded with guerrilla tactics.

In 1415, the English took still more territory, with Henry V's big victory at Agincourt. But rallied by the heavenly visions of young Joan of Arc, the French slowly drove the invaders out. Paris was liberated in 1436, and when Bordeaux fell to French forces (1453), the fighting ended without a treaty.

Passing through an iron gate near the high altar (closed during Mass, but often open on the opposite side even during Mass), you come to several **stone statues.** These figures were lifted from the facade during a recent cleaning and will eventually be installed in a museum. For us, it's a rare chance to stand toe-to-toe with a saint (weird feeling).

There are several stone tombs on your left, dating from when Rouen was the Norman capital. The first tomb is for Rollo—the first duke of Normandy in 933 (and great-great-great-great grandfather of William the Conqueror, seventh duke of Normandy, c. 1028). As the first duke, he was chief of the first gang of Vikings (the original "Normans") who decided to settle here. Called the "Father of Normandy," Rollo died at the age of 80, but is portrayed on his tomb as if he were 33 (as was the fashion, because Jesus died at that age). Because of later pillage and plunder, only Rollo's femur is inside the tomb.

And speaking of body parts, the next tomb contains the heart of Richard the Lionhearted. (The rest of his body lies in the Abbey of Fontevraud, described on page 327 in the Loire chapter.) A descendant of William the Conqueror, Richard was both a king of England and the 12th duke of Normandy.

• *Circle behind the altar. Look back above the entry to see a rare black-and-white rose window (its medieval colored glass is long gone). Continue a few paces, then look up to the ceiling over the nave.*

A violent 1999 storm blew the spire off the roof, sending it crashing to the cathedral floor. Looking directly above Rollo's femur, you can see the patchwork in the ceiling. Perhaps this might be a good time to exit? Pass through the small iron gate, turn right, and leave through the side door (north transept).

• *Stepping outside, look back at the **facade**.*

The fine, carved tympanum (the area over the door) shows a graphic Last Judgment. Jesus stands between the saved (on the left) and the damned (on the right). Notice the devil grasping a miser, who clutches a bag of coins. Look for the hellish hot tub, where even a bishop (pointy hat) is eternally in hot water.

Most of the facade has been cleaned—blasted with jets of water—but the fine limestone carving is still black. It's too delicate to survive the hosing, and instead awaits a more expensive laser cleaning (as do many other monuments in Rouen).

• *From this courtyard, a gate deposits you on a traffic-free street, rue St. Romain. Turn right and walk along...*

## Rue St. Romain

This street has half-timbered buildings and lanes worth a look. In a short distance, you can look through an arch, back at the cathedral's spire. Made of cast iron in the late 1800s—about the same time Gustave Eiffel was building his tower in Paris—the spire is, at 490 feet, the tallest in France. You can also see the former location of the missing smaller (green) spire—downed in that 1999 storm.

• *Farther down the street, find a shop that shows off a traditional art form in action.*

At **Fayencerie Augy** (at #26, with the blue facade), Monsieur Augy welcomes potential shoppers to browse his studio/gallery/shop and see Rouen's clay "china" being made the traditional way. First, the clay is molded and fired. Then it's dipped in white enamel, dried, lovingly hand-painted, and fired a second time. Rouen was the first city in France to make faience, earthenware with colored glazes. In the 1700s, the town had 18 factories churning out the popular product (closed Sun, 26 rue St. Romain, VAT tax refunds nearly pay for the shipping, www.fayencerie-augy.com). For more faience, visit the local Museum of Ceramics (see "Sights," later in this chapter).

• *Continue along rue St. Romain, which leads to the very fancy...*

## St. Maclou Church

This church's unique, bowed facade is textbook Flamboyant Gothic (sadly, its doorways are blackened by pollution). Notice the flame-like tracery decorating its gable. Since this was built at the very end of the Gothic age—and construction took many years—the doors are from the next age: the Renaissance (c. 1550). The interior is pretty, but skippable (Mon–Sat 10:00–12:00 & 14:00–18:00, Sun 10:30–17:30).

• *Leaving the church, turn right, and then take another right (giving the little boys on the corner wall a wide berth). Wander past a fine wall of half-timbered buildings fronting rue Martainville, to the end of St. Maclou Church.*

## Half-Timbered Buildings

Because the local stone—a chalky limestone from the cliffs of the Seine River—was of poor quality (your thumbnail is stronger), and because local oak was plentiful, half-timbered buildings became a Rouen specialty from the 14th through 19th centuries. Cantilevered floors were standard until the early 1500s. These top-heavy designs made sense: City land was limited, property taxes were based on ground-floor square footage, and the cantilevering minimized unsupported spans on upper floors. The oak beams provided the structural skeleton of the building, which was then filled in with a mix of clay, straw, pebbles...or whatever was available.

• *A block farther down, at 186 rue Martainville, a covered lane leads to the...*

## Plague Cemetery (Aître St. Maclou)

During the great plagues of the Middle Ages, as many as two-thirds of the people in this parish died. For the decimated community, dealing with the corpses was an overwhelming task. This half-timbered courtyard (c. 1520) was a mass grave, an ossuary where the bodies were "processed." Bodies would be dumped into the grave (where the well is now) and drenched in liquid lime to help speed decomposition. Later, the bones would be stacked in alcoves above the colonnades that line this courtyard. Notice the ghoulish carvings (c. 1560s) of gravediggers' tools, skulls, cross-bones, and characters doing the "dance of death." In this *danse macabre,* Death, the great equalizer, grabs people of all social classes (free, daily mid-March–Oct 8:00–20:00, Nov–mid-March 8:00–19:00). The place is now an art school. Peek in on the young artists. As you leave, find the dried black cat (died c. 1520, in tiny glass case to the left of the door). To overcome evil, it was buried during the building's construction.

• *Farther down rue Martainville, at place St. Marc, a colorful market blooms Sunday until 12:30 and all day Tuesday, Friday, and Saturday. If it's not market day, you can double back to the cathedral and rue du Gros Horloge, or continue with me to explore more of Rouen and find the Museum of Fine Arts (back toward the train station).*

**NORMANDY**

To reach the museum, turn right upon leaving the boneyard, then right again on rue Damiette, and hike up antique row to the vertical Church of St. Ouen (a seventh-century abbey turned church in the 15th century, fine park behind). Turn left at the church on rue des Faulx, cross the busy street, and continue down rue de l'Hôpital's traffic-free lane, which turns into rue Ganterie). A right on rue l'Ecrueuil leads to the **Museum of Fine Arts** and the **Museum of Ironworks** (both described next under "Sights") and the end of our tour. The tower where Joan of Arc was imprisoned is a few blocks uphill, on the way back to the train station.

# SIGHTS

## In Rouen

These three museums are within a block of each other, closed on Tuesdays, never crowded, and can all be visited with the same €5.40 combo-ticket (www.rouen-musees.com).

▲**Museum of Fine Arts (Musée des Beaux-Arts)**—Paintings from many periods are beautifully displayed in this museum, including works by Caravaggio, Peter Paul Rubens, Paolo Veronese, Jan Steen, Théodore Géricault, Jean-Auguste-Dominique Ingres, Eugène Delacroix, and the Impressionists. Don't miss Monet's painting of Rouen's Notre-Dame Cathedral, and the room dedicated to Géricault. Pick up the museum map at the ticket desk. Important rooms have excellent English descriptions on small, portable boards, and even have clever foldaway stools. The €2.50 audioguide is good, but spotty in its coverage (€3, occasional temporary exhibitions cost extra, Wed–Mon 10:00–18:00, 15th–17th-century rooms closed 13:00–14:00, closed Tue, 3 blocks below train station at 26 bis rue Jean Lecanuet, tel. 02 35 71 28 40).

**Museum of Ironworks (Musée le Secq des Tournelles, a.k.a. Musée de la Ferronnerie)**—This deconsecrated church houses iron objects, many of them more than 1,500 years old. Locks, keys, tools, coffee grinders—virtually anything made of iron is on display. You can duck into the entry area for a glimpse of a medieval iron scene without passing through the turnstile (€2.40, no English explanations, Wed–Mon 10:00–13:00 & 14:00–18:00, closed Tue, behind Museum of Fine Arts, 2 rue Jacques Villon, tel. 02 35 88 42 92).

**Museum of Ceramics**—Rouen's famous faience (earthenware), which dates from the 16th to the 18th centuries, fills this fine old mansion. Unfortunately, there is not a word of English (same hours and cost as Museum of Ironworks, above; 1 rue Faucon, tel. 02 35 07 31 74).

## Near Rouen

### The Route of the Ancient Abbeys (La Route des Anciennes Abbayes)—This route—punctuated with abbeys, apples, and Seine River views—provides a pleasing detour for drivers connecting Rouen and destinations farther west (if you're traveling *sans* car, skip it). Follow D-982 west of Rouen to Jumièges (visit its abbey), then cross the Seine on the car ferry at Duclair (about €2).

Drivers can stop to admire the gleaming Romanesque church at the **Abbey of St. Georges de Boscherville** (but skip the abbey grounds). The romantically ruined **Abbey of Jumièges** is the top sight to visit on this route. Founded in A.D. 654, it was destroyed by Vikings and rebuilt by William the Conqueror, only to be torn down again by French Revolutionaries (€5, helpful English handout, more detailed booklet for €6, daily mid-June–mid-Sept 9:30–13:00 & 14:30–18:30, mid-Sept–April until 17:30, last entry 30 min before closing, tel. 02 35 37 24 02). Several decent lunch options lie across the street from the abbey.

# SLEEPING

While I prefer Rouen in the day, sleeping here presents you with a mostly tourist-free city (most hotels cater to business travelers). These hotels are perfectly central, within two blocks of Notre-Dame Cathedral.

**$$$ Hôtel Mercure***, ideally situated a block north of the cathedral, is a concrete business hotel with a professional staff, a big lobby and bar, and 125 rooms loaded with modern comforts. Suites come with views of the cathedral, but are overpriced and not much bigger than a double. Look for frequent reduced rates (Db-€175, view Db-€190, suite-€270, air-con, elevator, pay Internet access and Wi-Fi, parking garage-€11/day, 7 rue Croix de Fer, tel. 02 35 52 69 52, fax 02 35 89 41 46, www.mercure.com, h1301@accor.com).

**$$ Hôtel de la Cathédrale** is run by friendly Nathalie and Alexandra, who welcome you with a flowery courtyard, a cozy, wood-beamed breakfast room, and frumpy but mostly country-French decor. Some rooms have hardwood floors, and most have basic bathrooms and poor sound insulation (Sb-€58–78, Db-€68–95, Tb-€98, Qb-€120, extra bed-€15, elevator, Internet access and Wi-Fi, overnight parking-€5, 24-hour parking-€10, 12 rue St. Romain, a block from St. Maclou Church, tel. 02 35 71 57 95, fax 02 35 70 15 54, www.hotel-de-la-cathedrale.fr, contact@hotel-de-la-cathedrale.fr). You can have lunch in its picturesque courtyard (restaurant closed Sun–Mon).

**$$ Hôtel Cardinal** offers rooms facing the cathedral, without the street appeal of the Hôtel de la Cathédrale. It's run by

## Sleep Code

(€1 = $1.50, country code: 33)
**S** = Single, **D** = Double/Twin, **T** = Triple, **Q** = Quad, **b** = bathroom, **s** = shower only, * = French hotel rating system (0-4 stars). Unless otherwise noted, credit cards are accepted and English is spoken.

To help you easily sort through these listings, I've divided the rooms into three categories based on the price for a standard double room with bath:

**$$$ Higher Priced**—Most rooms €90 or more.
**$$ Moderately Priced**—Most rooms between €60-90.
**$ Lower Priced**—Most rooms €60 or less.

English-speaking, born-and-raised-Rouennais Pascal and his wife Agnes. Nearly all of its 18 sufficiently comfortable rooms look right onto the cathedral, and a few are good for families. Rooms on the fourth floor are best, with small balconies and great cathedral views (Sb-€52–66, Db-€66–74, Db with balcony-€80–88, Tb-€92, Qb-€98, extra bed-€11, non-smoking rooms available, elevator, 1 place de la Cathédrale, tel. 02 35 70 24 42, fax 02 35 89 75 14, www .cardinal-hotel.fr, cardinalhotel.rouen@wanadoo.fr).

# EATING

## Near the Cathedral

**Crêperie le St. Romain,** between the cathedral and St. Maclou Church, is an excellent budget option. It's run by gentle Mr. Pegis, who serves filling €8 crêpes with small salads in a warm setting (lunch Tue–Sat, lunch and dinner Thu–Sat, closed Sun–Mon, 52 rue St. Romain, tel. 02 35 88 90 36).

**Dame Cakes** is ideal if it's lunchtime or teatime and you need a Jane Austen fix. The decor is from another, more precious era, and the baked goods are out of this world (salads and *plats*-€12–15, garden terrace in the back, Mon–Sat 12:00–15:00, closed Sun, 70 rue St. Romain, tel. 02 35 07 49 31).

**Chez Nous** is a sharp place with efficient owners serving well-prepared dishes at fair prices. There's lots of contemporary music and lots of yellow (€15 for 2-course *menu*, €18 for 3-course *menu*, closed Sun–Mon, 234 rue Martainville, tel. 02 35 89 50 02).

At **Flunch,** you'll find family-friendly, cheap, point-and-shoot, cafeteria-style meals in a fast-food setting (€9 *menu* includes salad bar, main course, and drink; good kids' menu, open daily until 22:00, a block from cathedral at 66 rue des Carmes, tel. 02 35 71 81 81).

## On Place du Vieux Marché

Two moderately priced restaurants that cater more to tourists than locals face place du Vieux Marché, across from the Joan of Arc Church. **Le Maupassant** is welcoming, with an outdoor terrace and three lively floors filled with orange leather booths. It's famous for its duck dishes and *moelleux au chocolat*—melted chocolate over ice cream and cake (regional *menus* from €18, daily, 39 place du Vieux Marché, tel. 02 35 07 56 90). **Le Terre-Neuvas** is all about seafood and has a modern interior (*menus* from €18, daily, 3 place du Vieux Marché, tel. 02 35 71 58 21).

# TRANSPORTATION CONNECTIONS

Rouen is well-served by trains from Paris, through Amiens to other points north, and through Caen to other destinations west and south.

**From Rouen by Train to: Paris'** Gare St. Lazare (20/day, 1–1.5 hrs), **Bayeux** (12/day, 3.5–4.5 hrs, change in Paris' Gare St. Lazare), **Pontorson–Mont St. Michel** (5/day, 4–7 hrs, 1 via Caen, most via Paris, change train stations from St. Lazare to Montparnasse, then TGV to Rennes, then 1.75-hr bus to Mont St. Michel).

**By Train and Bus to: Honfleur** (5/day Mon–Sat, 3/day Sun, 2 hr train to Le Havre, then 30-min bus over Normandy Bridge to Honfleur; Le Havre's bus station is right next to the train station, making connections easy; or train to Paris' Gare St. Lazare and transfer to Caen, 13/day, 2–3.5 hrs; then take 1–2-hr bus to Honfleur—either take express bus, 2/day, 1 hr, about €16; or the longer, more scenic *par la côte*—along the coast, 8/day, 2 hrs, about €13).

**NORMANDY**

# Honfleur

Gazing at its cozy harbor lined with skinny, soaring houses, it's easy to overlook the historic importance of this port. For more

than a thousand years, sailors have enjoyed Honfleur's (ohn-flur) ideal location, where the Seine River greets the English Channel. William the Conqueror received supplies shipped from Honfleur. Samuel de Champlain sailed from here in 1608 to North America, where he discovered the St. Lawrence River and founded

Quebec City. The town was also a favorite of 19th-century Impressionists: Eugène Boudin (boo-dan) lived and painted in Honfleur, attracting Monet and other creative types from Paris. In some ways, modern art was born in the fine light of idyllic little Honfleur.

Honfleur escaped the bombs of World War II, and today offers a romantic port enclosed on three sides with sprawling outdoor cafés. Long eclipsed by the gargantuan port of Le Havre just across the Seine, Honfleur happily uses its past as a bar stool...and sits on it.

# ORIENTATION

All of Honfleur's appealing streets and activities are within a short stroll of its old port (Vieux Bassin). The Seine River flows just east of the center, the hills of the Côte de Grâce form its western limit, and rue de la République slices north–south through the center to the port. Honfleur has one can't-miss sight (Ste. Catherine Church) and a handful of other tempting spots...but really, the town itself is its best sight.

## Tourist Information

The TI is in the flashy glass public library (Mediathéque) on quai le Paulmier, two blocks from Vieux Bassin toward Le Havre (July–Aug Mon–Sat 9:00–19:00, Sun 10:00–17:00; Sept–June Mon–Sat 9:30–12:30 & 14:00–18:30, Sun 10:00–17:00; free WCs inside, tel. 02 31 89 23 30, www.ot-honfleur.fr). Pick up the town map, as well as tourist maps of Normandy and the Calvados region. If you're headed to the D-Day beaches, ask for information here. Skip the useless museum pass. Ask about concerts, special events, and guided visits of Honfleur (tours usually Wed at 15:00, €6, 1.5 hrs, smart to reserve by calling TI).

## Arrival in Honfleur

**By Bus:** Get off at the small bus station *(gare routière)* near the TI (English-speaking information counter, confirm your departure, see "Transportation Connections," page 219). To reach the TI and old town, turn right out of the station and walk five minutes up quai le Paulmier.

**By Car:** Follow *Centre-Ville* signs, then find your hotel to unload your bags (double-parking is OK for a few minutes). Parking is a headache in Honfleur, especially on summer and holiday weekends. Some hotels offer parking...for a price (otherwise, your hotelier knows where you can park for free). The central Parking du Bassin (across from the TI) is monitored (€1.75/hour, €12/day). Parking du Môle is cheaper but less central, across the

# Honfleur

**P** PARKING
**B** BOAT EXCURSIONS

100 YARDS
100 METERS

MAISONS SATIE

TO **P** Ste. Cath., PARK, & JETTY WALK

JARDIN PUBLIC

BLVD. CHAR.

BOUDIN MUSEUM

RUE HAUTE

**11**

PLACE HAMELIN **2**

VIEW OF PONT NORMANDIE

**B**

AVANT PORT

**P** du Môle

RUE DE L'HOMME DE BOIS

**21**

RUE ALBERT 1er

**17**

**14** **13**

STE-CATHERINE

**+**

**1**

PLACE BERTH-ELOT

**18**

QUAI DES PAS...

**B**

QUAI DE LA QUARANTAINE

WC

LIEUTENANCE

**B**

QUAI DE LA VILLE

**19**

**P** du Bassin

**15**

VIEUX BASSIN

**3**

QUAI DE LA TOUR

BUS STN

RUE DES CAPUCINS

**8** **4**

RUE DU PUITS

**10**

RUE BRULEE

MUSEUMS OF OLD HONFLEUR

**16**

QUAI ST-ETIENNE

R. DES FOSSES

RUE BUCAILLE

RUE J. DOUBLET

**7**

PLACE DU PUITS

RUE MONTPENSIER

COURS

QUAI LE PAULMIER

**23**

**6**

TO COTE DE GRACE & **5**

RUE EUGENE BOUDIN

R. DELA CHAUSSÉE

RUE DE LA REPUBLIQUE

R. DES PRES

**20**

**i**

ST. LEONARD

**+**

TO **9**

DCH

RUE CACHIN

**24** **22**

NORMANDY

**1** Les Maisons de Léa
**2** Hôtel le Cheval Blanc
**3** L'Absinthe Hôtel & Le Bouilland Normand Rest.
**4** Hôtel du Dauphin
**5** Hôtel Monet
**6** Etap Hôtel
**7** La Cour Ste. Catherine B&B
**8** François and Sandra's Rooms
**9** To Sweet Madame Bellegarde's Rooms
**10** Le Bréard Restaurant
**11** P'tit Mareyeur Restaurant
**12** Le Vintage Café

**13** La Terrasse et l'Assiette Rest.
**14** La Cidrerie Bar & Crêperie
**15** Café de l'Hôtel de Ville
**16** Waterfront Crêpe Stand
**17** Late-Night Food to Go
**18** Le Perroquet Vert & L'Albatross Bars
**19** Tourist Train Stop
**20** Launderette
**21** Produits Regionaux Gribouille
**22** Internet Café
**23** Casino Grocery
**24** Champion Market

causeway (see map on previous page). Street parking, metered during the day, is free from 19:00 to 9:00.

## Helpful Hints

**Market Day:** The area around Ste. Catherine Church becomes a colorful open-air market every Saturday (9:00–13:00). A smaller organic food–only market takes place here on Wednesday mornings.

**Grocery Stores:** The **Champion Market** is the biggest in town (Mon–Sat 8:30–12:20 & 14:00–19:00, closed Sun except July–Aug 9:00–13:00, about a 10-min walk up rue de la République from Vieux Bassin, on place Sorel). There's also a good **Casino Grocery** near the TI (same hours as Champion Market, except closed Mon and open Sun year-round, 16 quai le Paulmier).

**Regional Products with Panache:** Visit **Produits Regionaux Gribouille** for any Normand delicacy you can dream up. Say *bonjour* to Monsieur Gribouille (gree-boo-ee) and watch your head—his egg-beater collection hangs from above (open 364 days a year, 9:30–13:00 & 14:00–19:00, 16 rue de l'Homme de Bois, tel. 02 31 89 29 54).

**Internet Access:** **Cyberpub** has unpredictable hours but plenty of computers (at Hôtel de la Diligence, 55 rue de la République, tel. 02 31 89 95 83).

**Laundry:** **Lavomatique** is a block behind the TI and toward the port (daily 7:00–20:00, 4 rue Notre-Dame).

**Taxi:** Call 06 18 18 36 36 or 06 08 60 17 98.

**Tourist Train:** Honfleur's *petit train* toots you up the Côte de Grâce—the hill overlooking the town—and back in about 50 minutes (€6, daily 10:30–11:30 & 14:30–17:30, departs from across gray swivel bridge that leads to Parking du Môle).

## SIGHTS AND ACTIVITIES

### In Honfleur

**Vieux Bassin**—Stand facing Honfleur's square harbor, with the merry-go-round across the lock to your left. Survey the town. The word Honfleur is Scandinavian, meaning the shelter *(fleur)* of Hon (a Norse settler). Eventually, the harbor was fortified by a wall with two gatehouses (the one surviving gatehouse is on your right) and a narrow boat passage protected by a chain. Those skinny houses on the right side were designed at a time when houses were taxed on their width, not height.

Just in front of the old, barrel-vaulted entry to the town (20 steps to your right), you can see a bronze bust of Samuel de Champlain—the explorer who sailed with an Honfleur crew 400 years ago to make his discoveries in Canada. The harbor, once crammed with fishing boats, is now home to local sailboats. Turn around to see various tour and fishing boats and the Normandy Bridge (described on page 215), a sleek suspension bridge, in the distance.

Fisherfolk catch flatfish, scallops, and tiny shrimp daily and bring them here. On the left, you may see fishermen's wives selling *crevettes* (shrimp). You can buy them *cuites* (cooked) or *vivantes* (alive and wiggly). They are happy to let you sample one (rip off the cute little head and tail, and pop the middle into your mouth—*délicieuse!*) or buy a cupful to go (€1.50, daily in season).

You're likely to see artists sitting at easels around the harbor, as Boudin and Monet did. Many consider Honfleur the birthplace of Impressionism. This was a time when people began to revere, not fear, the out-of-doors, and started to climb mountains "because they were there." Pretty towns like Honfleur and the nearby coast were ideal subjects to paint—and still are—thanks to what locals called the "unusual luminosity" of the region. Artists would set up easels on this side of the basin to catch the light playing on the line of buildings, slates, timbers, geraniums, clouds, and reflections in the water. Monet came here to visit the artist Boudin, a hometown boy, and the battle cry of the Impressionists—"Out of the studio and into the light!"—was born.

If you're an early riser, you can watch what's left of Honfleur's fishing fleet prepare for the day, and you just might experience that famous luminosity (bring your camera).

▲▲**Ste. Catherine Church (Eglise Ste. Catherine)**—The atypical wood-shingled exterior suggests that this church has a different story to tell than most. Walk inside. You'd swear that if it were turned over, it would float—the legacy of a community of sailors and fishermen, with plenty of boat-builders and no cathedral architects. When workers put up the first nave in 1466, it was immediately apparent that more space was needed—so the second was built in 1497. Because it felt too much like a market hall, they added side aisles. Notice the oak pillars. Since each had to be the same thickness, and since trees come in different sizes, some are full-length and others are supported by stone bases. In the last months of World War II, a bomb fell through the roof—but didn't explode. The pipe organ is popular for concerts, and half of the modern pews are designed to flip so that you can face the music. Take a close look at the many medieval instruments carved into the railing below the organ—a 16th-century combo band in wood (free, daily July–Aug 9:00–18:30, Sept–June 9:00–12:00 & 14:00–18:00).

The church's bell tower is equally unusual. It was not built atop the church, but across the square—to lighten the load of the wooden church's roof and to minimize fire hazards. Peek inside, where you'll find a tiny museum with a few church artifacts (€2—not worth it, free with your ticket to the Eugène Boudin Museum; April–Sept Wed–Mon 10:00–12:00 & 14:00–18:00, closed Tue; Oct–March Wed–Mon 14:00–18:00 only, closed Tue).

▲**Eugène Boudin Museum**—This pleasing little museum has three interesting floors with many paintings of Honfleur and the surrounding countryside. The first floor up displays Norman folk costumes; the second floor up has the Boudin collection; and the third floor houses the Hambourg/Rachet collection and the Katia Granoff room.

**Cost and Hours:** €4.70, €2 extra during special exhibits, English audioguide–€2 (no English explanations on display—but none needed); April–Sept Wed–Mon 10:00–12:00 & 14:00–18:00, closed Tue; Oct–Dec and mid-Feb–March Mon and Wed–Fri 14:00–17:00, Sat–Sun 10:00–12:00 & 14:00–17:00, closed Tue; closed Jan–mid-Feb; elevator, no photos, rue de l'Homme de Bois, tel. 02 31 89 54 00.

❍**Self-Guided Tour:** Pick up a map at the ticket counter, tip your beret to Eugène Boudin, and climb the stairs (or take the elevator).

**First Floor (Costumes):** Monsieur and Madame Louveau (see their photo as you enter) gave Honfleur this quality collection of local traditional costumes. The hats, blouses, and shoes are supported by paintings that place them in an understandable historical and cultural context. Of special interest are the lace bonnets, typical of 19th-century Normandy. You could name a woman's village by her style of bonnet. The dolls are not toys for tots, but marketing tools for traveling clothing merchants—designed to show off the latest fashions. The men's department is in the back of the room.

**Second Floor (Boudin Collection and More):** A right off the stairs leads into a large room of appealing 20th-century paintings and sculpture, done by artists who produced most of their works while living in Honfleur. A left off the stairs leads through a temporary exhibition hall into a fine gallery of 19th-century paintings (in the room on the left). Boudin's artwork here is arranged chronologically, from Romanticism through Realism to Impressionism (the heart of this museum). Find the glass display case in the rear titled *Précurseur de l'Impressionisme*, with little pastel drawings, and start here.

# Eugène Boudin
## (1824–1898)

Born in Honfleur, Boudin was the son of a harbor pilot. As an amateur teenage artist, he found work in an art-supply store that catered to famous artists from Paris (such as Jean-Baptiste-Camille Corot and Jean-François Millet) who came to paint the seaside. Boudin studied art in Paris, but kept his hometown roots. Thanks to his Paris connections, Boudin's work was exhibited at the Paris salons.

At age 30, Boudin met the teenage Claude Monet. Monet had grown up in nearby Le Havre, and, like Boudin, sketched the world around him—beaches, boats, and small-town life. Boudin encouraged him to don a scarf, set up his easel outdoors, and paint the scene exactly as he saw it. Today, we say: "Well, duh!" But "open-air" painting was unorthodox for artists trained to thoroughly study their subjects in the perfect lighting of a controlled studio setting. Boudin didn't teach Monet as much as he gave him the courage to follow his artistic instincts.

In the 1860s and 1870s, Boudin spent summers at his farm (St. Siméon) on the outskirts of Honfleur, hosting Monet, Edouard Manet, and others. They taught Boudin the Impressionist techniques of using bright colors, and building a figure with many individual brushstrokes. Boudin adapted those "strokes" to build figures with "patches" of color. In 1874, Boudin joined the renegade Impressionists at their "revolutionary" exhibition in Paris.

NORMANDY

Upon showing their work in Paris, Normandy artists—such as Eugène Boudin—created enough of a stir that Normandy came into vogue; many Parisian artists (including Monet and other early Impressionists) traveled to Honfleur to tune in to the action. Boudin himself made a big impression on the father of Impressionism. This collection of his paintings—which he gave to his hometown—provides a good study of the evolution from realistic portrayals of subjects (outlines colored in, like a coloring book) to masses of colors catching light (Impressionism). Boudin's beach scenes, showing aristocrats taking a healthy saltwater dip, helped fuel that trend. His skies were good enough to earn him the nickname "King of Skies."

**Third Floor (Hambourg/Rachet Collection):** There are two access points to the third floor. First follow the steps that lead from the Boudin room to the small Hambourg/Rachet collection (and a smashing painting of Honfleur). In 1988, André Hambourg and his wife, Nicole Rachet, donated their art to this museum. The collection is enjoyably Impressionistic, but with artwork from the mid-20th century.

**Third Floor (Salle Katia Granoff):** Retrace your steps back to the main stairway to reach the other third-floor room, where you'll find a worthwhile collection of 20th-century art by artists who lived and learned in Honfleur. Check out the few paintings by Raoul Dufy (a French Fauvist painter) and compare his imaginative scenes of Honfleur with others you've seen. Don't miss the brilliant view of the Normandy Bridge through the windows.

**Art Galleries**—Eugène Boudin ignited Honfleur's artistic tradition that still burns today. The town is a popular haunt of artists, many of whom display their works in Honfleur's terrific selection of art galleries. As you walk around the town, take the time to enjoy today's art.

▲**Maisons Satie**—This peaceful museum, housed in composer Erik Satie's birthplace, presents his music in a creative and enjoyable way. As you wander from room to room with your included audioguide, infrared signals transmit bits of Satie's music, along with a first-person story (in English). As if you're living as an artist in 1920s Paris, you'll drift past winged pears, strangers in the window, and small girls with green eyes. (If you like what you hear...don't move; the infrared transmission is sensitive, and the soundtrack switches every few feet.) The finale—performed by you—is the *Laboratory of Emotions* pedal-go-round. For a relaxing sit, enjoy the 12-minute movie (4/hr) featuring modern dance springing from Satie's collaboration with Picasso types (€5.50, includes audioguide; May–Sept Wed–Mon 10:00–19:00, closed Tue; Oct–Dec and mid-Feb–April Wed–Mon 11:00–18:00, closed Tue; closed Jan–mid-Feb; last entry one hour before closing, 5-min walk from harbor at 67 boulevard Charles V, tel. 02 31 89 11 11).

**Museums of Old Honfleur**—Two side-by-side museums combine to paint a picture of daily life in Honfleur since the Middle Ages. The curator creatively supports the artifacts with paintings, making the cultural context clearer.

The **Museum of the Navy** (Musée de la Marine) fills a small 15th-century church (facing Vieux Bassin) with an interesting collection of ship models and marine paraphernalia. The **Museum of Ethnography and Norman Popular Art** (Musée d'Ethnographie et d'Art Populaire), located in the old prison and courthouse, re-creates typical rooms from various eras and crams them with objects of daily life (€3.20 apiece or €4.40 for both; hours for both: April–Sept Tue–Sun 10:00–13:00 & 14:00–18:30, closed Mon; March and Oct–mid-Nov Tue–Fri 14:00–18:00, Sat–Sun 10:00–12:00 & 14:00–18:00, closed Mon; closed mid-Nov–Feb; ask for English explanation pages).

# Walks

**▲Côte de Grâce Walk**—For good exercise and a bird's-eye view of Honfleur and the Normandy Bridge, take the steep, 20-minute walk up to the Côte de Grâce viewpoint—best in the early morning or at sunset. Drivers follow rue du Puits, then turn right on rue des Capucins, following *Côte de Grâce* signs. On foot from Honfleur's main church, walk up rue du Puits, then turn right when you see the blue-on-white *piétons* sign and climb la Rampe du Mont Joli to see the splendid view. Two hundred yards past the top, the **Chapel of Notre-Dame de Grâce** merits a visit. Built in the early 1600s by the mariners and people of Honfleur, the church oozes with seafaring mementos. Model boats hang from the ceiling, pictures of boats balance high on the walls, and what's left is decorated by stained-glass images of sailors praying to the Virgin Mary while at sea. Even the holy water basins to the left and right of the entrance are in the shape of seashells.

Just below the chapel, a second lookout point gives a sweeping view of the super-industrial Le Havre, with the Manche (English Channel) to your left and the Normandy Bridge to your right.

**Jetty/Park Walk**—Take a level stroll in Honfleur along the water past the Hôtel le Cheval Blanc to see the mouth of the Seine River and big ships at sea. You'll pass kid-friendly parks, well-endowed with flowers and grass, and continue past the lock connecting Honfleur to the Seine and the sea. Grand and breezy vistas of the sea reward the diligent walker (allow one hour out and back for best views).

# Near Honfleur

**Boat Excursions**—Boat trips in and around Honfleur depart near Hôtel le Cheval Blanc (Easter–Nov usually about 11:00–17:00). The tour boat *Calypso* operates good 45-minute trips around Honfleur's harbor (€6, tel. 02 31 89 07 77). You'll also find several boats with cruises to the Normandy Bridge (see below) that unfortunately include two boring stops through the locks (about €8, 50 min, details at TI).

**▲Normandy Bridge (Pont de Normandie)**—The 1.25-mile-long pont de Normandie is the longest cable-stayed bridge in the Western world (€5 toll each way). This is a key piece of a super-expressway that links the Atlantic ports from Belgium to Spain. View the bridge from Honfleur (better from an excursion boat or above the town from the Côte de Grâce viewpoint—see above, and best at night, when bridge is floodlit) and consider visiting the bridge's free Exhibition Hall (under tollbooth on Le Havre side, daily 8:00–19:00). The Seine finishes its winding 500-mile journey here, dropping only 1,500 feet from its source. The river flows so slowly that in certain places, a stiff breeze can send it flowing upstream.

▲**Etretat**—Chalk-white cliffs soar high above a calm, crescent beach as France's answer to the White Cliffs of Dover. Walking trails lead hikers from the small seaside resort of Etretat along a vertiginous route with sensational views (and crowds of hikers in summers and on weekends). You'll recognize these cliffs from countless Impressionist paintings, including several at the Eugène Boudin Museum in Honfleur. Etretat is north of Le Havre, about an hour from Honfleur (you get to cross the pont de Normandie en route). This Coney Island–like small town holds plenty of cafés and a TI (place Maurice Guillard, tel. 02 35 27 05 21, www .etretat.net).

# SLEEPING

**(€1 = about $1.50, country code: 33)**

Honfleur is busy on weekends, holidays, and in the summer. English is widely spoken (Honfleur is a popular weekend getaway for Brits). A few moderate accommodations remain, but most hotels are pretty pricey. Budget travelers should consider the *chambres d'hôte* listed below.

## Hotels

**$$$ Les Maisons de Léa\*\*\***, Honfleur's most handsome hotel, charges dearly for its 30 adorable rooms with elaborate furnishings and Laura Ashley–esque decor. This hotel charms your socks off with its careful attention to detail—from country-French wood furnishings to antiques to a library room that may keep you inside even in good weather (Db-€145–180, suites-€260–400, 4-person cottage house-€430, skip the €15 continental breakfast, across from the church on place Ste. Catherine, tel. 02 31 14 49 49, fax 02 31 89 28 61, www.lesmaisonsdelea.com, contact@lesmaisonsdelea.com).

**$$$ Hôtel le Cheval Blanc\*\*\***, a Best Western, is a waterfront splurge with port views from all of its 32 sharp rooms (many with queen-size beds and high-tech showers), plus a rare-in-this-town elevator (small Db with lesser view-€90–120, Db with full port view-€135–160, bigger Db-€150–200, family rooms-€300–425, must cancel by 16:00 the day before or forfeit deposit, 2 quai des Passagers, tel. 02 31 81 65 00, fax 02 31 89 52 80, www.hotel -honfleur.com, lecheval.blanc@wanadoo.fr).

**$$$ L'Absinthe Hôtel\*\*\*** hides seven tastefully restored rooms behind the restaurant Le Bistro du Port. Whirlpool tubs, wood-beamed decor, and a cozy lounge with a fireplace make this place worthwhile. Five new rooms, all with port views, should be completed by your visit (Db-€120–150, Db suite-€250, extra bed-€25, 1 rue de la Ville, check in at L'Absinthe restaurant across alley, tel. 02 31 89 23 23, fax 02 31 89 53 60, www.absinthe.fr, reservation@absinthe.fr).

**$$ Hôtel du Dauphin\*\*** is Honfleur's best midrange value, with a colorful lounge/breakfast room, many stairs, an Escher-esque floor plan, and eager-to-please  Christian at the desk (afternoons and evenings). The 30 rooms— some with open-beam ceilings, most with queen- or king-size beds—are all quite comfortable and well-maintained (Db-€72– 100, Tb-€118–130, free Internet access and Wi-Fi, a stone's throw from Ste. Catherine Church at 10 place Pierre Berthelot, tel. 02 31 89 15 53, fax 02 31 89 92 06, www .hoteldudauphin.com, hotel.dudauphin@wanadoo.fr).

**$$ Hôtel Monet\*\***, on the road to the Côte de Grâce and a 10-minute walk down to the port (longer back up), is an overlooked find. This tranquil spot is an ivy-covered brick home with 10 good-value rooms facing a courtyard. Each room comes with a patio made for picnics, and you'll meet welcoming owners Christoph and Sylvie (Db-€64–74, Tb-€76–92, free and easy parking, Chartière du Puits, tel. 02 31 89 00 90, fax 02 31 89 97 16, www.motelmonet .fr, motelmonet@wanadoo.fr).

**$ Etap Hôtel** is modern, efficient, tight, and cheap, with antiseptically clean rooms (Db-€37–44, €6 for each extra person, reception is closed 11:00–17:00 & 21:00–6:00 but automatic check-in with credit card available 24 hrs, elevator, across from bus station and main parking lot on rue des Vases, tel. 08 92 68 07 81, fax 02 31 89 77 88, www.etaphotel.com).

## Chambres d'Hôte

The TI has a long list of Honfleur's many *chambres d'hôte* (rooms in private homes), but most are too far from the town center. These three are all fine values.

**$$ La Cour Ste. Catherine** is an enchanting bed-and-breakfast run by the open-hearted Madame Giaglis ("call me Liliane"). Her six big, modern rooms—each with firm beds and a separate sitting area—surround a perfectly Norman courtyard with a small terrace, fine plantings, and cool coffee shop. The rooms are as cheery as the owner (Db-€75, Tb-€90, Qb-€95, includes breakfast, cash only, Internet access, free parking in 2009 with this book, 200 yards up rue du Puits from Ste. Catherine Church at 74 rue du Puits, tel. 02 31 89 42 40, www.giaglis.com, coursainte catherine@orange.fr).

$ **François and Sandra's** five good-value *chambres* are above the Atelier Cédric Eudeline art gallery (though the gallery isn't affiliated with the rooms). The rooms are big, comfortable, and fairly priced (Db-€60, big Tb-€80, Qb-€100, cash only, no breakfast, behind Les Maisons de Léa at 8 rue du Puits, tel. 06 88 47 72 98, sandra-de-kerc@orange.fr). This place works closely with La Cour Ste. Catherine (previous page), where you are welcome to take breakfast for €5.

$ Sweet **Madame Bellegarde** offers two simple rooms in her traditional home (Db-€35–40, family-friendly Tb with great bathroom view-€60, cash only, 54 rue St. Léonard, 10-min uphill walk from TI, 3 blocks up from St. Léonard Church in untouristy part of Honfleur, look for small *chambres* sign in window, she'll try to hold a parking spot if you ask, tel. 02 31 89 06 52).

# EATING

Eat seafood or cream sauces here. It's a tough choice between the hard-to-resist waterfront tables of the many look-alike places lining the harbor, and eateries with more solid reputations elsewhere in town. Trust my dinner suggestions below and consider your hotelier's opinion. It's best to call ahead to reserve at most restaurants in Honfleur (particularly on weekends).

**Le Bouilland Normand** hides a block off the port on a pleasing square next to the recommended L'Absinthe Hôtel and serves a true Norman experience at reasonable prices (inside and out). Charming Annette serves while her chef-husband (who excels in sauces and seafood) manages *la cuisine*. Annette is happy to recommend some good options (€17–25 *menus*, closed Sun and Wed, on rue de l'Hôtel de Ville, tel. 02 31 89 02 41).

**Le Bréard** serves exquisite, modern French cuisine presented with care, style, and ingenuity. The chef has returned after several years in Paris' finer restaurants, bringing his considerable talent back to Honfleur. Come here to savor a fine, slow meal in a formal, yet appealing setting (€26–34 *menus*, closed Wed, 7 rue du Puits, tel. 02 31 89 53 40).

**P'tit Mareyeur** is whisper-formal, intimate, all about seafood, and a good value. Reservations are particularly smart here (€25 *menu*, try the bouillabaisse *honfleuraise*, closed Mon–Tue and Jan, 4 rue Haute, tel. 02 31 98 84 23, friendly owner Julie speaks some English).

**Le Vintage,** just off the port, is a happening bar/café with live piano and jazz most nights. Casual outside seating and a vigorous interior make this a good choice if you value liveliness over fine cuisine (€12–18 salads and *plats*, closed Tue, 8 quai des Passagers, tel. 02 31 89 05 28).

**La Terrasse et l'Assiette** is a higher-end, dress-up affair with a romantic red-brick-and-timbered interior and outdoor tables facing the church. Locals love this place, so book ahead (€30–50 *menus,* closed Mon–Tue, faces Ste. Catherine Church's left transept, 8 place Ste. Catherine, tel. 02 31 89 31 33).

**La Cidrerie** is a purely Norman cider bar with crêpes made in the traditional style, Calvados apple brandy, and an inviting atmosphere for adults and kids, closed Tue–Wed, set back on cathedral side of place Hamelin at #26, tel. 02 31 89 59 85).

*Along the Waterfront:* If the weather cooperates, or you just need to see the water, slide down to the harbor and table-shop the joints that line the high side. Several places have effective propane heaters that keep outdoor diners happy when it's cool. **Café de l'Hôtel de Ville** looks across to Honfleur's soaring homes with seafood and €12 pizza (daily, place de l'Hôtel de Ville, tel. 02 31 89 07 29).

*Breakfast:* If it's even close to sunny, skip your hotel breakfast and enjoy ambience for a cheaper price by eating on the port, where several cafés offer *petit déjeuner* for about €7–12, depending on the *menu* you select. Morning sun and views are best from the high side of the harbor.

*Dessert:* If you need an ice cream fix or a scrumptious dessert crêpe, find the waterfront stand at the southeast corner of Vieux Bassin.

*Late-Night Food to Go:* There's a salad, *frites,* and kebab place at 6 rue de l'Homme du Bois (until 22:00, closed Wed).

*Nightlife:* Nightlife in Honfleur centers on the old port. Two bar/cafés with different personalities sit 50 yards apart: **Le Perroquet Vert** entertains a somewhat higher-end crowd, while **L'Albatross** feels more down and dirty.

## TRANSPORTATION CONNECTIONS

Buses connect Honfleur with Le Havre, Caen, Deauville, and Lisieux (all with direct rail service to Paris), where you'll catch a train to other points. (Coming from Paris, the best train-to-bus transfers are usually in Lisieux or Deauville.) While train and bus service are usually coordinated, ask at Honfleur's bus station for the best connection for your trip (information desk open Mon–Fri 9:00–12:15 & 14:30–18:30, in summer also Sat–Sun 9:15–12:15, tel. 02 31 89 28 41, www.busverts.fr). Railpass-holders will save money by connecting through Deauville, as bus fares increase with distance.

**From Honfleur by Bus and/or Train to: Caen** (express buses 2/day, 1 hr, about €16; more scenic *par la côte* 8/day, 2 hrs, about €13), **Bayeux** (5/day, 2–3 hrs via bus and train, 1-hr express bus to

Caen, then 30-min train; or 2-hr bus via the coast to Caen, then 30-min train), **Rouen** (5/day Mon–Sat, 3/day Sun, 2 hrs via bus and train, bus over Normandy Bridge to Le Havre, then transfer to train to Rouen), **Paris'** Gare St. Lazare (13/day, 2–3.5 hrs; 1-hr bus to Lisieux, Deauville, or Le Havre, then 2-hr train to Paris; buses from Honfleur meet most Paris trains).

# Bayeux

Only six miles from the D-Day beaches, Bayeux was the first city liberated after the landing. Incredibly, the town was spared the bombs of World War II. After a local convent chaplain made sure London knew that this was not a German headquarters and of no strategic importance, a scheduled bombing raid was canceled—making Bayeux the closest city to the D-Day landing site not destroyed. Even without its famous tapestry and proximity to the D-Day beaches, Bayeux would be worth a visit for its enjoyable town center and awe-inspiring cathedral, beautifully illuminated at night. Bayeux makes a good home base for visiting the area's sights, particularly if you lack a car.

## ORIENTATION

### Tourist Information

The TI is on a small bridge two blocks north of the cathedral— conveniently located on the pedestrian street that connects place St. Patrice (with its recommended hotels and a Saturday market) and the tapestry. Pick up the *D-Day Landings* map, bus schedules to the beaches, and regional information (July–Aug Mon–Sat 9:00–19:00, Sun 9:00–13:00 & 14:00–18:00; April–June and Sept–Oct daily 9:30–12:30 & 14:00–18:00; Nov–March Mon–Sat 9:30–12:30 & 14:00–17:30, closed Sun; on pont St. Jean leading to rue St. Jean, tel. 02 31 51 28 28, www.bayeux-bessin-tourism.com).

For a **self-guided walking tour,** pick up the map called *Découvrez Vieux Bayeux* at the TI. Follow the bronze plates embedded in the sidewalk, and look for information plaques with English translations that correspond to the numbers on the map.

English-language **guided tours** of old Bayeux are offered in July and August, and sometimes also off-season (€4, 1.5 hours, usually at 15:00—call for times, tel. 02 31 92 14 21).

### Arrival in Bayeux

**By Train:** It's a 20-minute walk from the train station to the tapestry, and 15 minutes from the tapestry to place St. Patrice (and

# Bayeux

PUBLIC BUS STOP FOR D-DAY BEACHES

200 YARDS
200 METERS

CATHEDRAL

BAYEUX TAPESTRY

RUE CREMEL

BATTLE OF NORMANDY MUSEUM

TRAIN STATION

HALLE AUX GRAINS

**NORMANDY**

① Hôtel Churchill & Marché Plus Grocery
② Hôtel le Lion d'Or
③ Hôtel Tardif
④ Hôtel le Bayeux
⑤ Chambre d'Hôte Le Petit Matin
⑥ Hôtel d'Argouges
⑦ Hôtel Mogador
⑧ Hôtel le Maupassant & Café
⑨ La Chaumière Deli

⑩ La Fringale Restaurant
⑪ La Coline d'Enzo Rest.
⑫ L'Assiette Normande Rest.
⑬ Le Pommier Restaurant
⑭ Lace Conservatory
⑮ Baron Gérard Museum
⑯ Launderettes (3)
⑰ Scauto Car Rental
⑱ Bike Rental

several recommended hotels). To reach the tapestry, the cathedral, and the hotels, cross the street in front of the station and follow rue Cremel, then make a left on rue Nesmond (follow the huge spire). Allow €7 for a taxi from the train station to any recommended hotel or sight in Bayeux (taxi tel. 02 31 22 10 50).

**By Car:** Look for the cathedral spires and follow signs for *Centre-Ville,* and then signs for the *Tapisserie* (tapestry) or your hotel (individual hotels are well-signed from the ring road—wait for yours to appear).

## Helpful Hints

**Market Days:** The Saturday open-air market on place St. Patrice is much larger than the Wednesday market on pedestrian rue St. Jean. Both end by 13:00.

**Grocery Store: Marché Plus,** at rue St. Jean 14, is next to the recommended Hôtel Churchill (Mon–Sat 7:00–21:00, Sun 8:30–12:00).

**Internet Access:** Ask at your hotel or the TI (last year's cybercafé is this year's poodle-pampering shop).

**Laundry:** There's a launderette a block behind the TI, on rue Maréchal Foch. Two launderettes are near place St. Patrice: One is at 4 rue St. Patrice and the other is at 69 rue des Bouchers (both open daily 7:00–21:00).

**Bike Rental: Vélos Location,** run by amiable Mr. Decaen, has what you need and will deliver to outlying hotels (€10/half-day, €15/day, €5 picnic lunch, daily April–Oct 8:00–20:30, closes earlier off-season, across from the TI at Impasse de Islet, tel. 02 31 92 89 16).

**Taxi:** Call 06 70 40 07 96.

**Car Rental:** Bayeux offers few choices. **Scauto** is handiest, just below the train station at the BP gas station (16 boulevard Sadi-Carnot, tel. 02 31 51 18 51, fax 02 31 51 18 30, www.scauto.fr).

# SIGHTS

▲▲▲**Bayeux Tapestry (Tapisserie de Bayeux)**—Made of wool embroidered onto linen cloth, this precious-to-historians document is a 70-yard cartoon.

The tapestry tells the story of William the Conqueror's rise from duke of Normandy to king of England, and shows his victory over Harold at the Battle of Hastings in 1066. Long and skinny, it was designed to hang in the nave of Bayeux's cathedral.

# Bayeux History—The Battle of Hastings

Because of this pivotal battle, the most memorable date of the Middle Ages is 1066. England's king, Edward the Confessor, was about to die without an heir. The big question: Who would succeed him—Harold, an English nobleman and the king's brother-in-law, or William, duke of Normandy and the king's cousin? Edward chose William and sent Harold to Normandy to give William the news. On the journey, Harold was captured. To win his release, he promised he would be loyal to William and not contest the decision. To test his loyalty, William sent Harold to battle for him in Brittany. Harold was successful, and William knighted him. To further test his loyalty, William had Harold swear on the relics of the Bayeux cathedral that when Edward died, he would allow William to ascend the throne. Harold returned to England, Edward died... and Harold grabbed the throne.

William, known as William the Bastard, invaded England to claim the throne. Harold met him in southern England at the town of Hastings, where their forces fought a fierce 14-hour battle. Harold was killed, and his Saxon forces were routed. William—now "the Conqueror"—marched to London, claimed his throne, and became king of England as well as duke of Normandy.

The advent of a Norman king of England muddied the political waters and set in motion 400 years of conflict between England and France—not to be resolved until the end of the Hundred Years' War (about 1450). The Norman conquest of England brought that country into the European mainstream (but still no euros). The Normans established a strong central English government. Historians speculate that had William not succeeded, England would have remained on the fringe of Europe (like Scandinavia), and French culture (and language) would have prevailed in the New World. Hmmm.

Your visit consists of three separate parts that explain the basic story of the battle three times—which was about right for me. You'll start by visiting the actual tapestry with the help of an included audioguide that gives a top-notch, fast-moving, 20-minute, scene-by-scene narration complete with period music (if you lose your place, find subtitles in Latin). Next you'll climb upstairs into a room filled with mood-setting images and a reproduction of the tapestry, with extensive explanations. Your visit finishes with a 15-minute film in the cinema (up one flight) that gives a high-def dramatization of the battle.

Remember, this is Norman propaganda—the English (the bad guys, referred to as *les goddamns*, after a phrase the French kept hearing them say) are shown with mustaches and long hair; the

French (*les* good guys) are clean-cut and clean-shaven—with even the backs of their heads shaved for a better helmet fit.

**Cost and Hours:** €8, includes worthwhile audioguide for adults and a special kids' version, daily mid-March–Oct 9:00–18:30, Nov–mid-March 9:30–12:30 & 14:00–18:00, last entry 45 min before closing, tel. 02 31 51 25 50, www.tapisserie-bayeux.fr. Arrive by 9:00 or late in the day to avoid crowds. When buying your ticket, ask when they'll show the English version of the 15-minute battle film.

▲▲**Bayeux Cathedral**—This massive building dominates Bayeux. As you approach, notice its two towers—originally Romanesque, capped later with tall Gothic spires. The little rectangular stone house atop one tower (viewable from outside the church's transepts) was the watchman's home, from which he'd keep an eye out for incoming English troops during the Hundred Years' War... and for Germans five centuries later (it didn't work—the Germans took the town in 1940). Bayeux was liberated on D-Day plus one, June 7. About the only casualty was the German lookout—shot while doing just that from the window of this stone house. The west facade is structurally Romanesque, but with a decorative Gothic "curtain" added. There's an information board about the cathedral in the corner of the small square in front. The cathedral is beautifully illuminated after dark.

Walk inside (free, daily July–Aug 8:30–19:00, Sept–June 8:30–18:00). The view of the **nave** from the top of the steps shows a mix of Romanesque and Gothic. Historians believe the Bayeux tapestry originally hung here. Imagine it proudly circling the Norman congregation, draped around the nave from the arches. The nave's huge, round lower arches are Romanesque (11th century) and decorated with the same zigzag pattern that characterizes this "Norman" art in England. This section is so brightly lit because of the huge windows above, in the Gothic half of the nave. The glass was originally richly colored (see the rare surviving 13th-century bits in the high central window above the altar). The finest example of 13th-century "Norman" Gothic is in the choir (the fancy area behind the central altar). Each of the columns is decorated with Romanesque carvings. But those carvings lie under a Gothic-style stone exterior (with characteristic tall, thin lines adding a graceful verticality to the overall feel of the interior).

For maximum 1066 atmosphere, step into the spooky crypt (below the central altar), which was used originally as a safe spot for the cathedral's relics. The crypt displays two interesting columns and capitals with fine Romanesque carving. During a reinforcement of the nave, these two columns were replaced. Workers removed the Gothic veneer and discovered their true inner Romanesque beauty. Orange angel-musicians add color to this somber room.

NORMANDY

**Lace Conservatory (Conservatoire de la Dentelle)**—Notable for its carved 15th-century facade, the Adam and Eve house (find Adam, Eve, and the snake) offers a chance to watch workers design and weave intricate lace, just as artisans did in the 1600s. You can also see examples of lace from the past (free, daily 10:00–12:30 & 14:00–18:00, across from cathedral entrance, tel. 02 31 92 73 80).

**Baron Gérard Museum**—The museum, housed in Hôtel du Doyen outside the cathedral's south transept, has a modest painting gallery and a collection of porcelain and lace (€3.50, or free with ticket to tapestry, daily July–Aug 10:00–19:00, Sept–June 10:00–12:30 & 14:00–18:00).

▲**Battle of Normandy Memorial Museum (Musée Memorial de la Bataille de Normandie)**—This museum provides an excellent overview of WWII's Battle of Normandy with elaborate English explanations throughout. The fine exhibits cover everything from the historical context to the invasion's intense battles to the challenges that faced doctors and war correspondents. An enlightening 25-minute film is shown near the end (4/day, note the times as you enter). It's like a small, cheaper Caen Memorial Museum—but it's only worthwhile if you won't be visiting that more impressive museum (€6.50, included with Normandy Pass—see page 234, daily May–mid-Sept 9:30–18:30, mid-Sept–April 10:00–12:30 & 14:00–18:00, on Bayeux's ring road, 20 min on foot from center, tel. 02 31 51 46 90, www.normandiememoire.com).

Just beyond the museum is a **British War Cemetery** decorated with simple gravestones—the final resting place of 4,100 fallen soldiers.

# SLEEPING

## In Bayeux
**(€1 = about $1.50, country code: 33)**
Hotels are a good value here. Drivers should also see "Sleeping" under Arromanches, page 237. Remember, 2009 is the 65th anniversary of the D-Day landings, so prepare for big crowds from June 1–10.

## Near the Tapestry
**$$$ Hôtel Churchill***,** on a traffic-free street across from the TI, could not be more central. They have 32 plush rooms with fine furnishings, big beds, and tasteful art. The professional owners, the Heberts, were made for this business, and take excellent care of their clients (standard Db-€100, superior Db-€125, deluxe Db-€160, Tb-€160, Qb-€180, Internet access and Wi-Fi, comfortable bar/lounge, easy parking, at 14 rue St. Jean, tel. 02 31 21 31 80, fax 02 31 21 41 66, www.hotel-churchill.fr, info@hotel-churchill.fr). This

hotel also runs a shuttle van to Mont St. Michel (see "Transportation Connections," page 229).

**$$$ Hôtel le Lion d'Or*** is Bayeux's traditional Old World hotel, with a palm-tree-lined courtyard, easy €9 parking, professional service, comfy leather lounges, and an elegant restaurant (standard Db-€120, bigger Db-€135, still bigger Db-€170–190, suite Tb-€245, extra bed-€30, no elevator, 71 rue St. Jean, tel. 02 31 92 06 90, fax 02 31 22 15 64, www.liondor-bayeux.fr, lion.d-or .bayeux@wanadoo.fr).

**$$ At Hôtel Tardif,** you'll sleep like Napoleon in a central, six-room manor house that dates from the emperor's era but feels more like a bed-and-breakfast. It's at once *très elegant* and intimate, with traditional touches, a grand garden, and a smashing wooden spiral staircase (standard Db-€75, big Db-€120, massive Db-€180, Tb-€190, Qb-€210, Wi-Fi, 16 rue Nesmond, tel. 02 31 92 67 72, mobile 06 87 12 57 83, www.hoteltardif.com, hoteltardif @orange.fr).

**$$ Hôtel le Bayeux**,** the closest hotel I list to the train station (600 yards), is a quiet, simple place run by chatty Madame Bajum and her daughter Elodie (who will do your laundry for €5–10). It caters to student groups that enjoy its long halls, bright colors, and 29 sufficiently clean rooms. The room rates are impossible to pin down, though usually near the lower end of the following ranges (Db-€60–80, Tb-€75–120, Qb-€90–130, many family rooms with bunk beds, easy parking, a block from cathedral's right transept at 9 rue Tardif, tel. 02 31 92 70 08, fax 02 31 21 15 74, www.lebayeux.com, lebayeux@gmail.com).

**$$ Chambre d'Hôte Le Petit Matin** is a block above the cathedral, just off rue de la Maître, and has fine rooms and a lovely garden at good rates (Db-€65–75, Tb-€85, includes breakfast, cash only, €20 dinner if booked ahead, laundry-€10/load, 2 bis rue de Quincangrogne, tel. 02 31 10 09 27, mobile 06 08 28 65 59, www .lepetitmatin.com, lepetitmatin@hotmail.fr).

### Near Place St. Patrice

These three hotels are just off the big place St. Patrice (easy parking), but a 10-minute walk up rue St. Martin from the TI (a 15-min walk to the tapestry).

**$$$ Hôtel d'Argouges*** (dar-goo-zhah) makes an impression as you enter. Named for its builder, Lord d'Argouges, this tranquil retreat has a mini-château feel, with classy public spaces and a lovely private garden. The hotel is run by helpful and formal owners, Monsieur and Madame Ropartz, who have renovated every aspect of the hotel except the bathrooms (Db-€110–130, fine family suites-€190, deluxe mega-suite for up to 6 and good for two couples-€295, extra bed-€15, includes breakfast except in winter, parking-€2, just off huge place St. Patrice at 21 rue St. Patrice, tel. 02 31 92 88 86, fax 02 31 92 69 16, www.hotel-dargouges.com, dargouges@aol.com).

**$ Hôtel Mogador**** is a fine value, with engaging Monsieur Mencaroni at the helm. Choose between cozy, wood-beamed rooms on the busy square, or quiet, more colorful, modern rooms off the street. There are no public areas beyond the small breakfast room and tiny courtyard (Sb-€45, Db-€50–55, Tb-€65, Qb-€75, good breakfast-€6, 20 rue Alain Chartier at place St. Patrice, tel. 02 31 92 24 58, fax 02 31 92 24 85, hotel.mogador @wanadoo.fr).

**$ Hôtel le Maupassant** offers no-star, no-frills accommodations, but its few rooms above a central café are sufficiently comfortable. The bartender doubles as the receptionist (S-€30, Db-€41, 19 rue St. Martin, tel. 02 31 92 28 53, fax 02 31 92 35 40).

## Near Bayeux

Drivers will pass scads of good-value *chambres d'hôte* on the way from Bayeux to Arromanches, and on the road from Arromanches to the American Cemetery. (See also "D-Day Beaches," page 229.)

**$$ Château de Lignerolles** is run by Roel (pronounced "rule") and his charming wife Pia, who have followed their bliss and moved from Holland to Normandy. Their lovely and isolated inn (outside tiny Planquery, between Bayeux and St. Lô) has modern decor, with wonderful beds and linens in four rooms, three with bathroom down the hall. There are no restaurants nearby— though Bayeux is just a 15-minute drive (D-€70–75, Db-€80, Tb-€105, 2-night minimum, cash only, includes great breakfast; from Bayeux, take D-572 toward St. Lô and turn left to Balleroy, then stay left on D-13, heading toward Tilly-sur-Seulles; tel. 02 31 51 98 14, mobile 06 76 50 94 27, www.victorytours.com, ch.de .lignerolles@wanadoo.fr). Roel's "hobby" for the last 20 years has been the history of D-Day and the Battle of Normandy. (His 15 yards of history books on the subject are proof of his dedication.) Roel leads tours of the D-Day beaches (see "Victory Tours" under "Getting Around the D-Day Beaches," page 234).

**$$ La Ferme du Pressoir** is a lovely, traditional B&B on a big working farm, immersed in Norman landscapes about 15 minutes south of Bayeux. The five rooms filled with wood furnishings— along with the kind owners, Jacques and Odile—are vintage French (Db-€80, Tb-€100, Qb-€120, includes good breakfast, tel. 02 41 53 04 96, Le Haut St. Louet, just off A-84, exit at Villers-Bocage, www.bandbnormandie.com, lafermedupressoir @bandbnormandie.com).

**NORMANDY**

# EATING

Drivers can also consider the short drive to Arromanches for seaside options (see page 238).

## On or near Traffic-Free Rue St. Jean

This street is lined with cafés, *crêperies,* and inexpensive dining options.

**La Chaumière** is the best charcuterie (deli) in town; you'll find salads, quiches, and prepared dishes to go (Tue–Sun open until 19:30 except closed Sun 13:00–15:00, closed Mon; on rue St. Jean across from Hôtel Churchill). The grocery store across the street has what you need to complete your picnic.

**La Fringale** works for a simple, cheap meal on this pedestrian street (€9 salads, €15 *menu,* closed Wed, indoor and outdoor seating, 43 rue St. Jean, tel. 02 31 21 34 40).

**La Coline d'Enzo** is where discerning diners go for Norman nouvelle cuisine at fair prices. The dining room is an appealing blend of modern and traditional decor, overseen by gracious owner Delfine. A few tables line the side street outside (*menus* from €25, closed Sun–Mon, 2 rue des Bouchers, tel. 02 31 92 03 01).

## Near the Cathedral

**L'Assiette Normande** is a fun and popular eatery where you'll dine very well for a steal. It's kid-friendly and easygoing, and serves well-presented local dishes in lively rooms (€12, €17, and €32 *menus;* closed Mon, 3 rue des Chanoines, tel. 02 31 22 04 61).

**Le Pommier** is a fine place to sample regional products with clever twists in a relaxed yet refined atmosphere. Owner Thierry mixes old and new in his cuisine and decor. His *lotte* (whitefish) is excellent no matter how he prepares it, and his meat dishes are *très* tasty (*menus* from €24, open daily, 38 rue des Cuisiniers, tel. 02 31 21 52 10).

# TRANSPORTATION CONNECTIONS

**From Bayeux by Train to: Paris'** Gare St. Lazare (11/day, 2.5 hrs, 3 require change in Caen), **Amboise** (12/day, 5–6 hrs, change in Caen and Tours, or Paris-Montparnasse and Tours' St. Pierre des Corps), **Rouen** (12/day, 3.5–4.5 hrs, change in Paris' Gare St. Lazare), **Caen** (10/day, 15 min), **Honfleur** (5/day, 2–3 hrs via train and bus; 30-min train to Caen, then 1-hr express bus to Honfleur or more scenic 2-hr bus via the coast; or 1-hr train to Lisieux then 1-hr bus to Honfleur; for bus information, call 02 31 89 28 41), **Pontorson–Mont St. Michel** (2–3/day, 2 hrs to Pontorson, then bus to Mont St. Michel; also consider Hôtel Churchill's faster shuttle van—see next page).

By Bus to the D-Day Beaches: Bus Verts du Calvados offers minimal service to D-Day beaches with stops in Bayeux at place St. Patrice and at the train station (schedules at TI, tel. 08 10 21 42 14, www.busverts.fr). Lines #74 and #75 run east to Arromanches (2/day, 20 min), and line #70 runs west to the American Cemetery and Vierville-sur-Mer (4/day in summer, 2/day off-season, 35 min to American Cemetery, 40 min to Vierville-sur-Mer). The schedules leave you too long at either sight to make a round-trip by bus practical; consider one taxi one way and a bus the other. There's talk of a summer loop route serving the key D-Day sights; ask at the TI (but don't get your hopes up).

By Shuttle Van to Mont St. Michel: Hôtel Churchill (recommended under "Sleeping," page 225) runs a shuttle van to Mont St. Michel for €55 per person round-trip (€50 one-way, 1.5 hrs each way; available to the general public, though hotel clients get a small discount). The van leaves Bayeux at 9:00 and returns by 15:00, allowing travelers three hours at Mont St. Michel. For details, see www.hotel-churchill.fr.

# D-Day Beaches

The 75 miles of Atlantic coast north of Bayeux, stretching from Ste. Marie-du-Mont to Ouistreham, is littered with WWII museums, monuments, cemeteries, and battle remains left in tribute to the courage of the British, Canadian, and American armies that successfully carried out the largest military operation in history: D-Day (*Jour J* in French). It was on these serene beaches, at the crack of dawn on June 6, 1944, that the Allies finally gained a foothold in France, and Nazi Europe was doomed to crumble.

> *"The first 24 hours of the invasion will be decisive...The fate of Germany depends on the outcome...For the Allies, as well as Germany, it will be the longest day."*
> —Field Marshal Erwin Rommel to his aide, April 22, 1944 (from the movie *The Longest Day*)

## Planning Your Time

You'll want at least one full day to explore the D-Day beaches. If you only have one day, I'd spend it entirely on the beaches and—regretfully—miss the Caen Memorial Museum. (If you want to squeeze in the museum, visit it on your way to or from the beaches—but remember that the American Cemetery closes at 17:00.) I've listed the D-Day sights in the order of importance, with the most visit-worthy first. Naturally, most Americans prefer to

NORMANDY

# D-Day Beaches

ENGLISH CHANNEL

POINTE DU HOC

VIERVILLE-SUR-MER

US CEMETERY

ARROMANCHES

COURSEULLES + JUNO BEACH CENTER

SWORD BEACH

OUISTREHAM

5 MILES
10 KM

TO CABOURG

TO HONFLEUR (VIA COAST)

TO HONFLEUR (VIA AUTOROUTE), ROUEN + PARIS

D-515

D-514

D-7

D-79

D-404

CANADIAN CEMETERY

CAEN MEMORIAL MUSEUM (EXIT #7)

CAEN

RING FREEWAY

A-13

D-9

A-84

TO MONT ST MICHEL

TILLY-SUR-SEULLES

D-6

N-13

D-12

RYES +5

LONGUES-SUR-MER CLIFF

START

GUN BATTERY

OMAHA BEACH

GOLD BEACH

JUNO BEACH

3

5

2

BAYEUX

D-516

D-6

D-514

N-13

D-572

D-13

TO VILLERS-BOCAGE, A-84 +2

BALLEROY

1

TO ST. LO

ST. LAURENT

4

LA CAMBE

GERMAN CEMETERY

D-113

N-14

D-514

UTAH BEACH

ISIGNY-SUR-MER

TO STE. MERE EGLISE

1 Château de Lignerolles B&B
2 To La Ferme du Pressoir B&B
3 Le Mas Normand B&B
4 Hôtel du Casino
5 André & Madeleine Sebire B&B

— RECOMMENDED DRIVING ROUTE
— AUTOROUTE (TOLL)    — OTHER ROADS

focus on the American sector (west of Arromanches), rather than the British and Canadian sectors (east of Arromanches)—which have been overbuilt with resorts, making it harder to re-create the events of June 1944.

**By Car:** Begin on the cliffs above Arromanches and see the movie at the Arromanches 360° Theater to set your mood. Walk or drive a quarter-mile downhill to the town and visit Port Winston and the D-Day Landing Museum, then continue west to Longues-sur-Mer. Spend your afternoon visiting the American Cemetery, walking on the beach at Vierville-sur-Mer, and seeing the Pointe du Hoc Ranger Monument. Make a quick stop at the German Military Cemetery on your way back. Canadians may want to start at the Juno Beach Center and Canadian Cemetery (in Courseulles-sur-Mer, 10 min east of Arromanches), then pick up the itinerary described above.

***Sans* Car:** It's easiest to take a minivan tour from Bayeux or combine a visit to the Caen Memorial Museum with their guided minivan tour of the beaches for an excellent full day. Public transport is available, though limited to certain sights; it does not work for the Canadian sights. Many find that a one-day car rental works best.

## Getting Around the D-Day Beaches

**On Your Own:** Though the minivan excursions listed below offer superb history lessons—drawing Americans and Canadians out of their cars—**renting a car** is ideal, particularly for three or more people (see Bayeux's "Helpful Hints" for rental suggestions, page 222). Park in monitored locations at the sights, since break-ins have been a problem—particularly at the American Cemetery. Hardy souls can **bike** between the sights (though distances are enough to discourage most). Very limited **bus service** links Bayeux, the coastal town of Arromanches, and the most impressive sights of D-Day (see Bus Verts du Calvados information under Bayeux's "Transportation Connections," page 229). Consider a bus one way and taxi the other.

**By Taxi:** Taxi minivans shuttle up to seven people between the key sights at surprisingly fair rates. Approximate prices per taxi (not per person): €22 one-way from Bayeux to Arromanches, €38 round-trip with one hour of wait time; €33 one-way from Bayeux to the American Cemetery, €50 round-trip with one hour of wait time; and €70 round-trip for the American Cemetery and Pointe du Hoc with two hours of total wait time at the sights (other combinations possible, 50 percent surcharge after 19:00 and on Sun, taxi tel. 02 31 92 92 40).

**By Minivan Tour:** Several small companies offer all-day excursions to the D-Day beaches from Bayeux or nearby for about

## Countdown to D-Day

**1939**  On September 1, Adolf Hitler invades Poland, sparking World War II.

**1940**  Germany's "Blitzkrieg" ("lightning war") quickly overwhelms France, Nazis goose-step down the avenue des Champs-Elysées, and the country is divided into Occupied France (the north) and Vichy France (the south, ruled by right-wing French). Just like that, virtually the entire Continent is fascist.

**1941**  The Allies (Britain, the Soviet Union, and others) peck away at the fringes of "fortress Europe." The Soviets repel Hitler's invasion at Moscow, while the Brits (with American aid) battle German U-boats for control of the seas. On December 7, Japan bombs the US naval base at Pearl Harbor, Hawaii. The US enters the war against Japan and its ally Germany.

**1942**  Three crucial battles—at Stalingrad, El-Alamein, and Guadalcanal—weaken the German forces and their ally, Japan. The victorious tank battle at El-Alamein in the deserts of North Africa soon gives the Allies a jumping-off point (Tunis) for the first assault on the Continent.

**1943**  More than 150,000 Americans and Brits, under the command of George Patton and Bernard ("Monty") Montgomery, land in Sicily and begin working their way north through Italy. Meanwhile, Germany has to fend off tenacious Soviets on their eastern front.

**1944**  On June 6, 1944, the Allies launch "Operation Overlord," better known as D-Day. The Allies have amassed three million soldiers and six million tons of *matériel* in England to prepare for the biggest fleet-led invasion in history—across the English Channel to France, then eastward to Berlin. The Germans, hunkered down in

€85 per person or about €450 for groups of up to eight (prices usually include entry fees, some levy a surcharge of about €15 for Caen pickup). Only the **Caen Memorial Museum** offers half-day tours. Some companies provide excellent commentary to these moving sights, while others are so-so.

The following companies get rave reviews from my readers. Because they offer pick-up and drop-off at select train stations, these tours are popular with day-trippers from Paris. Book these tours well in advance, or hope for last-minute cancellations:

British-owned **Battlebus,** with its top-notch guides, offers a full slate of tour options from Bayeux (including family-friendly tours), and gets the best reviews from historians (full-day tours only, limited service during the winter, tel. 02 31 22 28 82 or 06 72 northern France, know an invasion is imminent, but the Allies keep it top secret. On the night of June 5, 150,000 soldiers board ships and planes, not knowing where they are headed until they're under way. Each one carries a note from General Dwight D. Eisenhower: "The tide has turned. The free men of the world are marching together to victory."

At 6:30 in the morning on June 6, 1944, Americans spill out of troop transports into the cold waters off a beach in Normandy, code-named Omaha. The weather is bad, seas are rough, and the prep bombing has failed. The soldiers, many seeing their first action, are dazed, confused, and weighed down by heavy packs. Nazi machine guns pin them against the sea. Slowly, they crawl up the beach on their stomachs. More than a thousand die. They hold on until the next wave of transports arrives.

All day long, Allied confusion does battle with German indecision—the Nazis never really counterattack, thinking D-Day is just a ruse, not the main invasion. By day's end, the Allies have taken several beaches along the Normandy coast and begun building artificial harbors, providing a tiny port-of-entry for the reconquest of Europe. The stage is set for a quick and easy end to the war. Right.

**1945** Having liberated Paris (August 26, 1944), the Allied march on Berlin from the west bogs down, hit by poor supply lines, bad weather, and the surprising German counterpunch at the Battle of the Bulge. Finally, in the spring, the Americans and Brits cross the Rhine, Soviet soldiers close in on Berlin, Hitler shoots himself, and—after nearly six long years of war—Europe is free.

02 50 74, www.battlebus.fr, tours@battlebus.fr).

**D-Day Battle Tours** is for true enthusiasts. British owner and zealot Ellwood von Seibold has realized his dream by moving here and living out his fantasy: teaching about the D-Day inva-

sion. He dresses in WWII army gear, drives a WWII Dodge Command Car (very cool), lives in a home where an American paratrooper landed in the garden, and owns a café in Ste. Mère Eglise (C-47 Café) that has the rudder of a WWII-era C-47 plane as its centerpiece.

His specialty is the American sector, particularly the American Cemetery, Omaha Beach, Pointe du Hoc, and Ste. Mère Eglise. His tours begin at the C-47 Café (where else?) on the town's main square, or he'll meet you at the train station in Carentan (1 person minimum, 8 maximum; 4 rue Eisenhower, tel. 02 33 94 44 13, mobile 06 32 67 49 15, www.ddaybattletours.com, ellwood @ddaybattletours.com).

**Victory Tours** is a one-man show run by friendly Dutchman Roel; he's informal but very informative, covering sights mostly in the American sector (departs from Bayeux only, www.victorytours .com; see Château de Lignerolles listing on page 227).

**Nigel Stewart** is another very capable guide who moonlights as an artist and "paints the history that surrounds him." Nigel can meet you anywhere in Normandy, and can drive his vehicle or guide using your vehicle (mobile 06 71 55 51 30, www.dday-guide .com, n.stewart@libertysurf.fr).

The **Caen Memorial Museum** offers well-done tours of the American and Canadian sectors in combination with a visit to their museum; it's handy for those who have limited time (see museum listing on page 245). They also have more guides, so are more likely to have availability when others don't.

## Helpful Hints

**Special Events:** The year 2009 marks the 65th anniversary of the D-Day landings; things will be very crowded from June 1–10.

**Normandy Pass:** If you plan to visit several sights, you can save some money by buying the Normandy Pass (€1 added to the full-price admission at your first sight). You'll save €1 at most subsequent sights and €4 at the Caen Memorial Museum— but for the best value, don't visit the Memorial first since you have to pay full price at your first sight.

# SLEEPING

## Along the D-Day Beaches
**(€1 = about $1.50, country code: 33)**

For more options, see "Sleeping" in the Arromanches section, page 237.

**$$ Le Mas Normand,** 10 minutes east of Arromanches in Ver-sur-Mer, is the child of *Provençale* Mylène and *Normand* Christian. Here you get a warm welcome and the best of both worlds: four lovingly decorated, Provence-style rooms wrapped in 18th-century Normand stone (a fifth room is in a renovated, four-person gypsy caravan). There's a lovely yard with ample grass, two dogs, some geese, and no smoking (Db-€60–80, Tb-€100, Qb-€120, includes breakfast and Wi-Fi; book ahead for Christian's home-cooked, gourmet dinner including wine, cider, and coffee-€40/person, requires 4 people, kids' menus available; drive to the east end of little Ver-sur-Mer, turn right at Hôtel P'tit Bouchon, take another right where the road ends at a T, and find the sign at 8 impasse de la Rivière; tel. & fax 02 31 21 97 75, www.lemasnormand.com, lemasnormand@wanadoo.fr).

**$$ Hôtel du Casino**\*\* is a good place to be one with the D-Day invasions and Omaha Beach. This average-looking hotel is surprisingly comfortable and sits alone, overlooking the beach in Vierville-sur-Mer, between the American Cemetery and Pointe du Hoc. There are pebble walls in the halls; all rooms have views, but the best face the sea—ask for *côté mer*. Introverted owner Madame Clémenceau will leave you alone with the sand, waves, seagulls, and your thoughts (Db-€72, extra bed-€16, view restaurant with *menus* from €23, café/bar on the beach below, tel. 02 31 22 41 02, fax 02 31 22 41 12, hotel-du-casino@orange.fr).

**$** At **André and Madeleine Sebire**'s B&B, you'll experience a real Normand farm. Its hardworking owners offer four modest, homey, and dirt-cheap rooms in the middle of nowhere (two miles from Arromanches). It's worth the effort to track it down in the tiny village of Ryes at Ferme du Clos Neuf (Sb-€30, Db-€35, Tb-€40, includes breakfast, tel. 02 31 22 32 34, emmanuelle.sebire@wanadoo.fr, little English spoken). Try these directions: Follow signs into Ryes, then locate the faded green *Chambres d'Hôte* sign opposite the village's lone restaurant. Follow that sign (rue de la Forge), cross a tiny bridge, turn right onto rue de la Tringale, and follow that for half a mile until you see a small sign on the right to *Le Clos Neuf*. Park near the tractors. If the Sebires prove too elusive, call from Ryes and they'll come get you.

# Arromanches

This small town was ground zero for the D-Day invasion. Almost overnight, it sprouted the immense Port Winston, which gave the Allies a foothold in Normandy, allowing them to begin their victorious push to Berlin and end World War II. The post-war period brought a decline. The population of tiny Arromanches finally reached 500 about five years ago...about the same as it was on June 5, 1944. Today, you'll find a good museum, an evocative beach and bluff (with an interesting film), and a touristy-but-fun little town that offers a pleasant cocktail of war memories, cotton candy, and beachfront trinket shops. Arromanches makes a great base for sightseeing (accommodations listed later in this section). Sit on the seawall after dark and listen to the waves lick the sand while you contemplate the events that took place here 65 years ago.

# ORIENTATION

## Tourist Information

The TI has the *D-Day Landings* map, bus schedules, a photo booklet of area hotels, a list of *chambres d'hôte,* and easy parking (daily June–Aug 9:30–18:00, Sept–May 10:00–12:00 & 14:00–17:00, opposite the recommended Hôtel d'Arromanches at 2 avenue Maréchal Joffre, tel. 02 31 22 36 45, www.ot-arromanches.fr).

## Arrival in Arromanches

The main parking lot, on the road toward Courseulles-sur-Mer, costs €2. If traffic seems bad, try the free lot at the Iveco market (across from Mountbatten Hôtel) and stroll three blocks down to the museum and town center; or try the free lot near the water past the mini-golf course.

## Helpful Hints

The main **post office** (PTT)—which has an **ATM**—is opposite the museum. There's a little **supermarket** a few blocks above the beach, just below the main post office. **Internet access** is possible at the TI. To get a local **taxi,** call 06 66 62 00 99.

# SIGHTS

**Artificial Harbor**—Start at the cliffs above the town, overlooking the site of the impressive World War II harbor.

**Getting There:** Drive two minutes toward Courseulles-sur-Mer and pay €2 to park; hike 10 min uphill from Arromanches; or take the free white train from the museum to the top of the bluff (runs daily June–Sept, Sat–Sun only Oct–May).

**○ Self-Guided Tour:** Wander left, to the cliffs overlooking the town and the beaches. Beyond Arromanches to the left is the American sector, with Omaha Beach and then Utah Beach (notice the cliffs); below and to the right lie the British and Canadian sectors (more level terrain).

Now think about this: At a makeshift harbor below, the Allies arrived in the largest amphibian attack ever, launching the liberation of Western Europe. On June 7, 1944, 17 old ships crossed the English Channel under their own steam. The crews sunk them so that the bow faced the next ship's stern, forming the first sea barrier. Then, 115 football-field-size cement blocks (called "Mulberries") were towed across the channel and sunk, creating a four-mile-long breakwater located a mile and a half offshore. Finally, engineers set up seven floating steel "pierheads" with extendable legs; they were linked to shore by four mile-long floating roads made of concrete pontoons. Soldiers then placed anti-aircraft guns on the pontoons, protecting a port the size of Dover, England. Within just six days of operation, 54,000 vehicles, 326,000 troops, and 110,000 tons of goods had crossed the English Channel. An Allied toehold on Normandy was secure. Eleven months later, Hitler was dead and the war was over.

The **Arromanches 360° Theater** shows a moving film, *The Price of Freedom*, with D-Day footage that flashes back from quiet farmlands and beaches to June 1944. It's a noisy montage of videos on a 360° screen—stand as near to the center as you can (€4.20, Feb–Dec daily 10:00–18:00, closed Jan, 2 shows/hr at :10 and :40 past the hour, 20 min, tel. 02 31 22 30 30).

**▲Port Winston and the D-Day Landing Museum (Musée du Débarquement)**—The world's first prefab harbor was created by the British in Arromanches. Since it was Churchill's brainchild, it was named Port Winston. The D-Day Landing Museum, which faces the surprisingly visible remains of what was intended to be a temporary harbor, provides an instructive hour-long visit. Take a good look at models and images illustrating the construction and use of the prefabricated harbor. Then gaze out the windows that look directly onto the harbor's remains, allowing you to mentally reconstruct this amazing accomplishment. Ponder the remarkable undertaking that resulted in this harbor being built in just 12 days, while battles raged. One video (8 min, ground floor) recalls D-Day. The other (15 min, upstairs) features the construction of the temporary port—ask for times when it is shown in English (€6.50, daily May–Aug 9:00–19:00, Sept–Dec and Feb–April 9:30–12:30 & 13:30–17:00, closed Jan, pick up English flier at door, tel. 02 31 22 34 31, www.arromanches-museum.com).

The most thought-provoking experience in town is to wander the beach among the concrete and rusted litter of the battle, and be thankful that all you hear are birds and surf.

# SLEEPING

**(€1 = about $1.50, country code: 33)**
Arromanches, with its pinwheels and seagulls, has a salty beach-town ambience that makes it a good overnight stop. For evening fun, try the cheery bar at **Hôtel d'Arromanches-Restaurant "Le Pappagall"** (see "Eating," page 238), or, for more of a nightclub scene, have a drink at **Pub Marie Celeste,** around the corner on rue de la Poste.

**$$$ Hôtel de la Marine\*\*\*** has one of the best locations for D-Day enthusiasts, with unobstructed views to the artificial harbor site from most of its 28 comfy, modern, non-smoking rooms (non-view Db-€75; view Db-€88–94, most about €90; Tb-€135; good family rooms for up to five-€150–180; elevator, view restaurant,

NORMANDY

half-board strongly encouraged—figure €85 per person, quai du Canada, tel. 02 31 22 34 19, fax 02 31 22 98 80, www.hotel-de-la -marine.fr, hotel.de.la.marine@wanadoo.fr).

**$$ Hôtel d'Arromanches-Restaurant "Le Pappagall"** (French slang for "parakeet") sits behind Hôtel de la Marine and is a great value, with nine smartly appointed rooms (some with water views), some tight stairways, and a cheery restaurant run by hard-working and fun-loving Alain and Rosa (Db-€69–76, Tb-€98, includes breakfast, Wi-Fi, 2 rue Colonel René Michel, tel. 02 31 22 36 26, fax 02 31 22 23 29, www.hoteldarromanches.fr, hotel darromanche@ifrance.com).

**$ Mountbatten Hôtel\*\***, located a long block up from the water, is an eight-room, two-story, motel-esque place with gener-ous-size, clean, and good-value lodgings. Upstairs rooms have a little view over the sea (Db-€65, Tb-€75, easy parking, short block below the main post office at 20 boulevard Gilbert Longuet, tel. 02 31 22 59 70, fax 02 31 22 50 30, www.hotelmountbatten.com, mountbattenhotel@wanadoo.fr).

## EATING

You'll find cafés, *crêperies*, and a few shops selling sandwiches to go (ideal for beachfront picnics). The two restaurants below offer reliable dining.

**Hôtel d'Arromanches-Restaurant "Le Pappagall"** has great mussels, filling fish *choucroute*, "*les* feesh and cheeps," salads, and a full menu at fair prices (€18–27 *menus*, may be closed on Thu, see hotel listing above).

**Hôtel de la Marine** allows you to dine or drink in style on the water. The cuisine gets mixed reviews, but the view doesn't (*menus* from €24, cool bar with same views, daily, see hotel listing above).

## TRANSPORTATION CONNECTIONS

**From Arromanches by Bus to Bayeux:** Catch buses #74 or #75 (4/day summer, 2/day off-season, 20-min ride). The bus stop is across from the main post office, four long blocks above the sea.

# American D-Day Sights
# West of Arromanches

The American sector is divided between Omaha and Utah beaches. Omaha Beach starts just west of Arromanches and has by far the most important sights for visitors, including the American Cemetery and Pointe du Hoc. Utah Beach sights are farther away, less impressive, and less visited—but no less important to the ultimate success of the Normandy invasion.

## Omaha Beach Sights

▲**Longues-sur-Mer Gun Battery**—Four German bunkers with guns intact, built to guard against seaborne attacks on the city, hunker down at the end of a 10-minute drive west of Arromanches (follow signs reading *Port en Bessin;* once in Longues-sur-Mer, follow *Batterie* signs). The guns, 300 yards inland, were arranged in a semicircle to maximize the firing range east and west, and are the only original guns remaining in place in the D-Day region. They formed a critical link in Hitler's Atlantic Wall defense, which ran from Norway to the Pyrénées. The guns could hit targets up to 13 miles away with great accuracy, and were a major obstacle to the landings at Omaha and Gold beaches. (American and British forces were pounded from this site.) The lone observation bunker (on the cliffs) directed the firing; field telephones connected the bunker to the gun batteries via underground wires. Walk to the bunker to appreciate the strategic view over the channel. From here, you can walk along the glorious Sentier du Littoral (coastal path) above the cliffs. Or enjoy great coastal views by driving five minutes down to the water and the remains of Port Winston at Arromanches (continue on the small road past the parking lot). This sight is always open and free (€5 booklet helpful, skip the €5 tour).

▲▲▲**WWII Normandy American Cemetery and Memorial**— Crowning a bluff just above Omaha Beach and the eye of the

D-Day storm, 9,387 brilliant white-marble crosses and Stars of David glow in memory of Americans who gave their lives to free Europe on the beaches below. You'll find this stirring sight in Colleville, near St. Laurent.

**Cost and Hours:** Free, daily 9:00–17:00, tel. 02 31 51 62 00, www.abmc.gov. Park carefully, as break-ins have been a problem.

❂ **Self-Guided Tour:** Your visit begins at the impressive **Visitors' Center.** Pass security, then pick up the well-written handout and allow time to appreciate the superb exhibit that spans two floors. You'll learn about the invasion preparations and the immense challenges they presented, and get a succinct overview of the actual landings. But the heart of the center highlights many individuals who gave their lives to liberate people they did not know. This adds a very personal touch to the D-Day landings and

NORMANDY

prepares visitors for the fields of white crosses and Stars of David outside. There are a manageable number of display cases, a few short videos, and a must-see 16-minute film (cushy theater chairs, on the half-hour, you can enter late). On the arrival floor, four computer terminals access a database that provides the story of any US serviceman who died in Normandy.

A path from the visitors' center leads to a bluff overlooking the piece of Normandy **beach** called "that embattled shore—portal of freedom." It's quiet and peaceful today, but the horrific carnage of June 6, 1944, is hard to forget. Steps lead down to the beautiful beach below. A walk on the beach is a powerful experience (also see "Vierville-sur-Mer," later in this section).

In the **cemetery,** you'll find a striking memorial, with giant reliefs of the Battle of Normandy and the Battle of Europe etched on the walls. Behind is the semicircular Garden of the Missing, with the names of 1,557 soldiers who were never found. A small metal knob next to the name indicates one whose body was eventually found—there aren't many.

Finally, wander among the peaceful and poignant sea of headstones. Notice the names, home states, and dates of death inscribed on each. Immediately after the war, all the dead were buried in temporary cemeteries. In the mid-1950s, the families of the soldiers decided whether their loved ones should remain with their comrades or be brought home (61 percent opted for repatriation). Officers (including General Theodore Roosevelt, Jr.) were disproportionately left  here. Their families knew they'd want to be buried alongside the men with whom they fought and died. Two of the Niland brothers, now famous from *Saving Private Ryan,* are buried here.

France has given the US permanent free use of this 172-acre site. It is immaculately maintained by the American Battle Monuments Commission.

▲**Vierville-sur-Mer**—This worthwhile detour for drivers allows direct access onto Omaha Beach. From the American Cemetery, drive west along D-514 into St. Laurent, then follow *Vierville par la Côte* signs to the beach. A right turn leads to **Le Ruquet** (where the road ends), a good place to appreciate the Allied soldiers' challenge on D-Day. The small German bunker and embedded gun protected this point, which has the easiest access inland from Omaha Beach. The bunker was finally destroyed by a ship's gun fired from less than one mile away. It was here that the Americans established their first road inland.

Find your way out to the beach and stroll to the right, below the American Cemetery, to better understand the assignment that American forces were handed on June 6. Imagine: You're already exhausted from a lack of sleep and nervous anticipation. Now you get seasick, too, and are about to land in a small, flat-bottomed boat, cheek-to-jowl with other soldiers. Your water-soaked pack feels like stone, and your gun feels even heavier. The boat door drops open, and you run for your life through water and sand onto this open beach, dodging bullets from above.

Twelve hundred American soldiers died on this beach the first day alone. As you walk, notice the scattered remains of rusted metal objects. At least 150,000 tons of metal were taken from these beaches after World War II, and they still didn't get it all.

Back in your car, retrace your route along the beach (look for worthwhile information boards along the sea) and continue heading toward the Pointe de la Percé cliff, which, from here, looks very Pointe du Hoc–like (American Army Rangers mistook this cliff for Pointe du Hoc, costing them time and lives).

Park near Hôtel Casino and walk to the beach. It was here that the Americans tried to assemble a floating bridge and their own artificial harbor (à la Arromanches), but the weather and tides scuttled those plans. Have a seaside drink or lunch at the Casino's café and consider a stroll along the beach toward the jutting Pointe de la Percé (best at lower tides). You may see tractors doing double duty pulling boats into and out of the sea.

As you leave Vierville-sur-Mer to the west, you'll pass the very pontoon bridge that was to be assembled at this beach. During the fighting, it was moved to Arromanches and used as a second off-loading ramp. It was discovered only a few years ago... in a junkyard.

▲▲**Pointe du Hoc Ranger Monument**—Here stood the Germans' most heavily fortified position along the coast (the strategic advantage is obvious). For the American landings to succeed, the Allies decided they had to take out this cliffside battery. For this task, 300 US Army Rangers were handpicked to attempt a castle-style assault of the cliffs, using grappling hooks and ladders borrowed from London fire departments. A massive fire-engine ladder extended from a bobbing boat that Rangers climbed to reach the top of the cliff in the heat of the battle. Only about a third of the Rangers survived the vertical assault. After finally succeeding in their task, the Rangers learned that the German guns had been moved. Nonetheless, the taking of this jutting cliff was important to securing the safe landing of American forces.

The large monument at the end of the bluff is the Ranger "Dagger," planted firmly in the ground. The German bunkers and the bombed-out landscape remain as they were found. This

NORMANDY

position was the most heavily bombarded of all on D-Day, receiving more than 10,000 tons of bombs (that equals 1,000 tons of TNT)—essential to the Rangers' ability to succeed in their mission. Picnicking is forbidden here—the bombed bunkers are considered gravesites. The new building at the parking lot was built for the 60th anniversary of the invasion. Inside you'll find fliers and an information desk (free, daily 9:00–17:00, 20 min by car west of American Cemetery just past Vierville-sur-Mer, tel. 02 31 51 62 00). A museum dedicated to the Rangers is in nearby Grandcamp-Maisy.

▲**German Military Cemetery**—To ponder German losses, drop by this somber, thought-provoking resting place of 21,000 German soldiers. While the American Cemetery is the focus of American travelers, visitors here speak in hushed German. The site seems appropriately bleak, with two graves per simple marker and dark crosses in groups of five. It's just south of Pointe du Hoc (daily April–Oct 8:00–19:00, Nov–March until 17:30; right off N-13 in village of La Cambe, 3.5 miles west of Bayeux, follow signs reading *Cimetière Allemand;* tel. 02 31 22 70 76).

# Utah Beach Sights

**Ste. Mère Eglise**—This celebrated village lies 30 minutes east of the Pointe du Hoc and was the first village to be liberated by the Allies. For *The Longest Day* movie buffs, this is a necessary pilgrimage. It was around Ste. Mère Eglise that many paratroopers landed off-target, most notably two Americans who dangled from the town's church while Germans took pot shots at them (a parachute has been reinstalled on the steeple where Private John Steele's became snagged—though not in the correct corner). While many paratroopers were killed before landing, those who survived played a critical role in the successful invasion by securing roads and bridges behind enemy lines. Today, the village greets travelers with 1940s music from street speakers, flag-draped streets, and a poorly organized museum (Musée des Troupes Aéroportées) about the paratroopers (€5.50, daily 9:00–18:30, tel. 02 33 41 41 35). To make the events surrounding this village come alive, hire WWII enthusiast Ellwood von Seibold for an all-day tour (look for C-47 Café on the main square; see page 233).

**Dead Man's Corner and Airborne Museum**—In 1944, the Germans used this French home as their local headquarters. Today, a tiny museum recounts the terrible battles that took place around the town of Carentan from June 6 through 11. A swampy inlet marked the division between Omaha and Utah beaches. It was critical for the Americans to take this land, allowing the armies on each beach to unite and move forward. But the Germans resisted, and a battle that was supposed to last one afternoon endured five days, leaving more than 2,000 Americans dead. American soldiers named the road below the museum "Purple Heart Lane."

The **Airborne Museum,** 15 minutes south of **Ste. Mère Eglise,** is ideal for enthusiasts (but overkill for the average traveler). Every display case shows incredible attention to detail. Dutch owner/collector/perfectionist Michel Detrez shows only original material. He acquired much of his impressive collection from American veterans who wanted their "souvenirs" to be preserved for others to see. The museum also offers a remarkable collection of D-Day paraphernalia for sale—both original items and replicas (€6, daily 9:00–18:30, in St. Côme du Mont, well-signed two exits north of Carentan on N-13, www.paratrooper-museum.org).

# Canadian D-Day Sights East of Arromanches

You'll need a car or taxi to get to either of these places, because they're not served by buses or trains.

## Juno Beach Center

Located on the beachfront in the Canadian sector, about 15 minutes east of Arromanches in Courseulles-sur-Mer, this center is dedicated to teaching travelers about the vital role Canadian forces played in the invasion, and about Canada in general (Canada declared war on Germany two years before the United States, a fact little recognized by most Americans today). After attending the 50th anniversary of the D-Day landings, Canadian veterans were saddened by the absence of information on their contribution (after the US and Britain, Canada contributed the largest number of troops—14,000), so they generated funds to build this center (the plaques in front honor key donors). Your visit includes a short film, then many thoughtful exhibits that bring to life Canada's unique ties with Britain, the US, and France, and explain how the war affected daily life in Canada. The center also has exhibits about Canada's geography, economy, and more (€6.50, €9 with guided tour, daily April–Sept 9:30–19:00, Oct and March 10:00–18:00, Nov–Feb 10:00–13:00 & 14:00–17:00, tel. 02 31 37 32 17).

The center's one-hour English guided **tours** of Juno Beach are worthwhile (€4.50 for tour alone, or €9 with center admission; June–Aug at 10:00, 12:00, and 15:00; Sept–May at 11:00 and 15:00;

verify times prior to your visit). Your charming guide will be one of four red-shirted young Canadians who each spend four months a year in France as a part of the center's plan to improve ties between France and Canada.

## Canadian Cemetery

This small, touching cemetery hides a few miles above the Juno Beach Center and makes a modest statement when compared with other, more grand cemeteries in this area. To me, it perfectly captures the understated nature of Canadians. Surrounded by farmland with distant views to the beaches, the graves are marked with the names of the soldiers, and all have live flowers planted in their honor. It's located between Courseulles-sur-Mer and Caen, just off D-79.

# Caen

Though it was mostly destroyed by WWII bombs, today's Caen (pronounced "kahn," population 115,000) is a thriving, workaday city packed with students and a few tourists. The brilliant WWII museum and the vibrant old city are the targets for travelers, though these sights come wrapped in a big city with rough edges. While Bayeux or Arromanches—which are smaller—make the best base for most D-Day sights, train travelers with limited time might find urban Caen more practical because of its buses to Honfleur and easy access to the Caen Memorial Museum.

## ORIENTATION

The looming château, built by William the Conqueror in 1060, sits across the street from the TI. West of the TI, modern rue St. Pierre is a popular shopping area and pedestrian zone. To the east of the TI, the more historic Vagueux quarter has many restaurants and cafés in half-timbered buildings. A marathon race in honor of the Normandy invasion is held every June 8th and ends at the Memorial Museum.

## Tourist Information

The TI is on place St. Pierre, 10 blocks across the canal from the train station. Pick up a map and free visitor's guide filled with practical information (Mon–Sat 9:30–18:00, closed Sun, free baggage storage at Memorial Museum; from the station, head right, take a right on rue Ste. Jean, cross the Vaucelles bridge and continue on rue St. Jean for 15 minutes—the TI is on your left across from the castle; drivers follow signs reading *Parking Château;* tel. 02 31 27 14 14, www.tourisme.caen.fr).

## Arrival in Caen

These directions assume you're headed for the town's main attraction, the Caen Memorial Museum.

**By Car:** Finding the memorial is quick and easy. It's a half-mile off the ring-road expressway (*périphérique nord,* take *sortie* #7, look for white signs reading *le Mémorial*). When leaving the museum, follow *Toutes Directions* back to the ring road.

**By Train:** Caen is two hours from Paris (14/day) and 15 minutes from Bayeux (10/day). From Caen's train station, take the tramway line #A or #B toward the castle. Buy tickets from the machine at the train station stop (about €1.20) and validate them on board (good for 1 hour). Get off at the Eglise St. Pierre stop and walk a block west to the bus stop (look for reader boards posting bus arrival times). Use the same ticket to take bus #2 (5/hr weekdays, 2/hr weekends) to *le Mémorial,* which is the last stop on that line. Taxis should cost about €15 one-way from the train station.

**By Bus:** Caen is one hour from Honfleur via express bus (2/day), or two hours by the scenic coastal bus (8/day). Buses stop near the train station (see "By Train," above).

# SIGHTS

## ▲▲▲Caen Memorial Museum (Le Mémorial de Caen)

Caen, the modern capital of lower Normandy, has the best and by far priciest WWII museum in France. Officially named the

"The Caen Memorial: History to Understand the World" *(Le Mémorial de Caen: L'histoire pour comprendre le monde),* it effectively puts the Battle of Normandy in a broader context. You'll see two video presentations and numerous exhibits on the lead-up to World War II, the actual Battle of Normandy, the Cold War, and the ongoing fight for peace (Nobel Prize Gallery and Peace Gardens).

**Cost:** €16, or €12 with a Normandy Pass purchased elsewhere (see page 234), free for all veterans and kids under 10 (ask about family rates).

**Hours and Information:** March–Oct daily 9:00–19:00 (mid-July–Aug until 20:00); Nov–Feb Tue–Sun 9:00–18:00, closed Mon; last entry 1.25 hours before closing, tel. 02 31 06 06 44—?  in June 6, 1944, fax 02 31 06 06 70, www.memorial-caen.fr.

**Planning Your Time:** Allow a minimum of 2.5 hours for visit, including an hour for the movies. You cou¹ˈ

all day here; in fact, tickets purchased after 13:00 are valid for 24 hours, so you can return the next day.

**Services:** There are no guided tours. The museum provides free baggage storage and free supervised babysitting for children under 10 (for whom exhibits may be too graphic). There's a large gift shop with plenty of books in English, an all-day cafeteria, and a restaurant with a garden-side terrace (lunch only, located in the Cold War wing). Picnicking in the gardens is also an option.

**Minivan Tours:** The museum offers good-value minivan tours covering the key sights along the D-Day beaches. Two identical half-day tours leave the museum: one at 9:00 (€55/person) and one at 13:00 (€69/person); both include entry to the museum (a €16 value). The "D-Day Tour" package is designed for day-trippers and includes pick-up from the Caen train station (with frequent service from Paris), a four-hour tour in English of the major Anglo-Canadian beaches, lunch, and then an afternoon at the Memorial Museum. Your day ends with a drop-off at the Caen train station in time to catch a train back to Paris or elsewhere (€100, includes English information book). Contact the museum for details, reservations, and advance payment.

❍ **Self-Guided Tour:** The museum is brilliant. Begin with a downward spiral stroll, tracing (almost psychoanalyzing) the path Europe followed from the end of World War I to the rise of fascism to World War II.

The lower level gives a thorough look at how World War II was fought—from General Charles de Gaulle's London radio broadcasts to Hitler's early missiles to wartime fashion to the D-Day landings.

You then see two powerful movies. *Jour J (D-Day)* is a 30-minute film that shows the build-up to D-Day itself and the successful campaign from there to Berlin (every 40 min from 10:00 to 19:00, works in any language, pick up schedule as you enter). While snippets come from the movie *The Longest Day,* most of the film consists of footage from actual battle scenes. The second movie, *Espérance (Hope),* is a thrilling sweep through the pains and triumphs of the 20th century (hourly, 20 min, also good in all languages).

The Cold War wing sets the scene with audio testimonies and photos of European cities destroyed during World War II. It continues with a helpful overview of the bipolar world that followed the war, with fascinating insights into the psychological battle waged by the Soviet Union and the US for the hearts and minds of their people until the fall of communism.

The next wing, titled "Worlds for Peace," has a white, space-ge design to encourage contemplation of a different future. The useum is the only place outside the US that displays building remains from the 9/11 attacks (you can see them at the end of the building, through the glass windows). The British Gardens, inaugurated in 2004 by Prince Charles, are located east of the Hall for Peace building.

The next section of the museum celebrates the irrepressible human spirit in the Gallery of Nobel Peace Prizewinners. It honors the courageous and too-often-inconspicuous work of people like Andrei Sakharov, Elie Wiesel, and Desmond Tutu, who understand that peace is more than an absence of war.

The finale is a walk through the US Armed Forces Memorial Garden (Vallée du Mémorial). On a visit here, I was bothered by the mindless laughing of lighthearted children unable to appreciate their blessings. Then I read on the pavement: "From the heart of our land flows the blood of our youth, given to you in the name of freedom." Then their laughter made me happy.

# Mont St. Michel

For more than a thousand years, the distant silhouette of this island abbey sent pilgrims' spirits soaring. Today, it does the same for tourists. Mont St. Michel, among the top four pilgrimage sites in Christendom through the ages, floats like a mirage on the horizon—though it does show up on film. Today, 3.5 million visitors—far more tourists than pilgrims—flood the single street of the tiny island each year.

## ORIENTATION

Mont St. Michel is connected by a two-mile causeway to the mainland and is surrounded by a vast mudflat. Your visit features a

one-street village that winds up to the fortified abbey. Between 10:00 and 16:00, tourists trample the dreamscape (much like earnest pilgrims did 800 years ago). A ramble on the ramparts offers mudflat views and an escape from the tourist zone.

While four tacky history-in-wax museums tempt visitors, the only worthwhile sights are the abbey at the summit of the island, and views from the ramparts and quieter lanes as you descend.

Daytime Mont St. Michel is a touristy gauntlet—worth a stop, but a short one will do. The tourist tide recedes late each afternoon. On nights from autumn through spring, the island stands serene, its floodlit abbey towering above a sleepy village.

Arrive late and depart early. The abbey interior should be open until 23:00 in July and August. To avoid the human traffic jam on the main drag, follow the detour path up or down the mount (see "The Village Below the Abbey" under "Sights and Activities," page 251).

## Tourist Information

The overwhelmed yet helpful TI and WC are to your left as you enter Mont St. Michel's gates. The TI has listings of *chambres d'hôte* on the mainland, English tour times for the abbey, tour times for walks outside the island, bus schedules, and the tide table *(Horaires des Marées)*, which is essential if you plan to explore the mudflats outside Mont St. Michel (July–Sept daily 9:00–19:00; Oct–June Mon–Sat 9:00–12:30 & 14:00–18:30, Sun 10:00–12:00 & 14:00–17:00; tel. 02 33 60 14 30, www.ot-montsaintmichel.com). A post office (PTT) and ATM are 50 yards beyond the TI.

## Arrival in Mont St. Michel

**By Train:** The nearest train station is in Pontorson (called Pontorson–Mont St. Michel), with an easy bus connection to Mont St. Michel (12/day July–Aug, 6/day Sept–June, 15 min). The few trains that stop here are met by a bus in front waiting to take passengers to Mont St. Michel. Winter evening trains may not have a bus connection (call Keolis-Emeraude for bus information in this region—tel. 02 99 19 70 70, www.keolis-emeraude.com). The bus drives to the entry gate of Mont St. Michel. Taxis from Pontorson to Mont St. Michel (or vice versa) cost about €18 (€25 after 19:00 and weekends/holidays, try to share a cab; see phone numbers under "Helpful Hints," later in this section).

From Bayeux, it's faster to arrive on Hôtel Churchill's minivan shuttle (see page 229).

**By Car:** Drive in slowly on the causeway, watching out for fine views and crossing sheep (the construction on your left is the new Couesnon river dam, part of an ambitious project to make the island an island again—described on page 250). Park in the pay lot near the base of the island (€4, free after 19:00). If sleeping on the island, you can park much closer; tell the attendant and you'll be instructed where to go. The highest tides rise to the edge of the causeway, which leaves the causeway driveable...but any cars parked below it are left underwater. (You'll be instructed where to park under high-tide conditions.) There's plenty of parking, except midday in high season. Jot down your parking sector and plan on a 10-minute walk to the island. Don't leave any luggage visible in your car.

If you'll be driving into Brittany from Mont St. Michel, see a suggested route in "Transportation Connections" on page 260.

## Helpful Hints

**Tides:** The tides here rise above 50 feet—the largest and most dangerous in Europe. High tides *(grandes marées)* lap against the TI door (where you'll find tide hours posted).

**Internet/Laundry/Groceries/Bike Rental:** The industrious **Hôtel Vert,** located at the beginning of the causeway on the right, has pay Internet access and Wi-Fi, a 24-hour self-service launderette, a grocery store, and bikes for rent (daily 8:00–20:00, see hotel listing under "Sleeping," on page 258).

**Taxi:** Call 02 33 48 24 09 or 02 33 60 33 23, or mobile 06 79 64 49 35.

**Guided Walks:** The TI has information on inexpensive guided walks across the bay (with some English). **La Traversée Traditionelle** traces the footsteps of pilgrims, starting across the bay at Le Bec d'Andaine and walking over the mudflat to Mont St. Michel (weekends only, May–Oct; €6, 4 miles—or 1.75 hours—each way, round-trip takes 4.5 hours, including one hour on Mont St. Michel; ask at TI or call 02 33 89 80 88, www.cheminsdelabaie.com). For a tour within the **abbey** itself, see my self-guided tour on page 253.

**Best Light:** Since Mont St. Michel faces west, morning light from the causeway is eye-popping. Take a memorable walk before breakfast. And don't miss the illuminated island after dark (also best from the causeway).

# SIGHTS AND ACTIVITIES

## Mont St. Michel

These sights are listed in the order you approach them from the mainland.

### Surrounding the Island

**The Bay of Mont St. Michel**—The vast Bay of Mont St. Michel has long played a key role. Since the sixth century, hermit monks in search of solitude lived here. The word "hermit" comes from an ancient Greek word meaning "desert." The next best thing to a desert in this part of Europe was the sea. Imagine the desert this bay provided as the first monk climbed the rock to get close to God. Add to that the mythic tide, which sends the surf speeding eight miles in and out with each tide cycle. Long before the causeway was built, when Mont St. Michel was an island, pilgrims would approach across the mudflat, aware that the tide swept in "at the speed of a galloping horse" (well, maybe a trotting horse...12 m.p.h., or about 18 feet per second).

Quicksand was another peril. But the real danger for adventurers today is the thoroughly disorienting fog and the fact that the

**NORMANDY**

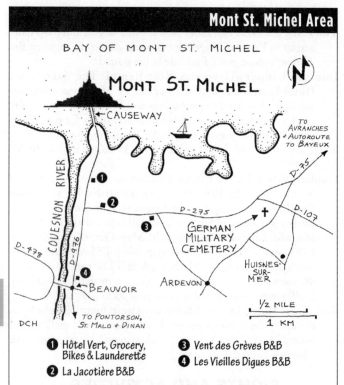

## Mont St. Michel Area

BAY OF MONT ST. MICHEL

MONT ST. MICHEL

← CAUSEWAY

TO
AVRANCHES
& AUTOROUTE
TO BAYEUX

D-75

COUESNON RIVER

D-976

D-478

D-275

D-107

GERMAN
MILITARY
CEMETERY

HUISNES-
SUR-
MER

ARDEVON

BEAUVOIR

TO PONTORSON,
ST. MALO & DINAN

DCH

½ MILE

1 KM

❶ Hôtel Vert, Grocery,
   Bikes & Launderette
❷ La Jacotière B&B

❸ Vent des Grèves B&B
❹ Les Vieilles Digues B&B

sea can encircle unwary hikers. (Bring a mobile phone.) Braving these devilish risks for centuries, pilgrims kept their eyes on the spire crowned by their protector, St. Michael, and eventually reached their spiritual goal.

**The Causeway**—In 1878 a causeway was built, letting pilgrims come and go without hip boots, regardless of the tide. While this increased the flow of visitors, it stopped the flow of water around the island. The result: Much of the bay has silted up, and Mont St. Michel is no longer an island. A new bridge and dam *(barrage)* on the Couesnon River should be completed by 2012 (dam construction is well underway), allowing the water to circulate—so Mont St. Michel will once again be an island (with a shuttle bus or train to zip visitors between the island and a 4,100-space parking lot, with modern hotels at the tip of the causeway). The gray door in the tower where the causeway meets Mont St. Michel is used in very high tides; otherwise, travelers enter on the wooden walkway to the left.

▲▲**Stroll Around Mont St. Michel**—To resurrect that Mont St. Michel dreamscape and evade all those tacky tourist stalls, you can walk out on the mudflats around the island. At low tide, it's reasonably dry and a great memory-maker. However, this can be hazardous, so be sure to double-check the tides or consider a tour (see "Guided Walks," earlier in this section). Remember the scene from the Bayeux tapestry where Harold rescues Normans from the quicksand? It happened somewhere in this bay.

## The Village Below the Abbey

Mont St. Michel's main street (rue Principale, or "Grande Rue"), lined with shops and hotels leading to the abbey, is grotesquely

touristy. It is some consolation to remember that, even in the Middle Ages, this was a commercial gauntlet, with stalls selling souvenir medallions, candles, and fast food. With only 30 full-time residents, the village lives solely for tourists. After visiting the TI, check the tide warnings posted on the wall and pass through the imposing doors.

Before the drawbridge, on your left, peek through the door of Restaurant la Mère Poulard. The original Madame Poulard (the maid of an abbey architect who married the village baker) made quick and tasty omelets here. These were popular for pilgrims, who needed to beat the tide to get out in pre-causeway days, and—even at the rip-off price of €30 *(omelette tradition)*—they're still a hit with tourists today (and much cheaper elsewhere). Pop in for a minute, just to enjoy the show as old-time-costumed cooks beat eggs.

Pass through the old drawbridge, join the main street, and begin your trudge through the crowds uphill past several gimmicky museums to the abbey (all island hotel receptions are located on this street). If the abbey's your goal, you can bypass the worst crowds and tourist kitsch by climbing the first steps on your right after the drawbridge and following the ramparts in either direction up and up to the abbey (quieter if you go right; ramparts described on page 256). Public WCs are next to the TI at the town entry, partway up the main drag, and at the abbey entrance.

You can attend Mass at the tiny St. Pierre Church (daily at 11:00, also Sat at 18:00, opposite Hôtel la Vieille Auberge).

## ▲▲Abbey of Mont St. Michel

Mont St. Michel has been an important pilgrimage center since A.D. 708, when the bishop of Avranches heard the voice of Archangel Michael saying, "Build here and build high." With brilliant foresight, Michael reassured the bishop, "If you build it...they will come." Today's abbey is built on the remains of a Romanesque

**Mont St. Michel**

BAY OF MONT ST. MICHEL

NORTH TOWER

50 YARDS
50 METERS

BOUCLE FORTRESS

ABBEY
W.C.

CLOISTERS

GARDENS

BOUCLE TOWER

LOWER TOWER

WEST TER-RACE

CHURCH

CEM.

GRAND RUE

RAMPARTS

WATCH

MONTÉE FANILS

VILLAGE

POST

W.C.

LIBERTY TOWER

W.C.

START

DCH

LOW TIDE ONLY!

ENTRY

CAUSEWAY

TO MAINLAND

ⓣ TAXI STAND   ⓟ PARKING
ⓑ BUS STOP    ⅄ VIEW
➡ RAMPARTS WALK UP TO ABBEY
-➡ DIRECT ROUTE UP TO ABBEY

❶ Hôtel des Terrasses Poulard
❷ Hôtel Croix Blanche
❸ Hôtel St. Pierre
❹ Hôtel le Mouton Blanc &
  Chez Mado Rest.

❺ Restaurant le
  St. Michel Rooms
❻ Hôtel la Vieille Auberge
❼ Entry to Abbey

NORMANDY

church, which stands on the remains of a Carolingian church. St. Michael, whose gilded statue decorates the top of the spire, was the patron saint of many French kings, making this a favored site for French royalty through the ages. St. Michael was particularly popular in Counter-Reformation times, as the Church employed his warlike image in the fight against Protestant heresy.

While this abbey has 1,200 years of history, much of its story was lost when its archives were taken to St. Lô for safety during World War II—only to be destroyed during the D-Day fighting.

As you climb the stairs, imagine the centuries of pilgrims and monks who have worn down the edges of these same stone steps.

**Cost and Hours:** €8.50; May–June daily 9:00–19:00; July–Aug Mon–Sat 9:00–23:00, Sun 9:00–19:00; Sept–April daily 9:30–18:00; last entry one hour before closing (tel. 02 33 89 80 00). Buy your ticket to the abbey and keep climbing. Mass is held daily except Monday at 12:15 in the abbey church.

**Visiting the Abbey:** Allow 20 minutes to hike at a steady pace from the TI. If visiting in the morning, arrive by 10:00 to minimize crowds, though late afternoons are usually less crowded in high season. In summer evenings, when the abbey is open until 23:00 and crowds are gone, visits come with music and mood lighting. It's worth paying a second admission to see the abbey so peaceful (nighttime program starts at 19:00; daytime tickets aren't valid for re-entry, but you can visit before 19:00 and stay on).

**Tours:** You'll find no English explanations in the abbey (except for a small leaflet). Follow my self-guided tour, below. For more detail, rent the well-done audioguide (€4/person, €6/2 people) or take a 1.25-hour English-language guided tour (free, tip requested, 4 tours/day, first tour usually at 10:00, last at 16:00, confirm tour times at TI, meet at top terrace in front of church). The guided tours, which can be good, come with big crowds. You can start a tour, then decide if it works for you—I'd skip them.

**◑ Self-Guided Tour:** Tour the abbey by following a one-way route. Keep climbing to the ticket booths and turnstile, then climb some more. Pass a public WC, a room with interesting models of the abbey through the ages, a guides' desk (posting the time of the next tour), and—finally—the terrace.

• *Walk to the round lookout at the far end and face the church.*

**West Terrace:** In 1776, a fire destroyed the west end of the church, leaving this grand view terrace. The original extent of the church is outlined with short walls (as well as the stonecutter numbers, generally not exposed like this—a reminder that they were paid by the piece). The buildings of Mont St. Michel are made of granite stones quarried from the Isles of Chausey (visible on a clear day, 20 miles away). Tidal power was ingeniously harnessed to load, unload, and even transport the stones, as barges hitched a ride with each incoming tide.

As you survey the Bay of Mont St. Michel, notice the polder land—farmland reclaimed by Normans in the 19th century with the help of Dutch engineers. The lines of trees mark strips of land used in the process. Today, this reclaimed land is covered by salt-loving plants and grazed by sheep whose salty meat is considered a local treat. You're standing 240 feet above sea level, at the summit of what was an island called "the big tomb." The small island just farther out is "the little tomb."

The bay stretches from Normandy to Brittany. The river below marks the historic border between the two lands. Brittany and Normandy have long vied for Mont St. Michel. In fact, the river used to pass Mont St. Michel on the other side, making the abbey part of Brittany. Today, it's just barely—but thoroughly—on Normand soil. You can see construction on the new dam across this river; it's the first phase of the project to return Mont St. Michel to being an island.

• *Now head back into the...*

**Abbey Church:** Sit on a pew near the front of the church, under the little statue of the Archangel Michael (with the spear to defeat dragons and evil, and the scales to evaluate your soul). Monks built the church on the tip of this rock in order to be as close to heaven as possible. The downside: There wasn't enough level ground to support a sizable abbey and church. The solution: Four immense crypts were built under the church to create a platform to support each of its wings. While most of the church is Romanesque (round arches, 11th century), the Gothic, light-filled apse behind the altar was built later. In 1421, the crypt that supported the apse collapsed, taking that end of the church with it. Almost none of the original windows survive (victims of fires, storms, lightning, and the Revolution).

• *Just outside the church, you'll find the...*

**Cloisters:** A standard feature of an abbey, this was the peaceful zone that connected various rooms where monks could meditate, read the Bible, and tend their gardens (growing food and herbs for medicine). The great view window is enjoyable today (what's the tide doing?), but it was of no use to the monks. The more secluded a monk could be, the closer he was to God. (A cloister, by definition, is an enclosed place.) Notice the carvings, which feature various plants and heighten the Garden-of-Eden ambience the cloister offered the monks. The statues of various saints, carved among some columns, were de-faced—literally—by French Revolutionary troops.

• *Continue on the tour to the...*

**Refectory:** This was the dining hall where the monks consumed both food and the word of God in silence—one monk read in a monotone from the Bible during meals (pulpit on the right near the far end). The monks gathered as a family here in one undivided space under one big arch (an impressive engineering feat in its day). The abbot ate at the head table; guests sat at the table in the middle. The clever columns are thin but very deep, allowing maximum light while offering solid support. From 966 until 2001, this was a Benedictine abbey. In 2001, the last three Benedictine monks checked out, and a new order of monks from Paris took over.

• *Stairs lead down to the…*

**Guests' Hall:** St. Benedict wrote that guests should be welcomed according to their status. That meant that when the king (or other VIPs) visited, they were wined and dined without a hint of monastic austerity. This room once exploded in color, with gold stars on a blue sky across the ceiling. (The painting of this room was said to be the model for Sainte-Chapelle in Paris.) The floor was of glazed red-and-green tiles. The entire space was bathed in glorious sunlight, made divine as it passed through a filter of stained glass. The big double fireplace, kept out of sight by hanging tapestries, served as a kitchen.

• *Hike the stairs to the…*

**Hall of the Grand Pillars:** Perched on a pointy rock, the huge abbey had four sturdy crypts like this to prop it up. You're standing under the Gothic portion of the abbey church—this was the crypt that collapsed in 1421. Notice the immensity of the columns (15 feet around) in the new crypt, rebuilt with a determination not to let it fall again.

• *To see what kind of crypt collapsed, walk on to the…*

**Crypt of St. Martin:** This simple, 11th-century Romanesque vault has minimal openings, since the walls needed to be solid and fat to support the buildings above. As you leave, notice the thickness of the walls.

• *Next, you'll find the…*

**Ossuary** (identifiable by its big treadwheel): The monks celebrated death as well as life. This part of the abbey housed the hospital, morgue, and ossuary. Because the abbey graveyard was small, it was routinely emptied, and the bones were stacked here.

During the Revolution, monasticism was abolished. Church property was taken by the atheistic government, and from 1793 to 1863, Mont St. Michel was used as an Alcatraz-type prison. Its first inmates were 300 priests who refused to renounce their vows. (Victor Hugo complained that using such a place as a prison was like keeping a toad in a reliquary.) The big treadwheel—the kind that did heavy lifting for big building projects throughout the Middle Ages—is from the decades when the abbey was a prison. Teams of six prisoners marched two abreast in the wheel—hamster-style—powering two-ton loads of stone and supplies up Mont St. Michel. Spin the rollers of the sled next to the wheel. Look down the steep ramp (another sled hangs just below). Notice the parking lot and the crowds down there. When the tide is very high, careless drivers can become carless drivers. A few years ago, a Scottish bus driver (oblivious to the time and tide, and very busy in a hotel room) lost his bus…destroyed by a salty bath. Local police tethered it to the lot so it wouldn't float away.

Finish your visit by walking through the Promenade of the Monks, under more Gothic vaults, and through the **Scriptorium Hall,** where monks decorated illuminated manuscripts. You'll then spiral down to the gift shop, turn right, and follow signs to *Jardin.* The room after the shop holds temporary exhibitions about the history and future of Mont St. Michel.

• *Exit the room and walk out into the rear garden. From here, look up at the miracle of medieval engineering.*

**The "Merveille":** This was an immense building project—a marvel back in 1220. Three levels of buildings were created: the lower floor for the lower class, the middle floor for VIPs, and the top floor reserved for the clergy. It was a medieval skyscraper, built with the social strata in mind. (Remember looking out of those top windows earlier?) The vision was even grander—the place where you're standing was to be built up in similar fashion, to support a further expansion of the church. But the money ran out, and the project was abandoned.

• *Stairs lead from here back into the village. To avoid the crowds on your descent, turn right when you see the sign for* Musée Historique *and find your own route down or, at the same place, follow chemin des Ramparts to the* left *and hike down via the...*

**Ramparts:** Mont St. Michel is ringed by a fine example of 15th-century fortifications. They were built to defend against a new weapon: the cannon. They were low, rather than tall—to make a smaller target—and connected by protected passageways, which enabled soldiers to zip quickly to whichever zone was under attack. The five-sided Boucle Tower (1481) was crafted with no blind angles, so defenders could protect it and the nearby walls in all directions. While the English conquered all of Normandy in the early 15th century, they never took this well-fortified island. Because of its stubborn success against the English in the Hundred Years' War, Mont St. Michel became a symbol of French national identity.

After dark, the island is magically floodlit. Views from the ramparts are sublime. For the best view, exit the island and walk out on the causeway a few hundred yards.

## Near Mont St. Michel

### German Military Cemetery (Cimetière Militaire Allemand)—Located three miles from Mont St. Michel, near tiny Huisnes-sur-Mer (drive east from Mont St. Michel on D-275, then follow signs), this somber but thoughtfully presented cemetery-mortuary houses the remains of 12,000 German soldiers. It offers insight into their lives with letters they sent home (English translations). From the lookout, take in the sensational views over Mont St. Michel.

# SLEEPING

**(€1 = about $1.50, country code: 33)**

Sleep on or near the island so that you can visit Mont St. Michel early and late. The key is simply being here before or after the crush of tourists. Sleeping on the island—inside the walls—is the best experience, though rooms just off the island are a good deal cheaper and require less walking between your car and the hotel. To reach a room on the island, you'll need to carry your bags about 10–15 minutes uphill, so consider taking only what you need for one night in a smaller bag. Leave no luggage visible in your car. Drivers can also consider the nearby and excellent-value *chambres d'hôte* listed below.

## On the Island

There are eight small hotels on the island, and because most visitors day-trip here, finding a room is generally no problem. While some pad their profits by requesting that guests buy dinner from their restaurant, *requiring* it is illegal. Higher-priced rooms generally have bay views. On arrival, remember to tell the parking attendant that you're staying at a hotel on the island, which allows you to park closer. Several hotels are closed from November until Easter.

The following hotels are listed in order of altitude, with the first hotel lowest on the island and closest to the parking.

**$$$ Hôtel des Terrasses Poulard***, 50 yards after the TI, rents the lowest, most polished, and priciest rooms on the island (standard Db with some view-€130, Db with better view-€200, Tb-€200–250, tel. 02 33 89 02 02, fax 02 33 60 37 31, www.terrasses-poulard.fr, hotel@terrasses-poulard.fr).

**$$$ Hôtel St. Pierre***** and **Hôtel Croix Blanche***,** which share the same owners and reception desk, sit side by side (reception at St. Pierre). Each has adequate rooms and some with good views. St. Pierre is warmer, sharper, and €15 pricier for view rooms (prices are the same for non-view rooms). Both have several family loft rooms (non-view Db-€110, view Db-€120–135, Tb-€145, rooms for up to 6-€175, Wi-Fi, tel. 02 33 60 14 03, fax 02 33 48 59 82, www.auberge-saint-pierre.fr, aubergesaintpierre@wanadoo.fr).

**$$ Hôtel le Mouton Blanc*** is a good value with 15 rooms that are split between two buildings: the main building *(bâtiment principal)* is cozier, with wood beams in most rooms; and the "annex" is brighter and more modern (Db-€85, loft Tb-€100, loft Qb-€125, tel. 02 33 60 14 08, fax 02 33 60 05 62, www.lemouton blanc.com, contact@lemoutonblanc.fr).

**$$ Restaurant le Saint Michel,** across from Hôtel le Mouton Blanc, rents the island's six cheapest and most basic, linoleum-floored rooms in a nearby annex. It's run by lighthearted Patricia

(Ds-€60, Db-€60–80, depends on view, extra person-€10, simple decor, no dinner requirements but a good restaurant, tel. & fax 02 33 60 14 37, www.lesaintmichelridel.com).

**$$ Hôtel la Vieille Auberge\*\***, recently purchased by Hôtel St. Pierre (see above), has 11 traditional rooms in two buildings. It requires the longest walk. The four rooms with large view terraces are exceptional if the weather cooperates—and if you don't mind hearing chimes regularly from the bell tower (Db-€80–90, Db with view and terrace-€135, extra bed-€20; contact through Hôtel St. Pierre, above).

## On the Mainland

Modern hotels gather at the mainland end of the causeway. These have soulless but cheaper rooms with easy parking and many tour groups. Hôtel Vert rents bikes, offering easy access to the island.

**$$ Hôtel/Motel Vert,** which offers many services (see "Helpful Hints," earlier in this chapter), is big and cheap. Hotel rooms provide standard comfort at good rates; the motel is a compound of funky little bungalows that are bare-bones simple, cheap, and fun for families (hotel: Db-€66, Tb-€80, Qb-€92; motel bungalows: Db-€56, Tb-€70, Qb-€82; tel. 02 33 60 09 33, fax 02 33 60 20 02, www.le-mont-saint-michel.com, stmichel@le-mont-saint-michel.com).

### Chambres d'Hôte

Simply great values, these converted farmhouses are near the village of Ardevon, a few minutes' drive from the island toward Avranches.

**$$ Les Vieilles Digues,** where delightful Danielle pampers you, is two miles toward Pontorson on the main road (on the left if you're coming from Mont St. Michel). There's a lovely garden and seven beautifully furnished, spotless, and homey rooms, all with showers and exterior entrances (but no views). Ground-floor rooms have patios on the garden (D-€60, Db-€70, Tb-€90, includes good breakfast, easy parking, 68 route du Mont St. Michel, tel. 02 33 58 55 30, fax 02 33 58 83 09, www.bnb-normandy.com, danielle.tchen@wanadoo.fr).

**$ La Jacotière,** charming Claudine Brault's stone farmhouse, is closest to Mont St. Michel and walkable to the causeway. She has six immaculate, three-star-quality rooms and views of the island from her side yard (Db-€60, studio with great view from private patio-€62, extra bed-€12, includes breakfast, tel. 02 33 60 22 94, fax 02 33 60 20 48, mobile 06 78 30 25 47, www.bedbreak.com/lajacotiere, la.jacotiere@wanadoo.fr).

**$ Vent des Grèves** is about 1.5 kilometers down D-275 from Mont St. Michel (green sign; if arriving from the north, it's just after Auberge de la Baie). Sweet Estelle (who speaks English) offers five bright, modern rooms with good views of Mont St. Michel and a common deck with tables to let you soak in the view (Sb-€35, Db-€45, Tb-€52, Qb-€62, includes breakfast, credit cards OK, tel. 02 33 48 28 89, ventdesgreves@orange.fr).

## EATING

Puffy omelets *(omelette montoise,* or *omelette tradition)* are Mont St. Michel's specialty, but usually require the most expensive fixed-price *menu* option to get. Also look for mussels (best with crème fraîche) and seafood platters, locally raised lamb (a saltwater-grass diet gives the meat a unique taste), and Muscadet wine (dry, white, and cheap). Several restaurants have outdoor seating with views along the ramparts walk—ideal when it's sunny (usually lunch only).

**Restaurant le St. Michel** is lighthearted, reasonable, family-friendly, and run by helpful Patricia (decent omelets, mussels, and pasta, open daily, check out the stone toilet, across from Hôtel du Mouton Blanc, tel. 02 33 60 14 37).

**Chez Mado** is a stylish, three-story café-*crêperie*-restaurant one door up from the Hôtel Mouton Blanc. It's worth considering for its upstairs terrace with views up to the abbey and down over the bay (open daily).

*Picnics:* The **supermarket,** located on the mainland at the Hôtel Vert, has what you need for a romantic picnic (see "Helpful Hints," page 249). You can also buy sandwiches, salads, and drinks to go on the island. Picnic in the small park below the abbey, to the left as you look up at it.

## TRANSPORTATION CONNECTIONS

### By Train and Bus

Bus and train service to Mont St. Michel is a challenge. Unless you're coming from Paris, you're likely to find that you must arrive and depart early or late—leaving you too much or too little time on the island.

**From Mont St. Michel to Paris:** There are three ways to get to Paris. Most travelers take the regional bus from Mont St. Michel to Rennes (€11, not covered by railpass, www.les courriersbretons.fr) and connect directly to the TGV (4/day, 4 hrs total from Mont St. Michel to Paris). You can also take the quick bus ride to Pontorson (see next page) and catch one of a very few trains from there (2/day, 5.5 hrs, transfer in Caen or Rennes). In summer, you can take the SNCF bus to Villedieu les Poêles, and transfer there to the train to Paris' Gare Montparnasse (4/day, 4 hrs total, bus and train covered by railpass).

**From Mont St. Michel to Pontorson:** The nearest train station to Mont St. Michel is five miles away, in Pontorson (called Pontorson–Mont St. Michel). It's connected to Mont St. Michel by bus (12/day July–Aug, 6/day Sept–June, 15 min) or taxi (€18 by day, €25 at night and on weekends; see "Helpful Hints," earlier in this section).

**From Pontorson by Train to: Bayeux** (2–3/day, 2 hrs; also see Hôtel Churchill's shuttle van from Mont St. Michelle to Bayeux—page 229), **Rouen** (5/day, 4–7 hrs, most via Paris, 1 via Caen), **Dinan** (3/day, 2 hrs, transfer in Dol), **St. Malo** (2–3/day, 1–2 hrs, transfer in Dol), **Amboise** (2–3/day; 5.5–7.5 hrs via transfers in Caen and Tours, or via Rennes, Le Mans, and Tours).

Pontorson also has a **bus station** with buses to several regional destinations (turn left out of the train station and walk 100 yards, verify stop location with your driver or at train station).

**From Mont St. Michel by Bus to: St. Malo** (2/day, usually about 9:20 and 15:45, 2 hrs with change in Pontorson; the 9:20 bus with transfer arrives in St. Malo at 11:00, where you can catch buses run to Dinan—TI has schedules, www.lescourriersbretons .fr), **Rennes** (4/day, 1.75 hrs).

## By Car
**From Mont St. Michel to Dinan, Brittany:** For a scenic drive into Brittany, take the following route: Head to Pontorson, then follow *St. Malo*, then *St. Malo par la Côte*, and join D-797, which leads along the *Route de la Baie* to D-155 and on to the oyster capital of Cancale. In Cancale, keep tracking *St. Malo par la Côte* and *Route de la Baie* signs. You'll be routed through the town's port (good lunch stop) then emerge on D-201. Take time to savor Pointe du Grouin, then continue west on D-201 as it hugs the coast to St. Malo. St. Malo merits a stop if time permits (see page 275 in Brittany chapter). From St. Malo, signs direct you to Rennes, then Dinan. This drive adds about 2.5 hours (with stops; takes longer on weekends and in summer) to the fastest path between Mont St. Michel and Dinan, but is well worth it when skies are clear. For more details on this drive, see "Scenic Drive Between Dinan and Mont St. Michel" on page 274 of the Brittany chapter.

**From Mont St. Michel to Bayeux:** Take the free and zippy A-84, and be ready to navigate if new signs to Bayeux are not yet in place (keep asking, "oo ay Bayeux?").

# BRITTANY

The broad peninsula of Brittany is wind-swept and rugged, with a forgotten interior, a well-discovered coast, strong Celtic ties, and a passion for crêpes and *cidre* (alcoholic apple cider served in bowls). This region of independent-minded locals is linguistically and culturally different from Normandy and, for that matter, the rest of France. The Couesnon River skirts the western edge of Mont St. Michel, and marks the border between Normandy and Brittany.

In 1491, the French King Charles VIII forced Brittany's 14-year-old Duchess Anne to marry him (at Château de Langeais in the Loire Valley). Their union made independent, feisty Brittany a part of France. Brittany lost its freedom, but with Anne as queen gained certain rights, such as free roads. (Even today, 500 years later, Brittany's highways come with no tolls... unique in France.)

Locals take great pride in their distinct Breton culture. In Brittany, music stores sell more Celtic music than anything else. It's hard to imagine that this music was forbidden as recently as the 1980s. During a more repressive time, many of today's big pop stars were underground artists. And not long ago, a child would lose French citizenship if christened with a Celtic name.

But the freckled locals are now free to wave their flag, sing their songs, and speak their language (there's a Breton TV station and radio station). Like their Irish counterparts, Bretons—many with red hair—are chatty, their music is alive with struggles against an oppressor, and the sea forms an integral part of their identity. The coastal route between Mont St. Michel and Dinan—through the town of Cancale (famous for oysters, and a good lunch stop),

Pointe du Grouin (fabulous ocean views), and the historic walled city of St. Malo—gives travelers with limited time a worthwhile glimpse at this photogenic province.

## Cuisine Scene in Brittany

While the endless coastline suggests otherwise, there is more than seafood in this rugged Celtic land. Crêpes are to Bretons what pasta is to Italians: a basic, reasonably priced, daily necessity. *Galettes* are savory buckwheat crêpes, commonly filled with ham, cheese, eggs, mushrooms, spinach, seafood, or a combination.

Oysters *(huîtres)* are the second food of Brittany, and are available all year. Mussels, clams, and scallops are often served as main courses. Look for crêpes with scallops and *moules marinières* (mussels steamed in white wine, parsley, and shallots). Farmers compete with fishermen for the hearts of locals by growing fresh vegetables, such as peas, beans, and cauliflower.

For dessert, look for *far breton,* a traditional custard often served with prunes. Dessert crêpes, made with white flour, are served with a variety of toppings.

Cider is the locally produced drink. Order *une bolée de cidre* (a traditional bowl of hard apple cider) with your crêpes.

Remember, restaurants serve only during lunch (11:30–14:00) and dinner (19:00–21:00, later in bigger cities); cafés serve food throughout the day.

BRITTANY

# Dinan

If you have time for only one stop in Brittany, do Dinan. Hefty ramparts corral its half-timbered and cobbled quaintness into Brittany's best medieval town center. While it has a touristic icing—plenty of *crêperies,* shops selling Brittany kitsch, and colorful flags—it's a workaday Breton town filled with people who appreciate the beautiful place they call home. This impeccably preserved ancient city (which escaped

the bombs of World War II) is peaceful and conveniently located (about a 45-minute drive from Mont St. Michel). For a memorable day, spend your morning exploring Dinan, and your afternoon walking, biking, or boating the Rance River.

# ORIENTATION

Dinan's old city, contained within its medieval ramparts, sits on a hill well above the Rance River. Cobbled lanes climb steeply from the river and Dinan's small port to the vast place du Guesclin (geklahn). There, you'll find lots of parking (see "Arrival in Dinan," below), Château de Dinan, and the TI. Place des Merciers, just north of place du Guesclin, is the center of most shopping activities.

## Tourist Information

Pick up a free map and bus and train schedules, and ask about boat trips on the Rance River (July–Aug Mon–Sat 9:00–19:00, Sun 9:00–12:30 & 14:30–18:00; Sept–June Mon–Sat 9:00–12:30 & 14:00–18:00, closed Sun; just off place du Guesclin near Château de Dinan on 9 rue du Château, tel. 02 96 87 69 76, www.dinan -tourisme.com).

## Arrival in Dinan

**By Train:** To get to the town center from Dinan's Old World train station (no lockers or baggage storage), find a taxi (see "Helpful Hints," below) or walk 20 minutes. If walking, head left out of the train station, make a right at Hôtel de la Gare up rue Carnot, turn right on rue Thiers, and then go left across big place Duclos-Pinot; from here, to get to the old center, go to the left of Café de la Mairie. To reach the TI and place du Guesclin, go to the right of this café (on rue du Marchix).

**By Bus:** Dinan's key inter-city bus stop is in front of the post office on place Duclos-Pinot, 10 minutes above the train station and five minutes below place du Guesclin (cross the square passing to the left of Café de la Mairie for the historic core).

**By Car:** Dinan is confusing for drivers; follow *Centre-Ville* signs and park on the massive place du Guesclin (free parking except July–Sept and on market days on Thu). If you enter Dinan by following signs for *la gare SNCF* (train station), drive the route described above (see "By Train") and keep to the right of Café de la Mairie to reach place du Guesclin. Check with your hotelier before leaving your car overnight on place du Guesclin; they will tow it before 8:00 on market or festival days.

## Helpful Hints

**Market Days:** On Thursday, a big open-air market is held on place du Guesclin (8:00–13:00). In July and August, Wednesday is flea-market day on place St. Sauveur.

**Supermarkets:** Groceries are upstairs in the **Monoprix** (Mon–Sat 9:00–19:30, closed Sun, 7 rue du Marchix). On Sundays, try

**Marché Plus,** on place Duclos-Pinot (Mon–Sat 7:00–19:00, Sun 9:00–13:00).

**Laundry:** **Pressing-Laverie's** Madame Heurlin can usually do your laundry in a few hours (€8/wash and dry, Tue–Fri 8:30–12:00 & 14:00–19:00, Sat 8:30–18:00, closed Sun–Mon, a few blocks from place Duclos at 19 rue de Brest, tel. 02 96 39 71 35).

**Bike Rental:** Try **Cycles Yves Gauthier,** which may change its name in 2009 (€15/day, Mon–Sat 9:00–12:00 & 14:00–19:00, closed Sun, near the train station at 15 rue Déroyer, tel. 02 96 85 07 60).

**Taxi:** Call 02 96 39 74 16 or 06 08 00 80 90 (8-seat minivans available).

**Tourist Train:** If the *petit train* is running (ask at the TI), it can get you down to the port easily (€6, daily 11:00–18:00, every 40 min, 40-min loop, departs from Théâtre des Jacobins; see self-guided walk of Dinan, below).

**Picnic-Park:** The small but flowery Jardin Anglais hides behind the Church of St. Sauveur.

# SELF-GUIDED WALK

## Welcome to Dinan

Frankly, I wouldn't go through a turnstile in Dinan. The attraction here is the town itself. Enjoy the old town center, ramble around the ramparts, and explore the old river-front harbor. Here are some ideas, laced together as a relaxed one-hour walk (not including exploring the port), starting near the TI. As you wander, notice the pride locals take in their Breton culture.

• *Start behind the TI in front of Château de Dinan.*

**Château de Dinan:** The nearby walls and the 120-foot-high *donjon* (keep) are all that's left of Dinan's once-intimidating castle. This was the centerpiece of Dinan's two miles of ramparts that once encircled the city. The museum inside (some English) and the view from the top are both disappointing unless you love looms.

• *Walk to the center of place du Guesclin, and find the statue of the horse-back rider.*

**Place du Guesclin:** This sprawling town square/parking lot is named after Bertrand du Guesclin, a native 14th-century knight and hero (described as small in stature but big-hearted) who became a great French military leader, famous for his daring victories over England during the Hundred Years' War (like Joan of

**Dinan**

OLD PORT

FRANCE

PATH TO LEHON

TO 25

OLD BRIDGE

VIADUCT

R. DU PORT

JARDIN ANGLAIS

St. CATH. Tower

PETIT FORT

Porte Jerzual

R. DU JERZUAL

ST. SAUVEUR

FINISH

PLACE ST. SAUVEUR

Porte Jerzual

R. DE BERTRAND

R. DE L'ÉCOLE

R. DU PETIT FORT

R. LECONTÉ DE L'ISLE

R. MICHEL

WC

R. BIG GUY

R. LINERIE

R. DE L'APPORT

CLAIRE

WALD. ROUSS.

GÉN. DE GAULLE

LEHON

R. DE L'HORLOGE

PLACE CHAMP

PLACE DU GUESCLIN

START

R. CHÂTEAU

T. RAG.

PLACE DES CORDELIERS

GRAND RUE

R. MERCIERS

R. CHAUX

R. FERRONNERIE

MARCHIX

MITT.

R. GARAVE

ST. MALO

R. CROIX

FOSSERIE

FOSSÉ

R. POST

PROMENADE DES PETITS FOSSES

R. CHATEAUBRIAND

CHÂTEAU

DCH

400 YARDS
400 METERS

RUE CARNOT

RUE THIERS

RUE PIVENTS

R. ROUAIRIES

PLACE DUCLOS-PINOT

R. LORD KITCHENER

R. BREST

TRAIN STATION

R. DEROYER

N

① Hôtel Arvor
② Chambres d'Hôtes Le Logis du Jerzual
③ Hôtel la Tour de l'Horloge
④ Hôtel du Théâtre
⑤ Hôtel d'Avaugour
⑥ Hôtel Ibis Dinan
⑦ Best Western Hôtel Jerzual
⑧ Hôtel de la Gare
⑨ Crêperie des Artisans
⑩ Au Vieux St. Sauveur
⑪ Crêperie Ahna
⑫ La P'tite Cantine
⑬ Le Cantorbery Restaurant
⑭ La Fleur de Sel Rest.
⑮ Le Cottage Restaurant
⑯ Launderette
⑰ Bike Rental
⑱ Monoprix (Groceries)
⑲ Marché Plus (Groceries)
⑳ Rue de la Cordonnerie Bars
㉑ Café de la Mairie
㉒ Clock Tower
㉓ Théâtre des Jacobins
㉔ Rampart Walk Gates (2)
㉕ To Hôtel Manoir de Rigourdaine & Bike Route to Port de Lyvet & St. Suliac

↗ WALKING TOUR ROUTE
✷ VIEW   Ⓑ BUS STOP

BRITTANY

Arc, he played a major role in defeating the English). On this very square, he defeated Sir Thomas of Canterbury in a nail-biter of a joust that locals still talk about to this day. The victory freed his brother, whom Thomas had taken prisoner in violation of a truce. For 700 years, merchants have filled this square to sell their produce and crafts (in modern times, it's Thursdays from 8:00–13:00).

• *With the statue of Guesclin behind you, follow rue Ste. Claire to the right, into the old town and to the...*

**Théâtre des Jacobins:** Fronting a pleasant little square, the theater was once one of the many convents that dominated the town. In fact, in medieval times, a third of Dinan consisted of convents. (They're still not uncommon in Brittany, which remains the most Catholic part of France.)

• *Turn left and walk down rue de l'Horloge ("Clock Street") toward the clock tower, where on your left, you'll see...*

**Anybody's Tombstone:** The tombstone without a head is a town mascot. It's actually a prefab tombstone, made during the Hundred Years' War, when there was more death than money in France. A portrait bust would be attached to this generic body for a proper, yet economical, burial.

• *Continue to the...*

**Clock Tower:** The old town spins around this clock tower, which has long symbolized the power of the town's merchants. The tower comes with 160 steps (the last few on a ladder) to a fine city view. Warning: Plug your ears at the quarter-hour, when the bells ring (€3, daily June–Sept 10:00–18:30, April–May 14:00–18:00, closed Oct–March).

• *Past the tower, take the first left into Dinan's historic commercial center, place des Merciers. Find a bakery selling* ker-y-pom *(about €1.50), traditional Breton shortbread biscuits with butter, honey, and an apple-pie filling. When warm, they're the best-tasting treat in town. Now, find the stone bench near the restaurant La Mère Pourcel.*

**Old Town Center:** The arcaded, half-timbered buildings in front of you are Dinan's oldest. They date from the time when property taxes were based on the square footage of the ground floor. To provide shelter from both the rain and taxes, buildings started with small ground floors, then expanded outward for their upper floors. Medieval shopkeepers sold goods in front of their homes under the shelter of leaning walls. Most streets are named for the key commerce that took place there. Picturesque rue de la Cordonnerie ("Shoe Street," to the left of La Mère Pourcel) is a good example of a medieval lane, with overhanging buildings whose roofs nearly touch. After a disastrous 18th-century fire, a law required that the traditional thatch be replaced by safer slate. The building with the arched stone facade at the opposite end of the square was a Franciscan monastery in the Middle Ages; today, it's a middle school—wrap your brain around that change.

• *Wander a short block up rue de la Cordonnerie, turn right, then double back on rue du Petit Pain, passing the unusual market-hall stalls. Continue around place des Merciers and turn right on rue de la Lainerie ("Street of Wool Shops"), staying on it as it turns into rue du Jerzual.*

**Rue du Jerzual:** This spiraling road was the primary medieval link to the port, and the focus of commercial activity in old Dinan. The steep cobbled street (slippery when wet) was chock-a-block with potential customers making their way between the port and the upper city. Notice the waist-high stone and wooden shelves that front many of the buildings. Here, medieval merchants could display their products and tempt passersby. You can continue all the way down to the port (for more on the port, look under "Sights"); it's a 10-minute walk down (remember, what goes down must come back up). If your knees disagree, follow the path described immediately below, to the ramparts.

• *For the best look at Dinan's impressive fortified wall, turn right after passing under the massive medieval gate (Porte du Jerzual) and work your way up the curving road. Turn right on rue Michel, then turn right again through the iron gate to walk along the...*

**Ramparts:** In the Middle Ages, this elevated walkway was connected with Château de Dinan (figure about a mile in either direction to the château from here). While the old port town was repeatedly destroyed, these ramparts were never taken by force. If an attacker got by the *contrescarpe* (second outer wall) and through the (dry) moat, he'd be pummeled by gross stuff dropped through the holes lining the ramparts. Today, the ramparts seem to guard only the town's residential charm and private gardens. Venture out on the (second) huge Governor's Tower to see how the cannon slots enabled defenders to shoot in all directions. The St. Malo tower lies to your left, and the farthest visible tower to your right is our next stop.

• *Double back to rue Michel and turn right. Take the first left, onto rue du Rempart. Walk to the round tower (in the corner of the park) called...*

**St. Catherine's Tower:** This was part of Dinan's medieval defense system, and today allows strategic views of the river valley and over the old port. To the right, find the medieval bridge and the path that leads along the river to Léhon (described under "Rance River Valley," next page). The English gardens behind you are picnic-pleasant.

• *Walk around the church behind you, and dip into the...*

**Church of St. Sauveur:** Enter this asymmetrical church (typical in Brittany) to see striking, modern, stained-glass windows and a beautifully lit nave. Pick up the English explanation and learn the church's raison d'être. The church is a thousand years old—the wood balcony in the entry looks even older, as it heaves under the weight of the organ above. When built, the church sat isolated on this hill as activity remained focused on and around the port.

• *Your tour is over. Good lunch cafés are across the square (see "Eating" on page 272), and you are a block below the main rue de l'Horloge.*

# SIGHTS

## Dinan's Old Port

Following the self-guided walk above, you can reach Dinan's modest little port by continuing down rue du Jerzual (which becomes rue du Petit Fort). Notice the unusual wood-topped building just before the port. This was a leather tannery. Those wooden shutters could open to dry the freshly tanned hides while the nearby river flushed the waste products (swimming was not in vogue then). The last business before the port is a memorable bakery highlighting local specialties. You deserve a baked break.

The port was the birthplace of Dinan a thousand years ago. For centuries, this is where people lived and worked. Once an important port, it was connected to the sea—15 miles away—by the Rance River. By taxing river traffic, the town grew prosperous. The tiny Vieux Pont (Old Bridge) dates to the 15th century. Because the port area was so exposed, the townsfolk retreated to the bluff behind its current fortifications. Notice the viaduct high above, built in 1850 to alleviate congestion and to send traffic around the town. Until then, the main road crossed the tiny Old Bridge, heading up rue du Jerzual to Dinan.

## ▲Rance River Valley

The best thing about Dinan's port is the access it provides to lush riverside paths that meander along the gentle Rance River Valley. You can walk, bike, drive, or boat in either interesting direction.

**On Foot:** For a breath of fresh Brittany air, visit the village of **Léhon.** Cross the Old Bridge in Dinan's port, turn right, and walk the level river trail for 30 minutes. You'll come to pristine Léhon. Visitors are greeted by a proud ninth-century abbey and church (find the cloisters), flowers along cobbled lanes, a town-topping medieval castle ruin (€4, good views, daily in summer only 10:00–19:00), and **La Marmite de l'Abbaye** café/restaurant (wood fire–grilled meats for lunch and dinner, drinks in between, July–Aug open daily, Sept–June closed Mon and maybe Tue, tel. 02 96 87 39 39).

**By Bike:** For bike rental, see "Helpful Hints," earlier in this section. Cyclists can follow the "On Foot" route (above), then cross Léhon's bridge and continue along the canal as far as they can pedal. You'll pass Breton cows, cute little lock houses, sublime scenery, and other nature-lovers. The villages of Evran and Treverien are both within reach (allow 45 min from Dinan to Evran, 25 min more to Treverien).

For another biking excursion, turn left rather than right at Dinan's port. Staying on the Dinan side of the river, bikers can join the parade of ocean-bound boats. It's a breezy and level 30-minute ride past rock faces, cornfields, and slate-roofed homes to the picturesque Port de Lyvet (cross small dam to reach village, trail ends a short distance beyond). **L'Effet Mer** café/restaurant is perfectly positioned in the village (open daily for lunch, dinner, or a refreshing drink, closed Wed off-season, tel. 02 96 83 21 10). Serious bikers should continue on to St. Suliac via La Vicomte (see "By Car," below).

**By Boat:** Boats depart from Dinan's port, at the bottom of rue du Jerzual, 50 feet to the left of the Old Bridge on the Dinan side (schedules depend on tides, get details at TI). The one-hour cruise on the *Jaman IV* boat comes with an English-speaking guide, plenty of scenery, and a chance to go through a lock (€8, runs April–Oct, 2–4/day, does not run Mon except July–Aug, tel. 06 07 87 64 90). A longer cruise with **Compagnie Corsaire** goes to St. Malo (€23 one-way, €29 round-trip, runs April–Sept, 1/day, slow and scenic 2.5 hrs one-way, schedule changes with the tide, tel. 08 25 16 81 20 or ask at TI). Enjoy St. Malo (described on page 275), then take the bus back (or bus to St. Malo, then boat back). Get the bus schedule before leaving Dinan (3/day, 50 min, no buses Sun). You can also rent a small motorboat from **Danfleurenn Nautic** (€38/hr, €80/half-day, 21 rue du Quai, tel. 06 07 45 89 97, book ahead for a half-day or full day).

**By Car:** Meandering the Rance River Valley by car requires a good map (the orange Michelin #309 worked for me). Drivers connecting Dinan and St. Malo can include this short Rance joyride detour: From Dinan, drop down to the port, then follow D-12 with the river to your right toward Taden, then toward Plouër-sur-Rance. Pass by La Hisse, then drop down and turn right, following signs to *Le Vicomte*. Cross the Rance on the small dam and find the cute **Port de Lyvet** (lunch café), then continue to La Vicomte and find D-29 north. Track your way to **St. Suliac,** a pretty little port town with a handful of restaurants, a small grocery store, and a photogenic *boulangerie*. Stroll the ancient alleys, find a bench on the grassy waterfront, and contemplate lunch. **La Ferme du Boucanier Bistrot** is a good bet (closed Tue–Wed, 2 rue de l'Hôpital, tel. 02 23 15 06 35). From here, continue on to St. Malo or return to Dinan.

# SLEEPING

Dinan is popular. Weekends and summers are tight; book ahead if you can. Dinan likes its nightlife, so be careful of loud rooms over bars, particularly on lively weekends.

## In the Old Center

**$$ Hôtel Arvor\*\***, well-located in the old city a block off place du Guesclin, has 24 modern and adequately comfortable rooms behind an old stone facade (standard Db-€58–78, Tb-€82, for larger rooms for up to 6 people add €15/person, elevator, free parking, 5 rue Pavie, tel. 02 96 39 21 22, fax 02 96 39 83 09, www .hotelarvordinan.com, hotel-arvor@wanadoo.fr).

**$$ Chambres d'Hôtes Le Logis du Jerzual** is just about as cozy as it gets. The ideal hostess, Sylvie Ronserray, welcomes guests with five warmly decorated rooms, period furnishings, and thoughtful touches throughout. Enjoy the terraced yard in this haven of calm so close to the action. It's just up from the port but a long, steep walk below the main town (Db-€80–90, extra bed-€20, includes breakfast, 25 rue du Petit Fort, tel. 02 96 85 46 54, fax 02 96 39 46 94, www.logis-du-jerzual.com, ronsseray@wanadoo.fr). Drive up rue du Petit Fort from the port (it's well-signed) and drop your bags. Parking is nearby.

**$ Hôtel la Tour de l'Horloge\*\*** is a good two-star bet burrowed deep in the town's center, with 12 imaginatively decorated and impeccably maintained rooms fronting the bar-lined rue de la Chaux. Madame Diard gives a warm welcome and runs the place with pride and grace. Some rooms can be noisy on weekends (Db-€60, Tb-€73, Qb-€85, 5 rue de la Chaux, ring doorbell to enter, tel. 02 96 39 96 92, fax 02 96 85 06 99, http://hoteltourdelhorloge .com, hotel.pbdelatour@orange.fr).

**$ Hôtel du Théâtre** is a budget traveler's dream, with seven good-enough rooms (when you consider the price) above a scrappy café/bar, across from Hôtel Arvor (S/D-€24, Db-€29, Tb-€39, 2 rue Ste. Claire, tel. 02 96 39 06 91, owner Patrick speaks some English).

## On Place du Guesclin

These hotels offer the easiest, closest parking on place du Guesclin (except on Wed night, since Thu is market day).

**$$$ Hôtel le d'Avaugour\*\*\***, facing a busy street, is Dinan's reliable three-star hotel, with an efficient staff, cozy lounges, and a backyard garden oasis near the town's medieval wall. The wood-furnished rooms have comfortable beds (all queen or king) and modern hotel amenities, including a TV sound system that works

## Sleep Code

**(€1 = $1.50, country code: 33)**
**S** = Single, **D** = Double/Twin, **T** = Triple, **Q** = Quad, **b** = bathroom,
**s** = shower only, * = French hotel rating system (0-4 stars).
Unless otherwise noted, credit cards are accepted and English
is spoken.

To help you sort easily through these listings, I've divided
the rooms into three categories based on the price for a
standard double room with bath:

$$$ **Higher Priced**—Most rooms €90 or more.
$$ **Moderately Priced**—Most rooms between €60–90.
$ **Lower Priced**—Most rooms €60 or less.

in the bathroom (street-side Db-€90–170, garden-side Db-€120–220, third person-€18, suites available, prices vary greatly by season, rooms over garden are best, elevator, bikes available, 1 place du Champ, tel. 02 96 39 07 49, fax 02 96 85 43 04, www.avaugour hotel.com, contact@avaugourhotel.com).

**$$ Hôtel Ibis Dinan**** stands tall a few minutes below place du Guesclin. A 10-minute walk from the train station, it offers shiny, predictable comfort in cookie-cutter rooms. They may have rooms when others don't (Db-€78, Tb-€105, Qb-€130, less on weekends, 1 place Duclos, tel. 02 96 39 46 15, fax 02 96 85 44 03, www.ibishotel.com, h5977@accor.com).

## At the Port

**$$$ Best Western Hôtel Jerzual**** fronts the port well below the old city and feels *très americain*, with a spacious lobby, a pool, a sauna, a café/bar, a restaurant, and comfortable rooms with big beds (standard Db-€106–126, bigger Db-€165–220, extra person-€22, 26 quai des Talard, tel. 02 96 87 02 02, fax 02 96 87 02 03, www.bestwestern.com, hotel-jerzual.dinan@wanadoo.fr).

## Near the Train Station

**$ Hôtel de la Gare*** faces the station and offers the "full Breton Monty," with *charmant* Laurence and Claude (who both love Americans), a local-as-it-gets café hangout, and surprisingly quiet, clean, and comfy rooms for a bargain. Don't let the hallways scare you. The hotel has no email of its own, but offers free Wi-Fi thanks to the owners' 13-year-old son (D-€28, Ds-€37, Db-€50, Tb/Qb-€50–65, place de la Gare, tel. 02 96 39 04 57, fax 02 96 39 02 29).

## Near Dinan

**$$ Hôtel Manoir de Rigourdaine**\*\* is *the* place to stay if you have a car and two nights, and want to savor Brittany. Overlooking a splendid scene of green mead-

ows and turquoise water, this well-renovated farmhouse comes with wood beams, pleas-ant public spaces, immaculate grounds, Internet access and Wi-Fi, and three-star rooms (many with views) for two-star prices. Run by ever-so-helpful Patrick and Anne-France, you won't want to leave (Db-€76–82, extra person-€15, I prefer the upstairs rooms, 15-min drive north of Dinan, tel. 02 96 86 89 96, fax 02 96 86 92 46, www.hotel-rigourdaine.fr, hotel.rigourdaine @wanadoo.fr). From Dinan, drop down to the port and follow D-12 toward Taden, then follow signs to Plouër-sur-Rance, then Langrolay, and look for hotel signs. If coming from the St. Malo area, take N-137 toward Rennes, then N-176 toward Dinan, take the Rance Plouër exit, and follow signs to Langrolay until you see hotel signs. From Rennes, take N-176 toward St. Brieuc, take the Plouër-sur-Rance exit, and follow the above directions.

# EATING

Dinan has good restaurants for every budget. Since *galettes* (savory crêpes) are the specialty, *crêperies* are a good and inexpensive choice, available on every corner. Crêpes with ham can be salty. Be daring and try the crêpes with scallops and cream, or go for the egg-and-cheese crêpes.

**Crêperie des Artisans** is well worth the walk for connoisseurs of fine crêpes and warm ambience. Sincere owner Patrick uses only traditional local ingredients. Try the *lait ribot* (a frothy, slightly sour milk drink) or the extra-dry cider from the wooden barrel in the corner (€9–14 *menus*, closed Mon, 6 rue du Petit Fort, halfway down to the port, tel. 02 96 39 44 10).

**Au Vieux St. Sauveur,** a local watering hole/café, has good prices and a hard-to-beat setting...if it's sunny (€6 for lunch salads and *plats*, daily, across from the church at 19 place St. Sauveur, tel. 02 96 85 30 20).

**Crêperie Ahna** is perennially busy satisfying its loyal clientele with tasty crêpes and salads (inside seating only, closed Sun, 7 rue de la Poissonnerie, tel. 02 96 39 09 13).

**La P'tite Cantine** offers a friendly greeting, fine salads, and meats grilled in the small fireplace (3 courses of crêpes-€12, closed

Sun–Mon, 17 rue de l'Apport, tel. 02 96 87 56 75).

**Le Cantorbery,** is a warm place (literally), where meats are grilled in the cozy dining-room fireplace *à la tradition.* The seafood is *très* tasty (*menus* from €25, closed Sun, just off place du Guesclin at 6 rue Ste. Claire, tel. 02 96 39 02 52).

**La Fleur de Sel** is named after sea salt, a prized local resource. It features well-prepared seafood and traditional fare, but lacks ambience (*menus* from €23, closed all day Mon and for dinner Sun and Wed, 7 rue Ste. Claire, tel. 02 96 85 15 14).

*At the Old Port:* You'll find several restaurants at the old port. Have a pre-dinner drink at one of the places on the river, then dine at **Le Cottage.** This spot merits the long walk along a cobbled lane, serving beautifully presented dishes to a happy clientele inside or out (*menus* from €18, daily, 78 rue du Petit Fort, tel. 02 96 87 96 70).

*Nightlife:* So many lively bars line the narrow, pedestrian-friendly **rue de la Cordonnerie** that the street is nicknamed "rue de la Soif" (Street of Thirst). When the weather is good, you can sit outside at the long, wooden tables and strike up a conversation with a friendly Breton.

# TRANSPORTATION CONNECTIONS

Locals take the bus to St. Malo or to Rennes, then catch trains from there; you'll find that trains from Dinan require several changes and take longer.

**From Dinan by Train to: Paris'** Gare Montparnasse (6/day, 4 hrs, change in Dol and Rennes), **Pontorson–Mont St. Michel** (3/day, 2 hrs, change in Dol, then bus or taxi from Pontorson, see "Transportation Connections" on page 260), **St. Malo** (5/day, 1 hr, change in Dol, bus is better—see below), **Amboise** (5/day, 5–6 hrs, via Rennes, then TGV to Paris with no station change needed in Paris; or cross-country via Rennes, Le Mans, and Tours—2/day, 5–6 hrs).

**By Bus to: Rennes** (with good train connections to many destinations, 8/day, 75 min), **St. Malo** (3/day, 1 hr; faster and better than train, as bus stops in both cities are more central), **Mont St. Michel** (3/day, 3–4 hrs, includes transfer with 1-hour wait in St. Malo or in Dol de Bretagne), **Dinard** (2/day, 1 hr). Buses leave from place Duclos-Pinot, by the main post office).

# Sights near Dinan

## ▲▲Scenic Drive Between Dinan and Mont St. Michel

This lovely ride is worth ▲▲▲ if it's clear. Dinan is ideally situated for a quick taste-of-Brittany driving tour that samples a bit of the rugged peninsula's coast. If you're connecting Dinan and Mont St. Michel, link the two with this worthwhile little detour. These directions are from Dinan to Mont St. Michel, but it works well in reverse order (see page 260). Allow 2.5 hours for the drive between Mont St. Michel and St. Malo, including stops (a more direct route takes 45 min). On a weekend or in summer, the drive will take longer—start early.

**St. Malo to the Emerald Coast:** From St. Malo (a worthwhile stop described on the next page), take the scenic road hugging the coast east on D-201 to Pointe du Grouin, where the appropriately named Emerald Coast (Côte d'Emeraude) begins. Leave St. Malo following *Cancale* signs and passing countless roundabouts, then look for signs to *Rothéneuf*, where you'll access D-201, which skirts in and out of film-gobbling views. Brown signs lead to short worthwhile detours to the coast; these are my two favorites:

**Ile Besnard and Dunes de Chevets:** A five-minute detour off D-201 leads to this glorious, sandy beach arcing alongside a crescent bay. There are rocks rising from the water to scramble on, a nature trail above the beach, and a view restaurant by the campground (Les Chevets Bar/Restaurant, closed Mon–Tue). From the hamlet of La Guimorais, a 10-minute drive above Rothéneuf, follow signs to *Ile Besnard* and *Dunes de Chevets* to the very end (past the campground), and park at the far end of the lot.

**Pointe du Grouin:** This striking rock outcrop yields views from easy trails in all directions. Park near Hôtel du Grouin (outdoor café with views), and continue on foot. Pass the *semaphore du grouin* (signal station), where paths lead everywhere. Breathe in the sea air. Can you spot Mont St. Michel in the distance? The big rock below is L'Ile des Landes, an island earmarked for a fort during the French Revolution. The fort was never built, and the island remains home to thousands of birds. What fool would build on an island in this bay?

**Cancale:** Return to your car and leave Pointe du Grouin, following signs to Cancale, Brittany's appealing oyster capital. Its harbor *(le port)* is lined with restaurants, all offering oysters and mussels. Upon arrival in Cancale, follow *par la côte* signs to arrive on the port side, where you'll find plenty of restaurants to choose from. Slurp oysters here.

**Cancale to Mont St. Michel:** Cancale is a 45-minute drive from Mont St. Michel. Head out of Cancale toward Mont St.

**Near Dinan**

AUTOROUTE
(TOLL EXCEPT BRITTANY)
— OTHER ROADS
— SCENIC DRIVE

ENGLISH CHANNEL

TO PLYMOUTH,
CHANNEL ISLANDS
+ PORTSMOUTH
(BRITAIN)

ILE
BESNARD
+
DUNES
DE
CHEVETS

N

TO CAEN
+ PARIS

AVRANCHES

ST.
MALO

EMERALD
COAST

POINTE
DU
GROUIN

MONT ST.
MICHEL

A-84

DINARD

ROTHE-
NEUF

D-201

CANCALE

TO
PARIS

D-355

D-976

N-175

D-168

N-137

D-155

D-797

NORMANDY

RANCE RIVER

E-401

PONTORSON

D-676

DOL

D-795

TO
BREST

E-401

DINAN

D-794

TO
FOUGERES

N-12

B R I T T A N Y

A-84

N-137

D-175

PARIS

TO RENNES

5 MILES

10 KM

DCH

**BRITTANY**

Michel on D-155, then D-797, and drive along *la Route de la Baie,*
which skirts the bay and passes big-time oyster farming, windmill
towers (most lacking their sails), flocks of sheep, and, at low tide,
grounded boats waiting for the sea to return. On a clear day, look
for Mont St. Michel in the distance. On a foggy day, look harder.

## ▲St. Malo

Come here to experience *the* Breton beach resort. The old center
(called Intra Muros) is your target, with powerful ramparts that hug
the entire town. The inner city has an eerie, almost claustrophobic
feeling, thanks to the concentration of tall, dark stone buildings
hemmed in by the tall ramparts. St. Malo is busy in summer, but if
you're game, it's an easy 45-minute drive—or a manageable bus or
train ride—from Mont St. Michel or Dinan. (However, there's no
baggage storage anywhere.)

St. Malo's **TI** is across from the main city gate on Esplanade St. Vincent (July–Aug Mon–Sat 9:00–19:30, Sun 10:00–18:00; Sept–June daily 9:00–12:30 & 13:30–18:30; tel. 08 25 13 52 00, www.saint-malo-tourisme .com). A ferry runs between St. Malo and Dinard (see "Dinard," later in this section).

**Getting There:** If you're arriving in St. Malo by **car,** follow *Centre-Ville* signs to the old center (signs lead to Intra-Muros), and park as close to the walls as you can. Parking is usually available on the port side of the walls (follow *Gare Maritime* signs) or near the TI, directly across from the main entrance gate (Porte St. Vincent). The main **bus** stops are across from the TI (buses to Dinan: 3/day, 50 min; and to Mont St Michel: 2/day, 2 hrs via easy Pontorson transfer).

**Sights:** The town feels better up top on the **walls.** It's a rewarding mile romp around the medieval fortifications; stairs provide access at each door *(porte)*. Drop down and walk on the beaches (if the tides allow), then find your way inside the walls to sample seafood. There's no shortage of restaurants here, many serving the local specialty of mussels *(moules)* and oysters *(huitres)*.

To turn this town into a ▲▲ sight (best by car), follow signs to *Centre-Ville,* then *Alet,* and park near the **Tour de Solidor.** The village of Alet is just a few minutes' drive past St. Malo's port (a 20-min walk to the old center), but feels a world apart. A splendid walking path above the tower leads around this small point with stunning views of crashing waves, the city of Dinard, the open sea, and finally, St. Malo (allow 30 min at a relaxed pace, go in a clockwise direction). WWII bunkers cap the small hill, and there's a memorial you can visit. Several popular cafés face the bay back near the Tour de Solidor.

*Sleeping in St. Malo:* Spending a night here gives you more time to enjoy the sunset and sea views from the town walls. Try the friendly **$ Hôtel le Nautilus**\**, inside the walls near the St. Vincent gate (Db–€49–59, elevator, free Wi-Fi, 9 rue de la Corne de Cerf, easiest to park outside walls and walk in through Porte St. Vincent, tel. 02 99 40 42 27, www.lenautilus.com, info@lenautilus .com, helpful Loïck).

## ▲Dinard

This upscale-traditional resort comes with a kid-friendly beach and plenty of old-time, Coney Island–style, beach-promenade ambience (2 buses/day from Dinan). The small passenger-only **ferry** from St. Malo provides the most scenic arrival (€6 round-trip, departs from below Promenade du Clair de Lune at Embarcadère).

The **TI,** between the casino and place de la République parking lot, is at 2 boulevard Féart (daily 9:30–12:30 & 14:00–18:00, July–Aug until 19:00, tel. 02 99 46 94 12, www.ot-dinard.com). To get to the TI from place de la République, walk toward the water, take your first right, and make another right onto boulevard Féart.

Dinard is a 10- to 20-minute drive from St. Malo. Leaving St. Malo, follow *Barrage de la Rance* signs through the unappealing port; in Dinard, follow *Centre-Ville* signs, and park on place de la République.

## ▲Fougères

This very Breton city is a handy stop for drivers traveling between the Loire châteaux and Mont St. Michel. Fougères has one of Europe's largest medieval castles, a fine old city center, and a panoramic park viewpoint. Drivers follow *Centre-Ville* signs, then *Château,* and park at the free lot just past the château.

For a memorable, leg-stretching stroll, start from the parking lot by the château. Walk into Fougères with the water-filled moat on your left, then follow *Jardin Public* signs. Stop for a peek in the handsome church of St. Sulpice (English handout inside); the woodwork is exceptional, from the paneled walls and ceiling to the choir stalls and the carved altar. Then let the *Jardin Public* signs lead you through back streets, passing gingerbread-like Breton homes, up into the lush park. Walk through manicured gardens to the base of St. Léonard Church and find the floral panorama. Double back most of the way you came, then veer right to the château and under the stone gate. There's no reason to enter the château unless you need more exercise or a town map (€4.20, daily 10:00–12:30 & 14:00–18:00). For a good view of the castle without the previous climb, walk a block above the castle (up rue de la Pinterie) and find the short ramparts across from the *crêperie* recommended below.

*Eating in Fougères:* You'll find a gaggle of cafés and crêperies near the castle with good choices and prices. **Le Bonheur Est Dans le Blé** is a notch above the others, serving tasty crêpes on a lovely little terrace overlooking the valley (a block up from the château at 3 rue Fourchette, tel. 02 99 94 99 72).

# THE LOIRE

The Loire River defines this popular tourist region as it glides gently east to west, officially separating northern from southern France. The importance of this river, and the valley's prime location in the center of the country just south of Paris, has made this an essential area to defend for more than a thousand years. And defended it was, as the Loire region is home to more than a thousand castles and palaces in all shapes and sizes. When a "valley address" became a must-have among 16th-century hunting-crazy royalty, rich Renaissance palaces replaced outdated medieval castles.

Hundreds of these castles and palaces are open to visitors, and they're the reason to visit the Loire (you'll see better villages and cities elsewhere). Today's Loire Valley is carpeted with fertile fields, crisscrossed by rivers, and laced with rolling hills. It's one of France's most important agricultural regions. It's also under significant development pressure, thanks to TGV bullet trains that link it to Paris in an hour, and cheap flights to England that make it a prime second-home spot for many Brits, including Mick Jagger.

## Choosing a Home Base

This is a big, unwieldy region for travelers, so I've divided it into two halves, each centered around a good, manageable town to use as a base: Amboise or Chinon. Châteaux-holics and gardeners stay longer and sleep in both towns.

**Amboise** is the best home base for first-timers to this area, as it offers handy access to these important châteaux: Chenonceau, Blois, Chambord, Cheverny, Fougères-sur-Bièvre, Chaumont-sur-Loire, Loches, and Valençay. Amboise also has better public

**The Loire**

CHATEAU    LOIRE RIVER
RAIL    OTHER RIVERS
AUTOROUTE (TOLL)    SEE DETAIL MAPS
OTHER ROADS

TO CHARTRES & PARIS
TO PARIS
TO PARIS
TO LE MANS, NORMANDY & BRITTANY
A-10
BLOIS
CHAMBORD
CHEVERNY
CHAUMONT
AMBOISE
FOUGERES-SUR-BIEVRE
A-85
CHER RIVER
CHENONCEAU
ST. AIGNAN
TO VIERZON & BOURGES
N-138
A-28
TGV
N-10
TOURS
VILLANDRY
LANGEAIS
D-35
TO SAUMUR
A-85
N-152
INDRE
A-85
AZAY-le-RIDEAU
USSE
CHINON
INDRE RIVER
A-10
LOCHES
VALENCAY
ABBAYE ROYALE DE FONTEVRAUD
VIENNE RIVER
TO POITIERS & DORDOGNE

10 MILES
10 KM

NOTE: NOT ALL ROADS SHOWN

DCH

transportation options, making it the preferable choice if you don't want to rent a car or bike.

**Chinon** and its nearby châteaux don't feel as touristy and appeal to road-less-traveled types. The key sights in this area include the châteaux of Azay-le-Rideau, Langeais, Villandry, Chatonnière, Rivau, Ussé, and the Abbaye Royale de Fontevraud. Chinon is also optimal for bikers, with quicker access to a bike path and more interesting destinations within pedaling distance.

**Loches** and **Azay-le-Rideau** are two possible home-base options for drivers, who should also consider the tempting rural accommodations listed throughout this chapter.

Amboise is east of the big city of Tours, and Chinon lies to Tours' west. It's about a 90-minute drive from Amboise to Chinon. If you sleep in or near Amboise and plan to visit châteaux west of Tours, you're looking at around a three-hour round-trip drive (and vice versa from Chinon)—certainly doable, but not my idea of good travel. Do what you can to avoid crossing the traffic-laden city of Tours (trust me).

## Planning Your Time

With convenient trains to Paris and Charles de Gaulle Airport, the Loire can be a good first or last stop on your French odyssey

(22 trains/day between Paris and Amboise, 1.5–2 hrs; 8 trains/day between Charles de Gaulle Airport and Tours, 2 hrs; easy car rental at Tours' St. Pierre-des-Corps station).

A day and a half is sufficient to sample the best châteaux. Don't go overboard. Two châteaux, possibly three (if you're a big person), make up the recommended daily dosage. Famous châteaux are least crowded early and late in the day. Most open at about 9:00 and close between 18:00 and 19:00. During the off-season, some close at 17:00, and midday from 12:00 to 14:00.

**Drivers:** For the single best day in the Loire, consider this plan: Sleep in or near Amboise and visit Chenonceau early (arrive by 9:00), when crowds are small; spend midday at Chambord (30-min drive from Chenonceau); enjoy Chaumont or Cheverny on the way back to your hotel (the hunting dogs are fed at 17:00 on most days at Cheverny—see page 311). Remember to allow time to visit Amboise. With a second full day, move to Chinon, visiting Villandry and Langeais en route, then devote your afternoon to Chinon. The best map of the area is Michelin #518, covering all the sights described in this chapter (the TI's free map of Touraine, the area surrounding Tours, is also quite good).

Try to see one château on your drive in (for example, if arriving from the north, visit Chambord, Cheverny, or Blois; if coming from the west or the south, see Azay-le-Rideau, Chinon, Langeais, or Villandry). If you're coming from Burgundy, don't miss the remarkable Château de Guédelon (see page 730 in Burgundy chapter). If you're driving to the Dordogne from the Loire, the A-20 autoroute via Limoges (near Oradour-sur-Glane) is fastest and toll-free until Brive-la-Gaillarde.

**Without a Car:** On a tight budget, bike or catch the bus from Amboise to the town of Chenonceaux (1–2/day), tour Chenonceau (the château), then spend the afternoon enjoying Amboise, its château, and Leonardo's last stand at Clos-Lucé. With a second day, the best (but pricier) option is a minivan excursion directly from Amboise to Chambord and Cheverny. If you're watching your wallet, you can take the train to Blois, tour its castle and old town, then take the excursion bus from there to Chambord and Cheverny (runs May–mid-Sept; for more train and bus specifics, see "Transportation Connections" from Amboise, page 299). Budget travelers based in Chinon can bike to Langeais, Ussé, and Villandry, and/or take the train via Tours to Azay-le-Rideau and Langeais (the train trips are long, and not a good option for most).

A limited visit to the Loire is doable as a day trip from Paris. Several minivan and bus tours make getting to the main châteaux a breeze (see "Getting Around the Loire Valley," next).

## Getting Around the Loire Valley

If you're looking to hunt down remote châteaux, it's best to have a car. Day rentals are easy in Amboise and at the St. Pierre-des-Corps train station in Tours (but not in Chinon). Trains, buses, bikes, or minivan tours help non-drivers reach the well-known châteaux (all described below). To get to the less famous châteaux without a car, you can take a taxi, arrange for a custom minivan excursion (affordable for small groups), or hop aboard a bike (gorgeous scenery, great option for those with enough time and stamina).

### By Train

With easy access from Amboise and Chinon, the big city of Tours is the transport hub for travelers bent on using the train or buses to explore the Loire (but has little else to offer visitors). Tours has two important train stations and a major bus station (with service to several châteaux). The main train station is called Tours SNCF, and the smaller, suburban TGV station is St. Pierre-des-Corps. Check the schedules carefully, as service is sparse on some lines. The châteaux of Amboise, Blois, Chenonceau, Langeais, Chinon, and Azay-le-Rideau have some train and/or bus service from Tours' main station (although Chenonceau is better by bus or bike from Amboise). Look under each sight for specifics, and seriously consider a minivan excursion (see below).

### By Bus or Minivan Excursion

A few bus and minivan excursions offer painless transportation to the valley's châteaux. These organized itineraries make life far easier for those without a car. TIs in the region should have details on the options listed here, and on others offering similar services.

While the minivan companies listed below don't visit all the castles in this chapter, they organize custom excursions to more remote châteaux, and will pick up your small group in Amboise, Chinon, or Azay-le-Rideau (€20–35/person for half-day itineraries from Tours, €45–50 for all day; figure €200 for groups of up to 7 for 4 hours, €380 all day).

**From Amboise to Châteaux East of Tours:** This area's three big-name castles—Chenonceau, Chambord, Cheverny—are reachable via bus; minivan tours offer visits to the same three, and quick glances at a few others.

***By Bus:*** If you're on a budget and visiting in summer, the region's buses aren't a bad option. Two bus routes described below run from the Blois train station, which is an easy train ride from Amboise (14/day, 20 min).

On weekdays year-round, the #2 city bus runs from Blois to Chambord (1/day, 30–40 min, leaves Blois train station at about

## Loire Valley Châteaux at a Glance

Which châteaux should you visit—and why? Here's a quick summary.

### Châteaux East of Tours

▲▲▲**Chenonceau** For sheer elegance arching over the Cher River, and for its lovely gardens. **Hours:** Daily mid-March–mid-Sept 9:00–19:00, closes earlier off-season. See page 300.

▲▲**Blois** For its urban setting, fine courtyard, and fun sound-and-light show. **Hours:** Daily April–Sept 9:00–18:30, Oct 9:00–17:30, Nov–March 9:00–12:30 & 14:00–17:30. See page 305.

▲▲**Chambord** For its grandeur (440 rooms), fun rooftop views, and evocative setting surrounded by a forest still popular with hunters. **Hours:** Daily April–Sept 9:00–18:15, Oct–March 9:00–17:15. See page 307.

▲▲**Cheverny** For its intimate feel, lavishly furnished rooms, and daily feeding of the hunting dogs. **Hours:** Daily July–Aug 9:15–18:45, April–June and Sept 9:15–18:15, Oct 9:45–17:30, Nov–March 9:45–17:00. See page 310.

▲▲**Chaumont-sur-Loire** For its imposing setting over the Loire River, intriguing rooms, and sensational Festival of the Gardens. **Hours:** Daily May–mid-Sept 10:00–18:00, April and late Sept 10:30–17:30, Oct–March 10:00–17:00. See page 312.

▲**Amboise** For terrific views over Amboise and Leonardo da Vinci memories. **Hours:** Daily April–June 9:00–18:30, July–Aug 9:00–19:00, Sept–Oct and March 9:00–18:00, Nov–Jan 9:00–12:00 & 14:00–16:45, Feb 9:00–12:00 & 13:30–17:30. See page 286.

**Fougères-sur-Bièvre** For its medieval architecture and presentation of castle-construction techniques. **Hours:** May–mid-Sept daily 9:30–12:30 & 14:00–18:30; mid-Sept–April Wed–Mon 10:00–12:30 & 14:00–17:00, closed Tue. See page 312.

THE LOIRE

noon, returns from Chambord at about 18:00, allow €3.50, no bus on Sun). Far better is the excursion bus that runs between Blois, Chambord, and Cheverny three times a day, allowing visits to both châteaux with your pick of three return times. This service runs from mid-May to early September (departures from Blois train station are at 9:10, 11:10, and 13:40). You can stay at Chambord (the first stop) for two, five, or seven hours, then catch the next bus to

**Valençay** For its Renaissance design, lovely gardens, and kid-friendly summer events. **Hours:** Daily July–Aug 9:30–19:30, April–June and Sept–Nov 9:30–18:00, closed Dec–March. See page 315.

### Châteaux West of Tours

▲▲**Azay-le-Rideau** For its magnificent setting in a romantic reflecting pond, and for its beautifully furnished rooms. **Hours:** Daily July–Aug 9:30–19:00, April–June and Sept–Oct 9:30–18:00, Nov–March 10:00–12:30 & 14:00–17:30. See page 322.

▲▲**Villandry** For the best gardens in the Loire Valley. **Hours:** Daily April–Sept 9:00–19:00, March and Oct 9:00–18:00, Nov–Feb 9:00–17:00. See page 325.

▲**Chinon** For its dramatic setting over the Vienne River, Joan of Arc history, and glorious views. **Hours:** Daily April–Sept 9:00–19:00, Oct–March 9:30–17:00. See page 315.

▲**Langeais** For its fortress-like setting above an appealing little village, handsome rooms, and parapet walk. **Hours:** Daily July–Aug 9:00–19:00, Feb–June and Sept–mid-Nov 9:30–18:30, mid-Nov–Jan 10:00–17:00. See page 324.

**Château de Chatonnière** For its overflowing flower display in spring and early summer. **Hours:** Daily mid-March–mid-Nov 10:00–19:00. See page 326.

**Château du Rivau** For its lovely vegetable and flower gardens based on designs from medieval tapestries. **Hours:** July–Aug daily 10:00–19:00; June and Sept Wed–Mon 10:00–12:30 & 14:00–19:00, closed Tue; May and Oct Wed–Sun 14:00–19:00, closed Mon–Tue; closed Nov–April. See page 326.

**Ussé** For an exterior look at its architecture, inspiration of the romantic Sleeping Beauty story. **Hours:** Daily July–Aug 9:30–19:00, mid-Feb–June and Sept–mid-Nov 10:00–18:00, closed mid-Nov–mid-Feb. See page 326.

Cheverny, or head back to Blois (€11.50 includes bus fare and good discounts on château entries, buy tickets and get schedule from TI or bus driver, look for bus marked *Chambord/Cheverny* in front of the restaurant at the Blois train station). When combined with a visit to the château in Blois, this makes a good, full-day side-trip from Amboise. For details, call the Blois TI at 02 54 90 41 41 (also see Blois section on page 305).

*By Minivan Excursion:* **Acco-Dispo** is a small minibus company based in Amboise with good all-day château tours from Amboise and Tours. Costs vary with the itinerary (€34/half-day, €52/day, daily, free hotel pick-ups, 18 rue des Vallées, Amboise, tel. 06 82 00 64 51, fax 02 47 57 67 13, www.accodispo-tours.com). English is the primary language. While on the road, you'll usually get a fun and enthusiastic running commentary covering each château's background, as well as the region's contemporary scene—but you're on your own at each château (and you pay the admission fee). All-day tours depart 8:30–10:30 (varies by itinerary); afternoon tours depart 13:20–13:50. Both return to Amboise at about 18:30. Several itineraries are available; most include Chenonceau, and some throw in a wine tasting. Reserve two or three days ahead, if possible. Groups are small, ranging from two to eight château-hoppers. (Day-trippers from Paris find this service convenient; after a 1-hour TGV ride to Tours, you're met near the central station and returned there at day's end.) Acco-Dispo also runs multiday tours of the Loire and Brittany.

**From Chinon to Châteaux West of Tours:** Tours is a one-hour train ride from Chinon (12 trains or SNCF buses/day). Minivan excursions leave from Tours' TI to many châteaux, including Azay-le-Rideau and Villandry. Try **Acco-Dispo** (described above) or **Quart de Tours**, with daily three-hour tours to Azay-le-Rideau and Villandry for about €20 (tel. 06 85 72 16 22, fax 02 47 49 98 57, www.quartdetours.com, also offers excursions to châteaux near Amboise from Tours).

## By Bike

Cycling options are endless in the Loire, where the elevation gain is generally manageable. (However, if you have only a day or two, rent a car or stick to the châteaux easily reached by buses and minivans.) Amboise, Blois, and Chinon all make good biking bases and have rental options. A network of nearly 200 miles of bike paths and well-signed small roads connect many châteaux between Chambord and Chaumont. Pick up the free bike-path map, *Le Pays des Châteaux à Vélo*, at any TI. (I also list several accommodations with easy access to these bike paths.) Biking specifics are listed per town for Amboise, Blois, and Chinon.

Near Chinon, a 30-mile bike path runs along the Loire River, passing by Ussé and Langeais, then meeting the Cher River at Villandry and continuing along the Cher to Tours and beyond. To follow this route, pick up the *La Loire à Vélo* brochure at any area TI.

Tours-based **Detours du Loire** can deliver rental bikes to most places in the Loire for reasonable rates (5 rue du Rempart, tel. 02 47 61 22 35, www.locationdevelos.com).

## Hot-Air Balloon Rides

In France's most popular regions, you'll find hot-air balloon companies eager to take you for a ride (Burgundy, the Loire, Dordogne, and Provence are best suited for ballooning). It's not cheap, but it's unforgettable—a once-in-a-lifetime chance to sail serenely over châteaux, canals, vineyards, Romanesque churches, and villages. Balloons don't go above 3,000 feet, and usually fly much lower than this, so you get a bird's-eye view of France's sublime landscapes.

Most companies offer similar deals and work this way: Trips range from 45 to 90 minutes of air time, to which you must add an hour for preparation, champagne toast, and transport back to your starting point. Deluxe trips add a gourmet picnic, making it a three-hour event. Allow about €150–180 for a short tour, and about €260 for longer flights. Departures are, of course, weather dependent, and are usually scheduled first thing in the morning or in early evening. If you've booked ahead and the weather turns bad, you can reschedule your flight, but you can't get your money back. Most balloon companies charge about €20 more for a bad-weather refund guarantee; unless your itinerary's very loose, it's a good idea.

Flight season is from April through October. It's smart to bring a jacket for the breeze, though temperatures in the air won't differ too much from those on the ground. Air sickness is usually not a problem, as the ride is typically slow and even. Baskets have no seating, so count on standing the entire trip. Group (and basket) size can vary from 4 to 16 passengers. Area TIs have brochures. France Montgolfières gets good reviews and offers flights in the areas that we recommend (tel. 08 10 60 01 53 or 02 54 32 20 48, fax 02 54 32 20 07, www.france-montgolfiere.com).

THE LOIRE

### By Car

You can rent a car in Amboise or at Tours' St. Pierre–des-Corps train station (see "Helpful Hints" for Amboise). I've listed specific driving instructions for each destination covered in this chapter.

## Cuisine Scene in the Loire Valley

Here in "the garden of France," locally produced food is delicious. Loire Valley rivers yield fresh trout *(truite)*, salmon *(saumon)*, and smelt *(éperlau)*, which are often served fried *(friture)*. *Rillettes*, a stringy pile of cooked and whipped pork, makes for a cheap, mouthwatering sandwich spread (use lots of mustard and add a baby pickle, called a *cornichon*). The area's fine goat cheeses include Crottin de Chavignol *(crottin* means horse dung, which is what this cheese, when aged, resembles), Saint-Maure Fermier (soft and creamy), and Selles-sur-Cher (mild). For dessert, try a delicious *tarte tatin* (upside-down caramel-apple tart).

The best and most expensive white wines are the Sancerres, made on the less-touristed western edge of the Loire. Less expensive, but still tasty, are Touraine Sauvignons and the sweeter Vouvray, whose grapes are grown near Amboise. Vouvray is also famous for its light and refreshing sparkling wines (called *vins pétillants*)—locals will tell you the only proper way to begin any meal in this region is with a glass of it, and I can't disagree (try the *rosé pétillant* for a fresh sensation). The better reds come from Chinon and Bourgueil.

Remember, restaurants serve food only during lunch (11:30–14:00) and dinner (19:00–21:00, later in bigger cities); bigger cafés offer eats throughout the day.

## *East of Tours*

# Amboise

Straddling the widest stretch of the Loire River, the town slumbers in the shadow of its hilltop château. A castle has overlooked the Loire from Amboise since Roman times. Leonardo da Vinci retired here...just one more fine idea of his.

As the royal residence of François I (r. 1515–1547), Amboise wielded far more importance than you'd imagine from a lazy walk through its pleasant, pedestrian-only commercial zone. In fact, its 14,000 residents are quite conservative, giving the town an attitude—as if no one told them they're no longer the second capital of France. The locals keep their wealth to themselves; consequently, many fine mansions hide behind nondescript facades. There's even a Royalist element in Amboise (and the duke of Paris, the guy who'd be king if there was one, lives here).

The half-mile-long "Golden Island" is the only island in the Loire substantial enough to be flood-proof and to have permanent buildings (including a soccer stadium and a 13th-century church). It was important historically as the place where northern and southern France, divided by the longest river in the country, came together. Truces were made here. The Loire marked the farthest point north that the Moors conquered as they pushed through Europe from Morocco. (Loire means "impassable" in Arabic.) Today, this region still divides the country—for example, weather forecasters say, "north of the Loire...and south of the Loire..."

With or without a car, Amboise is an ideal small-town home base for exploring the best of château country.

# ORIENTATION

Amboise (pop. 14,000) covers ground on both sides of the Loire, with the "Golden Island" (l'Ile d'Or) in the middle. The train station is on the north side of the Loire, but nearly everything else is on the south (château) side, including the TI and steady traffic.

Pedestrian-friendly rue Nationale parallels the river a few blocks inland and leads from the base of Château d'Amboise through the town center and past the clock tower—once part of the town wall—to the striking Romanesque Church of St. Denis.

## Tourist Information

The information-packed TI is in the round building on the riverbank, on quai du Général de Gaulle—though the office moves to its new digs across the street in late 2009 (May–Sept Mon–Sat 9:30–18:30, Sun 9:30–13:00 & 14:00–17:00; Oct–April Mon–Sat 10:00–13:00 & 14:00–18:00, Sun 10:00–13:00; tel. 02 47 57 09 28, www.amboise-valdeloire.com). Pick up a brochure featuring their self-guided walk of the city, pre-purchase tickets to key area châteaux (which saves time in ticket lines), and ask about sound-and-light shows in the region (generally summers only). The TI can also reserve a room for you in a hotel or *chambre d'hôte* (for a €2.50 fee), but first peruse the photo album of regional *chambres d'hôte*. Their free English service, SOS Chambres d'Hôte, can tell you what rooms are still available when the TI is closed (tel. 02 47 23 27 42). Public WCs are behind the TI.

## Arrival in Amboise

**By Train:** Amboise's train station, with a post office and taxi stand, is birds-chirping peaceful. Turn left out of the station, make a quick right, and walk down rue Jules Ferry five minutes to the bridge, which leads over the Loire River to the center city. Within three blocks of the station, you'll find some of my recommended accommodations (see "Sleeping," on page 293) and one of the bike-rental shops. It's a €6 taxi ride from the station to central Amboise.

**By Car:** Drivers set their sights on the flag-festooned château that caps the hill. Most recommended accommodations and restaurants cluster just downriver (west) and either have or can help you locate free parking. Warning: If driving through Amboise with the river on your left, be aware that some streets on your right have the right-of-way when merging.

## Helpful Hints

**Market Days:** Open-air markets are held on Friday (smaller, food only) and Sunday (bigger) in the parking lot behind the TI on the river (both 8:30–13:00).

**Supermarket: Marché Plus** is across from the TI (Mon–Sat 7:00–21:00, Sun 9:00–13:00), though the shops on pedestrian-only rue Nationale are infinitely more pleasing.

**Internet Access: Playconnect Cyber C@fe** has good rates (119 rue Nationale, tel. 02 47 57 18 04).

**Bookstore: Maison de la Presse** is a fine bookstore with a small selection of English novels and a big selection of maps and English guidebooks—such as Michelin's Green Guide *Châteaux of the Loire* (English version costs €15; bookstore open Mon 14:00–19:00, Tue–Sat 8:00–19:00, Sun 9:00–13:00, near TI at 5 quai du Général de Gaulle).

**Laundry:** The handy coin-op **Lav'centre** is near the TI, up allée du Sergent Turpin at #9 (allow €7/load, daily 7:00–20:00, last wash at 19:00, English instructions). The door locks at closing time; leave beforehand, or you'll trigger the alarm.

**Bike Rental:** You can rent a bike (roughly €11/half-day, €14/day, leave your passport or a photocopy) at either of these reliable places: **Locacycle** (daily 9:00–12:30 & 14:00–19:00, full-day rentals can be returned the next morning, near TI at 2 rue Jean-Jacques Rousseau, tel. 02 47 57 00 28) or **Cycles le Duc** (rents regular and electric bikes, Tue–Sat 9:00–12:00 & 14:30–19:00, closed Sun–Mon, 5 rue Joyeuse, tel. 02 47 57 00 17). The signed bike route to Chenonceaux leads past Leonardo's Clos-Lucé.

**Taxi:** Call 02 47 57 13 53 or 06 88 02 44 10 (allow €22 to Chenonceaux, €32 in the evening or on Sun). Taxis wait at the Avis car rental across from the TI.

**Car Rental: Garage Jourdain** rents cars (roughly €48/day for a small car with 100 kilometers/62 miles free, Mon–Fri 7:45–12:00 & 14:00–18:30, Sat 9:00–12:00, closed Sun, about a mile downriver from the TI at 105 avenue de Tours, tel. 02 47 57 17 92, fax 02 47 57 77 50). Pricier **Europcar** is just outside Amboise on route de Chenonceaux (about €65/day for a small car, they'll cover the taxi from the train station, tel. 02 47 57 07 64, fax 02 47 23 25 14).

**Chocolate Fantasy:** An essential and historic stop for chocoholics is **Bigot Pâtisserie & Chocolatier** (daily, one block off the river, where place Michel Debré meets rue Nationale, tel. 02 47 57 04 46).

THE LOIRE

# SIGHTS AND ACTIVITIES

## In Amboise

▲**Château du Clos-Lucé and Leonardo da Vinci Park**—In 1516, Leonardo da Vinci packed his bags (and several of his favorite paintings, including the *Mona Lisa*) and left an imploding Rome for better wine and working conditions here, in the Loire Valley. He accepted the position of engineer, architect, and painter to the French king. This "House of Light" is the plush palace where he spent his last three years. (He died May 2, 1519.) France's Renaissance king, François I, set Leonardo up here just so he could enjoy his intellectual company. François I was 22 when his 65-year-old mentor moved in.

**Cost and Hours:** The €12.50 entry price is steep, and worthwhile only for Leonardo fans with two hours to take full advantage of this sight. Open daily April–Oct 9:00–19:00, Nov–Dec and Feb–March 9:00–18:00, Jan 9:00–17:00, follow the helpful free English handout, tel. 02 47 57 00 73, www.vinci-closluce.com.

**Getting There:** It's a 10-minute walk uphill from Château d'Amboise, past troglodyte homes. If you drive, note that the parking lot at Clos-Lucé is unsafe—don't leave anything visible in the car.

**◯ Self-Guided Tour:** Your visit begins with a tour of Leonardo's elegant yet livable Renaissance home. Find the touching sketch in Leonardo's bedroom of François I comforting his genius pal on his deathbed. The house was built in 1450—just within the protective walls of the town—as a guest house to the Château d'Amboise. Today it thoughtfully re-creates (with helpful English information) the everyday atmosphere Leonardo enjoyed as he lived here—pursuing his passions to the very end.

The basement floor is filled with sketches recording the storm patterns of Leonardo's brain and models of his remarkable inventions (inspired by nature and built according to his notes). It's hard to imagine that this Roman candle of creativity died nearly 500 years ago. In the model room, notice the entry to the long tunnel that connected this house with the château—created so the king could come and go as he pleased. The adjacent garden café is reasonable and appropriately meditative; above it is a French-only 25-minute video about Leonardo.

Your visit finishes with a stroll through the whimsical park grounds, with life-size models of his inventions (including some that function, such as a "revolving bridge"), "sound stations" (in

THE LOIRE

**Amboise**

400 YARDS
400 METERS

VIEW
PARKING
BIKE RENTAL
BUS STOP

TRAIN STN.

TO PARIS

TO 17, BLOIS + PARIS

TO VOUVRAY + TOURS

L'ILE

CAMPING

D'OR

N-152

TO 13, NAZELLES, VOUVRAY + TOURS

LOIRE

CHATEAU

RUE AUG. THIERRY

CAVE HOMES

LE CLOS-LUCE
LEONARDO'S HOUSE

ST. DENIS

TO TOURS

TO D-31, BLERE, CHENONCEAUX, MINI-CHATEAUX

TO BLOIS, CHAUMONT

PCH

1 Le Manoir les Minimes
2 Hôtel le Clos d'Amboise & Au Charme Rabelaisien Chambres
3 Le Vieux Manoir
4 Hôtel Belle-Vue
5 Hôtel le Blason & L'Alliance Rest.
6 Hôtel Café des Arts
7 La Grange Chambres
8 Chambres Art-Thé
9 L'Iris des Marais Chambres
10 Hôtel la Brèche
11 L'Auberge de Jeunesse
12 To Château de Pray

13 To Château de Noizay, Château de Nazelles & Domaine des Bidaudieres Chambres
14 To Le Moulin du Fief Gentil & La Chevalerie
15 Le Pavillon des Lys Rest.
16 L'Epicerie & Chez Bruno Rests.
17 To L'Auberge de Launay Rest.
18 Bigot Pâtisserie & Chocolatier
19 Maison de la Presse Bookstore & Marché Plus Supermarket
20 Launderette
21 Internet Café
22 Bus Stop to Chenonceaux

THE LOIRE

English), and translucent replicas of some of his paintings. Here it's clear that everything that Leonardo observed and created was based on his intense study of nature.

▲**Château d'Amboise**—This historic royal residence was partially designed by Leonardo da Vinci. The king who did most of

the building (Charles VIII) is famous for accidentally killing himself by walking into a doorjamb on his way to a tennis match (seriously). Later occupants were shorter—including his successor, Louis XII, who moved the royal court to Blois. François I brought the Renaissance here in 1516 (through Leonardo da Vinci). The good English handout gives a credible tour and provides a helpful historical perspective. While several rooms are well-decorated, no one room stands out as exceptionally furnished or compelling, and this place pales when compared to other area châteaux. Still, it's handy, and offers terrific views over Amboise that alone almost merit the entry fee.

**Cost and Hours:** €9, daily April–June 9:00–18:30, July–Aug 9:00–19:00, Sept–Oct and March 9:00–18:00, Nov–Jan 9:00–12:00 & 14:00–16:45, Feb 9:00–12:00 & 13:30–17:30, tel. 02 47 57 00 98, www.chateau-amboise.com.

➋ **Self-Guided Tour:** After climbing the flower-lined ramp, our first stop is the lacy, petite chapel where Leonardo da Vinci is supposedly buried. This flamboyant little Gothic chapel comes with two fireplaces "to comfort the king" and two plaques "evoking the final resting place" of Leonardo (one in French, the other in Italian). Where he's actually buried, no one seems to know. Look up at the ceiling to appreciate the lacy design.

Views of rooftops and the Loire River escort you to the castle entry. Inside, you'll find red-brick rooms lined with high-backed chairs and massive stone fireplaces. At stop #2 ("the Sentry Walk"), several plans show the château's original size. From here, the strategic value of this site is clear—the visibility is great and the river below provided a natural defense. The bulky horsemen's tower climbs 130 feet in five spirals—designed for a mounted soldier in a hurry. Before entering the tower ramp, take a sharp right and walk on the outside passage around the same tower; mind the gargoyles' big mouths above.

The top-floor rooms are well-furnished from the post-Revolutionary 1800s and demonstrate the continued interest in this château among French nobility. What a difference in comfort a few hundred years make.

THE LOIRE

After touring the interior, wander the gardens for good views of the château.

▲**Château d'Amboise Sound-and-Light Show**—If you're into S&L, this is considered one of the best shows of its kind in the area. While it's entirely in French, you can buy the English booklet for €5. Volunteer locals from toddlers to pensioners re-create the life of François I with costumes, juggling, impressive light displays, and fireworks. Dress warmly, and be prepared for a long show (€14–18, Wed and Sat late June–July 22:30–24:00, Aug 22:00–23:30, get details at TI or call 02 47 57 14 47, www .renaissance-amboise.com). The ticket window is on the ramp to the château and opens at 20:30. While you may feel locked in, you're welcome to leave at any time.

**Mini-Châteaux**—This scruffy five-acre park on the edge of Amboise (on the route to Chenonceaux) shows the major Loire châteaux in 1:25-scale models, forested with 2,000 bonsai trees and laced together by a model TGV train and river boats. For children, it's a fun introduction to the real châteaux they'll be visiting (and there's a cool toy store). Essential English information is posted throughout the sight (adults-€13, kids-€9, daily June–Aug 10:00–19:00, Sept–Oct 10:00–18:00, April–May 10:30–19:00, closed Nov–March, last entry one hour before closing, tel. 02 47 23 44 44, www.mini-chateaux.com).

You'll find other kid-oriented attractions at Mini-Châteaux; skip the donkey show, but consider playing a round of mini-golf and feeding the fish in the moat (a great way to get rid of that old baguette).

**Caveau des Vignerons**—This small *cave* offers free tastings of cheeses and regional wines from 12 different vintners (mid-March–mid-Nov daily 10:00–19:00; under Château d'Amboise, across from recommended l'Epicerie restaurant—see "Eating," page 298; tel. 02 47 57 23 69).

**Biking from Amboise**—Allow an hour to Chenonceaux (about 8 miles one-way), but be warned: The first two miles are uphill, and the entire ride is on a road with light traffic. White-and-green biking signs will guide you past Clos-Lucé to Chenonceaux. Serious bikers can ride to Chaumont (see page 312) in 90 minutes, connecting Amboise, Chenonceaux, and Chaumont in an all-day, 37-mile pedal (see "Recommended Bike Route" on the map on page 302).

**River Cruise**—From May to September, a flat-bottomed boat chugs riders upriver toward Chaumont, then back to Amboise. You'll get good views of Amboise's château on this otherwise uneventful trip (€8.50, leaves on the hour from 11:00–18:00, 1 hr).

## Near Amboise

**Wine-Tasting in Vouvray**—In the nearby town of Vouvray, 10 miles toward Tours from Amboise, you'll find wall-to-wall opportunities for wine-tasting, including a convenient and top-quality winery, **Marc Brédif**. They have a good selection of Vouvray wines, as well as red wines from Chinon and Bourgeuil (the most reputed reds in the Loire). Reserve ahead for their wine and cheese tastings, where five wines are paired with different cheeses. You can also take a €5 tour of their impressive 1.2 miles of cellars dug into the hillside (free tasting room, Mon–Fri 9:00–12:00 & 14:00–18:00, Sat 10:30–12:00 & 13:00–18:00, Sun 10:30–13:00, tel. 02 47 52 61 44). Coming from Amboise, you'll pass it on N-152 after Vouvray in the direction of Tours; it's on the right, a few hundred yards after you enter Rochecorbon. (For tips on wine-tasting, see "French Wine-Tasting 101" on page 30.)

**ZooParc de Beauval**—If you need a zoo fix, this is France's biggest and most impressive one, with thousands of animals from the land and sea. It's about 30 minutes southeast of Amboise toward Vierzon—pick up details at the TI (tel. 02 54 75 50 00, www.zoo beauval.com).

# SLEEPING

## In Amboise

Amboise is busy in the summer, but there are lots of reasonable hotels and *chambres d'hôte* in and around the city; the TI can help with reservations.

### In the Center

**$$$ Le Manoir les Minimes**** is a good place to experience the refined air of château life in a 17th-century mansion, with antique furniture and precious art objects in the public spaces. Its 15 large, modern rooms work for those seeking luxury (tall folks take note: top-floor attic rooms have low ceilings). Several rooms have views of Amboise's château (standard Db-€125–140, larger Db-€175–190, suite-€270, 3- to 4-person suites-€460, extra bed-€25, air-con, Wi-Fi, 3 blocks upriver from bridge at 34 quai Charles Guinot, tel. 02 47 30 40 40, fax 02 47 30 40 77, www.manoirlesminimes.com, reservation@manoirlesminimes.com, helpful Patrice and Eric).

**$$$ Hôtel le Clos d'Amboise*** is a solid value if you want luxury without the financial hit. Amboise's best upper-range urban refuge is centrally located, with lovely gardens and well-designed rooms that mix a touch of modern with a classic, traditional look (Db-€73–130—most are €120, Db suite-€140–170, Tb-€140, big

---

## Sleep Code

**(€1 = about $1.50, country code: 33)**
**S** = Single, **D** = Double/Twin, **T** = Triple, **Q** = Quad, **b** = bathroom,
**s** = shower only, **\*** = French hotel rating system (0-4 stars).
Unless otherwise noted, credit cards are accepted and English
is spoken.

To help you easily sort through these listings, I've divided
the rooms into three categories based on the price for a
standard double room with bath:

**$$$  Higher Priced**—Most rooms €90 or more.
 **$$  Moderately Priced**—Most rooms between €60-90.
  **$  Lower Priced**—Most rooms €60 or less.

---

buffet breakfast for €11, Wi-Fi, heated swimming pool, fitness room, sauna, 27 rue Rabelais, tel. 02 47 30 10 20, fax 02 47 57 33 43, www.leclosamboise.com, contact@leclosamboise.com).

**$$$ Le Vieux Manoir\*\*\*** is an entirely different high-end splurge. American expats Gloria and Bob Belknap have lovingly restored this secluded but central one-time convent with an attention to detail that Martha Stewart could learn from. The gardens are flawless, as is the atrium-like breakfast room; the public spaces are oh-so-cozy; and the six bedrooms would make an antique collector drool. Eager-to-help Gloria is a one-person tourist office (Db-

€140-185, cottages-€215-305 and require 3-night minimum stay, includes hearty breakfast, non-smoking, air-con, Internet access and Wi-Fi, easy parking, 13 rue Rabelais, tel. & fax 02 47 30 41 27, www.le-vieux-manoir.com, info@le-vieux-manoir.com).

**$$ Hôtel Belle-Vue\*\*** is central and basic, overlooking the river where the bridge hits the town. This rambling, traditional hotel has spacious public areas, dark halls, and uninspired rooms, most with modern furnishings and effective double-paned windows. Half the rooms have views up to the château; four come with huge shared terraces (Db-€76, Tb-€95, Qb-€115, elevator, 12 quai Charles Guinot, tel. 02 47 57 02 26, fax 02 47 30 51 23, bellevuehotel.amboise@wanadoo.fr).

**$ Hôtel le Blason\*\*** has 25 rooms in a 15th-century, half-timbered building five blocks from the river on a busy street. It's run by eager-to-please owners Agnes and Thomas, who speak beautiful English. The rooms are tight, bright, and well-maintained, with ship-cabin-like bathrooms, double-paned windows, and air-conditioning on the top floor (Sb-€50, Db-€60, Tb-€70, Qb-€80, quieter rooms in back and on top floor, free Internet access and Wi-Fi, secure parking, 11 place Richelieu, tel. 02 47 23 22 41, fax 02 47 57 56 18, www.leblason.fr, hotel@leblason.fr).

**$ Café des Arts** feels more like a hostel, with seven spartan rooms lodged above a local bar/café next to the château (S-€25, D-€36, 32 rue Victor Hugo, tel. & fax 02 47 57 25 04, www.cafe desarts.net, cafedesarts@free.fr).

### Chambres d'Hôtes

The heart of Amboise offers several solid bed-and-breakfast options.

**$$$ Au Charme Rabelaisien** is a drop-dead-gorgeous place run by drop-dead-charming Madame Viard. Big doors from the street open onto a grand courtyard with manicured gardens, a heated pool, and three sumptuous rooms surrounding it (Db-€120–140, €80 for third person—child only, includes breakfast, air-con, private parking, 25 rue Rabelais, tel. 02 47 57 53 84, fax 02 47 57 53 84, www .au-charme-rabelaisien.com, aucharmerabelaisien@wanadoo.fr).

**$$ La Grange Chambres** welcomes with an intimate, flowery courtyard. Each of the four comfortable rooms has been tastefully restored with modern conveniences and big beds. There's also a common room with a fridge, couch, and tables for do-it-yourself dinners (Db-€73, Tb-€80, Qb-€95, includes breakfast, cash only, where rues Châptal and Rabelais meet at 18 rue Châptal, tel. 02 47 57 57 22, www.la-grange-amboise.com, yvelinesavin-lagrange @wanadoo.fr). Adorable Yveline Savin also rents a small two-room cottage (€430–550/week, 2–3-day stays possible).

**$$ At Chambres Art-Thé,** the Savignys hide three simple but reasonably priced and well-situated rooms above their small *salon de thé,* next to the château (Db-€65, Tb-€75, includes breakfast, 8 place Michel Debré, mobile 06 81 20 79 32, jeandesavigny@free.fr).

**$ L'Iris des Marais,** run by animated Katia Frain, offers two family-oriented *chambres* in a ramshackle building on a busy road. The rooms are modest and a good value, and the artsy garden will make you smile. The upstairs room provides basic comfort, while the garden accommodation is cushier and worth booking early (Db-€50–60, cash only, includes a good breakfast, 14 quai des Marais, tel. 02 47 30 46 51, www.irisdesmarais.com, vianney.frain@wanadoo.fr).

### Near the Train Station

**$$ Hôtel la Brèche\*,** a sleepy, inexpensive place near the station, has 14 unpretentious rooms with thin walls and small bathrooms. Many rooms overlook a neglected garden; those on the street are generally larger and louder (S-€48, Sb-€58, D-€60, Db-€68, Tb-€80, Qb-€96, room for up to five-€105, includes breakfast, a few good family rooms, 15-min walk from city center and 2-min walk from station, 26 rue Jules Ferry, tel. 02 47 57 00 79, fax 02 47 57 65 49, www.labreche-amboise.com, info@labreche-amboise.com).

**Hostel: $ L'Auberge de Jeunesse** (Centre Charles Péguy) is ideally located on the western tip of the "Golden Island," a 10-minute walk from the train station. Open to people of all ages, it's friendly and easy on the wallet. There are a handful of double rooms—some with partial views to the château—so book ahead (D-€22, bunk in 3- to 4-bed room-€11, sheets-€3.50, non-members pay €1.50 extra per night, breakfast-€3, reception open daily 15:00–20:00, Ile d'Or, tel. 02 47 30 60 90, fax 02 47 30 60 91, www.mjcamboise.fr, cis@mjcamboise.fr).

## Near Amboise

The area around Amboise is replete with good-value accommodations of every shape, size, and price range. This region offers drivers the best chance to experience château life at affordable rates—and my recommendations below justify the detour. You should also consider the accommodations in Chenonceaux and Hôtel du Grand St. Michel at Chambord (both listed later in this chapter).

**$$$ Château de Pray**** is a 750-year-old fortified castle with hints of its medieval origins revealed beneath its Renaissance elegance. The 14 rooms in the main château provide all the comforts, with appropriately heavy furniture. A more recent annex offers four additional rooms (that sleep up to three each), with lofts, terraces, and views of the castle. An overflowing pool and the

restaurant's vegetable garden lie below the château (small Db in main building-€140–170, larger Db-€190, Db in annex-€135, family room-€240, extra bed-€40, no air-con; 3-min drive upriver from Amboise toward Chaumont on D-751, look for turnoff just after passing under bridge; tel. 02 47 57 23 67, fax 02 47 57 32 50, http://praycastel.online.fr, praycastel@online.fr). The dining room is as splendid as the chef is talented (he recently earned a Michelin star, though rumors are he may retire), and the service is tops—it's a relaxing place to splurge and feel good about it. Reservations are required (*menus* from €49, reasonable wine list).

**$$$ Château de Noizay**** stands proudly over the village of Noizay. With 14 elegant rooms in a 16th-century castle and five rooms in a next-door annex, it's the most expensive place I list.

THE LOIRE

You'll enter a world of polished but relaxed service, with aristocratic public spaces, a big pool, a library room, and a *très* elegant dining room (*menus* from €48). It's worth considering if Château de Pray (above) is full or if you prefer being closer to Vouvray and Tours (standard Db-€150–195, larger Db-€250–300, extra bed-€25, American breakfast-€26, annex rooms have air-con, halfway between Amboise and Vouvray in little Noizay, tel. 02 47 52 11 01, fax 02 47 52 04 64, www.chateaudenoizay.com, noizay@relais chateaux.com).

**$$$ At Château de Nazelles Chambres,** friendly owners Veronique and Olivier Fructus have tastefully restored a five-room, 16th-century hillside manor house, once home to Chenonceau's original builder. You'll be treated to a cliff-sculpted pool, lush gardens with views over Amboise, and trails to the forest above. The three rooms in the main building are four-star quality, while the two rooms cut into the rock come with private terraces and rock-walled bathrooms (Db-€105, bigger Db-€140, includes breakfast, tel. & fax 02 47 30 53 79, www.chateau-nazelles.com, info@chateau-nazelles.com). From Amboise, take N-152 toward Tours, turn right on D-5, and then turn left in Nazelles-Négron on D-1. Quickly veer right above the post office (PTT) to 16 rue Tue-la-Soif. Look for the sign on your left, and enter through the archway on the right.

**$$$ Domaine des Bidaudieres Chambres,** just outside Vouvray, offers eight rooms in a gleaming 18th-century château overlooking a large pool, with a pond and the forest beyond. This kid-friendly place, with room to roam, features big (and air-conditioned) rooms and an even bigger pool. There's also ping-pong, a fitness room, and an elevator (Db-€125, Tb-€150, two-room troglodyte apartment that sleeps up to five-€170, small cottage ideal for four-€150, includes breakfast in a striking atrium, tel. 02 47 52 66 85, fax 02 47 52 62 17, www.bidaudieres.com, resa @bidaudieres.com). It's located off D-46 on the Amboise end of Vouvray—from N-152 at Vouvray, follow D-142, then D-46 toward Vernou.

**$$ Le Moulin du Fief Gentil,** a beautifully renovated, 16th-century mill house, offers a lovely experience that's just a 15-minute drive from Amboise and Chenonceaux. You get four acres, a backyard pond (fishing possible in summer, dinner picnics anytime), the possibility of home-cooked dinners (4-course dinner *menu* with wine-€28), and large, smartly decorated rooms (Db-€80, bigger Db-€100, 2-room apartment-€135, extra person-€20, includes breakfast, cash only, tel. 02 47 30 32 51, mobile 06 64 82 37 18, www.fiefgentil.com, contact@fiefgentil.com). It's located on the edge of Bléré; from Bléré, follow signs toward Luzille, and it's on the right.

$ **La Chevalerie** owner Martine Aleksic rents four simple, bargain *chambres* that are family-friendly in every way. Here, you'll get a warm reception and total seclusion in a farm setting, with a swing set, tiny fishing pond, shared kitchens, and connecting rooms (Db-€46, Tb-€60, Qb-€76, includes breakfast with fresh eggs, cash only, in La Croix-en-Touraine, tel. 02 47 57 83 64, lyoubisa.aleksic@orange.fr). From Amboise, take D-31 toward Bléré, and look for the *Chambres d'Hôte* sign on your left at about three miles, then turn left onto C-105.

# EATING

## In Amboise

Amboise is filled with inexpensive and forgettable restaurants, but a handful of places are worthy of your attention. Most of these eateries offer a good, end-of-meal cheese platter—a rarity in France these days. The focal point for much of the city's dining is across from the château entrance.

**Le Pavillon des Lys** is the talk of Amboise. It's where locals go for a dressy meal and formal service at affordable prices. Enjoy a drink on the terrace or in the candlelit lounge before sitting down to a special dinner in an intimate, elegant setting (*menus* from €40, closed Tue and late Nov–Jan, reserve ahead, 9 rue d'Orange, tel. 02 47 30 01 01, www.pavillondeslys.com).

**L'Epicerie,** across from the château entry, attracts a few locals and many hungry tourists. It serves traditional cuisine at fair prices outdoors facing the château, or beneath wood beams inside (*menus* from €22, closed Mon–Tue, reserve ahead, 46 place Michel Debré, tel. 02 47 57 08 94).

**L'Alliance** is a sharp restaurant run by a young couple (Pamela and Ludovica) trying to make their mark in Amboise. You'll dine well on creatively prepared regional specialties in a calming outdoor courtyard, almost outdoors in a glass "greenhouse," or in a pleasing interior dining room (*menus* from €18, closed Wed, next to the Hôtel le Blason at 14 rue Joyeuse, tel. 02 47 30 52 13).

**Chez Bruno** is the answer to budget travelers' prayers. You can dine indoors, or better yet, outside at this easygoing, popular, cheap wine bar/restaurant. You can also sample the well-priced fine wines, made by the owners (4-course *menu*-€16, 2-course-€12, single-course-€9, *menus* include good salad bar, open daily, 40 place Michel Debré).

## Near Amboise

Drivers should consider making the quick drive to **Château de Pray** or **Château de Noizay** for a royal experience—but reserve first (see "Near Amboise" under "Sleeping," page 296). It's also worth a call to see if Laurent has tables available in nearby Chenonceaux, at the recommended **Hôtel la Roseraie** (15-min drive, tel. 02 47 23 90 09; see page 304).

**L'Auberge de Launay** gets rave reviews for its warm welcome, cozy ambience, and delicious meals. Owners Françoise and Helene Bail are natural hosts (*menus* from €25, daily June–Sept, otherwise closed Sun–Mon, 9 rue de la Rivière in Limeray, about 4 miles from Amboise, across the river toward Blois, tel. 02 47 30 16 82).

# TRANSPORTATION CONNECTIONS

## By Bus and Taxi

**From Amboise to Nearby Châteaux:** For easiest access to area châteaux, see "Getting Around the Loire Valley," page 281.

**By Bus to: Chenonceaux** (1–2/day, Mon–Sat only, none on Sun, 15 min, one-way-€1.10; departs Amboise about 9:55, returns from Chenonceaux at about 12:25, allowing you about 80 min at the château; in summer, there's also an afternoon departure at about 14:55, with a return from Chenonceaux at about 17:10; the Amboise stop is on quai du Général de Gaulle on the non-river side of the street opposite the post office—look for the green-and-yellow sign at bus stop, confirm times with the TI; the Chenonceaux stop is across the street from the TI, tel. 02 47 05 30 49); **Tours** (8/day Mon–Sat, none on Sun, buses are cheaper than trains—about €2.50).

**By Taxi:** A cab from Amboise to Chenonceaux costs about €22, or €32 on Sundays and after 19:00. (Other châteaux are too expensive by cab.) Your hotel can call one for you (or call your own—see "Helpful Hints" on page 288). The meter doesn't start until you do.

## By Train

### Destinations Within the Loire

**From Amboise by Train to: Blois** (14/day, 20 min, bus excursions from there to Chambord and Cheverny—see "Getting Around the Loire Valley" on page 281), **Tours** (12/day, 25 min, allows connections to châteaux west of Tours), **Chinon** (9/day, 90 min, transfer in Tours).

### Beyond the Loire

Twelve 15-minute trains link Amboise daily to the regional train hub of St. Pierre-des-Corps (in suburban Tours). There, you'll find reasonable connections to distant points (including the TGV to Paris' Gare Montparnasse). Transferring in Paris can be the fastest way to reach many French destinations, even in the south.

THE LOIRE

**From Amboise by Train to: Paris** (12/day, 1.5 hrs to Paris' Gare Montparnasse with change to TGV at Tours' St. Pierre-des-Corps, requires TGV reservation; 10/day, 2 hrs direct to Paris' Gare d'Austerlitz, no reservation required), **Sarlat** (4/day, 5–6 hrs, several routes possible, best is to change at Tours' St. Pierre-des-Corps, then TGV to Libourne or Bordeaux–St. Jean, then train through Bordeaux vineyards to Sarlat; it's a bit slower on the route via Les Aubrais Orléans to Souillac then scenic SNCF bus to Sarlat), **Limoges** (near Oradour-sur-Glane, 9/day, 4 hrs, change at Tours' St. Pierre-des-Corps and Vierzon or at Les Aubrais–Orléans and Vierzon, then tricky bus connection from Limoges to Oradour-sur-Glane—see page 375), **Pontorson–Mont St. Michel** (2–3/day, 5.5–7.5 hrs via transfers at Caen and Tours or Rennes, Le Mans, and Tours), **Bayeux** (12/day, 5–6 hrs, change in Caen and Tours, or at Paris's Gare Montparnasse and Tours' St. Pierre-des-Corps), **Beaune** (8/day, 6 hrs, most with changes in Paris and in Dijon—arrive at Paris' Austerlitz station, then Métro to Gare de Lyon).

# Chenonceaux

This one-road, sleepy village—with a knockout château—makes a good home base for drivers. Note that Chenonceaux is the name of the town, and Chenonceau (no "x") is the name of the château, but they're pronounced the same: shuh-nohn-soh.

## ORIENTATION

### Tourist Information

The small TI is on the main road from Amboise as you enter the village (Mon–Sat 10:00–12:30 & 14:00–18:30, closed Sun, tel. 02 47 23 94 45). Warning: Because this parking lot is not patrolled, don't leave any luggage visible in your car. The bus stops are at the TI; the Amboise-bound stop is unsigned and across the street from the TI (1–2 buses/day to Amboise, Mon–Sat only, none on Sun, 15 min).

### Helpful Hints

**Money:** There's an ATM near the château ticket office.

**Internet Access:** The town's entrepreneurial **Tabac**, a few doors east of the recommended Hostel du Roy, has one computer (€3/20 min, open daily, on rue du Dr. Bretonneau). They also sell English-language newspapers.

**Picnic Supplies: La Maison des Pages** has some bakery items, cold drinks to go, and just enough groceries for a modest picnic (on the main drag between Hostel du Roy and Hôtel la Roseraie).

**Bike Rental:** The **Tabac** (see "Internet Access," previous page) has a few bikes for rent, as does the recommended **Relais Chenonceaux** (May–Sept daily 9:00–19:00, see "Sleeping," on page 305).

# SIGHTS

### ▲▲▲Château de Chenonceau

Chenonceau is the toast of the Loire. This 16th-century Renaissance palace arches gracefully over the Cher River and is impeccably maintained, with fresh flower arrangements in the summer and

roaring log fires in the winter. Understandably popular, Chenonceau is the third-most-visited château in France (after Versailles and Fontainebleau). Chenonceau's crowds are worth planning around; to beat them, arrive by 9:00 or after 17:00.

Plan on a 15-minute walk from the parking lot to the château.

**Cost and Hours:** Château–€10; audioguide–€4; château, audioguide, and wax museum–€15; daily mid-March–mid-Sept 9:00–19:00, closes earlier off-season; tel. 02 47 23 90 07, www .chenonceau.com. Consider a moonlit **evening walk**—"*promenade nocturne*"—on the château grounds (€5, July–Aug daily 21:30–23:30, only Fri–Sun in June, none Sept–May).

**Tours:** The interior is fascinating—but only if you take full advantage of the free and excellent 20-page **booklet** (included with entry), or rent an audioguide. Two different **iPod video/audioguide tours** are available (45 and 90 min); the 45-minute tour is plenty. There's also a 45-minute audioguide for kids (€4 for any audioguide, leave ID as deposit). Pay for the audioguide when you're buying your ticket (before entering the château grounds), then pick up the iPod just inside the château's door.

**Wax Museum (La Galerie des Dames–Musée de Cires):** This museum—located in the château stables—puts a waxy face on the juicy history of the château (€3, tickets only available at the château ticket office). It's well-described in English, with a focus on period clothing, and provides a good introduction before you sightsee.

**Cuisine Art:** A reasonable cafeteria is next door to the wax museum. Fancy meals are served in the orangery behind the stables. There's a cheap *crêperie*/sandwich shop at the entrance gate.

**Boat Trips:** In summer, the château has rental **rowboats**—an idyllic way to savor graceful château views (€2/30 min, July–Aug daily 10:00–19:00, 4 people/boat).

**Background:** While earlier châteaux were built for defensive purposes, Chenonceau was the first great pleasure palace.

**Châteaux near Amboise**

Nicknamed "the château of the ladies," it housed many famous women over the centuries. The original builder's wife oversaw the construction of the main part of the château. In 1547, King Henry II gave the château to his mistress, Diane de Poitiers, who added an arched bridge across the river to access the hunting grounds. She enjoyed her lovely retreat until Henry II died (pierced in a jousting tournament in Paris) and his vengeful wife, Catherine de Médicis, unceremoniously kicked her out (and into the château of Chaumont, described on page 312). Catherine added the three-story structure on Diane's bridge. She died before completing her vision of a matching château on the far side of the river, but not before turning Chenonceau into *the* place to see and be seen by local aristocracy. (Note that whenever you see a split coat of arms, it belongs to a woman—half her husband's and half her father's.)

○ **Self-Guided Tour:** Strut like an aristocrat down the tree-canopied path to the château. (There's a fun plant maze partway up on the left.) You'll cross three moats and two bridges, and pass an old round tower, which predates the main building. Notice the tower's fine limestone veneer, added so the top would better fit the new château.

The main château's original oak door greets you with Fs (for François I, r. 1515–1547), his fire-breathing salamander emblem, and coats of arms. The knocker is high enough to be used by visitors on horseback. The smaller door within the larger one could be for two purposes: to slip in after curfew, and to enter during winter without letting out all the heat.

As you continue, read your pamphlet or listen to your audioguide, and also pay attention to these details:

In the **guard room,** the best-surviving original tiles are near the walls. While the tapestries kept the room cozy, they also functioned to tell news or recent history (to the king's liking, of course).

The superbly detailed **chapel** survived the vandalism of the Revolution because the fast-thinking lady of the palace filled it with firewood. Angry masses were supplied with mallets and instructions to smash everything royal or religious. While this room was both, all they saw was stacked wood. The hatch door provided a quick path to the kitchen and an escape boat downstairs. The windows, blown out during World War II, are replacements from the 1950s.

The centerpiece of the **bedroom of Diane de Poitiers** is a severe portrait of Catherine de Médicis at 40 years old. After the queen booted out the mistress, she placed her own portrait over the fireplace, but she never used this bedroom. The 16th-century tapestries are among the finest in France. Each one took an average of 60 worker-years to make. Study the complex compositions of the *Triumph of Charity* and the violent *Triumph of Force*.

At 200 feet long, the three-story **gallery** spans the river. The upper stories house double-decker ballrooms and guest rooms. Notice how differently the slate and limestone of the checkered floor wear after 500 years. Imagine grand banquets here. Catherine, a contemporary of Queen Elizabeth I of England, wanted to rule with style. She threw wild parties and employed her ladies to circulate and soak up all the political gossip possible from the well-lubricated Kennedys and Rockefellers of her realm. Parties included grand fireworks displays and mock naval battles on the river.

For a quick walk outside (and more good palace views), cross the bridge, pick up a re-entry ticket, then stroll the other bank of the Cher (across the river from the château). The river you crossed marked the border between free and Nazi France in World War II.

Back then, Chenonceau witnessed many prisoner swaps. During World War I, the Grand Gallery also served as a military hospital, where more than 2,200 soldiers were cared for—picture hundreds of beds lining the gallery.

Back inside the gallery, the state-of-the-art (in the 16th century) **kitchen** is not to be missed. It was built near water (to fight the inevitable kitchen fires) and in the basement; since heat rises, the placement helped heat the palace. Beyond the fancy servants' dining room, there's a landing bay for goods to be ferried in and out.

The staircase leading **upstairs** wowed royal guests. It was the first non-spiral staircase they'd seen...quite a treat in the 16th century. The upper gallery usually contains a temporary modern-art exhibit. Small side rooms on the upper floor show fascinating old architectural sketches of the château. The walls, 20 feet thick, were honeycombed with the flues of 224 fireplaces and passages for servants to do their pleasure-providing work unseen. There was no need for plumbing. Servants fetched, carried, and dumped everything pipes do today. The balcony provides excellent views of the gardens—originally functional with vegetables and herbs. (Diane built the one to the right, Catherine the one to your left.) The estate is still full of wild boar and deer—the primary dishes of past centuries. The third floor is worth a peek for its black bedroom, designed by a widow whose husband was murdered by a monk.

## SLEEPING

**(€1 = about $1.50, country code: 33)**
Hotels are a good value in Chenonceaux.

**$$ Hôtel la Roseraie*** is like an Impressionist painting you can walk right into. It has a flowery terrace and 17 warmly decorated, French-country rooms. Laurent and Sophie try their best to spoil you in their entirely non-smoking hotel (standard Db-€70–85, big Db-€99–125, a few grand family rooms-€125–180, queen- or king-size beds, air-con, Internet access and Wi-Fi, free parking, heated pool, pleasant gardens, across from Hôtel du Bon Laboreur at 7 rue du Dr. Bretonneau, closed mid-Nov–March, tel. 02 47 23 90 09, fax 02 47 23 91 59, www.charmingroseraie.com, sfiorito @wanadoo.fr). The classy dining room and charming terrace are ideal for a nice dinner, available for guests and non-guests alike. Just be sure to reserve ahead (€27–47 *menus*, closed Mon).

**$$ Relais Chenonceaux\*\*\***, across from Hôtel la Roseraie, has a nice patio and unimaginative but wood-finished rooms at fair rates. The coziest—and warmest—rooms are on the top floor, but watch your head (Db-€62–70, Tb-€72–80, Qb-€100, tel. 02 47 23 98 11, fax 02 47 23 84 07, 10 rue du Dr. Bretonneau, www .chenonceaux.com, info@chenonceaux.com).

**$ Hostel du Roy\*\*** offers 32 simple rooms, some in a quiet garden courtyard, and a mediocre but inexpensive restaurant (Db-€42–60, Tb-€60, Qb-€64–92, room for up to 5-€110, 9 rue du Dr. Bretonneau, tel. 02 47 23 90 17, fax 02 47 23 89 81, www.hostel duroy.com, hostelduroy@wanadoo.fr).

## EATING

For a treat, reserve ahead for **Hôtel la Roseraie** (closed Mon). **Relais Chenonceaux,** with its pleasant interior and exterior terrace, serves up crêpes, salads, and *plats* at decent prices (daily). Both of these are listed under "Sleeping," previous page.

## TRANSPORTATION CONNECTIONS

**From Chenonceaux by Train to: Tours** (3/day, 30 min).

**By Bus to: Amboise** (1–2/day, Mon–Sat only, none on Sun, 15 min, one-way-€1.10, departs Chenonceaux at about 12:25, and in summer also at about 17:10, catch bus across the street from the TI, tel. 02 47 05 30 49).

**By Taxi to: Amboise** (€22, or €32 on Sun and after 19:00).

# Blois

Bustling Blois is a good mini-urban stop in this rural region.

Blois (pronounced "blah") owns a rich history, dolled-up pedestrian areas, a handsome château, good train service to Paris and Amboise, and quick access to Chambord and Cheverny by excursion bus or car (see "Getting Around the Loire Valley," page 281).

## ORIENTATION

Unlike most other châteaux, Blois' Château Royal is right in the city center, without a nearby forest, river, or lake. It's an easy walk from the train station, near ample underground parking, and just above the TI.

THE LOIRE

## Arrival in Blois

Train travelers can walk 10 minutes straight out of the station down avenue Jean Laigret to the TI and château (or take a taxi from in front of the station). Drivers follow signs reading *Centre-Ville* and *Château* (metered parking along avenue Jean Laigret or inside at Parking du Château—first 30 min free).

## Tourist Information

The TI is just across from the château entrance (May–Sept Mon–Sat 9:00–19:00, Sun 10:00–19:00; Oct–April Mon–Sat 9:30–12:30 & 14:00–18:00, Sun 10:00–13:00; 23 place du Château, tel. 02 54 90 41 41). Save time as you explore the center of Blois by using the TI's handy walking-tour brochure (skip the €6 audioguide). The brown and purple routes are best. The TI also has information on bike rentals.

# SIGHTS AND ACTIVITIES

▲▲**Château Royal**—Louis XII and François I each called this château home, and it's here where Catherine de Médicis spent her last night. At the castle's ticket office, pick up the helpful English brochure, then read the well-presented English displays.

Begin in the courtyard, where four different wings—ranging from Gothic to Neoclassical—underscore this château's importance over many centuries. (Find the model of the château to get your bearings.) Visit the interior counterclockwise. Begin to the right after entering the courtyard, in the dazzling Hall of the Estates-General; continue to a great display of gargoyles and models in a small lapidary museum; then go up through several richly tiled and decorated royal rooms (can you say busy?). Your visit ends with a walk through the ironworks room and a mini fine-arts museum, with a 16th-century who's-who portrait gallery where you can see what the château's inhabitants looked like.

**Cost and Hours:** €7.50, €12.50 combo-ticket with House of Magic—described below, daily April–Sept 9:00–18:30, Oct 9:00–17:30, Nov–March 9:00–12:30 & 14:00–17:30, tel. 02 54 55 26 26).

**Sound-and-Light Show:** Though usually in French, it's still worthwhile. An English version is planned for Wednesdays—confirm locally (€7, €11.50 combo-ticket also covers daytime château entry, €16.50 gets you both plus the House of Magic, next; daily April–Sept at about 22:00).

**House of Magic**—The home of Jean-Eugène Robert-Houdin, the illusionist whose name was adopted by Harry Houdini, offers an interesting but overpriced history of illusion and magic. Several daily shows have no words, so they work in any language (30 min, schedule posted at entry). Kids enjoy the gift shop (€7.50,

€12.50 combo-ticket with château; July–Aug daily 10:00–12:30 & 14:00–18:00; Sept–June Tue–Sun 10:00–12:30 & 14:00–18:00, closed Mon; at the opposite end of the square from the château).

**Biking from Blois**—Cycling from Blois to Chambord involves a level 75-minute, one-way ride, and allows connections to a good network of bike paths. Adding Cheverny makes a full-day, 30-mile round-trip (details available at TI).

## SLEEPING

**(€1 = about $1.50, country code: 33)**

If you need to bed down in Blois, do so at the warm and friendly **$ Hôtel Anne de Bretagne**** (Sb-€46, Db-€56–62, Tb-€74, Qb-€84, 150 yards uphill from Parking du Château, 5-min walk below the train station at 31 avenue Jean Laigret, tel. 02 54 78 05 38, fax 02 54 74 37 79, http://annedebretagne.free.fr, annedebretagne@free.fr).

## EATING

If you're stopping in Blois around lunchtime, plan on eating at **Le Marignan,** located on a breezy, traffic-free square in front of the château (daily, good salads, fast service, 5 place du Château, tel. 02 54 74 73 15). At the top of the hour, you can watch the stately mansion opposite the château become "the dragon house," as monsters crane their long necks out its many windows.

## TRANSPORTATION CONNECTIONS

**From Blois by Train to: Amboise** (14/day, 20 min), **Chinon** (9/day, 2 hrs, transfer in Tours), **Paris** (14/day, 1.5 hrs).

**By Bus:** The excursion bus to **Chambord** and **Cheverny** leaves from the train station in Blois (3/day in summer only; see "Getting Around the Loire Valley," page 281), as does the once-a-day bus #2 to **Chambord** (30–40 min, €3.50, no bus on Sun).

# Château de Chambord

With its huge scale and distinctly prickly silhouette, Château de Chambord, worth ▲▲, is the granddaddy of all châteaux in the Loire. It's surrounded by Europe's largest enclosed forest park, a game preserve defined by a 20-mile-long wall and teeming with wild deer and boar. Chambord (shahn-bor) began as a simple hunting lodge for bored Blois counts and became a monument to the royal sport and duty of hunting. (Apparently, hunting was considered important to keep the animal population under control and the vital forests healthy.)

The château, six times the size of most, has 440 rooms, and a fireplace for every day of the year. It consists of a keep in the shape of a Greek cross, with four towers and two wings surrounded by stables. It has four floors, with many stairs in between thanks to the high ceilings. The ground floor has reception rooms, the first floor up houses the royal apartments, the second floor up is mostly a hunting museum, and the rooftop offers a hunt-viewing  terrace. Because hunting visibility is best after autumn leaves fall, Chambord was a winter palace (which helps explain the number of fireplaces). Only 80 of Chambord's rooms are open to the public—and that's plenty. This place would be great for hide-and-seek.

**Cost and Hours:** €9.50 July–Aug, €8.50 Sept–June, parking-€3, daily April–Sept 9:00–18:15, Oct–March 9:00–17:15, last entry 30 min before closing (but you'll need more time there anyway), tel. 02 54 50 50 40, www.chambord.org. There are two ticket offices: one in the village in front of the château, and another inside the château. Call ahead to verify hours, guided tour times, horse shows, and evening visits.

**Getting There:** On weekdays, bus #2 connects Chambord with Blois' train station (1/day, 30–40 min, leave Blois at about noon, return from Chambord at about 18:00, allow €3.50, no bus on Sun). The Blois excursion bus is better (€11.50, three daily departures from Blois station mid-May–early Sept; for more info, see "Getting Around the Loire Valley," page 281).

**Information:** This château requires helpful information to make it come alive. All rooms except the hunting museum have good English explanations (the free brochure is useless). Overachievers can rent an audioguide (€4) for a thorough history of the château and its rooms.

**Services:** There's a fantastic bookshop in the château with a good selection of children's books. Among the collection of shops near the château, you'll find an ATM, WCs, local souvenirs, a wine-tasting room, and cafés. Bikes, rowboats, and electric boats can be rented across the tiny road by the canal. The canal is small, so room for boating is limited.

**Horse-Riding Demonstrations:** These take place daily in summer (€9.50; July–Aug daily at 11:45 and 16:30; May–June and Sept Tue–Fri at 11:45, Sat–Sun at 11:45 and 16:30, none on Mon; no demonstrations Oct–April; tel. 02 54 20 31 01).

**Views:** For the best views, cross the small river in front of the château and turn right toward the picnic perch. The Hôtel du

Grand St. Michel has a broad view terrace, ideal for post-château refreshment (see "Sleeping," later in this section).

○ **Self-Guided Tour:** Starting in 1518, François I created this "weekend retreat," using 1,800 workmen over 15 years. (You'll see his signature salamander symbol everywhere.) François I was an absolute monarch—with an emphasis on absolute. In 32 years of rule (1515–1547), he never once called the Estates-General to session (a rudimentary Parliament in *ancien régime* France). This grand hunting palace was another way to show off his power. Charles V—the Holy Roman Emperor and most powerful man of the age—was invited here and was, like, totally wowed. Here are the highlights:

The ground-floor **reception rooms** offer little to see, except for the subtitled video with helpful information on the château's construction.

Climb the monumental **double-spiral staircase,** which was likely inspired by Leonardo da Vinci, who died just as construction was starting. Allowing people to go up and down without passing each other (look up the center from the ground floor), it's a masterpiece of the French Renaissance. Peek at other visitors through the openings as you climb, and admire the ingenious design.

The first floor up offers the most interesting rooms: the very royal apartments in the **king's wing,** including François I's, Louis XIV's, and Maria Theresa's bedrooms. Gaze at their portraits and get to know them. I like François' bedroom the best—because he was a traveling king, his furniture was designed to be easily disassembled and moved with him (seems pretty thrifty for a king). The rooms devoted to the **Count of Chambord,** the final owner of the château, are also worth your time. This 19th-century count, last of the French Bourbons, was next in line to be the king when France decided it didn't need one. He was raring to rule. You'll see his coronation outfits and even souvenirs from the coronation that never happened. Check out his boyhood collection of little guns, including a working mini-cannon.

The second floor up has beautiful coffered ceilings (notice the "F" for you-know-who) and holds a series of ballrooms that once hosted post-hunt parties. It's now a **museum** with finely crafted hunting weapons and exhibits on myths, legends, traditions, and techniques from the 16th, 17th, and 18th centuries—unfortunately, with little information in English.

To see what happens when you put 365 fireplaces in your house (used to heat the palace in winter even today), climb to the **rooftop.** A pincushion of spires and chimneys decorates a viewing terrace, where the ladies would enjoy the spectacle of their ego-pumping hunters. On hunt day, a line of beaters would fan out and work inward from the distant walls, flushing wild game to the center, where the king and his buddies waited. Note the lantern tower of the tallest spire, which glowed with a nighttime torch when the king was in. From the rooftop, view the elegant king's wing—marked by *FRF (François Roi de France)* and bristling with fleurs-de-lis.

# SLEEPING

## Near Chambord and Cheverny
(€1 = about $1.50, country code: 33)

**$$ Hôtel du Grand St. Michel**\*\* lets you wake up with Chambord outside your window. It's an Old World, hunting-lodge kind of place with recently redone rooms and a trophy-festooned dining room (€22 and €28 *menus*). Sleep here, and you'll have a chance to roam the château grounds after the peasants have been run out (small Db-€55–66, standard Db-€65–75, Db with view of château-€75–90—worth the extra cost, extra bed-€12, tel. 02 54 20 31 31, fax 02 54 20 36 40, on place Saint Louis, www.saintmichel -chambord.com, hotelsaintmichel@wanadoo.fr).

**$$ Chambres la Flânerie,** on the bike route from Chambord to Cheverny, offers two family rooms in an adorable home. It's riddled with flowers, crawling with ivy, and surrounded by wheat fields and forests. The gentle Delabarres speak enough English, and have bikes to loan their fortunate guests (Db-€62, Tb-€80, Qb-€96, 25 rue de Gallerie, tel. 02 54 79 86 28, mobile 06 75 72 28 41, www.laflanerie.com, laflanerie@laflanerie.com). Coming from Blois on D-765, it's before Cheverny in the hamlet of Les Fées, right after the antique shop on the left. Turn right at the wooden bus shelter, where you'll see a sign to *Eric Auge Menuiserie,* then follow *Flânerie* signs.

THE LOIRE

# Cheverny

This stately hunting palace, a ▲▲ sight, is the most lavishly furnished of all the Loire châteaux. Those who complain that the Loire châteaux have stark and barren interiors missed Cheverny (shuh-vehr-nee). Because the palace was built and decorated from 1604 to 1634, and is immaculately preserved, it offers a unique architectural harmony and unity of style. From the start, this château has been in the Hurault family, and Hurault pride shows in its flawless preservation and intimate feel. The viscount's family still lives on the third floor. (You'll see some family photos.) Cheverny was spared by the French Revolution; the owners were popular then, as today, even among the village farmers.

The château is flanked by a pleasant village, with a small grocery, cafés offering good lunch options, and a few hotels. The town is easy to reach from Blois or Amboise by bus or minivan tour (see "Getting Around the Loire Valley," page 281).

**Cost and Hours:** €7, daily July–Aug 9:15–18:45, April–June and Sept 9:15–18:15, Oct 9:45–17:30, Nov–March 9:45–17:00, tel. 02 54 79 96 29, www.chateau-cheverny .fr. Get the English self-guided-tour brochure— which describes the interior beautifully—inside the château, not where you buy your ticket.

❍ **Self-Guided Tour:** Walking across the manicured grounds, you approach the gleaming château, with its row of Roman emperors, including Julius Caesar in the center. Inside, the private apartments upstairs were occupied until 1985 (the viscount's family now lives a floor above), and show the French art of living. In the **bedroom**—literally fit for a king—study the fun ceiling art, especially the "boys will be boys" cupids. You'll find a Raphael painting, a grandfather clock with a second hand that's been ticking for 250 years, a family tree going back to 1490, and a letter of thanks from George Washington to this family for their help in booting out the English. The attic of the orangery out back was filled during World War II with treasures from the Louvre, including the *Mona Lisa*.

Barking dogs remind visitors that the viscount still loves to hunt. The **kennel** (200 yards in front of the château, look for *Chenil* signs) is especially interesting at dinnertime, when the 70 hounds are fed (April–mid-Sept daily at 17:00, mid-Sept–March Mon and Wed–Fri at 15:00). The dogs—half English foxhound and half French Poitou—are bred to have big feet and bigger stamina. They're given food once a day, and the feeding *(la soupe des chiens)* is a fun spectacle that shows off their strict training. Before chow time, the hungry hounds fill the little kennel rooftop and watch the trainer bring in troughs stacked with delectable raw meat. He opens the gate, and the dogs gather enthusiastically around the food, yelping hysterically. Only when the trainer says to eat can they dig in. You can see the dogs at any time, but the feeding show is fun to plan for. The adjacent trophy room is stuffed with more than a thousand antlers and the heads of five wild boar.

THE LOIRE

# Fougères-sur-Bièvre

The feudal castle of Fougères-sur-Bièvre (foo-zher sewr bee-ehv) dominates its hamlet and is worth a stop, even if you don't go inside (but I would). Located a few minutes from Cheverny on the way to Chenonceaux and Amboise, Fougères-sur-Bièvre was constructed for defense, not hunting, and was built over the small river (to provide an unlimited water supply during sieges). Leveled in the Hundred Years' War, then rebuilt in the 1500s, it's completely restored. While there are no furnishings (there weren't many in the Middle Ages in any case), it gives a good look at how castles were built.

Follow the route with the helpful English handout (brief English explanations are also provided in most rooms). You'll see models of castle-construction techniques, including interesting exhibits on the making of half-timbered walls (oak posts and crossbeams provided the structural skeleton, and the areas between were filled in with a mix of clay, straw, and pebbles). Walk under medieval roof supports, gaze through loopholes, and stand over machicolations (holes for dropping rocks and scalding liquids on attackers) in the main tower. Seeing the main tower from within adds an entirely new appreciation of these structures' complexity, and the two medieval latrines demonstrate how little toilet technology has changed in 800 years.

**Cost and Hours:** €5; May–mid-Sept daily 9:30–12:30 & 14:00–18:30; mid-Sept–April Wed–Mon 10:00–12:30 & 14:00–17:00, closed Tue; last entry 30 min before closing, tel. 02 54 20 27 18, http://fougeres-sur-bievre.monuments-nationaux.fr).

**Getting There:** Fougères-sur-Bièvre has no easy public-transport link from Amboise...or anywhere else. If you're *sans* rental car or bike, arrange for a custom minivan tour—or skip it.

# Chaumont-sur-Loire

A castle has been located on this spot since the 11th century. The current version is a ▲▲ sight. The first priority here was defense. You'll appreciate the strategic location on the long climb up from the village below. (Drivers can avoid the uphill hike by going up and around to park at the higher *Annex du Château* entrance—follow *Stade du Tennis* signs as you climb.) Gardeners will appreciate the extraordinary Festival of Gardens (every year from mid-May to October, described below). Anglophones will miss the better English information provided at other châteaux.

**Cost and Hours:** €7.50, includes stables, daily May–mid-Sept 10:00–18:00, April and late Sept 10:30–17:30, Oct–March 10:00–17:00, last entry 30 min before closing, stables close daily 12:00–14:00, ticket office sometimes closes during lunch off-season, English handout available, tel. 02 54 51 26 26, www.domaine-chaumont.fr.

**Getting There:** There is no public transport to Chaumont; bikes and chartered minivans are the only means for non-drivers to visit this château (see "Getting Around the Loire Valley," page 281).

**Festival of Gardens:** This annual exhibit, with 25 elaborate gardens arranged around a different theme each year, draws rave reviews from international gardeners (€9, not included in château admission, May–mid-Oct only, tel. 02 54 20 99 22, www.chaumont-jardins.com).

**Background:** The Chaumont (show-mon) château you see today was built mostly in the 15th and 16th centuries. Catherine de Médicis forced Diane de Poitiers to swap Chenonceau for Chaumont; you'll see tidbits about both women inside. Louis XVI, Marie-Antoinette, Voltaire, and Benjamin Franklin all spent time here. Today's château offers a good look at the best defense design in 1500: on a cliff with a dry moat, big and small drawbridges with classic ramparts, loopholes for archers, and machicolations—hot oil, anyone?

**○ Self-Guided Tour:** Your walk through the palace—restored mostly in the 19th century—is poorly described in the flier you'll pick up as you enter. Here's some helpful information on what you'll see.

Start at the entry, littered with various coats of arms. As you walk in, take a close look at the two drawbridges. Inside, the heavy defensive feel is replaced with palatial luxury. Around 1700, a more stable age, the fourth wing was taken down to give the terrace its river-valley view. The 165-foot-deep well is fun for echoes. Study the entertaining spouts and decor on the courtyard walls.

A case contains **ceramic portrait busts** dating from 1770, when the lord of the house had a tradition of welcoming guests by having their portrait sketched, then giving them a ceramic bust made from this sketch when they departed. Find Ben Franklin's medallion.

The **dining room**'s fanciful limestone fireplace is exquisitely carved. Find the food (frog legs, snails, goats for cheese), the maid with the bellows, and even the sculptor with a hammer and chisel at the top (on the left).

The treasury box in the **guard room** upstairs is a fine example of 1600s-era locksmithing. The lord's wealth could be locked up here as safely as possible in those days, with a false keyhole, no handles, and even an extra box inside for diamonds.

The exquisitely tiled **Salle de Conseil** has wall-to-wall tapestries, and fireplaces designed to keep this meeting room warm.

The **bedroom** has a private balcony that overlooks the chapel, handy when the lord wanted to go to church on a bad-hair day. The sentimental glass, from 1880, shows scenes from the castle's history. The tiny balcony window has an original etching of Catherine de Médicis' favorite nephew. Gaze at him and imagine the elegance of 16th-century court life. Catherine de Médicis, who missed her native Florence, brought a touch of Italy to all her châteaux. As you leave, appreciate the nifty central handrail on the spiral staircase.

The **stables** *(ecuries)* were entirely rebuilt in the 1880s. The medallion above the door reads *pour l'avenir* (for the future), which shows off a real commitment to horse technology. Inside, circle clockwise—you can almost hear the horses walking about. Notice the deluxe horse stalls, padded with bins and bowls for hay, oats, and water, and complete with a strategically placed drainage gutter. The horses were named for Greek gods and great châteaux. The Horse Kitchen (Cuisine des Chevaux) produced mash twice weekly for the horses. The horse gear was rigorously maintained for the safety of carriage passengers. The covered alcove is where the horse and carriage were prepared for the prince, and the round former kiln was redesigned to be a room for training the horses.

The estate is a **tree garden,** set off by a fine lawn. Trees were imported from throughout the Mediterranean world to be enjoyed—and to fend off any erosion on this strategic bluff. The annual **Festival of Gardens** (described on previous page) takes place behind the stables.

THE LOIRE

# Loches and Valençay

The overlooked town of **Loches** (lohsh), located about 30 minutes south of Amboise, makes a good base for drivers wanting to visit sights east and west of Tours (in effect triangulating between Amboise and Chinon), but has no easy connections via train or bus. This pretty town sits on the region's loveliest river, the Indre, and holds an appealing mix of medieval monuments, stroll-worthy streets, and fewer tourists. Its château dominates the skyline and is worth a short visit. The Wednesday street market is small but lively. For an overnight stay, try **$$ Hôtel George Sand\*\*\***, located on the river, with a well-respected restaurant, idyllic terrace, and rustic, comfortable rooms (Db-€67, Tb-€74, Qb-€115, Wi-Fi, no elevator, 300 yards south of TI at 39 rue Quintefol, tel. 02 47 59 39 74, fax 02 47 91 55 75, www.hotelrestaurant-georgesand.com, contactGS@hotelrestaurant-georgesand.com).

The nearby Renaissance château of **Valençay** (vah-lahn-say) is a massive, luxuriously furnished structure with echoes of Talleyrand (Napoleon's prime minister), lovely gardens, and many kid-friendly summer events, such as fencing demonstrations (€10, ask about family rates, daily July–Aug 9:30–19:30, April–June and Sept–Nov 9:30–18:00, closed Dec–March, audioguide available, tel. 02 54 00 10 66).

## West of Tours

# Chinon

This pleasing town straddles the Vienne River and hides its ancient cobbles under a historic castle. Today's Chinon (shee-nohn) is better known for its popular red wines. But for me, it makes the best home base for seeing the sights west of Tours: Azay-le-Rideau (sound-and-light show), Langeais, Villandry, Chatonnière, Rivau, Ussé, and the Abbaye Royale de Fontevraud. Each of these worthwhile sights is no more than a 20-minute drive away. Trains provide access to many châteaux, but are time-consuming, so you're better off with a minivan excursion (see "Getting Around the Loire Valley," page 281, and "Transportation Connections," page 321).

The famous Renaissance writer and satirist François Rabelais was born here in the late 1400s—you'll see many references to him in his proud town. His best-known works, *Gargantua* and *Pantagruel,* describe the amusing adventures of father-and-son giants.

THE LOIRE

## ORIENTATION

Chinon stretches out along the Vienne River, and everything of interest to travelers lies between it and the hilltop château. Charming place du Général de Gaulle—ideal for café-lingering—is in the center of town.

### Tourist Information

The TI is in the center of town, near the base of the hill and a 15-minute walk from the train station. You'll find *chambre d'hôte* listings, wine-tasting details (wine-route maps available for the serious taster), bike-rental information, and an English-language, self-guided tour of the town (May–Sept daily 10:00–19:00; Oct–April Mon–Sat 10:00–12:00 & 14:00–18:00, closed Sun; in village center on place Hofheim, tel. 02 47 93 17 85, www.chinon.com). Free public WCs are around the back of the TI.

Chinon

TO AZAY, VILLANDRY, LANGEAIS, TOURS & USE BY BIKE

200 YARDS
200 METERS
View

Ste. Mexme
R. Buffon
Rue Hoche
Place J. d'Arc
St. Etienne
R. Ph. Comines
R. Marceau
R. du Coteaux St. Martin
Fort St. Georges
R. de Puits Bancs
WC's
Rousseau
Place Hof Heim
Rabelais
Jeanne d'Arc
Place de Gaulle
Rue Voltaire
Rue Jeanne d'Arc
Chateau
Route de Tours
R. Haute St. Maurice
Quai Pasteur
Charles VII
Commerce
Wow!
Vienne River
Rue de 11 Novembre
R. Descartes
Place de 11 Novembre
Blvd. Paul-Louis Courier
R. Docteur P. Labussière
Train Station
To Abbaye Royale de Fontevraud, Chateau de Riveau
Post
DCH

1. Hôtel Diderot
2. Best Western Hôtel de France & Le Café des Arts
3. Hôtel Agnès Sorel
4. To Le Clos de Ligré Chambres
5. Les Années 30 Rest.
6. L'Océanic Restaurant
7. Musée Animé du Vin Restaurant
8. Caves Plouzeau Wine-Tastings
9. La Cave Voltaire Wine-Tastings
10. Panoramic Elevator
11. Launderette
12. L'Etape en Chinonais (Bike Rental)
13. Canoe Rental
14. Grocery Store

THE LOIRE

## Helpful Hints

**Market Days:** On Thursday and Saturday mornings, a market takes place on place Jeanne d'Arc (western end of town). There's a smaller market on Sunday, around place du Général de Gaulle.

**Groceries: Shopi** is across from the Hôtel de Ville, on place du Général de Gaulle (closed for lunch 13:00–15:00 and on Sun afternoon).

**Laundry: Salon Lavoir** is near the bridge at #7 quai Charles VII (daily 7:00–21:00).

**Bike Rental:** Try **L'Etape en Chinonais,** a busy little café with bikes and picnic supplies (across from TI, €8/half-day, €15/day).

**Taxi:** Call 02 47 98 37 98.

**Car Rental:** It's best to book a car at the St. Pierre-des-Corps train station in Tours (see page 321).

**Best Views:** You'll find terrific rooftop views from rue du Coteaux St. Martin (between Ste. Mexme Church and the château—see map); and rewarding river views to Chinon by crossing the bridge in the center of town and turning right.

# SIGHTS AND ACTIVITIES

▲**Château de Chinon**—Don't underestimate this medieval castle, especially if you're looking for a contrast to all those softie

hunting-lodge palaces you've seen. The château's history, and the sensational views it affords, justify your visit. Henry II, Eleanor of Aquitaine, and their son, Richard the Lionhearted, all called this home at one time. Most importantly, it was in this castle that Joan of Arc pleaded with Charles VII to muster the courage to take the throne back from the nasty English. Charles had taken refuge in this well-fortified castle during the Hundred Years' War, making Chinon France's capital city during that period.

A three-year renovation, which should be complete by your visit, promises to deliver a thorough understanding of the castle's turbulent history and its key characters through films, videos, and posted information, all in English. Your visit will likely begin with a film presenting the castle's history, then continue on through the various towers and the new interior, which was in ruins prior to the ambitious renovation. You'll learn much about the castle's most famous inhabitant, Joan of Arc.

**THE LOIRE**

**Cost and Hours:** Likely €5, daily April–Sept 9:00–19:00, Oct–March 9:30–17:00. Because of the recent renovation, this information might change in 2009. Tel. 02 47 93 13 45.

**Getting There:** It's a steep walk up from town, though a new "panoramic" elevator should be running from behind the TI. Drivers can park near the entry at the top.

**Tours:** Try to join one of the excellent English-language tours of the château (45 min, free with entry ticket, 5/day in summer, 4/day off-season, call château for tour schedule). The tours focus on the big picture—why the castle was built here, how it differed from others in the Loire, the importance of Joan's visit, and how châteaux are rebuilt.

**Touring the Old City**—Chinon offers a tasty cocktail of quiet cobbled lanes, historic buildings, and few tourists. By following the TI's self-guided tour and reading plaques at key buildings, you'll gain a good understanding of this city's historic importance. Stop for a drink on place du Général de Gaulle and cross the river for best views to the castle.

**Wine-Tasting**—Chinon reds are among the most respected in the Loire, and there are a variety of ways to sample them. The most convenient is at **La Cave Voltaire,** where retired English-speaking sommelier Patrice would love to help you learn about his area's wines. He serves inexpensive appetizers and has wines from all regions of France (daily 10:00–22:00, near place du Général de Gaulle at 13 rue Voltaire, tel. 02 47 93 37 68).

At **Caves Plouzeau,** you'll walk through long, atmospheric caves—complete with mood lighting—that extend under the château to a (literally) cool tasting room and reasonably priced wines (€2, April–Sept Tue–Sat 11:00–13:00 & 15:00–19:00, closed Sun–Mon and Oct–March, at the western end of town on 94 rue Haute St-Maurice, tel. 02 47 93 16 34).

**▲Biking from Chinon**—Many good options are available from Chinon. Most bikers can do the pleasant bike ride from Chinon to Ussé—though you encounter a monumental hill when you're leaving Chinon. From there, you can join the bike path that crosses the Indre River, then follows the Loire River to Langeais and Villandry. After Villandry, the path follows the Cher River into Tours. Connecting these three châteaux is a full-day, 40-mile round-trip ride that only those in fit condition will enjoy.

**Canoeing from Chinon**—The campground across the lone bridge in Chinon rents plastic canoes and kayaks from May through September, and will shuttle you upriver for a relaxing float on the pretty Vienne River (€10/person for 2-hour float from Candes, tel. 06 23 82 96 33).

# SLEEPING

(€1 = about $1.50, country code: 33)

## In Chinon

If you stay overnight in Chinon, walk out to the river and cross the bridge for a floodlit view of the château walls. Hotels are a good value here.

**$$ Hôtel Diderot**\*\* is *the* place to stay in Chinon. This handsome 18th-century manor house on the eastern edge of town is

the closest hotel I list to the train station (drivers, look for signs from place Jeanne d'Arc). It's a family affair, run by spirited Laurent and his equally spirited sisters, Françoise and Martine, who will adopt you into their clan if you're not careful. The hotel surrounds a carefully planted courtyard, and has a full bar with a good selection of area wines. Rooms in the main building vary in size and decor, but all are well-maintained, with personal touches. Ground-floor rooms are a bit dark, but have private patios. The four good family rooms have connecting rooms, each with a private bathroom. Breakfast includes a rainbow of homemade jams (Sb-€45–55, Db-€55–77, extra bed-€12, Wi-Fi, limited parking-€6/day, 4 rue de Buffon, tel. 02 47 93 18 87, fax 02 47 93 37 10, www.hoteldiderot.com, hoteldiderot@hoteldiderot.com).

**$$ Best Western Hôtel de France**\*\*\* offers comfort without the personal touches of the other hotels I list. Still, I like the location—at Chinon's best square—as well as the open patios inside the hotel (Db-€78–110, most are about €88, Tb/Qb-€120–140, several rooms have balconies over the square, Wi-Fi, 49 place du Général de Gaulle, tel. 02 47 93 33 91, fax 02 47 98 37 03, www.bestwestern-hoteldefrance-chinon.com, elmachinon@aol.com).

**$$ Hôtel Agnès Sorel,** at the western end of town, is right on the river and handy for drivers, but a 30-minute walk from the train station. Of its 10 sharp rooms, three have river views, two have balconies, and five surround a small, flowery courtyard. A few are air-conditioned (Db-€52–75, most are €62, big Db suite-€100, T/Qb suite-€120, 4 quai Pasteur, tel. 02 47 93 04 37, fax 02 47 93 06 37, www.agnes-sorel.com, pierre.catin@orange.fr).

**$ Le Café des Arts** is ideal for budget travelers, with six simple, spotless rooms above Chinon's most atmospheric square (D-€38, Db-€42, 4 rue Jean-Jacques Rousseau, tel. & fax 02 47 93 09 84, frederic.giessinger@wanadoo.fr).

## Outside Chinon, near Ligré

$$$ **Le Clos de Ligré** lets you sleep in farmhouse silence, surrounded by vineyards and farmland. A 15-minute drive from Chinon, it has plenty of room to roam, a pool overlooking the vines, a billiards room with a baby grand piano, and stay-awhile indoor and outdoor spaces. Let English-speaking Martine Descamps spoil you with her cavernous and creatively decorated rooms that enclose a fine old courtyard (Db-€100, good family rooms, includes breakfast, €30 dinner includes the works, cash only, 37500 Ligré, tel. 02 47 93 95 59, mobile 06 61 12 45 55, www .le-clos-de-ligre.com, mdescamps@club-internet.fr). From Chinon, cross the river and go toward Richelieu on D-760, turn right on D-115, and continue for about five kilometers (3 miles). Turn left, following signs to *Ligré,* and look for signs to *Le Clos de Ligré* (see map on page 316).

# EATING

## In Chinon

For a low-stress meal with ambience, choose one of the cafés on the photogenic place du Général de Gaulle. The recommended **Le Café des Arts** hotel has a good, cheap restaurant with €10 salads, omelets, and €12 *plats* (closed Wed). But if food quality trumps outdoor ambience, try one of the next two restaurants. And for something really different and fun, visit Dédé la Boulange at the "Wine and Barrel Museum" (see below).

**Les Années 30** welcomes you with consistently good, classic French cuisine, attentive service (thanks to hostess Karine and chef Stephane), cozy interior rooms, and a small outdoor patio (*menus* from €27, closed Wed year-round and Tue–Wed in winter, at the western end of town at 78 rue Voltaire, tel. 02 47 93 37 18).

**L'Océanic,** in the thick of the pedestrian zone, is where locals go for seafood and tasty desserts. It has the best wine list in town, formal indoor or relaxed outdoor seating, and chic Marie-Poule to take your order (€22–38 *menus,* closed Sun–Mon, 13 rue Rabelais, tel. 02 47 93 44 55).

**Musée Animé du Vin et de la Tonnellerie** ("Wine and Barrel Museum") is a one-man show where mustachioed Dédé la Boulange dishes up all-you-can eat *fouées* (little pastry shells filled with a garlic paste, cheese, or a meat spread called *rillettes*) accompanied by a *mâche* salad (tossed with walnut oil), soft white beans stewed in goose fat, dessert *fouées,* wine, and coffee—all for €18. Watch Dédé slap the *fouées* in his rustic oven and let your hair down in this get-to-know-your-neighbor kind of place. There's no menu, because there's no need; sit down and let the food roll in (daily 10:00–22:00, 12 rue Voltaire, tel. 02 47 93 25 63).

THE LOIRE

## In Villandry, near Chinon

**Etape Gourmande at Domaine de la Giraudière** offers a rustic farmhouse dining experience a 25-minute drive away, in Villandry. Owner Beatrice provides great service and exquisite cuisine from her limited menu (ask her how she landed here). The *salade gourmande* makes a good lunch, or a hearty first course for dinner (consider splitting it). The *cochon au lait* (melt-in-your-mouth pork) weakened my defenses, and the nougat dessert finished me off (€16.50–33 *menus*, daily 12:00–15:00 & 19:30–21:00, closed mid-Nov–mid-March, a half-mile from Villandry's château toward Druye, tel. 02 47 50 08 60, fax 02 47 50 06 60). Domaine de la Giraudière works best for lunch, as it's between Villandry and Azay-le-Rideau. It also combines well with a visit to Azay-le-Rideau's sound-and-light show. For more on the town of Villandry, see page 325.

# TRANSPORTATION CONNECTIONS

## By Minivan

**From Chinon to Loire Châteaux: Acco-Dispo** and **Quart de Tours** offer fixed-itinerary minivan excursions from Tours. Take the train to Tours from Chinon, or get several travelers together to book your own van from Chinon (see "Getting Around the Loire Valley," page 281).

## By Train

Twelve trains and SNCF buses link Chinon daily with the city of Tours (1 hr, connections to other châteaux and minibus excursions from Tours—see "Getting Around the Loire Valley," page 281), and to the regional rail hub of St. Pierre-des-Corps in suburban Tours (TGV trains to distant destinations, and the fastest way to Paris). Traveling by train to the nearby châteaux (except for Azay-le-Rideau) requires a transfer in Tours and healthy walks from the stations to the châteaux. Fewer trains run on weekends.

**From Chinon to Loire Châteaux: Azay-le-Rideau** (7/day, 20 min direct, plus long walk to château), **Langeais** (5/day, 2 hrs, transfer in Tours), **Amboise** (9/day, 1.5 hrs, transfer in Tours), **Blois** (9/day, 2 hrs, transfer in Tours).

**To Destinations Beyond the Loire: Paris'** Gare Montparnasse (9/day, 2 hrs), **Sarlat** (4/day, 5–6 hrs, change at Tours' St. Pierre-des-Corps, then TGV to Libourne or Bordeaux–St. Jean, then train through Bordeaux vineyards to Sarlat), **Pontorson–Mont St. Michel** (3/day, 7 hrs, change at Tours main station and Caen, then bus from Pontorson; or via Paris TGV with changes at Tours' St. Pierre-des-Corps and Paris' Gare Montparnasse, then bus from Rennes), **Bayeux** (9/day, 5–6 hrs, change in Caen and Tours, or at Paris' Gare Montparnasse and Tours' St. Pierre-des-Corps).

## By Bus
**From Chinon to Langeais and Azay-le-Rideau:** Ask at the TI about buses to these towns (this service recently started, with 2/day to each).

# Azay-le-Rideau

About 30 minutes west of Tours, Azay-le-Rideau (ah-zay luh ree-doh) is a pleasant little town with a small but lively pedestrian zone and a château that gets all the attention. Azay-le-Rideau works as a base for visiting sights west of Tours by car, bike, or train (though the train station is a half-mile walk from the town center), and tempts travelers to bed down here with a fun sound-and-light show at its château (summer only in 2009).

## ORIENTATION

### Tourist Information
Azay-le-Rideau's TI is just below place de la République, a block to the right of the post office (Tue–Sat April–Oct 9:00–13:00 & 14:00–18:00, Nov–March 14:00–18:00, closed Sun–Mon year-round, 4 rue du Château, tel. 02 47 45 44 40). Pick up information on the sound-and-light show, and on bike rentals in Azay.

### Arrival in Azay-le-Rideau
It's about a 25-minute walk from the station to the town center (taxi tel. 06 60 94 42 00). Walk down from the station, turn left, and follow *Centre-Ville* signs. Drivers can head for the château and park there.

## SIGHTS

### ▲▲Château d'Azay-le-Rideau
This handsome 16th-century château is made magnificent by the way it seems to float in a romantic reflecting pond. Come for the serene setting, and enjoy the well-furnished rooms. You'll see more elaborately furnished châteaux elsewhere, but this one has that water thing going on. Big plans are afoot to re-do the gardens in 2009, so be prepared for some construction.

Azay-le-Rideau's builder—a government bureaucrat—wanted to design the most glorious castle of the time (not an unusual objective in this region 500 years ago). He came close enough to draw the attention of the king (François I). This was what he wanted, but not what he needed—the bureaucrat, who was France's treasurer, soon landed in jail for tax fraud.

Rooms are well-described in English, between the free

**Châteaux near Chinon**

Legend:
- Château
- Rail
- Autoroute (Toll)
- Other Roads
- Loire River
- Other Rivers
- Recommended Bike Route

1. Château de Chatonnière
2. Château du Rivau
3. Etape Gourmande Rest.
4. Le Clos de Ligré Chambres

DCH

THE LOIRE

handout and English plaques in most rooms. For the unabridged version, rent a €4 audioguide (€6 for two people). The château's manageable interior offers a collection of warmly furnished, I-could-live-here rooms. Try to recognize familiar faces among the portraits of those who stayed here. You'll see many bed-chambers and antechambers, a dining room, a kitchen, and a not-to-be-missed, 19th-century billiard room with a nifty scoring board. The gardens are a big grassy area with good views from benches to the château.

**Cost and Hours:** €8, daily July–Aug 9:30–19:00, April–June and Sept–Oct 9:30–18:00, Nov–March 10:00–12:30 & 14:00–17:30, last entry 45 min before closing, tel. 02 47 45 42 04, http://azay-le -rideau.monuments-nationaux.fr/en.

**Sound-and-Light Show:** The château hosts a sound-and-light show nightly in July and August (€10, call to see if times have been added for non-summer months). These shows allow you to stroll the grounds with interesting lighting and a musical background.

# SLEEPING

**(€1 = about $1.50, country code: 33)**

The town's appealing center may convince you to set up here (a good idea if you plan to see the sound-and-light show).

**$ Hôtel Biencourt\*\*** is ideally located on a traffic-free street between place de la République (easy parking) and the château. Owned by helpful Emmanuelle and Cédric, this modest hotel is a restored convent. Rooms are homey and comfortable enough, and there are a few big family rooms (Db-€50–55, Tb-€60–65, Qb-€70, air-con in some rooms, open March–mid-Nov, 7 rue de Balzac, tel. 02 47 45 20 75, fax 02 47 45 91 73, www.hotelbiencourt.com, biencourt@infonie.fr).

# EATING

For dining, consider **Ridelloise,** which is small, central, and budget-friendly (*menus* from €12, daily, 34–36 rue Nationale, tel. 02 47 45 46 53). For more serious, formal cuisine at fair prices, try **L'Aigle d'Or** (€29 for 4 courses, closed Wed and Sun, 10-min walk from place de la République toward Langeais at 10 avenue Adélaide-Riché, tel. 02 47 45 24 58). If you have a car, by all means drive it 10 minutes to **La Domaine de la Giraudière** in Villandry (see page 326).

# TRANSPORTATION CONNECTIONS

**From Azay-le-Rideau by Bus to: Chinon** and **Langeais** (this service recently started, 2/day, ask at TI).

**By Train to: Tours** (8/day, 30 min), **Chinon** (7/day, 20 min).

# Langeais

One of the most imposing fortresses of the Middle Ages, this sight—rated ▲—towers above its appealing little village. It comes with a moat, a drawbridge, lavish defenses, and turrets.

It's a well-furnished fort with enough rooms to hold your interest, many beautifully displayed tapestries, and useful English descriptions throughout. The attractive little town offers some respectably priced eating options near the château.

**THE LOIRE**

This castle was built on the ruins of a 10th-century fortress—you'll see the lone remnant in the garden as you enter. Langeais served a strategic role in the 1400s as a French outpost, facing the troublesome duchies of Anjou and Brittany. This castle's 15 minutes of fame came when it witnessed the secret marriage of King Charles VIII and 14-year-old Anne (the Duchess of Brittany), a union that brought independent Brittany into France's fold. You can witness the wedding in a large room outfitted with wax figures; a mini sound-and-light show explains the event (in English, ask for times at entry). The scene raises the obvious question: How could such a short person rule such a big country? Ponder that question as you walk along the parapet, with great views (through chicken wire) over the town.

**Cost and Hours:** €8.50, daily July–Aug 9:00–19:00, Feb–June and Sept–mid-Nov 9:30–18:30, mid-Nov–Jan 10:00–17:00, last entry one hour before closing, tel. 02 47 96 72 60, www.chateau-de-langeais.com).

**Getting There:** Nine trains a day link Langeais and Tours (20 min), with about five connections a day from there to **Chinon** (2 hrs total, faster by bike). Drivers should turn right at the foot of the castle and follow the road left (around the castle) to find the parking lot on the right.

# Villandry

Villandry (vee-lahn-dree) has an unremarkable castle, but its grounds make it a ▲▲ sight (worth ▲▲▲ for gardeners). Built in 1536 as the home of the finance minister, this château has the Loire's best gardens, immaculately maintained and arranged in elaborate geometric patterns. Pick up the well-done English handout that describes the four garden types and suggests a good walking route. The viewpoint behind the château is terrific. The 10-acre, Italian Renaissance–style garden (designed c. 1530) is full of symbolism. Even the herb and vegetable sections are artistic—design mattered to the monks who first planted these gardens (only vegetables used in the 16th century are still grown). Paying extra for the château interior isn't worth it, but it does include a 15-minute *Four Seasons of Villandry* slide show (with period music) that offers a look at the gardens throughout the year. You can stay as late as you like in the gardens, though you must enter before the ticket office closes.

**Cost and Hours:** €9, €6 for gardens only, daily April–Sept 9:00–19:00, March and Oct 9:00–18:00, Nov–Feb 9:00–17:00, tel. 02 47 50 02 09, www.chateauvillandry.com.

*Eating in Villandry:* The pleasant little village of Villandry offers several cafés and restaurants, a small grocery store, and a bakery. Consider combining your visit with a meal at the nearby Etape Gourmande at **La Domaine de la Giraudière** (follow signs to Druye from Villandry; see "Eating" in Chinon, page 324).

## More Château Gardens

Gardeners will be tempted by these untouristy "lesser châteaux" because of their pleasing plantings.

**Château de Chatonnière** features romantic paths through exquisitely tended gardens of various themes. Surrounded by fields of wild flowers (my favorite part), it's a must-visit for gardeners and flower fanatics in May to early July, when the place positively explodes in fragrance and color. At other times, when flowers are few, the entry fee is not worth it for most (€6, mid-March–mid-Nov daily 10:00–19:00, château interior

closed to visitors, between Langeais and Azay-le-Rideau just off D-57, tel. 02 47 45 40 29, www.lachatonniere.com).

**Château du Rivau** is well off the beaten path, a lovely 10-minute drive from Chinon. This gleaming-white château sits smack in the middle of wheat fields, with owners who are busily re-creating the fine gardens as they were 500 years ago (using medieval tapestries as models). Here you'll see vegetable and flower gardens and another castle interior—though you're here for the gardens (€8, July–Aug daily 10:00–19:00; June and Sept Wed–Mon 10:00–12:30 & 14:00–19:00, closed Tue; mid-April–May and Oct–mid-Nov Wed–Sun 14:00–19:00, closed Mon–Tue; closed mid-Nov–mid-April; in Lémeré on D-759—from Chinon follow *Richelieu* signs, then signs to the château; tel. 02 47 95 77 47, www.chateaudurivau.com).

## Ussé

This château, famous as an inspiration for Charles Perrault's classic version of the Sleeping Beauty story, is worth a quick photo stop for its fairy-tale turrets and gardens, but don't bother touring the interior of this pricey pearl. The best view, with reflections and a golden-slipper picnic spot, is from just across the bridge (€12, daily July–Aug 9:30–19:00, mid-Feb–June and Sept–mid-Nov 10:00–18:00, closed mid-Nov–mid-Feb, tel. 02 47 95 54 05, www .chateaudusse.fr).

# Abbaye Royale de Fontevraud

The Abbaye Royale de Fontevraud (fohn-tuh-vroh), a 15-minute drive west of Chinon, is worth ▲. This vast 12th-century abbey

provides the best look you'll get at medieval monastic life in this area. Here you can commune with Richard the Lionhearted and Eleanor of Aquitaine, and get a better grip on the important role medieval abbeys played in pulling Europe out of the Dark Ages. Europe's largest abbey feels like the economic engine it was 900 years ago—you can almost hear the gears grinding as you tour this elaborate monastic complex.

**Cost and Hours:** €6.50, daily June–Sept 9:00–18:00, Oct–May 10:00–17:30, tel. 02 41 51 71 41, www.abbaye-fontevraud.com.

**Tours:** This abbey is unusually well-presented for English-speakers. English-language **tours** depart four times a day from June to September (call for times in any season). If you miss the tour, the English leaflet and room-by-room explanations are quite informative. The best book on the abbey is *Fontevraud, Royal Abbey—Between Chinon and Saumur* by Francis Collombert (€12).

**❍ Self-Guided Tour:** Your visit begins in the bright church (Eglise Abbatiale). Sit on the entry steps, savor the ethereal light and the cavernous setting, and gaze down the nave. Two-thirds of the way down, Eleanor of Aquitaine lies next to her second husband, England's Henry II. Next to them lies their son Richard, Coeur de Lion ("Heart of Lion").

Exit through the right transept into the Grand Moutier Cloister. This was the focus of the monastery, where monks read, exercised, checked email, and washed. From here, keep left and you'll find a chapter house (Salle Capitulaire), where the monks' meetings took place, as well as the Chauffoir—the only heated room in the abbey, where monks could copy manuscripts when it was cold. You'll also see an open-beam-ceilinged dormitory (where most monks slept with little or no padding) currently used for expositions, plus an elegant refectory and a maze of underground tunnels *(accès souterrain)*. As you tour the abbey, remember that monastic life was dirt-simple: nothing but prayer, reading, and work. Daily rations were a loaf of bread and a quarter-liter of wine.

Your visit ends in the honeycombed 16th-century kitchen, with five chapel-chimneys and many holes for smoke to escape.

# SLEEPING AND EATING

(€1 = about $1.50, country code: 33)

$$$ **Hôtel la Croix Blanche**\*\*, 10 steps from the abbey, welcomes travelers with open terraces and will have you sleeping and dining in comfort. This traditional restaurant-hotel combines a hunting-lodge feel with polished service, comfortable open spaces, and rooms with classic French decor (perfectly comfortable Db-€75–120, "privilege" Db-€90–155, Tb-€120–160, grand suite-€130–190, place Plantagenets, tel. 02 41 51 71 11, fax 02 41 38 15 38, www.fontevraud.net, info@fontevraud.net). Their three restaurants meet every need: The elegant country restaurant has *menus* from €22, the brasserie has café fare, and the *crêperie* has...crêpes.

The **boulangerie** opposite the entrance to the abbey serves mouthwatering quiche and sandwiches at impossibly good prices. You'll also find a few *crêperies* and cafés near the abbey.

THE LOIRE

# DORDOGNE AND NEARBY

*Sarlat • Dordogne River Valley • Cro-Magnon Caves •*
*Oradour-sur-Glane • St. Emilion • Rocamadour*

The Dordogne River Valley is a rich brew of natural and man-made beauty. Walnut orchards, tobacco plants, and cornfields carpet the valley, while stone fortresses patrol the cliffs above. During much of the on-again, off-again Hundred Years' War, this strategic river—so peaceful today—separated warring Britain and France. Today's Dordogne River carries more travelers than goods, as the region's economy relies heavily on tourism.

The joys of the Dordogne include rock-sculpted villages, fertile farms surrounding I-should-retire-here cottages, film-gobbling vistas, lazy canoe rides, and a local cuisine worth loosening your belt for. But its big draw is its concentration of prehistoric artifacts. Limestone caves—decorated with prehistoric artwork—litter the Dordogne region.

## Planning Your Time

While tourists inundate the region in the summer, the Dordogne's charm is protected by its relative inaccessibility. Given the time it takes to get here, I'd allow a minimum of two nights and most of two days...or I'd skip it. Your sightseeing obligations, in order of priority, are: prehistoric cave art; the Dordogne River Valley, nearby villages, and castles; the town of Sarlat; and, if you have a bit more time, the less-traveled Lot River Valley (most efficiently done when heading to or from the south). Wine-lovers work in a pilgrimage to St. Emilion, two hours west.

If you're connecting the Dordogne with the Loire region by car, the fastest path is via the A-20 autoroute (exit at Souillac for Sarlat and nearby villages). Break up your trip from the north by stopping in Oradour-sur-Glane and/or Collonges-la-Rouge (see

"Oradour-sur-Glane and Nearby," page 374): Take autoroute A-20 to Limoges and follow *Angoulême* signs, then follow signs to *Oradour-sur-Glane*. If you need to spend the night in this area, consider tiny Mortemart (near Oradour-sur-Glane—see page 375). If you're connecting the Dordogne and Carcassonne, explore the Lot River Valley on your way south (see page 389). When heading west, take time to sample the Bordeaux wine region's prettiest town, St. Emilion (see page 376).

Those serious about visiting the Dordogne's best caves (especially with a relatively rare English-speaking tour) need to book well in advance (as explained on page 370).

The following three-day itinerary is designed to be done by car, but it's doable—if you're determined—via taxi rides, a canoe trip (the best way to see the Dordogne regardless of whether you've got a car or not), and an organized minivan tour.

**Day 1:** Enjoy a morning in Sarlat (ideally on a market day—Sat or Wed), then spend the afternoon on a canoe trip, with time at the day's end to explore Beynac and Castelnaud. If it's not market day in Sarlat, do the canoe trip, Beynac, and castle first, and enjoy the late afternoon and evening in Sarlat. (Since all of the town's essential sights are outdoors, my Sarlat self-guided walk works great after dinner.) The sensational views from Castelnaud's castle and Domme are best in the morning; visit Beynac's castle or viewpoint late in the day for the best light. With a little lead time, canoe-rental companies can pick up non-drivers in Sarlat. Taxis are also reasonable between Sarlat and the river villages.

**Day 2:** Drivers can begin at Lascaux II (the best cave art intro in the area, even though it's a replica). Then, follow the scenic Vézere River toward Les Eyzies-de-Tayac, stopping for lunch in idyllic little St. Léon and then on to the caves at La Roque St. Christophe (no reservations needed; doesn't close for lunch, unlike other caves). In Les Eyzies-de-Tayac, visit the museum of prehistory, then see the real thing at the cave or caves of your choice (I prefer Grotte de Font-de-Gaume and Grotte de Rouffignac). If you lack a car, this day's activities are only possible by taxi or minivan tour.

**Day 3:** Head east and upriver to explore Rocamadour, Gouffre de Padirac, and storybook villages such as Carennac, Autoire, and Loubressac. While Rocamadour is accessible by train and a short taxi ride, the rest of these places are feasible only with your own wheels, by taxi, or on a minivan tour.

## Choosing a Home Base

Sarlat is the only viable solution for train travelers, but those with a car should sleep riverside in La Roque-Gageac (a beautiful village with good hotels, see page 359) or Beynac (a spectacular

DORDOGNE

and photogenic village with good *chambres* and hotels, see page 359). For a grand château hotel experience that won't break the bank, sleep near the Lascaux caves, at Château de la Fleunie (30 min north of Sarlat, see page 369). And if you'd rather frolic on a real farm, sleep near Les Eyzies-de-Tayac at Auberge Veyret (see page 367). I recommend several other rural places that are good for drivers (see page 358). For a list of good *chambres d'hôte* near Sarlat, check www.chambres-perigord.com (in French, but easy to navigate—click *chambres d'hôte*).

## Getting Around the Dordogne

This region is a joy with a car, but tough without one. Consider renting a car for a day, renting a canoe or bike, or taking a minivan excursion (all described below). If you're up for a splurge, consider a hot-air balloon ride (see sidebar on page 285).

**By Train:** While it's possible to get into the region by train, connecting the Dordogne's sights by train once there is miserable. Trains run from Sarlat to the Grotte de Font-de-Gaume caves in Les Eyzies-de-Tayac (transfer in Le Buisson, 30-min walk from station to caves), but leave you in Les Eyzies-de-Tayac all day. Consider a taxi back (see below).

**By Car:** Roads are small, slow, and scenic. There is no autoroute near Sarlat, so you'll need more time than usual to get into, out of, and around this remote region. Little Sarlat is routinely snarled in traffic, so passing through it can slow you down. You can rent a car in Sarlat (see "Helpful Hints" on page 337), though bigger cites, such as Bordeaux and Brive-la-Gaillarde, offer greater drop-off flexibility. In summer (mid-June–mid-Sept), you'll pay to park in most riverfront lots between 10:00 and 19:00. Leave nothing in your car at night—thieves enjoy the Dordogne, too.

**By Taxi:** For taxi service from Sarlat to Beynac or La Roque-Gageac, allow €21 (€27 at night and on Sun); from Sarlat to Les Eyzies-de-Tayac, allow €32 one-way (€50 at night and on Sun) or €64 round-trip. Philippe (see below) can often pick you up within a few minutes if you call. Corrine, who runs Beynac-based **Taxi Corrine,** is helpful, speaks a little English, and is eager to provide good service to tourists (tel. 05 53 29 42 07, mobile 06 72 76 03 32, corrine.broqui@wanadoo.fr).

**By Custom Taxi/Minivan Excursion:** You have two good options. **Allô-Philippe Taxi** is run by amiable Philippe, who speaks English and has a comfortable minivan with raised seats for better viewing. Philippe will custom-design your tour, help with cave reservations, and provide some commentary during your excursion. He can pick you up anywhere—including Bordeaux's airport (€290) and remote train stations (€32/hr for up to 7 people—but 6 is more comfortable, €48/hr on Sun, €80 round-trip to Lascaux II from Sarlat area, book early, tel. 05 53 59 39 65, mobile 06 08 57 30 10, http://allophilippetaxi.monsite.wanadoo.fr, allophilippetaxi@wanadoo.fr).

**Decouverte et Loisirs** is run by Christine, who offers minivan tours for one to eight people. Compared to Philippe, she does more set tours and fewer custom ones. Her three weekly afternoon itineraries in English are: the Dordogne Valley villages and castles; the prehistoric-focused sights of Lascaux II, La Roque St. Christophe, and the National Museum of Prehistory in Les Eyzies-de-Tayac; and Rocamadour (allow €30–35/person, tel. 05 65 37 19 00, mobile 06 22 70 13 76, www.decouverte-loisirs.com, decouverte.loisirs @wanadoo.fr). While her fixed tours don't include Grotte de Font-de-Gaume, she can make a custom tour for you that does, and will make the necessary cave reservations if you book with her early enough.

**By Boat:** Non-drivers should rent a canoe, my favorite mode of transportation for exploring a slice of this region (see page 349 for rental information and suggested routes). A canoe offers easy access to the river's sights and villages, and canoe companies will pick you up in Sarlat for no extra charge. Since a canoe costs about €10/person (for the trip I recommend), and you can spend all day on and off the river touring sights I cover, this is a swimmingly good deal (see "Dordogne Canoe Trip," page 349). For the same scenery with less work, you can also take a boat cruise from Beynac (see page 357) or La Roque-Gageac (page 353).

**By Bike or Moped:** Cyclists find the Dordogne beautiful but hilly, with lots of traffic on key roads. Mopeds and electric bikes are an option. You can rent bikes and mopeds in Sarlat (see "Helpful Hints" on page 337).

## Cuisine Scene in the Dordogne

Gourmets flock to this area for its geese, ducks, and wild mushrooms. The geese produce (involuntarily) the region's famous foie gras. (They're force-fed, denied exercise, and slaughtered for their livers—see sidebar on page 356.) Foie gras tastes like butter and costs like gold. The duck specialty is *confit de canard* (duck meat preserved in its own fat— sounds terrible, but tastes great). *Pommes de terre sarladaises* are  mouthwatering, thinly sliced potatoes fried in duck fat and commonly served with *confit de canard*. Wild truffles are dirty black mushrooms that grow underground, generally on the roots of oak trees. Farmers traditionally locate them with sniffing pigs and

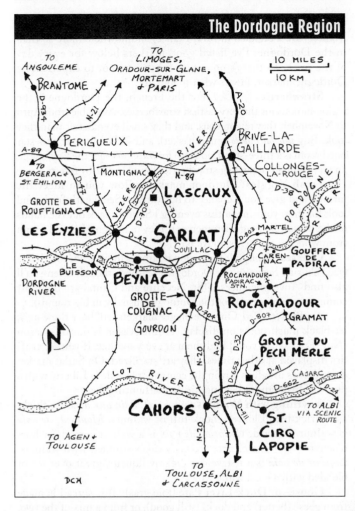

**The Dordogne Region**

TO ANGOULEME
BRANTOME
D-939
N-21
TO LIMOGES, ORADOUR-SUR-GLANE, MORTEMART & PARIS
A-20
10 MILES
10 KM
PERIGUEUX
A-89
TO BERGERAC & ST. EMILION
D-47
MONTIGNAC
N-89
BRIVE-LA-GAILLARDE
COLLONGES-LA-ROUGE
D-38
GROTTE DE ROUFFIGNAC
VEZERE RIVER
D-706
LASCAUX
D-704
DORDOGNE RIVER
LES EYZIES
D-47
SARLAT
D-803
MARTEL
SOUILLAC
CARENNAC
GOUFFRE DE PADIRAC
LE BUISSON
BEYNAC
ROCAMADOUR-PADIRAC STN.
ROCAMADOUR
DORDOGNE RIVER
GROTTE DE COUGNAC
D-704
GOURDON
D-807
GRAMAT
N-20
A-20
GROTTE DU PECH MERLE
D-32
D-653
D-41
CAJARC
LOT RIVER
D-662
D-24
TO ALBI VIA SCENIC ROUTE
CAHORS
D-911
ST. CIRQ LAPOPIE
N-20
A-20
TO AGEN & TOULOUSE
TO TOULOUSE, ALBI & CARCASSONNE
DCM

then charge a fortune for their catch (roughly $250 per pound). Native cheeses are Cabécou (a silver-dollar-size, pungent, nutty-flavored goat cheese) and Echourgnac (made by local Trappist monks). You'll find walnuts *(noix)* in salads, cakes, liqueurs, and salad dressings (also see "Anything with Walnuts," under "Dordogne Markets," next page). Wines to sample are Bergerac (red and white), Pecharmant (red, must be at least four years old), Cahors (a full-bodied red), and Monbazillac (sweet dessert wine). The *vin de noix* (sweet walnut liqueur) is delightful before dinner.

Remember, restaurants serve only during lunch (11:30–14:00) and dinner (19:00–21:00, later in bigger cities); bigger cafés serve food throughout the day.

## Dordogne Markets

Markets are a big deal in rural France, and nowhere more so than in the Dordogne. I've listed good markets below for every day of the week, so there's no excuse for drivers not to experience a Dordogne market. Here's what to look for:

**Strawberries** *(fraises):* For the French, the Dordogne is the region famous for the very tastiest strawberries. Available from April to November, they're gorgeous, and they smell even better than they look. Buy *une barquette* (small basket), and suddenly your two-star hotel room is a three-star. Look also for *fraises des bois,* the tiny, sweet, and less visually appealing strawberries found in nearby forests.

**Fresh Veggies:** Outdoor markets allow you to meet the farmer, and give you a chance to buy direct. (See what's fresh, and look for it on your menu this evening.) Subtly check out the hands of the person helping customers—if they're not gnarled and rough from working the fields, move on.

**Cheeses** *(fromages):* The region is famous for its Cabécou cheese (see "Cuisine Scene in the Dordogne," earlier), though often you'll also find Auvergne cheeses (St. Nectaire and Cantal are the most common) from just east of the Dordogne (usually in big rounds).

**Truffles** *(truffes):* Only the bigger markets will have these ugly, jet-black mushrooms on display. Truffle season is our off-season (Nov–Feb), when you'll find them at every market. If you see truffles displayed at other times, they are sterilized. On Sarlat market days, there's usually a guy in the center of place de la Liberté with a photo of his grandfather and his truffle-hunting dog.

**Anything with Walnuts** *(aux noix): Pain aux noix* are thick-as-a-brick bread loaves chock-full of walnuts. *Moutarde de noix* is walnut mustard. *Confiture de noix* is a walnut spread for hors d'oeuvres. *Gâteaux de noix* are tasty cakes studded with walnuts. *Liqueur de noix* is a marvelous creamy liqueur, great over ice or blended with a local white wine.

**Goose- or Duck-Liver Pâté** (foie gras): This spread is made from geese (better) and ducks (still good), or from a mix of the two. You'll see two basic forms: *entier* and *bloc.* Both are 100 percent foie gras; *entier* is a piece cut right from the product, while *bloc* has been whipped to make it easier to spread. Foie gras is best accompanied by a sweet white wine (like the locally produced Monbazillac, or Sauterne from Bordeaux). You can bring the unopened tins back into the US, *pas de problème.* For more on foie gras, see the sidebar on page 356.

**Confit de Canard:** At butcher stands, look for hunks of duck smothered in white fat, just waiting for someone to take them home and cook them up.

**Dried Sausages** *(saucissons secs):* Long tables piled high with dried sausages covered in herbs or stuffed with local goodies are a common sight in French markets. You'll always be offered a mouthwatering sample. Some of the variations you'll see include *porc, canard* (duck), *fumé* (smoked), *à l'ail* (garlic), *cendré* (rolled in ashes), *aux myrtilles* (with blueberries), *sanglier* (wild boar), and even *âne* (donkey)—and, but of course, *aux noix* (with walnuts).

**Olive Oil** *(huile d'olive):* You'll find stylish bottles of oil flavored with walnuts, chestnuts *(châtaignes),* and hazelnuts *(noisettes)*—good for cooking, ideal on salads, and great as gifts.

**Olives and Nuts** *(olives et noix):* These interlopers from Provence find their way to every market in France.

**Liqueurs:** While they're not made in this region, Armagnac, Cognac, and other southwestern fruit-flavored liquors are often available from a seller or two. Try the liqueur de pomme verte, and sample Armagnac in the tiny plastic cups.

## Dordogne Market Days

The best markets are in Sarlat (Sat and Wed, in that order), followed by the markets in Cahors on Saturday, St. Cyprien on Sunday, and Le Bugue on Tuesday. Markets usually shut down by 13:00.

**Sunday:** St. Cyprien (lively market, 10 min west of Beynac, difficult parking), Montignac (near Lascaux), and St. Genies (a tiny, intimate market with few tourists; halfway between Sarlat and Montignac)

**Monday:** Les Eyzies-de-Tayac (Grotte de Font-de-Gaume caves are here) and a tiny one in Beynac

**Tuesday:** Cénac (you can canoe from here—see "Dordogne Canoe Trip," page 349) and Le Bugue (great market 20 min west of Beynac)

**Wednesday:** Sarlat (big market)

**Thursday:** Domme

**Friday:** Souillac (transfer point to Cahors, Carcassonne)

**Saturday:** Sarlat and Cahors (both are excellent)

# Sarlat

Sarlat (sar-lah) is a pedestrian-filled banquet of a town, serenely set amid forested hills. There are no blockbuster sights—the only thing worth going inside for is the cathedral (and that just barely). Still, Sarlat features a seductive tangle of traffic-free, golden cobblestone lanes peppered with beautiful buildings, lined with foie gras shops (geese hate Sarlat), and stuffed with tourists. The town is warmly lit at night, and ideal for after-dinner strolls. It's just the right size—large enough to have a theater with four screens, but small enough so that everything is an easy meander

**DORDOGNE**

from the town center. While undeniably popular with tourists, it's the handiest home base for those without a car.

# ORIENTATION

Rue de la République slices like an arrow through the circular old town. Sarlat's smaller half has few shops and many quiet lanes. The action lies east of rue de la République. Make it a point to wander.

## Tourist Information

The TI, with English-speaking staff, is 50 yards to the right of the Cathedral of St. Sacerdos as you face the front entrance (April–June

and Sept–Oct Mon–Sat 9:00–12:00 & 14:00–18:00, Sun 10:00–13:00 & 14:00–17:00; July–Aug Mon–Sat 9:00–19:00, Sun 10:00–12:00 & 14:00–18:00; Nov–March closes at 18:00 and all day Sun, on rue Tourny, tel. 05 53 31 45 45, www.sarlat

-tourisme.com). Ask for an English version of the free city map, and pick up brochures on most regional sights. Their *Guide Pratique* booklet is good for car-, bike-, and canoe-rental information. They also sell the well-done, laminated *City of Sarlat* walking-tour map for €5, and booklets on sights throughout the region. For €2, the TI can also reserve you a hotel room or a time slot for a prehistoric cave visit (for more on cave reservations, see page 370). And for €5 you can take a TI-sponsored walking tour of Sarlat (May–Sept Wed at 11:00). The TI also has hiking guides in English, listing suggested trails through the hills and by the Dordogne River.

## Arrival in Sarlat

**By Train:** The sleepy train station keeps a lonely vigil (without a shop, café, or hotel in sight). It's a mostly downhill, 20-minute walk to the town center (consider a taxi, about €8—see "Helpful Hints," next page). To walk into town, turn left out of the station and follow the *Centre-Ville* sign down avenue de la Gare as it curves downhill, then turn right at the bottom on avenue Thiers. Some trains (such as those from Oradour and Cahors) arrive at nearby Souillac, which is connected to Sarlat's train station by an SNCF bus.

**By Car:** Sarlat's limited-access downtown funnels cars through narrow streets, creating long backups. Parking can be a headache, particularly on market days. Try parking along avenue Gambetta (at the north end of town), or in one of the signed lots on the ring road. The closest parking is metered.

## Helpful Hints

**Market Days:** Sarlat has been an important market town since the Middle Ages. Outdoor markets thrive on Wednesday morning and all day Saturday (see "Dordogne Market Days," on page 335). Saturday's market, which seems to swallow the entire town, is best in the morning (produce and food vendors leave at noon). Come before 8:00 to watch them set up, and once the market is under way, plant yourself at a well-positioned café to observe the civilized scene. Don't miss the market action in the former Church of Ste. Marie.

**Supermarket:** There's a **Petite Casino** grocery at 32 rue de la République (Tue–Sat 8:30–12:30 & 14:00–19:00, Sun 8:30–12:30, closed Mon).

**Internet Access: Easy Planet** is a five-minute walk north of the old town (Mon–Sat 10:00–19:00, closed Sun, 17 avenue Gambetta, tel. 05 53 29 23 48).

**Laundry:** Madame Mazzocato runs a good launderette across from the recommended Hôtel la Couleuvrine (self-serve daily 6:00–22:00, drop-off/pickup Mon–Fri only 8:00–12:30 & 14:00–18:30, 10 place de la Bouquerie). There's another self-service laundry near the recommended Hôtel de Selves (open daily 7:00–21:00, 74 avenue de Selves).

**Bike Rental:** Englishman Joel Caine runs **Bike Bus,** offering easy bike rental, delivery, and pickup; maps; and help in planning your route. Bike delivery is free with a minimum five-day rental in Sarlat or the St. Cyprien area (€20/day, €100/week; helmet, lock, and pump included; daily 9:00–12:00 & 14:00–19:00, tel. 06 08 94 42 01, www.multitravel.co.uk, info@multitravel.co.uk). My "Dordogne River Valley Scenic Loop," described on page 348, makes a good bike ride, or find excellent bike itineraries with detailed directions on the Bike Bus website (click on *Resources*). You can also rent bikes at the recommended hotel, **La Villa des Consuls** (bike rental called **CycleO,** tel. 05 53 29 80 65, www.cycleo.fr).

**Taxi:** Call Philippe of **Allô-Philippe Taxi** (tel. 05 53 59 39 65, mobile 06 08 57 30 10—see page 331 for information about using Philippe for regional day trips) or **Taxi Sarlat** (tel. 05 53 59 02 43, mobile 06 80 08 65 05).

**Car Rental:** Try **Europcar** (Le Pontet, at south end of avenue Leclerc on roundabout, place du Maréchal de Lattre de Tassigny, tel. 05 53 30 30 40, fax 05 53 31 10 39).

**Tours: Passion Périgord** is a two-man tour company run by passionate guides Jeff and Pierre. They offer €5 walks of Sarlat in English to small groups (even just two people). Call or email a few days ahead to book (countryside walks also possible, tel. 05 53 30 42 55, mobile 06 81 58 19 48, passionperigord@yahoo.fr).

# SELF-GUIDED WALK

## Welcome to Sarlat

This short walk starts facing the Cathedral of St. Sacerdos (a few steps from the TI). While it's designed to do by day (when the cathedral is open), it works beautifully after dinner, when the gas-lit lanes and candlelit restaurants twinkle.

**Place du Peyrou:** An eighth-century Benedictine abbey once stood where the Cathedral of St. Sacerdos does today. It provided the stability for Sarlat to develop into an important trading city during the Middle Ages. The old Bishop's Palace, built right into the cathedral (on the right, with its top-floor Florentine-style loggia), recalls Sarlat's Italian connection. The Italian bishop was the boyfriend of Catherine de Médicis (queen of France)—a connection that got him this fine residence. After a short stint here, he split to Paris with lots of local money. While his departure scandalized the town, it left Sarlat with a heritage of Italian architecture. (Notice the fine Italianate house of Etienne de la Boëtie on the opposite side of the square, and the similar loggia to its right.)

Another reason for Sarlat's Italian-flavored architectural zenith was its loyalty to the king during wartime. Sarlat's glory century was from about 1450 to 1550, after the Hundred Years' War (see sidebar on page 201). Loyal to the French cause—through thick and thin and a century of war—Sarlat was rewarded by the French king, who gave lots of money to rebuild the town in stone. Sarlat's new nobility needed fancy houses, complete with ego-boosting features. Many of Sarlat's most impressive buildings date from this prosperous era, when the Renaissance style was in vogue, and everyone wanted an Italian architect.

• *Take a closer look (opposite the cathedral) at...*

**The House of Etienne de la Boëtie:** This house was a typical 16th-century merchant's home—family upstairs and open ground floor (its stone arch now filled in) with big, fat sills to display retail goods. Pan up, scanning the crude-but-still-Renaissance carved reliefs. It was a time when anything Italian was trendy (when yokels "stuck a feather in their cap and called it macaroni"). La Boëtie (lah bow-ess-ee), a 16th-century bleeding-heart liberal who spoke and wrote against the rule of tyrannical kings, remains a local favorite.

Notice how the house just to the left arches over the small street. This was a common practice to maximize buildable space in the Middle Ages. Sarlat enjoyed a population boom after the Hundred Years' War ended in 1468.

• *If you're doing this walk during the day, head into the cathedral now. If you're doing this walk after hours, skip ahead to the Lantern of the Dead (below): Facing the cathedral, walk around it to the left, up the*

# Sarlat

TO ❶ AVE. GAMBETTA DE SELVES →

↑ TO ❻, ❻, LES EYZIES & 🅿
➡ WALKING TOUR ROUTE
🅿 PARKING

ST. CYPRIEN
AVE. DE GAULLE
BLVD. EUGENE LE ROY
🅿

❷
PLACE PETITE RIGAUDIE
❾
R. 8 MAI
BLVD.
MAGNANAT
NESSMAN
❷⓪
PLACE DE LA BOUQUERIE
🅿

PAPUCIE
CONSULS
FINISH
❶❸
PLACE DES OIES MARKET
❺
❽
RUE FENELON

STE-MARIE ✝
❶
RCE V. HUGO
PLACE LIBERTE
R. A. CADUET
SALAMANDRE
PRESIDIAL
R. D'ALBUSSE
R. LANDRY
BLVD. ARLET

COTE TOULOUSE
DE
LIBERTE
❹
❼
❶❽
❶⓪
R. MONTAIGNE

❶❼
PLACE P. P. GRASSE
R. J. J. ROUSSEAU
R. J. BOETIE
House of BOETIE
❶❾
PL. PEYROU
LIAR-SOU
START
ℹ
❶❺
LANTERN OF THE DEAD
ST. SACERDOS CATHEDRAL
🅿

BLVD. VOLTAIRE
RUE SIEGE
RUE REPUBLIQUE
R. TOURNY
RUE J. J. ESCANDE
PLACE GRANDE RIGAUDIE
BLVD. ARLET
🅿
JARDIN PUBLIC

PLACE 14 JUILLET
🅿
🅿
100 YARDS
100 METERS

POST
AVE. LECLERC
🅿
PLACE PASTEUR
TO TRAIN STN. BEYNAC, CAHORS & ❶❶
❸ ←
DCH

❶ Hôtel La Villa des Consuls & Bike Rental
❷ Hôtel de la Madeleine
❸ Hôtel Montaigne
❹ Hôtel de la Mairie
❺ Hôtel/Rest. la Couleuvrine
❻ To Hôtel de Selves, Hôtel de Compostelle & Hôtel Madrigal
❼ Chambres du Glacier & Brasserie
❽ Toulemon Rooms
❾ Les Cordeliers Rooms
❶⓪ La Lanterne Rooms
❶❶ To Hôtel le Relais de Moussidière & Europcar
❶❷ To Hôtel la Verperie
❶❸ La Mirandol Restaurant

❶❹ Le Petit Manoir Restaurant
❶❺ Chez le Gaulois Restaurant
❶❻ To Le Bistro de l'Octroi Rest. & Internet Café
❶❼ Pizzeria Romane
❶❽ Le Présidial Restaurant
❶❾ Petite Casino Grocery
❷⓪ Launderette

**DORDOGNE**

*lane, and through the little door in the wall to the rocket-shaped building on a bluff 30 yards behind the church.*

**Cathedral of St. Sacerdos:** While the cathedral's facade has a few well-worn 12th-century carvings, most of it dates from the 18th and 19th centuries.

Step inside the only historic Sarlat interior that merits a visit. The faithful believed that Mary delivered them from the great plague of 1348, so you'll find a full complement of Virgin Marys here and throughout the town. The Gothic interiors you'll see in this part of France are simple, with clean lines and nothing extravagant. The first chapel on the left is the baptistery. Locals would come here to give thanks after they made the pilgrimage to Lourdes for healing and returned satisfied. A column on the right shows a long list of hometown boys who gave their lives for France in World War I.

• *Exit the cathedral from the right transept (through a padded, brown, and unmarked door) into what was once the abbey's cloisters. Snoop through two quiet courtyards and then turn left making your way uphill toward the rear of the cathedral, hooking left through a stony passage along the back of the church. Climb the steps (through the monks' graveyard) to a bluff 30 yards directly behind the church. You'll find a bullet-shaped building ready for some kind of medieval take-off, known as the...*

**Lantern of the Dead (Lanterne des Morts):** Dating from 1147, this is the oldest monument in town. In four horrible days, a quarter of Sarlat's population died in a plague (1,000 out of 4,000). People prayed to St. Bernard of Clairvaux for help. He blessed their bread—and instituted hygiene standards while he was at it, stopping the disease. This lantern was built in gratitude. If it feels a bit eastern or Moorish, it's likely because of Bernard's Crusades experience in the Holy Land.

• *From the Lantern of the Dead, exit downhill and to the right, past an adorable house. Cross one street, and turn left a block later on impasse de la Vieille Poste, make a quick right on rue d'Albusse and then take a left onto...*

**Rue de la Salamandre:** The salamander—unfazed by fire or water—was Sarlat's mascot. Befitting its favorite animal, Sarlat was also unfazed by fire (from war) and water (from floods). Walk 10 yards down this "Street of the Salamander" and find the Gothic-framed doorway just below on your right. Step back and notice the tower that housed the staircase. Staircase towers like this (Sarlat has about 20) date from about 1600 (after the wars of religion between the Catholics and Protestants), when the new nobility needed to show off.

• *Continue downhill, passing under the salamander-capped arch, and pause near (or better, sit down at) the café on the...*

**Place de la Liberté:** This has been Sarlat's main market square since the Middle Ages. Sarlat's patriotic town hall stands behind you (with a café perfectly situated for people-watching). Top shops line the road between here and the cathedral. These tourist-pleasing stores are filled with the finest local products (truffles, liquors, foie gras, and so on).

You can't miss the dark **stone roofs** topping the buildings across the square. They're typical of this region: Called *lauzes* in French, the flat limestone rocks were originally gathered by farmers clearing their fields, then made into cheap, durable roofing material (today few people can afford them). The unusually steep pitch of the *lauzes* roofs—which last up to 300 years—helps distribute the weight of the roof over a greater area. Over time, most *lauzes* roofs have been replaced by more affordable roofing materials, but Sarlat retains a great number of stone-roofed homes. The small window is critical—it provides air circulation, allowing the lichen that coat the porous stone to grow, sealing gaps between the stones and effectively waterproofing the roof. Without that layer, the stone would crumble after repeated freeze-and-thaw cycles.

The bulky building with the fine *lauzes* roof (on the right) was the parish Church of Ste. Marie, which was converted into a gunpowder factory in 1789. Today, it's an indoor market (open daily 8:30–13:00). Marvel at its tall, strangely modern, seven-ton doors. Walk past the big doors and go up a few steps to meet the "boy of Sarlat"—marking the best view over place de la Liberté. Notice the cathedral's tower, with a salamander swinging happily from its spire.

• *Turn left (behind the boy) and trickle like medieval rainwater down the ramp into an inviting square. Here, you'll find a little gaggle of geese.*

**Place des Oies:** Feathers fly when geese are traded on this "Square of the Geese" on market days (Saturdays Nov–March). The birds are serious business here, and have been since the Middle Ages. Trophy homes surround this cute little square on all sides. Check out the wealthy merchant's home front and center, with a tower built big enough to match his ego. Off the square, a few steps to the right (before the recommended restaurant Le Mirandol), a 14th-century vault leads to a fountain. For generations, this was the town's only source of water, protected by the Virgin Mary. Opposite the restaurant and fountain, enter the wooden doorway (open only July–Aug) and pass through one room to find the massive Renaissance stairway. These show-off stairways, which replaced more space-efficient spiral ones, required a big house and a bigger income. Impressive.

• *Follow the cobbled gutter left on rue des Consuls, and enter the straight-as-an-arrow...*

DORDOGNE

**Rue de la République:** This modern thoroughfare dates from the mid-1800s, when blasting big roads through medieval cities was the fashion. It wasn't until 1963 that Sarlat's other streets would become off-limits to cars, thanks to France's forward-thinking minister of culture, André Malraux. The law that bears his name has served to preserve and restore important monuments and neighborhoods throughout France. Eager to protect the country's architectural heritage, private investors, cities, and regions worked together to create traffic-free zones, rebuild crumbling buildings, and make sure no cables or ugly wiring messed up the ambience of towns like this. Without the Malraux Law, Sarlat might well have more "efficient" roads like rue de la République slicing through what was once a charming old town center.

Your tour is over, but make sure you take time for a poetic ramble—ideally after dark—through this town. This is the only town in France illuminated by gas lamps, which cause the warm limestone to glow, turning the romance of Sarlat up even higher.

• *From here, you can cross rue de la République and wander through Sarlat's quiet, less commercial side, or find a café and raise a toast to Monsieur Malraux.*

# SLEEPING

## In Sarlat

Even with summer crowds, Sarlat is the train-traveler's best home base. Note that in July and August, some hotels require half-pension, and hotels in downtown Sarlat book up first. Parking can be a headache here—drivers will find rooms and parking more easily just outside of town (see "Near Sarlat," see page 345) or in the nearby villages and destinations described under "The Best of the Dordogne River Valley" (most a 15-minute drive away; see page 348).

## Hotels in the Town Center

**$$ La Villa des Consuls\*\*\*,** in an 18th-century home buried on Sarlat's quiet side, has 13 lovely and spacious rooms, several with a kitchen and a living room. Rooms surround a small courtyard, and come with wood floors, private decks, high ceilings, and no-expense-spared amenities such as Internet access, Wi-Fi, microwave ovens, and free washers and dryers. Helpful David helms the ship and prices his rooms to encourage longer stays. These rates are for stays of two to six nights (Db-€75–88, big Db/Tb/Qb-€115–142, 10 percent more for 1-night stays, less for 7 or more days, air-con, garage-€9/day, train station pickup-€6, 3 rue Jean-Jacques Rousseau, tel. 05 53 31 90 05, fax 05 53 31 90 06, www.villaconsuls.com, villadesconsuls@aol.com). David rents bikes to guests and non-guests alike.

---

# Sleep Code

**(€1= about $1.50, country code: 33)**

**S** = Single, **D** = Double/Twin, **T** = Triple, **Q** = Quad, **b** = bathroom, **s** = shower only, * = French hotel rating system (0–4 stars). Unless otherwise noted, credit cards are accepted and English is spoken.

To help you sort easily through these listings, I've divided the rooms into three categories based on the price for a standard double room with bath:

**$$$ Higher Priced**—Most rooms €95 or more.
**$$ Moderately Priced**—Most rooms between €65–95.
**$ Lower Priced**—Most rooms €65 or less.

---

**$$ Hôtel de la Madeleine*** is a central three-star value with professional service, elegant lounges, 39 well-maintained and air-conditioned rooms, and lots of tour groups (standard Db-€85–95, bigger Db-€100–150, Tb-€150–180, Qb-€160–200, elevator, Internet access and Wi-Fi, garage-€8/day, at north end of ring road at 1 place de la Petite Rigaudie, tel. 05 53 59 10 41, fax 05 53 31 03 62, www.hoteldelamadeleine-sarlat.com, hotel.madeleine @wanadoo.fr).

**$ Hôtel Montaigne****, Sarlat's best two-star value, is located a block south of the pedestrian zone. It's sharper than its simple lobby lets on, and is well-run by the welcoming Martinats. The rooms are spotless, spacious, and comfortable. Of the hotels I recommend, this one is nearest the train station (Db-€55–65, Tb-€65–75, easy parking, Internet access and Wi-Fi, place Pasteur, tel. 05 53 31 93 88, fax 05 53 31 99 71, www.hotelmontaigne.fr, contact@hotelmontaigne.fr).

**$ Hôtel de la Mairie** plays second fiddle to its café, which can keep hotel guests awake late. The hotel is young and basic, but well-located, with big rooms right on the main square (Ds-€50, Db-€58, Tb-€75, Qb-€90, rooms #3 and #6 have the best views, reception in café, place de la Liberté, tel. 05 53 59 05 71, fax 05 53 59 59 95, www.hotel-mairie-sarlat.com, contact@hotel-mairie -sarlat.com).

**$ Hôtel la Couleuvrine**** is in a historic building with a great location across from the launderette and near the park, with easy parking (for Sarlat). It offers medieval atmosphere in its two-star rooms, some of which could use new carpets. Families enjoy *les chambres familles* (#19 and #20 are in the tower) and there are three sharp suites. A few rooms have private terraces (Db-€65, Db suite-€85, Tb-€95, Qb-€110, elevator, some rooms have tight bathrooms, on ring road at 1 place de la Bouquerie, tel. 05 53 59 27 80, fax 05 53 31 26 83, www.la-couleuvrine.com, lacouleuvrine@wanadoo.fr). Half-pension is encouraged during busy periods and in the summer—figure €62 per person for room, breakfast, and a good dinner in the classy restaurant. The hotel also has a jazzy stone-vaulted wine bar that serves light meals and good wine by the glass.

### Hotels North of Town

The following hotels are a 10-minute walk north of the old town on avenue de Selves. All have easy parking.

**$$ Hôtel de Selves***,** with 40 well-equipped rooms in a modern shell, offers reliable comfort and amenities, including Internet access, Wi-Fi, sauna, a swimming pool, and a grand piano (Db-€85, bigger Db-€100, Db with balcony-€130, extra bed-€25, all rooms non-smoking, air-con, elevator, garage-€12/day, 93 avenue de Selves, tel. 05 53 31 50 00, fax 05 53 31 23 52, www.selves-sarlat.com, hotel@selves-sarlat.com).

**$$ Hôtel de Compostelle**** features a sleek, open lobby, and bright, modern, mostly spacious rooms, including several big ones for families (Db-€72–86, Tb-€140, Qb-€150 for 4–6 people, air-con, Wi-Fi in lobby, elevator is one floor up, backyard terrace, parking-€6, 64 avenue de Selves, tel. 05 53 59 58 53, fax 05 53 30 31 65, www.hotel-compostelle-sarlat.com, info@hotel-compostelle-sarlat.com).

**$ Hôtel Madrigal**,** one block past Hôtel Compostelle, is a well-maintained 11-room hotel with air-conditioning, Wi-Fi, a weight room, and solid two-star rooms, all with queen-size beds and small bathrooms (Db-€62–75, Tb/Qb-€88, parking-€6, 50 avenue des Selves, tel. 05 53 59 21 98, fax 05 53 30 31 65, www.hotel-madrigal-sarlat.com, info@hotel-madrigal-sarlat.com).

### Chambres d'Hôte

These *chambres d'hôte* are central, and compare well with the hotels listed above.

At **$ Chambres du Glacier,** gentle Monsieur Da Costa offers four cavernous and surprisingly elegant rooms above an outdoor café, in the thick of Sarlat's pedestrian zone (perfect for market days). Rooms come with café noise, sky-high ceilings, big windows over Sarlat's world, wood floors, and bathrooms you can get lost in (Db-€60, Tb-€70, Qb-€82, place de la Liberté, tel. 05 53 29 99 99, www.chambres-du-glacier-sarlat.com, carlos.da.costa.24@wanadoo.fr).

**$** Friendly, English-speaking **Pierre-Henri Toulemon** and French-speaking Diane have five large rooms with a private entry in a 17th-century home. They're located a few steps from the main square (Db-€45, €8 per extra person up to 5, breakfast-€6, cash only, no deposit required—simply call a day or two ahead to confirm your approximate arrival time, look for big steps from northeast corner of place de la Liberté, 4 rue Magnanat, tel. 05 53 31 26 60, mobile 06 08 67 76 90, www.toulemon.com, p-h.toulemon@wanadoo.fr). They also rent two cottages with living rooms and kitchens. One has one bedroom and sleeps four; the other cottage, just renovated, has three bedrooms (3-day minimum, easy parking).

**$$ Les Cordeliers,** owned by gentle Brits Chris and Amanda Johnson, offers four-star comfort at two-star prices. Most of the seven cushy rooms are cavernous; all are air-conditioned and beautifully furnished; and a small kitchen is at your disposal with serve-yourself snacks and drinks. Best of all, the price is unbeatable (Db-€79, 2-night minimum, big breakfast with eggs-€6, closed Nov–Feb, 51 rue des Cordeliers, tel. 05 53 31 94 66, www.hotelsarlat.com, info@hotelsarlat.com).

**$$ La Lanterne,** named for the monument it faces, is home to Brits Terri and Roy Bowen, who have restored a 500-year-old building that could not be more central or more welcoming. Rooms are thoughtfully appointed, and the guest living room was made for lounging (Db-€80–115, Tb apartment-€150, breakfast-€7, cash only, Wi-Fi, 9 bis rue Montaigne, tel. 05 53 59 17 79, mobile 06 31 57 18 23, www.sarlat.biz, info@sarlat.biz).

## Near Sarlat

Many golden stone hotels (with easy parking) surround Sarlat; these listings are good for drivers who prefer to be close to Sarlat, yet in a semi-rural location.

**$$$ Hôtel le Relais de Moussidière***,** a five-minute drive from Sarlat (on the way to Beynac), offers affordable luxury in a lush setting. This nontraditional hotel has a huge pool, private decks, and an almost tropical feel. Friendly husband-and-wife team Dominique and Dominique (no kidding) love Americans, and run the place with enthusiasm. Dominique (she) enjoys taking Americans on hikes and exploring little-known villages with them—just for the pleasure. Faye Dunaway stayed here for a month while filming *The Messenger: The Story of Joan of Arc* (fine standard Db-€112–122, bigger Db-€152, Tb-€144–174, includes buffet breakfast, most rooms have air-con; in Moussidière Basse: leave Sarlat to the south, direction Bergerac, watch for hotel sign on left just after Citroën garage; tel. 05 53 28 28 74, fax 05 53 28 25 11, www.hotel-moussidiere.com, contact@hotel-moussidiere.com).

**$ Hôtel la Verperie** (Green Fields) is aptly named, since it sits barely above Sarlat, surrounded by a park-like setting. Ideal for budget-minded families, the hotel has 25 rooms, a pool, table tennis, swings, restaurant, affordable rates, and adequate comfort in the bungalow-like rooms, each with a simple terrace (Db-€62, Tb-€75, Qb-€98, half-pension requested in high season-€65 per

**DORDOGNE**

adult per day, a 15-min walk just west of Sarlat, look for brown signs to *La Verperie* above the town's eastern side, tel. 05 53 59 00 20, fax 05 53 28 58 94, www.laverperie.com, hotellaverperie @wanadoo.fr).

# EATING

Sarlat is slammed with restaurants that cater to tourists, but you can still dine well and cheaply. The places described below have been very reliable; the last two are the most formal. If you have a car, consider driving to Beynac (page 354) or La Roque-Gageac (page 352) for a riverfront dining experience. Wherever you dine, sample a glass of sweet Monbazillac wine with your foie gras.

**La Mirandol,** a high-energy spot in a town of sleepy restaurants, satisfies local diners with several floors of jam-packed rooms. Those in the know come here for hearty, affordable regional cuisine, thanks to the owner's commitment to providing good food at fair prices. Cap your meal with a wander through their mysteriously lit *cave* (reasonable salads, *plats du jour,* terrific €13–29 *menus,* open daily, a block off rue de la République at 7 rue des Consuls, tel. 05 53 29 53 89).

**Le Petit Manoir** offers creative regional cuisine served in a quiet, elegant setting. Ambience is best in the lovely courtyard; prices are reasonable (€19 and €24 *menus*); and the desserts deserve your attention (closed Mon; just off rue de la République, near the western end of Sarlat, at 3 Passage Payen; tel. 05 53 29 82 14).

**Chez le Gaulois** is a welcome change from the many traditional Dordogne places. Pyrenees-raised Olivier serves a hearty mountain cuisine, with dishes such as fondue, raclette, and *tartiflette* (roasted potatoes mixed with ham and cheese—comes with a good salad for €12), and more. They have a few sidewalk tables, but the fun is inside and the service is English-fluent. The ceiling is cluttered with ham hocks and the soundtrack is jazz (good salads, daily April–Oct, Nov–March closed Sun–Mon, near the TI at 1 rue Tourny, tel. 05 53 59 50 64).

**Brasserie le Glacier** offers the best main square views from its outdoor tables and good café fare at reasonable prices. Come here for friendly service, a big salad or *plat,* and a view of the lights warming the town buildings (open daily, same contact info as Chambres du Glacier—see "Sleeping" section).

**Le Bistro de l'Octroi,** a few blocks north of the old town, is convenient to many hotels I list. Because it's a walk from the town center, it has to provide top cuisine and competitive prices to draw locals—and it does. This easygoing place serves fine bistro fare on a generous garden terrace and within the welcoming interior (daily, several cheap *menus*, 3-course *menu*–€15, 111 avenue des Selves, tel. 05 53 30 83 40).

**Pizzeria Romane** is a cheap, spacious, and family-friendly eatery where you can watch your pizza cook (closed Sun–Mon, on the quiet side of Sarlat at 3 côte de Toulouse, tel. 05 53 59 23 88).

**Hôtel la Couleuvrine** reeks of ambience, with heavy wood beams and white tablecloths. Choose between reliable regional cuisine in a fancy dining room or less-expensive, simpler fare in the jazzy bistro (€23 and €30 *menus,* open daily; also listed under "Sleeping," on page 343).

**Le Présidial** is a venerable place in a historic mansion, with lovely gardens, high ceilings, and almost-stuffy service. With Sarlat's most romantic garden setting, it's best on a balmy evening (allow €45 per person with wine, closed Sun, reservations smart, rue Landry, tel. 05 53 28 92 47).

# TRANSPORTATION CONNECTIONS

Sarlat's TI has train schedules. Souillac and Périgueux are the train hubs for points within the greater region. For all destinations below, you can go west, via the Libourne/Bordeaux line (transferring in either city, depending on your connection); or east, via SNCF bus to Souillac (covered by railpass, bus leaves from Sarlat train station). I've listed the fastest path in each case. Sarlat train info: tel. 05 53 59 00 21.

**From Sarlat by Train to: Paris** (7/day, allow 6 hrs: 3/day with change in Libourne or Bordeaux–St. Jean, then TGV; and 4/day via bus to Souillac, then train with possible change in Brive-la-Gaillarde), **Amboise** (4/day, 5–6 hrs, via Libourne or Bordeaux–St. Jean, then TGV to Tours' St. Pierre-des-Corps, then local train to Amboise), **Limoges/Oradour-sur-Glane** (slow and difficult trip with lots of changes, 5/day, 3–4 hrs: 3/day via bus to Souillac and train to Limoges, then bus to Oradour-sur-Glane; and 2/day with change in Le Buisson and Périgueux), **Cahors** (5/day, 2–3 hrs, bus to Souillac, then train to Cahors), **Albi** and **Carcassonne** (2/day, 4.5 hrs with changes in Le Buisson, Agen, and Toulouse; or 3/day, 6–7 hrs via bus to Souillac, then train with changes possible in Brive-la-Gaillarde and Toulouse), **St. Emilion** (4/day, 2–3 hrs, transfer in St. Foy; or 3/day to nearby Libourne, then bus or taxi to St. Emilion).

**To Beynac, La Roque-Gageac, Castelnaud, and Domme:** These are accessible only by taxi (allow €19–23) or bike (best rented in Sarlat). See Sarlat's "Helpful Hints," page 337, for specifics.

# The Best of the Dordogne River Valley

The most scenic stretch of the Dordogne lies between Carsac and Beynac. Traveling by canoe (see "Dordogne Canoe Trip," later in this section) is the best way to savor the highlights of the Dordogne River Valley, though several scenic sights lie off the river and require a car or bike. Following my "Dordogne River Valley Scenic Loop" directions, below, you can easily link Sarlat (described earlier) with La Roque-Gageac (see page 352), Beynac and its château (see page 354), and Castelnaud (see page 354) before returning to Sarlat.

## Planning Your Time

Vitrac Port (near Sarlat) is the best place to park for a canoe ride down the river. La Roque-Gageac, Beynac, and Domme have good restaurants (described later in this section). There are several good places to witness the *gavage* (feeding of the geese and ducks to make foie gras—see sidebar on page 356) between Beynac and Sarlat (their dinner time is generally about 18:00).

## SELF-GUIDED TOURS

### ▲▲Dordogne River Valley Scenic Loop

Following the directions below, you can see this area by car or bike (27 hilly miles) beginning and ending in Sarlat. Cyclists can cut 10 miles off this distance and see most of the highlights by aiming for La Roque-Gageac first (leave Sarlat to the south, then follow signs to *La Roque-Gageac*). For a longer bike trip that still avoids a busy road, follow the directions below, but skip Carsac and head first to Montfort (see map on page 351).

From Sarlat, drivers should follow signs along D-704 toward *Cahors* and *Carsac*. Cyclists heading to Montfort should start on the same route, then take the Montfort turn-off (well-signed at a roundabout). Just after leaving Sarlat, pass the foie gras outlet store, then the limestone quarry that gives the houses in this area their lemony color. The cornfields are busy growing food for ducks and geese—locals are appalled that humans would eat the stuff.

Drivers shouldn't miss the little signposted exit on the right to the **Eglise de Carsac (Church of Carsac),** just before Carsac. Set peacefully among cornfields, with its WWI monument, bonsai-like plane trees, and simple Romanesque exterior, the church is part of a classic rural French scene. Take a break here and enter the church if it's open.

From here drivers should continue on, following signs to *Montfort*. About a half-mile (1 kilometer) west of Carsac, pull over to enjoy the scenic viewpoint (overlooking a bend in the river known as Cingle de Montfort). Across the Dordogne River, fields of walnut trees stretch to distant castles, while the nearby hills are covered in oak trees. This region, Périgord, is nicknamed "black Périgord" for its thick blanket of oaks, which stay leafy throughout the winter. The fairy-tale castle you see is **Montfort.** While it was once the medieval home of Simon de Montfort—who led the Cathar Crusades in the early 13th century—today it's considered mysterious by locals. (The hometown rumor is that the castle is now the home of a brother of the emir of Kuwait.)

Continue on, passing under Montfort's castle (not worth a stop). If you're combining a canoe trip with this drive, cross the river following signs to *Domme*, and find my recommended canoe rental on the right side (see "Dordogne Canoe Trip," below). Otherwise, follow the signs to **La Roque-Gageac,** then on to **Castelnaud,** and finally to **Beynac,** with its imposing castle (all three towns are described in this chapter). From Beynac, it's a quick run back to Sarlat.

If you're driving, the charming, very touristy *bastide* (fortified village) of **Domme** is worth a side trip from Vitrac Port or La Roque-Gageac for its sensational views (see page 352). To resume your tour, return to La Roque-Gageac and follow signs downriver to Castelnaud.

## ▲▲▲Dordogne Canoe Trip

For a refreshing break from the car or train, explore the riverside castles and villages of the Dordogne by canoe (see my recommended canoe route, below).

You can rent plastic canoes—which are hard, light, and indestructible—from many outfits in this area. Whether a one-person kayak or a two-person canoe, they're stable enough for beginners. Many rental places will pick you up at an agreed-upon spot (even in Sarlat, provided that your group is big enough, or that they aren't too busy). All companies let you put in anytime between from 9:30 and 16:00 (if you start at 16:00, they'll pick you up at about 18:00). They all charge about the same (€10–15/person for two-person canoes, €15–20 for one-person kayaks). You'll get a life vest and, for a few extra euros, a watertight bucket in which to store your belongings. (The bucket is too big for just a camera, watch, wallet, and cell phone, so bring a resealable plastic baggie or something similar for dry storage on the canoe.) The trip is fun even in the rain (if you don't mind getting wet). Beach your boat wherever you want to take a break—it's light enough that you can simply drag it up high and dry to go explore. (The canoes aren't

**DORDOGNE**

worth stealing, since they're cheap and clearly color-coded for their parent company.) It's OK if you're a complete novice—the only whitewater you'll encounter will be the rare wake of passing tour boats...and your travel partner frothing at the views.

Of the region's many canoe companies, only **Copeyre Canoë** has a pull-out arrangement in Beynac (to get there, cross the river at Port Vitrac and turn right). Readers of this book get a 10 percent discount in 2009, and they'll even pick you up in Sarlat for free (this allows non-drivers a chance to explore the riverfront villages for the price of a canoe trip—tip the driver a few euros for this good service, tel. 05 53 28 23 82, www.canoe-copeyre.com).

**The Nine-Mile, Two-Hour Paddle from Vitrac Port to Beynac:** This is the most interesting, scenic, and handy trip if you're based in or near Sarlat. Vitrac Port, on the river close to Sarlat, is a handy starting point. And, with its mighty castle and pleasant hotels and restaurants, Beynac is a great place to end your journey.

Here's a rundown of the two-hour Vitrac–Beynac adventure: Leave Vitrac Port, paddling through lush, forested land. The fortified hill town of Domme will be dead ahead. Pass through Heron Gulch, and after about 45 minutes, you'll come to La Roque-Gageac (one of two easy and worthwhile stops before Beynac).

Paddle past La Roque-Gageac's wooden docks (where the tour boats normally tie up) to the stone ramp at the town. Do a 180-degree turn and beach thyself, dragging the boat high and dry. From there, you're in La Roque-Gageac's tiny town center, with a TI and plenty of restaurants nearby. Enjoy the town (described on page 352) before heading back to your canoe and into the water.

When leaving La Roque-Gageac, turn around to enjoy the village view. About 15 minutes farther downstream, you'll approach views of the feudal village and castle of Castelnaud. Look for the castle's huge model of a medieval catapult silhouetted menacingly against the sky (it's a steep but worthwhile climb to tour this castle—see page 354). Two grassy pullouts flank the bridge below the castle, and the bridge arches make terrific frames for castle views. Just past the grass there's a small market and charcuterie with all you need for a fine picnic, and a café/restaurant.

Another 15 minutes downstream brings views of Château de Fayrac on your left. The lords of Castlenaud built this to better spy on Beynac during the Hundred Years' War. Now on to your last stop: Beynac. The awesome Beynac castle—looming high above the town—gets better and better as you approach. Slow down and enjoy the ride (there's a snack stand with the same views at the bridge on the right). Head to the Copeyre canoe depot at the downstream end of town. You'll see the ramp just before the parking lot and wooden dock (where the tour boats generally tie up). Do another 180-degree turn, and beach yourself hard. The office

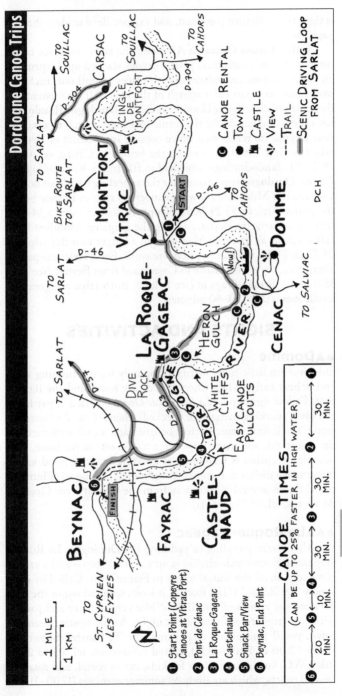

**Dordogne Canoe Trips**

TO SOUILLAC
TO SOUILLAC
CARSAC
D-704
CINGLE DE MONTFORT
TO CAHORS
TO SARLAT
D-704

**C** CANOE RENTAL
● TOWN
🏰 CASTLE
↘ VIEW
--- TRAIL
— SCENIC DRIVING LOOP FROM SARLAT

BIKE ROUTE TO SARLAT
MONTFORT
VITRAC
START
D-46
TO CAHORS
TO SARLAT
D-46
Wow!
LA ROQUE-GAGEAC
HERON GULCH
DOMME
TO SALVIAC
CENAC
DORDOGNE RIVER
WHITE CLIFFS
EASY CANOE PULLOUTS
DIVE ROCK
D-703
CASTEL-NAUD
FAYRAC
TO SARLAT
D-57
BEYNAC
Finish
TO ST. CYPRIEN + LES EYZIES

1 MILE
1 KM
N

**CANOE TIMES**
(CAN BE UP TO 25% FASTER IN HIGH WATER)

6 ← 20 MIN. ← 5 ← 10 MIN. ← 4 ← 30 MIN. ← 3 ← 30 MIN. ← 2 ← 30 MIN. ← 1

1 Start Point (Copeyre Canoes at Vitrac Port)
2 Pont de Cénac
3 La Roque-Gageac
4 Castelnaud
5 Snack Bar/View
6 Beynac, End Point

DCH

DORDOGNE

is right there. Return your boat, and explore Beynac (described on page 354).

**Other Canoe Options:** All along the river you'll see canoe companies, each with their plastic canoes stacked up. Depending on their location and relations with places to pull out, each one works best on a particular stretch of the river. All have essentially the same policies. Below Domme in Cénac, **Dordogne Randonées** has canoes and kayaks for the scenic two-hour stretch to a pullout near Beynac (to reach their office coming from Sarlat or Beynac, take the first left after crossing the bridge to Cénac, tel. 05 53 28 22 01, randodordogne@wanadoo.fr). In La Roque-Gageac, **Canoe-Dordogne** rents canoes for the appealing two-hour float to Château des Milandes, allowing canoers to stop in Beynac before the pullout (tel. 05 53 29 58 50). **Copeyre** also arranges a 14-mile trip from Carsac to Beynac, adding the gorgeous Montfort loop, called *Cingle de Montfort* (they also do a longer two-day trip, tel. 05 53 28 23 82, www.canoe-copeyre.com). For a lazier no-paddle alternative, try a river cruise to Castelnaud from Beynac (see page 354) or La Roque-Gageac (see below). Both trips are great for landlubbers (€8–9, 50–60 minutes).

# SIGHTS AND ACTIVITIES

## ▲▲Domme

This overrun little town merits a stop only for its stunning view, and is best early or late when crowds are fewer and the light is best. Follow signs up to *La Bastide de Domme.* Park at a pay lot in the town (parking meters are checked), then follow *Le Panorama* signs. You'll find picnic-perfect benches and a café with views at the panorama, and many forgettable restaurants in the town. One notable exception is **Cabanoix et Chataigne,** with good-value, imaginative dishes that combine traditional cuisine with international flavor (several blocks away from the view at 3 rue Geoffroy de Vivans, tel. 05 53 31 07 11).

## ▲▲▲La Roque-Gageac

Whether you're joyriding or paddling the Dordogne, La Roque-Gageac (lah rohk-gah-zhahk) is an essential stop—and a strong contender on all the "cutest towns in France" lists. Called by most simply "La Roque" ("The Rock"), it looks sculpted out of the rock between the river and the cliffs. While very touristy and packed with day-trippers, it's tranquil at night. At the upstream end of town, you'll find plenty of parking, the **TI** (Easter–Sept daily 10:00–12:00 & 14:00–18:00, closed off-season, tel. 05 53 29 17 01), a WC, swings and slides for kids, canoe rental, and *pétanque (boules)* courts, which are lively on summer evenings (17:00–21:00).

**DORDOGNE**

A small market brightens La Roque-Gageac on Friday mornings.

La Roque-Gageac is a one-street town stretching along the river. Cars and strollers compete for the same riverfront space. Walk above the river, past the boat docks and trees, and survey the town: The highest stone work (on the far right) was home to the town's earliest inhabitants in the 10th century. The 12th-century cave-dwellers' village (to the left, high above the Hôtel Belle Etoile) was built during the era of Norman (Viking) river raids. Long after the Vikings were tamed, French soldiers used this lofty perch as a barracks while fighting against England in the Hundred Years' War.

Now locate the exotic foliage by the church on the right. Tropical gardens (bamboo, bananas, lemons, and so on) are a village forte, since limestone absorbs heat.

Every winter, La Roque-Gageac endures a flood that would leave you (standing where you are now) underwater. When there's a big rain in central France, La Roque-Gageac floods two days later. The first floors of all the riverfront buildings are vacated off-season. (A house about five buildings down from Hôtel Belle Etoile shows various high-water marks—*inondation* means "flood.")

Looking farther downstream, notice the fanciful castle built in the 19th century by a British aristocrat (whose family still nurtures Joan of Arc dreams in its turrets). The old building just beyond that (downstream end of town) actually is historic—it's the quarantine house, where lepers and out-of-town visitors who dropped by in times of plague would be kept (after their boats were burned).

On the river you'll see small tour boats. While modern, they're modeled after the boats that were originally built here to take prized oak barrels down to Bordeaux. Unable to return against the river current, those boats were routinely taken apart for their lumber. Today, tourists, rather than barrels, fill the boats as they make a scenic round-trip on one-hour cruises to Castlenaud and back (€9, 2/hr, April–Nov daily, tel. 05 53 29 40 44). If you're experiencing a movie-based déjà vu, it's because these actual boats (dolled up, of course) were used by Johnny Depp, who delighted viewers and Juliette Binoche alike in the movie *Chocolat*.

Climb into the town by strolling up the cobbled lane to the right of the Hôtel Belle Etoile. The path ends where a right turn takes you to the exotic garden and viewpoint (in front of the simple church), and a left turn takes you to the privately owned and overpriced Fort Troglodyte (€5, daily 10:00–19:00). Fort Troglodyte—with lots of steps, grand views, and piles of rocks in caves evoking medieval paranoia—is worth the money and energy only if you won't be visiting the similar but much better La Roque St. Christophe (see page 373).

**DORDOGNE**

### ▲▲▲Castelnaud

This crumbling castle looks less mighty than Château de Beynac (across the river), but this sight packs a fine medieval punch. Now a museum, every room in the château has a story to tell. Several rooms
display weaponry and artifacts from
the Hundred Years' War, and others
have videos (with English subtitles),
interactive computers (in English),
and castle models. From the armory
to the kitchen, the whole experience
is designed to teach you about daily
castle life, from the battlefield to the dinner table. The upper court-yard has a 150-foot-deep well (drop a pebble). The rampart views are as unbeatable as the siege machines (located outside the walls) are formidable. Pick up the free and essential English explanations and follow *Suite de la Visite* signs to stay on course (€8, daily July–Aug 9:00–20:00, April–June and Sept 10:00–19:00, Oct and Feb–March 10:00–18:00, Nov–Jan 14:00–17:00, last entry one hour before clos-ing; from the river, it's a steep 20-min hike through the village, or drive to the €2 parking lot at the castle gate; daily demonstrations of medieval warfare mid-July–Aug, several restaurants near the castle's parking lot, tel. 05 53 31 30 00, www.castelnaud.com).

You can stop at Castelnaud on your canoe trip, or hike an hour from Beynac along a riverside path (while it's tricky to follow in parts—it hugs the river as it passes through campgrounds and farms—determined walkers do fine).

### ▲▲▲Beynac

The other must-see, picture-perfect Dordogne village, located four miles downstream from La Roque-Gageac, is Beynac (bay-nak).

It comes with a big, foreboding bonus: one of the most imposing castles in France.

The feudal village of Beynac tumbles down a steep hill from its majestic castle to the river far below. You'll have the Dordogne River at your doorstep and a perfectly pre-served medieval village winding, like a sepia-tone film set, from the beach to the castle above. Except for the castle, there's noth-ing to "tour." The purely stone village—with steep streets that still have their Languedoc (old French) names—is just plain pretty. The floodlit village is always open for evening strollers.

**Orientation:** The **TI** is across from the recommended Hôtel du Château (daily 10:00–12:30 & 14:00–17:30, tel. 05 53 29 43 08). Pick up the *Plan de Beynac* in English for a simple self-guided walking tour, and get information on hiking and canoes. A few steps down from the TI is the post office (which has an ATM). A nearby bakery has picnic fixings. If you need a lift, call Beynac-based **Taxi Corrine** (see "Getting Around the Dordogne," page 331). There's a sweet little market on Monday mornings in the river parking lot. In summer (mid-June–mid-Sept), drivers pay to park at lots located on the river, way up at the castle (follow signs to *Château de Beynac*), or halfway between. The same parking ticket works up at the château if you decide against the climb. Take everything out of your car.

**Hikes:** A too-busy road separates Beynac from its river. The village climbs steeply uphill from there to the château—the farther you get from the road, the more medieval the village feels. (You can drive up via a long lane looping around the back of town.) A trail, which begins across from Hôtel Bonnet at the eastern end of town, follows the river toward Castelnaud, with great views back toward Beynac and—for able route-finders—a healthy one-hour hike to Castelnaud. Find time to walk at least a few hundred yards along this trail to enjoy the view to Beynac.

**Château de Beynac:** Beynac's brooding, cliff-clinging château—worth ▲▲—soars 500 feet above the Dordogne River.

During the Hundred Years' War (see sidebar on page 201), the castle of Beynac housed the French, while the British set up camp across the river at Castelnaud. From the condition of the castles, it looks like France won. This sparsely furnished castle is most interesting for the valley views, but it still manages to evoke a powerful medieval feel. (These castles never had much furniture in any case.) Stone oil lamps light the way; swords, spears, and crossbows keep you honest; and the two stone WCs keep kids entertained. I like the soldiers' party room best—park your sword at the door and hang your crossbow on the hooks above, please. Notice the list across from the ticket window showing *Beynac et Ses Barons* (the barons of Beynac: *croisade* means Crusade, and *Coeur de Lion* means Lionheart—Richard the Lionhearted spent 10 years here). The current owner lives above the ticket booth. Authentic-looking wooden stockades were installed for the 1998 filming of the movie *The Messenger: The Story of Joan of Arc*. You're free to wander on your own, though after 17:00, you might be required to follow a tour. Pick up the English explanations (€0.15) or spring for the €5 well-done Château de Beynac pamphlet (€7, daily June–Sept 10:00–18:30, April–May and Oct closes at 18:00,

**DORDOGNE**

## Foie Gras and Force-Feeding the Geese

Force-feeding geese has the result of quickly fattening their livers, in order to make the Dordogne specialty, goose-liver pâté (foie gras). The practice is as controversial among animal rights' activists as bullfighting (a topic of much debate in Spain). While some view these geese as tortured prisoners, here's the (politically incorrect) perspective of those who produce and consume such farm-raised animals:

French enthusiasts of *la gavage* (as the force-feeding process is called) say the animals are calm, in no pain, and are designed to take in food in this manner, because of their massive gullets and expandable livers (used to store lots of fat for their long migrations). Geese do not have a gag reflex, and the linings of their throats are tough (they swallow rocks to store in their gizzards for grinding the food they eat). They can eat lots of food easily, without choking. They live lives at least as comfy as the chickens, cows, and pigs that many people have no problem eating, and are slaughtered as humanely as any non-human can expect in this food-chain existence.

The quality of foie gras depends on a stress-free environment; geese do best with the same human feeder and a steady flow of good corn. These mostly free-range geese live six months (most of our factory-farmed chickens in the US live less than two

Nov–March at 16:00 or 17:00—depending on weather and whim, last entry 45 min before closing, tel. 05 53 29 50 40).

**Viewpoints:** Even if you pass on the castle, hike or drive up to the town lookout for a commanding top-of-the-village view, which overlooks several castles and the river. Walk outside the village at the top (parking available), turn right (passing the little cemetery), and walk uphill until the view opens up. Castelnaud's castle hangs on the hill in the distance straight ahead; Château de Fayrac (owned by a Texan) is by the bridge just in front of Castelnaud, and was originally constructed by the lords of Castlenaud to keep a closer eye on the castle of Beynac. The Château de Marqueyssac is on a hill a bit to the left, and was built by the barons of Beynac to keep a closer eye on the boys at Castlenaud. More than a thousand such castles were erected in the Dordogne alone during the Hundred Years' War (1336–1453).

Two exceptional views of Beynac are nearby. The first lies along the riverside path that's opposite Hôtel Bonnet (walk as far as you can for great views back to Beynac); or drive about a months, and are plumped with hormones). Their "golden weeks" are the last three or four, when they go into the pen to have their livers fattened. With two or three feedings a day, their liver grows from about a quarter-pound to nearly two pounds. A goose with a fattened liver looks like he's waddling around with a full diaper under his feathers. (Signs and placards in the towns of the region show geese with this unique and, for foie gras lovers, mouth-watering shape.) The same process is applied to ducks to get the marginally less exquisite and less expensive duck-liver pâté.

The varieties of product you'll be tempted to buy (or order in restaurants) can be confusing. Here's a primer: first, *foie gras* means "fattened liver"; *foie gras d'oie* is from a goose, while *foie gras de canard* is from a duck (you'll also see a blend of the two). *Pâté de foie gras* is a "paste" of foie gras combined with other meats, fats, and seasonings (think of liverwurst). Most American consumers get the chance to eat foie gras only in the form of pâtés.

The *foie gras d'oie entier* (a solid chunk of pure goose liver) is the most expensive and prized version of foie gras, costing about €18 for 130 grams (about a tuna-can-size tin). The *bloc de foie gras d'oie* is made of chunks of pure goose liver that have been whipped to make them spreadable (figure €14 for 130 grams). The *medaillons de foie gras d'oie* must be at least 50 percent foie gras (the rest will be a pâté filler, about €8 for 130 grams). A small tin of blended duck-and-goose foie gras costs about €5.

After a week in the Dordogne, I leave feeling a strong need for foie gras detox.

half-mile toward La Roque-Gageac, and turn right at the Auberge du Château restaurant and follow the road to its end for similar views). But for the best (and easiest) village view, simply step up on the short wall between the parking lot and the river—just try fitting it all in your camera's viewfinder.

**Boat Trips:** Boats leave from Beynac's riverside parking lot for relaxing, 50-minute river cruises to Castlenaud and back (€8, nearly hourly, departures Easter–Oct daily 10:00–12:30 & 14:00–18:00, more frequent trips July–Aug, written English explanations, tel. 05 53 28 51 15).

## Foie Gras Farms

During the evenings, many farms in this area let you witness the force-feeding of geese for the "ultimate pleasure" of foie gras. Look for *Gavage* signs, but beware: It's hard for the squeamish to watch (read the sidebar above for a description before you visit). Of the three places listed below, the first is by far the best, with the only real tour. The second is a short walk from the Beynac castle (and therefore very handy), while the last is tiny, homey, and the most flexible in its hours. For locations, see the map on page 363.

**Elevage du Bouyssou,** a big homey goose farm a short drive from Sarlat, is run by a couple who enjoy their work. Denis Mazet (the latest in a long line of goose farmers here) spends five hours a day feeding his gaggle of geese. His wife Nathalie—clearly in love with country life—speaks wonderful English and enthusiastically shows guests around their idyllic farm. Each evening, she leads a one-hour, kid-friendly tour. You'll meet the geese babies, do a little unforced feeding, and hear how every part of the goose (except heads and feet) is used—even feathers (for pillows). Nathalie explains why locals see the force-feeding as humane (the same as raising any other animal for human consumption) before you step into the dark barn where about a hundred geese await another dinner. The tour finishes in the little shop. They raise and slaughter a thousand geese annually, producing about 1,500 pounds of foie gras—most of which is sold directly to visitors at good prices. In July and August, Nathalie includes a tasting of sweet wine on the tour (tours daily at 18:30 year-round, groups welcome, English tour on request at any time, tel. 05 53 31 12 31, elevagebouyssou@wanadoo.fr). To get to the farm, leave Sarlat on the Carsac-bound road (D-704), go about seven kilometers in the direction of Carsac, turn left at the cement plant, and follow *Bouyssou* signs until you reach the farm.

**Madame Gauthier,** a small farm where you can also observe the *gavage* and buy the product, is just down the road behind Château de Beynac. You can park there, or walk 10 minutes from the château through the parking lot and away from the river—you'll see signs (demonstrations 17:30–19:30, best to come at 17:30, no tour, tel. 05 53 29 51 45).

**La Ferme de l'Angle** is a tiny goose farm in the scenic middle of nowhere, a short distance north of Sarlat. Christiane (who speaks English) and Cyril (who speaks goose) are retired, and enjoy playing host to the guests who drop by. In July and August, they offer a small tasting *menu* in their yard. While there's no formal tour here and only a handful of geese, this is an easy way to see the *gavage* in action, since Cyril will demonstrate at just about any time (open daily, tel. 05 53 31 16 63). To get to the farm, located three miles from Sarlat, take D-704 (direction: Brive/Montignac), at Restaurant la Vieille Grange, take a left and follow signs.

# SLEEPING AND EATING

## Along the Dordogne River
**(€1= about $1.50, country code: 33)**

Those with a car can enjoy plush and tranquil rural accommodations at great prices. Here are a handful of good-value places located within a 15-minute drive of Sarlat. I like them for their locations in charming villages, the comfort they provide, the views they offer, or for a combination of these qualities. Read about the villages they're in (listed earlier), then make your choice—you can't go wrong.

## Sleeping and Eating in La Roque-Gageac

Along with Beynac, this is one of the region's most beautiful villages. Park in the lot at the eastern end of town if you're staying in any of these hotels, and take everything of value out of your car.

**$ Hôtel Belle Etoile**, located on the river in the center of La Roque-Gageac, is one of the best-run two-star hotel-restaurants in the region. Hostess Danielle and chef Régis (ray-geez)—who greets every diner—make the ideal team, with a loyal staff. Rooms are comfy and well-maintained; most have river views. The hotel is closed from November through March (non-riverview Db-€50, riverview Db-€66 or €76 for better view—I like the €66 rooms, gorgeous suite-€120–150, reserve private parking ahead, tel. 05 53 29 51 44, fax 05 53 29 45 63, www.belleetoile.fr, hotel.belle-etoile @wanadoo.fr). The hotel's **restaurant** is how I discovered this place—it's where locals go for a fine meal. They serve a memorable dinner of classic French cuisine in a romantic setting. The serving sizes are not great, but the quality is (*menus* from €27, closed for lunch Wed and all day Mon).

**$ Auberge des Platanes** has 13 rooms above a sprawling café and a restaurant across from the TI and parking lot. Service is less personal than at Hôtel Belle Etoile, as hotel guests take a back seat to café clients, but rooms are traditional, comfortable, and a good value (Sb-€35, Db-€45–50, Tb-€55–65, tel. 05 53 29 51 58, fax 05 53 31 19 32, www.aubergedesplatanes.com, contact @aubergedesplatanes.com).

**$ Hotel le Périgord** is a few strokes upriver from La Roque-Gageac. This newer hotel faces the hill town of Domme from across the river below, and rents traditional rooms at fair rates with nice gardens, a view pool, tennis courts, a game room, and a good restaurant (Db-€57–67, extra person-€16, Port de Domme, tel. 05 53 28 36 55, 05 53 28 38 73, www.hotelleperigord.eu, bienvenue @hotelleperigord.eu).

## Sleeping in Beynac

My favorite village on the river comes with some traffic noise and the region's greatest castle. Pay to park at the riverside lot (any day mid-June–mid-Sept) or park for free 300 yards up the road toward the castle. All parking is free overnight (19:00–10:00) and off-season. Parked cars are appealing to thieves.

**DORDOGNE**

**$ Hôtel du Château\*\***, on the river at Beynac's only—but busy—intersection, is run by an enterprising couple who are industriously transforming this hotel. There's a full café/bar, a good restaurant, free Internet access, Wi-Fi, and a small swimming pool. It's run by eager-to-please Sarissa and Christoph, a French-Dutch couple with two children and dog Max. The 16 rooms, most with queen-size beds, are bright and pleasant. Some have street noise, though air-conditioning (available in some rooms) solves that. Other rooms have terraces facing the river; four rooms can sleep up to four people and one has a full kitchen. Their half-pension is a good value (Sb-€45–65, Db-€50–70, price range is from mid- to high-season, tel. 05 53 29 19 20, fax 05 53 28 55 56, www.hotel duchateau-dordogne.com, info@hotelduchateau-dordogne.com).

**$ Chambres Residence Versailles** does its name justice, with five immaculate rooms that Louis himself would have appreciated. They have laundry facilities, Internet access, Wi-Fi, a quiet terrace and garden, and—best of all—the welcoming Fleurys, Jean-Claude and Françoise, who speak just enough English (Db-€60, three rooms have fine views, all have big beds, includes large English breakfast, cash only, no smoking anywhere, reserve ahead for a terrific home-cooked dinner-€20, route du Château, tel. & fax 05 53 29 35 06, www.lepetitversailles.fr, info@lepetitversailles .fr). With the river on your right, take the small road—wedged between the hill and Hôtel Bonnet—for a half-mile, turn right when you see their sign and continue 100 yards, then take a right down a steep driveway.

## Eating in Beynac

Beynac has a handful of worthwhile restaurants and a bakery with handy picnic-ready lunch items (across from the TI). Have a drink up high at the café opposite the castle entry, or down below at the café that hides right on the river (walk down the steps across from Hôtel du Château), and stay for dinner if the spirit moves you.

**Hôtel du Château** offers cozy dining in air-conditioned comfort, generous servings and reasonable prices (€16 salad/pasta bar, dinner *menus* from €18, daily, see hotel listing earlier).

**Taverne/Café des Remparts,** Beynac's scenic eatery, faces the castle at the top of the town and serves copious salads (try the *Paysanne* or *Gourmande*), good omelets, *plats*—or just a drink. I can't imagine leaving Beynac without relaxing at their view-perfect café for at least a drink; it's best at night, but call ahead to be sure they're open (July–Aug daily for lunch and dinner, otherwise open daily for lunch and Fri–Mon for dinner, across from castle, tel. 05 53 29 57 76).

**La Petite Tonnelle** has a romantic interior and a front terrace, and serves reliable and inviting cuisine at fair prices. It's a block up from Hôtel du Château (€16 two-course *menu,* €28 three-course *menu,* closed Tue–Wed except in summer, on the road to the castle, tel. 05 53 29 95 18).

## Sleeping near Castelnaud

This village, ideally situated between La Roque-Gageac and Beynac, has three excellent B&B choices nearby.

**$$ La Tour de Cause** is where California refugees Albert and Caitlin have found their heaven, amid their renovated farmhouse with five top-quality rooms, a well-tended garden, a big pool, Internet access, and, best of all, a *pétanque* court. Albert restores homes in California, and has taken his considerable talent to France (Sb-€70, Db-€85, includes breakfast, cash only, 2-night minimum mid-July–Aug, closed Nov–April, tel. 05 53 30 30 51, US tel. Nov–March 707/527-5051, www.latourdecause.com, info @latourdecause.com). From the Dordogne River, cross the bridge to Castelnaud, follow signs toward *Daglan,* and turn right in the hamlet of Pont de Cause; park at the blue gate.

**$$ Château Nineyrol** is a relaxed, welcoming place run by British expat Anne Penfold, who is as excited about this region as you are. She has five guest rooms with ramshackle personality: two big rooms (each sleeps up to four) and three smallish doubles; all the rooms have en-suite bathrooms. Enjoy the large pool and terrace with views of Castelnaud castle. Anne cooks a nice dinner—€25 for the works, including wine (Db-€65–75, Tb-€78–98, Qb-€86–136, laundry service available, bikes for rent, guided tours, tel. 05 53 30 46 01, mobile 06 33 61 34 63, www.nineyrol.com, nineyrol @wanadoo.fr). From Beynac it's on the road to La Roque-Gageac, 100 yards past the turnoff for Castelnaud, on your left.

**$ Le Lys de Castelnaud** is run by French medieval enthusiasts Nathalie and Dominque. Nathalie is a Joan of Arc fanatic and speaks sufficient English to explain her passion. The decor is steeped in the Middle Ages, with knights in armor, tapestries, and old swords. The four rooms are well priced (three have Castelnaud views) and have all the modern conveniences (Db-€55–60, Tb/ Qb-€80, Internet access, cash only, tel. 05 53 28 20 27, mobile 06 09 57 21 97, www.chambres-dordogne.com, lysdecastelnaud@aol .com). It's well-signed at the foot of the road that leads across the river to Castlenaud.

## Sleeping in Montfort

There's more to this castle-topped village than meets the eye— leave most tourists behind and find a few cafés, a pizzeria, and a handful of *chambres d'hôte,* including this recommended listing.

**$$ Chambres la Barde** is where Steve (he's British) and Bronwen (she's Welsh) offer five sumptuous rooms in their modern

**DORDOGNE**

and warm stone home. They have a swimming pool, cozy lounge, big grass yard, *pétanque,* game room, and views to Montfort castle from each room's terrace (Db-€65–85, €15 per extra person, breakfast-€6, one room sleeps five, cash only, below Montfort castle—green signs guide you there, tel. 05 53 28 24 34, mobile 06 21 96 51 90, www .perigord-dordogne-sarlat.com, steve.houghton@wanadoo.fr).

# Cro-Magnon Caves

The towns and sights of the Dordogne region—including Les Eyzies-de-Tayac, Grotte de Font-de-Gaume, Abri du Cap Blanc, Grotte de Rouffignac, Lascaux II, and Grotte de Cougnac—have a rich history of prehistoric cave art. The paintings you'll see here are famous throughout the world for their remarkably modern-looking technique, beauty, and mystery. To fully appreciate them, take time to read the following information, written by Gene Openshaw, on the purpose of the art and the Cro-Magnon style of painting.

## Cave Art 101

From 18,000 to 10,000 b.c., long before Stonehenge, before the pyramids, before metalworking, farming, and domesticated dogs, back when mammoths and saber-toothed cats still roamed the earth, prehistoric people painted deep inside limestone caverns in southern France and northern Spain. These are not crude doodles with a charcoal-tipped stick. They're sophisticated, costly, and time-consuming engineering projects planned and executed by dedicated artists supported by a unified and stable culture—the Magdalenians.

**The Magdalenians (c. 18,000–10,000 b.c.):** These hunter-gatherers of the Upper Paleolithic period (40,000–10,000 b.c.) were driven south by the Second Ice Age. (Historians named them after the Madeline archaeological site.) The Magdalenians flourished in southern France and northern Spain for eight millennia—long enough to chronicle the evolution and extinction of several animal species. (Think: Egypt lasted a mere 3,000 years; Rome lasted 1,000; America fewer than 250 so far.)

Physically, the people were Cro-Magnons. Unlike hulking, beetle-browed Neanderthals, Cro-Magnons were fully developed *Homo sapiens* who could blend in to our modern population. We know these people by the possessions found in their settlements: stone axes, flint arrowheads, bone needles for making clothes, musical instruments, grease lamps (without their juniper wicks), and cave paintings and sculpture. Many objects are beautifully decorated.

The Magdalenians did not live in the deep limestone caverns they painted (which are cold and inaccessible). But many

## Cro-Magnon Caves near Sarlat

PARIS

TO PÉRIGUEUX
& ST. EMILION
VIA A-89

TO N-89 & A-89:
PÉRIGUEUX

TO A-20:
LIMOGES,
ORADOUR-SUR-GLANE
& MORTEMART

MONTIGNAC

N

Grotte de
Rouffignac

ST.
LÉON

Lascaux
II

TO SOUILLAC
& A-20

VÉZÈRE

La Roque
St. Christophe

Les Eyzies
(Museum)

Abri du
Cap Blanc

LE
BUGUE

Grotte
de Font-
de-Gaume

LA FERME
DE L'ANGLE

SARLAT

ST.
CYPRIEN

MADAME
GAUTHIER'S

MONT-
FORT

ÉLEVAGE DU
BOUYSSOU

LE
BUISSON

BEYNAC

VITRAC

CARSAC

TO
BERGERAC
& ST. EMILION

CHÂTEAU
DES
MILANDES

LA
ROQUE-
GAGEAC

TO
SOUILLAC
& COLLONGES-
LA-ROUGE

CASTEL-
NAUD

DOMME

Grottes
de
Cougnac

**CASTLE**

**PREHISTORIC
SIGHTS**

**SCENIC LOOP**

**FOIE GRAS FARM**

CÉNAC

**DORDOGNE
RIVER**

TO CAHORS,
"EASTERN DORDOGNE"
& LOT RIVER VALLEY

5 MILES

5 KM

did live in the shallow cliffside caves that you'll see throughout your Dordogne travels, which were continuously inhabited from prehistoric times until the Middle Ages.

**The Paintings:** Though there are dozens of caves painted over a span of more than 8,000 years, they're all surprisingly similar. These Stone Age hunters painted the animals they hunted—bison or bulls (especially at Lascaux and Grotte de Font-de-Gaume, both listed below), horses, deer, reindeer, ibex (mountain goats), wolves, bears, and cats, plus animals that are now extinct—mammoths (the engravings at Grotte de Rouffignac, see page 371), woolly rhinoceros (at Grotte de Font-de-Gaume, see page 370), and wild oxen.

Besides animals, you'll see geometric and abstract designs, such as circles, squiggles, and hash marks. There's scarcely a *Homo sapiens* in sight (except the famous "fallen hunter" at Lascaux), but there are human handprints traced on the wall by blowing paint through a hollow bone tube around the hand. The hunter-gatherers painted

**DORDOGNE**

the animals they hunted...but none of the plants they gathered.

**Style:** The animals stand in profile, with unnaturally big bodies and small limbs and heads. Black, red, and yellow dominate (with some white, brown, and violet). The thick black outlines are often wavy, suggesting the animal in motion. Except for a few friezes showing a conga line of animals running across the cave wall, there is no apparent order or composition. Some paintings are simply superimposed atop others. The artists had clearly mastered the animals' anatomy, but they chose to simplify the outlines and distort the heads and limbs for effect, always painting in the distinct Magdalenian style.

Many of the cave paintings are on a Sistine Chapel–size scale. The "canvas" was huge: Lascaux's main caverns are more than a football field long; Grotte de Font-de-Gaume is 430 feet long; and Grotte de Rouffignac meanders six miles deep. The figures are monumental (bulls at Lascaux are 16 feet high). All are painted high up on walls and ceilings, like the woolly rhinoceros of Grotte de Font-de-Gaume.

**Techniques:** Besides painting the animals, these early artists also engraved them on the wall by laboriously scratching outlines into the rock with a flint blade, many following the rock's natural contour. A typical animal might be made using several techniques—an engraved outline that follows the natural contour, reinforced with thick outline paint, then colored in.

The paints were mixed from natural pigments dissolved in cave water and oil (animal or vegetable). At Lascaux, archaeologists have found more than 150 different minerals on hand to mix paints. Even basic black might be a mix of manganese dioxide, ground quartz, and a calcium phosphate that had to be made by heating bone to 700 degrees Fahrenheit, then grinding it.

No paintbrushes have been found, so artists probably used a sponge-like material made from animal skin and fat. They may have used moss or hair, or maybe even finger-painted with globs of pure pigment. Once they'd drawn the outlines, they filled everything in with spray paint—either spit out from the mouth or blown through tubes made of hollow bone.

Imagine the engineering problems of painting one of these caves, and you can appreciate how sophisticated these "primitive" people were. First, you'd have to haul all your materials into a cold, pitch-black, not-easily-accessible place. Assistants erected scaffolding to reach ceilings and high walls, ground up minerals with a mortar and pestle, mixed paints, tended the torches and oil lamps, prepared the "paintbrushes," laid out major outlines with a connect-the-dots series of points...then stepped aside for Magdalenian Michelangelos to ascend the scaffolding and create.

**Dating:** Determining exactly how old this art is—and even if it's authentic—is tricky. As different caves feature different animals, prehistorians can derive which caves are relatively older and younger, since climate changes caused various animal species to come and go. (Since much of the actual paint is mineral-based with no organic material, carbon-dating techniques are often ineffective.) In several cases, experts confirmed the authenticity of a painting because the portrayals of the animals showed anatomical details not previously known—until they were discovered by modern technology. (For instance, in Grotte de Rouffignac, the mammoths are shown with a strange skin flap over their anus, which was only discovered during the 20th century in a Siberian glacier.) They can also estimate dates by checking the amount of calcium glaze formed over the paint, which can sometimes only be seen by infrared photography.

**Why?** No one knows the purpose of the cave paintings. Interestingly, the sites the artists chose were deliberately awe-inspiring, out of the way, and special. They knew their work here would last for untold generations, as had the paintings that came before theirs. Here are some theories of what this first human art might mean:

It's no mystery that hunters would paint animals, the source of their existence. The first scholar to study the caves, Abbé Henri Breuil, thought the painted animals were magic symbols made by hunters to increase the supply of game. Or perhaps hunters thought that if you could "master" an animal by painting it, you could later master it in battle. Some scholars think the paintings teach the art of hunting, but there's very little apparent hunting technique shown. Did they worship animals? The paintings definitely depict an animal-centered (rather than a human-centered) universe.

The paintings may have a religious purpose, and some of the caverns are large and special enough that rituals and ceremonies could have been held there. But the paintings show no priests, sacrifices, rituals, or ceremonies. Scholars writing on primitive art in other parts of the world speculate that art was made by shamans in a religious or drug-induced trance, but France's paintings are very methodical.

The order of paintings on the walls seems random. Could it be that the caves are a painted collage of the history of the Magdalenians, with each successive generation adding their distinct animal or symbol to the collage, putting it in just the right spot that established their place in history?

The fact that styles and subject matter changed so little over the millennia might imply that the artists purposely chose timeless images to relate their generation with those before and after. Or they simply lived in a stable culture that did not value innovation. Or these people were too primitive to invent new techniques and topics.

**DORDOGNE**

Maybe the paintings are simply the result of the universal human drive to create, and these caverns were Europe's first art galleries, bringing the first tourists.

Very likely there is no single meaning that applies to all the paintings in all the caves. Prehistoric art may be as varied in meaning as current art.

Picture how a Magdalenian would have viewed these paintings: You'd be guided by someone into a cold, echoing, and otherworldly chamber. In the darkness, someone would light torches and lamps, and suddenly the animals would flicker to life, appearing to run around the cave, like a prehistoric movie. In front of you, a bull would appear, behind you a mammoth (which you'd never seen in the flesh), and overhead a symbol that might have tied the whole experience together. You'd be amazed that an artist could capture the real world and reproduce it on a wall. Whatever the purpose—religious, aesthetic, or just plain fun—there's no doubt the effect was (and is) thrilling.

Today, you can visit the caves and share a common experience with a caveman. Feel a bond with these long-gone people... or stand in awe at how different they were from us. Ultimately, the paintings are as mysterious as the human species.

## Helpful Hints

**Drivers Fare Best:** All of the prehistoric caves listed here are within a short drive of Sarlat. Considering the scarcity of public transit, if you don't have a car, you're a caveman without a spear (see page 331 for guided tours that connect some of these sights).

**Book Ahead:** July, August, and holiday weekends are busiest, so book as far ahead as you can during these times. Saturdays are generally quiet. Four caves take reservations (by phone, fax, or email): Lascaux II (July–Aug only), Grotte de Font-de-Gaume, Abri du Cap Blanc, and Grotte du Pech Merle (all described in this section). The rest are first-come, first-served. Remember that Sarlat's TI and some hotels can reserve cave visits for you (and are likely to be more effective in landing a reservation).

**Cave Tips:** Read "Cave Art 101" (page 362) to gain a better understanding of what you'll see. Dress warmly, even if it's hot outside. Tours can last up to an hour, and the caves are all a steady, chilly 55 degrees Fahrenheit, with 98 or 99 percent humidity.

DORDOGNE

While on tour, lag behind the group to have the paintings to yourself for a few moments. Photos, day packs, big purses, and strollers are not allowed. (You can take your camera—without using it—and check the rest at the site.)

**Local Guide:** Angelika Siméon is a qualified **local guide** eager to teach you about the caves (€145/half-day, €245/day—better, tel. 05 53 35 19 30, mobile 06 24 45 96 28, angelica.simeon @wanadoo.fr).

# SIGHTS

## Les Eyzies-de-Tayac

This single-street town is the touristy hub of a cluster of Cro-Magnon caves, castles, and rivers, and merits a stop only for its National Museum of Prehistory (see next page) and the Grotte de Font-de-Gaume cave (a 10-minute walk outside of town, described below).

Les Eyzies-de-Tayac is famous because it's where Monsieur Magnon first discovered the original Cro-Magnon man in 1870. That breakthrough set of bones was found just behind the hotel of Monsieur Magnon—Hôtel le Cro-Magnon, which is in business to this day on the main street in Les Eyzies. The name "Cro-Magnon" translates as "Mr. Magnon's Hole."

Les Eyzies-de-Tayac's **TI** rents bikes (Mon–Sat July–Aug 9:00–19:00, Sept–June 10:00–12:00 & 14:00–18:00, closed Sun except June–Sept 10:00–12:00 & 14:00–17:00; tel. 05 53 06 97 05, fax 05 53 06 90 79, www.leseyzies.com). The train station is a level 500 yards from the town center (turn right out of the station to get into town).

*Sleeping in and near Les Eyzies-de-Tayac:* Train travelers wanting to see the museum and famous cave will find Les Eyzies-de-Tayac a practical place to sleep, as will drivers interested in a fun farm experience.

**$$$ Auberge Veyret,** a 15-minute drive from Les Eyzies-de-Tayac, is as real a farm experience as it gets, with beefy cows and plump pigs. Mama greets you with a huge smile and nary a word of English, her son cooks, and her daughter (Laurence) and husband (Patrick) do everything else. The rooms are spotless and furnished like Grandma's, but with modern conveniences. You'll be expected to dine here—and you'd be a fool not to, since dinner includes everything from apéritif to *digestif,* with five courses in between and wine throughout (Db-€54 per person, lower rates for kids, includes breakfast and dinner, cash only, large pool, en route to Abri du Cap Blanc—look for any sign that says *Veyret,* tel. 05 53 29 68 44, fax 05 53 31 58 28, www.auberge-veyret.com, contact@auberge-veyret.com).

**DORDOGNE**

**$ Madame Bauchet** (call her "Nanou") owns the closest rooms to the train station, and they're a good clean value (Db-€38–42, Tb/Qb-€53, cash only, 200 yards from the station at 40 avenue de la Préhistoire—look for the brown *Chambres* sign, tel. 05 53 06 97 71, bauchetgerard@wanadoo.fr). Madame Bauchet does not speak English, but she's a creative communicator.

## ▲▲National Museum of Prehistory (Musée National de Préhistoire)

This modern museum houses more than 18,000 bones, stones, and crude little doodads that were uncovered locally. It takes you through prehistory, starting 400,000 years ago. With English info sheets provided along the way, it's a good first stop for learning about the age. While the museum does an excellent job presenting its exhibits, you have to be engaged and determined to learn to follow the museum's complex and serious teaching style.

Appropriately located on a cliff that's been inhabited by humans for 35,000 years (above Les Eyzies-de-Tayac's TI), the museum has a sleek design intended to help it blend into the surrounding rock. Videos demonstrate scratching designs, painting techniques, and how spearheads were made. Full-size models of Cro-Magnon people and animals stare at racks of countless arrowheads. The first floor sets the stage, describing human evolution and the importance of tools.

The second (and better) floor highlights prehistoric artifacts found in France. The most interesting things you'll see are in this order: a handheld arrow launcher, a 5,000-year-old flat-bottomed boat made from oak (pirogue), prehistoric fire pits, amazing cave-woman jewelry (including a necklace made of 70 stag teeth—pretty impressive, given that stags only have two teeth each—do the math), engravings on stone (don't miss the unflattering yet impressively realistic female figure), a handheld lamp used to light cave interiors *(lampe de Lascaux)*, and beautiful rock sculptures of horses (much like the paintings at the cave of Abri du Cap Blanc). Your visit ends on the cliff edge, with a Fred Flintstone–style photo op on a porch that some of our ancient ancestors once called home (€5; June–Sept daily 9:30–18:30; Oct–May Wed–Mon 9:30–12:00 & 14:00–17:30, closed Tue; tel. 05 53 06 45 65, www.musee-prehistoire-eyzies.fr).

## ▲▲Lascaux II

The region's—and the world's—most famous cave paintings are at Lascaux, 14 miles north of Sarlat and Les Eyzies. The Lascaux caves were discovered accidentally in 1940 by four kids and their dog. From 1948 through 1963, more than a million people climbed through this prehistoric wonderland. But these visitors tracked in fungus on their shoes and changed the temperature and humidity with their heavy breathing. In just 15 years, the precious art deteriorated more than during the 15,000 years before that. The original caves were closed. A copy cave—accurate to within one centimeter, reproducing the best 40-yard-long stretch, and showing 90 percent of the paintings found in Lascaux—was opened next to the original in 1983. Guides assure that the original is every bit as crisp and has just as much contrast as the facsimile you'll see.

At impressive Lascaux II, the reindeer, horses, and bulls of Lascaux I are painstakingly reproduced by top artists using the same dyes, tools, and techniques their predecessors did 15,000 years ago. Of course, seeing the real thing at the other caves is important, but come here first (taking one of the scheduled English-language tours) for a great introduction to the region's cave art. While it feels a bit rushed—40 people per tour are hustled through the two-room cave reproductions—the guides are committed to teaching, the paintings are astonishing, and the experience is mystifying. (Forget that they're copies, and enjoy being swept away by the prehistoric majesty of it all.)

**Cost and Hours:** €8.50; July–Aug daily 9:00–19:00; April–June and Sept daily 9:30–18:30; Oct–Dec and Feb–March Tue–Sun 10:00–12:00 & 14:00–17:30, closed Mon; closed Jan.

**Touring the Replica Cave:** You'll see Lascaux II with a 40-minute English tour (4–6/day May–Sept, usually at about 11:50 and 14:20, about 2/day off-season, call 05 53 51 96 23 for ticket availability and English tour times, reservations possible July–Aug only). Unless you're visiting in winter (Oct–March), you must buy your ticket before coming to Lascaux; the ticket office is next to the TI in Montignac, five minutes away by car. Deep-blue signs direct drivers to *La Billeterie* in Montignac (follow signs for *Centre-Ville*, then look for *La Billeterie,* and don't double-park); Lascaux is well-signed from there. In July and August, tours are usually sold out by 13:00, so book ahead. It's always 56 degrees in the cave, so dress warmly. Pleasant Montignac is worth a wander if you have time to kill.

*Sleeping near Lascaux:* **$$$ Château de la Fleunie*** offers regal 15th-century château accommodations surrounded by pastures and mountain goats, the biggest private pool I've seen in France, tennis courts, and a restaurant with *beaucoup d'ambiance* (Db in modern annex with terrace-€75–90, Db in château-€90–115, most are about €100, tower room for two-€155, €20 per extra person, prices rise an additional €20 July–Aug, *menus* from €30, half-pension required July–Aug-€80–90 per person, 10-min drive north of Montignac on road to Brive-la-Gaillarde, in Condat-sur-Vézère, tel. 05 53 51 32 74, fax 05 53 50 58 98, www.lafleunie.com, lafleunie@free.fr).

# ▲▲▲Grotte de Font-de-Gaume

Even if you're not a connoisseur of Cro-Magnon art, you'll dig this cave. It's the last cave in Europe with prehistoric multicolored (polychrome) painting still open to the public. (Lascaux—just down the road—and Spain's Altamira are closed, with copy caves for visitors instead.) The cave, made millions of years ago—not by a river, but by the geological activity that created the Pyrénées mountains—is entirely natural. It contains 15,000-year-old paintings of 230 animals, 82 of which are bison.

On a carefully guided and controlled 100-yard walk, you'll see about 20 red-and-black bison—often in elegant motion—painted with a moving sensitivity. When two animals face each other, one is black, and the other is red. Your guide, with a laser pointer and great reverence, will trace the faded outline of the bison and explain how, 15,000 years ago, cave dwellers used local minerals and the rock's natural contour to give the paintings dimension. Some locals knew about the cave long ago, when there was little interest in prehistory, but the paintings were officially discovered in 1901 by the village schoolteacher.

**Cost, Hours, Information:** €6.50, reservation fee-€1.50/group, Sun–Fri mid-May–mid-Sept 9:30–17:30, mid-Sept–mid-May 9:30–12:30 & 14:00–17:30, closed Sat, last departure 90 min before closing, no photography or large bags, tel. 05 53 06 86 00, fax 05 53 35 26 18, fontdegaume@monuments-nationaux.fr. Those planning to visit Abri du Cap Blanc can reserve and buy tickets here (see below).

**Getting a Ticket:** For the health of the precious and fragile art, the number of daily visitors allowable is strictly regulated (180 people per day, in groups of 12). Of the 180 spots available, 130 tickets are allotted to visitors who call or email to make advance reservations, and 50 are kept open for those wanting to enter badly enough to come early and wait for a ticket. In July and August (when spots get booked up months in advance), you'll need to reserve ahead by phone or email, or arrive by 8:00; the rest of the year, you should be OK if you pop in by 9:00. If you reserve by email, allow a few days for a response. They'll send you a form to fill out; provide your name and credit card number to hold your spot. Sundays are always first-come, first-served, with no reservations taken. You can call the site at certain times (10:30–12:00 and 14:30–16:00) to see if spots happen to be open (they often are) before doing the early-morning bit. You must check in 15 minutes before your tour, or you'll lose your place to the sightseeing vultures waiting to snatch up the spots of late arrivals. You can join this flock and try to snag a place given to standbys 15 minutes before the tour time (many don't show).

**Tours:** Since English tours are limited to two per day (usually at 11:30 and 15:30, May–Sept only), you'll likely make the visit with a French guide. While the English-info flier is useless, the actual tour is little more than pointing out legs, eyes, heads, and bellies of the bison, so don't fret if you're not on an English tour. Pierre Fanlac Editeur's *The Font-de-Gaume Cave* guidebook, sold for €6 in the shop, is an excellent substitute.

**Getting There:** The caves are a 10-minute walk from Les Eyzies-de-Tayac (toward Sarlat). From the ticket house, walk 400 yards on an uphill path to the cave entrance (where there's a free and safe bag check and a WC). There's easy parking on site, but drivers who can't get a ticket here (or who want to see completely different caves) should try the caves at Grotte de Rouffignac (see below), or aim for the more remote Grotte du Pech Merle, about 30 minutes east of Cahors (see page 392).

## ▲Abri du Cap Blanc

In this prehistoric cave (a 10-minute drive from Grotte de Font-de-Gaume), early artists used the rock's natural contours to add dimension to their sculpture. The small museum (with English explanations) will prepare you, and the useful English handout will guide you. Look for places where the artists smoothed or roughened the surfaces to add depth. In this single stone room, your French-speaking guide will spend 30 minutes explaining 14,000-year-old carvings. Impressive as these are, their subtle majesty is lost on some people. Free 45-minute tours leave on the half-hour (€6.50, hours in flux so call to verify, generally Sun–Fri mid-May–mid-Sept 9:30–17:30, mid-Sept–Oct and April–mid-May 9:30–12:30 & 14:00–17:30, closed Sat and Nov–March, no photos, walk 200 yards down from parking lot, tel. 05 53 59 21 74). Tickets and reservations are available at Font-de-Gaume cave, or at the site. Abri du Cap Blanc is well-signed, located two miles after Grotte de Font-de-Gaume (see above) on the road to Sarlat.

## ▲▲Grotte de Rouffignac

Rouffignac provides a different experience from other prehistoric caves in this area. Here, you'll ride a clunky little train down a giant subterranean riverbed, exploring about half a mile of this six-mile-long gallery. The cave was known to locals for decades—hence the oblivious graffiti (with dates going back to the 18th century) that litters the ceiling—but the 13,000-year-old paintings were discovered only in 1956.

**Cost, Hours, Information:** €6.50, daily July–Aug 9:00–11:30 & 14:00–18:00, April–June and Sept–Nov 10:00–11:30 & 14:00–17:00, closed Dec–March, tours 2/hr, no reservations, tel. 05 53 05 41 71, www.grottederouffignac.fr. Dress warmly; the visit lasts 60 minutes. It's really crowded only from mid-July through August—especially in the afternoons. Weekends tend to be quietest.

**DORDOGNE**

**Getting There:** Grotte de Rouffignac is well-signed from the route between Les Eyzies-de-Tayac and Périgueux; allow 25 minutes from Les Eyzies-de-Tayac.

**◐ Self-Guided Tour:** Your tour will likely be in French (guides may answer questions in English), but here's the gist of what they're saying on the stops of your train ride:

The cave was created by the underground river. It's entirely natural, but it was much shallower before the train-track bed was excavated. As you travel, imagine the motivation and determination of the painters who crawled so deep into this dark and mysterious cave. They left behind their art...and the wonder of people who crawled in centuries later to see it all.

All along the way, you'll see crater-like burrows made by hibernating bears long before the first humans painted here. There are hundreds of them—not because there were so many bears, but because year after year, a few of them would return, preferring to make their own private place to sleep (rather than using some other bear's den). After a long winter nap, bears would have one thing on their mind: Cut those toenails. The walls are scarred with the scratching of bears in need of clippers (look to the right as you ride).

**Stop 1:** The images of woolly mammoths etched into the walls can be seen only when lit from the side (as your guide will demonstrate). As the rock is very soft here, these were simply gouged out by the artists' fingers.

**Stop 2:** Look for images of finely detailed rhinoceroses in black paintings. The rock is harder here, so nothing is engraved.

**Stop 3:** On the left, you'll see woolly mammoths and horses engraved with tools in the harder rock. On the right is the biggest composition of the cave: a herd of peaceful mammoths. A mysterious calcite problem threatens to cover the paintings in ugly white splotches.

**Off the Train:** When you get off the train, notice how high the original floor was (the bear-crater level), and remember to imagine both the prehistoric makers and viewers of this art crawling back here with pretty lousy flashlight-substitutes. Here, the ceiling is covered with a remarkable gathering of animals. You'll see a fine 16-foot-long horse, a group of mountain goats, and a grandpa mammoth. Art even decorates the walls far down the big, scary hole. When the group chuckles, it's because the guide is explaining how the mammoth with the fine detail (showing a flap of skin over its anus) helped authenticate the paintings—these paintings couldn't be fakes, because no one knew about this anatomical detail until the remains of an actual mammoth were found in a Siberian ice field in modern times. (The discovery explained the skin flap that had long puzzled French prehistorians.)

## ▲La Roque St. Christophe

Five fascinating terraces carved by the Vézère River have provided shelter to people here for 50,000 years. While the terraces were inhabited in prehistoric times, there's no prehistoric art on display—the exhibit (except for one small cave) is entirely medieval. The official recorded history goes back to 976 A.D., when people settled here to steer clear of the Viking raiders who'd routinely sail up the river. (Back then in this part of Europe, the standard closing of a prayer wasn't "amen," but, "and deliver us from the Norseman, amen.")

A clever relay of river watchtowers kept an eye out for raiders. When they came, cave-dwellers gathered their kids, hauled up their animals (see the big, re-created winch), and pulled up the ladders. While there's absolutely nothing old here except for the carved-out rock (with holes for beams, carved out of the soft limestone), it's easy to imagine the entire village—complete with butcher, baker, and candlestick-maker—in this family-friendly exhibit. This place is a dream for kids of any age who hold fond tree-house memories.

It's simple to visit: There's a free parking lot across the stream, with picnic tables, a WC, and—adjacent to the babbling brook—a pondside café (providing good salads, omelets, and drinks—the nearby and pretty village of St. Léon provides more lunch choices). Borrow the English guide booklet (or buy it for €2) at the turnstile; stop to take in the picture showing its medieval buildings; and climb through the one-way circuit, which is slippery when damp (€7, daily April–Sept 10:00–18:30, March and Oct 10:00–18:00, Nov–Feb 11:00–17:00, last entry 45 min before closing, lots of steps, 5 miles north of Les Eyzies-de-Tayac, follow signs to *Montignac*, tel. 05 53 50 70 45). When planning your day, note that this is one of the rare sights that stays open through lunch.

## ▲Grottes de Cougnac

Located 19 miles south of Sarlat (and three well-signed miles north of Gourdon on D-704), this cave holds the oldest (14,000–25,000-year-old) paintings open to the public and fascinating rock formations. Less touristy than others, it provides a more intimate look at cave art, since guides have more time to explain the paintings (allow an hour for the visit). You'll get some explanations in English (unless it's high season), and see about 10 drawings of ibex and deer (with rust or black outlines) as well as a few representations of humans (€6.50, these hours correspond to first/last tour times: daily July–Aug 10:00–18:00, May–June and Sept 10:00–11:30 & 14:30–17:00, April and Oct 14:30–17:00, closed Nov–March, English book available, 70-min tours, some in English—call ahead, tel. 05 65 41 47 54, www.grottesdecougnac.com).

**DORDOGNE**

# Oradour-sur-Glane and Nearby

## ▲▲▲Oradour-sur-Glane

Located two hours north of Sarlat and 15 miles west of Limoges, this is one of the most powerful sights in France. French school-

children know this town well—most make a pilgrimage here. **Village des Martyrs,** as it is known, was machine-gunned and burned on June 10, 1944, by Nazi troops. The Nazis were either seeking revenge for the killing of one of their officers (by French Resistance fighters in a neighboring village) or simply terrorizing the populace in preparation for the upcoming Allied invasion (this was four days after D-Day). With cool attention to detail, the Nazis methodically rounded up the entire population of 642 townspeople. The women and children were herded into the town church, where they were tear-gassed and machine-gunned. Plaques mark the place where the town's men were grouped and executed. The town was then set on fire, its victims left under a blanket of ashes. Today, the ghost town, left untouched for more than 60 years, greets every pilgrim who enters with only one English word: Remember.

Follow *Village des Martyrs* signs and start at the rust-colored **underground museum** (Centre de la Mémoire), which provides a good social and political context for the event (with English explanations and audioguide), including home movies of locals before the attack and disturbing footage of similar events (don't miss the 12-minute film with English audioguide translations). Then, with hushed visitors, walk the length of Oradour's main street, past gutted, charred buildings in the shade of lush trees, to the underground memorial on the market square (rusted toys, broken crucifixes, town mementos under glass). The plaques on the buildings tell us the names and occupations of the people who lived there (*laine* means wool; a *sabotier* is a maker of wooden shoes; a *quincaillerie* is a hardware store; *cordonnier* means shoe repair; a *menuisier* is a carpenter; and *tissus* means fabrics). Visit the cemetery where most lives ended on June 10, 1944, and finish at the church, with its bullet-pocked altar.

**Cost, Hours, Information:** Entering the village is free, while the museum costs €7.50 (includes audioguide). Both are open daily mid-May–mid-Sept 9:00–19:00, off-season until 17:00 or 18:00, last visit one hour before closing, tel. 05 55 43 04 30, www.oradour.org.

**Getting There:** Public transport here is a challenge. Four daily buses connect Limoges with Oradour in 20 minutes (25-min walk from Limoges train station to bus stop on place Winston Churchill). Consider a taxi. Limoges is a stop on an alternative train route between Amboise and Sarlat.

*Sleeping and Eating in Oradour-sur-Glane:* **$ Hôtel La Glane\*\*** is the best hotel in the modern town, with the most respected restaurant. Both are cheap and good enough (Db-€47, *menus* from €11, next to Hôtel de Ville on place de la Mairie, tel. 05 55 03 10 43, fax 05 55 03 15 42).

## Mortemart

With a car and extra time, visit this bucolic village (15-min drive northwest of Oradour-sur-Glane on D-675). You'll find a medieval market hall, a smattering of appealing buildings, one café, and a sweet château (good picnic benches behind).

*Sleeping in Mortemart:* **$ Hôtel Relais\*\*** offers a tempting overnight stop. Located on the main road, it has five small but quite comfortable rooms over a fine restaurant. Formal Madame Pradeau speaks no English, but she'll work with you (Db-€42, Tb-€65, *menus* from €18, kids' *menu*-€10, closed Mon–Tue, tel. & fax 05 55 68 12 09).

## ▲Collonges-la-Rouge

Connoisseurs of beautiful villages need to visit this deep-red sandstone and slate-roofed village that curls down a friendly hill. Collonges-la-Rouge is a scenic 15-minute drive east of the A-20 autoroute (exit at Noailles), just south of Brive-la-Gaillarde and about a 50-minute drive from Sarlat. The **TI** has a brochure with English explanations and information on other nearby worth-a-wander villages (TI located near the top of town, tel. 05 55 25 32 25). Don't miss the church's Moorish entry, wavy floor, and holy dome. Like all adorable villages, Collonges-la-Rouge has plenty of shops and is busy at midday from June through September.

# St. Emilion and Bordeaux Wine Country

Two hours due west of Sarlat and just 40 minutes from Bordeaux, St. Emilion is another pretty face just waiting to flirt with you.

Unlike other French lookers, this one flirts in English—the historic presence of British interest in the wine industry has given the town an almost bilingual feel. It's a relaxing place for Americans.

Carved like an amphitheater in the bowl of a limestone hill, St. Emilion's handsome streets connect a few inviting squares with heavy cobbles and scads of well-stocked wine shops. There's little to do in this town of well-heeled and well-wined residents other than enjoy the setting, and, of course, sample the local sauce. (*Bien sur*, St. Emilion's primary sightseeing is for your palate.) Wine has been good to St. Emilion, though it accounts for barely 5 percent of Bordeaux's famous red-wine production (about 60 percent of the grapes you see are Merlot). Also try a tasty homemade macaroon, sold at many shops here. Sunday is market day in St. Emilion.

## ORIENTATION

### Tourist Information

The TI is a critical stop, at the top of the town on place des Créneaux, across from the high church bell tower. It's located in a one-time abbey and connected to pretty cloisters (that go ignored by most tourists—find the door in the rear of the TI and enter a peaceful place). The TI is well-armed with good information in English about anything you need. Check the bulletin board for English visits of the city, vineyard tours, and more. The TI rents bikes, has information on St. Emilion's few sights, and has a helpful booklet on *chambres d'hôte* (daily mid-June–mid-Sept 9:30–19:00, mid-Sept–mid-June 9:30–12:30 & 13:45–18:30, Nov–March closes at 18:00, place Pioceau, tel. 05 57 55 28 28, fax 05 57 55 28 29, www.saint-emilion-tourisme.com, st-emilion.tourisme@wanadoo.fr). A TI annex is near the entry to the underground church (see page 378, under "Activities").

## Arrival in St. Emilion

**By Train:** While there is a train station near St. Emilion, it's a 20-minute walk from town, and taxis don't wait here (6 trains/day Mon–Fri from Bordeaux, 4/day Sat–Sun). It's usually easier to get off in Libourne (five miles away, with good train service and easy car rental near the station). From Libourne, you can catch a cab (€15, see "Taxi and Local Guide," below) or take an infrequent bus to St. Emilion (3/day) from the bus station *(gare routière)* next to the train station.

**By Car:** If you're coming from Sarlat, take the autoroute from Périgueux and save 40 minutes over the local roads. If coming from the Loire, take the autoroute to Poitiers, then follow N-10 south toward Angouleme, then Bordeaux. You'll find parking (about €1/hour) in lots at the upper end of the town, or along the wall.

## Helpful Hints

**Taxi and Local Guide:** Jolly Robert Faustin, who drives a comfortable station wagon and speaks enough English, can advise you and arrange visits to wineries (he knows them all), and is an enjoyable person to spend time with (tel. & fax 05 57 25 17 59, mobile 06 77 75 36 64, www.taxi-saintemilion.com, robert.faustin@wanadoo.fr).

**Tourist Train:** A *petit train* toots you from St. Emilion through vineyards and back in 30 minutes (€6, 2/hr, stop is behind TI by vineyards).

# ACTIVITIES

**Wine-Tasting**—A fair starting point for oenophiles is the **Maison du Vin,** located next to the TI, where you get an introduction to wine, beginning with an hour-long video (played on the hour, English subtitles). In the next room, read the description of the winemaking process and sniff cool glass cylinders that let you smell elements in the wines before you taste them (free, daily 9:30–12:30 & 14:00–18:30, tel. 05 57 55 50 55, www.vins-saint-emilion.com).

While the TI offers various €10 guided bus excursion to the vineyards (in English and French, includes a tasting, usually departs TI at 15:00 mid-May–Sept), the many **wine shops** offer the best and easiest way to sample the array of local wines (see "French Wine-Tasting 101" on page 30). Keepers of small shops greet visitors in flawless English, with a central tasting table, maps of the vineyards, and several open bottles (most shops open daily 10:00–19:00, until 20:00 in summer). And while it's hard to distinguish these classy wine stores from each other, you'll be pleasantly surprised at the welcoming attitude that the passionate shopkeepers show for their wines. Americans may represent only

**DORDOGNE**

about 15 percent of the visitors, but we buy 40 percent of their wine. While the owners hope that you'll buy a bottle (particularly if you taste many wines) and shipping is easy (except to California and Texas), there's no pressure or fee for the tastings.

**Vignobles & Chateaux** is a polished wine shop with a self-proclaimed "dream-team" staff who will answer your every question. They also offer two-hour or full-day wine-tasting classes at their "Ecole de Vin" upstairs (€29/2 hours; €350/day with more extensive classes, gourmet lunch, and visits to prestigious wineries; 4 rue du Clocher, tel. 05 57 4 61 01, www.vignobleschateaux.com).

I also like the **Cercle des Oenophiles,** offering tastes and visits to their nearby cellars that have more than 400,000 stored bottles of wine (daily 10:00–19:00, at 12 rue Guadat, tel. 05 57 74 45 55).

**Views over St. Emilion**—You can climb the **bell tower** in front of the TI for a fine view (€1, give ID at TI in exchange for the key, daily same hours as TI—see earlier in this section). But the view is best from the **Tour du Donjon** several blocks below (€1, daily 11:00–18:00).

**Underground Tours of St. Emilion**—The TI offers frequent and somewhat interesting 45-minute tours with three stops: the catacombs (sorry, no bones); the underground monolithic church, which literally rocks; and Trinity Chapel. Learn who St. Emilion was, and be impressed that it took dedicated Benedictine monks 300 years to dig this monolithic church out of one big rock (9th–12th centuries). You'll also learn that there are about 125 miles of underground tunnels in the St. Emilion area originally dug as quarries. Today, they're ideal for wine storage. The tour is mandatory if you want to see these sights (€6, three English tours/day, more in French, English handout given on French tours is thorough). If time's limited and you can't get an English tour, I'd skip this sight.

# SLEEPING

**(€1 = about $1.50, country code: 33)**
There are no cheap hotels in St. Emilion. (Those that exist are fine, but they're more costly than elsewhere in France.) Seriously consider staying at a *chambre d'hôte* (see next page). Hotel prices skyrocket during the VinExpo festival at the end of June, and during harvest time (the end of Sept).

## Hotels
The first two places are a few doors apart, at the upper end of the city.

**$$$ Au Logis des Remparts\*\*\*** offers top comfort in tasteful rooms, plus a pool and a tranquil garden with vineyards to touch (standard Db-€110, nicer Db with bathtubs and garden views-€140–165, suites-€250–400, air-con, Wi-Fi, easy on-site parking, tel. 05 57 24 70 43, fax 05 57 74 47 44, www.logisdes remparts.com, contact@logisdesremparts.com).

**$$ L'Auberge de la Commanderie** welcomes visitors with a neon entry and Modernist decor in its two buildings—a main hotel and an annex. Run by amiable owner Henri, the hotel's 16 rooms are well-maintained and have ceiling fans. Rooms in the main building come with loud paintings, while annex rooms have more subtle stone walls and more space (small Db-€80, bigger Db-€90–110, Tb-€110, two-room apartment for up to four-€150, closed Jan–Feb, Internet access and Wi-Fi, free parking, tel. 05 57 24 70 19, fax 05 57 74 44 53, www.aubergedelacommanderie.com, contact@aubergedelacommanderie.com).

**$$ Le Logis de la Tourelle** rents five spacious rooms at the lower end of town for fair rates (Db-€65–75; check in at La Côte Braisée restaurant at 3 rue du Tertre de la Tente, and they'll escort you to rooms, which are several blocks away; tel. 05 57 24 79 65, fax 05 57 74 05 51, lacotebraisee@wanadoo.fr).

## Chambres d'Hôte

The vineyards that surround St. Emilion hide many good-value *chambres d'hôte*. Places below the town are scattered among the villages and are hard to find—get good directions before you go. You can meander the villages just outside St. Emilion's upper entry point, and pick the place you prefer (the village of Montagne has many good *chambres d'hôte*). Or stop by the TI for a long list with small photos (no room booking fee).

**$$ Moulin la Grangère,** dreamily wrapped in hills of vineyards, offers the perfect haven from which to appreciate the Bordeaux wine country. Charming Marie-Annick and Alain Noel rent three modern rooms in a well-renovated, blue-shuttered 19th-century mill with manicured gardens, a big pool, a *pétanque* court, and sublime scenery in every direction (Db-€70, Tb/Qb-€90–100, includes breakfast, cash only, Internet access, tel. 05 57 24 72 51, www.moulin-la-grangere.com, alain-noel@moulin-la-grangere.com). It's 10 minutes below St. Emilion: Follow D-122 from below St. Emilion and turn left on D-245. After two kilometers, look for signs on the left to *St. Christophe des Bardes,* then follow the small *Moulin la Grangère* signs.

**$ Château Meylet** is where Madame Favard rents four traditional rooms in her workaday wine *domaine*. The château is within a quarter-mile of St. Emilion's doorstep (Db-€56–62, Tb-€77, includes breakfast, cash only, shared kitchen, washer/dryer and bikes available; from the top of St. Emilion, follow D-243 toward Libourne, at 1.5 kilometers turn left at signs to *Château Meylet;* tel. 05 57 24 68 85, http://chateau.meylet.free.fr, chateaumeylet@free.fr).

# EATING

Skip the cafés lining the street by the TI and find the cafés on the melt-in-your-chair square, place du Marché.

**Amelia-Canta** is *the* happening spot on place du Marché for lunch or dinner on a warm evening. It has café fare, salads, and veggie options (€15–38 *menus*, open daily March–Nov, tel. 05 57 74 48 03).

**Les Girons'dines,** a few blocks down from the TI, is a charming place run by a mother-daughter team. The cuisine is traditional and reasonable, served in their fun, colorful interior or on their sweet terrace (5 rue des Girondins, tel. 05 57 24 77 72).

**L'Envers du Décor** wine bar–bistro is about fun, wine, and food, in that order. The restaurant's tabletops are wooden wine crates, and the floor is cool blue-and-brown tile. The feel of this place is perfect for this wine-happy town. Meat dishes are their forte (lunch *menus* from €19, dinner *menus* from €30, open daily, a few doors from the TI at 11 rue du Clocher, tel. 05 57 74 48 31).

# Rocamadour

An hour east of Sarlat, this historic pilgrimage town with its dramatic rock-face setting is a ▲▲ sight after dark. While once one of Europe's top pilgrimage sites (see sidebar on page 382), today it feels more tacky than spiritual. Still, if you can get into the medieval mind-set, its peaceful and dramatic setting—combined with the memory of the countless thousands of faithful who trekked from all over Europe to worship here—overwhelms the kitschy tourism, and it becomes a fine (short) stop.

Those who arrive late and spend the night enjoy fewer crowds and a floodlit spectacle. Those who visit only during the day might wonder why they did, as there's little to do here except to climb the pilgrims' steps (with people who aren't pilgrims) to a few churches, and then stare at the view.

## ORIENTATION

Rocamadour has three basic levels, connected by steps or elevators. The bottom level (La Cité Medievale or La Cité) is a single pedestrian street lined with shops and restaurants. The sanctuary level (Cité Religieuse) is up 223 holy steps. Its centerpiece is a church with seven chapels gathered around a small square. A switchback trail, the Way of the Cross (Chemin de la Croix), leads to the top level (called l'Hospitalet) and château (closed to the public) that crowns the cliff and offers a fine view and free parking. For most, the goal is the sanctuary at midlevel.

## Tourist Information

There are two TIs in Rocamadour: the glassy TI that drivers come to first, in the village of l'Hospitalet above Rocamadour (daily July–Aug 9:30–18:00, April–June and Sept–Oct 10:00–12:30 & 14:00–18:00, Nov–March until 17:00); and another on the level pedestrian street in La Cité Medievale (roughly same hours, tel. 05 65 33 22 00). On the same pedestrian street, you'll find an ATM next to the post office (PTT).

## Arrival in Rocamadour

**By Train:** Five daily trains (transfer in Brive-la-Gaillarde) leave you 2.5 miles from the village at an unstaffed station. It's a €10 taxi ride to Rocamadour (see "Helpful Hints—Taxi," next page). Start at the Cité Medievale (lower level), and visit from there.

**By Car:** Drivers have two options: You can park at the bottom of town (follow signs to *La Cité*), and walk to the end of the long pedestrian street (in La Cité Medievale), then either climb or take the elevator to the chapels. Or, for less walking, park above the town (from l'Hospitalet, follow *Château* signs) to a free lot and hike or take the elevator down.

**By Elevator:** With fewer pilgrims climbing steps on their knees, this very vertical town has added two handy if pricey elevators. *Ascenseur Cité* (€2 one-way, €3 round-trip) connects the lower town with the church, but skips the holy stairs. *Ascenseur Incliné* (€2.50 one-way, €4 round-trip) connects the church with the château and parking lot at the top, but skips the zigzag Way of the Cross. Each is run like any other elevator: on demand. Managed by two different companies, they're connected within 50 yards at the church level.

## Helpful Hints

**Views After Dark:** If you're staying overnight, don't miss the views of a floodlit Rocamadour from the opposite side of the valley (doable by car, on foot, or by tourist train; see below). It's best as a half-hour (round-trip) stroll. From the town's southeast end, follow the quiet road down, cross the bridge, and head up the far side of the gorge opposite the town. Leave before it gets dark, as the floodlighting is best at twilight. Wear light-colored or reflective clothing, or take a flashlight—it's a dark road with no shoulder. Within the town, climb the steps to just below the sanctuary, and consider a drink with a view at the Hôtel Sainte Marie.

**Tourist Train:** You can take the cheesy but convenient *petit train* to enjoy the view, complete with 50 other travelers, a bad sound

## Rocamadour's Religious History

Rocamadour was once one of Europe's top pilgrimage sights. Today, tourists replace the pilgrims, enjoying a dramatically situated one-street town under a pretty forgettable church—all because of a crude little thousand-year-old black statue of the Virgin Mary.

Of France's roughly 200 "Black Virgins," this was perhaps the most venerated. Black Virgins began at the end of the pagan era—when Europe was being forcefully Christianized. In Europe's pagan religions, black typically symbolized fertility and motherhood. For newly converted (and still reluctant) pagans, it was easier to embrace the Virgin if she was black.

Y2K was just a high-tech rerun of Y1K. A thousand years ago, many Europeans also expected the world to end, and pilgrimages became immensely popular. About that time, the first pilgrims came here—to a little cave in a cliff over a gorge created by the Alzou River—to pray to a crude statue of a Black Virgin. Then, in 1166, a remarkably intact body was found beneath the threshold of the troglodyte chapel. People assumed this could only be a hermit (certainly a saintly hermit) who had lived in this cave. He was given the name Amadour (servant of Mary) and the place was named Rocamadour (the rock of the servant of Mary).

Suddenly, this humble site was on the map. The Benedictines moved in to develop the spot, building a church over the cave. Like Mont St. Michel, a single-street town sprouted at its base to

system blaring worthless commentary in four languages, a flashing yellow light, and a rooftop crimping your view (€5, round-trip in 30 min, 2 trips/evening, departures starting at twilight—the first one is by far the best, check at the TI or call 05 65 33 67 84). You can walk its route in 30 minutes (see above), and take much better photos.

**Grocery Store:** It's on place de l'Europe, in the upper city (daily 8:00–20:00).

**Taxi:** Call 06 73 44 79 98, 06 81 60 14 60, or 05 65 50 14 82.

# SIGHTS

## In Rocamadour

### In the Upper Town (l'Hospitalet)

If you're coming from Sarlat or from the north, your first view of Rocamadour is the same one medieval pilgrims first saw—at the top of the gorge from the hamlet of **l'Hospitalet,** named for the hospitality it gave pilgrims. Stop here for the grand views (and its glassy TI). Imagine the impact of this sight in the 13th century, as awestruck pilgrims first gazed on the sanctuary cut out of the handle the needs of its growing pilgrim hordes. During Europe's great age of pilgrimages (12th and 13th centuries), the greatest of pilgrims (St. Louis, St. Dominique, Richard the Lionhearted, and so on) all trekked to this spot to pray. Rocamadour became a powerful symbol of faith and hope.

During the 14th-century Golden Age of Rocamadour, up to 8,000 people lived here, earning their living off of the pilgrims—who arrived in numbers of up to 20,000 a day. But with the 16th-century wars of religion and the Age of Enlightenment (in the 18th century), pilgrimages declined...and so did Rocamadour.

During the Romantic Age of the 19th century, pilgrimages were again in vogue, and Rocamadour rebounded. Local bishops rebuilt the château above the sanctuary, making it a pilgrims' reception center, and connecting it to the church with the Way of the Cross. (Most of the current buildings in the Sanctuary of Our Lady of Rocamadour date from the 19th century.) But there hasn't been a bona fide miracle here for eight centuries...and that hurts the pilgrimage business. Since the mid-20th-century, Rocamadour has become more of a tourist attraction, and today, Rocamadour's 650 inhabitants earn a living off its million visitors a year. The vast majority of those who climb the holy steps to the sanctuary are tourists—more interested in burning calories than incense.

limestone cliffs. It was through l'Hospitalet's fortified gate that medieval pilgrims gained access to the "Holy Way," which led from l'Hospitalet to Rocamadour.

**Château**—Dating from the 14th century, the "château" fortified a bluff that was an easy base for bandits to attack the wealthy church below. Today's structure is a 19th-century private house that was transformed to be a reception spot for pilgrims. It's *privé* unless you are a pilgrim (in which case you can sleep here). For tourists, all it offers is a short rampart walk for a grand view (probably not worth the €2.50 fee).

The zigzag **Way of the Cross** (Chemin de la Croix—a path marked with 14 Stations of the Cross, with a chapel for each station at each corner) gives religious purpose to the 15-minute hike between the château and the sanctuary below.

**Grottes Préhistorique des Merveilles**—This cave, located next to the upper TI, has the usual geological formations and a handful of small, blurred cave paintings. It's of no interest if you have seen or will see other prehistoric caves—its sole advantages are that it requires little effort to visit (with only about 10 steps down), and the guide can answer questions in English on the 40-minute tour

(€6, daily July–Aug 9:30–19:00, April–June and Sept 10:00–12:00 & 14:00–18:00, Oct–March until 17:00, decent handout available, tel. 05 65 33 67 92, www.grotte-des-merveilles.com).

## At the Sanctuary Level (La Cité Religieuse)

These sights form the heart of your rocky sightseeing. From the western end of the lower town, climb the steps as pilgrims did, passing a plaque listing key medieval pilgrimages starting with St. Bernard. From the upper town, take the Way of the Cross path down. Or take the easy way out, and take an elevator (from above or below). Either way, your destination will be signed *Sanctuaires*.

▲▲**The Sanctuary of Our Lady of Rocamadour**—Stand in the small square with the cliff to your left, and look up to the open door of the Church of St. Saveur. While the buildings originated much earlier, most of what you see was redone in the 19th century. Crammed onto a ledge on a cliff, the church couldn't follow the standard floor plan, so its seven chapels surround the square (called the *le parvis*) rather than the church. The Pope's palace sits behind you, the Bishop's palace is to your right, and a museum of sacred art (closed indefinitely) is to your left. There's also a small museum and shop selling various pilgrimage mementos, including modern versions of the medallions that pilgrims prized centuries ago as proof of their visit. The two most historic chapels are to your left on either side of the steps.

Walk up the flight of steps to the cliff, where a tomb is cut into the rock. This is where the miraculously preserved body of St. Amadour was found in 1166. Places of pilgrimage do better with multiple miracles. So, along with its Black Virgin and the miracle of St. Amadour's body (see sidebar on page 382), Rocamadour has the **Sword of Roland.** The rusty sword of Charlemagne's nephew sticks in the cliffside, 10 yards above Amadour's tomb. According to medieval sources, when Roland was about to die in battle, the great warrior didn't want his sword to fall into enemy hands. He hurled it from the far south of France, and it landed here—stuck miraculously into the Rocamadour cliffs just above the Black Virgin. (The sword is clearly from the 18th century, but never mind.)

**St. Michael's Chapel** is built around the original cave to your left (open only to pilgrims, with little to see inside). To your right, the **Chapel of the Virgin** (Chapelle Notre Dame) is the focal point of pilgrims. Step inside. High above the altar is the much-venerated Black Virgin, a 12th-century statue (covered with a thin plating of blackened silver—see sidebar on page 382) that depicts Mary presenting Jesus to the world. The oldest thing in the sanctuary—from the ninth century—is a simple rusted bell hanging from the ceiling. The suspended sailboat models are a reminder that sailors relied on Mary for safe passage.

**DORDOGNE**

The adjacent **Church of St. Saveur** is the sanctuary's main place of worship. In front of a central pillar, a copy of the Black Virgin is displayed to give visitors a closer look. The double wooden balcony (newly rebuilt) was for the monks. Imagine attending a Mass here in centuries past, when the church was filled with pilgrims, and monks lined the balconies. While Rocamadour's church seems more like a tourist attraction, it remains a sacred place of worship. A sign reminds tourists, "To admire, to contemplate, to pray. You're welcome to respectfully visit" (free, open daily generally 8:00–19:00).

From here you can walk under the Church of St. Saveur and find the Way of the Cross (Chemin de la Croix) and elevators up (Château par ascenseur) or down (La Cité par ascenseur).

### In the Lower Town (La Cité Medievale)

Rocamadour's town is basically one long street traversing the cliff below the sanctuary. For eight centuries, it has housed, fed, and sold souvenirs to the site's countless visitors. There's precious little here other than tacky trinket shops, but I enjoyed popping into the **Galerie le Vieux Pressoir** (named for its 13th-century walnut millstone). It fills a medieval vaulted room with the fine art of a talented couple: Richard Begyn and Veronique Guinard.

Seven of Rocamadour's 11 original **gates** survive. These were designed to control the pilgrim crowds. In the 14th century, as many as 20,000 would converge on this spot from all over Europe on a single day. From the western end of town, 223 steps lead up to the church at the sanctuary level. Traditionally, pilgrims kneel on each and pray an "Ave Maria" to Our Lady.

## Near Rocamadour

▲**Gouffre de Padirac**—Twenty minutes from Rocamadour is the huge sinkhole of Padirac, with its underground river and miles of stalagmites and stalactites (but no cave art). While it's an impressive cave, if you've seen caves already, it's slow in comparison, with an insufficient payoff (lots of climbing and not a word of English). While there's no attempt to help English-speakers, the mechanics of the visit are easy, and there's not much to communicate anyway. Here's the drill: After paying, hike the stairs (with big views of the sinkhole—a round shaft about 100 yards wide and deep), or ride the elevator to the river level. Line up and wait for your boat. Pack into the boat with about a dozen others for the slow row past a fantasy world of hanging cave formations. Get out and hike a big circle with your group and guide, enjoying lots of caverns, underground lakes, and mighty stalagmites and stalactites. Get back on the boat and retrace your course. Two elevators zip you back to the sunlight. The visit takes 90 minutes (crowds make it take longer in summer, when

**DORDOGNE**

I'd skip it). Dress warmly (€9, daily July–Aug 9:00–18:00, April–June and Sept 9:00–12:00 & 14:00–18:00, Oct–March 9:00–12:00 & 14:00–17:00, long lines at 14:00, tel. 05 65 33 64 56, www.gouffre-de-padirac.com). For knickknack Padirac, don't miss the shop.

# SLEEPING

## In Rocamadour

**(€1= about $1.50, country code: 33)**

Hotels are a deal here. You have two locations to choose from: the upper city, La Cité Religieuse (near l'Hospitalet), which has views down to Rocamadour; or below, within the medieval city, called La Cité Medievale. Parking is easier up top, but the spirit of St. Amadour is more present below. (I prefer the lower medieval city.) Every hotel—including the ones I recommend—has a restaurant where they'd like you to dine.

### In La Cité Medievale

**$ Hôtel-Restaurant le Terminus des Pèlerins**, at the western end of the pedestrian street in La Cité Medievale, has immaculate, comfortable rooms with wood furnishings; the best have balconies and face the valley. Helpful owner Geneviève was born in this hotel (Db–€50, Db with view and balcony–€70, Tb–€75, tel. 05 65 33 62 14, fax 05 65 33 72 10, www.terminus-des-pelerins.com, hotelterm.pelerinsroc@wanadoo.fr).

### In La Cité Religieuse

**$$ Hôtel Belvédère** has 18 well-maintained, modern, and appealing rooms, 12 of which have views over Rocamadour (rooms #14–18 have best views, Db with no view–€54–64, Db with view–€70–80, tel. 05 65 33 63 25, fax 05 65 33 69 25, www.lebelvedere-rocamadour.com, lebelvere@wanadoo.fr).

## Near Rocamadour

**$$ Moulin de Fresquet** is a dreamy *chambre d'hôte* five miles east of Rocamadour. Gracious Gérard and his wife Claude have lovingly restored an ancient mill in a lush, park-like setting. The four antique-furnished rooms come with wood beams and oodles of character. You're free to enjoy the outdoor terraces, chaise lounges, and duck pond—with ducks for pets, not for dinner. If you're really on vacation, stay here, and if Claude is cooking, eat here (dinner–€21, daily except Thu). Book as far ahead as possible, since this place is popular for a reason (Db–€60–92, fine Db suite–€110, Tb–€94, Qb–€99, includes breakfast, cash only, closed Nov–March, in Gramat, tel. 05 65 38 70 60, mobile 06 08 85 09 21, fax 05 65 33 60 13, www.moulindefresquet.com, info@moulindefresquet

**DORDOGNE**

.com). Go to Gramat, then follow signs through town to *Figeac;* the *chambre d'hôte* is well-signed at the east end of Gramat.

## EATING

### In Rocamadour

**Hôtel Belvédère,** in the upper town, has the best interior view from its modern dining room. Book ahead for a window-side table, ideally for a meal just before sunset (*menus* from €18, open daily, tel. 05 65 33 63 25; also listed under "Sleeping," above).

The **Bar l'Esplanade** hunkers cliffside below Hôtel Belvédère, and owns unobstructed views from the tables in its garden café. It's open for lunch, dinner, drinks, and snacks (daily, tel. 05 65 33 18 45).

---

# Near Rocamadour: The Overlooked Eastern Dordogne

Many find this remote, less-visited section of the Dordogne (Quercy *département*) even more beautiful than the area around Sarlat, and all find it less visited. For a good introduction to this area, follow this self-guided driving tour.

## SELF-GUIDED DRIVING TOUR

### Welcome to the Eastern Dordogne

Follow the Dordogne heading east, driving about an hour upriver from Souillac, to connect these worthwhile stops: Martel, Carennac, Château de Castelnau-Bretenoux, Loubressac, and Autoire. Rocamadour lies just beyond this area, as do the Tom Sawyer–like Gouffre de Padirac caves (both described earlier in this chapter). Allow 45 minutes from Sarlat to Souillac, then 15 minutes to Martel, and 20 minutes to Carennac (Château de Castelnau-Bretenoux and Loubressac are within 10 minutes of Carennac). From Carennac it's 25 minutes south to Rocamadour.

• *From Souillac's center, take D-803 east to...*

**Martel:** A well-preserved medieval town of 1,500 souls and seven towers, this peaceful place has a fine pedestrian area with many shops (good chance to stock up on picnic items). Neither on a river nor crowning a hilltop, it's largely overlooked by tourists. The town is named for Charles Martel (Charlemagne's grandfather and role model), who made his name by stopping the Moors as they marched into northern France in 732. A good walking tour of Martel starts at its fine main square (place des Consuls, with a medieval covered market), and connects the seven towers.

**Near Rocamadour**

• *From Martel, continue east on D-803 toward Castelnaud, Vayrac, and Bétraille, then cross the Dordogne on D-20 to find...*

**Carennac:** This riverside town demands to be photographed. Park along the river, by the fortified Prieuré St-Pierre. Explore the evocative church and examine its exquisitely carved tympanum. It was built as an outpost of the Cluny Abbey in the 10th century, then fortified in the 1500s during the wars of religion. For a memorable meal inside or out, head to **Le Prieuré Crêperie,** with a warm interior, fine salads, and filling crêpes (closed Mon, lunch served all day, across from the church, tel. 05 65 39 76 75). Cross the small bridge behind the *crêperie* for more village views.

• *From here, head east on D-30, tracking the Dordogne River. Turn left, following signs to...*

**Château de Castelnau-Bretenoux:** A splendidly situated and once-powerful military castle, this château has fine views in all directions and several well-furnished rooms. The reddish-golden stone and massive 12th-century walls make an impression, as does its height—almost 800 feet. Cross the moat to the castle courtyard, and climb the round military tower for sensational views, then join a 30-minute, mercifully brief French-only tour (meager English handout) to view the seven furnished rooms (€6.50, €2 to park, or park for free at the restaurant/café lot if you plan to have a snack or lunch, daily July–Aug 9:30–19:00, Sept–June 10:00–12:30 & 14:00–18:30, last entry one hour before closing, tel. 05 65 10 98 00).
• *Return to D-30, cross it, and continue straight up D-14. You'll come to...*

**Loubressac:** Arguably the most beautiful village in France, Loubressac hangs atop a beefy ridge, with outlandish views and a gaggle of adorable homes at its eastern end. You'll find an Old World café and modern hotel-restaurant, **$$$ Le Relais de Castelnau*****, which rents 40 rooms with a view terrace and pool (Db €80–110, tel. 05 65 10 80 90, fax 05 65 38 22 02, www.relais decastelnau.com).
• *From here, it's a short hop on D-118 to lovely little...*

**Autoire:** Arguably the *other* most beautiful village in France, this one lies a few minutes beyond Loubressac. Visit and decide which village is fairest of them all.
• *From here you can follow signs to Gramat, then on to Rocamadour.*

# Lot River Valley

Ninety minutes south of the Dordogne, the overlooked Lot River meanders under stubborn cliffs, past tempting villages, and through a strikingly beautiful valley.  The fortified bridge at Cahors, the prehistoric cave paintings at Grotte du Pech Merle, and the breathtaking town of St. Cirq Lapopie are worthwhile sights in this valley—each within a half-hour of the others. These sights can be combined to make a terrific day for travelers willing to invest the time (doable as a long day trip from the Sarlat area). They also work well as a day trip from Rocamadour, and are worthwhile for drivers connecting the Dordogne with Albi (see

DORDOGNE

page 458) or Carcassonne (see page 472). (If you're going to or coming from the south, you can scenically connect this area with Albi via Villefranche-de-Rouergue and Cordes-sur-Ciel.) With extra time, spend a night in St. Cirq Lapopie, since it makes a good base for visiting the area.

# St. Cirq Lapopie

This spectacularly situated village, clinging to a ledge sailing above the Lot River, knows only two directions—straight up and way down. In St. Cirq Lapopie, there's little to do but wander the rambling footpaths, inspect the flowers and stones, and thrill over the vistas. You'll find picnic perches, a handful of galleries and restaurants, and views from the bottom and top of the village that justify the pain.

St. Cirq Lapopie is well-signed 30 minutes east of Cahors, an hour south of Rocamadour, and just 20 minutes from the cave paintings of Grotte du Pech Merle (see page 392).

## ORIENTATION

While you need to be careful of weekend and high-season (July–Aug) crowds, St. Cirq Lapopie has not been blemished by too many boutiques. It remains pin-drop peaceful after-hours in any season. Arrive later in the day and spend the night to best appreciate where you are—your first views of St. Cirq Lapopie are eye-popping enough to convince you to stay.

### Tourist Information

The TI is located across from the recommended Auberge du Sombral (May–Sept daily 10:00–13:00 & 14:00–18:00, Oct–April closes at 17:00 and on Sun, tel. 05 65 31 29 06). Pick up the visitor's guide in English, with brief descriptions of 22 historic buildings, and ask for information on hikes in the area.

### Arrival in St. Cirq Lapopie

By Car: Arriving by car from the west, you'll pass the town across the Lot River, then cross a narrow bridge and climb. There are three well-signed parking options: a small, free, dirt parking lot partway up, leaving you with a hefty uphill walk; a much closer pay lot at village level (€3, exact change required); and a third lot that lies at the top (€3, great views from here). Pull over for photo stops as you climb.

DORDOGNE

# SIGHTS

**Chemin de Halage**—This is a beautiful riverside trail below St. Cirq Lapopie, originally used for pulling flat-bottomed boats upriver. Long sections of the trail are cut into the limestone cliff. Once riverside, walking downriver toward Cahors, you'll reach the cut-out section in about 20 minutes. It's a steep hike down and a long climb back up (trail leads from across from the TI or by walking through the village to the bottom). Get details at the TI.

# SLEEPING

**(€1= about $1.50, country code: 33)**
The village has all of 18 rooms, none of which is open off-season (mid-Nov–March).

**$$ At Hôtel de la Pélissaria\*\*\***, serene Marie-Françoise takes good care of her guests. Unfortunately, she's hanging up her hotelier gloves, and the hotel will close for good in mid-October of 2009. Ten tastefully appointed rooms are built into the hillside, so they're a bit dark (but cool when it's hot). The terraced gardens are just so, the pool is just tiny, and the views to the main village are just incredible. The hotel is at the lower end of the village, so be ready to earn your dinner (standard Db-€82, bigger Db-€100, superior Db-€130, tel. 05 65 31 25 14, fax 05 65 30 25 52, http://perso.wanadoo.fr/hoteldelapelissaria, hoteldelapelissaria@wanadoo.fr).

**$$ Auberge du Sombral\*\***, run with panache by Madame Haldeveled and daughter Marion (who speaks English), is a fine value in the town center below the TI. They'll welcome you with an oh-so-cozy lobby area and eight quite comfortable rooms above in various sizes, most with double beds (small Sb-€50, Db €75–80, tel. 05 65 31 26 08, fax 05 65 30 26 37, www.lesombral.com). The good restaurant serves lunch every day but Thursday, and dinners on Friday and Saturday nights.

# EATING

Dinner is tricky here; reliable help seems to be a problem, leaving restaurants understaffed at busy times. But this town was made for picnics; consider picking up dinner fixings in the hamlet of La Tour de Faure. (There's a small grocery store on the other side of the river just west of the bridge to St. Cirq Lapopie, and a bakery a short way east of the bridge.)

As restaurants go, **Lou Boulat Brasserie** works for me. It serves low-risk lighter meals (salads, crêpes, and *plats*) in a low-stress setting, with good views from the side terrace (closed Wed, located at the upper end of town, off the main road by the post office/PTT, tel. 05 65 30 29 04).

**L'Oustal** is the most traditional restaurant in town, with a handful of cozy tables inside and out on a little terrace (€16 and €32 *menus*, €15 *plats du jour,* closed Mon, below the towering church, tel. 05 65 31 20 17).

**Auberge du Sombral** serves reliable cuisine within a lovely dining room or out front on a photogenic terrace (see listing above, under "Sleeping").

# More Sights in the Lot River Valley

**Cahors and the Pont Valentré**—One of Europe's finest medieval monuments, this fortified bridge was built in 1308 to keep the English out of Cahors. It worked. Learn the story of the devil on the center tower. The steep trail on the non-city side leads to great views (views are actually better partway up, but be careful if the trail is wet) and was once part of the pilgrimage route to Santiago de Compostela in northwest Spain. Imagine that cars were allowed to cross this bridge until recently. Just past the city-side end of the bridge is **Le Cèdre,** a wine shop/café/souvenir stand with delightful owners; say *bonjour* to Marie-Danielle and Jean-Claude, and ask to sample Cahors' black wine and foie gras.

If you need an urban fix, stroll the pedestrian-friendly alleys between Cahors' cathedral and the river, a thriving place filled with good lunch options. To find this area by car, follow *Centre-Ville* and *St. Urcisse Eglise* signs, and park where you can.

▲▲**Grotte du Pech Merle**—This cave, about 30 minutes east of Cahors, has prehistoric paintings of mammoths, bison, and horses—rivaling the better-known cave art at Grotte de Font-de-Gaume. Grotte du Pech Merle is easier to view, as more people per day are allowed in (700), but that also makes the cave a bit less special. Still, it has brilliant cave art and interesting stalactite and stalagmite formations. I like the mud-preserved Cro-Magnon footprint. Allow a total of two hours for your visit, starting at the small museum, continuing with a 20-minute film subtitled in English, and finishing with the caves. It's smart to reserve your spot in advance (by phone or online) as private groups can fill the cave's quota. In summer, book a week ahead; if you visit without a reservation, arrive by 9:30 and line up. If you can't join an English tour, ask for the English-translation booklet (€7.50 admission mid-June–mid-Sept, otherwise €6; open daily March–mid-Nov 9:30–12:00 & 13:30–17:00, closes earlier off-season, tel. 05 65 31 27 05, fax 05 65 31 20 47, www.pechmerle.com). Before you visit, read "Cave Art 101" on page 362.

DORDOGNE

# BASQUE COUNTRY

*Euskal Herria*

Straddling two nations on the Atlantic Coast—stretching about 100 miles from Bayonne, France, south to Bilbao, Spain—lies the ancient, free-spirited land of the Basques. The Basque Country is famous for its sunny beaches and scintillating modern architecture...and for its feisty, industrious natives. It's also simply beautiful: Bright, white, chalet-style homes with deep-red-and-green shutters scatter across lush, rolling hills; the Pyrenees Mountains soar high above the Atlantic; and surfers and sardines share the waves.

Insulated from mainstream Europe for centuries, the plucky Basques have just wanted to be left alone for more than 7,000 years. An easily crossed border separates the French *Pays Basque* from the Spanish *País Vasco,* allowing you to sample both sides from a single base (in France, I hang my hat in cozy St. Jean-de-Luz; in Spain, I prefer fun-loving San Sebastián).

Much unites the French and Spanish Basque regions: They share a cuisine, Union Jack–style flag (green, red, and white), and common language (Euskara), spoken by about a half-million people. (Virtually everyone also speaks French or Spanish.) And both have been integrated by their respective nations, sometimes forcibly. The French Revolution quelled French Basque ideas of independence; 130 years later, Spain's Generalísimo Francisco Franco attempted to tame his own separatist-minded Basques.

But over the last generation, things have started looking up. The long-suppressed Euskara language is enjoying a resurgence. And, as the European Union celebrates regions rather than nations, the French and Spanish Basques are feeling more united. This heavily industrialized region is enjoying a striking 21st-century renaissance. In France, long-ignored cities such as Bayonne and the surfing mecca of Biarritz are being revitalized. And in Spain, the dazzling new architecture of the Guggenheim Bilbao modern-art museum and the glittering resort of San Sebastián are drawing enthusiastic crowds. At the same time, traditional small towns—like France's St. Jean-de-Luz and nearby mountain villages, and Spain's Lekeitio and Hondarribia—are also thriving, making the entire region colorful, fun, welcoming...and unmistakably Basque.

## Planning Your Time

One day is enough for a quick sample of the Basque Country, but two or three days lets you breathe deep and hold it in. Where you go depends on your interests: France or Spain? Cities (such as Bayonne, Bilbao, and San Sebastián) or resorts (including St. Jean-de-Luz, Biarritz, and...San Sebastián)?

If you want to slow down and focus on Spain, spend one day relaxing in San Sebastián and the second side-tripping to Bilbao (and possibly to Guernica and Lekeitio, especially if you have a car).

Better yet, sample Basque sights on both sides of the border. Sleep in one country, then side-trip into the other, devoting one day to France (St. Jean-de-Luz, Bayonne, and maybe Biarritz), and a second day to Spain (San Sebastián and maybe Bilbao).

Wherever you go, most of your sightseeing will be cultural, scenic, and culinary; in Basque Country, museum-going takes a backseat to relaxing.

## Getting Around the Basque Country

The tourist's Basque Country—from Bayonne to Bilbao—stays close to the coastline. Fortunately, everything is connected by good roads and public transportation.

**By Bus and Train:** In France, the three main towns (St. Jean-de-Luz, Bayonne, Biarritz) are connected by bus (trains also zip between St. Jean-de-Luz and Bayonne). To go between France and San Sebastián, a train—with a transfer in Hendaye—is your best bet (2/hr, takes 1 hour between St. Jean-de-Luz and San Sebastián; faster but less frequent by bus: 2/day direct, 45 min). From San Sebastián, the bus is the best way to reach Bilbao (and from there, Guernica and Lekeitio). Specific connections are explained in each section.

Note that a few out-of-the-way areas—France's Basque villages of the interior, Spain's Lekeitio and Bay of Biscay—are impractical by public transportation...but wonderful by car.

**By Car:** Bayonne, Biarritz, St. Jean-de-Luz, San Sebastián, and Bilbao are connected by a convenient expressway, called A-63 in France and A-8 in Spain (rough timings: St. Jean-de-Luz to Biarritz or Bayonne—30 min; St. Jean-de-Luz to San Sebastián—45 min; San Sebastián to Bilbao—1.25 hrs).

**Basque Country**

Language Warning: For the headers throughout this chapter, I've listed place names using the French or Spanish spelling first, and the Euskara spelling second. In the text, I use the spelling that prevails locally. While most people refer to towns by their French or Spanish names, road signs list places in the national language and in Euskara. The Spanish or French version is sometimes scratched out by independence-minded locals, so you might have to navigate by Euskara names.

Also note that in terms of linguistic priority (e.g., museum information), Euskara comes first, French and Spanish second, and English a distant third...and it sometimes doesn't even make the cut.

## Cuisine Scene in Basque Country

Mixing influences from the mountains, sea, Spain, and France, Basque food is reason enough to visit the region. The local cuisine—dominated by seafood, tomatoes, and red peppers—offers some spicy dishes, unusual in most of Europe. While you'll find similar specialties throughout the Basque lands, France is still France and Spain is still Spain. Here are some dishes you're most likely to find in each area.

French Basque Cuisine: The red peppers (called *piments*) hanging from homes in small villages end up in *piperade*, a dish that combines peppers, tomatoes, garlic, ham, and eggs. Look

# Who Are the Basques?

To call the Basques "mysterious" is an understatement. Before most European nations had ever set sail, Basque whalers competed with the Vikings for control of the sea. During the Industrial Revolution and lean Franco years, Basque steel kept the Spanish economy alive. In recent years, the separatist army ETA has given the Basques a reputation for rebellion and violence. And through it all, they've spoken a unique language that sounds to outsiders like gibberish or a secret code.

So, just who are the Basques? Even for Basques, that's a difficult question. According to traditional stereotypes, Basques are thought of as having long noses, heavy eyebrows, floppy ears, stout bodies, and a penchant for wearing berets. But widespread Spanish and French immigration has made it difficult to know who actually has Basque ethnic roots. (In fact, some of the Basques' greatest patriots have had no Basque blood.) And so today, anyone who speaks the Basque language, Euskara, is considered a "Basque."

Euskara, related to no other surviving tongue, has been used since Neolithic times—making it, very likely, the oldest European language that's still spoken. With its seemingly impossible-to-pronounce words filled with k's, tx's, and z's (rest rooms are *gizonak* for men and *emakumeak* for women), Euskara makes speaking French suddenly seem easy. (Some tips: *tx* is pronounced "ch," while *tz* is pronounced "ts." Other key words: *kalea* is "street," and *ostatua* is a cheap hotel.) Kept alive as a symbol of Basque cultural identity, Euskara is typically learned proudly as a second or third language. Many locals can switch effortlessly from Euskara to Spanish or French. Basques wave their language like a flag—look for Euskara street signs, menus, and signs in shops.

The Basque economy has historically been shaped by three factors: the sea, agriculture, and iron deposits.

Basque sailors were some of the first and finest in Europe, as they built ever-better boats to venture farther and farther

into the Atlantic in search of whales. (These long journeys were made possible by the invention of *bacalao*—dried, salted cod that could last for months to sustain whalers.) By the year 1000, Basque sailors were chasing whales a thousand miles from home, in the Norwegian fjords. Despite lack of physical evidence, many historians surmise that the Basques must have sailed to the Americas before Christopher Columbus.

When the "Spanish" era of exploration began, Basques continued to play a key role, as sailors and shipbuilders. Columbus' *Santa María* was likely Basque-built, and his crew included many Basques. History books teach that Ferdinand Magellan was the first to circumnavigate the globe, with the footnote that he was killed partway around. Who took over the ship for the rest of the journey, completing the circle? The Basque sailor Juan Sebastián de Elcano. And a pair of well-traveled Catholic priests, known for their far-reaching missionary trips that led to founding the Jesuit order, were also Basques: St. Ignatius of Loyola and St. Francis Xavier.

Later, the Industrial Age swept Europe, gaining a foothold in Iberia when the Basques began using their rich iron deposits to make steel. Pioneering Basque industrialists set the tempo as they dragged Spain into the modern world. Cities such as Bilbao were heavily industrialized, sparking an influx of workers from around Spain (which gradually diluted Basque blood in the Basque Country).

The independence-minded Basques are notorious for their stubbornness. In truth, as a culturally and linguistically unique island surrounded by bigger and stronger nations, the Basques have learned to compromise.

Historically Basques have remained on good terms with outsiders, so long as their traditional laws, the *Fueros,* were respected. While outdated, the *Fueros* continue to symbolize a self-governance that the Basques hold dear. It is only when foreign law has been placed above the *Fueros*—as many of today's Basques feel Spanish law does—that the people become agitated.

In recent years, most news of the Basques—especially in Spain—has been made by the terrorist organization ETA. (ETA stands for the Euskara phrase *Euskadi Ta Askatasuna,* or "Basque Country and Freedom"; *eta* also means "and" in Euskara.) ETA has been blamed for more than 800 deaths since 1968. The violence ebbs and flows, but ETA tends to focus on political targets, and their activities go largely unnoticed by tourists. While many people in Basque Country would like a greater degree of autonomy from Madrid, only a tiny minority supports ETA.

This is only a first glimpse into the important, quirky, and fascinating Basque people. To better understand the Basques, there's no better book than Mark Kurlansky's *The Basque History of the World*—essential pre-trip reading for historians.

for anything "Basque-style" *(basquaise)*—cooked with tomato, eggplant, red pepper, and garlic. Don't leave without trying *ttoro* (tchoo-roh), a seafood stew that is Basque Country's answer to bouillabaisse and cioppino. *Marmitako* is a hearty tuna stew. Local cheeses come from Pyrenean sheep's milk *(pur brebis)*, and the local ham *(jambon de Bayonne)* is famous throughout France. After dinner, try a shot of *izarra* (herbal-flavored brandy). To satisfy your sweet tooth, look for *gâteau basque*, a local tart filled with cream or jams, or chocolates from Bayonne. Hard apple cider is the locally made beverage, but the region's wine, Irouleguy, isn't worth its price.

**Spanish Basque Cuisine:** Hopping from bar to bar sampling *pintxos*—the local term for tapas—is a highlight of any trip (for details, see sidebar on page 434). On menus, you'll see *bacalao* (salted cod), best when cooked *à la bizkaina* (with tomatoes, onions, and roasted peppers); *merluza* (hake, a light whitefish prepared in a variety of ways); and *chipirones en su tinta* (squid served in their own black ink). Carnivores will find beef *(chuletas,* steaks) and lamb *(chuletillas,* lamb chops). Local brews include *sidra* (hard apple cider) and *txakolí* (cha-koh-LEE, a local light, sparkling white wine—often theatrically poured from high above the glass for aeration).

# French Basque Country (Le Pays Basque)

Compared to their cousins across the border, the French Basques seem French first and Basque second. (But don't tell them that.) You'll see less Euskara writing here. But these destinations have their own special spice, mingling Basque and French influences with beautiful rolling countryside and gorgeous beaches.

My favorite home base here is the central, comfy, and manageable resort village of St. Jean-de-Luz. It's a stone's throw to Bayonne (with its big-city bustle and fine Basque museum) and the snazzy beach town of Biarritz. A drive inland rewards you with a panoply of adorable French Basque villages. And St. Jean-de-Luz is a nice, relaxing place to "come home" to, with its mellow ambience, fine strolling atmosphere, and good restaurants.

# St. Jean-de-Luz / Donibane Lohizune

St. Jean-de-Luz (san zhahn-duh-looz) sits happily off the beaten path, cradled between its small port and gentle bay. Pastry shops serve Basque specialties, and store windows proudly display berets (a Basque symbol). Ice-cream lickers stroll traffic-free streets, while soft, sandy beaches tempt travelers to toss their itineraries into the bay. The knobby little mountain La Rhune towers above the festive scene. Locals joke that if it's clear enough to see La Rhune's peak, it's going to rain, but if you can't see it, it's raining already.

The town has precious little of sightseeing importance. But it's a fine base for exploring the Basque Country, and a relaxing beach and port town that provides the most enjoyable dose of Basque culture in France. In July and August, the town fills with French tourists from the north—especially the first two weeks of August, when it's practically impossible to find a room without a reservation made long in advance.

## ORIENTATION

St. Jean-de-Luz's old city lies between the train tracks, the Nivelle River, and the Atlantic. The main traffic-free street, rue Gambetta, channels walkers through the center, halfway between the train tracks and the ocean. The small town of Ciboure, across the river, holds nothing of interest.

The only sight worth entering in St. Jean-de-Luz is the church where Louis XIV and Marie-Thérèse tied the royal knot (Eglise St. Jean-Baptiste, described later in this section). St. Jean-de-Luz is best appreciated along its pedestrian streets, lively squares, and golden, sandy beaches. The park at the far eastern end of the beachfront promenade at Pointe Ste. Barbe makes a good walking destination, with views and walking trails.

### Tourist Information

The helpful TI is next to the big market hall, along the busy boulevard Victor Hugo (July–Aug Mon–Sat 9:00–19:30, Sun 10:00–13:00 & 15:00–19:00; Sept–June Mon–Sat 9:00–12:30 & 14:00–19:00, Sun 10:00–13:00—except Jan–March, when it's closed Sun; 20 boulevard Victor Hugo, tel. 05 59 26 03 16, www.saint-jean-de-luz.com or www.terreetcotebasque.com).

### Arrival in St. Jean-de-Luz

**By Train or Bus:** From the station, take the pedestrian underpass, then walk left along the busy street. To find the TI, take the first right turn (down Labrouche); the TI is at the far end of the market hall. Or, to reach the town center (place Louis XIV) from the busy road, stay straight around the traffic circle and carry on along avenue de Verdun, then turn right at the second traffic circle.

**By Car:** Follow signs for *Centre-Ville,* then *Gare* and *Office de Tourisme.* Parking (except on some peak summer days) is relatively easy: You can park in the big lot next to the bus station on the main road (about a five-minute walk to most hotels), or delve deeper into town looking for a smaller parking lot (at any lot, pre-pay at meter during daytime, free overnight). Hotels or the TI can advise you.

**By Plane:** The nearest airport is in Biarritz, 10 miles to the northeast. The tiny airport is easy to navigate, with a useful TI desk (airport tel. 05 59 43 83 83, www.biarritz.aeroport.fr). To reach St. Jean-de-Luz, you can take a public bus (€3, 7/day, fewer on Sun, 30 min, tel. 05 59 26 06 99 for schedule) or a 20-minute taxi ride (about €30).

## Helpful Hints

**Market Days:** Tuesday and Friday mornings (and Sat in summer), the farmers' stands spill through the streets from the Les Halles covered market on boulevard Victor Hugo, and seem to give everyone a whiff of "life is good" flavor.

**Supermarkets:** There's a **Petit Casino** grocery on rue Gambetta, just before boulevard Thiers (Mon–Sat 8:00–12:30 & 15:30–19:30, Sun 9:00–13:00 only, tel. 05 59 26 00 41). Or try the **Les Halles** market (above).

**Internet Access:** Run by friendly Irish expats Margaret and Peter, **Internet World** is best (July–Aug Mon–Sat 9:00–24:00, Sun 10:00–18:00; Sept–June Mon–Sat 10:00–18:00, closed Sun; 7 rue Tourasse, tel. 05 59 26 86 92).

**Laundry: Laverie du Port** at 5 place du Maréchal Foch (full-service for €12/load available Mon–Fri 9:30–12:30 & 14:30–19:00, Sat 9:30–13:00, closed Sun; cheaper self-service available daily 7:00–21:00).

**Car Rental: Avis,** at the train station, is handiest (Mon–Fri 8:00–12:00 & 14:00–18:00, Sat opens at 9:00, closed Sun, tel. 05 59 26 76 66, fax 05 55 26 19 42).

# SELF-GUIDED WALK

## Welcome to St. Jean-de-Luz

To get a feel for the town, take this self-guided, two-mile walk. You'll start at the port and make your way to the historic church. Allow about one hour.

**Port:** Begin at the little working port (at place des Corsaires, just beyond the parking lot). Pleasure craft are in the next port over. While fishing boats used to catch lots of whales, now they take in cod, sardines, tuna, and anchovies, and take out tourists (two boats advertise today's and tomorrow's mini–Atlantic cruises and fishing excursions, summer only). St. Jean-de-Luz feels cute and non-threatening now, but in the 17th century, it was home to the Basque Corsairs. With the French government's blessing, these pirates, who worked the sea—and enriched the town—moored here.

• *After you walk the length of the port, on your right is the tree-lined...*

**Place Louis XIV:** The town's main square, named for the king who was married here, is a hub of action. During the summer, the bandstand features traditional Basque music at 21:00 (almost nightly July–Aug, otherwise Sun and Wed). Facing the square is the City Hall (Herriko Etchea) and the "House of Louis XIV" (in which he lived for 40 festive days in 1660). A visit to this house is worthwhile only if you like period furniture (€5, open June–mid-Oct Wed–Mon, visits by guided tour only, 2–4/day, closed Tue and mid-Oct–May—when the privately owned mansion is occupied by the same family who've had it for over three centuries, tel. 05 59 26 27 58). The king's visit is memorialized by a small black equestrian statue at the entrance of the City Hall (a miniature of the huge one that marks the center of the Versailles courtyard).

• *Opposite the port on the far side of the square is...*

**Rue de la République:** From place Louis XIV, this historic lane—lined with mostly edible temptations—leads to the beach. Facing the square, the shop **Macarons Adam** still bakes (according to the family recipe) the macaroons Louis XIV enjoyed during his visit. You can try one (€0.90), or sample a less historic but just as tasty *gâteau basque,* a baked tart with a cream or jam filling (€1.70). Farther down rue de la République, you'll find the **Pierre Oteiza** shop, stacked with rustic Basque cheeses and meats from mountain villages (with a few samples generally out for the tasting). You'll likely eat on this lane tonight. **Kaiku,** the town's top restaurant, fills the oldest building in St. Jean-de-Luz (with its characteristic stone lookout tower), dating from the 1500s.

• *Continue to the...*

**Beach:** A high embankment protects the town from storm waters, but generally the Grande Plage—which is lovingly groomed daily—is the peaceful haunt of sun-seekers and happy children. Walk the elevated promenade (to the right). Various tableaux tell history in French. Storms (including a particularly disastrous one in 1749) routinely knocked down buildings until Napoleon III built the three breakwaters in the 1800s.

• *Stroll past the late Art Deco–style La Pergola, which houses a casino and the Hélianthal spa center (entrance around back), and overlooks the beach. Anyone in a white robe strolling the beach is from the spa. Beyond*

**BASQUE COUNTRY**

## St. Jean-de-Luz

ATLANTIC OCEAN

To Pointe Ste. Barbe

To Biarritz & Bayonne

La Pergola Spa + Casino

ST. JEAN

FISHING PORT

CIBOURE

NIVELLE RIVER

TRAIN STATION

Bus Stn.

PEDEST. UNDERPASS

To Hendaye & Spain

Place Corsaires

Place Louis XIV

Place M. Foch

BLVD. THIERS

BLVD. V. HUGO

BLVD. CHAUVIN

RUE THIBAUD

R. DELUC

RUE GAMBETTA

RUE GARAT

RUE TOURASSE

RUE REPUBLIQUE

RUE JACQUES

QUAI DE L'INFANTE

PROMENADE MAZARIN

QUAI MAURICE RAVEL

BLVD. MARECHAL FOCH

RUE VICTOR HUGO

RUE MARSPE

BLVD. MARECHAL PASSICOT

PONT DEGAILLE

200 YARDS
200 METERS

P PARKING

DCH

1. Hôtel de la Plage
2. Hôtel les Almadies
3. Hôtel Colbert
4. Hôtel Ohartzia
5. Hôtel le Petit Trianon
6. Hôtel le Verdun
7. La Ruelle & Le Kaiku Rests.
8. Chez Maya Petit Grill Basque
9. Muscade Tarterie
10. Launderette
11. Internet Café
12. Grocery
13. Les Halles Market

*La Pergola is the Neo-Romantic Grand Hôtel (c. 1900), with an inviting terrace for a coffee break. From here, dive back into town until you reach the bustling...*

**Rue Gambetta:** Turn right and circle back to your starting point, following the town's lively pedestrian shopping street. You'll notice many stores selling the renowned *linge Basque*—cotton linens such as tablecloths, napkins, and dishcloths, in the characteristic Basque red, white, and green.

• *Just before place Louis XIV, you'll see the town's main church...*

**Eglise St. Jean-Baptiste:** The marriage of Louis XIV and Marie-Thérèse put St. Jean-de-Luz on the map, and this church

is where it all took place. The ultimate in political marriages, the knot tied between Louis XIV and Marie-Thérèse in 1660 also cinched a reconciliation deal between Europe's two most powerful countries. The king of Spain, Philip IV—who lived in El Escorial Palace—gave his daughter in marriage to the king of France, who lived in Versailles. This marriage united Europe's two largest palaces, which helped end a hundred years of hostility and forged an alliance that enabled both to focus attention on other matters (like England). Little St. Jean-de-Luz was selected for its 15 minutes of fame because it was roughly halfway between Madrid and Paris, and virtually on the France–Spain border. The wedding cleared out both Versailles and El Escorial palaces, as anyone who was anyone attended this glamorous event.

The church, centered on the pedestrian street rue Gambetta, seems modest enough from the exterior...but step inside (daily 8:00–12:00 & 14:00–18:00). The local expertise was in shipbuilding, so the ceiling resembles the hull of a ship turned upside down. The dark wood balconies running along the nave segregated the men from the women and children (men went upstairs until the 1960s), and were typical of Basque churches. The number of levels depended on the importance of the church, and this church, with three levels, is the largest Basque church in France. The three-foot-long paddle-wheel ship hanging in the center was a gift from Napoleon III's wife, Eugènie. It's a model of an ill-fated ship that had almost sunk just offshore when she was on it. The 1670 Baroque altar feels Franco-Spanish, and features 20 French saints. Locals call it the finest in Basque Country. Drop €1 in the box to see it light up. The place has great acoustics, and the 17th-century organ is still used for concerts (€10, mostly in summer, ask for schedule and buy tickets at TI). As you leave the church, turn left

## Pelota

In keeping with their seafaring, shipbuilding, and metal-working heritage, Basque sports are often feats of strength: Who can lift the heaviest stone? Who can row the fastest and farthest?

But the most important Basque sport of all is *pelota*— similar to what you might know as jai alai. Players in white pants and red scarves or shirts use a long, hook-shaped wicker basket (called a *txistera* in Euskara, *chistera*

in French, *remonte* in Spanish) to whip a ball (smaller and far bouncier than a baseball) back and forth off walls at more than 150 miles per hour. This men's-only game can be played with a wall at one or both ends of the court. Most matches are not professional, but betting on them is common. It can also be played without a racket—this slow-motion handball version is used as a starter game for kids.

It seems that every small Basque town has two things: a church and a *pelota* court (called *fronton*). While some *frontóns* are simple and in poor repair, others are freshly painted as a gleaming sign of local pride.

The TI in St. Jean-de-Luz sells tickets and has a schedule of matches throughout the area; you're more likely to find a match in summer (21:00, almost daily July–mid-Sept, afternoon matches sometimes on Sat-Sun). The professional *cesta punta* matches on Tuesdays and Fridays often come with Basque folkloric halftime shows.

to find the bricked-up doorway—the church's original entrance. It was sealed after the royal marriage (shown on the wall to the right in a photo of a painting) to symbolize a permanent closing of the door on troubles between France and Spain.

## SLEEPING

Hotels are a reasonable value here. The higher prices are for peak season (generally June–Sept). In winter, some prices drop below those I've listed. Most hoteliers speak English. Breakfast costs extra, except for my first listing. Those wanting to eat and sleep for less will do slightly better just over the border, in San Sebastián.

**$$$ Hôtel de la Plage**\*** has the best location, right on the ocean. Its 22 rooms, 16 with ocean views, have a lively, yellow-and-blue, modern nautical decor (Db-€88–118, ocean view Db-€118–

## Sleep Code

**(€1 = about $1.50, France country code: 33, Spain country code: 34)**

**S** = Single, **D** = Double/Twin, **T** = Triple, **Q** = Quad, **b** = bathroom, **s** = shower only, * = French hotel rating system (0-4 stars). You can assume these places accept credit cards and speak English unless otherwise noted. Breakfast is generally not included (unless noted). This code applies to this chapter's listings in both Spain and France. The word *ostatua* (which you'll see throughout the Basque Country) means "pension."

To help you sort easily through these listings, I've divided the rooms into three categories based on the price for a standard double room with bath in peak season:

**$$$  Higher Priced**—Most rooms €90 or more.
**$$  Moderately Priced**—Most rooms between €60-90.
**$  Lower Priced**—Most rooms €60 or less.

158, prices fluctuate with demand, family rooms, includes breakfast, air-con, elevator, Wi-Fi, garage-€12, 33 rue Garat, tel. 05 59 51 03 44, fax 05 59 51 03 48, www.hoteldelaplage.com, reservation@hotel delaplage.com, run by friendly Pierre, Yannik, and Frederic).

**$$$ Hôtel les Almadies***, on the main pedestrian street, is a bright boutique hotel with seven flawless rooms, comfy public spaces with clever modern touches, a pleasant breakfast terrace, and an owner who cares (Sb-€75-105, Db-€90-130, higher prices are for rooms with tubs, try to request room with little balcony for no extra charge, child's bed-€20, buffet breakfast-€11, free Wi-Fi, parking-€9, 58 rue Gambetta, tel. 05 59 85 34 48, fax 05 59 26 12 42, www.hotel-les-almadies.com, hotel.lesalmadies@wanadoo .fr, Monsieur and Madame Hargous will charm you with their Franglish).

**$$$ Hôtel Colbert***, a Best Western, has 34 modern, tastefully appointed rooms across the street from the train station (Sb-€75-119, Db-€80-128, €10 extra for bigger "superior" rooms, breakfast-€13, air-con, elevator, free Wi-Fi, 3 boulevard du Commandant Passicot, tel. 05 59 26 31 99, fax 05 59 51 05 61, www .hotelcolbertsaintjeandeluz.com, contact@hotelcolbertsaint jeandeluz.com).

**$$ Hôtel Ohartzia** ("Souvenir"), one block off the beach, is comfortable, clean, peaceful, and characteristic, with the most charming facade I've seen. It comes with 17 simple but well-cared-for rooms, and generous, homey public spaces. The highlight for me is the bird-chirping, flower-petaled garden in the back; the higher prices listed here are for the four rooms with bathtubs and views over this little Eden (mid-July–Sept Sb/Db-€79–89, April–mid-July Sb/Db-€68–72, Oct–March Sb/Db-€60–68, extra bed-€15, 28 rue Garat, tel. 05 59 26 00 06, fax 05 59 26 74 75, www.hotel-ohartzia.com, hotel.ohartzia@wanadoo.fr). Their desk is technically open only 8:00–20:00, but owners Madame and Monsieur Audibert (who speak little English) live in the building; their son Benoît speaks good English.

**$$ Hôtel le Petit Trianon**\*\*, on a major street, is simple and traditional, with 26 nicely appointed rooms and accommodating staff (July–Sept Sb/Db-€75; mid-March–June and Oct–mid-Nov Sb-€58, Db-€62; even less off-season, air-con, free Wi-Fi on lower floors, garage-€10, 56 boulevard Victor Hugo, tel. 05 59 26 11 90, fax 05 59 26 14 10, www.hotel-lepetittrianon.com, lepetittrianon @wanadoo.fr). To get a room over the quieter courtyard, ask for *côté cours* (coat-ay coor).

**$ Hôtel le Verdun,** above a dreary restaurant facing the train station, rents 11 basic rooms (the cheapest beds in town). It's often full off-season, when it houses seasonal laborers (D-€28–40, Ds-€33–50, Db/Tb-€45–65, €5 breakfast at downstairs café, 13 avenue de Verdun, tel. 05 59 26 02 55, www.hotel-leverdun.com, hotel.leverdun@wanadoo.fr, Henri).

## EATING

St. Jean-de-Luz restaurants are known for offering good-value, high-quality cuisine. You can find a wide variety of eateries in the old center. For forgettable food with unforgettable views, choose from several places overlooking the beach. Most places serve from 12:15 to 14:00, and from 19:15 on. Remember, in France, *menu* means fixed-price, multi-course meal.

The traffic-free rue de la République, which runs from place Louis XIV to the ocean promenade, is lined with hardworking restaurants (two of which are recommended below). Places are empty at 19:30, but packed at 20:30. Making a reservation, especially on weekends or in summer, is wise. Consider a fun night of bar-hopping for dinner in San Sebastián instead (an hour away in Spain, described on page 420).

**La Ruelle** serves good, traditionally Basque cuisine—mostly seafood—in two tight little rooms jam-packed with tables, happy eaters, and kitschy Basque decor. André and his playful staff obviously enjoy their work, which gives this popular spot a relaxed and fun ambience. Portions are huge; their €18 *ttoro* (seafood stew) easily feeds two (€18–23 *menus*, closed Tue–Wed Oct–May, 19 rue de la République, tel. 05 59 26 37 80).

**Le Kaiku** is *the* gastronomic experience in town. They serve modern cuisine, specializing in "wild" (rather than farmed) seafood. The place is dressy, but offers a good time (*menus* for €35, €50, and €70; closed Tue–Wed, 17 rue de la République, tel. 05 59 26 13 20).

**Chez Maya Petit Grill Basque** serves hearty traditional Basque cuisine. Their €16 *ttoro* was a highlight of my day. They have €20 and €29 *menus*, but à la carte is more interesting. If you stick around in warm weather, you'll see the clever overhead fan system kick into action (closed all day Wed and Thu morning, 2 rue St. Jacques, tel. 05 59 26 80 76).

*Fast and Cheap:* Try the take-away crêpe stands on rue Gambetta. For a sit-down salad or a tart—either sweet or savory—consider **Muscade Tarterie** (€7–10 per slice, daily July–Aug, closed Mon Sept–June, 20 rue Garat, tel. 05 59 26 96 73).

## TRANSPORTATION CONNECTIONS

The train station in St. Jean-de-Luz is called St. Jean-de-Luz-Ciboure. Its clever departure board displays lights next to any trains leaving that day. Buses leave from the green building across the street. There is reduced bus and rail service on Sundays and off-season.

**From St. Jean-de-Luz by Train to: Bayonne** (hourly, 25 min), **St. Jean-Pied-de-Port** (4/day, 6/day in summer, 1.5 hrs, transfer in Bayonne), **Paris** (4 direct/day, 5.5 hrs), **Bordeaux** (11/day, 2 hrs), **Sarlat** (4/day, 4 hrs, transfer in Bordeaux), **Carcassonne** (5/day, 6 hrs, transfers likely in Bayonne and Toulouse).

**By Train to San Sebastián:** First, take the 10-minute train to the French border town of Hendaye (Gare SNCF stop, about 10/day). Or get to Hendaye by bus (3/day, 35 min); check the schedule to see which leaves first.

Leave the Hendaye station to the right, and look for the light-blue EuskoTren building, where you'll catch the commuter train into San Sebastián (2/hour, generally at :03 and :33 after the hour 7:00–22:00, 30-min trip—faster but less frequent by bus). This milk-run train is known as the Topo ("Mole") train, since it goes underground part of the time.

**By Bus:** Local bus #26 connects St. Jean-de-Luz either to **Bayonne** or **Biarritz** almost hourly. Confusingly, this one bus can run two different routes (one to Bayonne, the other to Biarritz Centre, 40 min to either one)—check the destination carefully. Another bus connects St. Jean-de-Luz to **Sare** (Mon–Tue and Thu–Fri 4/day, Wed 2/day, Sat 1/day, none Sun, 30 min). A Spanish bus runs to **San Sebastián** (2/day direct, Mon–Sat only, 45 min, runs only 1/week off-season, info in Spain tel. 902-101-210).

**By Taxi to: San Sebastián** will cost you about €75 for up to four people, but it's convenient (tel. 05 59 26 10 11 or 06 25 76 97 69).

**By Excursion Bus:** The TI has information and sells tickets for popular day-trip excursions, including **Guggenheim Bilbao** (€35 round-trip, includes €12.50 museum admission, Wed only, departs 9:30 from bus terminal next to train station, returns 19:30). Other day trips are available (Ainhoa, Espelette, St. Jean-Pied-de-Port, and San Sebastián) on different days of the week.

## Route Tips for Drivers

A one-day side-trip to both Bayonne and Biarritz is easy from St. Jean-de-Luz—these three towns form a sort of triangle (depending on traffic, each one is less than a 30-minute drive from the other). Hop on the autoroute to Bayonne, sightsee there, then take the N-10 road into Biarritz. Leaving Biarritz, continue along the coastal N-10. In Bidart, watch (on the right) for the town's proud *frontón* (*pelota* court). Consider peeling off to go into the village center of Guéthary, with another *frontón*. If you're up for a walk on the beach, cross the little bridge in Guéthary, park by the train station, and hike down to the walkway along the surfing beach (lined with cafés and eateries). When you're ready to move on, you're a very short drive from St. Jean-de-Luz.

# Bayonne / Baiona

To feel the urban pulse of French Basque Country, visit Bayonne—modestly but honestly nicknamed "your anchor in the Basque Country" by its tourist board. With frequent, fast connec-

tions with St. Jean-de-Luz (25 min by train, 40 min by bus), Bayonne makes an easy half-day side-trip.

Come here to browse through Bayonne's atmospheric and well-worn yet lively Old Town, and to admire its impressive

Museum of Basque Culture. Known for establishing Europe's first whaling industry and for inventing the bayonet, Bayonne is more famous today for its ham *(jambon de Bayonne)* and chocolate.

Get lost in Bayonne's Old Town. In pretty Grand Bayonne, tall, slender buildings climb above cobbled streets, decorated in Basque fashion with green-and-red shutters. Make sure to stroll the streets around the cathedral and along the banks of the smaller Nive River, where you'll find the market (Les Halles).

# ORIENTATION

Bayonne's two rivers, the grand Adour and the petite Nive, divide the city into three parts: St. Esprit, with the train station; and the more interesting Grand Bayonne and Petit Bayonne, which together make up the Old Town.

## Tourist Information

The TI is in a modern parking lot a block off the mighty Adour River, on the northeastern edge of Grand Bayonne. They have very little in English other than a map and a town brochure (Mon–Fri 9:00–18:30, Sat 10:00–18:00, closed Sun except 10:00–13:00 in July–Aug, place des Basques, tel. 08 20 42 64 64).

## Arrival in Bayonne

**By Train:** The TI and Grand Bayonne are a 10-minute walk from the train station: Walk straight out of the station, cross the traffic circle, and then cross the imposing bridge (pont St. Esprit). Once past the big Adour River, continue across a smaller bridge (pont Mayou), which spans the smaller Nive River. Stop on pont Mayou to orient yourself: You just left Petit Bayonne (left side of Nive River). Ahead of you is Grand Bayonne (spires of cathedral straight ahead, TI a few blocks to the right). The Museum of Basque Culture is in Petit Bayonne, facing the next bridge up the Nive River.

**By Car and Bus:** The handiest parking is also where buses arrive in Bayonne: next to the TI at the modern parking lot on the edge of Grand Bayonne. To reach the town center from here, first walk with the busy road on your left to the big park. Then turn right and walk with the park on your left-hand side. After a few blocks, you'll see atmospheric streets leading up to the cathedral on your right; if you continue straight, you'll reach the bridge over the Nive River called pont Mayou (described above).

To reach this parking lot, **drivers** take the *Bayonne Sud* exit from the autoroute, then follow green *Bayonne Centre* signs, then white *Centre-Ville* signs (with an *i* for tourist information). You'll see the lot on your right. In high season, when this lot can be full, use one of the lots just outside the center (follow signs to *Glain* or *Porte d'Espagne* as you arrive in town), then catch the little orange *navette* (shuttle bus) to get into the center (free, find route maps posted at stops in town, every 7 min, Mon–Sat 7:30–19:30, closed Sun).

# SIGHTS

**Museum of Basque Culture (Musée Basque)**—This superb museum (in Petit Bayonne, facing the Nive River at pont Marengo) explains French Basque culture from cradle to grave—in French,

Euskara, and Spanish. The only English you'll read is "do not touch" (unless you buy their informative English booklet for €5). Artifacts and videos take you into traditional Basque villages and sit you in the front row of time-honored festivals (€5.50, July–Aug daily 10:00–18:30, also open and free Wed evenings 18:30–21:30; Sept–June Tue–Sun 10:00–18:30, closed Mon; last entry one hour before closing, 37 quai des Corsaires, tel. 05 59 59 08 98, www.musee-basque.com).

On the ground floor, you'll begin by walking through some 16th-century gravestones, then you'll see a display of carts and tools used in rural life. Look for the *laiak*—distinctive forked hoes used to work the ground. At the end of this section, you'll watch a grainy film on Basque rural lifestyles.

The next floor up begins by explaining that the house *(etxea)* is the building block of Basque society. More than just a building, it's a social institution—Basques are named for their house, not vice-versa. You'll see models and paintings of Basque houses, then domestic items, a giant door, kitchen equipment, and furniture (including a clever combination bench-table, near the fireplace). After an exhibit on Basque clothing, you'll move into the nautical life, with models, paintings, and actual boats. The little door leads to a model of the port of Bayonne in 1805, back when it was a highly strategic walled city.

Upstairs, you'll learn that the religious life of the Basques was strongly influenced by the Camino de Santiago pilgrim trail, which passed through their territory. One somber room explains Basque funeral traditions. The section on social life includes a video of Basque dances (typically accompanied by a flute and drums). These are improvised, but according to a clearly outlined structure—not unlike a square dance. The prominence given to the sport of *pelota* (see sidebar on page 404) indicates its importance to this people. One dimly lit room shows off several types of baskets *(chistera)*, gloves, and balls used for the game, and videos show how these items are made. The museum wraps up with a short lesson on the region's history from the 16th to the 20th centuries, including exhibits on the large Jewish population here (who had fled from a hostile Spain) and the renaissance of Basque culture in the 19th century.

**Cathédrale Ste. Marie**—Bankrolled by the whaling community, this cathedral sits dead-center in Grand Bayonne and is worth a peek (free, Mon–Sat 10:00–11:45 & 15:00–17:45, Sun 15:30–18:00). Find the unique keystones on the ceiling along the nave, then circle behind the church to find the peaceful 13th-century cloisters (free, daily 9:00–12:30 & 14:00–17:00, until 18:00 mid-May–mid-Sept).

**Sweets Shops**—With no more whales to catch, Bayonne turned to producing mouthwatering chocolates and marzipan; look for shops on the arcaded rue du Port Neuf (running between the cathedral and the Adour River).

**Ramparts**—The ramparts around Grand Bayonne are open for walking and great for picnicking (access from park at far end of TI parking lot). However, the ramparts do not allow access to either of Bayonne's castles—both are closed to the public.

## EATING

**Le Bayonnais,** next door to the Museum of Basque Culture, serves traditional Basque specialties à la carte. Sit in the blue-tiled interior, or out along the river (€15–25 main dishes, €16 lunch *menu*, closed Sun–Mon, quai des Corsaires 38, tel. 05 59 25 61 19).

**La Cidrerie Txotx** (pronounced "choch") has a Spanish-bodega ambience under a chorus line of hams. Or you can sit outside, along the river just past the market hall (€7–10 Basque tapas or €12–16 *plats*, daily, 49 quai Jauréguiberry, tel. 05 59 59 16 80).

**A la Bolée** serves up €6–9 sweet and savory crêpes in a cozy atmosphere along the side of the cathedral (daily, 10–11 place Pasteur, tel. 05 59 59 18 75).

If the weather is good, consider gathering a **picnic** from the pedestrian streets and head for the park around the ramparts below the *Jardin Botanique* (benches galore).

## TRANSPORTATION CONNECTIONS

From Bayonne, you can reach **St. Jean-de-Luz** by bus (#26, almost hourly, 40 min) or by train (hourly, 25 min). To **Biarritz,** the bus is best (take the unfortunately named "STAB" bus #1 to reach Biarritz Centre, departs every 10 min, takes 20 min). There's also a train from Bayonne up to **St. Jean-Pied-du-Port** (4/day, 6/day in summer, 1 hr). Bus #23 takes you to the inland Basque villages of **Espelette** and **Ainhoa** (4/day Mon–Fri only, none Sat–Sun, 25 min to Espelette, 35 min to Ainhoa).

# Biarritz / Biarritz

A glitzy resort town steeped in the belle époque, Biarritz (BEE-ah-ritz) is where the French Basques put on the ritz. In the 19th century, this simple whaling harbor became, almost overnight, a high-class aristocrat-magnet dubbed the "beach of kings." While St. Jean-de-Luz and Bayonne are more fully French and more fully Basque, the made-for-international-tourists, jet-set scene of Biarritz is not without its charms.

Perched over a popular surfing beach, anchored by grand hotels and casinos, hemmed in by jagged and picturesque rocky islets at either end, and watched over by a lighthouse on a distant promontory, Biarritz offers perhaps the most picturesque stretch of the French Basque coastline.

## ORIENTATION

Biarritz feels much bigger than its population of 30,000. The town sprawls, but virtually everything we're interested in lines up along the waterfront: the beach, promenade, hotel and shopping zone, and TI.

### Arrival in Biarritz

**By Car:** Drivers follow signs for *Centre-Ville*, then carefully track signs for specific parking garages. The most central garages are called *Grande Plage, Casino, Bellevue,* and *St. Eugénie.* Signs in front of each one tell you if it's full *(complet),* in which case, move on to the next one.

**By Bus:** Buses stop at "Biarritz Centre," a parking lot next to the TI (STAB buses to/from Bayonne stop along the side of the lot, while buses to/from St. Jean-de-Luz stop at the end of the lot). If you're taking a bus, be aware that some stop at the outskirts of town—only take one to "Centre."

Don't bother taking the **train** to or from Biarritz, as the station is about two miles from the tourist area (buses #2 and #9 connect the train station to the city center).

There is no baggage storage in Biarritz.

### Tourist Information

The TI is in a little pink castle two blocks up from the beach (just above the beach and casino, hiding behind the city hall/*hôtel de ville*—look for signs). Pick up the free map and get details on any sightseeing that interests you (July–Aug daily 9:00–19:00; Sept–June Mon–Fri 9:00–18:00, Sat–Sun 10:00–17:00; Square d'Ixelles, tel. 05 59 22 37 10, www.biarritz.fr).

## SIGHTS

There's little of "sightseeing" value in Biarritz. The TI can fill you in on the town's four museums (Marine Museum—described below; Chocolate Planet and Museum—intriguing, but a long walk from the center; Oriental Art Museum—large and diverse collection of art from across Asia; and Biarritz Historical Museum—really?).

Your time is best spent strolling along the various levels that climb up from the sea. From the TI, you can do a loop: First head west on the lively **pedestrian streets** that occupy the plateau above the water, which are lined with restaurants, cafés, and high-class, resorty "window-licking." (Place Georges Clemenceau is the grassy "main square" of this area.)

Work your way out to the point with the **Marine Museum** (Musée de la Mer). The most convenient of Biarritz's attractions, this pricey museum/aquarium wins the "best rainy-day option" award, with a tank of seals and a chance to get face-to-teeth with live sharks (€8, hours vary based on season, daily April–Oct, closed Mon Nov–March, tel. 05 59 22 33 34, www.museedelamer.com).

Whether or not you're visiting the museum, it's worth hiking down to the entrance, then wandering out on the walkways that connect the big offshore rocks. These lead to the so-called **Virgin Rock** (Rocher de la Vierge), topped by a statue of Mary. Spot any surfers? Europe generally isn't known for its surfing...but Biarritz is the exception.

From here, stick along the water as you head back toward the TI. After a bit of up and down over the rocks, don't miss the trail down to **Fishermen's Wharf** (Port des Pêcheurs), a little pocket of salty authenticity that clings like a barnacle to the cliff below the hotels. The remnants of an aborted construction project from the town's glory days, this little fishing settlement of humble houses and rugged jetties seems to faintly echo the Basque culture that thrived here before the glitz hit. Many of the houses have been taken over by the tourist trade (gift shops and restaurants).

Continuing along the water (and briefly back up to street level), make your way back to the town's centerpiece, the **big beach**

(Grande Plage). Dominating this inviting stretch of sand is the Art Deco casino, and the TI is just above that. If you haven't yet taken the time on your vacation to splash, wade, or stroll on the beach...now's your chance.

## TRANSPORTATION CONNECTIONS

Biarritz is connected by bus #26 to **St. Jean-de-Luz** (nearly hourly, 40 min). Buses run by the company called "STAB" take you to **Bayonne** (#1, departs every 10 min, takes 20 min).

---

# Villages in the French Basque Country

Traditional villages among the green hills, with buildings colored like the Basque flag, offer the best glimpse at Basque culture. Cheese, hard cider, and *pelota* players are the primary products of these villages, which attract few foreigners but many French summer visitors. Most of these villages have welcomed pilgrims bound for Santiago de Compostela since the Middle Ages. Today's hikers trek between local villages or head into the Pyrenees. The most appealing villages lie in the foothills of the Pyrenees, spared from beach-scene development.

Use St. Jean-de-Luz as your base to visit the Basque sights described in this section. You can reach some of these places by public transportation, but the hassle outweighs the rewards.

Do a circuit of these towns in the order they're listed here (and, with time, also add St. Jean-Pied-de-Port at the end). Assuming you're driving, I've included route instructions, as well.

• *From St. Jean-de-Luz, follow signs for* Ascain, *then* Sare. *On the road toward Sare, you'll pass the station for the train up to...*

## La Rhune / Larrun

Between the villages of Ascain and Sare, near the border with Spain, a small cogwheel train takes tourists to the top of La Rhune, the region's highest peak (2,969 feet). You'll putt-putt up the hillside for 30 minutes in an open-air train car to reach panoramic views of land and sea (€14 round-trip for adults, €8 for kids, runs mid-March–mid-Nov, departures weather-dependent—so the trip is worthless if it's not clear, departures every 35 min when busiest in July–Aug, tel. 05 59 54 20 26, www.rhune.com).

• *Continue along the same road to...*

## Sare / Sara

Sare, which sits at the base of the towering mountain La Rhune, is among the most picturesque villages—and the most touristed. It's easily reached from St. Jean-de-Luz by bus or car. The small TI is on the main square (Mon–Fri 9:30–12:30 & 14:00–18:00, Sat 9:30–12:30, closed Sun, tel. 05 59 54 20 14). Nearby is a cluster of hotels and the town church (which has an impressive interior, with arches over the altar and Basque-style balconies lining the nave). At the far end of the square is the town's humble *frontón*.

• *Leaving Sare, first follow signs for* St. Pée, *then watch for the turn-off to...*

## Ainhoa / Ainhoa

Ainhoa is a colorful, tidy, picturesque one-street town that sees fewer tourists (which is a good thing). Its chunks of fortified walls

and gates mingle with red-and-white, half-timbered buildings. The 14th-century church—with a beautiful golden *retable* (screen behind the altar)—and the *frontón* (*pelota* court) share center stage.

Ainhoa is also a popular starting point for hikes into the hills. For a spectacular village-and-valleys view, drive five minutes (or walk 90 sweaty minutes) up the steep dirt road to the Chapelle de Notre-Dame d'Aranazau ("d'Aubepine" in French). Start in the parking lot directly across the main street from the church, then head straight uphill. Follow signs for *oratoire*, then count the giant white crosses to the top.

• *As you leave Ainhoa, you'll have to backtrack the way you came in to find the road to...*

## Espelette / Ezpeleta

Espelette won't let you forget that it's the capital of the region's AOC red peppers *(piments d'Espelette)*, with strands of them dangling like good-luck charms from many houses and storefronts. After strolling the charming, cobbled center, wander downhill at the end of town to find the town church and the well-restored château and medieval tower, which now houses the town hall, an exhibition, and the TI (Mon–Fri 8:30– 12:30 & 14:00–18:00, Sat 9:30–12:30, closed Sun, tel. 05 59 93 95 02).

**BASQUE COUNTRY**

## *Ventas* Shops

Dancing between France and Spain and along the foothills of the Pyrenees, you'll see many signs for *ventas* (from the Spanish *vender,* "to sell"). Follow one of these signs to a cultural detour. Originally used as contraband outposts, *ventas* shops operate as café, bar, restaurant, grocery store, gas station, cheap boutique, and more. Most are lost in the hills and hard to find, and many still don't have signs—locals just know where they are. Today, they are legal in a borderless Europe, and still offer inexpensive products—customers are mostly the French Basque, who cause traffic jams on weekends driving to the border to do cheap shopping or fill the gas tank. In most *ventas,* gas is cheaper by 25 percent, cigarettes and alcohol leave by the case, and the Spanish, French, and Euskara languages mingle as locals enjoy a coffee or beer among hanging garlands of cheap hams.

*Sleeping and Eating:* For a good regional meal, consider the **$ Hôtel Euzkadi** restaurant, with a *muy* Spanish ambience (€25–32 *menus,* daily 12:30–14:00 & 19:30–21:00, closed Mon–Sun off-season, 285 Karrika Nagusia, tel. 05 59 93 91 88). The hotel has 27 rooms with modern touches and a swimming pool (Sb-€41–43, Db-€52–65, air-con, elevator, free Wi-Fi, www.hotel-restaurant -euzkadi.com).

• *From Espelette, if you have time, you can simply follow signs to* St. Jean-Pied-de-Port.

## St. Jean-Pied-de-Port / Donibane Garazi

Just five miles from the Spanish border, the walled town of St. Jean-Pied-de-Port (sahn zhahn-pee-duh-por) is the most popular village in all the French Basque countryside. Traditionally, St. Jean-Pied-de-Port has been the final stopover in France for pilgrims undertaking the Camino de Santiago ("Way of Saint James")—the medieval pilgrimage route that runs from here 500 miles across the north of Spain to the city

of Santiago de Compostela. After centuries of obscurity, the pilgrimage has become more popular again recently, as thousands of modern travelers each year follow that ancient trail on foot, bike, or horseback. From St. Jean-Pied-de-Port, Santiago-bound pilgrims cross the Pyrenees together and continue their march through

Spain. The scallop shell of "St. Jacques" (French for "James") is etched on walls throughout the town.

Visitors to this town are equal parts pilgrims and French tourists. Gift shops sell a strange combination of pilgrim gear (such as quick-drying shirts and shorts) and Basque souvenirs. This place is packed in the summer (so come early or late).

**Tourist Information:** The TI, on the main road along the outside of the walled Old Town, can give you a town map (hours vary, generally July–Aug Mon–Sat 9:00–19:00, Sun 10:00–12:00; Sept–June Mon–Sat 9:00–12:00 & 14:00–18:00, Sun 10:00–12:00; maybe less in winter; tel. 08 10 75 36 71). For Camino information, you'll do better at the Pilgrim Friends Office (described below).

**Arrival in St. Jean-Pied-de-Port: Parking** is ample and well-signed from the main road. If arriving by **train,** exit the station to the left, then follow the busy road at the traffic circle toward the city wall.

**Sights:** There's little in the way of sightseeing here, other than pilgrim-spotting. But St. Jean-Pied-de-Port feels like the perfect "Welcome to the Camino" springboard for the upcoming journey. Many modern pilgrims begin their Camino in this traditional spot because of its easy train connection to Bayonne, and because—as its name implies ("St. John at the Foot of the Pass")—it offers a very challenging but rewarding first leg: up, over, and into Spain.

Cross the old bridge over the Nive River (the same one that

winds up in Bayonne) to the **Notre-Dame Gate,** which was once a drawbridge. Then head up the main walking drag, **rue de la Citadelle.** With its rosy-pink buildings and ancient dates above its doorways, this lane simply feels old. Notice lots of signs for *chambres* (rooms) and *refuges*—humble, hostel-like pilgrim bunkhouses.

Partway up, on the left at #39, look for the **Pilgrim Friends Office** (Les Amis du Chemin de Saint-Jacques, daily 7:30–12:00 & 13:30–20:30 & 21:30–22:30, tel. 05 59 37 05 09). This is where pilgrims check in before their long journey to Santiago; 32,000 pilgrims started out here last year (compared to just 4,000 a decade ago). For €2, a pilgrim can buy the official credential *(credenciel)* that she'll get stamped at each stop between here and Santiago to prove she walked the whole way and earn her *compostela* certificate. Pilgrims also receive a warm welcome, lots of advice, and help finding a bunk (the well-traveled staff swears that no pilgrim ever

## It Happened at Hendaye

If taking the train between the Spanish and French Basque regions, you'll change trains at the nondescript little Hendaye station. While it seems innocent enough, this was a site of a fateful meeting between two of Europe's most notorious 20th-century dictators.

In the days before World War II, Adolf Hitler and Francisco Franco maintained a diplomatic relationship. But after the fall of France, they decided to secretly meet here in Hendaye to size each other up. On October 23, 1940, Hitler traveled through Nazi-occupied France, then waited impatiently on the platform for Franco's delayed train. The over-eager Franco hoped the Führer would invite him to join in a military alliance with Germany (and ultimately share in the expected war spoils).

According to reports of the meeting, Franco was greedy, boastful, and misguided, leading Hitler to dismiss him as a buffoon. Franco later spun the situation by claiming that he had cleverly avoided being pulled into World War II. In fact, his own incompetence is what saved Spain. Had Franco made a better impression on Hitler here at Hendaye, it's possible that Spain would have entered the war...which could have changed the course of Spanish, German, and European history.

goes without a bed in St. Jean-Pied-de-Port).

A few more steps up, you'll pass the skippable €3 Bishop's Prison (Prison des Evêques, on the left). Continue on up to the **citadel,** dating from the mid-17th century—when this was a highly strategic location, keeping an eye on the easiest road over the Pyrenees between Spain and France. While not open to the public (it houses a school), the grounds around this stout fortress offer sweeping views over the French Basque countryside.

*Sleeping in St. Jean-Pied-du-Port:* Lots of humble pilgrim dwellings line the main drag, rue de la Citadelle. If you're looking for a bit more comfort, consider these options.

**$$ Hotel Ramuntcho**\*\* is the only real hotel option in the Old Town, located partway up rue de la Citadelle. Its 16 rooms above a restaurant are straightforward but modern (Sb-€64–74, Db-€70–79, 1 rue de France, tel. 05 59 37 03 91, fax 05 59 37 35 17, http://perso.wanadoo.fr/hotel.ramuntcho, hotel.ramuntcho@wanadoo.fr).

**$$ Itzalpea,** a café and tea house, rents five rooms along the main road just outside the Old Town (Db-€60–76 depending on size, includes breakfast, air-con, 5 place du Trinquet, tel. 05 59 37 03 66, fax 05 59 37 33 18, www.maisondhotes-itzalpea.com, itzalpea@wanadoo.fr).

**$ Chambres Chez l'Habitant** has five old-fashioned, pilgrim-perfect rooms along the main drag. Welcoming Maria and Jean Pierre speak limited English, but their daughter can help translate (€20 per person in D, Db, Q, or Qb, includes breakfast, 15 rue de la Citadelle, tel. 05 59 37 05 83).

**Transportation Connections:** A scenic train conveniently links St. Jean-Pied-de-Port to **Bayonne** (4/day, 6/day in summer, 1 hr), and from there to **St. Jean-de-Luz** (about 30 min beyond Bayonne). It's about a 1.25-hour drive from St. Jean-de-Luz.

# Spanish Basque Country (El País Vasco)

Four of the seven Basque territories lie within Spain. Many consider Spanish Basque culture to be feistier and more colorful than the relatively integrated French Basques—you'll hear more Euskara spoken here than in France.

For 40 years, the figure of Generalísimo Franco loomed large over the Spanish Basques. Franco depended upon Basque industry to keep the floundering Spanish economy afloat. But even as he exploited the Basques economically, he so effectively blunted Basque culture that the language was primarily Spanish by default. Franco kicked off his regime by offering up the historic Basque town of Guernica as target practice to his ally Hitler's air force. The notorious result—the wholesale slaughter of innocent civilians—was immortalized by Pablo Picasso's mural *Guernica*.

But Franco is long gone, and today's Basques are looking to the future. The iron deposits have dried up, prompting the Basques to re-imagine their rusting cities for the 21st century. True to form, they're rising to the challenge. Perhaps the best example is Bilbao, whose iconic Guggenheim Museum—built on the former site of an industrial wasteland—is the centerpiece of a bold new skyline.

San Sebastián is the heart of the tourist's *País Vasco*, with its sparkling beach picturesquely framed by looming green mountains and a charming old town with gourmet *pintxos* (tapas) spilling out of every bar. On-the-rise Bilbao is worth a look for its landmark Guggenheim and its atmospheric Old Town. For small-town fun, drop by the fishing village of Lekeitio (near Bilbao) and little Hondarribia near the French border. And for history, Guernica has some intriguing museums.

# San Sebastián / Donostia

Shimmering above the breathtaking bay of La Concha, elegant and prosperous San Sebastián (Donostia in Euskara) has a favored

location with golden beaches capped by twin peaks at either end, and a cute little island in the center. A delightful beachfront promenade runs the length of the bay, with an intriguing Old Town at one end and a smart shopping district in the center. It has 180,000 residents and almost

that many tourists in high season (July–Sept). With a romantic setting, a soaring statue of Christ gazing over the city, and a late-night lively Old Town, San Sebastián has a Rio de Janeiro aura. While the "sightseeing" isn't too compelling, the scenic city provides a pleasant introduction to Spain's Basque Country. And as a culinary capital of Spain, it dishes up some of the top tapas anywhere.

In 1845, Queen Isabel II's doctor recommended she treat her skin problems by bathing here in the sea. (For modesty's sake, she would go inside a giant cabana that could be wheeled into the surf—allowing her to swim far from prying eyes, never having to set foot on the beach.) Her visit mobilized Spain's aristocracy, and soon the city was on the map as a seaside resort. By the turn of the 20th century, San Sebastián was the toast of the belle époque, and a leading resort for Europe's beautiful people. Before World War I, Queen María Cristina summered here and held court in her Miramar Palace overlooking the crescent beach (the turreted, red-brick building partway around the bay). Hotels, casinos, and theaters flourished. Even Franco enjoyed 35 summers in a place he was sure to call San Sebastián, not Donostia.

## Planning Your Time

San Sebastián's sights can be exhausted in a few hours, but it's a great place to be on vacation for a full, lazy day (or longer). Stroll the two-mile-long promenade and scout the place you'll grab to work on a tan. The promenade leads to a funicular that lifts you to the Monte Igueldo viewpoint. After exploring the Old Town and port, walk up to the hill of Monte Urgull. With more time, art-lovers can venture to the Chillida-Leku Museum on the outskirts. A key ingredient of any visit to San Sebastián is enjoying tapas in the Old Town bars.

# Dipping into Spain

If you're heading from France to Spain, you don't have to worry about border stops or currency changes (both countries use the euro). But here are a few other practicalities:

**Phones:** Spain's telephone country code is 34. Remember that French phone cards and stamps will not work in Spain.

**Hours:** Most Spanish sights and stores close for a "siesta" from about 13:00 to 16:00, and dinner doesn't begin until 21:00 or 22:00 (though tapas are always available).

**Eating Tips:** Most Spaniards have their big meal at lunch, then build a light dinner out of appetizer portions called tapas (or, in Basque Country, *pintxos*). Rather than choosing one restaurant for the evening, eaters hop from bar to bar sampling these tasty snacks. For tips on this ritual, see "Do the *Txiquiteo* Tango" on page 435.

**Spanish Survival Phrases:** While many Spanish Basques speak Euskara, most speak Spanish in everyday life. You'll find these phrases useful:

| English | Spanish | Pronounced |
|---|---|---|
| Good day. | *Buenos días.* | **bway**-nohs **dee**-ahs |
| Mr. / Mrs. | *Señor / Señora* | sayn-**yor** / sayn-**yor**-ah |
| Please. | *Por favor* | por fah-**bor** |
| Thank you. | *Muchas gracias.* | **moo**-chahs **grah**-thee-ahs |
| You're welcome. | *De nada.* | day **nah**-dah |
| Excuse me. | *Perdone.* | pehr-**doh**-nay |
| Yes. / No. | *Sí. / No* | see / noh |
| Cheers! | *¡Salud!* | sah-**lood** |
| men | *hombres, caballeros* | **ohm**-brays, kah-bah-**yay**-rohs |
| women | *mujeres, damas* | moo-**hehr**-ays, **dah**-mahs |
| one / two / three | *uno / dos / tres* | **oo**-noh / dohs / trays |
| coffee with milk | *café con leche* | kah-**feh** kohn **lay**-chay |
| sandwich | *bocadillo* | boh-kah-**dee**-yoh |
| Where is...? | *¿Donde está...?* | **dohn**-day ay-**stah** |
| tourist office | *turismo* | too-**rees**-moh |
| city center | *centro ciudad* | **thehn**-troh thee-oo-**dahd** |
| Do you speak English? | *¿Habla usted inglés?* | **ah**-blah oo-**stehd** een-**glays** |

# ORIENTATION

The San Sebastián that we're interested in surrounds Concha Bay (Bahía de la Concha). It can be divided into three areas: Playa de la Concha (best beaches), the shopping district (called Centro), and the skinny streets of the grid-planned Old Town (called Parte Vieja, to the north of the shopping district). Centro, just east of Playa de la Concha, has beautiful turn-of-the-20th-century architecture, but no real sights. A busy drag called Alameda del Boulevard (or just "Boulevard") separates the Centro from the Old Town, and is also where you'll find the TI.

It's all bookended by mini-mountains: Monte Urgull to the north and east, and Monte Igueldo to the south and west. The river (Río Urumea) divides central San Sebastián from the district called Gros (which—contrary to its name—is actually quite nice, with a lively night scene and surfing beach).

## Tourist Information

San Sebastián's TI, conveniently located right on the Boulevard, has information on city and regional sights, as well as bus and train schedules. Pick up the free map and the *Holiday Guide* booklet, which has English descriptions of the three walking tours—the Old Town/Monte Urgull walk is best (July–Sept Mon–Sat 8:30–20:00, Sun 10:00–14:00 & 15:30–19:00; Oct–June Mon–Sat 9:00–13:30 & 15:30–19:00, Sun 10:00–14:00; Boulevard 8, tel. 943-481-166, www.sansebastianturismo.com). Skip the **San Sebastián Card** unless you plan to use the bus a lot (€10 for 3 days of free bus transport plus minor sightseeing discounts).

## Arrival in San Sebastián

Neither train station has luggage storage. Near the bus station, you can check bags at the Alsa ticket office; downtown, try the CyberWorld Internet café (€3/4 hrs, €5/8 hrs, €8/24 hrs, daily 11:00–13:00 & 16:00–22:00, Aldamar 3, tel. 943-420-651).

**By Train:** If you're coming on a regional Topo train from Hendaye/Hendaia on the French border, get off at the **EuskoTren station** (end of the line, called Amara). It's a level 15-minute walk to the center: Exit the station and walk across the long plaza, then veer left and walk eight blocks down Calle Easo (toward the statue of Christ hovering on the hill) to the beach. The Old Town will be ahead on your right, with Playa de la Concha to your left. To speed

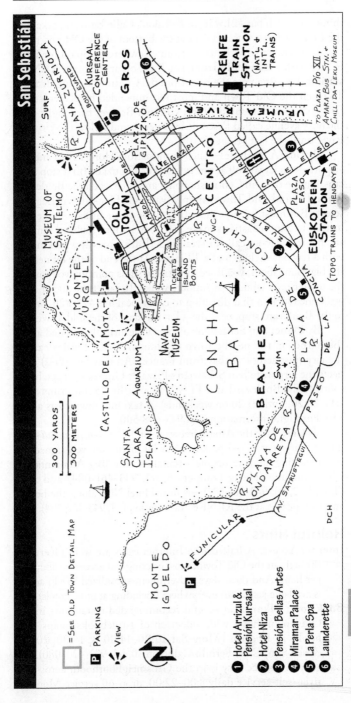

San Sebastián

KURSAAL
CONFERENCE CENTER

SURF

R PLAYA ZURRIOLA

BOULEVARD

GROS

PLAZA DE GIPUZKOA

RENFE
TRAIN
STATION
(NAT'L. +
INT'L.
TRAINS)

URUMEA RIVER

To Plaza Pío XII,
AMARA BUS STN. +
CHILLIDA-LEKU MUSEUM

MUSEUM OF
SAN TELMO

OLD TOWN

ALAMEDA DEL BOULEVARD

LEGAZPI

CITY HALL

CENTRE

SAN MARTÍN

SAN CALLE

PLAZA
EASO

PASO

EUSKOTREN
STATION

(TOPO TRAINS TO HENDAYE)

CASTILLO DE LA MOTA

MONTE
URGULL

Tickets for
Island Boats

WC

R ZUBIETA

LA CONCHA

AQUARIUM

NAVAL
MUSEUM

CONCHA
BAY

BEACHES

SWIM

PLAYA DE LA CONCHA

SANTA-
CLARA
ISLAND

PLAYA DE ONDARRETA

AV. SATRUSTEGUI

DCH

300 YARDS
300 METERS

MONTE
IGUELDO

FUNICULAR

P

N

= SEE OLD TOWN DETAIL MAP

P PARKING

VIEW

❶ Hotel Arrizul &
 Pensión Kursaal
❷ Hotel Niza
❸ Pensión Bellas Artes
❹ Miramar Palace
❺ La Perla Spa
❻ Launderette

things up, catch bus #21, #26, or #28 along Calle Easo and take it to the Boulevard stop, near the TI at the bottom of the Old Town.

If you're arriving by train from elsewhere in Spain (or from France with a transfer in Irún), you'll get off at the main **RENFE station.** It's just across the river from the Centro shopping district. To reach the Old Town and most recommended hotels, cross the fancy, dragon-decorated María Cristina Bridge, turn right onto the busy avenue called Paseo de los Fueros, and follow the Urumea River until the last bridge.

**By Bus:** A few buses—such as those from Hondarribia and the airport—can let you off at pretty Plaza de Gipuzkoa (first stop after crossing the river, in Centro shopping area). To reach the Boulevard (with TI) and Old Town, simply walk one block down Legazpi street. But most buses—including those from Bilbao—take you instead to San Sebastián's makeshift "bus station" (dubbed Amara) at a big roundabout called Plaza Pío XII. It's basically a parking lot with a few bus shelters and a TI kiosk. At the end of the lot nearest the big roundabout, you'll see directional signs pointing you toward the town center (about a 30-minute walk). To save time and energy, walk one block in that direction to catch local bus #21, #26, or #28 to the Boulevard stop, near the TI at the start of the Old Town.

**By Plane:** San Sebastián's airport is beautifully situated along the harbor in the nearby town of Hondarribia, 12 miles east of the city (just across the bay from France). An easy bus (#I-2) connects the airport to San Sebastián's Plaza de Gipuzkoa, just a block south of the Boulevard and TI (€2, about 3/hr, 25 min, runs daily 7:45–20:20, until 21:20 on weekends). A taxi into town costs about €30. For flight information, call 943-668-500.

**By Car:** Take the Amara freeway exit, follow *centro ciudad* signs into the city center, and park in a pay lot (many are well-signed). If you're picking up or returning a rental car, the "Big Autorental"—which includes Hertz (Zubieta 5, tel. 943-461-084) and Avis (Triunfo 2, tel. 943-461-527)—is near Hotel Niza along the beach, and Europcar is at the RENFE train station (tel. 943-322-304).

## Helpful Hints

**Internet Access:** A half-dozen Internet cafés are well-advertised throughout the Old Town, most offering fast access for about €2 per hour. And these days, government-subsidized Wi-Fi access is available just about everywhere (including at most hotels).

**Bookstore: Elkar,** near several recommended restaurants in the Old Town, has a wide selection of guidebooks, maps, and books in English (Mon–Sat 10:00–14:00 & 16:00–20:00, closed Sun, Calle Fermín Calbetón 30, tel. 943-420-080).

**Laundry: Wash & Dry** is in the Gros neighborhood, across the river (self-service daily 8:00–22:00, drop-off service Mon–Fri

9:30–13:00 & 16:00–20:00, Iparragirre 6, tel. 943-293-150). Unfortunately, there are no launderettes in the Old Town.

**Bike Rental:** Try **Bici Rent Donosti** (also rents scooters, Avenida de Zurriola 22, 3 blocks across the river from the TI, mobile 655-724-458), or **Bicicletas Alai,** behind the Amara bus station (Avenida de Madrid 24, tel. 943-470-001).

## Getting Around San Sebastián

**By Bus:** Along the Boulevard at the bottom edge of the Old Town, you'll find a line of public buses ready to take you anywhere in town; give any driver your destination, and he'll tell you the number of the bus to catch (€1.20, pay driver).

Some handy bus routes: #21, #26, and #28 connect the Amara bus and EuskoTren stations to the TI (get off at the Boulevard stop); #16 begins at the Boulevard/TI stop, goes along Playa de la Concha and through residential areas, and eventually arrives at the base of the Monte Igueldo funicular. The TI has a good bus-route map (or see www.ctss.es).

**By Taxi:** Taxis start at €3, then charge €0.50 per kilometer. You can't hail a taxi on the street—you must call one (tel. 943-404-040 or 943-464-646) or find a taxi stand (most convenient along the Boulevard).

# TOURS

The TI runs English-language **walking tours** of the Old Town (Parte Vieja), Monte Urgull, and Centro (€5, 90 min, July–Aug daily at 10:00, Sept–June weekends only at 11:00, confirm schedule with TI). The TI also rents **audioguides** (€10/2 hrs).

Gabriella Ranelli, an American who's lived in San Sebastián for 20 years, is a **local guide** specializing in culinary tours. She can take you on a sightseeing spin around the Old Town, along with a walk through the market and best *pintxo* bars (€135/half-day, €180/day, more for driving into the countryside, mobile 609-467-381, www.tenedortours.com, info@tenedortours.com). She also does cooking classes, where you shop at the market then cook up some tasty *pintxos* of your own (€115 per person for a small group).

Two tour options on wheels (following a similar route around the bay) are available, but most travelers won't find them necessary in this walkable city: The **"txu-txu"** tourist train (€4.50, daily July–mid-Sept 11:00–21:00, mid-Sept–June 11:00–13:00 & 14:00–19:00, 40-min round-trip, tel. 943-422-973); and the **Donosti Tours** hop-on, hop-off bus tour (follows two different routes—one along the bay and the other around the city; €12/route, or €14 for both, about 1 hour each, ticket good for 24 hours, leaves from Victoria Eugenia theater on the Boulevard, tel. 696-429-847).

# SIGHTS AND ACTIVITIES

## ▲▲Old Town (Parte Vieja)

Huddled in the shadow of its once-protective Monte Urgull, the Old Town is where San Sebastián was born about 1,000 years ago. The grid plan of streets hides heavy Baroque and Gothic churches, surprise plazas, and fun little shops, including venerable pastry stores, rugged produce markets, Basque-independence souvenir shops, and seafood-to-go delis. "THC shops" offer the latest from the decriminalized marijuana scene in Spain—adults are allowed to grow two plants. Be sure to wander out to the port to see the fishing industry in action (described later in this section).

The highlight of the Old Town is its array of incredibly lively tapas bars—though here, these snacks are called *pintxos* (PEEN-chohs; see "Eating" later in this section).

**▲Plaza de la Constitución**—The Old Town's main square is where bullfights used to be held. Notice the seat numbering on the balconies: Even if you owned an apartment here, the city retained rights to the balconies, which it could sell as box seats. (The residents could peek over the paying customers' shoulders.)

Above the clock, notice the seal of San Sebastián: A merchant ship with sails billowing in the wind. The city was granted trading rights by the crown—a reminder of the Basque Country's importance in Spanish seafaring.

Inviting café tables spill into the square from all corners. But one thing you won't see are the "private eating clubs" on this square (and others that dot the city center). Basque society is matrilineal and very female-oriented. A husband brings home his paycheck and hands it directly to his wife, who controls the house's purse-strings (and everything else). Basque men felt they needed a place where they could congregate and play "king of the castle." They formed eating clubs, where members could reserve a table to cook for their friends. While the clubs used to be exclusively male, women are now allowed as invited guests...but never in the kitchen, which remains the men's domain.

**Museum of San Telmo**—This humble museum will likely be closed for renovation through 2010. When open, it displays exhibits and paintings in rooms arranged around the peaceful cloister of a former Dominican monastery. There are a few exhibits on Basque folk life, and a small collection of 19th- and 20th-century paintings by Basque artists that offers an interesting peek into the spirit, faces, and natural beauty of this fiercely independent region (other featured artists include El Greco and Rubens; Plaza Zuloaga 1, tel. 943-481-580).

▲**Bretxa Public Market (Mercado de la Bretxa)**—Wandering through the public market is a fun way to get in touch with San Sebastián and with Basque culture. The big, white market building on the Boulevard has been converted into a modern shopping mall inside, but the fish and meat market still thrives underground (enter by going down escalators in smaller glass building behind the market hall; most stalls open Mon–Fri 8:00–14:00 & 17:00–20:00, Sat 8:00–14:00 only, Plaza de Sarriegi).

At the bottom of the escalator, notice the **fish stall** on the left (marked *J. Ma. Mujika*). In the case, you'll see different cuts of *bacalao* (cod). Entire books have been written about the importance of cod to the evolution of seafaring in Europe. The fish could be preserved in salt to feed sailors on ever-longer trips into the North Atlantic, allowing them to venture beyond the continental shelf (where they could catch fresh fish). Cod was also popular among Catholic landlubbers on Fridays. Today cod remains a Basque staple. People still buy the salted version, which must be soaked for 48 hours (and the water changed three times) to become edible. If you're in a rush, you can buy de-salted cod...for a price.

Continue into the market and turn left down the meat aisle, checking out the different types of ham. The best ham in this region (and in all of France) comes from across the border, in Bayonne. Then enter the fresh-fish market—often with the catch of the day set up in cute little scenes.

Head back up to street level and cross the street to the **Ailor Lasa Gaztategi** cheese shop (Mon–Fri 8:30–14:00 & 17:15–20:00, Sat 8:30–14:30, closed Sun, Aldamar 12, tel. 943-430-354). Pass the fragrant piles of mushrooms at the entrance and head back to the display case, showing off the Basque specialty of *idiazábal*—raw sheep's milk cheese. Notice the wide variety, which depends on the specific region it came from, whether it's smoked or cured, and for how long it's been cured *(curación)*. If you're planning a picnic, this is a very local (and expensive) ingredient.

## The Port

At the west end of the Old Town, protected by Monte Urgull, is the port. To reach the first three sights, take the passage through the wall at the appropriately named Calle Puerto, and jog right along the level, portside Paseo del Muelle. You'll pass fishing boats unloading the catch of the day (with hungry locals looking on), salty sailors' pubs, and fisherfolk mending nets. Also along this strip are the Naval Museum and the Aquarium. The trails to the top of Monte Urgull are just above this scene, near Santa María Church (or climb up the stairs next to the aquarium).

**Cruise**—Small boats cruise from the Old Town's port to the island in the bay (Isla Santa Clara), where you can hike the trails and have lunch at the lone café, or pack a picnic before setting sail (€8 round-trip; departures hourly on the hour 12:00–13:00 & 16:00–20:00, boats don't run Oct–May).

**Naval Museum (Museo Naval)**—This museum's two floors of exhibits describe the seafaring city's history, revealing the intimate link between the Basque culture and the sea. The well-presented exhibit changes each year. As the closest thing to a Basque culture museum the city has, this is quite good, but suffers from a lack of English information (€1.20, free on Thu, ask if they have any English info at entry, Tue–Sat 10:00–13:30 & 16:00–19:30, Sun 11:00–14:00, closed Mon, just before aquarium at Paseo del Muelle 24, tel. 943-430-051).

▲**Aquarium**—San Sebastián's aquarium is small and expensive, but surprisingly good. Exhibits include a history of the sea, a collection of naval vessels, models showing various drift-netting techniques, a petting tank filled with nervous fish, a huge whale skeleton, and a 45-foot-long tunnel that allows you to look up at floppy rays and menacing sharks (€10, €6 for kids under 13, some English explanations; July–Aug daily 10:00–21:00; Easter–June and Sept Mon–Fri 10:00–20:00, Sat–Sun 10:00–21:00; Oct–Easter Mon–Fri 10:00–19:00, Sat–Sun 10:00–20:00; at the end of Paseo del Muelle at Carlos Blasco de Imaz Plaza 1, tel. 943-440-099, www.aquariumss.com).

▲**Monte Urgull**—The once-mighty castle (Castillo de la Mota) atop the hill deterred most attackers, allowing the city to prosper in the Middle Ages. The museum located within the castle, featuring San Sebastián history, is mildly interesting. The best views from the hill are not from the statue of Christ, but from the ramparts on the left side (as you face the hill), just above the port's aquarium. **Café El Polvorín,** nestled in the park, is a friendly place with salads, sandwiches, and good sangria.

A new walkway allows you to stroll the mountain's entire perimeter near sea level. This route is continuous from Hotel Parma to the aquarium, and offers an enjoyable after-dinner wander. You can also walk a bit higher up over the port (along the white railing)—called the *paseo de las curas,* or "priest's path," where the clergy could stroll unburdened by the rabble in the streets below. These paths are technically open only from sunrise to sunset (daily May–Sept 8:00–21:00, Oct–April 8:00–19:00), but you can often access them later.

## The Beach

▲▲**La Concha Beach and Promenade**—The shell-shaped Playa de la Concha, the pride of San Sebastián, has one of Europe's loveliest stretches of sand. Lined with a two-mile-long promenade,

it allows even backpackers to feel aristocratic. While pretty empty off-season, in summer, sunbathers pack its shores. But year-round, it's surprisingly devoid of eateries and money-grubbing businesses. There are free showers, and *cabinas* provide lockers, showers, and shade for a fee. For a century, the lovingly painted wrought-iron balustrade that stretches the length of the promenade has been a symbol of the city; it shows up on everything from jewelry to headboards. It's shaded by tamarisk trees, with branches carefully pruned into knotty bulbs—another symbol of the city.

The Miramar palace and park, which divides the crescent in the middle, was where Queen María Cristina held court when she summered here. Her royal changing rooms are used today as inviting cafés, restaurants, and a fancy spa.

**La Perla Spa**—The spa attracts a less royal crowd today and appeals mostly to visitors interested in sampling "the curative properties of the sea." You can enjoy its Talasso Fitness Circuit, featuring a hydrotherapy pool, relaxation pool, panoramic Jacuzzi, cold-water pools, seawater steam sauna, dry sauna, and a relaxation area. For those seriously into spas, they offer additional services, from Dead Sea mud wraps to massages to day-long "personalized programs" (€21 for 1.75-hour fitness circuit, €27 for 3-hour circuit, daily 8:00–22:00, caps sold and towels rented, bring or buy a swimsuit, on the beach at the center of the crescent, Paseo de La Concha, tel. 943-458-856, www.la-perla.net).

## More Sights

**Monte Igueldo**—For commanding city views (if you ignore the tacky amusements on top), ride the funicular up Monte Igueldo, a

mirror image of Monte Urgull. The views over San Sebastián, along the coast, and into the distant green mountains are sensational day or night. The entrance to the funicular is on the road behind the tennis club on the far western end of Playa de Ondarreta, which extends from Playa de la Concha to the west (funicular-€2.30 round-trip; July–mid-Sept daily 10:00–22:00; April–June and mid-Sept–Oct daily 11:00–20:00; Nov–March Mon–Tue and Thu–Fri 11:00–18:00, Sat–Sun 11:00–20:00, closed Wed). If you drive to the top, you'll pay €1.70 to enter. The #16 bus takes you here from the Old Town in about 10 minutes, stopping at the funicular station.

**Kursaal Conference Center**—These two Lego-like boxes (just east and across the river from the Old Town, in Gros) mark the spot of what was once a grand casino, torn down by Franco to discourage gambling. Many locals wanted to rebuild it as it once was, in a similar style to the turn-of-the-20th-century buildings in the Centro. But, in an effort to keep up with the postmodern trends in Bilbao, city leaders opted instead for Rafael Moneo's striking contemporary design. The complex is supposed to resemble the angular rocks that make up the town's breakwater. The Kursaal houses a theater, conference facilities, some gift shops and travel agencies, and a restaurant.

## Near San Sebastián: Chillida-Leku Museum

Eduardo Chillida (1924–2002), a popular Basque sculptor, is the focus of this enjoyable museum on the outskirts of town. Chillida worked rough, heavy materials (such as iron and marble) into huge but delicate-seeming abstract sculptures. You might not have heard of Chillida, but you've likely seen his big, blocky works, which decorate cities around Spain and throughout Europe. In San Sebastián, among the rocks at the west end of the beachfront promenade, you'll find one of Chillida's most famous works: the "wind combs" *(peine del viento)*.

The museum has three parts: The entry area shows a 45-minute loop film of the artist at work; the grounds—with beautiful, grassy rolling hills and trees—display his larger works, mostly of iron or rose marble; and a 16th-century farmhouse—which the artist renovated expressly for this purpose—shows off some of his smaller works (of bronze, felt, clay, alabaster, and so on).

As you explore, notice the way Chillida began with imposing chunks of media, then carved passages into them to allow light and air to penetrate an otherwise impenetrable block. This has the unexpected effect of making big, clumsy things seem light and graceful. Most of his works are carved from a single piece. The artist believed that works should be unique and evolve organically—he'd contemplate the medium and listen to what it had to say before carving it up. As you stroll the grounds surveying the works, imagine both the intense pressure and the delicate touch required to persuade these materials to become art.

Because it takes some effort to get here, the museum is best for people who know Chillida and appreciate his work. Art-lovers in the region to visit the Guggenheim might find this to be the perfect complement.

**Cost and Hours:** €8.50, good €4 audioguide; July–Aug Mon–Sat 10:30–20:00, Sun 10:30–15:00; Sept–June Wed–Mon 10:30–15:00, closed Tue; Barrio Jáuregui 66, Hernani, tel. 943-336-006, www.eduardo-chillida.com.

**Getting There:** It's on the edge of San Sebastián, about a €10 taxi ride from the Old Town. You can also take bus #G-2 from near the Perla Spa along the beach (2/hr, €1.25).

## SLEEPING

Rates in San Sebastián fluctuate with the season. When you see a range, the top end is for summer (roughly July–Sept), and the low end is for the shoulder season (May–June and Oct); outside of these times, you'll pay even less. Since breakfast is often not included, I've recommended some good options elsewhere in town (see "Eating," later in this section).

### In or near the Old Town

**$$$ Hotel Parma** is a business-class place with 27 fine rooms and family-run attention to detail and service. It stands on the edge of the Old Town, away from the bar-scene noise, and overlooks the river and a surfing beach (Sb-€63–86, windowless interior Db-€93–130, view Db-€113–144, air-con, modern lounge, pay Internet access, free Wi-Fi, Paseo de Salamanca 10, tel. 943-428-893, fax 943-424-082, www.hotelparma.com, hotelparma@hotelparma.com; Iñaki, Pino, and Maider).

**$$ Pensión Edorta** ("Edward") elegantly mixes wood, brick, and color into 12 modern, stylish rooms (S/D-€40–60, Sb/Db-€60–80, extra bed-€20–25, elevator, Calle Puerto 15, tel. 943-423-773, fax 943-433-570, www.pensionedorta.com, info@pensionedorta.com).

**$ Pensión Amaiur** is a flowery and inviting place buried deep in the Old Town, with great-value rooms. Kind Virginia gives the justifiably popular *pensión* a homey warmth—and it's absolutely spotless. Her 13 colorful, cozy rooms share seven bathrooms (S-€28–42, quiet interior D-€38–50, exterior D-€45–60, T-€60–80, Q-€75–95, family room, kitchen facilities, pay Internet access, free Wi-Fi, next to Santa María Church at Calle 31 de Agosto 44, tel.

BASQUE COUNTRY

# San Sebastián's Old Town

1 Hotel Parma
2 Pensión Edorta
3 Pensión Amaiur
4 Hotel Adore Plaza
5 Bar Goiz-Argi & Bodégon Alejandro
6 Bar Sport & Bar Borda-Berri
7 Ganbara Bar
8 La Cuchara de San Telmo
9 A Fuego Negro
10 Casa Urola
11 Sebastián & La Rampa Rests
12 Kanpai Deli
13 Barrenetxe
14 Bar Gorriti
15 Santa Lucia
16 Ailor Lasa Gaztategi
17 Elkar Bookstore
18 CyberWorld (Left Luggage)

943-429-654, www.pensionamaiur.com, amaiur@telefonica.net).

**$ Hotel Adore Plaza,** run by young and energetic Santi, offers bright and good-value rooms overlooking the Old Town's centerpiece, Plaza de la Constitución. If Santi isn't around, his parents will offer a warm, friendly welcome. Seven rooms—four with balconies and views of the plaza, and three interior rooms with less noise—share four bathrooms (D-€50–60, one Db-€65–75, T-€66–81, Q-€80–100, includes tax, elevator, free Wi-Fi, Plaza de la Constitución 6, tel. & fax 943-422-270, mobile 610-521-092 or 610-521-532, www.adoreplaza.com, adoreplaza@yahoo.es).

## Across the River, in Gros

The pleasant Gros district—San Sebastián's "uptown"—is marked by the super-modern, blocky Kursaal conference center. The nearby beach is popular with surfers. These hotels are less than a 10-minute walk from the Old Town.

**$$$ Hotel Arrizul** is new and fresh, with sleek, mod decor in each of its 12 rooms (Sb-€65–88, Db-€99–129, breakfast-€6, air-con, elevator, free Wi-Fi, Peña y Goñi 1, tel. 943-322-804, fax 943-326-701, www.arrizulhotel.com, info@arrizulhotel.com).

**$$ Pensión Kursaal** has 10 basic but colorful rooms (Db-€63–82, elevator, pay Internet, free Wi-Fi, Peña y Goñi 2, tel. 943-292-666, fax 943-297-536, www.pensionesconencanto.com, kursaal@pensionesconencanto.com).

## On the Beach

**$$$ Hotel Niza,** set in the middle of Playa de la Concha, is understandably often booked well in advance. Half of its 40 rooms (some with balconies) overlook the bay. From its chandeliered and plush lounge, a classic elevator takes you to its comfortable, pastel rooms with wedding-cake molding (tiny interior Sb-€58–64, Db-€123–139, view rooms cost the same—requests with reservation considered...but no promises, extra bed-€22, only streetside rooms have air-con, great buffet breakfast-€11, free Internet access and Wi-Fi, parking-€14/day—must reserve in advance, Zubieta 56, tel. 943-426-663, fax 943-441-251, www.hotelniza.com, niza @hotelniza.com). The breakfast room has a sea view and doubles as a bar with light snacks throughout the day (Bar Biarritz, daily 7:30–24:00, food service ends at 22:30). The cheap and cheery restaurant downstairs, called La Pasta Gansa, serves good pizzas and salads (Wed–Mon 13:30–15:30 & 20:30–24:00, closed Tue).

## Near the EuskoTren Station

**$$ Pensión Bellas Artes,** while farther from the Old Town than my other listings, is worth the 15-minute walk. Lively Leire, who lived in New York and runs her *pensión* with pride, rents 10 small, well-appointed, tidy rooms with all the thoughtful extra touches you might hope for. Leire and her mother love to give their guests sightseeing and dining tips (Sb-€47–58, Db-€72–79, extra bed-€35, €3 breakfast available nearby, non-smoking, elevator, free Internet access and Wi-Fi, very near the EuskoTren station in a pleasant urban neighborhood at Urbieta 64, tel. 943-474-905, fax 943-463-111, www.pension-bellasartes.com, info@pension-bellasartes.com).

# EATING

Basque food is regarded as some of the best in Spain...and San Sebastián is the culinary capital of Basque Country. What the city lacks in world-class museums, it more than makes up for in food. You could spend months here, eat somewhere different each night, and never have the same meal twice. (For tips on Spanish Basque cuisine, see page 398.)

San Sebastián is proud of its many Michelin-rated fine dining establishments. But these require a big commitment of time and money, so I've listed only a few restaurants. Instead, most casual visitors will prefer to hop from pub to pub through the Old Town, following the crowds between Basque-font signs.

## *Pintxo* Bar-Hopping

San Sebastián's Old Town pro-vides the ideal backdrop for tapas-hopping; just wander the streets and straddle up to the bar in the liveliest spot. Calle Fermín Calbetón has about the best con-centration of bars; the streets San Jerónimo and 31 de Agosto are also good.

## On Calle Fermín Calbetón

I've listed these in order, as you progress deeper into the Old Town. There are plenty of other options along here, but these are top-notch.

**Bar Goiz-Argi** ("Morning Light"), every local's top rec-ommendation, serves its tiny dishes with pride and attitude. Advertising *pintxos calientes,* they cook each treat for you, allow-ing you a montage of petite gourmet snacks; try their *tartaleta de txangurro* (spider-crab spread on bread) or their wonderful shrimp kebab. Wash it all down with a glass of whichever wine you like—open bottles are clearly priced and displayed on the shelf. You stand at the bar since there are no chairs (closed Mon–Tue, Calle Fermín Calbetón 4, tel. 943-425-204).

## Do the *Txiquiteo* Tango

*Txiquiteo* (chih-kee-TAY-oh) is the word for hopping from bar to bar, enjoying characteristically small sandwiches and

tiny snacks (*pintxos*, PEEN-chohs) and glasses of wine. Local competition drives small bars to lay out the most appealing array of *pintxos*, and the selection is amazing. Watch the locals to see what they're eating and find out what's best. But don't get carried away at one place—there will be more you'll want to try at the next bar.

Later in the evening, the best spreads get picked over (20:30 is prime time). As the night progresses, bars get more crowded and bartenders bounce around. If

you can't get the bartender's attention to serve you a particular *pintxo*, don't be shy—just grab it and a napkin, and munch away. Most bars operate on the honor system, so keep a mental note of the number of tapas you've eaten.

If you want a meal instead of *pintxos*, note that some bars—even ones that look only like bars from the street—have attached restaurants (usually with an entrance from the bar). If you're hungry, ask if there's a restaurant.

At **Bar Sport,** they may offer to *calentar* (heat up) some of your selections, such as the toothpick-towering *jamón* and mushroom *pintxo*. They have a few tables, but don't expect service. Order at the bar and take it to your table...if you're lucky enough to get one (daily, Calle Fermín Calbetón 10, tel. 943-426-888).

**Bar Borda-Berri** (loosely "Mountain Hut"), a couple doors down, features a more low-key ambience and top-quality €3 *pintxos*. There are only a few items at the bar; check out the chalkboard menu for today's options (ask for English translation), order, and they'll make it fresh. The specialty here is melt-in-your-mouth beef cheeks *(carrillera de tenera)* in a tangy sauce (closed Mon, Calle Fermín Calbetón 12, tel. 943-430-342).

### Other *Pintxo* Bars in the Old Town

**Ganbara** serves little croissant-sandwich *pintxos*, and also heaps piles of peppers and mushrooms—whatever's in season—on its bar. They'll sauté you a tasty *ración* for a steep price; for example, a plate of grilled *hongos a la plantxa*—grilled giant mushrooms—will run you about €13 (closed Mon, San Jerónimo 21, tel. 943-422-575).

La Cuchara de San Telmo, with cooks taught by a big-name Basque chef, is a cramped place that devotes as much space to its thriving kitchen as its bar. It has nothing pre-cooked and set on the bar—you order your mini-gourmet plates with a spirit of adventure from the constantly changing blackboard. Their foie gras with apple jelly is rightfully famous (€3 *pintxos,* closed Mon, tucked away on a lonely alley called Santa Corda behind Museum of San Telmo at 31 de Agosto 28, tel. 943-420-840).

A Fuego Negro is cool and upscale compared to the others, with a hip, slacker vibe and a blackboard menu of *pintxos* and drinks (closed Mon, 31 de Agosto 31, mobile 650-135-373).

## Sit-Down Restaurants

Bodégon Alejandro is a good spot for modern Basque cuisine in a dark and traditional setting (3-course fixed-price meal-€35, from 13:00 and 20:30, closed Mon–Tue except in Aug, no dinner Sun, in the thick of the Old Town on Calle Fermín Calbetón 4, tel. 943-427-158).

Casa Urola, a block away, is a fine option for a traditional, sit-down Basque meal (more expensive, €16–22 entrées, from 13:00 and 20:00, reservations smart, Calle Fermín Calbetón 20, tel. 943-423-424).

*Seafood Along the Port:* For seafood with a salty sailor's view, check out the half-dozen hardworking, local-feeling restaurants that line the harbor on the way to the aquarium. Along here, locals like Sebastián (more traditional, closed Tue) and La Rampa (more upscale, closed Tue afternoon and all day Wed).

## Picnics and Take-Out

A picnic on the beach or atop Monte Urgull is a tempting option. These places are a memorable place to assemble a bang-up spread.

Kanpai, a high-quality deli serving Basque and international cuisine, offers tempting, well-presented food. Davíd (who runs the place with his mother) carefully crafts each dish. Step up to the display case and get something "to go" for an easy and tasty picnic, or enjoy it at one of their little tables, and ask them to *calentar*—heat it up (€10 3-course meal offered Mon–Fri only, fancier foods on weekends, also wine-tastings, open daily 10:00–15:00 & 17:00–21:00, San Lorenzo 4, tel. 943-423-884).

Explore the Bretxa Public Market at Plaza de Sarriegi (described on page 427).

Upscale picnickers can tempt their tastebuds at Barrenetxe for an amazing array of breads, prepared foods, and some of the best desserts in town. In business since 1699, the somewhat formal service is justified (open daily, hours vary but always closed Sun afternoon, Plaza de Guipúzcoa 9, tel. 943-424-482).

## Breakfast

If your hotel doesn't provide breakfast—or even if it does—consider one of these places. The first is a traditional stand-up bar, while the second is a greasy spoon.

**Bar Gorriti,** delightfully local, is packed with market workers and shoppers starting their busy day. You'll stand at the bar and choose a hot-off-the-grill *tortilla* (omelet) sandwich and other goodies (€2 each). This and a cup of coffee makes for an energizing and very Basque breakfast (bar open long hours daily, breakfast served 6:30–10:00, facing the side of the big white market building at San Juan 3, tel. 943-428-353).

**Santa Lucía,** a 1950s-style diner, is ideal for a cheap Old Town breakfast or *churros* break (*churros* are like deep-fried, sweet French fries that can be dipped in pudding-like hot chocolate). Photos of two dozen different breakfasts decorate the walls, and plates of fresh *churros* with sugar keep patrons happy. Grease is liberally applied to the grill...from a squeeze bottle. To counteract this place's heart-attack potential, get a glass of O.J., fresh-squeezed by the clever machine (daily 8:00–21:00, Calle Puerto 6, tel. 943-425-019).

# TRANSPORTATION CONNECTIONS

## By Train

Remember that San Sebastián has two train stations: RENFE and EuskoTren (described in "Arrival in San Sebastián," earlier in this chapter). The station you use depends on your destination.

**RENFE Station:** This station handles long-distance destinations within Spain (most of which require reservations). Connections include **Irún** (12/day, 25 min), **Hendaye,** France (9/day, 30 min), **Madrid** (3/day, 5–7 hrs), **Burgos** (4/day, 3–3.5 hrs), **León** (1/day, 5 hrs), **Pamplona** (3/day, 2 hrs), **Salamanca** (1/day, 6 hrs), **Vitoria** (5/day, 1.75 hrs), **Barcelona** (1/day, 8.5 hrs; also 1 night train/day except Sat, 10 hrs), and **Santiago de Compostela** (1/day, 11 hrs, final destination A Coruña).

**EuskoTren Station:** If you're going into France, it's best to take the regional Topo train (which leaves from the EuskoTren station) over the French border into **Hendaye** (2/hr, 30 min, departs EuskoTren station at :15 and :45 after the hour 6:15–21:45). From Hendaye, connect to France's SNCF network, including **Paris** (from Hendaye: 4/day, 5.5 hrs, or 8.5-hr night train, reservations required). Unfortunately, San Sebastián's EuskoTren station doesn't have information on Paris-bound trains from Hendaye (except sometimes in summer). Don't buy the Spanish ticket too far in advance—EuskoTren tickets to Hendaye must be used within two hours of purchase (or else they expire).

Also leaving from San Sebastián's EuskoTren station are

slow regional trains to destinations in Spain's Basque region, including **Bilbao** (hourly, €10.50 round-trip ticket saves €2, 2.25–2.75 hrs—the bus is faster; EuskoTren info: tel. 902-543-210, www.euskotren.es). Although the train ride from San Sebastián to Bilbao takes twice as long as the bus, it passes through more interesting countryside. The Basque Country shows off its trademark green and gray: lush green vegetation and gray clouds. It's an odd mix of heavy industrial factories, small homegrown veggie gardens, streams, and every kind of livestock you can imagine.

## By Bus

There is no real bus station in San Sebastián—it's more a congregation of bus parking spots next to the big Hotel Amara Plaza, at the roundabout called Plaza Pío XII (on the river, four blocks south of EuskoTren station). The "station" is called Amara (for the neighborhood it's in). Some schedules are posted at various stops, but confirm departure times and buy your tickets in advance at any of the bus companies with offices on either side of the block north of the station area (toward downtown, along Avenida de Sancho el Sabio and Paseo de Vízcaya). Pesa, which serves St. Jean-de-Luz and Bilbao, is located on the same side as the "station," at Avenida de Sancho el Sabio 33 (tel. 902-101-210, www .pesa.net). The Alsa office—which serves Madrid, Burgos, and León, and also has baggage storage—is at Paseo de Vízcaya 16 (tel. 902-422-242, www.alsa.es).

From San Sebastián, buses go to **Bilbao** (get ticket from Pesa office, 2/hr, hourly on weekends, 6:30–22:00, 1.25 hrs, €9.20, departs from Amara; morning buses fill with tourists, commuters, and students so consider buying your ticket the day before; once in Bilbao, buses leave you at Termibús stop with easy tram connections to the Guggenheim modern-art museum), **Pamplona** (La Roncalesa office, 8/day, 1 hr, €6.50), **León** (Alsa office, 1/day, 6 hrs, €28), **Madrid** (Alsa office, 8/day, 6 hrs direct, otherwise 7 hrs, €30–42; same bus stops at **Burgos**), and **Barcelona** (Vibasa office, 2/day and 1 at night, 7.5 hrs, €27).

To visit **Hondarribia** (described on page 439), you can catch bus #I-2 much closer to the center at Plaza Gipuzkoa (1 block south of TI; about 3/hr, 30 min, €2, same bus goes to airport en route to Hondarribia).

**Buses to French Basque Country:** A bus goes from San Sebastián's Amara bus station to **St. Jean-de-Luz** (Mon–Sat only, 2/day at 9:00 and 14:30, 45 min, €4.20 one-way, €7.50 round-trip, get ticket from Pesa office, runs only 1/week off-season), then continues directly to **Biarritz** (1.25 hrs from San Sebastián) and **Bayonne** (1.5 hrs from San Sebastián).

# Between San Sebastián and St. Jean-de-Luz: Hondarribia

Just 45 minutes apart by car, San Sebastián and St. Jean-de-Luz bridge the Spanish and French Basque regions. Between them you'll find the functional towns of Irún (Spain), Hendaye (France)...and the delightful hill town of Hondarribia, which is worth a visit if you have time to spare.

## Fuenterrabía / Hondarribia

For a taste of small-town *País Vasco,* dip into this enchanting, seldom-visited town (commonly known by its Euskara name rather than the Spanish version, Fuenterrabía). Much smaller and easier to manage than San Sebastián, and also closer to France (across the picturesque Bay of Txingudi from Hendaye), Hondarribia allows travelers a stress-free opportunity to enjoy Basque culture. While it's easy to think of this as a border town (between France and Spain), culturally it's in the middle of Basque Country.

The town comes in two parts: the lower port town and the historic, balcony-lined streets of the hilly and walled upper town. The upper town, which feels quite manicured, is a delightful place to poke around if you have time. The main square is fronted by Charles V's austere, oddly squat castle (now a parador inn—see below). You can follow the TI's self-guided tour of the old town (English brochure available) or just lose yourself within the walls to explore the plazas.

In the modern lower town, straight shopping streets serve a local clientele and a pleasant walkway takes strollers along the beach.

**Arrival in Hondarribia:** Drivers can use the metered parking by the port (marked with blue lines, pre-pay for parking at machine). Buses into town stop near the TI.

**Tourist Information:** The TI is located where the lower town and the upper town meet, two blocks up from the port on Jabier Ugarte 6 (July–Sept daily 10:00–14:00 & 15:00–19:00; Oct–June Mon–Fri 9:00–13:30 & 16:00–18:30, Sat–Sun 10:00–14:00; tel. 943-645-458).

*Sleeping:* Accommodations are pricey here, but it's a nice small-town alternative to San Sebastián. **$$$ Parador El Emperador,** with 36 rooms housed in a former imperial fortress, is the town's splurge (Sb-€165, Db-€205, elevator, free Wi-Fi, Plaza

de Armas 14, tel. 943-645-500, fax 943-642-153, www.parador
.es, hondarribia@parador.es). Tourists are allowed to have sangria in the *muy* cool bar, though the terraces are for guests only.
**$$$ Hotel San Nicolas,** facing the parador from across the square,
offers a more affordable alternative, with 18 nicely appointed rooms
(many with views) above a smoky local café (Sb–€70–90, Db–€90–
100, higher price is for mid-July–mid-Sept, can be even cheaper
Mon–Thu outside of summer, breakfast not included, elevator,
free Wi-Fi, Plaza de Armas 6, tel. 943-644-278, fax 943-646-217,
www.hotelsannikolas.com, info@hotelsannikolas.com).

## TRANSPORTATION CONNECTIONS

**From Hondarribia by Bus to: San Sebastián** (about 3/hr, 30 min
on express bus, departs from near TI—same bus also stops at air-
port; or twice as long on local public bus), **Hendaye** on the French
border (2/hr, 20 min, June–Sept only). A bus stop in Hondarribia
is across from the post office, one block below the TI.

  **By Boat to: Hendaye** (4/hr in summer, 2/hr off-season, 10
min, runs about 11:00–19:00 or until dark).

# Between San Sebastián and Bilbao: The Bay of Biscay

Between the two Spanish Basque
cities of San Sebastián and Bilbao
is a beautiful countryside of roll-
ing green hills, and a scenic, jag-
ged coastline that looks almost
Celtic. Aside from a scenic joy-
ride, this area merits a visit for
the cute fishing and resort town
of Lekeitio.

## Route Tips for Drivers

San Sebastián and Bilbao are connected in about an hour and a
quarter by the A-8 expressway (the toll between the cities is about
€7.50). While speedy and scenic, this route is nothing compared to
some of the free, but slower, back roads connecting the two towns.

  If side-tripping from San Sebastián to Bilbao, you can drive
directly there on A-8 in the morning. But coming home to San
Sebastián, consider this more scenic route: Take A-8 until the
turnoff for Guernica, then head up into the hills on B-635. After
visiting Guernica (described on page 442), follow signs along the
very twisty road to Lekeitio (about 40 min). Leave Lekeitio on the

road just above the beach; after crossing the bridge, take the left fork and follow B-3428 to Ondarroa (with a striking modern bridge and nice views back into the steep town), Mutriku, and Deba to hug the coastline east to San Sebastián. There's a fine photo-op pull-out as you climb along the coast just after Deba. Soon after, you'll have two opportunities to get on the A-8 (blue signs) for a quicker approach to San Sebastián; but if you've enjoyed the scenery so far, stick with the coastal road (white signs, N-634) through Zumaia and Getaria, re-joining the expressway at Zarautz.

## Lequeitio / Lekeitio

A small fishing port with an idyllic harbor and a fine beach, Lekeitio (leh-KAY-tee-oh) is just over an hour by bus from Bilbao and an

easy stop for drivers. It's protected from the Bay of Biscay by a sand spit that leads to the lush and rugged little San Nicolás Island. Hake boats fly their Basque flags and proud Basque locals black out the Spanish translations on street signs.

Lekeitio is a teeming resort during July and August (when its population of 7,000 triples as big-city Basque folks move in to their vacation condos), and it's a backwater fishing village the rest of the year. It's isolated from the modern rat race by its location down a long, windy little road.

While sights are humble here, the 15th-century St. Mary's Parish Church is a good example of Basque Gothic, with an

impressive altarpiece (Mon–Sat 8:00–12:00 & 17:00–19:30, closed Sun). The town's back lanes are reminiscent of old days when fishing was the only industry. Fisherwomen sell their husbands' catches each morning from about 10:30 along the port. The golden crescent beach is as inviting as the sandbar, which—at low tide—challenges you to join the seagulls out on San Nicolás Island.

**Getting There:** Buses connect Lekeitio with **Bilbao** (hourly, 1.25 hrs; same bus stops at **Guernica**, 40 min) and **San Sebastián** (4/day Mon–Fri, 2/day Sat–Sun, 1.25 hrs). But this stop is most logical for those with a car. Drivers can park most easily in the lot near the bus station. Exit the station left, walk along the road, then take the first right (down the steep, cobbled street) to reach the harbor. There is no luggage storage in town.

**Tourist Information:** The TI faces the fish market next to the harbor (July–Aug daily 10:00–14:00 & 16:00–20:00; Sept–June Tue–Sat 10:30–13:30 & 16:00–19:00, Sun 10:00–14:00, closed Mon; tel. 946-844-017).

*Sleeping:* **$$ Emperatriz Zita Hotel** is the obvious best bet for your beach-town break. It's named for Empress Zita (who lived here in exile after her Habsburg family lost World War I and was booted from Vienna). While Zita's mansion burned down, this 1930s rebuild still has a belle époque aristocratic charm, solid classy furniture in 42 spacious rooms, real hardwood floors, and an elegant spa in the basement. Located on the beach a few steps from the harbor, with handy free parking and a view restaurant, it's a fine value (Sb-€46–59, Db-€60–77, Db suite-€90–107, views—ask for *vistas del mar*—are worth the extra €6, high prices are for mid-June–mid-Sept and Fri–Sat all year, extra bed-€20, breakfast-€8, elevator, free Wi-Fi, Santa Elena Etorbidea, tel. 946-842-655, fax 946-243-500, www.aisiahoteles.com, zita@aisiahoteles.com). The hotel also has a thermal seawater pool, Jacuzzi, and full-service spa (all available at reasonable prices).

*Eating:* Although it's sleepy in the off-season, the harbor promenade is made-to-order in summer for a slow meal or a tapas crawl. **Restaurante Zapirain,** hiding in the narrow streets a few blocks up from the harbor, is a local favorite for fancy seafood. This cozy, white-tablecloth eatery fills one small room with 10 tables of happy eaters (€15 starters, €20 main dishes, closed Tue, Igualdegi 3, tel. 946-840-255).

# Guernica / Gernika

The workaday market town of Guernica (GEHR-nee-kah) is near and dear to Basques and pacifists alike. This is the site of the Gernikako Arbola (oak tree of Gernika), which marked the assembly point where the regional Basque leaders, the Lords of Bizkaia, met through the ages to assert their people's freedom. Long the symbolic heart of Basque separatism, it was also a natural target for Franco (and his ally Hitler) in the Spanish Civil War—resulting in an infamous bombing raid that left the town in ruins (see the sidebar "The Bombing of Guernica"), as immortalized by Picasso in his epic work *Guernica*. Today, Guernica—while nothing special at first glance—holds some of

the Basque Country's more compelling museums. And Basque bigwigs have re-claimed the town as a meeting point—they still elect their figurehead leader on that same ancient site under the oak tree.

# ORIENTATION

Guernica is small (about 15,000 inhabitants) and compact, focused on its large market hall (Mon market 9:00–14:00).

## Arrival in Guernica

Drivers will find a handy parking lot near the train tracks at the end of town. Buses drop off along the main road skirting the town center. No matter where you enter, the TI is well-signed (look for yellow *i* signs)—head there first to get your bearings.

## Tourist Information

The TI is in the town center (Mon–Sat 10:00–14:00 & 16:00–19:00—no lunch break in summer, Sun 10:00–14:00, Artekalea 8, tel. 946-255-892, www.gernika-lumo.net). Pick up the free, good town map. If you'll be visiting both the Peace Museum and the Basque Country Museum, buy the €5.25 combo-ticket here.

# SIGHTS

I've arranged Guernica's sights in the order of a handy sightseeing loop from the TI.

• *Exit the TI to the left, cross the street, and walk up the left side of the square, where you'll find the...*

▲**Gernika Peace Museum**—Because of the brutality of the Guernica bombing, and the powerful Picasso painting that documented the atrocities of war, the name "Guernica" has become synonymous with pacifism. This thoughtfully presented exhibit has taken a great tragedy of 20th-century history and turned it into a compelling cry for peace in our time. Borrow the English translations at the entry, request an English showing of the movie upstairs, and head up through the two-floor exhibit. The first floor begins by considering different ways of defining "peace." You'll then enter an apartment and hear Begoña describe her typical Guernica life in the 1930s...until the bombs dropped (a mirror effect shows you the devastating aftermath). You'll exit into an exhibit about the town's history, with a special emphasis on the bombing. Finally, a 10-minute movie shows grainy footage of the destruction, and ends with a collage of peaceful reconciliations in recent history—in Ireland, South Africa, Guatemala, Australia, and Berlin. On the second floor, Picasso's famous painting is superimposed on three transparent panels to highlight different themes. The exhibit concludes with a survey of the recent history of conflicts in the Basque Country (€4; July–Aug Tue–Sat 10:00–20:00, Sun 10:00–15:00, closed Mon; Sept–June Tue–Sat 10:00–14:00 & 16:00–19:00, Sun 10:00–14:00, closed Mon; Foru Plaza 1, tel.

**BASQUE COUNTRY**

## The Bombing of Guernica

During the Spanish Civil War, Guernica was the site of one of history's most reviled wartime acts.

Monday, April 26, 1937, was market day, when the town was filled with farmers and peasants from the countryside selling their wares. At about four-forty in the afternoon, a German warplane appeared ominously on the horizon, and proceeded to bomb bridges and roads surrounding the town. Soon after, more planes arrived. Three hours of relentless saturation bombing followed, as the German and Italian air forces pummeled the city with incendiary "firebombs." People running through the streets or along the green hillsides were strafed with machine-gun fire. As the sun fell low in the sky and the planes finally left, hundreds—or possibly thousands—had been killed, and many more wounded. (Because Guernica was filled with refugees from other besieged towns, nobody is sure quite how many perished.)

Hearing word of the attack in Paris, Pablo Picasso—who had been commissioned to paint a mural for the 1937 world's fair—was decimated at the news of what had gone on in Guernica. Inspired, he painted what many consider the greatest anti-war work of art, ever.

Why did the bombings happen? Reportedly, Adolf Hitler wanted an opportunity to try out his new saturation-bombing attack strategy (these days, we'd call it "shock and awe"). Francisco Franco, who was fed up with the independence-minded Basques, offered up their historic capital as a candidate for the experiment.

There's no doubt that Guernica, a gateway to Bilbao, was strategically located. But historians believe most of the targets here were far from strategic. Why attack so mercilessly, during the daytime, on market day, when innocent casualties would be maximized? Like the famous silent scream of Picasso's *Guernica* mother, this question haunts pacifists everywhere to this day.

946-270-213, www.peacemuseumguernica.org).

• *Continue uphill to the big church. At the road above the church, you can turn right and walk a block and a half to find a tile replica of* **Picasso's Guernica** *(left-hand side of the street). Or you can head left to find the next two attractions.*

▲**Basque Country Museum (Euskal Herria Museoa)**—This well-presented, newly renovated exhibit offers a good overview of Basque culture and history. Follow the suggested route and climb chronologically up through Basque history, with the help of an included audioguide. You'll find exhibits about traditional Basque architecture and landscape, and a region-by-region run-down of the Basque Country's seven parts. One interesting map shows Basque emigration over the centuries—including to the US. The top floor is the most engaging, highlighting Basque culture: sports, dances, cuisine, myths and legends, music, and language, plus a wrap-around movie featuring images of a proud people living the Basque lifestyle (€3, Tue–Sat 10:00–14:00 & 16:00–19:00, Sun 11:00–15:00, closed Mon, Allendesalazar 5, tel. 946-255-451).

▲▲**Gernika Assembly House and Oak Tree**—In the Middle Ages, the meeting point for the Basque general assembly was under the old oak tree on the gentle hillside above Guernica. The tradition continues today, as the tree stands at the center of a modest but interesting complex celebrating Basque culture and self-government (free, daily 10:00–14:00 & 16:00–18:00, until 19:00 in summer, on Allendesalazar, tel. 946-251-138).

As you enter the grounds, the **old trunk** in the small colonnade dates from the 1700s. Basque traditions have lived much, much longer than a single tree's life span. When one dies, it's replaced with a new one. This is the oldest surviving trunk.

Once inside the big building, the exhibit has three parts. The **stained-glass window room** features a gorgeous ceiling rife with

Basque symbolism. The elderly leader stands under the oak holding a book with the "Old Law" *(Lege Zarra).* These are the *Fueros,* which the Basques lived by for centuries. Below him are groups representing the three traditional skills of this industrious people: sailors and fishermen, miners and steel-workers, and farmers. Behind them all is a classic Basque land-scape: on the left is the sea, and on the right are rolling green hills dotted with red-and-white homes.

Out back, a tribune surrounds the fateful **oak tree.** This little fella is from 2005, planted here when the earlier one "finished out its life cycle" after standing here for nearly a century and a half. This tree is a descendant of that one, and (supposedly) of all the trees here since ancient times. This is where Basque leaders have met in solidarity across the centuries. In the Middle Ages, after Basque lands became part of Castile, Castilian kings came here to pledge respect to the old Basque laws. When Basque independence came under fire in the 19th century, patriots rallied by singing a song about this tree ("Ancient and holy symbol / Let thy fruit fall worldwide / While we gaze in adoration / Upon thee, our blessed tree"). After the 1937 bombing, in which this tree was miraculously unscathed, hundreds of survivors sought refuge under its branches. Today, while official representatives in the Spanish government are elected at the polls, the Basques choose their figurehead leader, the Lehendakari ("First One"), in this same spot.

Finally, the **assembly chamber** is like a mini-parliament for the region of Bizkaia ("Vízcaya" in Spanish, "Biscay" in English; one of the seven Basque territories). Notice the holy water and the altar—a sign that there's no separation of church and state in Basque politics. The paintings show the Lords of Bizkaia swearing allegiance to the *Fueros*.

## TRANSPORTATION CONNECTIONS

Guernica is well-connected to **Bilbao** (1–2 trains/hr to Bilbao's Atxuri station, 40 min; also 2 buses/hr, 40 min) and to **Lekeitio** (hourly buses, 40 min). Connections are much less on weekends. The easiest way to connect to San Sebastián is via Bilbao, though you can also get there on the slow Topo train (transfer in Lemoa).

# Bilbao / Bilbo

In recent years, Bilbao (bil-BOW, rhymes with "cow") has seen a transformation like no other Spanish city. Entire sectors of the industrial city's long-depressed port have been cleared away to allow construction of a new opera house, convention center, and the stunning Guggenheim Museum.

Bilbao feels at once like a city of the grim industrial past...and of an exciting new future. It mingles beautiful but crumbling old buildings; eyesore high-rise apartment blocks; brand-new, super-modern additions to the skyline (such as the Guggenheim); and, draping the lush green hillsides on the horizon all around, typical whitewashed Basque homes with red roofs. Bilbao enjoys a vitality and well-worn charm befitting its status as a regional capital of culture and industry.

## Planning Your Time

For most visitors, the Guggenheim is the main draw (and many could spend the whole day just there). But with a little more time, it's worth hopping on a tram to also explore the atmospheric Old Town (Casco Viejo).

Don't bother coming to Bilbao on Monday, when virtually all its museums—including the almighty Guggenheim—are closed (except in July–Aug).

# ORIENTATION

When you're in the center, Bilbao feels smaller than its popula-

tion of 500,000. The city, nestled amidst green hillsides, hugs the Bilbao River as it curves through town. The Guggenheim is more or less centrally located near the top of that curve; the bus station is to the west; the Old Town (Casco Viejo) and train stations are to the east; and a super-convenient (and actually enjoyable-to-ride) green tram called the EuskoTran ties it all together.

## Tourist Information

Bilbao's handiest TI is next to the Guggenheim (July–Aug Mon–Sat 10:00–19:00, Sun 10:00–18:00; Sept–June Tue–Fri 11:00–18:00, Sat 11:00–19:00, Sun 11:00–15:00, closed Mon; Avenida Abandoibarra 2, tel. 944-710-301, www.bilbao.net). There are also branches at the airport and at Arriaga Theater near the Old Town. Pick up a city map and the bimonthly *Bilbao Guide*. If you're interested in something beyond the Guggenheim, ask about walking tours and grab the museum brochure (describing museums dedicated to everything from bullfighting and seafaring to sports and Holy Week processionals).

## Arrival in Bilbao

Most travelers—whether arriving by train, bus, or car—will want to go straight to the museum. Thanks to a perfectly planned tram

system (EuskoTran), this couldn't be easier. From any point of entry, simply buy a €1.15 single-ride ticket at a user-friendly green machine (€3.15 for an all-day pass), hop on a green-and-gray tram, enjoy the Muzak, and head for the Guggenheim stop (there's only one line so you can't get lost, trams come every 10–15 min, www.euskotran.es). When you buy your ticket, validate it immediately at the machine (follow the red arrow), since you can't do it once on board.

The Metro system, designed by prominent architect Lord Norman Foster, is a work of art...but not practical for most visitors.

If you get lost, ask: *"¿Dónde está el museo Guggenheim?"* (DOHN-day ay-STAH el moo-SAY-oh "Guggenheim").

Note that the only luggage storage in town is at the Termibús station (not at either train station).

**By Train:** Bilbao's **RENFE station** (trains from most parts of Spain) is on the river in central Bilbao. The train station is on top of a small shopping mall. To reach the tram to the Guggenheim, descend into the stores. Leave from the exit marked *Hurtado de Amézaga,* and go right to find the BBK bank. Enter, find the *Automatikoa* door on the right, and buy your ticket at the green machine marked *Abando* (the machine is mixed in with a bunch of ATMs). Leave the bank and continue right around the corner. Validate your ticket at the machines at the tram stop before boarding the tram marked *Basurto.*

Trains coming from San Sebastián arrive at the riverside **Atxuri station,** southeast of the museum. Buy and validate your ticket, hop on a tram (direction: Basurto), and follow the river to the Guggenheim stop.

**By Bus:** Buses stop at the **Termibús station** on the western edge of downtown, about a mile southwest of the museum. The station has luggage lockers and a left-luggage desk (€2/bag, Mon–Fri 7:00–22:00, Sat 8:00–21:00, Sun 7:00–21:00). The tram (San Mamés station) is on the road just below the station—look for the steel *CTB* sign, buy and validate a ticket at the machine, and hop on the tram (direction: Atxuri) to Guggenheim.

**By Plane:** Bilbao's compact, modern, user-friendly airport is about six miles north of downtown. Everything branches off of a light-and-air-filled main hall, designed by prominent architect Santiago Calatrava. A handy bus (#3247) takes you directly to the center (€1.25, pay driver, 3/hr, 20-min trip, makes 3 stops downtown—the first one is closest to the Guggenheim—before ending at the Termibús station). To find the bus, turn right out of the terminal. A taxi into town costs about €20. Note that there is no direct connection from Bilbao's airport to San Sebastián—you'll have to take the bus to Termibús to transfer to a San Sebastián–bound bus (2/hr). A taxi directly to San Sebastián will run you €150.

**By Car:** Parking at the museum itself is a hassle; the closest option is the garage two blocks in front (Calle Iparraguirre 18). But to avoid stressful city traffic and frustrating one-ways, the best plan is this: Use the expressway exit marked *Centro,* following signs to *Guggenheim.* You'll pass the long train station on your right; continue straight through the traffic circle, veer left at the river, and park at the big garage (called Pío Baroja). Walk 10 minutes to the museum, or hop on the tram (direction: Basurto).

**Bilbao**

TRAM
METRO STATION
PARKING

1 Gran Hotel Domine Bilbao
2 Hotel Bilbao Jardines
3 Iturrienea Ostatua
4 Hotel Arriaga
5 Pensión Ladero
6 La Estrella Ostatu

GUGGENHEIM BILBAO

NERVION RIVER

EUSKALDUNA BRIDGE
SALVE BRIDGE
ZUBIZURI BRIDGE
AYUNTAMIENTO BRIDGE
ARENAL BRIDGE

TO AIRPORT

OLD TOWN
BASQUE MUSEUM
RIBERA MARKET
ATXURI TRAIN STN.
CATHEDRAL

TO SAN SEBASTIÁN

S. ANTON BRIDGE
SAN FRAN.
DCH

OPERA HOUSE
ART MUSEUM
GRAN VIA

ALAMEDA RECALDE
ALAMEDA DE MAZZARREDO
DE MAZZARREDO
Pio Baroja
PLAZA CIRC.
DIEGO LÓPEZ
PLAZA MOYÚA
DE DON DIEGO
URQUIJO
MAIN TRAIN STN.

PLAZA INDAUTXU
ALAMEDA DE URQUIJO
AUTONOMIA
BULL-RING

SAN MAMÉS STADIUM
CONVENTION CENTER
TERMIBÚS BUS STN.
GURT

SABINO
ARANA

TO A-8 FREEWAY & SAN SEBASTIÁN

¼ MILE
400 METERS

**BASQUE COUNTRY**

# SIGHTS

## ▲▲▲Guggenheim Bilbao

While the collection of art in this museum is no better than that in Europe's other great modern-art museums, the building itself—designed by Frank Gehry and opened in 1997—is the reason why so many travelers happily splice Bilbao into their itineraries.

**Cost, Hours, Information:** €12.50, includes excellent audioguide; July–Aug daily 10:00–20:00; Sept–June Tue–Sun 10:00–20:00, closed Mon; same-day re-entry allowed—get bracelet on your way out; café—see "Eating," later in this section, no photos inside, tram stop: Guggenheim, Metro stop: Moyua, Avenida Abandoibarra 2, tel. 944-359-080, www.guggenheim-bilbao.es. For guided tours in English, call 944-359-090 for a schedule.

**Background:** Frank Gehry's groundbreaking triumph offers a fascinating look at 21st-century architecture. Using cutting-edge technologies, unusual materials, and daring forms, he created a piece of sculpture that smoothly integrates with its environment and serves as the perfect stage for some of today's best art. Clad in limestone and titanium, the building connects the city with its river. Gehry meshed many visions. To him, the building's multiple forms  jostle like a loose crate of bottles. The building is inspired by a silvery fish...and also evokes wind-filled sails heading out to sea. Gehry keeps returning to his fish motif, reminding visitors that, as a boy, he was inspired by carp...even taking them into the bathtub with him.

**❍ Self-Guided Tour:** The audioguide will lead you room-by-room through the collection, but this information will get you started.

Guarding the main entrance is artist Jeff Koons' 42-foot-tall **West Highland Terrier.** Its 60,000 plants and flowers, which blossom in concert, grow through steel mesh. A joyful structure, it brings viewers back to their childhood...perhaps evoking humankind's relationship to God...or maybe it's just another notorious Koons hoax. One thing is clear: It answers to "Puppy."

Descend to the **main entrance.** After buying your ticket, be sure to pick up a free audioguide—it explains Gehry's architecture in vivid detail and describes the exhibits (both permanent and temporary). Also pick up the English brochure explaining the architecture and museum layout (at the information desk), and the monthly bulletin detailing the art currently on display.

After presenting your ticket, enter the **atrium.** This acts as the heart of the building, pumping visitors from various rooms on three levels out and back, always returning to this central area before moving on to the next. The architect invites you to caress the sensual curves of the walls. There are virtually no straight lines (except the floor). Notice the sheets of glass that make up the elevator shaft—overlapping each other like a fish's scales. The various glass and limestone panels are each unique, designed by a computer and shaped by a robot...as will likely be standard in constructing the great buildings of the future.

From the atrium, step out onto the riverside **terrace.** The "water garden" lets the river symbolically lap at the base of the building. This pool is home to two unusual sculptures (which appear occasionally throughout the day): a five-part "fire fountain" (notice the squares in the pool to the right) and a "fog sculpture" that billows up from below.

Still out on the terrace, notice the museum's commitment to public spaces: On the right, a grand **staircase** leads under a big green bridge to a tower; the effect wraps the bridge into the museum's grand scheme. The 30-foot-tall **spider,** called *Maman* ("Mommy"), is a French artist's depiction of her mother: She spins a beautiful and delicate web of life...which is used to entrap her victims. (It makes a little more sense if you understand that the artist's mother was a weaver. Or maybe not.)

Gehry designed the vast **ground floor** mainly to house often-huge modern-art installations. Computer-controlled lighting adjusts for different exhibits. Surfaces are clean and bare, so you can focus on the art.

Speaking of which...because this museum is part of the Guggenheim "family" of museums, the **collection** perpetually rotates among the sister Guggenheim galleries in New York, Venice, and Berlin. The best approach to your visit is simply to immerse yourself in a modern-art happening, rather than to count on seeing a particular piece or a specific artist's works.

Twenty galleries occupy three floors. Use the handy touch-screens scattered throughout the museum to figure out exactly where you are and what's left to see, since the organic floor plan can be confusing. If you've always confused Klimt with Matisse, be sure to visit the *espacio didáctico* (learning area) on the third floor for its brilliantly concise timeline of all major art movements since the mid-19th century.

Or, if you're not turned on by this kind of art, just rattle around the inside of the remarkable building for a while. Especially around the atrium, every angle morphs the building into a whole new experience.

A great way to really enjoy the **exterior** is to take a circular stroll up and down each side of the river, along the handsome promenade and over the two modern pedestrian bridges. (After you tour the museum, you can borrow a free "outdoor audioguide" to learn more—but it doesn't take you across the river.) The building's skin—shiny, metallic, with a scale-like texture—is made of thin titanium, carefully created to give just the desired color and reflective quality. The external appearance tells you what's inside: the blocky limestone parts contain square-shaped galleries, while the titanium sections hold non-linear spaces.

As you look out over the rest of the city, think of this: Gehry designed his building to reflect what he saw here in Bilbao. Now other architects are, in turn, creating new buildings that complement his. It's an appealing synergy for this old city.

## Old Town (Casco Viejo)

Bilbao's Old Town is worth a stroll, with tall, narrow lanes lined with thriving shops and tapas bars. Because the weather is wetter here than in many other parts of Spain (hence the green hillsides), the little balconies that climb the outside walls of buildings are glassed in, creating cozy little breakfast nooks. Approaching on the tram, hop off at the Arriaga stop, near the dripping-Baroque riverfront theater of the same name. From here, it's a short stroll into the twisty Old Town.

Whether you want to or not, you'll eventually wind up at Old Bilbao's centerpiece, the **Santiago Cathedral**, a 14th-century Gothic church with a tranquil interior that's recently been scrubbed clean inside and out (free, €1 to dip into cloister, Mon–Sat 10:00–13:00 & 17:00–19:30, closed Sun).

Various museums (including those dedicated to diocesan art and the Holy Week processions) are in or near the Old Town, but on a quick visit only one is worth considering...

**Basque Museum (Euskal Museoa)**—As a leading city of Spain's Basque region, it's fitting that Bilbao would have a museum dedicated to its unique culture. Unfortunately, the almost complete lack of English leaves the exhibits, much like the Basques themselves, shrouded in mystery. Around a ground-floor cloister, you'll see old stone monuments. The first floor delves into the Basque cultural heritage, displaying ceramics, guns, looms, and other tools. Special emphasis is given to nautical artifacts from this seafaring people; Basque settlers in the American West; and the pastoral lifestyles of rural Basques. The top floor is dedicated to archaeology, with exhibits about old tools and settlements (€3, Tue–Sat 11:00–17:00,

Sun 11:00–14:00, closed Mon, Miguel de Unamuno Plaza 4, tel. 944-155-423, www.euskal-museoa.org).

# SLEEPING

**(€1 = about $1.50, country code: 34)**

Bilbao merits an overnight stay. Even those who are only interested in the Guggenheim find that there's much more to see in this historic yet quickly changing city. Unless otherwise noted, the 7 percent tax is not included in the prices listed below.

## Near the Guggenheim Museum

**$$$ Gran Hotel Domine Bilbao** is *the* place for wealthy modern-art fans looking for a handy splurge. It's right across the street from the Guggenheim, with decor (by a prominent Spanish designer) clearly inspired by Gehry's masterpiece. The hotel is gathered around an atrium with a giant "stone tree" and other artsy flourishes. Its 145 plush rooms are distinctly black, white, steel, and very postmodern (standard Db-€135, museum-view "executive" rooms for €20 more, rates can vary widely—can be much higher during conferences and cheaper during summer, no breakfast, non-smoking rooms, air-con, elevator, free Internet and Wi-Fi, great museum-view breakfast terrace, Alameda Mazarredo 61, tel. 944-253-300, fax 944-253-301, www.granhoteldominebilbao.com, recepcion.domine@hoteles-silken.com).

## In the Old Town

To reach the Old Town, take the tram to the Arriaga stop. Note that the rates at these places can fluctuate by about €5 from season to season; I've listed the average rate.

**$$ Hotel Bilbao Jardines,** a fresh new place buried in the Old Town, is the most hotelesque option, with 32 modern but basic rooms (Sb-€58, Db-€75, cheaper off-season, breakfast-€4.50, quieter rooms in back, air-con, elevator, free Wi-Fi, Calle Jardines 9, tel. 944-794-210, fax 944-794-211, www.hotelbilbaojardines .com, info@hotelbilbaojardines.com).

**$ Iturrienea Ostatua,** on a pedestrian street in the Old Town, is a tidy pension renting 21 rooms packed with brick, stone, and antiques (Sb-€50, Db-€60, twin Db-€66, Tb-€80, prices include taxes, €10–15 more July–Aug, breakfast-€8, free Wi-Fi, Santa María 14, tel. 944-161-500, fax 944-158-929, www .iturrieneaostatua.com, info@iturrieneaostatua.com). From the main train station, cross the bridge and go past the big theater. Where the river bends, turn left and walk a block and a half up quaint Santa María street.

**BASQUE COUNTRY**

**$ Hotel Arriaga** offers 21 traditional but well-maintained rooms and a spirited reception (Sb-€48, Db-€60, extra bed-€11, some rooms overlook a busy street—request a quiet back room, free Wi-Fi, parking-€11, Ribera 3, tel. 944-790-001, fax 944-790-516). As you cross the bridge from the station, it's just behind the big theater of the same name.

**$ Pensión Ladero,** renting ramshackle but cheap rooms, is a fine budget option in the Old Town. They don't accept reservations, but you can call when you arrive to check availability (S-€24, D-€36, T-€53, Q-€63, up 4 flights of stairs; 7 rooms up a very tight spiral staircase share 1 bathroom, while 11 rooms use the other 3 bathrooms on the main floor; cash only, Lotería 1, tel. 944-150-932, www.pensionladero.es). You'll find the *pensión* just before the cathedral at the center of the Old Town. This is a better value than the more prominent Pensión Roquefer across the street.

**$ La Estrella Ostatu** has 26 simple but neat rooms up a twisty staircase near the Basque Museum (Sb-€35, Db-€60 in summer including tax, cheaper off-season, breakfast-€3–4, María Muñoz 6, tel. 944-164-066, fax 944-150-731, www.laestrellaostatu.com, laestrellabilbao@yahoo.es, just enough English spoken).

# EATING

## Near the Guggenheim Museum

The easiest choice is the good cafeteria right in the museum itself (upper level, separate entry above museum entry; Tue–Sun 9:00–21:00, closed Mon, €15 lunch deal offered 13:00–15:15). The streets in front of the museum have a handful of both sit-down and carry-out eateries (cafés, pizzerias, sandwich shops) to choose from.

## In the Old Town

Bilbao has a thriving restaurant and tapas-bar scene. For pointers on Basque food, see page 398. You'll find the best options on three streets near the cathedral. Most restaurants around the Old Town advertise a fixed-price lunch for around €10.

**Perro street** is tops for the tasty little tapas called *pintxos* (PEEN-chohs). This is the place to do a tapas-bar crawl. Along here, Bar Irrintzi (open daily, at #8) and Gatz Bar (closed Sun afternoon, at #10) have the best reputation, but locals also enjoy Santa María and Kasko (all of these are within a few yards of each other).

**Santa María street** is better for a sit-down restaurant meal. Browse the menus and interiors and choose your favorite. Well-regarded options include three places virtually next door to each other (at #4): Egiluz (€10 meals, closed Tue afternoon and all day Wed), Río-Oja (€8 specialties, focus on shareable traditional dishes called *kazuelitas*, closed Mon), and Rotterdam (€10–15 meals).

Finally, more eateries abound on **Jardines street,** including the popular Breton (meals and *pintxos,* at #11, closed Mon).

# TRANSPORTATION CONNECTIONS

**From Bilbao by Bus to: San Sebastián** (2/hr, hourly on weekends, 6:00–22:30, 1.25 hrs, arrives at San Sebastián's Amara station), **Guernica** (2/hr, 40 min), **Lekeitio** (hourly, 1.25 hrs), **Burgos** (4–5/day, 2 hrs), **Santander** (hourly, 90 min, transfer there to bus to **Santillana del Mar** or **Comillas** in Cantabria). These buses depart from Bilbao's Termibús station.

**By RENFE Train to: Madrid** (2/day, 6 hrs), **Barcelona** (2/day, 9.25 hrs), **Burgos** (5/day, 3 hrs), **Salamanca** (1/day, 5.5 hrs), **León** (1/day, 5 hrs), **Santiago de Compostela** (1/day, 11 hrs). Remember, these trains leave from the RENFE station, across the river from the Old Town. Note that in a few years, a planned new train line will connect Bilbao to other cities in a snap (30 min to San Sebastián, 2.25 hrs to Madrid, 5.5 hrs to Paris)—but it's still slow trains for now.

**By EuskoTren to: San Sebastián** (hourly, long and scenic 2.25–2.75-hr trip to San Sebastián's EuskoTren station, €6.20), **Guernica** (1–2/hr, 40 min). These trains depart from Bilbao's Atxuri station, just beyond the Old Town.

# LANGUEDOC

From the 10th to the 13th centuries, this mighty and independent region controlled most of southern France. The ultimate in mean-spirited crusades against the Cathars (or Albigensians) began here in 1208, igniting Languedoc's meltdown and eventual incorporation into the state of France.

The name *languedoc* comes from the *langue* (language) that its people spoke: *Langue d'oc* ("language of Oc," *Oc* for the way they said "yes") was the dialect of southern France; *langue d'oïl* was the dialect of northern France (where *oïl* later became *oui*, or "yes"). Languedoc's language faded with its power.

The Moors, Charlemagne, and the Spanish have all called this area home. The Spanish influence is still present in this region, particularly in the south, where restaurants serve paella and the siesta is still respected.

While sharing many of the same attributes as Provence (climate, wind, grapes, and sea), this sunny, intoxicating, southwesternmost region of France is allocated little time by most travelers. Lacking Provence's cachet and sophistication, Languedoc feels more real. Pay homage to Henri de Toulouse-Lautrec in Albi; spend a night in Europe's greatest fortress city, Carcassonne; scamper up to a remote Cathar castle; and sift through sand in Collioure. That wind you feel is called *la tramontane* (trah-mohn-tahn-yuh), Languedoc's version of Provence's mistral wind.

## Planning Your Time

Albi makes a good day or overnight stop between the Dordogne region and Carcassonne (figure about 2 autoroute hours from Albi to either place). Plan your arrival in Carcassonne carefully:

If you arrive late in the afternoon, spend the night, and leave by 11:00 the next day, you'll miss most day-trippers. Collioure lies a few hours from Carcassonne and is your Mediterranean beach-town vacation from your vacation, where you'll want two nights and a full day. To find the Cathar castle ruins and the village of Minerve, you'll need wheels of your own and a good map. If you're driving, the most exciting Cathar castles—Peyrepertuse and Quéribus—work well as day stops between Carcassonne and Collioure. And if nature beckons, the Gorges du Tarn makes an idyllic joyride a few hours east of Albi. No matter what kind of transportation you use, Languedoc is a logical stop between the Dordogne and Provence—or on the way to Barcelona, which is just over the border.

## Getting Around Languedoc

Albi, Carcassonne, and Collioure are all accessible by train, but a car is essential for seeing the remote sights. Pick up your rental car in Albi or Carcassonne, and buy the Michelin Local maps #344 and #338. Roads can be pencil-thin, and traffic slow.

For a scenic one-hour detour route connecting Albi and points north (such as the Dordogne), take D-964 between Caussade (30 min south of Cahors), Bruniquel, Gaillac, and Albi. With a bit more time, link Caussade, Saint-Antonin-Noble-Val (D-926), Bruniquel, Castelnau-de-Montmiral, Gaillac, and Albi (using D-115 and D-964; see "Route of the Bastides," page 468). If you really want to joyride, take a half-day drive through the glorious Lot River Valley via Villefranche-de-Rouergue, Cajarc, and St. Cirq Lapopie (covered in the "Dordogne and Nearby" chapter— see page 390). If speed is of the essence, connect the Dordogne with Albi via the autoroute to Montauban.

## Cuisine Scene in Languedoc

Hearty peasant cooking and full-bodied red wines are Languedoc's tasty trademarks. Be adventurous. Cassoulet, an old Roman concoction of goose, duck, pork, mutton, sausage, and white beans, is the main-course specialty. You'll also see *cargolade*, a satisfying stew of snail, lamb, and sausage. Local cheeses are Roquefort and Pelardon (a nutty-tasting goat cheese). Corbières, Minervois, and Côtes du Roussillon are the area's good-value red wines. The locals distill a fine brandy, Armagnac, which tastes just like cognac and costs less.

Remember, restaurants serve only during lunch (11:30–14:00) and dinner (19:00–21:00, later in bigger cities); some cafés serve food throughout the day.

# Albi

Albi, an enjoyable river town of sienna-tone bricks and half-timbered buildings, is worth a stop for two world-class sights: its towering cathedral and the Toulouse-Lautrec Museum. Lost in the Dordogne-to-Carcassonne shuffle and overshadowed by its big brother Toulouse, unpretentious Albi rewards the stray tourist well.

# ORIENTATION

Albi's cathedral is home base. For our purposes, all sights, pedestrian streets, and hotels fan out from here, and are less than a five-minute walk away. The Tarn River hides below and behind the cathedral. The best city view is from the 22 Août 1944 bridge. Albi is dead quiet on Sundays and Monday mornings.

## Tourist Information

The helpful TI is on the square in front of the cathedral, next to the Toulouse-Lautrec Museum (July–Aug Mon–Sat 9:00–19:30, Sun 10:30–12:30 & 14:00–18:30; Sept–June Mon–Sat 9:00–12:30 & 14:00–18:00, Sun 10:30–12:30 & 14:00–18:30; tel. 05 63 49 48 80, www.albi-tourisme.fr). Ask about concerts, pick up a map of the city center with the walking-tour brochure, and get the map of *La Route des Bastides Albigeoises* (hill towns near Albi).

## Arrival in Albi

**By Train:** There are two stations in Albi; you want Albi-Ville (no baggage storage, but you can check luggage for the day at the Toulouse-Lautrec Museum). It's a level, 15-minute walk to the town center. Take the second left out of the station onto avenue Maréchal Joffre, and then take another left on avenue du Général de Gaulle. Go straight across place Lapérouse and find the traffic-free street to the left that leads into the city center. This turns into rue Ste. Cécile, which takes you to my recommended hotels and the cathedral.

**By Car:** Follow *Centre-Ville* and *Cathédrale* signs (if you lose your way, follow the tall church tower). There's a big, free lot on avenue du Général de Gaulle, just before place Lapérouse. Metered parking (free 19:00–8:00 and all day Sun) is close to the old city along boulevard Général Sibille (also near place Lapérouse).

## Helpful Hints

**Market Day:** The town's outdoor market is held Saturday mornings on place Lapérouse (until 12:30), and every day except Monday in the Art Nouveau market hall, a block past the cathedral square.

**Groceries:** The store **8 à Huit** is across from the recommended Hôtel Lapérouse (Tue–Sat 8:00–20:00, plus Sun mornings and Mon afternoons, 14 place Lapérouse).

**Wine Shop: Au Roussillon** has a fine selection of this area's surprisingly tasty wines; try a wine from Gaillac (Tue–Sat 10:00–12:00 & 14:00–18:00, closed Sun–Mon, 2 rue de Saunal).

**Internet Access: Ludi.com** is at 62 rue Séré de Rivières (Mon–Sat 14:00–24:00, closed Sun, tel. 05 63 43 34 24).

**LANGUEDOC**

**Albi**

7 VIEW

P PARKING

★ PLACE ST. CECILE

TO CORDES

RUE RINALDI

TARN RIVER

PONT 22 AOUT

OLD BRIDGE

TOULOUSE-LAUTREC MUSEUM

R. ENG.

R. EMILE GRAND

GEORGES POMPIDOU

MALROUX

R. RHONE

CATHEDRAL

ST. MARIES

CEC.

ST. SALVY CHURCH & CLOISTER

BLVD. GEN. SIBILLE

PEUCH.

VERDUSSE

R. HOTEL DE VILLE

PLACE DU VIGAN

R. L'ORT SALVY

ROQUE

R. SEL

PORTE-NEUVE

SERE POST

LICES JEAN MOULIN

PLACE LAPEROUSE

R. SAVERY

GENEVE

BUS STN.

200 YARDS

200 METERS

AVE. DE GAULLE

TO TRAIN STN.

DCH

1. Hostellerie du Santoine
2. Hôtel Chiffre
3. Le Vieil Alby Hôtel-Restaurant
4. Hôtel Lapérouse
5. La Viguière & Le Papillon Restaurants
6. Le Tournesol Restaurant
7. Au Roussillon Wine Shop
8. Market Hall
9. Internet Café
10. 8 à Huit Grocery
11. Launderette

**Laundry:** Do your washing at **Lavotop,** above the river at 10 rue Emile Grand (daily 7:00–21:00).

**Taxi:** Call **Albi Taxi Radio** at 05 63 54 85 03.

**Car Rental: Europcar** is closest to the train station (24 avenue François Verdier, walk 1 long block down avenue Général Leclerc from the station and turn right, tel. 05 63 48 88 33). All others require a taxi ride.

# SIGHTS

## In Albi

Everything of sightseeing interest is within a few blocks of the towering cathedral. (I've included walking directions to connect some of the key sights.) Get oriented on the main square.

▲▲▲**Place Ste. Cécile**—Grab a bench on the far side of place Ste. Cécile and face the church. With the church directly in front of you, the bishop's palace (along with the Toulouse-Lautrec Museum, river view, and TI) is a bit to the right. The market is a block behind you on your right. And the sleepy St. Salvy cloister is a block behind on your left.

Why the big church? At its peak, Albi was the administrative center for 465 churches. Back when tithes were essentially legally required taxes, everyone gave their 10 percent, or "*dime*" (dee-may), to the church. The local bishop was filthy rich, and with all those *dimes,* he had money to build a dandy church. In medieval times, there was no interest in making a space so people could step back and get a perspective on such a fine building. A clutter of houses snuggled right up to the church's stout walls, and only in the 19th century were things cleared away. Just in the last few years were the cars cleared out (another triumph for the European pedestrian).

Why so many bricks? Because there were no stone quarries nearby. Albi is part of a swath of red-brick towns from here to Toulouse (nicknamed "the pink city" for the way its bricks dominate that townscape). Notice on this square the buffed brick addresses next to the sluggish stucco ones. As late as the 1960s, the town's brickwork was considered low-class, and was covered by stucco. Today, the stucco is being peeled away, and Albi has that brick pride again.

▲▲▲**St. Cécile Cathedral (Cathédrale Ste. Cécile)**—When the heretical Cathars were defeated in the 13th century, this massive cathedral was the final nail in their coffin. Big and bold, it made clear who was in charge. The imposing exterior and the stunning interior drive home the message of the Catholic (read: "universal") Church in a way that would have stuck with any medieval worshipper. This place oozes power—get on board, or get run over.

## The Cathars

The Cathars were a heretical group of Christians who grew in numbers from the 11th through the 13th centuries under tolerant rule in Languedoc. They saw life as a battle between good (the spiritual) and bad (the material), and they considered material things evil and of the devil. While others called them "Cathars" (from the Greek word for "pure") or "Albigensians" (for their main city, Albi), they called themselves simply "friends of God." Cathars focused on the teachings of St. John, and recognized only baptism as a sacrament. Because they believed in reincarnation, they were vegetarians.

Travelers encounter traces of the Cathars in their Languedoc sightseeing because of the Albigensian Crusades (1209–1240s). The king of France wanted to consolidate his grip on southern France. The pope needed to make a strong point that the only acceptable Christianity was Roman style. Both found self-serving reasons to wage a genocidal war against the Cathars, who never amounted to more than 10 percent of the local population and coexisted happily with their non-Cathar neighbors. After a terrible generation of torture and mass burnings, the Cathars were wiped out. There were many thousands of victims in this tragedy (Cathar and others). The last Cathar was burned in 1321.

Today, tourists find haunting castle ruins (once Cathar strongholds) high in the Pyrénées, and eat hearty *salade Cathar*.

**Cost and Hours:** Free, daily June–Sept 9:00–18:30, Oct–May 9:00–12:00 & 14:00–18:30. Once inside, you'll pay €1 to enter the choir (worthwhile). The treasury (a single room of reliquaries and church art) is not worth the €3 fee or the climb.

**Organ Concerts:** The cathedral hosts frequent concerts (the TI has a schedule); free organ concerts are usually offered in July and August (Sun at 16:00 and Wed at 17:00).

**⊘ Self-Guided Tour:** Visit the cathedral using the following self-guided commentary. Begin facing the...

**Exterior:** The cathedral looks less like a church and more like a fortress. In fact, it was a central feature of the town's defensive walls. Notice how high the windows are (out of stone-tossing range). The simple Gothic style was typical of this region—designed to be sensitive to the anti-materialistic tastes of the local Cathars.

The top (from the gargoyles and newer, brighter bricks upward) is a fanciful, 19th-century, Romantic-era renovation. The church was originally as plain and austere as the bishop's palace (the similar, bold brick building to the right, now housing the

Toulouse-Lautrec Museum). Imagine the church with a rooftop more like that of the bishop's palace.

• *Climb up to the extravagant Flamboyant Gothic entry porch.*

**Entry and Interior:** The entry was built about two centuries after the original plain church (1494), when concerns about Cathar sensitivities were long passé. Originally colorfully painted, it provided one fancy entry.

The interior, also far from plain, looks essentially as it did in 1500. The highlights are the vast *Last Judgment* painting (west wall, under the organ) and the ornate choir (east end).

• *Walk to the front of the altar and face the...*

**Last Judgment:** The oldest art in the church (1474), this is also the biggest Last Judgment painting from the Middle Ages. The dead come out of the ground, then line up (above) with a printed accounting of their good and bad deeds displayed in ledgers on their chests. Judgment, here we come. Those on the left (God's right) look confident and comfortable. Those on the right—the hedonists—look edgy. Get closer. Below, on both sides of the arch, are seven frames illustrating a wonderland of gruesome punishments sinners could suffer through while attempting to earn a second chance at salvation. Those who fail end up in the black clouds of Hell (upper right). But where's Jesus—the key figure in any Judgment Day painting? The missing arch in the middle (cut out in late-Renaissance times to open the way to a new chapel) once featured Christ overseeing all the action. (While no one knows for sure, a good guess at how this painting would have looked is on a small stand near the last pew back where you entered.) The assembly above (on the left) shows the heavenly hierarchy: The pope and bishops sit closest to (the missing) Jesus, then more bishops and priests—before kings—followed by monks, and then, finally, commoners like you and me.

The **altar** is the newest art in the church. But this is not the front of the church at all—you're facing west. Turn 180 degrees and head east, for Jerusalem (where medieval churches almost always point).

• *Stop first at the choir—a fancy, more intimate room within the finely carved stone "screen."*

**The Choir:** In the Middle Ages, nearly all cathedrals had ornate Gothic choir screens like this one. These highly decorated walls divided the church into a private place for clergy and a general zone for the common rabble. The screen enclosed the altar and added mystery to the Mass. In the 16th century, with the success of the Protestant movement and the Catholic Church's Counter-Reformation, choir screens were removed. (In the 20th century, the Church took things one step further, and priests actually turned and faced their parishioners.) Later, French Revolutionary atheists destroyed most of the choir screens that remained—Albi's is a rare survivor. Pay €1 to stroll around it. You'll see Old Testament figures in the Dark Ages exterior, and New Testament figures in the enlightened interior. Stepping inside, marvel at the fine limestone carving. Scan each of the 72 unique little angels. Check out the brilliant ceiling, which hasn't been touched or restored in 500 years. A bishop, impressed by the fresco technique of the Italian Renaissance, invited seven Florentine artists to do the work. Good call.

• *Exit through the side door, next to where you paid for the choir. You'll pass a WC on your way to the...*

▲▲**Toulouse-Lautrec Museum (Musée Toulouse-Lautrec)**—The Palais de la Berbie (once the fortified home of Albi's archbishop) has the world's largest collection of Henri de Toulouse-Lautrec's paintings, posters, and sketches.

**Cost and Hours:** €5, audioguide-€3; July–Aug daily 9:00–18:00; June and Sept daily 9:00–12:00 & 14:00–18:00; April–May daily 10:00–12:00 & 14:00–18:00; Oct and March Wed–Mon 10:00–12:00 & 14:00–17:30, closed Tue; Nov–Feb Wed–Mon 10:00–12:00 & 14:00–17:00, closed Tue; tel. 05 63 49 48 70, www.musee-toulouse-lautrec.com.

**Background:** Henri de Toulouse-Lautrec, born here in 1864, was crippled from youth. After he broke both legs, the lower half of his body never grew correctly. His father, once very engaged in parenting, lost interest in his son. Because of this, Henri was on the fringe of society, and therefore had an affinity for people who didn't quite fit in. He later made his mark painting the dregs of the Parisian underclass with an intimacy only made possible by a man with his life experience.

◐ **Self-Guided Tour:** The museum displays more than 1,000 of Toulouse-Lautrec's pieces chronologically. As you tour, use the dates of the paintings (always indicated) to tie Henri's evolution as an artist to his work. The museum underwent a major renovation in 2008 to create even more space, so expect changes to some of the information below.

**1870s:** First, you'll see the works of his youth *(jeunesse)* in a glass case—the impressive doodles of an 11-year-old.

**1880:** During his later, yet still pre-Paris, years, Henri lived far from any artistic action (in Albi) and could only be inspired by magazines. This was his Impressionistic stage.

**1882:** Henri moved to the big city to pursue his passion. In his early Paris works, we see his trademark shocking colors and down-and-dirty, street-life scenes emerge. Compare his art-school work and his street work: Henri augmented his classical training with vivid life experience. His subjects were from bars, brothels, and cabarets...we're not in Albi anymore. Henri was particularly fascinated by cancan dancers (whose legs moved with an agility he'd never experience), and captured them expertly.

**1880–1889:** These were his exploratory years—dabbling in any style he encountered.

**1890s:** Henri started making some money by illustrating for magazines and newspapers. Back then, the daily happy hour included brothel visits—1892 to 1894 was his prostitution period. He respected the ladies, feeling both fascination and empathy toward them. The prostitutes accepted him the way he was and let him into their world...and he sketched great portraits.

Notice the big *Au Salon de la Rue des Moulins* (1894). There are two versions: the quick sketch, then the finished studio version. With this piece, Toulouse-Lautrec arrived—no more sampling. The artist has established his unique style: colors (garish), subject matter (hidden worlds), moralism (none), oblivious to society's norms. Henri's trademark use of cardboard was simply his quick, snapshot way of working: He'd capture these slice-of-life impressions on the fly on cheap, disposable material, intending to convert them to finer canvas paintings later, in his studio. But the cardboard quickies survive as Toulouse-Lautrec masterpieces.

Toulouse-Lautrec's bread and butter were his **advertising posters,** and the room containing these posters is the museum's highlight. He was an innovative advertiser, creating simple, bold, and powerful lithographic images for printing posters. Displays show his original lithograph blocks (simply prepare the stone with a backwards image, apply ink—which sticks chemically to the black points—and print posters). Four-color posters meant creating four different blocks. The Moulin Rouge poster established his business reputation in Paris—strong symbols, bold and simple: just what, where, and when.

Toulouse-Lautrec's cane (in a glass case) gives additional insight into this tortured artistic genius. To protect him from his self-destructive lifestyle, loved ones had him locked up in a psychiatric hospital. But, with the help of this clever hollow cane, he still got his booze. Friends would drop by with hallucinogenic absinthe, his drink of choice—also popular among many other artists of the time. With these special deliveries, he'd restock his cane, which even came equipped with a fancy little glass.

In 1901, at age 37, alcoholic, paranoid, depressed, and syphilitic, Henri de Toulouse-Lautrec returned to his mother—the only woman who ever really loved him—and died in her arms. The art world didn't mourn. Obituaries, speaking for the art establishment, basically said good riddance to Toulouse-Lautrec and his ugly art. Although no one in the art world wanted Henri's pieces, thankfully his mother and best friend recognized his genius and

LANGUEDOC

saved his work. They first offered it to the Louvre, which refused. Finally, in 1922, the mayor of Albi accepted the collection and hung Toulouse-Lautrec's work here in what, for more than a century, had been a boring museum of archaeology.

• *Facing the Toulouse-Lautrec Museum, go left, leaving the courtyard and rounding the building for a good city view over the Tarn River.*

▲**Albi Town View**—Albi was situated here because of its river access to Bordeaux (which connected the town to the rest of the trading world). In medieval times, the fastest and most economical way to transport goods was down rivers like this. The lower, older bridge (pont Vieux) was first built in 1020. Prior to its construction, the weir (which you can see just beyond this first bridge) provided a series of stepping stones that enabled people to cross the river. Look at the bishop's palace. The garden below dates from the 17th century (when the palace at Versailles was inspiring people all over France to create fancy gardens). The palace itself grew from the 13th century until 1789, when the French Revolution ended the power of the bishops and the state confiscated the building. Since 1905, it's been a museum.

**St. Salvy Church and Cloister (Eglise St. Salvi et Cloître)**— While this church (the oldest in town) is nothing special, the cloister creates a delightful space. Delicate arches surround an enclosed courtyard (open all day), providing a peaceful interlude from the shoppers that fill the pedestrian streets. Notice the church wall from the courtyard. It was the only stone building in Albi in the 11th century; the taller parts, added later, are made of brick. This is just one of many appealing little courtyards hiding throughout town. In the rough-and-tumble Middle Ages, many buildings faced inward. If doors are open, you're welcome to pop into courtyards. The Hôtel Décazes (8 rue Toulouse-Lautrec, across from La Viguière restaurant) is another good example.

**Market Hall (Marché Couvert)**—Albi's quiet Art Nouveau market, just renovated, is good for picnic-gathering and people-watching (Tue–Sun until 13:00, closed Mon, 2 blocks from cathedral).

# SLEEPING

**$$$ Hostellerie du Santoine*** is Albi's oldest hotel (established in 1784), and the most comfortable and traditional place I list. Guests enter an inviting and spacious lobby that opens onto an enclosed garden. Rooms are Old World cozy with all the comforts (Db-€125, big Db-€185, suites-€185, a block above big place du Vigan at 17 rue Santoine, tel. 05 63 54 04 04, fax 05 63 47 10 47, www.saint-antoine-albi.com, courriel@hotel-saint-antoine-albi.com).

**$$$ Hôtel Chiffre*** is a safe bet, with 38 comfortable and well-appointed rooms (Db-€90–115, some with queen-size beds,

**LANGUEDOC**

## Sleep Code

**(€1 = about $1.50, country code: 33)**

**S** = Single, **D** = Double/Twin, **T** = Triple, **Q** = Quad, **b** = bathroom, **s** = shower only, * = French hotel rating system (0–4 stars). Unless otherwise noted, credit cards are accepted and English is spoken.

To help you sort easily through these listings, I've divided the rooms into three categories based on the price for a standard double room with bath:

**$$$** **Higher Priced**—Most rooms €90 or more.
**$$** **Moderately Priced**—Most rooms between €60–90.
**$** **Lower Priced**—Most rooms €60 or less.

air-con, elevator, garage-€9/day, traditional restaurant, near place du Vigan at 50 rue Séré de Rivières, tel. 05 63 48 58 48, fax 05 63 47 20 61, www.hotelchiffre.com, hotel.chiffre@yahoo.fr).

**$ Le Vieil Alby Hôtel-Restaurant**, in the heart of Albi's pedestrian area, has modern, well-maintained, non-smoking rooms, run by helpful Monsieur Sicard (Db-€48–64, Tb-€69, garage-€7/day, 25 rue Toulouse-Lautrec, tel. 05 63 54 14 69, fax 05 63 54 96 75, levieilalby@wanadoo.fr).

**$ Hôtel Lapérouse** is a work in progress, one block from the old city and a 10-minute walk to the train station. The hotel offers simple rooms; some are renovated and cheery, though I'd skip the rooms on the busy street. There's easy parking, a quiet garden, a big pool, and *très* friendly owners. Spring for a room with a balcony over the garden and pool (Sb/Db on street-€42, Sb/Db on garden-€54, Sb/Db on garden with deck-€64, Internet access and Wi-Fi, 21 place Lapérouse, tel. 05 63 54 69 22, fax 05 63 38 03 69, www.hotel-laperouse.com, hotel.laperouse@wanadoo.fr).

## EATING

Albi is filled with reasonable restaurants that serve a rich local cuisine. Be warned: "Going local" here is likely to get you *tripe* (cow intestines), *andouillette* (sausages made from pig intestines), *foie de veau* (calf liver), and *tête de veau* (calf's head). Choose a restaurant or select one of the many cafés on the lively place du Vigan. For a choice of traditional restaurants, survey the places along rue Toulouse-Lautrec (2 blocks from Hôtel St. Clair).

**La Viguière** is *the* place to go for a fine, slow meal, served in a nice interior or a pleasant courtyard. The cuisine is classic French, with a dash of local specialties tossed in. It's best to sit in the courtyard, where a wall of windows allows you to watch owner/chef Thierry and his charming wife Evelynne prepare your meal (€18, €25, and €42 *menus;* closed Wed off-season, 7 rue Toulouse-Lautrec, tel. 05 63 54 76 44).

**Le Papillon Restaurant,** a jazzy, six-table, Cathar-cool eatery under medieval stones and timbers, fuses Californian and French cuisines. It's the dream come true for two guys from California—while Michael Gabel cooks, his partner, Rick Perry, serves. Seafood is their forte, there are good vegetarian options, and the salads are tops. Reserve for both lunch and dinner (€10–15 evening *plats,* open Thu–Sat for dinner, Tue–Sat for lunch, 1 rue Toulouse-Lautrec, tel. 05 63 43 10 77).

**Le Tournesol** is a good lunch option for vegetarians, since that's all they do. The food is delicious, the setting is bright with many windows, and the service is friendly (open Fri–Sat for lunch and dinner, Tue–Thu for lunch only, closed Sun–Mon, 11 rue de l'Ort en Salvy, tel. 05 63 38 38 14).

## TRANSPORTATION CONNECTIONS

You'll connect to just about any destination through Toulouse.

**From Albi by Train to: Toulouse** (11/day, 70 min), **Carcassonne** (9/day, 2.5 hrs, change in Toulouse), **Sarlat** (2/day, 4.5 hrs with changes in Toulouse, Agen, and Le Buisson; or 3/day, 6–7 hrs with changes possible in Brive-la-Gaillarde and Toulouse, then bus from Souillac), **Paris** (6/day, 6–7.5 hrs, change in Toulouse, also night train).

---

# Near Albi

## West of Albi
▲**Route of the Bastides**—The hilly terrain north of Albi was tailor-made for medieval villages to organize around for defensive purposes. Here, scores of fortified villages *(bastides)* spill over hilltops, above rivers, and between wheatfields, creating a worthwhile detour for drivers. These planned communities were the medieval product of community efforts organized by local religious or military leaders. Most *bastides* were built during the Hundred Years' War (see sidebar on page 201) to establish a foothold for French or British rule in this hotly contested region, as well as to provide stability to benefit trade. Unlike other French hill towns, *bastides* were not the product of a safe haven provided by a castle. Instead, they were a premeditated effort by a community to collectively construct houses as a planned defensive unit, *sans* castle.

Connect these *bastides* as a day trip from Albi, or as you drive

**Near Albi**

between Albi and the Dordogne. For a good loop route from Albi, cross the 22 Août 1944 bridge and follow signs to *Cordes-sur-Ciel* (allow 30 min). The view of Cordes as you approach is memorable, but that's as close as I'd get to this often-packed town (see description later in this section). From Cordes, follow signs to *Saint-Antonin-Noble-Val*, an appealing, flat "hill town" on the river, with few tourists. Then pass vertical little Penne, Bruniquel (signed from Saint-Antonin-Noble-Val), Larroque, Puycelci (my favorite—see below), and finally, Castelnau-de-Montmiral (with a fine main square), before returning to Albi. Each of these places is worth exploring if you have the time.

For a scenic route north to the Dordogne that includes many of the same *bastides*, leave Albi on N-88 to Gaillac, then follow D-964 to Castelnau-de-Montmiral, Puycelci, and on to Bruniquel. Then either head directly to Caussade (tricky turnoff shortly after leaving Bruniquel) and Cahors, or continue scenically north on D-115 to Saint-Antonin-Noble-Val through the Gorges de l'Aveyron. From Saint-Antonin, follow D-5 and D-926 to Caussade, then take N-20 to Cahors.

▲**Puycelci**—This town crowns a bluff surrounded only by green (15 minutes north of Gaillac). Drive to the top, where you'll find easy parking and an unspoiled, level village with a couple of cafés, one "serious" restaurant, a small grocery, a few *chambres d'hôte*, and one sharp little hotel. The park-like ramparts come with picnic benches and grand vistas—a good place to listen to the birds and the wind. As you wander, consider the recent history of an ancient town like this. In 1900, 2,000 people lived here with neither running water nor electricity. Then things changed. Half of all French men were casualties of World War I, and Puycelci didn't escape—as the monument (by the parking lot) attests. In 1968, when the village was down to three families, running water replaced the venerable cisterns, and things started looking up. Today, while still with almost no commercial activity, the town has a stable population of 100, all marveling at how the value of their land has skyrocketed.

Stroll through the village, starting at the parking lot. Enter the village, passing the recommended Puycelci Roc Café. At the opposite side of town, a rampart walk circles you counterclockwise back to the parking lot, where an orientation table explains what's in the distance. As you stroll this sleepy little place, look for photos of the town at the turn of the 20th century.

***Eating and Sleeping in Puycelci:*** **Puycelci Roc Café,** at the parking lot, has good café fare, a warm interior, and pleasant outdoor tables (daily for dinner, Sat–Wed for lunch, tel. 05 63 33 13 67).

A night in Puycelci is my idea of a vacation. **$$ L'Ancienne Auberge** is the place to eat and sleep, with eight surprisingly smart and comfortable rooms, a country-elegant restaurant, a cozy *bistrot* with a fireplace you could walk into, and two outdoor patios (*plats* from €13, *menus* from €24). Owner/chef Dorothy moved here from New Jersey many years ago and is eager to share her cuisine and her passion for this region (Db-€70–95, air-con, place de l'Eglise, tel. 05 63 33 65 90, fax 05 63 33 21 12, www.ancienne-auberge.com, caddack@aol.com).

**$$ Delphine de Laveleye Chambres** is another fine choice, with two cozy rooms around a small garden and pool, and a three-room *gîte* (Db-€60–75, Tb-€125, *gîte*-€600/week, tel. 05 63 33 13 65, www.chezdelphine.com, delphine@chezdelphine.com).

**Bruniquel**—This overlooked, *très* photogenic, but less-tended village will test your thighs as you climb the lanes upward to the château (€2.50, April–Sept daily 10:00–12:30 & 14:00–18:00, closed Oct–March). Several cheap but adequately comfortable rooms can be found at the mellow **$ L'Etape du Château** (Db-€50, Tb-€60, Qb-€70, tel. 05 63 67 25 00, www.etapeduchateau.com, etapeduchateau@orange.fr). You can also get good food here (€10 salads, €12–17 *plats, menus* from €17).

**Cordes-sur-Ciel**—It's hard to resist this brilliantly situated hill town just 15 miles north of Albi, but I would. Enjoy the fantastic view on the road from Albi, but go no closer. Cordes, once an important Cathar base, has slipped over the boutique-filled edge to the point where it's hard to find the medieval town, and it's jammed on weekends and in the summer.

## East of Albi

Two hours east of Albi lies a hauntingly beautiful region unknown to most Americans. Mountains, rivers, and Brigadoon-like villages conspire to give the adventurous nature lover a true experience of *la France profonde.*

**Gorges du Tarn**—Adventure-lovers can canoe, hike, or drive the beautiful Tarn River Gorge by heading east from Albi to Millau, then following the gorge all the way to St. Enimie. Roads are slow but spectacular.

The best base for canoeing is from tiny La Malène (on the way to St. Enimie, 25 miles northeast of Millau). In La Malène, **Company Canoë 2000** rents what you need to run the mellow river (down the path to the right of bridge, tel. 04 66 48 57 71); the 8- or 11-kilometer trips (about 5 or 7 miles) have the best views. Take your lunch and picnic along the way. If you'd rather not paddle a canoe, you can take a Batelier boat (leaves from bridge, seats 5–6 people, ask for a boatman who speaks a leetle English).

*Sleeping in La Malène:* Stay at the simple but comfortable **$ Auberge de l'Embarcadère** (Db-€45, Tb-€52, tel. 04 66 48 51 03, fax 04 66 48 58 94) or in the country-luxurious **$$$ Manoir de Montesquiou,** run entirely by one family. Dad manages the hotel, Mom is the head chef, the three sisters serve your meals, and son-in-law Greg runs the bar (Db-€68–106, suites fit for a queen-€131–139, extra bed-€16, you'll be expected to dine at its great restaurant, *menus* from €24, tel. 04 66 48 51 12, fax 04 66 48 50 47, www.manoir-montesquiou.com, montesquiou@demeures -de-lozere.com).

**Millau Bridge (Viaduc de Millau)**—Completed in 2005, the sleek and futuristic 1.5-mile-long suspension bridge, which shoots across the Tarn River Valley, is the world's highest at 885 feet. A modern-day Pont du Gard (see page 544), the Millau Bridge was built as a critical link in the A-75 autoroute, which connects Paris with the Mediterranean and Barcelona. A quarter-million tons of concrete were used to set the supporting pillars, with the tallest rising 1,125 feet—taller than the Eiffel Tower. It was built by the same construction company that erected the Eiffel Tower in 1889. The bridge's British architect, Lord Norman Foster, also designed London's egg-shaped City Hall, as well as Berlin's equally glassy Reichstag Parliament dome (bridge always open; current car toll about €6, or €7.50 in July–Aug; bridge is 70 miles northeast of Albi on A-75).

# Carcassonne

Medieval Carcassonne is a 13th-century world of towers, turrets, and cobblestones. It's Europe's ultimate walled fortress city—stuffed with too many tourists. At 10:00, salespeople stand at the doors of their main-street shops, a gauntlet of tacky temptations poised and ready for their daily ration of customers. But early, late, or off-season, a quieter Carcassonne is an evocative playground for any medievalist. Forget midday...spend the night.

Locals like to believe that Carcassonne got its name this way: 1,200 years ago, Charlemagne and his troops besieged this fortress-town (then called La Cité) for several years. A cunning townsperson named Madame Carcas saved the town. Just as food was running out, she fed the last few bits of grain to the last pig and tossed him over the wall. Splat. Charlemagne's bored and frustrated forces, amazed that the town still had enough food to throw fat party pigs over the wall, decided they would never succeed in starving the people out. They ended the siege, and the city was saved. Madame Carcas *sonne*-d (sounded) the long-awaited victory bells, and La Cité had a new name: Carcas-sonne. It's a cute story...but historians suspect that Carcassonne is a Frenchified version of the town's original name (Carcas).

As a teenager on my first visit to Carcassonne, I wrote this in my journal: "Before me lies Carcassonne, the perfect medieval city. Like a fish that everyone thought was extinct, somehow Europe's greatest Romanesque fortress city has survived the centuries. I was supposed to be gone yesterday, but here I sit imprisoned by choice—curled in a cranny on top of the wall. The wind blows away the sounds of today, and my imagination 'medievals' me. The moat is one foot over and 100 feet down. Small plants and moss upholster my throne." Let this place make you a kid on a rampart.

# ORIENTATION

Contemporary Carcassonne is neatly divided into two cities: The magnificent La Cité (the fortified old city, with 200 full-time residents taking care of lots more tourists) and the lively Ville Basse (modern lower city). Two bridges, the busy pont Neuf and the traffic-free pont Vieux, both with great views, connect the two parts.

## Tourist Information

Carcassonne's TI has three locations. The main TI, in **Ville Basse,** is useful only if you're walking to La Cité (28 rue de Verdun, tel. 04 68 10 24 30). A far more convenient branch is in **La Cité,** to your right as you enter the main gate (Narbonne Gate—or porte Narbonnaise, tel. 04 68 10 25 35). Both TIs have the same hours (daily July–Aug 9:00–19:00, until 18:00 April–June and Sept–Oct, until 17:00 Nov–March). The tower across from La Cité's TI has information on walking tours of the walls, a good book selection, and a fine wooden model of La Cité (notice that no house rises above the fortified walls). If you're arriving by train, the most convenient TI is the small kiosk across the canal from the **train station**—though its opening times are limited and vary off-season (generally daily July–Aug 9:00–19:00, April–June and Sept–Oct 14:00–18:00, closed Nov–March, tel. 04 68 25 94 81).

At any of these TI locations, pick up the map of La Cité, which includes a fine self-guided tour, and ask about festivals (www.carcassonne-tourisme.com).

From mid-June through mid-September, the TI offers a few **excursion vans or buses** each week to less-famous Cathar castles (see "Near Carcassonne," later in this chapter; €35/half-day, €50/day, check with TI for dates and times).

## Arrival in Carcassonne

**By Train:** The train station (which has no baggage storage) is located in the Ville Basse, a 30-minute walk from La Cité. You have three options for reaching La Cité: taxi, shuttle bus (in high season), or on foot.

**Taxis** charge €8 for the short but worthwhile trip to La Cité, but cannot enter the city walls (taxis wait in front of the train station, or find the taxi stand one block across the canal).

A **shuttle bus** *(navette)* whisks you from boulevard Omer Sarraut (a block in front of the train station) to La Cité (€1.50,

4/hr, mid-June–Sept daily 9:30–19:30, no bus off-season, ticket good for round-trip—so hang onto it).

The 30-minute **walk** to La Cité is pleasant, though it ends with a good uphill climb. Walk straight out of the station, cross the canal, then the busy ring road, and keep straight on rue Clémenceau for about seven blocks. After place Carnot (frequent markets), turn left on rue de Verdun, walk three blocks, and turn right on the vast square Gambetta. Angle across the square, turn right after Hôtel Ibis, then cross pont Vieux (great views). Signs will guide you up rue Trivalle and rue Nadaud to La Cité.

**By Car:** Follow signs to *Centre-Ville,* then *La Cité.* You'll come to a large parking lot at the entry to the walled city (first 30 min free, €4.50/3–6 hrs, €8/24 hrs) and a drawbridge at the Narbonne Gate, at the walled city's entrance. If staying inside the walls, you can park for free in the castle moat (facing the Narbonne Gate, turn left, then right after the small cemetery). You must show your reservation (verbal assurances won't do; hôtels le Donjon and de la Cité will pick you up—see "Sleeping," page 481). You are allowed to drive into the city after 18:00. Theft is common—leave nothing in your car at night.

## Helpful Hints

**Market Days:** Pleasing place Carnot in Ville Basse hosts a nontouristy open market (Tue, Thu, and Sat mornings until 13:00; Sat is the biggest).

**Summer Festivals:** Carcassonne becomes colorfully medieval during many special events each July and August. Highlights are the *spectacle équestre* (jousting matches) and July 14 (Bastille Day) fireworks. The TI has details.

**Internet Access:** Most hotels have Internet access. In La Cité, find **Cité Sandwich,** near the Château Comtal entrance (daily 9:00–20:00, later in high season, place du Château—see map on page 477). In the Ville Basse, **Alerte Rouge** is best, with lots of computers, free Wi-Fi, and a small bar (Mon–Sat 10:00–23:00, closed Sun, 73 rue de Verdun—see map on page 475, tel. 04 68 25 20 39).

**Laundry:** Try **Laverie Express** (daily 8:00–22:00, 5 square Gambetta at Hôtel Ibis; from La Cité, cross pont Vieux and turn right).

**Bike Rental: Evasion 2 Roues** has bikes to go (closed Sun–Mon, 85 allée d'Iéna, tel. 04 68 11 90 40). The TI can recommend other bike rentals. Canalside rides are a fun and level way to spin your wheels.

## Carcassonne Overview

**TO ALBI VIA D-118**

**CANAL DU MIDI**

**TRAIN STATION**

**ANTOINE MARTY**

**BLVD. O. SARRAUT**

**ALLE D'IENA**

**VILLE BASSE**
(NEW CITY)

**PLACE CARNOT**

**RUE VERDUN**

**BLVD. JAURES**

**RUE CLEM.**

**SQUARE GAMBETTA**

**PONT NEUF**
(NEW BRIDGE)

**PLAY-GROUND**

**AVE LECLERC**

**BLVD. BARBES**

**BLVD. ROUMENS**

**TO CATHAR CASTLES VIA D-118**

**PONT VIEUX**
(OLD BRIDGE)

**R. DE LA BARBACANE**

**TRIVALLE**

**TO N-113**

**TO AUTO-ROUTE A-61**

**AUDE RIVER**

**LA CITE**
(OLD CITY)
See detail map

**VIEW**    **(B) BUS STOP**

1/4 MILE

.5 KM

DCH

1. Hôtel des Trois Couronnes & Restaurant le Richepin
2. Hôtel du Soleil le Terminus
3. Hôtel Astoria
4. Hertz Car Rentals
5. Avis Car Rental
6. Launderette
7. Internet Café
8. Bike Rental
9. Canal Cruise

**Taxi:** Call 04 68 71 50 50 or 04 68 71 36 36.

**Car Rental:** The **Avis** agency is at 52 rue A. Martyet (from train station, cross canal, then turn left on boulevard Omer Sarraut), but with a prior reservation, you can pick up your car at the train station (tel. 04 68 25 05 84). **Hertz** is two blocks straight out of the station (turn right on boulevard Omer Sarraut to #33, tel. 04 68 25 41 26, closed 12:00–14:00).

LANGUEDOC

# SELF-GUIDED WALK

## ▲▲▲Carcassonne's Medieval Walls and La Cité

While the tourists shuffle up the main street, this walk introduces you to the city with history and wonder, rather than tour groups and plastic swords. We'll sneak into the town on the other side of the wall...through the back door.

Start outside La Cité's main entrance, the Narbonne Gate (porte Narbonnaise). You're welcomed by a contemporary-looking bust of Madame Carcas—which is actually modeled after a 16th-century original of the town's legendary first lady (for her story, see page 472).

• *Cross the bridge toward the...*

**Narbonne Gate:** Pause at the drawbridge and survey this immense fortification. When forces from northern France finally conquered Carcassonne, it was a strategic prize. Not taking any chances, they evicted the residents, whom they allowed to settle in the lower town (Ville Basse)—as long as they stayed across the river. (While called "new," this lower town actually dates from the 13th century.) La Cité remained a French military garrison until the 18th century.

The drawbridge was made crooked to slow any attackers' rush to the main gate. (It's just as effective today with tourists.)

• *After crossing the drawbridge, lose the crowds and follow the cobbled path to the left and uphill, between the walls. (The only reason to continue straight is to visit the TI—just inside the next gate to the right, with fine Gothic vaulting and a medieval cistern.)*

*At the first short set of stairs, climb to the outer-wall walkway and linger while facing the inner walls.*

**Wall View:** These massive walls—nearly two miles around, with 52 towers—defended an important site near the intersection of north–south and east–west trade routes. People have occupied this spot since Neolithic times. The Romans built Carcassonne's first wall, upon which the bigger medieval wall was constructed. Identify the ancient Roman bits by finding the smaller rocks mixed with narrow stripes of red bricks (and no arrow slits). The outer wall was not built until the 1300s.

Look over the wall and down at the moat below. Like most medieval moats, it was never filled with water (or even alligators). A ditch like this—which was originally even deeper—effectively stopped attacking forces from rolling up against the wall in their mobile towers and spilling into the city. Another enemy tactic was to "undermine" (tunnel underneath) the wall, causing a section to cave in. Notice the small, square holes at foot level along the ramparts. Wooden extensions of the rampart walkways (which we'll see later at the castle) once plugged into these holes, so that

# Carcassonne's La Cité

100 YARDS

100 METERS      DCH

→ WALKING TOUR ROUTE

**P** PARKING

❶ Hôtel de la Cité & Barbacane Restaurant

❷ Best Western Hôtel le Donjon

❸ Chambres l'Echappée Belle

❹ Auberge des Lices Rooms & Rest.

❺ Chambres le Grand Puits

❻ Auberge de Jeunesse & Comptoir des Vins et Terroirs

❼ Hôtels du Château & le Montmorency

❽ To Hôtel Mercure

❾ Hôtel Espace Cité

❿ Notre-Dame de l'Abbaye Rooms

⓫ Au Comte Roger Restaurant

⓬ Le Tour Davejean Restaurant

⓭ L'Auberge du Grand Puits Rest.

⓮ Le St. Jean Restaurant

⓯ Le Bar à Vins Café & Jazz Bar

⓰ Tiny Grocery

⓱ Gérard Sion Galerie (Photos)

⓲ Hotel Parking Entrance (Daytime Only)

⓳ Internet Café

townsfolk could drop nasty and sticky things on anyone tunneling in. In peacetime, the area between the two walls was used for medieval tournaments, jousting practice, and markets.

During La Cité's Golden Age, the 1100s, independent rulers with open minds allowed Jews and Cathars to live and prosper within the walls, while troubadours wrote poems of ideal love. This liberal attitude made for a rich intellectual life, but also proved to be La Cité's downfall. The Crusades aimed to rid France of the dangerous Cathar movement (and their liberal sympathizers), which led to Carcassonne's defeat and eventual incorporation into the kingdom of France.

The walls of this majestic fortress were partially reconstructed in 1855 as part of a program to restore France's important monuments. The tidy crenellations and the pointy tower roofs are generally 19th-century. As you continue your wall walk to higher elevations, the lack of guardrails is striking. This would never happen in the US; in France, if you fall, it's your own fault (so be careful). Note the lights embedded in the walls. This fortress, like most important French monuments, is beautifully illuminated every night (for directions to a good nighttime view, see "Night Wall Walk to Pont Vieux," page 480).

• *You could keep working your way around the walls, and finish with the five Roman towers just before you return to the starting point. Walking the entire circle between the inner and outer gate is a terrific 20–30-minute stroll (and fantastic after dark).*

*But for this tour, we'll stop at the first entrance possible into La Cité, the...*

**Inner Wall Gate:** The wall has the same four gates it had in Roman times. Before entering, notice the squat tower on the outer wall—this was a "barbican" (placed opposite each inner gate for extra protection). Barbicans were always semicircular—open on the inside to expose anyone who breached the outer defenses. Invading today is far easier than in the good old days. Make note of the holes in the barbican for supporting a wood catwalk (you'll see a good example soon). As you leave the square gate room to enter the town, look up, and you'll see slots and holes (used for dumping things on intruders), a slot for the portcullis (the big iron grate), and the frame for a heavy wooden door.

Once safely inside, look back up at the inner wall tower to view *beaucoup* narrow arrow slits—even if enemies got this far, they still weren't home free.

• *Opposite the tower is...*

**St. Nazaire Church (Basilique St. Nazaire):** This was a cathedral until the 18th century, when the bishop moved to the lower town. Today, due to the depopulation of the basically dead-except-for-tourism Cité, it's not even a functioning parish church. Notice the Romanesque arches of the nave and the delicately vaulted Gothic arches over the altar and transepts. After its successful conquest of this region in the 13th-century Albigensian Crusades, France set out to destroy all the Romanesque churches and replace them with Gothic ones—symbolically asserting its northern rule with this more northern style of church. With the start of the Hundred Years' War in 1337, the expensive demolition was abandoned. Today, the Romanesque remainder survives, and the destroyed section has been rebuilt Gothic, which makes it one of the best examples of Gothic architecture in southern France. When the lights are off (as they often are), the interior—lit only by candles and 14th-century stained glass—is evocatively medieval (daily 9:00–11:45 & 14:00–18:30, until 17:00 in winter).

**Hôtel de la Cité:** Located across from St. Nazaire Church, this beyond-posh hotel sits where the Bishop's Palace did 700 years ago. Today, it's a worthwhile detour to see how the privileged few travel. You're free to wander, so find the library-cozy bar, then the rear garden, and turn right for super wall views that you can't see from anywhere else.

• *From here, follow the main road (rue St. Louis) several blocks, merge right, then find a small castle-view terrace on your left.*

**Château Comtal:** Carcassonne's third layer of defense, while originally built in 1125, was completely redesigned in later reconstructions. From this fine viewpoint, you can see the wooden rampart extensions that once encircled the entire city wall. (Notice the empty peg holes to the left of the bridge.) When *Robin Hood: Prince of Thieves,* starring Kevin Costner, was filmed here in 1990, the entire city was turned into a film set. Locals enjoyed playing bit parts and seeing their château labeled "Nottingham Castle" in the fanciful film.

The castle is open to the public and provides a predictable medieval interior, a modest museum, and a romp on the inner wall and up a tower (€8, daily April–Sept 10:00–18:30, Oct–March 9:30–17:00, last entry 45 min before closing, audioguide for two-€6, tel. 04 68 11 75 87).

• *Fifty yards away, opposite the entrance to the castle, is...*

**Place du Château:** This busy little square sports a modest statue remembering the man who saved the city from deterioration and neglect in the 19th century. The bronze model circling the base of the statue shows Carcassonne's walls as they looked before the 1855 reconstruction by Eugène Viollet-le-Duc.

• *Facing the château entry, place du Grand Puits lies a block to your right. It's named for the oldest of Carcassonne's 22 wells that served the city in the Middle Ages. Behind you, the main drag leads down to the Narbonne Gate, where you began this walk.*

# SIGHTS AND ACTIVITIES

**▲▲▲Night Wall Walk to Pont Vieux**—Save post-dinner energy for a don't-miss walk around the same walls you visited today (great dinner picnic sites as well). The effect at night is mesmerizing: The embedded lights become torches and unfamiliar voices, the enemy. End at the pont Vieux for a floodlit fantasy, and you can do no better. The best route is a partial circumnavigation clockwise between the walls. Start at the Narbonne Gate, and follow my self-guided walk (described earlier) to the Inner Wall Gate. Don't enter through this gate; instead, continue your walk between the walls around La Cité. In about five minutes, you'll pass through a narrow passage behind Château Comtal, and come to a ramp leading down; look for a hard left at the bottom of a cobbled decline, just before the path rises back up. This ramp leads all the way down to rue de la Barbacanne, where you'll turn right to reach the pont Vieux and exceptional views of floodlit Carcassonne. Return from the pont Vieux the same way you came, then complete your clockwise walk between the walls back to the Narbonne Gate. For an easier return climb, cross the bridge and continue straight on rue Trivalle, then veer right up rue Nadaud and track the walls.

**Comptoir des Vins et Terroirs**—Slip into this attractive wine bar to sample a good selection of local wines. Prices are reasonable, and you'll need something to sip on the ramparts tonight (hours vary, generally about 10:00–13:00 & 14:00–21:00, often later in summer, across from Auberge de Jeunesse hostel at 3 rue du Comte Roger, tel. 04 68 26 44 76).

**Gérard Sion Galerie**—Duck into this impressive photo gallery before selecting which Cathar castles you want to visit (brilliant shots of many monuments in Languedoc, generally open daily 10:00–19:00, just up from place Marcou at 27 rue du Plô).

**Canal du Midi**—Completed in 1681, this sleepy, 155-mile canal connects France's Mediterranean and Atlantic coasts and runs right by the train station in Carcassonne. Before railways, Canal du Midi was clogged with commercial traffic—today, it entertains only pleasure craft. Look for the slow-moving hotel barges strewn with tanned and well-fed vacationers. Small boats that ferry tourists along the canal leave from in front of the train station (€8/1.5 hrs, €10/2.5 hrs, 2–3/day, April–Oct, closed Mon, tel. 06 07 74 04 57). A better way to experience the canal is on a relaxed bike ride along the level towpath (for bike rental, see "Helpful Hints," earlier in this chapter).

# NIGHTLIFE

For relief from all the medieval kitsch, savor a drink in four-star library-meets-bar ambience at the **Hôtel de la Cité** bar (€8 for a glass of wine or beer, place de l'Eglise). To taste the liveliest square, with loads of tourists and strolling musicians, sip a drink or nibble a dessert on place Marcou. To be a medieval poet, share a bottle of wine in your own private niche somewhere remote on the ramparts. **Le Bar à Vins** offers jazz, good wines by the glass (€2), and a young crowd enjoying a garden in the moonshadow of the wall...without any tourists (daily, 6 rue du Plô; described under "Eating," later in this section). For a fine before- or after-dinner drink with floodlit wall views, stop by the recommended **Hotel du Château's** broad terrace, below the porte Narbonnaise (2 rue Camille Saint-Saëns).

# SLEEPING

**(€1 = about $1.50, country code: 33)**
Sleep within or near the old walls, in La Cité. Hôtel du Terminus and Hôtel Astoria have lodgings near the train station. In the summer, when La Cité is jammed with tourists, think of sleeping in quieter Caunes-Minervois (see "Near Carcassonne, in Caunes-Minervois," later in this section). Top prices listed are for July and August, when the town is packed. At other times of the year, prices drop and there are generally plenty of rooms.

## In Carcassonne's La Cité

Two pricey hotels, three good B&Bs, and an excellent youth hostel offer a full range of rooms inside the walls.

**$$$ Hôtel de la Cité**** offers 61 rooms with deluxe everything in a beautiful building next to St. Nazaire Church. Peaceful gardens, a swimming pool, royal public spaces, an elegant restaurant, and reliable luxury are yours—for a price (Db-€420–570, suites-€600–1,400, extra adult-€60, breakfast-€28, 20 percent winter discount, air-con, garage-€21/day, place de l'Eglise, tel. 04 68 71 98 71, fax 04 68 71 50 15, www.hoteldelacite.com, reservations@hoteldelacite.com).

**$$$ Best Western Hôtel le Donjon**** offers 75 overpriced and smallish—but well-appointed—rooms, a polished lobby, and a great location inside the walls. Rooms are split between three different buildings in La Cité. Most prefer the main building (standard Sb/Db-€120–160, Db suite-€250–350, standard Tb-€145–185, Tb suite-€165–220, Qb-€185–240, air-con, elevator, pay Wi-Fi, private parking-€10, 2 rue Comte Roger, tel. 04 68 11 23 00, fax 04 68 25 06 60, www.hotel-donjon.fr, info@bestwestern-donjon.com).

**$$ Chambres l'Echappée Belle** is an oasis of peace in the center of La Cité, complete with small garden. Four traditional, comfy rooms have wood floors, queen-size beds, jet showers, and air-conditioning. Serious owners Bruce and Johanna sold their B&B in Scotland and moved here for a change of pace (Db-€75–125, May–Sept, 2 nights minimum, includes breakfast, credit cards OK, a few blocks past youth hostel at 5 rue Raymond Roger Trencavel, tel. 04 68 25 33 40, www.lechappeebelle.co.uk, info@lechappeebelle.co.uk).

**$$ Auberge des Lices** hides two lovely rooms above its restaurant, with tile floors, high ceilings, exposed beams, and stone walls (Db-€80, larger Db-€140, €20/extra person up to five, 3 rue Raymond Roger Trencavel, tel. 04 68 72 34 07, fax 04 68 72 61 55, www.blasco.fr, leslices@blasco.fr).

**$ Chambres le Grand Puits,** across from Hôtel des Remparts, is a splendid value. It has one cute double room and two cavernous apartment-like rooms that could sleep five, with kitchenette, private terrace, and nice personal touches. Inquire in the small boutique, and say *bonjour* to happy-go-lucky Nicole (Sb/Db-€50–65, Tb-€60–75, Qb-€80–90, includes self-serve breakfast, cash only, 8 place du Grand Puits, tel. & fax 04 68 25 16 67, http://legrandpuits.free.fr, Nicole.trucco@club-internet.fr).

**$ The Auberge de Jeunesse** youth hostel is big, clean, and well-run, with an outdoor garden courtyard, self-service kitchen, TV room, bar, washer/dryer, bike rental, Internet access, and a welcoming ambience that begins with jolly Michele at the reception. If you ever wanted to bunk down in a hostel, do it here—all ages are welcome. Only summer is tight; reserve ahead. Non-members pay €3 extra per night (bunk in 4- to 6-bed dorm-€17; a few double rooms available for same price—first come, first served; includes sheets and breakfast, open all day, rue du Vicomte Trencavel, tel. 04 68 25 23 16, fax 04 68 71 14 84, www.fuaj.org or www.hihostels.com, carcassonne@fuaj.org).

## Just Outside La Cité

Sleeping just outside La Cité offers the best of both worlds: quick access to the ramparts, less claustrophobic surroundings, and easy parking.

At **$$$ Hôtel du Château\*\*\*** and **$$ Hôtel le Montmorency\*\***, Cécile, Stéphane, Nicole, dog Opus, and lazy cat Minet are perfect hosts and offer the best hotel value in Carcassonne, with very comfortable rooms knocking at the door of La Cité's drawbridge. The two hotels are separated by a small street and have different personalities, but share a reception lobby, stylish swimming pool with views to the ramparts (heated all year), whirlpool tub, airy terrace tables with fine views, and free Internet access and Wi-Fi. The *très* smart **Hôtel du Château** occupies the main building, selling four-star comfort at three-star prices, with 15 over-the-top gorgeous rooms (standard Db-€140–160, superior Db-€180–200, Db with terrace on pool-€200–220, €20 less in winter, 2 rue Camille Saint-Saëns, tel. 04 68 11 38 38, fax 04 68 11 38 39, www.hotelduchateau.net, contact@hotelduchateau.net). The **Hôtel le Montmorency** annex, behind Hôtel du Château, is no slouch, with 20 tight but well-designed rooms, Provençal decor, firm beds, and air-conditioning (Db-€75–95, Tb-€115, 2 rue Camille Saint-Saëns, tel. 04 68 11 96 70, fax 04 68 11 96 79, www .lemontmorency.com, le.montmorency@wanadoo.fr). Private parking for both hotels is €6.

**$$$ Hôtel Mercure**\*\*\* hides a block behind the Hôtel le Montmorency, a five-minute walk to La Cité. It rents 61 snug-but-comfy, air-conditioned rooms and has a refreshing garden, a good-sized pool, big elevators, and a warm bar-lounge. A few rooms have views of La Cité (small Db-€135, moderate Db-€150, big Db-€185, Tb-€200, pay Internet access and Wi-Fi, includes parking, 18 rue Camille Saint-Saëns, tel. 04 68 11 92 82, fax 04 68 71 11 45, h1622@accor.com).

**$$$ Hôtel des Trois Couronnes**\*\*\* offers 40 good rooms with terrific views up to La Cité (and 40 non-view rooms that you don't want), all trapped in an ugly concrete shell. It's a 15-minute walk below La Cité, and 20 minutes on foot from the train station (Db with view-€110–120, air-con, elevator, pay Wi-Fi, indoor pool with views, garage-€8, 2 rue des Trois Couronnes—see map on page 475, tel. 04 68 25 36 10, fax 04 68 25 92 92, www.hotel -destroiscouronnes.com, hotel3couronnes@wanadoo.fr). The reasonably priced restaurant also has good views.

**$$ Hôtel Espace Cité**\*\*, two blocks downhill from Hôtel le Montmorency, is a good value (though a bit soulless, particularly compared to the next listing). With 48 small, modern, shiny rooms, this place is well-run and handy for drivers (Db-€62–78, Tb-€78–93, Qb-€93–110, air-con, free Internet access and Wi-Fi, includes parking, 132 rue Trivalle, tel. 04 68 25 24 24, fax 04 68 25 17 17, www.hotelespacecite.fr, infos@hotelespacecite.fr).

**$ At Notre-Dame de l'Abbaye,** you can sleep like a monk. A 10-minute walk below La Cité, this abbey rents spotless and sim-ple-yet-cheery rooms—some with good views to the ramparts—that surround a quiet cloister. Lots of school groups stay here, but they sleep in the other wing (D-€45, Db with tiny bathroom-€60, Tb/Qb-€80, includes breakfast, credit cards OK, €9 dinners, 20-min walk from train station at 103 rue Trivalle, tel. 04 68 25 16 65, fax 04 68 11 47 01, ndaa@wanadoo.fr).

## Near the Train Station

**$$$ Hôtel du Soleil le Terminus\*\*\***, across from the train station, is turn-of-the-century faded-grand. The lobby reminds me of a train-station waiting hall. Rooms are big and comfortable, with high ceilings (standard Db-€90–115, superior Db-€110–135, Db-suite-€140–160, air-con, elevator, pay Internet access and Wi-Fi, basement pool, secure parking-€9, lots of groups, 2 avenue Maréchal Joffre, tel. 04 68 25 25 00, fax 04 68 72 53 09, www.hotels-du-soleil.com, reservation@hotels-du-soleil.com). They have six bikes to rent to guests.

**$ Hôtel Astoria\*\*** offers the cheapest hotel beds that I list in town, divided between a main hotel and an annex across the street. The shiny tiled rooms are modern and clean, with foam mattresses, and the owners are helpful. Call ahead—it's popular. From the train station, walk across the canal, turn left, and go two blocks (D-€34–40, Ds-€42–50, Db-€44–60, Tb/Qb-€64–74, parking-€6, 18 rue Tourtel, tel. 04 68 25 31 38, fax 04 68 71 34 14, www.astoriacarcassonne.com, hotel-astoria@wanadoo.fr).

## Near Carcassonne, in Caunes-Minervois

To experience unspoiled, tranquil Languedoc, sleep surrounded by vineyards in the authentic-feeling village of Caunes-Minervois. Comfortably nestled in the foothills of the Montagne Noire, Caunes-Minervois—a 25-minute drive from Carcassonne—offers an eighth-century abbey (complete with Internet access), two cafés, a good pizzeria, a few wineries, and very few tourists. My two recommendations sit side-by-side in the heart of the village, and their owners are eager to help you explore their region.

**$$ Hôtel d'Alibert\*\***, in a 15th-century home with ambience galore, has a mix of nicely renovated and Old World traditional rooms. It's managed with a relaxed *je ne sais quoi* by Frédéric "call me Fredo" Dalibert (small Db-€52, standard Db-€72, huge Db-€82, extra person-€10, place de la Mairie, tel. 04 68 78 00 54, frederic.dalibert@wanadoo.fr). Eat lunch or dinner in his terrific restaurant (closed Sun–Mon).

**$$ L'Ancienne Boulangerie** is a relaxed place with thoughtfully appointed rooms and a breakfast terrace that will slow your pulse. Retired Irishmen Garreth and Roy run the joint while their wives work back home—these are two happy blokes (Sb-€50, Db-€65, lofty family room-€70/couple and €10/child, includes breakfast, rue St. Genes, tel. 04 68 78 01 32, www.ancienne boulangerie.com, ancienne.boulangerie@free.fr).

# EATING

## In La Cité

For a social dinner, take your pick from a food circus of basic eateries on a leafy courtyard—often with strolling musicians in the summer—on lively **place Marcou** (just inside the front gate and up to the left). While cassoulet (described under "Cuisine Scene" on page 458) is the traditional must, big salads can provide a light yet rich alternative.

Hôtel de la Cité's **Barbacane Restaurant** owns Carcassonne's only Michelin star (€80 *menus*; see "Sleeping," earlier in this section).

**Au Comte Roger**'s quiet elegance seems out of place in this touristy town. For half the price of the Barbacane, you can celebrate a special occasion memorably. Chef Roger specializes in fresh products and Mediterranean cuisine. Ask for a table in the courtyard or dine inside with modern art, but book ahead (€40 *menus*, closed Sun–Mon, 14 rue St. Louis, tel. 04 68 11 93 40). Don't confuse this place with a part of the Hôtel le Donjon, called Le Comte Roger.

**Auberge des Lices,** a shy yet popular place hidden down a quiet lane, has a feminine interior, a peaceful courtyard, and the best balance of price and quality for traditional cuisine I found (€17 and €24 *menus*, closed Tue–Wed, 3 rue Raymond Roger Trencavel, tel. 04 68 72 34 07).

**Le Tour Davejean**—surprisingly, not named for its owners (or a musical duo), but for the tower it hides—is a brown, wicker-warm, intimate escape. Diners climb one level to enjoy a decent meal at fair prices, either inside or on a quiet terrace (*menus* from €16, €2.50 wines by the glass, good cassoulet and desserts, closed Tue–Wed, 32 rue du Plô, tel. 04 68 71 60 63).

**L'Auberge du Grand Puits** is cheap and easy. You'll sit (best outside) in a flimsy chair to eat a copious meal served by a mellow Jerome (many choices, €16 *menu* is enough for two, open daily, cool music, 1 place des Grands Puits, tel. 04 68 71 27 88).

**Le St. Jean** has the best château-view tables on a quiet square away from the fray. It attracts a loyal following with its well-presented bistro fare at reasonable prices (€16–24 *menus*, daily, place St. Jean, tel. 04 68 47 42 43).

**Restaurant le Richepin,** in Hôtel des Trois Couronnes (described under "Sleeping," earlier in this section), gives you a panorama of Carcassonne—from the top floor of a concrete hotel (*menus* from €24, open daily, 2 rue des Trois Couronnes).

**Le Bar à Vins,** popular with the twentysomething set, is tucked away in a pleasant garden just inside the wall, but away from the crowds. It serves an enticing selection of open wines and €12 tapas—open-faced sandwiches, along with various appetizers (€2 glasses of wine, mid-June–mid-Sept daily 10:00–2:00 in the morning, closes earlier off-season, 6 rue du Plô, tel. 04 68 47 38 38).

**Picnics:** Basic supplies can be gathered at the shops along the main drag (generally open until at least 19:30). For your beggar's banquet, picnic on the city walls. For fast, cheap, hot food, look for places on the main drag that have quiche and pizza to go.

## TRANSPORTATION CONNECTIONS

**From Carcassonne by Train to: Collioure** (9/day, 2 hrs, most require change in Narbonne), **Sarlat** (2/day, 4.5 hrs with changes in Toulouse, Agen, and Le Buisson; or 3/day, 6–7 hrs with changes possible in Brive-la-Gaillarde and Toulouse, then bus from Souillac), **Arles** (10/day, 3 hrs, most with transfer in Narbonne or Nîmes), **Nice** (6/day, 6–9 hrs, fastest via change in Marseille), **Paris'** Gare Montparnasse (14/day, 6.5 hrs, most require changes in Toulouse or Montpellier, direct trains take 8 hrs, night train also available), **Toulouse** (hourly, 1 hr), **Barcelona** (3/day, 5–7 hrs, change in Narbonne and Port Bou, the border town).

# Near Carcassonne

The land around Carcassonne is carpeted with vineyards and littered with romantically ruined castles, ancient abbeys, and photogenic villages. The castle remains of Peyrepertuse and Quéribus make terrific stops between Carcassonne and Collioure (allow 1.5–2 hrs from Carcassonne on narrow, winding roads). The gorge-sculpted village of Minerve, 45 minutes east of Carcassonne, works well for Provence-bound travelers.

**Getting There:** While public transportation is hopeless, taxis capable of seating six cost €150–200 for a day-long excursion (taxi tel. 04 68 71 50 50). The Carcassonne TI provides occasional excursion buses to these places (call for dates and times, tel. 04 68 10 25 35 or 04 68 10 24 30; see "Tourist Information" on page 473).

## ▲▲▲Châteaux of Hautes Corbières

About two hours south of Carcassonne, in the scenic foothills of the Pyrénées, lies a series of surreal, mountain-capping castle ruins. Like a Maginot Line of the 13th century, these sky-high castles were strategically located between France and the Spanish kingdom of Roussillon. As you can see by flipping through the picture books in Carcassonne tourist shops, these castles' crumbled ruins are an impressive contrast to the restored walls of La Cité. Bring a good map (lots of tiny roads) and sturdy walking shoes—prepare for a vigorous climb, and be wary of slick stones.

The most spectacular is the château of **Peyrepertuse**, where

## Near Carcassonne

AUTOROUTE (TOLL)
OTHER ROADS
CASTLES

the ruins seem to grow right out from the narrow splinter of cliff. The views are sensational—you can almost reach out and touch Spain. Let your imagination soar, but watch your step as you try to reconstruct this eagle's nest (€5, daily July–Aug 9:00–20:30, April–June and Sept 10:00–19:00, Oct 10:00–18:00, Nov–March 10:00–17:00, tel. 04 68 45 40 55 or 06 71 58 63 36, www.chateau-peyrepertuse.com). Canyon-lovers will enjoy the detour to the nearby and narrow **Gorges de Galamus,** just north of St. Paul de Fenouillet. Closer to D-117, impressive **Quéribus** towers above the road and requires a steep hike. It's famous as the last Cathar castle to fall and was left useless after 1659, when the border between France and Spain was moved farther south into the high Pyrénées (same cost and hours as Peyrepertuse).

## Near Caunes-Minervois

The next two Cathar sights tie in well with a visit to Caunes-Minervois (described under "Sleeping—Near Carcassonne, in Caunes-Minervois," page 484), and provide an easy excursion from Carcassonne, offering you a taste of this area's appealing countryside.

## Châteaux of Lastours

Ten miles north of Carcassonne, these four ruined castles cap a barren hilltop and give drivers a handy (if less dramatic) look at the region's Cathar castles. From Carcassonne, follow signs to *Mazamet*, then *Conques-sur-Orbiel*, then *Lastours*. In Lastours, you can hike to the castle or drive to a viewpoint.

Hikers park at the lot as they enter the village, walk 10 minutes upriver to the glass entry (look for *Accueil* signs), then walk 20 minutes uphill to the castles (allow at least an hour for a reasonable tour). The castles, which once surrounded a fortified village, date from the 11th century. The village welcomed Cathars (becoming a bishop's seat at one point) but paid for this "tolerance" with destruction by French troops in 1227. Everyone should make the short drive to the belvedere for a smashing panorama over the castles (€5 for access to castles and belvedere viewpoint, €2 for belvedere viewpoint only, July–Aug daily 9:00–20:00, April–June and Sept daily 10:00–18:00, Oct daily 10:00–17:00, Nov–March Sat–Sun 10:00–17:00 only. An idyllic lunch awaits near the lower entry at **Le Moulin,** where a small bakery has arranged a few tables serenely overlooking the river (good quiche, sandwiches, drinks, closed Thu).

## ▲Minerve

A one-time Cathar hideout, the spectacular village of Minerve is sculpted out of a deep canyon that provided a natural defense.

Strong as it was, it couldn't keep out the Pope's armies, and the village was razed during the vicious Albigensian Crusades. The view from the small parking lot alone (€2) justifies the detour. Cross the bridge on foot, then wander into the village to its upper end and a ruined tower. A worthwhile path leads

across from the tower, around the village, and down to the river (watch your step as you descend); you can re-enter the village from the riverbed at its lower end.

Minerve has two cool cafés, one hotel, a nifty little bookshop, a few wine shops, and a smattering of art galleries. You'll also find two small museums: a prehistory museum and the compact **Hurepel de Minerve,** with models from the Cathar era that effectively describe this terrible time (€2.50, excellent English explanations, interesting for kids, daily April–Oct 10:00–12:45 &

14:00–18:00, rue des Martyrs, tel. 04 68 91 12 26).

*Sleeping and Eating in Minerve:* Stay here and melt into southern France (almost literally, if it's summer). **$ Relais Chantovent's** unpretentious and spotless rooms are designed for those who came to get away from it all—no phones and no TV, but generous quiet (Db-€43–55, tel. 04 68 91 14 18, fax 04 68 91 81 99, www.relaischantovent-minerve.fr). Its sharp restaurant deserves your business and is popular, so reserve ahead (*menus* from €20, closed Sun–Mon). The **Café de la Place** provides the perfect break and has a pool for anyone's use (€3, tel. 05 68 91 22 94).

**Getting There:** Minerve is between Carcassonne and Béziers, nine miles northeast of Olonzac and 40 minutes by car from Carcassonne. It's a good stop between Provence and Carcassonne.

**Wine-Tasting:** In the mood to sample some wine? Stop at **Domaine de Pech d'André** and visit my friends Monsieur and Madame Remaury. They offer a good selection and an exquisite setting in which to sample the local product (coming from Minerve, it's just past Azillanet, look for *Domaine* signs on your left, tel. 04 68 91 22 66, a leetle English spoken).

# Collioure

Surrounded by less-appealing resorts, lovely Collioure is blessed with a privileged climate and a romantic setting. By Mediterranean standards, this seaside village should be overrun—it has everything. Like an ice-cream shop, Collioure offers 31 flavors of pastel houses and six petite, scooped-out, pebbled beaches sprinkled with visitors. This sweet scene, capped by a winking lighthouse, sits under a once-mighty castle in the shade of the Pyrénées. Evenings are best in Collioure—as the sky darkens, yellow lamps reflect warm pastels and deep blues.

Just 15 miles from the Spanish border, Collioure (Cotlliure in Catalan) shares a common history and independent attitude with its Catalan siblings across the border. Happily French yet proudly Catalan, it flies the yellow-and-red flag of Catalunya, displays street names in French and Catalan, and supports business names with *el* and *els,* rather than *le* and *les.* Sixty years ago, most villagers spoke Catalan, and today the language is enjoying a resurgence as Collioure rediscovers its roots.

Come here to unwind and regroup. Even with its crowds of vacationers in peak season (July and Aug are jammed), Collioure is what many look for when they head to the Riviera—a sunny, relaxing splash in the Mediterranean.

## Planning Your Time

Check your ambition at the station. Enjoy a slow coffee on *le Med*, lose yourself in the old town's streets, compare the *gelati* shops on rue Vauban, and snuggle into a pebble-sand beach (waterproof shoes are helpful). And if you have a car, don't miss a drive into the hills above Collioure (described below).

# ORIENTATION

Most of Collioure's shopping, sights, and hotels are in the old town, across the drainage channel from Château Royal. There are good views of the old town from across the bay near the recommended Hôtel Boramar, and brilliant views from the hills above.

## Tourist Information

The TI hides behind the main beachfront cafés at 5 place du 18 Juin (July–Aug Mon–Sat 9:00–20:00, Sun 10:00–18:00; April–June and Sept Mon–Sat 9:00–12:00 & 14:00–19:00, closed Sun; Oct–March Tue–Sat 9:00–12:00 & 14:00–19:00, closed Sun–Mon; tel. 04 68 82 15 47, www.collioure.com).

## Arrival in Collioure

**By Train:** Walk out of the station (which has no baggage storage), turn right, and follow the road downhill for about 10 minutes until you see Hôtel Fregate (directions to hotels are listed from this reference point—see "Sleeping," later in this section). The station ticket office has irregular hours; if they're open, pick up a schedule for any Spain side-trips or for your next destination.

**By Car:** Collioure is 16 miles south of Perpignan. Take the *Perpignan–Sud Sortie* exit from the autoroute and follow signs to *Argelès-sur-Mer* (also called simply *Argelès*), then *Collioure*. Parking is tricky, and almost impossible in summer—arrive early or late. Follow *Collioure Centre-Ville* signs, turn left onto rue de la République when you see the *Garage Renault* sign, and look for any available spots. There's a big pay lot (Parking Glacis) off rue de la République (stay right at the bottom of rue de la République and pass through a metered lot, about €1.50/hour, €9/24 hours). Ask your hotelier for parking suggestions, and take everything of value out of the car.

# Collioure

TO
MADELOC TOWER,
AUTOROUTE &
CARCASSONNE

TRAIN STN.

100 YARDS
100 METERS

**P** PARKING
**↘** VIEW

TO
OVERFLOW
PARKING

ROUTE ARGE-LES

PLACE LECLERC

AVE. MAILLOL

RUE REPUBLIQUE

AVE. MIRADOU

ONE WAY

AVE. DE GAULLE

Parking
Glacis

Post

ONE WAY

WC

AVE. PASTEUR

AVE. PELLETAN

AVE. FERRY

AVE. MIRADOU

CHATEAU
ROYAL

WC

KIDS
PLAY
AREA

RUE DEMOCRATIE

Boules

TRAIL
TO
WINDMILL
& ST. ELME

PORT
D'AVALL
BEACH
(SANDY)

JAUBAN

BLVD. BORAMAR

ARAGO

NORD
BEACH
(ROCKY)

RUE JEAN BART

MUSEUM

BORAMAR
BEACH
(ROCKY)

NOTRE-DAME
DES ANGES

ST. VINCENT
BEACH
(SANDY)

CHAPELLE
ST.
VINCENT

LA
BALETTE
BEACH
(QUIET)

MEDITERRANEAN
SEA

DCH

TO BANYULS
& SPAIN

1 Hôtel Casa Pairal
2 Hôtel les Templiers
3 Hôtel Princes de Catalogne
4 Peroneille's Chambres
5 Hôtel les Caranques
6 Hôtel Boramar
7 Café Copacabana
8 Le Tremail Restaurant
9 La Marinade Restaurant

10 Brasserie au Casot
11 La Neptune Restaurant
12 Côté Terroir Wine Shop
13 Launderettes (2)
14 Promenade sur Mer Cruises
15 Garage Renault (Car Rental)
16 Café Sola (Internet)
17 Espace Fauve

## Helpful Hints

**Market Days:** Markets are held on Wednesday and Sunday mornings on place Maréchal Leclerc, across from Hôtel Fregate.

**Internet Access:** Try the lighthearted **Café Sola,** next to the recommended Hôtel Casa Pairal (daily, about 7:00–21:00 or later, free Wi-Fi if you buy a drink, or use their computers, 2 avenue de la République, tel. 04 68 82 55 02).

**Laundry: Laverie 3L** will do your laundry while you do your relaxing (daily July–Aug 9:00–19:00, otherwise 9:00–12:00 & 15:00–18:00, at roundabout at 28 rue de la République, tel. 04 68 98 04 17; the sign tells you to drop laundry next door at Immosud). There's also a **self-serve launderette** a block away (daily 7:00–21:00, across from bike shop, near 10 rue de Gaulle).

**Taxi:** Call 04 68 82 27 80 or 04 68 82 09 30.

**Car Rental: National** is pricey but central, located in Garage Renault, opposite the launderette on rue de la République (allow €90/day with 250 kilometers, tel. 04 68 82 08 34).

## SIGHTS AND ACTIVITIES

There's no important sight here except what lies on the beach and the views over Collioure. Indulge in a long seaside lunch, inspect the colorful art galleries, catch up on your postcards, and maybe take a hike. Don't be surprised to see French Marines playing commando in their rafts; Collioure's bay caters to more than just sun-loving tourists.

**View from the Beach**—Walk out to the jetty's end, past the church and past the little chapel, and find a seat above the beach. Collioure has been a popular place since long before your visit. For more than 2,500 years, people have fought to control its enviable position on the Mediterranean at the foot of the Pyrénées. The mountains that rise behind Collioure provide a natural defense, while its port gives it a commercial edge, making Collioure a simply irresistible target. A string of forts defended Collioure's landlocked side. To the left, you can see the still-standing Fort St. Elme (built by powerful Spanish king Charles V, the same guy who built El Escorial near Madrid). The 2,100-foot-high observation tower of Madeloc rises high above, front and center, and scattered ruins crown several other hilltops. To the far right, the 18th-century *citadelle*, Fort Mirador, is now home to a French Marine base. Back to the left, that ancient windmill (1344) was originally used for grain; today it grinds out olive oil.

Collioure's medieval town gathers between its church and royal château, sandwiched defensively and spiritually between the two. The town was batted back and forth between the French and Spanish for centuries. Locals just wanted to be left alone—as Catalans—and most still do (notice the yellow-and-red Catalan flag flying above the château). It was Spanish for nearly 400 years before becoming definitively French in 1659 (*merci* to Louis XIV). After years of neglect, Collioure was rediscovered by artists drawn to its pastel houses and lovely setting. Henri Matisse, André Derain, Pablo Picasso, Georges Braque, Raoul Dufy, and Marc Chagall all parked their brushes here at one time or another. You're likely to recognize Collioure in paintings in many museums across Europe.

**Château Royal (Royal Castle)**—The 800-year-old castle, built over Roman ruins, served as home over the years to Majorcan kings, Crusaders, Dominican monks, and Louis XIV (who had the final say on the appearance we see now). Today, it serves tourists, offering great rampart walks, views, and mildly interesting local history exhibits (€4, daily June–Sept 10:00–18:00, Oct–May 9:00–17:00, last entry 45 min before closing, tel. 04 68 82 06 43).

**Notre-Dame des Anges (Our Lady of the Angels Church)**—This waterfront church is worth a gander (daily 9:00–12:00 & 14:00–18:00). Find a pew and listen to the waves to calm your soul. Supporting a guiding light (in more than one way), the church's foundations are built into the sea, and its one-of-a-kind lighthouse–bell tower helped sailors return home safely. The highlight is its over-the-top golden altar, unusual in France but typical of Catalan churches across the border. Drop €1 in the box to the left of the altar: lights, cameras, reaction—ooh la la!

**Path of Fauvism (Chemin du Fauvisme)**—As you stroll Collioure's lanes, you'll occasionally see prints hanging on the walls. You're on the "Chemin du Fauvisme," where you'll find 20 copies of Derain's and Matisse's works, inspired by their stays in Collioure in 1905. The **Espace Fauve** office, across from the château at the foot of the footbridge, sells well-done booklets that feature postcard-size images of the works and identify where the copies are mounted in Collioure (June–Sept daily 9:30–12:00 & 15:00–19:00, Oct–May closed Mon and weekend mornings, quai de l'Amirauté, tel. 04 68 98 07 16). As with Arles and Vincent van Gogh, there are no original paintings by Derain or Matisse here for the public to enjoy. However, the museum in Céret has a good collection (page 495), as does the recommended Hôtel les Templiers (page 496).

**Beaches (Plages)**—You'll usually find the best sand-to-stone ratio at plage St. Vincent and at plage de Port d'Avall (sporadically open paddleboat/kayak rental–€11/hr). The tiny plage de la Balette is quietest, with views of Collioure.

**Wine-Tasting**—Collioure and the surrounding area produce well-respected wines, and many shops offer informal tastings of the sweet Banyuls and Collioure reds and rosés. Try **Côté Terroir,** with a fine selection from many wineries and good prices (daily 10:00–13:00 & 15:00–20:00, next to Hôtel Fregate at 6 place Maréchal Leclerc, tel. 08 73 76 00 12).

**Cruise**—Mildly interesting **Promenades sur Mer** boat excursions provide views of Collioure from the Mediterranean as they cruise toward Spain and back (€8, 60-min tour, 3–5/day, Easter–Sept weather permitting, leaves from breakwater near château, commentary in French only, tel. 04 68 81 43 88).

## Hikes

The three views described below offer different perspectives of this splendid area.

▲**Stone Windmill**—Stone steps lead 10 minutes up behind Collioure's museum to a 13th-century windmill with magnificent views that are positively peachy at sunset. Find the museum behind Hôtel Triton, walk through its stony backyard, and follow the paved path marked with yellow dashes. Bring your own beverage.

▲**Hike to Fort St. Elme**—This vertical hike (one hour each way) is best done early or late (there's no shade) and is worth the sweat, even if you don't make it to the top (trail starts from windmill described above). You can't miss the square castle lurking high above Collioure. The view from the top is grand, though the privately owned castle is not open to the public.

Cheaters can do it by car. Drive to Port Vendres, then find the small sign marked *Fort St. Elme* on your right just before leaving the port (the road also leads to a supermarket). Continue on the small road that leads up from behind the train station.

▲▲▲**Drive/Hike Through Vineyards to Madeloc Tower (Tour de Madeloc)**—Check your vertigo at the hotel, fasten your seatbelt, and take this drive-and-hike combination high above Collioure. The narrow road, hairpin turns, and absence of guardrails only add to the experience, as Collioure shrinks to Lego-size and the clouds become your neighbors. (Expect some small changes from the route described below, as road improvements are planned.)

Leave Collioure, head toward Perpignan, and look for signs reading *Tour de Madeloc* at the roundabout above the town. Climb through impossibly steep and rocky terraced vineyards, following *Tour* and *Balcon de Madeloc* signs. After about 20 minutes, you'll come to a fork in the road with a paved path (marked by a "no entry" symbol that applies to cars) and a road leading downhill (the sign identifies it as *La Route des Vignobles*—The Route of the Vineyards). Park at the fork in the road, and walk 10–15 minutes up the paved path to the first ruined structure (the *Balcon*). The views everywhere are magnificent—the Pyrénées on one side, and the beach towns of Port Vendres and Collioure on the other (scenic picnic tables provided). While this satisfies most, you can continue hiking up and up the tiny road to *la Tour* (the Tower) and commune with the gods. Allow an hour at a slow yet steady pace along the splintered ridgetop, and you'll reach the eagle's-nest setting of this ancient tower, now fitted with communication devices. There's no shade, so do this hike early or late in the day. Once you're back down among mortals, you can return to Collioure following *La Route des Vignobles* to Banyuls-sur-Mer, then take coastal N-114 to Collioure and your hotel.

## Near Collioure

**Day Trip to Spain**—The 15-mile, 40-minute coastal drive via the Col de Banyuls into Spain is beautiful and well worth the countless curves, even if you don't venture past the border.

Train travelers can day-trip to Spain, either to **Barcelona** (4/day, 2.75–4.25 hrs one-way, change in Cerbère or Port Bou) or to the closer **Figueres** (3/day, 1.5 hrs one-way, transfer in Cerbère or Port Bou) and its Salvador Dalí museum (€11; July–Sept daily 9:00–20:00; June daily 9:30–18:00; Oct and March–May Tue-Sun 9:30–18:00, closed Mon; Nov–Feb Tue–Sun 10:30–18:00, closed Mon; last entry 45 minutes before closing, Spanish tel. 972-677-500, www.salvador-dali.org). Get train schedules at the station. Since Figueres is just off the autoroute, it works well for drivers, too.

**Céret**—To see the art that Collioure inspired, you'll have to drive 25 windy miles inland to this pleasing town, featuring fountains and mountains at its doorstep. Céret's claim to fame is its modern-art museum, with works by some of Collioure's more famous visitors, including Picasso, Joan Miró, Chagall, and Matisse (€5.50, daily mid-June–mid-Sept 10:00–19:00, otherwise 10:00–18:00, tel. 04 68 87 27 76). Allow 40 min to Céret by car, or take a train to nearby Perpignan and a bus from there—get details at TI.

# SLEEPING

**(€1 = about $1.50, country code: 33)**

Collioure has a fair range of hotels at favorable rates. You have two good choices for your hotel's location: central, in the old town (closer to train station); or across the bay, with views of the old town (10-min walk from the central zone, with easier parking).

## In the Old Town

Directions to the following places are given from the big Hôtel Fregate, at the edge of the old town, a 10-minute walk down from the train station. Price ranges reflect low versus high season.

**$$$ Hôtel Casa Pairal\*\*\***, opposite Hôtel Fregate and hiding down a short alley (behind Café Sola), is Mediterranean-elegant and Collioure's best splurge. Enter to the sounds of a fountain gurgling in the flowery courtyard. Reclining lounges await in the garden and by the pool. The rooms are quiet, comfortable, and tastefully designed. "Medium" rooms, on the first floor, have high ceilings and small balconies over a courtyard (small Db-€95–105, medium Db-€125–170, big Db suite with terrace-€180–210, extra bed-€25, air-con, parking-€8, impasse des Palmiers, tel. 04 68 82 05 81, fax 04 68 82 52 10, www.hotel-casa-pairal.com, contact @hotel-casa-pairal.com, reserve ahead for room and parking).

**$$ Hôtel les Templiers\*\***, in the thick of things in the old town, has wall-to-wall paintings squeezed in every available space, a perennially popular café-bar, and good-value rooms. The paintings are payments in kind and thank-yous from artists who have stayed here—find the black-and-white photo in the bar of the hotel's owner with Picasso. The rooms—some of which have views—are either new and modern, or older and characteristic (standard Db-€60–75, bigger Db-€80–105, ask about connecting family rooms, pass on the annex rooms unless they're next to main hotel block, air-con, a block toward beach from Hôtel Fregate along drainage canal at 12 quai de l'Amirauté, tel. 04 68 98 31 10, fax 04 68 98 01 24, www.hotel-templiers.com, info@hotel-templiers.com).

**$$ Hôtel Princes de Catalogne\*\*\*** offers 29 comfortable, spacious, American-style rooms. Get a room on the mountain side, or *côté montagne* (koh-tay mon-tan-yah), for maximum quiet (Db-€70–80, extra person-€12, air-con, next to Casa Pairal, rue des Palmiers, tel. 04 68 98 30 00, fax 04 68 98 30 31, www.hotel-princescatalogne.com, contact@hotel-princescatalogne.com).

**$ Monsieur and Madame Peroneille's Chambres,** on the pedestrian street two blocks past Hôtel Fregate, are the cheapest rooms in the old town. The rooms are simple, clean, and mostly spacious. The more serious Monsieur (who speaks Catalan) and bubbly Madame are both in their late 80s and have rented these rooms for more than 30 years without learning a word of English—so don't hold your breath. The rooms in the main building *(la maison principale)* are better than the cheaper rooms in the annex, but both are acceptable. Ask to see the rooftop terrace (Sb-€32, D-€42, Db-€47, Tb-€66, Qb-€70, cash only, 20 rue Pasteur, tel. 04 68 82 15 31, fax 04 68 82 35 94).

## Across the Bay

**$$ Hôtel les Caranques\*\***, a few curves toward Spain from Collioure's center, tumbles down the cliffs and showcases million-dollar sea views from each of its small, spotless, modestly decorated rooms (most with balconies beyond sliding glass doors). Enjoy the view terraces with mod plastic furniture, and the four-star breakfast-room panorama. This idyllic place, run by gentle Monsieur and Madame Sarrazin, is a steal (D-€47, Db-€73–82, most are about €75, route de Port Vendres, 30-min walk from train station, tel. 04 68 82 06 68, fax 04 68 82 00 92, www.les-caranques.com, contact@les-caranques.com). To scenically walk to Collioure's center, follow the sidewalk, then turn right down the steps just after the *Relais des Trois Mas* sign.

**$$ Hôtel Boramar**\*\*, across the bay from Collioure's center, is understated and modest, but well-maintained. Get a room with a terrace facing the sea and smile...or sleep elsewhere (Db without view-€60, Db with view-€70, Tb with view-€75, rue Jean Bart, tel. 04 68 82 07 06, www.hotel-boramar.com).

# EATING

Try the local wine and eat anything Catalan, including the fish and anchovies (hand-filleted, as no machine has ever been able to accomplish this precise task).

All of my recommended restaurants have indoor and outdoor tables, and most are in the old town (the first three are within 50 yards of each other). Your task is to decide whether you want to eat well or with a view. Several delicious *gelati* shops and a Grand Marnier crêpe stand next to the Café Copacabana fuel after-dinner strollers with the perfect last course. If you're traveling off-season, call ahead, since many restaurants here are closed December through February.

**Café Copacabana,** on the main beach (Boramar), offers big salads and a few seafood dishes in its sandy café. Skip their sidewalk-bound restaurant (which has a bigger selection but smaller view) and find a red sway-back chair beachside. The quality is good enough, considering the view, and it's family-friendly—kids can play on the beach while you dine (daily mid-March–mid-Dec, plage Boramar, tel. 04 68 82 06 74, best at sunset).

**Le Tremail** is *the* place to go for contemporary seafood and Catalan specialties served outside or in. It's a small, popular place one block from the bay, where rue Arago and rue Mailly meet. Reserve ahead if you can (€23–35 *menus,* open daily, 16 bis rue Mailly, tel. 04 68 82 16 10).

**La Marinade,** across from the TI, is a consistently good bet for seafood served in a lively outdoor setting (€22–28 *menus,* daily, 14 place du 18 Juin, tel. 04 68 82 09 76).

**Brasserie au Casot** owns the best setting away from the crowds, past the church on plage St. Vincent, and serves salads and *plats* with views for a fair price. Matisse would dig the decor

(June–Sept daily 11:00–20:00 weather permitting, lunch only Oct and May, closed on Thu in winter, plage St. Vincent, tel. 04 68 22 42 46).

**La Neptune,** across the bay, dishes up top seafood and views of Collioure to discerning diners. Dress up a bit, cross the bay, and ask for a table with a view (*menus* from €40, closed Tue–Wed, 9 route de Port Vendres, tel. 04 68 82 02 27).

Small places sell a variety of meals to go (*à emporter;* ah em-pohr-tay) for budget-minded romantics wanting to dine on the bay.

For post-dinner fun, head to one of the bayfront cafés on plage Boramar, or try the recommended **Hôtel les Templiers** and get down with the locals (daily, 12 quai de l'Amirauté, tel. 04 68 98 31 10).

# TRANSPORTATION CONNECTIONS

**From Collioure by Train to: Carcassonne** (9/day, 2 hrs, most require change in Narbonne), **Paris** (5/day, 6 hrs, changes in Perpignan or Montpellier and Lyon, then TGV to Gare Montparnasse, one direct train to Gare d'Austerlitz in 10 hrs, plus a handy night train), **Barcelona,** Spain (4/day, 2.75–4.25 hrs, change in Cerbère or Port Bou), **Figueres,** Spain (3/day, 1.5 hrs, transfer in Cerbère or Port Bou), **Avignon/Arles** (7/day, 3.5 hrs, many transfer points possible). Consider handy night trains to Paris, key Italian destinations, and Geneva, Switzerland. The train station's ticket office closes at 17:45 (tel. 04 68 82 05 89).

# PROVENCE

This magnificent region is shaped like a giant wedge of quiche. From its sunburned crust, fanning out along the Mediterranean coast from Nîmes to Nice, it stretches north along the Rhône Valley to Orange. The Romans were here in force and left many ruins—some of the best anywhere. Seven popes, artists such as Vincent van Gogh and Paul Cézanne, and author Peter Mayle all enjoyed their years in Provence. This destination features a splendid recipe of arid climate (except for occasional vicious winds, known as the mistral), oceans of vineyards, dramatic scenery, captivating cities, and adorable hill-capping villages.

Explore the ghost town that is ancient Les Baux and see France's greatest Roman ruin, the Pont du Gard. Spend your starry, starry nights where Van Gogh did, in Arles. Uncover its Roman past, then find the linger-longer squares and café corners that inspired Vincent. Youthful but classy Avignon bustles in the shadow of its brooding Palace of the Popes. It's a short hop from Arles or Avignon into the splendid scenery and villages of the Côtes du Rhône and Luberon regions that make Provence so popular today.

## Planning Your Time

Make Arles or Avignon your sightseeing base, particularly if you have no car. Arles has a blue-collar quality and good-value hotels, while Avignon (three times larger than Arles) feels sophisticated and offers more nightlife and shopping. Italophiles prefer smaller Arles, while poodles pick urban Avignon.

To measure the pulse of Provence, spend at least one night in a smaller town. Vaison la Romaine is ideal for those heading to/from the north, and Isle-sur-la-Sorgue is centrally located between Avignon and the Luberon. Most destinations are accessible by public transit, though bus service can be sketchy.

You'll want a full day for sightseeing in Arles (best on Wed or Sat, when the morning market rages), a half-day for Avignon, and a day or two for the villages and sights in the countryside.

## Getting Around Provence

**By Car:** The region is made-to-order for a car. The yellow Michelin Local maps #332 and #340 are a godsend. Avignon (pop. 100,000) is a headache for drivers; Arles (pop. 35,000) is easier. Be wary of thieves: Park only in well-monitored spaces and leave nothing valuable in your car. If you're heading north from Provence, consider a three-hour detour through the spectacular Ardèche Gorges (see page 571).

**By Train or Bus:** Travelers relying on public transportation might find their choices limited. Public transit is good between cities and decent to some towns, but marginal at best to the villages.

Frequent trains link Avignon and Arles (about 20 min between each). Orange is easy from Avignon by train. Buses connect smaller towns (including Les Baux in July–Aug, which otherwise can be reached only by taxi or tour).

Isle-sur-la-Sorgue offers the most accessible small-town experience (an easy hop by train or bus from Avignon). The Pont du Gard—and, to a lesser extent, Vaison la Romaine and some Côtes du Rhône villages—are also connected by bus from Avignon.

While a tour of the villages of the Côtes du Rhône or Luberon is best on your own by car, excellent minivan tours and basic bus excursions are available (TIs in Arles and Avignon have information on bus excursions to regional sights that are hard to reach *sans* car; see "Tours of Provence," next).

## Tours of Provence

**Wine Safari**—Dutchman Mike Rijken runs a one-man show, taking travelers through the region he adopted 20 years ago. Mike came to France to train as a chef, later became a wine steward, and has now found his calling as a driver/guide. His English is fluent, and while his focus is wine and wine villages, Mike knows the region thoroughly and is a good teacher of its history (€55/half-day, €100/day, priced per person; tel. 04 90 35 59 21, mobile 06 19 29 50 81, www.winesafari.net, mikeswinesafari@wanadoo.fr).

**Imagine Tours**—Unlike most tour operators, this is a non-profit organization with a focus on cultural excursions. It offers personalized tours allowing visitors to discover the "true heart of Provence." The itineraries adapt to your interests, and the volunteer guides will meet you at your hotel or the departure point of your choice

**Provence**

(€150/half-day, €275/day, prices are for up to 4 people, tel. & fax 04 90 24 84 26, mobile 06 89 22 19 87, www.imagine-tours.net).

**Wine Uncovered**—Passionate Englishman (is that an oxymoron?) Oliver Hickman takes small groups on focused tours of selected wineries in the villages near Vaison la Romaine. Oliver is serious about French wine, knows his subject matter inside and out, and wants to help you learn. He offers in-depth tastings at two wineries for €40 per person (his minimum fee is €110) and full-day tours for €70 per person. If you need transportation, he can help arrange it (tel. 06 75 10 10 01, www.wine-uncovered.com, oliver.hickman @wine-uncovered.com).

**François Marcou**—For a fun and distinctly French perspective on wines of the Côtes du Rhône region, François offers different itineraries each day. He is based in Avignon and will pick up travelers at their hotel, the TI, or the train station (€75 per person for all-day wine tours that include 4–5 tastings, tel. 06 28 05 33 84, www.avignon-wine-tour.com, avignon.wine.tour @modulonet.fr).

**Visit Provence**—Based in Avignon, this company provides a variety of guided tours to most destinations covered in this book. They have eight-seat minivans and English commentary (about €60/half-day, €100/day; they'll pick you up at your hotel in Avignon). Ask about their cheaper big-bus excursions, or consider hiring a van and driver for your own private use (plan on €210/half-day, €400/day, tel. 04 90 14 70 00, check website for current destinations, www.provence-reservation.com).

## Cuisine Scene in Provence

The almost extravagant use of garlic, olive oil, herbs, and tomatoes makes Provence's cuisine France's liveliest. To sample it, order anything *à la proven-* *çale.* Among the area's spicy specialties are ratatouille (a thick mixture of vegetables in an herb-flavored tomato sauce), *brandade* (a salt cod, garlic, and cream mousse), aioli (a garlicky mayonnaise, often served atop fresh vegetables, potatoes, fish, or  whatever), tapenade (a paste of pureed olives, capers, anchovies, herbs, and sometimes tuna), *soupe au pistou* (vegetable soup with basil, garlic, and cheese), and *soupe à l'ail* (garlic soup). Look also for *riz camarguaise* (rice from the Camargue) and *taureau* (bull meat). Banon (wrapped in chestnut leaves) and Picodon (nutty taste) are the native cheeses. The region's sheep's milk cheese, Brousse, is creamy and fresh. Provence also produces some of France's great wines at relatively reasonable prices. Look for Gigondas, Sablet, Côtes du Rhône, and Côte de Provence. If you like rosé, try the Tavel. This is the place to splurge for a bottle of Châteauneuf-du-Pape.

Remember, restaurants serve only during lunch (11:30–14:00) and dinner (19:00–21:00, later in bigger cities), but some cafés serve food throughout the day.

## Le Mistral

Provence lives with its vicious mistral winds, which blow 30-60 miles per hour, about 100 days out of the year. Locals say it blows in multiples of threes: three, six, or nine days in a row. The mistral clears people off the streets and turns lively cities into ghost towns. You'll likely spend a few hours or days taking refuge—or searching for cover. The winds are strongest between 12:00 and 15:00.

When the mistral blows, it's everywhere, and you can't escape. Author Peter Mayle said it could blow the ears off a donkey (I'd include the tail). Locals say it ruins crops, shutters, and roofs (look for the stones holding tiles in place on many homes). They'll also tell you that this pernicious wind has driven many people crazy (including young Vincent van Gogh). A weak version of the wind is called a *mistralet*.

The mistral starts above the Alps and Massif Central mountains and gathers steam as it heads south, gaining momentum as it screams over the Rhône Valley (which acts like a funnel between the Alps and Pyrénées) before exhausting itself as it hits the Mediterranean. While this wind rattles shutters throughout the Riviera and Provence, it's strongest over the Rhône Valley...so Avignon, Arles, and the Côtes du Rhône villages bear its brunt. While wiping the dust from your eyes, remember the good news: The mistral brings clear skies.

## Provence Market Days

Provençal market days offer France's most colorful and tantalizing outdoor shopping. The best markets are on Monday in Cavaillon, Tuesday in Vaison la Romaine, Wednesday in St. Rémy, Thursday in Nyons, Friday in Lourmarin, Saturday in Arles, Uzès, and Apt, and, best of all, Sunday in Isle-sur-la-Sorgue. Crowds and parking problems abound at these popular events—arrive by 9:00, or, even better, sleep in the town the night before.

**Monday:** Cavaillon, Bedoin (between Vaison la Romaine and Mont Ventoux)

**Tuesday:** Vaison la Romaine, Gordes, and Lacoste

**Wednesday:** St. Rémy, Arles, Uzès, Sault, and Malaucène (near Vaison la Romaine)

**Thursday:** Nyons, Vacqueyras, Roussillon, and Isle-sur-la-Sorgue

**Friday:** Lourmarin, Carpentras, Bonnieux, and Châteauneuf-du-Pape

**Saturday:** Arles, Uzès, Apt, and Valréas (north of Vaison la Romaine)

**Sunday:** Isle-sur-la-Sorgue, Coustellet

# Arles

By helping Julius Caesar defeat Marseille, Arles (pronounced "arl") earned the imperial nod and was made an important port city. With the first bridge over the Rhône River, Arles was a key stop on the Roman road from Italy to Spain, the Via Domitia. After reigning as the seat of an important archbishop and a trading center for centuries, the city became a sleepy backwater of little importance in the 1700s. Vincent van Gogh settled here a hundred years ago, but left only a chunk of his ear (now gone). American bombers destroyed much of Arles in World War II as the townsfolk hid out in its underground Roman galleries. But today Arles thrives again, with its evocative Roman ruins, an eclectic assortment of museums, made-for-ice-cream pedestrian zones, and squares that play hide-and-seek with visitors. It's an understandably popular home base from which to explore Provence.

## ORIENTATION

Arles faces the Mediterranean, turning its back on Paris. While the town is built along the Rhône, it almost completely ignores the river. That's all for the best, since it is the part of Arles most damaged by Allied bombers in World War II (and is therefore the least appealing today).

Landmarks hide in Arles' medieval tangle of narrow, winding streets. Virtually everything is close—but first-time visitors can walk forever to get there. Hotels have good, free city maps, and Arles provides helpful street-corner signs that point you toward sights and hotels. Racing cars enjoy Arles' medieval lanes, turning sidewalks into tightropes and pedestrians into leaping targets.

### Tourist Information

The **main TI** is on the ring road boulevard des Lices, at esplanade Charles de Gaulle (April–Sept daily 9:00–18:45; Oct–March Mon–Sat 9:00–16:45, Sun 10:00–13:00; tel. 04 90 18 41 20, www.arlestourisme.com). There's also a **train station TI** (Mon–Fri 9:00–13:00 & 14:00–16:45, closed Sat–Sun). At either TI, pick up the city map, note the bus schedules (in books on the TI desks), and get English information on nearby destinations such as the Camargue wildlife area (described on page 516). Ask about "bullgames" (Provence's more humane version of bullfights—see page 514) and walking tours of Arles. They sell a €1 brochure describing several walks in Arles, including one that locates Van Gogh's "easels" (also explained on page 514). Both TIs charge €1 to reserve hotel rooms.

## Arrival in Arles

**By Train:** The train station is on the river, a 10-minute walk from the town center (baggage storage nearby—see "Helpful Hints," below). Before heading into town, get what you need at the train station TI (see above).

To reach the town center, turn left out of the train station and walk 10 minutes; or wait for the free Starlette bus (3/hr, Mon–Sat only) at the shelter across the street. Taxis generally wait out front, but if you don't see any, call the posted telephone numbers (rates are fixed, allow about €10 to any of my recommended hotels).

**By Bus:** The central Centre-Ville bus station is a few blocks below the main TI, located on the ring road at 16–24 boulevard Georges Clemenceau.

**By Car:** Arles' only parking garage is Parking des Lices, near the TI on boulevard des Lices (€7/24 hrs). Most hotels have parking nearby—ask for detailed directions (it's only €3/24 hrs at most meters). For most hotels, first follow signs to *Centre-Ville*, then *Gare SNCF* (train station). You'll come to a big roundabout (place Lamartine) with a Monoprix department store to the right. You can park for free along the city wall and find your hotel on foot; the hotels I list are no more than a 10-minute walk away (best not to park here overnight due to theft concerns and markets on Wed and Sat). Courageous drivers can plunge into the narrow streets between the two stumpy towers via rue de la Calade, and follow signs to their hotel. Again, theft is a big problem; leave nothing in your car, and trust your hotelier's advice on where to park.

## Helpful Hints

**Market Days:** The big markets are on Wednesdays and Saturdays. For all the details, see page 513.

**Meetings and Festivals:** An international photo event jams hotels in early July.

**Internet Access: Cyber Café Taxiphone** will make you feel like you've gone to Morocco (daily 10:00–22:00, 31 rue Augustin Tardieu).

**Baggage Storage and Bike Rental:** Recommended Hôtel Régence (see page 519) will store your bags for €3–5 each (7:30–22:00 mid-March–mid-Nov, closed in winter). They also rent bikes (€6/hr, €14/day, one-way rentals within Provence possible, same hours as baggage storage). Ask about their electric bikes—handy on windy days. From Arles, you can ride to Les Baux (20 miles round-trip, very steep climb) or into the Camargue (40 miles round-trip, forget it in the wind)—provided you're in great shape.

**Laundry:** There's a launderette at 12 rue Portagnel (daily 7:00–21:30, you can stay later to finish if you're already inside, English instructions).

**Car Rental: Avis** is at the train station (tel. 04 90 96 82 42), and **Europcar** and **Hertz** are downtown (2 bis avenue Victor Hugo, Europcar tel. 04 90 93 23 24, Hertz tel. 04 90 96 75 23).

**Local Guide:** Charming **Jacqueline Neujean,** an excellent guide, knows Arles and nearby sights intimately and loves her work (€90/2 hrs, tel. 04 90 98 47 51).

**English Book Exchange:** A small exchange is available at **Soleilei** ice-cream shop (see "Eating," later in this chapter).

**Language and Cooking Courses:** Food- or language-lovers enjoy classes offered by outgoing American (and Arles resident) Madeleine Vedel and her French husband, Eric. In addition to renting out rooms (see Maison d'Hôtes en Provence under "Sleeping," later in this section), they present a wide range of cooking and language-learning experiences: Pick wild asparagus, hunt mushrooms, harvest grapes at an organic winery, or make chocolate (www.cuisineprovencale.com).

**Public Pools:** Arles has three public pools (indoor and outdoor). Ask at the TI or your hotel.

**Boules:** The local "*boul*ing alley" is by the river on place Lamartine. After their afternoon naps, the old boys congregate here for a game of *pétanque*—it's fun to watch (see page 837 for details on this popular local pastime).

## Getting Around Arles

In this flat city, everything's within walking distance. Only the Ancient History Museum requires a long walk (take a taxi for €10, or a public bus for €0.80—details on page 507). The elevated riverside promenade provides Rhône views and a direct route to the Ancient History Museum (to the southwest) and the train station (to the northeast). Keep your head up for *Starry Night* memories, but eyes down for decorations by dogs with poorly trained owners.

Arles' **taxis** charge a set fee of about €10, but nothing except the Ancient History Museum is worth a taxi ride. To call a cab, dial 04 90 96 90 03.

The free **Starlette bus** circles the town (3/hr, Mon–Sat only), but is useful only for access to the train station.

## SIGHTS

The worthwhile **Monument Pass** *(le pass monuments)* covers almost all of Arles' sights (adults-€13.50, kids under 18-€12, sold at each sight except the Arlaten Folk Museum; Fondation Van

Gogh discounted, but not fully covered). The less-tempting €9 *Circuit Romain* ticket covers Arles' four Roman sights, but not the Ancient History Museum. With no pass, you'll pay €3–6 per sight. While any sight is worth a few minutes, many aren't worth the individual admission.

Start at the Ancient History Museum for a helpful overview (drivers should try to do this museum on their way into Arles), then dive into the city-center sights. Remember, many sights stop selling tickets 30–60 minutes before closing (both before lunch and at the end of the day).

## ▲▲Ancient History Museum (Musée de l'Arles et de la Provence Antiques)

Begin your town visit here—it's Roman Arles 101. Located on the site of the Roman chariot racecourse (the arc of which is built into the parking lot), this air-conditioned, all-on-one-floor museum is just west of central Arles along the river. Models and original sculptures (with almost no English translations) re-create the Roman city, making workaday life and culture easier to imagine.

**Cost, Hours, Location:** €5.50, daily April–Oct 9:00–19:00, Nov–March 10:00–17:00, presqu'île du Cirque Romain.

**Information:** Ask for the English booklet, which provides some background on the collection, and find out whether there are any free English tours (usually daily July–Sept at 17:00, 90 min). Tel. 04 90 18 88 88, www.arles-antique.cg13.fr.

**Getting There:** To reach the museum by **foot** from the city center (a 25-min walk), turn left at the river and take the riverside path to the big, modern building just past the new bridge. The **taxi** ride costs €10 (museum can call a taxi for your return). **Bus** #1 gets you within a five-minute walk (€0.80, 3/hr, daily except Sun). Catch the bus in Arles on boulevard des Lices, then get off at the Musée de l'Arles Antique stop and follow the signs (to your left as you step off the bus).

**❺Self-Guided Tour:** Find the impressive row of pagan and early-Christian sarcophagi (from the second to fifth centuries). These would have lined the Via Aurelia outside the town wall. In the early days of the Church, Jesus was often portrayed beardless and as the good shepherd, with a lamb over his shoulder (see relief at end of ramp, #41).

Next, you'll see models of every Roman structure in (and near) Arles. These are the highlight for me, as they breathe life into buildings as they looked

2,000 years ago. Find the Forum (still the center of town, though only two columns survive today); the floating bridge (over the widest, and therefore slowest, part of the river); the Arena (with its movable stadium cover, which sheltered spectators from sun or rain); and the Circus, or chariot racecourse. While long gone, the racecourse must have been like Rome's Circus Maximus in its day—its obelisk is now the centerpiece of Arles' place de la République.

Finally, check out the 3-D model of the aqueduct of Barbegal, with its 16 waterwheels and eight grain mills cascading down a nearby hillside (well worth a side-trip if you have a car).

The model of the Roman city shows that an emphasis on sports—with the Arena and huge racecourse—is not unique to modern America. It also illustrates how little Arles seems to have changed over two millennia, with warehouses still on the opposite side of the river and houses clustered around the city center.

All of the museum's statues are original, except for the greatest—the *Venus of Arles*, which Louis XIV took a liking to and had moved to Versailles. It's now in the Louvre—and, as locals say, "When it's in Paris...bye-bye." Jewelry, fine metal and glass artifacts, and well-crafted mosaic floors make it clear that Roman Arles was a city of art and culture.

## In Central Arles

Ideally, visit these sights in the order listed below. I've included some walking directions to connect the dots.

▲▲**Forum Square (Place du Forum)**—Named for the Roman forum that once stood here, this square was the political and religious center of Roman Arles. Still lively, this café-crammed square is a local watering hole and popular for a *pastis* (see "Eating," later in this section). The bistros on the square, while no place for a fine dinner, can put together a good-enough salad or *plat du jour*—and when you sprinkle on the ambience, that's €10 well spent.

At the corner of Grand Hôtel Nord-Pinus, a plaque shows how the Romans built a foundation of galleries to make the main square level. The two columns are all that survive from the upper story of the entry to the Forum. Steps leading to the entrance are buried (the Roman street level was about 20 feet below you).

The statue on the square is of **Frédéric Mistral** (1830–1914). This popular poet, who wrote in the local dialect rather than in French, was a champion of Provençal culture. After receiving the Nobel Prize in Literature in 1904, Mistral used his prize money to preserve and display the folk identity of Provence. He founded the regional folk museum (see "Arlaten Folk Museum," page 512) at a time when France was rapidly centralizing. (The local mistral wind—literally, "master"—has nothing to do with his name.)

The **bright-yellow café**—called Café Van Gogh today, but

# Arles

**Van Gogh Sights**

1. Place Lamartine
2. Starry Night Over the Rhône View Easel
3. Fondation Van Gogh
4. Place du Forum (Café Van Gogh)
5. Espace Van Gogh

**Other**

6. Europcar & Hertz Car Rentals
7. Launderette
8. Avis Car Rental & Bike Rental
9. Internet Café

PROVENCE

100 YARDS
100 METERS

← VAN GOGH WALKING TOUR
★ FORUM SQUARE
P PARKING
B BUS STOP
View

previously named Café la Nuit—is famous as the subject of one of Vincent van Gogh's most famous works in Arles. While his painting showed the café in a brilliant yellow from the glow of gas lamps, the facade was bare limestone, just like the other cafés on this square. The café's current owners have painted it to match Van Gogh's version...and to cash in on the Vincent-crazed hordes who pay too much to eat or drink here.

• *Walk a block to rue du Hôtel de Ville, turn right, and you'll find the big...*

**Republic Square (Place de la République)**—This square used to be called "place Royale"...until the French Revolution. The obelisk was the centerpiece of Arles' Roman Circus. The lions at its base are the symbol of the city, whose slogan is (roughly) "the gentle lion." Find a seat and watch the peasants—pilgrims, locals, and street musicians. There's nothing new about this scene.

• *Overlooking this square is...*

**▲▲St. Trophime Church**—Named after a third-century bishop of Arles and located on a large square, this church sports the finest Romanesque main entrance (west portal) I've seen anywhere.

Like a Roman triumphal arch, the church facade trumpets the promise of Judgment Day. The tympanum (the semicircular area above the door) is filled with Christian symbolism. Christ sits in majesty, surrounded by symbols of the four evangelists: Matthew (the winged man), Mark (the winged lion), Luke (the ox), and John (the eagle). The 12 apostles are lined up below Jesus. It's Judgment Day...some are saved and others aren't. Notice the condemned (on the right)—a chain gang doing a sad bunny-hop over the fires of hell. For them, the tune trumpeted by the three angels above Christ is not a happy one. Below the chain gang, St. Stephen is being stoned to death, with his soul leaving through his mouth and instantly being welcomed by angels. Ride the exquisite detail back to a simpler age. In an illiterate medieval world, long before the vivid images of our Technicolor time, this was a neon billboard over the town square.

There's no charge to enter the church (daily April–Sept 9:00–12:00 & 14:00–18:30, Oct–March 9:00–12:00 & 14:00–17:00). Just inside the door on the right, a handy chart locates the interior highlights and helps explain the carvings you just saw on the tympanum.

Tour the church counterclockwise. The tall, 12th-century Romanesque nave is decorated by a set of tapestries showing scenes from the life of Mary (17th-century, from French town of Aubusson). Amble around the Gothic apse. Just to the left of the high altar, check out the relic chapel—with its fine golden boxes that hold long-venerated bones of obscure saints. Farther down is a chapel built on an early-Christian sarcophagus from Roman Arles (dated about A.D. 300). The heads were lopped off during the French Revolution.

This church is a stop on the ancient pilgrimage route to Santiago de Compostela in northwest Spain. For 800 years, pilgrims on their way to Santiago have paused here...and they still do today. As you leave, notice the modern-day pilgrimages advertised on the far right near the church's entry.

PROVENCE

• *Leaving the church, turn left, then left again through a courtyard to enter the cloisters.*

The adjacent **cloisters** are interesting, with many small columns that were scavenged from the ancient Roman theater. Enjoy the sculpted capitals, the rounded 12th-century Romanesque arches, and the pointed 14th-century Gothic ones. On the second floor, you'll walk an angled rooftop designed to catch rainwater—notice the slanted gutter that channeled the water into a cistern (€3.50, daily March–Oct 9:00–18:00, Nov–Feb 10:00–17:00).

• *To get to the next sight, face the church, walk left, then take the first right on rue de la Calade.*

**Classical Theater (Théâtre Antique)**—This first-century B.C. Roman theater once seated 10,000. In the Middle Ages, it served as a convenient town quarry—precious little of the original theater survives (though considerable effort is ongoing to rebuild sections of the seating area). For more on Roman theaters, see page 749.

Walk to a center aisle and pull up a stone seat. To appreciate its original size, look to the upper-left side of the tower and find the protrusion that supported the highest of three seating levels. Today, 3,000 can attend events here. Two lonely Corinthian columns look out from the stage over the audience. The orchestra section is defined by a semicircular pattern in the stone. Stepping up onto the left side of the stage, look down to the slender channel that allowed the curtain to disappear below, like magic. Go backstage and browse through broken bits of Rome, and loop back to the entry behind the grass (€3; June–Aug daily 9:30–12:30 & 14:00–18:30; April–May and Sept Tue–Sun 9:00–12:00 & 14:00–17:30, closed Mon; Oct–March Tue–Sun 9:00–12:00 & 14:00–16:30, closed Mon). Budget travelers can peek over the fence from rue du Cloître, and see just about everything for free.

• *A block uphill is the...*

**▲▲▲Roman Arena (Amphithéâtre)**—Nearly 2,000 years ago, gladiators fought wild animals here to the delight of 20,000 screaming fans. Today, local daredevils still fight wild animals here—"bullgame" posters around the Arena advertise upcoming spectacles (see "Bullgames," under "Events in Arles," later in this section). A lengthy restoration process is well underway, giving the amphitheater an almost bleached-teeth whiteness.

In Roman times, games were free (sponsored by city bigwigs) and fans were seated by social class. The many exits allowed for rapid dispersal after the games—fights would break out among frenzied fans if they couldn't leave quickly. Through medieval times and until the early 1800s, the arches were bricked up and the stadium became a fortified town—with 200 humble homes crammed within its circular defenses. Three of the medieval towers survive (the one above the ticket booth is open and rewards those who climb it with a good view). To see two still-sealed arches—complete with cute medieval window frames—turn right as you leave, walk to the Andaluz restaurant, and look back to the second floor (€5.50, daily May–Sept 9:00–18:00, March–April and Oct 9:00–12:00 & 14:00–18:00, Nov–Feb 10:00–12:00 & 14:00–16:30).

• *Turn left out of the Arena and walk uphill to find the...*

**▲▲Fondation Van Gogh**—A refreshing stop for any art-lover, and especially interesting to Van Gogh fans, this small gallery features works by contemporary artists who pay homage to Vincent through thought-provoking interpretations of his works. Many pieces are explained in English by the artists. The black-and-white photographs (both art and shots of places that Vincent painted) complement the paintings. Unfortunately, this collection is often on the road July through September, when non–Van Gogh material is on display here (€7, €5 with Monument Pass; great collection of Van Gogh souvenirs, prints, and postcards for sale in gift shop; April–June daily 10:00–18:00; July–Sept daily 10:00–19:00; Oct–March Tue–Sun 11:00–17:00, closed Mon; facing Arena at 24 bis rond-point des Arènes, tel. 04 90 49 94 04, www.fondationvan gogh-arles.org). For more on Vincent, see the "Van Gogh in Arles" sidebar on page 514.

• *The next two sights are back across town. The Arlaten Folk Museum is close to place du Forum, and the Réattu Museum is near the river.*

**▲Arlaten Folk Museum (Musée Arlaten/Museon Arlaten)**—Built on the remains of the Roman Forum (first century A.D., see the courtyard), this museum houses the treasures of daily Provençal life. It was given to Arles by Nobel Prize winner Frédéric Mistral (see "Forum Square," earlier in this section). Mistral's vision was to give locals an appreciation of their cultural roots, presented in tableaux that unschooled villagers could understand—"a veritable poem for the ordinary people who cannot read." The museum offers a unique and intimate look at local folk culture from the 18th and 19th centuries. As it's undergoing a massive renovation, only about a quarter of the collection is on display. A visit is still worthwhile, and a well-done English handout explains the entire collection (€1; June–Aug daily 9:30–12:30 & 14:00–18:30; April–May and Sept Tue–Sun 9:00–12:00 & 14:00–17:30, closed Mon; Oct–March Tue–Sun 9:00–12:00 & 14:00–16:30, closed Mon; last entry one hour before closing, 29 rue de la République, tel. 04 90 96 08 23, www.museonarlaten.fr).

A one-way route takes you through several rooms showing old costumes, religious objects, and popular traditions, watched over by guards in traditional dress. The last room holds two dioramas, the museum's pride and joy. The first diorama shows "the great supper"—a Provençal feast served on Christmas Eve before midnight Mass. It's 1860, and everything on the table is locally produced. Traditionally, 13 sweets—for Jesus and the 12 apostles—were served. Grandma and grandpa warm themselves in front of the fireplace; grandpa pours wine on a log for good luck in the coming year. In the second display, a wealthy mom is shown with her newborn. Her friends visit with gifts that represent the four physical and moral qualities hoped for in a new baby—good as bread, full as an egg, wise as salt, and straight as a match. The cradle is fully stocked with everything needed to raise an infant in 1888.

**Réattu Museum (Musée Réattu)**—Housed in a beautiful 15th-century mansion, this mildly interesting, mostly modern art collection includes 57 Picasso drawings (some two-sided and all done in a flurry of creativity—I liked the bullfights best), a room of Henri Rousseau's Camargue watercolors, and an unfinished painting by the Neoclassical artist Jacques Réattu...but none with English explanations (€4, €2 extra for special exhibits, daily July–mid-Sept 10:00–19:00, March–June and mid-Sept–Oct 10:00–12:30 & 14:00–17:30, Nov–Feb 13:00–17:00, last entry 30 min before closing for lunch or at end of day, 10 rue du Grand Prieuré, tel. 04 90 96 37 68).

# EVENTS IN ARLES

▲▲**Wednesday and Saturday Markets**—Twice a week in the morning, Arles' ring road erupts into an open-air market of fish, flowers, produce, and you-name-it. The Wednesday market runs along boulevard Emile Combes, between place Lamartine and bis avenue Victor Hugo; the segment nearest place Lamartine is all about food, and the upper half features clothing, tablecloths, purses, and so on. On the first Wednesday of the month, it's a flea market,

## Van Gogh in Arles

*The whole future of art is to be found in the south of France.*
—Vincent van Gogh, 1888

Vincent was 35 years old when he came to Arles in 1888, and it was here that he discovered the light that would forever change him. Coming from the gray skies and flatlands of the Netherlands and Paris, he was bowled over by everything Provençal—jagged peaks, gnarled olive trees, brilliant sunflowers, and the furious wind. Van Gogh worked in a flurry in Arles, producing more paintings than at any other period in his too-brief career—more than 200 in just a few months. (The fact that locals pronounced his name "vahn-saw van gog" had nothing to do with his psychological struggles here.)

Sadly, none of Van Gogh's paintings remain in Arles—but you can still visit the places that inspired him. Around downtown Arles, you'll find about a dozen steel-and-concrete Van Gogh **"easels"** that mark places Vincent painted, including the *Café at Night* on Forum Square. Each comes with a photo of the actual painting (see photo above) and provides fans with a fun opportunity to compare the scene then and now. The TI has a €1 brochure that locates all the easels. Small stone markers with yellow accents embedded in the pavement lead to the easels. Here is a quick summary of the places that inspired a few of his most famous paintings.

Vincent arrived in Arles on February 20, 1888, to a foot of snow. He rented a small house on the north side of **place Lamartine.** The house was destroyed in 1944 by an errant, bridge-seeking bomb, but the four-story building behind it—where you see the Civette Arlesienne—still stands (find it in the painting).

with less produce. The Saturday market is along boulevard des Lices near the TI. Join in, buy flowers, try the olives, sample some wine, and swat a pickpocket. Both markets are open until 12:00.

▲▲**Bullgames (Courses Camarguaises)**—Occupy the same seats that fans have used for nearly 2,000 years, and take in Arles' most memorable experience—the *courses camarguaises* in the ancient Arena. These nonviolent "bullgames" are more sporting than bloody Spanish bullfights. The bulls of Arles (who, locals stress, "die of old age") are promoted in posters even more boldly than their human foes. In the bullgame, a ribbon *(cocarde)* is laced between the bull's horns. The *razeteur,* with a special hook, has

From place Lamartine, walk to the river (passing a new monument in honor of two American pilots killed in action during the liberation of Arles), then look toward the town to find where Vincent set his easel for this ***Starry Night over the Rhône*** painting, where stars boil above the skyline of Arles. The original bridge in the painting (see the remains on the right), along with many riverfront cafés, were destroyed in World War II. Come back at night to match his painting with today's scene. (Note: This painting is not the *Starry Night* you're thinking of, which Van Gogh painted at a hospital in nearby St. Rémy.)

Vincent—who dreamed of making Arles a magnet for fellow artists—persuaded his friend Paul Gauguin to come. At first, the two got along well. They spent days side-by-side, rendering the same subject in their two distinct styles. At night, they hit the bars and brothels. Van Gogh's well-known *Café at Night* captures the glow of an absinthe buzz at the Café du Terrace (now Café Van Gogh) on **place du Forum** (look for the easel here).

After two months together, the two artists clashed over art and personality differences. One December night, they were drinking absinthe at the café when Vincent suddenly went ballistic. He threw his glass at Gauguin. Gauguin left. Walking through place Victor Hugo, Gauguin heard footsteps behind him and turned to see Vincent coming at him, brandishing a razor. Gauguin quickly fled town. Later that night, Van Gogh sliced off his own earlobe and gave it to a prostitute.

Vincent was checked into the local hospital, today's **Espace Van Gogh** cultural center. It surrounds a garden that the artist loved (and the only flower garden that I've seen in Arles). Only the courtyard is open to the public; find the "easel" to see what Vincent painted here (free, near the Arlaten Museum on rue President Wilson).

In the spring of 1890, Vincent left Provence to be cared for by a doctor in Auvers-sur-Oise, north of Paris. On July 27, he wandered into a field and shot himself. He died two days later.

15 minutes to snare the ribbon. Local businessmen encourage a *razeteur* (dressed in white with a red cummerbund) by shouting out how much money they'll pay for the *cocarde*. If the bull pulls a good stunt, the band plays the famous "Toreador" song from *Carmen*. The following day, newspapers report on the games, including how many *Carmens* the bull earned.

Three classes of bullgames—determined by the experience of the *razeteurs*—are advertised in posters: The *course de protection* is for rookies. The *trophée de l'Avenir* comes with more experience. And the *trophée des As* features top professionals. During Easter and the fall rice harvest festival *(Féria du Riz)*, the Arena hosts actual Spanish bullfights (look for *corrida*) with outfits, swords, spikes, and the whole gory shebang. Bullgame tickets run €5–15, while bloody bullfights *(corrida)* are pricier (€12–80). Schedules change every year—ask at the TI or check online at www.arenes-arles .com (in 2008, the bullgames were every Wed at 17:00 July–Aug).

Don't pass on a chance to see *Toro Piscine*, a silly spectacle for warm summer evenings where the bull ends up in a swimming pool (uh-huh...get more details at TI). Nearby villages stage *courses camarguaises* in small wooden bullrings nearly every weekend; the TI has the latest schedule.

## Near Arles

**The Camargue**—Knocking on Arles' doorstep, this is one of the few truly "wild" areas of France, where pink flamingos, wild bulls, and the famous white horses wander freely amid rice fields, lagoons, and mosquitoes. It's a ▲▲▲ sight for nature-lovers, but uneventful for others. While possible by public transportation, it's ideal by car. The best route to follow is toward Salin de Giraud: Leave Arles on D-570 toward Stes-Maries-de-la-Mer, passing the D-36 turnoff to Salin de Giraud. Turn left on D-37 toward Salin de Giraud and follow it as it skirts the Etang de Vaccarès lagoon. The lagoon itself is off-limits, but this area has views and good opportunities to get out of the car and smell the marshes. Turn right off D-37 onto the tiny road at Villeneuve, following La Capelière and La Fiélouse. The best part of the Camargue (particularly in spring) awaits at La Digue de la Mer, about 10 scenic kilometers (6 miles) past La Capelière. A rough dirt road rising above water on both sides greets travelers; it's time to get out of your car and stroll (though you can drive on for a few miles to Phare de la Gacholle). This is a critical reproduction area for flamingos (about 5,000 offspring annually), so it's your best chance to see groups of mamas and papas up close and personal.

**Stes-Maries-de-la-Mer**—At the western end of the Camargue lies this whitewashed, Spanish-feeling seafront town with flamingos, bulls, and miles of horses on its outskirts. The place feels like a French Coney Island and is so popular that it's best avoided on weekends and during holidays. The town has little to offer except its beachfront promenade, bullring, and towering, five-belled, fortified church. Most tourists come to take a horse, jeep, or bike into the Camargue—and there's no lack of outfits ready to take you for a ride. The TIs in Arles (see page 504) and Stes-Maries-de-la-Mer have long lists (Stes-Maries-de-la-Mer TI open daily April–Sept

**Near Arls**

PROVENCE

9:00–19:00, until 20:00 in summer, Oct–March 9:00–17:00, tel. 04 90 97 82 55, www.saintesmaries.com).

## SLEEPING

### In Arles

Hotels are a great value here; many are air-conditioned, though few have elevators. The Calendal, Musée, and Régence hotels offer exceptional value.

**$$$ Hôtel le Calendal\*\*\*** is a seductive place located between the Arena and Classical Theater. You enter through a handsome

## Sleep Code

**(€1 = about $1.50, country code: 33)**
**S** = Single, **D** = Double/Twin, **T** = Triple, **Q** = Quad, **b** = bathroom, **s** = shower only, **\*** = French hotel rating system (0-4 stars). Unless otherwise noted, credit cards are accepted and English is spoken.

To help you sort easily through these listings, I've divided the rooms into three categories based on the price for a standard double room with bath:

**$$$ Higher Priced**—Most rooms €80 or more.
  **$$ Moderately Priced**—Most rooms between €55–80.
    **$ Lower Priced**—Most rooms €55 or less.

terrace into an expertly run hotel with comfy lounges and a lovely palm-shaded courtyard. Enjoy the great €11 buffet breakfast, and have lunch in the courtyard or at the inexpensive sandwich bar (daily 12:00–15:00). There's a children's play area, and a new pool and "spa" with a Jacuzzi and a Turkish bath—and they even have my Provence video on DVD in the lobby. The comfortable rooms come in all shapes and sizes (smallest Db-€54, standard Db-€80–95, Db with balcony-€98–115, price depends on room size, air-con, Wi-Fi and four free laptops for guests, reserve ahead for parking-€10, just above Arena at 5 rue Porte de Laure, tel. 04 90 96 11 89, fax 04 90 96 05 84, www.lecalendal.com, contact @lecalendal.com).

**$$$ Hôtel d'Arlatan\*\*\*,** built on the site of a Roman basilica, is classy in every sense of the word. It has sumptuous public spaces, a tranquil terrace, a designer pool, a turtle pond, and antique-filled rooms, most with high, wood-beamed ceilings and stone walls. In the lobby of this 15th-century building, a glass floor looks down into Roman ruins (smallest Db-€90, standard Db-€105–125, bigger Db-€125–160, Db/Qb suites-€180–250, excellent buffet breakfast-€13, air-con, bathrobes, ice machines, elevator, Wi-Fi, parking-€13–16, 1 block below place du Forum at 26 rue Sauvage, tel. 04 90 93 56 66, fax 04 90 49 68 45, www.hotel-arlatan.fr, hotel -arlatan@wanadoo.fr).

**$$ Hôtel du Musée\*\*** is a quiet and affordable manor-home hideaway tucked deep in Arles (tricky to find by car). This delightful refuge comes with 28 air-conditioned rooms, a flowery two-tiered courtyard, and snazzy art-gallery lounges. Lighthearted Claude and English-speaking Laurence, the gracious owners, are eager to help (Sb-€45–50, Db-€55–70, Tb-€70–80, Qb-€85, Wi-Fi and a laptop available for guests, garage-€10, follow signs to *Réattu Museum* to 11 rue du Grand Prieuré, tel. 04 90 93 88 88, fax 04 90 49 98 15, www.hoteldumusee.com, contact@hoteldu musee.com).

**$$ Hôtel de la Muette**\*\*, with reserved owners Brigitte and Alain, is a good choice. Located in a quiet corner of Arles, this low-key hotel is well-kept, with stone walls, wood beams, and air-conditioning. The just-renovated rooms are very sharp (Db-€65–70, Tb-€68–75, Qb-€85, buffet breakfast with eggs-€8, Internet access and Wi-Fi, garage-€7, 15 rue des Suisses, tel. 04 90 96 15 39, fax 04 90 49 73 16, www.hotel-muette.com, hotel.muette@wanadoo.fr).

**$$ Maison d'Hôtes en Provence,** run by engaging American Madeleine and her soft-spoken French husband Eric, combines an interesting B&B experience—four spacious and funky-but-comfy rooms—with optional Provençal cooking workshops. Foodies should check out their website for its affordable range of gourmet classes (Db-€70–75, extra person-€15, good family room, across from launderette at 11 rue Portagnel, tel. & fax 04 90 49 69 20, www.cuisineprovencale.com, actvedel@wanadoo.fr).

**$$ Hôtel le Cloître**\*\* was originally the cloister provost's residence. Caring owners Jean-François and Agnes run a warm, ramshackle place with 30 simple but homey rooms. The best rooms are on the first floor, while cheaper rooms are on the second floor (Ss or Ds-€44, Sb or Db-€51, bigger Db-€65–70, Tb-€75, Qb-€85, no air-con, no elevator, Internet access and Wi-Fi, parking-€5, closed Nov–mid-March, 16 rue du Cloître, tel. 04 90 96 29 50, fax 04 90 96 02 88, www.hotelcloitre.com, hotel_cloitre@hotmail.com).

**$$ Hôtel Acacias**\*\*, just off place Lamartine and inside the old city walls, is a modern pastel paradise. Its smallish, well-maintained, well-priced rooms have all the comforts (Sb or Db-€48–58, larger Db-€62–72, extra bed-€15, air-con, elevator, Wi-Fi, 1 rue Marius Jouveau, tel. 04 90 96 37 88, fax 04 90 96 32 51, www .hotel-acacias.com, contact@hotel-acacias.com).

**$ Hôtel Régence**\*\*, about the best deal in Arles, has a riverfront location, immaculate and comfortable Provençal rooms, good beds, safe parking, and easy access to the train station (Db-€45–55, Tb-€55–65, Qb-€65–75, good buffet breakfast-€6, choose river view or quieter courtyard rooms, most rooms have showers, air-con, no elevator but only two floors, Internet access and Wi-Fi; from place Lamartine, turn right immediately after passing between towers to reach 5 rue Marius Jouveau; tel. 04 90 96 39 85, fax 04 90 96 67 64, www.hotel-regence.com, contact @hotel-regence.com). The gentle Nouvions also rent bikes.

**$ Hôtel Voltaire**\* rents 12 small and spartan rooms with ceiling fans and nifty balconies overlooking a caffeine-stained square. Located a block below the Arena, it's perfect for starving artists. Smiling owner "Mr." Ferran (fur-ran) loves the States (his dream

PROVENCE

# Arles Hotels and Restaurants

1 Hôtel le Calendal
2 Hôtel d'Arlatan
3 Hôtel du Musée
4 Hôtel de la Muette
5 Maison d'Hôtes en Provence
6 Hôtel le Cloître
7 Hôtel Régence
8 Hôtel Acacias
9 Hôtel Voltaire
10 To Mas du Petit Grava

11 Restaurants Le 16, Au Bryn du Thym & La Paillotte
12 Bistrot à Vins Restaurant
13 La Cuisine de Comptoir Rest.
14 Café de la Major (Coffee/Tea)
15 Le Grillon Rest.
16 L'Atelier & A Côté Restaurants
17 Soleilei Ice Cream

100 YARDS
100 METERS

★ FORUM SQUARE
P PARKING
B BUS STOP
↳ VIEW

TO LES BAUX, FONTVIEILLE & AVIGNON
TO TRAIN STATION
AVE. STALIN
MONO-PRIX
PLACE LAM.
PETANQUE
GATE
RUE JULES FERRY
RUE JOUVEAU
CAVALERIE
RHONE
R.L. BLUM
PLACE VOLTAIRE
R. CONDOR.
REATTU MUSEUM
QUAI LAMARTINE
R. AMPH.
R. PORTAGNEL
R. TARDIEU
TO ANCIENT HISTORY MUSEUM
DORMOY
DU
GRAND PRIEURE
RUE DU QUATRE SEPT.
R. VOLTAIRE
QUAI MARX
RUE
RUE DE HOTEL DE VILLE
SAUVAGE
SUISSES
RUE REFUGE
DR. FANTON
RUE DES ARENES
ROMAN ARENA
R. LIBERTE
R. DIDEROT
FOND. V.G.
R. BALZE
RUE CALADE
ANCIENT CITY WALLS
RUE
WC
ST. TROPHIME
PLACE REPUB.
RUE DE CLOITRE
PORTE DE LAURE
CLASSICAL THEATER
RUE REPUBLIQUE
ARLATEN FOLK MUSEUM
RUE DE
JARDIN D'ETE
CLOISTER
MONTEE VAUBAN
BD. E. COMBES
B BUS STN.
BLVD. DES LICES
POST & TAXIS
PLAYGROUND
V. HUGO
TO ANCIENT HISTORY MUSEUM
R. E. FASSIN
DCH
TO LES AYLSCAMPS CEMETERY
TO

is to travel there), and hopes you'll add to his postcard collection (D-€30, Ds-€34, Db-€40, 1 place Voltaire, tel. 04 90 96 49 18, fax 04 90 96 45 49, levoltaire@aol.com). They also serve lunch and dinner (see "Eating," later in this section).

## Near Arles

Many drivers, particularly those with families, prefer staying outside Arles in the peaceful countryside, with easy access to the area's sights. See also "Sleeping—In or near Les Baux" on page 553.

**$$$ Le Peiriero***,** 15 minutes from Arles in the town of Fontvieille, is a pooped parent's dream-come-true, with a grassy garden, massive pool, table tennis, badminton, massage parlor, indoor children's play area, and even a few miniature golf holes. The spacious family-loft rooms, capable of sleeping up to five, have full bathrooms on both levels. This complete retreat also comes with a terrace café and a well-respected restaurant (streetside Sb or Db-€96–116, gardenside Db-€130, Db with terrace-€140, loft-€210, dinner *menu*-€29, €35 for breakfast and dinner, air-con, Wi-Fi, free parking, just east of Fontvieille on road to Les Baux, 34 avenue des Baux, tel. 04 90 54 76 10, fax 04 90 54 62 60, www.hotel-peiriero.com, info@hotel-peiriero.com). Just a short drive from Arles and Les Baux (and 20 minutes from Avignon), little Fontvieille slumbers in the shadows of its big-city cousins (though it has its share of restaurants and boutiques).

**$$$ Mas du Petit Grava** is a vintage Provençal farmhouse 15 tree-lined minutes east of Arles. Here California refuge Jim and his friend Ike offer four large and well-cared-for rooms with tubs, tiles, and memories of Vincent (Jim is a huge Van Gogh fan). A lovely garden surrounds a generously sized pool, but what draws most here is Jim and Ike (Db-€100–120, includes a fine breakfast, tel. 04 90 98 35 66, www.masdupetitgrava.net). From Arles, drive east on D-453 toward St. Martin de Crau; 2.5 kilometers (about 1.5 miles) after passing through Raphèle, veer left—not hard left—at the blue Massa Garage.

# EATING

You can dine well in Arles on a modest budget—in fact, it's hard to blow a lot on dinner here (most of my listings have *menus* for €22 or less). The bad news is that restaurants here change regularly, so double-check my suggestions. Most places I list have outdoor seating. Before dinner, go local on place du Forum and enjoy a *pastis*. This anise-based apéritif is served straight in a glass with ice, plus a carafe of water—dilute to taste.

For **picnics,** a big, handy Monoprix supermarket/department store is on place Lamartine (Mon–Sat 8:30–19:25, closed Sun).

## On or near Place du Forum

Great atmosphere and mediocre food at fair prices await on place du Forum. By all accounts, the garish, yellow Café Van Gogh is worth avoiding. A half-block below the Forum, on rue du Dr. Fanton, lies a lineup of more tempting restaurants (including the first four listed below).

**Le 16,** with warm ambience inside and out, is an affordable place to enjoy a fresh salad (€9, bright and creative) or a one-course dinner (their "bull and red rice" is popular). They also offer a daily *plat du jour,* a two-course €14 *formule,* and a seasonal *menu* (closed Sat–Sun, 16 rue du Dr. Fanton, tel. 04 90 93 77 36).

**Au Bryn du Thym,** almost next door, has long been reliable and specializes in traditional Provençal cuisine. Arrive early for an outdoor table, and let Madame Colombaud take care of you (€19 *menu,* closed Tue, 22 rue du Dr. Fanton, tel. 04 90 49 95 96).

**La Paillotte,** a few doors down, features soft tablecloths under wood-beamed comfort inside, a terrace outside, and fine regional cuisine at affordable prices. It's quite popular with tourists (€18–30 *menus,* closed Wed, 28 rue du Dr. Fanton, tel. 04 90 96 33 15).

**Bistrot à Vins** is for wine addicts who enjoy matching food and drink. You'll dine to light jazz at this cozy *bistrot,* which is well-run by affable Ariane. She speaks enough English and offers simple, tasty dishes (€10–16) designed to highlight her reasonably priced wines—many available by the glass. Try the veal with mashed potatoes (indoor dining only, closed Mon–Tue, 2 rue du Dr. Fanton, tel. 04 90 52 00 65).

At **La Cuisine de Comptoir,** locals abandon Provençal décor and pretend they're urbanites in Paris. This cool little bistro (indoor tables only) serves light €9 *tartine* dinners—a cross between pizza and bruschetta served with soup or salad (closed Sun, just off place du Forum's lower end at 10 rue de la Liberté, tel. 04 90 96 86 28).

**Café de la Major** is the place to go to recharge with some serious coffee or tea (closed Sun, 7 bis rue Réattu, tel. 04 90 96 14 15).

## Near the Roman Arena

For about the same price as on place du Forum, you can enjoy regional cuisine with a point-blank view of the Arena. Because they change regularly, the handful of (mostly) outdoor eateries that overlook the Arena are pretty indistinguishable.

**Le Grillon**—with good salads, crêpes, and *plats du jour* for €9–12—has been the most reliable (closed Wed, at the top of Arena on rond point des Arènes, tel. 04 90 96 70 97).

**Hôtel le Calendal** (recommended in "Sleeping," earlier in this section) serves lunch in its lovely courtyard (€15, daily 12:00–15:00) or delicious little sandwiches for €2 each (three makes a good meal) at its small café.

**Hôtel Voltaire** (recommended in "Sleeping," earlier in this section) serves a nothing-fancy three-course dinner (or lunch) for €11 and hearty salads for €8–10—try the *salade fermière* (1 place Voltaire, tel. 04 90 96 49 18).

## A Gastronomic Dining Experience

One of France's most recognized chefs, Jean-Luc Rabanel, has created a sensation with two different-as-night-and-day dining options 50 yards from place de la République (at 7 rue des Carmes). They sit side by side, both offering indoor and terrace seating.

**L'Atelier** is so intriguing that people travel great distances just for the experience. Diners fork over €80 (at lunch, you'll spoon out €50) and trust the chef to create a memorable meal...which he does. There is no menu, just an onslaught of delicious taste sensations served on artsy dishes. Don't plan on a quick dinner and don't come for the setting—it's a contemporary, shoebox-shaped dining room, but several outdoor tables are also available. The get-to-know-your-neighbor atmosphere means you can't help but join the party (closed Mon–Tue, best to book ahead, friendly servers will hold your hand through this palate-widening experience, tel. 04 90 91 07 69, www.rabanel.com).

**A Côté** saddles up next door offering a wine bar/bistro ambience and top-quality cuisine for far less. Here you can sample the famous chef's talents for as little as €6 (tapas plate) or as much as €30 (3-course *menu*). You'll also find reasonable prices for wine (from €3 a glass) and a helpful staff (daily, tel. 04 90 47 61 13).

## And for Dessert...

**Soleilei** has Arles' best ice cream, with all-natural ingredients and unusual flavors such as *fadoli*—olive oil. There's also a shelf of English books for exchange (open daily, across from recommended Le 16 restaurant at 9 rue du Dr. Fanton).

# TRANSPORTATION CONNECTIONS

**From Arles by Train to: Paris** (17/day, 2 direct TGVs—4 hrs, 15 with transfer in Avignon—5 hrs), **Avignon Centre-Ville** (11/day, 20 min, less frequent in the afternoon), **Nîmes** (9/day, 30 min), **Orange** (4/day direct, 35 min, more frequently with transfer in Avignon), **Aix-en-Provence Centre-Ville** (10/day, 2 hrs, requires at least 1 transfer in Marseille), **Marseille** (20/day, 1–2 hrs), **Cassis** (7/day, 2 hrs), **Carcassonne** (10/day, 3 hrs, most with transfer in

Nîmes or Narbonne), **Beaune** (10/day, 4.5 hrs, 9 with transfer in Nîmes or Avignon and Lyon), **Nice** (11/day, 3.75–4.5 hrs, most require transfer in Marseille), **Barcelona** (2/day, 6 hrs, transfer in Montpellier), **Italy** (3/day, transfer in Marseille and Nice; from Arles, it's 4.5 hrs to Ventimiglia on the border, 8 hrs to Milan, 9.5 hrs to Cinque Terre, 11 hrs to Florence, and 13 hrs to Venice or Rome).

**From Arles Train Station to Avignon TGV Station:** If you're connecting from Arles to the TGV in Avignon, it's easiest to take the bus directly from Arles' train station to Avignon's TGV station (11/day, 1 hr). Another option—which takes the same amount of time, but adds more walking—is to take the regular train from Arles to Avignon's Centre-Ville station, then catch the *navette* (shuttle bus) to the TGV station from there.

**From Arles Bus Station to**: **Nîmes** (6/day, 1 hr), **St. Rémy-de-Provence** (3/day Mon–Sat only, none Sun or Nov–March, 50 min), **Fontvieille** (6/day, 10 min), **Camargue/Stes-Maries-de-la-Mer** (5/day Mon–Sat, 3/day Sun, 1 hr). The bus station is at 16–24 boulevard Georges Clemenceau (2 blocks below main TI, next to Café le Wilson). Bus info: tel. 04 90 49 38 01 (unlikely to speak English).

**To Les Baux:** The bus to **Les Baux** runs only in July and August (6/day, 35 min, €5 one-way). For other ways to reach Les Baux, see "Getting to Les Baux" on page 548.

# Avignon

Famous for its nursery rhyme, medieval bridge, and brooding Palace of the Popes, contemporary Avignon (ah-veen-yohn) bustles and prospers behind its mighty walls. During the 68 years (1309–1377) that Avignon starred as the *Franco Vaticano,* it grew from a quiet village into a thriving city. With its large student population and fashionable shops, today's Avignon is an intriguing blend of medieval history, youthful energy, and urban sophistication. Street performers entertain the international crowds who fill Avignon's ubiquitous cafés and trendy boutiques. If you're here in July, be prepared for big crowds and higher prices, thanks to the rollicking theater festival. (Reserve  your hotel far in advance.) Clean, sharp, and popular with tourists, Avignon is more impressive for its outdoor ambience than for its museums and monuments. See the Palace of the Popes, and then explore the city's thriving streets and beautiful vistas from the parc des Rochers des Doms.

# ORIENTATION

The cours Jean Jaurès, which turns into rue de la République, runs straight from the Centre-Ville train station to place de l'Horloge and the Palace of the Popes, splitting Avignon in two. The larger eastern half is where the action is. Climb to the parc des Rochers des Doms for the town's best view, tour the pope's immense palace, lose yourself in Avignon's back streets, and find a shady square to call your own. Avignon's shopping district fills the traffic-free streets where rue de la République meets place de l'Horloge.

## Tourist Information

The main TI is between the Centre-Ville train station and the old town, at 41 cours Jean Jaurès (April–Oct Mon–Sat 9:00–18:00—until 19:00 in July, Sun 9:00–17:00; Nov–March Mon–Fri 9:00–18:00, Sat 9:00–17:00, Sun 10:00–12:00; tel. 04 32 74 32 74, www.avignon-tourisme.com). From April through mid-October, a branch TI office, called Espace Ferruce, is open at St. Bénezet Bridge (daily 10:00–13:00 & 14:00–18:00, but it can be slow with just one person working).

At either TI, get the good tear-off map and pick up the free and handy *Guide Pratique* (info on car and bike rentals, hotels, apartment rentals, and museums). Also pick up the free **Avignon Passion Pass** (valid 15 days, for up to five people). Get the pass stamped when you pay full price at your first sight, and then receive reductions at the others (for example, €2 less at the Palace of the Popes and €3 less at the Petit Palais). The discounts add up—always show your Passion Pass when buying a ticket. The pass comes with the Avignon "Passion" map and guide, which includes several good (but tricky-to-follow) walking tours.

## Arrival in Avignon
### By Train

Avignon has two train stations: TGV (linked to downtown by frequent shuttle buses) and Centre-Ville.

**TGV Station (Gare TGV):** This shiny new station is on the outskirts of town. There is no baggage storage here (though you can store your bags at the Centre-Ville station, described later in this section). To pick up a **rental car,** take the south exit *(sortie sud)* to find the *location de voitures* (for driving directions to other destinations from this station, see "By Car," on page 527).

To get to the city center, the best and most inexpensive

PROVENCE

# Avignon

ILE DE LA BARTHELASSE

ST. BENEZET BRIDGE

Petit Palais Museum

RIVER

TO LYON VIA D-225 & A-7

RHONE

PARK (ROCHERS DES DOMS)

POND

BLVD. ST-LAZARE

PALACE SQUARE

PALACE OF THE POPES

TO

DALADIER BRIDGE

TO VILLE-NEUVE

OLD CITY WALLS

BLVD DU RHONE

PLACE CRILLON

R. GROTTES

ST. ETIENNE

R. BALANCE

PLACE DE L'HORLOGE

V. LEGAT

PEYROL

ST. PIERRE

CROIX

RUE CARNOT

PASSAGE L'ORAT.

ST. AGRICOL

RUE JOSEPH VERNET

MARCHANDS

ROUG.

SYNAGOGUE

PL. PIE

PL. PIG.

MARKET

R. THIERS

R. CARN.

VIEUX

R. BONNETERIE

CALVET MUSEUM

R. DE LA REPUBLIQUE

R. FOURB.

R. ROI RENE

PLACE ST. DIDIER

FONDATION ANGLADON

R. DES LICES

R. TEINT.

WATER-WHEEL

200 YARDS
200 METERS

BLVD. RASPAIL

R. JAURES

JACQ. CONS.

FABRE

PERD.

RUE DES LICES

PLACE DES CORPS-SAINTS

OLD CITY WALLS

TO NIMES VIA A-9

POST

COURS JFK

BLVD.

ST. MICHEL

ST. ROCH

DCH

BUS & STN.

↖ VIEW
--- PED. PATH
Ⓟ PARKING
Ⓑ MAIN BUS STOP
➡ WALKING TOURS

TRAIN STN.
"CENTRE-VILLE"

TO ARLES & TGV TRAIN STN.

① Start of Welcome to Avignon Walk
② Views & Orientation Table
③ Best View of Bridge & Stairs to Ramparts
④ Hôtel la Mirande (Start of Discovering Back Streets Walk)
⑤ TGV Shuttle & Bus #11 Stop
⑥ Launderette
⑦ To Shakespeare Bookshop
⑧ Chez W@M Internet Café
⑨ Provence Bike Rental
⑩ Shopi Grocery
⑪ City Hall
⑫ Tourist Train Stop
⑬ Shuttle Boat Stops (2)

option is to take the ***navette*/shuttle bus** (marked *Navette/Avignon Centre;* €1.10, buy ticket from driver, 3/hr, 15 min). To find the bus stop, leave the station by the north exit *(sortie nord),* walk down the stairs, and find the long bus shelter to the left. In downtown Avignon, you'll arrive at a stop located three blocks from the city's main TI and two blocks from Centre-Ville station (just inside the city walls, in front of the post office on cours Président Kennedy—see map on page 526). A **taxi** ride between the TGV station and downtown Avignon costs about €14.

If you're heading from the Avignon TGV station to the **Arles train station,** you can catch a direct SNCF bus from the same TGV stop (11/day, 1 hr, schedule available at any information booth inside the TGV station).

**Centre-Ville Station (Gare Avignon Centre-Ville):** All non-TGV trains (and a few TGV trains) serve the central station. You can store bags here—exit the station to the left and look for *consignes* sign (daily May–Sept 6:00–22:00, Oct–April 7:00–19:00). To reach the town center, walk out of the train station and through the city walls onto cours Jean Jaurès. The TI is three blocks down, at #41.

### By Bus

The dingy bus station *(gare routière)* is 100 yards to the right of Centre-Ville station as you leave (beyond and below Ibis Hôtel).

### By Car

Drivers entering Avignon follow *Centre-Ville* and *Gare SNCF* (train station) signs. Park in the garage next to Centre-Ville station, or at the new Parking Jean Juarès under the ramparts across from the train station (about €10/half-day, €13/day). Some free parking is available near the city walls (on boulevard Saint-Roch near Porte de la République). To park in the underground garage at the Palace of the Popes, follow the signs from the riverside road (boulevard St. Lazare) just past St. Bénezet Bridge. Leave nothing in your car. Hotels have advice for smart overnight parking.

If you're renting a car at the TGV station and heading to Arles, Les Baux, or the Luberon, leave the TGV station following signs to *Avignon Sud,* then *La Rocade.* You'll soon see exits to Arles (best for Les Baux as well) and Cavaillon (for Luberon villages).

### Helpful Hints

**Book Ahead for July:** During the July theater festival, rooms are rare—reserve very early or stay in Arles (see page 517) or in or near Les Baux (page 553).

**Internet Access:** The TI has a current list, or ask your hotelier. **Chez W@M** is near Les Halles market hall (Mon–Thu

8:00–20:00, Fri–Sat 8:00–23:00, Sun 8:00–18:00, 34 rue Bonneterie, tel. 04 90 86 19 03).

**English Bookstore:** Try **Shakespeare Bookshop** (Tue–Sat 9:30–12:00 & 14:00–18:30, closed Sun–Mon, 155 rue Carreterie, in Avignon's northeast corner, tel. 04 90 27 38 50).

**Baggage Storage:** You can leave your bags at the Centre-Ville train station (see "Arrival in Avignon," earlier in this section).

**Laundry:** The launderette at 66 place des Corps-Saints, where rue Agricol Perdiguier ends, has English instructions and is handy to most hotels (daily 7:00–20:00).

**Grocery Store: Shopi** is central and has long hours (Mon–Sat 7:00–21:00, Sun 9:00–12:00, 2 blocks from the TI, toward place de l'Horloge on rue de la République).

**Bike Rental:** The TI has the latest on bike rentals. You can rent a bike or a scooter near the bus station at **Provence Bike** (52 boulevard Saint-Roch, tel. 04 90 27 92 61). You'll enjoy riding on the Ile de la Barthelasse, but biking is better in Isle-sur-la-Sorgue (page 575) and Vaison la Romaine (page 563).

**Car Rental:** The TGV station has the car-rental agencies (open long hours daily).

**Shuttle Boat:** A free shuttle boat plies back and forth across the river (as it did in the days when the town had no functioning bridge) from near St. Bénezet Bridge (daily July–Aug 11:00–21:00, Sept–June roughly 10:00–12:30 & 14:00–18:00, 3/hr). It drops you on the peaceful Ile de la Barthelasse, with its riverside restaurant (see page 542), grassy walks, and bike rides with city views. If you stay on the island for dinner, check the schedule for the last return boat—or be prepared for a pleasant 25-minute walk back to town.

**Commanding City Views:** Walk or drive across Daladier Bridge (pont Daladier) for a great view of Avignon and the Rhône River (there's a good walking path across the bridge, along the river). You can enjoy other impressive vistas from the top of parc des Rochers des Doms, from the tower cafeteria in the Palace of the Popes, and from the end of the famous, broken St. Bénezet Bridge.

# TOURS

**Walking Tours**—The TI offers informative, two-hour English walking tours of Avignon (€10, discounted with Avignon Passion Pass, €15 includes a tour of the Pope's Palace; April–Oct daily at 10:00, Nov–March on Sat only; depart from main TI, Sun departures from ticket room at Palace of the Popes; themes vary daily).

**Tourist Trains**—Two little trains, designed for tired tourists, leave regularly from the Palace of the Popes (mid-March–mid-Oct daily

10:00–19:00). One does a town tour (€7, 3/hr, 45 min, English commentary) and the other choo-choos you sweat-free to the top of the park, high above the river (€1 one-way, schedule depends on demand, no commentary).

**Guided Excursions**—Several minivan tour companies based in Avignon offer tours to destinations described in this chapter, including the Pont du Gard, the Luberon, and the Camargue (about €60–75 per person for all-day tours). See "Tours of Provence" on page 500, or ask the TI to book you a tour.

PROVENCE

# SELF-GUIDED WALK

## ▲▲Welcome to Avignon

Before starting this walk—which connects the city's top sights—be sure to pick up the Avignon Passion Pass at the TI, then show it when entering each attraction to receive discounted admission (explained on page 525).

• *Start your tour where the Romans did, on place de l'Horloge, in front of City Hall (Hôtel de Ville).*

### Place de l'Horloge

This café square was the town forum during Roman times and the market square through the Middle Ages. (Restaurants here come with ambience, but marginal-quality meals.) Named for a medieval clock tower that the City Hall now hides, this square's present popularity arrived with the trains in 1854.

• *Walk uphill past the carousel (public WCs behind). You'll see the Palace of the Popes looming large over the buildings. Veer right at the street's end, and continue into...*

### Palace Square (Place du Palais)

This grand square is surrounded by the Palace of the Popes, the Petit Palais, and the cathedral. In the 1300s, the Vatican moved the entire headquarters of the Catholic Church to Avignon. The Church bought Avignon and gave it a complete makeover. Along with clearing out vast spaces like this square and building this three-acre palace, the Church erected more than three miles of protective wall, with 39 towers, "appropriate" housing for cardinals (read: mansions), and residences for the entire Vatican bureaucracy. The city was Europe's largest construction zone. Avignon's population grew from 6,000 to 25,000 in short order. (Today, 13,000 people live within the walls.) The limits of pre-papal Avignon are outlined on city maps: Rues Joseph Vernet, Henri Fabre, des Lices, and Philonarde all follow the route of the city's earlier defensive wall.

The Petit Palais (Little Palace) seals the uphill end of the square and was built for a cardinal; today, it houses medieval paintings (museum described below). The church just to the left of the Palace of the Popes is Avignon's cathedral. It predates the Church's purchase of Avignon by 200 years. Its small size reflects Avignon's modest, pre-papal population. The gilded Mary was added in 1854, when the Vatican established the doctrine of her Immaculate Conception. Mary is purposefully taller than the Palace of the Popes. The Vatican never accepted what it called the "Babylonian Captivity," and had a bad attitude about Avignon long after the pope was definitively back in Rome.

Directly across the square from the palace's main entry stands a cardinal's residence built in 1619. Its fancy Baroque facade was a visual counterpoint to the stripped-down Huguenot aesthetic of the age. During this time, Provence was a hotbed of Protestantism—but, buried within this region, Avignon was a Catholic stronghold.

Notice the stumps in front of the Conservatoire National de Musique. Nicknamed *bites,* slang for the male anatomy, they effectively keep cars from double-parking in areas designed for people. Many of the metal ones slide up and down by remote control to let privileged cars come and go.

• *You can visit the massive Palace of the Popes (described later in this section) now, but it works better to visit that palace at the end of this walk.*

*Now is a good time to take in the...*

## Petit Palace Museum (Musée du Petit Palais)

This palace displays the Church's collection of mostly medieval Italian painting (including one delightful Botticelli) and sculpture. All 350 paintings deal with Christian themes. A visit here before going to the Palace of the Popes helps furnish and populate that otherwise barren building (€6; June–Sept Wed–Mon 10:00–13:00 & 14:00–18:00, closed Tue; Oct–May Wed–Mon 9:30–13:00 & 14:00–17:30, closed Tue; at north end of Palace Square, tel. 04 90 86 44 58).

• *From Palace Square, we'll head up to the rocky hilltop where Avignon was first settled, then down to the river. With this short loop, you can enjoy a park, hike to a grand river view, walk a bit of the wall, and visit Avignon's beloved **broken bridge**—an experience worth ▲▲. Begin by hiking (or taking the tourist train—see "Tours," earlier in this section) up to the...*

## ▲▲Parc des Rochers des Doms

While the park itself is a delight—with a sweet little café and public WCs—don't miss the climax: a panoramic view of the Rhône River Valley and the broken bridge. You'll find a huge terrace in the north side of the park, with an orientation table and information plaques, but views that are inferior to the smaller viewpoint described below (park gates open daily April–Sept 7:30–20:00, Oct–March 7:30–18:00).

For the best views (and the favorite make-out spot for local teenagers), find the small terrace across the grass from the park café and behind the odd zodiac display. An orientation table explains the view. On a clear day, the tallest peak you see, with its white limestone cap, is Mont Ventoux ("Windy Mountain"). St. André Fortress (across the river) was built by the French in 1360, shortly after the pope moved to Avignon, to counter the papal incursion into this part of Europe. The castle was in the kingdom of France. Avignon's famous bridge was a key border crossing, with towers on either end—one French and one Vatican. The one across the river is the Tower of Phillip the Fair (described under "Sights," later in this chapter).

• *From this viewpoint, take the stairs to the left (closed at night) down to the tower. As the stairs spiral down, just before St. Bénezet Bridge, catch a glimpse of the...*

## Ramparts

The only bit of the rampart you can walk on is just beyond the tower (access from St. Bénezet Bridge). When the pope came in the 1360s, small Avignon had no town wall...so he built one. What you see today was restored in the 19th century.

• *When you come out of the tower on street level, exit outside the walls and walk left, going under the bridge to find the bridge's entrance.*

## ▲▲St. Bénezet Bridge (Pont St. Bénezet)

This bridge, whose construction and location were inspired by a shepherd's religious vision, is the "pont d'Avignon" of nursery-rhyme fame. The ditty (which you've probably been humming all day) dates back to the 15th century: *Sur le pont d'Avignon, on y danse, on y danse, sur le pont d'Avignon, on y danse tous en rond* ("On the bridge of Avignon, we will dance, we will dance, on the bridge of Avignon, we will dance all in a circle").

But the bridge was a big deal even outside of its kiddie-tune fame. Built between 1171 and 1185, it was the only bridge crossing the mighty Rhône in the Middle Ages. It was damaged several times by floods and subsequently rebuilt, until 1668, when most of it was knocked down by a disastrous icy flood. The townsfolk decided not to rebuild this time, and for more than a century, Avignon had no bridge across the Rhône. While only four arches survive today, the original bridge was huge:

PROVENCE

Imagine a 22-arch, 3,000-foot-long bridge extending from Vatican territory to the lonely Tower of Philip the Fair, which marked the beginning of France. A Romanesque chapel on the bridge is dedicated to St. Bénezet. While there's not much to see on the bridge, the audioguide included with your ticket tells a good story. It's also fun to be in the breezy middle of the river with a fine city view.

**Cost and Hours:** €4, €12 combo-ticket includes Palace of the Popes, same hours as the Palace of the Popes (see below), last entry one hour before closing, tel. 04 90 27 51 16. The ticket booth is housed in what was a medieval hospital for the poor (funded by bridge tolls). Admission includes a small museum about the song of Avignon's bridge and your only chance to walk a bit of the ramparts (enter both from the tower).

• *To get to the Palace of the Popes from here, exit left, then turn left again back into the walls and walk to the end of the short street, then turn right following signs to* Palais des Papes. *After a block, look for the brown signs leading you left under the passageway, and up the stairs to Palace Square and the...*

## ▲▲Palace of the Popes (Palais des Papes)

In 1309, a French pope was elected (Pope Clement V). At the urging of the French king, His Holiness decided he'd had enough of unholy (and dangerous) Italy. So he loaded up his carts and moved to Avignon for a secure rule under a supportive king. The Catholic Church literally bought Avignon (then a two-bit town), and popes resided here until 1403. Meanwhile, Italians demanded a Roman pope, so from 1378 on, there were twin popes—one in Rome and one in Avignon—causing a schism in the Catholic Church that wasn't fully resolved until 1417.

A visit to the mighty yet barren papal palace comes with an audioguide that leads you along a one-way route and does a credible job of overcoming the lack of furnishings. It teaches the basic history while allowing you to tour at your own pace.

As you wander, ponder that this palace—the largest surviving Gothic palace in Europe—was built to accommodate 500 people as the administrative center of the Vatican and home of the pope. This was the most fortified palace of the age (remember, the pope left Rome to be more secure). You'll walk through the pope's personal quarters (frescoed with happy hunting scenes), see models of how the various popes added to the building, and learn about its state-of-the-art plumbing. The rooms are huge. The "pope's chapel" is twice the size of the adjacent Avignon cathedral.

While the last pope checked out in 1417, the Vatican owned Avignon until the French Revolution in 1789. During this interim period, the pope's "legate" (official representative...normally a nephew) ruled Avignon from this palace. Avignon residents, many of whom had come from Rome, spoke Italian for a century after the pope left, making it a linguistic island within France. In the Napoleonic age, the palace was a barracks, housing 1,800 soldiers. You can see cuts in the wall where high ceilings gave way to floor beams. Climb the tower (Tour de la Gâche) for a grand view and windswept café.

A room at the end of the tour (called *la boutellerie*) is dedicated to the region's wines, of which they claim the pope was a fan. Sniff "Le Nez du Vin"—a black box with 54 tiny bottles designed to develop your "nose." (Blind-test your travel partner.) The nearby village of Châteauneuf-du-Pape is where the pope summered in the 1320s. Its famous wine is a direct descendant of his wine. You're welcome to taste here (€6 for three fine wines and souvenir tasting cup).

**Cost and Hours:** €9.50, €12 combo-ticket includes St. Bénezet Bridge, daily mid-March–Oct 9:00–19:00, until 20:00 July and Sept, until 21:00 in Aug, Nov–mid-March 9:30–17:45, last entry one hour before closing, tel. 04 90 27 50 74, www.palais-des -papes.com.

• *After you finish, you'll exit at the rear of the palace. To return to Palace Square, make two rights after exiting the palace.*

# SIGHTS

## Avignon's Back Streets

Most of the following sights line Avignon's back streets, an enjoyable wander from the exit of the Palace of the Popes.

**Avignon's Synagogue**—Jews first arrived in Avignon with the Diaspora (exile) of the first century. Avignon's Jews were nick-named "the Pope's Jews" because of the protection that the Vatican offered to Jews expelled from France. While this synagogue dates from the 1220s, in the mid-19th century it was completely rebuilt in a Neoclassical, Greek-temple style by a non-Jewish architect. This is the only synagogue under a rotunda that you'll see any-where. The ark holding the Torah is in the east, next to a list of the Jews who were deported from here to Auschwitz in 1942, after Vichy France was overtaken by the Nazis. To visit the synagogue, press the buzzer and friendly Rabbi Moshe Amar will be your guide (Mon–Fri 10:00–12:00 & 15:00–17:00, closed Sat–Sun, 2 place Jerusalem, tel. 04 90 55 21 24).

**Rue des Teinturiers**—This "Street of the Dyers" is Avignon's headquarters for all that's hip. You'll pass the Grey Penitents cha-pel about three small bridges down. The upper facade shows the

GPs, who dressed up in robes and pointy hoods to do their anonymous good deeds back in the 13th century (long before the KKK dressed this way).

As you stroll, you'll see the work of amateur sculptors, who have carved whimsical car barriers out of limestone. Earthy cafés, galleries, and a small stream (a branch of the Sorgue River) with waterwheels line this tie-dyed street. This was the cloth industry's dyeing and textile center in the 1800s. Those stylish Provençal fabrics and patterns you see for sale everywhere started here, after a pattern imported from India.

For trendy restaurants on this atmospheric street, see "Eating," later in this section.

• *Farther down rue des Teinturiers, you'll come to the...*

**Waterwheel**—Standing here, imagine the Sorgue River—which hits the mighty Rhône in Avignon— being broken into several canals in order to turn 23 such wheels. In about 1800, waterwheels powered the town's industries. The little cogwheel above the big one could be shoved into place, kicking another machine into gear behind the wall. (For more on the Sorgue River and its waterwheels, see "Wandering Isle-sur-la-Sorgue," page 574.) Across from the wheel at #41 is

**La Cave Breysse,** offering regional wines by the glass and good lunch fare (see "Eating," later in this section).

## Elsewhere in Avignon

**Fondation Angladon-Dubrujeaud**—Visiting this museum is like being invited into the elegant home of a rich and passionate art collector. It mixes a small but enjoyable collection of art from Post-Impressionists (including Paul Cézanne, Vincent van Gogh, Honoré Daumier, Edgar Degas, and Pablo Picasso) with re-created art studios and furnishings from many periods. It's a quiet place with a few superb paintings (€6; May–Nov Tue–Sun 13:00–18:00, closed Mon; Dec–April Wed–Sun 13:00–18:00, closed Mon–Tue; 5 rue Laboureur, tel. 04 90 82 29 03, www.angladon.com).

**Calvet Museum (Musée Calvet)**—This fine-arts museum impressively displays its good collection, and now provides an English-language audioguide with admission (€6; June–Sept Wed–Mon 10:00–18:00, closed Tue; Oct–May Wed–Mon 10:00–12:00 & 13:00–18:00, closed Tue; in the quieter western half of town at 65 rue Joseph Vernet, antiquities collection a few blocks away at 27 rue de la République—same hours and ticket, tel. 04 90 86 33 84, www.musee-calvet.org).

## Near Avignon, in Villeneuve-lès-Avignon

▲**Tower of Philip the Fair (Tour Philippe-le-Bel)**—Built to protect access to St. Bénezet Bridge in 1307, this massive tower offers the finest view over Avignon and the Rhône basin. It's best late in the day (€2; April–Sept daily 10:00–12:30 & 14:00–18:30; March and Oct–Nov Tue–Sat 10:00–12:30 & 14:00–17:00, closed Sun–Mon; closed Dec–Feb; tel. 04 32 70 08 57). To reach the tower from Avignon, you can drive (5 min, cross Daladier Bridge, follow signs to *Villeneuve-lès-Avignon*); take a boat (Bateau-Bus departs from Mireio Embarcadère near Daladier Bridge); or take bus #11 (2/hr, catch bus in front of post office on cours Président Kennedy—see map on page 526).

# SLEEPING

Hotel values are better in Arles. Avignon is particularly popular during its July festival, when you must book ahead (expect inflated prices). Also note that only a few hotels have elevators—specifically, the first three listed near place de l'Horloge.

## Near Avignon's Centre-Ville Station

The first three listings are a 10-minute walk from the Centre-Ville train station; turn right off cours Jean Jaurès on rue Agricol Perdiguier.

**$$ Hôtel Colbert**** is Avignon's best two-star hotel and a good midrange bet, with well-maintained and nicely decorated rooms in many sizes. Your efficient hosts—Patrice, Annie, and *le chien* Brittany—care for this restored manor house, with its warm public spaces and sweet little patio (Sb-€45–60, small Db-€60, bigger Db-€78, Tb-€98, air-con, Wi-Fi, parking-€9, 7 rue Agricol Perdiguier, tel. 04 90 86 20 20, fax 04 90 85 97 00, www.lecolbert -hotel.com, contact@avignon-hotel-colbert.com).

**$$ Hôtel le Splendid*** rents 17 simple but cheery rooms with wood floors and small but sharp bathrooms (Sb-€42–48, Db-€60, bigger Db with air-con-€70, Tb with air-con-€80, three Db apartments-€90, extra person-€10, discounts for stays longer than one week, 17 rue Agricol Perdiguier, tel. 04 90 86 14 46, fax 04 90 85 38 55, www.avignon-splendid-hotel.com, contacthotel @infonie.fr).

**$ Hôtel du Parc*** is a spotless value with white walls, tiny bathrooms, and stone accents. It's scrupulously managed by entertaining Avignon native Madame Rous, who bakes her own bread and pastries for breakfast—and even made the bedspreads by hand (S-€29, Ss-€39, D-€40, Ds-€48–56, Ts-€67, no TVs or phones, tel. 04 90 82 71 55, fax 04 90 85 64 86, hotel.parc@modulonet.fr). This place is cheaper and homier than Hôtel le Splendid, across the street.

# Avignon Hotels

ILE DE LA BARTHELASSE

RIVER

TO LYON VIA D-225 & A-7 & ⓫

St. Benezet Bridge

Petit Palais Museum

BLVD. ST-LAZARE

PARK (ROCHERS DES DOMS)

POND

RHONE

BLVD. DU RHONE

R. FER.

PALACE SQUARE

Palace OF THE Popes

TO VILLE-NEUVE

DALADIER BRIDGE

⓬

CITY WALLS

ST. ETIENNE

R. B. LANCE

R. GROTTES

⓻

LOULLE

⓹

RUE

PLACE DE L'HORLOGE

PEY.

LEGAT

⓺

CROIX

R. CARNOT

⓼

PASSAGE L'ORAT.

RUE

ST. AGRICOL

JOSEPH

⓾

MARCH.

ROUG.

St. Pierre

SYN.

PL. VIEUX PIE

R. FOUR B

R. THIERS

Market

TO VILLE-NEUVE

P

RUE REMPART

CALVET MUSEUM

VERNET

R. DE LA REPUBLIQUE

⓼

PLACE ST.-DIDIER

R. FAUCONS

R. BONNETERIE

R. Roi RENE

R. TEINT

Fondation Angladon

DES LICES

WATER-WHEEL

N

200 YARDS
200 METERS

BLVD. RASPAIL

FABRE

RUE

⓸

PLACE DES CORPS-SAINTS

OLD CITY WALLS

View
Ped. Path
P Parking
Ⓑ Main Bus Stop

TO NIMES VIA A-9

POST Ⓑ

COURS JFK

JAURES

PERP.

⓷ ⓵

ST. MICHEL

ROCH

DCH

BUS STN.

BLVD.

ST.

TRAIN STN. "CENTRE-VILLE"

TO ARLES & TGV TRAIN STN.

⓵ Hôtel Colbert
⓶ Hôtel du Parc
⓷ Hôtel le Splendid
⓸ Hôtel Boquier
⓹ Hôtel d'Europe
⓺ Hôtel Mercure Cité des Papes
⓻ Hôtel Pont d'Avignon

⓼ Hôtel de Blauvac
⓽ Hôtel Médiéval
⓾ Villa Agapè B&B
⓫ To Le Clos du Rempart Rooms & Lumani B&B
⓬ To Jardin de Bacchus Rooms & Auberge Bagatelle Hostel

**$** At **Hôtel Boquier\*\***, engaging Madame Sendra offers 12 quiet, good-value rooms under wood beams (small Db-€55, bigger Db-€68, Tb-€78, Qb-€90, extra bed-€10, air-con, Internet access and Wi-Fi, parking-€7, near the TI at 6 rue du portail Boquier, tel. 04 90 82 34 43, fax 04 90 86 14 07, www.hotel-boquier.com, contact@hotel-boquier.com).

## In the Center, near Place de l'Horloge

**$$$** **Hôtel d'Europe\*\*\*\***, with Avignon's most prestigious address, lets peasants sleep royally—if you get one of the 10 surprisingly reasonable "standard rooms." Enter a fountain-filled courtyard, linger in the lounges, and savor every comfort. The hotel is located on the handsome place Crillon, near the river (standard Db-€175, first-class Db-€350, superior Db-€495, breakfast-€25, elevator, Internet access, garage-€16, near Daladier Bridge at 12 place Crillon, tel. 04 90 14 76 76, fax 04 90 14 76 71, www.heurope.com, reservations@heurope.com). The hotel's restaurant is Michelin-rated (one star) and serves an upscale €50 *menu* in its formal dining room or front courtyard.

**$$$** **Hôtel Mercure Cité des Papes\*\*\*** is a modern chain hotel within spitting distance of the Palace of the Popes. It has 89 smartly designed small rooms (Sb-€115, Db-€130–170, many rooms have views over place de l'Horloge, air-con, elevator, 1 rue Jean Vilar, tel. 04 90 80 93 00, fax 04 90 80 93 01, www.mercure .com, h1952@accor.com).

**$$$** **Hôtel Pont d'Avignon\*\*\***, just inside the walls near St. Bénezet Bridge, is part of the same chain as the Hôtel Mercure Cité des Papes, with the same prices for its 87 rooms (direct access to a garage makes parking easier than at the other Mercure hotel, elevator, on rue Ferruce, tel. 04 90 80 93 93, fax 04 90 80 93 94, www.mercure.com, h0549@accor.com).

**$$** At **Hôtel de Blauvac\*\***, friendly owner Veronica manages 16 mostly spacious, plush-carpeted, high-ceilinged rooms (many with an additional upstairs loft). It's a faded old manor home with a sky-high atrium. Its location near the pedestrian zone means reliable noise at night (Sb-€70–80, Db-€75–85, Tb-€90–100, Qb-€105, €10 less off-season, Internet access, 1 block off rue de la République at 11 rue de la Bancasse, tel. 04 90 86 34 11, fax 04 90 86 27 41, www.hotel-blauvac.com, blauvac@aol.com).

**$$** **Hôtel Médiéval\*\*** is burrowed deep a few blocks from the Church of St. Pierre. Built as a cardinal's home, this massive stone mansion has a small garden and friendly-as-they-get Mike at the helm. It has 35 wood-paneled, air-conditioned, unimaginative rooms (Sb-€49, Db-€59–74, bigger Db or Tb-€83–90, kitchenettes available but require 3-night minimum stay, Wi-Fi, 5 blocks east of place de l'Horloge, behind Church of St. Pierre at 15 rue Petite

Saunerie, tel. 04 90 86 11 06, fax 04 90 82 08 64, www.hotel
medieval.com, hotel.medieval@wanadoo.fr).

## Chambres d'Hôte

$$$ **Villa Agapè,** just off busy place de l'Horloge (right in the
center of town), is an oasis of calm and good taste. Run by friendly
Madame de La Pommeraye, the villa has three handsomely deco-
rated rooms, a peaceful courtyard, lovely public spaces, and a
soaking pool to boot (Db-€100–150, extra person-€30, includes
breakfast, 2-night minimum, closed in July, Internet access and
Wi-Fi, from place de l'Horloge it's one block down on left above
the pharmacy at 13 rue St. Agricol—ring buzzer, tel. & fax 04 90
85 21 92, mobile 06 07 98 71 30, www.villa-agape.com, michele
@villa-agape.com). For a weeklong stay, ask about renting her
entire house, where you get Madame's room, study, and kitchen
(€2,500–3,300).

$$$ At **Le Clos du Rempart,** Madame Assad, another
Parisian refugee, rents two rooms and one apartment on a pleas-
ant courtyard decorated in a Middle Eastern theme, complete
with a hammock. It's less central but close enough for many (Db-
€100–140 depending on season and room size, 2-bedroom apartment for 4 with kitchen-€175–230, apartment cheaper by the week,
includes breakfast, air-con, Wi-Fi, 1 parking spot in garage, inside
the walls east of the Pope's Palace at 35–37 rue Crémade—call
or check website for directions, tel. & fax 04 90 86 39 14, www
.closdurempart.com, aida@closdurempart.com).

$$$ **Lumani** provides the ultimate urban refuge just inside
the city walls, a 15-minute walk from the Pope's Palace. In this
graceful old manor house, gentle Elisabeth and Jean welcome
guests to their art-gallery-cum-bed-and-breakfast that surrounds a
fountain-filled courtyard with elbow room. She paints, he designs
buildings, and both care about your experience in Avignon. The
five rooms are decorated with flair; no two are alike and all overlook
the shady garden (small Db-€100, big Db-€130, Db suites-€160,
extra person-€25, includes breakfast, Internet access and Wi-Fi,
music studio, parking-€10 or easy on street, 37 rue de Rempart
St Lazare, tel. 04 90 82 94 11, www.avignon-lumani.com, lux
@avignon-lumani.com).

## On the Outskirts of Town

$ **Auberge Bagatelle's hostel** offers dirt-cheap beds, a lively atmo-
sphere, café, grocery store, launderette, great views of Avignon,
and campers for neighbors (D-€40, dorm bed-€17, across Daladier
Bridge on Ile de la Barthelasse, bus #10 from main post office,
tel. 04 90 86 71 31, fax 04 90 27 16 23, www.aubergebagatelle.fr,
auberge.bagatelle@wanadoo.fr).

## Near Avignon
**$$** At **Jardin de Bacchus,** just 15 minutes northwest of Avignon and convenient to the Pont du Gard, enthusiastic and English-speaking Christine and Erik offer three rooms in their rural farmhouse overlooking little Tavel's famous vineyards (Db-€75–80, 2-night minimum or add €20, fine dinner possible, Wi-Fi, tel. 04 66 90 28 62, www.provence-escapade.fr, jardindebacchus@free.fr). Ask about their cooking classes.

# EATING

Skip the overpriced places on place de l'Horloge (L'Opéra Café and La Civette near the carousel are the least of the evils here) and find a more intimate location for your dinner. Avignon has many delightful squares filled with tables ready to seat you.

## Near the Church of St. Pierre
The church divides two enchanting squares. One is quiet and intimate, the other is lively.

**L'Epicerie,** sitting alone on an intimate square, serves the highest-quality and highest-priced cuisine around the Church of St. Pierre (€20–25 *plats,* closed Sun off-season, cozy interior good in bad weather, 10 place St. Pierre, tel. 04 90 82 74 22).

*On Place des Châtaignes:* Pass under the arch by L'Epicerie restaurant and enter enchanting place des Châtaignes, with a tasty commotion of tables from four restaurants. The first you'll come to is **La Goulette,** featuring Tunisian specialties like couscous and *tagine* (slow-cooked meals in a special pot from €15, closed Mon, tel. 04 90 86 06 69). **Crêperie du Cloître** sells cheap salads and dinner crêpes (closed Sun–Mon, cash only). **Restaurant Nem,** tucked in the corner, is Vietnamese and family-run (*menus* from €12, cash only). **Pause Gourmande** is a small lunch-only eatery with €9 *plats du jour* and always has a veggie option (closed Sun).

## Place Crillon
This large and trendy square just off the river attracts a stylish crowd. Several cafés offer inexpensive bistro fare with *menus* from €16, *plats* from €12, and many tables to choose from. **Restaurant les Artistes** seems most popular (€16 *menu,* daily until 22:30, 21 place Crillon, tel. 04 90 82 23 54), while **Café Le Crillon** is most refined and more pricey (closed Sun).

PROVENCE

# Avignon Restaurants

ILE DE LA BARTHELASSE

RIVER

TO LYON VIA D-225 & A-7

PETIT PALAIS MUSEUM

ST. BENEZET BRIDGE

BLVD. ST-LAZARE

PARK (ROCHERS DES DOMS)

POND

RHONE

BLVD. DU RHONE

R. FER

R. GROTTES

PALACE SQUARE

PALACE OF THE POPES

DALADIER BRIDGE

CITY WALLS

R. B. LANCE

PLACE DE L'HORLOGE

PER. LEGAT

CROIX

TO VILLE-NEUVE

RUE LOULLE

ST. ETIENNE

RUE JOSEPH

ST. AGRICOL

R. CARNOT

ST. PIERRE

OLD CITY WALLS

PASSAGE L'ORAT.

MARCH.

ROUG.

SYN.

VIEUX

PL. PIE

R. THIERS

MARKET

CALVET MUSEUM

RUE VERNET

R. DE LA RE PUBLIQUE

R. FOURB.

R. BONNETERIE

R. Roi RENE

R. TENT.

WATER-WHEEL

FONDATION ANGLADON

DES LICES

TO

FABRE

RUE

RASPAIL

BLVD.

ST. JAURES

PERD.

PLACE DES CORPS-SAINTS

OLD CITY WALLS

200 YARDS
200 METERS

TO NIMES VIA A-9

POST
B

COURS JFK

ST. MICHEL

ST. ROCH

DCH

VIEW
PED. PATH
P PARKING
B MAIN BUS STOP

COURS
BLVD.

ST.

BUS STN.

TRAIN STN. "CENTRE-VILLE"

TO ARLES & TGV TRAIN STN.

**1** Restaurants near Church of St. Pierre

**2** Place de Crillon Restaurants

**3** La Cave Breysse Wine Bar & Restaurant l'Empreinte

**4** Woolloomooloo Restaurant

**5** To Restaurant Numéro 75

**6** L'Isle Sonnante Restaurant

**7** La Compagnie des Comptoirs Restaurant

**8** Le Caveau du Théâtre Rest.

**9** Hôtel la Mirande Restaurant

**10** Le Bercail Restaurant

**11** Place des Corps-Saints Restaurants

## Place des Corps-Saints

You'll find several relaxed and reasonable eateries with tables sprawling under big plane tress on this shady square. **Cuisine et Comptoire** attracts the café crowd (closed Sun, tel. 04 90 82 18 39), though I enjoy the €10 pizzas and friendly service at **Le Pili** (daily, tel. 04 90 27 39 53).

## Rue des Teinturiers

This "happening" street has a wonderful concentration of eateries popular with the natives, and justifies the long walk. It's a youthful and trendy area, recently spiffed up with a canalside ambience and little hint of tourism. I'd survey the eateries listed here before choosing.

**La Cave Breysse** is a fun and colorful pause before dinner. Midday or evening, Christine and Tim would love to serve you a fragrant €2.50 glass of regional wine. Choose from the blackboard by the bar that lists all the bottles open today, then join the gang outside by the canal. In the evening, this place is a hit with the young local crowd for its wine (flexible hours, usually Tue–Sat 12:00–14:30 & 18:00–22:30, closed Sun–Mon, no food in evening; across from waterwheel at 41 rue des Teinturiers).

**L'Empreinte** is good for North African cuisine. Choose a table in its tent-like interior, or sit canalside on the cobbles (copious couscous for €13–20, take-out and veggie options available, open daily, 33 rue des Teinturiers, tel. 04 32 76 31 84).

**Woolloomooloo** was named, Dada-style, for the aboriginal term for "little black kangaroo." It's a funky and young-spirited eatery...think Van Gogh drunk on rum-and-fruit punch. The food—while slopped together from a precooked buffet—is hearty, creative, and a fair value. You'll mix and match from a very fun menu (2 courses-€22, 3 courses-€28, 3 courses matched with 3 wines-€36, open daily, frequent jazz evenings, 16 rue des Teinturiers, tel. 04 90 85 28 44).

**Restaurant Numéro 75** is worth the walk (just past where the cobbles end on rue de Teinturiers), filling the Pernod mansion (of *pastis* liquor fame) and a large, romantic courtyard with outdoor tables. The menu is limited to Mediterranean cuisine, but everything's *très* tasty. It's best to go with the options offered by your young, black-shirted server (2-course lunch *menu* with wine and coffee-€20; dinner *menus:* appetizer and main course or main course and dessert-€27, 3 courses-€33; Mon–Sat 12:00–14:00 & 20:00–22:00, closed Sun, 75 rue Guillaume Puy, tel. 04 90 27 16 00).

## Elsewhere in Avignon

At **L'Isle Sonnante,** join chef Boris and his wife Anne to dine intimately in their formal and charming one-room *bistrot.* You'll

**PROVENCE**

choose from a small menu offering only fresh products and be served by owners who care (*menus* from €27, closed Sun–Mon, 100 yards from the carousel on place de l'Horloge at 7 rue Racine, tel. 04 90 82 56 01, best to book ahead).

**La Compagnie des Comptoirs** is the brainchild of famous twin-brother chefs who established a following in southern France with their inventive cuisine. Enter a white world of cool bars, sleek interiors, and a grand courtyard (the restaurant's highlight). This is where young Avignon professionals meet to enjoy foods from the Mediterranean basin (allow €45 for dinner with wine, or enjoy the same cuisine and ambience for far less at lunch—€10–12 *plats du jour,* 83 rue Joseph Vernet, tel. 04 90 85 99 04).

**Le Caveau du Théâtre** invites relaxed diners to share a glass of wine or dinner at one of their sidewalk tables, or to come inside and enjoy the carefree interior (€13 *plats,* €18 *menus,* fun ambience for free, closed Sun, 16 rue des Trois Faucons, tel. 04 90 82 60 91).

**Hôtel la Mirande** is the ultimate Avignon splurge. Reserve ahead here for understated elegance and Avignon's top cuisine (€35 lunch *menu,* €105 dinner tasting *menu;* closed Tue–Wed—but for a price break, dine in the kitchen with the chef on these "closed" days for €85 including wine; behind Palace of the Popes, 4 place de la Mirande, tel. 04 90 86 93 93, fax 04 90 86 26 85).

## Across the River

**Le Bercail** offers a fun opportunity to get out of town (barely) and take in *le fresh air* with a terrific riverfront view of Avignon, all while enjoying inexpensive Provençal cooking served in big portions. Book ahead, as this restaurant is popular (*menus* from €16, serves late, daily April–Oct, tel. 04 90 82 20 22).

To get there, take the small shuttle boat (located near St. Bénezet Bridge) to the Ile de la Barthelasse, turn right, and walk five minutes. As the boat usually stops running at about 18:00 (except in July–Aug, when it runs until 21:00), you can either taxi home or walk 25 minutes along the pleasant riverside path and over Daladier Bridge.

# TRANSPORTATION CONNECTIONS

## Trains

Remember, there are two train stations in Avignon: the suburban TGV station and the Centre-Ville station in the city center (€1.10 shuttle buses connect to both stations, buy ticket from driver, 3/hr, 15 min). Only the Centre-Ville station has baggage storage (see "Arrival in Avignon," earlier in this section). Car rental is available at the TGV station. Some cities, such as Paris, are served both by slower local trains (including some slower TGV trains) from the Centre-Ville station and by faster TGV trains from the TGV station; I've listed the most convenient stations for each trip.

**From Avignon's Centre-Ville Station by Train to: Arles** (11/day, 20 min, less frequent in the afternoon), **Orange** (10/day, 15 min), **Nîmes** (14/day, 30 min), **Isle-sur-la-Sorgue** (10/day on weekdays, 5/day on weekends, 30 min), **Lyon** (10/day, 2 hrs, also from TGV station—see below), **Carcassonne** (8/day, 7 with transfer in Narbonne, 3 hrs), **Barcelona** (2/day, 6 hrs, transfer in Montpellier).

**From Avignon's TGV Station to: Arles** (by SNCF bus, 11/day, 1 hr), **Nice** (20/day, 13 of which are via TGV, 4 hrs, most require transfer in Marseille), **Marseille** (10/day, 1 hr), **Aix-en-Provence TGV** (10/day, 25 min), **Lyon** (12/day, 1.5 hrs, also from Centre-Ville station—see above), **Paris'** Gare de Lyon (9/day in 2.5 hrs, 6/day in 3–4 hrs with change), **Paris'** Charles de Gaulle airport (7/day, 3 hrs).

## Buses

The bus station *(gare routière)* is just past and below the Ibis Hôtel, to the right as you exit the train station (information desk open Mon–Fri 10:15–13:00 & 14:00–18:00, Sat 8:00–12:00, closed Sun, tel. 04 90 82 07 35). Nearly all buses leave from this station. The biggest exception is the SNCF bus service from the Avignon TGV station to Arles (see above). The Avignon TI has schedules. Service is reduced or nonexistent on Sundays and holidays. Check your departure time beforehand and make sure to verify your destination with the driver.

**From Avignon to Pont du Gard:** Buses go to this famous old aqueduct (3/day, 50 min, departs from bus station, usually from stall #11), but the schedule doesn't work well for day-trippers from Avignon; instead, consider a taxi one-way and bus back (see page 544).

**By Bus to Other Regional Destinations: Uzès** (4/day Mon–Sat, none Sun, 1 hr); **St. Rémy-de-Provence** (6/day Mon–Sat, none Sun, 50 min, handy way to visit its Wed market); **Orange** (hourly, 45 min); **Isle-sur-la-Sorgue** (6/day Mon–Sat, fewer on Sun, 45 min); **Vaison la Romaine, Nyons, Sablet,** and **Séguret** (2–3/day during school year, called *période scolaire*, 1/day otherwise and 1/day from TGV station, 75–90 min); **Gordes** (via Cavaillon, 1/day, not on Wed or Sun, 2 hrs, spend the night or taxi back to Cavaillon); **Lourmarin** (3/day, 90 min).

PROVENCE

# Pont du Gard, Les Baux, and Orange

The countryside around Arles and Avignon is littered with world-class sightseeing opportunities. Below I've described key sights and a half-day excursion into the countryside ("Côtes du Rhône Scenic Loop," page 568). Les Baux works well by car from Avignon or Arles, and by bus from Arles in July and August. The town of Orange ties in tidily with a trip to the Côtes du Rhône villages. The Pont du Gard is a short hop west of Avignon and on the way to/from Languedoc for drivers. Travelers relying on public transportation will find their choices very limited. Isle-sur-la-Sorgue in the Luberon (page 572) is the most accessible small town.

## Pont du Gard

Throughout the ancient world, aqueducts were like flags of stone that heralded the greatness of Rome. A visit to this sight still works to proclaim the wonders of that age. This perfectly preserved Roman aqueduct was built as the critical link of a 30-mile canal that, by dropping one inch for every 350 feet, supplied nine million gallons of water per day (about 100 gallons per second) to Nîmes—one of ancient Europe's largest cities. Though most of the aqueduct is on or below the ground, at the Pont du Gard it spans a canyon on a massive bridge—one of the most remarkable surviving Roman ruins anywhere.

### Getting to the Pont du Gard

The famous aqueduct is between Remoulins and Vers-Pont du Gard on D-981, 17 miles from Nîmes and 13 miles from Avignon.

**By Car:** Pont du Gard is an easy 25-minute drive due west of Avignon on N-100 and D-981 (follow signs to *Nîmes*, then *Pont du Gard*) and 45 minutes northwest of Arles (via Tarascon). The handy Rive Gauche parking is off D-981 (the road from Remoulins to Uzès). (Parking is also available on the Rive Droite side, but it's farther away from the museum.) If going to Arles from Pont du Gard, follow signs to *Nîmes* (not Avignon), then follow D-986.

**By Bus:** Buses run to the Pont du Gard (on the Rive Gauche side) from Avignon, Nîmes, and Uzès, but schedules are not well-coordinated. Consider this plan: Take the 12:05 bus from Avignon, arriving at Pont du Gard at 12:50, then take the 14:45 bus from there to Nîmes (where trains run hourly back to Avignon).

Most buses stop at the traffic roundabout 300 yards from the aqueduct. In summer and on weekends, however, buses usually drive into the Pont du Gard site and stop at the parking lot's ticket booth. You can confirm where the bus stops at the parking booth inside the Pont du Gard site.

At the roundabout, the stop for buses coming from Avignon and Nîmes is on the side opposite of Pont du Gard; the stop for buses to Nîmes and to Avignon is on the same side as Pont du Gard (see map on page 546). Make sure you're waiting for the bus on the correct side of the traffic circle, and use your hand to signal the bus to stop for you (otherwise, it'll chug on by). Buy your ticket when you get on, and verify your destination with the driver.

**By Taxi:** From Nîmes or Avignon, it's about €42 for a taxi ride to Pont du Gard (tel. 04 66 29 40 11). If you're staying in Avignon and only want to see the Pont du Gard (and not Nîmes or Uzès), consider splurging on a taxi to the aqueduct in the morning, then take the early afternoon bus back.

## ORIENTATION

There are two riversides to Pont du Gard: the Left Bank (Rive Gauche) and Right Bank (Rive Droite). Park on the Rive Gauche, where you'll find the museums, ticket booth, ATM, cafeteria, WCs, and shops—all built into a modern plaza. You'll see the aqueduct in two parts: first the fine museum complex, then the actual river gorge spanned by the ancient bridge.

**Cost:** While it's free to see the aqueduct itself, the optional activities cost extra: parking (€5), museum (€7), corny film (€4), and a kids' space called *Ludo* (€5, scratch-and-sniff experience in English of various aspects of Roman life and the importance of water). The extensive outdoor *garrigue* natural area, featuring historic crops and landscapes of the Mediterranean, is free (though €4 buys you a helpful English booklet). All these attractions are designed to give the sight more meaning—and they do—but for most visitors, only the museum is worth paying for. Those on a budget can skip the pay sights, just pay €5 for parking, and enjoy the aqueduct for free.

The €12 **combo-ticket** (€9 for kids ages 6–17) covers all sights and parking, and includes the €4 booklet to the *garrigue* natural area. If you want to see all the sights, this is a good value. Families save with the €24 **family ticket** (covers 2 parents and up

**Pont du Gard**

- ROAD
--- PATH
7 VIEW
P PARKING

PONT DU GARD

GARRIGUE
NATURAL
AREA

TO
REMOULINS
& NIMES

P (RIVE DROITE)
DON'T PARK
HERE

MUSEUM
COMPLEX
CINEMA, LUDO (KIDS' SPACE),
INFO, SHOP, WC &
RESTAURANT

GARDON RIVER

❸

P (RIVE GAUCHE)
PARK HERE

D-981
TO
UZES

D-981

❷

❶

ROUNDABOUT

TO REMOULINS,
NIMES, AVIGNON, ARLES
& A-9 FREEWAY

NOT TO SCALE:
MUSEUM TO PONT DU GARD
IS A 5-MINUTE WALK

❶ Bus Stop from Avignon & Nîmes
❷ Bus Stop to Avignon & Nîmes
❸ Bus Stop (Summer & Weekends)

DCH

to 4 kids). If you get a combo-ticket, check the movie schedule; the romancing-the-aqueduct 25-minute film is silly, but it offers good information in a flirtatious French-Mediterranean style...and a cool, entertaining, and cushy break.

For an extra €6, you can rent an **audioguide** for detailed explanations of the aqueduct in English.

**Hours:** The museum is open May–Sept Tue–Sun 9:30–19:00, Mon 13:00–19:00; Oct–April closes at 17:00; closed two weeks in Jan. The aqueduct itself is free and open until 1:00 in the morning, as is the parking lot. Tel. 08 20 90 33 30, www .pontdugard.fr.

**Canoe Rental:** Consider seeing Pont du Gard by canoe. Collias Canoes will pick you up at Pont du Gard (or elsewhere, if prearranged) and shuttle you to the town of Collias. You'll float down the river to the nearby town of Remoulins, where they'll pick you up and take you back to Pont du Gard (€18/person, €9/ child under 12, usually 2 hrs though you can take as long as you like, good idea to reserve the day before in July–Aug, tel. 04 66 22 85 54).

**Plan Ahead for Swimming:** Pont du Gard is perhaps best enjoyed on your back and in the water—bring along a swimsuit, and sandals for the rocks.

# SIGHTS

▲**Museum**—The state-of-the-art museum's multimedia approach (well-presented in English) shows how water was an essential part of the Roman "art of living." You'll see examples of lead pipes, faucets, and siphons; walk through a rock quarry; and learn how they moved those huge rocks into place and how those massive arches were made. While actual artifacts from the aqueduct are few, the exhibit shows the immensity of the undertaking as well as the payoff. Imagine the excitement as this extravagant supply of water finally tumbled into Nîmes. A relaxing highlight is the scenic video helicopter ride along the entire 30-mile course of the structure, from its start at Uzès all the way to the Castellum in Nîmes.

▲▲▲**Viewing the Aqueduct**—A park-like path leads to the aqueduct. Until a few years ago, this was an actual road—adjacent to the aqueduct—that had spanned the river since 1743. Before you cross the bridge, pass under it and hike about 300 feet along the riverbank for a grand viewpoint from which to study the second-highest standing Roman structure. (Rome's Colosseum is only 6 feet taller.)

This was the biggest bridge in the whole 30-mile-long aqueduct. It seems exceptional because it is: The arches are twice the width of standard aqueducts, and the main arch is the largest the Romans ever built—80 feet (so it wouldn't get its feet wet). The bridge is about 160 feet high and was originally about 1,100 feet long. Today, 12 arches are missing, reducing the length to 790 feet.

While the distance from the source (in Uzès) to Nîmes was only 12 miles as the eagle flew, engineers chose the most economical route, winding and zigzagging 30 miles. The water made the trip in 24 hours with a drop of only 40 feet. Ninety percent of the aqueduct is on or under the ground, but a few river canyons like this required bridges. A stone lid hides a four-foot-wide, six-foot-tall chamber lined with waterproof mortar that carried the stream for more than 400 years. For 150 years, this system provided Nîmes with good drinking water. Expert as the Romans were, they miscalculated the backup caused by a downstream corner, and had to add the thin extra layer you can see just under the lid to make the channel deeper.

The appearance of the entire gorge changed in 2002, when a huge flood flushed lots of greenery downstream. Those floodwaters put Roman provisions to the test. Notice the triangular-shaped buttresses at the lower level—designed to split and divert the force of any flood *around* the feet of the arches rather than *into*

PROVENCE

them. The 2002 floodwaters reached the top of those buttresses. Anxious park rangers winced at the sounds of trees crashing onto the ancient stones...but the arches stood strong.

The stones that jut out—giving the aqueduct a rough, unfinished appearance—supported the original scaffolding. The protuberances were left, rather than cut off, in anticipation of future repair needs. The lips under the arches supported wooden templates that allowed the stones in the round arches to rest on something until the all-important keystone was dropped into place. Each stone weighs four to six tons. The structure stands with no mortar—taking full advantage of the innovative Roman arch, made strong by gravity.

Walk across the bridge for a closer look. Across the river, a high trail (marked *panorama*) leads upstream and offers commanding views. On the exhibit side of the structure, a trail marked *Accès l'Aqueduc* leads up to surviving stretches of the aqueduct. For a peaceful walk alongside the top of the aqueduct (where it's on land and no longer a bridge), follow the red-and-yellow markings. Remains of this part are scant because of medieval cannibalization—frugal builders couldn't resist the precut stones as they constructed local churches. The ancient quarry (about a third of a mile downstream on the exhibit side) may be open to the public in 2009.

# Les Baux

The hilltop town of Les Baux crowns the rugged Alpilles (ahl-pee) Mountains, evoking a tumultuous medieval history. Here, you can imagine the struggles of a strong community that lived a rough-and-tumble life—thankful more for their top-notch fortifications than for their dramatic views. While mobbed with tourists most of the day, Les Baux rewards those who arrive by 9:00 or after 17:30. (While the hilltop citadel's entry closes at the end of the day, once you're inside, you're welcome to live out your fondest medieval fantasies all night long.) Sunsets are dramatic, the castle is brilliantly illuminated after dark, and nights in Les Baux are pin-drop peaceful.

## Getting to Les Baux

**By Car:** Les Baux is a 20-minute drive from Arles: Follow signs for *Avignon*, then *Les Baux*. Parking costs €4. As you enter, take a ticket, then drive as close to the top of the parking lot as you can. Pay at the machine just below the town entry (next to telephone, WC, and bakery).

**By Bus:** From Arles, the direct bus service to Les Baux runs only during July and August (6/day, 35 min, €5 one-way, via Abbey of Montmajour, Fontvieille, and Paradou). You can also get from Arles or Avignon to Les Baux via St. Rémy (this town is worth exploring, or just use it as a transit point). From either city, take the bus to St. Rémy (50 min, €4 one-way; from Arles: 3/day Mon–Sat April–Oct, none Sun or Nov–March; from Avignon: 6/day Mon–Sat, none Sun); then take a taxi to Les Baux; then taxi back to your home base (for fares, see below).

**By Taxi:** Count on €37 for a taxi one-way from Arles (€45 after 19:00), and allow €15 one-way from St. Rémy (tel. 06 80 27 60 92).

**By Minivan Tour:** The best option for many is a minivan tour, which can be both efficient and economical (easiest from Avignon; see "Tours of Provence" on page 500).

## ORIENTATION

Les Baux is actually two visits in one: castle ruins perched on an almost lunar landscape, and a medieval town below. Savor the castle, then tour—or blitz—the lower streets on your way out. The town, which lives entirely off tourism, is packed with shops, cafés, and tourist knickknacks. This polished-stone gauntlet of boutiques is a Provençal dream-come-true for shoppers.

### Tourist Information

The TI is immediately on the left as you enter the village (daily May–Sept 9:00–18:30, Oct–April 9:30–12:30 & 14:00–17:30, tel. 04 90 54 34 39, www.lesbauxdeprovence.com). Ask about combo-ticket deals, such as the castle ruins and Cathédrale d'Images for €12.50 (saves about €3), and the €15 **Les Baux Jours pass,** which covers the castle ruins, the Cathédrale d'Images, and the Yves Brayer Museum (saves €4). The TI can also call a cab for you.

### Arrival in Les Baux

Walk up the cobbled street into town, where you're greeted first by the TI. From here, the main drag leads directly to the castle—just keep going uphill (a 10-min walk).

## SIGHTS

### The Castle Ruins (The "Dead City")

The sun-bleached ruins of the "dead city" of Les Baux are carved into, out of, and on top of a rock 650 feet above the valley floor. Many of the ancient walls of this striking castle still stand as a testament to the proud past of this once-feisty village.

**Les Baux**

1 Le Mas d'Aigret
2 Le Mas de l'Esparou B&B
3 Hostellerie de la Reine Jeanne
4 To Le Mazet des Alpilles B&B

NOT TO SCALE

TO ST REMY VIA MOST SCENIC ROUTE

CAVES DE SARRAGAN

CATHEDRALE D'IMAGES

D-17

MUSEUM OF SANTONS

TO ARLES & FONTVIEILLE

CHAPEL OF PENITENTS

EYGUIERES GATE

YVES BRAYER MUSEUM

PLACE LOUIS JOU

R. PORTE MAGE

WC

P

C.E.M.

WC

ST. VINCENT

RUE DE LA CALADE

UPHILL!

i

P

T O W N

RUE NEUVE

GRAND RUE F. MISTRAL

CASTLE RUINS

CHAPEL

RUE TRENCAT

RUE DU CHATEAU

DES FOURS

CITY HALL

RENAISSANCE WINDOW

TICKETS & ENTRY TO "DEAD CITY"

R. DE LORME

TO ST REMY

D-5A

C   L   I   F   F   S

DCH

P PARKING

VIEW

LOWER TOWN WALK

TO MAUSSANE, PARADOU, ABBEY DE MONTMAJOUR, ARLES, & BARBEGAL

**Cost and Hours:** €7.70, includes good audioguide; daily July–Aug 9:00–20:00, Easter–June and Sept–Oct 9:00–19:00, Nov–Easter 9:30–17:00. If you are inside the castle when the entry closes, you can stay as long as you like. From mid-July through late August, medieval pageantry and tournaments enliven the mountaintop. If you bring your lunch, enjoy the picnic tables.

**History:** Imagine the importance of this citadel in the Middle Ages, when the Lords of Baux were notorious warriors. (How many feudal lords could trace their lineage back to one of the "three kings" of Christmas-carol fame, Balthazar?) In the 11th century, Les Baux was a powerhouse in southern France, controlling about 80 towns. The Lords of Baux fought the counts of Barcelona for control of Provence...and eventually lost. But while in power, these guys were mean. One ruler enjoyed forcing unransomed prisoners to jump off his castle walls.

In 1426, Les Baux was incorporated into Provence and France. Not accustomed to subservience, Les Baux struggled with the French king, who responded by destroying the fortress in 1483. Later, Les Baux regained some importance and emerged as a center of Protestantism. Arguing with Rome was a high-stakes game in the 17th century, and Les Baux's association with the Huguenots brought destruction again in 1632 when Cardinal Richelieu (under King Louis XIII) demolished the castle. Louis rubbed salt in the wound by billing Les Baux's residents for his demolition expenses. The once-powerful town of 4,000 was forever crushed.

In the old olive mill where you buy your ticket, study the models of the town before its 17th-century destruction. Take full advantage of the audioguide—it narrates 30 stops while you wander where you like, keying in the number for any sight that interests you.

As you walk on the windblown field, past kid-thrilling medieval siege weaponry, try to imagine 4,000 people living up here. Notice the water-catchment system (a slanted field that caught rainwater and drained it into a cistern—necessary during a siege).

If you need to take a break, the little chapel across from the entry runs videos with Provençal themes (plays constantly; no words—just images and music).

For the most sensational views, climb to the blustery top of the citadel. Hang on. The mistral wind just might blow you away.

## Lower Town

After your castle visit, you can shop and eat your way back through the new town. Or you can escape the crowds by taking the second left as you leave the castle, continuing downhill, and checking out these minor but worthwhile sights as you descend.

• *On the main drag (grand rue Frédéric Mistral), a few blocks below the castle, is…*

**Manville Mansion City Hall**—The 15th-century city hall flies the red-and-white flag of Monaco, a reminder that the Grimaldi family (which has long ruled the tiny principality of Monaco) owned Les Baux until the French Revolution (1789). In fact, in 1982, Princess Grace Kelly and her royal husband, Prince Rainier Grimaldi, came to Les Baux to receive the key to the city.

Twenty yards up rue Neuve, the fine 1571 **Renaissance window,** marking the site of a future Calvinist museum, stands as a reminder of this town's Protestant history. This was probably a place of Huguenot worship—the words carved into the lintel, *Post tenebras lux,* were a popular Calvinist slogan: "After the shadow comes the light."

• *At the end of rue Neuve, head right on rue des Fours to get to the …*

**Yves Brayer Museum (Musée Yves Brayer)**—This enjoyable museum lets you peruse three floors of paintings (Van Gogh–like Expressionism, without the tumult) by Yves Brayer (1907–1990), who spent his final years here in Les Baux. Like Van Gogh, Brayer was inspired by all that surrounded him. Brayer picked up inspiration from his travels through Morocco, Spain, and the rest of the Mediterranean world (€4, daily 10:00–12:30 & 14:00–18:30, tel. 04 90 54 36 99). Pick up the descriptive English sheet at the entry.

• *Next door is...*

**St. Vincent Church**—This 12th-century Romanesque church was built short and wide to fit the terrain. The center chapel on the right (partially carved out of the rock) houses the town's traditional Provençal processional chariot. Each Christmas Eve, a ram pulled this cart—holding a lamb, symbolizing Jesus, and surrounded by candles—through town to the church.

• *Around the corner (to the left as you leave the church) are public WCs. Directly in front of the church is a vast view, making clear the strategic value of this rocky bluff's natural fortifications. A few steps away is the...*

**Chapel of Penitents**—Notice the nativity scene painted by Yves Brayer, illustrating the local legend that says Jesus was born in Les Baux. Leaving the church, turn left. Wash your shirt in the old-town "laundry"—with a pig-snout faucet and 14th-century stone washing surface designed for short women.

• *Heading downhill on rue de la Calade, you'll pass cafés with wonderful views, the town's fortified wall, and one of its two gates. After passing a free (and curiously evangelical) "museum of aromas and perfumes," you hit the awe-inspiring...*

**Museum of Santons**—This free museum displays a collection of *santons*, popular folk figurines that decorate local Christmas mangers. Notice how the nativity scene "proves" once again that Jesus was born in Les Baux. These painted clay dolls show off local dress and traditions. Find the old couple leaning heroically into the mistral.

## Near Les Baux

A half-mile beyond Les Baux, D-27 (toward Maillane) leads to dramatic views of the hill town. There are pullouts and walking trails at the pass, and two sights that fill cool, cavernous caves in former limestone quarries dating back to the Middle Ages. (The limestone is easy to cut, but gets hard and nicely polished when exposed to the weather.) Speaking of quarries, in 1821, the rocks and soil of this area were found to contain an important mineral for the making of aluminum. It was named after the town: bauxite.

**Caves de Sarragan**—The best views of Les Baux are from this parking lot, occupied by the Sarragan Winery (which invites you in for a taste). While this place looks like it's designed for groups, the friendly, English-speaking staff welcomes individuals (free, daily April–Sept 10:00–12:00 & 14:00–19:00, Oct–March until 18:00, tel. 04 90 54 33 58).

▲**Cathédrale d'Images**—This similar cave nearby offers a mesmerizing sound-and-slide show. Its 48 projectors flash countless images set to music on the quarry walls as visitors wander around. The 2009 program features the life of Pablo Picasso (€7.60, daily March–Dec 10:00–18:00, closed Jan–Feb, tel. 04 90 54 42 65). Dress warmly, since the cave is cool.

## SLEEPING

### In or near Les Baux

$$$ **Le Mas d'Aigret***, barely east of Les Baux on the road to St. Rémy, is a well-run, lovely refuge that crouches under Les Baux. Lie on your back and stare up at the castle walls rising beyond the swimming pool or enjoy valley views from the groomed terraces (Db with no view-€95, larger Db with balcony and view-€150, Tb/Qb-€210–240, two cool troglodyte rooms-€200–240, half-pension option with big breakfast and good dinner-€40 per person, air-con, rooms have some daytime road noise, tel. 04 90 54 20 00, fax 04 90 54 44 00, www.masdaigret.com, contact@masdaigret.com, Dutch Marieke and French Eric).

$$ **Le Mas de l'Esparou** *chambre d'hôte*, a few minutes below Les Baux toward Paradou, is welcoming and kid-friendly, with three spacious rooms, a big swimming pool, table tennis, and distant views of Les Baux. Sweet Jacqueline loves her job, and her lack of English only makes her more animated (Db-€64, extra bed-about €16, includes breakfast, cash only, between Les Baux and Maussane les Alpilles on D-5, look for white sign with green lettering, tel. & fax 04 90 54 41 32).

$$ **Hostellerie de la Reine Jeanne****, an exceptional value, is a good place to watch the sun rise and set. Run by Gaelle and Marc, this place offers a handful of comfy rooms are above a busy (and good-value) restaurant (standard Ds-€52, standard Db-€58, Db with view deck-€62–72, cavernous family suite-€105, air-con in most rooms, ask for *chambre avec terrasse*, good *menus* from €16, 150 feet to your right after entry to the village of Les Baux, tel. 04 90 54 32 06, fax 04 90 54 32 33, www.la-reinejeanne.com, reine .jeanne@wanadoo.fr).

$ **Le Mazet des Alpilles** is a small home with three tidy, air-conditioned rooms just outside the unspoiled village of Paradou, five minutes below Les Baux. It may have space when others don't (Db-€55, ask for largest room, includes breakfast, cash only, air-con, child's bed available, pleasant garden, follow brown signs from D-17, in Paradou look for route de Brunelly, tel. 04 90 54 45 89, www.alpilles.com/mazet.htm, lemazet@wanadoo.fr). Sweet Annick speaks just enough English.

# Orange

Orange is notable for its Roman arch and grand Roman Theater. Orange was a thriving city in ancient times—strategically situated on the Via Agrippa, connecting the important Roman cities of Lyon and Arles. It was actually founded as a comfortable place for Roman army officers to enjoy their retirement. Even in Roman times, career military men retired after only 20 years. Does the emperor want thousands of well-trained, relatively young guys hanging around Rome? No way. What to do? "How about a nice place in the south of France...?"

## ORIENTATION

### Tourist Information

The unnecessary TI is located next to the fountain and parking area at 5 cours Aristide Briand (April–Sept Mon–Sat 9:30–19:00, Sun 10:00–13:00 & 14:00–18:30; Oct–March Mon–Sat 10:00–13:00 & 14:00–17:30, closed Sun; tel. 04 90 34 70 88).

### Arrival in Orange

**By Train:** Orange's **train station** is a level 15-minute walk from the Roman Theater (or a €8 taxi ride, tel. 06 09 51 32 25). The recommended Hôtel de Provence across from the station will keep your bags (see "Sleeping," later in this section). To walk into town from the train station, head straight out of the station (down avenue Frédéric Mistral), merge left onto Orange's main shopping street (rue de la République), then turn left on rue Caristie; you'll run into the Roman Theater's massive stage wall.

**By Bus:** Buses drop you at place Pourtoules, two blocks from the Roman Theater (walk to the hill and turn right to reach the theater, bus station tel. 04 90 24 15 59).

**By Car:** Drivers follow *Centre-Ville* signs, then *Théâtre Antique* signs, and park as close to the Roman Theater's huge wall as possible; the easiest option is Parking Théâtre Antique (by the fountain and the TI). Those coming from the autoroute will land here by following *Centre-Ville* signs; others should follow *Centre-Ville* signs, then *Office du Tourisme* signs, to find this parking. To reach the theater, walk to the hill and turn left.

# SIGHTS

**▲▲Roman Theater (Théâtre Antique)**—Orange's ancient theater is the best-preserved in existence, and the only one in Europe with its acoustic wall still standing. (Two others in Asia Minor also survive.)

**Cost, Hours, Information:** €8, daily April–Sept 9:00–18:00, until 19:00 in summer, Oct–March 9:00–17:00, tel. 04 90 51 17 60. Your ticket includes an informative audioguide, the 13-minute film, and entrance to the small museum across the street (Musée d'Art et d'Histoire). Pop in to see a few theater details and a rare grid used as the official property-ownership registry—each square represented a 120-acre plot of land.

**Cheap Trick:** Vagabonds wanting to see the theater for free can hike up nearby stairs (*escalier est* off rue Pourtoules is closest) to view it from the bluff high above.

**Cafés:** A shaded café-filled square (place de la République) is hidden away two blocks from the theater up rue Ségond Weber.

**⊙Self-Guided Tour:** After you enter (to the right of the actual theater), you'll see a huge dig—the site of the Temple to the Cult of the Emperor. Look for signs to the worthwhile 13-minute movie (English subtitles) that gives you a good visual sense of the how the theater looked to the Romans.

Enter the theater, then climb the steep stairs to find a seat high up to appreciate the acoustics (eavesdrop on people by the

stage). Contemplate the idea that 2,000 years ago, Orange residents enjoyed grand spectacles with high-tech sound and lighting effects—such as simulated thunder, lightning, and rain.

A grandiose Caesar overlooks everything, reminding attendees of who's in charge. If it seems like you've seen this statue before, you probably have. Countless sculptures identical to this one were mass-produced in Rome and shipped throughout the empire to grace buildings like this theater for propaganda purposes. To save money on shipping and handling, only the heads of these statues were changed with each new ruler. The permanent body wears a breastplate emblazoned with the imperial griffon (body of a lion, head and wings of an eagle) that only the emperor could wear. When a new emperor came to power, new heads were made in Rome and shipped off throughout the empire to replace the pop-off heads on all these statues. (Imagine George W. Bush's head on Bill Clinton's body.)

**Orange**

TO GAP

ARC DE TRIOMPHE

AVE ARTAUD

N

200 YARDS

200 METERS

P PARKING

V. VIEW

AVE. DE L'ARC DE TRIOMPHE

PLACE ST. JEAN

RUE ST. JEAN

MEYNE RIVER

R. LA COUR

R. VICTOR-HUGO

BLVD. PALADIER

RUE DU NOBLE

RUE DU TANNEURS

A. BRIAND

CATHEDRAL

PL. CLEM.

R. CARISTIE

TO A-7 FREEWAY

RUE ST-MARTIN

COURS A. BRIAND

PL. REB.

R. PONT NEUF

R. DE LA REPUBLIQUE

AVE. FABRE

TO VAISON LA ROMAINE

AVE DES THERMES

PL. HERBES

R. PONTILLAC

PLACE FRERES-MOUNET

ENTER

R. ST. FLOR.

PL. LIB.

AVE. FRED. MISTRAL

RUE CONTRA SCARPE

TO TRAIN STN. & HOTEL DE PROVENCE

EXCA-VATIONS

MONTEE DU CHALONS

V.

ESCALIER EST

RUE POURTOULES

COURS POURTOULES

Post

P

BUS STN.

RUE DE TOURRE

ROMAN THEATER

ST. EUTROPE HILL

RUE A. BLANC

(D-68)

AVE. GEN LECLERC

TO CHATEAUNEUF-DU-PAPE

TO AVIGNON VIA N-7

DCH

Archaeologists believe that a puny, vanquished Celt was included at the knee of the emperor, touching his ruler's robe respectfully—a show of humble subservience to the emperor. It's interesting to consider how an effective propaganda machine can con the masses into being impressed by their leader.

The horn has blown. It's time to find your seat: row two, number 30. Sitting down, you're comforted by the "EQ GIII" carved into the seat (*Equitas Gradus* #3...three rows for the Equestrian order). You're not comforted by the hard limestone bench (thinking it'll probably last 2,000 years). The theater is filled with 10,000 people. Thankfully, you mix only with your class, the nouveau riche—merchants, tradesmen, and city big shots. The people seated above you are the working-class, and way up in the "chicken roost" section are the scum of the earth—slaves, beggars, prostitutes, and youth hostellers. Scanning the orchestra section (where the super-rich sit on real chairs), you notice the town dignitaries hosting some visiting VIPs.

Okay, time to worship. They're parading a bust of the emperor from its sacred home in the adjacent temple around the stage. Next is the ritual animal sacrifice called *la pompa* (so fancy, future generations will use that word for anything full of such...pomp). Finally, you settle in for an all-day series of spectacles and dramatic entertainment. All eyes are on the big stage door in the middle—where the Julia Roberts and Tom Hanks of the day will appear. (Lesser actors come out of the side doors.)

The play is good, but many come for the halftime shows—jugglers, acrobats, and striptease dancers. In Roman times, the theater was a festival of immorality. An ancient writer commented, "The vanquished take their revenge on us by giving us their vices through the theater."

With an audience of 10,000 and no amplification, acoustics were critical. A roof originally covered the stage, somewhat like the glass-and-iron stage roof you see today (recently installed to protect the stage wall). The original was designed not to protect the stage from the weather, but to project the voices of the actors into the crowd. For further help, actors wore masks with leather caricature mouths that functioned as megaphones. The side walls originally rose as high as the stage wall and supported a retractable roof that gave the audience some protection from the sun. After leaving the theater, look up to the stage wall from the outside and notice the supports for poles that held the roof in place.

The Roman Theater was all part of the "give them bread and circuses" approach to winning the support of the masses (not unlike today's philosophy of "give them tax cuts and *American Idol*"). The spectacle grew from 65 days of games per year when the theater was first built (and when Rome was at its height) to about 180 days each year by the time Rome finally fell.

▲**Roman "Arc de Triomphe"**—Technically the only real Roman arches of triumph are in Rome's Forum, built to commemorate various emperors' victories. The great Roman arch of Orange is actually a municipal arch erected (about A.D. 19) to commemorate a general, named Germanicus, who protected the town. The 60-foot-tall arch is on a noisy traffic circle (north of city center, on avenue Arc de Triomphe).

# SLEEPING

**(€1 = about $1.50, country code: 33)**
**$$ Hôtel de Provence**\*\***, at the train station, is air-conditioned, quiet, comfortable, and affordable. Friendly Madame Verbe runs this traditional place with grace (Db–€60–65, small rooftop pool, café, 60 avenue Frédéric Mistral, tel. 04 90 34 00 23, fax 04 90 34 91 72, www.hoteldeprovence84.com, hoteldeprovence84@orange.fr).

# TRANSPORTATION CONNECTIONS

**From Orange by Train to: Avignon** (10/day, 15 min), **Arles** (4/day direct, 35 min, more with transfer in Avignon), **Lyon** (16/day, 2 hrs).

**By Bus to: Vaison la Romaine** (2–3/day, 45 min), **Avignon** (hourly, 45 min). Buses to Vaison la Romaine and other wine villages depart from the big square, place Pourtoules (turn right out of the Roman Theater and right again on rue Pourtoules).

---

# Villages of the Côtes du Rhône

The sunny Côtes du Rhône wine road—one of France's best—starts at Avignon's doorstep. It winds north through a mountainous landscape carpeted with vines, peppered with warm stone villages, and presided over by the Vesuvius-like Mont Ventoux. The wines of the Côtes du Rhône (grown on the *côtes*, or hillsides, of the Rhône River Valley) are easy on the palate and on your budget. But this hospitable place offers more than famous wine—its hill-capping villages inspire travel posters, and its vistas are unforgettable. Yes, there are good opportunities for enjoyable wine-tasting, but there is also a soul to this area...if you take the time to look.

## Planning Your Time

Vaison la Romaine is the small hub of this region, offering limited bus connections with Avignon and Orange, bike rental, and a mini-Pompeii in the town center. Nearby, you can visit the impressive Roman Theater in Orange (described earlier), drive to the top of Mont Ventoux, follow my self-guided "Côtes du Rhône Scenic Loop" driving tour (described later in this section), and pedal to nearby towns for a breath of fresh air. The vineyards' centerpiece, the Dentelles de Montmirail mountains, are laced with a variety of exciting trails ideal for hikers.

To explore this area, allow two nights for a good start. Drivers should head for the hills. Those without wheels find that Vaison la

Romaine is the only practical home base (or, maybe better, consider a minivan tour for this area; see "Getting Around the Côtes du Rhône—By Tour," below).

## Getting Around the Côtes du Rhône

**By Car:** Pick up the Michelin Local maps #332 or #528 to navigate your way around the Côtes du Rhône. (Landmarks like Dentelles de Montmirail and Mont Ventoux make it easy to get your bearings.) I've described my favorite driving route on page 568. If your plan is to connect the Côtes du Rhône with the Luberon, do it scenically via Mont Ventoux (follow signs to *Malaucène*, then to *Mont Ventoux*, allowing 2 hours to Roussillon). This route is one of the most spectacular in Provence. If continuing north toward Lyon, consider the worthwhile detour via the Ardèche Gorges (described on page 571).

**By Bus:** Buses run to Vaison la Romaine from Orange and Avignon (2–3/day, 45 min from Orange, 90 min from Avignon) and connect several wine villages (including Gigondas, Sablet, and Beaumes de Venise) with Vaison la Romaine and Nyons to the north. Another line runs from Vaison la Romaine to Carpentras, serving Crestet (below Le Crestet), Malaucène, and Le Barroux (2/day, tel. 04 90 36 09 90). Both routes provide scenic rides through this area.

**By Train:** Trains get you as far as Orange (from Avignon: 10/day, 15 min), where buses make the 45-minute trip to Vaison la Romaine (see above).

**By Tour:** Various minivan tours leave from Avignon offering all-day excursions to this area. For a wine-focused tour, I recommend three individuals who can expertly guide you through region. For all tours to this area, see "Tours of Provence," on page 500.

# Vaison la Romaine

With quick access to vineyards, villages, and Mont Ventoux, this lively little town of 6,000 makes a great base for exploring the Côtes du Rhône region by car or by bike. You get two villages for the price of one: Vaison la Romaine's "modern" lower city has worthwhile Roman ruins and a lone pedestrian street (but a disappointing main square, place Montfort). The car-free medieval hill town looms above, with meandering cobbled lanes, a dash of art galleries and cafés, and a ruined castle with a good view from its base.

## ORIENTATION

The city is split in two by the Ouvèze River. The Roman Bridge connects the more modern lower town (Ville-Basse) with the hill-capping medieval upper town (Ville-Haute).

PROVENCE

## Tourist Information

The superb TI is in the lower city, between the two Roman ruin sites, at place du Chanoine Sautel (Mon–Sat 9:00–12:00 & 14:00–17:45, Sun 9:00–12:00, closed Sun Oct–April, tel. 04 90 36 02 11, www.vaison-en-provence.com). Say *bonjour* to *charmante* and ever-so-patient Valerie—get bus schedules, ask about festivals and evening programs, and pick up information on walks from Vaison la Romaine. Ask for the English pamphlets on biking and hiking—they have maps and instructions for several bike and walking loops, ranging from easy half-day trips to all-day affairs.

## Arrival in Vaison la Romaine

**By Bus:** The unmarked bus stop to Orange and Avignon is in front of the Cave la Romaine winery. Buses from Orange or Avignon drop you across the street (2–3/day, 45 min from Orange, 90 min from Avignon). Tell the driver you want the stop for the *Office de Tourisme*. When you get off the bus, walk five minutes down avenue Général de Gaulle to reach the TI and recommended hotels.

**By Car:** Follow signs to *Centre-Ville*, then *Office de Tourisme;* park free across from the TI. Most parking is free in Vaison la Romaine.

## Helpful Hints

**Market Day:** Sleep in Vaison la Romaine on Monday night, and you'll wake to an amazing Tuesday market. But be warned: Mondays are quiet during the day, as many shops close (but sights are open). If you spend a Monday night, avoid parking at market sites or you won't find your car where you left it (if signs indicate *Stationnement Interdit le Mardi,* don't park there—ask your hotel where you can park).

**Internet Access:** The TI has a good list. The most central is **Brasserie du Siècle** near the recommended Hôtel Burrhus on place Montfort (daily 7:00–1:00 in the morning, tel. 04 90 36 00 19).

**Laundry:** The self-service **Laverie la Lavandière** is on cours Taulignan, near avenue Victor Hugo (daily 8:00–22:00). The friendly owners, who work next door at the dry cleaners, will do your laundry while you sightsee—when you pick up your laundry, thank them with a small tip (dry cleaners open Mon–Sat 9:00–12:00 & 15:00–19:00, closed Sun).

**Bike Rental:** Try **Mag 2 Roues,** in the lower town on cours Taulignan (tel. 04 90 28 80 46).

**Taxi:** To get a taxi, call 04 90 36 00 04 or 06 22 28 24 49.

**Car Rental:** Wallgreen has a few cars for rent at **Vaison Pneus** (closed Sun, avenue Marcel Pagnol, tel. 04 90 28 73 54).

**Local Guide:** Let sincere and knowledgeable **Anna-Marie Melard**

PROVENCE

bring those Roman ruins to life for you (€55/80-min tour, tel. 04 90 36 50 48).

# SIGHTS AND ACTIVITIES

## In Vaison la Romaine

**Roman Ruins**—Ancient Vaison la Romaine had a treaty that gave it the preferred "federated" relationship with Rome (rather than simply being a colony). This, along with a healthy farming

economy (olives and vineyards), made it a most prosperous place... as a close look at its sprawling ruins demonstrates. About 6,000 people called Vaison la Romaine home 2,000 years ago. When the barbarians arrived, the Romans were forced out, and the townspeople fled into the hills. Here's something to ponder: The town has only recently reached the same population as during its Roman era.

Vaison la Romaine's Roman ruins are split by a modern road into two sites: Puymin and La Villasse. Each is well-presented, offering a good picture of life during the Roman Empire. Visit **Puymin** first. Inside the site, climb the hill to the museum (exhibits explained in English loaner booklet). Behind the museum is a 6,000-seat theater (just enough seats for the number of residents). Nearest the entry are the scant but impressive remains of a sprawling mansion. Back across the modern road in **La Villasse,** you'll explore a "street of shops" and the foundations of more houses.

**Cost and Hours:** €8 Roman ruins combo-ticket includes both ruins, a helpful audioguide, and the cloister at the Notre-Dame de Nazareth Cathedral (see below); daily April–Sept 9:30–18:00, Oct–March 10:00–12:00 & 14:00–17:00.

**Lower Town (Ville-Basse)**—Vaison la Romaine's nondescript modern town stretches from its car-littered main square, place Montfort. A few blocks away, the stout **Notre-Dame de Nazareth Cathedral**—with an evocative cloister—is a good example of Provençal Romanesque (cloister entry-€1.50, covered by €8 Roman ruins combo-ticket—see above). The pedestrian-only Grand Rue is a lively shopping street leading to the small river gorge and the Roman Bridge.

**Roman Bridge**—The Romans cut this sturdy, no-nonsense vault into the canyon rock 2,000 years ago, and it has survived ever since. Until the 20th century, this was the only way to cross the Ouvèze River. The metal plaque on the wall *(Crue du 22-09-92)*

PROVENCE

# Vaison la Romaine

- B  Bus Stop
- P  Parking
- --  Trail

① Hôtel le Beffroi
② L'Evêché Chambres
③ Hôtel la Fête en Provence
④ Hôtel Burrhus
⑤ La Bartavelle Restaurant
⑥ Le Bateleur Restaurant
⑦ Le Tournesol & La Lyriste Restaurants
⑧ Bistro du'O Restaurant
⑨ Internet Café
⑩ Bike Rental
⑪ Launderette
⑫ To Car Rental
⑬ Bus to Avignon/Orange
⑭ Bus from Avignon/Orange
⑮ To Séguret by Bike or Car

shows the high-water mark of the record flood that killed 30 people and washed away the valley's other bridges. The flood swept away the modern top of this bridge...but couldn't budge the 55-foot Roman arch.

**Upper Town (Ville-Haute)**—While there's nothing of particular importance to see in the fortified medieval old town atop the hill, the cobbled lanes and enchanting fountains make you want to break out a sketchpad. Vaison la Romaine had a prince-bishop since the fourth century. He came under attack by the Count of Toulouse in the 12th century. Anticipating a struggle, the prince-bishop abandoned the lower town and built a château on this rocky outcrop (about 1195). Over time, the rest of the townspeople followed, vacating the lower town and building their homes at the base of the château behind the upper town's fortified wall.

To reach the upper town, hike up from the Roman Bridge (passing memorials for both world wars) through the medieval gate, under the lone tower crowned by an 18th-century wrought-iron bell cage. The château is closed, but a steep, uneven trail to it rewards you with a fine view.

▲**Market Day**—In the 16th century, the pope gave Vaison la Romaine market-town status. Each Tuesday since then, the town has hosted a farmers' market. Today, merchants gather with gusto, turning the entire place into a festival of produce and Provençal products. This Tuesday-morning market is one of France's best, but it can challenge claustrophobes. Be warned that parking is a real headache unless you arrive early (see "Helpful Hints" on page 560, and "Provence Market Days" on page 503).

**Wine-Tasting**—Cave la Romaine, a five-minute walk up avenue Général de Gaulle from the TI, offers a variety of great-value wines from nearby villages in a pleasant, well-organized tasting room (daily 8:30–13:00 & 14:00–19:00, avenue St. Quenin, tel. 04 90 36 55 90).

**Hiking**—The TI has good information on relatively easy hikes into the hills above Vaison la Romaine. It's about 75 minutes to the tiny hill town of Le Crestet, though views begin immediately. To find this trail, drive or walk past the upper town (with the castle just on your left), find the *chemin des Fontaines,* and stay the course as far as you like. Cars are not allowed on the road after about a mile. Consider taking a taxi to Le Crestet, and walking back (see "Le Crestet," page 568). The TI also has information on a loop hike from Vaison la Romaine to Crestet (a newer village below the older hillside town of Le Crestet)—it follows the same path to Le Crestet, with a different return route.

**Biking**—This area is not particularly flat, and it's often hot and windy, making bike-riding a dicey option. But if it's calm, the five-mile ride to cute little Villedieu (recommended restaurant described under "Eating," later in this section) is a delight. The bike route is signed along small roads; you'll find signs from Vaison la Romaine to Villedieu at the roundabout by Cave La Romaine (see map page 562). With a little more energy, you can pedal beyond Villedieu on the lovely road to Mirabel (ask in Villedieu for directions). Or get a good map and connect the following villages for an enjoyable 11-mile loop ride: Vaison la Romaine, St. Romain-en-Viennois, Puyméras (with a recommended restaurant—see page 567), Faucon, and St. Marcellin-lès-Vaison. The TI and bike shop have good information on mountain-biking trails.

# SLEEPING

## In Vaison la Romaine

Hotels in Vaison la Romaine are a good value. Those in the medieval upper town (Ville-Haute) are quieter, cozier, cooler, and a 15-minute walk uphill from the parking lot next to the TI (some hotels also offer closer parking). If you have a car, consider staying in one of the charming Côtes du Rhône villages near Vaison la Romaine (see next page). If staying at one of the first three places, follow signs to *Cité Médiévale* and park just outside the upper village entry (driving into the Cité Médiévale itself is a challenge, with tiny lanes and nearly impossible parking).

$$$ **Hôtel le Beffroi*** hides deep in the upper town, just above a demonstrative bell tower (you'll hear what I mean). It offers 16th-century, red-tile-and-wood-beamed-cozy lodgings with nary a level surface. The rooms—split between two buildings a few doors apart—are Old World comfy, and some have views. You'll also find tasteful public spaces, a garden with view tables (light meals available in the summer), a small pool with more views, and animated Nathalie at the reception (standard Db-€95–115, superior Db-€145, Tb-€170, rue de l'Evêché, tel. 04 90 36 04 71, fax 04 90 36 24 78, www.le-beffroi.com, info@le-beffroi.com). The hotel's restaurant offers *menus* from €29.

$$$ **L'Evêché Chambres,** almost next door to le Beffroi in the upper town (look for the ivy), is a five-room, melt-in-your-chair B&B. The owners (the Verdiers) own the art boutique across the street, have an exquisite sense of interior design, and are passionate about books, making this place feel like a cross between a library and an art gallery (Sb-€75–90, standard Db-€85–100, Db suite-€115–145, the *solanum* suite is worth every euro, Tb-€125–155, Internet access and Wi-Fi, rue de l'Evêché, tel. 04 90 36 13 46, fax 04 90 36 32 43, http://eveche.free.fr, eveche@aol.com).

$$ **Hôtel la Fête en Provence,** conveniently located for drivers at the entry to the medieval upper town, has a variety of room shapes and sizes. All the rooms are chiffon-comfortable, and several have small kitchenettes. Rooms are located around

a calming courtyard, and there's a pool and Jacuzzi next door (standard Db-€75, bigger Db with king-size bed and bath-€105, extra person-€15, Cité Médiévale, tel. & fax 04 90 36 36 43, www.hotellafete-provence.com, fete-en-provence@wanadoo.fr). Their apartment (€115) sleeps up to six people, and comes with a kitchenette and sitting area.

**$ Hôtel Burrhus**\*\* is part art gallery, part funky hotel—and the best value in the lower town. It's a central, laid-back, go-with-the-flow place, with a broad terrace over the raucous place Montfort (the double-paned windows are effective, but for maximum quiet, request a back room). Its floor plan will confound even the ablest navigator. The bigger, newer rooms—with contemporary decor, bigger bathrooms, and air-conditioning—are worth the extra euros for most travelers (Db-€52–58, newer Db-€62–85, extra bed-€15, air-con in some rooms, free Internet access and Wi-Fi, 1 place Montfort, tel. 04 90 36 00 11, fax 04 90 36 39 05, www.burrhus.com, info@burrhus.com).

## Near Vaison la Romaine

These four accommodations are within a 10-minute drive of Vaison la Romaine.

**$$$ Domaine de Cabasse**\*\*\* is a lovely spread flanked by vineyards at the foot of Séguret (with a walking path to the village). Winemaking is their primary business (tastings possible), though the hotel is well-run by its relaxed staff. The 13 rooms have retained a simple Old World feel. All the rooms have decks, and a big pool is at your disposal. From the entry gate—which opens automatically...and slowly—the place appears more formal than it is (Db-€125–150, breakfast-€12.50, on D-23 between Sablet and Séguret, tel. 04 90 46 91 12, fax 04 90 46 94 01, www.cabasse.fr, info@cabasse.fr). The restaurant offers a satisfying, though limited, €29 dinner *menu* served inside or out.

**$$$ Hôtel Les Florets**\*\*, a half-mile above Gigondas, is surrounded by pine trees at the foothills of the Dentelles de Montmirail. It comes with a huge terrace that Van Gogh would have loved, thoughtfully designed rooms, and an exceptional restaurant (Db-€100–110, Tb-€115–135, annex rooms are best, tel. 04 90 65 85 01, fax 04 90 65 83 80, www.hotel-lesflorets.com, accueil@hotel-lesflorets.com). For more details about the hotel's restaurant, see page 567.

**$$$ Domaine de Tilleuls**\*\*\*, 10 minutes from Vaison la Romaine in workaday Malaucène, is a winning, well-priced refuge, and the most family-friendly place I list. (Welcoming owners Arnaud and Dominique have three kids.) Its 20 country-modern rooms fill an old farmhouse overlooking lovely grounds with namesake linden trees *(tilleuls)*, a sandbox, toys, and a large pool. If you missed market day in Vaison la Romaine, sleep here Tuesday night and wake to a bustling market (Db-€80–100, Tb/Qb-€115, Wi-Fi, Internet café nearby, well-signed in Malaucène on the route to Mont Ventoux, tel. 04 90 65 22 31, fax 04 90 65 16 77, www.hotel-domainedestilleuls.com, info@hotel-domainedestilleuls.com).

**$$ L'Ecole Buissonnière Chambres** is run by an engaging Anglo-French team, Monique and John, who share their peace and quiet 10 minutes from Vaison la Romaine. This creatively restored farmhouse has three character-filled, half-timbered rooms, and convivial public spaces. Getting to know John, who has lived all over the south of France and even worked as a *gardian* (cowboy) in the Camargue, is worth the price of the room; he's also generous with his knowledge of the area. The outdoor kitchen allows guests to picnic in high fashion in the tranquil garden (Db-€56–65, Tb-€75–79, Qb-€90–97, includes breakfast, cash only, between Villedieu and Buisson on D-75, tel. 04 90 28 95 19, ecole.buissonniere@wanadoo.fr). If they're full, they'll work hard to find you a room nearby at comparable rates.

# EATING

## In Vaison la Romaine

Vaison la Romaine offers a handful of excellent places—arrive by 19:30 or reserve ahead, particularly on weekends. And while you can eat very well on a moderate budget in Vaison, it's well worth venturing to nearby Côtes du Rhône villages to eat (see "Near Vaison la Romaine," next page). Wherever you dine, begin with a fresh glass of Muscat from the nearby village of Beaumes de Venise.

**La Bartavelle** is a fine place to savor traditional French cuisine in the lower town. Owner Berangère (bear-ahn-zher) has put together a tourist-friendly mix-and-match menu of local options. You get access to the top-end selections even on the €20 bottom-end *menu*—just fewer courses. Be sure to reserve ahead (closed Mon, small terrace outside, air-con and pleasant interior, 12 place de Sus Auze, tel. 04 90 36 02 16).

**Le Bateleur,** almost on the river, serves refined Provençal cuisine in a more formal setting. English-speaking owners, Jean-François and his wife Fabienne, are popular hosts (€18 lunch *menu*, €30 and €40 dinner *menus*, closed Mon year-round and Thu Oct–May, air-con, near Roman Bridge at 1 place Théodore Aubanel, tel. 04 90 36 28 04).

**Le Tournesol** offers a good €18 dinner, with mostly Provençal dishes and friendly service. I love the *aubergine feuilleté* (eggplant puff pastry) and lamb with cheese. Show this book in 2009 to get a free *kir* (daily June–Oct, Nov–May closed Tue–Wed, 30 cours Taulignan, tel. 04 90 36 09 18, owner Patrick speaks a little English).

**La Lyriste** sits opposite le Tournesol, offering a delectable *menu* for €20 and indoor or outdoor seating (45 Cours Taulignan, tel. 04 90 36 04 67).

**Bistro du'O,** in the upper village, is the buzz of Vaison. Reserve ahead and you'll dine on soft leather chairs under soaring stone arches and enjoy mouthwatering cuisine that is creatively presented yet affordable. The lamb is terrific (*menus* from €25, closed Sun, rue du Château, tel. 04 90 41 72 90).

**Hôtel le Beffroi's** garden is just right for a light dinner in the summer (€15 *menus* in garden, *menus* from €29 inside restaurant, recommended under "Sleeping," earlier in this chapter).

## Near Vaison la Romaine

Drivers enjoy a wealth of country-Provençal dining opportunities in rustic settings, handy to many of the rural accommodations. Most are within a 10-minute drive of Vaison la Romaine. Other eateries are described along the "Côtes du Rhône Scenic Loop," next page.

**La Girocedre** is an enchanting place to eat lunch or dinner if you have a car and it's nice outside. Just three picturesque miles from Vaison la Romaine in adorable Puyméras, this place offers a complete country-Provençal package: outdoor tables placed just-so in a lush garden, warm interior decor, and mouthwatering Provençal cuisine (€13–16 *plats, menus* from €25, closed Mon, tel. 04 90 46 50 67).

**Hôtel les Florets,** in Gigondas, is a traditional, family-run place that's worth the drive. Dinners are a sumptuous blend of classic French cuisine and Provençal accents, served with class by English-speaking Thierry. The marvelous terrace makes your meal even more memorable (*menus* from €29, restaurant closed Wed, service can be slow; see hotel listing under "Sleeping," earlier in this section).

**La Maison Bleue,** on Villedieu's adorable little square, is a pizza-and-salad place with great outdoor ambience. Skip it if the weather forces you inside (open for lunch and dinner, closed Wed, tel. 04 90 28 97 02).

# TRANSPORTATION CONNECTIONS

The most central bus stop is at Cave Vinicole.

**From Vaison la Romaine by Bus to: Avignon** (2–3/day during school year, called *période scolaire;* otherwise 1/day, plus 1/day to Avignon TGV station, 90 min), **Orange** (2–3/day, 45 min), **Nyons** (2–3/day, 45 min), **Crestet** (lower village below Le Crestet, 2/day, 5 min), **Carpentras** (2/day, 45 min). Bus info: tel. 04 90 36 05 22.

# Côtes du Rhône
# Sights near Vaison la Romaine

PROVENCE

## ▲▲▲Côtes du Rhône Scenic Loop

With a car or minivan tour and a half-day, you can experience this glorious loop clockwise around the Dentelles de Montmirail, visiting the mountaintop village of Le Crestet, adorable little Suzette, and the famous wine villages of Beaumes-de-Venise, Gigondas, and Séguret. I've listed a few wineries *(domaines)* along the way. This easy loop is a shame to miss even if wine isn't your thing.

Leave Vaison la Romaine following signs toward Carpentras on D-938, detour up to Le Crestet, then return to D-938 and turn right onto D-90 just before entering Malaucene. Follow D-90 to Beaumes de Venise (passing Suzette and later, a turnoff to Domaine de Durban), then find D-8 and then D-7, which will take you back to Vaison la Romaine passing Gigondas, Sablet, and Séguret.

Here are the key stops on this route:

## ❶ Le Crestet

This hilltop village—founded after the fall of the Roman Empire, when laws were lost and people banded together in high places like this for protection from marauding barbarians—followed the usual hill town evolution. The outer walls of the village did double duty as ramparts and house walls. The castle above (dating about A.D. 850, closed to the public) provided a final safe haven if attacked. With about 500 residents in 1200, Le Crestet was a very important town in this region. The village reached its zenith in the mid-1500s, when 660 people called Le Crestet home. The village began its gradual decline in the 1600s, though the population remained fairly stable until WWII. Today, about 35 people live within the walls year-round (about 55 during the summer). The village's only business, café-restaurant **Le Panoramic,** has an upstairs terrace with a view that justifies the name...even if the food is overpriced (open daily for lunch and dinner, tel. 04 90 28 76 42).

## ❷ Suzette

Tiny Suzette floats on its hilltop (midway along D-90), with a small 12th-century chapel, one café, a handful of residents, and the gaggle of houses where they live. Find the big orientation board above the lot and find the broad shoulders of Mont Ventoux. At 6,000 feet, it always seems to have some clouds hanging around. The top looks like it's snow-covered; if you drive up there, you'll see it's actually white stone. Suzette's homes once

## Côtes du Rhône Scenic Loop

5 MILES
10 KM

TO NYONS
D-94

MIRABEL

TO ARDECHE GORGES
D-94

VILLEDIEU

PUYMERAS

FAUCON

VAISON LA ROMAINE
ROAIX

D-8
RASTEAU
CAIRANNE · D-69
SEGURET
D-88
SABLET

D-938
BIKE LOOP
D-5
LE CRESTET

PATH ①

D-975
D-90
MALAUCENE

DENTELLES DE MONTMIRAIL

TO ORANGE & AVIGNON
D-977
GIGONDAS ④
② SUZETTE

D-979
TO MONT VENTOUX

VACQUEYRAS
③
LAFARE
D-19
BEDOIN

LA ROQUE ALRIC
LE BARROUX
D-974

TO ORANGE & A-7
BEAUMES-DE-VENISE
D-938
D-7
D-474
TO MONT VENTOUX

D-950
CARPENTRAS
D-942

TO AVIGNON
D-942
D-49
D-938

TO ISLE-SUR-LA-SORGUE & LUBERON

DCH

① Le Crestet
② Suzette
③ Domaine de Durban Winery
④ Gigondas
⑤ Séguret

huddled in the shadow of an imposing castle, destroyed during the religious wars of the mid-1500s. **Les Coquelicots,** a tiny eatery surrounded by vines and views, is a sweet spot for lunch or a drink. The food is scrumptious (owner/chef Frankie insists on fresh products) and the setting is memorable. Try the €14 *Assiette Provençale,* or any of his grilled meats and fish (usually closed Tue–Wed May–Sept, then open weekends only Oct–April, tel. 04 90 65 06 94). Good picnic tables lie just past Suzette for those who brought their own food. Back across the road from the orientation table is a tasting room for **Château Redortier** wines (English brochure and well-explained list of wines provided; skip their whites, but try the good rosés and reds).

## ❸ Domaine de Durban

In this stunning setting, *charmante* Nathalie or her assistant will take your taste buds on a tour. This *domaine* produces appealing whites, reds, and Muscats. Start with the 100 percent Viognier, then try their Viognier-Chardonnay blend. Their rosé is light and refreshing (and cheap). Their two reds are very different from each other: One is fruity, and the other—aged in oak—is tannic. Finish with their popular Muscat de Venise (wines cost €4–10 per bottle, Mon–Sat 9:00–12:00 & 14:00–18:30, closed Sun, tel. 04 90 62 94 26). Picnics are not allowed, though strolling amid the gorgeous vineyards is. To find the winery, drive to Beaumes de Venise on D-90 and keep right at the first *Centre-Ville* sign as the road bends left, then carefully track *Domaine de Durban* signs for three incredibly scenic miles.

## ❹ Gigondas

This town produces some of the region's best reds and is ideally situated for hiking, mountain-biking, and driving into the mountains. The **TI** has a list of wineries, *chambres d'hôte,* and good hikes or drives (Mon–Sat 10:00–12:30 & 14:00–18:00, likely closed Sun, place du Portail, tel. 04 90 65 85 46). Take a walk up through the town (best after wine-tasting)—the church is an easy destination with good views over the heart of the Côtes du Rhône vineyards. Several good tasting opportunities sit side-by-side on the main square. **Le Caveau de Gigondas** is best, where Sandra and Barbara await your visit with a large and free selection of tiny bottles for sampling, filled directly from the barrel (daily 10:00–12:00 & 14:00–18:30, 2 doors down from TI, tel. 04 90 65 82 29). Here you can compare wines from a variety of private producers in an intimate, low-key surrounding. There's a small grocery store and several eating options in the village. Diagonally across from the TI, the shaded red tables of **Du Verre à l'Assiette** ("From Glass to Plate") entice lunchtime eaters (also good interior ambience, €10 salads, €14 *plats*, €15 mixed plate of meats and salad, daily, place du Village, tel. 04 90 12 36 64). To dine very well or sleep nearby, find **Hôtel les Florets,** a half-mile above town (restaurant closed Wed, see page 565).

## ❺ Séguret

Blending into the hillside with a smattering of shops, two cafés, made-to-stroll lanes, and a natural spring, this village is understandably popular. Try to visit early or late in the day (Séguret works well for a breakfast stop or a pre-dinner stroll). The bulky entry arch just above the parking area came with a massive gate, which kept bad guys out for centuries. To appreciate how the homes' outer walls provided security in those days, stroll down the main drag, keep right, then take one of the tunnel exits to the right. These exit passages, or *poternes,* were needed in periods of peace to allow the town to expand below. Find Séguret's open washbasin—a hotbed of social activity and gossip over the ages—and the community bread oven *(four banal),* used for festivals and celebrations. At Christmas, this entire village transforms itself into one big crèche scene (a Provençal tradition that has long since died out in other villages).

## ▲Ardèche Gorges (Gorges de l'Ardèche)

These gorges, which wow visitors with abrupt chalky-white cliffs, follow the Ardèche River through immense canyons and thick forests. This drive is a scenic way to go north (to Lyon, for example). To reach the gorges from Vaison la Romaine, drive west 45 minutes, passing through Bollène and Pont Saint-Esprit to Vallon Pont d'Arc (the tourist hub of the Ardèche Gorges). From Vallon Pont d'Arc, you can canoe along the peaceful river through some of the canyon's most spectacular scenery and under the rock arch of Pont d'Arc (half-day, all-day, and 2-day trips possible), and learn about hiking trails that get you above it all (**TI** tel. 04 75 88 04 01, www.vallon-pont-darc.com). If continuing north toward Lyon, connect Privas and Aubenas, then head back via the autoroute. Endearing little Balazuc—a village north of the gorges, with narrow lanes, flowers, views, and a smattering of cafés and shops—makes a fine stop.

# Hill Towns of the Luberon

Just 30 miles east of Avignon, the Luberon region hides some of France's most captivating hill towns and sensuous landscapes. Those intrigued by Peter Mayle's books love joyriding through the region, connecting I-could-live-here villages, crumbled castles, and meditative abbeys. Mayle's bestselling *A Year in Provence* describes the ruddy local culture from an Englishman's perspective as he buys a stone farmhouse, fixes it up, and adopts the region as his new home. His book is a great read while you're here.

The Luberon terrain in general (much

of which is a French regional natural park) is as appealing as its villages. Gnarled vineyards and wind-sculpted trees separate tidy stone structures from abandoned buildings—little more than rock piles—that seem to challenge city slickers to fix them up. Mountains of limestone bend along vast ridges, while colorful hot-air balloons survey the sun-drenched scene from above.

## Getting Around the Luberon

**By Car:** Luberon roads are scenic and narrow. With no major landmarks, it's easy to get lost in this area—and you will get lost, trust me—but getting lost is the point. Pick up the Michelin Local map #332 to navigate.

**By Bus:** Isle-sur-la-Sorgue is easy by bus from Avignon, with several daily trips and a central stop at the post office (6/day Mon–Sat, fewer on Sun, 45 min). Without a car or minivan tour, I'd skip the more famous hill towns of the Luberon.

**By Train:** Trains get you to Isle-sur-la-Sorgue (station called "L'Isle–Fontaine de Vaucluse") from Avignon (10/day on weekdays, 5/day on weekends, 30 min) or from Marseille (8/day, 1–2 hours). If you're day-tripping by train, check return times before leaving the station.

**By Minivan Tour:** Dutchman Mike Rijken, who runs **Wine Safari,** offers tours of this area, as do several other Avignon-based companies (see "Tours of Provence" on page 500).

**By Bike:** Hardy bikers can ride from Isle-sur-la-Sorgue to Gordes, then to Roussillon, connecting other villages in a full-day loop ride (30 miles round-trip to Roussillon and back, with lots of hills). Many appealing villages are closer to Isle-sur-la-Sorgue and offer easier biking options (see "Biking" on page 575).

# Isle-sur-la-Sorgue

This sturdy market town—literally, "Island on the Sorgue River"—sits within a split in its crisp, happy little river. After

the arid cities and villages elsewhere in Provence, the presence of water at every turn is a welcome change. In Isle-sur-la-Sorgue—called the "Venice of Provence"—the Sorgue River's extraordinarily clear and shallow flow divides like cells, producing water, water everywhere. Every other shop seems to sell some kind of antique.

# ORIENTATION

While Isle-sur-la-Sorgue is renowned for its market days (Sun and Thu), it's otherwise a pleasantly average town with no important sights and a steady trickle of tourism. It's calm at night and downright dead on Mondays.

## Tourist Information

The TI has information on hiking and biking, and a line on rooms in private homes, all of which are outside the town (Mon–Sat 9:00–12:30 & 14:30–18:00, Sun 9:00–12:30, in town center next to church, tel. 04 90 38 04 78, www.oti-delasorgue.fr).

## Arrival in Isle-sur-la-Sorgue

**By Car:** Traffic is a mess and parking is a headache on market days (all day Sun and Thu mornings). Circle the ring road and look for parking signs, or give up and find the pay lot behind the post office (PTT). There are several lots just west of the roundabout at Le Bassin. You'll also pass freestyle parking on roads leaving the city. Don't leave anything visible in your car.

**By Train:** Remember that the train station is called "L'Isle–Fontaine de Vaucluse." To reach my recommended hotels, walk straight out of the station and turn right on the ring road.

**By Bus:** The bus from Avignon drops you at the post office (PTT), a block from the recommended Hôtel les Névons.

## Helpful Hints

**Shop Hours:** The antique shops this town is famous for are open Saturday to Monday only.

**Internet Access:** Try **Internet Station,** across from the church and TI and a block down rue Danton at #3 (tel. 04 90 20 03 28).

**Bookstore:** You'll find a handful of English novels at **Librairie** where the pedestrian street rue de la République meets Notre-Dame des Anges church (Tue–Sat 7:00–12:00 & 14:00–19:00, Sun–Mon 7:00–12:00).

**Laundry:** It's just off the rue de la République, at 23 impasse de l'Hôtel de Palerme (daily 7:00–20:00).

**Supermarket:** A well-stocked **Spar** market is on the main ring road, near the Peugeot Car shop and the train station (Mon–Sat 8:30–12:30 & 15:00–19:00, Sun 15:00–19:00). A smaller **Casino** market is more central on pedestrian rue de la République (Tue–Sun 7:30–12:30 & 15:30–19:30, closed Mon).

**Bike Rental: Isles 2 Roues,** by the train station, rents bikes (€14/day, must show your passport, 10 avenue de la Gare, tel. 04 90 38 19 12).

**Taxi:** Call 06 84 64 32 67.

**Public WC:** There's a good WC in the parking lot between the post office (PTT) and the Hôtel les Névons.

**Hiking:** The TI has good information on area hikes; most trails are accessible by short drives, and you can use a taxi to get there.

## SIGHTS AND ACTIVITIES

**Wandering Isle-sur-la-Sorgue**—The town has crystal-clear water babbling under pedestrian bridges stuffed with flower boxes, and its old-time carousel is always spinning. Navigate by the town's splintered streams and nine mossy waterwheels, which, while still turning, power only memories of the town's wool and silk industries. Here are key sights along the way.

**The Sorgue River:** With its source (a spring) a mere five miles away, the Sorgue River never floods and has a constant flow and temperature in all seasons. Despite its exposed location, Isle-sur-la-Sorgue prospered in the Middle Ages, thanks to the natural protection this river provided. Walls with big moats once ran along the river, but they were destroyed during the French Revolution. Find Le Bassin, where the Sorgue River enters the town and separates into many branches (carefully placed lights make this a beautiful sight after dark). Fishing provided Isle-sur-la-Sorgue's economic base until the waterwheels took over. Fishermen trapped fish in nets or speared them while standing on skinny, flat-bottomed boats.

The clumsy-looking **waterwheels** that you'll see at various points on the river have been in business since the 1200s, when they were used for grinding flour. Paper, textile, silk, and woolen mills would later find their power from this river. At its peak, the town had 70 waterwheels and in the 1800s, Isle-sur-la-Sorgue competed with Avignon as Provence's cloth-dyeing and textile center. Those stylish Provençal fabrics and patterns you see for sale everywhere were made possible by this river.

**Notre-Dame des Anges:** This 12th-century church has a festive Baroque interior and seems overgrown for today's town. Walk in. The curls and swirls and gilded statues date from an era that was all about Louis XIV, the Sun King. This is propagandist architecture, designed to wow the faithful into compliance.

**▲▲Market Days**—The town erupts into a carnival-like market frenzy each Sunday and Thursday, with hardy crafts and local produce. The Sunday market is astounding and famous for its antiques; the Thursday market is more intimate (see market tips on page 503). Find a table across from the church at the Café de France and enjoy the scene.

**Antique Toy and Doll Museum (Musée du Jouet et de la Poupée Ancienne)**—The town's lone sight is a fun and funky toy museum with more than 300 dolls displayed in three small rooms (€3.50, kids-€1.50; July–Sept Mon–Sat 10:30–18:30, Sun 11:00–18:00; Oct–June Tue–Fri 13:00–18:00, Sat–Sun 11:00–17:00, closed Mon; 26 rue Carnot).

**Biking**—These towns make easy biking destinations from Isle-sur-la-Sorgue: Velleron (5 miles north, flat, a tiny version of Isle-sur-la-Sorgue with waterwheels, fountains, and an evening farmer's market Mon–Sat 18:00–20:00); Lagnes (3 miles east, a pretty and well-restored hill town with views from its ruined château); and Fontaine-de-Vaucluse (5 miles northeast, a touristy village at the source of the Sorgue River, gently uphill). Allow 30 miles and many hills for the round-trip ride to Roussillon (see "Bike Rental" under "Helpful Hints," earlier in this section).

# SLEEPING

## In and near Isle-sur-la-Sorgue

**$$$ Chambres Sous l'Olivier,** located five minutes east of Isle-sur-la-Sorgue, is well-situated for exploring the hill towns of the Luberon and Isle-sur-la-Sorgue. Its six lovely rooms are housed in a massive, 150-year-old farmhouse with lounges that you and your entire soccer team could spread out in. Julien and Carole take care of your every need, and they'll cook you a full-blown dinner with wine for €29 per person (Db-€90–130, 3-room suite for up to 6 people-€220, prices include breakfast; credit cards not accepted—pay with cash, euro travelers checks, or bank transfer; pool, route d'Apt, tel. 04 90 20 33 90, www.chambresdhotesprovence.com, souslolivier@orange.fr). It's below Isle-sur-la-Sorgue, about 25 minutes from Avignon toward Apt on D-900 (near Petit Palais—don't go to Lagnes by mistake). Look for signs 200 yards after the big sign to *le Mas du Grand Jonquier,* on the right.

**$$ Hôtel les Névons**\*\*, two blocks from the center of Isle-sur-la-Sorgue (behind the post office), is concrete motel–modern outside, but a good value within. The staff is eager to please, and you have two wings to choose from: the new wing, with cavernous (by local standards) and well-appointed rooms; or the old wing, with more modest, cheaper (but fine) rooms. There are several family suites and a roof deck with 360-degree views around a small pool (old wing—Db-€58–65; new wing—huge Db-€68–80, Tb-€80–90, Qb-€90–100; air-con, Internet access, Wi-Fi in lobby, easy parking, 205 chemin des Névons, push and hold the gate button a bit on entry, tel. 04 90 20 72 00, fax 04 90 20 56 20, www.hotel-les-nevons.com, info@hotel-les-nevons.com).

# EATING

## In Isle-sur-la-Sorgue

Inexpensive restaurants are easy to find in Isle-sur-la-Sorgue, but consistent quality is another story. The restaurants I list offer good value, but none of them is really "cheap." For inexpensive meals, troll the riverside cafés for today's catch. Dining on the river is a unique experience in this arid land famous for its hill towns, and shopping for the perfect table is half the fun. Riverside picnics work well here (the Fromenterie bakery, next to the post office, stocks mouthwatering quiche and more).

Begin your dinner with a glass of wine at the cozy **Le Caveau de la Tour de l'Isle** (part wine bar, part wine-and-cheese shop, Tue–Sat until about 20:00, closed Sun–Mon, 12 rue de la République, tel. 04 90 20 70 25).

**Les Terrasses du Bassin,** a new player in town, shows great promise with moderate prices, good choices, and a cool riverfront location (terrace dining available). The affable owners are working hard to provide a good value and welcoming service. Say hello to Max and come for a full meal or just a *plat* (€9 lunch salads and good pasta, €16 dinner *plats*, €25 dinner *menu*, closed Tue–Wed, 2 avenue Charles de Gaulle, tel. 04 90 38 03 16).

**La Prévôté** is a place to really do it up. Its dining room is covered in wood beams, the outdoor patio is peaceful, and the ambience is country-classy but not stuffy. A branch of the Sorgue runs under the restaurant, visible through glass windows (*menus* from €43, save room for amazing cheese platter, closed Tue–Wed, 4 rue J. J. Rousseau, on narrow street that runs along left side of church as you face it, tel. 04 90 38 57 29).

**L'Ousteau de l'Isle,** a mile from the town center, dishes up regional cuisine with a modern twist and a friendly welcome. Skip the modern interior and ask for a table *sur la terrasse* (dinner *menus* from €27, lunch *menu* for €18, closed Tue–Wed, 147 chemin de Bosquet, tel. 04 90 20 81 36). From Isle-sur-la-Sorgue's center, follow signs toward *Apt,* and turn right at Pain d'Antan Boulangerie; or walk 20 minutes along the river and cross the small bridge to chemin de Bosquet.

# Roussillon

With all the trendy charm of Santa Fe on a hilltop, photogenic Roussillon requires serious camera and café time (and €3 for parking). Roussillon has been a protected village since 1943 and has benefited from a complete absence of modern development. An enormous deposit of ochre gives the earth and its buildings that distinctive red color and provided this village with its economic base until shortly after World War II. This place is popular; it's best to visit early or late in the day.

# ORIENTATION

Roussillon sits atop Mont Rouge (Red Mountain) at about 1,000 feet above sea level, and requires some uphill walking to reach. Exposed ochre cliffs form the village's southern limit.

## Tourist Information

The little TI is in the center, between the two parking lots and across from the David restaurant. Walkers should get info on trails from Roussillon to nearby villages (April–Oct Mon–Sat 10:00–12:00 & 14:00–18:00, closed Sun except in summer; Nov–March Mon–Sat 14:00–17:30, closed Sun; tel. 04 90 05 60 25).

## Arrival in Roussillon

Parking lots are available at every entry to the village. The closest two lots are on the northern edge (Parking St. Michel, by the recommended Hôtel Rêves d'Ocres) and on the southern flank, closer to the ochre cliffs (Parking Sablons). If you approach from Gordes or Joucas, you'll end up at the northern lot. If you're coming from N-100 and the south, you'll park at the southern lot (but don't park there on Wednesday night, because Thursday is Roussillon's market day). Leave nothing valuable showing in your car.

## Helpful Hints

An ATM is next to the TI. Internet access and a modest selection of English books are available at the delightful **Librairie** book-store on the main square (daily 10:00–18:00; its good café is also described in "Eating," later in this section).

# SIGHTS

## ▲The Village

Climb to the village top and find the orientation plaque and the

dramatic viewpoint, often complete with a howling mistral wind. During the Middle Ages, a castle stood where you are, on the top of Mont Rouge. While nothing remains of the castle today, the strategic advantage of this site is clear: You can see forever. Notice how little sprawl is

Roussillon

NOT TO SCALE—
TOURIST INFO TO ST. MICHEL
CHURCH IS A 5-MIN. UPHILL WALK

1 Le Clos de la Glycine

2 Hôtel Rêves d'Ocres

3 To Madame Cherel,
Hôtel Les Sables d'Ocre
& Le Clos des Cigales

4 Le Bistrot de Roussillon,
Café Couleur & Le Castrum

5 Librairie Bookshop
(Café & Internet)

6 Orientation Plaque,
View & Start of Walk

STEPPED STREETS

P PARKING

VIEW

PROVENCE

TO OCHRE CLIFFS

DCH

POSTE AVE. BURLIERE

P (Ocres)

P (Pasquier) WC

1

TO D-227
ST-SATURNIN-LES-APT
& RUSTREL

RUE DE LA POSTE

POST

5

4

Ochre Conservatory,
D-104 to Gault + Apt
& N-100 to Bonnieux

RUE CASTEAU

+ RUE DE L'ARCADE

PLACE MAIRIE

P (Fontaine)

PLACE MATHIEU

BELL TOWER

6

MONT ROUGE

ST. MICHEL

RUE RONDE

RUE DES R. BOURGADES

RUE DES R. LAURIERS

D-2

TO MURS,
JOUCAS & GORDES
VIA D-2

P

WC

(St. Michel)

RUE DE LA PORTE HEUREUSE

P (Sablons) WC

2

D-169

TO GORDES & JOUCAS

N

in the valley below. Because the Luberon is a natural reserve (Parc Naturel Régional du Luberon), development is strictly controlled.

A short stroll down leads to the church. Duck into the pretty 11th-century Church of St. Michel, and appreciate the well-worn center aisle and the propane heaters—winters can be frigid in this area. The white interior tells us that the stone came from elsewhere.

Examine the different hues of yellow and orange in the village. These lime-finished exteriors, called *chaux* (limes), need to be redone about every 10 years. Locals choose their exact color...but in this town of ochre, it's never white. The church tower you walk under marked the entrance to the fortified town.

See how local (or artsy) you can look in what must be the most scenic village square in Provence (place de la Mairie) and watch the river of shoppers. Is anyone playing *boules* at the opposite end? You could paint the entire town without ever leaving the red-and-orange corner of your palette. Many do. While Roussillon receives its share of day-trippers, evenings are romantically peaceful on this square.

### ▲▲Ochre Cliffs

Roussillon was Europe's capital for ochre production until World War II. A stroll to the south end of town, beyond the upper parking lot, will show you why: Roussillon sits on the world's largest known ochre deposit. A brilliant orange path leads through the richly colored ochre canyon, explaining the hue of this village (€2, daily 9:00–17:30, until 19:00 in summer; beware—light-colored clothing and orange powder don't mix).

The value of Roussillon's ochre cliffs was known even in Roman times. Once excavated, the clay ochre was rinsed with water to separate it from sand, and bricks of the stuff were dried and baked for deeper hues. The procedure for extracting the ochre did not change much over 2,000 years, until ochre mining became industrialized in the late 1700s. Used primarily for wallpaper and linoleum, ochre use reached its zenith just before World War II. (After that, cheaper substitutes took over.)

## SLEEPING

(€1 = about $1.50, country code: 33)

### In Roussillon

The TI posts a list of hotels and *chambres d'hôte*. Parking is free if you sleep in Roussillon—ask your hotelier where to park. The village offers three good-value accommodations—conveniently, one for each price range.

**$$$ Le Clos de la Glycine*** provides Roussillon's four-star accommodations at three-star prices, with nine gorgeous rooms located dead-center in the village (Db-€140–155, big Db-€180, loft suite with deck and view-€275, Wi-Fi, located at the refined restaurant David, across from the TI on place de la Poste, tel. 04 90 05 60 13, fax 04 90 05 75 80, www.luberon-hotel.com, le.clos .de.la.glycine@wanadoo.fr).

**$$ Hôtel Rêves d'Ocres**\*\*** is a solid two-star value, run by eager-to-help Sandrine and Yvan. It's ochre-colored, warm, and comfortable, with 16 mostly spacious and tastefully designed rooms (eight have view terraces, none have TV) and a lovely lounge where you can stretch out (Sb-€56, Db without balcony-€76, Db with balcony-€82, Tb-€95, meek air-con, Internet access, route de Gordes, tel. 04 90 05 60 50, fax 04 90 05 79 74, www.hotel -revesdocres.com, hotelrevesdocres@wanadoo.fr). Coming from Gordes and Joucas, it's the first building you pass in Roussillon.

**$ Madame Cherel** rents ramshackle rooms that are barely this side of a youth hostel. A common view terrace and good reading materials are available, and the beds have firm mattresses (D-€42–46, includes breakfast, cash only, 3 blocks from upper parking lot, between the gas station and school, La Burlière, tel. 04 90 05 71 71, mulhanc@hotmail.com). Chatty and sincere Cherel speaks English, is a wealth of regional travel tips, and rents mountain bikes to guests (€15/day).

## Near Roussillon, in or near Joucas

The tiny village of Joucas lies a few minutes below Roussillon and hides a handful of good-value accommodations. Each of the three hotels listed below comes with a good restaurant.

**$$$ La Ferme de la Huppe**\*\*\*** has a Gordes address, but it's closer physically and spiritually to Joucas. This small, farmhouse-elegant hacienda makes an excellent mini-splurge. Ten low-slung rooms gather on two levels behind the stylish pool. The decor is understated and rustic. Dinners poolside or in the cozy dining room have been memorable, though new owners take over in 2009, so you'll have to judge for yourself; expect some changes to these prices (small Db-€90, bigger Db-€110–130, much bigger Db-€150–170, includes breakfast, air-con, Wi-Fi; between Joucas and Gordes on D-156 road to Goult, just off D-2; tel. 04 90 72 12 25, fax 04 90 72 01 83, www.lafermedelahuppe.com).

**$$$ Le Mas du Loriot** is another worthwhile almost-in-Joucas value. Gentle owners Alain and Christine have carved the ideal escape out of an olive grove, with eight soothing rooms, private terraces, a generous pool, and home-cooked dinners—all at fair prices and with a view to remember (Db-€100–130, extra bed-€20, €28 four-course dinners available three nights a week, Internet access, on D-102 between Joucas and Murs, tel. 04 90 72 62 62, fax 04 90 72 62 54, www.masduloriot.com, hotel@masduloriot.com).

**$$ Hostellerie des Commandeurs\*\***, run by soft Sophie, has modern, comfortable, and clean rooms in the village of Joucas. It's kid-friendly, with a big pool and a sports field/play area next door. The relaxed restaurant offers tasty cuisine at very fair prices (*menus* from €18). Ask for a south-facing room *(coté sud)* for the best views (Db-€55–58, extra bed-€16, above park at village entrance, tel. 04 90 05 78 01, fax 04 90 05 74 47, www.lescommandeurs.com, hostellerie@lescommandeurs.com).

PROVENCE

# EATING

## In Roussillon

Choose ambience over cuisine if dining in Roussillon, and enjoy any of the eateries on the main square. It's a festive place, where children dance while parents dine, and dogs and cats look longingly for leftovers. Restaurants change with the mistral here—what's good one year disappoints the next. Consider my suggestions and go with what looks best. The first three places listed below share the same square and offer similar values. One should always be open.

At **Le Bistrot de Roussillon,** David and Yann offer the most consistent value on the square, with excellent salads (try the *salad du bistrot*) and *plats* for the right price. There's a breezy terrace in back and a comfy interior (daily, tel. 04 90 05 74 45).

**Café Couleur** and **Le Castrum** flank Le Bistrot de Roussillon, offering similar atmosphere and prices, but less-steady quality.

The **Librairie** bookstore, opposite the above-listed restaurants on the square, hides a slick, top-floor café/*salon de thé* where you can have lunch or a drink outside on the splendid terrace, or inside surrounded by books (€12 salads, €19 *plats*, café closed Mon, bookstore hours listed in "Helpful Hints," earlier in this section).

---

# More Luberon
# Hill Towns and Sights

*Le Lubéron* is packed with appealing villages and beautiful scenery, but it has only a handful of must-see sights. If you don't have a car, skip this area. If you do, pick up an in-depth local map (Michelin Local map #332 works fine) and explore. And remember, getting lost in the Luberon is half the fun.

## Gordes

For the last 40 years, Gordes has been the most touristy and trendy town in the Luberon—creating gridlock and parking headaches (come early). In the 1960s, Gordes was a virtual ghost town of derelict buildings. But now it's thoroughly renovated and filled with people who live in a world without calluses. Many Parisian big shots and wealthy foreigners have purchased and restored older homes here, putting property values out of sight for locals. As you approach Gordes, make a hard right at the impressive view of the village (you'll find some parking along the small road). Beyond here, the village has little of interest, except its many boutiques and its Tuesday market (which ends at 13:00). The town's 11th-century castle houses a mildly interesting collection of contemporary art. The more interesting Abbey Notre-Dame de Sénanque (listed next) is nearby and well-marked from Gordes.

## Abbey Notre-Dame de Sénanque

This still-functioning and beautifully situated Cistercian abbey was built in 1148 as a back-to-basics reaction to the excesses of

Benedictine abbeys. The Cistercians strove to be separate from the world, and to recapture the simplicity, solitude, and poverty of the early Church. To succeed required industrious self-sufficiency—a skill that these monks had. Their movement spread and colonized Europe with a new form of Christianity. By 1200, there were more than 500 such monasteries and abbeys in Europe.

The abbey is best appreciated from the outside, and is worth the trip for its splendid and remote setting alone. Come early or late, stop at a pullout for a bird's-eye view as you descend, then wander the abbey's perimeter with fewer tourists. In late June through much of July, the lavender fields that surround the abbey make a breathtaking picture.

The abbey interior is open only for attending Mass (Sun at 10:00, Mon at 8:30, Tue–Sat at 12:00) and for tours (€4.60 admission includes tour in French only, about 6/day Mon–Sat, 1 hour, limited to 50 people so call ahead or check their website, good bookshop open Mon–Sat 10:00–12:00 & 13:30–18:00, Sun 14:00–18:00, tel. 04 90 72 05 72, www.senanque.fr).

## Museum of Lavender (Musée de la Lavande)

Located halfway between Gordes and Isle-sur-la-Sorgue in Coustellet, this surprisingly interesting museum does a fine job explaining the process of lavender production with interesting exhibits and good English information (via an audioguide, a film, and posted explanations at the exhibits). It's popular with tour groups, smells great inside, and offers the ultimate "if they made it with lavender, we sell it" gift shop (€5, daily 10:00–12:00 & 14:00–18:00, in Coustellet just off N-100 toward Gordes, tel. 04 90 76 91 23).

The next three listings are all located just below N-100, near the hill town of Bonnieux.

## St. Julien Bridge (Pont St. Julien)

This small, three-arched bridge survives as a testimony to Roman engineers—and to the importance of this rural area 2,000 years ago. It's the only surviving bridge on what was once the main road from northern Italy to Provence—the primary route used by Roman armies. This 215-foot-long Roman bridge was built from 27 B.C. to A.D. 14. Mortar had not yet been invented, so (as with the Pont du Gard) stones were carefully set in place. Amazingly, the bridge survives today, having outlived Roman marches, hundreds of floods, and decades of automobile traffic. A new bridge finally rerouted traffic from this beautiful structure in 2005.

## Bonnieux

Spectacular from a distance, this town disappoints up close. It lacks a pedestrian center, though the Friday-morning market briefly creates one. The main reason to visit here is to enjoy its excellent restaurants.

*Eating in Bonnieux:* The two Bonnieux eateries I list are next to the TI. Eat outside at the first place, and inside at the second: **Le Fournil** has marvelous food, a postcard-perfect terrace, and outdoor tables around a tranquil fountain. The interior is uninviting (unless you dig caves and modern decor), so book an outdoor table or skip it (€15 lunch *plats,* €42 dinner *menus;* closed for dinner Mon; closed for lunch Mon–Tue and Sat; tel. 04 90 75 83 62). **Le Tenil** sits across from Le Fournil, with fabulous Luberon views and cuisine to match (€30 *menu,* closed Sun, book ahead for a window table, tel. 04 90 75 61 28).

## Lacoste

Little Lacoste slumbers across the valley from Bonnieux in the shadow of its looming castle. Climb through this photogenic village of arches and stone paths, passing American art students (from the Savannah College of Art and Design) showing their work. Support an American artist, learn about their art, and then keep climbing and climbing to the ruined castle base. The view of Bonnieux from the base of Lacoste's castle is as good is it gets.

The Marquis de Sade (1740–1814) lived in this castle for more than 30 years. Author of dirty novels, he was notorious for hosting orgies behind these walls, and for kidnapping peasants for scandalous purposes. He was eventually arrested and imprisoned for 30 years, and thanks to him, we have a word to describe his favorite hobby—sadism.

**Eating in Lacoste:** If it's time for lunch, find the **Bar/Restaurant de France**'s outdoor tables overlooking Bonnieux and savor the view (inexpensive, daily, lunch only off-season, tel. 04 90 75 82 25).

# THE FRENCH RIVIERA

*La Côte d'Azur*

A hundred years ago, celebrities from London to Moscow flocked to the French Riviera to socialize, gamble, and escape the dreary weather at home. Belle époque resorts now also cater to budget vacationers at France's most sought-after fun-in-the-sun destination.

Some of the Continent's most stunning scenery and intriguing museums lie along this strip of land—as do millions of heat-seeking tourists. Nice has world-class museums, a grand beachfront promenade, a seductive old town, and all the drawbacks of a major city (traffic, crime, pollution, etc.). But the day trips possible from Nice are easy and varied: Monte Carlo welcomes everyone, with cash registers open; Antibes has a romantic port and silky-sandy beaches; and the hill towns present a breezy and photogenic alternative to the beach scene. Evenings on the Riviera, a.k.a. the Côte d'Azur, were made for a promenade and outdoor dining.

## Choosing a Home Base

My favorite home bases are Nice, Antibes, and Villefranche-sur-Mer.

**Nice** is the region's capital and France's fifth-largest city. With convenient train and bus connections to most regional sights, this is the most practical base for train travelers. Urban Nice also has a full palette of museums (most of which are now free), a beach scene that rocks, the best selection of hotels in all price ranges, and good nightlife options.

A car is a headache in Nice, though it's easily stored at one of the many pricey parking garages.

Nearby **Antibes** is smaller, with a bustling center, terrific nightlife, great sandy beaches, grand vistas, good walking trails, and a much-admired Picasso Museum. Antibes has frequent train service to Nice and Monaco, and it's easy for drivers.

**Villefranche-sur-Mer** is the romantic's choice, with a serene setting and small-town warmth. It has finely ground pebble beaches, quick public transportation to Nice and Monaco, easy parking, and hotels in most price ranges.

## Planning Your Time

Most should plan a full day for Nice, a full day for Monaco and the Corniche route that connects it with Nice, and a half-day for Villefranche-sur-Mer or Antibes. Monaco and Villefranche-sur-Mer have good energy at night (sights are closed, but crowds are few; consider dinner there), and Antibes is good day or night (good beaches and hiking, plus lively nightlife). Hill-town- and nature-lovers should allow a day to explore the hill-capping hamlets near Vence (but for most, these are a lower priority).

## Helpful Hints

**Medical Help: Riviera Medical Services** has a list of English-speaking physicians for anywhere along the Riviera. They can help you make an appointment or call an ambulance (tel. 04 93 26 12 70, www.rivieramedical.com).

**Sightseeing Schedules:** On Mondays, the following sights are closed—the Modern and Contemporary Art Museum, Fine Arts Museum, and cours Saleya market in Nice, along with Antibes' Marché Provençal. On Tuesdays, the Chagall, Matisse, and Archaeological museums in Nice are closed.

**Events:** The Riviera is famous for staging major events. Unless you're actually taking part in the festivities, these events give you only room shortages and traffic jams. Here are the three biggies in 2009: Nice Carnival (Feb 13–March 1), Grand Prix of Monaco (May 21–24), and Festival de Cannes, better known as the Cannes Film Festival (May 13–24).

## Getting Around the Riviera

Nice is perfectly situated for exploring the Riviera by public transport. Eze-le-Village, Villefranche-sur-Mer, Antibes, St-Paul-de-Vence, and Cannes are all within a one-hour bus or train ride of each other. Boats go from Nice to Monaco and St-Tropez.

**By Bus and Train:** Many key Riviera destinations are connected by direct bus or train service from Nice, and some are served by both. Since bus fare is only €1, the pricier train is a better choice only when it saves you time (which it generally does—there is no faster way to move about the Riviera than by train). All trains serving Nice arrive at and depart from the Nice-Ville station.

You make the call—both modes of transportation work well. All prices are one-way. The following bus frequencies are for Monday–Saturday. Sundays either have limited or no service.

| Destination | Bus from Nice | Train from Nice |
|---|---|---|
| Villefranche | 4/hr, 20 min | 2/hr, 10 min, €1.80 |
| Cap Ferrat | every 40 min, 30 min (no service on Sun) | none |
| Monaco | 4/hr, 45 min | 2/hr, 20 min, €3.40 |
| Menton | 4/hr, 1 hr | 2/hr, 25 min, €3.60 |
| Antibes | 2–4/hr, 1–1.5 hrs | 2/hr, 15–30 min, €3.90 |
| Cannes | 2–4/hr, 1.5–1.75 hrs | 2/hr, 30–40 min, €6 |
| St-Paul-de-Vence | every 40 min, 45 min | none |
| Vence | every 40 min, 50 min | none |
| Grasse | every 40 min, 1.25 hrs | 1/hr, 1.25 hrs, €7 |
| Eze-le-Village | 16/day, 25 min | none |
| La Turbie | 4/day, 45 min | none |

Buses also run from Monaco to Eze-le-Village and to La Turbie, allowing travelers to triangulate Nice, Monaco, and Eze-le-Village or La Turbie for a good all-day excursion—ending up back in Nice (see page 641 for details).

**By Minivan Excursion:** The TI and most hotels have information on minivan excursions from Nice (€50–60/half-day, €80–110/day). **Med-Tour** is one of many (tel. 04 93 82 92 58 or 06 73 82 04 10, www.med-tour.com); **Tour Azur** is a bit pricier (tel. 04 93 44 88 77, www.tourazur.com); and **Revelation Tours** specializes in English excursions (tel. 04 93 53 69 85, www.revelation-tours .com). All companies also offer private tours by the day or half-day (check with them for their outrageous prices, about €90/hr).

**By Boat:** From June to mid-September, Trans Côte d'Azur offers scenic trips from Nice to Monaco and Nice to St-Tropez. Boats leave in the morning and return in the evening, giving you all day to explore your destination. Drinks and WCs are available on board. Boats to **Monaco** depart at 9:30 and return at 18:00 (€28 round-trip, 45 min each way, June–Sept Tue, Thu, and Sat only). Boats to **St-Tropez** depart at 9:00 and return at 19:00 (€50 round-trip, 2.5 hrs each way; July–Aug Tue–Sun, no boats Mon; late June and early Sept Tue, Thu, and Sun only). Reservations are required for both boats, and tickets for St-Tropez often sell out, so book a few days ahead (tel. 04 92 00 42 30, fax 04 92 00 42 31,

The French Riviera

www.trans-cote-azur.com). The boats leave from Nice's port, bassin des Amiraux, just below Castle Hill—look for the blue ticket booth *(billeterie)* on quai de Lunel (see map on page 591). The same company also runs one-hour round-trip cruises along the coast to Cap Ferrat (see "Tours," later in this chapter).

## Cuisine Scene in the Riviera

The Riviera adds a Mediterranean flair to the food of Provence. While many of the same dishes served in Provence are available throughout the Riviera (see "Cuisine Scene in Provence," page 502), there are differences, especially if you look for anything Italian or from the sea.

Local specialties are bouillabaisse (the spicy seafood stew that seems worth the cost only for those with a seafood fetish), *bourride* (a creamy fish soup thickened with aioli, a garlic sauce), and *salade niçoise* (nee-swaz; a tomato, potato, olive, anchovy, and tuna salad). You'll also find these tasty bread treats: *pissaladière* (bread dough topped with onions, olives, and anchovies), *fougasse* (a spindly, lacelike bread), *socca* (a thin chickpea crêpe), and *pan bagnat* (like a *salade niçoise* stuffed into a huge hamburger bun). Italian cuisine is native (ravioli was first made in Nice), easy to find, and generally a good value (*pâtes fraîches* means "fresh pasta"). White and rosé Bellet and the rich reds and rosés of Bandol are the local wines.

Remember, restaurants serve only during lunch (11:30–14:00) and dinner (19:00–21:00, later in bigger cities); cafés—except for the smaller ones—serve food throughout the day.

## The Riviera's Art Scene

The list of artists who have painted the Riviera reads like a Who's Who of 20th-century art. Pierre-Auguste Renoir, Henri Matisse, Marc Chagall, Georges Braque, Raoul Dufy, Fernand Léger, and Pablo Picasso all lived and worked here—and raved about the region's wonderful light. Their simple, semi-abstract, and—most importantly—colorful works reflect the Riviera. You'll experience the same landscapes they painted in this bright, sun-drenched region, punctuated with views of the "azure sea." Try to imagine the Riviera with a fraction of the people and development you see today.

But the artists were mostly drawn to the uncomplicated lifestyle of fishermen and farmers that has reigned here since time began. As the artists grew older, they retired in the sun, turned their backs on modern art's "isms," and painted with the wide-eyed wonder of children, using bright primary colors, basic outlines, and simple subjects.

A dynamic concentration of well-organized modern- and contemporary-art museums (many described in this book) litter the Riviera, allowing art-lovers to appreciate these masters' works while immersed in the same sun and culture that inspired them. Many of the museums were designed to blend pieces with the surrounding views, gardens, and fountains, thus highlighting that modern art is not only stimulating, but sometimes simply beautiful.

# Nice

Nice (sounds like "niece"), with its spectacular Alps-to-Mediterranean surroundings, eternally entertaining seafront promenade, and intriguing museums, is an enjoyable big-city highlight of the Riviera. In its traffic-free old city, Italian and French flavors mix to create a spicy Mediterranean dressing. Nice may be nice, but it's hot and jammed in July and August—reserve ahead and get a room with air-conditioning *(une chambre avec climatisation)*.

Everything you'll want to see in Nice is within walking distance, or a short bus or tram ride away.

# ORIENTATION

Most recommended sights and hotels are between the train station and the beach, near avenue Jean Médecin or boulevard Victor Hugo. It's a 20-minute walk (or a €10 taxi ride) from the train station to the beach, and a 20-minute walk along the promenade from the fancy Hôtel Negresco to the heart of Old Nice.

You can also hop aboard the new tramway (the first of three planned lines is finally running). A quick 10-minute (€1) ride takes you through the center of the city, connecting the train station, Old Nice, and the bus station. All city and regional buses cost only €1 per trip, making this one of the cheapest and easiest cities in France to get around (see "Getting Around Nice," later in this section).

## Tourist Information

Nice's helpful TI has three locations: at the **airport** (in Terminal 1, daily 8:00–21:00, closed Sun off-season), next to the **train station** (usually busy; summer Mon–Sat 8:00–20:00, Sun 9:00–18:00; rest of year Mon–Sat 9:00–19:00, Sun 10:00–17:00), and facing the **beach** at 5 promenade des Anglais (usually quiet, daily 9:00–18:00, until 20:00 July–Aug, closed Sun off-season, tel. 08 92 70 74 07—costs €0.34/min, www.nicetourisme.com). Pick up the thorough *Practical Guide to Nice,* information on day trips (such as city maps and details on boat excursions), and a free Nice map (or find a better one at your hotel).

## Arrival in Nice

**By Train:** All trains stop at Nice's main station, Nice-Ville (also called Gare Thiers, baggage storage at the far right with your back to the tracks, lockers open daily 7:00–21:45, left luggage desk Mon–Sat 8:45–12:00 & 14:00–15:45, closed Sun). This is one busy station, and theft is a problem, so never leave your bags unattended.

Turn left out of the station to find a branch of the **TI** a few steps away. Continue a few more blocks for the Gare Thiers **tram stop** (this will take you to place Masséna, the old city, and bus station). Board the tram on the near side of the street (the one heading toward the right, direction Pont Michel; see "Getting Around Nice," page 593). Many of my recommended **hotels** are a 10- to

**Nice**

1/4 MILE
400 METERS

🚃 TRAM
🅿 PARKING

CIMIEZ

MATISSE MUSEUM
ROMAN RUINS
ARCHAEOLOGICAL MUSEUM

CHAGALL MUSEUM

GARE DE SUD TRAIN STN.

TO ENTRE-VAUX

RUSSIAN CATH.

FREEWAY

NOTRE-DAME

TRAIN STN.

RUE MASSENA

MASSENA MUSEUM

HOTEL NEGRESCO

TO AIRPORT

PROMENADE DES ANGLAIS

MODERN ART MUSEUM

PLACE MASSENA

BUS STN.

OLD NICE

CASTLE HILL

PLACE GARI-BALDI

PORT

COURS SALEYA

QUAI D. ETATS-UNIS

ELEVATOR

B E A C H E S

TOURIST TRAIN PICK-UP

BELLANDA TOWER

TO ANTIBES, CANNES & VENCE

TO VILLEFRANCHE, MONACO & ITALY

DCH    M E D I T E R R A N E A N    S E A

**FRENCH RIVIERA**

1 To High Corniche (sky-high route to Monaco)
2 To Middle Corniche (middle route, best for Monaco & Eze-le-Village)
3 To Low Corniche (low route to Villefranche-sur-Mer & Cap Ferrat)
4 To Fine Arts Museum
5 World War II Monument

6 US Embassy
7 Trans Côte d'Azur Cruises
8 Le Grand Tour Bus Departure Point & Albert I Park
9 Bus #22 Stops (3)
10 Bus #17 Stops

15-minute walk down the same street (see "Sleeping—Between Nice Etoile and the Sea" on page 610).

To find **car rental** offices and more recommended **hotels,** turn right out of the station. To get to the hotels, cross avenue Thiers, then walk down the steps by Hôtel Interlaken (see "Sleeping—Between the Train Station and Nice Etoile," page 608). If you'd rather head to the beach, continue past these hotels and keep walking down avenue Durante as it turns into rue des Congrés to reach the heart of Nice's beachfront promenade.

For **taxis** or for **buses to the airport,** walk straight out of the train station. You'll find taxis in the first lane, express airport bus #99 in the second lane, and local airport bus #23 in the third lane.

**By Bus:** Nice's bus station *(gare routière)* is sandwiched between boulevard Jean Jaurès and avenue Félix Faure, next to the old city. The station has no baggage storage. Cross boulevard Jean Jaurès and enter teeming Old Nice, or cross avenue Félix Faure to get to my recommended hotels near Nice Etoile.

**By Car:** Driving into the city on the autoroute from the west, take the first Nice exit (for the airport—called Côte d'Azur, Central) and follow signs for *Nice Centre* and *Promenade des Anglais.* (Be ready to cross three left lanes of traffic as soon as you get off the autoroute.) Try to avoid arriving at rush hour (usually Mon–Fri 8:00–9:30 & 17:00–19:30), when promenade des Anglais grinds to a halt. Hoteliers know where to park (allow €14–20/day). The parking garage at the Nice Etoile shopping center on avenue Jean Médecin is pricey but near many of my recommended hotels (ticket booth on third floor, about €20/day, €10–12 20:00–8:00). All on-street parking is metered (9:00–18:00 or 19:00), but usually free all day on Sunday.

**By Plane:** For information on Nice's handy airport, see "Transportation Connections," at the end of this section.

## Helpful Hints

**Theft Alert:** Nice has more than its share of pickpockets. Have nothing important on or around your waist, unless it's in a money belt tucked out of sight (thieves target fanny packs); don't leave anything visible in your car; be wary of scooters when standing at intersections; don't leave things unattended on the beach while swimming; and stick to main streets in Old Nice after dark.

**Museums:** Some Nice museums (Chagall, Matisse, Archaeological) are closed Tuesdays, while others (Modern and Contemporary Art, Fine Arts) close on Mondays. As of 2008, city museums became free of charge (except the Chagall Museum and the Russian Cathedral). Rainy-day options just got cheaper.

**Internet Access:** There's no shortage of places to get online in

Nice—they're everywhere. Ask at your hotel, or just look up as you walk (keep your eye out for the @ symbol).

**English Bookstore: The Cat's Whiskers** has an eclectic selection of novels and regional travel books, including mine. Say *bonjour* to mellow owner Linda (Tue–Sat 10:00–12:00 & 14:00–19:00, closed Sun–Mon, 26–30 rue Lamartine—see map on page 609, tel. 04 93 80 02 66).

**Laundry:** You'll find launderettes everywhere in Nice—ask your hotelier for the nearest one. The self-service **Point Laverie** is centrally located (daily 8:00–20:00, at the corner of rue Alberti and rue Pastorelli, next to Hôtel Vendôme—see map on page 609).

**Grocery Store:** The big **Monoprix** on avenue Jean Médecin and rue Biscarra has it all, including a deli counter, bakery, and cold drinks (closed Sun, see map on page 616). You'll also find many small grocery stores (some open Sun and/or until late hours) near my recommended hotels.

**Renting a Bike (and Other Wheels): Roller Station** rents bikes (*vélos*, €5/hr, €10/half-day, €15/day), inline skates (*rollers*, €6/day), Razor-type scooters (*trotinettes*, €6/half-day, €9/day), and skateboards (€6/half-day, €9/day). You'll need to leave your ID as a deposit (daily 9:30–19:00, July–Aug until 20:00, next to yellow awnings of Pailin's Asian restaurant at 49 quai des Etats-Unis—see map on page 611, another location at 10 rue Cassini near place Garibaldi, tel. 04 93 62 99 05, owner Eric).

**Car Rental:** Renting a car is easiest at Nice's airport, which has offices for all the major companies. You'll also find most companies represented at Nice's train station.

**English Radio:** Tune into Riviera-Radio at FM 106.5.

**Views:** For panoramic views, climb Castle Hill (see page 601), or take a one-hour boat trip (see page 595).

**Rocky Beaches:** To make life tolerable on the rocks, swimmers should buy a pair of the cheap plastic beach shoes sold at many shops (flip-flops fall off in the water). Try **Go Sport** (daily 10:00–19:00, 13 place Masséna—see map on page 611).

## Getting Around Nice

While you can walk to most attractions in Nice, the bus and tram can be useful. Both are covered by the same single-ride €1 ticket (good for 74 min in one direction, including transfers between bus and tram; can't be used for a round-trip). An all-day pass is €4 (valid on local buses and trams, as well as buses to nearby destinations—see "Getting Around the Riviera," earlier in this chapter).

The **bus** is handy to reach the Chagall and Matisse museums and maybe to the Russian Cathedral. Make sure to validate your

FRENCH RIVIERA

ticket in the machine just behind the driver—watch to see how locals do it.

Nice's new **tramway** runs along avenue Jean Médecin and boulevard Jean Jaurès. This handy tram connects the main train station (Gare Thiers stop), place Masséna (Masséna stop, a few blocks' walk from the sea), Old Nice (Opéra–Vieille Ville), the bus station (Cathédrale–Vieille Ville), and the Modern and Contemporary Art Museum (Place Garibaldi). It also comes within a few blocks of the Gare du Sud station (Libération stop),

from where the scenic Chemins de Fer de Provence trains depart (see page 657). Taking the tram in the direction of Pont Michel will take you from the train station toward the beach and bus station (direction Las Planas goes the other way). Buy tickets at the machines on the platforms (coins only, no credit cards, choose the English flag to change the display language, spin the round knob and push the green button, red button to cancel). Once you're on the tram, don't forget to validate your ticket by inserting it into the top of the white box, then reclaiming it.

**Taxis** are handy for getting to Nice's outlying sights, and worth it if you're nowhere near a bus or tram stop (figure €10–12 from promenade des Anglais). They normally pick up only at taxi stands *(tête de station)*, or you can call 04 93 13 78 78.

The hokey **tourist train** gets you up Castle Hill (see "Tours," next).

## TOURS

**Bus Tour**—Le Grand Tour Bus provides a hop-on, hop-off service on an open-deck bus with headphone commentary. There are two routes: The red route (2/hr, about 90 min) includes promenade des Anglais, old port, Cap de Nice, and the Chagall and Matisse museums on Cimiez Hill. The less-frequent blue route (6/day) includes the Russian Cathedral, the promenade, and more of modern Nice (€20/1-day pass, €23/2-day pass, cheaper for seniors and students, €10 for last tour of the day at about 18:00, some hotels offer €2 discounts—ask at your hotel, buy tickets on bus, main stop is near where promenade des Anglais and quai des Etats-Unis meet, across from plage Beau Rivage—look for signs, tel. 04 92 29 17 00). This tour is a pricey way to get to the Chagall and Matisse museums, but it's a good option if you also want a city overview tour. If you want to use this bus to go to the Russian Cathedral, make sure to check the schedule, as it may be faster to walk.

**Tourist Train**—For €7 (or €3 for children under 9), you can spend 40 embarrassing minutes on the tourist train tooting along the promenade, through the old city, and up to Castle Hill. This is a sweat-free way to get to Castle Hill...but so is the elevator, which is much cheaper (every 30 min, daily 10:00–18:00, June–Aug until 19:00, recorded English commentary, meet train near Le Grand Tour Bus stop on quai des Etats-Unis, tel. 04 93 62 85 48).

**▲Boat Cruise**—Here's your chance to join the boat parade and see Nice from the water. On this one-hour, star-studded tour, you'll cruise in a comfortable, yacht-size vessel to Cap Ferrat and past Villefranche-sur-Mer, then return to Nice with a final lap along promenade des Anglais. It's a scenic trip (the best views are from the seats on top), worthwhile if you won't be hiking along the Cap Ferrat trails that provide similar views. French (and sometimes English-speaking) guides play Robin Leach, pointing out mansions owned by some pretty famous people, including Elton John (just as you leave Nice, it's the soft-yellow square-shaped place right on the water), Sean Connery (on the hill above Elton, with rounded arches and tower), Microsoft mogul Paul Allen (in saddle of Cap Ferrat hill, above yellow-umbrella beach with sloping red-tile roof), and Mick Jagger (between Cap Ferrat and Villefranche-sur-Mer, pink place hidden by trees). I wonder if this gang ever hangs out together...(€13; May–Oct Tue–Sun 2/day, usually at 11:00 and 15:00, no boats Mon; March–April Tue–Wed, Fri, and Sun at 15:00; no boats Nov–Feb; call ahead to verify schedule, arrive 30 min early to get best seats, drinks and WCs available). For directions to the dock and contact information, see "Getting Around the Riviera—By Boat," page 587.

**Walking Tours**—The TI on promenade des Anglais organizes weekly walking tours of Old Nice in French and English (€12, May–Oct only, usually Sat morning at 9:30, 2.5 hours, reservations necessary, depart from TI, tel. 08 92 70 74 07).

Nice's cultural association (Centre du Patrimoine) offers incredibly cheap €3 on-demand walks on varying themes (in English, minimum 3 people). Call 04 92 00 41 90 or 06 76 98 67 82 a few days ahead to make a reservation. Most tours start at their office at 75 quai des Etats-Unis; look for the red plaque next to Musée des Ponchettes (see map on page 611).

**Les Petits Farcis Cooking Tour and Classes**—Canadian food-journalist-turned-Francophile Rosa Jackson is making a Mediterranean splash with her one- and four-day cooking classes in Old Nice. Her single-day classes include a morning trip to the open-air market for picking up ingredients, and an afternoon session, where you'll learn what to do with your purchases. Her four-day courses focus exclusively on the art of cooking (1 day-€200, 4

FRENCH RIVIERA

days—€480, tel. 06 81 67 41 22, www.petitsfarcis.com). Ask about the farm tours she organizes to meet the producers themselves.

# SELF-GUIDED WALK

## A Scratch-and-Sniff Walk Through Old Nice

• *See the map on page 611, and start at Nice's main market square, the...*

**Cours Saleya** (koor sah-lay-yuh): Named for its broad exposure to the sun *(soleil)*, this commotion of color, sights, smells, and people has been Nice's main market square since the Middle Ages (produce market held Tue–Sun until 13:00—on Mon, an antique market takes center stage). Amazingly, part of this square was a parking lot until 1980, when the mayor of Nice had an underground garage built.

Stroll down the center of the cours. The first section is devoted to the plants and flowers that seem to grow effortlessly and everywhere in this ideal climate. Carnations, roses, and jasmine are local favorites in what has been the Riviera's biggest flower market since the 19th century. The boisterous produce section trumpets the season with mushrooms, strawberries, white asparagus, zucchini flowers—whatever's fresh gets top billing.

Place Pierre Gautier (also called Plassa dou Gouvernou—bilingual street signs include the old Niçoise language, an Italian dialect) is where the actual farmers set up stalls to sell their produce and herbs directly.

Continue down the center of cours Saleya, stopping when you see La Cambuse restaurant on your left. In front, hovering over the black barrel fire with the paella-like pan on top, is the self-proclaimed Queen of the Market, Thérèse (tehr-ehz). When she's not looking for a husband, Thérèse is cooking *socca*, Nice's chickpea crêpe specialty. Spend €2 for a wad of *socca* (careful—it's hot, but good). If she doesn't have a pan out, that means it's on its way (watch for the frequent scooter deliveries). Wait in line...or else it'll be all gone when you return.

• *Continue down cours Saleya. The fine golden building at the end is where Henri Matisse lived for 17 years. Turn left at the Café des Ponchettes, and head down...*

**Rue de la Poissonnerie:** Look up at the first building on your right. Adam and Eve are squaring off, each holding a zucchini-like gourd. This scene (post-apple) represents the annual

## Nice at a Glance

▲▲▲**Chagall Museum** The world's largest collection of Chagall's work, popular even with people who don't like modern art. **Hours:** Wed-Mon 10:00-17:00, May-Oct until 18:00, closed Tue. See page 601.

▲▲**Promenade des Anglais** Nice's four-mile, sunstruck seafront promenade. **Hours:** Always open. See page 599.

▲▲**Old Nice** Charming old city offering enjoyable atmosphere and a look at Nice's French-Italian cultural blend. **Hours:** Always open. See page 596.

▲**Matisse Museum** A worthwhile collection of Henri Matisse's paintings. **Hours:** Wed-Mon 10:00-18:00, closed Tue. See page 603.

▲**Russian Cathedral** Finest Orthodox church outside of Russia. **Hours:** Daily 9:00-12:00 & 14:30-18:00, until 17:00 off-season. See page 605.

**Modern and Contemporary Art Museum** Ultramodern museum with enjoyable collection from the 1960s-1970s, including Warhol and Lichtenstein. **Hours:** Tue-Sun 10:00-18:00, closed Mon. See page 604.

**Molinard Perfume Museum** Small museum tracing the history of perfume. **Hours:** Daily 10:00-19:00, sometimes closed Mon off-season. See page 604.

**Castle Hill** Site of an ancient fort, today it boasts great views—especially in early mornings and evenings. **Hours:** Park closes at 20:00 in summer, earlier off-season. Elevator runs daily 10:00-19:00, until 20:00 in summer. See page 601.

rapprochement in Nice to make up for the sins of a too-much-fun Carnival (Mardi Gras). Nice residents have partied hard during Carnival for more than 700 years. A few doors down, on the left, find the small church dedicated to St. Rita, the patron saint of desperate causes. She holds a special place in locals' hearts, and this church is the most popular in Nice.

• *Turn right on the next street, where you'll pass Old Nice's most happening café/bar (Distilleries Ideales), with a lively happy hour (18:00–20:00) and a* Pirates of the Caribbean*-style interior. Now turn left on "Right" Street (rue Droite), and enter an area that feels like a Little Naples.*

**Rue Droite:** In the Middle Ages, this straight, skinny street provided the most direct route from wall to wall, or river to sea. Stop at Esipuno's bakery (at place du Jésus) and say *bonjour* to the friendly folks. Thirty years ago, this baker was voted the best in France—the trophies you see were earned for bread making, not bowling. His son now runs the place. Notice the firewood stacked by the oven. Farther along, at #28, Thérèse (whom you met earlier) cooks her *socca* in the wood-fired oven before she carts it to her barrel on cours Saleya. The balconies of the mansion in the next block mark the Palais Lascaris (1647, gorgeous at night), a rare souvenir from one of Nice's most prestigious families (free, Wed–Mon 10:00–18:00, closed Tue, worth touring for a peek at 1700s Baroque Italian high life). Look up and make faces back at the guys under the balconies.

• *Turn left on the rue de la Loge, then left again on rue Centrale, to reach...*

**Place Rossetti:** The most Italian of Nice's piazzas, place Rossetti feels more like Rome than Nice. This square comes alive after dark. Fenocchio is popular for its many gelato flavors. Walk to the fountain and stare back at the church. This is the Cathedral of St. Réparate—an unassuming building for a major city's cathedral. The cathedral was relocated here in the 1500s, when Castle Hill was temporarily converted to military-only use. The name comes from Nice's patron saint, a teenage virgin named Réparate whose martyred body floated to Nice in the fourth century, accompanied by angels. The interior gushes Baroque. Remember that Baroque was a response to the Protestant Reformation. With the Catholic Church's "Counter-Reformation," the theatrical energy of churches was cranked up—with reenergized, high-powered saints and eye-popping decor.

• *Our walk is over. Castle Hill is straight up the stepped lane opposite the cathedral (see page 601).*

## ACTIVITIES

**▲Wheeling the Promenade—** Get a bike and ride along the coast in both directions (about 30 min each way). **Roller Station** rents bikes, in-line skates, and mini-scooters (see "Helpful Hints," earlier in this chapter). Both of the following paths start along promenade des Anglais.

The path to the west stops just before the airport at perhaps the most scenic *boules* courts in France. Stop and watch the old-timers while away their afternoon tossing those shiny metal balls (see page 837).

Heading east, you'll round the hill—passing a scenic cape and the town's memorial to both world wars—to the harbor of Nice, with a chance to survey some fancy yachts. Pedal around the harbor and follow the coast past the Corsica ferry terminal (you'll need to carry your bike up a flight of steps). From there, the path leads to an appealing tree-lined residential district.

**Relaxing at the Beaches**—Nice is where the masses relax on the rocks. After settling into the smooth pebbles, you can play beach

volleyball, table tennis, or *boules;* rent paddleboats, personal watercraft, or windsurfing equipment; explore ways to use your zoom lens as a telescope; or snooze on comfy beach beds with end tables. To rent a spot on the beach, compare rates, as prices vary—beaches on the east end of the bay are usually cheaper (mattress and *chaise longue*-€12–18,

umbrella-€5, towel-€3). Many hotels have special deals with certain beaches for discounted rentals (check with your hotel for details). Consider lunch in your bathing suit (€10–12 salads and pizzas in bars and restaurants all along the beach). For a peaceful cup of coffee by the sea, stop here first thing in the morning before the crowds hit. *Plage Publique* signs explain the 15 beach no-nos (translated in English).

While Nice's beaches are traditionally rocky, a few years ago a small sandy area appeared toward the Italy end of the bay.

# SIGHTS

## ▲▲▲Along the Promenade des Anglais

Welcome to the Riviera. There's something for everyone along this four-mile-long seafront circus. Watch the Europeans at play, admire the azure Mediterranean, anchor yourself on a blue seat, and prop your feet up on the made-to-order guardrail. Later in the day, come back to join the evening parade of tans along the promenade.

The broad sidewalks of promenade des Anglais ("walkway of the English") were financed by wealthy English tourists who wanted a safe place to stroll and admire the view. In 1822, the walk was paved in marble for aristocrats who didn't want to dirty their shoes or smell the fishy gravel. For now, stroll like the belle époque English aristocrats for whom the promenade was built.

Start at the pink-domed Hôtel Negresco, then cross to the

sea and end your promenade at Castle Hill. The following sights are listed in the order you'll pass them. This walk is ideally done at sunset (as a pre-dinner stroll).

**Hôtel Negresco**—Nice's finest hotel (also a historic monument) offers the city's most expensive beds (€460 minimum for a sea view, see "Sleeping," later in this section), and a free "museum" interior (always open—provided you're dressed decently, absolutely no beach attire). March straight through the lobby (as if you're staying there) into the exquisite Salon Royal. The chandelier hanging from the Eiffel-built dome is made of 16,000 pieces of crystal. It was built in France for the Russian czar's Moscow palace...but because of the Bolshevik Revolution in 1917, he couldn't take delivery. Read the explanation of the dome and saunter around counterclockwise: The bucolic scene, painted in 1913 for the hotel, sets the tone. Nip into the toilets for either a turn-of-the-century powder room or a Battle of Waterloo experience. The chairs nearby were typical of the age (cones of silence for an afternoon nap sitting up).

**Bay of Angels (Baie des Anges)**—Grab a blue chair and face the sea. The body of Nice's patron saint, Réparate, was supposedly escorted into this bay by angels in the fourth century. To your right is where you might have been escorted into France—Nice's airport, built on a massive landfill. On that tip of land way beyond the runway is Cap d'Antibes. Until 1860, Antibes and Nice were in different countries—Antibes was French, but Nice was a protectorate of the Italian kingdom of Savoy-Piedmont, a.k.a. the Kingdom of Sardinia. (During that period, the Var River—just west of Nice—was the geographic border between these two peoples.) In 1850, locals spoke Italian and ate pasta. As Italy was uniting, the region was given a choice: Join the new country of Italy or join France (which was enjoying good times under the rule of Napoleon III). The vast majority voted in 1860 to go French...and voilà!

The green hill to your left is Castle Hill. Farther left lies Villefranche-sur-Mer (marked by the tower at land's end, and home to lots of millionaires), then Monaco (which you can't see, with more millionaires), then Italy (with lots of, uh, Italians). Behind you are the foothills of the Alps (Alpes Maritimes), which gather threatening clouds, ensuring that the Côte d'Azur enjoys sunshine more than 300 days each year. While half a million people live here, pollution is carefully treated—the water is routinely tested and very clean. Stroll the promenade with the sea starboard, and read about "Relaxing at the Beaches" (under "Activities," later in this section).

**Albert I Park**—The park was named for the Belgian king who enjoyed wintering here. While the English came first, the Belgians and Russians were also huge fans of 19th-century Nice. The 1960 statue in the park commemorates Nice's being part of France for 100 years. If you detour from the promenade into the park and continue down the center of the grassy strip, you'll be walking over Nice's river, the Paillon (covered since the 1800s). For centuries, this river was Nice's natural defense to the north and west (the sea protected the south, and Castle Hill defended the east). Imagine the fortified wall ran along its length from the hills behind you to the sea. With the arrival of tourism in the 1800s, Nice expanded over and beyond the river.

**Castle Hill (Colline du Château)**—This hill—in an otherwise flat city center—offers sensational views over Nice, the port (to the east), the foothills of the Alps, and the Mediterranean. The city of Nice was first settled here by Greeks circa 400 B.C. In the Middle Ages, a massive castle stood there, with turrets, high walls, and soldiers at the ready. With the river guarding one side and the sea the other, this mountain fortress seemed strong—until Louis XIV leveled it in 1706. Nice's medieval seawall ran along the lineup of two-story buildings below. Today, you'll find a waterfall, a playground, two cafés (fair prices), and a cemetery—but no castle—on Castle Hill. The views are best early or at sunset, or whenever the weather's really clear (park closes at 20:00 in summer, earlier off-season). You can get to the top by foot, by elevator (€0.70 one-way, €1.10 round-trip, runs daily 10:00–19:00, until 20:00 in summer, next to beachfront Hôtel Suisse), or by tourist train (described under "Tours," earlier in this section). Up top, you'll find cafés and an extensive play area for kids.

Nice's port, where you'll find Trans Côte d'Azur's boat cruises (described on page 587), is just below on the east edge of Castle Hill.

## Museums

To bring culture to the masses, the city of Nice has nixed the entry fee to all municipal museums—so it's free to enter any of the sights listed below, except the Chagall Museum and the Russian Cathedral. Amazing. The first two museums (Chagall and Matisse) are a long walk northeast of Nice's city center, and because they're on the same bus line (in the same direction), it makes sense to visit them at the same time. From place Masséna, the Chagall Museum is a 30-minute walk, and the Matisse Museum is a 60-minute walk.

**▲▲▲Chagall Museum (Musée National Marc Chagall)**—Even if you're suspicious of modern art, this museum—with the largest collection of Chagall's work in captivity anywhere—is a delight. After World War II, Chagall returned from the US to settle in nearby Vence. Between 1954 and 1967, he painted a cycle of 17 large murals designed for, and donated to, this museum. These paintings, inspired by the biblical books of Genesis, Exodus, and the Song of Songs, make up the "nave," or core, of what Chagall

## Chagall's Style

Chagall uses a deceptively simple, almost childlike style to paint a world that's hidden to the eye—the magical, mystical world below the surface. Here are some of his techniques:

- **Deep, radiant colors,** inspired by Expressionism and Fauvism (an art movement pioneered by Matisse and other French painters).
- **Personal imagery,** particularly from his childhood in Russia—smiling barnyard animals, fiddlers on the roof, flower bouquets, huts, and blissful sweethearts.
- **A Hasidic Jewish perspective,** the idea that God is everywhere, appearing in everyday things like nature, animals, and humdrum activities.
- **A fragmented Cubist style,** multifaceted and multidimensional, a perfect style to capture the multifaceted, multidimensional complexity of God's creation.
- **Overlapping images,** like double-exposure photography, with faint imagery that bleeds through, suggesting there's more to life under the surface.
- **Stained-glass-esque technique** of dark, deep, earthy, "potent" colors, and simplified, iconic, symbolic figures.
- **Gravity-defying compositions,** with lovers, animals, and angels twirling blissfully in midair.
- **Happy, not tragic mood** depicting a world of personal joy, despite the violence and turmoil of world wars and revolution.
- **Childlike simplicity,** drawn with simple, heavy outlines, filled in with Crayola colors that often spill over the lines. Major characters in a scene are bigger than the lesser characters. The grinning barnyard animals, the bright colors, the magical events presented as literal truth...Was Chagall a lightweight? Or a lighter-than-air-weight?

called the "House of Brotherhood."

Each painting is a lighter-than-air collage of images that draw from Chagall's Russian-folk-village youth, his Jewish heritage, biblical themes, and his feeling that he existed somewhere between heaven and earth. He believed that the Bible was a synonym for nature, and that color and biblical themes were key ingredients for understanding God's love for his creation. Chagall's brilliant blues and reds celebrate nature, as do his spiritual and folk themes. On your way out, be sure to visit the three Chagall stained-glass windows in the auditorium (depicting God's creation of the universe).

**Cost, Hours, Location:** €7, free first Sunday of the month (but crowded), can cost a little more during special exhibits; open Wed–Mon 10:00–17:00, May–Oct until 18:00, closed Tue year-round; avenue Docteur Ménard, tel. 04 93 53 87 20, www .musee-chagall.fr.

**Services:** An idyllic garden café (open April–Oct) with fair prices awaits in the corner of the museum grounds. A spick-and-span WC is next to the ticket desk (there's one inside, too).

**Getting to the Chagall Museum:** You can reach the museum by bus or on foot. **Bus #22** serves the Chagall Museum from place Masséna (5/hr Mon–Sat, 3/hr Sun, €1; stop faces eastbound on rue Gioffredo, a block east of Galeries Lafayette—see map on page 611). The museum's bus stop (called Musée Chagall, shown on the bus shelter) is on boulevard de Cimiez (walk uphill from the stop to find the museum). To **walk** from central Nice to the Chagall Museum, go to the train-station end of avenue Jean Médecin and turn right onto boulevard Raimbaldi. Walk four long blocks along the elevated road, then turn left onto avenue Raymond Comboul, and follow *Musée Chagall* signs.

**Leaving the Museum: Taxis** usually wait outside the museum. To take **bus #22** back to downtown Nice, turn right out of the museum, then make another right down boulevard de Cimiez, and catch the bus on the near side of the street. To continue on to the Matisse Museum, catch bus #22 using the uphill stop, located across the street. To **walk** to the train station from the museum, turn left out of the museum, then left again on the street behind it. Look for the staircase on your left (leading down), cross under the freeway, then turn right to reach the station.

▲**Matisse Museum (Musée Matisse)**—This museum, worth ▲▲▲ for his fans, contains the world's largest collection of Henri Matisse paintings. It offers a painless introduction to the artist, whose style was shaped by Mediterranean light and by fellow Côte d'Azur artists Pablo Picasso and Pierre-Auguste Renoir. The collection is scattered through several rooms with a few worthwhile works, though it lacks a certain *je ne sais quoi* when compared to the Chagall Museum.

Henri Matisse, the master of leaving things out, could suggest a woman's body with a single curvy line—leaving it to the viewer's mind to fill in the rest. Ignoring traditional 3-D perspective, he used simple dark outlines saturated with bright blocks of color to create recognizable but simplified scenes, all composed into a decorative pattern to express nature's serene beauty. You don't look "through" a Matisse canvas, like a window; you look "at" it, like wallpaper.

Matisse understood how colors and shapes affect us emotionally. He could create either shocking, clashing works (Fauvism) or geometrical, balanced, harmonious ones (later works). While other modern artists reveled in purely abstract design, Matisse (almost) always kept the subject matter at least vaguely recognizable. He used unreal colors and distorted lines not just to portray what an object looks like, but to express the object's inner nature (even inanimate objects). Meditating on his paintings helps you connect with nature—or so Matisse hoped.

**Cost, Hours, Location:** Free, Wed–Mon 10:00–18:00, closed Tue, 164 avenue des Arènes de Cimiez, tel. 04 93 81 08 08, www.musee-matisse-nice.org. The museum is set in an olive grove amid the ruins of the Roman city of Cemenelum.

**Getting to the Matisse Museum:** It's a long uphill walk from the city center. Take the bus (details below) or a cab (about €12 from promenade des Anglais). Once here, walk into the park to find the pink villa. **Buses #22** and **#17** offer frequent service to the Matisse Museum from just off place Masséna on rue Gioffredo (Masséna Guitry stop, a block east of the Galeries Lafayette department store—see map on page 611; €1 for the trip). Get off at the Arènes–Matisse bus stop.

**Leaving the Museum:** When leaving the museum, find the stop for bus #22 (which has more frequent service downtown and stops en route at the Chagall Museum) by exiting the park and crossing boulevard de Cimiez, where the two roads meet (the stop is on boulevard de Cimiez, not avenue des Arènes de Cimiez—see map on page 591). The stop for bus #17 (less frequent, no Chagall stop) also faces downhill, but it's on avenue des Arènes de Cimiez. Confusing, I know.

**Modern and Contemporary Art Museum (Musée d'Art Moderne et d'Art Contemporain)**—This ultramodern museum features an explosively colorful, far-out, yet manageable permanent collection (on the second floor) of mostly American and European art from the 1960s and 1970s. The exhibits include a few works by Andy Warhol, Roy Lichtenstein, and Jean Tinguely, and small models of Christo's famous wrappings. Several of Niki de Saint Phalle's works are almost huggable. The temporary exhibits can be as appealing to modern-art-lovers as the permanent collection—ask the TI what's playing.

**Cost, Hours, Location:** Free, Tue–Sun 10:00–18:00, closed Mon, about a 15-minute walk from place Masséna, near bus station on promenade des Arts, tel. 04 93 62 61 62, www.mamac-nice.org.

**Molinard Perfume Museum**—The Molinard family has been making perfume in Grasse (about an hour's drive from Nice) since 1849. Their Nice store has a small museum in the back that illustrates the story of their industry. Back when people believed water spread the plague (Louis XIV supposedly bathed less than once a year), doctors advised people to rub fragrances into their skin and then powder their body. Back then, perfume was a necessity of everyday life.

Room 1 shows photos of the local flowers used in perfume production. Room 2 shows the earliest (18th-century) production method. Petals would be laid on a bed of animal fat. After baking in the sun, the fat would absorb the essence of the flowers. Petals would be replaced daily for two months until the fat was saturated. Models and old photos show the later distillation process (660 pounds of lavender would produce only a quarter-gallon of essence). Perfume is "distilled like cognac and then aged like wine." Room 3 shows the desk of a "nose" (top perfume creator). Of the 150 real "noses" in the world, more than 100 are French. You are welcome to enjoy the testing bottles before heading into the shop.

**Cost, Hours, Location:** Free, daily 10:00–19:00, sometimes closed Mon off-season, just between beach and place Masséna at 20 rue St. François de Paule—see map on page 611, tel. 04 93 62 90 50, www.molinard.com.

**Other Nice Museums**—All of these museums are acceptable rainy-day options, and free of charge.

The **Fine Arts Museum** (Musée des Beaux-Arts), located in a sumptuous villa with lovely gardens, houses 6,000 works from the 17th to 20th centuries, and will satisfy your need for a fine-arts fix (free, Tue–Sun 10:00–18:00, closed Mon, 3 avenue des Baumettes, western end of Nice, take bus #38 from the bus station, tel. 04 92 15 28 28, www.musee-beaux-arts-nice.org).

The **Archaeological Museum** (Musée Archéologique) displays various objects from the Romans' occupation of this region. It's convenient—just below the Matisse Museum—but has little of interest to anyone but ancient Rome aficionados. You also get access to the Roman bath ruins...which are, sadly, overgrown with weeds (free, very limited information in English, Wed–Mon 10:00–18:00, closed Tue, near Matisse Museum at 160 avenue des Arènes de Cimiez, tel. 04 93 81 59 57, www.musee-archeologique-nice.org).

The **Masséna Museum** (Musée Masséna) re-opened in 2008 after a long renovation. It features 18th- and 19th-century paintings (mostly by artists from Nice), local porcelain, and other collections relevant to the city's tumultuous history (free, Wed–Mon 10:00–18:00, closed Tue, 35 promenade des Anglais, tel. 04 93 91 19 10).

## ▲Russian Cathedral

Nice's Russian Orthodox church—claimed to be the finest outside Russia—is worth a visit. Five hundred rich Russian families wintered in Nice in the late 19th century. Since they couldn't pray in a Catholic church, the community needed a worthy Orthodox house of worship. Czar Nicholas I's widow provided the land (which required tearing down her house), and Czar Nicholas II gave this church to the Russian community in 1912. (A few years later, Russian comrades—who didn't winter on the Riviera—assassinated him.) Here in the land of olives and anchovies, these proud onion domes seem odd. But, I imagine, so did those old Russians.

Step inside (pick up English info sheet). The one-room interior is filled with icons and candles, and the old Russian music adds to the ambience. The wall of icons (iconostasis) divides things between the spiritual world and the temporal world of the worshippers. Only the priest can walk between the two worlds, by using the "Royal Door." Take a close look at items lining the front (starting in the left corner). The angel with red boots and wings—the protector of the Romanov family—stands over a symbolic tomb of Christ. The tall, black, hammered-copper cross commemorates the massacre of Nicholas II and his family in 1918. Notice the Jesus icon to the right of the Royal Door. According to a priest here, as worshippers meditate, staring deep into the eyes of Jesus, they enter a lake where they find their soul. Surrounded by incense, chanting, and your entire community...it could happen. Farther to the right, the icon of the unhappy-looking Virgin and Child is decorated with semiprecious stones from the Ural Mountains. Artists worked a triangle into each iconic face—symbolic of the Trinity.

**Cost, Hours, Location:** €3, daily 9:00–12:00 & 14:30–18:00, until 17:00 off-season, chanted services Sat at 17:30 or 18:00, Sun at 10:00, no tourist visits during services, no short shorts, 17 boulevard du Tzarewitch, tel. 04 93 96 88 02. The park around the church stays open at lunch and makes a fine setting for picnics.

**Getting to the Russian Cathedral:** From the train station, it's a 10-minute walk; exit the station to the right onto avenue Thiers, turn right on avenue Gambetta, and follow signs to the cathedral. Or, from the station, take any bus heading west on avenue Thiers and get off at avenue Gambetta (a few stops away).

# NIGHTLIFE

Promenade des Anglais, cours Saleya, and rue Masséna are all worth an evening walk. Nice's bars play host to one of the Riviera's most happening late-night scenes, full of jazz, rock, and heat-seeking singles. Most activity focuses on Old Nice, near place Rossetti and along rue Droite. **Distilleries Ideales** is a fine place to start or end your evening, with a lively, international crowd and a fun interior (where rues de la Poissonnerie and Barillerie meet, happy hour 18:00–20:00). Just down the street, **Wayne's Bar** is a happening spot for the younger, English-speaking backpacker crowd (15 rue Préfecture). The plush bar at **Hôtel Negresco** is fancy-cigar old English.

Plan on a cover charge or expensive drinks when music is involved. If you're out very late, avoid walking alone. Nice is well-known for its lively after-dark action; for more relaxed and accessible nightlife, consider nearby Antibes (described later in this chapter).

## SLEEPING

Don't look for charm in Nice. Go for modern and clean, with a central location and, in summer, air-conditioning. The rates listed here are for April through October. Prices generally drop €10–20 from November through March, but go sky-high during the Nice Carnival (Feb 13–March 1 in 2009), Monaco's Grand Prix (May 21–24 in 2009), and the Cannes Film Festival (May 13–24 in 2009). Between the Grand Prix and the film festival, the second half of May is very tight every year. June is convention month, and Nice is one of Europe's top convention cities. Reserve early if visiting May through August, especially during these times. For parking, ask your hotelier (several have limited private parking), or see "Arrival in Nice—By Car," earlier in this chapter.

I've divided my sleeping recommendations into three areas: between the train station and Nice Etoile shopping center (easy access to the train station and Old Nice via the sleek new tramway, 20-min walk to promenade des Anglais); between Nice Etoile and the sea (east of avenue Jean Médecin, great access to Old Nice and the sea at quai des Etats-Unis); and between boulevard Victor Hugo and the sea (a somewhat classier area, offering better access to promenade des Anglais but longer walks to the train station and Old Nice). I've also listed a hotel near the airport.

Most hotels I list have public Internet access in the lobby and/or Wi-Fi for laptop users.

---

### Sleep Code

**(€1 = about $1.50, country code: 33)**

**S** = Single, **D** = Double/Twin, **T** = Triple, **Q** = Quad, **b** = bathroom, **s** = shower only, **\*** = French hotel rating (0–4 stars). Hotels speak English, have elevators, and accept credit cards unless otherwise noted.

To help you sort easily through these listings, I've divided the rooms into three categories based on the price for a standard double room with bath:

**\$\$\$  Higher Priced**—Most rooms €100 or more.
**\$\$  Moderately Priced**—Most rooms between €70-100.
**\$  Lower Priced**—Most rooms €70 or less.

---

**FRENCH RIVIERA**

## Between the Train Station and Nice Etoile

This area offers Nice's cheapest sleeps, though most hotels near the station ghetto are overrun, overpriced, and loud. These are the pleasant exceptions (most are near avenue Jean Médecin). They're listed in order of proximity from the train station, going toward the beach.

**$ Hôtel la Belle Meunière,** in a fine old mansion built for Napoleon III's mistress, offers cheap beds and private rooms just a block below the train station. Lively and youth-hostel-esque, this place attracts budget-minded travelers of all ages with frumpy-but-adequate rooms and charismatic Madame Marie-Pierre presiding. Tables in the front yard greet guests and provide opportunities to meet other travelers (bunk in 4-bed dorm–€23 with private bath, €18 with shared bath, Db–€60, includes breakfast, 21 avenue Durante, tel. 04 93 88 66 15, fax 04 93 82 51 76, www.belle meuniere.com, hotel.belle.meuniere@cegetel.net).

**$$ Hôtel Durante**,** run by smiling Nathalie, feels like a Mediterranean villa, with its cheery and way-orange facade, spacious central courtyard, and cool bathroom tiles. Rooms are good enough, and the price is right (Db–€71–79, bigger Db–€100–150, Tb–€130–150, air-con, 16 avenue Durante, tel. 04 93 88 84 40, fax 04 93 87 77 76, www.hotel-durante.com, info@hotel-durante.com).

**$$ Hôtel St. Georges**** is big and bright, with a backyard garden, reasonably clean and comfortable high-ceilinged rooms, orange tones, blue halls, fair rates, and friendly reception (Sb–€78, Db–€93, Tb with 3 separate beds–€115, extra bed–€20, air-con, 7 avenue Georges Clémenceau, tel. 04 93 88 79 21, fax 04 93 16 22 85, www.hotelsaintgeorges.fr, contact@hotelsaintgeorges.fr).

**$$ Star Hotel**** is a fair budget option. Rooms are small and bare-bones, with air-conditioning and surprisingly firm beds (Sb–€55–60, Db–€65–80, Tb–€85–95, no elevator—rooms on 4 floors, 14 rue Biscarra, tel. 04 93 85 19 03, fax 04 93 13 04 23, www.hotel -star.com, info@hotel-star.com).

**$ Auberge de Jeunesse les Camélias** is a laid-back youth hostel in a grand building with a fine location. Rooms accommodate between four and seven people (136 beds in all) and come with showers and sinks—WCs are down the hall. Reservations must be made via the website in advance, or on the same day by phone. In high season, call by 10:00 (€21/bed, €3 extra without hostel membership, rooms closed 11:00–15:00 but can leave bags, includes breakfast, Internet access, laundry, kitchen, safes, bar, 3 rue Spitalieri, tel. 04 93 62 15 54,www.hihostels.com, nice -camelias@fuaj.org, Isabelle at the desk and Bernard at the helm).

**$ B&B Nice Home Sweet Home** is a great value. Gentle Genevieve Levert rents out three spacious rooms and one small single in her home. Her rooms are simply decorated, with high

# Nice Hotels

1. Hôtel la Belle Meunière
2. Hôtel Durante
3. Hôtel St. Georges
4. Star Hotel
5. Auberge de Jeunesse les Camélias
6. B&B Nice Home Sweet Home
7. Hôtel Masséna
8. Hôtel Suisse
9. Hôtel Mercure Marché aux Fleurs
10. Hôtel Lafayette
11. Hôtel de la Mer
12. Hôtel Negresco
13. Hôtel le Royal
14. Hôtel Windsor
15. Hôtel les Cigales
16. Hôtels Splendid & Gounod
17. Hôtel Villa Victoria
18. To Hôtel Ibis
19. Hôtel Vendôme & Launderette
20. Cat's Whiskers Bookstore

FRENCH RIVIERA

ceilings, big windows, lots of light, and sitting areas where you can spread out. One room comes with private bath; otherwise, it's just like at home...down the hall (S-€31–38, D-€61–70, Db-€65–75, Tb-€74–84, Q-€80–90, includes breakfast, air-con units available in summer, no elevator, washer/dryer-€5, use of fridge, 35 rue Rossini at intersection with rue Auber, 2nd floor, tel. 06 19 66 03 63, www.nicehomesweethome.com, glevert@free.fr).

## Between Nice Etoile and the Sea

**$$$ Hôtel Masséna\*\*\*\***, in a classy building a few blocks from place Masséna, is a stylish business hotel showcasing 100 rooms with every amenity at almost-reasonable rates (small Db-€120–150, larger Db-€140–190, still larger Db-€200–270, extra bed-€30, some non-smoking rooms, check website or call same day for special rates—prices drop when hotel is not full, reserve parking ahead-€25/day, 58 rue Gioffredo, tel. 04 92 47 88 88, fax 04 92 47 88 89, www.hotel-massena-nice.com, info@hotel-massena-nice.com).

**$$$ Hôtel Suisse\*\*\***, below Castle Hill, has Nice's best ocean and city views for the money, and is surprisingly quiet given the busy street below. Rooms are quite comfortable, the decor is classy, and the staff is professional. There's no reason to sleep here if you don't land a view, so I've listed prices only for view rooms—many of which have balconies (Db-€155–195, extra bed-€36, breakfast-€15, 15 quai Rauba Capeu, tel. 04 92 17 39 00, fax 04 93 85 30 70, www.hotels-ocre-azur.com, hotel.suisse@hotels-ocre-azur.com).

**$$$ Hôtel Mercure Marché aux Fleurs\*\*\*** is a chain hotel ideally situated across from the sea and behind cours Saleya. It offers smallish yet tastefully designed rooms (some with beds in a loft). Prices are reasonable, though rates vary dramatically over the season (Db-€115–140, Db suite-€200, sea view-€50 extra, air-con, 91 quai des Etats-Unis, tel. 04 93 85 74 19, fax 04 93 13 90 94, h0962@accor.com). Don't confuse this Mercure with the six others in Nice.

**$$$ Hôtel Vendôme\*\*\*** gives you a whiff of the belle époque, with pink pastels, high ceilings, and grand staircases in a mansion set off the street. That whiff could be sharper (many tour groups stay here and the rooms seem a tad tired), but the location is decent, prices are almost fair, and rooms are modern and come in all sizes. The best have balconies (on floors 4 and 5)—request *une chambre avec balcon* (Sb-€111, Db-€144, Tb-€159, air-con, book ahead for limited parking-€12/day, 26 rue Pastorelli, tel. 04 93 62 00 77, fax 04 93 13 40 78, www.vendome-hotel-nice.com, contact @vendome-hotel-nice.com).

**$$$ Hôtel Lafayette\*\*\***, in a nice location a block behind the Galeries Lafayette department store, looks average from the outside. But inside it's homey, with 18 well-designed, mostly spacious

## Old Nice Hotels and Restaurants

1. Hôtel Suisse
2. Hôtel Mercure Marché aux Fleurs
3. Hôtel de la Mer
4. La Cambuse Rest.
5. La Festival de la Moule
6. Nissa Socca Rest.
7. L'Univers Rest.
8. Restaurant Castel
9. Chez Palmyre Rest.
10. L'Acchiardo Rest.
11. Oliviera Shop/Rest.
12. Restaurant du Gesù
13. Lou Pilha Leva Rest.
14. Fenocchio's Gelato (2)
15. Distilleries Ideales
16. Wayne's Bar
17. Bike Rental
18. Go Sport
19. Centre du Patrimoine (Walking Tours)

**FRENCH RIVIERA**

rooms, all one floor up from the street. Kind Sandrine and Georges take darned good care of you—all in all, a fine value (standard Db-€100–115, spacious Db-€105–125, extra bed-€24, coffee service in rooms, central air-con, no elevator, 32 rue de l'Hôtel des Postes, tel. 04 93 85 17 84, fax 04 93 80 47 56, www.hotellafayettenice.com, info@hotellafayettenice.com).

**$$ Hôtel de la Mer\*\*** sits in an enviable position between place Masséna and Old Nice (in fact, it's one of the closest listings here to the old town). This small, modest, *très* traditional place is run by gracious Madame Ferry (Db-€75–95, Tb-€85–140, top prices are for July–Aug, air-con, 4 place Masséna, tel. 04 93 92 09 10, fax 04 93 85 00 64, www.hoteldelamernice.com, hotel.mer@wanadoo.fr).

## Between Boulevard Victor Hugo and the Sea

**$$$$ Hôtel Negresco\*\*\*\*** owns Nice's most prestigious address on promenade des Anglais and knows it. Still, it's the kind of place that, if you were to splurge just once in your life... Rooms are opulent (see page 600 for further description), and tips are expected (viewless Db-€360, Db with sea view-€460–580, view suite-€770–1,900, breakfast-€35, cool bar, 37 promenade des Anglais, tel. 04 93 16 64 00, fax 04 93 88 35 68, www.hotel-negresco-nice.com, reservations@hotel-negresco.com).

**$$$ Hôtel le Royal\*\*\*** stands shoulder-to-shoulder on promenade des Anglais with the big boys (the Negresco, Concorde, and Westminster hotels). With 140 rooms, big lounges, and hallways that stretch forever, it feels a bit institutional. But the prices are reasonable considering the solid, air-conditioned comfort and terrific location—and they sometimes have rooms when others don't (viewless Db-€112–132, Db with sea view-€142–162, bigger view room-€162–182 and worth the extra euros, extra person-€25, 23 promenade des Anglais, tel. 04 93 16 43 00, fax 04 93 16 43 02, www.hotel-royal-nice.cote.azur.fr, royal@vacancesbleues.com).

**$$$ Hôtel Windsor\*\*\*** is a snazzy garden retreat that feels like a cross between a modern-art museum and a health spa. Some of the contemporary rooms, designed by modern artists, defy explanation. It has a full-service bar, a small outdoor swimming pool and gym (both free for guests), an €11 sauna, €55 massages, and light, full meal service in the cool, shaded garden area (standard Db-€120, bigger Db-€150, big Db with balcony-€175, extra bed-€20, rooms over garden worth the higher price, air-con, Internet access, 11 rue Dalpozzo, tel. 04 93 88 59 35, fax 04 93 88 94 57, www.hotelwindsornice.com, reservation@hotelwindsornice.com).

**$$$ Hôtel les Cigales\*\*\*** is one of my favorites. It's a smart little pastel place with tasteful decor, 19 plush rooms (most with tub-showers), air-conditioning, and a nifty upstairs terrace, all well-managed by friendly Mr. Valentino, with Veronique and Elaine. Book directly through the hotel and show this book for a surprise treat on arrival (standard Db-€90–129, big Db-€115–140, Tb-€150, €30 more during major events, extra bed-€20, 16 rue Dalpozzo, tel. 04 97 03 10 70, fax 04 97 03 10 71, www.hotel -lescigales.com, info@hotel-lescigales.com).

**$$$ Hôtel Splendid****** is a worthwhile splurge if you miss your Marriott. The panoramic rooftop pool, Jacuzzi, bar, restaurant, and breakfast room almost justify the cost...but throw in comfortable rooms (four of the six floors are non-smoking), a free gym, spa services, and air-conditioning, and you're as good as home. Check their website for deals (Db-€225, deluxe Db with terrace-€265, suites-€355–395, free breakfast if you stay at least 3 nights, 10 percent off for weeklong stays, parking-€22/day, 50 boulevard Victor Hugo, tel. 04 93 16 41 00, fax 04 93 16 42 70, www.splendid-nice.com, info@splendid-nice.com).

**$$$ Hôtel Gounod*****\* is behind Hôtel Splendid, and because the two share the same owners, Gounod's guests are allowed free access to Splendid's pool, Jacuzzi, and other amenities. Don't let the lackluster lobby fool you. Most rooms are richly decorated, with high ceilings and air-conditioning—though quality can vary (Db-€155, palatial 4-person suites-€250, parking-€15/day, 3 rue Gounod, tel. 04 93 16 42 00, fax 04 93 88 23 84, www.gounod -nice.com, info@gounod-nice.com).

**$$$ Hôtel Villa Victoria*****\* is nicely managed by cheery Marlena, who welcomes travelers into this classy old building with a green awning and an attractive lobby overlooking a generous garden. Rooms are traditional and well-kept, with space to stretch out (Db-€115–160, Tb-€135–175, suites-€160–210, pricier rooms face the garden, breakfast-€15, air-con, parking-€15, 33 boulevard Victor Hugo, tel. 04 93 88 39 60, fax 04 93 88 07 98, www.villa-victoria.com).

## Closer to the Airport

**$$ Hôtel Ibis**** offers a handy port-in-the-storm outlet for those with early flights or just stopping in for a single night (Db-€75–90 when no special events in town, 359 promenade des Anglais, tel. 04 89 88 30 30, fax 04 93 21 19 43, reception@ibisnice.com).

# EATING

Remember, you're in a resort. Go for ambience and fun, and lower your palate's standards. Italian is a low-risk and local cuisine. The restaurants listed below are concentrated in neighborhoods close to my recommended hotels, though you should focus your dining energy on Old Nice. Promenade des Anglais is ideal for picnic dinners on warm, languid evenings. Old Nice has the best and busiest dining atmosphere, while the Nice Etoile area is more convenient and offers a good range of choices. To feast cheaply, eat on rue Droite in Old Nice, or explore the area around the train station. For a more peaceful meal, head for nearby Villefranche-sur-Mer (described later in this chapter). For terribly touristy trolling, wander the wall-to-wall places lining rue Masséna. Yuck.

## In Old Nice

Nice's dinner scene converges on cours Saleya (koor sah-lay-yuh), which is entertaining enough in itself to make the generally mediocre food a good deal. It's a fun, festive place to compare tans and mussels. Even if you're eating elsewhere, wander through here in the evening. For locations, see the map on page 611.

**La Cambuse** is a small island of refinement for those who want to dine on cours Saleya—and the one place along here that doesn't try to reel in passersby. Owner Gregory is swimming upstream in his effort to provide quality cuisine with attentive service in this touristy area. Split a starter like the filling *petits farcis niçois* (stuffed vegetables), then order your own *plat* (€13 starters, €18–24 *plats,* open daily, 5 cours Saleya, tel. 04 93 80 82 40).

**La Festival de la Moule** is a relatively cheap place that's all about mussels. For just €11, you get all-you-can-eat mussels and fries (across the square from la Cambuse, 20 cours Saleya, tel. 04 93 62 02 12).

**Nissa Socca** offers good, cheap Italian cuisine and a lively atmosphere in a small room a few blocks from cours Saleya. Indoor tables are usually steamy—arrive early to land a table outside (€9 pizza, €10 pastas, €15–24 *menus,* Mon–Sat from 19:00, closed Sun, a block off place Rossetti on rue Ste. Réparate, tel. 04 93 80 18 35).

**L'Univers,** a block off place Masséna, earned a Michelin star while maintaining a warm ambience. This elegant place is as relaxed as a "top" restaurant can be, from its casual decor to the tasteful dinnerware. When the artfully presented food arrives, you know this is high cuisine (*menus* from €44, closed Sun, 53 boulevard Jean Jaurès, tel. 04 93 62 32 22, plumailunivers@aol.com).

**Restaurant Castel** is your best eat-on-the-beach option. Dining here, you almost expect Don Ho to grab a mic. You're right on the beach below Castle Hill, perfectly positioned to watch evening swimmers get in their last laps as the sky turns pink and city lights flicker on. The views are unforgettable; you can even have lunch at your beach chair if you've rented one (€10/half-day, €14/day). Dinner here is best, so arrive before sunset and linger long enough to merit the few extra euros the place charges (€13–16 salads and pastas, €20–24 main dishes, open daily, 8 quai des Etats-Unis, tel. 04 93 85 22 66).

### Dining Cheap *à la Niçoise*

Try at least one of these five places—not just because they're terrific budget options, but primarily because they offer authentic *niçoise* cuisine.

**Chez Palmyre** is as real as it gets. Your hostess Madame Palmyre shuffles between her small kitchen and the seven-table dining room. The four-course *menu* is only €13, and the cuisine could not be more homemade (closed Sun, cash only, 5 rue Droite, tel. 04 93 85 72 32).

**L'Acchiardo,** in the heart of Old Nice, does a good job mixing a loyal local and tourist clientele. Its simple, hearty, *niçoise* cuisine is served for fair prices in a homey setting overseen by gentle Monsieur Acchiardo (€13 dinner *plats,* cash only, closed Sat–Sun, 38 rue Droite, tel. 04 93 85 51 16).

**Oliviera** is all about the French olive. This shop/restaurant sells a wide variety of oils, offers free tastings, and serves a menu of dishes paired with specific oils (just like a wine pairing). Owner Nadim, who speaks excellent English, knows all of his producers personally and provides great "Olive Oil 101" explanations with his tastings (it's nice if you buy something afterwards). You'll feel how passionate he is about his products, and once you come to taste, you'll want to stay and eat (€14–22 main dishes, Tue–Sat 10:00–22:00, closed Sun–Mon, 8 bis rue du Collet, tel. 04 93 13 06 45, www.oliviera.com).

**Restaurant du Gesù,** a happy-go-lucky budget eatery, squeezes plastic tables into a slanting square deep in the old city (sailors accustomed to dining at an angle will feel right at home). Arrive early or join the mobs waiting for an outside table; better yet, have fun in the soccer-banner–draped interior. The *raviolis sauce daube* is popular (€9 pizzas, €10 pastas, closed Sun, 1 place du Jésus, tel. 04 93 62 26 46).

**Lou Pilha Leva** offers a fun, *très* cheap lunch or dinner option with *niçoise* specialties and outdoor-only benches. Order your food from one side and drinks from the other (open daily, located where rue de la Loge and Centrale meet in Old Nice).

### And for Dessert...

Gelato-lovers should save room for the tempting ice cream stands in Old Nice. For instance, **Fenocchio** serves up 86 flavors, from tomato to lavender to avocado—which is actually pretty good (daily until 23:30, two locations in Old Nice: on place Rossetti and on rue de la Poissonnerie).

### Eating near Nice Etoile

If you're not up for eating in Old Nice, try one of these spots around the Nice Etoile shopping mall.

FRENCH RIVIERA

## Nice Restaurants

1. Rue Biscarra Eateries
2. Bistrot les Viviers
3. L'Ovale Rest. & La Cantine de Lulu
4. La Maison de Marie Rest.
5. La Part des Anges Wine Bar
6. Il Vino Ino Rest. & Cave de L'Origine Wine Bar
7. Chantecler Restaurant
8. Restaurant d'Angleterre
9. Voyageur Nissart Rest.
10. Monoprix Grocery Store
11. Bus #98 to Airport
12. Bus #22 to Chagall & Matisse Mus. & Bus #17 to Matisse Museum
13. Buses #99 & 23 to Airport

TO CHAGALL & MATISSE MUSEUMS

Rue Massena PEDEST. ZONE
TRAM

1/4 MILE
.5 KM

MODERN ART MUSEUM

TRAIN STATION

NICE ETOILE SHOPPING MALL

BUS STN.

OLD NICE

CASTLE HILL
ELEVATOR

HOTEL NEGRESCO

PROMENADE DES ANGLAIS

QUAI DES ETATS-UNIS

B E A C H E S

Tourist Train PICK-UP

*On Rue Biscarra:* Laid-back cafés line up along the broad sidewalk on rue Biscarra (just east of avenue Jean Médecin behind Nice Etoile, all closed Sun). **L'Authentic, Le Vin sur Vin,** and **Le Cenac** are all reasonable enough. **Le Vin sur Vin** seems most popular as a restaurant and wine bar (tel. 04 93 92 93 20), though **L'Authentic** is also good, with memorable owners (burly Philippe and sleek Laurent), daily specials, €19 *menus*, and reasonable pasta dishes (live music some Fri and Sat nights, 18 bis rue Biscarra, tel. 04 93 62 48 88).

**Bistrot les Viviers** appeals to those who require attentive service, silver warming covers, and authentic *niçoise* cuisine. At this cozy splurge, allow €65 per person for wine and three courses, or consider lunch (€17 *menus*). It has two different settings (with the same prices): a formal restaurant and a more relaxed *bistrot* next door. Reserve for the atmospheric *bistrot*. Fish is the chef's forte (closed Sun, 5-min walk west of avenue Jean Médecin at 22 rue Alphonse Karr, tel. 04 93 16 00 48).

**L'Ovale** is a find. How this ever-so-local and rugby-loving café survives in a tourist mecca, I'll never know. It's run by Nice's nicest couple, Jean-Marc and Jacqueline, who serve quality food at respectable prices. Join the lively local crowd and dine inside on big *plats* for €11. Consider their specialty, *cassoulet* (€36 for two people), or enjoy *la planche de charcuterie* as a meaty, filling first course (excellent €15 3-course *menu*, closed Sun, air-con, 29 rue Pastorelli, tel. 04 93 80 31 65).

**La Maison de Marie** is a surprisingly high-quality refuge off touristy rue Masséna, where most other places serve mediocre food to tired travelers. Enter through a deep-red arch to a bougainvillea-draped courtyard, and enjoy the fair prices and good food that draw locals and out-of-towners alike. The interior tables are as appealing as those in the courtyard (*menus* from €21, open daily, look for the square red flag at 5 rue Masséna, tel. 04 93 82 15 93).

**La Cantine de Lulu** is small and charming. This Czech-owned restaurant serves homemade recipes from Nice and Prague (closed Sat–Mon, 26 rue Alberti, tel. 04 93 62 15 33).

**La Part des Anges,** an atmospheric wine shop with a few tables in the back, serves a decent but limited menu and a large selection of wines (open daily for lunch, Fri–Sat only for dinner, reserve ahead, 17 rue Gubernatis, tel. 04 93 62 69 80).

## Near Promenade des Anglais

**Il Vino Ino,** a block from promenade des Anglais, has street appeal. This lively, reasonably priced eatery serves only Italian food amid cheery decor, either indoors or out (closed Sun, 33 rue de la Buffa, tel. 04 93 87 94 25).

**Cave de L'Origine,** run by kind Isabelle and Carlo, is a quality food shop *(épicerie)* and wine bar that also serves a small menu selection. Carlo enjoys talking about his all-natural wines and other products, as he knows all the farmers personally. Stop by for a glass of wine, to peruse the shop, or to reserve a table for a meal (open Tue–Sat for lunch, Thu–Sat for dinner, reservations smart; shop open Tue–Sat 10:00–20:00, closed Sun–Mon; 3 rue Dalpozzo, tel. 04 83 50 09 60).

**Chantecler** has Nice's most prestigious address—inside the Hôtel Negresco. This is everything a luxury restaurant should be: elegant, soft, and top-quality. If your trip is ending in Nice, call or email for reservations—you've earned this splurge *(menus* from €90, closed Mon–Tue, 37 promenade des Anglais, tel. 04 93 16 64 00, chantecler@hotel-negresco.com).

## Near the Train Station

These two places are hardly undiscovered—they're listed in many other guidebooks—but they deserve their acclaim.

**Restaurant d'Angleterre** is ideal for hungry travelers on a tight budget. For €15, you get a filling three-course dinner with tasty choices and great service (indoor and outdoor tables, closed Sun–Mon, 25 rue d'Angleterre, tel. 04 03 88 64 48).

**Voyageur Nissart** has blended budget cuisine with cool Mediterranean ambience and friendly service since 1908 (€17 *menus,* closed Mon, 19 rue d'Alsace-Lorraine, tel. 04 93 82 19 60).

# TRANSPORTATION CONNECTIONS

For basic train, bus, and boat schedules from Nice to nearby towns, see "Getting Around the Riviera," earlier in this chapter. Note that most long-distance train connections to other French cities require a change in Marseille.

**From Nice by Train to: Marseille** (18/day, 2.5 hrs), **Cassis** (14/day, 3 hrs, transfer in Toulon or Marseille), **Arles** (11/day, 3.75–4.5 hrs, most require transfer in Marseille or Avignon), **Avignon** (20/day, 13 of which are via TGV, 4 hrs, a few direct, most require transfer in Marseille), **Paris'** Gare de Lyon (10/day, 6 hrs, may require change; 11-hr night train goes to Paris' Gare d'Austerlitz), **Aix-en-Provence** TGV station (10/day, 3.5 hrs, may require transfer in Marseille or Toulon), **Chamonix** (4/day, 10 hrs, 3 transfers), **Beaune** (7/day, 7 hrs, 1–2 changes), **Munich** (4/day, 12–13 hrs with 2–4 transfers, night trains possible via Italy), **Interlaken** (6/day, 9–11 hrs, 2–5 transfers), **Florence** (6/day, 7–9 hrs, 1–3 transfers), **Milan** (7/day, 5–5.5 hrs, 4 with transfers), **Venice** (5/day, 8–9 hrs, all require transfers), **Barcelona** (2/day, 11–12 hrs).

## Nice's Airport

Nice's easy-to-navigate airport (Aéroport de Nice Côte d'Azur) is on the Mediterranean, a 20–30-minute drive west of the city center. Planes leave about hourly to Paris (1-hr flight, about the same price as a train ticket, check www.easyjet.com for the cheapest flights to Paris' Orly airport). The two terminals (Terminal 1 and Terminal 2) are connected by frequent shuttle buses *(navettes)*. Both terminals have banks, ATMs, taxis, baggage storage, and buses to Nice. The TIs for Nice and Monaco are in Terminal 1 (tel. 08 20 42 33 33 or 04 89 88 98 28, www.nice.aeroport.fr).

**Taxis** into the center are expensive, charging €30 to Nice hotels and €50 to Villefranche-sur-Mer (10 percent more from 19:00–7:00 and all day Sunday). Taxis stop outside door *(Porte)* A-1 at Terminal 1 and outside *Porte* A-3 at Terminal 2. Notorious for overcharging, Nice taxis are not always so nice. If your fare for a ride into town is much higher than €30 (or €33 at night or on Sun), refuse to pay the overage. If this doesn't work, tell the cabbie to call a *gendarme* (police officer). It's always a good idea to ask for a receipt *(reçu)*.

**Airport shuttle vans** work with some of my recommended hotels, but they only make sense when going *to* the airport, not when arriving. Unlike taxis, shuttle vans offer a fixed price that doesn't rise on Sundays, early mornings, or evenings. Prices are best for groups (figure €25 for one person, and only a little more for additional people). Keet Business is a good option (€25/shuttle for 2–4 people, tel. 06 60 33 20 54, www.keet-business.com), or ask your hotelier for recommendations.

Three bus lines connect the airport with the city center, offering good alternatives to high-priced taxis and shuttles. **Bus #99** (airport express) runs from both terminals to Nice's main train station (€4, 2/hr, 8:00–21:00, 30 min, drops you within a 10-min walk of many recommended hotels). To take this bus *to* the airport, catch it right in front of the train station (departs on the half-hour). If your hotel is within walking distance of the station, #99 is a breeze. **Bus #98** serves both terminals, and runs along promenade des Anglais to Nice's main bus station *(gare routière)*, which is near Old Nice (€4, 3/hr, from the airport 6:00–23:00, to the airport until 21:00, no service on Sun, 30 min). The slower, cheaper local **bus #23** serves only Terminal 1, and makes every stop between the airport and train station (€1, 3/hr, 6:00–20:00, 40 min, direction: St. Maurice). For all buses, buy tickets in the information office just outside either terminal, or from the driver. To reach the bus information office and stops at Terminal 1, turn left after passing customs and exit the doors at the far end. Buses serving Terminal 2 stop across the street from the exit. If you take bus #98 or #99, hang on to your €4 ticket—it's good all day on any public bus and the tramway in Nice, and for buses between Nice and nearby towns (see page 586 for details).

To get to **Villefranche-sur-Mer** from the airport, take bus #98 to Nice's bus station *(gare routière)*, then transfer to the Villefranche-sur-Mer bus (bus #100, use same ticket).

To reach **Antibes** and **Cannes,** take line #200 from Terminal 1 (€1, about 2/hr, 40–45 min to Antibes, 1–1.25 hrs to Cannes—duration depends on traffic). Pricey express buses (line #110) run directly to **Monaco** from the airport (€16.50, hourly, 50 min), but you'll save money by transferring in Nice to a Monaco-bound bus.

# Villefranche-sur-Mer

Located halfway between the world-famous resorts of Nice and Monaco, Villefranche-sur-Mer offers travelers an easygoing slice of small-town Mediterranean life. In 30 minutes or less, you can be gambling in style in Monaco or sauntering the promenade des Anglais in Nice. This town feels Italian, with soft-orange buildings; steep, narrow streets spilling into the sea; and pasta *con* pesto. Luxury sailing yachts glisten in the bay—an inspiration to those lazing along the harborfront to start saving when their trips are over. Sand-pebble beaches and a handful of interesting sights keep visitors just busy enough.

## ORIENTATION

### Tourist Information

The TI is in the park named jardin François Binon, below the main bus stop, labeled *Octroi* (July–Aug daily 9:00–19:00; Sept–June Mon–Sat 9:00–12:00 & 14:00–18:00, closed Sun; a 20-min walk or €10 taxi from train station, tel. 04 93 01 73 68, www.villefranche -sur-mer.org). Pick up the brochure detailing a self-guided walking tour of Villefranche-sur-Mer and information on boat rides (usually mid-June–Sept).

### Arrival in Villefranche-sur-Mer

**By Bus:** Buses from Nice and Monaco drop you next to jardin François Binon, at the Octroi bus stop just above the TI. The old town and most hotels are downhill. The stop for buses going back to Nice is across the street from where you were dropped off (buses run every 10–15 min).

**By Plane:** Allow an hour from the airport to Villefranche. The express bus #98 runs between Nice's airport and bus station (€4, 3/hr, no service on Sun, 30 min); there you can transfer to bus #100 to Villefranche (4/hr, 20 min). One €4 ticket covers the whole trip.

**By Train:** Villefranche-sur-Mer's train station is a 15-minute walk along the water from the old town and many of my recommended hotels. Find the staircase leading down toward the water, and turn right to walk straight into town. Taxis to my recommended hotels cost €10, but they don't wait here and prefer longer rides; call instead, and pray the phone is working (tel. 06 09 33 36 12 or 06 39 32 54 09).

**By Car:** From Nice's port, follow signs for *Menton, Monaco,* and *Basse Corniche.* In Villefranche-sur-Mer, turn right at the TI (first signal after Hôtel la Flore) for parking and hotels. For a quick visit to the TI, park at the nearby pay lot. A bit farther down, you'll find free parking in the moat areas within the boundaries of the citadel—better for longer visits and well-signed from main road *(Parking Fossés).* There's a safer pay lot on the water across from Hôtel Welcome, and some hotels also have their own parking.

## Helpful Hints

**Market Day:** An antiques market enlivens Villefranche-sur-Mer on Sundays (on place Amélie Pollonnais by Hôtel Welcome and in jardin François Binon by the TI). On Saturday mornings, a small food market sets up near the TI (only in jardin François Binon).

**Internet Access:** Two options sit side-by-side on place du Marché. **Chez Net,** an "Australian International Sports Bar Internet Café," has American keyboards but no printers, while **L'Ex Café** has printers but only French keyboards. Either place lets you enjoy a late-night drink while surfing the Internet (both open daily).

**Electric Bike Rental:** If you plan to explore the area and you don't feel like walking, consider renting an electric bike from **Eco-Loc.** The adventurous can also try this as an alternative to taking the bus into Nice (€7/hr, €20/4 hrs, €30/day, April–Sept daily 9:00–17:30, deposit and ID required, best to call for reservations 24 hrs in advance; helmets, locks, baskets, and child seats available; on port near parking lot and Hôtel Welcome, tel. 06 63 91 16 77, Christophe and Sebastian speak English).

**Laundry:** The town has two launderettes—both owned by Laura and located just below the main road on avenue Sadi Carnot. At the upper *pressing moderne,* Laura does your wash for you, but it's expensive (Tue–Sun 8:00–12:30 & 14:00–18:30, closes

Sat at 17:00, closed Mon, next to Hôtel Riviera, tel. 04 93 01 73 71). The lower *laverie* is self-service only (daily 7:00–20:00, opposite 6 avenue Sadi Carnot).

**Taxi:** Beware of taxi drivers who overcharge—the normal weekday, daytime rate to central Nice is about €35; to the airport, figure €50; to Eze-le-Village, about €35. The five-minute trip from the waterfront up to the main street level (to bus stops on the Low Corniche) should be less than €10. Ask your driver to write down the price before you get in, and get a receipt when you pay (tel. 06 09 33 36 12 or 06 39 32 54 09).

**Minibus:** Little minibus #80 will save you the sweat of going from the harbor up the hill, but it only runs once per hour (€1). It travels from the port to the top of the hill, stopping near La Fiancée du Pirate (see "Sleeping," later in this section) before going over the hill to the outlying, suburban Nice Riquier train station (only convenient if you're already on minibus, must transfer to train to downtown Nice).

**Sports Fans:** Lively *boules* action takes place each evening just below the TI and the huge soccer field (see page 837).

## SIGHTS

**The Harbor**—Browse Villefranche-sur-Mer's minuscule harbor. Only eight families still fish to make money. Gaze out to sea and marvel at the beautiful sailing yachts that call this bay home. (You might see well-coiffed captains being ferried in by dutiful mates to pick up their statuesque call girls.) Local guides keep a list of the world's 100 biggest yachts and talk about some of them as if they're part of the neighborhood.

Parallel to the beach and about a block inland, you can walk the mysterious rue Obscura—a covered lane running 400 feet along the medieval rampart.

**Chapel of St. Pierre (Chapelle Cocteau)**—This chapel, decorated by artist, poet, and filmmaker Jean Cocteau, is the town's cultural highlight. A brooding fisherwoman collects a €2 donation for the fishermen's charity, and then sets you free to enjoy the chapel's small but intriguing interior. In 1955, Jean Cocteau covered the barrel-vaulted chapel with heavy black lines and pastels. Each of Cocteau's works—the Roma (Gypsies) of Stes-Maries-de-la-Mer who dance and sing to honor the Virgin, girls wearing traditional outfits, and three scenes from the life of St. Peter—are explained in English. Is that Villefranche-sur-Mer's citadel in

**FRENCH RIVIERA**

# Villefranche-sur-Mer

1. Hôtel Welcome & Souris Gourmande Rest.
2. Hôtel Villa Vauban
3. Hôtel la Flore
4. To Hôtel la Fiancée du Pirate & Minibus Route
5. Hôtel de la Darse
6. Michel's & Le Cosmo Rest.
7. La Mère Germaine Rest.
8. La Grignotière Rest.
9. Le Roxy Rest.
10. La Serre Rest.
11. Casino Grocery
12. Internet: Chez Net Bar & L'Ex Café
13. Boat Rides & Electric Bike Rental
14. Launderette
15. Octroi Bus Stop (from Nice; to Monaco & Cap Ferrat)
16. Octroi Bus Stop (to Nice; from Monaco & Cap Ferrat)

TO EZE + MONACO VIA LOW CORNICHE ROAD

TRAIN STATION

BLVD NAPOLEON

GEORGES CLEMENCEAU

PONCHARD.

QUAI AM. COURBET

BEACH

TO CAP FERRAT ON FOOT

**N**

P PARKING
T TAXI STAND
H STEPPED STREETS

AVE. 1er

AVE. ALBERT

AVE. GALLIENI

R. VOLTI
R. BARON
R. DU POILU
RUE OBSCURE

Post

AVE. SADI

AVE. CH. JEUN.

AVE. JOFFRE

RUE CARNOT

OLD TOWN

CHAPEL OF ST. PIERRE

GARE MARITIME

AVE. FOCH

AVE. VERDUN

ALLEE DUVAL

PLAY AREA

ATM

CITADEL

SCENIC WALKWAY

AVE. PRINCESSE GRACE

AVE. DE GAULLE

QUAI CORPERIE

AVENUE

PLAY AREA

TO NICE

PORT DE LA DARSE

200 YARDS
200 METERS

MEDITERRANEAN SEA

DCH

the scene above the altar? (€2 donation, Tue–Sun 10:00–12:00 & 15:00–19:00, closed Mon and when fisherwoman is tired, below Hôtel Welcome.)

**Citadel**—The town's mammoth castle was built in the 1500s by the Duke of Savoy to defend against the French. When the region joined France in 1860, it became just a barracks. In the 20th century, the city had no military use for the space, and started using the citadel to house its police station, City Hall, and two art galleries.

**Church**—The town church features a fine crucifix—carved, they say, from a fig tree by a galley slave in the 1600s.

**Boat Rides (Promenades en Mer)**—These little cruises, with English handouts, are offered sporadically, usually on Wednesdays and Fridays (€11 for 1-hour cruise around Cap Ferrat, €16 for 2-hour cruise as far as Monaco—but doesn't actually stop there, 5/week July–Aug, 1/week June and Sept, none off-season, boats depart from the harbor across from Hôtel Welcome, call to confirm the ever-changing schedule, reservations a must, tel. 04 93 76 65 65, www.amv-sirenes.com).

**Beach Walk**—A seaside walkway leads under the citadel and connects the old town with the yacht harbor, where you'll find one hotel and a few cafés. This scenic walk turns downright romantic after dark. Even if you're sleeping elsewhere, take an ice-cream-licking stroll here. You can also wander along Villefranche-sur-Mer's waterfront and continue beyond the train station for postcard-perfect views back to Villefranche-sur-Mer (ideal in the morning—go before breakfast). You'll come to a quieter beach with good picnic benches. You can even extend your walk to Cap Ferrat (the wooded peninsula across the bay from Villefranche).

# SLEEPING

**(€1 = about $1.50, country code: 33)**
You have a handful of good hotels to choose from in Villefranche-sur-Mer. The ones I list have sea views from at least half of their rooms—well worth paying extra for.

$$$ **Hôtel Welcome*** easily has the best location in Villefranche-sur-Mer, anchored right on the water in the old town, with all 32 balconied rooms overlooking the harbor. You'll pay top price for all the comforts in this smart hotel. Skip the claustrophobic sixth-floor rooms ("comfort" Db-€200, bigger "superior" Db-€230, suites-€335–380, extra bed-€35, air-con, no Wi-Fi, elevator, parking garage-€20/day, 3 quai Amiral Courbet, tel. 04 93 76 27 62, fax 04 93 76 27 66, www.welcomehotel.com, resa @welcomehotel.com).

$$$ **Hôtel Villa Vauban\*\*\*** is a small villa two blocks below the TI, with nine well-maintained rooms. Many have balconies and sea views, and most come with Old World bathrooms. Amiable British expat Alan Powers adds a personal touch that's rare in this area. He's happy to answer your questions (Db with small view-€95–130, Db with big sea view-€125–170, Db suite with sea view-€140–190, air-con, Wi-Fi, 11 avenue Général de Gaulle, tel. & fax 04 93 55 94 51, www.hotelvillavauban.com, info@hotelvillavauban.com).

$$$ **Hôtel la Flore\*\*\*** is suitable if your idea of sightseeing is to enjoy the view from your spacious bedroom deck (most rooms have one), or the pool. The free parking couldn't be easier, but the staff is a tad formal, and it's a 10-minute uphill walk from the old town (Db with no view-€85–135, Db with view and deck-€135–150, larger Db for up to five people with even better view and bigger deck-€170–210, Db mini-suite-€220, Qb loft with huge terrace-€240, extra bed-€34, 10–15 percent cheaper Oct–March, air-con, elevator; just off main road high above harbor—go 2 blocks from TI toward Nice, near the bus stop to Nice and Monaco at 5 boulevard Princesse Grace de Monaco; tel. 04 93 76 30 30, fax 04 93 76 99 99, www.hotel-la-flore.fr, hotel-la-flore@wanadoo.fr).

$$ **Hôtel la Fiancée du Pirate** is only feasible if you have a car, as it's high up in Villefranche-sur-Mer on the Middle Corniche (parking is no problem). Don't let the streetside appearance deter you. Friendly Eric and Laurence offer 15 bright and comfortable rooms, along with a pool, Jacuzzi, lush garden, roomy lounge area, and breakfast terrace with partial views of Cap Ferrat and the sea. Choose between rooms in the main building (Db-€88–110, Tb/Qb-€130–165), or view rooms on the garden patio (standard Db-€85–95, Tb/Qb-€110–125). From June to September, they require a three-night minimum stay and offer lunch, salads, and snacks by the pool (air-con, Wi-Fi, 8 boulevard de la Corne d'Or, Moyenne Corniche N7, tel. 04 93 76 67 40, fax 04 93 76 91 04, www.fianceedupirate.com, info@fianceedupirate.com).

$$ **Hôtel de la Darse\*\*** is a shy and unassuming little hotel burrowed in the shadow of its highbrow neighbors. This low-profile alternative right on the water at Villefranche-sur-Mer's old port (a 5-min level walk to the harbor) offers the best value in town. Most rooms have been renovated, but the ones facing the sea are worth the extra few euros for their million-dollar-view balconies (view Db-€85, view Tb-€97, most with air-con and some noise on weekend nights, book well ahead for these). Rooms on the quieter garden side are sharp and have air-con but no view (Db-€80; extra bed-€10, 4 floors, no elevator, from TI walk or drive down avenue Général de Gaulle to the old Port de la Darse, parking usually available nearby, tel. 04 93 01 72 54, fax 04 93 01 84 37, www.hotel-dela-darse-villefranche-sur-mer.cote.azur.fr, hoteldeladarse@wanadoo.fr).

# EATING

Comparison-shopping is half the fun of dining in Villefranche-sur-Mer. Make an event out of a pre-dinner stroll through the old city. Check what looks good on the lively place Amélie Pollonnais (next to Hôtel Welcome), saunter the string of pricey candlelit places lining the waterfront, and consider the smaller, wallet-friendlier eateries embedded in the old city's walking streets. I like eating on place Amélie Pollonnais, where the whole village seems to converge at night.

**Le Cosmo Restaurant/Café** takes center stage on place Amélie Pollonnais, with great tables overlooking the harbor and the Cocteau chapel's facade (after some wine, Cocteau pops). It serves nicely presented and tasty meals, along with great Bandol red wine. Ask for the daily suggestions and consider the €10 *omelette niçoise* (€10–14 fine salads and pastas, €13–21 *plats*, open daily, place Amélie Pollonnais, tel. 04 93 01 84 05).

**Michel's,** on the other side of the fountain, is more romantic and stylish, and can be a decent splurge (allow €35/person, closed Tue and in Nov, tel. 04 93 76 73 24).

**La Mère Germaine,** right on the harborfront, is the only place in town classy enough to lure a yachter ashore. It's dressy, with fine service and a harborside setting. The name comes from when the current owner's grandmother fed hungry GIs in World War II. Try the bouillabaisse, served with panache (€68/person with 2-person minimum, ask about the less-expensive but ample mini-version, €39 *menu*, open daily, reserve harborfront table, tel. 04 93 01 71 39).

Disappear into Villefranche-sur-Mer's walking streets and find cute little **La Grignotière,** serving a €31 *gourmet menu,* an €18 couscous, and plenty of pizza and pasta options (daily May–Oct, closed Wed Nov–April, cozy in bad weather, 3 rue Poilu, tel. 04 93 76 79 83).

**Le Roxy,** on the main road just above the TI, is a *très* local, friendly, and cheap diner with hardworking Monique and chef-hubbie Bebert. They make excellent pizza (€8.50) and salads, and their killer *soup de poisson* (€11) makes for a good meal. Ask for seconds (closed Mon–Tue, 2 avenue de Grande Bretagne, tel. 04 93 76 71 80).

**La Serre,** nestled next to the church in the old town halfway up the hill, has a hardworking owner serving well-priced meals to a loyal local clientele. Choose from the many pizzas (all named after US states and €10 or less), salads, or meats (open daily, cheap house wine, 16 rue du May, tel. 04 93 76 79 91).

**Souris Gourmande** ("Gourmet Mouse") is handy for a made-to-order sandwich, either to take away or to eat there. Just be patient and get to know your chef, Albert (€5 sandwiches, daily 11:30–19:30, closed Fri in winter, at base of steps behind Hôtel

Welcome). Sandwich in hand, you'll find plenty of great places to enjoy a harborside sit.

There's a handy **Casino market/grocery store** a few blocks above Hôtel Welcome at 12 rue Poilu (Thu–Tue 7:30–13:00 & 15:00–19:30, Wed 7:30–13:00 only).

*For Drivers:* If you have a car and are staying a few nights, consider the short drive up to Eze-le-Village or, better still, La Turbie (recommendations listed under each destination, later in this chapter).

If it's summer (June–Sept) and you have a car, live the consummate Mediterranean experience by driving 10 minutes to Cap Ferrat and lunch or dine beachside at the **Restaurant de la Plage Passable,** located across the bay from Villefranche-sur-Mer. Enjoy sensational views, and a surprisingly elegant dining experience to the sounds of children still at play on the beach. Watch as darkness descends and lights flicker over Villefranche-sur-Mer's heavenly setting. Follow signs to *Cap Ferrat* and *Villa Ephrussi,* then look for signs pointing down to *Plage de Passable* (€15 starters, €18–25 *plats,* open daily late June–Sept, until 20:00 in good weather April–May and Oct, tel. 04 93 76 06 17).

## TRANSPORTATION CONNECTIONS

The last bus leaves Nice for Villefranche-sur-Mer at about 19:45; the last bus from Villefranche-sur-Mer to Nice departs at about 20:50; and one train runs later (24:00).

**From Villefranche-sur-Mer by Bus:** Bus #100 leaves every 15 minutes and heads east to **Monaco** (25 min) or west to **Nice** (20 min); remember, any ride costs €1. In Villefranche-sur-Mer, all bus stops are along the main drag; the most convenient is the Octroi stop, just above the TI.

**By Train to: Monaco** (2/hr, 10 min), **Nice** (2/hr, 10 min), **Antibes** (2/hr, 40 min).

# The Three Corniches: Villefranche to Monaco

Nice, Villefranche-sur-Mer, and Monaco are linked by three coastal routes: the Low, Middle, and High Corniches. The roads are nicknamed for the decorative frieze that runs along the top of a building (cornice). Each Corniche offers sensational views and a different perspective on this exotic strip of land. You can find the three routes from Nice by driving up boulevard Jean Jaurès past the bus station *(gare routière)*. For the Low Corniche, follow signs to N-98 *(Monaco par la Basse Corniche)*, which leads past Nice's port. Shortly after the turnoff to the Low Corniche, you'll see signs for the N-7 *(Moyenne Corniche)* leading to the Middle Corniche. Signs for the High *(Grande)* Corniche appear a bit after that; follow D-2564 to Col des 4 Chemins and the Grande Corniche.

**Low Corniche:** The Basse Corniche (also called "Corniche Inférieure") strings ports, beaches, and villages together for a traffic-filled ground-floor view. It was built in the 1860s (along with the train line) to bring people to the casino in Monte Carlo. When this Low Corniche was finished, many hill-town villagers descended to the shore and started the communities that line the sea today. Before 1860, the population of the coast between Villefranche-sur-Mer and Monte Carlo was zero. Think about that as you make the trip today.

**Middle Corniche:** The Moyenne Corniche is higher, quieter, and far more impressive. It runs through Eze-le-Village (described later in this section) and provides breathtaking views over the Mediterranean, with several scenic pullouts. (The ones above Villefranche-sur-Mer are particularly stunning.)

**High Corniche:** Napoleon's crowning road-construction achievement, the Grande Corniche caps the cliffs with staggering views from almost 1,600 feet above the sea. It is actually the Via Aurelia, used by the Romans to conquer the West.

**Villas:** Driving from Villefranche-sur-Mer to Monaco, you'll come upon impressive villas. A particularly grand entry leads to the sprawling estate built by King Leopold II of Belgium in the 1920s. Those driving up to the Middle Corniche from Villefranche-sur-Mer can look down on this yellow mansion and its lush garden, which fill an entire hilltop. This estate was later owned by the Agnelli family (of Fiat fame and fortune), and then by the Safra family (American bankers).

**The Best Route:** For a ▲▲▲ route, **drivers** should take the

**Villefranche, Monaco, and the Corniches**

N · VIEW

3 MILES
5 KM

TO PEILLON

ROQUEBRUNE

TO ITALY

MENTON

LA TROPHÉE
DES ALPES

A-8 FREEWAY

EZE-LE-
VILLAGE

TRAIL

MONACO

CAP D'AIL

TO
ANTIBES

EZE-BORD-DE-MER

VILLEFRANCHE-
SUR-MER

BEAULIEU-SUR-MER & VILLA KERYLOS

VILLA EPHRUSSI DE ROTHSCHILD

N. 7

MEDITERRANEAN
SEA

TO
AIRPORT +
ANTIBES

NICE

ST. JEAN-
CAP FERRAT

CAP FERRAT

DCH

❶ Low Corniche Road
(Basse Corniche
or Corniche Inférieure
& Bus #100 Route)

❷ Middle Corniche Road
(Moyenne Corniche)

❸ Great or High Corniche Road
(Grande Corniche)

Middle Corniche from Nice or Villefranche-sur-Mer to Eze-le-Village; from there, follow signs to the Grande Corniche and La Turbie, then finish by dropping down into Monaco. **Buses** travel each route; the higher the Corniche, the less frequent the buses (4/hr on Low, roughly 5–6/day on Middle and High; get details at Nice's bus station). There are no buses between Eze-le-Village and La Turbie, though buses do connect Nice and Monaco with La Turbie.

## SIGHTS

The following two sights—Eze-le-Village and La Trophée des Alpes monument—are listed in the order you'll reach them, traveling from Villefranche-sur-Mer to Monaco.

### ▲Eze-le-Village

Floating high above the sea, flowery and flawless Eze-le-Village (don't confuse it with the seafront town of Eze-Bord-de-Mer) is entirely consumed by tourism. This *village d'art et de gastronomie* (as it calls itself) houses perfume outlets, upscale boutiques, steep cobbled lanes, and magnificent views. Touristy as this place certainly Eze, its stony state of preservation and magnificent hilltop setting over the Mediterranean justify a visit.

Bus stops and parking lots weld the town to the highway (Middle Corniche) that passes under its lowest wall. The helpful **TI** is in the far corner of the car park below the town; ask them about English-language tours of the village and gardens (TI open April–Oct daily 9:00–19:00; Nov–March Mon–Sat 9:00–18:30, closed Sun; place de Gaulle, tel. 04 93 41 26 00, www.eze-riviera .com). Public WCs are located just behind the TI and in the village behind the church.

At the **Jardins d'Eze,** you'll find a prickly festival of cactus. Since 1949, these ruins have been home to 400 different plants 1,300 feet above the sea (well-described in English, €5, open daily, hours change frequently but usually May–Sept 9:00–19:00, Oct–April until dusk, tel. 04 93 41 10 30). At the top, you'll be treated to a commanding 360-degree view, with a helpful *table d'orientation.* On a really clear day, you can see Corsica.

The **Perfume Factory Fragonard,** 350 feet below Eze-le-Village, is designed for tour groups—it cranks them through all day long. Drop in for a free 20–40 minute tour (daily 9:00–18:00, but best Mon–Fri 9:00–11:00 & 14:00–15:30, when the "factory" actually has people working, tel. 04 93 41 05 05). You'll see how the perfume and scented soaps are made and bottled before you're herded into the gift shop. For a more personal and intimate look at perfume, cross the main road in Eze-le-Village to visit the **Gallimard** shop.

*Eating in Eze-le-Village:* To enjoy Eze-le-Village in relative peace, visit at sunset and stay for dinner. You'll dine well at the stone-cozy **Le Troubador** (€33 *menu,* closed Sun–Mon, 4 rue du Brec, tel. 04 93 41 19 03), or for less, at the basic **Nid de l'Aigle** ("Eagle's Nest," open Thu–Tue for lunch, April–Oct also open for dinner Fri–Mon, tel. 04 93 41 19 08).

*Getting to Eze-le-Village:* There are two Ezes: Eze-le-Village (the spectacular hill town) and Eze-Bord-de-Mer (a modern beach resort far below Eze-le-Village). Eze-le-Village is about 20 minutes east of Villefranche-sur-Mer on the Middle Corniche. Two bus lines (#82 and #112) provide 16 buses per day from Nice to Eze-le-Village (eight on Sun, 25 min, €1). You can also take the train or Nice–Monaco bus to Eze-Bord-de-Mer. From there, take the #83 shuttle bus straight up to Eze-le-Village from the Gare SNCF stop (€1, 8/day, daily 9:45–18:00; you can also take a taxi between the two Ezes—allow €22 one-way, tel. 06 09 84 17 84). To connect Eze-le-Village directly with Monte Carlo in Monaco, take bus #112 (7/day Mon–Sat, none on Sun, 15 min). There are no direct buses from Villefranche-sur-Mer to Eze-le-Village or between La Turbie and Eze-le-Village.

## Tourist Information

Antibes has two TIs. The most convenient is in the old town, just inside the walls at 32 boulevard d'Aguillon (Mon–Sat 10:00–12:00 & 13:30–18:00, closed Sun, tel. 04 93 34 65 65). The *Maison de Tourisme* is in the newer city, where the fountains squirt at 11 place Général de Gaulle (where boulevard Albert 1er and rue de la République meet; July–Aug daily 9:00–19:00; Sept–June Mon–Sat 9:00–12:30 & 13:30–18:00, Sun 9:00–12:00; tel. 04 97 23 11 11, www.antibesjuanlespins.com). At either TI, pick up the excellent city map and the self-guided walking tour of old Antibes, and get details on the hikes described below. The Nice TI has Antibes maps—plan ahead.

## Arrival in Antibes

**By Train:** To get to the port and the old town (10-min walk), cross the street in front of the station, skirting left of the Piranha Café, and follow avenue de la Libération downhill. As you come to the end of the street, the port will be on the left and the old town to the right. To reach the main TI in the modern city (10-min walk), exit right from the station on avenue Robert Soleau; follow *Centre Ville* and *Office du Tourisme* signs to place Général de Gaulle. The last train back to Nice leaves at about 21:00.

**By Bus:** Handy bus #200 stops a few blocks from the TI (turn right as you leave the TI to find the stops just off boulevard Dugommier: buses from Nice and to Cannes stop on avenue Aristide Briand; buses to Nice and from Cannes stop on boulevard Gustave Chancel). Buses from other destinations use the bus station at the edge of the old town on place Guynemer, a block below the old town TI (info desk open Mon–Sat 8:30–12:00 & 14:30–17:30, closed Sun).

**By Car:** Day-trippers follow signs to *Centre-Ville*, then *Port Vauban*, and park near the old town walls (first 30 min free, then about €2/hr). Walk into the old town through the last arch on the right.

If you're sleeping here, follow signs to your hotel, and get advice from your hotelier on where to park. (Most hotels have free parking.) The most appealing hotels in Antibes are only reachable by car. Luckily, Antibes works well for drivers. Compared to Nice, it's a breeze to navigate and a convenient springboard for the Inland Riviera. Pay parking is usually available at Antibes' train station, so drivers can ditch their cars and day-trip from Antibes by train.

## Helpful Hints

**Internet Access:** The TI keeps an updated list of Internet cafés.

**English Bookstore: Heidi's English Bookshop** has a welcoming vibe and a great selection of new and used books, including my guidebooks (daily May–Sept 10:00–19:00, Oct–April 11:00–18:00, 24 rue Aubernon).

**Laundry:** Smiling Madame Hallepau will do your laundry while you swim. Her launderette is above the market hall on rue de la Pompe (Mon–Fri 8:30–12:00 & 15:30–18:30, closed Sat–Sun).

**Grocery Store:** Picnickers will appreciate **Epicerie de la Place** (daily until 22:00 in summer, until 21:00 off-season, where rue Sade meets place Nationale).

**Taxi:** Call 08 25 56 07 07 or 04 93 67 67 67.

**Car Rental:** The big-name agencies have offices in Antibes—the most central are **Avis** (32 boulevard Albert 1er, tel. 04 93 34 65 15) and **Hertz** (across from the train station at 129 boulevard Wilson, tel. 04 93 61 18 15).

**Airport Bus:** Bus #200 runs from near the main TI to Nice's airport (2–3/hr, 40–45 min depending on traffic; to find the bus stop, see "Arrival in Antibes," earlier in this section).

## Getting Around Antibes

Walking works fine to get between Antibes' train station and most of its sights and beaches. The lone destination I recommend that requires wheels is Cap d'Antibes, which is served by bus #2 (leaves from bus station; see "Cap d'Antibes Hike" under "Sights and Activities," later in this section).

A **tourist train** offers circuits around old Antibes, the port, the ramparts, and to Juan-les-Pins (€7, departs from place de la Poste, tel. 06 03 35 61 35).

# SELF-GUIDED WALK

## Welcome to Antibes

This 40-minute amble will help you get your bearings, and works well day or night. Begin at the old port (Vieux Port) along avenue de Verdun (below the train station—parking right there). This is among the oldest of Europe's yachting harbors and was the model for many to come. Locals claim that this is Europe's first and biggest pleasure-boat harbor, with 1,600 stalls. That old four-pointed structure crowning the opposite end of the port is **Fort Carré** (described under "Sights and Activities," later in this section), which protected Antibes from foreigners for more than 500 years.

Near the end of the yachts, opposite the arch that leads into the old town, you'll see the pathetic

## Antibes Hotels and Restaurants

**FRENCH RIVIERA**

TRAIN STN.

TO ③, FORT CARRE & NICE

PORT VAUBAN

VIEUX PORT

AVE. DU 11 NOV.

AVE. DE LA LIBERATION

BEST PARKING

START  AVE. DE VERDUN

ARCH

PLAGE DE LA GRAVETTE

AVE. ROBERT SOLEAU

AVE. THIERS

BLVD. D'AGUILLON

ANDRE

BLVD. GAMBETTA

RUE VAUBAN

RUE DE LA REPUBLIQUE

TOURIST TRAIN PICK-UP

PLACE NAT.

SALEURS

PALM.

CLEM.

CHURCH OF IMMACULATE CONCEPTION

SADE

CLOSE

REEL

MARKET HALL

PICASSO MUSEUM

CHATEAU GRIMALDI

COURS MASSENA

PROM. AMIRAL DE GRASSE

HISTORY & ARCHAEOLOGY MUSEUM

PLACE DE GAULLE

AVE. BRIAND

BLVD. CHANCEL

BLVD. WILSON

J. BLVD. ALBERT

BLVD. ALBERT M.

BLVD. FOCH

BLVD. GEN. MAIZIERES

200 YARDS
200 METERS

TO ①

RUE BOURGEOIS

BLVD. GEN. LECLERC

PLACE ALBERT 1er  FINISH

MEDITERRANEAN SEA

TO PLAGE SALVIS, CAP D'ANTIBES & ②

→ WALKING TOUR
Ⓑ MINIBUS STOP
Ⓟ PARKING
→ ONE-WAY STREET

① To Hôtel Pension le Mas Djoliba
② To Hôtels La Jabotte, Beau Site, Restaurant de Bacon & Beach-Front Dining
③ Bastide de la Brague
④ Modern Hôtel
⑤ Hôtel Relais du Postillon
⑥ Hôtel le Cameo
⑦ La Marmite Restaurant
⑧ Le Jardin & L'Aubergine Rest.
⑨ Le Brulot & Le Brulot Pasta
⑩ Les Vieux Murs Rest.
⑪ Epicerie de la Place Grocery
⑫ Heidi's English Bookshop
⑬ The Office Internet Café
⑭ Launderette
⑮ Bus #200 from Nice & to Cannes
⑯ Bus #200 from Cannes to Nice/Nice Airport
⑰ Avis Car Rental
⑱ Hertz Car Rental

remains of a once-hearty **fishing fleet.** The Mediterranean is pretty much fished out. Most of the seafood you'll eat here comes from fish farms or the Atlantic.

Pass the sorry fleet and keep walking along the harbor, then find the entry—through the wall on your right—to the shell-shaped **plage de la Gravette,** a normally quiet public beach tucked right in the middle of old Antibes. Wander up the ramp to the round lookout to better appreciate the scale of the ramparts that protected this town. Because Antibes was the last fort before the Italian border, the French king made sure the ramparts were strong and well-defended. The twin towers crowning the old town are the church's bell tower and the tower topping Château Grimaldi (today's Picasso Museum). Before leaving the beach, check out the saltwater showers.

Backtrack and enter Antibes' **old town** through the arch under the rampart. Today, the town is the haunt of a large community of English, Irish, and Aussie boaters who help crew the giant yachts of the rich and famous. (That helps explain the Irish pubs and English bookstores.) Continue straight ahead and uphill, and you'll arrive at Antibes' **market hall** (Tue–Sun until 13:00, closed Mon except June–Aug). Like many other places in Antibes, this hall does double duty...it's filled with café tables at night.

If you take a left where the market starts, you'll run into Antibes' pretty, pastel **Church of Immaculate Conception,** built on the site of a Greek temple (worth a peek inside). The little church served as the area's cathedral until the mid-1200s.

Looming above the church on prime real estate is the white-stone **Château Grimaldi,** home to Antibes' prized **Picasso Museum.** This site has been home to the acropolis of the Greek city of Antipolis, a Roman fort, and a medieval bishop's palace (once connected to the cathedral below). The château was the home of the Grimaldi family (who still rule Monaco). Its proximity to the cathedral symbolized the sometimes too-cozy relationship between society's two dominant landowning classes: the Church and the nobility. (In 1789, the French Revolution changed all that.)

Find your way to the water and, heading right, follow the ramparts and views to the **History and Archaeology Museum.** From the terrace above the museum, you'll get a clear view of the forested **Cap d'Antibes,** crowned by its lighthouse and studded with mansions (see "Cap d'Antibes Hike" later in this section). The Cap was long the refuge of Antibes' rich and famous, and a favorite haunt of F. Scott Fitzgerald and Ernest Hemingway. After a quick tour of the museum (described under "Sights and Activities," next page), continue hugging the coast past place Albert 1er until you see the terrific views back to old Antibes. Benches and soft sand await. You're on your own from here—strong walkers can continue to the view from the Phare de la Garoupe (see

"Sights and Activities," below); others can return to old Antibes and poke around in its peaceful back lanes.

# SIGHTS AND ACTIVITIES

▲▲**Picasso Museum (Musée Picasso)**—Sitting serenely where the old town meets the sea, this small, three-floor museum offers a remarkable collection of Picasso's paintings, sketches, and ceramics. Picasso lived in the castle for four months in 1946, when he cranked out an amazing amount of art. The resulting collection (donated by Picasso) put Antibes on the tourist map. You'll see many of his ceramics: plates with faces, bird-shaped vases, woman-shaped bottles, bull-shaped statues, and colorful tiles. But the highlight is his lively, frolicking *La Joie de Vivre* painting. This large (4 feet by 8 feet) Greek bacchanal sums up the newfound freedom in a newly liberated France (1946) and sets the tone for the rest of the collection. You'll also see several Cubist-style nudes *(nus couchés)*, plus the *Antipolis Suite*—a series of 25 (mostly reclining) nudes, very simplified and stripped-down in style, and works that demonstrate his cartoonist and caricaturist skills (€6, Tue–Sun 10:00–18:00, maybe until 20:00 some evenings in summer, closed Mon, off-season probably closed 12:00–14:00; check hours at TI, as they may change in 2009).

**History and Archaeology Museum (Musée d'Histoire et d'Archéologie)**—More than 2,000 years ago, Antibes was the center of a thriving maritime culture. It was also an important Roman city, featuring many of the hallmarks of Roman civilization—aqueducts, theaters, baths, and so on. This museum—the only place to get a sense of the city's ancient roots—displays Greek, Roman, and Etruscan odds and ends in two easy-to-visit rooms (no English descriptions, though the small museum brochure offers some background in English). Your visit starts at an 1894 model of Antibes and continues past displays of Roman coins, cups, plates, and scads of amphorae. The curious, long lead pipe connected to a center box was used as a bilge pump; nearby is a good display of Roman anchors (€3, daily 10:00–12:00 & 14:00–18:00, on the water between Picasso Museum and place Albert 1er).

▲**Market Hall (Marché Provençal)**—The daily market bustles under a 19th-century canopy, with flowers, produce, Provençal products, and beach accessories (in the old town, behind Picasso Museum on cours Masséna). The market wears many appealing hats: produce daily until 13:00, handicrafts Thursday through Sunday in the afternoon, and fun outdoor dining in the evenings (market closed Mon in Sept–May).

**Other Markets**—Antibes' lively antique/flea market fills place Nationale and place Audiberti (next to the port) on Saturdays (7:00–18:00). Its clothing market winds through the streets around the post office (rue Lacan) on Thursdays (9:00–18:00).

**Fort Carré**—This impressively situated citadel, dating from 1487, was the last fort inside France. It protected Antibes from Nice, which until 1860 was part of Italy. You can tour this unusual four-pointed fort, but there's little to see inside. People visit for the fantastic views (€3, includes tour, Tue–Sun June–Sept 10:00–18:00, Oct–May 10:00–16:30, closed Mon).

**Beaches (Plages)**—The best beaches stretch between Antibes' port and Cap d'Antibes, and the very best (plage de la Salis and plage du Ponteil) are just south of place

Albert 1er. All are groomed and beautifully sandy. Plage de la Salis is busy but manageable in summer and on weekends, with snack stands and views of the old town. The closest beach to the old town is at the port (plage de la Gravette), which seems calm in any season.

## Walks and Hikes

From place Albert 1er (where boulevard Albert 1er meets the beach), you get a good view of plage de la Salis and Cap d'Antibes. That tower on the hill is your destination for the first walk described below. The longer "Cap d'Antibes Hike" begins on the next beach, just over that hill.

▲▲**Chapelle et Phare de la Garoupe**—The territorial views—good at sunset, best at sunrise, skippable if hazy—from this viewpoint more than merit the 25-minute uphill climb from the plage de la Salis (a few blocks after Maupassant Apartments, follow the rough, cobbled chemin du Calvaire up to lighthouse tower). An orientation table explains that you can see from Nice to Cannes and up to the Alps. By car, follow signs for *Cap d'Antibes,* then look for *Chapelle et Phare de la Garoupe* signs.

▲**Cap d'Antibes Hike (Sentier Touristique Piétonnier de Tirepoil)**—At the end of the mattress-ridden plage de la Garoupe (over the hill from Phare de la Garoupe lighthouse), you'll find a remarkable trail around Cap d'Antibes. The beautiful path undulates above a splintered coastline splashed by turquoise water and

peppered with exclusive mansions. You'll walk for two miles, then head inland along small streets, ending at the recommended Hôtel Beau-Site (and bus stop). You can walk as far as you'd like and then double back, or do the whole loop (allow 2.5 hours at most, use the TI's Antibes map). Bring good shoes, as footing is uneven and slippery in places. Sundays are busiest.

To get to the trail from Antibes, take **bus #2** from the bus station for about 15 minutes to the La Fontaine stop at Hôtel Beau-Site (about every 40 min Mon–Sat, 8/day Sun, return stop is 50 yards down on opposite side, get return times at station). Walk 10 minutes down to plage de la Garoupe and start from there. By **car,** follow signs to Cap *d'Antibes,* then *plage de la Garoupe,* and park there. The trail begins at the far-right end of plage de la Garoupe.

## Near Antibes
**Juan-les-Pins**—This village, across the Cap d'Antibes isthmus from Antibes, is where the action is in the evenings. It's a modern beach resort with good beaches, plenty of lively bars and restaurants, and a popular jazz festival in July. Buses, trains, and even a tourist train (see "Getting Around Antibes," earlier in this section) make the 10-minute trip to and from Antibes constantly.

# SLEEPING

(€1 = about $1.50, country code: 33)
My favorite Antibes hotels require a car or taxi. Pickings are slim when it comes to centrally located hotels in this city, where restaurants are a dime a dozen but hotels play hard to get.

## Outside the Town Center
**$$$ Hôtel Pension le Mas Djoliba**\*** is a good splurge, best for drivers (since it's a 15–20-min walk from the beach and old Antibes, and a 25-min walk from the train station). Reserve early for this tranquil, bird-chirping, flower-filled manor house where no two rooms are the same. From May to September, they definitely prefer (but won't insist) that you dine here. It's hard to pass up once you see the setting—after a busy day of sightseeing, dinner by the pool is a treat. The bigger rooms are well worth the small additional cost (Db with breakfast and dinner-€160–220, Db only-€100–160, several excellent family rooms-€170–240, breakfast-€11, air-con, Wi-Fi, cool *boules* court and loaner balls, 29 avenue de Provence; from boulevard Albert 1er, look for blue signs as you approach the beach and turn right up avenue Gaston Bourgeois; tel. 04 93 34 02 48, fax 04 93 34 05 81, www.hotel-djoliba.com, contact@hotel-djoliba.com).

**$$$ Hôtel La Jabotte**\** defies the rules. Hiding down an ignored alley just a block from the famous beaches and a 20-minute walk from the old town, this small, cozy place is run by owners who care. Yves, Claude, and dog Tommy have turned a small beach villa into a boutique hotel with personality: The colors are rich, the decor shows a personal touch, and most rooms have individual terraces that face a small, central garden (Db-€105–115, includes good breakfast and a few parking spots, no air-con, Wi-Fi, 13 avenue Max Maurey, take the third right after passing the big Hôtel Josse, tel. 04 93 61 45 89, fax 04 93 61 07 04, www.jabotte.com, info@jabotte.com).

**$$ Hôtel Beau Site\*\*\*** is my only listing on Cap d'Antibes, a 10-minute drive from the old town (look for the blue sign). It's a terrific value if you want to get away...but not *too* far away. (But if you don't have a car, you'll feel isolated.) This place is a sanctuary, with sweet Nathalie in charge, a pool, a comfy patio garden, and easy parking. Eleven rooms have balconies (standard Db-€82–90, bigger Db-€100–115, even bigger Db-€134–148, family rooms-€160–210, extra bed-€25; incredible boaty-breakfast-€12.50, continental breakfast-€6.50, air-con, Wi-Fi, bikes available, 141 boulevard Kennedy, tel. 04 93 61 53 43, fax 04 93 67 78 16, www.hotelbeausite.net, hbeausit@club-internet.fr). From the hotel, it's a 10-minute walk down to the crowded plage de la Garoupe and a nearby hiking trail (see "Walks and Hikes," earlier in this section).

**$$ Bastide de la Brague** is an easygoing, seven-room bed-and-breakfast hacienda in no-man's-land, up a dirt road above Marineland (10-min drive east of Antibes). But the place is a find as it's central to Riviera sights and run by a fun-loving family (wife Isabelle, who speaks English, hubby Frank, and Mama). Rooms are new, quite comfortable, air-conditioned, and affordable; several are made for families. Request the €22 home-cooked dinner and you'll get the works—from apéritif to coffee and everything in between (costs less for kids). There's enough space to stretch out, and they love families (Db-€75–95, Tb/Qb-€95–115, includes breakfast, 55 avenue No. 6, Antibes 06600, tel. 04 93 65 73 78, www.bbchambreantibes.com, bb06@wanadoo.fr). Frank is happy to take guests on a private boat tour of the coast (allow €30 per person for all afternoon, 4 people minimum). From Antibes, drive toward Nice par Bord de la Mer, turn left toward Brague and Marineland, then right at the roundabout (toward Groules), then take the first left and follow signs.

## In the Town Center

**$$ Modern Hôtel\*\***, in the pedestrian zone near the bus station, is a fine value for budget travelers. The 17 standard-size rooms—each with air-conditioning, bright decor, and Wi-Fi—are simple, spick-and-span, and well-run by Laurence (Sb-€58–69, Db-€65–84, 1 rue Fourmillière, tel. 04 92 90 59 05, fax 04 92 90 59 06, www.modernhotel06.com, modern-hotel@wanadoo.fr).

**$$ Hôtel Relais du Postillon\*\***, on a central, thriving square, offers 15 rooms with great potential above a peaceful café. All of the rooms need a facelift. They have three true singles and several rooms with small balconies, but no air-conditioning (Sb-€46, Db-€64–90, price varies by room size, most have tight bathrooms, Wi-Fi, 8 rue Championnet, tel. 04 93 34 20 77, fax 04 93 34 61 24, www.relaisdupostillon.com, relais@relaisdupostillon.com).

**$ Hôtel le Cameo**** is a busy café that rents a few bare-bones rooms upstairs for desperate travelers. All open onto the boisterous place Nationale, which means you don't sleep until the restaurant sleeps (Ds-€62, Db-€66, Tb-€74, Qb-€82, 5 place Nationale, tel. 04 93 34 24 17, fax 04 93 34 35 80, no English spoken).

# EATING

Antibes is a fun place to dine out. You can eat on a budget, enjoy a fine meal at an acceptable price, or join the party just inside the walls on boulevard d'Aguillon, under the festive Marché Provençal, or on place Nationale (all filled with tables and tourists—I prefer the Marché Provençal). The options are endless. Take a walk and judge for yourself, and be tempted by these good suggestions. Romantics should picnic at the beach. Everyone should stroll along the ramparts after dinner.

**La Marmite** offers diners an honest, unpretentious budget value in old Antibes, with eight tables, helpful service, and fine seafood (*menus* from €15, closed Mon, 20 rue James Close, tel. 04 93 34 56 79).

**Le Jardin** is reliable and reasonable, with tables filling a pretty and peaceful garden courtyard. Arrive early to secure a table outside and enjoy good regional cooking (€19–27 *menus* and tasty €17 *plats,* closed Wed, 5 rue Sade, tel. 04 93 34 64 74).

**L'Aubergine,** right next door, offers Antibes' only real vegetarian option, and at fair prices (*menus* from €21, closed Wed, 7 rue Sade, tel. 04 93 34 55 93).

**Le Brulot** is an Antibes institution with two restaurants—Le Brulot and Le Brulot Pasta—that sit almost side-by-side a short block below Marché Provençal on rue Frédéric Isnard. Join locals at the very popular **Le Brulot,** known for its Provençal cuisine and meats cooked on an open fire. It's a small place, overflowing onto the street, with a few outside tables and a dining room below. Try the aioli (€19 *menus,* closed Sun, at #2, tel. 04 93 34 17 76). **Le Brulot Pasta** is family-friendly and goes Italian with excellent pizza (the €11 *printanière* is tasty and huge) and big portions of pasta, served in air-conditioned comfort under stone arches (open daily, at #3, tel. 04 93 34 19 19).

**Les Vieux Murs** is *the* place to splurge in Antibes for regional specialties. Its candlelit, red-tone, *très romantique* interior overlooks the sea, and the outside tables are worth booking ahead—but pass on the upstairs room (€43 dinner *menu*, €30 lunch *menu*, open daily June–mid-Sept, closed Mon off-season, valet parking available, along ramparts beyond Picasso Museum at 25 promenade Amiral de Grasse, tel. 04 93 34 06 73).

**Restaurant de Bacon** is the locals' pick as Antibes' best restaurant, thanks to its top-notch bouillabaisse and views of Antibes. Located on Cap d'Antibes, past the plage de la Salis, it's simple from the outside (no sign), but lovely on the inside, and made for seafood-lovers (*menus* from €50, allow €70 for bouillabaisse, closed Mon–Tue and Oct–Feb, boulevard de Bacon, tel. 04 93 61 50 02, www.restaurantdebacon.com).

## TRANSPORTATION CONNECTIONS

**From Antibes by Train:** TGV and local trains serve Antibes' little station. Trains go to **Cannes** (2/hr, 15 min), **Nice** (2/hr, 15–30 min, €3.90), **Grasse** (1/hr, 40 min), **Villefranche-sur-Mer** (2/hr, 40 min), **Monaco** (2/hr, 45–60 min), **Marseille** (16/day, 2.5 hrs).

**By Bus:** Handy bus #200 ties everything together (runs Mon–Sat 4/hr, Sun 2–3/hr, any ride costs €1). Because of busy Riviera roads, trip durations depend on traffic. This bus goes west to **Cannes** (35 min), and east to **Nice** (1–1.5 hrs). Some eastbound buses also stop at **Nice Airport** (2–3/hr, 40–45 min).

# Inland Riviera

For a verdant, rocky, fresh escape from the beaches, head inland and upward. Some of France's most perfectly perched hill towns and splendid scenery hang overlooked in this region that's more famous for beaches and bikinis. Driving is the easiest way to get around, though the bus gets you to many of the places described. Vence and St-Paul-de-Vence are well-served by bus from Nice every 40 minutes (see "Getting Around the Riviera," earlier in this chapter).

## Vence

Vence is a well-discovered yet appealing town set well above the Riviera. While growth has sprawled well beyond Vence's old walls, and cars jam its roundabouts, the mountains are front and center and the breeze is fresh in this engaging town that bubbles with workaday life and ample tourist activity. Vence is best at night and makes a handy base for travelers wanting the best of both worlds: a hill-town refuge near the sea.

# ORIENTATION

## Tourist Information

Vence's fully loaded and eager-to-help TI faces the main square at 8 place du Grand Jardin. They have bus schedules, brochures on the cathedral, and a city map with a well-devised self-guided walking tour (25 stops, incorporates informative wall plaques). They also publish a list of Vence art galleries with English descriptions of the collections. To properly engage you in French culture, the TI also has information on French-language classes, and—even better—*pétanque* instruction with *boules* to rent for €3 per person (TI open June–Sept Mon–Sat 9:00–19:00, Sun 10:00–18:00; Oct–May Mon–Sat 9:00–18:00, closed Sun; tel. 04 93 58 06 38, www.ville-vence.fr).

**Market day** in the Cité Historique is on Tuesday and Friday mornings on place Clemenceau. There's a big, all-day antique market on place du Grand Jardin every Wednesday.

## Arrival in Vence

**By Bus:** The bus stop is on place du Grand Jardin, next to the TI (schedules are posted in the window of the travel agency by the bus stop).

**By Car:** Follow signs to *cité historique*, and park where you can. A central pay lot is under place du Grand Jardin, across from the TI. Park here if you're spending the night somewhere other than Hôtel Miramar (which has its own parking).

# SIGHTS

Explore the narrow lanes of the old town *(cité historique)* using the TI's worthwhile self-guided tour map. Connect the picturesque streets, enjoy a drink on a quiet square, inspect an art gallery, and find the small, 11th-century cathedral with its colorful Chagall mosaic of Moses. If you're here later in the day, enjoy the *boules* action across from the TI (consider renting a set from the TI).

**Château de Villeneuve**—This 17th-century mansion, adjoining an imposing 12th-century watchtower, bills itself as "one of the Riviera's high temples of modern art," with a rotating collection. Check with the TI to see what's playing in the temple (€5, Tue–Sun 10:00–12:30 & 14:00–18:00, closed Mon, tel. 04 93 58 15 78).

**▲Chapel of the Rosary (Chapelle du Rosaire)**—The chapel, a 20-minute walk from town, was designed by an elderly and ailing Henri Matisse in thanks to the Dominican sister who had taken care of him (he was 81 when the chapel was completed). The modest chapel is a simple collection of white walls laced with yellow, green, and blue stained-glass windows and charcoal black-on-white tile sketches. The sunlight filters through the glass and does a

FRENCH RIVIERA

cheery dance across the sketches. While the chapel is the ultimate pilgrimage for serious Matisse fans, the experience may underwhelm others. For more on Chagall, see Nice's Chagall Museum listing, earlier in this chapter.

**Cost and Hours:** €3, Mon, Wed, and Sat 14:00–17:30, Tue and Thu 10:00–11:30 & 14:00–17:30, Sun only open for Mass at 10:00 followed by tour of chapel, closed Fri and mid-Nov–mid-Dec, tel. 04 93 58 03 26.

**Getting There:** To reach the chapel from the Vence TI, turn right out of the TI and walk down avenue Henri Isnard, then right on avenue de Provence, following signs to *St-Jeannet* (allow 20 min).

## SLEEPING

**(€1 = about $1.50, country code: 33)**

Hôtel Miramar is a 10-minute walk above the old town. Both of the latter two places are a short walk from the TI, next to the Château de Villeneuve; to reach them, turn right out of the TI, then right again, then left.

**$$$ Hôtel Miramar\*\*\*** is a relaxed 18-room Mediterranean villa perched on a ledge with grand panoramas. Friendly owner Daniel welcomes you into this refuge, which he's filled with many personal touches. The Old World rooms come in soothing colors, with firm beds and worn furnishings. The pool and view terrace could make you late for dinner, or seduce you into skipping it altogether—picnics are allowed (Sb-€68–88, standard Db-€88–108, Db with balcony-€98–128, Db with great view and balcony-€128–158, family suite-€130–185, some rooms have air-con, most don't need it, bar, table tennis, parking, turn left out of the TI and follow the brown signs to 167 avenue Bougearel, tel. 04 93 58 01 32, fax 04 93 58 20 22, www.hotel-miramar-vence.com, resa@hotel-miramar-vence.com).

**$$$ La Maison du Frêne** is an art-packed B&B with four sumptuous rooms located behind the TI. Energetic Thierry combines his passion for contemporary art and hosting travelers in his lovingly restored manor house (Db-€140, includes breakfast, air-con, 1 place du Frêne, tel. 04 93 24 37 83, www.lamaisondufrene.com, lamaisondufrene@wanadoo.fr).

**$$ L'Auberge des Seigneurs**\*\* is a shy little place just inside the old town. Its six simple yet character-filled rooms—above a cozy restaurant—have wood furnishings, red-tile floors, and good-enough bathrooms (spacious Sb-€65, Db-€85–100, place du Frêne, tel. 04 93 58 04 24, fax 04 93 24 08 01, www.auberge -seigneurs.com).

## EATING

Tempting outdoor eateries litter the old town; they all look good to me. Embedded lights in the old-town cobbles light the way after dark.

*On Place Clemenceau:* These two restaurants serve tasty Provençal cuisine a few doors apart on the charming place Clemenceau: **La Cassolette,** at #10, is an intimate place with reasonable prices and a romantic terrace across from the floodlit church (€25 *menus,* €13–15 *plats,* closed Tue, tel. 04 93 58 84 15). **Le P'tit Provençal,** at #4, offers limited outdoor seating, a lovely upstairs dining room, and a menu that stays fresh with each season (€25 and €30 *menus,* closed Mon all year, also closed Tue off-season, tel. 04 93 58 50 64).

At nearby **La Peyra,** enjoy a dinner salad or pasta dish outdoors to the sound of the town's main fountain (€15 "maxi salads" and *plats,* daily, 13 place du Peyra, tel. 04 93 58 67 63).

**L'Auberge des Seigneurs** feels more alpine than Mediterranean, and is good for a cooler day, when you can sit by the fire and watch your meat being cooked. The choices are limited and filling. Sandrine will help you decide (*menus* from €32, closed Sun–Mon; also recommended under "Sleeping," earlier in this section).

# Near Vence

## St-Paul-de-Vence

The most famous of Riviera hill towns, and the most-visited village in France, feels that way—like an overrun and over-restored artist-shopping-mall. Its attraction is understandable, as every cobble

and flower seems *just-so,* and the setting is remarkable. Avoid visiting between 11:00 and 18:00, particularly on weekends. Arriving early will make it easier to find a parking space near the village (cars are not allowed inside St-Paul). Consider skipping breakfast at your hotel and eating it instead at the local hangout, **Café de la Place.**

The **TI,** just through the gate into the old city on rue Grande, has maps with minimal explanations of key buildings (daily 10:00–18:00, tel. 04 93 32 86 95, www.saint-pauldevence.com). If the entrance to the old city is jammed, take the road that veers left just before the entrance, and enter the town through its side door. Meander deep into St-Paul-de-Vence's quieter streets to find the panoramic views. See if you can find the hill town of Vence at the foot of an impressive mountain.

▲**Fondation Maeght**—This inviting, pricey, far-out, private museum is situated a steep walk or short drive above St-Paul-

de-Vence. Fondation Maeght (fohn-dah-shown mahg) offers an excellent introduction to modern Mediterranean art by gathering many of the Riviera's most famous artists under one roof. The founder, Aimé Maeght, long envisioned the perfect exhibition space for the artists he supported and befriended as an art dealer. He purchased a dry piece of hilltop land, planted more than 35,000 plants, and hired an architect (José Luis Sert) with the same vision.

A sweeping lawn laced with amusing sculptures and bending pine trees greets visitors. On the right, a chapel designed by Georges Braque—in memory of the Maeghts' young son, who died of leukemia—features a moving, purple stained-glass work over the altar. The unusual museum building is purposefully low-profile, to let its world-class modern-art collection take center stage. Works by Fernand Léger, Joan Miró, Alexander Calder, Georges Braque, and Marc Chagall are thoughtfully arranged in well-lit rooms. The backyard of the museum has views, a Gaudí-esque sculpture labyrinth by Miró, and a courtyard filled with the wispy works of Alberto Giacometti. The only permanent collection in the museum consists of the sculptures, though the museum tries to keep a good selection of paintings by the famous artists here year-round. There's also a great gift shop and cafeteria.

**Cost and Hours:** €11, €2.50 to take photos, daily July–Sept 10:00–19:00, Oct–June 10:00–18:00, tel. 04 93 32 81 63, www .fondation-maeght.com.

**Getting There:** The museum is a steep, uphill-but-doable, 20-minute walk from St-Paul-de-Vence and the bus stop. Blue signs indicate the way (parking is available at the top, though the lot can be full).

## La Route Napoléon: North to the Alps

After getting bored in his toy Elba empire, Napoleon gathered his entourage, landed on the Riviera, bared his breast, and told his fellow Frenchmen, "Strike me down or follow me." France followed. But just in case, he took the high road, returning to Paris along the route known today as La Route Napoléon. (Waterloo followed shortly afterward.)

**By Car:** The route between the Riviera and the Alps is beautiful (from south to north, follow signs: Digne, Sisteron, and Grenoble). An assortment of pleasant villages with inexpensive hotels lies along this route, making an overnight easy. Little Entrevaux feels forgotten and still stuck in its medieval shell. Cross the bridge, meet someone friendly, and consider the steep hike up to the citadel (€2). Sisteron's Romanesque church and view from the citadel above make this town worth a quick leg-stretch.

**By Narrow-Gauge Train (Chemins de Fer de Provence):** Leave the tourists behind and take your kids on the scenic train-bus-train combination that runs between Nice and Digne through canyons, along whitewater rivers, and through many tempting villages (Nice to Digne: 4/day, 3.5 hours, about €19, 25 percent discount with railpass, departs Nice from the South Station—Gare du Sud—about 10 blocks behind the main train station, two blocks from the Libération tram stop, 4 rue Alfred Binet, tel. 04 97 03 80 80, www.trainprovence.com).

Start with an 8:50 departure and go as far as you want. Little **Entrevaux** is a good destination that feels forgotten and still stuck in its medieval shell (two or so scenic hours from Nice, about €10). Climb high to the citadel for great views.

The train ends in **Digne-les-Bains,** where you can catch a main-line train (covered by railpasses) to other destinations—or better, continue scenically to **Annecy** following this plan (assuming you've taken the 8:50 train from Nice): Take the bus (quick transfer if you get the 8:50 train from Nice, free with railpass) to **Veynes** (4/day, 90 min). From there you can catch the most scenic two-car train to **Grenoble** (5/day, 2 hours), then take a train to **Annecy** (arriving about 18:50).

To do the entire trip from Nice to Annecy in one day, you must start with the 8:50 departure, but I'd spend a night in one of the tiny villages en route. Clelles has a decent hotel: **Hôtel Ferrat**** is a basic, family-run mountain hacienda at the base of Mont Aiguille, with a swimming pool and a good restaurant (Sb-€40–52, Db-€53–60, tel. 04 76 34 42 70, fax 04 76 34 47 47, hotel .ferrat@wanadoo.fr).

# THE FRENCH ALPS

*Alpes-Savoie*

Savoie grows Europe's highest mountains and is the top floor of the French Alps (the lower Alpes-Dauphiné lie to the south). More than just a pretty-peaked face, stubborn Savoie maintained its independence from France until 1860, when mountains became targets, rather than obstacles, for travelers. Its borders once extended south to the Riviera and far west across the Rhône River Valley. Home to skier Jean-Claude Killy and the first winter Olympics (1924 in Chamonix), today's Savoie is France's mountain-sports capital, featuring 15,771-foot Mont Blanc as its centerpiece. With wood chalets overflowing with geraniums and cheese fondue in every restaurant, Savoie feels more Swiss than French.

The scenery is drop-dead spectacular. Serenely self-confident Annecy is a postcard-perfect blend of natural and man-made beauty. In Chamonix, it's just you and Madame Nature—there's not a museum or important building in sight. If the weather's right, take Europe's ultimate cable-car ride to the 12,600-foot Aiguille du Midi in Chamonix.

## Planning Your Time

Lakefront Annecy has boats, bikes, and hikes with mountain views for all tastes and abilities. Its trademark arcaded walking streets and good transporta-tion connections (most trains to Chamonix pass through Annecy) make it a convenient stopover. But if you're pressed

## The French Alps

TO ZERMATT + MILAN

VERNAYAZ

MARTIGNY

ARGENTIERE

LES PRAZ

CHAMONIX

SWITZ.

TO GENEVA

LA ROCHE

TO PARIS

CULOZ

ANNECY

MENTHON

HIKE

ST. GERVAIS

LES BOSSONS

LIFTS

LA PALUD

COURMAYEUR

TALLOIRES

DUINGT

COL DE LA FORCLAZ

LAC D'ANNECY

MT. BLANC

ITALY

AIX LES BAINS

ALBERTVILLE

PRÉ ST. DIDIER

AOSTA

TO TORINO

TO LYON & NICE

FRANCE

DCH

10 MILES
10 KM

N

☐ SEE DETAIL MAPS

++ RAIL   — ROAD   ·········· LIFT   --- BORDER

for time and antsy for Alps, get thee to Chamonix. There you can skip along alpine ridges, glide over mountain meadows, zip down the mountain on a luge (wheeled bobsled), or meander along riverside paths on a mountain bike. Plan a minimum of two nights and one day in Chamonix, and try to work in a night in Annecy. Since weather is everything in this area, get the forecast by calling Chamonix's TI (tel. 04 50 53 00 24) or the weather-report line (in English, dial from anywhere in France, tel. 08 92 68 02 74). If it looks good, make haste to Chamonix; if it's gloomy, Annecy offers more distraction. Both Chamonix and Annecy are mobbed with tourists in summer. (If you're driving or taking the train from here to the Riviera, see "La Route Napoléon" tips at the end of the previous chapter.)

The Alps have twin peaks: the summer and winter seasons, when hotels and trails are slammed. June and November are deadquiet in Chamonix (many hotels and restaurants close) as locals recover from one high season and prepare for the next.

## Getting Around the Alps

Annecy and Chamonix are well-connected by trains. Buses run from Chamonix to nearby villages, and the Aiguille du Midi lift takes travelers from Chamonix to Italy over Europe's most scenic border crossing.

## Cuisine Scene in Savoie

Savoie cuisine is mountain-hearty. Its Swiss-similar specialties include *fondue savoyarde* (melted Beaufort and Comté cheeses and local white wine, sometimes with a dash of Cognac), raclette (chunks of semi-melted cheese served with potatoes, pickles, sausage, and bread), *tartiflettes* (hearty scalloped potatoes with melted cheese), *poulet de Bresse* (the best chicken in France), *Morteau* (smoked pork sausage), *gratin savoyard* (a potato dish with cream, cheese, and garlic), and fresh fish. Local cheeses are Morbier (look for a charcoal streak down the middle), Comté (like Gruyère), Beaufort (aged for two years, hard and strong), Reblochon (mild and creamy), and Tomme de Savoie (mild and semi-hard). Evian water comes from Savoie, as does Chartreuse liqueur. Apremont and Crépy are two of the area's surprisingly good white wines. The local beer, Baton de Feu, is more robust than other French beers.

Remember, restaurants serve only during lunch (11:30–14:00) and dinner (19:00–21:00, later in bigger cities); some cafés serve food throughout the day.

# Annecy

There's something for everyone in this lakefront city that knows how to be popular: mountain views, flowery lanes, romantic canals, a hovering château, and swimming in—or boating on, or biking around—the translucent lake. Sophisticated yet outdoors-oriented and bike-crazy, Annecy (ahn-see) is France's answer to Switzerland's Luzern, and, while you may not have glaciers knocking at your door as in nearby Chamonix, the distant peaks paint  a darn pretty picture with Annecy's lakefront setting. Annecy has a few museums, but don't kid yourself—you're here for its lovely setting and strollable streets.

## ORIENTATION

Modern Annecy (pop. 50,000) sprawls for miles, but we're interested only in its compact old town, hunkered on the southwest corner of the lake. The old town is split by the Thiou River and bounded by the château to the south, the TI and rue Royale to the north, rue de la Gare to the west, and the lake to the east.

**Annecy**

1. Splendid Hôtel
2. Hôtel du Palais de l'Isle
3. Hôtel Ibis
4. Jardins du Château B&B
5. Hôtel du Château
6. Auberge du Lyonnais Hôtel/Rest.
7. Hôtel des Alpes
8. Hôtel Central
9. Le Cochon a l'Oreille Rest.
10. Le Freti & Café l'Estaminet
11. Chez Mama Lise Rest.
12. To Le Bistro du Port Rest.
13. Launderette
14. Monoprix (Groceries)
15. Bike Rentals (3)
16. Museum of Annecy

THE FRENCH ALPS

## Tourist Information

The TI is a few blocks from the old town, across from the big grass field, inside the brown-and-glass Bonlieu shopping center (daily mid-May–mid-Sept 9:00–18:30, mid-Sept–mid-May 9:00–12:30 & 13:45–18:00, closed Sun Nov–March, 1 rue Jean Jaurès, tel. 04 50 45 00 33, www.lac-annecy.com). Get a city map, the *Town Walks* walking-tour brochure (several mildly interesting walks described), the map of the lake showing the bike trail, and, if you're spending a few days, the helpful *Annecy Guide,* with everything a traveler needs to know. Ask about walking tours in English (€6, July–Aug only, normally Tue and Fri at 16:00). You'll also find TIs in most villages on the lake.

## Arrival in Annecy

**By Train:** To reach the old town and TI, leave the station, veer left at street level, and cross the big road to the pinkish Hôtel des Alpes. Continue a few blocks down rue de la Poste, then turn left on rue Royale for the TI and some hotels, or continue straight to more recommended hotels. There is no baggage storage in Annecy.

**By Car:** Annecy is a traffic mess; in high season (July–Aug), try to arrive very early, during lunch, or late. Avoid most of the snarls by taking the Annecy Sud exit from the autoroute and following *Albertville* signs. Upon entering Annecy, turn left at the roundabout below the hospital for the city center. (Don't follow signs for *Annecy-le-Vieux,* which is another town entirely.)

Refer to the map on page 661 to find these pay parking lots: You can park right on the lake with the buses opposite the boat dock at Parking Stade Nautique (few spaces for cars, but this might be your lucky day), or follow signs to the underground Parking Hôpital-Clinique, where you should find a spot. There are also handy lots near the train station. If you're staying at a hotel in town, you can park overnight for free at a public lot—but only if you ask at your hotel. If you're staying at the Hôtel du Château or Les Jardins du Château Bed & Breakfast, pull up to the barrier at the Parking du Château, press the little button, and tell the person that you are a hotel guest, and they will raise the bar to let you drive in (staffed 24/7).

## Helpful Hints

**Market Days:** The biggest market in Annecy is on Saturday, with food, clothes, and crafts (until 12:30, around boulevard Taine). A thriving outdoor food market occupies most of the old town center on Tuesday, Friday, and Sunday mornings.

**Department Store:** The **Monoprix** is at the corner of rue du Lac and rue Notre-Dame (Mon–Sat 8:30–19:50, closed Sun, supermarket upstairs).

THE FRENCH ALPS

**Internet Access:** Most hotels have Internet access; otherwise Annecy is an Internet desert for travelers. Ask at the TI.

**Laundry:** The launderette is at the western edge of the old town near where rue de la Gare meets rue Ste. Claire (daily 7:00–21:00, 6 rue de la Gare).

**Bike Rental:** Across from the lake steamers, **Roul' ma Poule** rents bikes (€10/half-day, €15/day, includes helmet and basket, leave ID as deposit, mid-May–mid-Oct daily 9:00–12:00 & 13:30–19:00, closed mid-Oct–mid-May, 4 rue Marquisats, tel. & fax 04 50 27 86 83, www.annecy-location-velo.com, helpful owner Stefan). **Localoisirs** will deliver and pick up a bike at your hotel for free (€15/day, 47 avenue du Petit Port, tel. 06 08 86 81 59). You can also rent a bike at **Vélonecy** at the train station (€10/half-day, €15/day; less for students, seniors, and train travelers; includes helmet and basket, requires credit-card deposit, Mon–Sat 9:00–12:00 & 13:00–18:30, closed Sun, tel. 04 50 51 38 90).

**Bad Weather:** If it's raining, consider a day trip to Lyon (7 trains/day, 2 hours; see Lyon chapter). The last train to Annecy usually leaves Lyon at about 20:00, allowing a full day in the big city.

# SIGHTS AND ACTIVITIES

**Strolling**—Most of the old city is wonderfully traffic-free. The river, canals, and arcaded streets are made for ambling. The TI's *Town Walks* brochure describes Annecy with basic historical information. Get lost—the water is your boundary. Surrender to the luscious ice cream shops and waterfront cafés.

**Museum of Annecy (Palais de l'Isle)**—This serenely situated 13th-century building cuts like the prow of a ship through the heart of the Thiou River. Once a prison, now a boring museum, it held French Resistance fighters during World War II (€4, June–Sept Wed–Mon 10:30–18:00, Oct–May Wed–Mon 10:00–12:00 & 14:00–18:00, closed Tue).

**Château Museum (Musée-Château d'Annecy)**—The castle was built in the late 1100s by aristocrats from nearby Geneva. Today, it houses a modestly interesting museum that mixes local folklore, anthropology, natural history, and modern and fine art with great views over the lake and city. The only compelling reason to enter the château is for the view (€5, same hours as Museum of Annecy).

**▲Boating**—To tool around the lake, rent a paddleboat (*pédalos,* some equipped with a slide, about €10/30 min, €14/hour) or a motorboat (*hors-bord,* no license needed, for 2 people about €28/30 min, €44/hour, each extra person about €1, up to 7 people, several companies all have the same rates). This is one of Europe's cleanest, clearest lakes, and the water is warmer than you'd think.

**Compagnie des Bateaux du Lac d'Annecy** offers worthwhile lake cruises. The one-hour cruise makes no stops but has frequent departures (€12, 8–10/day May–Aug, 6–8/day April and Sept). The two-hour cruises, called *Circuit Omnibus,* make stops at several villages around the lake (€15, 3–5/day); these are ideal for hikers and bikers (see below). The elaborate dinner (€50–75) and dancing cruises look like fun. Get schedules and prices for all boat trips at the TI or on the lake behind Hôtel de Ville (tel. 04 50 51 08 40, www.annecy-croisieres.com).

**Boat and Hike**—For a scenic workout and a rewarding full-day excursion, take the 10:30 boat to **Menthon–St. Bernard** (€4.90), hike 2.5 hours to lovely **Talloires,** then catch the boat back to Annecy (€8.60). From the boat dock in Menthon–St. Bernard, walk to the right along the shore toward the large palace and follow the signposts for Roc de Chère. The path leads up and over the Roc, passing the Golf de Talloires. The last stretch into Talloires drops steeply—wear good shoes. Cross Talloires to the port and beach (swim and lunch there), then catch the 15:00 boat back to Annecy to arrive at about 16:15 (the last boat for Annecy from Talloires leaves at 17:30).

▲**Biking**—Annecy was made for biking; it's an ain't-it-great-to-be-alive way to poke around the lake and test waterfront cafés and parks. A popular bike trail *(piste cyclable)* runs along the west side of the lake (some sections of the trail are on a roadway); it's smart to wear sunglasses and bring water. The small village of Duingt is seven level miles away and makes a good destination. Steady bikers make it in 45 minutes, and smell-the-roses cyclists need at least an hour. You can ride to Duingt and take the *Omnibus* boat back to Annecy (€6, 3 departures per day from Duingt, normally at 11:45, 15:30, and 18:00, verify at boat dock or TI, bikes allowed).

To get to Duingt, leave Annecy on the main road (N-508) with the lake on your left and join the bike trail after about a mile. Once the painted bike lane ends in Sévrier, you'll see a sign for the trail *(piste cyclable)* to the left. Follow it to Duingt (exit the trail just before the tunnel for Duingt, ride down to main road and turn right, then find the small, green boat-dock shelter just after the castle). The trail beyond Duingt is beautiful, as the lake narrows—hardy cyclists can make it all the way around the lake in about three hours (no bike path on opposite side of lake, just narrow roads, with one good hill).

This route also works well in reverse: Take the *Omnibus* boat to Duingt and pedal back (turn right when you get off the boat and join the bike trail behind Duingt's tall church).

**Driving**—For the best car-accessible views overlooking Annecy, drive 12 miles to Col de la Forclaz (3,600 feet, restaurants with view terraces). Take D-508 south along the lake past Duingt and turn left on D-42 a few minutes after leaving the lake (allow 45 min one-way with traffic). This also ties in easily with the scenic route to Chamonix via N-508.

# SLEEPING

Annecy is popular—particularly on weekends and during the summer. Hotel rates drop from about mid-October through late April and generally increase in summer. Most hotels can help you find free overnight parking (in lots, after 18:00 until 9:00). Unless otherwise noted, these hotels do not have elevators. If a hotel does not have a website listed below, try the site for Annecy's TI: www .lac-annecy.com.

## In the Town Center
This part of town is pedestrian-friendly and comes with some noise.

**$$$ Splendid Hôtel*** makes a striking impression with its grand facade and flags. This business hotel, with every comfort (including elevators, bar, terrace, and free Internet access and Wi-Fi), sits on Annecy's busiest street across from the park and the TI. Rooms are handsome, with parquet floors (Sb-€100–110, Db-€112–122, Tb-€158, Qb-€173, breakfast buffet-€14, air-con, big beds, 4 quai Eustache Chappuis, tel. 04 50 45 20 00, fax 04 50 45 52 23, www.splendidhotel.fr, info@splendidhotel.fr).

**$$$ Hôtel du Palais de l'Isle*** offers a romantic canalside location in the thick of the old town and 33 stylish, contemporary rooms—several with canal or rooftop views (Sb-€80–130, Db-€99–115, deluxe Db-€148, grand suites-€210–260, air-con, elevator, pricey Internet access, 13 rue Perrière, tel. 04 50 45 86 87, fax 04 50 51 87 15, www.hoteldupalaisdelisle.com, palisle@wanadoo.fr).

**$$$ Hôtel Ibis** is a cheery place and a decent chain-hotel option, with narrow rooms, a canalside lounge, and easy underground parking. It's well-situated on a modern courtyard on the edge of the old town, a few blocks from the train station (Sb/Db-€90, extra bed-€10, buffet breakfast-€8, air-con, elevator, 12 rue de la Gare, tel. 04 50 45 43 21, fax 04 50 52 81 08, www.ibis hotel.com, H0538@accor.com).

**$$ Auberge du Lyonnais** has 10 good-value, alpine-decorated rooms above a bustling restaurant (recommended under "Eating," later in this section). It's as central as you can get with adequately comfortable rooms; the rooms on the canal are worth the few extra euros (Db-€65–75, 9 rue de la République, walk through the restaurant to the small reception, tel. 04 50 51 26 10, fax 04 50 51 05 04, www.auberge-du-lyonnais.com, aubergedulyonnais @wanadoo.fr).

THE FRENCH ALPS

## Sleep Code

**(€1 = about $1.50, country code: 33)**
**S** = Single, **D** = Double/Twin, **T** = Triple, **Q** = Quad, **b** = bathroom,
**s** = shower only, **\*** = French hotel rating system (0-4 stars).
Unless otherwise noted, credit cards are accepted and English
is spoken.

To help you sort easily through these listings, I've divided
the rooms into three categories based on the price for a
standard double room with bath:

**$$$   Higher Priced**—Most rooms €85 or more.
**$$   Moderately Priced**—Most rooms between €65-85.
**$   Lower Priced**—Most rooms €65 or less.

**$ Hôtel des Alpes\*\*,** an excellent budget option, has 32
immaculate, comfortable, bright rooms at a busy intersection just
across from the train station. Rooms on the courtyard are quieter
but darker; those on the street have effective double panes (Sb-
€48–54, Db-€54–60, Tb-€75–79, Qb-€82–89, €7 more for a bathtub, free Wi-Fi, 12 rue de la Poste, tel. 04 50 45 04 56, fax 04 50 45
12 38, www.hotelannecy.com, info@hotelannecy.com).

**$ Hôtel Central\*** is just that. This modest and homey place,
behind an ivy-covered courtyard off a big pedestrian street, is just
this side of a youth hostel (Ds-€41, Db-€46, extra person-€8, 6
bis rue Royale, tel. 04 50 45 05 37, fax 04 50 51 80 19, www.hotel
centralannecy.com, stefanpicollet@hotmail.com, informal owners
Stefan and mama Parel).

## At the Foot of the Château

These are in a quiet area a steep five-minute walk up from the old
town on rampe du Château (for parking information, see "Arrival
in Annecy," earlier in this section).

At **$$$ Les Jardins du Château Bed & Breakfast,** welcoming
Anne-Marie and Jean-Paul have created Annecy's highest urban
refuge (near the château entry). Their chalet *chambre d'hôte* comes
with a small garden and eight modern yet comfy rooms, all with
kitchenettes and some with views and balconies. Jean-Paul doubles
as a mountain guide and offers a wealth of information (small
Db-€70, bigger Db-€88–140—most are about €88, good family
rooms-€82–122, includes breakfast except Nov–March when rooms
are cheaper, cash only, bike rental, free parking, 1 place du Château,
tel.04 50 45 72 28, jardinduchateau@wanadoo.fr).

**$$ Hôtel du Château\*\*,** just below the château, comes with a
great view terrace and 15 simple, bright, and spotless rooms; about

half have views, and all have updated bathrooms with showers. It's first-come, first-get for the precious few free parking spots (Db-€60–70, Tb-€75, Qb-€85, free Internet access and Wi-Fi, 16 rampe du Château, tel. 04 50 45 27 66, fax 04 50 52 75 26, www .annecy-hotel.com, hotelduchateau@noos.fr).

# EATING

While the touristy old city is well-stocked with forgettable restaurants, I've found a few worthy places. And though you'll pay more to eat with views of the river or canal, the experience is uniquely Annecy. The ubiquitous and sumptuous *gelati* shops remind us how close Italy is. If it's sunny, assemble a gourmet picnic at the arcaded stores and dine lakeside. Wherever you eat, don't miss an ice-cream-licking stroll along the lake after dark.

**Le Cochon à l'Oreille** ("The Pig's Ear") is a meat-lover's nirvana. Just off the Thiou canal, it welcomes with a leafy courtyard and a warm interior. Amicable owners "Fred" and Jean speak English and are serious about their cooking. The accent is on fresh products and meat dishes, not on melted cheese (€18 *menu* that changes weekly, daily for lunch and dinner, quai du Perrière, tel. 04 50 45 92 51).

**Le Freti,** with a lighthearted waitstaff, is the most reliable restaurant for local cuisine I've found in Annecy. It's the place to go for mouthwatering fondue, raclette, or anything with cheese. Each booth comes with its own outlet for melting raclette (€13 fondue, good salads and onion soup and cheap wine, open daily; walk through door at 12 rue Ste. Claire, it's upstairs; tel. 04 50 51 29 52).

If Le Freti sounds cheesy, go next door to **Café l'Estaminet** for a Belgian welcome. You'll get salads, omelets, pasta, mussels, fries, and more for fair prices and a sliver of a backyard deck hanging over the river (open daily in summer, closed Sun off-season, 8 rue Ste. Claire, tel. 04 50 45 88 83).

**Chez Mama Lise** is like eating in an alpine folk museum, with stuffed mountain animals, rusted tools, tourists, and knickknacks everywhere. The cuisine—fondue, raclette, and other cheese dishes—is as alpine as the decor (open daily, 11 rue Grenette, tel. 04 50 45 41 18).

**Auberge du Lyonnais** is a well-respected and classy eatery that specializes in seafood with a sweet setting on the river (indoor and outdoor seating). The outgoing owners love Americans; ask Dominique about his many trips to the States, and about his Ford pickup (*menus* from €39, less on weeknights, open daily, 9 rue de la République, tel. 04 50 51 26 10).

Many cafés and restaurants ring Annecy's postcard-perfect lake. If you have a car and need views, prowl the many lakefront villages. **Le Bistro du Port,** a nautical place with blue deck chairs, is beautifully situated at the boat dock in Sévrier (€10–12 salads, €16–22 main courses, open daily, Port de Sévrier, tel. 04 50 52 45 00).

## TRANSPORTATION CONNECTIONS

**From Annecy by Train to: Chamonix** (8/day, 2.5 hrs, change in St. Gervais), **Lyon** (7/day, 2 hrs, most change in Aix-les-Bains, some by bus), **Beaune** (7/day, 5–6 hrs, change in Lyon), **Nice** (8/day, 7–9 hrs, at least 3 changes), **Paris'** Gare de Lyon (13/day, 4–5 hrs, many with change in Lyon).

# Chamonix

THE FRENCH ALPS

Bullied by snow-dipped peaks, churning with mountain lifts, and littered with hiking trails, the resort of Chamonix (shah-

moh-nee) is France's best base for alpine exploration. Officially called Chamonix–Mont Blanc, it's the largest of five villages at the base of Mont Blanc, with about 10,000 residents. Chamonix's purpose in life has always been to accommodate

visitors with some of Europe's top alpine thrills—it's slammed from mid-July through mid-August and on winter holidays, but it's *très* peaceful at other times. Chamonix's sister city is Aspen, Colorado.

## Planning Your Time

Ride the lifts early (crowds and clouds roll in later in the morning) and save your afternoons for lower altitudes. If you have one sunny day, spend it this way: Start with the Aiguille du Midi lift (go early, reservations possible and recommended July–Aug), take it all the way to Helbronner (linger around the rock needle longer if you can't get to Helbronner), double back to Plan de l'Aiguille, hike to Montenvers and the Mer de Glace (only with good shoes and snow level permitting), and take the train down from there. End your day with a well-deserved drink at a view café in Chamonix. If the weather disappoints or the snow line's too low, hike the Petit Balcon Sud or Arve River trails.

**Chamonix Valley Overview**

MT. BLANC
15,771

"Wow!"

ITALY

LE BREVENT
8,284

PANORAMIC DU MONT ↓ ↓ BLANC

AIGUILLE DU MIDI
12,605

GARE HELBRONNER
11,371

GLACIER DU GEANT

PLAN DE L'AIGUILLE
7,556

ARVE R.

PLAN-PRAZ
6,562

LES GRANDS MONTETS
10,745

MER DE GLACE

LUGE

MONTENVERS
6,276

CHAMONIX TOWN
3,399

LA FLEGERE
6,158

❶
❷
❺
❹
❸

N

LAC BLANC

LES PRAZ
4,108

ELEVATIONS IN FEET

ARGENTIERE

❶ Grand Balcon Nord Hike
   (2-3 Hrs One-Way, Moderate)
❷ Grand Balcon Sud Hike
   (2-3 Hrs One-Way, Moderate)
❸ La Flégère to Lac Blanc Hike
   (3 Hrs Round-Trip, Difficult)
❹ Petit Balcon Sud Hike
   (2 Hrs One-Way, Easy-Moderate)
❺ Arve Riverbank Stroll
   (1-2 Hr Loop, Easy)

THE FRENCH ALPS

# ORIENTATION

Eternally white Mont Blanc is Chamonix's southeastern limit; the Aiguilles Rouges mountains form the northwestern border. The frothy Arve River splits Chamonix in two. The thriving pedestrian zone, just west of the river along rues du Docteur Paccard and Joseph Vallot, is Chamonix's core. The TI is just above the pedestrian zone, and the train station is east of the river.

## Tourist Information

Visit the TI to prepare your attack. Get the weather forecast, pick up the free town and valley map and the "panorama" map of all the valley lifts, and consider the €4 hiking map called *Carte des Sentiers* (see "Chamonix Area Hikes," later in this section). Ask about hours of lifts (important), the Multipass for lifts (described under "Getting Around (and Up and Down) the Valley,"

## Chamonix Quick History

**1786**  Jacques Balmat and Michel-Gabriel Paccard are the first to climb Mont Blanc (find the statue in Chamonix's pedestrian zone).

**1818**  First ascent of Aiguille du Midi.

**1860**  The Savoie region (including Chamonix) becomes part of France. After a visit by Napoleon III, the trickle of nature-loving visitors to Chamonix turns to a gush.

**1901**  Train service reaches Chamonix, unleashing its tourist appeal forever.

**1908**  The cogwheel train to Montenvers is completed.

**1924**  First Winter Olympics held in Chamonix.

**1930**  Le Brévent *téléphérique* (gondola lift) opens to tourists.

**1955**  Aiguille du Midi *téléphérique* opens to tourists.

**2009**  You visit Chamonix.

next page), biking information, and help with hotel reservations. Their helpful website has updated sightseeing info, weather forecasts, and more (July–Aug daily 8:30–19:00; Sept–June Mon–Sat 9:00–12:30 & 14:00–18:30, Sun 9:00–12:00; hours may vary—call ahead, free 24-hour Wi-Fi outside the TI, tel. 04 50 53 00 24, fax 04 50 53 58 90, www.chamonix.com).

Grab a beachy sling chair outside the TI and plan a hike or check your email. Also outside is a huge monitor showing which lifts are operating, weather conditions, and other helpful information. Check the Compagnie du Mont Blanc's website (www.compagniedumontblanc.com) for current lift information and to book the Aiguille du Midi lift.

For a quick mountain overview, leave the TI and walk between the church and the Office de la Haute Montagne. Climb the stone steps that lead over a road, then up more steps to a small park-like area (good picnic spot). Mont Dru, the dominant peak to the left, sits alone and towers above the Mer de Glace glacier. Burly, rounded Mont Blanc stands high to the right. The menacing glacier below seems to threaten Chamonix—but is actually in hasty retreat.

## Arrival in Chamonix

**By Train:** Walk straight out of the station (no baggage check available) and up avenue Michel Croz. In three blocks, you'll reach the town center; turn left at the big clock, then right for the TI.

**By Bus:** The long-distance bus station is at the train station (see arrival instructions, above).

**By Car:** For most of my recommended hotels and the TI, take the Chamonix Nord turnoff (second exit coming from Annecy). Most parking is metered and well-signed, though your hotel can direct you to free parking.

The Mont Blanc tunnel (7.2 miles long, about a 12-min drive) allows quick access between Chamonix and Italy (one-way-€32, round-trip-€40 with return valid for 1 week, €360 if you're driving a truck, www.tunnelmb.com).

**By Plane:** The nearest international airports are in Lyon (linked by 10 trains/day, 4 hrs; 3 hrs by car) and in Geneva, Switzerland (hourly trains, 3.5 hrs; 3/day, 2 hrs by shuttle—see "Transportation Connections" at the end of this section; 1.5 hrs by car).

## Helpful Hints

**Beat the Crowds:** In high season, take the first lift to beat the crowds and afternoon clouds. Consider breakfast at *le* top.

**Be Prepared:** Snow abounds up high, making the glare unbearable, so bring your sunglasses. Be sure your camera has enough battery power and storage space for those perfect alpine shots. For Chamonix's weather, check at the TI or at www.chamonix .com. For a five-day weather forecast in English, call 08 92 68 02 74 from anywhere in France for a small charge.

**Supermarkets:** Little **Casino** markets are omnipresent in Chamonix, though the **Super U** market is big and central (Mon–Sat 8:15–19:30, Sun 8:30–12:00, rue Joseph Vallot). Supplement your run-of-the-mill groceries with gourmet local specialties from **Le Refuge Payot** (two locations: 166 rue Joseph Vallot and 255 rue du Docteur Paccard).

**Internet Access:** The TI has free Wi-Fi and a good list of Internet cafés.

**Laundry:** **Laverie Alpina** (look for *Pressing* sign) is in the rear of Galerie Alpina shopping center. Marie-Paule will do your laundry for the cost of the washer and dryer (allow €9 for a load, leave a small tip and fold your clothes yourself, Mon–Sat 8:00–18:00, until 19:00 in summer, closed Sun, tel. 04 50 53 30 67). Another *laverie* is one block up from the Aiguille du Midi lift at 174 avenue de l'Aiguille du Midi (daily 9:00–20:00, instructions in English).

## Getting Around
## (and Up and Down) the Valley

Note that lifts and cogwheel trains are named for their highest destination (e.g., Aiguille du Midi, Montenvers, and Le Brévent).

**By Lift:** Gondolas *(téléphériques)* climb mountains all along the valley, but the best one leaves from Chamonix (see "Sights and Activities," later in this section). While sightseeing is optimal from the Aiguille du Midi gondola, there are more hiking options from the Le Brévent gondola.

The lift to Aiguille du Midi is open summer and winter (closures possible in May and late Oct–early Dec). The *télécabines* on the Panoramic Mont Blanc lift to Helbronner (Italy) run only from May to late September, and even then only in good weather (call the TI to confirm). Other area lifts are generally open from January to mid-April and from mid-June to late September. For all lifts, because maintenance closures can occur anytime, it's always smart to verify at the TI.

If you're spending two or more days in the Chamonix valley, a **Multipass** saves time and money. It allows unlimited access to all the lifts and trains (except the Helbronner gondola to Italy), and includes all reservation fees (both Aiguille du Midi and Montenvers) and the elevator at the top of Aiguille du Midi. Best of all, it allows you to bypass lift-ticket lines after your first purchase. You'll pay a €3 refundable deposit for a "smart card" that will allow you to scan your way to the top (€47/1 day, €53/2 days, €66/3 days, €80/4 days, €90/5 days, available for up to 15 days; days are consecutive, though you can also buy a more expensive pass for non-consecutive days; kids age 12–15 and adults over 60 pay about 15 percent less, kids age 4–11 pay 30 percent less, kids under 4 usually not allowed, www.compagniedumontblanc.com).

Families can benefit from reduced fares by asking for family tickets (2 adults and 2 children under 15).

**By Foot:** See "Chamonix Area Hikes," later in this section.

**By Bike:** The TI has a brochure showing bike-rental shops and the best biking routes. The peaceful river valley trail is ideal for bikes and pedestrians.

**By Bus or Train:** One road and one scenic rail line lace together the towns and lifts of the valley. Local buses run hourly off-season, and twice an hour in summer, to valley villages (main stop is 200 yards to the right when you leave the TI, past Hôtel Mont Blanc, look for the bus shelters). Direction "Le Tour" takes you toward Les Praz (for Hike #2) and Switzerland; direction "Les Houches" takes you the opposite direction.

To help reduce traffic pollution in the valley, hotels distribute free Chamonix Guest Cards providing free travel on all Chamonix area buses (except the night bus) and the valley train between Serves and Vallorcine for the duration of your hotel stay. This is a great value for those with time to explore the valley. The train ride toward Martigny in Switzerland is gorgeous, and villages such as Les Praz and Tines (10 min by bus) offer quiet village escapes from busy Chamonix.

# Chamonix Activities at a Glance

▲▲▲**Aiguille du Midi Gondola** The valley's most spectacular and popular lift, taking you to magnificent views at 12,600 feet. From here, you can ride the cute *télécabines* over the Alps to Italy and back, take Chamonix's greatest hike to the Mer de Glace (from the halfway-up stop at Plan de l'Aiguille), or just enjoy the views.

▲▲**Train to Montenvers** Cogwheel train to the Mer de Glace, an eight-mile-long glacier where you can walk inside the glacier, admire jagged mountain peaks, have lunch with a view (or sleep) at the Montenvers hotel, and hike to the Aiguille du Midi lift (though the hike is best done in the other direction).

▲▲▲**Le Brévent Gondola** Second-most spectacular lift from Chamonix, allowing access to the mountain range on the opposite side of the valley from Mont Blanc. Get off halfway at the Planpraz station for the Grand Balcon Sud hike to the La Flégère lift, or go all the way to Le Brévent for sky-high views and a restaurant.

▲▲▲**La Flégère Lift** Starting point for hikes to Lac Blanc and to the Grand Balcon Sud trail back to Planpraz (on the Le Brévent Gondola). Refuge-Hôtel La Flégère, at the station, offers drinks, snacks, and accommodations, all with a view.

**Arve River Valley Stroll** Several trails allow a level walk or bike ride in the woods between Chamonix and Les Praz. See paragliders make dramatic landings and enjoy mountain views outside Chamonix to the sound of the Arve River.

# SIGHTS AND ACTIVITIES

## ▲▲▲Aiguille du Midi

This is easily the valley's (and arguably, Europe's) most spectacular and popular lift. If the weather's clear, the price doesn't matter. Pile into the *téléphérique* (gondola) and soar to the tip of a rock needle 12,600 feet above sea level. Chamonix shrinks as trees fly by, soon replaced by whizzing rocks, ice, and snow until you reach the top. No matter how sunny it is, it's cold. The air is thin. People are giddy (those prone to altitude sickness are less giddy). Fun things can happen at Aiguille du Midi (ay-gwee doo mee-dee) if you're not too winded to join the locals in the halfway-to-heaven tango.

From the top of the lift station, you have several options. Follow *ascenseur* signs through a tunnel, then ride the elevator through the rock to the summit of this pinnacle (€3 in high

**Over the Alps—France to Italy**

MT. BLANC
15,771

"WOW!"

AIGUILLE
DU MIDI
12,605

HEL-
BRONNER
11,371

RIFUGIO
TORINO
11,073

PLAN DE
L'AIGUILLE
7,572

PAVILLION
6,988

ITALIA | FRANCE

GLACIER

VALLEE
BLANCHE
11 MILE
SKI RUN!

TO
COURMAYEUR
+ AOSTA

7 MILE TUNNEL

TO
PARIS +
MARTIGNY
(SWITZ)

**LA PALUD**
4,495

**CHAMONIX**
3,399

MAP NOT TO SCALE
DCH

SOUTH ←→ NORTH

ELEVATIONS IN FEET

season, free off-season and when the *télécabines* to Helbronner are not running). Missing the elevator is a kind of Alpus-Interruptus I'd rather not experience. The Alps spread out before you. In the distance and behind a broader mountain, you can see the bent little Matterhorn—the tall, shady pyramid listed in French on the observation table as "Cervin—4,505 meters" (14,775 feet). And looming just over there is **Mont Blanc,** the Alps' highest point at 4,810 meters (15,771 feet). Use the telescopes to spot mountain climbers; more than 2,000 scale this mountain each year. That rusty tin-can needle above you serves as a communication tower. Check the temperature next to the elevator. Plan on 32 degrees Fahrenheit, even on a sunny day. Sunglasses are essential.

Back down, explore Europe's tallest lift station. More than 150 yards of tunnels lead to a cafeteria (fair prices—have lunch or coffee with a view), toilets, gift shop, and an icicle-covered gateway to the glacial world. Follow *la Vallée Blanche* signs to an "ice tunnel" where skiers and mountain climbers make their exit. The views are sensational, and merely observing is exhilarating. Peek down the icy cliff and ponder the value of an ice ax. Skiers make the 11-mile run from here to the Mer de Glace (described later in this section) in about half a day (in winter they can ski 13 miles all the way back to the valley at Argentière).

Next, for your own private glacial dream world, get into the little red *télécabine* (called Panoramic Mont Blanc) and sail south to **Helbronner Point,** the Italian border station. This line stretches three miles with no solid pylon. (It's propped by a "suspended pylon," a line stretched between two peaks 1,300 feet from the Italian end.) In a gondola for four, you'll dangle silently for 40 minutes as you glide over glaciers and past a forest of peaks to Italy. Hang your head out the window; explore every corner of your view. From Helbronner Point, you can continue down into Italy (see "Day Trips—A Little Italy," later in this chapter), but there's really no point unless you're traveling that way.

From Aiguille du Midi, you can ride all the way back to Chamonix, or better (if you like to hike and are wearing good shoes, or just want a break), get off halfway down at **Plan de l'Aiguille.** You'll find a small bar with outdoor tables at the lift station; paragliders jumping off cliffs; and, a 15-minute walk below, the Plan de l'Aiguille refuge (snacks, drinks, and views). But the best reason to get off here is to follow the trail to the Mer de Glace. From Plan de l'Aiguille, walk 15 minutes down to the refuge, go right, and hike the spectacularly scenic, undulating, and at times quite strenuous two- to three-hour trail to Montenvers (overlooking the Mer de Glace glacier—described later). From here, you'll catch the train back into Chamonix (for all the hike details, see "Chamonix Area Hikes—Hike #1," later in this section). Don't hike all the way down to Chamonix from Plan de l'Aiguille or Montenvers–Mer de Glace; it's a long, steep walk through thick forests with few views.

**Hours:** Lift hours are weather- and crowd-dependent, but generally run daily July–Aug 6:00–16:30, late May–June and Sept 8:00–16:30, and Oct–late May 8:00–15:30. The last return from the Aiguille du Midi lift is generally one hour after the last ascent. The last *télécabine* departure to Helbronner Point is about 14:00–15:00, and the last train down from Montenvers is about 17:00–18:00.

**Strategy:** To beat the hordes and clouds, ride the Aiguille du Midi lift (up and down) as early as you can. To beat major delays in summer, leave no later than 7:00 or reserve ahead (first lift departs at about 6:00). If the weather has been bad and turns good, expect big crowds in any season (even worse on weekends). If it's clear, don't dillydally.

In peak season, smart travelers reserve the Aiguille du Midi lift in advance (€2 fee). You can reserve at the information booth next to the lift (open mid-June–mid-Sept), online at www.compagnie dumontblanc.com, or by telephone (year-round, tel. 04 50 53 22 75, automated reservations in English). Reservations are taken up to 10 days in advance (six days in winter); pick them up at the lift station at least 30 minutes before departure. Reservations are free with a Multipass (see "Getting Around (and Up and Down) the Valley," earlier in this chapter), and are not possible for the *télécabines* to Helbronner.

**Costs:** The following prices are for ages 16 and over; kids age 4–11 are 30 percent less and kids age 12–15 and adults over 60 are

15 percent less (family rates for 2 adults and 2 children under 15 are also available). From Chamonix to: Plan de l'Aiguille—round-trip-€21 (one-way-€18); Aiguille du Midi—round-trip-€38 (one-way-€35, not including parachute); the Panoramic Mont Blanc *télécabine* to Helbronner—round-trip-€55 (one-way-€46). If you are planning to stop at Plan de l'Aiguille on the way back down and hike to Montenvers, ask about a *"spécial randonée"* ticket for about €35.

Tickets just for the stretch from Aiguille du Midi to Helbronner are sold at both base and summit lift stations with no difference in price (round-trip-€18, one-way-€12). It's €25 to drop into Italy (sold at Helbronner). *Oui* and *si*, you can bring your luggage.

**Time to Allow:** Chamonix to Aiguille du Midi—20 minutes one-way, two hours round-trip, three to four hours in peak season; Chamonix to Helbronner—90 minutes one-way, three to four hours round-trip, longer in peak season. On busy days, minimize delays by making a reservation for your return lift time upon arrival at the top. (For information on Aiguille du Midi, call 04 50 53 30 80.)

## ▲▲Mer de Glace (Montenvers)

From Gare de Montenvers (the little station over the tracks from Chamonix's main train station), the cute cogwheel Train du Montenvers toots you up to tiny Montenvers (mohn-tuh-vehr). There you'll see a dirty, rapidly receding glacier called the Mer de Glace (mayr duh glahs, "Sea of Ice"), and fantastic views up the white valley (Vallée Blanche) of splintered, snow-capped peaks (2–3/hr, 20 min, round-trip-€20, one-way-€17, family rates available, prices include gondola and ice caves entry, daily 8:30–17:00, July–Aug 8:00–18:00, confirm times with TI or call 04 50 53 12 54).

France's largest **glacier,** at eight miles long, is impressive from above and below. Walk to the view deck. The glacier extends under the dirt about a half-mile downhill to the left. Imagine that it recently rose as high as the vegetation below (note the mounds of dirt—called moraines—left in its retreat). In 1860, this glacier stretched all the way down to the valley floor. They say this fast-moving glacier is just doing its cycle thing, growing and shrinking—a thousand years ago, cows grazed on grassy fields here. Al Gore thinks differently.

Now look up to the peaks (find the orientation charts). **Monsieur Dru**'s powerful spire, at about 11,700 feet, makes an irresistible target for climbers. It was first scaled in 1860 (long before the train you took here was built) and was recently free-climbed (no ropes, belays, etc.); see the colored lines indicating different routes taken—one by an *Américain*. Those guys are nuts. The smooth snow field to the left of Dru's spire (Les Grands Montets) is the top of Chamonix's most challenging ski run, with a vertical drop of about 6,500 feet.

The glacier's **ice caves** are below you (take the small gondola down and prepare to walk 280 steps each way). If you've already seen a glacier up close, you might skip this one, though I found it a relevant trip given the attention being paid to global warming *(le rechauffement climatique)*. This is also where skiers end their run from the Aiguille du Midi (you might recognize someone if you rode that lift earlier).

Walking left to **Refuge-Hôtel du Montenvers** leads to a full-service restaurant, view tables (fair prices, limited selection), and a warm interior (for information on sleeping here, see "Sleeping," later in this section). The hotel was built in 1880, when "tourists" arrived on foot or by mule. The three-hour trail to Plan de l'Aiguille begins from above the hotel. For terrific views, hike toward Plan de l'Aiguille—via the trail that veers left—even just a short distance. The views get better fast, and the higher you climb, the better the view (follow signs on the stone building opposite the hotel; you want *sentier gauche* to *Signal Montenvers*). Bring a picnic and join the locals.

## ▲▲▲Gondola Lifts *(Téléphériques)* to Le Brévent and La Flégère

While Aiguille du Midi gives a more spectacular ride, the Le Brévent and La Flégère lifts offer different hiking and viewing options with unobstructed panoramas across to the Mont Blanc range. Le Brévent (luh bray-vahn) lift is in Chamonix; La Flégère (lah flay-zhair) lift is in nearby Les Praz (lay prah). The lifts are connected by a scenic hike or by bus along the valley floor (free with Chamonix Guest Card, see "Chamonix Area Hikes—Hike #2," later in this section); both have sensational view cafés for non-hikers.

**Le Brévent lift** is a steep, 10-minute walk up the road above Chamonix's TI. This *téléphérique* stops halfway up at Planpraz station (round-trip-about-€12, one-way-€10, nice restaurant, great views and hiking) and continues to Le Brévent station at the top with more views and hikes, though Planpraz offers plenty for me (round-trip-€22, one-way from Chamonix-€17, daily 9:00–16:00, July–Aug 8:00–17:00, last return from Planpraz 1 hour after last ascent, closed late April–mid-June and Oct, tel. 04 50 53 13 18).

**La Flégère lift** runs from the neighboring village of Les Praz, with just one stop at La Flégère station (round-trip-€12, one-way-€10, daily 8:40–16:00, summer 7:40–17:00, last return from La Flégère 50 min after last ascent, closed late April–mid-June and mid-Sept–Oct, tel. 04 50 53 18 58). Hikes to Planpraz and Lac

## Kid Activities

Chamonix provides a wealth of fun opportunities for kids—consider these options.

**Parc de Loisirs des Planards** Chamonix's most ambitious activities for kids of all ages, including a luge (summer only—see "Other Activities" under "Chamonix Area Hikes," later in this section) and a Parc d'Aventure with tree courses, Tarzan swings, trampolines, electric motorbikes, Jet Skis, and more (Parc d'Aventure-€23, under 18-€19, early July–Aug daily 10:00–19:30, mid-June–early July and early Sept daily 14:00–18:00, May–mid-June and mid-Sept–Oct generally weekends only 13:30–18:00, 15-min walk from town center, over the tracks from train station and past Montenvers train station, tel. 04 50 53 08 97, www.planards.com).

**Le Paradis des Praz** Pleasant activity park ideal for 4- to 10-year-olds, with donkey rides, zip-wire rides, and more. It's in the small village of Les Praz, by the lift to Flégère (mid-June–mid-Sept daily 10:00–18:30, otherwise Wed and weekend afternoons, tel. 06 61 73 23 00, www.paradis-des-praz.com). Rent a bike in Chamonix and ride along the level Arve River trail to reach this park, or take the free bus (see "Getting Around (and Up and Down) the Valley," earlier in this section).

**Parc de Merlet** Animal sanctuary with trails that let you discover mountain animals (marmots, mountain goats, llamas, deer, and more). It's located in Coupeau above Les Houches, and offers exceptional views. You can get there by car or a two-hour hike (€5, ages 4-12-€3, May–Sept daily 10:00–18:00, July–Aug until 19:30, tel. 04 50 53 47 89, www.parcdemerlet.com).

**Maison de la Montagne** Daily or weekly outdoor programs for kids (rafting, hiking, mountain biking, etc.) allow parents time alone in the mountains (ages 8-12-€67/day, ages 13-17-€90/day, tel. 04 50 53 00 88 or 04 50 53 55 70).

Blanc leave from the top of this station (see hikes #2 and #3 under "Chamonix Area Hikes," later in this section).

## Chamonix Area Hikes

Your first stop should be at the full-service **Maison de la Montagne,** across from the TI. On the third floor, the **Office of the High Mountain** (Office de Haute-Montagne) can help you plan your hikes and tell you about trail and snow conditions (daily 9:00–12:00 & 15:00–18:00, tel. 04 50 53 22 08, www.ohm-chamonix.com). The staff speaks enough English, has vital weather reports and maps, and some English hiking guidebooks (you can photocopy key pages). Ask to look at the trail guidebook (sold in many stores, includes the extremely helpful €4 *Carte des Sentiers,* the region's hiking map—also sold at the TI). You can also use the handy restroom here on the second floor.

At **Compagnie des Guides de Chamonix** on the ground floor, you can hire a guide to take you hiking for the day (about €300), help you scale Mont Blanc, or hike to the Matterhorn and Zermatt (about €800 for the 2-day climb up Mont Blanc; open daily 9:00–12:00 & 15:30–19:00, closed Sun–Mon off-season, tel. 04 50 53 00 88, fax 04 50 53 48 04, www.chamonix-guides.com).

I've described three big hikes (Hikes #1, #2, and #3) and two easier walks (Hikes #4 and #5); see the map on page 680. These hikes give nature-lovers of any ability good options for enjoying the valley in most seasons. Start early, when the weather's generally best. This is critical in summer; if you don't get to the lifts by 8:30, you'll meet a conveyor belt of hikers. If starting later or walking longer, confirm lift closing hours, or prepare for a long, steep hike down.

For your hike, pack sunglasses, sunscreen, rain gear, water, and snacks. Wear warm clothes and good shoes. Trails are rocky and uneven. Take your time, watch your footing, don't take shortcuts, and say *"Bonjour!"* to your fellow hikers.

**▲▲▲Hike #1: Plan de l'Aiguille to Montenvers–Mer de Glace (Grand Balcon Nord)**—This is the most efficient way to incorporate a two- to three-hour high-country hike into your ride down from the valley's greatest lift, and check out a world-class glacier to boot. The well-used trail rises but mostly falls (dropping 1,500 feet from Plan de l'Aiguille to Montenvers–Mer de Glace) and is moderately difficult, provided the snow is melted (generally covered by snow until June; get trail details at the Office of the High Mountain, above). Some stretches are steep and strenuous, with uneven footing and slippery rocks. From the Aiguille du Midi lift, get off halfway down at Plan de l'Aiguille and follow signs to the unmarked wooden refuge (reasonably priced food and drinks, closed off-season). From there, take a right and follow *Montenvers* signs for about an hour. If you don't see signs, ask for the way to Montenvers: *"Quelle direction pour Montenvers?"* (kell dee-reck-shown poor mohn-ton-vare). When the trail splits, follow signs up the steep trail to Signal Montenvers (more scenic and easier), rather than to the left toward Montenvers (it may look easier at first, but it becomes difficult). At this point, you'll grind it out up and up to the best views of the trail. It's a long, steep, and memorable drop to Montenvers and the Mer de Glace (described earlier in this section). In Montenvers, take the train back to Chamonix. Don't walk the rest of the trail down from Montenvers (long, steep, disappointing views).

**▲▲Hike #2: La Flégère to Planpraz (Grand Balcon Sud)**—This glorious hike undulates above Chamonix Valley

# Chamonix Area Hikes and Lifts

ELEVATIONS IN FEET

LAC BLANC

HIKE 3

LA FLEGERE 6,158

L'INDEX

TO ARGENTIERE, LE BUET & MARTIGNY (SWITZ.)

N-506

SUD

LES TINES

HIKE 5

Le Paradis du Praz

HIKE 2

GRAND BALCON SUD

LES PRAZ STN.

PLAN-PRAZ 6,562

LE BREVENT 8,284

LE PETIT BALCON SUD

TO MONTENVERS STN. & MER DE GLACE

HIKE 4

LAC DU BREVENT 6,978

LES MOUSSOUX

LUGE!

LES PLANARDS

TOWN OF CHAMONIX 3,399 (See detail map)

HIKE 1

LES BOSSONS & HOTEL DU MIDI

ARVE RIVER

N-506

MT. BLANC TUNNEL

PLAN DE L'AIGUILLE 7,572

TO PARC DE MERLET, SERVOZ, GENEVA & ANNECY

TO LA PALUD, COURMAYEUR & AOSTA (ITALY)

AIGUILLE DU MIDI 12,605

TO GARE HELBRONNER & LA PALUD (ITALY)

———— ROAD

+-+-+-■ RAIL & STATION

•—•—• LIFT & STATION

------ TRAIL     DCH

▲ MTN. REFUGE

1 MILE

2 KM

THE FRENCH ALPS

with staggering views of Mont Blanc and countless other peaks, glaciers, and wildflowers. There's just 370 feet of difference in elevation between La Flégère and Planpraz lift stations—so this hike, while not without its ups and downs, is manageable, but still requires serious stamina. You can do it in either direction, but I prefer starting at La Flégère, which is how I've described the hike.

From Chamonix, drive five minutes, walk 40 minutes along the Arve River (see Hike #5, below), or take the Chamonix bus (every 30–60 min, 10-min ride, free with Chamonix Guest Card) to the tiny village of Les Praz and its La Flégère lift station. Ride the lift up to La Flégère (€10) and walk down to the Refuge-Hôtel La Flégère. Find the signs to *Planpraz* (you don't want Les Praz–Chamonix—that's straight down), then hike the rolling Grand Balcon Sud to Planpraz station, the midway stop on the Le Brévent lift line (allow 2.5 hours). Take the Planpraz lift down to Chamonix (€10) and skip the steep hike down. Ask for the round-trip rate allowed with La Flégère and Planpraz (Le Brévent) lifts, available at either lift (saves about €6).

▲▲**Hike #3: La Flégère to Lac Blanc**—This is the most demanding hiking trail of those I list; it climbs steeply and steadily over a rough, boulder-strewn trail for 90 minutes to snowy Lac Blanc (pronounced "lock blah"). Some footing is tricky and good shoes or boots are essential. I like this trail, as it gets you away from the valley edge and opens views to peaks you don't see from other hikes. The destination is a snow-white lake surrounded by peaks and a nifty chalet-refuge offering good lunches (and dinners with accommodations). The views on the return trip are breathtaking. Check for snow conditions on the trail and go early (particularly in summer), as there is no shade and this trail is popular. Follow directions from Hike #2 to La Flégère station (above), then walk out the station's rear door past the orientation table and view area, and follow signs to *Lac Blanc*. The trail is well-signed and improves in surface quality as you climb. While you can eliminate a good portion of the uphill hiking by riding the lift up to L'Index from La Flégère, beware: the trail from L'Index can require serious skill and equipment because of snow; ask before you go on.

▲**Hike #4: Petit Balcon Sud**—This trail runs above the valley on the Brévent side from the village of Servoz to Argentière, passing Chamonix about halfway, and is handy when snow or poor weather make other hikes problematic. No lifts are required—just firm thighs to climb up to and down from the trail. Access paths link villages below. Once you're up, the trail rises and falls with some steep segments and uneven footing, but is generally easy to walk. Check with the TI about the directions given here, as maintenance work on Le Brévent lift in 2008 could have changed the trail's access.

To reach the trail from Chamonix, walk up to Le Brévent lift station, then follow the asphalt road to the left of the lift leading uphill; it turns into a dirt road that signs mark as the *Petit Balcon Sud* trail. After about 20 minutes on the dirt road, a sign for the *Petit Balcon Sud* points left and up a smaller trail. This segment of the hike doubles back above Chamonix, taking you toward Servoz (keep following *Petit Balcon Sud*). Go as far as you like, taking any trail down (signed to the village below). For an easier hike to **Les Praz** (where you can take the Arve River trail back to Chamonix), bypass this Petit Balcon turnoff and stay on the dirt road. After about 30 minutes, follow *la Floria* signs right and join the Petit Balcon Sud trail, then find *Les Praz* signs to get down the hill (a worthwhile 20-min round-trip detour leads to **La Floria chalet,** which has drinks, snacks, tables, flowers, and views, open mid-June–late Sept; at about the same junction, you'll see a shortcut back to Chamonix through the woods). Continuing to Les Praz, when you reach the asphalt road below, turn left to explore the village and to connect with the river trail back to Chamonix (turn right immediately after the bridge), or turn right for the bus stop back to Chamonix (figure it takes the bus 20 min to reach Les Praz from the time point posted in Le Tour).

### Hike #5: Arve Riverbank Stroll and Paragliding Landing Field

—For a level, forested-valley stroll, follow the Arve River toward Les Praz. Find Chamonix's Hôtel Alpina, then follow the path upstream past red-clay tennis courts and find the green arrow to *Les Praz*. Cross two bridges to the left and turn right along the rushing Arve River, and then follow Promenade des Econtres. Several trails loop through these woods; if you continue walking straight, you'll reach Les Praz—an appealing destination with several cafés and a pleasing village green.

If you keep right after the tennis courts (passing the piles of river sediment excavated to keep the river from flooding), you'll come to a grassy landing field, signed *Parapente*, where paragliders hope to touch down. Walk to the top of the little grassy hill for fine Mont Blanc views and a great picnic spot. The recommended Micro Brasserie de Chamonix is nearby (see "Eating," later in this section).

## Other Activities

▲**Luge (Luge d'Eté)**—Here's something for thrill-seekers— ride a chairlift up the mountain and then scream down a twisty, banked, concrete slalom course on a wheeled sled. Chamonix has two roughly parallel luge courses. While each course is just longer than a half mile and about the same speed, one is marked for slower sledders and the other for speed demons. Young or old, hare or tortoise, any fit person can manage a luge. *Freinez* signs tell you when to brake. Don't take your hands off your stick; the course is fast and slippery. The luge courses are set in a grassy park with kids' play areas—see the "Kid Activities" sidebar earlier in this section (1 hour of "unlimited" runs—figure you'll get three-€12.50, 1.5 hours-€15, 1 ride-€5, 6 rides-€25, 12 rides-€42, rides can be split with companions and tickets are good for a month; daily early July–late Aug 10:00–19:30; daily mid-June–early July and late Aug–mid-Sept 13:30–18:00; otherwise weekend and holiday afternoons only, call for spring and fall hours, covered with snow in winter, 15-min walk from town center over the tracks from train station, follow signs to Planards, tel. 04 50 53 08 97).

▲▲▲**Paragliding (Parapente)**—When it's sunny and clear, the skies above Chamonix sparkle with colorful parachute-like sails that circle the valley like birds of prey. For €90, launch yourself off a mountain in a tandem paraglider with a trained, experienced pilot and fly like a bird for about 20 minutes. Try **Summits Parapente** (smart to reserve a day ahead, open year-round, tel. 04 50 53 50 14, mobile 06 84 01 26 00, fax 04 50 55 94 16, across from Galerie Alpina at 27 allée du Savoy, www.summits.fr /parapente_chamonix).

For a sneak preview, walk to the main landing area and watch paragliders perfect their landings (see "Chamonix Area Hikes—Hike #5," earlier in this section).

## Rainy-Day Options

If the weather disagrees with your plans, stay cool and check out the options below, which are both included in one €5 ticket. Although neither offers a word of English, the exhibits are fairly straightforward.

**Alpine Museum (Musée Alpin)**—Situated in one of Chamonix's oldest "palaces," this place has good exhibits about Chamonix's evolution from a farming area to one focused on skiing. The museum shows off Chamonix's mountaineering, skiing, and mineralogical history (explanations in French only) and has exhibits on the first Winter Olympics held right here (€5, includes Espace Tairraz, daily 15:00–19:00, 89 avenue Michel Croz, tel. 04 50 53 25 93).

**Espace Tairraz**—This fascinating collection features crystals from the region in every color, shape, and size (€5, includes Alpine Museum, daily 14:00–19:00).

# DAY TRIPS

**A Day in French-Speaking Switzerland**—Plenty of tempting alpine and cultural thrills await just an hour or two away in Switzerland. A road-and-train line sneaks you scenically from Chamonix to the Swiss town of Martigny. While train travelers cross without formalities, drivers are charged a one-time fee of 40 Swiss francs (about €25) for a permit to use Swiss autobahns (valid for one calendar year).

**A Little Italy**—The remote Valle d'Aosta and its historic capital city of Aosta are the finale to a spectacular gondola ride over the Mont Blanc range. The side-trip is worthwhile if you'd like to taste Italy (spaghetti, gelato, and cappuccino), enjoy the town's great evening ambience, or view the ancient ruins in Aosta (often called the "Rome of the North").

Take the spectacular lift (Aiguille du Midi–Helbronner) to Italy, described on page 674. From Helbronner, catch the lift down to La Palud and take the bus to Aosta (hourly, change in Courmayeur). Aosta's train station has connections to anywhere in Italy (usually on slow trains via Turin, about every 2 hours).

For a more down-to-earth experience, you can take the bus from Chamonix to Aosta (€14 one-way, €24 round-trip, reservation required in summer, 5/day July–mid-Sept, 2/day mid-Sept–June). Get schedules at Chamonix's bus station (located at train station, tel. 04 50 53 01 15). For buses using the Mont Blanc tunnel, it's a two-hour trip to Aosta (otherwise it's three hours via Martigny). Drivers can simply drive through the Mont Blanc tunnel (round-trip-€40, one-way-€32, www.tunnelmb.com).

# SLEEPING

**(€1 = about $1.50, country code: 33)**

Reasonable hotels and dorm-like chalets abound in Chamonix with easy parking and quick access from the train station. With the helpful TI, you can find budget accommodations anytime. Outside winter, mid-July to mid-August is most difficult, when some hotels have five-day minimum-stay requirements. Prices tumble off-season (outside July–Aug and Dec–Jan). Many hotels and restaurants are closed in April, June, and November, but you'll still find a room and a meal. If you want a view of Mont Blanc, ask for *côté Mont Blanc* (coat-ay mohn blah). Summertime travelers should seriously consider a night high above in a refuge-hotel.

All hoteliers speak English. Price ranges usually reflect low-to-high season rates. Ask at your hotel about the Chamonix Guest Card, which provides free use of most buses and trains during your stay (see "Getting Around (and Up and Down) the Valley," earlier in this section). The TI can help you book a room—either in person or by email (reservation@chamonix.com).

## Hotels in the City Center

**$$$ Hôtel Gourmets et Italy*** is run by quiet Erique and effervescent Christine, and is a sharp, 40-room place with cozy public spaces, a cool riverfront terrace, balcony views from many of its appealing rooms, and a small pool (standard Db with shower-€80–100, larger Db with bath and Mont Blanc view-€95–125, extra person-€16, closed late April–early June, 2 blocks from casino on Mont Blanc side of river, 96 rue du Lyret, tel. 04 50 53 01 38, fax 04 50 53 46 74, www.hotelgourmets-chamonix.com, hgicham@aol.com).

**$$$ Hôtel Richemond**** is a grand place with a retirement-home feel in its faded-alpine-elegant public spaces. The same family has run this hotel since it was built in 1914, and the rooms are traditional, comfortable, and generally spacious, with period furniture. There's also an outdoor terrace and a game room with a pool table, "flipper" (pinball), and table tennis (Sb-€60–68, Db-€93–108, Tb-€113–136, Qb-€126–150, includes good buffet breakfast, free parking, 228 rue du Docteur Paccard, tel. 04 50 53 08 85, fax 04 50 55 91 69, www.richemond.fr, richemond @wanadoo.fr, Claire and brother Bruno make fine hosts).

**$$$ Hôtel l'Oustalet*** is a modern chalet hotel that makes me feel like I'm in Austria. It's warmly run by two sisters who understand the importance of good service. The place is family-friendly with lots of grass, a pool, and six family suites. All rooms are sharp, with wood paneling, views, and balconies (Sb-€75–115, Db-€106–135, Qb family rooms-€150–195, free parking, near Aiguille du Midi lift at 330 rue du Lyret, tel. 04 50 55 54 99, fax 04 50 55 54 98, www.hotel-oustalet.com, infos @hotel-oustalet.com).

**$$$ Chalet Beauregard,** an upscale *chambre d'hôte,* is a short but steep walk above the TI. It's relaxed and peaceful, with a private garden, table tennis, and swings. Five of its seven cushy rooms have balconies with great views (Sb-€49–89, Db-€69–99, Tb-€89–129, ask about amazing top-floor suite-€135–195, cash only upon arrival or pay with PayPal in advance, may require 4-night minimum stay in summer, includes breakfast, free parking, often closed in May, on road to Le Brévent lift, 182 rue de La Mollard, tel. 04 50 55 86 30, www.chalet-beauregard.com, infos@chalet-beauregard.com, friendly Manuel and Laurence).

**$$ Hôtel de l'Arve**** has a contemporary alpine feel, with 37 comfortable rooms, some right on the Arve River looking up at Mont Blanc. Owners Isabelle and Beatrice, wood accents, fireplace lounge, pool room, pleasant garden, sauna, climbing wall, Internet access, free Wi-Fi, and easy parking add to the appeal. When available, the half-pension option is a good value at €20 extra per person for a buffet breakfast and simple four-course dinner; let them know ahead if you want it (standard Db-€61–88, larger or view Db-€71–103, big view room-€81–118, extra person-€15, breakfast-€10, free parking, around the corner from huge Hôtel Alpina, 60 impasse des

# Chamonix Town

1/4 MILE
400 METERS

**P** PARKING

★ CHAMONIX TOWN CENTER

TO LES PRAZ (HIKE #4) & Switz.

PARAPENTE LANDING

TENNIS COURTS

TO LES PRAZ STN. & SWITZ.

AVE. PLAGE

TO HIKE #2 & #3

HIKE #4

LE BREVENT LIFT

MAISON DE LA MONTAGNE

BEGIN HIKE #5

LES PLANARDS LIFT (LUGE)

LA MOLLARD

RUE MOUSSOUX

PAYOT

RUE DR. PACCARD

RUE VALLOT

CASINO

RUE WHYMPER

AVE. DU BOUCHET N-506

CACHAT LE GEANT

BUS STN.

MICHEL CROZ

CHEMIN CRIST.

MOUILLES

TRAIN STN.

MONTENVERS TRAIN STN.

TO MER DE GLACE

ALLEE

RUE DE LYRET

AVE. AIGUILLE DU MIDI

ROUTE BLANCHE N-506

TO LES BOSSONS

ROUTE PECLES

ARVE RIVER

TO MT BLANC TUNNEL

AIGUILLE DU MIDI LIFT & HIKE #1

TO AIGUILLE DU MIDI & ITALY

DCH

N

1 Hôtel Gourmets et Italy
2 Hôtel Richemond
3 Hôtel l'Oustalet
4 Chalet Beauregard
5 Hôtel de l'Arve
6 Hôtel les Crêtes Blanches
7 Hôtel le Chamonix
8 To Hôtel l'Aiguille du Midi
9 La Calèche & Midnight Express Rest.
10 Le Boccalatte Brasserie
11 Le Bivouac, Le Panier des 4 Saisons & Le Refuge Payot

12 La Cabolée Restaurant
13 L'Impossible Restaurant
14 Le Refuge Payot
15 Bistro des Sports
16 Micro Brasserie de Chamonix (MBC)
17 Super U Grocery
18 Launderettes (2)
19 Summits Parapente (Paragliding)
20 Parc de Loisirs des Planards
21 Alpine Museum
22 Espace Tairraz (Crystals)

THE FRENCH ALPS

Anémones, tel. 04 50 53 02 31, fax 04 50 53 56 92, www.hotelarve
-chamonix.com, contact@hotelarve-chamonix.com).

**$$ Hôtel les Crêtes Blanches**** is a sweet little place wrapped
around a peaceful courtyard (with outdoor tables) just off rue Joseph
Vallot (next to the Super U grocery). Rooms are well-designed
with appealing wood paneling. Most have small balconies and all
come with views of Mont Blanc. A ceramic wood stove and stylish
couches anchor the comfy lounge area (Db-€60–88, Tb-€87–102,
Qb-€100–116, an adorable dollhouse-sized chalet sleeps 6 and
comes with a kitchen for €115–135, 16 impasse du Génépy, tel. 04
50 53 05 62, fax 04 50 53 67 25, www.cretes-blanches.com, cretes
-blanches@wanadoo.fr).

**$$ Hôtel le Chamonix****,** centrally located across from the
TI and above a café, offers red carpets and wood paneling with 16
good-value rooms, but no elevator. The rooms facing Mont Blanc
have great views, are larger and brighter, and have little balconies...
but also attract noise from *le café* below, which closes at 20:00 (standard Db-€55–80, standard Db with Mont Blanc view-€62–90,
Tb-€75–100, Qb-€90–115, no elevator, 11 rue de l'Hôtel de Ville,
tel. 04 50 53 11 07, fax 04 50 53 64 78, www.hotel-le-chamonix
.com, hotel-le-chamonix@wanadoo.fr).

## Near Chamonix

If Chamonix overwhelms you, spend the night in one of the valley's overlooked, lower-profile villages.

**$$ Hôtel l'Aiguille du Midi**** lies in the village of Les
Bossons, about two miles from Chamonix toward Annecy. The
English-speaking Farini family runs this mountain retreat in a
park-like setting, with a swimming pool, tennis court, whirlpool
tub, table tennis, and a laundry room to boot. The alpine-comfort-
able rooms aren't big...and you won't care. The classy restaurant
offers good à la carte and *menu* options (Db-€70–82, Tb-€99,
Qb-€118, these discounted prices guaranteed for Rick Steves read-
ers through 2009, elevator, €23–48 *menus*, easy by train, get off at
Les Bossons, tel. 04 50 53 00 65, fax 04 50 55 93 69, www.hotel
-aiguilledumidi.com, hotel-aiguille-du-midi@wanadoo.fr).

## Refuges and Refuge-Hotels near Chamonix

Chamonix has the answer for hikers who want to sleep high above,
but aren't into packing it all in: refuge-hotels (generally open
mid-June to mid- or late September, depending on snow levels).
Refuge-hotels usually have some private rooms (and dorm rooms),
hot showers down the hall, and restaurants. Reserve in advance
(a few days are generally enough), then pack your small bag for a
memorable night among new international friends. The **Office of
the High Mountain** in Chamonix can explain your options (see

"Chamonix Area Hikes," earlier in this section).

**\$\$ Refuge-Hôtel du Montenvers,** Chamonix's oldest refuge, is a cool experience at the Montenvers train stop. It was built in 1880 as a climbing base for mountain guides before the train went there, so materials had to be gathered from nearby. The five simple wood-cozy rooms and dining room feel as though they haven't been modified since then (half-pension in a double room about €56 per person, €40 per person in dorm room, good showers down the hall, tel. 04 50 53 87 70, fax 04 50 55 38 55, restauration. montenvers@compagniedumontblanc.fr). For directions, see "Chamonix Area Hikes—Hike #1," earlier in this section.

**\$ Refuge-Hôtel La Flégère** hangs on the edge and is also at the lift station. It's simple, but ideally located for hiking to Lac Blanc or Planpraz (3 private rooms with 5 beds, many dorm beds, half-pension-€42 per person, fireplace, cozy bar-café, right at La Flégère lift, tel. 06 03 58 28 14). For directions, see "Chamonix Area Hikes—Hike #2," earlier in this section.

# EATING

You have two basic dining options in Chamonix—cozy, traditional *savoyarde* restaurants serving fondue, raclette, and the like, or big cafés in central locations serving a wide variety of dishes (including regional specialties) that allow you to watch rivers of hikers return from a full day in the mountains. Prices are roughly the same—you choose. If it's a beautiful day, take an outdoor table at a central café; if you're dining inside, go local and consider these places (most are closed between lunch and dinner).

## In the Town Center

**La Calèche** presents delectable regional dishes in a warm, hyperdecorated alpine setting. You'll dine amid antique dolls, cuckoo clocks, copper pots, animal trophies, and more. It's centrally located just off place Balmat. Try the *croziflette*—buckwheat pasta cut into tiny flat squares, baked with cream, onion, and cheese, then topped with cured ham (€23 *menu,* the €28 *menu* is much better, open daily, 18 rue du Docteur Paccard, tel. 04 50 55 94 68). Don't leave without a visit to the WCs.

**Le Boccalatte Brasserie** serves a simple but good-value lunch or dinner with a pleasing atmosphere, a few blocks above the Aiguille du Midi lift. The place is family-friendly with a playful waitstaff. Try the €18 or €28 *menus,* or choose from a large selection of local specialties, big €10 salads, and 20 kinds of beer. It's run by English-speaking Thierry, a friendly Alsatian (daily 12:00–22:00, 59 avenue de l'Aiguille du Midi, tel. 04 50 53 52 14).

**Le Bivouac** is an unassuming, shoebox-sized place where you'll eat cheaply and well in an informal setting. It's a family affair run by gregarious owner-chef Jean-Guy (who should sing opera), along with son Chris and sweet Cloé. Salads are a meal in themselves, and the *plats* are tasty. Ask *le chef*'s opinion—he likes his souvlaki and *roulée savoyarde* (266 rue Docteur Paccard, tel. 04 50 53 34 08).

**Le Panier des 4 Saisons** is where locals go for traditional French (not local) cuisine like *Grand-mère* used to make. The place is charmingly elegant, and deserves its good reputation (*menus* from €24, located on the first floor in Galerie Blanc Neige at 266 rue Docteur Paccard, tel. & fax 04 50 53 98 77).

*Sandwiches:* **Midnight Express** serves fine sandwiches until late and has a few outside tables across from the recommended La Calèche restaurant. Try a *pain rond-rustique* (round-bread rustic sandwich), served hot *(chaud)* or cold *(froid)*.

## Away from the Pedestrian Center

These eateries, each a 10-minute walk from Chamonix's center, merit the detour if they strike your fancy.

**La Cabolée,** next to La Brévent station, is a small, hip eatery with great omelets and a wonderful view from its outdoor tables. This is a Slow Food place—everything is cooked fresh—so be patient if the restaurant is full and the service feels slow (daily 10:00–14:00 & 18:00–22:00, may be closed mid-May–mid-June and Nov, tel. 04 50 55 97 28).

**L'Impossible,** housed in a beautiful 150-year-old farmhouse, mixes alpine coziness with soft elegance, and is a fine bet for traditional alpine cuisine (*menus* from €23, €18 gourmet fondue, open daily, 5-min walk from Aiguille du Midi lift on route des Pélerins, tel. 04 50 53 20 36).

*Après Hike:* The **Bistro des Sports** is where locals hang their ice picks after a hard day in the mountains. Drinks are cheap, the crowd is loud, and the ambience works (daily until late, 176 rue Joseph Vallot). **Micro Brasserie de Chamonix,** a knock-off of the microbrew pubs back home, is a cool place to hang out after a day of paragliding or rappelling. It's not central, across from the *parapente* landing strip (see "Chamonix Area Hikes—Hike #5," earlier in this section), but it's reasonable and lively. Come here for a homemade brew, a glass of wine, or a pub dinner, and expect crowds of twenty- and thirtysomethings (daily 16:00–1:00 in the morning, 350 route du Bouchet, look for *MBC* sign, tel. 04 50 53 61 59).

# TRANSPORTATION CONNECTIONS

Bus and train service to Chamonix is surprisingly good. You'll find helpful bus and train information desks at the train station. Some train routes pass through Switzerland to reach Chamonix (such as from Paris and Colmar) and require a supplement if you have a France-only railpass. You can avoid passing through Switzerland if you plan ahead.

**From Chamonix by Train to: Annecy** (8/day, 2.5 hrs, change in St. Gervais), **Beaune** and **Dijon** (7/day, 6–7 hrs, changes in St. Gervais and Lyon), **Nice** (4/day, 10 hrs, change in St. Gervais and Lyon), **Arles** (5/day, 7–8 hrs, change in St. Gervais and Lyon), **Paris'** Gare de Lyon (8/day, daily July–Aug and Dec–April, Fri–Sun only May–June and Sept–Nov, may be more frequent in May, 6–8 hrs, some change in Switzerland), **Martigny, Switzerland** (nearly hourly, 2 hrs, scenic trip), **Geneva, Switzerland** and its airport (roughly hourly, 3–4 hrs, two changes).

**From Chamonix by Bus and Shuttle:** Airport shuttles provide fast service from €25 per person to the city center and airport in **Geneva,** Switzerland (3/day, 2 hrs, www.chamonixshuttles .com, or www.geneva-chamonix-transfers.com). You can also take the bus to **Courmayeur** via Mont Blanc tunnel, with connections to Aosta and Milan (2/day, 45 min). Long-distance buses depart from the train station, not from local bus stops. Get information at the TI or at the bus station (tel. 04 50 78 05 33).

**To Italy:** See "Day Trips—A Little Italy," page 684.

# BURGUNDY

The rolling hills of Burgundy gave birth to superior wine, fine cuisine, spicy mustard, and a sublime countryside. This deceptively peaceful region witnessed Julius Caesar's defeat of the Gauls, then saw the Abbey of Cluny rise from the ashes of the Roman Empire to vie with Rome for religious influence in the 12th century. Burgundy's last hurrah came in the 15th century, when its powerful dukes controlled an immense area stretching north to Holland.

Today, bucolic Burgundy runs from about Auxerre in the north to near Lyon in the south, and it's crisscrossed with canals and dotted with quiet farming villages. It's also the transportation funnel for eastern France and makes a convenient stopover for travelers (car or train), with quick access north to Paris or Alsace, east to the Alps, and south to Provence.

Traditions are strong here. Only a small part of Burgundy is covered by vineyards, but grapes are what they do best. The white cows you see everywhere are Charolais. France's best beef ends up in *bœuf bourguignon*. This is a calm, cultivated, and serene region, where nature is as sophisticated as the people. If you're looking for quintessential French culture, you'll find it in Burgundy.

## Planning Your Time

With limited time, stay in or near Beaune. It's conveniently located for touring; plan on a half-day in Beaune and a half-day for the vineyards and countryside. With a full day, spend the morning in Beaune and the afternoon exploring the surrounding vineyards and wine villages (good by bike, car, or minibus tour). If you have a car (cheap rentals are available), or strong legs and a bike, the best way to spend your afternoon is by following my scenic vineyard drive to La Rochepot (see page 716).

To explore off-the-beaten-path Burgundy, visit unspoiled Semur-en-Auxois and France's best-preserved medieval abbey complex at Fontenay (they're on the way to Paris, or doable as a long day trip from Beaune). The magnificent church at Vézelay is harder to reach, and is best done as a day-trip from Semur-en-Auxois, or en route to Paris or the Loire Valley. If you're connecting Burgundy with the Loire, don't miss the medieval castle construction at Guédelon. And if you're driving between Beaune and Lyon (see next chapter), take the detour to adorable Brancion and once-powerful Cluny.

## Getting Around Burgundy

Trains link Beaune with Dijon to the north and Lyon to the south. Ten buses per day cruise between vineyards on N-74, linking Dijon, Beaune, and Chalon-sur-Saône (the bus detours into some wine villages, and serves others from N-74—see page 713). Bikes, minibus tours, and short taxi rides get non-drivers from Beaune into the countryside. Buses connect Semur-en-Auxois with the Dijon and Montbard train stations.

## Cuisine Scene in Burgundy

Arrive hungry. Considered by many to be France's best, Burgundian cuisine is peasant cooking elevated to an art, and entire lives are spent debating the best restaurants and bistros.

Several classic dishes were born in Burgundy: *escargots de Bourgogne* (snails served sizzling hot in garlic butter), *bœuf bourguignon* (beef simmered for hours in red wine with onions and mushrooms), *coq au vin* (rooster stewed in red wine), and *œufs en meurette* (poached eggs in a red wine sauce, often served on a large crouton), as well as the famous Dijon mustards. Look also for *jambon persillé* (cold ham layered in a garlic-parsley gelatin), *pain d'épices* (spice bread), and *gougères* (light, puffy cheese pastries). Native cheeses are Époisses and Langres (both mushy and great) and my favorite, Montrachet (a tasty goat cheese). *Crème de cassis* (black currant liqueur) is another Burgundian specialty; look for it in desserts and snazzy drinks (try a *kir*).

Remember, restaurants serve only during lunch (11:30–14:00) and dinner (19:00–21:00, later in bigger cities); some cafés serve food throughout the day.

## Burgundy's Wines

Along with Bordeaux, Burgundy is why France is famous for wine. From Chablis to Beaujolais, you'll find great fruity reds, dry whites, and crisp rosés. The three key grapes are Chardonnay (dry white wines), Pinot Noir (medium-bodied red wines), and Gamay (light, fruity red wines, such as Beaujolais). Every village produces its own distinctive wine, from Chablis to Meursault to Chassagne-Montrachet. Road maps read like fine-wine lists. If the wine village has a hyphenated name, the latter half of its name often comes from the town's most important vineyard (e.g., Gevrey-Chambertin, Aloxe-Corton, and Vosne-Romanée). Look for *Dégustation Gratuite* (free tasting) signs, and prepare for serious wine-tasting—and steep prices, if you're not careful. For a more easygoing tasting, head for the hills: The less prestigious Hautes-Côtes (upper slopes) produce some terrific, inexpensive, and overlooked wines. The least expensive (but still tasty) wines are *Bourgogne* and *Passetoutgrain* (both red), and whites from the Mâcon and Chalon areas. If you like rosé, try Marsannay, considered one of France's best. For tips on tasting, see "French Wine-Tasting 101" on page 30, and for good places to taste, try my suggestions.

# Beaune

You'll feel comfortable right away in this prosperous and popular little wine capital, where life centers on the production and consumption of the prestigious, expensive Côte d'Or wines. *Côte d'Or* means "golden hillside," and such hillsides are a spectacle to enjoy in late October as the leaves turn.

Medieval monks and powerful dukes of Burgundy laid the groundwork that established this town's prosperity. The monks cultivated wine and cheese, while the dukes cultivated wealth. The townscape of Beaune is as French as you'll find anywhere. The ring road keeps out the traffic, so, rather than parking spots, the town squares host fountains, gardens, carousels, and markets. Today, one of the world's most important wine auctions takes place here during the third weekend of November.

## ORIENTATION

Beaune is compact (pop. 25,000), with a handful of interesting monuments and vineyards on its doorstep. Limit your Beaune ramblings to the town center, lassoed within its medieval walls and circled by a one-way ring road, and leave time to stroll into the vineyards. All roads and activities converge on the perfectly French square, place Carnot (as do Wednesday and Saturday markets). Beaune is quiet on Sundays and Monday mornings.

### Tourist Information

The TI is located across from the post office on the ring road's southeastern corner (look for *Porte Marie de Bourgogne* on the red banner (daily 9:00–18:00, tel. 03 80 26 21 30, www.beaune-tourisme .com). The TI has extensive information on wine-tasting in and near Beaune, a room-finding service, a list of *chambres d'hôte*, and bus

## Beaune's Best Wine and Food Stores

Beaune overflows with wine boutiques eager to convince you that their wines are best. Here are a few to look for.

The wine shop **Denis Perret** has a good selection in all price ranges and a helpful, English-speaking staff managed by friendly owner Alain. If you've tasted a wine elsewhere that you like, they can usually find a less costly bottle with similar qualities. They can chill a white for your picnic (Mon–Sat 9:00–12:00 & 14:00–19:00, closed Sun, 40 place Carnot, tel. 03 80 22 35 47, www.denisperret.fr).

For an exquisite selection of fruit liquors (such as crème de cassis), fruit syrups, and Burgundian brandy, find **Védrenne** at 28 rue Carnot (closed Sun).

The low-key wine hardware store **Comptoir Viticole** is good for wine paraphernalia (Mon–Sat 8:00–12:45 & 13:45–19:00, closed Sun, where rue d'Alsace runs into place Carnot).

For food, **Alain Hess** beautifully displays fine cheeses, mustards, and other gourmet food products (7 place Carnot). A few doors down, welcoming **Mulot-Petitjean Pain d'Epices** shows off exquisite packages of this tasty and local spice bread, also handy as gifts (1 place Carnot).

schedules. The town model outside the TI merits your attention.

Ambitious sightseers can benefit by buying the **Pass Beaune,** which can get you a discount at most sights listed in this chapter (including Hôtel Dieu, Wine Museum, Abbey of Fontenay, Bacchus Wine Tours, Abbey of Cluny, and most major wine cellars in Beaune). The catch: You're technically pre-paying for discounted admission to individual sights...so once you buy the pass, you're committed to visiting those attractions. Buy this pass only if your plans are set in stone (5 percent off 2 sights, 10 percent off 3 sights, 15 percent off 4 or more sights; buy at the TI).

## Arrival in Beaune

**By Train:** To reach the city center from the train station (no baggage storage), walk straight out of the station up avenue du 8 Septembre, cross the busy ring road, and continue up rue du Château. Follow it as it angles left and pass the mural, veering right onto rue des Tonneliers. A left on rue de l'Enfants leads to Beaune's pedestrian zone and place Carnot.

**By Bus:** Beaune has no bus station—only several stops along the ring road. Ask the driver for *le Centre-Ville.* The Jules Ferry (zhul fair-ee) stop is closest to the train station; the Clemenceau stop is best for visiting Château de la Rochepot (described under "The Beaune Region," later in this chapter). Bus #44 connects Beaune with other wine villages along the famous Route du Vin, and runs to Dijon's train station (about 6/day, bus info: tel. 03 80 42 11 00).

**By Car:** Follow *Centre-Ville* signs to the ring road. Once on the ring road, turn right at the first signal after the modern post office (rue d'Alsace), and park for free a block away in place Madeleine. If the lot is full—which it often is on market days—look for spaces on surrounding streets or along the ring road.

## Helpful Hints

**Market Days:** Beaune hosts a smashing Saturday market and a little Wednesday market on its central squares (both until 12:30). The Saturday market animates the entire town and is worth planning ahead for (for more on market days, see the sidebar on page 26). Locals watch the action from the Baltard Café on place de la Halle, then have lunch at an outdoor café (many good choices—see my "Eating" listings, later in this section, for ideas—but sit down by 12:30 or forget it).

**Supermarket: Supermarché Casino** has a great selection, a deli, and fair prices (Mon–Sat 8:30–20:00, closed Sun, through the arch off place Madeleine).

**Internet Access:** The **Baltard Café,** across from the main TI, has pricey Internet access and Wi-Fi (€1/15 min, computer terminals upstairs, 14 place de la Halle, tel. 03 80 24 21 86).

**Laundry:** Beaune's two launderettes are both open daily 7:00–21:00. One is in the town center at 65 rue Lorraine; the other is between the train station and place Madeleine at 17–19 rue du Faubourg St. Jean.

**Bike Rental:** See "Getting Around the Beaune Region," on page 713, for information.

**Taxi:** Call Gerard Rebillard for Beaune's friendliest taxi (cabbies speak English, tel. 06 11 83 06 10, allo-beaune.taxi@liberty surf.fr). For other taxis, call 06 09 35 63 12 or 03 80 24 21 73.

**Car Rental: ADA** is cheap and closest to the train station (allow €50/day for a small car with 100 kilometers/62 miles free, Mon–Sat 8:00–12:00 & 14:00–18:00, closed Sun, 26 avenue 8 Septembre, tel. 03 80 22 72 90). **Avis** is five blocks away on the ring road, near place Madeleine (hours vary, but generally Mon–Sat 9:00–13:00 & 14:00–17:30, closed Sun, 48 bis Jules Ferry, tel. 03 80 24 96 46).

**Best Souvenir Shopping:** The **Athenaeum** has a great variety of souvenirs, including wine and cooking books in English, with a great children's section upstairs (daily 10:00–19:00, across from Hôtel Dieu at 7 rue de l'Hôtel Dieu). And you won't find a bookstore with a better wine bar.

# TOURS

**Tourist Train**—A TGV-esque little train will show you Beaune and nearby vineyards (€5, runs April–Oct 11:00–17:00, almost hourly departures from near Hôtel Dieu, no morning trips on Wed and Sat market days, 40 min).

**Local Guides**—You have two great choices. For Beaune and nearby, consider Canadian **Sarah Bird**—she's married to a local and knows Beaune thoroughly. She can do tours of Beaune only, or can include a sample of the vineyards and countryside, by bike, foot, or car (€100/90 min, €250/half-day). She and her husband also rent bikes (see "Bourgogne Randonnées" on page 713).

For tours that focus on vineyards, **Colette Barbier,** a professor of gastronomy and wines at the University of Dijon, is an engaging guide and fluent in English. She knows Burgundy like a local—because she is one (her family has lived in the region for 250 years). Book well in advance, though last-minute requests sometimes work out (€195/half-day, €350/day, tel. & fax 03 80 23 94 34, mobile 06 80 57 47 40, www.burgundy-guide.com, cobatour@aol.com).

# SIGHTS

## ▲▲▲Hôtel Dieu

This medieval charity hospital is now a museum. The Hundred Years' War and the plague called the Black Death devastated Beaune, leaving three-quarters of its population destitute. Nicholas Rolin, chancellor of Burgundy (enriched, in part, by his power to collect taxes), had to do something for "his people" (or, more likely, was getting old and wanted to close out his life on a philanthropic, rather than a greedy, note). So, in 1443, Rolin paid to build this hospital. It was completed in just eight years.

**Cost, Hours, Location:** €6, daily April–mid-Nov 9:00–18:30, mid-Nov–March 9:00–11:30 & 14:00–17:30, last ticket sold one hour before closing. It's right in the center of Beaune, dominating place de la Halle (across from the TI).

**❷ Self-Guided Tour:** While the English flier and English descriptions throughout are helpful, this self-guided tour gives your visit more meaning. Tour the rooms, which circle the courtyard in a clockwise direction, starting from near the turnstile.

**Courtyard of Honor:** Honor meant power, and this was all about showing off. While the exterior of the hospital and the town side of the courtyard are less ostentatious (because there was no point in attracting the pesky 15th-century brigands who looted whatever looked most rewarding), the inner rooftop is dazzling. The colorful glazed tile roof established what became a style recognized in France as typically "Burgundian." The tiles, which

**BURGUNDY**

last 300 years, are fired three times: once to harden, then to burn in the color, and finally for the glaze. They were redone in 1902. The building is lacy Flamboyant Gothic with lots of decor—and more weathervanes than any other building in France.

**Paupers' Ward:** This grandest room of the hospital was the ward for the poorest patients. The vault, typical of big medieval rooms, was constructed like the hull of a ship. The screen separates the ward from the chapel. Every three hours, the door was opened, and patients could experience Mass from their beds. Study the ceiling. Crossbeams are held by the mouths of creatively carved monsters—each mouth is stretched realistically, and each face has individual characteristics. Between the crossbars are busts of real 15th-century townsfolk—leading citizens, with animals humorously indicating their foibles (e.g., a round-faced glutton next to a pig). This room housed patients until 1949 (see painting, middle left). During epidemics, there were two to a bed.

The carved wooden statue over the door shows a bound Christ—demonstrating graphically to patients that their savior suffered and was able to empathize with their ordeal. Its realism shows that Gothic art had moved beyond the stiff formality of Romanesque carving. Behind the little window, next to the statue, was the nuns' dorm. The sisters would check on patients from here. Notice the scrawny candleholder; if a patient died in the night, the candle would be extinguished. Study the glass display cases near the beds. Rolin, who believed every patient deserved dignity, provided each patient with a pewter jug, mug, bowl, and plate. But the ward didn't get heat until the 19th century (notice the heating grates on the floor).

**Chapel:** The hospice was not a place of hope. People came here to die. Care was more for the soul than the body. (Local guides are routinely instructed in writing by American tour companies not to use the word "hospice," because it turns off their clients. But this was a hospice, plain and simple, and back then, death was apparently less disturbing.) The stained glass shows Nicolas Rolin (lower left) and his wife, Guigone (lower right)—dressed as a nun to show her devotion. Nicolas' feudal superior, the Duke of Burgundy, is portrayed above him. Notice the action on Golgotha. As Jesus is crucified, the souls of the two criminals crucified with him (portrayed as miniature naked humans) are being snatched up—one by an angel and the other by a red devil. You're standing on tiles with the love symbol (or "gallant device") designed by Nicolas and Guigone to celebrate their

BURGUNDY

# Beaune

1. Hôtel le Cep
2. Hôtel Athanor
3. Hôtel des Remparts
4. Hôtel Ibis
5. To Hôtel de France
6. Hôtel La Villa Fleurie
7. Hôtel de la Paix
8. L'Auberge Bourguignonne Rooms
9. Hôtel Rousseau
10. Les Jardins de Loïs B&B
11. To Hôtels Villa Louise & le Home
12. To Other Chambres d'Hôte
13. Launderettes (2)
14. Bike Rental
15. Bus to Pommard & La Rochepot
16. ADA Car Rental
17. Avis Car Rental
18. Internet Café
19. Museum of the Wine of Burgundy
20. Mustard Mill
21. Athenaeum Bookstore
22. Tourist Train Departures

///// Pedestrian Zone
▥ Stairs
↔ ↑ Ramparts Walk, One-Way
P Parking

\* Not to scale—Place Madeleine to Hôtel Dieu is a 10 min. walk

BURGUNDY

TO ⑪, N-74, SAVIGNY + DIJON

RUE FAUBOURG ST. NICHOLAS →

TO TRAIN STATION

AVE 8 SEPT.

BLVD. COLBERT

BLVD. JOFFRE

R. SPULLER

CHATEAU

RUE ROUSSEAU

RUE LORRAINE

R. COLLEGE

RUE THIERS

STE. MARG.

R. MAREY

PLACE MONGE

RUE TONNELIERS

RUE TRIBUNAL

RUE THIERS

FAUB. ST. JEAN

BLVD. FERRY

PLACE MADELEINE

P. JOIGNEUX

R. FAUB. MADELEINE

SUPER-MARKET

R. FAUB.

RUE D'ALSACE

PLACE CARNOT

HOTEL-DIEU

RUE LOUIS VERY

HOTEL DIEU

NOTRE DAME

AVE REPUBLIQUE

RUE CLOUTIER

RUE PARADIS

AVE GARDIN

ST. MART

R. MAUROUX

START

BLVD. ST. JACQUES

POST

TO A-6 FREEWAY

BLVD. BRET.

RUE FAUB. BRET.

BLVD. CLEMENCEAU

AVE JAFFELIN

PARK DE LA BOUZAISE + VINEYARDS

TO CHATEAUNEUF-EN-AUXOIS + BLIGNY

TO D-973 + N-74 LA ROCHEPOT, POMMARD, CHALONS-SUR-SAONE + ⑫

DCH

love (as noble couples often did). The letters N and G are entwined in an oak branch, meaning that their love was strong. The word *seule* ("only one") and the lone star declare that Guigone is the only star in Nicolas' cosmos.

**St. Hugue Ward:** In the 17th century, this smaller ward was established for wealthy patients. They were more likely to survive, and the decor displays themes of hope, rather than resignation: The series of Baroque paintings lining the walls show the biblical miracles that Jesus performed. As the wealthy would lie in their beds, they'd stare at the ceiling—a painting with the bottom of an angel's foot, surrounded by the sick waiting to be healed by Jesus in his scarlet robe. The syringes in the display case are as delicate as caulking guns.

**St. Nicolas Room:** Originally part of the kitchen, this room now exhibits more tools of the doctoring trade (amputation saws, pans for blood-letting, and so on). Notice the nearby hatch in the floor, showing the river running below; the hole provided a primitive but convenient disposal system.

**Kitchen:** The kitchen display here shows a 16th-century rotisserie. When fully wound, the cute robot would crank away, and the spit would spin slowly for 45 minutes. The 19th-century stove provided running hot water, which spewed from the beaks of swans.

**Pharmacy:** The nuns grew herbs out back, and strange and wondrous concoctions were stored in pottery jars. The biggest jar (by the window) was for *theriaca* ("panacea"). The most commonly used medicine back then, it was a syrup of herbs, wine, and opium.

**St. Louis Ward:** A maternity ward until 1969, this room is lined with fine 16th- and 17th-century tapestries illustrating mostly Old Testament stories. Dukes traveled with tapestries to cozy up the humble places they stayed in while on the road. The 16th-century pieces have better colors, but inferior perspective. (The most precious tapestries here are from the 15th century and are displayed in the next room, where everyone is enthralled by the great van der Weyden painting.)

**Roger van der Weyden's *Last Judgment*:** This exquisite painting, the treasure of the Hôtel Dieu, was commissioned by Rolin in 1450 for the altar of the Paupers' Ward. He spared no cost, hiring the leading Flemish artist of his time. The entire altarpiece survives. The back side (on right wall) was sliced off so everything could be viewed at the same time. The painting is full of symbolism. Christ presides over Judgment Day. The lily is mercy, the sword is judgment, the rainbow promises salvation, and the jeweled globe at Jesus' feet symbolizes the universality of Christianity's message. As four angels blow their trumpets, St. Michael the archangel—very much in control—determines which souls are heavy with sin. Mary and the apostles pray for the souls of the dead as they emerge from their graves. But notice how both Michael and Jesus are expressionless—at this point, the cries of the damned and their loved ones are useless. In the back row are real people of the day.

The intricate detail, painted with a three-haired brush, is typical of Flemish art. While Renaissance artists employed mathematical tricks of perspective, these artists captured a sense of reality by painting minute detail upon detail. Stare at Michael's robe and wings. Check out John's delicate feet and hands. Study the faces of the damned; you can almost hear the gnashing of teeth. The feet of the damned show the pull of a terrible force. On the far left, notice those happily entering the pearly gates. On the far right—it's the flames of hell (no, this has nothing to do with politics).

Except for Sundays and holidays, the painting was kept closed and people saw only the panels that now hang on the right wall: Nicolas and Guigone piously at the feet of St. Sebastian—invoked to fight the plague—and St. Anthony, whom patients called upon for help in combating burning skin diseases.

## More Sights in Beaune

**Collégiale Notre-Dame**—Built in the 12th and 13th centuries, Beaune's cathedral was a "daughter of Cluny" (built in the style of the Cluny Abbey, described on page 735). Except for the 14th-century Gothic front porch addition, it's a fine example of Cluny-style Romanesque architecture. Enter to see the 15th-century tapestries (behind the altar), a variety of stained glass, and what's left of frescoes depicting the life of Lazarus (tapestry open daily 9:30–12:30 & 14:00–19:00).

To get to the Museum of Wine (listed below) from here, walk 30 steps straight out of the cathedral, turn left down a cobbled alley (rue d'Enfer, or "Hell Street"—named for the fires of the Duke's kitchens once located on this street), keep left, and enter the courtyard of Hôtel des Ducs.

**Museum of the Wine of Burgundy (Musée du Vin de Bourgogne)**—From this folk-wine museum, which fills the old residence of the Dukes of Burgundy, it's clear that the history and culture of Burgundy and its wine were fermented in the same bottle. Wander into the free courtyard for a look at the striking palace, antique wine presses (in the *cuverie*, or vatting shed; good English explanations), and a concrete model of Beaune's 15th-century street plan (a good chance to understand the town's impressive fortified wall). Inside the museum, you'll see a model of the region, with tools, costumes, and scenes of Burgundian wine history—but no tasting. English explanations are in each room (€5.40, ticket also includes the Musée des Beaux-Arts et Musée Marey art museum; April–Nov daily 9:30–18:00; Dec–March Wed–Mon 9:30–17:00, closed Tue; tel. 03 80 22 08 19).

**BURGUNDY**

**Cave des Aromes**—In the summer months, an engaging exhibit on the sense of smell awaits at Beaune's Chambre de Commerce. You'll sniff glass containers holding a great range of aromas and try to associate these aromas with those you find in wine. It's a fun place to drop in and sniff (free, July–early Sept daily 10:00–12:30 & 14:00–18:00, closed mid-Sept–June, on rue Vergnette de la Motte, near where rue d'Alsace meets place Carnot).

**The Mustard Mill (La Moutarderie Fallot)**—The last of the independent mustard mills in Burgundy opens its doors for bilingual guided tours in French and English. The tour is pricey (€10), yet informative—you'll learn why Burgundy was the birthplace of mustard (it's about wine juice), and where they get their grains today (Canada)—but it takes over an hour to explain what could be done in half that time. Still, for mustard enthusiasts, it's well-presented—you'll see a short film, learn about the key machines used in processing mustard (with the help of audioguides), and finish with a mustard tasting (€10, open Mon–Sat with tours at 10:00 and 11:30, additional tours at 15:30 and 17:00 July–Aug, closed Sun, call TI to reserve or book online, across ring road in the appropriately yellow building at 31 rue du Faubourg Bretonniere, www.fallot.com).

**Ramparts Walk, Parc de la Bouzaise, and Vineyards**—Stroll above Beaune along its 13th-century wall to get a sense of its once-commanding medieval defenses, then wander into nearby vineyards. Most of the rampart is accessible from inside the town, but much has melted into peaceful residential lanes. Walk out rue Maufoux past Hôtel le Cep, and find the ramp leading to the ramparts (Remparts des Dames) on the right. Wander north along the fortification to the next street (avenue de la République), drop down and turn left, and cross the ring road and leave town, following the same stream that runs under the Hôtel Dieu for three blocks to the park. The vineyards are behind the park, with narrow lanes, paths, and great early-morning and sunset views (walkers need 15 min from Beaune's center to reach the vineyards; drivers need only about 2 min).

# WINE-TASTING

## In Beaune

Countless opportunities exist for you to learn the fine points of Burgundy's wines. Shops everywhere offer free, informal, and informative tastings (with the expectation that you'll buy at least one bottle). For tips on wine-tasting, see "French Wine-Tasting 101," page 30.

A few large cellars *(caves)* charge an entry fee, allowing you to taste a variety of wines (with less expectation that you'll buy). Most of these *caves* offer some form of introduction or self-guided tour (see also "Minibus and Walking Tours of Vineyards near Beaune," page 706). Don't mind the mossy ceilings. Many cellars have spent centuries growing this "angel's hair"—the result of humidity created by the evaporation of the wines stored there.

Here are a few good places to learn about Burgundy wines in Beaune.

**Bouchard Aîné**—This place has been in business since 1753, and offers the best traditional cellar tour and introduction to wine-tasting, with a well-done tour highlighting the five senses. You'll stop at several stations to taste as you visit the cellars, and learn about why each sense matters when it comes to wine (€9.50, daily bilingual tours usually at 10:30, 11:30, 14:30, 15:30, 16:30, and 17:30, on the ring road at 4 boulevard Maréchal Foch, tel. 03 80 24 06 66, www.bouchard-aine.fr, magasin@bouchard-aine.fr).

**Domaine Lois Dufouleur**—Welcoming Philippe and Anne-Marie add a personal touch at this beautiful, family-run cellar, and are happy to teach you about their wines (€8 for 4 wines, call ahead for easy-to-get appointment, 8 boulevard Bretonnière, tel. 03 80 22 41 97, mobile 06 73 85 11 06; their B&B, Les Jardins de Loïs, is listed under "Sleeping," later in this section).

**Sensation Vin**—The short, relaxed, and informative wine classes here provide a terrific introduction to Burgundy wines. You'll gather around a small counter in the comfortable wine bar/classroom and learn while you taste. Since the owners do not make wine, you'll get an objective education (with blind tastings) and sample from a variety of producers. While you can pop in anytime, it's best to call ahead to arrange a class/tasting (€9 for 4 wines in 30-min class, €19 for 6 wines and more info in 60-min class, €35 for 12 wines in 2-hour class—aspirin provided; 2-person minimum, daily 10:00–19:00, near Collégiale Notre-Dame at 1 rue d'Enfer, tel. 03 80 22 17 57, www.sensation-vin.com, contact @sensation-vin.com).

## Outside of Beaune

The TI has a long list of area vintners. The famous Route des Grands Crus that connects Burgundy's most prestigious wine villages between Aloxe-Corton and Nuits St. Georges is disappointing, as you're forced onto unappealing N-74. North of Vougeot, the route improves (locals call this section the "Champs-Elysées of Burgundy"). But I find the beautiful routes connecting villages between Beaune and La Rochepot and south to Santenay more easygoing and enjoyable (for example, Monthelie, Nantoux, St. Romain, and St. Aubin are all off the famous path and offer ample tastings).

I've listed a few favorites below. Taxis are a practical way to sample village life and prowl the vineyards. (La Cave de Pommard,

# Burgundian Wine Quality, 1999-2007

**1999** This is an outstanding vintage, especially for reds, which are supple and easy to drink now, and for the next several years.

**2000** This year is a less impressive vintage than the previous two years; reds should be consumed soon, as they lack concentration for aging purposes. Whites are much better.

**2001** A difficult growing season, with rain and a late frost, producing reds that are thinner, less consistent, and more tannic than in previous years. Whites fared much better.

**2002** Called the "vintage of the decade" by some, the reds have recently been released. The whites are excellent, with good structure, balance, and pure, clean fruit flavors.

**2003** A most unusual year due to the extreme summer heat. The harvest was a month early, so the grapes were small, with thick skins, and produced only about half the usual yield. The reds are deeper in color and taste very different from usual Pinot Noirs. All wines need to be drunk sooner—the average time you can keep this year's vintage is about half the normal (10 years at most for reds; whites should be consumed right away).

**2004** A lousy summer (rain, hail, and wind) but a brilliant September (three weeks of bright sunshine). The good

just two miles from Beaune, is the closest place that I describe.) Transco bus #44 serves Pommard (4/day, 5 min) and Puligny Montrachet (4/day, 20 min) from Beaune (Beaune TI has schedules, only afternoon buses work). Note that at free tastings, you're expected to buy a bottle or two, unless you're with a group tour.

**Caveau de Montrachet**—This wine bar–like tasting room, 10 minutes south of Beaune in Puligny Montrachet (pool-ee-nee mohnt-rah-shay) on the scenic route to Château de la Rochepot (see driving tips on page 716), represents many local white-wine vintners. They offer a great selection from this area that's known as *the* king of white wines (these kings are pricey but worth it). Knowledgeable Julien is happy to answer your every question (€7 for 4 wines, free if you buy 6 bottles; March–Oct daily 9:30–12:00 & 14:00–19:00; Nov–Feb Tue–Sat 10:00–12:00 & 15:00–18:00, closed Mon; tel. 03 80 21 96 78). Transco bus #44 from Beaune stops near the *cave*.

**Domaines d'Aloxe Corton**—Here you can sample from eight makers of the famous Aloxe-Corton; prices are affordable, and the *domaines* produced reds that are very fruity, clean, supple, and "flattering" (according to my friend). They can be drunk and appreciated early, though they will last a long time. The whites are excellent, with a precise acidity giving them the freshness and pure fruitiness of a great vintage.

**2005** Has the makings of a great vintage: The harvest was healthy and balanced, with great natural sugar. A local magazine called 2005 "the vintage of dreams." The reds are superb—rich, plain, concentrated, full-bodied, and intense. They will age magnificently. The whites may be a little less impressive, but are still good.

**2006** Challenged even the most experienced winemakers with capricious weather that didn't allow an idle moment in the vineyards or the cellar. The whites look to be of high quality with good consistency from Chablis to Mâcon. Supple and fresh, they are already fruity with consider-able richness. The reds are excellent across the board, with beautiful and intense color. Some are delicate and elegant, while others are robust and full-bodied. Their aromas vary from red fruits to cherry, spices, and cocoa.

**2007** A hot spring, combined with the worst Burgundian sum-mer in 30 years, meant a light vintage for the reds—so drink them sooner rather than later. Whites will probably be subpar as well, so you may want to skip this vintage.

BURGUNDY

easygoing staff speaks enough English (small fee for tasting, free if you buy 2 bottles, Thu–Mon 10:00–13:00 & 15:00–19:00, usually closed Tue–Wed, tel. 03 80 26 49 85). You'll find the *caveau* a few steps from the church on the little square in Aloxe-Corton. For directions on reaching this by car or bike, see "Bike (or Drive) the Vineyards" under "The Beaune Region," later in this chapter.

**La Cave de Pommard**—A short drive (or a level two-mile bike ride) from Beaune leads to this good cellar in Pommard (on the way to or from Château de la Rochepot—see driving tips on page 716). The ambience is good, tastings are free and easy-going, and the prices are reasonable (bottles from €5–65, most €15–20). The young staff speaks English well enough and tries hard. From Beaune's ring road, follow signs for *Chalon-sur-Saône*, then *Autun*, to reach Pommard. The cellars are on the right, just after the Château de Pommard's long wall; park in the village and walk back (free, daily 10:00–19:00, ask to visit the small *caves* below, 3 route de Beaune, tel. 03 80 24 99 00, www.cavede pommard.com).

**Minibus and Walking Tours of Vineyards near Beaune**—**Bacchus Wine Tours** offers minibus tours of the villages and vineyards around Beaune. These English-speaking tours get you into the countryside and smaller wineries, though you won't do much tasting (generally one tasting per tour). There are three two-hour minivan itineraries (€36–42, tour #2 is best for beginners, tours depart from TI generally at 12:00, 14:30, and 17:00, tel. 03 80 24 79 12, www.burgundy-tourism-safaritours.com, or call TI to reserve). Ask about their new walking tours. **Transco** buses also run from Beaune through or near many of the great wine villages (see "Getting Around the Beaune Region," page 713).

# SLEEPING

## In the Center of Beaune

**$$$ Hôtel le Cep\*\*\*\*** is the venerable place to stay in Beaune, if you have the means. Buried in the town center, this historic building comes with fine public spaces inside and out, and 62 gorgeous wood-beamed and traditionally decorated rooms in all sizes (standard Db-€175, deluxe Db-€215, suites-€255–500, continental breakfast-€21, air-con, king-size beds, Internet access and Wi-Fi, fitness center, parking-€15/day, 27 rue Maufoux, tel. 03 80 22 35 48, fax 03 80 22 76 80, www.hotel-cep-beaune.com, resa@hotel-cep-beaune.com).

**$$$ Hôtel Athanor\*\*\*** charges top euro for its central location a block from the cathedral, and mixes modern comfort with a touch of old Beaune (small Db-€100, *superieure* Db-€118, deluxe Db-€155, extra bed-€18, skip overpriced breakfast, some rooms with air-con, elevator, pay Wi-Fi, garage-€10/day but a long walk away, 9–11 avenue de la République, tel. 03 80 24 09 20, fax 03 80 24 09 15, www.athanor-hotel-bourgogne.com, hotel.athanor@wanadoo.fr).

**$$$ Hôtel des Remparts\*\*\***, a peaceful oasis in a manor house, features rustic-classy, affordable rooms with beamed ceilings, period furniture, a quiet courtyard, and a few great family suites (Db-€88–108—pricier rooms are bigger with elaborate bathrooms, Db suite-€116–135, Tb-€89–118, Qb-€148, cozy attic rooms, Internet access and pay Wi-Fi, laundry service, bike rental, garage-€9/day, just inside ring road between train station and main square at 48 rue Thiers, tel. 03 80 24 94 94, fax 03 80 24 97 08, www.hotel-remparts-beaune.com, hotel.des.remparts@wanadoo.fr, run by the formal Epaillys and friendly Chantal).

**$$$ Les Jardins de Loïs\*\*\*\***, run by welcoming winemakers Philippe and Anne-Marie, is a four-star B&B. The four big rooms all overlook gargantuan gardens lined with fruit trees, and show a no-expense-spared attention to detail and comfort. There's also a

BURGUNDY

# Sleep Code

**(€1 = about $1.50, country code: 33)**
**S** = Single, **D** = Double/Twin, **T** = Triple, **Q** = Quad, **b** = bathroom,
**s** = shower only, * = French hotel rating system (0–4 stars).
Unless otherwise noted, credit cards are accepted and English
is spoken.

To help you easily sort through these listings, I've divided
the rooms into three categories based on the price for a
standard double room with bath:

**$$$ Higher Priced**—Most rooms €90 or more.
**$$ Moderately Priced**—Most rooms between €60-90.
**$ Lower Priced**—Most rooms €60 or less.

nice lounge area and a Turkish bath (Db-€100, Tb-€150, includes
breakfast, air-con, Wi-Fi, on the ring road a block after Hôtel de
la Poste at 8 boulevard Bretonnière, tel. 03 80 22 41 97, mobile 06
73 85 11 06, www.jardinsdelois.com, contact@jardinsdelois.com).
Their atmospheric wine cellar, Domaine Lois Dufouleur, also
offers tastings (€8 for 4 wines, arrange ahead, see page 703).

**$$ Hôtel Ibis**,** modern with 73 efficient rooms, is an accept-
able last resort for most, but a good first resort if you have kids and
want a pool. The bigger "Club" rooms are worth the extra euros
(standard Db-€80, "Club" Db-€88, extra person-€10, non-smok-
ing floor, air-con, free parking, you'll pass it as you enter Beaune
from the autoroute, tel. 03 80 22 75 67, fax 03 80 22 77 17, www
.hotelibis.com, h1363@accor.com). There's another, cheaper Ibis
Hôtel—along with a gaggle of Motel 6–type places—closer to the
autoroute.

**$$ Hôtel de France**,** is a well-run place and easy for train
travelers and drivers (parking across from the train station).
It comes with clean rooms and outgoing owners Tita and Eric.
Half-board is required on Saturday (Sb-€50–77, Db-€57–77—most
are about €67, Tb-€67–77, air-con, Internet access and Wi-Fi,
garage-€9/day, 35 avenue du 8 Septembre, tel. 03 80 24 10 34, fax
03 80 24 96 78, www.hoteldefrance-beaune.com, hoteldefrance
.beaune@wanadoo.fr).

**$$ Hôtel la Villa Fleurie***,** an adorable 10-room refuge, is
run by affable Madame Chartier on a plain street a few blocks out-
side the ring road (15-min walk from the center). Most rooms are
wood-floored, plush, and *très* traditional, and come with big bath-
rooms and air-conditioning (small Db-€70, bigger Db-€80, nifty
Tb/Qb loft-€110–120, Wi-Fi, easy and free parking, 19 place Col-
bert, tel. 03 80 22 66 00, fax 03 80 22 45 46, www.lavillafleurie.fr,

**BURGUNDY**

la.villa.fleurie@wanadoo.fr). From Beaune's ring road, turn right in front of the Bichot winery.

## Place Madeleine

These hotels are a few blocks from the city center and train station, with easy parking.

**$$ Hôtel de la Paix***,** a few steps off place Madeleine, is a fine choice, with 24 modern and well-appointed rooms (some with small balconies), several good family rooms, and a snazzy bar with a pool table (Db-€82–92, loft Tb-€105, Qb-€122–135, air-con, Internet access and Wi-Fi, private parking, 45 rue du Faubourg Madeleine, tel. 03 80 24 78 08, fax 03 80 24 10 18, www.hotelpaix.com, contact@hotelpaix.com).

**$ L'Auberge Bourguignonne's** restaurant hides 10 comfortable and well-priced rooms with no public spaces (Db-€56–60, bigger Db with air-con-€73, Tb-€75, check in at restaurant, 4 place Madeleine, tel. 03 80 22 23 53, fax 03 80 22 51 64, www.auberge-Bourguignonne.fr, contact@auberge-bourguignonne.fr).

**$ Hôtel Rousseau** is a good-value, no-frills, frumpy manor house that turns its back on Beaune's sophistication. Cheerful, quirky, and hard-to-find owner Madame Rousseau, her pet birds, and the quiet garden will make you smile, and the tranquility will help you sleep. The cheapest rooms are a godsend for budget travelers. The rooms with showers are like Grandma's, with enough comfort (S-€30, D-€39, D with toilet-€48, Db-€59, T with toilet-€54, Tb-€65, Q-€60, Qb-€70, showers down the hall-€3, cash only, reservations preferred by email, free parking, 11 place Madeleine, tel. 03 80 22 13 59, fax 03 80 22 67 55, hotelrousseau beaune@orange.fr). Check-ins after 19:00 and morning departures before 7:30 must be arranged in advance.

## Near Beaune

You'll find some exceptional and family-friendly values within a short drive of Beaune. Hotels in famous wine villages are generally pricey and overrated.

### Hotels

**$$$ Hôtel Villa Louise*** is a romantic place burrowed in the prestigious wine hamlet of Aloxe-Corton, five minutes north of Beaune. Many of its 13 *très* cozy and tastefully decorated rooms overlook the backyard vineyards, a small covered pool, and a large, grassy garden made for sipping the owner's wine (sadly, no picnics allowed). The serious owners—the Perrins—will show you their vaulted cellars (Db-€110–152—most are about €110–130, Db suite-€195, buffet breakfast-€15, Internet access and Wi-Fi, sauna, next to the château at 9 rue Franche, tel. 03 80 26 46 70, fax 03 80 26 47

16, www.hotel-villa-louise.fr, hotel-villa-louise@wanadoo.fr).

**$$ Hôtel le Home**,** just off busy N-74 a half-mile north of Beaune, is a good value, with comfy rooms in an old mansion. Engaging owner Mathilde (mah-teel-dah), who has lived in Los Angeles, runs the place in an easygoing manner. The rooms in the main building are Laura Ashley–soft (Db-€68–75, Tb-€73–83, Qb-€90, top-floor rooms have the most character). Rooms on the parking courtyard (only Db-€66) come with stone floors, small terraces, and bright colors, but can be dark (free parking and Wi-Fi, 138 route de Dijon, tel. 03 80 22 16 43, fax 03 80 24 90 74, www.lehome.fr, info@lehome.fr).

### Chambres d'Hôte

The Côte d'Or has scads of *chambres d'hôte;* get a list at the TI and reserve ahead in the summer. The wine villages south of Beaune, such as Paligny Montrachet, and the cliff-dwelling villages near La Rochepot, such as St. Romain and Orches, make great non-Beaune bases, with several *chambres d'hôte* (well-signed in the villages). You'll need a car to get to any of these. Families should make a beeline for Isabelle Raby's place.

**$$$ Château de Melin,** run by friendly Hélène, is a semi-restored château that offers comfort, though no interior public spaces. Four huge rooms play second fiddle to their winery (don't expect prompt service). Outside you can enjoy a small pond, vineyards (tastings available), and gardens to stretch out in (Db-€92–110, Tb-€125, Qb-€145, includes good breakfast, cash only, 10 min from Beaune toward La Rochepot, between villages of Auxey-Duresses and La Rochepot, tel. 03 80 21 21 19, fax 03 80 21 21 72, www.chateaudemelin.com, chateaumelin@free.fr).

**$$ La Domaine de Corgette** is hunkered below a hillside in lovely little St. Romain. Welcoming Véronique has restored an old vintner's home with style. A stay-a-while terrace, private parking, cozy common rooms, and wine-tastings are at your disposal (Db-€70–90, Qb-€100, cash only, follow signs from Auxey-Duresses, on rue de la Perrière, tel. & fax 03 80 21 68 08, www.domaine corgette.com, maisondhotescorgette@yahoo.fr).

**$ La Clé des Vignes** sits on the vineyard's edge in Puligny Montrachet. It's a find, with four spacious, tastefully furnished, and peaceful rooms with good public spaces, outdoor tables, and great rates. Anne-Sophie is a pleasant host (Db-€60, includes breakfast, cash only, a few blocks from the recommended Caveau des Vignerons and the central roundabout toward St. Aubin at 14 rue Poiseul, Puligny-Montrachet, tel. 03 80 22 65 49, mobile 06 75 09 00 27, la-cle-desvignes@wandoo.fr).

**$ Isabelle Raby** rents three good rooms at fair rates a half-mile above Baubigny in rocky little Orches. She offers the best setup for families, including a pretty pool, table tennis, swings, and fine views from her manicured backyard. Reserve ahead for a homemade dinner for €25 (Db-€60, Tb-€70, Qb-€80, Quint-€90, includes big breakfast, cash only, tel. 03 80 21 78 45).

# EATING

For a small town, Beaune offers a wide range of reasonably priced restaurants. Review my suggestions below carefully before setting out, and reserve ahead to avoid frustrations (especially on weekends). Many places are closed Sunday and Monday.

## In the Center of Beaune

**La Ciboulette,** intimate and family-run with petite Helene as your hostess, offers fine cuisine that mixes traditional Burgundian flavors with creative dishes and lovely presentation. It's worth the longer walk—and you can do your laundry next door while you dine (€20 and €25 *menus*, closed Mon–Tue; from place Carnot, walk out rue Carnot to 69 rue Lorraine, tel. 03 80 24 70 72).

**Brasserie le Carnot** is Beaune's vintage café, with good interior and great exterior seating in the pedestrian zone. It serves excellent pizza, good salads, pasta dishes, and the usual café fare (open daily, where rue Carnot and rue Monge meet).

**Bistrot Bourguignon** is a relaxed wine bar–bistro with a lengthy wine list and 15 wines available by the glass (order by number from display behind bar). The bon vivant owner, Jean-Jacques, and son Virgil offer the same affordable prices at either bar or table. Come for a glass of wine or to enjoy a light dinner. Dine at the counter, the tables, or in the living room-like interior (€10 starters, €15 *plats*, closed Sun–Mon, on a pedestrian-only street at 8 rue Monge, tel. 03 80 22 23 24).

**Caveau des Arches** offers fair prices and a chance to dine underground with atmosphere in stone cellars (€22 *menu* with the classics, closed Sun–Mon, where the ring road crosses rue d'Alsace—which leads to place Madeleine—at 10 boulevard Perpreuil, tel. 03 80 22 10 37).

**Palais des Gourmets' Salon de Thé** provides the best-value outdoor lunch on place Carnot, with delicious quiche, omelets, crêpes, and memorable desserts (open daily until 18:30, next to The Athenaeum's back door entrance at 14 place Carnot, tel. 03 80 22 13 39).

**Le Jardin des Remparts** is a fine Burgundian splurge. This dressy stone manor house is elegant inside and out (leafy terrace dining in summer), yet the service is casual and attentive. The excellent nouvelle cuisine proudly works with regional products. Always reserve ahead here (€35–60 *menus*, eight-course "discovery

BURGUNDY

*menu"* for €90, closed Sun–Mon, just past Hôtel Dieu on ring road at 10 rue de l'Hôtel Dieu, tel. 03 80 24 79 41, lejardin@club -internet.fr).

## On Place Madeleine

**Les Caves Madeleine** is a wine shop that keeps its cozy little dining room busy. Diners are surrounded by shelves of this week's wines with prices chalked onto bottles. Choose a private table, or join the convivial communal table, where good food and wine kindle conversation, then lubricate new friendships. The owners are wine merchants who pass their savings on to you. (As you choose a bottle at store prices and add €5 to drink here, top-end wines become affordable.) This small place is family-run by "Lo-lo," who enjoys sharing his love of wine (good wines by the glass, €14 and €24 *menus,* closed Thu and Sun, 8 rue du Faubourg Madeleine, tel. 03 80 22 93 30).

**Le Comptoir des Tontons** is a 10-table place where the focus is on the quality of the food rather than ambience. Come here to savor a slow dinner featuring organic foods and creative combinations (€23 *menu,* 22 rue du Faubourg Madeleine, tel. 03 80 24 19 64).

**L'Auberge Bourguignonne** is decidedly Burgundian, with serious service and proudly displayed awards. Choose from the dressy dining room; the folksy, more traditional dining room; or tables outside on the square (*menus* from €21, some seafood, daily, air-con, reservations smart, 4 place Madeleine, tel. 03 80 22 23 53).

## After Dinner

If you're tired of speaking French, pop into the late-night-lively **Pickwicks Pub** (Mon–Sat 17:00–05:00, closed Sun, behind church at 2 rue Notre-Dame).

## Near Beaune

**Le Relais de la Diligence,** a five-minute drive from Beaune, serves budget Burgundian cuisine, with many *menu* options. The dressy dining room with sliding-glass walls has you feeling like you're sitting in the vineyard. Or, on a balmy evening, you can eat on the terrace (*menus* from €18, the €2.50 *Menu Tutu* for dogs—I'm serious—includes ground hamburger and pâté, June–Sept open daily, Oct–May closed Tue–Wed, take N-74 toward Chagny/ Chalon and turn left at L'Hôpital Meursault on D-23, tel. 03 80 21 21 32).

# TRANSPORTATION CONNECTIONS

**From Beaune by Train to: Dijon** (14/day, 25 min), **Paris'** Gare de Lyon (nearly hourly, 2.5 hrs, most require change in Dijon), **Colmar** (6/day, 4–5 hrs, changes in Dijon and in Besançon, Mulhouse, or

**BURGUNDY**

## Beaune Restaurants and Wine Cellars

1. La Ciboulette Restaurant
2. Brasserie le Carnot
3. Bistrot Bourguignon
4. Caveau des Arches Rest.
5. Palais des Gourmets' Salon de Thé
6. Le Jardin des Remparts Rest.
7. Les Caves Madeleine Rest.
8. Le Comptoir des Tontons
9. L'Auberge Bourguignonne Rest.
10. Pickwicks Pub
11. To Le Relais de la Diligence Rest.
12. Denis Perret Wine Shop
13. Comptoir Viticole Wine Hardware
14. Alain Hess Deli & Mulet Pain d'Epices
15. Bouchard Aîné Wine Cellar
16. Domaine Lois Dufouleur Wine Cellar
17. Sensation Vin Wine Bar
18. Védrenne Liquors

BURGUNDY

**Legend:**

//// Pedestrian Zone
||| Stairs
→ One-Way
P Parking

* Not to Scale—
Place Madeleine
To Hotel Dieu Is
A 10 Min. Walk

To N-74, Savigny & Dijon

Rue Faubourg
St. Nicholas

To Train Station

Ave 8 Sept.

Chateau

Blvd. Joffre

Colbert

R. Spuller

Rousseau

Tonneliers

Tribunal

Rue Thiers

Faub. St. Jean

Blvd. Ferry

Place Madeleine

R. Faub.

Supermarket

DCH

Rue Lorraine

Place Monge

Paradis

Ste. Marg.

R. College

R. Marey

Ateliers

Rue d'Alsace

Place Carnot

Verne

Notre-Dame

Hotel Dieu

Blvd. St. Jacques

Post

To A-6 Freeway

Rue Republique

Clonier

Gardin

P Mauroux

Louis Very

Blvd. Foch

St. Mart.

Ave. Pal. Mart.

Ave. Taffelin

Ave. Tafelin

Blvd. Clemenceau

Faub. Bret.

To Park de la Bouzaise & Vineyards

To Chateauneuf-en-Auxois & Bligny

To D-973 & N-74
La Rochepot, Pommard,
Chalons-sur-Saone &

Belfort), **Arles** (10/day, 4.5 hrs, 9 with transfer in Lyon and Nîmes or Avignon), **Chamonix** (7/day, 6–7 hrs, change in Lyon and St. Gervais, some require additional changes), **Annecy** (7/day, 5–6 hrs, change in Lyon), **Amboise** (8/day, 6 hrs, most with changes in Dijon and in Paris, arrive at Paris' Gare de Lyon, then Métro to Austerlitz or Montparnasse stations).

# The Beaune Region

## Getting Around the Beaune Region
**By Bus:** Transco bus #44 runs from Beaune through the vineyards and villages south to Chalon-sur-Saône, west to La Rochepot, and north to Dijon. About seven buses per day link Beaune and Dijon via several famous wine villages; ask at the TI for schedules and stops, or call for information (tel. 03 80 42 11 00).

**By Bike:** Well-organized, English-speaking Florent and Sarah at **Bourgogne Randonnées** offer good bikes, bike racks, maps, and detailed itineraries (their advice inspired the trips described below). Ask about their favorite routes that follow only small roads and dedicated bike paths. I like the *Discovering the Chardonnay Kingdom* tour. It departs from Beaune's parc de la Bouzaise and connects the wine villages of Pommard, Meursault, and Volnay in a scenic, mostly level, 14-mile loop ride (can be extended to Puligny Montrachet for a level 22-mile loop). They can deliver your bike to your hotel anywhere in France (bikes–€4/hr, €17/day, Mon–Sat 9:00–12:00 & 13:30–19:00, Sun 10:00–12:00 & 14:00–19:00, near train station at 7 avenue du 8 Septembre, tel. 03 80 22 06 03, fax 03 80 22 15 58, www.detours-in-france.com, info@bourgogne-randonnees.com).

# SIGHTS

## ▲Bike (or Drive) the Vineyards
Hop on a bike in Beaune, and in minutes, you can be immersed in the lush countryside and immaculate vineyards of the Côte d'Or. The bike lane that circles Beaune's ring road, and the many little-traveled roads (along with the friendly bike-rental place in Beaune—described above), make this area good for biking. Just beware of loose gravel. For an easy and very rewarding roll through wine paradise, follow this relatively

# The Beaune Region

**Legend:**
- ━━━ AUTOROUTE (TOLL)
- ─── OTHER ROADS
- ▬▬▬ SCENIC VINEYARD DRIVE
- ═══ SELF-GUIDED BIKE TOUR
- ↘✦ VIEW
- ⛫ CASTLE

TO HAUTES COTES DE BEAUNE

TO DIJON

TO VEZELAY & PARIS

PERNAND-VERG.

ALOXE-CORTON

A-6 SAVIGNY

D-18

CHOREY

A-31

D-970

TO BLIGNY-SUR-OUCHE, & CHATEAUNEUF EN-AUXOIS

TO IVRY

D-17

ST. ROMAIN

POMMARD

**BEAUNE**

D-973

D-973

N-74

ORCHES

D-973

AUXEY-DURESSES

MEURSAULT

EVELLE

L' HOPITAL

BAU-BIGNY

TO AUTUN

**LA ROCHEPOT**

D-113b

AUTOROUTE

A-6

TO CHALON & LYON

D-33

ST. AUBIN

N-74

PULIGNY MONTRACHET

N-6

3 MILES

3 KM

N-6

CHAGNY

D-981

TO CHALON & LYON

SCENIC ROUTE TO BRANCION

DCH

**1** Château de Melin B&B

**2** La Domaine de Corgette B&B & Wine Barrel Fabrication

**3** Isabelle Raby B&B

**4** La Clé des Vignes B&B

BURGUNDY

level 10-mile half-day loop from Beaune. It laces together three renowned wine villages—Aloxe-Corton, Pernand Verge-lesses, and Savigny-les-Beaune—connecting you with the best of Burgundian nature and village wine culture. (Bikers needn't be shy about tasting like a professional—spitting rather than swallowing.) Bring water and snacks, as there is precious little available until the end of this route. Your tour concludes in Savigny-les-Beaune, where you'll find several attractions, including a recommended café-restaurant, wine-tasting, a small grocery, and a unique château. This route, while best by bike, also works well by car.

**○ Self-Guided Tour:** From Beaune's ring road bike lane, take N-74 north toward Dijon; soon after, follow signs leading left to *Savigny-les-Beaune.* Cross over the freeway, then follow signs to *Pernand Vergelesses* on D-18 (at the roundabout). Turn right at signs to *Aloxe-Corton,* and ride gently down to **Aloxe-Corton** (keep following its church spire in the distance to your left). This tiny town, with a world-class reputation among wine enthusiasts, has many tasting opportunities (but no cafés). Within a few steps of the church is the main square (like a small parking lot). The easygoing **Domaines d'Aloxe Corton** offers tastings (see page 704). A block farther, the grand **Château Corton-André** is open daily and offers a visit of its cellars with wine tastings (daily 10:00–13:00 & 14:00–19:00, tel. 03 80 26 44 25, www.pierre-andre.com).

Back on your bike, leave Aloxe's little square and head up the hill to **Pernand Vergelesses.** There's no compelling reason to stop at this quiet village (though drivers, or bikers in need of a challenge, can climb above the village to the panorama: Turn right into Pernand Vergelesses and go up and up past the church until you see small *Panorama* signs).

Most will turn left on the road back to Beaune, then veer right into the vineyards on the first lane. Make a quick left and follow this vineyard service road, keeping right for about 1.5 miles until you see a *5T* sign (watch for loose gravel on this section). Turn left before the sign, then right, and right again, and ride into **Savigny-les-Beaune.**

You'll come to a three-way intersection. The left fork leads back to Beaune. The middle fork leads to *Centre-Ville,* where you'll find the good **New Rock Café** on a pleasant little square (good salads and beef, outdoor tables, closed Mon, tel. 03 80 21 50 00); a grocery shop a few blocks past the café (closed 12:30–15:00); and a four-towered collectors' château, **Le Château de Savigny** (with 80 fighter jets parked in the side yard, 2,000 models of planes inside, Abarth antique cars, and 300 motorcycles to boot—but little English information; €8, daily April–Oct 9:00–18:30, Nov–March 9:00–12:00 & 14:00–17:30, last entry 1.5 hours before closing, tel. 03 80 21 55 03). The leftmost road leads back to Beaune.

For a more scenic and very rigorous all-day ride, consider biking the route below (ideal by car). Bikers can shortcut this ride by following Bourgogne Randonnées' *Chardonnay Kingdom* itinerary (see "By Bike," earlier in this section).

## ▲▲Scenic Vineyard Drive to/from La Rochepot

Take this pretty, peaceful detour for the best approach to La Rochepot's romantic castle, and to glide through several of Burgundy's most reputed vineyards. Bikers may prefer doubling back to Beaune after visiting Puligny Montrachet. Read ahead and note that if you want to see the wine-barrel-makers at work, you need to get there by 15:00—if that's a push, reverse this loop.

➔ **Self-Guided Tour:** Leave Beaune's ring road following signs for *Chalon-sur-Saône,* then follow signs to *Pommard,* where you'll see the user-friendly winery **La Cave de Pommard** (see page 705) and the fun (and *très* local) lunch café, **Hotel du Pont** (€13 lunch *menus,* €8 salads, good terrace, closed Sun, tel. 03 80 22 03 41). South of Pommard, the road climbs gradually through fine views. From here, follow signs to *Meursault,* then work your way through this world-famous wine town by following small signs to *Centre-Ville* (not N-74). When you reach the main square, stay right and find the bike-route signs (to the right of the Casino store). Once out of Meursault, keep straight and merge onto D-113b to Puligny Montrachet.

You'll pass through low-slung vineyards, then come to a round-about in the center of Puligny Montrachet with a cool bronze sculpture of vineyard workers. Across from the sculpture, the **Caveau de Montrachet** offers a chance to sample the world's best whites (see page 704). Signs from here lead through more manicured vineyards to St. Aubin. A hard right takes you on N-6 for a short distance; find *La Rochepot* signs as you bypass St. Aubin. Follow signs for *La Rochepot* (D-33) over hills and through the vineyards of the Hautes-Côtes (upper slopes), and you'll come to a drop-dead view of the castle (stop mandatory). Turn right when you reach La Rochepot, and follow *Le Château* signs to the castle (described below).

After visiting the castle, turn right out of its parking lot and mosey through Baubigny, Evelles, and rock-solid Orches. After Orches, climb to the top of Burgundy's world—keeping straight on D-17, you'll pass several exceptional lookouts (the village of St. Romain swirls below, and if it's really clear, look for Mont Blanc). Then drive down through St. Romain, and follow signs for *Auxey-Duresses,* then *Beaune* (you'll pass Burgundy's most important wine-barrel-maker, François Frères, in St. Romain—described below; notice the wood slats used for barrel-making).

## ▲Château de la Rochepot

This very Burgundian castle rises above the trees and its village, eight miles from Beaune. It's accessible by car, bike (hilly), or infrequent bus. Cross the drawbridge under the Pot family coat of arms and knock three times with the ancient knocker to enter. If no one comes, knock harder, or find a log and ram the gate. This pint-size castle is splendid inside and out. Tour half on your own and the other half with a French guide (get the English handout, some tours in English—call ahead, most guides speak some English and can answer questions). This castle's construction began during the end of the Middle Ages (when castles were built to defend) and was completed during the Renaissance (when castles were transformed into luxury homes). So it's neither a purely defensive structure (as in the Dordogne) nor a palace (as in the Loire)—it's a little of both.

The furnishings are surprisingly elaborate given the military look of the exterior. I could sleep like a baby in the Captain's Room, surrounded by nine-foot-thick walls. Don't miss the 15th-century alarmed safe. Notice the colorful doorjamb. These same colors were used to paint many buildings (including castles and churches) and remind us that medieval life went beyond beige and stone. The kitchen will bowl you over; the dining room sports a 15th-century walnut high-chair. Climb the tower and see the Chinese room, sing chants in the resonant chapel, and make ripples in the 240-foot-deep well. (Can you spit a bull's-eye?) Paths outside lead around the castle and make a worthwhile walk. Don't leave without driving, walking, or pedaling up D-33 a few hundred yards toward St. Aubin (behind Hôtel Relais du Château) for a romantic view.

**Cost and Hours:** €7.50, €9.50 if you add tour of exterior offered Sundays at 11:30, private tours in English-€60, call to confirm times, open Wed–Mon June–mid-Sept 10:00–18:00, April–May 10:00–11:45 & 14:00–17:30, mid-Sept–Oct 10:00–11:45 & 14:00–16:45, closed Tue and Nov–March, tel. 03 80 21 71 37, www.larochepot.com.

**Getting There:** To reach the château from Beaune, follow signs for *Chalon-sur-Saône* from Beaune's ring road, then follow signs to *Autun* along a lovely 15-minute drive to La Rochepot. Once in the town, turn right a block before the Relais du Château Hôtel to reach the castle.

## Tonnellerie François Frères (Wine Barrel Fabrication)

Here you can pop in and observe one of France's most important barrel-makers at work. Park in the lot above St. Romain and walk to the left end of the parking lot, then follow the hammer noise up a few steps and take in the almost medieval scene. Well-stoked fires heat the oak staves to make them flexible, sweaty workers pound iron rings around the barrels, and no one slacks in this hardworking factory where demand seems strong. Work starts early and ends by about 15:00 (open Mon–Fri, closed Sat–Sun, tel. 03 80 21 23 33, http://francoisfreres.com).

# Between Beaune and Paris

North of Beaune, you'll find a handful of appealing places that string together well for a full-day excursion: towering Châteauneuf-en-Auxois, sleepy Semur-en-Auxois, remote Fontenay's abbey, pretty little Flavigny-sur-Ozerain, and Julius Caesar's victorious Alise Ste. Reine.

As a bonus, following my self-guided driving tour of this area (below) takes you along several stretches of the **Burgundy Canal** (Canal de Bourgogne). Like much of France, Burgundy is laced by canals dug in the early Industrial Age. Two hundred years ago, canals like these provided the cheapest way to transport cargo. The Burgundy canal was among the most important of France's canals, as it enabled Paris to be connected with the Mediterranean Sea. The canal is 145 miles long, with 209 locks, and rises over France's continental divide in Pouilly-en-Auxois, just below Châteauneuf-en-Auxois (where the canal runs underground for about two miles). Digging began on the canal in 1727 and was not completed until 1832—just in time for the invention of steam engines on rails that would soon replace the need for canals.

## Self-Guided Driving Tour

This all-day loop links Châteauneuf-en-Auxois, Semur-en-Auxois, Fontenay, Flavigny-sur-Ozerain, and Alise Ste. Reine. The trip includes vineyards, pastoral landscapes, the Burgundy canal, a Cistercian abbey, Gallic-Roman history, and two medieval villages. (If you're heading to/from Paris, this scenic tour can be done en route or as an overnight stop; accommodations are listed.) It requires a car, Michelin Local map #520, and navigational patience. Stops that are bolded are described in greater detail later in this chapter.

**➋ Self-Guided Tour:** Here's your itinerary for a full day in Back Door Burgundy. Leave Beaune, following signs for *Auxerre* and *Bligny-sur-Ouche;* from Bligny-sur-Ouche, take D-33 to Pont d'Ouche (following signs to *Pont du Pany* and *Dijon*), where you'll turn left along the canal, following signs to *Château de Châteauneuf.* In five minutes, you'll see **Châteauneuf-en-Auxois** castle looming above. From Châteauneuf, drop back down to the canal to Vandenesse (nice picnic spot on its "port," with good views of Châteauneuf), then follow signs for *Pouilly-en-Auxois,* then *Semur-en-Auxois* on D-970. From **Semur-en-Auxois,** follow *Montbard,* then *Fontenay* signs to reach the **Abbey of Fontenay.** The abbey is your goal today; allow at least an hour here. With no stops, this one-way drive from Beaune to Fontenay should take about 75 minutes.

Return to Beaune along D-905, following signs for *Venary les Laumes,* and contemplate short detours to **Alise Ste. Reine** (the "Alésia" battlefield where Caesar defeated the Gauls) and lovely little **Flavigny-sur-Ozerain** (of *Chocolat* film fame). If you're doing this trip on your way to or from Paris, visit Flavigny and Alise Ste. Reine between Semur-en-Auxois and Fontenay, or skip them. Better yet, sleep in Semur-en-Auxois or Châteauneuf-en-Auxois, and do it all at a sane pace (see below).

Non-drivers can get as far as Semur-en-Auxois by bus (3/day from Montbard or Dijon—early morning, noon, and evening; rail-pass gets you a free ticket, ask TI in Semur about where to get bus ticket). There are no trains to Semur.

# Châteauneuf-en-Auxois

This purely medieval castle monitored passage between Burgundy and Paris, with hawk's-eye views from its 2,000-foot setting. *Châteauneuf* means "new castle," so you'll see many in France. This one is in the Auxois area, so it's Châteauneuf-en-Auxois (not to be confused with the famous Châteauneuf-du-Pape in Provence). The living hill town hunkers in the shadow of its pit-bull château and merits exploring. Park at the lot in the upper end of the village; don't miss the panoramic viewpoint nearby. The military value of this site is powerfully clear from here. Find the Burgundy Canal and the three reservoirs that have maintained the canal's flow for more than 300 years. The small village below is Châteauneuf's port, Vandenesse-en-Auxois—you'll be there shortly. If not for phylloxera—the vine-loving insect that ravaged France in the early 1900s, killing all of its vineyards—you'd see more vineyards than wheat fields.

Saunter into the village, where every building feels historic and stocky farmers live side-by-side with slim artists. Walk into the courtyard, but skip the château's interior (€5, Tue–Sun 10:00–12:00 & 14:00–19:00, closed Mon, get English handout). You'll get better moat views and see the more important castle entry by walking below the Hostellerie du Château, and then turning right, following *Eglise* signs. If you're hungry, Châteauneuf has several affordable cafés and restaurants along its main drag.

## SLEEPING

### In or near Châteauneuf-en-Auxois

**$$ Lady A Barge,** in the canalside village of Vandenesse-en-Auxois, has tight but sufficiently comfortable rooms on a handsome hotel barge at two-star prices, with views of Châteauneuf's castle. Catherine entertains, while Sami cooks an elaborate dinner upon request for €25, including some wine (Sb-€60, Db-€65, one-night stay-€10 extra, includes breakfast, book ahead in summer, ask about cruises on the canal—although the barge usually stays put, open all year, cash only, bikes available, Lady A, Bord du Canal, tel. 03 80 49 26 96, fax 03 80 49 27 00, www.peniche-lady -a.com, ladyabarge@yahoo.fr). From the freeway exit in Pouilly-en-Auxois, take D-18 to Vandenesse-en-Auxois to find the canal.

$ **Hostellerie du Château\*\*** is a modest but cozy place for a good night's sleep in Châteauneuf. It houses an enticing budget-vacation ensemble: nine homey, inexpensive rooms with a garden overlooking a brooding castle. The managers change annually, making it hard to recommend the appealing restaurant (Db-€46–76 depending on size, plumbing, and view—showers cheaper than baths; extra bed-€10, *menus* from €28, closed Nov–Feb, tel. 03 80 49 22 00, fax 03 80 49 21 27, www.hostellerie-chateauneuf.com, infos@hostellerie-chateauneuf.com). Their "Residence" nearby has bigger rooms, but with less character.

# Semur-en-Auxois

This happy town feels real. There are few tourists and no important sights to digest—just a pleasing jumble of Burgundian alleys perched above the meandering Armançon River and behind the town's four massive towers, all beautifully illuminated after dark.

Semur-en-Auxois (suh-moor-ahn-ohx-wah) works well as a base to visit the sights described in this day trip, or as a handy lunch or dinner stop. Semur is also about 45 minutes from the famous church in Vézelay (see page 726) and two hours from Paris, making it an easy first- or last-night stop on your trip. Don't miss the smashing panorama of Semur (best at night) from the viewpoint by the Citroën shop where D-980 and D-954 intersect (see "View over Semur-en-Auxois" under "Sights," later in this section).

## Tourist Information

The **TI** is across from Hôtel Côte d'Or, at Semur's medieval entry (July–Aug Mon–Sat 9:00–12:00 & 14:00–18:00, closed Sun and Sept–June, 2 place Gaveau, tel. 03 80 97 05 96, www.ville-semur -en-auxois.fr). Pick up their city-walking brochure, information on the regional sights, and bike-rental information and suggested routes (hilly terrain).

# SIGHTS

You can connect the following sights (and see everything of importance in Semur) with a short stroll. Begin at the TI, then stop under the Sauvigny gate.

**Sauvigny and Guiller Gates**—These two impressive gates provided safe entry to Semur in the Middle Ages. Look up at the Sauvigny gate and see the indentations for posts that held a drawbridge in place. The Guiller gate, 100 years older, marked the town's limit in the 1300s.

• *From here, enter charming rue Buffon, Semur's oldest commercial street. At the end of this street is the...*

**Church of Notre-Dame**—The town's main sight, the 13th-century church that dominates its small square, is worth a quick look. Walk counterclockwise around the ambulatory behind the altar. The first chapel on the right is dedicated to St. Eloi, and has unusual stained-glass windows honoring Semur's WWI soldiers. Then notice the rich colors in the next chapel. Gothic churches were usually brightly painted, not as you see them today—somber and gray. The bits of stained glass around Mary's statue date from the 13th century and are the only originals left. Before leaving the church, glance at the second-to-last chapel on your right, with a large plaque honoring American soldiers who lost their lives in World War I (Mon–Sat 9:00–12:00 & 14:00–18:30, Sun 14:00–18:30, decent English handout).

• *Leave with the church to your back and walk down the square, then turn left at the bottom on rue du Rempart and see...*

**Semur's Towers**—You'll pass three of Semur's four burly towers. In the Middle Ages, 18 towers were connected by defensive ramparts to encircle the center city. Caught in a crossfire between the powerful Dukes of Burgundy and the king of France, Semur's defenses were first destroyed by Louis XI in 1478, then finished off during the wars of religion in 1602.

• *Keep straight for several blocks, and find the park where Semur's outer defenses once stood. Walk down the road that drops below the walls, turn left at the bottom, and follow the road for views up to Semur. Just after the medieval bridge, look for steps up to your left (rue du Fourneau) to return to the town center. For even better vistas, consider the classic...*

**▲▲View over Semur-en-Auxois**—Drive or hike downhill from the TI, cross the river, then head uphill and turn left at the top roundabout. Just after the Citroën dealership, there's a lookout with an orientation table and a memorable view of the red roofs, spires, and towers—especially striking at night. Walkers don't need to go the distance; views are great well before this viewpoint.

**BURGUNDY**

## SLEEPING AND EATING

If Semur-en-Auxois seduces you into spending a night, try **$$ Hôtel les Cymaises\*\***, where you get three-star comfort for the price of two, with comfortable rooms and big beds in a manor house with a quiet courtyard (Db-€65, Tb-€76, 2-room Qb-€95, private parking, 7 rue du Renaudot, tel. 03 80 97 21 44, fax 03 80 97 18 23, www.hotelcymaises.com, hotel.cymaises@wanadoo.fr).

**L'Entracte** is where everybody goes for pizza, pasta, salads, and more in a relaxed atmosphere (daily, below the church on 4 rue Fevret). The historic **charcuterie** (delicatessen) across from the church can supply your picnic needs.

# Abbey of Fontenay

The entire ensemble of buildings making up this isolated Cistercian abbey, rated ▲▲, has survived, giving visitors perhaps the best

picture of medieval abbey life in France. In the Middle Ages it was written, "To fully grasp the meaning of Fontenay and the power of its beauty, you must approach it trudging through the forest footpaths...through the brambles and bogs...in an October rain." But even if you use the parking lot, Fontenay's secluded setting, blanketed in birdsong with a garden lovingly used "as a stage set," is truly magical.

**Cost and Hours:** €9, daily 10:00–18:00, tel. 03 80 92 15 00.

**Getting There:** The abbey is a 20-minute drive from Semur by way of Montbard. There's no bus service—allow about €20 round-trip for a taxi from Montbard's train station (taxi tel. 06 08 26 61 55 or 06 08 99 21 13, Montbard TI tel. 03 80 92 53 81).

**Background:** This abbey—one of the oldest Cistercian abbeys in France—was founded in 1118 by St. Bernard as a back-to-basics reaction to the excesses of Benedictine abbeys, such as Cluny. The Cistercians worked to recapture the simplicity, solitude, and poverty of the early Church. Bernard created "a horrible vast solitude" in the forest, where his monks could live like the desert fathers of the Old Testament. They chose marshland ("Cistercian" is derived from "marshy bogs") and strove to be separate from the world (which required the industrious self-sufficiency these abbeys were so adept at). The movement spread, essentially colonizing Europe religiously. In 1200, there were more than 500 such monasteries and abbeys in Europe.

Like the Cistercian movement in general, Fontenay flourished through the 13th to 15th centuries. A 14th-century proverb said, "Wherever the wind blows, to Fontenay money flows." Fontenay thrived as a prosperous "mini-city" for nearly 700 years, until the French Revolution, when it became the property of the nation and was eventually sold.

❍ **Self-Guided Tour:** Like visitors centuries ago, you'll enter through the abbey's **gatehouse.** The main difference: Anyone with a ticket gets in, and there's no watchdog barking angrily at you (through the small hole on the right). Pick up the English self-guided tour flier with your ticket. Your visit follows the route below (generally clockwise). Arrows keep you on course, and signs tell you which sections of the abbey are private (as its owners still live here).

The **abbey church** is pure Romanesque and built to St. Bernard's specs: Latin cross plan, no fancy stained glass, unadorned columns, nothing to distract from prayer. The lone statue is the 13th-century *Virgin of Fontenay,* a reminder that the church was dedicated to St. Mary. Enjoy the ethereal light. You can almost hear the brothers chanting.

Stairs lead from the front of the church to a vast, 16th-century, oak-beamed **dormitory** where the monks slept—together, fully dressed, on thin mats. Monastic life was pretty simple: prayer, reading, work, seven services a day, one meal in the winter, two in the summer. Daily rations: a loaf of bread and a quarter-liter of wine.

Back down the stairs, enter the **cloister,** beautiful in its starkness. This was the heart of the community, where monks read, exercised, washed, did small projects—and, I imagine, gave each other those silly haircuts. The shallow alcove (next to the church door) once stored prayer books; notice the slots for shelves. Next to that, the chapter room was where the abbot led discussions and community business was discussed. The adjacent monks' hall was a general-purpose room, likely busy with monks hunched over tables copying sacred texts (a major work of abbeys). The dining hall, or refectory, also faced the cloister (closed to the public).

Across the garden stands the huge abbey **forge.** In the 13th century, the monks at Fontenay ran what many consider Europe's first metalworking plant. Iron ore was melted down in ovens with big bellows. Tools were made and sold for a profit. The hydraulic hammer—which became the basis of industrial manufacturing of iron throughout Europe—was first used here. Leaving the building, walk left around the back to see the stream, which was diverted to power the wheels that operated the forge. Water was vital to abbey life. The pond—originally practical, rather than decorative—was a fish farm (some whoppers survive to this day). Leave through the gift shop, which was the public chapel in the days when visitors were not allowed inside the abbey grounds.

# Flavigny-sur-Ozerain

Ten minutes from Semur and five minutes from Alise Ste. Reine, little Flavigny-sur-Ozerain (flah-veen-yee-sur-oh-zuh-rain) had its 15 minutes of fame in 2000 when the movie *Chocolat* was filmed here. Taking its *chocolat*-covered image in stride, this unassuming and serenely situated village feels permanently stuck in the past, with one café, one *crêperie*, and two boutiques.

There's little to do here other than appreciate the setting (best from the grassy ramparts) and try the little *anis* (anise) candies. Pick up a map at the **TI** (May–Sept daily 10:00–12:30 & 13:00–18:30; April and Oct Tue–Sat 10:30–12:30 & 13:00–18:00, closed Sun–Mon; closed Nov–March; down rue de l'Église in front of church).

*Chocolat*-lovers will have to be satisfied with a few of the building facades featured in the film; there are no souvenirs or posters to be found, and nary a chocolate shop (locals, who prefer their homemade *anis* candies, weren't thrilled with the movie). There are four buildings that fans might recognize. Most significant is the one used as the *chocolaterie* (chocolate shop); it's across the square from the church entry, just past La Grange restaurant on rue du Four (look for the arched window). The Count's home is today's *mairie* (city hall), also opposite the church entry, but to the left as you leave the church. The *coiffure* (hairdresser) is one door down from the TI—look for the white shutters. And what was the Café de la République is three doors up from the TI, with an austere facade. Johnny Depp never visited Flavigny (his loss), and there is no river here (the river scene was filmed in the Dordogne, near Beynac).

Elsewhere in Flavigny, you can buy the locally produced *anis* candies in pretty tins. They make great souvenirs (see them being made Mon–Fri 9:00–11:00 in the Abbey of St. Pierre). You can also visit the ancient Church of St. Genest (daily 14:00–17:45; if it's closed, ask the town hall next door to open it). The grassy ramparts are worth a stroll for the view (behind the church, down rue de la Poterne, and out the gate).

## SLEEPING AND EATING

**(€1 = about $1.50, country code: 33)**
**$$ L'Ange Souriant Chambre d'Hôte** is comfortable and intimate (Sb-€50, Db-€65, Tb-€90, Qb-€98, on rue Voltaire, tel. & fax 03 80 96 24 93, www.ange-souriant.com, a.souriant@wanadoo.fr).

**$ Le Relais de Flavigny,** next door, is an appealing little restaurant with seven basic, bargain rental rooms above (S/D-€28, Ss/Ds-€33, *menus* from €16, €10 hearty summertime lunch salads, open daily, at bottom of rue de l'Église from church, tel. 03 80 96 27 77, www.le-relais.fr, relais-de-flavigny@wanadoo.fr).

**La Grange** ("The Barn") serves farm-fresh fare, including luscious quiche, salad, fresh cheeses, pâtés, and fruit pies (July–mid-Sept Tue–Sun 12:30–18:00, closed Mon; April–June and mid-Sept–Nov open only on Sun, closed Dec–March; across from church, look for brown doors and listen for lunchtime dining, tel. 03 80 35 81 78).

## TRANSPORTATION CONNECTIONS

To reach Flavigny, leave Semur following *Venary les Laumes* signs, and look for the turnoff to Flavigny (at the village of Pouillenay). The approach to Flavigny from Pouillenay via D-9 is picture-perfect. Park at the gate or in the lot just below. From this lot, signs lead to *Alise Ste. Reine*, described below (great views back to Flavigny as you leave).

---

# Alise Ste. Reine

*A united Gaul forming a single nation animated by the same spirit could defy the universe.*
　　　　　　　　　　　　—Julius Caesar, *The Gallic Wars*

A five-minute drive from Venary les Laumes, above the vertical little village of Alise Ste. Reine, is where historians think Julius Caesar defeated the Gallic leader Vercingétorix in 52 B.C., thus winning Gaul for the Roman Empire and forever changing France's destiny.

Follow the *Statue de Vercingétorix* signs leading up through Alise Ste. Reine to the park with the huge statue of the Gallic warrior overlooking his Waterloo. Stand as he did, imagine yourself trapped on this hilltop, and read about...

### The Dying Gauls

In 52 B.C., General Julius Caesar and his 60,000 soldiers surrounded Alésia (today's Alise Ste. Reine), hoping to finally end the uprising of free Gaul and establish Roman civilization in France. Holed up inside the hilltop fortress were 80,000 die-hard (long-haired, tattooed) Gauls under their rebel chief, Vercingétorix (pronounced something like "verse in Genesis"). Having harassed Caesar for months with guerrilla-war attacks, they now called on their fellow Gauls to converge on Alésia to wipe out the Romans.

Rather than attack the fierce-fighting Gauls, Caesar's soldiers patiently camped at the base of the hill and began building a wall. In six weeks, they completed a 12-foot-tall stone wall all the way around Alésia (11 miles around), and then a second larger one (13 miles around), trapping the rebel leaders and hoping to starve them out. If the Gauls tried to escape, not only would they have to breach the two walls, they'd first have to cross a steep no-man's-land dotted with a ditch, a moat, and booby traps (like sharp stakes in pits and buried iron spikes).

The starving Gauls inside Alésia sent their women and children out to beg mercy from the Romans. The Romans (with little food themselves) refused. For days, the women and children wandered the unoccupied land, in full view of both armies, until they starved to death.

After months of siege, Vercingétorix's reinforcements finally came riding to save him. With 90,000 screaming Gallic warriors (Caesar says 250,000) converging on Alésia, and 80,000 more atop the hill, Caesar ordered his men to move between the two walls to fight a two-front battle. The Battle of Alésia raged for five days—a classic struggle between the methodical Romans and the impetuous "barbarians." When it became clear the Romans would not budge, the Gauls retreated.

Vercingétorix surrendered, and Gallic culture was finished in France. During the three-year rebellion, one in five Gauls had been killed, enslaved, or driven out. Roman rule was established for the next 500 years, strangling the Gallic/Celtic heritage. Vercingétorix spent his last years as a prisoner, paraded around as a war trophy. In 46 B.C., he was brought to Rome for Caesar's triumphal ascension to power, where he was strangled to death in a public ritual.

# Between Burgundy and the Loire

These two sights—Vézelay and its Romanesque Basilica of Ste. Madeleine, and the under-construction Château de Guédelon—make good stops for drivers connecting Burgundy and the Loire Valley, or linking Burgundy and Paris, though you'll want to leave by 9:00 to fit in both. (Allow five to six hours of driving from Beaune to Paris or the Loire, plus time to visit each sight.)

## Vézelay and the Basilica of Ste. Madeleine

For over eight centuries, travelers have hoofed it up through this pretty little town to get to the famous hilltop church, the Basilica of Ste. Madeleine. In its 12th-century prime, Vézelay welcomed the medieval masses. Cultists of Mary Magdalene came to file past her (supposed) body. Pilgrims rendezvoused here to march to Spain to venerate St. James' (supposed) relics in Santiago de Compostela. Three Crusades were launched from this hill: the Second Crusade (1146), announced by Bernard of Clairveaux, the Cluny abbot with pope-like powers; the Third Crusade (1190), under Richard the Lionheart and King Philippe Auguste; and the Seventh Crusade (1248), by King (and Saint) Louis IX. Today, tourists flock to Vézelay's basilica, famous for its place in history, its soul-stirring Romanesque architecture—reproduced in countless art books—and for the relics of Mary Magdalene.

**Tourist Information:** Vézelay's **TI,** which has Internet access, is at the lower end of the village (on rue St. Etienne, which turns into rue St. Pierre; June–Oct daily 10:00–13:00 & 14:00–18:00; Nov–May Fri–Wed 10:00–13:00 & 14:00–18:00, closed Thu; tel. 03 86 33 23 69).

# SIGHTS

## ▲Basilica of Ste. Madeleine

To accommodate the growing crowds of medieval pilgrims, the abbots of Vézelay enlarged their original church (1104), then rebuilt it after a disastrous 1120 fire. The building we see today—one of the largest and best-preserved Romanesque churches—was done in stages: nave (1120–1140), narthex (1132–1145), and choir (1215). The construction spanned the century-long transition from the Romanesque style (round barrel arches like the ancient Romans', thick walls, small windows) to Gothic (pointed arches, flying buttresses, high nave, lots of stained glass). Vézelay blends elements of both styles.

**Cost and Hours:** Free entry, daily 8:00–19:30.

**Tours and Information:** Eager volunteers offer one-hour English guided tours that depart from inside the narthex (donation requested, no tours 12:00–14:00, call to get times or to arrange a private tour, tel. 03 86 33 39 50). For extra credit, buy the €5 guidebook as you enter. The view from the park behind the church is sublime.

**◑ Self-Guided Tour:** The **facade**—with one tower missing its original steeple, another that's unfinished altogether, and an inauthentic tympanum—isn't why you came. Step inside.

The **narthex,** or entrance hall, served several functions. Religiously, it was a place to cross from the profane to the sacred. Practically, it gave shelter to overflow pilgrim crowds (even overnight, if necessary) as they shuffled through one of the three doorways. And aesthetically, the dark narthex prepares the visitor for the radiant nave.

BURGUNDY

# Mary Magdalene

France has a special affection for Mary Magdalene (La Madeleine), and Vézelay is one of several churches dedicated to her—a rarity in Europe, where most churches honor Jesus' mother, the Virgin Mary.

The Bible says that Mary Magdalene, one of Jesus' followers, was exorcised of seven demons (Luke 8:2), witnessed the Crucifixion (Matthew 27:56), and was the first mortal to see the resurrected Jesus (Mark 16:9-11)—the other disciples didn't believe her.

Some theologians have fleshed out Mary's reputation by associating her with biblical passages that don't specifically name her: e.g., the sinner who washed Jesus' feet with her hair (Luke 7:36-50), the forgiven adulteress (John 8), or the woman with the alabaster jar who anointed Jesus (Matthew 26:7-13).

In medieval times, legends appeared (especially in France) that, after the Crucifixion, Mary Magdalene fled to southern France, lived devoutly in a cave, converted locals, performed miracles, and died in Provence. Renaissance artists portrayed her as a fanciful blend of Bible and legend: a red-headed, long-haired prostitute who was rescued by Jesus, symbolizing the sin of those who love too much.

In recent times, feminists have claimed Mary Magdalene a victim of male-dominated Catholic suppression. Bible scholars cite passages in two ancient (but non-canonical) gospels that cryptically allude to Mary as Jesus' special "companion." The Da Vinci Code—a popular if unhistorical novel—seizes on this, slathers it with medieval legend, and asserts that Mary Magdalene was actually Jesus' wife who bore him descendants, and that her relics lie not in Vézelay but in a shopping mall in Paris.

The **tympanum** (carved relief) over the central doorway is one of Romanesque's signature pieces. It shows the risen Christ, ascending to heaven in an almond-shaped cloud, shooting Holy Ghost rays at his apostles and telling them to preach the Good News to the ends of the Earth. The whole diversity of humanity (appropriate, considering Vézelay's function as a gathering place) appears beneath: hunters, fishermen, farmers, pygmies, and men with long ears, feathers, and dog heads. The signs of the zodiac arch over the scene.

Gaze through the central doorway into the **nave** at the rows and rows of arches that seem to recede into a luminous infinity—the effect is mesmerizing. The nave is long, high, and narrow (200' x 60' x 35'), creating a tunnel effect formed by 10 columns-and-arches on each side. Overhead is the church's most famous feature—barrel vaults (wide arches) built of stones alternating between creamy-white and pink-brown. The side aisles have low ceilings, while the nave rises up between them, lined with slender, floor-to-ceiling columns that unite both stories. The interior glows with an even light from the unstained glass of the clerestory windows. The absence of distractions or bright colors makes this simple church perfect for meditation.

The capitals of the nave's columns are carved masterpieces by several sculptors of saints and Bible scenes. All are worth studying (the guidebook sold at the entry identifies each scene, starting in the narthex), but some you might easily recognize are David and Goliath (fourth column on left), Moses and the Golden Calf (sixth column), Adam and Eve (ninth column), Peter Freed from Prison (10th and final column on the left), and the well-known "Mystical Mill" (fourth column on right), showing Old Testament Moses and New Testament Paul working together to fill sacks with grain (and, metaphorically, the Bible with words).

The light at the end of the tunnel-like nave is the **choir** (altar area), radiating a brighter, blue-gray light. Constructed when Gothic was the rage, the choir has pointed arches and improved engineering, but the feel is monotone and sterile.

In the right transept stands a statue of the woman this church was dedicated to—not the Virgin Mary (Jesus' mother) but one of Jesus' disciples, Mary Magdalene. She cradles an alabaster jar of ointment she used (according to some Bible interpretations) to anoint Jesus.

Drop into the **crypt** for the ultimate medieval experience in one of Europe's greatest medieval churches. You're entering the foundations of the earlier, ninth-century church that monks built here on the hilltop after Vikings had twice pillaged their church at the base of the hill.

File past the small container with the **relics of Mary Magdalene.** In medieval times, Vézelay claimed to possess Mary's entire body, but the relics were later damaged and scattered by anti-Catholic Huguenots (16th century) and Revolutionaries (18th century), leaving only a few pieces.

Are they really her mortal remains? We only have legends—many different versions—that first appeared in the historical record around A.D. 1000. The most popular legends say that Mary Magdalene traveled to Provence where she died, and that her bones were brought from there by a monk to save them from Muslim pirates. In the 11th century, the abbots of Vézelay heavily marketed the notion that these were Mary's relics, and when the pope authenticated it in 1058, tourism boomed.

Vézelay prospered until the mid-13th century, when King Charles of Anjou announced that Mary's body was not in Vézelay, but had been found in another town. Vézelay's relics suddenly looked bogus, and pilgrims stopped coming. For the next five centuries, the church fell into disrepair and then was vandalized by secularists in the Revolution. The church was restored (1840–1860) by a young architect named Eugène Viollet-le-Duc, who would later revamp Notre-Dame in Paris.

After visiting the chapter house and cloisters (out the right transept), make sure you catch the view from behind the church of the Cure River Valley.

## SLEEPING AND EATING

**(€1 = about $1.50, country code: 33)**
You'll find pleasant cafés with reasonable food all along the street leading to the church.

**$$ Hôtel de la Poste et du Lion d'Or** has the best moderate, country-classy rooms in Vézelay (good Db-€74–80, bigger Db-€85–100, easy parking, at the foot of the village, place du Champ-de-Foire, tel. 03 86 33 21 23, fax 03 86 32 30 92, www.laposte-liondor.com, contact@laposte-liondor.com).

**La Dent Creuse** has the best terrace tables at the lower end of the village (left side), with salads, pizza, and more (daily until 21:30, place du Champ-de-Foire, tel. 03 86 33 36 33).

**Auberge de la Coquille** is a cozy place to eat inside and out, with reasonable prices (daily until 21:30, halfway up to the church at 81 rue St. Pierre, tel. 03 86 33 35 57).

## TRANSPORTATION CONNECTIONS

Vézelay is about 45 minutes northwest of **Semur-en-Auxois** (20 min off the autoroute to Paris). Train travelers go to **Sermizelles** (by way of Auxerre or Avallon, 5/day) and taxi from there (6 miles, allow €17 one-way, taxi tel. 03 86 32 31 88 or 06 85 77 89 36).

# Château de Guédelon

A historian's dream (worth ▲▲, or ▲▲▲ for kids), this medieval castle is being built by 35 enthusiasts using only the tools, techniques, and materials available in the 13th century. The project is the dream of two individuals and is based on plans drafted in 1228. When complete, it will include four towers surrounding a central courtyard with a bridge and a moat. The goal of this exciting project is to give visitors a better appreciation of medieval construction, and for the builders to learn about medieval techniques as they work. Ground was broken in 1997, but the castle won't be complete for another 14 years (the castle is currently about 10–20 feet tall). When the castle is done, the ambitious owners plan to build a medieval abbey.

Enter the project to the sound of chisels chipping rock and the sight of people dressed as if it were 800 years ago. A human-powered hamster wheel hoists carefully dressed stone up tower walls (the largest tower will reach six stories when completed). Carpenters whack away at massive beams, creating supports for stone arches, while weavers demonstrate how clothing was made (a sheep's pen provides the raw material). Thirteen workstations help visitors learn about castle construction, from medieval rope-making to blacksmithing. Feel free to ask the workers questions, since some speak English.

Kids can't get enough of Guédelon—it was my son's favorite place in France. It's a favorite for local school field trips, so expect lots of kids. And if it's been raining, expect a muddy mess—you are, after all, in a construction site.

**Cost and Hours:** €9, excellent English handout, picnic area and lunch café inside; castle open July–Aug daily 10:00–19:00; mid-March–June Thu–Tue 10:00–18:00, Sun until 19:00, closed Wed; Sept Thu–Tue 10:00–17:30, Sat–Sun until 18:00, closed Wed; Oct Thu–Tue 10:00–17:30, closed Wed; closed Nov–mid-March; tel. 03 86 45 66 66, www.guedelon.fr.

**Guided Tours:** To make the most of this sight—easily worth it if you have kids—contact Guédelon expert and American expat Julie Sonveau (€100/90 min, tel. 03 86 74 64 75 or 06 63 54 86 88, julie.son@hotmail.com).

**Getting There:** Guédelon is an hour west of Vézelay on D-955, between St. Amand-en-Puisaye and St. Saveur-en-Puisaye.

*Sleeping near Guédelon:* Guédelon is remote. If you need to sleep nearby, try **$$ Hôtel Les Grands Chênes,** where British Rachael and French Alain have restored a pretty manor home among trees, lakes, and waves of grass (Db-€72, Tb-€72–87, Qb-€110, on D-18 between St. Fargeau and St. Amand-en-Puisaye, tel. 03 86 74 04 05, fax 03 86 74 11 41, www.hotel-de-puisaye.com, contact@hotel-de-puisaye.com).

# Between Burgundy and Lyon

Drivers traveling south from Beaune should think about detouring into the lovely and unspoiled Mâconnais countryside. Brancion, Chapaize, Cluny, and Taizé gather a few minutes from each other, about 25 minutes west of the autoroute between Mâcon and Tournus. Those day-tripping from Beaune should allow most of a day. To connect these towns scenically from Beaune, follow N-74 south to Chagny (Burgundy's ugliest town), find nearby Remigny (just east of Chagny), and follow D-109 to Aluze. Then follow D-978 east and D-981 south through Givry, Buxy, and on to Chapaize. Michelin map #520 is helpful.

## Brancion and Chapaize

An hour south of Beaune by car (12 miles west of Tournus on D-14) are two tiny villages, each with "daughters of Cluny"—churches that owe their existence and architectural design to the nearby and once-powerful Cluny Abbey. Between the villages you'll pass a Stonehenge-era menhir (standing stone) with a cross added on top at a later point—evidence that this was sacred ground long before Christianity (from Brancion, it's on the right just after passing the bulky Château de Nobles).

### Brancion

This is a classic feudal village. Back when there were no nations in Europe, control of land was delegated from lord to vassal. The Duke of Burgundy ruled here through his vassal, the Lord of Brancion. His vast domain—much of south Burgundy—was administered from this tiny fortified town.

Within its walls, the feudal lord had a castle, church, and all the necessary administrative buildings to provide justice, collect taxes, and so on. Strategically perched on a hill between two river valleys, he enjoyed a complete view of his domain. Brancion's population peaked centuries ago at 60. Today, it's home to only four full-time residents.

The castle, part of a network of 17 castles in the region, was destroyed in 1576 by Protestant Huguenots. After the French Revolution, it was sold to be used as a quarry and spent most of the 19th century being picked apart. While the flier gives a brief tour, the small castle is most enjoyable for its evocative angles and the lush views from the top of its keep (€4, daily 10:00–13:00 & 14:00–18:30).

Wandering from the castle to the church, you'll pass the town's lone business, a 15th-century market hall demonstrating France's boundless love affair with the market day (used by farmers from the surrounding countryside until 1900), plus several other buildings from that period.

The 12th-century warm-stone church (with faint paintings surviving from 1330) is the town's highlight. Circumnavigate the small building—this is Romanesque at its pure, unadulterated, fortress-of-God best (thick walls, small windows, once colorfully painted interior, no-frills exterior). Notice the stone roof; inside, find the English explanations of the paintings. From its front door, enjoy a lord's view over one glorious Burgundian estate.

*Sleeping and Eating in or near Brancion:* You have two good choices. In the center of the village, **$ L'Auberge du Vieux Brancion** serves traditional Burgundian fare (€14 lunch *menu,* €22 dinner *menu*) and also offers a perfectly tranquil place to spend the night (very simple and frumpy rooms, Ds-€37, Db-€50–56, family rooms-€55–72, tel. & fax 03 85 51 03 83, www.brancion.fr, josserand@brancion.fr).

For a much more upscale experience, including the best Burgundian view rooms that I've found, drive a mile south of the village, following the sign to **$$$ Hôtel la Montagne de Brancion***. A vine-covered paradise awaits...for a price. Every one of the 19 sharp, deck-equipped rooms faces a territorial view over vineyards, hills, and pastures. The garden comes with sway-back view chairs, and a pool lies below. The owners pride themselves on their "gourmet restaurant" and expect you to dine there (Db-€110–140, Tb-€170, suites-€215, breakfast-€15, *menus* from €48 or à la carte, tel. 03 85 51 12 40, fax 03 85 51 18 64, www.brancion.com, reservation@brancion.com).

## Chapaize

This hamlet, a few miles closer to Beaune, grew up around its Benedictine monastery—only its 11th-century church survives. It's a pristine place (cars park at the edge of town), peppered with flowers and rustic decay, and surrounded by grassy fields. A ghost-town café faces the village's classic Romanesque church—study the fine stonework by Lombard masons. (Its lean seems designed to challenge the faith of parishioners.) The WWI monument near the entry—with so many names from such a tiny hamlet—is a reminder that half of all young French men were casualties in the war that *didn't* end all wars. Wander around the back for a view of the belfry, and then ponder Chapaize across the street while sipping a *café au lait.*

# Cluny

People come from great distances to admire Cluny's great abbey that is no more. This mother of all abbeys once vied with the Vatican as the most important power center in Christendom (Cluny's abbot often served as mediator between Europe's kings and the pope). The building was destroyed during the French Revolution, and there's precious little to see today. Still, the abbey makes a worthwhile visit for history buffs looking to get some idea of the scale of this vast complex.

The pleasant little town that grew up around the abbey maintains its street plan, with plenty of original buildings, and even the same population it had in its 12th-century heyday (4,500). As you wander the town, which claims to be the finest surviving Romanesque town in France, enjoy the architectural details on everyday buildings. Much of the town's fortified walls, gates, and towers survive.

## ORIENTATION

Everything of interest is within a few minutes' walk of the **TI** (daily June–Sept 10:00–12:30 & 14:30–18:45, May and Oct closes at 18:00, Nov–April closes at 17:00, pick up the "helpful practical guide," 6 rue Mercière, tel. 03 85 59 05 34).

The TI is at the base of the **"Cheese Tower,"** so named because it was used to age cheese (or perhaps for the way tourists smell after climbing to the top). The tower offers a fine city view (€1.25, same hours as TI).

A **farmers' market** animates the old town each Saturday.

### Arrival in Cluny

Drivers park at designated lots and follow *Centre-Ville* signs on foot. Bus connections are meager (3–4/day from Chalon-sur-Saône, 75 min; 6/day from Mâcon, 50 min), and there's no train station.

## SIGHTS

Cluny has two sights—a museum and the abbey—but most visitors will be satisfied without paying to enter either. The museum's highlight (a big model of medieval Cluny) is free to view from the entry, and the abbey itself is easily viewed from outside (€6.50 ticket covers both museum and abbey entrance, both open daily May–Aug 9:30–18:30, Sept–April 9:30–12:00 & 13:30–17:00, tel. 03 85 59 15 93). Historians should invest in the €7 *The Abbey of Cluny* guidebook, sold in the museum.

**Museum of Art and Archaeology (Musée Ochier)**—The small abbey museum fills the Palace of the Abbot with bits from

# History of Cluny and its (Scant) Abbey

In 1964, St. Benedict (480–547), founder of the first monastery (Montecassino, south of Rome) from which a great monastic movement sprang, was named the patron saint of Europe. Christians and non-Christians alike recognize the impact that monasteries had in establishing a European civilization out of the dark chaos that followed the fall of Rome.

The Abbey of Cluny was the ruling center of the first great international franchise, or chain, of monasteries in Europe. It was the heart of an upsurge in monasticism, of church reform, and an evangelical revival that spread throughout Europe—a phenomenon historians call the Age of Faith (11th and 12th centuries). From this springboard came a vast network of abbeys, priories, and other monastic orders that kindled the establishment of modern Europe.

In 910, 12 monks founded a house of prayer at Cluny, vowing to follow the rules of St. Benedict. The cult of saints and relics was enthusiastically promoted, and the order was independent and powerful. From the start, the Abbot of Cluny answered only to the pope (not to the local bishop or secular leader). The abbots of the other Cluniac monasteries were answerable only to the Abbot of Cluny (not to their local bishop or prince). This made the Abbot of Cluny arguably the most powerful person in Europe.

The abbey's success has been attributed to a series of wise leaders, or abbots. In fact, four of the first six abbots actually became saints. They didn't answer to kings or bishops, but directly to the pope. They preached the principles of piety and the art of shrewd fundraising. Concerning piety, the abbots got people to stop looting the monasteries. Regarding shrewd fundraising, they convinced Europe's wealthy landowners to will their estates to the monasteries in return for perpetual prayers for the benefit of their needy and frightened souls.

From all this grew the greatest monastic movement of the High Middle Ages. A huge church was built at Cluny, where in 1100, it was the headquarters of 10,000 monks who ran nearly a thousand monasteries and priories across Europe. Cluny peaked in the 12th century, then faded in influence (though monasteries continued to increase in numbers and remain a force until 1789).

medieval Cluny and a very helpful model of the abbey complex (visit this before you explore the ruins). I like seeing the stone carvings eye-to-eye, though the museum holds little else of interest.

**Site of Cluny Abbey**—Much of today's old town stands on the site of what was the largest church in Christendom. It was 555 feet long, and soared high with five naves. The whole complex (church plus monastery) covered 25 acres. Revolutionaries destroyed it in

1790. Today, only the tower and part of the transept still stand. The visitor's challenge: Visualize it. Get a sense of its grandeur. The National Stud Farm and a big school obliterate much of the floor plan of the abbey.

The best point from which to appreciate the abbey's awesome dimensions is atop the steps across from the museum. Look out to the remaining tower (there used to be three). You're standing above the end of the nave that stretched all the way to those towers. Down the steps, a marble table shows the original floor plan (*vous êtes ici* means "you are here"). Walk past the nubs that remain of the once-massive columns.

You can use the English flier to tour what little of the abbey still stands (entrance between the Hôtel de Bourgogne—see below—and the cool Café du Nord). Along the way, you'll find helpful English information posted. Still, there's not much to see. The best reason to enter the site is to watch the 10-minute 3-D film. It's in French only, but still worthwhile, offering a virtual tour of the 1,000-year-old church that helps you grasp the tragedy of its destruction. If you tour the abbey, you'll exit at the flour mill (Tour de Farine), where you can loop back along the town's pleasing main drag, rue de Mercière (cafés, shops, and the TI line this pedestrian-friendly street).

**National Stud Farm (Les Haras Nationaux)**—Napoleon (who needed *beaucoup de* horses for his army of 600,000) established this horse farm in 1806. Today, 50 thoroughbred stallions kill time in their stables. If the stalls are empty, they're out doing their current studly duty...creating fine racehorses. The gate is next to Hôtel de Bourgogne (€5, visits only by guided tour, usually in the afternoon, guides speak some English, get schedule from TI).

# SLEEPING

**(€1 = about $1.50, country code: 33)**
If you're spending the night, bed down at the cushy and traditional **$$$ Hôtel de Bourgogne\*\*\***, which is built into the wall of the abbey's right transept and is as central as can be for enjoying the town (standard Db-€88–100, bigger Db-€130, garage-€9, place de l'Abbaye, tel. 03 85 59 00 58, fax 03 85 59 03 73, www.hotel-cluny.com, contact@hotel-cluny.com). It also has a fine restaurant (*menus* from €26).

# Taizé

To experience the latest in European monasticism, drop by the booming Christian community of Taizé (teh-zay), a few miles north of Cluny on the road to Brancion. The normal, un-cultlike ambience of this place—with thousands of mostly young, European pilgrims asking each other, "How's your soul today?"—is remarkable. Even if this sounds a tad airy, you might find the 30 minutes it takes to stroll from one end of the compound to the other—amid ancient abbeys and noble Romanesque churches—a worthwhile detour. A visit to Taizé can be a thought-provoking experience, particularly after a visit to Cluny. A thousand years ago, Cluny had a similar power to draw the faithful in search of direction and meaning in life.

The Taizé community welcomes visitors who'd like to spend a few days getting close to God through meditation, singing, and simple living. While designed primarily for youthful pilgrims in meditative retreat (there are about 5,000 here in a typical week), people of any age are welcome to pop in for a meal or church service.

Taizé is an ecumenical movement—prayer, silence, simplicity—welcoming Protestant as well as Catholic Christians. While it feels Catholic, it isn't. (But, as some of the brothers are actually Catholic priests, Catholics may take the Eucharist.) The Taizé style of worship is well-known among American Christians for its hauntingly beautiful chants—songbooks and CDs are the most popular souvenirs from here.

Three times a day, the bells ring and worshippers file into the long, low, simple, and modern Church of Reconciliation. It's dim—candlelit with glowing icons—as the white-robed brothers enter. The service features responsive singing of chants (from well-worn songbooks that list lyrics in 19 languages), reading of biblical passages, and silence, as worshippers on crude kneelers stare into icons. The aim: "Entering together into the mystery of God's presence." (Secondary aim: Helping Lutherans get over their fear of icons.)

**Getting There:** Drivers follow *La Communauté* signs and park in a dirt lot. Buses serve Taizé from Chalon-sur-Saône to the north and from Mâcon to the south (3/day, 60 min from each).

**Orientation:** At the southern (Cluny) end, the Welcome Office provides an orientation and daily schedule, and makes a good first stop (pick up a copy of the bimonthly *Letter from Taizé* and the single-page information leaflet, *The Taizé Community*). Time your visit for a church service (Mon–Sat 8:15, 12:20, and 20:30; Sun 10:00 and 20:30; Catholic and Protestant communion available daily). The Exposition (next to the church) is the thriving community shop, with books, CDs, sheet music, handicrafts, and

**BURGUNDY**

other souvenirs. The Oyak (near the parking lot) is where those in a less monastic mood can get a beer or burger.

**Staying at Taizé:** Those on retreat fill their days with worship services; workshops; simple, relaxed meals; and hanging out in an international festival of people searching for meaning in their lives. Visitors are welcomed free. The cost for a real stay is €10–20 per day (based on a sliding scale; those under 18 stay for less) for monastic-style room and board. Adults (over age 30) are accommodated in a more comfortable zone, but count on simple dorms. Call or email first if you plan to stay overnight (reception open Mon–Fri 10:00–12:00 & 18:00–19:00, tel. 03 85 50 30 02). The Taizé community website explains everything—in 29 languages (www.taize.fr).

# LYON AND THE RHONE VALLEY

*Rhône-Alpes*

The Rhône Valley links Provence and Burgundy and is the gateway to the high Alps. The region is bordered to the west by the soft hills of the Massif Central and by the rolling foothills of the Alps just to the east. The mighty Rhône River rumbles through the valley from its origin in Lake Geneva to its final resting place 500 miles away in the Mediterranean near Arles.

Vineyards blanket the western side of the Rhône Valley, from those of the Beaujolais just north of Lyon, to the steep slopes of Tain-Hermitage below Lyon. On the eastern side of the river and closer to Avignon are the vineyards of the famous Côtes du Rhône.

The Rhône Valley has always provided the path of least resistance for access from the Mediterranean to northern Europe, and today Roman ruins litter the valley between Lyon and Orange.

This overlooked region is dominated by the energetic metropolis of Lyon, a center of industry and culture. Just 70 minutes south of Beaune, two hours north of Avignon, and 90 minutes west of Annecy, Lyon is France's best-kept urban secret, and deserves at least one night and a full day.

## Cuisine Scene in Lyon

For the people of Lyon, eating out is a passion. It's all the buzz—a favorite conversation topic likely to generate heated debate. Here, great chefs are more famous than professional soccer players. (Paul Bocuse is the most famous chef.) Restaurants seem to outnumber cars, and all are busy. With an abundance of cozy, excellent restaurants in every price range, it's hard to go wrong—unless you order *tripes* (cow intestines, also known as *tablier de sapeur*), *foie de veau* (calf's liver), or *tête de veau* (calf's head). Beware: These questionable dishes are very common in small bistros *(bouchons)* and can be the only choices on cheaper *menus*. Look instead for these classics: St. Marcellin cheese, *salade lyonnaise* (croutons, ham, and a poached egg on a bed of lettuce), green lentils *(lentilles)* served on a salad or with sausages, *quenelles de brochet* (fish dumplings in a creamy sauce), and *filet de sandre* (local whitefish).

# Lyon

Straddling the Rhône and Saône rivers between Burgundy and Provence, Lyon has been among France's leading cities since Roman times. Today, overlooked Lyon is one of France's big-city surprises. In spite of its workaday, business-first facade, Lyon is France's most historic and culturally important city after Paris. You'll experience two different-as-night-and-day cities: the Old World cobbled alleys, Renaissance mansions, and colorful facades of Vieux Lyon; and the more staid but classy, Parisian-feeling shopping streets of Presqu'île. Once you're settled, this big city feels small, welcoming, and surprisingly untouristy. It seems everyone's enjoying the place—and they're all French.

## Planning Your Time

Lyon makes a handy day visit for train travelers, as many trains pass through Lyon and both stations have baggage storage and easy connections to the city center. But those who spend the night can experience the most renowned cuisine in France at appetizing prices, and enjoy one of Europe's most beautifully floodlit cities.

For a full day of sightseeing, start on Fourvière Hill (to get here, take the funicular near St. Jean Cathedral in Vieux Lyon), visit the Notre-Dame Basilica, and tour the Roman Theaters and Gallo-Roman Museum. Catch the funicular back down to Vieux Lyon and have lunch, then explore the old town and its hidden passageways. Finish your day touring the Museum of Fine Arts, Resistance Center, or Lumière Museum (on early films). Many of Lyon's important sights are closed on Mondays, Tuesdays, or both. Dine well in the evening and cap your day enjoying a stroll through the best-lit city in France.

Drivers connecting Lyon with southern destinations should consider the scenic detour via the Ardèche Gorges (see Lyon's "Transportation Connections," at the end of this section), and those connecting to Burgundy should consider taking the Beaujolais Wine Route, then visiting Brancion and Cluny (see page 762).

# ORIENTATION

Despite being France's third-largest metropolitan area (after Paris and Marseille), Lyon is peaceful and manageable. Traffic noise is

replaced by pedestrian friendliness in the old center—listen to how quiet this big city is. Notice the emphasis on environmentally friendly transport: Electric buses have replaced many diesel buses, and pedal taxis (called *"cyclopolitains,"* seek-loh-poh-lee-tan) are used instead of traditional taxis for short trips for a cost of just €1

per kilometer. A network of more than 1,000 city-owned bikes is available for locals' use (you'll see these black-and-red bikes everywhere—unfortunately, they require a European credit card to use).

Lyon provides the organized traveler with a full day of activities. Sightseeing can be done on foot from any of the recommended hotels, though it's handy to make use of the funiculars and Métro. Most of the town's attractions can be conveniently linked in an easy walking-tour route. Lyon's sights are concentrated in three areas: Fourvière Hill, with its white Notre-Dame Basilica glimmering over the city; historic Vieux Lyon, which lies below on the bank of the Saône River; and the Presqu'île (home to my recommended hotels), lassoed by the Saône and Rhone rivers. Huge place Bellecour lies in the middle of the Presqu'île, and always seems to be hosting an event.

## Tourist Information

The well-equipped TI is generous with helpful, free information, and can reserve a hotel for you at no charge (daily 9:00–18:00, tel. 04 72 77 69 69, www.lyon-france.com, corner of place Bellecour, free public WCs behind the TI building). Pick up the English version of the city map (with museum information, good enlargements of central Lyon and Vieux Lyon, and all public parking lots); an event schedule (ask about concerts in the Roman Theaters during *Les Nuits de Fourvière*—early June–early Aug—and events at the Opera House); and the *Only Lyon* booklet (with a directory of shopping and eateries, as well as articles on special aspects of the city). For information on the TI's audioguide and guided walks, see "Tours," later in this section.

The TI sells a useful **Lyon City Card** for serious sightseers (€19/1 day, €29/2 consecutive days, €39/3 consecutive days, under 18 half-price). This pass includes all Lyon museums, free use of the Métro/bus system, a river cruise (April–Oct), a walking tour of Lyon with a live guide, and a 50 percent discount on the TI's audioguide. If you visit the Gallo-Roman Museum and the Resistance and Deportation History Center, plus take a guided walking tour and use public transit, the one-day pass pays for itself.

## Arrival in Lyon

**By Train:** Lyon has two train stations—Lyon-Perrache and Part-Dieu. Many trains stop at both, and through-trains connect the two stations every 10 minutes. Both have baggage storage (daily 6:00–23:00) and are well-served by Métro, bus, airport shuttle, and taxi.

The **Perrache station** is more central and within a 20-minute walk of place Bellecour (follow *Porte/Place Carnot* signs, then cross place Carnot and walk straight up pedestrian rue Victor Hugo). Or take the Métro (direction: Laurent Bonnevay) two stops to Bellecour and follow *sortie rue République* signs.

The **Part-Dieu station** is a bit smaller, but has the same services as Perrache. To get to the city center, follow *sortie Vivier Merle* signs outside the station to the Métro. Take the Métro toward Stade de Gerland, transfer at Saxe-Gambetta to the Gare de Vaise route, get off at Bellecour, and follow signs reading *sortie rue République* (see "Getting Around Lyon," later in this section, for Métro help).

Figure €12 for a **taxi** from either train station to the hotels listed near place Bellecour.

**By Car:** The city center has good signage and is relatively easy to navigate, though you'll encounter traffic on the surrounding freeways. To get from the freeways to the center, follow *Centre-Ville* and *Presqu'ile* signs, and then follow *place Bellecour* signs. Park in the lots under place Bellecour or place des Célestins (yellow *P* means "parking lot") or get advice from your hotel. The TI's map identifies all public car parks. Overnight parking (generally 19:00–8:00) is only €3.50, but day rates are nearly €2 per hour.

**By Plane:** Lyon's sleek little airport, Saint-Exupéry—15 miles from the city center—is a breeze to navigate (ATMs, English information booths, tel. 08 26 80 08 26, www.lyon .aeroport.fr). It has connections to most major European cities, including two flights per hour to Paris' Charles de Gaulle Airport, and has its own TGV station (9 trains/day from downtown Paris, 2 hrs). Car rental is a snap. Three shuttles *(navettes)* per hour make the 40-minute trip from the airport to both Lyon train stations for €9 (tel. 04 72 68 72 17, www.satobus.com). Allow €50–60 for a taxi.

## Helpful Hints

**Consulates:** The **US Consulate** is near the Rhône River, east of the Cordeliers Métro stop at 1 quai Jules Courmant (tel. 04 78 38 36 88), and the **Canadian Consulate** is at 17 rue Bourgelat (tel. 04 72 77 64 07).

**Market Days:** A small market stretches along the Saône River between pont Bonaparte and passerelle du Palais de Justice (daily until 12:30). Tuesday through Saturday, it's produce; Sunday morning, it's crafts and contemporary art on the other side of the bridge near the Court of Justice; and Monday, it's textiles. There's another bustling morning produce market on boulevard de la Croix-Rousse every day except Monday (see "La Croix-Rousse," on page 753).

**Supermarket:** The little **Casino** below the recommended Hôtel des Célestins is handy to most of my hotels (Mon–Fri 8:00–20:00, Sat 15:00–19:30, closed Sun).

**Festivals:** Lyon celebrates the Virgin Mary with candlelit windows during the Festival of Lights each year on December 8 (www.lumieres.lyon.fr).

**Internet Access:** Nearly all hotels I list have Internet access. **Raconte Moi La Terre** is a way-cool travel bookstore with Internet access near the Cordelier Métro stop (where rues Grolée and Thomassin meet, tel. 04 78 92 60 62).

**Laundry:** A launderette is at 7 rue Mercière on the Presqu'île near the Alphonse Juin bridge (daily 6:00–21:00); another is between place Bellecour and Perrache station, a few steps off rue Victor Hugo (daily 7:30–20:30, 19 rue Ste. Helene).

**SNCF Train Office:** The **SNCF Boutique**, at 2 place Bellecour, is handy for train info, reservations, and tickets (Mon–Fri 9:00–18:45, Sat 10:00–18:30, closed Sun).

**Children's Activities:** The Parc de la Tête d'Or is vast, with rental rowboats, a miniature golf course, and ponies to ride (across Rhône River from La Croix-Rousse neighborhood, Métro: Masséna, tel. 04 72 69 47 60).

## Getting Around Lyon

Lyon has a user-friendly public transit system, with two sleek streetcar lines (tramways T-1 and T-2), four underground Métro lines (A, B, C, and D), an extensive bus system, and two funiculars (there are two directions heading uphill: *Fourvière* for the basilica and *Saint-Just* for the Roman Theaters). The subway is similar to Paris' Métro in many ways (e.g., routes are signed by *direction* for the last stop on the line) but is more automated (you buy tickets at coin-op machines), cleaner, and less crowded. You can transfer between Métro and tramway lines with the same ticket (€1.60/1 hr, €2.20/2 hrs, €4.40/1 day, €12.80/10 rides, all tickets cover funicular). The €4.40 one-day ticket is a great deal if you use the funicular and visit either the Resistance Center or the Lumière Museum. Change the display language to English by choosing the British flag option. Use the black roller to *selectionner* your ticket, firmly push the top button twice to *confirmer* your request, and then insert coins. If you're using the Métro, insert your ticket in the turnstile, then reclaim it. If the stop has no turnstile, you must validate your ticket by punching it in a nearby chrome machine (tramway users always validate on the trams). Study the wall maps to be sure of your *direction;* ask a local if you're not certain. Yellow signs are directional, and green signs lead to exits.

## TOURS

The TI's handy **audioguide** (€8/half-day) offers good, self-guided walking tours of Vieux Lyon.

Live **guided walks** of Vieux Lyon are offered most days at 14:30 (€9, 2 hours, in French, in English if demand justifies, depart from the TI, no need to reserve—just show up, generally 5 days a week in summer, verify days and times with TI). Other, less-frequent English-language walks include tours of the Opera House, La Croix-Rousse district, and silk workshops.

## SELF-GUIDED SPIN-TOUR

### Bonaparte Bridge (Pont Bonaparte)

This central bridge, just a block from place Bellecour, is made-to-order for a spin-tour.

• *Stand on the bridge and face the golden statue of the Virgin Mary marking the Notre–Dame Basilica on Fourvière Hill. (It's actually capping the smaller chapel, which predates the church by 500 years.) The basilica is named for the Roman Forum* (Fourvière) *upon which it sits. Now begin to look clockwise.*

The Metallic Tower (called La Tour Métallique—not La Tour Eiffel), like the basilica, was finished just before World War I. It was originally an observation tower but today functions only as a TV tower. The husky church on the riverbank below (St. Jean Cathedral) marks the center of the old town. Upstream, the Neoclassical columns are part of the Court of Justice (where Klaus Barbie, head of the local Gestapo—a.k.a. "the Butcher of Lyon"—was sentenced to life in prison in the 1980s). Farther upstream, the hill covered with tall, pastel-colored houses is the La Croix-Rousse district, former home of the city's huge silk industry. With the invention of the "Jacquard looms," which required 12-foot-tall ceilings, new factory buildings were needed and the new weaving center grew up on this hill. In 1850, it was thriving with 30,000 looms.

# Lyon at a Glance

▲▲**Roman Theaters and Gallo-Roman Museum** Terrific museum covering Roman Lyon. **Hours:** Tue-Sun 10:00-18:00, closed Mon. See page 749.

▲▲**Resistance and Deportation History Center** Displays and videos telling the inspirational story of the French Resistance. **Hours:** Wed-Fri 9:00-17:30, Sat-Sun 9:30-18:00, closed Mon-Tue. See page 755.

▲**Museum of Fine Arts** France's second-most important fine-arts museum (after the Louvre). **Hours:** Wed-Thu and Sat-Mon 10:00-18:00, Fri 10:30-18:00, closed Tue. See page 753.

▲**Lumière Museum** Museum of film, dedicated to the Lumière brothers' pivotal contribution. **Hours:** Tue-Sun 11:00-18:30, closed Mon. See page 756.

**Notre-Dame Basilica** Lyon's ornate version of Paris' Sacré-Cœur. **Hours:** Daily 8:00-19:00, Sun Mass usually at 7:00, 9:30, 11:00, and 17:00. See page 746.

**St. Jean Cathedral** Gothic church with 700-year-old astronomical clock. **Hours:** Mon-Fri 8:00-12:00 & 14:00-19:30, Sat-Sun 14:00-17:00. See page 750.

**Traboules** Cool covered passageways in Vieux Lyon. **Hours:** Daily 8:00-20:00. See page 750.

**Atelier de la Soierie** Workshop demonstrating handmade silk printing and screen painting. **Hours:** Mon-Fri 9:00-12:00 & 14:00-19:00, Sat 9:00-13:00 & 14:00-18:00, closed Sun. See page 752.

**Museums of Fabrics and Decorative Arts** Museum of Fabrics tracing development of textile weaving over 2,000 years; Museum of Decorative Arts featuring 18th-century decor in a mansion. **Hours:** Tue-Sun 10:00-17:30, closed Mon, Museum of Decorative Arts closes 12:00-14:00. See page 755.

LYON

The place Bellecour side of the river is the district of Presqu'île (*presqu'île* means "peninsula" in French, or literally "almost-an-island"). This strip of land created where the Saône and Rhône rivers come together is home to Lyon's Opera House, City Hall, theater, top-end shopping, banks, and all of my recommended hotels. A morning market sets up daily under the trees (just beyond the red bridge), and the riverfront café (La Buvette du

Pont Bonaparte) to your right is ideal for a drink with a view (best at night).

Speaking of bridges, all of Lyon's bridges—including the one you're standing on—were destroyed by the Nazis as they checked out in 1944. Looking downstream, you can see the stately mansions of Lyon's well-established families. Across the river again, the Neo-Gothic St. Georges church marks the neighborhood of the first silk weavers. The ridge behind St. Georges is dominated by a big building—once a seminary for priests, now a state high school—and leads us back to Mary.

• *Walk across the bridge and continue toward the hill two blocks to find the funicular station, where you can ride up Fourvière Hill to the basilica (catch the train marked* Fourvière, *not* St. Just; *sit up front and admire the funicular's funky old technology). From there, you can tour the basilica, enjoy the city view, and visit the Roman Theaters and Gallo-Roman Museum, then catch another funicular back down and explore the old town (Vieux Lyon). I've listed key sights (below) in this order. Otherwise, it's a 20-minute walk upriver to place des Terreaux, where you'll find the City Hall (Hôtel de Ville) and Museum of Fine Arts.*

# SIGHTS

## Fourvière Hill
### Notre-Dame Basilica
### (Basilique Notre-Dame de Fourvière)

Bam!—this ornate church is right in your face as your exit the funicular. About the year 1870, the bishop of Lyon vowed to build a magnificent tribute to the Virgin Mary if the Prussians spared his city. (Similar deal-making led to the construction of the basilica of Sacré-Cœur in Paris.) Building began in 1872, and the church was ready for worship by World War I.

**Cost and Hours:** Free, daily 8:00–19:00, Sun Mass usually at 7:00, 9:30, 11:00, and 17:00.

**◐ Self-Guided Tour:** Before entering, step back to view the fancy facade, the older chapel on the right (supporting the statue of Mary; open daily 7:00–19:00), and the top of the Eiffel-like TV tower on the left.

Go inside. You won't find a more Mary-centered church. Everything—floor, walls, ceiling—is covered with fine **mosaics.** Scenes glittering on the walls tell stories of the Virgin (in Church history on the left, and in French history on the right). Amble down the center aisle at an escargot's pace and examine some of these scenes:

First scene on the left: In 431, the Council of Ephesus declared Mary to be the "Mother of God."

Across the nave, first on the right: The artist imagines

## Illuminated Lyon

The golden statue of Mary above Notre-Dame Basilica was placed atop a 16th-century chapel on December 8, 1852. Spontaneously, the entire city welcomed her with candles in their windows. Each December 8 ever since, the city glows softly with countless candles.

This tradition has spawned an actual industry. Lyon is famous as a model of state-of-the-art floodlighting, and the city hosts conventions on the topic. Each night, more than 200 buildings, sites, and public spaces are gloriously flood-lit. Go for an after-dinner stroll and enjoy the view from Bonaparte Bridge after dark. Paris calls itself the City of Light—but actually Lyon is.

Lugdunum (Lyon)—the biggest city in Roman Gaul, with 50,000 inhabitants—as the first Christian missionaries arrive. The first Christian martyrs in France (killed in A.D. 177) dance across heaven with palm branches.

Next left: In 1571, at the pivotal sea battle of Lepanto, Mary provides the necessary miracle as the outnumbered Christian forces beat the Turks.

Opposite (from right to left): Joan of Arc hears messages from Mary, rallies the French against the English at the Siege of Orléans in 1429 (find the Orléans coat of arms above), and is ultimately burned at the stake in Rouen at age 19 (1431).

On the left: In 1854, Pope Pius I proclaims the dogma of the Immaculate Conception in St. Peter's Square (establishing the belief among Catholics that Mary was born without the "Original Sin" of apple-eating Adam and Eve). To the left of the Pope, angels carry the tower of Fourvière Church; and to the right is the image of the Virgin of Lourdes (who miraculously appeared in 1858).

Finally, on the right: Louis XIII offers the crown of France to the Virgin Mary. (The empty cradle hints that while he had her on the line, he asked, "Could I please have a son?" Louis XIV was born shortly thereafter.) Above marches a parade of pious French kings, from Clovis and Charlemagne to Napoleon (on the far right—with the white cross and red coat). Below are the great Marian churches of France (left to right)—Chartres, Paris' Sacré-Cœur and Notre-Dame, Reims (where most royalty was crowned), and this church. These six scenes in mosaic all lead to the altar where Mary reigns as Queen of Heaven.

Exit under Joan of Arc and descend to the **lower church,** dedicated to Mary's earthly husband, Joseph. Priorities here are painfully clear, as money ran out for Joseph's church. Today, it's used as a concert venue (notice the spongy-yellow acoustic material

# Lyon

P   PARKING
M   METRO STATION
T   TRAMWAY
++  FUNICULAR
☆   VIEW

SEE Old Lyon & Presqu'ile Detail Map

TO PARK DE LA TETE D'OR

TO LA CROIX-ROUSSE

SILK WORKSHOP

OPERA

PLACE DES TERREAU

HOTEL DE VILLE

Hôtel de Ville

SAONE

PLACE ST. PAUL

ALGERIE

MUSEUM OF FINE ARTS

HERRIOT   REPUB.   GARET

FOOT BRIDGE

FOURVIERE

PLACE CHANGE

PRESQU'ILE

PONT LAFAY.

NOTRE-DAME

VIEUX LYON

A. JUIN

R. MERCIERE   BREST   RUE PRES.

Cordeliers

RUE

PONT

Fourvière

GALLO-ROMAN MUSEUM

ST. ART   ST. JEAN

FOOT BRIDGE

ST. JEAN

US CONSULATE

PONT.

ROMAN THEATERS

TRAMAS.

Vieux Lyon

SNCF TICKETS

ZOLA   GASP.

PLACE DE LA REPUBLIQUE

WILSON

TO PART DIEU TRAIN STN.

Minimes

ST. JUST

PLACE BELLECOUR

Bellecour

RUE BARRE

PONT GUILL.

TO LUMIERE MUSEUM

RUE DU PLAT   RUE SALA

i   WC

RIVER

N

TO BEAUJOLAIS & WINE ROUTE

A-6 AUTOROUTE

Ampère

RUE VICTOR HUGO

DE LA CHARITE

STE-HEL.   PONT DE L'UNIV.

BERNARD

RHONE

MUSEUMS OF FABRICS & DECORATIVE ARTS

PLACE AMPERE

RUE

PLACE CARNOT

QUAI DR. GUILLETON   RUE GUILLETON

QUAI

PERRACHE TRAIN STN.

M  T

PONT GALLIENI

TO RESISTANCE MUSEUM & AIRPORT

DCH

1/4 MILE
400 METERS

❶ Hôtel Iris
❷ Brasserie Georges
❸ Chez Abel Rest.
❹ Les Muses de l'Opéra Rest.

❺ La Buvette du Pont Bonaparte Café
❻ Launderette (2)
❼ Bonaparte Bridge (Walk Starts Here)

LYON

covering the vaulting). Return on the same stairs to the humble 16th-century chapel to the Virgin; outside, look up to see the glorious statue of Mary that overlooks Lyon.

Just around this chapel (past the church museum and the recommended Restaurant Panoramique—described under "Eating," later in this section) is a commanding **view** of Lyon. You can see from La Croix-Rousse district to the Bonaparte Bridge, with greater Lyon (pop. 1.3 million) spread out before you in the distance. The black barrel-vaulted structure to the left is the Opera House, and the rose-colored skyscraper in the distance is appropriately called "Le Crayon" (the pencil). On a clear afternoon, you'll get a glimpse of Mont Blanc (the highest point in Europe, just left of the pencil-shaped skyscraper), looking as *blanc* as can be.

• *To get to the Roman Theaters and the Gallo-Roman Museum (described below), walk back toward the funicular station and turn left down rue Roger Radisson. The museum hides down the steps where rue Roger Radisson meets rue Cléberg. Before entering the museum, get the best overview of the ancient site by taking a short left on the road leading downhill (rue Cléberg). Then find the ramp that leads to the museum's rooftop (open the gate). A red banner marks the museum entry.*

## ▲▲Roman Theaters and Gallo-Roman Museum (Musée de la Civilisation Gallo-Romaine)

Constructed in the hillside with views of the two Roman Theaters, this museum makes clear Lyon's importance in Roman times. Lyon (founded in A.D. 43) was an important transportation hub for the administration of Roman Gaul (and much of modern-day France). Emperors Claudius and Caracalla were both born in Lugdunum (Roman Lyon).

The fascinating **Gallo-Roman Museum** is wonderfully explained in English, and takes you on a chronological stroll through ancient Lyon. All the artifacts are local ("Gallo-Roman"). The fine bronze chariot dates from the seventh century B.C. The model of Roman Lyon shows a town of 50,000 in its second-century A.D. glory days. (The forum stands where the basilica does today.) Curved stones in an arena were actual seats—inscribed with the names of big shots who sat there. A speech by Emperor Claudius carved into a big, black-bronze tablet recalls how, in A.D. 48, he worked to integrate Gauls into the empire by declaring that they were eligible to sit in the Roman Senate (English translation on the wall). A mosaic shows a *Ben Hur*–type chariot race and, with the push of a button, you can see the mechanics of a Roman theater stage curtain in action...raised instead of lowered (€4, €6 if special exhibits, free on Thu, open Tue–Sun 10:00–18:00, closed Mon, tel. 04 72 38 49 30, www.musees-gallo-romains.com).

• *Exit the museum into the theaters...*

**LYON**

The **big theater** (which originally held 10,000) today seats 3,000 for concerts. The **smaller theater,** an "odeon" (from the Greek "ode" for song), was acoustically designed for speeches and songs. The ground is peppered with gravestones and sarcophagi (free, open daily until 19:00). From early June through early August, the theaters host *Les Nuits de Fourvière,* an open-air festival of concerts, theater, dance, and film. Check programs at the TI and purchase tickets here at the theaters (box office at gate exit toward the Minimes funicular station, Mon–Sat 11:00–18:00, closed Sun), or online at www.nuitsdefourviere.org.

• *The ancient road between the Roman Theaters leads down and out, where you'll find the Minimes funicular station (to the right as you leave the theaters). Take the funicular to Vieux Lyon (go to the side of the tracks labeled* Vieux Lyon, *not* St. Just*), where it will deposit you only a few steps from St. Jean Cathedral.*

## Vieux Lyon (Old Lyon)

**St. Jean Cathedral**—Stand back in the square for the best view. This mostly Gothic cathedral took 200 years to build. It doesn't soar as high as its northern French counterparts. Influenced by their Italian neighbors, churches in southern France are less vertical than those in the north. This cathedral, while unremarkable inside (except for its 700-year-old astronomical clock that performs several times a day), is the "primate cathedral of Gaul," serving what's considered the oldest Christian city in France (Mon–Fri 8:00–12:00 & 14:00–19:30, Sat–Sun 14:00–17:00).

Outside (make two right turns as you leave) are the ruins of a mostly 11th-century church, destroyed during the French Revolution (the cathedral was turned into a "temple of reason"). What's left of a baptistery from an early Christian church (c. A.D. 400) is under glass.

▲**Old Lyon and Covered Passageways (Traboules)**—Lyon offers the best concentration of well-preserved Renaissance buildings in the country. The city grew rich from its trade fairs and banking, and was the king of Europe's silk industry from the 16th to 19th centuries, humming with some 30,000 looms. The fine buildings of the old center were inspired by Italy and financed by the silk industry.

Rue St. Jean, leading from the cathedral to place du Change, is the main drag, flanked by parallel pedestrian streets. (The rue de Bœuf is quieter and more appealing than touristy rue St. Jean.) The city's trademark serpentine passageways *(traboules)* were essentially shortcuts linking the old town's three main streets. These hidden paths give visitors a hide-and-seek opportunity to discover pastel courtyards, lovely loggias, and delicate arches. Spiral staircases were often shared by several houses. The *traboules* provided shelter

# Old Lyon

1. La Machonnerie Restaurant
2. Les Lyonnais Restaurant
3. Les Retrouvailles Rest.
4. Le Tire-Bouchon Rest.
5. Nardone René Glacier
6. La Basoche Renaissance Building
7. Traboules Entrance at #54 Rue St. Jean

- ::::: TRABOULES (PASSAGEWAYS)
- +++ FUNICULAR
- ;> VIEW
- M METRO STATION
- P PARKING

when silk was being moved from one stage to the next.

Detour a few steps from rue St. Jean and make a left up rue de la Bombarde. You'll find a well-restored Renaissance building (La Basoche) that gives you a good idea of what hides behind many facades in old Lyon (note the black-and-white photos showing this structure before its 1968 renovation). As you stroll along rue St. Jean, notice the heavy doors leading to the *traboules*. The longest is #54, which links to rue du Bœuf. When a doorway is open, you can wander in and explore inner courtyards. Only a few of Lyon's 315 *traboules* are open to the public, and some of those are open mornings only (press top button next to street-front door to release door when entering, push lit buttons to illuminate dark walkways, and slide door-handle levers when leaving). You're welcome to explore from 8:00 until 20:00 if you are quiet, respectful of the residents, and don't go up any stairs.

As you wander Vieux Lyon, look for door plaques giving a history of each building and *traboule*. After walking through a few *traboules*, you'll understand why Lyon's old town was an ideal center for the Resistance fighters to slip in and out of as they confounded the Nazis.

The place du Change, at the north end of rue St. Jean, was the banking center of medieval Lyon. This money scene developed after the city was allowed to host trade fairs in 1420. Its centerpiece is France's first stock exchange.

• *From here it's a short walk across the river to place des Terreaux and the Museum of Fine Arts (cross pont de la Feuillée and continue straight four blocks). Ice-cream connoisseurs must stop at* **Nardone René Glacier** *before crossing the river (daily 10:00–24:00, on river near place du Change, 3 place Ennemond Fousseret).*

## Presqu'île

This bit of land (French for "peninsula," and literally meaning "almost-an-island") between the two rivers is Lyon's shopping spine, with thriving pedestrian streets. The neighborhood's northern focal point is...

**Place des Terreaux**—This grand square hosts the City Hall (Hôtel de Ville), the Museum of Fine Arts, and a grand fountain by Frédéric-Auguste Bartholdi (the French sculptor who designed America's Statue of Liberty). Its most important function for locals is allowing the last rays of sun to penetrate the café tables near the City Hall. Join the crowd for a late-afternoon sip.

The fountain features Marianne (the Lady of the Republic) riding a four-horse-powered chariot. The square itself is pretty wet, with 69 fountains spurting playfully in a vast grid.

**Atelier de la Soierie**—This silk workshop, just off place des Terreaux (behind Café le Moulin Joli, a Resistance hangout during

World War II), welcomes the public to drop in to see silk printing and screen painting by hand. Keep in mind that this is a lost
art that today has mostly been replaced by machines. Within the
shop, you'll see stretched silk canvases, buckets of dye, and artists
in action. Climb the staircase to visit a boutique selling handmade
silk creations. Prices range from €25 to €250 (free entry, Mon–Fri
9:00–12:00 & 14:00–19:00, Sat 9:00–13:00 & 14:00–18:00, closed
Sun).

**La Croix-Rousse**—Hilly, untouristy, and Soho-esque, this
neighborhood was home to 30,000 silk looms in the 1800s. Today
this part of town is popular with Lyon's hippies and hipsters. The
smartest way to visit is to take the Métro straight to the top, then
follow a series of scenic slopes and stairs that gradually bring you
back down to the Presqu'île (described below). Or—to burn off
last night's *Lyonnaise* feast—follow this suggested route in reverse.

Begin by exiting the Métro at the La Croix-Rousse stop.
Every day but Monday, a lively produce market stretches down
boulevard de la Croix-Rousse. Start your downhill stroll along
rue des Pierres Plantées, pausing to appreciate the impressive view
from the Jardin de la Grande Côte. Head down the stairs and follow the main drag, montée de la Grande Côte. Swing a right on
rue des Tables Claudiennes, and take the next left down a set of
stairs overlooking the Amphitheater of the Three Gauls—another
of Lyon's fine Roman ruins. Cross the street and climb down your
last set of stairs into leafy place Sathonay. You may see giddy brides
and grooms lining up outside the Salle des Mariage. This pretty
park is an understandably popular place to tie the knot. From here,
Lyon fans out in front of you, with the Rhône to your left and the
Saône to your right.

▲**Museum of Fine Arts (Musée des Beaux-Arts)**—Located
in a former abbey, which was secularized by Napoleon in 1803
and made into a public museum, this fine-arts museum has an
impressive collection, ranging from Egyptian antiquities to
Impressionist paintings.

The first floor offers a stroll through a fine collection of
ancient (especially Egyptian) art, medieval art, and Art Nouveau
(furniture). The adjacent chapel is a dreamy Orsay-like display of
19th- and 20th-century statues (including work by Auguste Rodin
and Bartholdi).

The second floor displays a pretty selection of paintings from many ages and countries (with no famous works,
but a fine Impressionist collection). The highlight is a series of
pre-Raphaelite-type works called *Le Poème de l'Âme* ("The Poem
of the Soul") by Louis Janmot. This cycle of 18 paintings and 16
charcoal drawings traces the story of the souls of a boy and a girl as
they journey through childhood, adolescence, and into adulthood.

## Old Lyon and Presqu'île

Legend:

**M** Metro Station
**---†** Funicular
**∴** View
**P** Parking
**▢** See Old Lyon Detail Map

1 Hôtel des Artistes
2 Hôtel Globe et Cecil
3 Hôtel des Célestins & Casino Supermarket
4 Hotel du Théâtre
5 Hôtel la Residence
6 Youth Hostel
7 La Machonnerie Restaurant
8 Les Lyonnais Restaurants (2)
9 Les Retrouvailles Rest.
10 Le Tire-Bouchon Rest.
11 Rest. Panoramique de la Fourvière
12 Nardone René Glacier
13 Le Bouchon aux Vins Rest.
14 Le Mercière Rest.
15 La Francotte Bistro
16 Grand Café des Négociants
17 Launderette
18 Internet Café

LYON

They struggle with fears and secular temptations before gaining spiritual enlightenment on the way to heaven. The boy loses his faith and enjoys a short but delicious hedonistic fling that leads to misery in hell. But a mother's prayers intercede, and he reunites with the girl to enjoy heavenly redemption.

**Cost and Hours:** €6, Wed–Thu and Sat–Mon 10:00–18:00, Fri 10:30–18:00, closed Tue, first floor closes 11:55–13:05, second floor closes 13:05–14:15, pick up museum map on entering, picnic-perfect courtyard, 20 place des Terreaux, Métro: Hôtel de Ville, tel. 04 72 10 17 40, www.mba-lyon.fr. A bar/café with calming terrace seating is on the first floor, next to the bookstore.

**Museums of Fabrics and Decorative Arts (Musées des Tissus et des Arts Décoratifs)**—These museums, south of place Bellecour, fill two buildings (sharing a courtyard and connected with an interior hallway). While packed with exquisite exhibits, they provide little information in English (descriptive sheets upstairs in the Museum of Fabrics, nothing in Museum of Decorative Arts). The Museum of Fabrics traces the development of textile weaving over 2,000 years and shows off some breathtaking silk work. The Museum of Decorative Arts, billed as "an ambience museum," is a luxurious mansion decorated to the hilt with 18th-century furniture, textiles, and tapestries in a plush domestic setting (€5 covers both museums, Tue–Sun 10:00–17:30, closed Mon, Museum of Decorative Arts closes 12:00–14:00, 34 rue de la Charité, Métro: Bellecour, tel. 04 78 38 42 00, www.musee-des-tissus.com).

**Enjoying Presqu'île**—There's more to this "almost-an-island" than the sights listed here. Join the treadmill of shoppers on sprawling rue de la République (north of place Bellecour) and the teeming rue Victor Hugo pedestrian mall (south of place Bellecour). Peruse the *bouchons* (characteristic bistros—especially characteristic in the evening) of rue Mercière.

**Grand Café des Négociants** is ideal for a break. This *grand café*, which has been in business since 1864, feels like it hasn't changed since then, with its soft leather chairs, painted ceilings, and glass chandeliers (daily, 1 place Francisque Régaud, near Cordeliers Métro stop, tel. 04 78 42 50 05).

## Away from the Center

**▲▲Resistance and Deportation History Center (Centre d'Histoire de la Résistance et de la Déportation)**—Located near Vichy (capital of the French puppet state) and neutral Switzerland, Lyon was the center of the French Resistance from 1942 to 1945. These ordinary heroes fought the Nazis—they were the "underground," or Resistance. Bakers hid radios inside loaves of bread to secretly contact London. Barmaids passed along tips from tipsy Nazis. Communists in black berets cut telephone lines.

Farmers hid downed airmen in haystacks. Housewives spread news from the front with their gossip. Printers countered Nazi propaganda with anonymous pamphlets.

This well-done museum, which once served as a Nazi torture chamber, uses audioguides, videos, and easy-to-follow English descriptions to tell the inspirational story of the French Resistance (€4, Wed–Fri 9:00–17:30, Sat–Sun 9:30–18:00, closed Mon–Tue, 14 avenue Berthelot).

**Getting There:** You have a few options: Ride the **Métro** to Jean Macé, exit toward the elevated train line, turn right on avenue Berthelot, and walk back five blocks; **walk** 15 minutes from Perrache station across pont Gallieni, then three blocks to 14 avenue Berthelot; or, easiest, take the T-2 **tramway** from below Perrache station to Centre Berthelot.

▲**Lumière Museum (Musée Lumière)**—Antoine Lumière and his two sons Louis and Auguste—the Eastman-Kodaks of France—ran a huge factory with 200 workers in the 1880s, producing four million glass photographic plates a day. Then, in 1895, they made the first *cinématographe*, or movie. In 1903, they pioneered the "autochrome" process of painting frames to make "color photos." This museum tells their story.

The highlights are the many screens playing the earliest "movies." The first film reels held about 950 frames, which played at 19 per second, so these first movies were only 50 seconds long. About 1,500 Lumière films are catalogued between 1895 and 1907. (Notice that each movie is tagged with its "Catalog Lumière" number.) The very first movie ever made features workers piling out of the Lumière factory at the end of a work day.

The museum fills the Villa Lumière, the family's belle époque mansion, built in 1902. The ground floor shows movies and the earliest cameras and projectors. Upstairs are exhibits on still photography and the Lumière living quarters (furnished c. 1900). Across the park from the mansion is a shrine at what's left of the warehouse where the first movie was actually shot. In a wonderful coincidence, *lumière* is the French word for "light."

En route to the museum, enjoy your ride on the futuristic (and driverless) Métro D. Sit in the front and command your own underground starship (€6.60, Tue–Sun 11:00–18:30, closed Mon, half a block from the Monplaisir-Lumière Métro stop at 25 rue du Premier-Film, tel. 04 78 78 18 95, www.institut-lumiere.org).

# NIGHTLIFE

Lyon has France's second-largest cultural budget after Paris, so there are always plenty of theatrical productions and concerts to attend. The TI has the latest information and schedules. From mid-June through mid-September, the Opera House terrace hosts an outdoor jazz café with free concerts (usually Mon–Sat at 19:00, 20:00, and 22:00; no Sun concerts, www.opera-lyon.com).

After dinner, a stroll through Lyon's old town and a walk along the river affords a chance to savor the city's famous illuminations (see sidebar on page 747). For a lively bar and people-watching scene, prowl rue de la Monnaie (angles off "restaurant row," rue Mercière to the south) and the streets between place des Terreaux and the Opera House.

# SLEEPING

Hotels in Lyon are a steal compared to those in Paris. Weekends are generally discounted in this city that lives off business travelers (some hotels even offer 2-for-1 deals if booked ahead—ask about weekend packages). Be aware that prices rise and rooms disappear when trade fairs are in town (which is not uncommon), so it's smart to reserve your room in advance. If you have trouble, the TI can help for free in person or by email (resa@lyon-france.com). All hotels listed below are on the Presqu'île. Hotels have elevators unless otherwise noted, and air-conditioning is a godsend when it's hot.

## On or near Place des Célestins

It's well worth booking ahead to sleep in this classy yet unpretentious neighborhood (Métro: Bellecour). Just a block off the central place Bellecour and a block to the Saône River, travelers have easy access to Lyon's sights, can join shoppers perusing the upscale boutiques, or can watch children playing in the small square fronting the Théâtre des Célestins. Warning: Weekend nights can be noisy if you score a room facing place des Célestins.

**$$$ Hôtel des Artistes***, ideally located on place des Célestins, is red-velvet plush, comfortable, professional, and the best value in its price range (Sb-€85–105, standard Db-€95–105, larger Db-€115–125, standard rooms are plenty comfortable, air-con, Internet access and Wi-Fi, 8 rue Gaspard-André, tel. 04 78 42 04 88, fax 04 78 42 93 76, www.hoteldesartistes.fr, hartiste @club-internet.fr).

**$$$ Hôtel Globe et Cecil***, the most elegant of my listings, offers refined comfort on a refined street with traditionally decorated and generously sized rooms. The lounge areas are spacious (Sb-€130, Db-€160, free breakfast, air-con, pay Wi-Fi, 21 rue Gasparin, tel. 04 78 42 58 95, fax 04 72 41 99 06, www.globeetcecil hotel.com, accueil@globeetcecilhotel.com).

**$$ Hôtel des Célestins**, just off place des Célestins, is warmly run by Stephanie and Cornell-grad Laurent. Its cheery, immaculate rooms are filled with thoughtful touches. Streetside

## Sleep Code

**(€1 = about $1.50, country code: 33)**
**S** = Single, **D** = Double/Twin, **T** = Triple, **Q** = Quad, **b** = bathroom,
**s** = shower only, **\*** = French hotel rating system (0–4 stars).
Unless otherwise noted, credit cards are accepted and English
is spoken.

To help you sort easily through these listings, I've divided
the rooms into three categories based on the price for a
standard double room with bath:

**$$$** **Higher Priced**—Most rooms €95 or more.
**$$** **Moderately Priced**—Most rooms between €65–95.
**$** **Lower Priced**—Most rooms €65 or less.

rooms have more light and weekend noise (Sb-€69–85, Db-€85–95, bigger Db-€100 and worth the extra euros, Tb-€105–125, apartments-€110–150, €8.50 buffet breakfast served 7:00–12:00, completely non-smoking, air-con, Internet access, pay Wi-Fi, 4 rue des Archers, tel. 04 72 56 08 98, fax 04 72 56 08 65, www.hotel celestins.com).

**$$ Hotel du Théâtre\*\*** requires a tromp up two flights of stairs to reach the lobby and does not have air-conditioning, but it's well-located on place des Célestins (enter from the hotel's rear). It comes with firm beds, mostly spacious rooms, and simple but thoughtful touches (S-€45, Sb-€60, Db-€66–72, Tb-€90, place des Célestins, tel. 04 78 42 33 32, fax 04 72 40 00 61, www.hotel -du-theatre.fr, contact@hotel-du-theatre.fr).

## South of Place Bellecour

This hotel is my closest listing to the Perrache train station.

**$$ Hôtel la Residence\*\*\*** feels big and institutional, but its 67 rooms are air-conditioned, well cared for, and a fine value. Most are spacious, with high ceilings (Sb/Db-€80, Tb-€95, Qb-€100, most rooms have bathtubs, Internet access, 18 Victor Hugo, tel. 04 78 42 63 28, fax 04 78 42 85 76, www.hotel-la-residence.com, hotel-la-residence@wanadoo.fr).

## Near the Opera House

**$ Hôtel Iris,** tucked away near the Opera House, is the most basic and cheap budget deal I found in Lyon. The location is good for night owls, but edgy for others. The owners are slowly transforming this historic building (with a striking 16th-century inner courtyard stairway) into a little 14-room hotel. For now, rooms are somber, with brown tones and an African motif. Access to most rooms is through a smelly back alley (D-€39, Db-€47–56, breakfast-€5, 36 rue de l'Arbre Sec, Métro: Hôtel de Ville, tel. 04 78 39 93 80, fax 04 72 00 89 91, www.hoteliris.freesurf.fr).

**$ Vieux Lyon Youth Hostel** is impressively situated a 10-minute walk above Vieux Lyon. Open 24 hours daily, it has a lively common area with kitchen access and cheap meals (bed in 4- to 6-bed room-€17, includes sheets and breakfast, small safes available, 45 montée du Chemin, Métro: Hôtel de Ville, tel. 04 78 15 05 50, fax 04 78 15 05 51, www.fuaj.org, lyon@fuaj.org). Book only by email. Take the funicular to Minimes, exit the station and make a left U-turn, and follow the station wall downhill to montée du Chemin.

# EATING

Dining is a ▲▲▲ attraction in Lyon, and it comes at a bearable price. Half the fun is joining the procession of window-shoppers mulling over where they'll *diner ce soir*. At dinner, the city's population seems to double as locals emerge to stretch their stomachs.

Lyon's characteristic *bouchons* are small bistros that evolved from the days when Mama would feed the silk workers after a long day. True *bouchons* are simple places with limited selection and seating (just like Mama's), serving only traditional fare and special 46-centiliter *pot* (pronounced "poh") wine pitchers. The lively pedestrian streets of Vieux Lyon and rue Mercière on the Presqu'île are *bouchon* bazaars, worth strolling even if you dine elsewhere. While food quality may be better away from these popular restaurant rows, you can't beat the atmosphere. Many of Lyon's restaurants close on Sunday and Monday, except along rue Mercière. If you plan to dine somewhere special, reserve ahead.

## Vieux Lyon

Come to Old Lyon for maximum ambience. For the epicenter of restaurant activity, go to place Neuve St. Jean, and survey the scene and menus before sitting down.

**La Machonnerie,** a block opposite the cathedral, serves traditional cuisine that draws in the locals—try to reserve in advance. Expect to be greeted by gregarious owner-chef Félix, whose €25 *menu* is well worth the upgrade (*menus* from €20, closed Sun, air-con, 36 rue Tramassac, tel. 04 78 42 24 62).

**Les Lyonnais,** a block north, is lighthearted with rich colors, wood tables, and a photo gallery of loyal customers lining the walls (€19 and €22 *menus*, closed Sun, 1 rue Tramassac, tel. 04 78 37 64 82). A second location (described under "On or near rue Mercière," next page) faces the Saône River.

**Les Retrouvailles** serves tasty, but less traditional, Lyonnais cuisine in a charming setting under wood-beam ceilings. Here your dining experience is carefully managed by friendly owners Pierre *(le chef)* and Odile (€20 and €27 *menus*, closed Sun, 38 rue du Bœuf, tel. 04 78 42 68 84).

**Le Tire-Bouchon** ("The Corkscrew") is a tiny, simple, and fun *bouchon*, with low ceilings, ample wallpaper, and flowers (*menus* from €19, closed Sun–Mon, 2 floors, 16 rue de Bœuf, tel. 04 78 37 69 95).

**Restaurant Panoramique de la Fourvière,** atop Fourvière Hill with a spectacular view overlooking Lyon, serves traditional cuisine in a superb setting, but service can be slow. Choose from the non-smoking interior or the leafy terrace, both with views (*menus* from €25, lunch *plat du jour*–€12, daily until 22:00, 9 place de Fourvière, near Notre-Dame Basilica, tel. 04 78 25 21 15).

*Ice Cream:* **Nardone René Glacier,** on the river near place du Change, serves up Lyon's best ice cream with pleasant outdoor seating (daily 10:00–24:00, 3 place Ennemond Fousseret).

## On the Presqu'île

The pedestrian rue Mercière is the epicenter of *bouchons* on the Presqu'île. Along this street, an entertaining cancan of restaurants stretches four blocks from place des Jacobins to rue Grenette. Enjoy surveying the scene and choose whichever eatery appeals.

### On or near rue Mercière

**Le Bouchon aux Vins** bustles with authentic Lyonnais atmosphere, plus good meals at fair prices. It must be famed chef-owner Jean-Paul Lacombe's least expensive establishment (*menus* from €25, open daily, 62 rue Mercière, tel. 04 78 38 47 40).

**Le Mercière,** at #56, fills two shoebox-size rooms and the *passage* between them with down and dirty, get-to-know-your-neighbor *bouchon* character (*menus* from €22, open daily, 56 rue Mercière).

**Les Lyonnais** (recommended earlier) has a second location facing the Saône River, with a generous terrace and stellar views up to the basilica—particularly at night (closed Sun–Mon, 1 quai des Célestins, tel. 04 78 37 41 80).

### On Place des Célestins

**La Francotte**'s worn tile floor and appealing zinc-topped bar give this place a casual atmosphere—unless the theater has just let out, when it's jam-packed. Try anything served with their mouth-watering roasted garlic potatoes (*menus* from €24, closed Sun–Mon, near many recommended hotels at 8 place des Célestins, tel. 04 78 37 38 64).

LYON

## Worth a Detour

**Brasserie Georges,** next to Perrache station and almost as big, offers a forest of tables; dozens of frantic, aproned waiters; and decor from another time. It's been a Lyon institution since 1836, and makes a lively place to celebrate (*menus* from €22, *plats* from €15, good French onion soup, daily 11:30 until late, 30 cours de Verdon, tel. 04 72 56 54 54).

**Chez Abel** is the ultimate local *bouchon*, far away from restaurant rows and tourists, and catering to one kind of client only: local residents. It has a warm, chalet-like interior and a welcoming red-cheeked owner. Servings are generous; the *quenelle de brochet* is downright massive. Consider a *plat du jour* and maybe a salad. Reserve ahead (*menus* from €25, closed Sat–Sun and in Aug, about a 15-min walk south of place Bellecour, Métro: Ampère, a short block from Saône River, 25 rue Guynemer, tel. 04 78 37 46 18).

**Les Muses de l'Opéra** is an intriguing option for lunch or dinner (after 20:00) with a great view (and average quality). Ride the elevator to the seventh floor of the Opera House (€30 dinner *menu*, closed Sun, tel. 04 72 00 45 58).

# TRANSPORTATION CONNECTIONS

After Paris, Lyon is France's most important rail hub. Train travelers find this gateway to the Alps, Provence, the Riviera, and Burgundy an easy stopover. Two main train stations serve Lyon: Part-Dieu and Perrache. Most trains officially depart from Part-Dieu, though many also stop at Perrache, and trains run between the stations every 10 minutes. Double-check which station your train departs from.

**From Lyon by Train to: Paris** (at least hourly, 2 hrs), **Annecy** (7/day, 2 hrs, most change in Aix-les-Bains, some by bus), **Chamonix** (8/day July–Aug and Dec–April, Fri–Sun only May–June and Sept–Nov, can be more frequent in May, 6–8 hrs, some change in Switzerland), **Strasbourg** (5/day, 5 hrs), **Dijon** (12/day, 2 hrs), **Beaune** (10/day, 2 hrs, many change in Mâcon), **Avignon** (22/day; 12 to TGV station in 1.5 hrs, 10 to main station in 2 hrs), **Arles** (14/day, 2.5 hrs, most change in Avignon, Marseille, or Nîmes), **Nice** (6/day, 5 hrs), **Carcassonne** (6/day, 4 hrs), **Venice** (6/day, 11–13 hrs, most change in Geneva and Milan, night train), **Rome** (4/day, 10–12 hrs, at least one change in Milan, night train), **Florence** (3/day, 10 hrs), **Geneva** (8/day, 2 hrs), **Barcelona** (1 day train, 7 hrs, change in Perpignan; 2 night trains with transfers).

**Route Tips for Drivers:** En route to Provence, consider a three-hour detour through the spectacular Ardèche Gorges: Exit the A-6 autoroute at Privas and follow the villages of Aubenas, Vallon Pont d'Arc (offers kayak trips), and Pont Saint-Esprit (for more on this route, see page 571). En route to Burgundy, consider a Beaujolais detour (see below).

# Beaujolais Wine Route

Just south of Cluny and north of Lyon, the beautiful vineyards and villages and relaxed wine-tastings of the Beaujolais region make for an appealing detour. The most scenic and interesting section lies between Mâcon and Villefranche-sur-Saône, a few minutes west of A-6 on N-6. The route runs from the Mâconnais wine region and the famous village of Pouilly-Fuissé south through Beaujolais' most important villages: Chiroubles, Fleurie, and Juliénas. Look for *Route de Beaujolais* signs, and expect to get lost a few times. Trains running between Lyon and Macon stop at several wine villages, including Romanèche-Thorins (described below; 6 trains/day from Lyon).

For a pricey but thorough introduction to this region's wines, visit **Le Hameau du Vin** in Romanèche-Thorins. The king of Beaujolais, Georges DuBœuf, has constructed a Disney-esque introduction to wine at his wine museum, which immerses you into the life of a winemaker and features impressive models, exhibits, films, and videos. You'll be escorted from the beginning of the vine to present-day winemaking, with a focus on Beaujolais wines (several visits possible, best is €16 and includes a small tasting and free English headphones, daily April–Oct 10:00–18:00, Nov–March 10:00–17:00; in Romanèche-Thorins, look for signs labeled *Le Hameau du Vin* from N-6, then *La Gare* signs, and look for the old train-station-turned-winery; tel. 03 85 35 22 22, www.hameauduvin.com).

LYON

# ALSACE

The province of Alsace stands like a flower-child referee between Germany and France. Bounded by the Rhine River on the east and the Vosges Mountains on the west, this is a green region of Hansel-and-Gretel villages, ambitious vineyards, and vibrant cities. Food and wine are the primary industry, topic of conversation, and perfect excuse for countless festivals.

Alsace has changed hands several times between Germany and France because of its location, natural wealth, naked vulnerability—and the fact that Germany considered the mountains as the natural border, while the French saw the Rhine as the dividing line.

Having been a political pawn for 1,000 years, Alsace has a hybrid culture: Natives who curse do so bilingually, and the local cuisine features sauerkraut with fine wine sauces. If you're traveling in December, come here for France's most celebrated Christmas markets and festivals.

Colmar is one of Europe's most enchanting cities—with a small-town warmth and world-class art. Strasbourg is a big-city version of Colmar, worth a stop for its remarkable cathedral and to feel its high-powered and trendy bustle.

## Planning Your Time

Set up for two nights in or near Colmar. Allow one day for Colmar and another for Strasbourg and the Route du Vin (Wine Road). If you have only one day, spend your morning in Colmar and your afternoon along the Route du Vin. Urban Strasbourg, with its soaring cathedral and vigorous center, is a headache for drivers but a quick 30-minute train ride from Colmar—do it by train as a day trip from Colmar.

## Alsace

The humbling World War I battlefields of Verdun and the bubbly vigor of Reims in northern France (both described in the next chapter) are closer to Paris than to Alsace, and follow logically only if your next destination is Paris. The newest high-speed TGV-Est train links Paris with Reims, Verdun, Strasbourg, Colmar, and destinations farther east, bringing the Alsace within 2.5 hours of Paris and giving train travelers easier access to Reims or Verdun en route between Paris and Alsace.

---

### Early Crockpots

For old-school Alsatian comfort food, order the ubiquitous *baeckeoffe,* which is still served at your table in traditional pottery. The dish gets its name from where it was cooked—in the "baker's oven." For centuries, Alsatian women combined the week's leftover pork, beef, and veal with potatoes, onions, and leeks in a covered clay pot, then added white wine. Carrying the pot on their way to church on Sunday, the women would pass by the baker's and put their pot in one of the large stone ovens, still warm from baking the morning bread. During the three-hour Mass, the meat would simmer, and be perfectly stewed in time for lunch. The pottery, which is still produced and sold locally, remains an integral part of every Alsatian household.

---

## Getting Around Alsace

Frequent trains make the trip between Colmar and Strasbourg a snap (2/hr, 35 min). Buses and minivan excursions radiate from Colmar to villages along the Route du Vin, and you can rent bikes in Colmar and Turckheim if you prefer to pedal (for details on all of these options, see "Route du Vin," later in this chapter).

## Cuisine Scene in Alsace

Alsatian cuisine is a major tourist attraction in itself. The German influence is obvious: sausages, potatoes, onions, and sauerkraut. Look for *choucroute garnie* (sauerkraut and sausage—although it seems a shame to eat it in a fancy restaurant), the more traditionally Alsatian *baeckeoffe* (potato, meat, and onion stew), *rösti* (an oven-baked potato-and-cheese dish), fresh trout, and foie gras. At lunch, or for a lighter dinner, try a *tarte à l'oignon* (like an onion quiche, but better) or *tarte flambée* (like a thin-crust pizza with onion and bacon bits). If you're picnicking, buy some stinky Munster cheese. Dessert specialties are *tarte alsacienne* (fruit tart) and *glace kugelhopf* (a light cake mixed with raisins, almonds, dried fruit, and cherry liqueur).

Remember, restaurants serve only during lunch (11:30–14:00) and dinner (19:00–21:00, later in bigger cities), but some cafés serve food throughout the day.

## Alsatian Wines

Alsatian wines are named for their grapes—unlike in Burgundy or Provence, where wines are commonly named after villages, or in Bordeaux, where wines are often named after châteaux. White wines dominate in the Alsace. The following wines are made entirely of their namesake grape variety: Sylvaner (fairly light, fruity, and inexpensive), Riesling (more robust than Sylvaner, but drier than the German style you're probably used to), Gewürztraminer (spicy, with a powerful bouquet; good with pâtés and local cheeses), Muscat (very dry, with a distinctive bouquet and taste; best as a before-dinner wine), Tokay Pinot Gris (more full-bodied than Riesling, but fine with many local main courses), Pinot Noir (the local red is overpriced; very light and fruity, generally served chilled), and the tasty Crémant d'Alsace (the region's good and inexpensive sparkling wine). You'll also see *eaux-de-vie,* powerful fruit-flavored brandies; try the *framboise* (raspberry) flavor.

# Colmar

Colmar is a well-pickled old place of 70,000 residents, offering a few heavyweight sights in a comfortable, midsize-town package.

Historic beauty was usually a poor excuse for being spared the ravages of World War II, but it worked for Colmar. The American and British military were careful not to bomb the half-timbered old burghers' houses, characteristic red- and green-tiled roofs, and cobbled lanes of Alsace's most beautiful city. The town's distinctly French shutters combined with the ye-olde German half-timbering give Colmar an intriguing ambience.

Today, Colmar is alive with colorful buildings, impressive art treasures, and German tourists. Schoolgirls park their rickety horse carriages in front of City Hall and are ready to give visitors a clip-clop tour of the old town. Antiques shops welcome browsers, and hoteliers hurry down the sleepy streets to pick up fresh croissants in time for breakfast.

## ORIENTATION

Assume you will get lost, as there isn't a straight street in Colmar. Thankfully, most streets are pedestrian-only, and it's a lovely town to be lost in. Navigate by the high church steeples and the helpful signs that seem to pop up whenever you need them (directing visitors to the various sights). For tourists, the town center is place Unterlinden (a 15-min walk from the train station), where

ALSACE

you'll find the TI, Colmar's most important museum, and a big Monoprix supermarket/department store. Every city bus starts or finishes on place Unterlinden.

Colmar is most crowded from May through September and during its festive Christmas season (www.noel-colmar.com). Weekends are busy all year (reserve ahead). The impressive music festival fills hotels the first two weeks of July (www.festival-colmar .com), and the local wine festival rages for 10 days in early August. Open-air markets bustle next to the Dominican Church and St. Martin Cathedral on Thursdays and Saturdays.

## Tourist Information

The TI, next to the Unterlinden Museum on place Unterlinden, is generous with printed material (April–Oct Mon–Sat 9:00–18:00—or until 19:00 July–Aug, Sun 10:00–13:00; Nov–March Mon–Sat 9:00–12:00 & 14:00–18:00, Sun 10:00–13:00; tel. 03 89 20 68 92, www.ot-colmar.fr). Pick up the excellent city map (describing a good town walk), a map of the Route du Vin (Wine Road), information on bike rental, and *Colmar Actualités,* a booklet with bus schedules. Get information about concerts and festivals in Colmar and in nearby villages, and ask about Colmar's Folklore Tuesdays (with folk dancing at 20:30 every Tue mid-May–mid-Sept on place de l'Ancienne Douane). Drivers exploring the Route du Vin can buy the *Blay Foldex Alsace* map (€6), and cyclists can ask for a biking map. The TI also reserves hotel rooms and has *chambre d'hôte* listings for Colmar and the region. A public WC is 20 yards left of the TI.

You'll come across a few high-tech TI computer terminals at key locations throughout Colmar, offering 24/7 access to their website and hotel information (one is just outside the TI, and is a good alternative if there's a line at the counter).

## Arrival in Colmar

**By Train:** Colmar's old train station and new TGV station have been fused into a large single station, with separate entrances connected by an underground passageway. Because both TGV and non-TGV trains depart from the same station now, make sure you're boarding the right train (the trains have different access points).

The old train station was built during Prussian rule with the same plans for the station in Danzig (now Gdańsk, Poland). Check out the charming 1991 window that shows two local maidens about to be run over by a train and rescued by an artist. Opposite, he's shown painting their portraits.

To reach the town center from either station (15-min walk), walk straight out past Hôtel Bristol (keeping the hotel on your

**ALSACE**

left), turn left on avenue de la République, and keep walking. Buses #1, #2, and #3 (to the left outside of the old station) all go to the TI (€1.10, pay driver). Buses to Route du Vin villages leave from the stop to the right as you leave the old station. Allow €8 for a taxi to any hotel in central Colmar (the taxi stand is on the left as you leave the station).

**By Car:** Follow signs for *Centre-Ville*, then *place Rapp*. There's a 900-spot pay-parking garage under place Rapp, and free lots at Parking du Musée d'Unterlinden (across from Hôtel Primo) and off the ring road near Hôtel St. Martin (follow signs from the ring road to *Parking de la Vieille Ville*). Several hotels have private parking, and those that don't can advise you where to park. When entering or leaving on the Strasbourg side of town, look for the big Statue of Liberty replica erected on July 4, 2004, to commemorate the 100th anniversary of the death of the sculptor Frédéric-Auguste Bartholdi.

## Helpful Hints

**Market Days:** Markets take place Thursdays on place de l'Ancienne Douane, and Saturdays on place St. Joseph (both mornings only). Textiles are on sale Thursdays on place de la Cathédrale (all day) and Saturdays on place des Dominicains (afternoons only), and fish and produce are featured in the old market hall in the Tanners' Quarter on Thursday mornings. There's also a flea market every Friday from June to August on place des Dominicains.

**Department Store:** The big **Monoprix,** with a supermarket, is across from the TI and Unterlinden Museum (Mon–Sat 8:00–19:45, closed Sun).

**Internet Access:** Try **Infr@reseau,** near the TI at 12 rue du Rempart (Mon–Sat 10:00–21:00, Sun 14:00–20:00, tel. 03 89 23 98 45), or **Cyber Didim,** across the street at 9 rue du Rempart (above snack shop, daily 9:30–24:00, tel. 03 89 29 01 41).

**Laundry:** There's a launderette near the recommended Maison Jund *chambre d'hôte* at 1 rue Ruest, just off the pedestrian street rue Vauban (usually open daily 7:00–21:00). Or try **5 à Sec,** across from the post office and Champs de Mars (same-day service, Mon–Sat 8:30–19:00, closed Sun, 32 avenue de la République).

**Bike Rental: Kiosque Colmarvélo** is the cheapest around, with the most extensive hours (€5/half-day, €6/day; bikes have 5 speeds, medium-width tires, basket, and lock; baby seats and helmets on request, €50 cash deposit and passport required, April–Oct daily 8:30–12:15 & 13:15–19:15, closed Nov–March, look for the orange-and-green kiosk in the park at place Rapp—near the carousel, tel. 03 89 41 37 90). Before you head out, buy a biking map either at the TI or a *librarie* (bookstore).

**Taxis:** At the train station, call 03 89 41 40 19; otherwise, call 03 89 27 08 31 or 06 09 42 60 75.

**Car Rental:** The least expensive is **ADA** (Mon–Fri 8:00–12:00 & 14:00–18:30, Sat 8:00–12:00, closed Sun, 22 rue Stanislas, tel. 03 89 23 90 30, www.ada.fr). **Avis** is at the old train station (Mon–Fri 8:00–12:00 & 14:00–19:00, Sat until 17:00, closed Sun, tel. 03 89 23 21 82). The TI has a long list of other options.

**Poodle Care:** To give your poodle a shampoo and a haircut (or just watch the action), drop by **Quatt Pattes** (near Hôtel Rapp at 8 rue Berthe Molly).

# TOURS

There are no city tours in English, but private English-speaking **guides** are available through the TI (about €120/3 hours).

Colmar has two competing **tourist trains.** Le Petit Train Blanc, the better of the two, departs across from the Monoprix, near the Dominican church (€6, 45-min tours, departs every 30 min 9:00–18:00, recorded commentary, hop on or off as you please). In the summer, **horse-drawn carriages** do a similar route (€6, 30-min tours).

For **minivan tours** of the Route du Vin, see page 783.

# SELF-GUIDED WALK

## Welcome to Colmar's Old Town

This walk—good by day or by night—is a handy way to link the city's three worthwhile sights. Supplement this information by reading the sidewalk information plaques that describe every point of interest in town. Allow an hour for this walk at a peaceful pace (more if you enter sights).

The importance of 15th- to 17th-century Colmar is clear as you wander its pedestrian-friendly old center. It's decorated with 45 buildings classified as historic monuments. In the Middle Ages, most of Europe was fragmented into chaotic little princedoms and dukedoms. Merchant-dominated cities, natural proponents of the formation of large nation-states (a.k.a. globalization), banded together to form "trading leagues" (the World Trade Organizations of their day). The Hanseatic League was the super-league of northern Europe. Prosperous Colmar was the leading member of a smaller league of 10 Alsatian cities, called the Decapolis (founded 1354). The names of the streets you'll walk along bear witness to the merchants' historic importance to Colmar.

**ALSACE**

# Colmar

200 YARDS
200 METERS

TO STRASBOURG VIA N-83

TO KAYSERSBERG VIA N-415

||| PEDESTRIAN ZONE
Ⴎ VIEW
P PARKING
→ ONE-WAY STREET
⇒ WALKING TOUR ROUTE

RUE DE LA CAVALERIE

RUE 5e DIVISION

RUE DES ANCÊTRES

RUE DES INGERSHEIM

RUE DE RIBEAUVILLE

R. GOLBERY

RUE UNT:

RUE DU REMPART

RUE DU NORD

POST

UNTERLINDEN MUSEUM
FINISH

MONOPRIX STORE

MAISON DES TÊTES

RUE DES CLEFS

RUE RAPP

RUE ETROITE

RUE VAUBAN

AVE DE GAULLE

RUE STAN.

RUE DES BOULANGERS

DOMINICAN CHURCH

TO MUNSTER

LA REPUBLIQUE

PLACE RAPP

BLVD DU CHAMP DE MARS

RUE DES MARCHANDS

RUE MOLLY

BERTHE

ST. MARTIN CATH.

RUE DE L'EGLISE

GRAND RUE

R. PREISS

PLAY AREA

POST

CHAMP DE MARS

R. WEIN.

BARTHOLDI MUSEUM

AVE BRUAT

RUE DES AUGUSTINS

RUE CHAUFFOUR

R. PFEFFEL

BLES

PLACE DE L'ANCIENNE DOUANE

RUE DES TANNEURS

GRAND RUE

RUE DES ECOLES

TANNERS QUARTER

CUSTOMS HOUSE
START

MARKET HALL

LAUCH RIVER

RUE POISSON.

QUAI

TO ①,
TRAIN STATIONS,
EGUISHEIM,
& BELFORT
VIA D-30

RUE TURENNE

PETITE VENISE

RUE SCHWENDI

BLVD. ST. PIERRE

DCH

1 Hôtel St. Martin
2 Hostellerie le Maréchal
3 Hôtel/Restaurant le Rapp
4 Hôtel Turenne
5 Hôtel Ibis
6 Maison Jund Rooms
7 Hôtel Primo
8 To Grand Hôtel Bristol & B&B Chez Leslie
9 La Krutenau Restaurant
10 Le Comptoir de Georges Rest.
11 L'un des Sens Wine Bar

12 Winstub Schwendi
13 La Maison Rouge Restaurant
14 Wistub Flory
15 Chez Hansi
16 Internet Cafés (2)
17 Launderette (2)
18 Bike Rental
19 ADA Car Rental
20 Quatt Pattes Dog Grooming
21 Maison Pfister
22 Le Petit Train Blanc Departure Point

ALSACE

• *Start your tour at the old...*

**Customs House (Koïfhus):** Here, delegates of the Decapolis would meet to sort out trade issues, much like the European Union does in nearby Strasbourg today. Walk under its archway to place de l'Ancienne Douane and face the Frédéric-Auguste Bartholdi statue—arm raised, à la Statue of Liberty—and do a 360-degree spin to appreciate a gaggle of gables. This was the center of business activity in Colmar, with trade routes radiating to several major European cities. All goods that entered the city were taxed here. Today, it's the festive site of outdoor wine-tastings on many summer evenings.

• *The half-timbered commotion of higgledy-piggledy rooftops on the downhill side of the fountain marks the...*

**Tanners' Quarter:** These vertical 17th- and 18th-century rooftops competed for space in the sun to dry their freshly tanned hides, while the nearby river channel flushed the waste products. This neighborhood, restored in about 1970, was a pioneer in the government-funded renovation of old quarters. Residents had to play along or move out. Follow the statue's left elbow and walk down petite rue des Tanneurs (not just "rue des Tanneurs"). Turn right at the end of the street (walking along the city's first wall— c. 1230, now built into the row of houses), then take the first left along the stream. On your right is the old market hall (fish, produce, and other products were brought here by flat-bottom boat). Today, it's Colmar's main market hall, where locals buy produce, meat, and fish on Thursday mornings.

• *Cross the canal and turn right on quai de la Poissonnerie ("Wharf of the Fish Market"), and you'll enter...*

**Petite Venise:** This neighborhood, a collection of Colmar's most colorful houses lining the small canal, is popular with tourists during the day. But at night it's romantic, with a fraction of the crowds. It lies between the town's first wall (built to defend against arrows) and its later wall (built in the age of gunpowder). The local river was canalized for medieval industry—to provide water for the tanners, to allow farmers to barge their goods into town, to power mills, and so on. Walk several blocks along the flower-box-lined canal to the end of rue de la Poissonnerie. Turn right, walk to the center of the bridge, and enjoy the view. To the right, you'll see examples of the flat-bottom gondolas used to transport goods on the small river. Today, they give tourists sleepy and scenic 30-minute, €6 canal tours (departure on demand, buy tickets at the bar/restaurant La Krutenau—see page 781).

• *Cross the bridge, take the second right on Grande Rue, and stroll several blocks back to the Customs House (green-tiled roof). Turn left and, with your back to the Customs House, walk uphill along rue des Marchands ("Merchants' Street")—one of the most scenic stretches in town. (The ruler of Malaysia was so charmed by this street that he had it re-created in Kuala Lumpur.) In two blocks you come face-to-face with the...*

**Maison Pfister (Pfister House):** The richly decorated merchant's house from 1537, with its external spiral-staircase turret and painted walls, illustrates the city folks' taste for Renaissance humanism (a fine little wine shop fills the ground floor). The man carved into the side of the building the next door up (at #9) was a drape maker; he's shown holding a bar, Colmar's measure of about one meter. In the Middle Ages, it was common for cities to have their own units of length; one reason merchants supported the "globalization" of their time was to get rid of different measuring systems.

• *Look closely at the architecture.*

**Half-Timbered Houses:** House #9 (with the guy holding the bar) shows off the classic half-timbered design—the beams (upright, cross, angular supports) are grouped in what's called (and looks like) "a man." Typical houses are built with a man in the middle flanked by two "half men." While houses of the rich were made of stone, anyone on a budget built half-timbered structures (though all homes here sit on a stone base to prevent them from sinking into the marshy ground). Originally, proud townsfolk would plaster over their cheap half-timbered walls to create the illusion of a stone house. Then, in the 20th century, half-timbered became charming, so they peeled away the plaster to reveal the old beams. You can identify true stone homes by their windowsills: Wooden sills mean they're half-timbered, while stone sills indicate the entire building is built of stone. As you explore the town, notice how upper floors are cantilevered out. This was both a structural trick and a tax dodge. A single supporting wall could support more if it rested in from the upper floor's edge. And real-estate taxes were based on the square footage of the ground floor.

If you wander at night, you'll notice that Colmar is not only beautifully pedestrianized, but also wonderfully floodlit. Countless small floodlights set in amid the cobbles illuminate the town after dark. They can be changed to give different intensities and colors, keeping Colmar fresh and inviting after dark.

One more block along on the left is the **Bartholdi Museum** (see page 776). Next door (#28) is Au Pain Dorée, with its charming Art Nouveau facade and interior. Art Nouveau was rare in Colmar. During the style's heyday in the early 20th century—which was also just after this region was taken from France by Germany—Art Nouveau was considered an anti-German statement, and therefore controversial.

• *A passage to the right leads to...*

**St. Martin Cathedral:** The city's golden cathedral (erected in 1235), with its lone tower (two were planned) and gleaming tiles, was inspired by the Hôtel Dieu in Beaune. Walk left around the cathedral. Notice that the relief over the main door depicts not your typical Last Judgment scene, but the Three Kings who visited Baby Jesus. The Magi, whose remains are in the Rhine city of Köln, Germany, are popular in this region. Just past the cathedral, head left up the pedestrian-only rue des Serruriers ("Locksmiths' Street") to the **Dominican Church** (worth entering and described under "Sights," later in this section). Compare the impressive St. Martin Cathedral with this low-slung, sober structure that perfectly symbolizes Dominican austerity. These two very different houses of worship were built at the same time.

• *Continue past the Dominican Church (rue des Serruriers becomes rue des Boulangers—"Bakers' Street"). Then make a right on rue des Têtes (notice the beautiful swan sign over the* pharmacie *at the corner). Walk a block to the fancy old house with all the heads (on the right).*

**Maison des Têtes ("House of Heads"):** Colmar's other famous merchant's house, built in 1609 by a big-shot winemaker, is playfully decorated with 105 faces and masks (on the ground floor, the guy in the center has pig's feet).

Four houses to the right, a 1947 bakery sign (look above the big pretzel) shows the *boulangerie* basics in Alsace: croissant, *kugelhopf*, and baguette. Across the street, study the fine early-20th-century store sign trumpeting the wonders of a butcher (including pork and foie gras—with the traditional maiden chasing a goose about to be force-fed), all hung on the beak of a chicken.

• *Angle down rue de l'Eau ("Water Street") opposite Maison des Têtes for a shortcut to the TI and the Unterlinden Museum, with its namesake linden trees lining the front yard (popular locally for making the calming "Tilleul" tea).*

# SIGHTS

## ▲▲▲Unterlinden Museum

Colmar's touristic claim to fame is one of my favorite museums in Europe. Its extensive yet manageable collection ranges from Roman Colmar to medieval winemaking exhibits, and from traditional wedding dresses to paintings that give vivid insight into the High Middle Ages. Plan on spending extra time in this museum, as its collection is so unique and varied, and the excellent audioguide (included with your admission) makes the curator your best friend. The museum is one of the most visited in all of France for its devastatingly beautiful *Isenheim Altarpiece,* so it can be crowded and loud. (The best time to visit is about 12:00–14:00—when most are lunching—or at the end of the day.)

**Cost, Hours, Location:** €7, €6 for seniors, price includes indispensable audioguide; May–Oct daily 9:00–18:00; Nov–April

Wed–Mon 9:00–12:00 & 14:00–17:00, closed Tue; 1 rue d'Unterlinden, tel. 03 89 20 15 58, www.musee-unterlinden.com.

● **Self-Guided Tour:** Use this commentary to supplement the information provided by the included audioguide.

**Gothic Statues (Room 1):** Room 1 features 14th-century Gothic statues from St. Martin Cathedral's facade. Study the faces. Even though they endured the elements outdoors for more than 500 years, it's still clear that they were sculpted carefully. Take a close look at the 15th-century stained glass; fine details are painted into the glass that no one would ever see. The glass is essentially a jigsaw puzzle connected by lead. Around here, glass this old is rare—most of it was destroyed by rampaging Protestants in the Reformation wars.

**Cloister:** Step into the soothing cloister (the largest 13th-century cloister in Alsace) and walk right, passing the WCs in the corner. This was a Dominican convent founded for noblewomen in 1230. It functioned until the French Revolution, when the building became a garrison. Rooms with museum exhibits branch off from here. Don't miss the wine room (next corner) with its 17th-century oak presses and finely decorated casks. Wine revenue was used to care for Colmar's poor. The nuns owned many of the best vineyards around, and production was excellent. So was consumption. Notice (on the first cask on left) the Bacchus with the distended tummy straddling a keg. The quote from 1781 reads: "My belly's full of juice. It makes me strong. But drink too much and you lose dignity and health."

**Painting Gallery:** Left of the wine-press room, enter the painting gallery marked *art médiéval*. Stop first by the spinning case of engravings by Martin Schongauer, Albrecht Dürer's master. Throughout the museum, you'll see small photos of engravings illustrating how painters were influenced by other artists' engravings. Most German painters of the time were also engravers (that's how they made money—making lots of copies for sale). The following rooms are filled with paintings that are wonderfully described by the audioguide. As you enjoy the art, remember that Alsace was historically German and part of the upper Rhine River Valley. (This museum boasts France's only painting by Lucas Cranach.) Remember those Three Kings (of Bethlehem fame) from St. Martin Cathedral? They're prominently featured throughout this region, because their heads ended up as relics in Köln's cathedral (on the Rhine).

These rooms lead to the...

***Isenheim Altarpiece:*** The highlight of the museum (and, for me, the city) is Matthias Grünewald's gripping *Isenheim Altarpiece* (c. 1515), actually a series of three different paintings on hinges that pivot like shutters (study the little model on the wall, explained in English). Designed to help people in a medieval hospital endure horrible skin diseases (such as St. Anthony's Fire, later called rye ergotism)—long before the age of painkillers—it's one of the most

powerful paintings ever produced. Germans know this painting like Americans know the *Mona Lisa*.

Stand in front of the centerpiece as if you were a medieval peasant, and let the agony and suffering of the Crucifixion drag its fingers down your face. It's an intimate drama. The point—Jesus' suffering—is drilled home: the weight of his body bends the crossbar (unrealistically, creating to some eyes an almost crossbow effect). His elbows are pulled from their sockets by the weight of his dead body. People who are crucified die of asphyxiation, as Jesus' chest implies. His mangled feet are swollen with blood. The grief on Mary's face is agonizing. In hopes that the intended viewers (the hospital's patients) would know that Jesus understood their suffering, Jesus himself was even painted to appear as if he had a skin disease. Study the faces and the Christian symbolism. Mary is wrapped in the shroud that will cover Jesus. The sorrowful composition on the left is powerful. On the far left stands St. Sebastian (called upon by those with the plague) and on the right is St. Anthony (the Red Adair of rotten rye). Walk to the back of this panel.

The Resurrection scene is unique in art history (Grünewald had no master and no students). Jesus rockets out of the tomb as man is transformed into God. As if proclaiming once again, "I am the Light," he is radiant. His shroud is the color of light: Roy G. Biv. Around the rainbow is the "resurrection of the flesh." Jesus' pink and perfect flesh would appeal to the patients who meditated on the scene. The right half of this panel depicts the Annunciation.

In the nativity scene on the next panel—set in the Rhineland—much-adored Mary is tender and loving, true to the Dominican belief that she was the intercessor for all in heaven. The three scenes of the painting changed with the church calendar. The happy ending—a psychedelic explosion of Resurrection joy—is the spiritual equivalent of jumping from the dentist's chair directly into a whirlpool tub. The last two panels show the Temptation of St. Anthony and his visit to St. Paul the hermit. The final scene, carved in wood by Nikolaus Hagenauer, is St. Anthony on his throne.

**The Rest of the Museum:** Downstairs, you'll find a modern-art section, and Roman and prehistoric artifacts. The upstairs rooms contain local and folk history, with everything from 19th-century Romantic paintings, old armoires, and medieval armor to old-time toys.

## ▲▲▲Dominican Church (Eglise des Dominicains)

Here's another medieval mindblower. In this church, you'll find Martin Schongauer's angelically beautiful *Virgin in the Rosebush* holding court, dating from 1473 but looking as if it were painted yesterday. Here, graceful Mary is shown as a welcoming mother. Jesus clings to her, reminding the viewer of the warmth of his relationship with Mary. The Latin on her halo reads, "Pick me also for your child, O very Holy Virgin." Rather than telling a particular Bible story, this is a general scene, designed to meet the personal devotional needs of any worshipper. Here, nature is not a backdrop; Mary and Jesus are encircled by it. Schongauer's robins, sparrows, and goldfinches bring extra life to an already impressively natural rosebush. The white rose anticipates Jesus' crucifixion. The frame, with its angelic orchestra, dates only from 1900. The contrast provided by the simple Dominican setting heightens the flamboyance of this Gothic masterpiece. Dominican churches were intentionally austere, symbolic of their zeal to purify their faith and compete with the growing popularity of 13th-century heretical movements, such as Catharism, which preached a simpler faith (€1.50, mid-March–Dec daily 10:00–13:00 & 15:00–18:00, last entry 15 min before closing, closed Jan–mid-March, no photos).

## ▲Bartholdi Museum

This little museum recalls the life and work of the local boy who gained fame by sculpting America's much-loved Statue of Liberty. Frédéric-Auguste Bartholdi (1834–1904) was a dynamic painter/photographer/sculptor with a passion for the defense of liberty and freedom. Because Prussia took Alsace in 1871, he spent most of his career in Paris, unable to move back to his home of Colmar without becoming a German. He devoted years of his life to realizing the vision of a statue of liberty for America that would stand in New York City's harbor. Closer to home, several Bartholdi statues grace Colmar's squares.

**Cost, Hours, Location:** €4.50, March–Dec Wed–Mon 10:00–12:00 & 14:00–18:00, closed Tue and Jan–Feb, pick up English flier, in heart of old town at 30 rue des Marchands, tel. 03 89 41 90 60, www.musee-bartholdi.com.

**◑ Self-Guided Tour:** Curiously, there is no English in this museum. The following commentary will help make things meaningful.

Behind the ticket desk, study Bartholdi's photo (actually six photos in a line) of New York City's harbor in 1876. The first piling of the Brooklyn Bridge is up. Bartholdi added the tiny Statue of Liberty on the far left (along with the boats).

The main floor hosts mostly temporary exhibits of Alsatian works. Upstairs to the left, rooms re-create Bartholdi's high-society flat in Paris. The dining room is lined with portraits of his aristocratic family. In the next room hangs a fine portrait of the sculptor, facing his mother (on a red chair). He was very close to his mom, writing her daily letters. Many see her features in the Statue of Liberty. Find the gloomy painting of the Statue of Liberty at the top of the stairs.

The rest of this first floor shows off Bartholdi's French work. Notice how his patriotic pieces tend to have one arm raised—*Vive la France,* God bless America, *Deutschland über alles*...you can fill in the flag-waving blank.

Bartholdi's most famous French work, the *Lion of Belfort,* celebrates the Alsatian town that fought so fiercely in 1871 that it was never annexed into Germany. Photos show the red sandstone lion sitting regally below the mighty Vauban fortress of Belfort—a symbol of French spirit standing strong against Germany.

The second floor up (top floor) is dedicated to Bartholdi's American works—the paintings, photos, and statues that Bartholdi made during his many travels to the States. You'll see statues of Columbus and Lafayette (who was only 19 years old when he came to America's aid) with George Washington. Then the exhibit traces the evolution and completion of the dream of a Statue of Liberty. Fascinating photos show the Eiffel-designed core, the frame being covered with plaster, and then the hand-hammered copper plating, which was ultimately riveted to the frame. The statue was assembled in Paris, then un-riveted and shipped to New York, in 1886...10 years late. The big ear is half-size.

While the statue was a gift from France, the US had to come up with the cash to build a pedestal. This was a tough sell, but Bartholdi was determined to see his statue erected. On 10 trips to the US, he worked to raise funds and lobbied for construction, bringing with him this painting and a full-size model of the torch—which the statue would ultimately hold. (Lucky for Bartholdi and his cause, his cousin was the French ambassador to the US.) Eventually, the project came together—the pedestal was built, and the Statue of Liberty has welcomed waves of immigrants into New York ever since.

# SLEEPING

Hotels are busy on weekends in May, June, September, and October, and every day in July and August. But there are always rooms—somewhere. Should you have trouble finding a bed, ask the TI for help, or look in a nearby village, where small hotels and bed-and-breakfasts are plentiful (see my recommendations in nearby Eguisheim, later in this chapter).

## In the Center

$$$ Hôtel St. Martin***, near the old Customs House, is a family-run place that began as a coaching inn (since 1361). Its 40 traditional yet well-equipped rooms, with air-conditioning and big beds, are woven into its antique frame. The hotel has three sections (young, middle-aged, and elderly) joined by a peaceful courtyard. All rooms offer good comfort and character, though the best rooms are in the new (young) wing, with traditional furnishings and stone walls (Db-€90–109). The cheapest rooms are the oldest, with showers instead of tubs and no elevator (Sb-€79, standard Db-€89–99, bigger Db-€109, still bigger Db-€149, Tb/Qb-€129, breakfast-€12, air-con in some rooms, free Internet access and Wi-Fi, free public parking nearby at Parking de la Vieille Ville, 38 Grand Rue, tel. 03 89 24 11 51, fax 03 89 23 47 78, www.hotel-saint-martin.com, colmar@hotel-saint-martin.com).

At $$$ Hostellerie le Maréchal****, you'll pay top euro for Colmar's most famous and characteristic digs in the heart of La Petite Venise. While rooms are small for the price, the setting is romantic and the service is ever so professional (standard Db-€105–140, Db with whirlpool tub-€160–225, suite Db-€255, breakfast-€14, free Wi-Fi, parking-€14, 4 place des Six Montagnes Noires, tel. 03 89 41 60 32, fax 03 89 24 59 40, www.le-marechal.com, info@le-marechal.com). Their well-respected restaurant will melt a romantic's heart, and they'll heartily encourage you to dine here (€38–78 *menus*, reserve ahead).

$$$ Hôtel le Rapp***, ideally located off place Rapp, offers a variety of rooms for many budgets. The cheapest rooms are small but adequate; the larger rooms are tastefully designed, with queen-size beds. There's also a small basement pool, sauna, Turkish bath, and an indoor/outdoor bar-café. It's well-run and family-friendly, with a big park one block away and lazy Pastaga, the hotel hound (Sb-€76, standard Db-€90, bigger Db-€100, junior suite for 2–4 people-€140, good buffet breakfast-€10, air-con, elevator, free Internet access and Wi-Fi, 1 rue Weinemer, tel. 03 89 41 62 10, fax 03 89 24 13 58, www.rapp-hotel.com, rapp-hot@calixo.net). Its restaurant serves a classy Alsatian *menu* with impeccable service (closed Thu–Fri).

ALSACE

### Sleep Code

**(€1 = about $1.50, country code: 33)**
**S** = Single, **D** = Double/Twin, **T** = Triple, **Q** = Quad, **b** = bathroom,
**s** = shower only, * = French hotel rating system (0–4 stars).
Unless otherwise noted, credit cards are accepted and English
is spoken.

To help you sort easily through these listings, I've divided
the rooms into three categories based on the price for a
standard double room with bath:

$$$ **Higher Priced**—Most rooms €90 or more.
$$ **Moderately Priced**—Most rooms between €50–90.
$ **Lower Priced**—Most rooms €50 or less.

**$$ Hôtel Turenne**** is a fair value, though less central. The hotel capitalizes on its charming historic facade, though most of its 83 rooms are in a less-inspired, modern wing. It's a 10-minute walk from the city center, a 15-minute walk from the train station, and is located on a busy street with easy parking underneath. Rooms vary in size and some have tight bathrooms (Sb-€50–70, Db-€65–70, Tb-€72, family-friendly studios-€115, park for free on the street or pay €7 to park in their lot, air-con, elevator for most rooms, nice bar and breakfast room, Internet access and free Wi-Fi, 10 rue de Bâle; from train station walk straight out to avenue Raymond Poincaré, then turn left on rue des Americains; tel. 03 89 21 58 58, fax 03 89 41 27 64, www.turenne.com, infos@turenne.com).

**$$ Hôtel Ibis****, on the ring road, sells hospital-white, efficient comfort with tiny bathrooms (Sb/Db-€70, bigger Db-€80, Tb-€85, breakfast-€8, air-con, inside parking-€7, 10 rue St. Eloi, tel. 03 89 41 30 14, fax 03 89 24 51 49, www.ibishotel.com, h1377@accor.com).

**$ Maison Jund** holds my favorite budget beds in Colmar. This ramshackle yet historic half-timbered house—the home of a likeable winemaker and his wife (André and Myriam)—feels like a medieval tree house soaked in wine and filled with flowers. The rooms are bare-bones simple but comfortable enough, spacious, and equipped with kitchenettes (D-€35, Db/Tb-€45–55; huge family apartment with steep staircase-€80 for 2, sleeps up to 6, €5/additional person; no breakfast, affordable organic wine for sale in their tasting room below, Internet access and free Wi-Fi, 12 rue de l'Ange, tel. 03 89 41 58 72, fax 03 89 23 15 83, www.martinjund.com, martinjund@hotmail.com). Leave your car at the lot across from Hôtel Primo. Train travelers can take bus #1, #2, or #3 from the station to the TI, walk from Unterlinden

ALSACE

Museum past Monoprix, and veer left on rue des Clefs, left on rue Etroite, and right on rue de l'Ange. This is not a hotel, so there is no real reception—though good-natured Myriam seems to be around, somewhere, most of the time (call if you plan to arrive after 21:00).

$ **Hôtel Primo\*\***, near the Unterlinden Museum, is an efficient, bright, nothing-but-the-plastic-and-concrete-basics place to sleep for those who consider ambience a four-letter word. The friendly staff will hold a room for you until 18:00 if you call. Rooms facing the big square *(grand place)* are far quieter (S/D/T-€29, Sb-€39–55, Db-€45–55, Tb/Qb-€65, small discount for Rick Steves readers in 2009, foam mattresses, Internet access and free Wi-Fi, free parking in big square in front, 5 rue des Ancêtres, tel. 03 89 24 22 24, fax 03 89 24 55 96, www.hotel-primo.com, hotel-primo@villes-et-vignoble.com). Half the beds have footboards—a problem if you're more than six feet tall.

## Near the Train Station

$$$ **Grand Hôtel Bristol\*\*\*** couldn't be closer to the station. In spite of its Best Western plaque and its popularity with groups, it retains some character, with pleasant public spaces and 91 good, if pricey, rooms (Sb-€95, standard Db-€100–120, big Db-€139–149, 7 place de la Gare, tel. 03 89 23 59 59, fax 03 89 23 92 26, www.grand-hotel-bristol.com, reservation@grand-hotel-bristol.com).

$$ **Bed-and-Breakfast Chez Leslie** is a vintage B&B in a residential neighborhood (a five-minute walk from the station, 20-minute walk from the city center). The rooms are bright and whimsically decorated, and the garden makes for a refreshingly flowery place to relax. San Franciscan Leslie Collins loves hosting visitors in her home (Sb-€57, Db-€74, family room €84–105, €5 cheaper for stays more than 1 night, includes breakfast, ask about apartment rental in town, 31 rue de Mulhouse, tel. 03 89 79 98 99, mobile 06 82 58 91 98, www.chezleslie.com, info@chezleslie.com). From the train platform, exit down the stairs into the underground passageway toward rue du Tir (away from station), walk up the stairs at the end, go left down the street, and turn right at the first corner (rue de Soultz). Continue up to the square and turn left on rue de Mulhouse.

**ALSACE**

# EATING

Colmar is full of good restaurants offering traditional Alsatian *menus* for €17–25, and expensive places with lighter fare. (Also see "Eating" in nearby Eguisheim, later in this chapter.)

## In Petite Venise

For dining with a canalside view, head into Petite Venise and make your way to the photo-perfect bridge on rue Turenne, where you'll find several picturesque places.

**La Krutenau**'s wood tables sprawl along the canal, offering many desserts and only *tartes flambées*. Come for a light meal with ambience (inside or out), a dessert, or a drink on a warm evening (closed Sun–Mon, 1 rue de la Poissonnerie, tel. 03 89 41 18 80).

**Le Comptoir de Georges** serves traditional Alsatian dishes alongside French classics. The atmosphere is low-key, and your paper placemat doubles as the menu. The best seats are on the tiny terrace that hangs off the back side of the restaurant, overlooking the canal (closed Sun–Mon; serves food all day—breakfast, lunch, and dinner; 1 place des Six Montagnes Noires, tel. 03 89 20 60 72).

## In the Old City Center

**L'un des Sens** is a welcoming and happening little wine bar with a long list of wines and a short list of foods (meat plates, fancy foie gras, cheese plates, and a few salads). The colorful interior and upbeat waitstaff make this a fun place for a light meal, or to start your evening on the right foot (food served Tue–Sat 11:00–21:00, closed Sun–Mon, 18 rue Berthe Molly, tel. 03 89 24 04 37).

**Winstub Schwendi** has the lively feel of a German pub inside (with 10 beers on tap) and a terrace outside. Choose from a dozen different filling, robust Swiss *rösti* plates or *tarte flambées;* I like the *strasbourgoise* (€10–18 main dishes, daily 10:00–24:00, very popular on weekends, facing old Customs House at 3 Grand Rue, tel. 03 89 23 66 26).

**La Maison Rouge** has a folk-museum interior and noisy sidewalk seating with good, reasonably priced, traditional Alsatian cuisine. You'll be greeted by the *jambon à l'os*—ham cooking on the bone (€20–35 *menus,* try the endive salad and *tarte flambée forestière,* closed Sun–Mon, 9 rue des Ecoles, tel. 03 89 23 53 22).

**Winstub Flory,** hiding in a small alley, is known for its large portions and reliable Alsatian specialties. There's some outdoor seating and a warm, half-timbered interior (€15–23 *plats,* €22 *menus,* daily 18:30–21:45, 1 rue Mangold, tel. 03 89 41 78 80).

**Hôtel-Restaurant le Rapp** is a traditional place to savor a slow, elegant meal served with grace and fine Alsatian wine. If you want to order high on the menu, this is a fine place to do it (great *baeckeoffe* for €16 that makes a whole meal, *menus* from €24, good salads, they take their vegetarian options seriously, closed Thu–Fri, air-con, 1 rue Berthe Molly, tel. 03 89 41 62 10).

**ALSACE**

**Chez Hansi,** next to the Customs House, is a popular place with something for every appetite. Try local specialties (such as chicken in Riesling sauce) or medieval "pub grub" like *choucroute garnie* (€13–25 main dishes, €18–44 *menus*, daily 11:45–13:45, Fri–Tue also open for dinner 18:45–21:30, 23 rue des Marchands, tel. 03 89 41 37 84).

## TRANSPORTATION CONNECTIONS

**From Colmar by Train to: Strasbourg** (2/hr, 35 min), **Reims** (via TGV: 10/day, 3 hrs, most change in Strasbourg), **Verdun** (8/day, 4–5 hrs, possible changes in Metz, Saverne, and Strasbourg), **Beaune** (6/day, 4–5 hrs, changes in Besançon, Mulhouse, or Belfort and Dijon), **Paris'** Gare de l'Est (via TGV: 12/day, 3 direct, others change in Strasbourg, 3.5 hrs; via non-TGV train: 8/day, 5.5 hrs, change in Strasbourg, Dijon, or Mulhouse), **Amboise** (via TGV: 8/day, 5 hrs, most with transfer in Strasbourg and Paris; via non-TGV train: 8/day, 9 hrs, via Paris), **Basel,** Switzerland (13/day, 1 hr), **Karlsruhe,** Germany (10/day, 2.5 hrs, best with change in Strasbourg; from Karlsruhe, it's 90 min to Frankfurt, 3 hrs to Munich).

# Route du Vin (Wine Road)

Alsace's Route du Vin is an asphalt ribbon that ties 90 miles of vineyards, villages, and feudal fortresses into an understandably popular tourist package. This is a sun belt that gets less rain than many parts of southern France.  The generally dry climate has made for good wine and happy tourists since Roman days. Colmar and Eguisheim are ideally located for exploring the 30,000 acres of vineyards blanketing the hills from Marlenheim to Thann.

If you have only a day, focus on towns within easy striking range of Colmar. Top stops are Eguisheim, Kaysersberg, Hunawihr, Ribeauvillé, and the too-popular Riquewihr. Be careful not to overdose on all the half-timbered cuteness. Two, maybe three villages meet the needs of most. As you tour this region, you'll see storks' nests on many church spires and city halls, thanks to a campaign to reintroduce the birds to this area. (Nests can weigh as much as 1,000 pounds.)

Get a map of the Route du Vin from any TI. For background,

review "French Wine-Tasting 101" (page 30) and information on half-timbered architecture (page 772).

Most towns have wineries that give tours (some charge a fee), and many small producers open their courtyards with free tastings. The modern cooperatives at Eguisheim, Bennwihr, Hunawihr, and Ribeauvillé, created after the destruction of World War II, provide a good look at modern and efficient methods of production.

Learn to recognize the basic grapes: Riesling is the king of Alsatian grapes. The name comes from the German word that describes its slightly smoky, gasoline smell. Gewürztraminer is "the lady's wine"—its bouquet is like a rosebush, its taste is fruity, and its aftertaste is spicy. In fact, it's named for the German word for "spicy." Crémant d'Alsace, the Alsatian sparkling wine, is very good—and much cheaper. The French term for headache, if you really get "Alsauced," is *mal à la tête*.

Towns are most alive during their weekly morning (until noon) farmers' markets (Monday-Kaysersberg; Tuesday-Munster; Friday-Turckheim; Saturday-Ribeauvillé and Colmar—behind train station near St. Joseph's Church). Riquewihr and Eguisheim have no market days.

## Getting Around the Route du Vin

If you're driving, buy a good regional map (1:200,000 scale or better) before heading out.

**By Bus:** Several companies run buses connecting Colmar's train station with most villages along the Route du Vin (except on Sundays, when there are none). Kaysersberg has good weekday service and makes an easy day trip from Colmar; Riquewihr, Hunawihr, and Ribeauvillé have decent service, but service to Eguisheim is minimal (Mon–Sat schedules from Colmar to Eguisheim: 3/day, usually at 12:00, 16:00, and 17:00, 20 min; to Kaysersberg: almost hourly, 25–40 min; to Riquewihr, Bennwihr, Hunawihr, Turckheim, and Ribeauvillé: 6/day, 30–45 min). Allow €1.50-3.50 one-way to these villages. Most schedules are posted where buses stop. Pick up schedules and get help deciphering them at the TI. Buy tickets from the driver.

**By Taxi:** Allow €15 from Colmar to Eguisheim, and €25–30 from Colmar or Eguisheim to Kaysersberg (call friendly William at 06 14 47 21 80, another taxi at 03 89 80 71 71, or ask the TI to call).

**By Minivan Tour:** Cheerful Jean-Claude Werner leads **Les Circuits d'Alsace** day trips in a comfortable seven-person minivan (small groups: 2-person minimum, larger groups possible, solo travelers may be able to squeeze in with another group, in English and/or Japanese, great sound system on comfy air-con minibus). His informative tours include a few enjoyable, very short vineyard walks. Jean-Claude's enthusiasm and personal touches add to the experience. Wine-tastings and gourmet excursions can be arranged on request. Half-day tours visit three towns, generally Kaysersberg, Turckheim, and Eguisheim (€53 per person). For €3 more per person, Jean-Claude can extend your half-day visit by 30 minutes to include Haut-Kœnigsbourg castle. Full-day tours for €99 per person add a couple more towns and Haut-Kœnigsbourg (5 percent discount with this book in 2009, castle admission extra, reserve directly with Jean-Claude, pick-up at your hotel, tel. 03 89 41 90 88, mobile 06 72 37 17 11, www.alsace-travel.com, werner @alsace-travel.com).

**Regioscope** is another good option, with full- and half-day tours in a 15-seat, air-conditioned minivan led by Frédéric Albert (departures from Colmar and Strasbourg possible). Morning departures leave Colmar at 9:15; afternoon departures leave at 13:45. Half-day trips return by 12:15 or 18:30. On Tuesday, Thursday, Friday, and Sunday mornings, they go to Ribeauvillé and Kaysersberg (€50 per person); then in the afternoon, they head to Haut-Kœnigsbourg and Riquewihr (€59 includes wine-tasting, €104 for both morning and afternoon tours). On Wednesday and Saturday, morning tours visit Eguisheim and Turckheim (€50), and afternoon tours go to Titisee in Germany's Black Forest (€69; or €115 for both tours). Excursions from Strasbourg include a morning tour of Mont Sainte-Odile and Obernai (€50), and an afternoon tour of Haut-Kœnigsbourg and Riquewihr (€75; or €120 for both). All prices include entrance fees and guided tours of the castles. In December, ask about Christmas Market excursions (tel. 06 88 21 27 15, www.regioscope.com, info@regioscope.com).

**By Bike:** The Route du Vin's more-or-less-level terrain and abundance of bike trails make biking a reasonable option, particularly once you get to the villages (see "Helpful Hints," page 768, for bike rental in Colmar). To save yourself the ride out of Colmar, rent a bike in Turckheim (84 Grand Rue, tel. & fax 03 89 27 06 36). While there is no bike rental in Eguisheim, the Auberge Alsacienne has bikes for guests (see page 790). Colmar to Eguisheim to Turckheim and back makes a manageable 15-mile, half-day circuit; add Kaysersberg for a full day's outing, but beware—the road to Kaysersberg is busy.

Most key roads leaving Colmar have a painted bike lane. One of those lanes leads to **Eguisheim** and is a level snap, though it's entirely on busy roads. For a quieter route, leave Colmar along avenue de la République, using the painted bike lane. After the shopping malls, turn right onto chemin Laenderweg, where you'll join fellow bikers and tractors. Follow this road past cornfields to a busy roundabout, carefully join the traffic, and exit straight out the other side to the Route du Vin. Turn left onto rue Marbache and follow it to Eguisheim. If you ask for directions, don't confuse

## Alsace's Route de Vin

TO STRASBOURG
& PARIS VIA
AUTOROUTE

PARIS
ALSACE
FRANCE

HAUT-
KŒNIGGSBOURG
CASTLE

TO
MARLENHEIM

SCENIC
LOOP

ST.
HIPP.

N

BERGHEIM

D-1083

**RIBEAUVILLE**

**HUNAWIHR**

ZELLENBERG

TO
NANCY &
PARIS VIA
COL DU
BONHOMME

**RIQUEWIHR**

N-415

KIENTZHEIM

PANORAMA

**BENNWIHR**

**KAYSERSBERG**

SIGOLSHEIM

N-415

AMMERSCHWIHR

INGERSHEIM

VOSGES

**COLMAR**

N-415

**TURCKHEIM**

TO
FREIBURG
& BLACK
FOREST
(GERMANY)

MOUNTAINS

WINTZENHEIM

TO
MUNSTER   D-417

**EGUISHEIM**

D-1

HUSSEREN
LES CHATEAUX

D-14

TO
THANN

N-83

TO
MULHOUSE
& BASEL
(SWITZ.)

DCH

TO BELFORT
DIJON &
BEAUNE

ALSACE

~ ROUTE DU VIN

🏰 CASTLES

✳ VIEWPOINT

5   MILES

8 KM

Eguisheim (say "aye-gush-I'm") with Ingersheim ("anger-shime").

From Colmar to **Kaysersberg,** figure on pedaling steadily for 60 minutes on mostly busy roads (bike lane on the main road from Colmar, *route du Colmar*). Get advice and a good map from the TI or a bike shop and avoid major roads—except for those you use to leave Colmar (see below).

The roads between Ingersheim, Wintzenheim, and Eguisheim are peaceful.

**By Car:** To reach the Route du Vin north of Colmar, leave Colmar's train station following signs to *Epinal.* In Wintzenheim, follow signs to *Turckheim,* then find D-10 (Route du Vin) to Ingersheim (Kaysersberg is a short detour from here), Riquewihr, Hunawihr, Ribeauvillé, and Château du Haut-Kœnigsbourg. Look for *Route du Vin* signs. For Eguisheim, leave Colmar on N-83 toward Belfort.

**By Foot:** Well-signed walking trails *(sentiers viticoles)* connect Route du Vin villages through the vineyards (get info at local TIs and under "Sights," below). Hikers can climb high to the ruined castles of the Vosges mountains (Eguisheim and Ribeauvillé are good bases). The *sentier viticole* connecting Kaysersberg and Riquewihr is a good two-hour walk that works well with buses from Colmar (see page 792).

# SIGHTS

## Along the Route du Vin, North of Colmar

These sights are listed from south to north, in the order you'll encounter them if you're heading north out of Colmar.

**Eguisheim**—This is the most charming village of the region (described on page 788).

**Turckheim**—With a fine square and garden-filled moat, this pleasant town is refreshingly untouristy, just enough off the beaten path to be overlooked. WWII buffs appreciate its "Colmar Pocket" museum, chronicling the American push to take Alsace from the Nazis. Turckheim is ideal for renting a bike and pedaling along the virtually traffic-free paved trail to Munster (Munster's market day is Tue).

**Kaysersberg**—This town has WWII sights, Dr. Albert Schweitzer's house, and plenty of hiking opportunities (described on page 792).

**Riquewihr**—This little village is so picturesque today because it was so rich centuries ago; you can recognize its old wealth because it has the most stone houses of any place in Alsace. The walled village is crammed with tourist shops, cafés, galleries, cobblestones, and flowers. Sharpen your elbows if you arrive with the many groups in the afternoon. The **TI** is at 2 rue de la 1ère Armée

(Mon–Sat 9:30–12:00 & 14:00–18:00, Sun 10:00–13:00, tel. 03 89 73 23 23, www.ribeauville-riquewihr.com, info@ribeauville -riquewihr.com).

You'll enter at the lower end under the Hôtel de Ville (City Hall). Within a few yards, you'll see the tourist train (€6, next departure time posted, 30 min, recorded tour through vineyards). Try the excellent and free wine-tasting at Caves Dopff et Irion (uphill from Hôtel de Ville, daily 10:00–19:00, tel. 03 89 47 92 51). The wonderful "air-conditioning" is completely natural—you're in a cave.

Shop and browse—sampling fresh local baked goods given free to tourists—to the top of town, where you'll find one of the best bell towers in the region (1291). The Dolden Museum (at the tower) shows off farm and winemaking tools (daily in summer, weekend afternoons only off-season). Check out the engraving of 13th-century Riquewihr by the fountain. Walks both inside and outside the ramparts begin from here. (The best walk is to the left, or south.)

**Zellenberg**—This town has an impressive setting and is worth a quick stop for the views from either side of its narrow perch.

**Hunawihr**—This bit of wine-soaked Alsatian cuteness is far less visited than its more famous neighbors, and features a 16th-century fortified church that today is shared by Catholics and Protestants (the Catholics are buried next to the church; the Protestants are buried outside the church wall). Park below in the village at the sheltered picnic tables and follow the trail up to the church, then loop back through the village. Kids enjoy Hunawihr's small park, Parc des Cigognes, where they'll spot otters and over 150 storks (April–Sept daily 10:00–12:00 & 14:00–18:00, no midday closing June–Aug, until 17:00 March and Oct–Nov, closed Dec–Feb, other animals take part in the afternoon shows, tel. 03 89 73 72 62, www.cigogne-loutre.com). Eat well at **Winstub Suzel** near the church (€18–25 *menus,* serves lunch and dinner, closed Mon and Wed nights, 2 rue de l'Eglise, tel. 03 89 73 30 85).

**Ribeauvillé**—Come here to hike. Two brooding castles hang above this pleasant town seldom visited by Americans. The steep castle trail leaves from the top of the town (at Hôtel Trois Châteaux, park in city lot here). Allow 45 minutes one-way, or just climb 10 minutes for a view over the town (www.ribeauville -riquewihr.com).

▲**Château du Haut-Kœnigsbourg**—This granddaddy of Alsatian castles, strategically situated on a rocky spur high above the flat Rhine plain, protected the passage between Alsace and Lorraine for centuries. Its pink stones were quarried from the Vosges Mountains. Rebuilt in the early 20th century, the well-furnished castle highlights Germanic influence in Alsatian history with decorations that illustrate castle life from the 15th through 17th centuries. There's little English, so you'll want the informative 60-minute audioguide (€7.50, under 18 free, audioguide-€4, daily June–Aug 9:30–18:00, March–May and Sept–Oct 9:30–17:00, Nov–Feb 9:45–12:00 & 13:00–16:30, last entry 30 min before closing, about 15 min north of Ribeauvillé above St. Hippolyte, tel. 03 88 82 50 60).

**Vieil-Armand WWI Memorial**—This powerful memorial evokes the slaughter of the Western Front in World War I, when Germany and France bashed heads for years in a war of attrition. It's up a windy road above Cernay (20 miles south of Colmar). From the parking lot, walk 10 minutes to the vast cemetery, and walk 30 more minutes through trenches to a hilltop with a grand Alsatian view. Here you'll find a stirring memorial statue of French soldiers storming the trenches in 1915–1916, facing near-certain death.

# Eguisheim

Just a few miles south of Colmar's suburbs, this circular, flower-festooned little wine town (pop. 1,600) is pretty darn cute. Eguisheim ("aye-gush-I'm") is ideal for a relaxing lunch and vineyard walks, and makes a good small-town base for exploring Alsace. It's a cinch by car (easy parking) and manageable by bike (see "Getting Around the Route du Vin—By Bike," page 784), but barely accessible by bus. Consider taking the bus one-way and taxi the other to Colmar or other villages (bus schedules available at TIs and posted at key stops). Eguisheim's stop is at the lower end of the village, by the post office.

**Tourist Information:** The TI has information on accommodations, festivals, vineyard walks, and Vosges mountain hikes (Mon–Fri 9:30–12:00 & 14:00–18:00, Sat 9:30–12:00 & 13:30–17:30, closed Sun, 22 Grand Rue, tel. 03 89 23 40 33, www.ot-eguisheim.fr). They're happy to call a taxi for you.

**Internet Access: Le Café** has Internet access, lattes, and delicious baked goodies (daily 10:00–19:00, impasse Allmend, behind 2C rue du Rempart Nord, tel. 03 89 41 14 30).

## SELF-GUIDED WALK

### Welcome to Eguisheim

While Eguisheim's wall is gone, the rue des Remparts (Nord and Sud) survives, scenically circling the village. The main drag, Grand Rue, bisects the circle leading to a town square that's as darling as a Grimm fairy tale.

Start your visit at the bottom of town (near the TI) and circle the ramparts clockwise, walking up rue du Rempart Sud. The most enchanting and higgledy-piggledy view in town is right at the start of the loop (at the tight Y in the road; go left and uphill). Rue du Rempart Sud is more picturesque than rue du Rempart Nord, but I'd walk the entire circle. After going about a quarter of the circle, when you see a church on your right, you may want to cut into the town center to enjoy the little square, place de l'Eglise.

Back on the rue des Remparts, you'll see that what was once the moat is now lined with 13th- to 17th-century houses—a cancan of half-timbered charm. You're actually walking a lane between the back of fine homes (on the left) and their barns (on the right). Look for emblems of daily life, religious and magical symbols, dates on lintel stones, and so on. (The government pays 15 percent of the cost of any work locals do on their exteriors.) For more on half-timbered architecture, see page 772.

Once you've finished the loop, walk up Grand Rue to Eguisheim's main square, **place du Château St. Léon,** and lose all sense of discipline sampling the shops, cafés, and fruits of the local vine. This square, lined with fine Renaissance houses, marks the heart of the old town. The castle is privately owned and closed to the public. Surviving bits of its 13th-century, eight-sided wall circle the chapel, built in Neo-Romanesque style on the site of the castle's keep in 1895. While it is of little historic importance, it's worth a peek to see how a Romanesque chapel may have been painted (drop any coin into the €0.50 box for light). The 19th-century fountain sports a statue of St. Leo IX (1048–1054), the only Alsatian pope. Equisheim's most famous son was a saint, to boot.

Exploring the town, you may come upon some of its 20 "tithe courtyards." Farmers who worked on land owned by the church used to come to these courtyards to pay their tithes (10 percent of their production). With so many of these courtyards, it's safe to conclude that the farming around here was excellent.

## ACTIVITIES

**Wine-Tasting**—Don't leave without visiting one of Eguisheim's countless cozy wineries or the big and modern **Wine Cooperative** (Wolfberger, Cave Vinicole d'Eguisheim, Mon–Sat 8:00–12:00 & 14:00–18:00, Sun from 10:00, 6 Grand Rue, tel. 03 89 22 20 20).

**Views over Eguisheim**—If you have a car, follow signs up to *Husseren Les Cinq Châteaux,* then walk 20 minutes to the ruined castle towers for a good view of the Vosges Mountains above and vineyards below.

By mountain bike or on foot, find any path through vineyards above Eguisheim for nice views (the TI has a free map, *Canton de Wintzenheim en Balade*). For a bracing and scenic 90-minute round-trip hike, walk uphill on Grande Rue, cross the ring road leaving

**ALSACE**

Eguisheim's town center, and turn left at the *Camping* arrow. Pass the campground, then follow *Sentier Viticole* signs past the little Stork Park and keep straight. The five châteaux of Husseren float above on your right. *Sentier Viticole* signs will lead you on a loop trip through the vineyards to the village of Husseren at the base of those castles, then back to Eguisheim.

# SLEEPING

**(€1 = about $1.50, country code: 33)**

## Hotels

**$$$ Hôtel St. Hubert\*\*\*** offers 15 rooms with polished, modern, German-hotelesque comfort (and strict management to match), and an indoor pool and sauna (€7). The 10-minute walk from the town center is rewarded with vineyards out your window (big Db-€111, family suite for four-€182, extra bed-€16, four rooms have patios, free pickup at Colmar's train station if reserved a day in advance, reception open 8:00–12:00 & 15:00–22:00, 6 rue des Trois Pierres, tel. 03 89 41 40 50, fax 03 89 41 46 88, www.hotel-st -hubert.com, reservation@hotel-st-hubert.com).

**$$$ Hostellerie du Château\*\*\***—part art gallery, part hotel— provides stylish, contemporary luxury on the pleasant main square (Db-€81–99, Db with "view" over square-€95–114 and worth the splurge, suite with whirlpool tub-€135–165, extra bed-€20, pay Wi-Fi, garage €10/day, 2 place du Château St. Léon IX, tel. 03 89 23 72 00, fax 03 89 41 63 93, www.hostellerieduchateau.com, info@hostellerieduchateau.com).

**$$ Auberge Alsacienne\*\*\*** is conveniently located near the bus stop, with small, tastefully designed rooms in a picturesque building and rental bikes for guests (Db-€55–75, Tb-€90, 12 Grand Rue, tel. 03 89 41 50 20, fax 03 89 23 89 32, www.auberge -alsacienne.net, auberge-alsacienne@wanadoo.fr).

**$$ Auberge du Rempart** is atmospheric, with white, bright, and airy rooms above a lively café/restaurant deep inside the town. The reception desk is in the restaurant and is usually open only during lunch and after 18:00 (standard Db-€51, bigger Db-€70, great family suite-€119, 3 rue du Rempart Sud, near TI, tel. 03 89 41 16 87, fax 03 89 41 06 50, www.auberge-du-rempart.com, auberge-du-rempart@wanadoo.fr).

## Chambres d'Hôte

Three of these owners speak no English, but they're creative at communicating. Please remember to cancel if you reserve a room and can't use it.

ALSACE

**$$ Madame Hertz-Meyers,** your Alsatian grandmother who wishes you spoke French so she could chat with you, offers mostly big rooms in a mansion surrounded by vineyards, only 200 feet from the village. Rooms in the main house are great for families and better than her two modern apartments (Sb-€50–55, Db-€60–70, Tb-€80, includes breakfast, cash only, 3 rue du Riesling; look for sign *Albert-Hertz, Dégustation-Vente,* walk into courtyard and ring bell at *Chambres* sign; check-in after 18:00 unless otherwise prearranged by fax, tel. & fax 03 89 23 67 74).

**$ Alexandre Freudenreich** rents spacious, light, and decent rooms at a good price. He speaks English and has four rooms in the village center and two more modern rooms in another building up in the vineyards. He can pick you up in Colmar if you book ahead (Db-€42, includes breakfast, cash only, take 2 rights out of the TI to 4 cour Unterlinden, tel. & fax 03 89 23 16 44, maisonhote @aol.com).

**$ Madame Dirringer** has a formal place with four comfortable rooms facing a traditional courtyard (Db-€35, good family room, breakfast-€6, cash only, 11 rue du Riesling, tel. 03 89 41 71 87).

**$ Madame Bombenger** has a modern, graceful home that sits just above Eguisheim with three rooms, nice views into the vineyards and over Eguisheim, and sweet Madame Bombenger—who speaks some English—to welcome you (Sb-€35, Db-€45, €2 less for more than 1 night, includes breakfast, 3 rue des Trois Pierres, tel. & fax 03 89 23 71 19, mobile 06 61 94 31 09, bombenger.marie -therese@wanadoo.fr).

# EATING

The **charcuterie** on place du Château has killer quiche to go and everything you need for a fine picnic (daily until 19:00, Mon–Fri closes 12:30–14:00). You can picnic on the wooden benches by the fountain, or listen to the trickling of the square's fountain at their adjacent restaurant and order directly from the menu (daily, €8–12 *tartes flambées* and quiche).

**Auberge de Trois Châteaux** is very Alsatian, with cozy ambience and traditional cuisine (€16–22 *menus* and affordable *plats du jour,* closed Tue–Wed, 26 Grand Rue, tel. 03 89 23 70 61).

**Auberge Alsacienne** offers regional cuisine in a more refined setting (€21 two-course *menu,* €27 three-course *menu,* closed Sun eve and Mon, 12 Grand Rue, tel. 03 89 41 50 20).

**Auberge du Rempart** is best for outdoor dining in a pleasant courtyard around a fountain. Come here for less expensive and lighter meals and good *tartes flambées* (€8–17 *plats,* closed Mon, closed Sun and sometimes Thu evenings Sept–June, 3 rue du Remparts Sud, near TI, tel. 03 89 41 16 87).

ALSACE

**Au Vieux Porche** is a wood-beamed, white-tablecloth affair, ideal for a leisurely meal or a special occasion (€15–25 *plats,* closed Tue–Wed, upper end of town at 16 rue des Trois Châteaux, tel. 03 89 24 01 90).

# Kaysersberg

Philosopher-physician Albert Schweitzer's hometown offers a cute jumble of 15th-century homes under a romantically ruined castle with easy vineyard trails at its doorstep, and plenty of tourists. Frequent buses from Colmar make Kaysersberg an easy day trip. Catch buses back to Colmar across the road from the bus shelter where riders are dropped coming from Colmar (a block from post office).

The **TI** is inside the Hôtel de Ville (City Hall) near the town's main entry (June–Sept Mon–Sat 9:00–12:30 & 14:00–18:00, Sun 10:00–12:30; Oct–May Mon–Sat 9:30–12:00 & 14:00–17:30, closed Sun; tel. 03 89 78 22 78, www.kaysersberg .com, WCs out the door to left under arch). Walkers can pick up the free *Sentier Viticole* map for hiking between wine villages, and check bus schedules (from their destination back to Colmar). Serious walkers can buy the trail map (see "Walking Trails from Kaysersberg," later in this section). The TI also has information on bike rental.

Strolling through Kaysersberg is a treat. Walking up the main drag through the town, you'll see **St. Croix Church** (daily 9:00–16:00, sometimes open later, unique crucifix in front of a fine 1518 altarpiece—push button for light); colorful shops (pop into the Moulin des Arts—a touristy shopping mall with waterwheels); the humble town museum (€2, July–Aug Wed–Mon 14:00–18:00, closed Tue and Sept–June); and its 16th-century bridge. As the Nazis were preparing to evacuate, they planned to destroy the bridge. Locals reasoned with the commander, agreeing to dig an anti-tank ditch just beyond the bridge—and the symbol of the town was saved. At the top end of town, you'll come to **Dr. Albert Schweitzer's house,** a small and disappointing museum. It has two rooms of scattered photos and artifacts from his time in Africa, without a word of English (€2, Easter–Oct daily 9:00–12:00 & 14:00–18:00, closed Nov–Easter, 126 rue du Général de Gaulle). The square across the street hosts a thriving market each Monday until noon.

**Walking Trails from Kaysersberg:** Trails depart from just outside the TI (get details at the TI). To find the main trail, turn left out of the TI and walk under the arch. A left on the trail leads up to the **castle** (free, fine views and benches, 113 steps up a dark stairway to the tower). Hikers can continue past the castle for more

ALSACE

views and walks on vineyard roads. This also leads to the longer route to Riquewihr (2.5 hours).

For an easier hike to Riquewihr, turn right on the main trail back down by the TI. You'll start on a bike path *(piste cyclable)* to Kientzheim, then join the trail (follow *Sentier Viticole* and blue crosses) to Riquewihr, where buses can take you back to Colmar.

**WWII Sights:** The hill just north of Kaysersberg is soaked in WWII blood. Towns around it have gray- rather than red-tiled roofs (indicating they were entirely destroyed and rebuilt). **Kientzheim** has an American-made tank parked in its front yard (and a wine museum in its castle grounds). In 2004, the refreshing network of tiny streams trickling down its streets (standard before World War II) was restored. Both Sigolsheim (scene of fierce fighting—note its sterile rebuilt Romanesque church) and Bennwihr are modern, as they were taken and lost a dozen times by the Allies and Nazis, and entirely destroyed. The hill above is still called "Bloody Hill," as it was nicknamed by German troops. Between its cemeteries, you'll find some of the best vines on the Route du Vin.

A **WWII Monument** stands atop Bloody Hill. The spectacular setting, best at sunset, houses a monument to the American divisions that helped liberate Alsace in World War II (find the American flag). Up the lane, a beautiful cemetery is the final resting place of 1,600 men who fought in the French army (many gravestones are Muslim, for soldiers from France's North African colonies—Morocco, Algeria, and Tunisia). From this brilliant viewpoint, you can survey the entire southern section of the Route du Vin and into Germany. The road to the memorial leaves from the center of Sigolsheim (follow *Necropole* and *Cimitière* signs turning at Pierre Sparr winery, then keep straight and climb into the vineyards).

# Strasbourg

Strasbourg is urban Alsace at its best—it feels like a giant Colmar with rivers and streetcars. It's a progressive, livable city,

with generous space devoted to pedestrians, scads of bikes, mod trams, meandering waterways, and a young, lively mix of university students, Eurocrats, and street people. This place has an Amsterdam-like feel. Situated just west of the Rhine River,

Strasbourg provides the ultimate blend of Franco-Germanic culture, architecture, and ambience. A living symbol of the perpetual peace between France and Germany, Strasbourg was selected as home to the European Parliament, the European Council (sharing administrative responsibilities for the European Union with Brussels, Belgium), and the European Court of Human Rights.

## Planning Your Time

Strasbourg makes a good day trip from Colmar. And, thanks to new high-speed TGV-train service, it also makes a handy stop for train travelers en route to or from Paris (baggage storage available). None of its museums are essential (though the Alsatian Museum is well-done)—you're here to see the cathedral, wander the waterways, and take a bite out of the big city. Plan on three hours to hit the highlights, starting at Strasbourg's dazzling cathedral (arrive in Strasbourg by 11:30 so you can comfortably make the 12:30 cathedral clock performance—see "Sights and Activities," later in this section) and ending with the district called La Petite France (ideally for lunch).

# ORIENTATION

## Tourist Information

Strasbourg's main TI faces the cathedral (daily 9:00–19:00, 17 place de la Cathédrale, tel. 03 88 52 28 28, www.ot-strasbourg.fr, info@ot-strasbourg.fr). A smaller TI is located in the train station's south hall (same hours). Buy the €1 city map (which describes a decent walking tour in English), or pay €5.50 for an **audioguide** that covers the cathedral and old city in more detail than most need (available only at the main TI, includes a cute little map of the route, allow 90 min). The TI also has bike maps for the city and surrounding areas.

The €11.40 **Strasbourg Pass,** valid three days, is a good value for many travelers. It includes one free museum entry and half-off coupons for others, a discount on the town audioguide, a free half-day bike rental, the boat cruise, and free entry to the cathedral narthex view and the astrological clock tour.

## Arrival in Strasbourg

**By Train:** TGV trains serve Strasbourg's handsome train station. The station has baggage storage, located at platform 1 (daily 7:45–20:30, €4–8.50, depends on locker size, coins only, airport-type security screening so allow time, WCs nearby-€0.50). A helpful TI is in the station's south hall. Rental bikes are available in the lower level of the glass atrium (see "Helpful Hints," page 797).

To **walk** to the cathedral in 15 urban minutes, go straight out

ALSACE

**Strasbourg**

N

200 YARDS
200 METERS

TRAIN STATION

To PLACE DE HAGENAU
AUTOROUTES A-4 + A-35

To PLACE DE LA RÉPUBLIQUE

CATHEDRAL

PALAIS ROHAN

ALSATIAN MUSEUM

LA PETITE FRANCE

MODERN ART MUSEUM

BARRAGE VAUBAN

PONTS COUVERTS

To AUTOROUTES A-4 (PARIS) + A-35 (COLMAR)

**ALSACE**

1 Hôtel Cathédrale
2 Hôtel Cardinal de Rohan
3 Hôtel Suisse
4 Hôtel des Arts
5 Chez Yvonne Rest.
6 Le Clou Winstub
7 Poêles de Carottes
8 Galeries Lafayette
9 Place Benjamin Zix
10 Quai de la Bruche
11 Bike Rental
12 Pharmacy
13 To European Parliament
14 Mus. of the Cathedral
15 Astronomical Clock
16 Internet Café
17 SNCF Boutique

WALKING LOOP ROUTE BETWEEN THE TRAIN STATION + CATHEDRAL

View
P PARKING

of the station, cross the big square (place de la Gare), and walk past Hôtel Vendôme and up rue du Maire Kuss. Cross the river, and continue up serpentine, pedestrian-friendly rue du 22 November all the way to place Kleber. Cross bustling place Kleber, maintaining the same direction, then turn right on the huge pedestrian street (rue des Grandes Arcades). Turn left on rue des Hallebardes, then follow that spire.

To get from the train station to the city center by **public transportation,** catch the caterpillar-like tram that leaves from under the station (buy €1.30 one-way ticket or €2.50 day pass from machines on platforms, coins only, then validate in skinny machines). Take Tram #A (direction: Illkirch) three stops to Grande Rue, two blocks from the cathedral. (You can return to the station, Gare Centrale, from same stop, direction: Hautepierre.)

**By Car:** Pay to park safely in Strasbourg. Follow *Gare Centrale* signs, then *Parking Aurélie* signs (it's on boulevard de Metz—to the right with your back to the station). To park even closer to the center (and encounter more traffic), follow *Centre-Ville/Cathédrale* signs. Parking lots are well-marked—place Gutenberg and place du Château are close to the cathedral, though the larger Austerlitz *parking* works fine. Skip the train station's pricey underground lot (€3/hr).

**By Plane:** The user-friendly Strasbourg-Entzheim airport (tel. 03 88 64 67 67), with frequent and often inexpensive flights to Paris, is easily accessible via tram and shuttle bus: From the airport, catch the shuttle bus (*navette,* about €5.50 one-way, €10 round-trip, 2/hr) to the Baggersee stop, where Tram #A (transfer included in *navette* ticket) runs frequently to the city center, stopping at the train station and cathedral (allow 40 min total).

## Helpful Hints

**Quiet Transportation:** Beware of quiet streetcars and bicycles—look both ways before crossing streets. Bikes are allowed on pedestrian streets.

**US Consulate:** It's at 15 rue d'Alsace (tel. 03 88 35 31 04, fax 03 88 24 06 95).

**Internet Access:** Several cybercafés lie on the main street into town from the station, rue du Maire Kuss. **Milk,** a flashy 24/7 Internet café, is at 34 rue du Vieux-Marché aux Vins.

**Post Office:** It's at the cathedral (Mon–Fri 8:00–18:30, Sat 8:00–17:00).

**Pharmacy:** It's located just opposite the train station; ask for an English-speaking pharmacist (Mon–Fri 8:30–19:15, Sat 8:30–12:30 & 14:00–17:00, closed Sun).

**Laundry:** You'll find a handy launderette on rue des Veaux, near the recommended hotels.

ALSACE

**Bike Rental:** You can rent bikes at **Vélocation,** in the lower level of the train station (€5/half–day—either 7:00–13:00 or 13:00–20:00, €8/day; open Mon–Fri 7:00–20:00, Sat–Sun 9:30–12:30 & 13:30–19:30; follow signs for *Bike Parking lot,* Place de la Gare, tel. 03 88 23 56 75, www.velocation.net).

**Taxi:** Call 03 88 36 13 13.

**Train Tickets:** The SNCF Boutique at 7 quai de Paris sells train tickets and makes reservations.

# SIGHTS AND ACTIVITIES

## ▲▲Strasbourg Cathedral (Cathédrale de Notre-Dame)

Stand in front of Hôtel de la Cathédrale and crane your neck up. If this church, with its cloud-piercing spire and pink sandstone color, wows you today, imagine its impact on medieval tourists. The delicate Gothic style of the cathedral (begun in 1176, not finished until 1429) is another Franco-German mixture that somehow survived the French Revolution, the Franco-Prussian War, World War I, and World War II. The square in front of the cathedral makes the ideal stage for street performers—it's like a medieval fair.

Before entering the cathedral, survey the scene. This square was Roman 2,000 years ago. Then, as now, it was the center of activity. The dark half-timbered building to your left, next to the TI, was the home of a wealthy merchant in the 16th century, and symbolizes the virtues of capitalism that Strasbourg has long revered. Goods were sold under the ground-floor arches; owners lived above. Strasbourg made its medieval mark as a trading center, taking advantage of its position at the crossroads of Europe and its access to the important Rhine River to charge tolls for the movement of goods. Its robust economy allowed for the construction of this remarkable cathedral. Strasbourg's location also made it susceptible to new ideas. Martin Luther's theses were posted on its main doors, and after the wars of religion, this cathedral was Protestant for more than 100 years. (Louis XIV returned it to Catholicism in 1621.)

As you enter the cathedral (free, daily 7:00–11:40 & 12:45–19:00), notice the sculpture over the left portal (complacent, spear-toting Virtues getting revenge on those nasty Vices). Enter and walk down the center. The stained glass on the lower left shows various rulers of Strasbourg, while the stained glass on your right depicts Bible stories. An ornate, gold-leafed organ hangs above the second pillars. Walk to the choir and stare at the stained-glass image of Mary; find the European Union flag at the top.

In the right transept is a high-tech, 15th-century **astronomical**

ALSACE

**clock** (restored in 1883) that gives a ho-hum performance every 15 minutes (keep your eye on the little angel about 15 feet up, slightly left of center), better on the half-hour (angel on the right), and best at 12:30 (everybody gets in the act, including a rooster and 12 apostles—for the 12 hours). Arrive by 11:45 outside the right transept, buy your €2 ticket, then enter and hear an explanation of the clock's workings—and beware of pickpockets.

For €4.60, you can climb 332 steps to the **top of the narthex** for an amazing view (free first Sun of the month, access on right side of cathedral, daily April–Sept 9:00–19:30, June–Aug Fri–Sat nights sometimes until 22:00, Oct–March 10:00–17:30).

Before leaving this area, investigate the network of small pedestrian streets that connect the cathedral with the huge place Kleber (home to various outdoor markets depending on the day of the week). Each street is named for the primary trade that took place there.

## Museums near the Cathedral

These museums lie outside the cathedral's right transept and are interesting only for aficionados with particular interests or a full day in Strasbourg. They're all free on the first Sunday of the month (www.musees-strasbourg.org).

**Palais Rohan**—This stately palace houses three museums: the **Museum of Decorative Arts** (big rooms with red velvet chairs), the **Museum of Fine Arts** (a small, well-displayed collection of paintings from Middle Ages to Baroque, some by artists you would recognize), and the **Archaeological Museum,** the best of the three, with a stellar presentation of Alsatian civilization through the millennia and English explanations (€4 each, under 18 free, Wed–Mon 10:00–18:00, closed Tue, 2 place du Château, tel. 03 88 52 50 00).

**Museum of the Cathedral (Musée de l'Oeuvre Notre-Dame)**—This well-organized museum has plenty of artifacts from the cathedral (€4, includes English audioguide, under 18 free, Tue–Sun 10:00–18:00, closed Mon, 3 place du Château, tel. 03 88 32 88 17).

**Alsatian Museum**—One of Strasbourg's oldest and most characteristic homes hosts this extensive, well-presented collection of Alsatian folk art. You'll see scenes from daily life, traditional home interiors (including a close-up look at half-timbered construction), lots of tools, and a good overview of the life of a winemaker. Ask for the English handout (€4, Wed–Mon 12:00–18:00, Sun from 10:00, closed Tue, across the river and down 1 block to the right from the boat dock at 23 quai St. Nicholas, tel. 03 88 52 50 01).

## Boat Ride on the Ill River

To see the cityscape from the water, take a loop cruise around Strasbourg. The glass-topped boats are air-conditioned and sufficiently comfortable—both sides have fine views. You'll pass through two locks as you circle the old city clockwise. The highlight for me was cruising by the European Parliament buildings and the European Court of Human Rights (adults-€8, under 18-half-price, 70 min, good English commentary with live guide or audioguide, 2 boats/hour, daily April–Oct 9:30–21:00, May–Sept until 22:00; Nov–March boats depart only at 10:30, 13:00, 14:30, and 16:00; dock is 2 blocks outside cathedral's right transept, where rue Rohan meets the river, tel. 03 88 84 13 13, www.batorama.fr).

## ▲La Petite France

The historic home to Strasbourg's tanners, millers, and fishermen, this awfully charming area is laced with canals, crowned with magnificent half-timbered homes, carpeted with cobblestones, and filled with tourists.

From the cathedral, walk down rue des Hallebardes to the merry-go-round, then continue straight following rue Gutenberg. Cross big rue des Francs Bourgeois and keep straight (now on Grande Rue). Turn left on the third little street (rue du Bouclier, street signs are posted behind you), and make your way to the middle of the bridge (pont St. Martin). Gaze at the various locks and the channels that meet here. Find your way down to the river and follow the walkway over the lock deep into La Petite France. Make friends with a leafy café table on place Benjamin Zix, or find the siesta-perfect parks between the canals across the bridge at rue des Moulins. Climb the once-fortified grassy wall (Barrage Vauban) for a decent view—the glass structure behind you is the new modern-art museum (interesting more for its architecture than its collection).

La Petite France's coziest cafés line the canal on **quai de la Bruche** near the barrage. From here, it's a 10-minute walk back to the station: With the river on your left, walk along quai de Turckheim, cross the third bridge, and find rue du Maire Kuss.

# SLEEPING

(€1 = about $1.50, country code: 33)

**$$$ Hôtel Cathédrale*** is comfortable and contemporary, with a Jack-and-the-beanstalk spiral stairway (elevator begins one floor up) and a hopelessly confusing floor plan. This modern yet atmospheric place lets you stare at the cathedral point-blank from your room. Skip the cheaper rooms *sans* view (small Db with no

**ALSACE**

view-€85–110, medium Db with no view-€120, larger Db with view-€150, prices sometimes lower on weekends, buffet breakfast-€13, air-con, laundry service, free Wi-Fi, free bicycles can be reserved for up to 2 hours, book ahead for one of 5 parking spaces, 12–13 place de la Cathédrale, tel. 03 88 22 12 12, toll-free in France 08 00 00 00 84, fax 03 88 23 28 00, www.hotel-cathedrale.fr, reserv@hotel-cathedrale.fr).

**$$ Hôtel Cardinal de Rohan\*\*\*** has a classy address in the pedestrian zone just steps from the cathedral, with royal public spaces and 36 well-appointed rooms (standard Db-€75, bigger Db-€139–149, Tb-€159, buffet breakfast-€13, air-con, free Internet access and Wi-Fi, book ahead for one of 6 parking spaces-€17, 17 rue du Maroquin, tel. 03 88 32 85 11, fax 03 88 75 65 37, www .hotel-rohan.com, info@hotel-rohan.com).

**$$ Hôtel Suisse\*\*,** across from the cathedral's right transept and off place du Château, is a low-profile, dark, central, serious, and solid two-star value (Sb-€59–79, Db-€79–99, prices €10 less in Jan–Feb and July–Aug—when parliament isn't in session, extra person-€10, buffet breakfast-€9.50, elevator, free Wi-Fi, 2 place de la Râpe, tel. 03 88 35 22 11, fax 03 88 25 74 23, www.hotel-suisse .com, info@hotel-suisse.com).

**$$ Hôtel des Arts\*\*,** above a busy café, is a simple, bare-bones place with microscopic bathrooms and air-conditioning. Rooms overlooking the square in front are fun but noisy (Sb/Db-€66–72, Tb-€78, entirely non-smoking, 10 place du Marché aux Cochons de Lait, tel. 03 88 37 98 37, fax 03 88 37 98 97, www.hotel-arts.com, info@hotel-arts.fr).

# EATING

Atmospheric *winstubs* (wine bars) serving affordable salads and *tarte flambée* are a snap to find. If the weather is nice, head for **La Petite France** and choose ambience over cuisine—dine outside at any café/*winstub* that appeals to you. Alternatively, stock up on picnic supplies at the terrific grocery store on the main floor of the **Galeries Lafayette** department store (Mon–Sat 9:00–20:00, closed Sun, place Kleber).

For a real meal, skip the touristy restaurants on the cathedral square and along rue de Maroquin. Consider these nearby places instead; both are one block behind the TI (go left out of the TI, then take the first left through the passageway and keep walking): **Chez Yvonne** (marked *S'Burjerstuewel* above windows) has a tradition of good food, pleasant staff, and affordable prices (allow €25–30, reservations smart on weekends and holidays, open daily until late, 10 rue du Sanglier, tel. 03 88 32 84 15). Half a block left down rue du Chaudron at #3 lies **Le Clou Winstub,** with €12

ALSACE

salads and €14 *plats du jour*. This place often looks closed from the outside, but don't be shy (closed Wed lunch and all day Sun, tel. 03 88 32 11 67).

Vegetarians find respite from porky Alsatian cuisine at **Poêles de Carottes** (big €10 salads and stir-fries, closed Sun–Mon, 2 place de Meuniers, tel. 03 88 32 33 23).

## TRANSPORTATION CONNECTIONS

Strasbourg makes a good side-trip from Colmar or a stop on the way to or from Paris.

**From Strasbourg by Train to: Colmar** (2/hr, 35 min), **Reims** (via TGV: 10/day, 2 hrs, change at Gare Champagne-Ardennes), **Paris'** Gare de l'Est (via TGV: hourly, 2.5 hrs; via non-TGV train: 10/day, 4 hrs), **Lyon** (5/day, 5 hrs), **Karlsruhe,** Germany (via TGV: 4/day, 40 min; via non-TGV train: 12/day, 1–1.5 hrs, most with change in Appenweier or Wissembourg), **Basel,** Switzerland (via TGV: 4/day, 70 min; via non-TGV train: hourly, 2 hrs).

# REIMS AND VERDUN

Different as night and day, bubbly Reims and brooding Verdun offer worthwhile stops between Paris and Alsace. The administrative capital of the Champagne region, bustling, modern Reims greets travelers with cellar doors wide open. It features a lively center, a historic cathedral, and of course, Champagne tasting. Often overlooked, quiet Verdun is famous for the lengthy and brutal World War I battles that surrounded the city and leveled the countryside, and offers an exceptional opportunity to learn about the Great War. With new high-speed TGV trains, both of these destinations are now more easily accessible to travelers (particularly if coming from Paris).

## Planning Your Time

Organized travelers in a hurry can see Reims and Verdun as they travel between Paris and the Alsace, though most will want an overnight (both destinations work) to best appreciate the sights. Plan on most of a day for Reims and a half-day for Verdun. It's about 70 miles between the two towns, making a day trip from Reims to Verdun worth considering (if you have a car—it's too difficult by train). Day trips by train from Paris to Reims are a breeze, but day trips to Verdun require careful planning.

## Getting Around Reims and Verdun

Driving is a breeze, even in the bigger city of Reims, and many find this a good place to pick up a rental car for a longer trip after leaving Paris. Reims offers excellent public transportation, with handy buses linking its major sights. But public transit is non-existent in Verdun, where it's best to rent a car for the day or take a

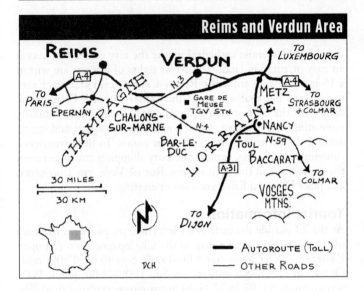

**Reims and Verdun Area**

private tour to visit the battlefields.

Frequent high-speed TGV trains link Paris and Reims in 45 minutes, while rare TGV trains link Paris and Verdun in an hour and 45 minutes. Trains between Reims and Verdun are slow thanks to required transfers.

# Reims

With its Roman gate, Gothic cathedral, Champagne caves, and vibrant pedestrian zone, Reims (pronounced "rance," which rhymes with "France") feels both historic and youthful. Reims has a turbulent history: This is where 26 French kings were coronated, where Champagne first bubbled, where WWI devastation (all but 70 buildings were damaged in 1918) met miraculous reconstruction during the Art Deco age, and where the Germans officially surrendered in 1945, bringing World War II to a close in Europe. The town's sights give you an entertaining peek at the entire story.

## Planning Your Time

You can see Reims' essential sights in less than a day. Twelve daily TGV trains make the trip from Paris a snap—take a morning train from Paris and explore the cathedral and city center before lunch, then spend your afternoon below ground, in a cool, chalky Champagne cellar. You can be back at your Parisian hotel in time for a rest before dinner.

REIMS

# ORIENTATION

Reims' hard-to-miss cathedral marks the city center and makes an easy orientation landmark. Most sights of interest are within a 15-minute walk from the Reims-Centre train station. Easy-to-use loop bus routes connect the harder-to-reach Champagne *caves* with the train station and cathedral. The city is ambitiously renovating its downtown, and is converting the square and streets around the cathedral into pedestrian zones. To best experience contemporary Reims, explore the busy shopping streets between the cathedral and the train station. Rue de Vesle, rue Condorcet, and place Drouet d'Erlon are most interesting.

## Tourist Information

At the TI outside the cathedral's left transept, pick up a free map of the town center and a map of the Champagne *caves* (TI open Easter–mid-Oct Mon–Sat 9:00–19:00, Sun 10:00–18:00; mid-Oct–Easter Mon–Sat 9:00–17:00, Sun 11:00–16:00; public WCs across street, tel. 03 26 77 45 00, www.reims-tourisme.com). The TI can book a visit to any *cave* that accepts visitors, and can call a taxi to get you there. Better yet, go by *cyclopolitain* (tricycle taxi) or bus (for more on both, see "Getting Around Reims," later in this section). The TI also rents pricey audioguide tours covering the cathedral, city center, and Art Deco architecture (single-€5, each additional set-€4).

## Arrival in Reims

**By Train:** From Paris, you'll arrive at the easy-to-navigate Reims-Centre station (no baggage check). You can reach the cathedral by foot in 15 minutes: Walk straight out of the station (passing Avis), cross the tree-lined boulevards Joffre and Foch, and stroll up the pedestrian place Drouet d'Erlon. Turn left on rue Condorcet, then right on rue de Talleyrand. The time-saving Citadine bus runs from the station (see "Getting Around Reims," later in this section) to the cathedral and to the Taittinger and Martel *caves* (described in "Champagne Tours," page 810).

**By Car:** Follow *Centre-Ville* and *Cathédrale* signs and park on the street approaching the cathedral (rue Libergier) or in the well-signed Parking Cathédrale structure (€1.40/hour).

## Helpful Hints

**Internet Access:** You can surf and snack at **Clique et Croque** (€4/hr, Mon–Sat 10:00–24:00, Sun 14:00–20:00, near the cathedral at 19 rue Chanzy, tel. 03 26 86 93 92).

**Laundry: Laverie Chanzy** is a few blocks in front of the cathedral (daily 7:00–21:30, 59 rue Chanzy).

**Taxi:** Call 03 26 47 05 05. A taxi from the train station to the farthest Champagne *cave* will cost about €8.

**Car Rental: Avis** is at the train station (cours de la Gare, tel. 08 20 05 05 05); **Europcar** is at 76 boulevard Lundy (tel. 08 25 04 52 82); and **Hertz** is at 26 boulevard Joffre (tel. 03 26 47 98 78; all three usually open Mon–Sat 8:00–12:00 & 14:00–19:00, closed Sun).

**Local Guide:** British expat Jon Catt can show you around the city, its champagne *caves,* and the battlefields near Reims. Jon does not drive so you must have your own transport if you go beyond Reims (€120/half-day, €200/day, plus expenses, tel. & fax 03 25 73 74 52, mobile 06 17 44 49 67, http://tourguide champagne.blogspot.com, jon.catt@wanadoo.fr).

## Getting Around Reims

**By Citadine Bus:** While most sights are close, two Champagne *caves* (Taittinger and Martel) are a 30-minute walk from the station. Two Citadine bus lines link the historic center with these far-flung cellars, with circular routes starting and ending at the Reims-Centre train station (every 12 min, none on Sun, €1, pay driver). Line #1 does the route clockwise; line #2 does it counterclockwise. To catch the bus, cross the parking lot in front of the train station and look for the yellow Citadine bus stop before crossing the boulevard. From in front of the station, Citadine #1 runs to the cathedral and TI (stop: Cathédrale) in five minutes, and to Taittinger and Martel (stop: St. Niçaise) in 10 minutes. To return, board the same bus and continue the loop back to the station. Bus line #K also runs from the station (catch it just across the street from Hertz car rental, direction Béthany), getting you close to the Mumm Champagne *cave* (stop: Justice).

**By *Cyclopolitain* Tricycle:** These modern lightweight electric tricycles carry one or two passengers and function like taxis, but for shorter trips. The young drivers (called Cyclonautes) speak English and are happy to take you anywhere within the city limits (€2/person per kilometer, €20 for 30-min tour; flag one down, have the TI call for you, or call direct at 06 27 95 54 72). If you take a tour, it'd be nice to tip €2–3; otherwise there's no need to tip for simple point-to-point transport.

# SIGHTS

## ▲▲▲Reims Cathedral

The cathedral of Reims, begun in 1211, is a glorious example of Gothic architecture, and one of Europe's greatest churches.

**Cost and Hours:** Free, daily 7:30–19:30.

**Background:** Clovis, the first king of the Franks, was baptized at a church on this site in A.D. 496, establishing France's Christian roots that hold firm today. Since Clovis' baptism, Reims' cathedral has served as *the* place for the coronation of 25 French kings and queens—allowing it to play a more important role in France's political history than Paris' Notre-Dame cathedral. A self-assured Joan of Arc led a less-assured Charles VII to be crowned here in 1429. The French rallied around their new king to push the English out of France and to finally end the Hundred Years' War. During the French Revolution, the cathedral was converted to a

temple of reason (as was Notre-Dame in Paris). After the restoration of the monarchy, the cathedral hosted the crowning of Charles X in 1825—the last coronation in France. During World War I, it was devastated by severe bombing. Then it was completely rebuilt, thanks in large part to John D. Rockefeller...just in time for the start of World War II.

**◑ Self-Guided Tour:** Stand on the square in front of the cathedral and admire perhaps the best west portal anywhere, with more than 2,000 statues festooning its walls inside and out. (Since medieval churches face east, toward the Holy Land, you enter through the west portal.) Like the cathedrals in Paris and in Chartres, this church is dedicated to "Our Lady" (Notre-Dame). Statues depicting the crowning of the virgin take center-stage on the facade. For eight centuries, Catholics have prayed to the "Mother of God," kneeling here to ask her to intervene with God on their behalf. In 1429, Joan of Arc received messages from Mary encouraging her to rally French troops against the English at the Siege of Orléans.

Notice the flying buttresses soaring from the sides of the church. These massive "beams" are critical to supporting this structure. The pointed arches inside the church push the weight of the roof outward, rather than downward. The "flying" buttresses support the roof by pushing back inward, creating a delicate balance between the two forces. Gothic architects learned by trial and error—many church roofs caved in as they tested their theories and strove to build ever higher. Work on this cathedral began decades after the Notre-Dame cathedrals in Paris and Chartres, allowing architects to take advantage of what they'd learned from those magnificent earlier structures.

Contemplate the lives of the people who built this huge building, starting in 1211. Construction on a scale like this required a wholesale community effort—all hands on deck. Most townsfolk who participated donated their money or their labor knowing

# Reims

Ⓑ Citadine Bus Stops

Ⓟ Parking

▨ Pedestrian Zone

1. Grand Hôtel Continental & Micro Brasserie les 3 Brasseurs
2. Latino Hôtel
3. Bénédicte et Claude Philippon B&B
4. Grand Hôtel du Nord & L'Apostrophe Rest.
5. Brasserie du Boulingrin
6. Au Plat du Jour
7. Café du Palais
8. Europcar Car Rental
9. Hertz Car Rental
10. Museum of the Surrender
11. Parking Cathédrale
12. Launderette & Internet Café

**REIMS**

that neither they, nor their children, nor their children's children, would ever see it completed—such was their pride, dedication, and faith. Imagine the effort it took to raise the funds and manage the workforce. Master masons supervised, while the average Jean did much of the sweat work. Labor was something even the poorest medieval peasant could donate generously.

Walk inside. The weight of the roof is supported by a few towering columns that seem to sprout crisscrossing pointed arches. This technique allowed the church to grow higher, and liberated the walls to become window frames. Now, look back at the entry wall with 120 statues filling the niches. The rose window (high above on this wall) contains the best original stained glass in the church (from 1255, removed during World War I to be spared destruction). Most of the windows are clear and newer: 18th- and 19th-century tastes called for more light, and the original, dark stained glass was replaced.

The south transept windows, destroyed in World War I, were replaced in 1954 by the local Champagne-makers. The windows show the connection of the Champagne industry to this town and its church with scenes portraying the tending of vines (left), the harvest (center), and the time-honored double-fermentation process (right). Notice, around the edges, the churches representing all the grape-producing villages in the area.

The apse (east end, behind the altar) holds a luminous set of Marc Chagall stained-glass windows from 1974. Chagall's inimi-table style lends itself to stained glass and he enjoyed opportunities to adorn great churches with his windows. The left window shows scenes from the Old Testament, and the center features the resurrection of Christ. On the right the tree of Jesse is extended to symbolically include the royalty of France—both affirming the divine power of the monarchs and stressing the responsibility to rule with wisdom and justice.  Helpful English explanations offer historical detail.

## More Sights

**Palais du Tau**—This former Archbishop's Palace houses artifacts from the cathedral (with scant English information). You'll look into the weathered eyes of original statues from the cathedral's facade (taken in from the acidic open air for their own preservation). A set of precious tapestries, telling stories from the life of Mary, are the originals that warmed the walls of the cathedral's choir in the 16th century. As mentioned earlier, Reims hosted the last French coronation—that of Charles X in 1825. Since the coronation jewels, vestments, and other garb were lost a generation earlier in the French Revolution, what you see here was mostly made especially for this event (€6.50; May–Aug Tue–Sun 9:30–18:30, closed Mon; Sept–April Tue–Sun 9:30–12:30 & 14:00–17:30, closed Mon; tel. 03 26 47 81 79).

**▲Museum of the Surrender (Musée de la Reddition)**—World War II buffs enjoy visiting the historic room where the

Germans signed the document of surrender of all German forces in the early morning of May 7, 1945. The news was announced the next day, turning May 8 into Victory in Europe (V-E) Day. Anyone interested in World War II will find the extensive collection of artifacts fascinating (particularly the ticker tape with the happy news, old photos, and a 10-minute video shown on request). The room of the signing still has the maps with troop positions on the walls and the 13 chairs with name tags, each in their original spots (€3, Wed–Mon 10:00–12:00 & 14:00–18:00, closed Tue, 12 rue Franklin Roosevelt, tel. 03 26 47 84 19).

**Porte de Mars**—The last vestige of Reims' ancient Roman heritage—an entry gate—is a short walk from the Reims-Centrale train station. The Porte de Mars, built in the second century A.D., was one of four principal entrances into the ancient Gallo-Roman town and the only one still standing. Inspired by triumphal arches that Rome built to herald war victories, this one was constructed to celebrate the Pax Romana (a period of peace and stability—after all of Rome's foes were vanquished). Unlike most of the rest of town, the Porte was undamaged in World War I but bears the marks of other eras, such as its integration into the medieval ramparts. Find the ruts under the arcade which guided chariots, and look for the depiction of the legend of Romulus and Remus (extremely faint on ceiling under left arch), complete with suckling she-wolf, from which Reims gets its name (free, always open, place du Boulingrin).

**▲Carnegie Library (Bibliotheque Carnegie)**—The legacy of the Carnegie Library network, funded generously by the 19th-century American millionaire Andrew Carnegie and his steel fortune (notice the American flag above the main entrance on the left), extends even to Reims. Built in the flurry of inter-war reconstruction, this beautiful Art Deco building still houses the city's public library. Since entrance is free and it's just behind the cathedral, it's worth a quick look. Visitors are welcome to admire the mosaics, onyx-laden entrance hall, and Jacque Simon chandelier, but are asked not to enter the reading room (some come here to study). Peek through reading room door to admire the stained-glass windows of this temple of thinking. The gorgeous wood-paneled card-catalogue room takes older visitors back to

their childhoods (notice how each card is tediously typed), or even back to 1928, the year the library was inaugurated (free, Tue–Sat 10:00–13:00 & 14:00–19:00, closed Thu morning and Sun–Mon, place Carnegie).

**Art Deco on Place Drouet d'Erlon**—Place Drouet d'Erlon is a long street-like square marking the commercial center of town. (From the train station, it's directly across the park-like boulevards.) The square's centerpiece, a fountain with a winged figure of victory at the top, celebrates the major rivers of this district. It hasn't worked as a fountain since WWI bombings—a reminder of the devastation brought on this city. All around you'll see the stylized features—geometric reliefs, motifs in iron work, rounded corners, and simple concrete elegance—of Art Deco. The only hints that this was once a medieval town are the narrow lots that struggle to fit today's buildings. Pop into the Waida Patisserie (3 place Drouet d'Erlon) for a pure, typical Art Deco interior. As you stroll about, keep an eye open for "Biscuits Roses"—light, rose-colored egg-and-sugar cookies that date from 1756. They're the locals' favorite munchie to accompany a glass of Champagne (most places that sell the treat offer free samples).

## Champagne Tours and Sights

### In Reims

**▲▲Champagne Tours**—While the bubbly stuff's birthplace is closer to Epernay, you can tour several interesting Champagne *caves* right in Reims, the administrative capital of the Champagne region. All charge for tastings and are open daily. Most have daily English tours (often booked for groups) and sometimes allow individuals to join these tours. Call in advance for the schedule and to secure a spot on a tour (Martel offers the most personal and best-value tour). Bring a sweater, even in summer, as the *caves* are cool and clammy.

Mumm (pron. "moome") is closest to the train station (15-minute walk) and welcomes the public. Its "traditional visit" (€8, 1 hour) includes a good 10-minute video, a small museum of old Champagne-making contraptions, and a tour of its industrial-size, modern-feeling chalk cellars where 25 million bottles are stored. The video explains the place's history back to 1827 and the Champagne-making process with the enthusiasm of an advertisement ("Cordon Rouge is dedicated to the audacity and passion of exceptional men and women, with a subtle balance between freshness and intensity"). The tour ends with a glass of bubbly Cordon Rouge. You can pay more for the same tour with extra "guided" tastings—€14 for two tastes, or €20 for three (tours depart March–Oct daily 9:00–11:00 & 14:00–17:00, Nov–Feb weekend afternoons and weekdays by reservation, tel. 03 26 49 59 69, www.mumm.com, guides@mumm.com). Mumm is four blocks left out of the train station, on the other side of place de la République at 34 rue du Champ de Mars (also accessible by bus line #K from the train station). Visits begin in the building on the right, #34, at the end of the courtyard. Follow *Visites des Caves* signs.

**Taittinger** (tay-tan-zhay) is one of the biggest, priciest, and most renowned of Reims' *caves*. They run three morning and three afternoon tours in English through their impressive cellars (call for times and to reserve a spot, about 20–30 people per tour). After seeing their 10-minute promo-movie (hooray for Taittinger!), follow your guide—mine reminded me of an old-time airline hostess—for 45 chilly minutes and 80 steps down to a chalky underworld of *caves*, the deepest of which were dug by ancient Romans. You'll tour part of the three miles of *caves*, pass some of the three million bottles stored here, and learn all you need to know about the Champagne process from your well-informed guide. Popping corks signal when the tour's done and the tasting's begun (€10, includes tasting, 1 hour, tours daily mid-March–mid-Nov 9:30–12:00 & 14:00–16:30, closed weekends off-season, 9 place St. Nicaise, tel. 03 26 85 84 33, www.taittinger.com).

**Martel** gives a homey contrast to Taittinger's big-business style. It's a small operation with less extensive *caves* and is *sans* doubt the best deal in town. Call to set up a visit and expect a small group that might be yours alone. Friendly Emmanuel runs the place. Only 20 percent of their product is exported (mostly to Europe), so you won't find much of their Champagne in the US. Their €8, 45-minute visit focuses on the basics and includes an informative 10-minute film and a tour of their small cellars peppered with rusted old winemaking tools. It culminates with a tasting of three different Champagnes in a casual living-room atmosphere (daily 10:00–19:00, open through lunch, 17 rue des Créneaux, tel. 03 26 82 70 67, www.champagnemartel.com).

**Getting to Taittinger and Martel:** These two places are a few blocks apart, about 30 minutes by foot southeast of the cathedral. It's easiest and cheap (€1) to get there by Citadine bus (see "Getting Around Reims," earlier in this section). A handy Citadine stop is just behind the cathedral (find the yellow stop a block to the left at the rear of the cathedral and take #1). Get off at the stop St. Nicaise (stops are digitally displayed on the bus or ask driver) and you'll see the long walls of Taittinger and the green sign to little Martel. If you take a taxi from the train station, figure on €8 one-way (cellars will call a cab for you after the tour). By *cyclopolitain* tricycle, it's €6 per person. If you walk, take rue de l'Université (from behind the cathedral's right transept), then rue du Barbâtre.

### Near Reims
**Epernay**—Champagne purists may want to visit Epernay (16 miles away, well-connected to Paris and Reims), where the grand-daddy of Champagne companies, **Moët et Chandon,** offers tours with three pricey tasting possibilities (€13 for single tasting, €18 for 2 tastes, €25 for 3, no reservation needed, daily mid-March–mid-Nov 9:30–11:30 & 14:00–16:30, closed weekends off-season, tel. 03 26 51 20 20, www.moet.com). From the Epernay train station, walk five minutes straight up rue Gambetta to place de la République, and take a left on avenue de Champagne (how fitting). According to the story, it was near here in about 1700 that the monk Dom Perignon, after much fiddling with double fermentation, stumbled onto this bubbly treat. On that happy day, he ran through the abbey shouting, "Brothers, come quickly...I'm drinking stars!"

**Route de la Champagne**—Drivers can joyride through the scenic and prestigious vineyards just south of Reims (the TI has maps). Follow D-9 south to Cormontreuil, then Louvois, then Bouzy, to see the chalky soil and vines that produce Champagne's costly wines. Many of the villages have small hotels if you'd like to sleep surrounded by vineyards.

# SLEEPING

The first three of my listings are on place Drouet d'Erlon.

**$$ Grand Hôtel Continental\*\*\*** is a fine old hotel with well-priced, three-star comfort; stay-awhile public spaces; and helpful Maxeme at the desk (standard Db-€63–76, "junior suite" Db-€98–112, "superior suite" Db-€165–185, apartments for 3–8 available, 10 percent discount for Rick Steves readers on all but standard rooms, some non-smoking rooms, air-con, elevator, laundry service, pricey Wi-Fi, parking-€6, 5-min walk from the train station at 93 place Drouet d'Erlon, tel. 03 26 40 39 35, fax 03 26 47 51 12, www.grand hotelcontinental.com, grand-hotel-continental@wanadoo.fr).

## Sleep Code

**(€1 = about $1.50, country code: 33)**
**S** = Single, **D** = Double/Twin, **T** = Triple, **Q** = Quad, **b** = bathroom,
**s** = shower only, **\*** = French hotel rating system (0–4 stars).
Unless otherwise noted, credit cards are accepted and English is spoken.

To help you sort easily through these listings, I've divided the rooms into two categories based on the price for a standard double room with bath:

**$$** **Higher Priced**—Most rooms €50 or more.
**$** **Lower Priced**—Most rooms less than €50.

**$$ Latino Hôtel** lives up to its name with spicy music and 11 colorful, funky rooms at fair rates. It's above a bar so it can be noisy on weekends. Rooms facing the back are quieter but smaller and face the adjacent building (Db-€54–74, 33 place Drouet d'Erlon, tel. 03 26 47 48 89, fax 03 26 86 92 67, www.latinocafe.fr, latinocafe@latinocafe.fr).

**$$ Grand Hôtel du Nord\*\*** delivers basic two-star comfort in high-ceilinged rooms (Db-€65, 75 place Drouet d'Erlon, tel. 03 26 47 39 03, fax 03 26 40 92 26).

**$ Bénédicte et Claude Philippon Chambres d'Hôte** is Reims' best lodging value. This delightful couple offers two comfortable, homey, and centrally located rooms on place du Chapitre (#21), 100 yards from the cathedral's left transept. Look for the yellow *Chambres d'Hôte* sign (S-€40, D-€50, T-€65, shared bathroom, includes French breakfast, fourth floor with elevator, parking on square, tel. 03 26 91 06 22, mobile 06 77 76 20 13, claude.philippon@tele2.fr).

# EATING

Find good people-watching opportunities—if not high cuisine—with the many restaurants on place Drouet d'Erlon. All of these recommendations make good lunch or dinner options.

**L'Apostrophe,** an appealing place with a snazzy-cozy interior, offers a well-presented, creative cuisine that draws a loyal clientele (€15 *plats*, €26 *menu*, look for specials, daily, 59 place Drouet d'Erlon, tel. 03 26 79 19 89).

**Micro Brasserie les 3 Brasseurs** is a rollicking, Alsatian-flavored micro-brewery with copper vats and a young, inviting feel. You'll get good brasserie fare and (for once in France) more beer than wine (€8 salads, €10–13 *plats*, €16 choucroute, 73 place Drouet d'Erlon, tel. 03 26 47 86 28).

**Brasserie du Boulingrin** is the oldest brasserie in town, gushing with Art Deco. A Reims institution, it serves traditional French cuisine at blue-collar prices (€15–18 *plats*, €18–25 *menus*, closed Sun; 10-min walk north of the TI or central train station at 49 rue de Mars, or take the Citadine bus #2, stop Boulingrin; tel. 03 26 40 96 22).

**Au Plat du Jour,** near the Martel and Taittinger *caves*, makes a useful pre- or post-Champagne-tasting option. Casually elegant, with old posters and Champagne labels adorning the walls, this is a good spot to enjoy hearty, classic French cuisine (€14–19 *plats*, €16–21 *menus*, closed Sun, 219 rue Barbâtre, tel. 03 26 85 27 60).

**Café du Palais** is appreciated by older locals who don't mind paying a premium to eat a meal or sip coffee wrapped in 1930s ambience. Reims' most venerable café-bistro stands across from the Grand Theater (14 place Myron Herrick, tel. 03 26 47 52 54).

## TRANSPORTATION CONNECTIONS

There are two train stations in Reims (Reims-Centre and Gare Champagne-Ardennes). All trains to/from Paris (TGV and other) use the Reims-Centre station, while TGV trains to/from points east (i.e., Strasbourg or Colmar) use Gare Champagne-Ardennes (3 miles from the center of Reims, frequent shuttle-train connections to Reims-Centre station).

**From Reims by Train to: Paris'** Gare de l'Est (via TGV: 12/day, 45 min), **Epernay** (non-TGV: 12/day, 30 min), **Verdun** 8/day, 2–4 hrs, most with change in Châlons or Metz), **Strasbourg** (via TGV: 10/day, 2 hrs, change at Gare Champagne-Ardennes), **Colmar** (via TGV: 10/day, 3 hrs, most change at Gare Champagne-Ardennes and in Strasbourg).

# Verdun

Few traces of World War I remain in Europe today, but the battlefields of Verdun provide an appropriately hard-hitting tribute to the 800,000 lives lost here in the horrific war of 1914–1918. The lunar landscape left by World War I battles is today buried under thick forests. Millions of live bombs are scattered in vast cordoned-off areas—it's not unusual for French farmers or hikers to be injured by unexploded mines. Drive or ride through the eerie moguls surrounding Verdun, stopping at melted-sugar-cube forts and plaques marking where towns once existed. With three hours and a car, a tour (operated by the TI), or easy taxi rides, you can see the most important sights and appreciate the horrific scale of the battles. The town of Verdun is not your destination, but a starting point for your visit into the nearby battlefields.

## Tourist Information

The TI is just across the river (cross pont Chaussée) east of Verdun's city center on place de la Nation (May–Sept Mon–Sat 8:30–18:30, Sun 10:00–17:00; Oct–April Mon–Sat 9:00–12:00 & 14:00–17:00, Sun 10:00–13:00; tel. 03 29 86 14 18, www.verdun-tourisme.com, verduntourisme@wanadoo.fr). They have books in English, maps of the city center with English descriptions of key monuments, and maps of the battlefields. Most importantly for non-drivers, this is where tours to the battlefields depart (see page 816; drivers don't need to stop here). The pleasant park across the street provides a good picnic setting and a more cheerful break from the heavy sights.

## Arrival in Verdun

**By Train:** Scarce TGV trains serve the new **Gare Meuse TGV station,** where a 30-minute shuttle bus ride takes you to Verdun' central station (described below). This high-speed service puts the city of Verdun within 1.75 hours of Paris, but with only two high-speed, direct trips a day, it's critical to confirm the schedule in advance.

Several slower trains are also available (see "Transportation Connections" at the end of this section). These non-TGV trains arrive at Verdun's **central station,** 15 minutes by foot from the TI.

To reach the town center, walk straight out of the station (no baggage check), cross the parking lot and the roundabout and keep straight down avenue Garibaldi, then follow to *Centre-Ville* signs on rue St. Paul. (You'll pass a grocery store and a recommended car-rental agency soon after leaving the station.) Turn left on the first traffic-free street in the old center (rue Chaussée, good lunch options) and walk past the towers and across the river to the TI.

**By Car:** Drivers can bypass the town center and TI and drive straight for the battlefields. Follow signs reading *Verdun Centre-Ville,* then signs toward *Longwy,* then find signs to *Douaumont* and *Champs de Bataille* (battlefields) on D-112, then D-913. By following signs to *Fort de Douaumont* and *Ossuaire,* you'll pass Mémorial–Musée de Fleury, your first stop. To reach the TI, follow signs to *Centre-Ville,* then *Office du Tourisme* (you'll pass the TI just before crossing the river).

## Getting Around the Verdun Battlefields

The battlefield remains are situated on both sides of the Meuse River; the *rive droite* (right bank)—where we'll go—has more sights.

Verdun has sparse train service—plan your arrival and departure carefully. Once there, you have three choices for touring the battlefields:

**By Car:** Dirt-cheap car rental is available a block from the train station at **AS Location** (about €44/day with 100 km/80 miles included—easily enough to do the battlefields, Mon–Sat 7:45–11:45 & 14:00–18:00, closed Sun, 22 rue Louis Maury, tel. & fax 03 29 86 58 58). Book ahead if possible, though they normally have cars available.

**By Tour:** Verdun's TI offers four-hour tours of the battle sites described in this section. Though the tour is in French, the guides usually speak a little English (€27, includes entry fees, reserve ahead, May–mid-Sept daily departures at 14:00, see "Tourist Information," previous page).

Far better and more personal are tours offered by battlefield historians **Tony Noyes** and **Christina Holstein.** Tony, a Brit, has made a lifelong study of the Great War. Christina is from nearby Luxembourg and provides local color. They can custom-design your tour to include walking and driving the Verdun battlefields and other WWI sights (€310 for 2-person, all-day tour including transportation from Verdun; larger groups possible, from France call 00-35 26 21 22 38 48, www.verdun-tours.com, verduntours @verdun-tours.com).

**By Taxi:** For about €40 round-trip, taxis can drop a carload at one sight and pick up at another (walk between sights). Ask to be dropped off at the Mémorial–Musée de Fleury and picked up at the Fort de Douaumont four hours later (visiting l'Ossuaire in between); it's about two miles from one sight to the other, so expect to walk a minimum of four miles for this plan. For less walking, ask to be dropped off at l'Ossuaire and picked up at either Fort de Douaumont or Mémorial–Musée de Fleury. Taxis normally meet trains at the station; otherwise they park at the TI (taxi tel. 06 07 02 24 16 or 03 29 86 05 22). It's easiest to arrange a taxi with the help of the TI.

# SELF-GUIDED TOUR

## ▲▲The Battlefields of Verdun

Verdun's battlefields are littered with monuments and ruined forts. For most travelers, a half-day is enough, though historians could spend days here. We'll concentrate on the three most important sights: Mémorial–Musée de Fleury, l'Ossuaire de Douaumont, and Fort de Douaumont. Each offers a different perspective on the war.

**Information:** All sights are adequately described in English. If you want more, the TI and all sights sell helpful books in English describing the Battle of Verdun. The simple but adequate €5

booklet *Verdun: Images of War* provides
helpful details (in three languages) and
black-and-white photos. More readable
is *The Battle of Verdun* by Yves Buffetaut
(about €12). The best is Alistair Horne's
*The Price of Glory*, which sorts through
the complex issues surrounding Verdun
and offers perspectives from both sides
of the conflict—if you can, read it ahead
of your visit (about €14).

**Background:** After the annexation of Alsace and Lorraine following
the German victory in the Franco-
Prussian War in 1871, Verdun found itself just 25 miles from the
German border. This was too close for comfort for the French,
who invested mightily in the fortification of Verdun, hoping to
discourage German thoughts of invasion. The plan failed. World
War I erupted in August of 1914, and after a lengthy stalemate,
the Germans elected to strike a powerful knockout punch at the
heart of the French defense, to demoralize them and force a quick
surrender. They chose Verdun as their target. By defeating the best
of the French defenses, the Germans would cripple the French
military and morale. The French chose to fight to the bitter end.
Three hundred days of non-stop trench warfare ensued.

Soft, forested lands hide the memories of World War I's longest battles, which raged here for over 300 days in 1916. Thirteen
villages were caught in the middle and obliterated, never to be
resurrected (signed as *Villages Détruits*). Only small monuments
remind us that they ever existed. It's difficult to imagine today's
lush terrain as it was generations ago...a gray, treeless, crater-filled
landscape, smothered in mud and shattered in stone.

**◑ Self-Guided Tour:** Drivers (and cabbies) leave Verdun on
N-3, then take a left on D-112. Take the first turnoff possible (see
map on page 818) into the...

**Massif Fortifié de Souville:** At this parking and picnic area,
find a curving trench and craters that mark so much of the land
here. A few communication trenches like this remain (see below),
though all fortified trenches were destroyed during the battles or
have since been filled in. After leaving the parking area, you'll soon
pass a monument to André Maginot, the creator of the Maginot
Line of forts that were erected following World War I to defend
France against all future attacks from the east. He was wounded
during the battle of Verdun.

• *Continue following signs to* Ossuaire *and* Douaumont.

**Mémorial–Musée de Fleury:** This museum makes a good
first visit. It's built on the site of a village (Fleury) destroyed during

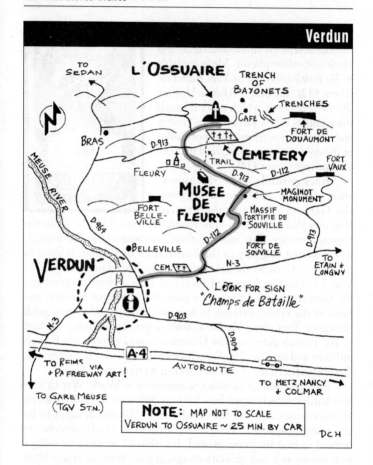

**Verdun**

TO SEDAN

L'OSSUAIRE

TRENCH OF BAYONETS

TRENCHES

CAFE

FORT DE DOUAUMONT

BRAS

D.913

CEMETERY

FORT VAUX

TRAIL

FLEURY

D.913

D.112

MEUSE RIVER

MUSEE DE FLEURY

MAGINOT MONUMENT

FORT BELLE-VILLE

MASSIF FORTIFIE DE SOUVILLE

D.964

D.112

D.913

BELLEVILLE

FORT DE SOUVILLE

VERDUN

CEM.

N-3

TO ETAIN & LONGWY

LOOK FOR SIGN "Champs de Bataille"

D.903

D.904

N-3

A-4

AUTOROUTE

TO REIMS VIA PA FREEWAY ART!

TO METZ, NANCY & COLMAR

TO GARE MEUSE (TGV STN.)

**NOTE:** MAP NOT TO SCALE
VERDUN TO OSSUAIRE ~ 25 MIN. BY CAR

DCH

the fighting. This museum provides a helpful visual presentation of this war that would see the potential of mankind's destructive creativity—machine guns, flamethrowers, poisonous gas, airplanes, and observation balloons were all first used in World War I. The museum houses a manageable number of displays of weapons, uniforms (note the French colonies' contributions), models, and photos. Its centerpiece is the re-creation of a battlefield (built by veterans of the battle), and a faded-but-worthwhile 15-minute movie (request English version or read English subtitles; less important if you see the better film at l'Ossuaire—next page). Look for the model of the unblemished Fort de Douaumont, and remember this when you visit the fort. While basic information is posted in English, the €2 guide to the museum is informative and easy to follow for much of the museum (€7, daily April–Aug 9:00–18:00, Sept–March 9:00–12:00 & 14:00–18:00, closed mid-Dec–Jan).

• *Continue to the next sight. For walkers, a trail leads from across the street and through the woods to that tall, missile-like building…*

**L'Ossuaire de Douaumont:** This is the tomb of 130,000 French and Germans whose last homes were the muddy trenches of Verdun. The artillery shell–shaped tower and cross design of this building symbolizes war and peace. Drivers can park at the rear and look through the low windows for a bony memorial to those whose political and military leaders asked them to make the "ultimate sacrifice" for their countries. Enter down the steps and start with the thought-provoking 20-minute film that seems particularly relevant today (€3, ask for English headphones—you can adjust volume). The little picture boxes in the gift shop are worth a look if you don't visit Mémorial–Musée de Fleury. Climb upstairs and experience a humbling and moving tribute to the soldiers who were convinced that this war would end all wars and that their children would grow up in a world at peace. The red lettering on the walls lists a soldier's name, rank ("Lt" is lieutenant, "Cal" is corporal, "St" is sergeant), regiment, and dates of birth and death. Skip the 204 steps up the tower (daily May–Aug 9:00–18:30, April and Sept 9:00–12:00 & 14:00–18:30, mid-Feb–March and Oct 9:00–12:00 & 14:00–17:30, Nov 9:00–12:00 & 14:00–17:00, Dec 14:00–17:00 only, closed Jan–mid-Feb, tel. 03 29 84 54 81).

Walk out to the cemetery and listen for the eerie buzz of silence and peace. Reflect on a war that ruined an entire generation, leaving half of all Frenchmen aged 15 to 30 dead or wounded. Rows of 15,000 Christian crosses and Muslim headstones (oriented toward Mecca), all with roses, decorate the cemetery. Moroccan soldiers were instrumental in France's ultimate victory at Verdun, a fact often overlooked by right-wing politicians in France.

Looking over the cemetery from above, the road on the lower left leads 1.5 miles to Fort de Douaumont (see below). Also to the left, but behind you, a road leads to a good little café, **Abri des Pelerins** (salads, omelets, €13 *menu*, March–Nov daily until 18:00, tel. 03 29 85 50 58). While it's too far for walkers and there's not much to see there now, those interested can continue down the road to **Tranchée des Baïonnettes** (Trench of Bayonets). Here, an entire company of soldiers was buried alive in their trench (the soldiers' bayonets remained aboveground for decades). The bulky concrete monument to this sad event was donated by the US.

• *Now head for…*

**Fort de Douaumont:** This was the most important stronghold in the network of forts built to protect Verdun after the annexation of Alsace and Lorraine to Germany in 1871. Built into the hillside, it served as a strategic command center for both sides at various times. Inside, there's little to see except two miles of cold, damp hallways. Experiencing these corridors will add to your sympathy for the soldiers who were forced to live like moles (€3, ask for English descriptions, daily April–Sept 10:00–18:00, Oct–Dec 10:00–17:00, Feb–March 10:00–12:00 & 14:00–17:00, closed Jan). Climb to the bombed-out top of the fort and check out the round, iron-gun emplacements that could rise and revolve.

Between l'Ossuaire and Fort de Douaumont, on either side of the road, you'll pass what remains of the **London Communication Trench.** This served as a means of communication and resupply for the Fort de Douaumont. Notice the concrete-reinforced sides. You'll see the ruins of several *abri* (shelters) on the hillside above the trench—these provided safe haven for the trench's soldiers.

## SIGHTS

### In Verdun

Unless you're arriving by train and have some time to spare, there's no reason to visit central Verdun's sights. The severe **Victory Monument** (Monument à la Victoire) is a block from the river overlooking the pedestrian zone. Seventy-three steps follow a watery path to a crypt storing records of the soldiers who fought here (both French and German). The **Citadelle Souterraine** offers a disappointing walk through the tunnels of the French Command. While it tries to re-create the Battle of Verdun scene, it's not worth your time or money (€6, daily April–Sept 9:00–18:00, Oct–Dec and Feb–March 10:00–12:00 & 14:00–17:00, closed Jan).

## SLEEPING AND EATING

Hotels in Verdun are cheap. A good bet is Monsieur Poirot's friendly, easygoing **$ Hôtel Montaulbain**\*\* (Ss-€29, Sb-€33, Ds-€36, Db-€42, Tb-€50, near the Victory Monument, 10-min walk from the station at 4 rue de la Vieille Prison, tel. 03 29 86 00 47, fax 03 29 84 75 70). You'll find several inexpensive restaurants in the pedestrian zone and along the river. On rue Chausée, find the great take-away **Charcuterie Artisanale.** There's also a good café near l'Ossuaire in the battlefields, **Abri des Pelerins** (see page 819).

## TRANSPORTATION CONNECTIONS

Remember, a few high-speed TGV trains serve the Verdun area from the Gare Meuse TGV station, 30 minutes south of Verdun, while more-frequent non-TGV trains continue to use Verdun's central station. For TGV connections listed below, allow an additional 30 minutes to reach Verdun's central station by shuttle bus.

**From Verdun by Train to: Colmar** (8/day, 4–5 hrs, possible changes in Metz, Saverne, and Strasbourg), **Reims** (8/day, 2–4 hrs, most with change in Châlons or Metz), **Paris'** Gare de l'Est (via TGV: 2/day, 1.25 hrs; via non-TGV train with change in Châlons or Metz: 6/day, 3–3.5 hrs).

# FRANCE:
## Past and Present

### "La Marseillaise"

There's a movement in France to soften the lyrics of their national anthem. Sing it now...before it's too late.

*Allons enfants de la Patrie,* (Let's go, children of the motherland,)
*Le jour de gloire est arrivé.* (The day of glory has arrived.)
*Contre nous de la tyrannie* (The blood-covered flag of tyranny)
*L'étendard sanglant est levé.* (Is raised against us.)
*L'étendard sanglant est levé.* (Is raised against us.)
*Entendez-vous dans les campagnes* (Do you hear these ferocious
　soldiers)
*Mugir ces féroces soldats?* (Howling in the countryside?)
*Qui viennent jusque dans nos bras* (They're nearly in our grasp)
*Egorger vos fils et vos compagnes.* (To slit the throats of your sons
　and your women.)
*Aux armes citoyens,* (Grab your weapons, citizens,)
*Formez vos bataillons,* (Form your battalions,)
*Marchons, marchons,* (March on, march on,)
*Qu'un sang impur* (So that their impure blood)
*Abreuve nos sillons.* (Will fill our trenches.)

### French History in an Escargot Shell

About the time of Christ, Romans "Latinized" the land of the Gauls. With the fifth-century fall of Rome, the barbarian Franks and Burgundians invaded. Today's France evolved from this unique mix of Latin and Celtic cultures.

While France wallowed with the rest of Europe in medieval darkness, it got a head start in its development as a nation-state. In 507, Clovis established Paris as the capital of his Christian Merovingian dynasty. Clovis and the Franks would eventually become Louis and the French. Charles Martel stopped the spread of Islam by beating the Spanish Moors at the Battle of Poitiers. And Charlemagne ("Charles the Great"), the most important of the "Dark Age" Frankish kings, was crowned Holy Roman Emperor by the pope in 800. Charlemagne presided over the "Carolingian Renaissance" and effectively ruled a vast-for-the-time empire.

The Treaty of Verdun (843), which divided Charlemagne's empire among his grandsons, marks what could be considered the birth of Europe. For the first time, a treaty was signed in vernacular languages (French and German), rather than in Latin. This split established a Franco-Germanic divide, and heralded an age of fragmentation. While petty princes took the reigns, the Frankish king ruled only Ile de France, a small region around Paris.

Vikings, or Norsemen, settled in what became Normandy. Later, in 1066, these "Normans" invaded England. The Norman king, William the Conqueror, consolidated his English domain, accelerating the formation of modern England. But his rule also muddied the political waters between England and France, kicking off a centuries-long struggle between the two nations.

In the 12th century, Eleanor of Aquitaine (a separate country in southwest France) married Louis VII, king of France, bringing Aquitaine under French rule. They divorced, and she married Henry of Normandy, soon-to-be Henry II of England. This marital union gave England control of a huge swath of land from the English Channel to the Pyrénées. For 300 years, France and England would struggle over control of Aquitaine. Any enemy of the French king would find a natural ally in the English king.

In 1328, a French king (Charles IV) died without a son. The English king (Edward III) was his nephew and interested in the throne, but the French resisted. This quandary pitted France, the biggest and richest country in Europe, against England, which had the biggest army. They fought from 1337 to 1453 in what was modestly called the Hundred Years' War.

Regional powers from within France actually sided with England. Burgundy took Paris, captured the royal family, and recognized the English king as heir to the French throne. England controlled France from the Loire north, and things looked bleak for the French king.

Enter Joan of Arc, a 16-year-old peasant girl driven by religious voices. France's national heroine left home to support Charles VII, the dauphin (boy prince, heir to the throne but too young to rule). Joan rallied the French, ultimately inspiring them to throw out the English. In 1430, Joan was captured by the Burgundians, who sold her to the English, who convicted her of heresy and burned her at the stake in Rouen. But the inspiration of Joan of Arc lived on, and by 1453, English holdings on the Continent had dwindled to the port of Calais.

HISTORY

# A Typical Medieval Church

History comes to life when you visit a medieval church. Knowing a few simple terms will make your church visit a lot richer. Not every church will have every feature. Note that a "cathedral" isn't a type of church architecture, but rather a governing center for a local bishop.

**Nave:** The long, central section of the church (running east to west, from the entrance to the altar) where the congregation stood through the service.

**Transept:** The north–south part of the church, which crosses (perpendicularly) the east–west nave. In a traditional Latin cross-shaped floor plan, the transept forms the "arms" of the cross.

**Aisles:** The long, generally low-ceilinged arcades that flank the nave.

**Altar:** The raised area with a ceremonial table (often adorned with candles or a crucifix), where the priest prepares and serves the bread and wine for Communion.

**Choir:** A cozy area, often screened off, located within the church nave and near the high altar where services are sung in a more intimate setting.

**Apse:** The space beyond the altar, generally bordered with small chapels.

**West Portal:** The main entry to the church (on the west end, opposite the main altar).

**Facade:** The outer wall of the church's main (west) entrance, viewable from outside and generally highly decorated.

**Groin Vault:** An arched ceiling formed where two equal barrel vaults meet at right angles. Less common usage: term for a medieval jock strap.

By 1500, a strong, centralized France had emerged, with borders similar to today's. Its kings (from the Renaissance François I through the Henrys and all those Louises) were model divine monarchs, setting the standards for absolute rule in Europe.

Outrage over the power plays and spending sprees of the kings, coupled with the modern thinking of the Enlightenment—whose leaders were the French *philosophes*—led to the French Revolution (1789). In France, it was the end of the *ancien régime,* as well as its notion that some are born to rule, while others are born to be ruled.

The excesses of the Revolution in turn led to the rise of Napoleon, who ruled the French empire as a dictator. Eventually, *his* excesses ushered him into a South Atlantic exile, and the French settled on a compromise role for their leader. The modern French king was himself ruled by a constitution. Rather than dress in leotards and powdered wigs, he went to work in a suit with a briefcase.

The 20th century spelled the end of France's reign as a military and political superpower. Devastating wars with Germany in 1870, 1914, and 1940—and the loss of her colonial holdings—left France with not quite enough land, people, or production to be a top player on a global scale. But the 21st century may see France rise again: Paris is once more the cultural capital of Europe, and France—under the EU banner—is a key player in integrating Europe as one unified economic power. And when Europe is a superpower, Paris may yet be its capital.

## Contemporary Politics in France

The five key political issues in France today are high unemployment (about 8 percent), high taxes (about 44 percent of the gross domestic product), a steadily increasing percentage of ethnic minorities (almost 10 percent of France's population is Muslim), what to do about the European Union, and the balancing act between maintaining cushy workers' benefits with the need to compete in a global marketplace. The challenge is to address these issues while maintaining the social benefits that the French expect from their government.

Today, France is part of the 27-member European Union (a kind of "United States of Europe") that has successfully dissolved borders and implemented a single currency, the euro. However, while France's governments have been decidedly pro-EU, its people are somewhat skeptical. In 2005, the French voted against ratifying an EU constitution that would have increased the EU's political powers. Many French fear that a more powerful EU would ultimately result in a loss of job security and social benefits (a huge issue in France).

# Top French Notables in History

**Madame and Monsieur Cro-Magnon:** Prehistoric hunter-gatherers who moved to France (c. 30,000 B.C.), painted cave walls at Lascaux and Font-de-Gaume, and eventually settled down as farmers (c. 10,000 B.C.).

**Vercingétorix (72–46 B.C.):** This long-haired warrior rallied the Gauls against Julius Caesar's invading Roman legions (52 B.C.). Defeated by Caesar, France fell under Roman domination, enduring 500 years of peace, prosperity, the establishment of cities, building of roads, education in Latin, and conversion to Christianity.

**Charlemagne (A.D. 742–814):** For Christmas in A.D. 800, the pope gave King Charlemagne the title of Emperor, thus uniting much of Europe under the leadership of the Franks ("France"). Charlemagne stabilized France amid centuries of barbarian invasions. After his death, the empire was split, carving the outlines of modern France and Germany.

**Eleanor of Aquitaine (c. 1122–1204):** The beautiful, sophisticated ex-wife of the King of France married the King of England, creating an uneasy union between the two countries. During her lifetime, French culture was spread across Europe by roving troubadours, theological scholars, and skilled architects pioneering "the French style"—Gothic.

**Joan of Arc (1412–1431):** When France and England fought the Hundred Years' War to settle who would rule (1337–1453), teenage Joan of Arc—guided by voices in her head—rallied the French troops. Though Joan was captured and burned as a heretic, the French eventually drove England out of France for good, establishing the current borders. Over the centuries, the church upgraded Joan's status from heretic to saint (canonized 1920).

**François I (1494–1547):** This Renaissance king ruled a united, modern nation, making it a cultural center that hosted the Italian Leonardo da Vinci. François set the tone for future absolute monarchs, punctuating his commands with the phrase, "for such is our pleasure."

**Louis XIV (1638–1715):** Charismatic and cunning, the "Sun King" ruled Europe's richest, most populous, most powerful nation-state. Educated Europeans spoke French, dressed in Louis-style leotards and powdered wigs, and built Versailles-like palaces. Though Louis ruled as an absolute monarch (distracting the nobility with courtly games), his reign also fostered the arts and philosophy, sowing the seeds of democracy and revolution.

**Marie-Antoinette (1755–1793):** As the wife of Louis XVI, she came to symbolize (probably unfairly) the decadence of France's ruling class. When Revolution broke out (1789), she was arrested, imprisoned, and executed—one of thousands who were guillotined on Paris' place de la Concorde as an enemy of the people.

**Napoleon Bonaparte (1769–1821):** This daring young military man became a hero during the Revolution fighting Europe's royalty. He went on to conquer much of Europe, became leader of France, and eventually ruled as a dictator with the title of Emperor. In 1815, an allied Europe defeated and exiled Napoleon, reinstating the French monarchy—though future kings (including Napoleon's nephew, who ruled as Napoleon III) were subject to democratic constraints.

**Claude Monet (1840–1926):** Monet's Impressionist paintings capture the soft-focus beauty of the belle époque—middle-class men and women enjoying drinks in cafés, walks in gardens, and picnics along the Seine. At the turn of the 20th century, French culture reigned supreme while its economic and political clout was fading, soon to be shattered by the violence of World War I.

**Charles de Gaulle (1890–1970):** A career military man, de Gaulle helped France survive occupation by Nazi Germany during World War II with his rousing radio broadcasts and unbending faith in France. As president, he led the country through its postwar rebuilding, through divisive wars in Vietnam and Algeria (trying to preserve France's colonial empire), and through turbulent student riots in the 1960s.

**Contemporary French:** Which recent French people will history remember? President François Mitterand (1916–1996), the driving force behind La Grande Arche and Opéra Bastille? Marcel Marceau (1923–2007), white-faced mime? Chef Paul Bocuse (b. 1926), inventor of nouvelle cuisine? Brigitte Bardot (b. 1934), film actress, crusader for animal rights, and popularizer of the bikini? Yves Saint Laurent (1936–2008), one of the world's greatest fashion designers? Jean-Marie Le Pen (b. 1928), founder of the far-right National Front party, with staunch anti-immigration policies? Bernard Kouchner (b. 1939), co-founder of Doctors without Borders and minister of foreign affairs under President Sarkozy? Or Zinédine Zidane (b. 1972), France's greatest soccer player ever, whose Algerian roots helped raise the status of Arabs in France?

French national politics are complex but fascinating. While only two parties dominate American politics, France has seven major parties and several smaller ones. From left to right, the major parties include: the Ligue Communiste Révolutionnaire (LCR), which is as far left as you get in France; the more moderate reformed Communists (PCF, or Parti Communiste Français); the environmental party (Les Verts, a.k.a. "The Greens"); the middle-of-the-road Socialists (PS, or Parti Socialiste); the aristocratically conservative MoDem (Mouvement Démocrate, formerly the Union pour la Démocratie Française); the center right UMP (Union pour la Majorité Présidentielle); and the racist, isolationist Front National party. In general, the MoDem and UMP split the conservative middle ground, and the Socialists dominate the liberal middle ground. But in France, unlike in the US, informal coalitions are generally necessary for any party to "rule."

You've likely read about the Front National party, led by Jean-Marie Le Pen. His infamous "France for the French" platform calls for the expulsion of ethnic minorities and broader police powers. The situation was especially tense in fall 2005, when Muslim youths rioted in Parisian suburbs, protesting discrimination. Although the Front National has a staunch voter base of about 15 percent, the recent rise in unemployment and globalization worries have increased its following, allowing Le Pen to nudge the political agenda to the right. On the far left, the once powerful Communists (PCF) draw only about 5 percent of the popular vote, forcing them to work more flexibly with the less radical Socialists and the environmental party (Les Verts). The left end of the political spectrum in France has seen its fortunes rise when the economy is strong, and fall when it's weak.

The French president is elected by popular vote every five years, while the more powerful prime minister is chosen by the president, then confirmed by the parliament (Assemblée Nationale). With five major parties, a single majority is rare, so it takes a coalition to elect a prime minister. Over the past 15 years, the right has been more successful in marshaling its supporters than the left. Previous President Jacques Chirac (two terms, 1995–2007) and current President Nicolas Sarkozy (elected in 2007) are both conservatives.

Sarkozy is pro-US (though he doesn't speak English) and pro-EU. He is tough on crime and on unchecked immigration. To address a sluggish economy, he proposes a tough-love, carrot-and-stick approach—limiting the power of unions and cutting workers' benefits, while offering tax incentives to workers who put in overtime (above the current 35–39-hour work week). His policies are generating predictable resistance from unions—expect at least one major strike somewhere in France during your trip.

It's his personal life, however, that has raised more French eyebrows. Sarkozy likes to jog, and wears sweats when relaxing *(quelle horreur!)*. Moreover, within a year of becoming president, he divorced his wife of 11 years and married sexy Italian model-turned-singer Carla Bruni (who has been linked romantically with Mick Jagger and Eric Clapton, and one of your co-authors). The press has nicknamed Sarkozy "Bling Bling" for his love of celebrities and celebrity status.

# APPENDIX

## CONTENTS

Resources . . . . . . . . . . . . . . . . . . . . 831
Telephones, Email, and Mail . . . . 838
Transportation . . . . . . . . . . . . . . . . . 848
Recommended Itinerary
   by Train/Bus . . . . . . . . . . . . . . . 850
Recommended
   Itinerary by Car . . . . . . . . . . . . . 858
Holidays and Festivals . . . . . . . . . 867
Conversions and Climate . . . . . . 869
Essential Packing Checklist . . . . . 872
Hotel Reservation Form . . . . . . . . 873
Pronunciation Guide for
   Place Names . . . . . . . . . . . . . . . 874
French Survival Phrases . . . . . . . . 879

## RESOURCES

### Tourist Offices

#### In the US

France has a national tourist information office (abbreviated **TI** in this book) that is a wealth of information. Before you go, you can contact the TI to briefly describe your trip and request any information (such as city maps and schedules of upcoming festivals). If you want tourist materials sent to you, there's a small fee.

**Contact:** Tel. 514/288-1904, info.us@franceguide.com. To download brochures free of charge, see www.franceguide.com (read the options carefully to avoid signing up for promotional emails).

APPENDIX

## Tourist Offices in France

Except in Paris, where they aren't very necessary, your best first stop in any new city is the local TI. Throughout France, you'll find TIs are usually well-organized and have English-speaking staff, offering useful maps, special events information, English-language tour information, lists of inexpensive bed-and-breakfasts, and more. If you're arriving in town after the office closes, call ahead or pickup a map in a neighboring town. To call any TI in France, dial 3265 and say the city with your best French accent. Theoretically, you'll be connected (€0.34/min).

Most TIs will help you find a room by calling hotels (for free or a small fee) or by giving you a complete listing of available bed-and-breakfasts. Towns with a lot of tourism generally have English-speaking guides available for private hire (about $140 for a 2-hour guided town walk).

The French call TIs by different names. *Office de Tourisme* and *Bureau de Tourisme* are used in cities, while *Syndicat d'Initiative* or *Information Touristique* are used in small towns. Also look for *Accueil* signs in airports and at popular sights. These are information booths staffed with seasonal helpers who provide tourists with limited, though generally sufficient, information. Smaller TIs are often closed from 12:00 to 14:00.

## Resources from Rick Steves
### Guidebooks and Online Updates

This book is updated every year in person. The telephone numbers and hours of sights listed in this book are accurate as of mid-2008—but even with annual updates, things change. For the very latest, visit www.ricksteves.com/update. Also at my website, you'll find a valuable list of reports and experiences—good and bad—from fellow travelers (www.ricksteves.com/feedback).

This book is one of more than 30 titles in my series on European travel, which includes country guidebooks, city and

regional guidebooks (including Paris, and Provence & the French Riviera), and my budget-travel skills handbook, *Rick Steves' Europe Through the Back Door*. My phrase books—for French, Italian, German, Spanish, and Portuguese—are practical and budget-oriented. My other books are *Europe 101* (a crash course on art and history, newly expanded and in full color), *European Christmas* (on traditional and modern-day celebrations), and *Postcards from Europe* (a

# Begin Your Trip at www.ricksteves.com

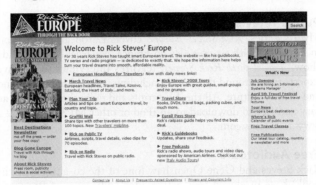

At our travel website, you'll find a wealth of free information on European destinations, including fresh monthly news and helpful tips from thousands of fellow travelers.

Our **online Travel Store** offers travel bags and accessories specially designed by Rick Steves to help you travel smarter and lighter. These include Rick's popular carry-on bags (wheeled and rucksack versions), money belts, totes, toiletries kits, adapters, other accessories, and a wide selection of guidebooks, planning maps, and DVDs.

Choosing the right **railpass** for your trip—amidst hundreds of options—can drive you nutty. We'll help you choose the best pass for your needs, plus give you a bunch of free extras.

Rick Steves' Europe Through the Back Door travel company offers **tours** with more than two dozen itineraries and about 450 departures reaching the best destinations in this book...and beyond. Our France tours include Paris and the South of France in 15 days, Paris and the Heart of France in 11 days (focusing on the best of the north; a kid-friendly version of this tour is also available), the Best of Paris and London in eight days, and the one-week Paris city tour. You'll enjoy great guides, a fun bunch of travel partners (with small groups of generally around 26), and plenty of room to spread out in a big, comfy bus. You'll find European adventures to fit every vacation length. For all the details, and to get our Tour Catalog and a free Rick Steves Tour Experience DVD (filmed on location during an actual tour), visit www.ricksteves.com or call the Tour Department at 425/608-4217.

fun memoir of my travels). For a complete list of my books, see the inside of the last page of this book.

## Public Television and Radio Shows

My TV series, *Rick Steves' Europe,* covers European destinations in 70 shows, with six episodes on France. My weekly public radio show, *Travel with Rick Steves,* features interviews with travel experts from around the world, including several hours on France and French culture. All the TV scripts and radio shows (which are easy and free to download to an iPod or other MP3 player) are at www.ricksteves.com.

## Free Audiotours

Rick Steves and Gene Openshaw (one of the co-authors of this book) have produced free, self-guided audiotours of Paris—for the Louvre, Musée d'Orsay, Versailles, and Historic Paris—as well as for major sights in Florence, Rome, and Venice. Created for users of iPods and other MP3 players, the tours allow you to focus on what you're seeing rather than what you're reading.

RICK STEVES
EUROPE
PODCAST

The tours are available through iTunes and at www.ricksteves.com. Simply download them onto your computer and transfer them to your MP3 player. (Remember to bring a Y-jack and extra set of ear buds for your travel partner.)

## Maps

The black-and-white maps in this book, drawn by Dave Hoerlein, are concise and simple. Dave, who is well-traveled in France, designed the maps to help you locate recommended places and reach TIs, where you'll find more in-depth (and often free) maps of cities or regions. Better maps are sold at newsstands—take a look before you buy to be sure the map has the level of detail you want.

Michelin maps are available throughout France at bookstores, newsstands, and gas stations (about €5 each, cheaper than in the US). The Michelin #528 map (1:1,000,000 scale) covers this book's destinations with good detail for drivers. Drivers should consider the soft-cover Michelin France atlas (the entire country at 1:200,000, well-organized in a €20 book with an index and maps of major cities). Spend a few minutes learning the Michelin key to get the most sightseeing value out of these maps.

Train travelers do fine with a simple rail map (such as the one that comes with a railpass) and city maps from the TI offices.

## Other Guidebooks

For most travelers, this book is all you need. But if you're heading beyond my recommended destinations, you might want some supplemental information. Considering the improvements they'll make in your $4,000 vacation, $40 for extra maps and books is money well spent. Note that none of the following guidebooks are updated annually; check the publication date before you buy.

I like Cadogan guides for their well-presented background information and coverage of cultural issues. Their recommendations suit upscale travelers. Lonely Planet's *France* is well-researched, with good maps and hotel recommendations for low- to moderate-budget travelers. But because it tries to cover every city in France, you'll likely find too little information on the most important places and too much information on the minor places you don't care about. The highly opinionated *Let's Go: France* (St. Martin's Press) is ideal for students and vagabonds traveling by train and staying in hostels. The popular, skinny, green Michelin guides are dry but informative, especially for drivers. They're known for their city and sightseeing maps, and for their succinct, helpful information on all major sights. English editions, covering most of the regions you'll want to visit, are sold in France for about €14 (or $20 in the US).

## Recommended Books and Movies

To get a feel for France past and present, consider reading some of these books or seeing these films:

### Non-Fiction

For a good introduction to the French culture and people, read *Sixty Million Frenchmen Can't Be Wrong* (Jean-Benoit Nadeau and Julie Barlow), *Culture Shock: France* (Sally Adamson Taylor) and/or *French or Foe* (Polly Platt).

For a readable history of the country, try *The Course of French History* (Pierre Goubert). *Portraits of France* (Robert Daley) is an interesting travelogue that roams from Paris to the Pyrénées. A mix of writers explore French culture in *Travelers Tales: France* (edited by James O'Reilly, Larry Habegger, and Sean O'Reilly).

Many great memoirs take place in Paris. Consider reading Ernest Hemingway's *A Moveable Feast*, Art Buchwald's *I'll Always Have Paris*, and/or *Paris to the Moon*, by *New Yorker* writer Adam Gopnik, who takes his young son for a carousel ride in the Luxembourg Garden.

If you'll be visiting Provence, pick up Peter Mayle's memoirs, *A Year in Provence* and *Toujours Provence*. Ina Caro's *The Road from the Past* is filled with enjoyable essays on her travels through France, with an accent on history. *The Da Vinci Code* fans will enjoy reading the book that inspired that book—*Holy Blood, Holy Grail* (Michael Baigent, Richard Leigh, and Henry Lincoln)—which takes place mostly in southern France. *Labyrinth* (Kate Mosse) is an intriguing tale, much of which takes place in medieval southern France during the Cathar crusade.

War buffs may want to read these classics before visiting the D-Day Beaches: *The Longest Day* (Cornelius Ryan) and *Wine & War: The French, the Nazis, and the Battle for France's Greatest Treasure* (Donald and Petie Kladstrup). *Is Paris Burning?*, set in the post-WWII years, tells the story of Paris during its recovery from the Occupation (Larry Collins).

If you'll be enjoying an extended stay in France, consider reading *Living Abroad in France* (Terry Link). Gourmands appreciate the *Marling Menu-Master for France* (William E. Marling).

## Fiction

"It was the best of times, it was the worst of times," begins Charles Dickens' gripping tale of the French Revolution, *A Tale of Two Cities*. In *Les Misérables* (Victor Hugo), a Frenchman tries to escape his criminal past, fleeing from a determined police captain and becoming wrapped up in the Revolutionary battles between the rich and the starving. Another recommended book set during this time is *City of Darkness, City of Light*, by Marge Piercy.

Ernest Hemingway was a fan of Georges Simenon, a Belgian who wrote mysteries based in Paris, including *The Hotel Majestic*. Other mysteries using Paris as the backdrop are *Murder in Montparnasse* (Howard Engel), *Murder in the Marais* (Cara Black), and *Sandman* (J. Robert Janes).

*A Very Long Engagement* (Sebastien Japrisot) is a love story set during the bleak years when World War I raged. Using a similar timeframe, *Birdsong* (Sebastian Faulks) follows a 20-year-old Englishman into France, and into the romance that follows.

*Chocolat* (Joanne Harris)—a book and a 2000 movie with Johnny Depp and Juliette Binoche—charms readers with its story of magic and romance.

*Suite Française* (Irène Némirovsky) plunges readers into the chaos of the evacuation of Paris during World War II, as well as daily life in a small rural town during the ensuing German occupation. The author, a Russian Jew living in France, wrote her account within weeks of the actual events, and died at Auschwitz in 1942.

## Films

In *The Grand Illusion* (1937, directed by Jean Renoir), WWI prisoners of war hatch an escape plan. Considered a masterpiece of French film, the movie was later banned by the Nazis for its anti-fascism message.

## The Rules of *Boules*

Throughout France, you'll see citizens playing *boules* (also known as *pétanque*). Each player starts with three iron balls, with the object of getting them close to the target, a small wooden ball called a *cochonnet*. The first player tosses the *cochonnet* about 30 feet, then throws the first of his iron balls near the target. The next player takes a turn. As soon as a player's ball is closest, it's the other guy's turn. Once all balls have been thrown, the score is tallied—the player with the closest ball gets one point for each ball closer to the target than his opponent's. The loser gets zero. Games are generally to 15 points.

A regulation *boules* field is 10 feet by 43 feet, but the game is played everywhere—just scratch a throwing circle in the sand, toss the *cochonnet,* and you're off. Strategists can try to knock the opponent's balls out of position, knock the *cochonnet* itself out of position, or guard their best ball with the other two.

Stanley Kubrick's *Paths of Glory* (1957) is a WWI story about the futility and irony of war. François Truffaut, a filmmaker of the French New Wave school, shows the Parisian streets in *Jules and Jim* (1962). Wander the streets of Paris with a small boy as he chases *The Red Balloon* (1956).

*Jean de Florette* (1986), a marvelous tale of greed and intolerance, follows a hunchback as he fights for the property he inherited. Its sequel, *Manon of the Spring* (1986), continues with his daughter's story. *Blue/White/Red* (1990s) is a stylish trilogy of films by Krzystof Kieslowski, based on France's national motto—"Liberty, Equality, and Fraternity."

*Cyrano de Bergerac* (1990) is about a homely, romantic poet who woos his love with the help of another, better-looking man. Fans of crime films—and Robert De Niro—will like *Ronin* (1998), with multiple scenes shot in France. *Saving Private Ryan* (1998) is Steven Spielberg's intense and brilliant story of the D-Day landings.

*The Gleaners & I* (2000)—a quiet, meditative film by Agnès Varda—follows a few working-class men and women as they gather sustenance from what's been thrown away. In *Amélie* (2001), a charming young waitress in Paris searches for love. If you'll be heading to Versailles, consider seeing *Marie Antoinette* (2006), which stars Kirsten Dunst as the infamous French queen (with a California accent).

# TELEPHONES, EMAIL, AND MAIL

## Telephones

Smart travelers learn the phone system and use it daily to reserve or reconfirm rooms, get tourist information, reserve restaurants, confirm tour times, or phone home. When spelling out your name on the phone, it's essential to use French letter pronunciation: *a* is pronounced "ah," *e* is pronounced "ewh," and *i* is pronounced "ee." To avoid confusion, say "*a*, Anne," "*e*, euro," and "*i*, Isabelle."

## Types of Phones

You'll encounter various kinds of phones in France:

**Card-operated phones**—in which you insert a locally bought phone card into a public pay phone—are common in Europe.

**Coin-operated phones** are becoming increasing rare in France. You might see them at gas stations and in big hotel lobbies.

**Hotel room phones** are sometimes cheap for local calls (confirm at the front desk first), but can be a rip-off for long-distance calls ($1–2/minute unless you use an international phone card—described below). But incoming calls are free, making this a cheap way for friends and family to stay in touch, provided they have a good long-distance plan for calls to Europe.

**American mobile phones** work in Europe if they're GSM-enabled, tri-band or quad-band, and on a calling plan that includes international calls. They're convenient, but pricey. For example, with a T-Mobile phone, you'll pay $1 per minute for calls and about $0.35 for text messages.

**European mobile phones** are affordable to buy and come without contracts. These phones are loaded with prepaid calling time that you can recharge as you use up the minutes. As long as you're not "roaming" outside the phone's home country, incoming calls are free. On my last trip, I bought a good phone for €40 (which included five minutes of time) and added 30 minutes for €25. For €65 (about $100), I had more than enough time for making and receiving calls from home during my three weeks in France. If you're traveling to multiple countries within Europe, make sure the phone is electronically "unlocked," so that you can swap out its SIM card (a fingernail-size chip that holds the phone's information) for a new one in other countries. For more information on mobile phones, see www.ricksteves.com/phones.

## Using Phone Cards

Get a phone card for your calls. Prepaid phone cards come in two types: international and insertable (both described below). Look for these cards at any post office and most newsstands and tobacco shops *(tabacs)*, which you'll find everywhere, including at train stations and airports.

Both types of phone cards work only in France. While traveling in France, you can share either type of card with your companions (and, in the case of an international phone card, your buddy doesn't even need the actual card—just the numbers on it). If you have time left on a card when you leave the country (as you likely will), simply give it to another traveler—anyone can use it.

**International phone cards,** called *cartes à code international* (cart ah code an-tehr-nah-see-oh-nahl), enable you to make calls to the US for as little as three cents per minute. They come with a dial-up code that can be used from nearly any phone, including the one in your hotel room (if it's set on "pulse," switch it to "tone"; remember to ask at the desk about hidden fees on toll-free calls). Cards are marked as national (for France) or international. All cards work for local or international calls, but you get far better rates if you use the card for the purpose it was intended—so if you plan to use your card mostly for calls home, ask for an international card (denominations in €7 and €15 amounts). They're all good values—on one trip, my €15 international card lasted for four weeks of regular calls home.

These *cartes à code international* are simple to use, generally all work the same way, and come with English instructions. You usually need to scratch the card to reveal your code, although some shops also sell cardless codes, printed right on your receipt. Dial the free number; if the four-digit access code on the card doesn't work from your hotel-room phone, try the card's 10-digit, toll-free code that starts with 08. A voice in French (but sometimes followed by English) tells you to enter your code. Before or after entering your code, you may need to press (or *"touche,"* pronounced "toosh") either the pound key (#, *dièse,* dee-ehz) or the star key (*, *étoile,* eh-twahl)—this varies per card. At the next message, dial the number you're calling (possibly followed by the pound or star key; you don't have to listen through the entire sales pitch).

**Insertable phone cards,** called *télécartes* (tay-lay-kart), can only be used at pay phones. While international per-minute rates are much cheaper with an international phone card than with an insertable phone card, the international cards are slower to use (more numbers to dial). Use a *télécarte* for quick local calls from a phone booth. There are two denominations: *une petite* costs about €7.50; *une grande* about €15. While you can use a *télécarte* to call anywhere in the world, it's only a good deal for making local calls.

## Using Hotel-Room Phones, VoIP, or US Calling Cards

The best way to call home is using an international phone card, but here are some other alternatives.

The phone in your **hotel room** is convenient...but expensive. While incoming calls (made by folks back home) can be an affordable way to keep in touch, charges for *outgoing* calls can be a very unpleasant surprise. Dialing direct from your hotel room—without using an international phone card (described above)—is usually quite pricey for international calls. Before you dial, get a clear explanation from the hotel staff of the charges, even for local and (supposedly) toll-free calls.

If your family has an inexpensive way to call Europe, either through a long-distance plan or prepaid calling card, have them call you in your hotel room. Give them a list of your hotels' phone numbers before you go. Then, as you travel, send them an email or cell-phone text message, or make a quick pay-phone call to set up a time for them to give you a ring.

If you're traveling with a laptop, consider trying **VoIP (Voice over Internet Protocol)**. With VoIP, two computers act as the phones, allowing for a free Internet-based call. The major providers are Skype (www.skype.com) and Google Talk (www.google.com/talk).

**US Calling Cards** (such as the ones offered by AT&T, MCI, or Sprint) are the worst option. You'll nearly always save a lot of money by paying with a phone card (see above).

## How to Dial

Calling from the US to Europe, or vice versa, is simple—once you break the code. The European calling chart on page 842 will walk you through it.

### Dialing Within France

France has a direct-dial 10-digit phone system (no area codes). To call anywhere within France, just dial the number. For example, the number of one of my recommended hotels in Arles is 04 90 96 11 89. That's the number you dial whether you're calling it from the Arles train station or from Paris.

France's toll-free numbers start with 0800 (like US 800 numbers, though in France you don't dial a 1 first). In France, these 0800 numbers—called *numéro vert* (green number)—can be dialed free from any phone without using a phone card. But you can't call France's toll-free numbers from America, nor can you count on reaching America's toll-free numbers from France.

Note that any 08 number that does not have a 00 directly following is a toll call, generally costing €0.10–€0.50 per minute.

### Dialing Internationally

If you want to make an international call, follow these steps:

Dial the international access code (00 if you're calling from Europe, 011 from the US or Canada). Europeans often write their phone numbers with + at the front—if you see a phone number that begins with +, replace it with the country's international access code.

Dial the country code of the country you're calling (see European calling chart on next page).

Dial the local number, keeping in mind that calling many countries requires dropping the initial zero of the phone number (see chart on next page for specifics per country).

So, to call the recommended Arles hotel from the US, dial 011 (the US international access code), 33 (France's country code), then 4 90 96 11 89.

To call my office in Edmonds, Washington, from France, I dial 00 (Europe's international access code), 1 (the US country code), 425 (Edmonds' area code), and 771-8303.

## Useful Phone Numbers

### Consulates and Embassies

**US Consulate and Embassy in Paris:** tel. 01 43 12 22 22, passport services open Mon–Fri 9:00–12:00, closed Sat–Sun (4 avenue Gabriel, to the left as you face Hôtel Crillon, Mo: Concorde, http://france.usembassy.gov)

**Canadian Consulate and Embassy in Paris:** tel. 01 44 43 29 02, open Mon–Fri 14:30–16:30, closed Sat–Sun (35 avenue Montaigne, Mo: Franklin D. Roosevelt, www.amb-canada.fr)

**Australian Consulate in Paris:** tel. 01 40 59 33 00, open Mon–Fri 9:00–12:00 & 14:00–16:00, closed Sat–Sun (4 rue Jean Ray, Mo: Bir-Hakeim, www.france.embassy.gov.au)

**US Consulate in Lyon:** tel. 04 78 38 36 88 (1 quai Jules Courmant)

**Canadian Consulate in Lyon:** tel. 04 72 77 64 07 (21 rue Bourgelat)

**US Consulate in Marseille:** tel. 04 91 54 92 00, fax 04 91 55 09 47 (place Varian Fry)

**US Consulate in Nice:** tel. 04 93 88 89 55, fax 04 93 87 07 38 (7 avenue Gustave V, does *not* provide visa services—Paris is the nearest office for these services)

**Canadian Consulate in Nice:** tel. 04 93 92 93 22, fax 04 93 92 55 51 (10 rue Lamartine)

**US Consulate in Strasbourg:** tel. 03 88 35 31 04, fax 03 88 24 06 95 (15 rue d'Alsace)

# European Calling Chart

Just smile and dial, using this key:
AC = Area Code, LN = Local Number.

| European Country | Calling long distance within... | Calling from the US or Canada to... | Calling from a European country to... |
|---|---|---|---|
| Austria | AC + LN | 011 + 43 + AC (without the initial zero) + LN | 00 + 43 + AC (without the initial zero) + LN |
| Belgium | LN | 011 + 32 + LN (without initial zero) | 00 + 32 + LN (without initial zero) |
| Bosnia-Herzegovina | AC + LN | 011 + 387 + AC (without initial zero) + LN | 00 + 387 + AC (without initial zero) + LN |
| Britain | AC + LN | 011 + 44 + AC (without initial zero) + LN | 00 + 44 + AC (without initial zero) + LN |
| Croatia | AC + LN | 011 + 385 + AC (without initial zero) + LN | 00 + 385 + AC (without initial zero) + LN |
| Czech Republic | LN | 011 + 420 + LN | 00 + 420 + LN |
| Denmark | LN | 011 + 45 + LN | 00 + 45 + LN |
| Estonia | LN | 011 + 372 + LN | 00 + 372 + LN |
| Finland | AC + LN | 011 + 358 + AC (without initial zero) + LN | 999 + 358 + AC (without initial zero) + LN |
| France | LN | 011 + 33 + LN (without initial zero) | 00 + 33 + LN (without initial zero) |
| Germany | AC + LN | 011 + 49 + AC (without initial zero) + LN | 00 + 49 + AC (without initial zero) + LN |
| Greece | LN | 011 + 30 + LN | 00 + 30 + LN |
| Hungary | 06 + AC + LN | 011 + 36 + AC + LN | 00 + 36 + AC + LN |
| Ireland | AC + LN | 011 + 353 + AC (without initial zero) + LN | 00 + 353 + AC (without initial zero) + LN |

| European Country | Calling long distance within ... | Calling from the US or Canada to ... | Calling from a European country to ... |
|---|---|---|---|
| Italy | LN | 011 + 39 + LN | 00 + 39 + LN |
| Montenegro | AC + LN | 011 + 382 + AC (without initial zero) + LN | 00 + 382 + AC (without initial zero) + LN |
| Netherlands | AC + LN | 011 + 31 + AC (without initial zero) + LN | 00 + 31 + AC (without initial zero) + LN |
| Norway | LN | 011 + 47 + LN | 00 + 47 + LN |
| Poland | LN | 011 + 48 + LN (without initial zero) | 00 + 48 + LN (without initial zero) |
| Portugal | LN | 011 + 351 + LN | 00 + 351 + LN |
| Slovakia | AC + LN | 011 + 421 + AC (without initial zero) + LN | 00 + 421 + AC (without initial zero) + LN |
| Slovenia | AC + LN | 011 + 386 + AC (without initial zero) + LN | 00 + 386 + AC (without initial zero) + LN |
| Spain | LN | 011 + 34 + LN | 00 + 34 + LN |
| Sweden | AC + LN | 011 + 46 + AC (without initial zero) + LN | 00 + 46 + AC (without initial zero) + LN |
| Switzerland | LN | 011 + 41 + LN (without initial zero) | 00 + 41 + LN (without initial zero) |
| Turkey | AC (if no initial zero is included, add one) + LN | 011 + 90 + AC (without initial zero) + LN | 00 + 90 + AC (without initial zero) + LN |

The instructions above apply whether you're calling a land line or mobile phone.

The international access codes (the first numbers you dial when making an international call) are 011 if you're calling from the US or Canada, or 00 if you're calling from virtually anywhere in Europe (except Finland, where it's 999).

To call the US or Canada from Europe, dial 00, then 1 (the country code for the US and Canada), then the area code and number. In short, 00 + 1 + AC + LN = Hi, Mom!

## Emergency/Medical Needs

**Police:** tel. 17
**Emergency Medical Assistance:** tel. 15
**Ambulance in Paris:** tel. 01 45 67 50 50, message asks for your address and name

## Travel Advisories

**US Department of State:** tel. 202/647-5225, www.travel.state.gov
**Canadian Department of Foreign Affairs:** Canadian tel. 800-267-6788, www.dfait-maeci.gc.ca
**US Centers for Disease Control and Prevention:** tel. 877-FYI-TRIP, www.cdc.gov/travel

## Trip Planning Assistance

**Detours in France:** tel. 03 80 22 06 03 (can assist with planning and rooms anywhere in France, www.detours-in-france.com)

## Directory Assistance

**Directory Assistance for Paris and France** (some English spoken): tel. 12
**Tourist Information Offices:** To call any TI in France, dial 3265 and say the name of the city in your best French accent (€0.34/min)
**Collect Calls to the US:** tel. 00 00 11

## Paris Information

**Tourist Information:** tel. 08 92 68 30 00 (recorded info with long menu, €0.34/min), www.parisinfo.com
**American Church:** tel. 01 40 62 05 00 (65 quai d'Orsay, Mo: Invalides), www.acparis.org
**American Hospital:** tel. 01 46 41 25 25 (63 boulevard Victor Hugo, in Neuilly suburb, Mo: Porte Maillot, then bus #82), www.american-hospital.org

## Trains

**Train (SNCF) Reservations and Information:** tel. 3635 (in French only)

## Airports

**Paris:** Charles de Gaulle and Orly Airports share the same numbers—tel. 3950 (€.34/min), www.adp.fr. For Beauvais Airport, call 08 92 68 20 66, www.aeroportbeauvais.com.
**Lyon:** Saint-Exupéry Airport—tel. 08 26 80 08 26 (€0.15/min), www.lyon.aeroport.fr
**Marseille:** Aéroport Marseille–Provence—tel. 04 42 14 14 14, www.marseille.aeroport.fr

**Nice:** Aéroport de Nice—tel. 08 20 42 33 33 (€0.12/min), www
.nice.aeroport.fr

### Airlines

The following 08 numbers are toll calls; the per-minute fee generally ranges from €0.10 to €0.50.

**Aer Lingus:** tel. 08 21 23 02 67
**Air Canada:** tel. 08 25 88 29 00
**Air France:** tel. 08 20 82 08 20 or 08 20 82 36 54
**Alitalia:** tel. 08 20 31 53 15
**American Airlines:** tel. 01 55 17 43 41
**Austrian Airlines:** tel. 08 02 81 68 16
**bmi British Midland Airways:** tel. 08 90 71 00 81
**British Airways:** tel. 08 25 82 54 00
**Continental:** tel. 01 71 23 03 35
**Delta:** tel. 08 11 64 00 05
**easyJet:** tel. 08 26 10 33 20
**Iberia:** tel. 08 25 80 09 65
**Icelandair:** tel. 01 44 51 60 51
**KLM:** tel. 08 90 71 07 10
**Lufthansa:** tel. 08 26 10 33 34
**Northwest:** tel. 08 90 71 07 10
**Olympic:** tel. 01 44 94 58 58
**Royal Air Maroc:** tel. 08 20 82 18 21
**SAS:** tel. 08 25 32 53 35
**Swiss:** tel. 08 20 04 05 06
**United:** tel. 08 10 72 72 72
**US Airways:** tel. 08 10 63 22 22

### Car Leasing in France

**Europe by Car:** US tel. 800-223-1516, US fax 212/246 1458, www
.europebycar.com
**Auto France:** US tel. 800-572-9655, US fax 201/393-7800, www
.autofrance.net

### Hotel Chains

**Huge Chain of Hotels:** www.accorhotels.com (handles Ibis,
Mercure, and Novotel hotels); US tel. 800-515-5679
**Ibis Hotels:** www.ibishotel.com, tel. 08 92 68 66 86; from US dial
011 33 8 92 68 66 86 (message tells you to push the * button)
**Formule 1 Hotels:** www.hotelformule1.com, tel. 08 92 68 56 85
(€0.34/min)
**Mercure Hotels:** www.mercure.com, tel. 08 25 88 33 33, US tel.
800-221-4542
**Kyriad Hotels:** www.kyriad.com, tel. 08 25 02 80 38; from US dial
011 33 1 64 62 59 70

## The Language Barrier and That French Attitude

You've no doubt heard that the French are "mean and cold and refuse to speak English." This is an out-of-date preconception left over from the days of Charles de Gaulle. Be reasonable in your expectations: Waiters are paid to be efficient, not chatty. And postal clerks are every bit as speedy, cheery, and multilingual as ours are back home.

The biggest mistake most Americans make when traveling to France is trying to do too much with limited time. This approach is a mistake in the bustling north, and a virtual sin in the relaxed south. Hurried, impatient travelers who miss the subtle pleasures of people-watching from a sun-dappled café often misinterpret French attitudes. By slowing your pace and making an effort to understand French culture by living it, you're much more likely to have a richer experience. With the five weeks of paid vacation and 35-hour work week that many French workers consider as non-negotiable rights, your hosts can't comprehend why anyone would rush through their vacation.

The French take great pride in their customs, clinging to their belief in cultural superiority despite the fact that they're no longer a world superpower. Let's face it: It's tough to keep on smiling when you've been crushed by a Big Mac, Mickey Moused by Disney, and drowned in instant coffee. Your hosts are cold only if you decide to see them that way. Polite and formal, the French respect the fine points of culture and tradition. Here,

**Best Western Hotels:** www.bestwestern.com, tel. 08 00 90 44 90, US tel. 800-780-7324

**Château Hotels:** www.chateaucountry.com

**Country Home Rental:** www.gites-de-france.fr/eng or www.gite.com

### Youth Hostels
**Hostelling International, US Office:** www.hiayh.org
**Hostelling International, Canada Office:** www.hostellingintl.ca

### Hotel Barges
**Papillon Barge:** www.hotelbarge.com, US tel. 781/631-5414, tel. 06 86 28 11 55
**Barge Nilaya:** www.bargenilaya.com, tel. 06 70 82 47 60

## Email and Mail
**Email:** Many travelers set up a free email account with Yahoo, Microsoft (Hotmail), or Google (Gmail). Email use among European hoteliers is quite common.

strolling down the street with a big grin on your face and saying hello to strangers is a sign of senility, not friendliness (seriously). They think that Americans, while friendly, are hesitant to pursue more serious friendships. Recognize sincerity and look for kindness. Give them the benefit of the doubt.

French communication difficulties are exaggerated. To hurdle the language barrier, bring a small English/French dictionary, a phrase book (look for mine, which contains a dictionary and menu decoder), a menu reader (if you're a gourmet eater), and a good supply of patience. In transactions, a small notepad and pen minimize misunderstandings about prices; have vendors write the price down. If you learn only five phrases, learn and use these: *bonjour* (good day), *pardon* (pardon me), *s'il vous plaît* (please), *merci* (thank you), and *au revoir* (goodbye). The French place great importance on politeness. Begin every encounter with *"Bonjour (or S'il vous plaît), madame/monsieur"* and end every encounter with *"Au revoir, madame/monsieur."*

When you do make an effort to speak French, expect to be politely corrected—*c'est normal*. The French are language perfectionists—they take their language (and other languages) seriously. Often they speak more English than they let on. This isn't a tourist-baiting tactic, but timidity on their part about speaking another language less than fluently. Start any conversation with, *"Bonjour, madame/monsieur. Parlez-vous anglais?"* and hope they speak more English than you speak French.

In France's key cities—such as Paris, Nice, Lyon, and Avignon—you'll find plenty of coffee shops offering wireless connections (Wi-Fi, pronounced "wee-fee" by the French) to travelers with laptop computers. You'll find little hole-in-the-wall Internet-access shops throughout France, though fewer in small towns. If you can't find an Internet café, post offices that offer Internet access *(cyberposte)* can be a good solution; buy a chip-card (about same prices as phone cards, rechargeable for €4 per hour) and you're in business.

Many hotels now offer their guests Internet access in their lobbies from a terminal (which may be free or operated with coins or a telephone card); the access is usually slow, though you'll probably be slow, too, getting used to a French keyboard. Every year, more hotels offer Wi-Fi (sometimes free, sometimes for a charge). And some even have laptop loaners. Ask if your hotel has access. If it doesn't, your hotelier will direct you to the nearest place to get online.

**Mail:** French post offices are sometimes called PTT, for "Post, Telegraph, and Telephone"—look for *La Poste* signs. Hours vary, though most are open weekdays 8:00–19:00 and Saturday morning 8:00–12:00. Stamps and phone cards are also sold at *tabac* (tobacco) shops. It costs about €1 to mail a postcard to the US. While you can arrange for mail delivery to your hotel (allow 10 days for a letter to arrive), phoning and emailing are so easy that I've dispensed with mail stops altogether. Federal Express makes pricey two-day deliveries.

A convenient, if pricey, way to send packages home is by using the PTT's Colissimo XL postage-paid mailing box. It costs about €33 for the International version, which allows you to send home all the goodies you can stuff into an 18" × 12" × 8" box (no weight limit).

# TRANSPORTATION

## By Car or Train?

Cars are best for three or more traveling together (especially families with small kids), those packing heavy, and those scouring the countryside. Trains and buses are best for solo travelers, blitz tourists, and city-to-city travelers. Train stations are usually centrally located in cities, which makes hotel-hunting and sightseeing easy. But in France, many of your destinations are likely to be small, remote places, such as Honfleur, Mont St. Michel, D-Day beaches, Loire châteaux, Dordogne caves, and villages in Provence and Burgundy. In such places, trains and buses can require great patience, planning, and time. If relying on public transportation, seriously consider the value of the minivan excursion tours listed throughout this book and focus more time on fewer key destinations. You won't regret it.

## Trains

France's rail system (SNCF) sets the pace in Europe. Its super TGV (tay zhay vay; *train à grande vitesse*) system has inspired bullet trains throughout the world. The TGV runs at 170–220 mph. Its rails are fused into one long, continuous track for a faster and smoother ride. The TGV has changed commuting patterns in much of France by putting most of the country within day-trip distance of Paris.

## Schedules

Schedules change by season, weekday, and weekend. Verify train times shown in this book—on the Web, check http://bahn.hafas .de/bin/query.exe/en. Bigger stations have helpful information agents roaming the station and at *Accueil* offices or booths. They can answer rail questions more quickly than the information or ticket windows. Make use of these people; don't stand in a ticket line if all you need is a train schedule.

# France Train Terms and Abbreviations

**SNCF** *(Société Nationale Chemins de Fer):* This is France's national railway system, operating all national train lines that link cities and towns.

**TGV** *(Train à Grande Vitesse):* SNCF's network of high-speed trains (twice as fast as regular trains) that connect major cities in France. These trains always require a reservation.

**CORAIL:** These trains are next best compared to the TGV in terms of speed and comfort.

**TER** *(Trains Express Régionale):* These trains serve smaller stops within a region. For example, you'll find trains called TER de Bourgogne (trains operating only in Burgundy) and TER Provence (Provence-only trains).

## Paris Region Only

For more on Paris transit, see "Getting Around Paris," page 44.

**RATP** *(Réseau Autonome de Transport Parisienne):* This organization operates subways and buses within Paris.

**Le Métro:** This network of subway lines serves central Paris.

**RER** *(Réseau Express Régional):* This commuter rail and subway system links central Paris with suburban destinations.

**Transilien:** It's similar to the RER system, but travels farther afield, serving the Ile de France region around Paris. Railpasses cover these lines.

## Coping with Strikes

Going on strike *(en grève)* is a popular pastime in this revolution-happy country. President Sarkozy is pushing unions to their limits, and since bargaining between management and employees is not standard procedure, workers strike to get attention. Truckers and tractors block main roads and autoroutes (they call it Opération Escargot: "Operation Snail's Pace"), baggage handlers bring airports to their knees, and museum workers make Mona Lisa off-limits to tourists. Métro and train personnel seem to strike every year—perhaps during your trip. What does the traveler do? You could *jetter l'éponge* (literally, throw in the sponge) and go somewhere less strike-prone (Switzerland's nice), or learn to accept certain events as out of your control. Strikes in France generally last no longer than a day or two, and if you're aware of them, you can usually plan around them. Your hotelier will know the latest (or can find out). Make a habit of asking your hotel receptionist about strikes, and check online for English-language updates at www.americansinfrance.net /DailyLife/Strike.cfm.

# Whirlwind Three-Week Tour of France by Train and Bus

This itinerary is designed for train travelers. To do this trip by train and bus, make liberal use of minivan tours and taxis. A France Flexipass with nine train days—buying tickets in France for days 5, 7, and 14 (short and cheap trips)—works fine. A France Rail and Drive Pass is another good option. A car is especially handy for exploring Normandy, the Dordogne, and Provence. If you only have two weeks, end your tour in Nice and skip Honfleur. *Bonne route* and *bon courage!*

| Day | Plan |
|---|---|
| 1 | Fly into Paris. |
| 2 | Sightsee Paris. |
| 3 | More time in Paris. |
| 4 | Train and bus to Mont St. Michel via Rennes (4 hrs, arrive on Mont St. Michel about 13:00). Afternoon and night on Mont St Michel. |
| 5 | Train to Bayeux (2 hrs, arrive about 11:45). Afternoon for visiting Bayeux. Sleep in Bayeux. |
| 6 | All day for D-Day beaches by minivan, taxi, bike, bus, or a combination of these. Sleep in Bayeux. |
| 7 | Train to Caen, then bus to Honfleur (2 hrs). Sleep in Honfleur. |
| 8 | Bus to Lisieux or Deauville then train to Paris. Transfer to Gare d'Austerlitz and take the train to Amboise (7 hrs total). Sleep in Amboise. |
| 9 | All day for touring Loire châteaux (good options by bus, bike or minivan tour). Sleep in Amboise. |

## Railpasses

Long-distance travelers can save money with a France Railpass, sold only outside Europe (through travel agents or Europe Through the Back Door; see "Cost of Railpasses" on page 852). For less than the cost of a Paris–Avignon–Paris ticket, the France Railpass offers three days of travel (within a month) anywhere in France. You can add up to six additional days for the cost of a two-hour ride each. Save money by getting the second-class instead of the first-class version and/or travel with a companion (the Flexi Saverpass gives 2 people traveling together a 20 percent discount). Each day of use allows you to take as many trips as you want on one calendar day (you could go from Paris to Beaune in Burgundy, enjoy wine-tasting, then continue to Avignon, stay a few hours, and end in Nice—though I wouldn't recommend it). Buy second-class tickets in France for shorter trips, and save your valuable pass days for longer trips. Note that if you're connecting the French Alps with

| 10 | Train to Sarlat (5 hrs, arrive about 15:00). Afternoon and evening in Sarlat. Sleep in Sarlat. |
|----|----|
| 11 | All day for caves and canoes by train and bike or minivan/taxi tour. Sleep in Sarlat. |
| 12 | Train to Carcassonne (5.5 hrs, leaving about noon is best, though earlier trips are possible). Dinner and evening wall walk. Sleep in Carcassonne. |
| 13 | Morning wall walk, then train to Arles (2.5 hrs). Afternoon in Arles. |
| 14 | Train to Nîmes, then bus to Pont du Gard. Tour the Pont du Gard, then bus to Avignon and spend your afternoon/evening there (consider dinner). Train back to Arles. Sleep in Arles. |
| 15 | Morning in Arles or Les Baux (by taxi or tour), afternoon train to Nice (4 hrs), set up in Nice. Sleep in Nice. |
| 16 | All day for Nice and Monaco. Sleep in Nice. |
| 17 | Morning train to Lyon (4 hrs). Afternoon and night in Lyon. |
| 18 | Train to Chamonix (4 hrs, consider a halfway stopover in Annecy—easy bag check). Sleep in Chamonix. |
| 19 | With clear weather, take the mountain lifts up to Aiguille du Midi and beyond. Sleep in Chamonix. |
| 20 | Early train to Paris (arrive about 13:30). Last afternoon and night in Paris. (Or make it a 23-day tour with a scenic, 6.5-hr train through Switzerland to Colmar, spend two nights there, then take the TGV back to Paris.) |
| 21 | Fly home. |

Alsace, you might travel through Switzerland, requiring France railpass holders to buy a ticket for that segment (about €50).

## Buying Tickets

If traveling *sans* railpass, inquire about the many point-to-point discount fares possible (for advance purchase, for youths, those over 60, married couples, families/Discovery fares, travel during off-peak hours, and more). Remember that second-class tickets provide the same transportation for up to 33 percent less (and many regional trains to less-trafficked places often have only second-class cars).

**TGV:** While there's no deadline to buy any train ticket, the fast, reserved TGV trains can fill up. It's wise to book ahead for any TGV you cannot afford to miss, especially on the busy Paris–Avignon–Nice line. Tickets go on sale 90 days in advance, and the cheapest tickets sell out early. To buy tickets online, visit www.tgv.com; if you select English as your language and choose any country

# Cost of Railpasses

Prices listed are for 2009 and are subject to change. For the latest prices, details, and train schedules (and easy online ordering), see my comprehensive *Guide to Eurail Passes* at www.ricksteves.com/rail.

"Saver" prices are per person for two or more people traveling together. "Youth" means under age 26. The fare for children 4–11 is half the adult individual fare or Saver fare. Kids under age 4 travel free.

## FRANCE PASS

|  | Adult 1st Class | Adult 2nd Class | Senior 1st Class | Youth 1st Class | Youth 2nd Class |
|---|---|---|---|---|---|
| 3 days in 1 month | $293 | $250 | $268 | $217 | $186 |
| Extra rail days (max 6) | 45 | 37 | 40 | 33 | 28 |

Senior = 60 and up.

## FRANCE SAVERPASS

|  | 1st Class | 2nd Class |
|---|---|---|
| 3 days in 1 month | $249 | $215 |
| Extra rail days (max 6) | 39 | 31 |

## FRANCE RAIL & DRIVE PASS

Any 2 rail days and 2 car days in 1 month.

| Car Category | 1st Class | Extra Car Day |
|---|---|---|
| Economy | $264 | $47 |
| Compact | 267 | 50 |
| Intermediate | 277 | 60 |
| Full Size | 306 | 89 |
| Premium Automatic | 322 | 105 |
| Minivan | 335 | 118 |

Prices are per person, two traveling together. Solo travelers pay about $100 extra; third and fourth adults pay $207 per person. Extra rail days (3 max) cost $36 per day. To order a Rail & Drive pass, call your travel agent or Rail Europe at 800-438-7245. *This pass is not sold by Europe Through the Back Door.*

**Map key:**
Approximate point-to-point one-way second-class rail fares in US dollars. First class costs 50 percent more. Add up fares for your itinerary to see if a railpass will save you money.

APPENDIX

# SELECTPASS

This pass covers travel in three adjacent countries. For four- and five-country options, please visit **www.ricksteves.com/rail**.

| | Individual 1st Class | Saver 1st Class | Youth 2nd Class |
|---|---|---|---|
| 5 days in 2 months | $435 | $370 | $284 |
| 6 days in 2 months | 481 | 410 | 315 |
| 8 days in 2 months | 570 | 487 | 370 |
| 10 days in 2 months | 660 | 559 | 427 |

# FRANCE–SWITZERLAND PASS

| | Individual 1st Class | Saver 1st Class | Youth 2nd Class |
|---|---|---|---|
| 4 days in 2 months | $376 | $320 | $265 |
| Extra rail days (max 6) | 43 | 37 | 30 |

# FRANCE–ITALY PASS

| | Individual 1st Class | Individual 2nd Class | Saver 1st Class | Saver 2nd Class | Youth 2nd Class |
|---|---|---|---|---|---|
| 4 days in 2 months | $351 | $307 | $307 | $271 | $232 |
| Extra rail days (max 6) | 42 | 35 | 35 | 30 | 27 |

**Be aware of your route.** Many daytime connections from Paris to Italy pass through Switzerland (e.g., connecting in Basel, Geneve, or Lausanne) which costs an additional $60 or more in second class if Switzerland is not covered by your pass. Direct Paris-Italy day or night trains are covered by the pass, regardless of their route. Routes via Nice, Torino, or Modane will bypass Switzerland (consult a good timetable for details).

# FRANCE–SPAIN PASS

| | Individual 1st Class | Individual 2nd Class | Saver 1st Class | Saver 2nd Class | Youth 2nd Class |
|---|---|---|---|---|---|
| 4 days in 2 months | $351 | $307 | $307 | $271 | $232 |
| Extra rail days (max 6) | 42 | 35 | 35 | 30 | 27 |

If you're only dipping into a bit of Spain, you may not need the France-Spain pass. For instance, a ticket from the French border at Cerbere to Barcelona costs only $30. From the border at Hendaye to Madrid costs $75, but if you cover this ground via the fancy Paris–Madrid "Elipsos" night train, the same passholder fares ($70 and up) apply whether your pass covers one or both countries.

# FRANCE–GERMANY PASS

| | Individual 1st Class | Individual 2nd Class | Saver 1st Class | Saver 2nd Class | Youth 2nd Class |
|---|---|---|---|---|---|
| 4 days in 2 months | $387 | $349 | $349 | $315 | $271 |
| 5 days in 2 months | 427 | 385 | 385 | 348 | 299 |
| 6 days in 2 months | 468 | 421 | 421 | 376 | 329 |
| 8 days in 2 months | 549 | 495 | 495 | 431 | 385 |
| 10 days in 2 months | 631 | 568 | 568 | 495 | 446 |

# FRANCE–BENELUX PASS

| | Individual 1st Class | Individual 2nd Class | Saver 1st Class | Saver 2nd Class | Youth 2nd Class |
|---|---|---|---|---|---|
| 4 days in 2 months | $346 | $301 | $295 | $255 | $224 |
| 5 days in 2 months | 377 | 334 | 321 | 284 | 252 |
| 6 days in 2 months | 413 | 366 | 352 | 312 | 280 |
| 8 days in 2 months | 482 | 437 | 410 | 371 | 335 |
| 10 days in 2 months | 549 | 507 | 549 | 432 | 390 |

other than the US or France, you'll be able to print tickets at home or pick up in the station (if instead you choose "France," the site will be in French, and if you choose "US," you'll be redirected to www.raileurope.com). The US company, RailEurope, delivers tickets to your home but doesn't always have the lowest rates.

**On the Train:** You can buy tickets on the train for a €4 surcharge, but you must find the conductor immediately on boarding; otherwise it's a €35 minimum charge.

**Automatic Train Ticket Machines:** Available at most stations, these are great time-savers for short trips when ticket window lines are long (but your American credit card won't work so you'll need euro coins or bills). Some have English instructions, but for those that don't, here is what you are prompted to do. (The default is usually what you want; turn the dial or move the cursor to your choice, and press *"Validez"* to agree to each step.)

1. *Quelle est votre destination?* (What's your destination?)
2. *Billet Plein Tarif* (Full-fare ticket—yes for most.)
3. *1ère ou 2ème* (First or second class; normally second is fine.)
4. *Aller simple ou aller-retour?* (One-way or round-trip?)
5. *Prix en Euro* (The price should be shown if you get this far.)

## Reservations

Reservations, while generally unnecessary for non-TGV trains, are advisable during busy times (e.g., Fri and Sun afternoons, Sat mornings, weekday rush hours, and particularly holiday weekends; see "Major Holidays and Weekends," page 5). Reservations are required for any TGV train (usually €3, more during peak periods), for selected other routes, and for *couchettes* (berths, €15) on night trains. Railpass-holders need reservations for the TGV trains and should book ahead because a limited number of seats are set aside for railpass users. To avoid the more expensive fares, avoid traveling at peak times; ask at the station. You are required to validate (*composter*, kohm-poh-stay) all train tickets and reservations. Before boarding any SNCF train, look for a yellow machine nearby to stamp your ticket or reservation. (Do not *composte* your railpass, but do validate it at a ticket window before the first time you use it.) Watch others and imitate.

## Baggage Check

*Consigne* or *Espaces Bagages* is available only at the biggest train stations (about €4–10 per bag depending on size), and is noted where available in this book (depends on security concerns, so be prepared to keep your bag). For security reasons, all luggage must carry a tag with the traveler's first and last name and current address. This applies to hand luggage as well as bigger bags that are stowed. Free tags are available at all trains stations in France.

## The French Rail System

### Train Tips

• Arrive at the station with plenty of time before your departure to find the right platform, confirm connections, and so on. In small towns, your train may depart before the station opens; if so, go directly to the tracks and find the overhead sign that confirms your train stops at that track.

• Larger stations have platforms with monitors showing each car's layout (numbered forward or backward) so you can figure out where your *voiture* will stop on the long platform and where to board each car. Notice the low baggage area placed every two cars—people use it to avoid hoisting their suitcases to the high overhead rack.

• Check schedules in advance. Upon arrival at a station, learn your departure possibilities. Large stations have a separate information window or office; at small stations, the ticket office gives information.

• If you have a rail flexipass, write the date on your pass each day you travel (before you board your first train).

• Validate tickets (not passes) and reservations in yellow machines before boarding. If you're traveling with a pass and have a reservation for a certain trip, you must validate the reservation.

• Reservations for all TGV trains are required and often sell out. You can reserve any train at any station or through SNCF Boutiques (small offices in city centers). A limited number of reservations are allocated for railpass users during peak times—reserve as far ahead as you can, especially for Friday and Sunday afternoons and Saturday mornings.

• Before getting on a train, confirm that it's going where you think it is. For example, if you want to go to Bayeux, ask the conductor or any local passenger, *"A Bayeux?"* (ah bah-yuh; meaning, "To Bayeux?").

• Some trains split cars en route. Make sure your train car is continuing to your destination by asking, for example, *"Cette voiture va à Bayeux?"* (set vwah-toor vah ah bah-yuh; meaning, "This car goes to Bayeux?").

• If a non-TGV train seat is reserved, it will usually be labeled *réservé,* with the cities to and from which it is reserved.

• Verify with the conductor all of the transfers you must make: *"Correspondance à?",* meaning, "Transfer to where?"

• To guard against theft, it's best to keep your bags right overhead. If you store them at the end of the car, make sure you can see them from your seat (they're most vulnerable to theft when the train stops).

• Note your arrival time, so you'll be ready to get off.

• Use the trains' free WCs before you get off (but not while the train is stopped).

• If you want to mix train and bike travel, ask at stations for information booklets *(Train + Vélo).*

## Buses

Regional bus service takes over where the trains stop. You can get nearly anywhere in France by rail and bus...if you're well-organized, patient, and not in a hurry. Review my bus schedule information and always verify times at the local tourist office or bus station; call ahead when possible. A handful of bus lines are run by SNCF (France's rail system) and are included with your railpass (show railpass at station to get free bus ticket), but most bus lines are independent of the rail system and are not covered by railpasses. Train stations often have bus information where train-to-bus connections are important—and vice versa for bus companies. On Sunday, regional bus service virtually disappears.

## Key Travel Phrases

*Bonjour, monsieur/madame, parlez-vous anglais?*
**Pron:** bohn-zhoor, muhs-yur/mah-dahm, par-lay-voo
ahn-glay?
**Meaning:** Hello, sir/madam, do you speak English?

*Je voudrais un départ pour* (destination), *pour le* (date), *vers*
(general time of day), *la plus direct possible.*
**Pron:** zhuh voo-dray uhn day-par poor (destination), poor luh
(date), vehr (time), lah ploo dee-rehk poh-see-bluh.
**Meaning/Example:** I would like a departure for Avignon, on
23 May, about 9:00, the most direct way possible.

## Bus Tips

- Read the train tips above, and use those that apply.
- TIs often have regional bus schedules and can help plan your
trip.
- Remember that service is sparse or even nonexistent on
Sunday. Wednesday bus schedules are often different during
the school year, since school is out this day.
- Be at stops at least five minutes early.
- On schedules, *en semaine* means Monday through Saturday,
*dimanche* is Sunday, and *jours fériés* are holidays.

## Regional Minivan Excursions

Worthwhile day tours are generally available in regions where bus
and train service is sparse. For the D-Day beaches, châteaux of the
Loire Valley, Dordogne Valley villages and caves, Provence's villages and vineyards, the Route du Vin (Wine Road) in Alsace, and
wine-tasting in Burgundy, I list reliable companies that provide
this helpful service at fair rates. Some of these minivan excursions
offer just transportation between the sights; others add a running
commentary and information on regional history.

## Renting a Car

To rent a car in France, you must be at least 18 years old and have
held your license for one year. Although an International Driving
Permit (IDP) is not required if your driver's license has been
renewed within the last year, play it safe and get one anyway ($15
through AAA, plus the cost of two passport-type photos, www
.aaa.com).

Drivers under the age of 25 may incur a young-driver surcharge, and some rental companies do not rent to anyone 75 and
over. If you're considered too young or old, look into leasing, which

# Whirlwind (Kamikaze) Three-Week Trip Through France for Drivers

| Day | Plan |
|---|---|
| 1 | Fly into Paris, pick up your car, visit Giverny and overnight in Honfleur (1 night). Save Paris sightseeing for the end of your trip. |
| 2 | Spend today at D-Day sights: Arromanches, American Cemetery, and Pointe du Hoc (and Caen Memorial Museum, if time allows). Dinner and overnight in Bayeux (1 night). |
| 3 | Bayeux Tapestry and church, Mont St. Michel, sleep on Mont St. Michel (1 night). |
| 4 | Spend your morning on Mont St. Michel, then head for châteaux country in the Loire Valley. Tour Chambord, then stay in Amboise (2 nights). |
| 5 | Do a day trip, touring Chenonceaux and Cheverny or Chaumont. Save time at the end of the day for Amboise and its sights. |
| 6 | Head south to the Dordogne region, stopping at Oradour-sur-Glane en route. End in a Dordogne village—your choice of the handful I recommend (2 nights). |
| 7 | Browse the town and market of Sarlat, take a canoe trip, and tour Font-de-Gaume cave. |
| 8 | Head to the Languedoc region, lunch in Puycelci or Albi, and spend the evening in Carcassonne (1 night). |
| 9 | Morning in Carcassonne, then on to Provence with a stop at the Pont du Gard aqueduct. Stay in or near Arles (2 nights). |
| 10 | All day for Arles and Les Baux. |
| 11 | Visit Avignon or a Provençal hilltown such as Roussillon, then depart for the Riviera, staying in Nice or Villefranche-sur-Mer (2 nights). |
| 12 | Sightsee in Nice and Monaco. |
| 13 | Make the long drive north to the Alps, and sleep in Chamonix (2 nights). |
| 14 | With clear weather, take the mountain lifts up to Aiguille du Midi and beyond. |
| 15 | A half-day for the Alps (in Chamonix or Annecy). Then head for Burgundy, ending in Beaune for a wine-tasting. Sleep in Beaune (1 night). |

**16** Spend the morning in Beaune, then move on to Colmar (2 nights).

**17** Enjoy Colmar and the Route du Vin villages.

**18** Return to Paris, visiting Verdun or Reims en route. Collapse in Paris hotel (4 nights).

**19** Sightsee Paris.

**20** More time in Paris.

**21** Finish up your sightseeing in Paris, and consider side-tripping to Versailles.

has less-stringent age restrictions (see "Leasing," page 861).

Research car rentals before you go. It's cheaper to arrange most car rentals from the US. Call several companies and look online to compare rates, or arrange a rental through your hometown travel agent. Two reputable companies among many are Auto Europe (www.autoeurope.com) and Europe by Car (www.europebycar.com). For the best rental deal, rent by the week with unlimited mileage. I normally rent the smallest, least-expensive model with a stick-shift (cheaper than an automatic). Almost all rentals are manual by default, so if you need an automatic, you must request one in advance. If you want to save money on gas, ask for a diesel car.

For a three-week rental, allow $900 per person (based on two people sharing a car), including insurance, tolls, gas, and parking. For long trips, consider leasing (see next page); you'll save money on insurance and taxes. Compare pick-up costs (downtown can be cheaper than the airport) and explore drop-off options. Returning a car at a big-city train station can be tricky; get precise details on the car drop-off location and hours. Except in major cities, rental offices are usually closed during lunch and on Sundays.

When picking up the car, check it thoroughly and make sure any damage is noted on your rental agreement. Find out how your car's lights, turn signals, wipers, and gas cap function. When you return the car, make sure the agent verifies its condition with you.

If you want a car for only a day or two (e.g., for the D-Day beaches or Loire châteaux), you'll likely find it cheaper to rent it in France—most US-arranged rentals make financial sense only for three days or more. You can rent a car on the spot just about anywhere in France. In many cases, this is a worthwhile splurge. All you need is your American driver's license and a major credit card (figure €55–80/day, including 100 kilometers, or 60 miles, per day).

A **rail-and-drive pass** (such as a EurailDrive, Selectpass Drive, or France Rail and Drive) allows you to mix car and train travel economically (sold only outside France, from your travel agent). Generally big-city connections are best done by train, and rural regions are best done by car. With a rail-and-drive pass, you can take advantage of the speed and comfort of the TGV trains for longer trips, and rent a car for as little as one day at a time for day trips that can't be done without one (such as the Loire, the Dordogne, and Provence).

The basic France Rail and Drive Pass comes with two days of car rental and two days of rail in one month. You can pick up a car in one city and drop it off in another. Though you're only required to reserve the first car day, it's safer to reserve all days, as cars are not always available on short notice.

## Car Insurance Options

When you rent a car, you are liable for a very high deductible, some-times equal to the entire value of the car. There are various ways you can limit your financial risk in case of an accident. For France, you have three options: buy Collision Damage Waiver (CDW) cover-age from the car-rental company (figure roughly 25 percent extra), a travel insurance company, or get coverage through your credit card (free, if your card automatically includes zero-deductible coverage).

**CDW** includes a very high deductible (typically $1,000–1,500). When you pick up the car, you'll be offered the chance to "buy down" the deductible to zero (for $10–30/day; this is often called "super CDW").

If you opt for credit-card coverage, there's a catch. You'll tech-nically have to decline all coverage offered by the car-rental com-pany, which means they can place a hold on your card for the full deductible amount. In case of damage, it can be time-consuming to resolve the charges with your credit-card company. Before you decide on this option, quiz your credit-card company about how it works and ask them to explain the worst-case scenario.

Buying CDW insurance (plus "super CDW") is the easier but pricier option. Using the coverage that comes with your credit card saves money, but can involve more hassle. For longer trips, leasing—which includes taxes and insurance—is worthwhile.

Finally, you can buy CDW insurance from Travel Guard ($9/day plus a one-time $3 service fee covers you up to $35,000, $250 deductible, tel. 800-826-4919, www.travelguard.com). It's valid throughout Europe, but some car-rental companies refuse to honor it (especially in Italy and the Republic of Ireland). Oddly, residents of Washington state aren't allowed to buy this coverage.

For more fine print about car-rental insurance, see www.rick steves.com/cdw.

## Leasing

For trips of two and a half weeks or more, leasing (which auto-matically includes zero-deductible collision and theft insurance) is the best way to go (and your only option if your age excludes you from standard car rental). By technically buying and then selling back the car, you save lots of money on tax and insurance. Leasing provides you a brand-new car with unlimited mileage and a 24-hour emergency assistance program. You can lease for little as 17 days to as long as six months. Car leases must be arranged from the US. Two reliable companies offering 17-day lease packages from about $1,100 for a small car ($1,400 for a midsize) are Auto France (US tel. 800-572-9655, fax 201/393-7800, www.autofrance .net) and Europe by Car (US tel. 800-223-1516, www.europeby car.com). Anyone age 18 or over with a driver's license is eligible, and you can pick up and/or drop off at several cities in France and throughout Europe.

## Driving in France

Get an International Driving Permit (see "Renting a Car," page 857) and bring your driver's license. Seat belts are mandatory for all, and children under age 10 must be in the back seat.

Gas *(essence)* is expensive, costing about $9 per gallon. Diesel *(gazole)* is less (about $8 per gallon), and since diesel cars get better mileage, rent one if you can. Gas is most expensive on autoroutes and cheapest at big supermarkets (closed at night and on Sun). Many gas stations close on Sunday. US credit and debit cards won't work at self-service gas pumps and automated stations, but are accepted at staffed stations.

Four hours on the autoroute costs about €25 in tolls (for which you'll need to pay cash, since US credit and debit cards won't work), but the alternative to these super "feeways" usually means being marooned behind sluggish tractors in countryside traffic. Autoroutes save enough time, gas, and nausea to justify the splurge. Mix high-speed "autorouting" with scenic country-road rambling. You'll usually take a ticket when entering an autoroute and pay when you leave. Shorter autoroute sections have periodic unstaffed toll booths, where you can pay by dropping coins into a basket (change given, but keep a good supply of coins handy to avoid waiting). Autoroute gas stations usually come with well-stocked mini-marts, clean restrooms, sandwiches, maps, local products, and cheap vending-machine coffee (€1.20, I dig the *cappuccino sucré*). Many have small cafés or more elaborate cafeterias with reasonable prices.

Roads are classified into departmental (D), national (N), and autoroutes (A). D routes (usually yellow lines on maps) are usually slower, but often the most scenic. N routes (usually red lines) are the fastest after autoroutes (orange lines). Green road signs are for national routes; blue are for autoroutes. There are plenty of good facilities, gas stations (many closed Sun), and rest stops along most French roads.

Because speed limits are by road type, they typically aren't posted, so it's best to memorize them:
- Two-lane D and N routes outside cities and towns: 90 km/hour
- Divided highways outside cities and towns: 110 km/hour
- Autoroutes: 130 km/hour

If it's raining, subtract 10 km/hour on D and N routes and 20 km/hour on divided highways and autoroutes. Speed limit signs are a red circle around a number; when you see that same number

**AND LEARN THESE ROAD SIGNS**

STOP

50 — Speed Limit (km/hr)

50 — Speed Limit No Longer Applies

No Passing

End of No Passing Zone

SENS UNIQUE — One Way

Intersection

Main Road

Freeway

Danger

No Entry

No Entry for Cars

All Vehicles Prohibited

P — Parking

No Parking

DOUANE — Customs

Yield

again in gray with a broken line diagonally across it, this means that limit no longer applies. Speed limits drop to 30–50 km/hour in villages (always posted) and must be respected. France loves photo ticketing and carefully places moveable cameras to trap unsuspecting drivers, particularly in 30–50 km/hour zones. You can get busted for going even a few kilometers over the limit (believe me).

Parking is a headache in larger cities, and theft is a problem. Ask your hotelier for ideas, and pay to park at well-patrolled lots (blue *P* signs direct you to parking lots in French cities). Parking garages usually require that you take a ticket with you and prepay at a machine (called a *caisse*) on your way back to the car. Overnight parking (usually 19:00–8:00) is generally reasonable (except in Paris and Nice). Curbside metered parking also works (usually free 12:00–14:00 & 19:00–9:00, and all day and night in Aug). Look for a small machine selling time (called *horadateur,* usually one per block), plug in a few coins (€1.50 buys about an hour, though this varies by city), push the green button, get a receipt showing the amount of time you have, and display it inside your windshield.

## Driving Tips

- Be aware that in city and town centers, traffic merging from the right normally has the right-of-way *(priorité à droite),* even when merging on to a major road. In contrast, cars entering the many suburban roundabouts must yield *(cédez le passage).*
- Be ready for many roundabouts—navigating them is an art. The key is to know your direction and be ready for your turn-off. If you miss it, take another lap.
- When navigating through cities, approach intersections cautiously, stow the map, and follow the signs to *Centre-Ville* (city center). From there, head to the TI *(Office de Tourisme).*
- When leaving or just passing through cities, follow the signs for *Toutes Directions* or *Autres Directions* (meaning "anywhere else") until you see a sign for your specific destination.

# Road Signs and Driving Tips

## Instructional Signs That You Must Obey

| | |
|---|---|
| *Cédez le Passage* | Yield |
| *Priorité à Droite* | Right-of-way is for cars coming from the right |
| *Vous n'avez pas la priorité* | You don't have the right of way (when merging) |
| *Rappel* | Remember to obey the sign |
| *Déviation* | Detour |
| *Allumez vos feux* | Turn on your lights |
| *Doublage Interdit* | No passing |
| *Parking Interdit/ Stationnement Interdit* | No parking |

## Signs for Your Information

| | |
|---|---|
| *Route Barrée* | Road blocked |
| *Sortie des Camions* | Work truck exit |
| *Centre Commercial* | Grouping of large, suburban stores (not city center) |
| *Centre-Ville* | City center |
| *Feux* | Traffic signal |
| *Horadateur* | Remote parking meter, usually at the end of the block |
| *Parc de Stationnement* | Parking lot |
| *Rue Piétonne* | Pedestrian-only street |
| *Sauf Riverains* | Local access only |

## Signs Unique to Autoroutes

| | |
|---|---|
| *Aire* | Rest stop with WCs, telephones, and sometimes gas stations |
| *Bouchon* | Traffic jam ahead |
| *Fluide* | No slowing ahead (fluid conditions) |
| *Péage* | Toll |
| *Télépéage* | Toll booths—automatic toll payment only |
| *Toutes Directions* | All directions (leaving city) |
| *Autres Directions* | Other directions (leaving city) |
| *Par temps de Pluie* | When raining (modifies speed limit signs) |

**Driving in France: Distance and Time**

*m = miles*
*h = hours*

Note: Your times may vary based on traffic, construction, and road conditions.

- Driving on any roads but autoroutes will take longer than you anticipated, so allow yourself plenty of time for slower traffic (tractors, trucks, traffic, and hard-to-decipher signs require patience). First-timers should estimate how long they think a drive will take...then double it. I pretend that kilometers are miles (for distances) and base my time estimates accordingly.
- While locals are eating lunch (12:00–14:00), many sights (and gas stations) are closed, so you can make great time driving—but keep it slow when passing through villages.
- U-turns are illegal throughout France, and you cannot turn right on red lights.
- Be very careful when driving on smaller roads—many are narrow, flanked by little ditches that are easy to slide into. I've met several readers who "ditched" their cars (and were successfully pulled out by local farmers).

- On autoroutes, keep to the right lanes to let fast drivers by, and be careful when merging into a left lane, as cars can be coming at very high speeds. Cars and trucks commonly keep their left blinker on while in a passing lane, indicating that they plan to get back over to the right.
- Motorcycles will scream between cars in traffic. Be ready—they expect you to keep to the right in your lane to let them pass.
- Gas can be tricky to find in rural areas on Sunday, so fill up on Saturday. Autoroute filling stations are always open and always staffed.
- Keep a stash of coins in your ashtray for parking and small autoroute tolls.

## Biking

Throughout France, you'll find areas where public transportation is limited and bicycle touring might be a good idea. For many, biking is a romantic notion whose novelty wears off after the first hill or headwind—realistically evaluate your physical condition and be clear on the limitations bikes present. Start with an easy pedal to a nearby village or through the vineyards, then decide how ambitious you feel. Most find that two hours on a narrow, hard seat is enough. I've listed bike-rental shops where appropriate and suggested a few of my favorite rides. Local TIs always have addresses for bike-rental places. For a good touring bike, figure about €10 for a half-day and €16 for a full day. You'll pay more for better equipment; generally the best is available through bike shops, not at train stations or other outlets. French bikers often do not wear helmets, though most rental outfits have them (for a small fee). Some shops even rent electric bikes.

## Cheap Flights

If you're visiting one or more French cities on a longer European trip—or linking up far-flung French cities (such as Paris and Nice)—consider intra-European airlines. While trains are still the best way to connect places that are close together, a flight can save both time and money on long journeys. When comparing a flight to a train trip, consider the time it takes to get to the airport and how early you'll need to arrive to check in before the flight. Most flights make sense only as an alternate to a train ride five or more hours in length.

One of the best websites for comparing inexpensive flights is www.skyscanner.net. Other comparison search engines include www.kayak.com, www.mobissimo.com, www.sidestep.com, and www.wegolo.com.

Well-known cheapo airlines include easyJet (www.easyjet .com), Ryanair (www.ryanair.com), and Vueling (www.vueling .com). Be aware of the potential drawbacks of flying on the cheap:

nonrefundable and nonchangeable tickets, rigid baggage restrictions (and fees if you have more than what's officially allowed), use of airports far outside town, tight schedules that can mean more delays, little in the way of customer assistance if problems arise, and, of course, no frills. To avoid unpleasant surprises, read the small print—especially baggage policies—before you book.

# HOLIDAYS AND FESTIVALS

This list includes major festivals, plus national holidays observed throughout France. Many sights close down on national holidays, and weekends around those holidays are often wildly crowded with vacationers (book your hotel room for the entire holiday weekend well in advance). Note that this isn't a complete list; holidays often strike without warning. For more information, contact the France TI (listed at the beginning of the appendix).

| | |
|---|---|
| **Jan 1** | New Year's Day |
| **Jan 6** | Epiphany |
| **Feb 13–March 1** | Nice Carnival (Mardi Gras, parades, fireworks, www.nicecarnaval.com) |
| **March** | Grenoble Jazz Festival, near Lyon (www.jazzgrenoble.com) |
| **April 12** | Easter Sunday |
| **Late April–Mid-Oct** | Festival of Gardens, Chaumont-sur-Loire (www.chaumont-jardin.com) |
| **May** | Versailles Festival (arts), Versailles; Festival Jeanne d'Arc (pageants), Rouen |
| **May 1** | Labor Day |
| **May 8** | VE Day |
| **May 21** | Ascension |
| **May 31** | Pentecost |
| **May 13–24** | Cannes Film Festival, Cannes (www.festival-cannes.fr) |
| **May 21–24** | Monaco Grand Prix (auto race), Monaco |
| **June 6** | 65th Anniversary of the D-Day Landing, Normandy (also expect crowds before and after this date). |
| **June** | Marais Festival (arts), Paris |
| **Mid-June** | Le Mans Auto Race, Le Mans—near Loire Valley (www.lemans.org) |
| **June 21** | Music Festival (Fête de la Musique), concerts and dancing in the streets throughout France (www.fetedelamusique.culture.fr) |

# 2009

### JANUARY

| S | M | T | W | T | F | S |
|---|---|---|---|---|---|---|
|  |  |  |  | 1 | 2 | 3 |
| 4 | 5 | 6 | 7 | 8 | 9 | 10 |
| 11 | 12 | 13 | 14 | 15 | 16 | 17 |
| 18 | 19 | 20 | 21 | 22 | 23 | 24 |
| 25 | 26 | 27 | 28 | 29 | 30 | 31 |

### FEBRUARY

| S | M | T | W | T | F | S |
|---|---|---|---|---|---|---|
| 1 | 2 | 3 | 4 | 5 | 6 | 7 |
| 8 | 9 | 10 | 11 | 12 | 13 | 14 |
| 15 | 16 | 17 | 18 | 19 | 20 | 21 |
| 22 | 23 | 24 | 25 | 26 | 27 | 28 |

### MARCH

| S | M | T | W | T | F | S |
|---|---|---|---|---|---|---|
| 1 | 2 | 3 | 4 | 5 | 6 | 7 |
| 8 | 9 | 10 | 11 | 12 | 13 | 14 |
| 15 | 16 | 17 | 18 | 19 | 20 | 21 |
| 22 | 23 | 24 | 25 | 26 | 27 | 28 |
| 29 | 30 | 31 |  |  |  |  |

### APRIL

| S | M | T | W | T | F | S |
|---|---|---|---|---|---|---|
|  |  |  | 1 | 2 | 3 | 4 |
| 5 | 6 | 7 | 8 | 9 | 10 | 11 |
| 12 | 13 | 14 | 15 | 16 | 17 | 18 |
| 19 | 20 | 21 | 22 | 23 | 24 | 25 |
| 26 | 27 | 28 | 29 | 30 |  |  |

### MAY

| S | M | T | W | T | F | S |
|---|---|---|---|---|---|---|
|  |  |  |  |  | 1 | 2 |
| 3 | 4 | 5 | 6 | 7 | 8 | 9 |
| 10 | 11 | 12 | 13 | 14 | 15 | 16 |
| 17 | 18 | 19 | 20 | 21 | 22 | 23 |
| 24/31 | 25 | 26 | 27 | 28 | 29 | 30 |

### JUNE

| S | M | T | W | T | F | S |
|---|---|---|---|---|---|---|
|  | 1 | 2 | 3 | 4 | 5 | 6 |
| 7 | 8 | 9 | 10 | 11 | 12 | 13 |
| 14 | 15 | 16 | 17 | 18 | 19 | 20 |
| 21 | 22 | 23 | 24 | 25 | 26 | 27 |
| 28 | 29 | 30 |  |  |  |  |

### JULY

| S | M | T | W | T | F | S |
|---|---|---|---|---|---|---|
|  |  |  | 1 | 2 | 3 | 4 |
| 5 | 6 | 7 | 8 | 9 | 10 | 11 |
| 12 | 13 | 14 | 15 | 16 | 17 | 18 |
| 19 | 20 | 21 | 22 | 23 | 24 | 25 |
| 26 | 27 | 28 | 29 | 30 | 31 |  |

### AUGUST

| S | M | T | W | T | F | S |
|---|---|---|---|---|---|---|
|  |  |  |  |  |  | 1 |
| 2 | 3 | 4 | 5 | 6 | 7 | 8 |
| 9 | 10 | 11 | 12 | 13 | 14 | 15 |
| 16 | 17 | 18 | 19 | 20 | 21 | 22 |
| 23/30 | 24/31 | 25 | 26 | 27 | 28 | 29 |

### SEPTEMBER

| S | M | T | W | T | F | S |
|---|---|---|---|---|---|---|
|  |  | 1 | 2 | 3 | 4 | 5 |
| 6 | 7 | 8 | 9 | 10 | 11 | 12 |
| 13 | 14 | 15 | 16 | 17 | 18 | 19 |
| 20 | 21 | 22 | 23 | 24 | 25 | 26 |
| 27 | 28 | 29 | 30 |  |  |  |

### OCTOBER

| S | M | T | W | T | F | S |
|---|---|---|---|---|---|---|
|  |  |  |  | 1 | 2 | 3 |
| 4 | 5 | 6 | 7 | 8 | 9 | 10 |
| 11 | 12 | 13 | 14 | 15 | 16 | 17 |
| 18 | 19 | 20 | 21 | 22 | 23 | 24 |
| 25 | 26 | 27 | 28 | 29 | 30 | 31 |

### NOVEMBER

| S | M | T | W | T | F | S |
|---|---|---|---|---|---|---|
| 1 | 2 | 3 | 4 | 5 | 6 | 7 |
| 8 | 9 | 10 | 11 | 12 | 13 | 14 |
| 15 | 16 | 17 | 18 | 19 | 20 | 21 |
| 22 | 23 | 24 | 25 | 26 | 27 | 28 |
| 29 | 30 |  |  |  |  |  |

### DECEMBER

| S | M | T | W | T | F | S |
|---|---|---|---|---|---|---|
|  |  | 1 | 2 | 3 | 4 | 5 |
| 6 | 7 | 8 | 9 | 10 | 11 | 12 |
| 13 | 14 | 15 | 16 | 17 | 18 | 19 |
| 20 | 21 | 22 | 23 | 24 | 25 | 26 |
| 27 | 28 | 29 | 30 | 31 |  |  |

**July**   Nice Jazz Festival (www.nicejazzfest.com); Avignon Festival (theater, dance, music, www.festival-avignon.com); Beaune International Music Festival; Music and Opera Festival, Orange (performed in Roman theater, www.choregies.asso.fr); "Jazz at Juan" International Jazz Festival, Antibes/Juan-les-Pins; Classical Music Festival, Cannes; Jousting matches and medieval festivities, Carcassonne; Nights of Fourvière, Lyon (theater and music in a Roman theater, www.nuits-de-fourviere .org); Colmar International Music Festival, www.festival-colmar.com); Aix-en-Provence International Music and Opera Festival, (www.festival-aix.com)

| July 4–26 | Tour de France, the national bicycle race culminating on the Champs-Elysées (www.letour.fr) |
| July 14 | Bastille Day (fireworks, dancing, and revelry all over France) |
| Aug | International Fireworks Festival, Cannes |
| Aug 15 | Assumption of Mary |
| Late Aug | Jazz at La Villette Festival, Paris (www .villette.com) |
| Sept | Fall Arts Festival (Fête d'Automne), Paris; Wine harvest festivals in many towns |
| Early Oct | Grape Harvest Festival in Montmartre, Paris (www.commanderiemont.com) |
| Nov 1 | All Saints' Day |
| Early Nov | Dijon International and Gastronomic Fair, Dijon, Burgundy |
| Nov 11 | Armistice Day |
| Nov 19–22 | Wine Auction and Festival (Les Trois Glorieuses), Beaune |
| Late Nov–Dec 24 | Christmas Markets, Strasbourg |
| Dec 8 | Festival of Lights (celebration of Virgin Mary, candlelit windows), Lyon |
| Dec 20–Jan 4 | Winter holidays |
| Dec 25 | Christmas Day |

APPENDIX

# CONVERSIONS AND CLIMATE

## Numbers and Stumblers

- Europeans write a few of their numbers differently than we do. 1 = 1, 4 = 4, 7 = 7.
- In Europe, dates appear as day/month/year, so Christmas is 25/12/09.
- Commas are decimal points and decimals commas. A dollar and a half is 1,50, and there are 5.280 feet in a mile.
- When pointing, use your whole hand, palm down.
- When counting with fingers, start with your thumb. If you hold up your first finger to request one item, you'll probably get two.
- What Americans call the second floor of a building is the first floor in Europe.
- On escalators and moving sidewalks, Europeans keep the left "lane" open for passing. Keep to the right.

## Metric Conversions (approximate)

| | |
|---|---|
| 1 foot = 0.3 meter | 1 square yard = 0.8 square meter |
| 1 yard = 0.9 meter | 1 square mile = 2.6 square kilometers |

1 mile = 1.6 kilometers    1 ounce = 28 grams
1 centimeter = 0,4 inch    1 quart = 0.95 liter
1 meter = 39.4 inches    1 kilogram = 2.2 pounds
1 kilometer = 0.62 mile    32°F = 0°C

## Clothing Sizes

When shopping for clothing, use these US-to-France comparisons as general guidelines (but note that no conversion is perfect).

- Women's dresses and blouses: Add 30 (US women's size 10 = French size 40)
- Men's suits and jackets: Add 10 (US size 40 regular = French size 50)
- Men's shirts: Multiply by 2 and add about 8 (US men's size 15 collar = French size 38)
- Women's shoes: Add about 31 (US size 8 = French size 39)
- Men's shoes: Add 32–34 (US size 9 US = French size 43; US size 11 = French size 45)

## Climate

First line, average daily high temperature; second line, average daily low; third line, days without rain. For more detailed weather statistics for destinations in this book (as well as the rest of the world), check www.worldclimate.com.

| | J | F | M | A | M | J | J | A | S | O | N | D |
|---|---|---|---|---|---|---|---|---|---|---|---|---|
| **Paris** | | | | | | | | | | | | |
| | 43° | 45° | 54° | 60° | 68° | 73° | 76° | 75° | 70° | 60° | 50° | 44° |
| | 34° | 34° | 39° | 43° | 49° | 55° | 58° | 58° | 53° | 46° | 40° | 36° |
| | 14 | 14 | 19 | 17 | 19 | 18 | 19 | 18 | 17 | 18 | 15 | 15 |
| **Nice** | | | | | | | | | | | | |
| | 50° | 53° | 59° | 64° | 71° | 79° | 84° | 83° | 77° | 68° | 58° | 52° |
| | 35° | 36° | 41° | 46° | 52° | 58° | 63° | 63° | 58° | 51° | 43° | 37° |
| | 23 | 22 | 24 | 23 | 23 | 26 | 29 | 26 | 24 | 23 | 21 | 21 |

APPENDIX

## Temperature Conversion:
## Fahrenheit and Celsius

*Europe takes its temperature using the Celsius scale, while we opt for Fahrenheit. For a rough conversion from Celsius to Fahrenheit, double the number and add 30. For weather, remember that 28°C is 82°F—perfect. For health, 37°C is just right.*

# Essential Packing Checklist

Whether you're traveling for five days or five weeks, here's what you'll need to bring. Remember to pack light to enjoy the sweet freedom of true mobility. Happy travels!

- ☑ 5 shirts
- ☑ 1 sweater or lightweight fleece jacket
- ☑ 2 pairs pants
- ❏ 1 pair shorts
- ❏ 1 swimsuit (women only—men can use shorts)
- ☑ 5 pairs underwear and socks
- ☑ 1 pair shoes
- ☑ 1 rain-proof jacket
- ☑ Tie or scarf
- ❏ Money belt
- ❏ Money—your mix of:
    - ❏ Debit card for ATM withdrawals
    - ❏ Credit card
    - ❏ Hard cash in US dollars
- ❏ Documents (and back-up photocopies)
- ❏ Passport
- ❏ Airplane ticket
- ❏ Driver's license
- ❏ Student ID and hostel card
- ❏ Railpass/car rental voucher
- ❏ Insurance details
- ❏ Daypack
- ❏ Sealable plastic baggies
- ❏ Camera and related gear
- ❏ Empty water bottle
- ❏ Wristwatch and alarm clock
- ❏ Earplugs
- ❏ First-aid kit
- ❏ Medicine (labeled)
- ❏ Extra glasses/contacts and prescriptions
- ❏ Sunscreen and sunglasses
- ❏ Toiletries kit
- ❏ Soap
- ❏ Laundry soap (if liquid and carry-on, limit to 3 oz.)
- ❏ Clothesline
- ❏ Small towel
- ❏ Sewing kit
- ❏ Travel information
- ❏ Necessary map(s)
- ❏ Address list (email and mailing addresses)
- ❏ Postcards and photos from home
- ❏ Notepad and pen
- ❏ Journal

# Hotel Reservation

To: _____  _____
         **hotel**                              **email or fax**

From: _____  _____
           **name**                              **email or fax**

Today's date: _____ /_____ /_____
                       **day**    **month**    **year**

Dear Hotel _____ ,
Please make this reservation for me:

Name: _____

Total # of people: _____  # of rooms: _____  # of nights: _____

Arriving: _____ /_____ /_____  My time of arrival (24-hr clock): _____
              **day  month   year**     (I will telephone if I will be late)

Departing: ____ /____ /____
                **day  month  year**

Room(s): Single____  Double ____  Twin ____  Triple ____  Quad____

With: Toilet _____  Shower_____  Bath _____  Sink only_____

Special needs: View____  Quiet____  Cheapest ____  Ground Floor____

Please email or fax confirmation of my reservation, along with the type of
room reserved and the price. Please also inform me of your cancellation
policy. After I hear from you, I will quickly send my credit-card information
as a deposit to hold the room. Thank you.

_____
*Name*

_____
*Address*

_____
*City*                              **State**        **Zip Code**    **Country**

*Before hoteliers can make your reservation, they want to know the informa-
tion listed above. You can use this form as the basis for your email, or you can
photocopy this page, fill in the information, and send it as a fax (also available
online at www.ricksteves.com/reservation).*

# Pronunciation Guide for Place Names

When using the phonetics: Try to nasalize the n sound (let the sound come through your nose). Note that the "ah<u>n</u>" combination uses the "ah" sound in "father," but the "a<u>n</u>" combination uses the "a" sound in "sack." Pronounce the "ī" as the long "i" in "light." If your best attempt at pronunciation meets with a puzzled look, just point to the place name on the list.

## In Paris

**Arc de Triomphe** ark duh tree-oh<u>n</u>f

**arrondissement** ah-roh<u>n</u>-dees-moh<u>n</u>

**Bateaux-Mouches** bah-toh moosh

**Bon Marché** boh<u>n</u> mar-shay

**Carnavalet** kar-nah-vah-lay

**Champ de Mars** shah<u>n</u> duh mar

**Champs-Elysées** shah<u>n</u>-zay-lee-zay

**Conciergerie** kon-see-ehr-zhuh-ree

**Ecole Militaire** eh-kohl mee-lee-tehr

**Egouts** ay-goo

**Fauchon** foh-shoh<u>n</u>

**Galeries Lafayette** gah-luh-ree lah-fay-yet

**gare** gar

**Gare d'Austerlitz** gar doh-stehr-leets

**Gare de l'Est** gar duh less

**Gare de Lyon** gar duh lee-oh<u>n</u>

**Gare du Nord** gar dew nor

**Gare St. Lazare** gar sa<u>n</u> lah-zar

**Garnier** gar-nee-ay

**Grand Palais** grah<u>n</u> pah-lay

**Grande Arche de la Défense** grah<u>n</u>d arsh duh lah day-fah<u>n</u>s

**Ile de la Cité** eel duh lah see-tay

**Ile St. Louis** eel sa<u>n</u> loo-ee

**Jacquemart-André** zhahk-mar-ah<u>n</u>-dray

**Jardin des Plantes** zhar-da<u>n</u> day plah<u>n</u>t

**Jeu de Paume** juh duh pohm

**La Madeleine** lah mah-duh-lehn

**Le Hameau** luh ah-moh

**Les Halles** lay ahl

**Les Invalides** lay-za<u>n</u>-vah-leed

**Orangerie** oh-rah<u>n</u>-zhuh-ree

**Louvre** loov-ruh

**Marais** mah-ray

**marché aux puces** mar-shay oh poos

**Marmottan** mar-moh-tah<u>n</u>

**Métro** may-troh

**Monge** moh<u>n</u>zh

**Montmartre** moh<u>n</u>-mart

**Montparnasse** moh<u>n</u>-par-nahs

**Moulin Rouge** moo-la<u>n</u> roozh

**Musée de l'Armée** mew-zay duh lar-may

**Musée d'Orsay** mew-zay dor-say

**Notre-Dame** noh-truh-dahm

**Orsay** or-say

**palais** pah-lay

**Palais de Justice** pah-lay duh zhew-stees

**Palais Garnier** pah-lay gar-nee-ay

**Palais Royal** pah-lay roh-yahl

**Parc de la Villette** park duh la vee-leht

**Parc Monceau** park moh<u>n</u>-soh

**Père Lachaise** pehr lah-shehz

**Petit Palais** puh-tee pah-lay

**Pigalle** pee-gahl

**Place Dauphine** plahs doh-feen

**Place de la Bastille** plahs duh lah bah-steel

**Place de la Concorde** plahs duh lah koh<u>n</u>-kord

**Place de la République** plahs duh lah ray-poo-bleek

**Place des Vosges** plahs day vohzh

**Place du Tertre** plahs dew tehr-truh

**Place St. André-des-Arts** plahs sa<u>n</u> tah<u>n</u>-dray day-zart

**Place Vendôme** plahs vah<u>n</u>-dohm

**Pompidou** pohn-pee-doo
**Pont Alexandre III** pohn ah-leks-ahn-druh twah
**Pont Neuf** pohn nuhf
**Promenade Plantée** proh-mehn-ahd plahn-tay
**quai** kay
**Rive Droite** reeve dwaht
**Rive Gauche** reeve gohsh
**Rodin** roh-dan
**rue** rew
**Rue Cler** rew klehr
**Rue Daguerre** rew dah-gehr
**Rue de Rivoli** rew duh ree-voh-lee
**Rue des Rosiers** rew day roz-ee-ay
**Rue Montorgueil** rew mohn-tor-goy
**Rue Mouffetard** rew moof-tar
**Sacré-Cœur** sah-kray-koor
**Sainte-Chapelle** sant-shah-pehl
**Seine** sehn
**Sèvres-Babylone** seh-vruh-bah-bee-lohn
**Sorbonne** sor-buhn
**St. Germain-des-Prés** san zhehr-man-day-pray
**St. Julien-le-Pauvre** san zhew-lee-ehn-luh-poh-vruh
**St. Séverin** sahn say-vuh-ran
**St. Sulpice** sahn sool-pees
**Tour Eiffel** toor ee-fehl
**Trianon** tree-ahn-ohn
**Trocadéro** troh-kah-day-roh
**Tuileries** twee-lay-ree
**Venus de Milo** vuh-news duh mee-loh

## Outside of Paris
**Abri du Cap Blanc** ah-bree dew cah blahn
**Aiguille du Midi** ah-gwee dew mee-dee
**Aïnhoa** an-oh-ah
**Albi** ahl-bee
**Alet** ah-lay
**Alise Ste. Reine** ah-leez sant rehn
**Aloxe-Corton** ah-lohx kor-tohn
**Alsace** ahl-sahs
**Amboise** ahm-bwahz
**Annecy** ahn-see
**Antibes** ahn-teeb
**Aosta (Italy)** ay-oh-stah

**Apt** ahp
**Aquitaine** ah-kee-tehn
**Arles** arl
**Arromanches** ah-roh-mahnsh
**Autoire** oh-twahr
**Auvergne** oh-vehrn
**Avignon** ah-veen-yohn
**Azay-le-Rideau** ah-zay luh ree-doh
**Balazuc** bah-lah-zook
**Bayeux** bī-yuh
**Bayonne** bī-yuhn
**Beaucaire** boh-kehr
**Beaujolais** boh-zhoh-lay
**Beaune** bohn
**Bedoin** buh-dwan
**Bennwihr** behn-veer
**Beynac** bay-nak
**Biarritz** bee-ah-reetz
**Blois** blah
**Bonnieux** bohn-yuh
**Bordeaux** bor-doh
**Brancion** brahn-see-ohn
**Brittany** bree-tah-nee
**Bruniquel** brew-nee-kehl
**Caen** kahn
**Cahors** kah-or
**Cajarc** kah-zhark
**Calais** kah-lay
**Camargue** kah-marg
**Cambord** kahn-bor
**Cancale** kahn-kahl
**Carcassonne** kar-kah-suhn
**Carennac** kah-rehn-ahk
**Carsac** kar-sahk
**Castelnaud** kah-stehl-noh
**Castelnau-de-Montmiral** kah-stehl-noh-duh-mohn-mee-rahl
**Caussade** koh-sahd
**Cavaillon** kah-vī-ohn
**Cénac** say-nahk
**Céret** say-ray
**Chambord** shahn-bor
**Chamonix** shah-moh-nee
**Champagne** shahn-pahn-yuh
**Chapaize** shah-pehz
**Chartres** shart
**Château de Chatonnière** shah-toh duh shah-tuhn-yehr
**Château de Rivau** shah-toh duh ree-voh
**ChâteauduHaut-Kœnigsbourg** shah-toh dew oh-koh-neegs-boorg

**Châteauneuf-du-Pape** shah-toh-nuhf-dew-pahp
**Châteauneuf-en-Auxois** shah-toh-nuhf-ehn-ohx-wah
**Chaumont-sur-Loire** shoh-mohn-sewr-lwahr
**Chenonceau** shuh-nohn-soh
**Chenonceaux** shuh-nohn-soh
**Cherbourg** shehr-boor
**Cheverny** shuh-vehr-nee
**Chinon** shee-nohn
**Cluny** klew-nee
**Colleville** kohl-veel
**Collioure** kohl-yoor
**Collonges-la-Rouge** koh-lohnzh-lah-roozh
**Colmar** kohl-mar
**Cordes-sur-Ciel** kord-sewr-see-yehl
**Côte d'Azur** koht dah-zewr
**Cougnac** koon-yahk
**Courseulles-sur-Mer** koor-suhl-sewr-mehr
**Coustellet** koo-stuh-lay
**Digne** deen-yuh
**Dijon** dee-zhohn
**Dinan** dee-nahn
**Dinard** dee-nar
**Domme** dohm
**Dordogne** dor-dohn-yuh
**Eguisheim** eh-geh-shīm
**Entrevaux** ahn-truh-voh
**Epernay** ay-pehr-nay
**Espelette** eh-speh-leht
**Eze-Bord-de-Mer** ehz-bor-duh-mehr
**Eze-le-Village** ehz-luh-vee-lahzh
**Faucon** foh-kohn
**Flavigny-sur-Ozerain** flah-veen-yee-sewr-oh-zuh-ran
**Font-de-Gaume** fohn-duh-gohm
**Fontenay** fohn-tuh-nay
**Fontevraud** fohn-tuh-vroh
**Fontvieille** fohn-vee-yeh-ee
**Fougères** foo-zher
**Fougères-sur-Bièvre** foo-zher-sewr-bee-ehv
**Gaillac** gī-yahk
**Gigondas** zhee-gohn-dahs
**Giverny** zhee-vehr-nee
**Gordes** gord
**Gorges de l'Ardèche** gorzh duh lar-dehsh

**Grenoble** gruh-noh-bluh
**Grouin** groo-an
**Guédelon** gway-duh-lohn
**Hautes Corbières** oht kor-bee-yehr
**Hendaye** ehn-dī
**Honfleur** ohn-flur
**Huisnes-sur-Mer** ween-sewr-mehr
**Hunawihr** uhn-ah-veer
**Ile Besnard** eel bay-nar
**Isle-sur-la-Sorgue** eel-sewr-lah-sorg
**Juan-les-Pins** zhwan-lay-pan
**Kaysersberg** kī-zehrs-behrg
**Kientzheim** keentz-īm
**La Charente** lah shah-rahnt
**La Rhune** lah rewn
**La Rochepot** lah rohsh-poh
**La Roque St. Christophe** lah rohk san kree-stohf
**La Roque-Gageac** lah rohk-gah-zhahk
**La Trophée des Alpes** lah troh-fay dayz ahlp
**La Turbie** lah tewr-bee
**Lacoste** lah-kohst
**Langeais** lahn-zhay
**Languedoc** long-dohk
**Lascaux** lah-skoh
**Lastours** lahs-toor
**Le Bugue** luh bewg
**Le Crestet** luh kruh-stay
**Le Havre** luh hah-vruh
**Le Ruquet** luh rew-kay
**Lémeré** lay-muh-ray
**Les Baux** lay boh
**Les Eyzies-de-Tayac** lay zay-zee-duh-tī-yahk
**Les Praz** lay prah
**Les Vosges** lay vohzh
**Limoges** lee-mohzh
**Loches** lohsh
**Loire** lwahr
**Longues-sur-Mer** long-sewr-mehr
**Loubressac** loo-bruh-sahk
**Lourmarin** loo-mah-ran
**Luberon** lew-beh-rohn
**Lyon** lee-ohn
**Malaucène** mah-loh-sehn
**Marne-la-Vallée-Chessy** marn-lah-vah-lay-shuh-see
**Marseille** mar-say
**Martel** mar-tehl**

**Mausanne** moh-sahn
**Ménerbes** may-nehrb
**Millau** mee-yoh
**Minerve** mee-nerv
**Mirabel** mee-rah-behl
**Modreuc** mohd-rewk
**Mont Blanc** moh<u>n</u> blah<u>n</u>
**Mont St. Michel** moh<u>n</u> sa<u>n</u> mee-shehl
**Mont Ventoux** moh<u>n</u> vehn-too
**Montenvers** moh<u>n</u>-tuh-vehr
**Montfort** moh<u>n</u>-for
**Montignac** moh<u>n</u>-teen-yahk
**Mortemart** mort-mar
**Munster** mewn-stehr
**Nantes** nah<u>n</u>t
**Nice** nees
**Normandy** nor-mah<u>n</u>-dee
**Nyons** nee-yoh<u>ns</u>
**Oradour-sur-Glane** oh-rah-door-sewr-glahn
**Orange** oh-rahnzh
**Padirac** pah-dee-rahk
**Paris** pah-ree
**Pech Merle** pehsh mehrl
**Peyrepertuse** pay-ruh-per-tewz
**Pointe du Hoc** pwa<u>n</u>t dew ohk
**Pont du Gard** poh<u>n</u> dew gahr
**Pontorson** poh<u>n</u>-tor-soh<u>n</u>
**Provence** proh-vah<u>ns</u>
**Puycelci** pew-suhl-cee
**Puyméras** pwee-may-rahs
**Queribus** kehr-ee-bews
**Reims** ra<u>ns</u> (rhymes with France)
**Remoulins** ruh-moo-la<u>n</u>
**Rennes** rehn
**Ribeauvillé** ree-boh-vee-yay
**Riquewihr** reek-veer
**Rocamadour** roh-kah-mah-door
**Rouen** roo-ah<u>n</u>
**Rouffignac** roo-feen-yahk
**Roussillon** roo-see-yoh<u>n</u>
**Route du Vin** root dew va<u>n</u>
**Sablet** sah-blay
**Sare** sahr
**Sarlat** sar-lah
**Savigny-les-Beaune** sah-veen-yee-lay-bohn
**Savoie** sah-vwah
**Séguret** say-goo-ray
**Semur-en-Auxois** suh-moor-eh<u>n</u>-ohx-wah

**Sigolsheim** see-gohl-shīm
**Souillac** soo-ee-yahk
**St. Suliac** sa<u>n</u> soo-lee-ahk
**St. Cirq Lapopie** sa<u>n</u> seerk lah-poh-pee
**St. Cyprien** sa<u>n</u> seep-ree-<u>ehn</u>
**St. Emilion** sa<u>n</u> tay-meel-yoh<u>n</u>
**St. Geniès** sa<u>n</u> zhuh-nyehs
**St. Jean-de-Luz** sa<u>n</u> zhah<u>n</u>-duh-looz
**St. Jean-Pied-de-Port** sa<u>n</u> zhah<u>n</u>-pee-yay-duh-por
**St. Malo** sa<u>n</u> mah-loh
**St. Marcellin-lès-Vaison** sa<u>n</u> mar-suh-la<u>n</u>-lay-vay-zoh<u>n</u>
**St. Rémy** sa<u>n</u> ray-mee
**St. Romain-en-Viennois** sa<u>n</u> roh-ma<u>n</u>-eh<u>n</u>-vee-eh<u>n</u>-nwah
**St-Paul-de-Vence** sa<u>n</u>-pohl-duh-vah<u>ns</u>
**Ste. Mère Eglise** sa<u>n</u>t mehr ay-gleez
**Stes-Maries-de-la-Mer** sa<u>n</u>t-mah-ree-duh-lah-mehr
**Strasbourg** strahs-boorg
**Suzette** soo-zeht
**Taizé** teh-zay
**Tarascon** tah-rah-skoh<u>n</u>
**Tours** toor
**Turckheim** tewrk-hīm
**Ussé** oo-say
**Uzès** oo-zehs
**Vacqueyras** vah-kee-rahs
**Vaison la Romaine** vay-zoh<u>n</u> lah roh-mehn
**Valançay** vah-lah<u>n</u>-say
**Valréas** vahl-ray-ahs
**Vence** vah<u>ns</u>
**Verdun** vehr-duhn
**Versailles** vehr-sī
**Veynes** vay-nuh
**Vézelay** vay-zuh-lay
**Vierville-sur-Mer** vee-yehr-veel-sewr-mehr
**Villandry** vee-lah<u>n</u>-dry
**Villefranche-de-Rouergue** veel-frah<u>n</u>sh-duh-roo-ehrg
**Villefranche-sur-Mer** veel-frah<u>n</u>sh-sewr-mehr
**Villeneuve-lès-Avignon** veel-nuhv-lay-zah-veeh-yoh<u>n</u>
**Vitrac** vee-trahk
**Vouvray** voo-vray
**Villedieu** vee-luh-dyuh

## French Survival Phrases

When using the phonetics, try to nasalize the n sound.

| Good day. | **Bonjour.** | bohn-zhoor |
| Mrs. / Mr. | **Madame / Monsieur** | mah-dahm / muhs-yur |
| Do you speak English? | **Parlez-vous anglais?** | par-lay-voo ahn-glay |
| Yes. / No. | **Oui. / Non.** | wee / nohn |
| I understand. | **Je comprends.** | zhuh kohn-prahn |
| I don't understand. | **Je ne comprends pas.** | zhuh nuh kohn-prahn pah |
| Please. | **S'il vous plaît.** | see voo play |
| Thank you. | **Merci.** | mehr-see |
| I'm sorry. | **Désolé.** | day-zoh-lay |
| Excuse me. | **Pardon.** | par-dohn |
| (No) problem. | **(Pas de) problème.** | (pah duh) proh-blehm |
| It's good. | **C'est bon.** | say bohn |
| Goodbye. | **Au revoir.** | oh vwahr |
| one / two | **un / deux** | uhn / duh |
| three / four | **trois / quatre** | twah / kah-truh |
| five / six | **cinq / six** | sank / sees |
| seven / eight | **sept / huit** | seht / weet |
| nine / ten | **neuf / dix** | nuhf / dees |
| How much is it? | **Combien?** | kohn-bee-an |
| Write it? | **Ecrivez?** | ay-kree-vay |
| Is it free? | **C'est gratuit?** | say grah-twee |
| Included? | **Inclus?** | an-klew |
| Where can I buy / find...? | **Où puis-je acheter / trouver...?** | oo pwee-zhuh ah-shuh-tay / troo-vay |
| I'd like / We'd like... | **Je voudrais / Nous voudrions...** | zhuh voo-dray / noo voo-dree-ohn |
| ...a room. | **...une chambre.** | ewn shahn-bruh |
| ...a ticket to ___. | **...un billet pour ___.** | uhn bee-yay poor |
| Is it possible? | **C'est possible?** | say poh-see-bluh |
| Where is...? | **Où est...?** | oo ay |
| ...the train station | **...la gare** | lah gar |
| ...the bus station | **...la gare routière** | lah gar root-yehr |
| ...tourist information | **...l'office du tourisme** | loh-fees dew too-reez-muh |
| Where are the toilets? | **Où sont les toilettes?** | oo sohn lay twah-leht |
| men | **hommes** | ohm |
| women | **dames** | dahm |
| left / right | **à gauche / à droite** | ah gohsh / ah dwaht |
| straight | **tout droit** | too dwah |
| When does this open / close? | **Ça ouvre / ferme à quelle heure?** | sah oo-vruh / fehrm ah kehl ur |
| At what time? | **À quelle heure?** | ah kehl ur |
| Just a moment. | **Un moment.** | uhn moh-mahn |
| now / soon / later | **maintenant / bientôt / plus tard** | man-tuh-nahn / bee-an-toh / plew tar |
| today / tomorrow | **aujourd'hui / demain** | oh-zhoor-dwee / duh-man |

## In the Restaurant

| | | |
|---|---|---|
| I'd like / We'd like... | **Je voudrais / Nous voudrions...** | zhuh voo-dray / noo voo-dree-c |
| ...to reserve... | **...réserver...** | ray-zehr-vay |
| ...a table for one / two. | **...une table pour un / deux.** | ewn tah-bluh poor uhn / duh |
| Non-smoking. | **Non fumeur.** | nohn few-mur |
| Is this seat free? | **C'est libre?** | say lee-bruh |
| The menu (in English), please. | **La carte (en anglais), s'il vous plaît.** | lah kart (ahn ahn-glay) see voo play |
| service (not) included | **service (non) compris** | sehr-vees (nohn) kohn-pree |
| to go | **à emporter** | ah ahn-por-tay |
| with / without | **avec / sans** | ah-vehk / sahn |
| and / or | **et / ou** | ay / oo |
| special of the day | **plat du jour** | plah dew zhoor |
| specialty of the house | **spécialité de la maison** | spay-see-ah-lee-tay duh lah may-zohn |
| appetizers | **hors-d'oeuvre** | or-duh-vruh |
| first course (soup, salad) | **entrée** | ahn-tray |
| main course (meat, fish) | **plat principal** | plah pran-see-pahl |
| bread | **pain** | pan |
| cheese | **fromage** | froh-mahzh |
| sandwich | **sandwich** | sahnd-weech |
| soup | **soupe** | soop |
| salad | **salade** | sah-lahd |
| meat | **viande** | vee-ahnd |
| chicken | **poulet** | poo-lay |
| fish | **poisson** | pwah-sohn |
| seafood | **fruits de mer** | frwee duh mehr |
| fruit | **fruit** | frwee |
| vegetables | **légumes** | lay-gewm |
| dessert | **dessert** | duh-sehr |
| mineral water | **eau minérale** | oh mee-nay-rahl |
| tap water | **l'eau du robinet** | loh dew roh-bee-nay |
| milk | **lait** | lay |
| (orange) juice | **jus (d'orange)** | zhew (doh-rahnzh) |
| coffee | **café** | kah-fay |
| tea | **thé** | tay |
| wine | **vin** | van |
| red / white | **rouge / blanc** | roozh / blahn |
| glass / bottle | **verre / bouteille** | vehr / boo-teh-ee |
| beer | **bière** | bee-ehr |
| Cheers! | **Santé!** | sahn-tay |
| More. / Another. | **Plus. / Un autre.** | plew / uhn oh-truh |
| The same. | **La même chose.** | lah mehm shohz |
| The bill, please. | **L'addition, s'il vous plaît.** | lah-dee-see-ohn see voo play |
| tip | **pourboire** | poor-bwar |
| Delicious! | **Délicieux!** | day-lee-see-uh |

For more user-friendly French phrases, check out *Rick Steves' French Phrase B and Dictionary* or *Rick Steves' French, Italian & German Phrase Book*.

# INDEX

## A

Abbeys: Cluny, 734–736; Fontenay, 722–723; Jumièges, 205; Mont St. Michel, 251–256; Notre-Dame de Sénanque, 582; Royale de Fontevraud, 327; St. Georges de Boscherville, 205

Abri du Cap Blanc: 371

Accommodations: *See* Sleeping; and *specific destinations*

Aiguille du Midi (Alps): 673–675

Ainhoa: 415

Airborne Museum (Ste. Mère Eglise): 243

Airfares: 3, 866–867

Airlines: 845; carry-on restrictions, 6

Airports: 844–845; Paris, 159–165. *See also specific airports*

Aître St. Maclou (Rouen): 203

Albert I Park (Nice): 600–601

Albi: 458–468; map, 460

Alet: 276

Alise Ste. Reine: 719, 725–726

Aloxe-Corton: 704–705, 715; sleeping, 708–709

Alpes-Savoie: 658–690; map, 659. *See also* Chamonix

Alpilles Mountains: 548

Alpine Museum (Chamonix): 683

Alsace: 762–801; map, 764

Alsatian Museum (Strasbourg): 798

Alsatian wines: 765–766, 782–793; map, 785; tours, 783–784

Amboise: 286–300; eating, 298–299; map, 290; sights/activities, 289–293; sleeping, 293–298; transportation, 287–288, 299–300

Amboise Château: 282, 291–292

American Art Museum (Giverny): 184

American Cemetery and Memorial (Colleville): 239–240

American Church (Paris): 41, 43, 71, 107, 111

American Express: 10–11

Amphithéâtre (Arena) (Arles): 511–512

Amsterdam: train travel, 158

*Anis* candies: 724

Annecy: 660–668; map, 661

Annecy Museum: 663

Antibes: 642–652; eating, 651–652; map, 645; sights/activities, 644–649; sleeping, 649–651; transportation, 643, 644, 652

Antibes History and Archaeology Museum: 647

Aosta (Italy): 684

Apartment rentals: 22–23

Apt: market, 503

Aquariums: Monaco, 638; San Sebastián, 428

Aqueduct (Pont du Gard): 544–548

Arc de Triomphe (Orange): 557

Arc de Triomphe (Paris): 66, 92, 108

Archaeological museums: Antibes, 647; Arles, 507–508; Cluny, 734–735; Les Eyzies-de-Tayac, 368; Lyon, 745, 749–750; Nice, 605; Paris, 85–86; Strasbourg, 798

Archaeological sites: Cro-Magnon caves, 362–373, 383–384, 392. *See also* Roman sites

Ardèche Gorges: 571

Argentière: 681

Arlaten Folk Museum (Arles): 512–513

Arles: 504–524; eating, 521–523; maps, 509, 517, 520; market, 503; sights/activities, 506–517; sleeping, 517–521; transportation, 505, 506, 523–524

Arles Ancient History Museum: 507–508

Army Museum (Paris): 66, 84

Arromanches: 235–238

Art: Cro-Magnon caves, 362–373, 383–384, 392; of the Riviera, 589. *See also* Impressionism; *and specific artists*

Art museums: sightseeing tips, 14–15. *See also specific museums*

Art Nouveau: 64, 466, 772

Arve River: 669, 673, 682

Atelier de la Soierie (Lyon): 745, 752–753

ATM machines: 10, 11

Attitude, French: 846–847

Au Lapin Agile (Paris): 106
Autoire: 389
Autun: 705
Avignon: 524–543; eating, 539–542; maps, 526, 536, 540; sights/activities, 529–535; sleeping, 535–539; tours, 528–529; transportation, 525, 527, 542–543
Avignon Synagogue: 533

## B

Back Door travel philosophy: 37
Baie des Anges (Nice): 600
Ballooning, Loire Valley: 285
Barcelona: train travel, 495
Baron Gérard Museum (Bayeux): 225
Bartholdi, Frédéric-Auguste: 752, 771; Museum (Colmar), 772, 776–777
Basque Country: 393–455; French, 398–419; map, 395; Spanish, 419–455; transportation, 394–395
Basque Country Museum (Guernica): 444–445
Basque Culture, Museum of (Bayonne): 409–410
Basque Museum (Bilbao): 452–453
Basques: 396–397
*Basse Corniche:* 628–630
*Bastides:* 468–469
*Bateaux-Mouches* (Paris): 52–53, 152
Battle of Hastings: 223
Battle of Normandy Memorial Museum (Bayeux): 225
Baubigny: 716; sleeping, 709–710
Bayeux: 220–229; map, 221
Bayeux Cathedral: 224
Bayeux Tapestry: 222–224
Bay of Angels (Nice): 600
Bay of Biscay: 440–442
Bay of Mont St. Michel: 249–250
Bayonne (Baiona): 408–411
Beaches: Annecy, 664; Antibes, 646, 648; Biarritz, 413–414; Collioure, 492–493; Dinard, 276; Ile Besnard, 274; Juan-les-Pins, 649; Lekeitio, 441; Nice, 593, 599; Paris, 65; St. Jean-de-Luz, 401; St. Malo, 275; San Sebastián, 429; Villefranche-sur-Mer, 624. *See also* D-Day beaches
Beaujolais Wine Route: 762

Beaune: 694–713; eating, 710–711; maps, 699, 712; sights/activities, 697–706; sleeping, 706–710; tours, 697; transportation, 695–696, 711, 713
Beaune region: 713–717; map, 714
Beauvais Airport (Paris): 164–165, 844
Bed-and-breakfasts *(chambres d'hôte):* 20–22. *See also specific destinations*
Bedoin: market, 503
Bennwihr: 783, 793
Bernard, Saint: 384, 722–723
Berthillon (Paris): 147
Beynac: 349, 354–357; eating, 360–361; market, 335; sleeping, 359–360
Beynac Château: 355–356
Biarritz: 412–414
Bibliotheque Carnegie (Reims): 809–810
Biking: 866; Amboise, 288, 292; Annecy, 663, 664; Arles, 505; Avignon, 528; Bayeux, 222; Beaune, 713–715; Blois, 307; the Camargue, 516–517; Carcassonne, 474; Chamonix, 672; Chenonceaux, 300–301; Chinon, 317, 318; Colmar, 768–769; Dinan, 264, 268–269; Dordogne, 332, 348; Giverny, 185–186; Isle-sur-la-Sorgue, 573, 575; Les Eyzies-de-Tayac, 367; Loire Valley, 284; Luberon, 572; Nice, 593, 598–599; Paris, 51–52, 55–56; Route du Vin, 784, 786; San Sebastián, 425; Sarlat, 337; Strasbourg, 797; Vaison la Romaine, 560, 563–564; Versailles, 174–175; Villefranche-sur-Mer, 621
Bilbao: 446–455; map, 449
Bird Market (Paris): 64
Black Virgin: 382–385
Bléré: sleeping, 297
Blois: 305–307
Blois Royal Castle: 282, 306–307
Boat cruises: Amboise, 292; Annecy, 664; Avignon, 528; Beynac, 357; Carcassonne, 480; Collioure, 494; Dinan, 269; Dordogne, 332; Honfleur, 215; Nice, 595; Paris, 52–54, 152; Riviera, 587–588; San Sebastián, 428; Strasbourg, 799;

Villefranche-sur-Mer, 624
Boating: Annecy, 663–664. *See also* Canoeing and kayaking
Bonaparte: *See* Napoleon Bonaparte
Bonaparte Bridge (Lyon): 744–746
Bon Marché (Paris): 103
Bonnieux: 583; market, 503
Books, recommended: 835–836
Bordeaux: 376–380
Boudin, Eugène: 208, 211, 213; Museum (Honfleur), 212–214
*Boules:* 506, 623, 837
Bouzy: 812
Brancion: 732–733
Brayer (Yves) Museum (Les Baux): 552
Bretxa Public Market (San Sebastián): 427
British War Cemetery (Bayeux): 225
Brittany: 261–277
Bruniquel: 470
Brussels: train travel, 158
Budgeting: 3–4
Bullfights, in Arles: 514–516
Burgundy: 691–738; map, 693
Burgundy Canal: 718
Burgundy wines: 693–694, 695, 702–706, 713–717; museum (Beaune), 701; tours, 697, 706
Burgundy Wine Museum (Beaune): 701
Business hours: 8
Bus travel: 856–857; whirlwind three-week tour, 850–851. *See also specific destinations*

**C**
Caen: 244–247
Caen Memorial Museum: 234, 245–247
Cafés (brasseries): overview, 28–29; tipping, 12. *See also specific destinations*
Cahors: 389, 392; market, 335
Calder, Alexander: 95, 656
Calvet Museum (Avignon): 534
Camargue, the: 516–517
Camembert cheese: 190, 192
Camino de Santiago: 410, 416–418
Camping (campgrounds): 22, 274, 318, 790
Canadian Cemetery (Courseulles): 244
Canal du Midi (Carcassonne): 480

Canal St. Martin (Paris): 150
Cancale: 274–275
Cannes Film Festival: 586, 607
Canoeing and kayaking: Ardèche Gorges, 571; Chinon, 318; Dordogne River, 332, 349–352; Pont du Gard, 546; Tarn River Gorge, 471
Cap d'Antibes: 646–649
Cap Ferrat: 595, 624, 627
Carcassonne: 472–486; maps, 475, 477
Carennac: 388
Car insurance: 861
Car leasing: 845, 861–862
Carnavalet Museum (Paris): 67, 100
Carnegie Library (Reims): 809–810
Carpentras: market, 503
Car rentals: 6, 857, 860–861. *See also specific destinations*
Carsac Church: 348
Car travel: 848, 862–866; distance and time, 865; road signs, 863, 864; three-week trip, 858–859. *See also specific destinations*
Casinos: 414; Monte Carlo, 639–640
Castelnau-Bretenoux Château: 389
Castelnaud: 349, 354; sleeping near, 361
Castelnau-de-Montmiral: 458, 469
Castle Hill (Nice): 597, 601
Castles: *See* Châteaux
Catacombs of Paris: 89
Cathars: overview, 462
Cathédrale d'Images (Les Baux): 553
Cathédrale Russe (Nice): 597, 605–606
Caunes-Minervois: 487–489; sleeping, 484
Caussade: 458, 469
Cavaillon: market, 503
Caves (caverns): 362–373, 383–384, 392, 552–553
Cell (mobile) phones: 838
Cemeteries: 67, 101, 203, 225, 239–240, 242, 244, 256
Cénac: canoeing, 352; market, 335
Centre d'Histoire de la Résistance et de la Déportation (Lyon): 745, 755–756
Centre Pompidou (Paris): 67, 97
Ceramics Museum (Rouen): 204
Céret: 495
Chagall, Marc: 92–93, 97, 98, 493,

495, 602, 656, 808; Museum
(Nice), 597, 601–603
Chagny: 732
Chalon-sur-Saône: 705, 716
Chambord Château: 282, 307–310
Chamonix: 668–690; eating, 688–
689; maps, 669, 674, 680, 686;
sights and activities, 673–684;
sleeping, 684–688; transportation,
670–672, 689–690
Champagne: 810–812
Champ de Mars (Paris): 108
Champs-Elysées (Paris): 67, 90–92,
108
Changing of the Guard (Monaco):
638
Chapaize: 733
Chapelle Cocteau (Villefranche):
622, 624
Chapelle du Rosaire (Vence): 653–654
Chapelle et Phare de la Garoupe
(Antibes): 648
Charlemagne: 472, 823, 826
Charles de Gaulle Airport (Paris):
159–163, 844
Chartres: 180–183
Chartres Cathedral: 180–182
Châteauneuf-du-Pape: market, 503
Châteauneuf-en-Auxois: 718,
719–720
Châteaux (castles): Amboise,
291–292; Annecy, 663; Azay-
le-Rideau, 322–323; Beynac,
355–356; Blois Royal Castle,
306–307; Carcassonne, 479;
Castelnau-Bretenoux, 389;
Castelnaud, 354; Chambord,
282, 307–310; Châteauneuf-en-
Auxois, 719; Chatonnière, 326;
Chaumont-sur-Loire, 312–314;
Chenonceau, 301–304; Cheverny,
310–311; Chinon, 317–318; Clos-
Lucé (Amboise), 289; Collioure
Royal Castle, 493; Corton-André
(Aloxe-Corton), 715; Dinan, 264;
Fayrac, 350, 356; Fougères-sur-
Bièvre, 312; Guédelon, 730–731;
Hautes Corbières, 486–487;
Haut-Konigsbourg, 787–788;
Husseren, 789–790; la Fleunie,
369; Langeais, 324–325; La
Rochepot, 716–717; Lastours,
488; Lignerolles, 227; Loches,
314–315; Meylet, 379; Montfort,

349; Nazelles, 297; Nineyrol, 361;
Noizay, 296–297; Peyrepertuse,
486–487; Pray, 296; Quéribus,
487; Rivau, 326; Rocamadour,
383; Savigny, 715; Ussé, 326;
Valençay, 283, 315; Versailles,
66, 167–176; Villandry, 325–326;
Villeneuve (Vence), 653
Chatonnière Château: 283, 326
Chaumont-sur-Loire: 282, 312–314
Cheeses: 190, 192, 292, 334, 427
Chemin de Halage (St. Cirq
Lapopie): 391
Chemin du Fauvisme (Collioure): 493
Chemins de Fer de Provence: 657
Chenonceau Château: 282, 301–304
Chenonceaux: 300–305
Cheverny Château: 282, 310–311
Children, traveling with: 20–21
Chillida-Leku Museum (San
Sebastián): 430–431
Chinon: 315–322; map, 316
Chinon Château: 283, 317–318
Chiroubles: 762
Chocolat (movie): 724
Chocolate: 104, 198, 288, 411, 724
Chunnel (Channel Tunnel): 158–159
Churches: architecture, 824. See also
specific churches
Cimetière du Père Lachaise (Paris):
67, 101
Citadelle Souterraine (Verdun): 820
Clelles: 657
Clignancourt flea market (Paris): 104
Climate: 5–6, 870
Clos-Lucé Château (Amboise): 289,
291
Clothing sizes: metric conversions,
870
Cluny: 734–736
Cluny Abbey: 735–736
Cluny Museum (Paris): 67, 85–86
Cluny Museum of Art and
Archaeology: 734–735
Cocteau (Jean) Chapel
(Villefranche): 622, 624
Col de Banyuls: 495
Col de la Forclaz: 664–665
Collégiale Notre-Dame (Beaune): 701
Colleville: 239–240
Colline du Château (Nice): 597, 601
Collioure: 489–498; map, 491
Collioure Royal Castle: 493
Collonges-la-Rouge: 375

Colmar: 766–782; eating, 780–782; information, 767; map, 770; sights/activities, 769–777; sleeping, 778–780; tours, 769; transportation, 767–768, 782

Colmar Dominican Church: 773, 776

Comtal Château (Carcassonne): 479

Conciergerie (Paris): 64–65

Condat-sur-Vézère: sleeping, 369

Consulates: 841

Cooking classes: Arles, 506; Nice, 595–596; San Sebastián, 425

Cordes-sur-Ciel: 470

Corton-André Château (Aloxe-Corton): 715

Costs of trip: 3–4

Côte de Grâce (Honfleur): 215

Côte d'Or wines: 694, 713–717

Côtes du Rhône: 558–571

Cougnac caves: 373

Courses Camarguaises (Arles): 514–516

Courseulles-sur-Mer: 243–244

Cours Saleya (Nice): 596, 606, 614

Cousteau Aquarium (Monaco): 638

Coustellet: 582–583; market, 503

Credit cards: 6, 10–11; lost or stolen, 11–12

Cro-Magnon caves: 362–373, 383–384, 392; map, 363

Crown of Thorns: 62–63

Cruises: See Boat cruises

Cuisine: 33–35; Alsace, 765; Basque Country, 395, 398; Brittany, 262; Burgundy, 692; Dordogne, 332–335; Languedoc, 458; Loire Valley, 285–286; Lyon, 739; Normandy, 190, 192; Provence, 502–503; Riviera, 588–589; Savoie, 660

Curie, Marie: 88

Currency and exchange: 10, 11

Customs House (Colmar): 771

Customs regulations: 13

**D**

Dalí (Salvador) Museum (Paris): 102

Da Vinci, Leonardo: 74–75, 289, 291

*Da Vinci Code:* 54, 55, 86, 728, 835–836

D-Day beaches (Normandy): 229–247; map, 230; tours, 231–234

D-Day Landing Museum (Arromanches): 237

Dead Man's Corner (Ste. Mère Eglise): 242–243

Deba: 441

Degas, Edgar: 77, 534

De Gaulle, Charles: 92, 827

De Gaulle Airport (Paris): 159–163, 844

Delacroix, Eugène: 76, 204

Dentelles de Montmirail: 568–571

Department stores: 27; Annecy, 662; Arles, 521; Colmar, 768; Paris, 103, 107; Strasbourg, 800

Deportation Memorial (Paris): 59–60

Diane de Poitiers: 302–303, 313

Digne-les-Bains: 657

Dinan: 262–273; map, 265

Dinan Château: 264

Dinan Clock Tower: 266

Dinard: 276–277

Dining: See Eating; and *specific destinations*

Disneyland Paris: 186–188

Dolden Museum (Riquewihr): 787

Doll Museum (Isle-sur-la-Sorgue): 575

Domaine de Durban: 570

Domaines d'Aloxe Corton: 704–705, 715

Domme: 349, 350, 352; market, 335; sleeping, 359

Donostia: See San Sebastián

Dordogne: 329–389; cuisine, 332–333; map, 333; markets, 334–335; transportation, 331–332. See also *specific destinations*

Dordogne River Valley: 348–362; map, 351

Driving: See Car travel

Duclair: 205

Dufy, Raoul: 214, 493

Duingt: 664–665

Dunes de Chevets: 274

**E**

Eating: 25–35; budgeting, 3–4; glossary of terms, 27, 28, 880; tipping, 12. See also Cuisine; Markets; and *specific destinations*

Economy: xviii–xix

Egouts de Paris: 83

Eguisheim: 786, 788–792

Eiffel Tower (Paris): 66, 80–83, 108

Eleanor of Aquitaine: 317, 327, 823, 826

Electricity: 9
El País Vasco (Spanish Basque Country): 419–455
Email: 846–847. *See also specific destinations*
Embassies: 841
Emerald Coast: 274
Emergencies: 844
Entrevaux: 657
Epernay: 812
Equestrian Performance Academy (Versailles): 178
Erotic Art Museum (Paris): 102–103
Espace Tairraz (Chamonix): 683
Espelette (Ezpeleta): 415–416
Etretat: 216
*Eurostar:* 158–159
Evelles: 716
Evran: 269
Exchange rate: 11
Eze-Bord-de-Mer: 630
Eze-le-Village: 629–630

**F**
Fabrics and Decorative Arts Museums (Lyon): 745, 755
Faience: 202, 204
Fashion boutiques, in Paris: 103–104
Faucon: 564
Fauvism Museum (Collioure): 493
Fayencerie Augy (Rouen): 202
Fayrac Château: 350, 356
Festivals: 867–869
Figueres: train travel, 495
Fishermen's Wharf (Biarritz): 413
Flag, French: xix
Flavigny-sur-Ozerain: 719, 724–725
Fleunie Château: 369
Fleurie: 762
Flower Markets: Nice, 596; Paris, 64
Foie gras: 34, 334, 356–358
Fondation Angladon-Dubrujeaud (Avignon): 534
Fondation Maeght (St-Paul-de-Vence): 656
Fondation Van Gogh (Arles): 512
Fontaine-de-Vaucluse: 575
Font-de-Gaume caves: 370–371
Fontenay Abbey: 722–723
Fontevraud Royal Abbey: 327
Fontvieille: sleeping, 521
Food: *See* Cheeses; Chocolate; Cuisine; Eating; Foie gras; Markets; Olive oil

Fort Carré (Antibes): 644, 648
Fort de Douaumont (Verdun): 819–820
Fort St. Elme (Collioure): 492, 494
Forum Square (Arles): 508, 510
Fougères: 277
Fougères-sur-Bièvre Château: 282, 312
Fouquet's (Paris): 91–92
Fourvière Hill (Lyon): 746–747, 749
Fragonard Perfume Factory (Eze): 630
Fragonard Perfume Museum (Paris): 93
François I: 74–75, 286, 289, 291–292, 306, 309, 826
French Alps: *See* Alpes-Savoie
French Basque Country: 398–419
French language: *See* Language
French Resistance: *See* Resistance
French Riviera: *See* Riviera
Fuenterrabía: 439–440

**G**
Gaillac: 458, 469
Galamus Gorge: 487
Galeries Lafayette: Paris, 93, 103, 107; Strasbourg, 800
Gallimard (Eze-le-Village): 630
Gallo-Roman Museum (Lyon): 745, 749–750
Gare d'Austerlitz (Paris): 158
Gare de l'Est (Paris): 157
Gare de Lyon (Paris): 156–157
Gare du Nord (Paris): 154
Gare Montparnasse (Paris): 154, 156
Gare St. Lazare (Paris): 157
Garnier Opéra (Paris): 67, 92–93, 107
Gay travelers, in Paris: 145–146
Gehry, Frank: 450–452
Gérard Sion Galerie (Carcassonne): 480
Géricault, Théodore: 76, 204
German Military Cemeteries (Normandy): 242, 256
Gernika Assembly House (Guernica): 445
Gernika Peace Museum (Guernica): 443–444
Gigondas: 570; eating, 567; sleeping, 565
Giverny: 184–186; map, 185
Gondolas, in Chamonix: 671–675, 677–678

Gordes: 581–582; market, 503
Gorges de Galamus: 487
Gorges de l'Ardèche: 571
Gorges du Tarn: 471
Gouffre de Padirac: 385–386
Government: xix, 825, 828–829
Grand Balcon Nord: 679
Grand Balcon Sud: 679, 681
Grande Arche de la Défense (Paris): 67, 94–95
*Grande Corniche:* 628–632
Grand Palais (Paris): 94
Grand Prix de Monaco: 586, 632
Grenoble: 657
Grimaldi Château (Antibes): 646, 647
Grotte de Font-de-Gaume: 370–371
Grotte de Rouffignac: 371–372
Grotte du Pech Merle: 392
Grottes de Cougnac: 373
Grottes Préhistoriques des Merveilles (Rocamadour): 383–384
Grünewald, Matthias: 774–775
Guédelon Château: 730–731
Guernica: 442–446
Guernica Oak Tree: 445–446
Guggenheim Bilbao: 450–452
Guidebooks: 835; Rick Steves, 832, 834
Guiller Gate (Semur-en-Auxois): 721

**H**
Hamlet (Versailles): 175–176
Hautes Corbières Château: 486–487
Haut-Konigsbourg Château: 787–788
Helbronner Point: 674–675
Hendaye: 418
High Corniche: 628–632
Hiking (walking): Ainhoa, 415; Annecy, 663; Antibes, 648–649; Beynac, 355; the Camargue, 516–517; Carcassonne, 480; Chamonix, 678–682; Collioure, 494–495; Dinan, 268; Etretat, 216; Galamus Gorge, 487; Honfleur, 215; Isle-sur-la-Sorgue, 574; Kaysersberg, 792–793; Lastours, 488; Mont St. Michel, 250–251; Pont du Gard, 548; Ribeauvillé, 787; Route du Vin, 786, 789–790; St. Cirq Lapopie, 391; Semur-en-Auxois, 721;

Tarn River Gorge, 471; Vaison la Romaine, 563
Hill Towns of the Luberon: 571–584
History: 822–825
Holidays: 5, 867–869
Holocaust Memorial (Paris): 98
Hondarribia: 439–440
Honfleur: 207–220; eating, 218–219; map, 209; sights/activities, 210–216; sleeping, 216–218; transportation, 208, 210, 219–220
Horseback riding: Versailles, 178
Hostels *(auberges de jeunesse):* overview, 22, 846. *See also specific destinations*
Hot-air ballooning, Loire Valley: 285
Hotels: 16–20; hotel chains, 845–846; reservations, 23–24; reservation form, 873. *See also specific destinations*
Hôtel de la Cité (Carcassonne): 479, 481, 485
Hôtel de Sully (Paris): 97
Hôtel Dieu (Beaune): 697–698, 700–701
Hôtel Negresco (Nice): 600, 606, 612, 618
House of Etienne de la Boëtie (Sarlat): 338
House of Magic (Blois): 306–307
Hugo, Victor: 88, 96–97, 836
Huisnes-sur-Mer: 256
Hunawihr: 787
Hundred Years' War: 201, 224, 266, 317, 329, 354, 355, 806, 823
Hurepel de Minerve: 488–489
Husseren Les Cinq Châteaux: 789–790

**I**
Ile Besnard: 274
Ile de la Cité (Paris): 56–59, 134; sleeping, 124–125
Ile St. Louis (Paris): 60, 108; eating, 146–147; map, 61; sleeping, 124
Ill River: cruises, 799
Impressionism: 77–80, 85, 184, 211, 212–214
Information sources: 831–832. *See also specific destinations*
Internet access: 846–847. *See also specific destinations*
Ironworks Museum (Rouen): 204

*Isenheim Altarpiece* (Grünewald): 774–775

Isle-sur-la-Sorgue: 572–576; market, 503, 574

Italy: 684

**J**

Jacquemart-André Museum (Paris): 67, 93–94

Jardin des Plantes (Paris): 88

Jardin du Luxembourg (Paris): 87, 125–126

Jardin Exotique (film): 639

Jardins d'Eze: 630

Jazz music: 105–106, 481, 606, 649, 867–868

Jeu de Paume (Paris): 70

Jewish Art and History Museum (Paris): 67, 97–98

Jewish Quarter (Paris): 98; eating, 144–145

Joan of Arc: 196–198, 317, 747, 806, 823, 826; Museum (Rouen), 197–198

Joan of Arc Church (Rouen): 198

Joucas: sleeping, 580–581

Juan-les-Pins: 649

Juliénas: 762

Jumièges Abbey: 205

Juno Beach Center (Courseulles): 243–244

**K**

Kayaking: *See* Canoeing and kayaking

Kaysersberg: 786, 792–793

Kids, traveling with: 20–21

Kientzheim: 793

King's Vegetable Garden (Versailles): 176–178

Kursaal Conference Center (San Sebastián): 430

**L**

La Cambe: 242

La Cave de Pommard: 705, 716

Lac Blanc: 681

Lace Conservatory (Bayeux): 225

La Cité (Carcassonne): 473, 476–479; eating, 485–486; map, 477

La Concha Beach (San Sebastián): 429

Lacoste: 583–584; market, 503

La Croix-Rousse (Lyon): 753

La Défense (Paris): 67, 94–95

La Digue de la Mer: 516

Ladurée (Paris): 92

*Lady and the Unicorn* tapestries: 85–86

La Flégère Lift: 677–678, 679, 681

La Fleunie Château: 369

Lagnes: 575

La Grande Arche (Paris): 67, 94–95

La Guimorais: 274

La Malène: 471; sleeping, 471

"La Marseillaise" (song): 822

La Moutarderie Fallot (Beaune): 702

Langeais: 283, 324–325

Language: 846–847; Basque, 395; classes, in Arles, 506; coffee and tea lingo, 28; hotel accommodations, 18; pronunciation guide, 875–878; restaurant phrases, 880; road signs, 864; Spanish phrases, 421; survival phrases, 879–880; travel phrases, 857; wine lingo, 31

Languedoc: 456–498; map, 457

Lantern of the Dead (Sarlat): 340

La Perla Spa (San Sebastián): 429

La Petite France (Strasbourg): 799

La Rhune (Larrun): 414

La Rochepot: 716–717; sleeping, 709

La Rochepot Château: 716–717

La Roque-Gageac: 349, 350, 352–353; sleeping and eating, 359

La Roque St. Christophe: 373

La Route des Anciennes Abbayes: 205

La Route Napoléon: 657

Larroque: 469

Lascaux II: 368–369

*Last Judgment* (van der Weyden): 700–701

Lastours Châteaux: 488

Latin Quarter (Paris): 60–62, 145

La Trophée des Alpes: 631–632

La Turbie: 631–632

Lavender Museum (Coustellet): 582–583

La Villasse: 561

Le Brévent Gondola: 677–678

Le Bugue: market, 335

Le Crestet: 568

Left Bank (Paris): 39, 85–89; map, 87

Le Hameau du Vin (Romanèche-Thorins): 762

Le Havre: 215
Léhon: 268–269
Lekeitio: 440–442
Le Mémorial de Caen: 234, 245–247
Le Mistral: 503
Leonardo da Vinci Park (Amboise): 289, 291
Le Paradis des Praz (Les Praz): 678
Le Pays Basque: 398–419
Lequeitio: 440–442
Le Ruquet: 240–241
Les Baux: 548–554; map, 550
Les Bossons: sleeping, 687
Les Eyzies-de-Tayac: 367–368; market, 335
Les Halles (Paris): 400
Les Haras Nationaux (Cluny): 736
Les Larmes de Jeanne d'Arc de Rouen: 198
L'Espace Dalí (Paris): 102
Les Praz: 677–678, 682
L'Hospitalet (Rocamadour): 382–383
Lido de Paris: 90–91
Lignerolles Château: 227
Ligré: sleeping near, 320
Loches Château: 314–315
Loire River: cruises, 292
Loire Valley: 278–328; cuisine, 285–286; map, 279; transportation, 281–285
London: train travel, 158–159
London Communication Trench (Verdun): 820
Longues-sur-Mer Gun Battery: 239
L'Orangerie (Paris): 66, 77
L'Ossuaire de Douaumont (Verdun): 819
Lot River Valley: 389–392
Loubressac: 389
Louis Vuitton (Paris): 91
Louis XIV (Sun King): 90, 166, 176–177, 399, 826; Versailles, 66, 167–178
Lourmarin: market, 503
Louvois: 812
Louvre Museum (Paris): 66, 70, 72–76
Low Corniche: 628–630
Lower Town (Les Baux): 551–552
Luberon Hill Towns: 571–584
Luge: 678, 682–683
Lumière Museum (Lyon): 745, 756
Luxembourg Garden (Paris): 87, 125–126

Luzille: sleeping, 297
Lyon: 739–762; cuisine, 739–740; eating, 759–761; information, 741–742; maps, 748, 751, 754; nightlife, 756–757; sights/activities, 744–756; sleeping, 757–759; tours, 744; transportation, 742, 743–744, 761–762
Lyon Museum of Fine Arts: 745, 753, 755

**M**
Mâcon: 762
Madeloc Tower: 494–495
Maeght Foundation (St-Paul-de-Vence): 656
Mail: 847–848. *See also specific destinations*
Maison de la Montagne (Chamonix): 678–679
Maison des Têtes (Colmar): 773
Maison du Chocolat (Paris): 104
Maison Pfister (Colmar): 772
Maisons Satie (Honfleur): 214
Malaucène: market, 503; sleeping, 565–566
Manville Mansion City Hall (Les Baux): 551
Maps: about, 834. *See also specific destinations*
Marais (Paris): 95–101, 117–119; eating, 140–146; maps, 96, 99, 120, 141; nightlife, 145–146; sleeping, 119–123
Marc Brédif (Vouvray): 293
*Marché: See* Markets
Marie-Antoinette: 64–65, 90, 167–168, 173–177, 827
Marine Museum (Biarritz): 413
Markets: 26; Albi, 459, 466; Amboise, 288; Annecy, 662; Antibes, 647–648; Arles, 505, 513–514; Bayeux, 222; Bayonne, 408; Beaune, 696; Bonnieux, 503; Carcassonne, 474; Chinon, 317; Cluny, 734; Collioure, 492; Colmar, 768; Dinan, 263; Dordogne, 334–335; Honfleur, 210; Isle-sur-la-Sorgue, 503, 574; Kayserberg, 792; La Roque-Gageac, 353; Loches, 314; Lyon, 743; Nice, 596; Paris, 104–105, 111, 118, 126; Provence, 503; Rouen, 194, 203; Roussillon,

577; St. Jean-de-Luz, 400; San Sebastián, 427; Sarlat, 335, 337, 341; Vaison la Romaine, 560, 563; Vence, 653; Villefranche-sur-Mer, 621

Marmottan Museum (Paris): 67, 85

Marne-la-Vallée-Chessy: 187

Martel: 387, 811–812

Martigny (Switzerland): 683–684

Mary Magdalene: 728, 729

Masséna Museum (Nice): 605

Massif Fortifié de Souville (Verdun): 817

Matisse, Henri: 77, 97, 493, 495; Museum (Nice), 597, 603–604; Rosary Chapel (Vence), 653–654

Matterhorn: 679

Mayle, Peter: 21, 499, 503, 571, 835

Medical needs: 844

Mémorial de Caen: 234, 245–247

Mémorial de la Déportation (Paris): 59–60

Mémorial de la Shoah (Paris): 98

Mémorial-Musée de Fleury (Verdun): 817–818

Menthon-St. Bernard: 664

Menton: 632

Mercedes-Benz (Paris): 90

Mer de Glace: 676–677, 679

Merveilles caves (Rocamadour): 383–384

Metric conversions: 869–870

Métro (Paris): 45–47; Cité "Métropolitain" Stop, 64

Meylet Château: 379

Middle Corniche: 628–630

Millau Bridge: 471

Minerve: 488–489

Mini-Châteaux (Amboise): 292

Minivan excursions: 857

Mirabel: 564

Miró, Joan: 95, 495, 656

Mistral, Frédéric: 508, 512–513

Mistral winds: 503

Modern and Contemporary Art Museum (Nice): 597, 604

Moët et Chandon: 812

Molinard Perfume Museum (Nice): 597, 604–605

Monaco: 632–641; map, 633

Monaco Cathedral: 638

Monaco Grand Prix: 586, 632

*Mona Lisa* (Da Vinci): 74–75

Monet, Claude: 77, 827; Giverny, 184; Marmottan Museum (Paris), 67, 85

Money: 10–13; budgeting, 3–4

Monsieur Dru: 676–677

Mont Blanc: 668–669, 674

Mont Dru: 670

Monte Carlo Casino: 639–640

*Monte Carlo Story* (film): 639

Monte Igueldo (San Sebastián): 429–430

Montenvers: 676–677, 679

Monte Urgull (San Sebastián): 428

Montfort: 349; sleeping, 361–362

Montignac: 369; market, 335

Montmartre (Paris): 101–103; eating, 151

Montmartre Museum (Paris): 102

Montparnasse Tower (Paris): 88–89

Montrachet's Cave (Puligny Montrachet): 704

Mont Rouge: 577, 579

Mont St. Michel: 247–260, 274–275; maps, 250, 252

Mont St. Michel Abbey: 251–256

Mont St. Michel Bay: 249–250

Mortemart: 375

Moulin Rouge (Paris): 102

Movies, recommended: 836–837

*Moyenne Corniche:* 628–630

Mumm: 810–811

Musée Alpin (Chamonix): 683

Musée Archéologique (Nice): 605

Musée Arlaten (Arles): 512–513

Musée Basque (Bayonne): 409–410

Musée Calvet (Avignon): 534

Musée Carnavalet (Paris): 67, 100

Musée-Château d'Annecy: 663

Musée d'Art Américain (Giverny): 184

Musée d'Art et Histoire du Judaïsme (Paris): 67, 97–98

Musée d'Art Moderne et d'Art Contemporain (Nice): 597, 604

Musée de la Civilisation Gallo-Romaine (Lyon): 745, 749–750

Musée de la Lavande (Coustellet): 582–583

Musée de la Reddition (Reims): 809

Musée de l'Arles et de la Provence Antiques: 507–508

Musée de l'Armée (Paris): 66, 84

Musée de l'Erotisme (Paris): 102–103

Musée de l'Orangerie (Paris): 66, 77

Musée de Montmartre (Paris): 102

Musée des Beaux-Arts: Lyon, 745, 753, 755; Nice, 605; Paris, 94; Rouen, 204; Strasbourg, 798

Musée d'Ethnographie et d'Art Populaire (Honfleur): 214

Musée d'Histoire et d'Archéologie (Antibes): 647

Musée d'Orsay (Paris): 66, 77–80

Musée du Débarquement (Arromanches): 237

Musée du Jouet et de la Poupée Ancienne (Isle-sur-la-Sorgue): 575

Musée du Louvre (Paris): 66, 70, 72–76

Musée du Petit Palais (Avignon): 530

Museé du Quai Branly (Paris): 83

Musée du Vin de Bourgogne (Beaune): 701

Musée Jacquemart-André (Paris): 67, 93–94

Musée le Secq des Tournelles (Rouen): 204

Musée Lumière (Lyon): 745, 756

Musée Marmottan Monet (Paris): 67, 85

Musée Masséna (Nice): 605

Musée Matisse (Nice): 597, 603–604

Musée Memorial de la Bataille de Normandie (Bayeux): 225

Musée National de la Marine (Paris): 83

Musée National de Préhistoire (Les Eyzies-de-Tayac): 368

Musée National du Moyen Age (Paris): 67, 85–86

Musée National Marc Chagall (Nice): 597, 601–603

Musée Océanographique (Monaco): 638

Musée Ochier (Cluny): 734–735

Musée Picasso (Antibes): 646, 647

Musée Picasso (Paris): 67, 98, 100

Musée Réattu (Arles): 513

Musée Rodin (Paris): 66, 84–85

Musées des Tissus et des Arts Décoratifs (Lyon): 745, 755

Musée Toulouse-Lautrec (Albi): 464–466

Musée Yves Brayer (Les Baux): 552

Museo Naval (San Sebastián): 428

Museum of American Art (Giverny): 184

Museum of Annecy: 663

Museum of Basque Culture (Bayonne): 409–410

Museum of Ceramics (Rouen): 204

Museum of Erotic Art (Paris): 102–103

Museum of Ethnography and Norman Popular Art (Honfleur): 214

Museum of Ironworks (Rouen): 204

Museum of San Telmo (San Sebastián): 426–427

Museum of Santons (Les Baux): 552

Museum of the Navy (Honfleur): 214

Museum of the Surrender (Reims): 809

Museum of the Wine of Burgundy (Beaune): 701

Museums: sightseeing tips, 14–15. *See also specific museums*

Museums of Fabrics and Decorative Arts (Lyon): 745, 755

Mustard Mill (Beaune): 702

Mutriku: 441

**N**

Napoleon Bonaparte: 76, 92, 100, 180, 657, 736, 827; Tomb (Paris), 66, 84

Napoleon Collection (Monaco): 638

Narbonne Gate (Carcassonne): 476

National Maritime Museum (Paris): 83

National Museum of Prehistory (Les Eyzies-de-Tayac): 368

National Stud Farm (Cluny): 736

Naval Museum (San Sebastián): 428

Navy Museum (Honfleur): 214

Nazelles Chambres Château: 297

Newspapers: 9–10

Nice: 589–620; eating, 613–618; helpful hints, 592–593; information, 590; maps, 591, 609, 611, 616; nightlife, 606–607; sights/activities, 596–606; sleeping, 607–613; tours, 594–596; transportation, 590, 592, 593–594, 618–620

Nice Airport: 619–620, 845

Nice Archaeological Museum: 605

Nice Carnival: 586, 597

Nice Modern and Contemporary Art Museum: 597, 604

Nineyrol Château: 361

Noizay Château: 296–297

Normandy: 189–260; map, 191; transportation, 190. *See also* D-Day beaches

Normandy American Cemetery and Memorial (Colleville): 239–240

Normandy Bridge: 215–216

Notre-Dame Cathedral (Chartres): 180–182

Notre-Dame Cathedral (Paris): 57, 59, 66, 108

Notre-Dame Cathedral (Rouen): 200–202

Notre-Dame Church (Semur-en-Auxois): 721

Notre-Dame de Fourvière (Lyon): 745, 746–747, 749

Notre-Dame de Grâce Chapel (Honfleur): 215

Notre-Dame de Nazareth Cathedral (Vaison la Romaine): 561

Notre-Dame des Anges (Collioure): 493

Notre-Dame des Anges (Isle-sur-la-Sorgue): 574

Notre-Dame de Sénanque Abbey: 582

Nyons: market, 503

**O**

Ochre Cliffs of Roussillon: 579

Old Lyon: 750–754; eating, 759–760

Old Nice: 596–598; eating, 614–615

Old Town (Bilbao): 452–453

Old Town (Colmar): 769–773

Old Town (San Sebastián): 422, 426–427

Old Town Center (Dinan): 266–267

Olive oil: 335, 615

Omaha Beach: 238–242

Ondarroa: 441

Opéra Bastille (Paris): 107

Opéra Garnier (Paris): 67, 92–93, 107

Oradour-sur-Glane: 374–375

Orange: 554–558; map, 556

Orangerie Museum (Paris): 66, 77

Orches: 716; sleeping, 709–710

Orly Airport (Paris): 163–164, 844

Orsay Museum (Paris): 66, 77–80

Our Lady of Rocamadour: 384

Our Lady of the Angels Church (Collioure): 493

**P**

Packing checklist: 872

Padirac: 385–386

País Vasco (Spanish Basque Country): 419–455

Palace of Justice (Rouen): 200

Palais de Justice (Paris): 64

Palais de l'Isle (Annecy): 663

Palais des Papes (Avignon): 532–533

Palais du Tau (Reims): 808–809

Palais Rohan (Strasbourg): 798

Palais Royal (Paris): 76, 134

Panthéon (Paris): 67, 88

Paradou: sleeping, 553–554

Paragliding: 682, 683

Parc de la Bouzaise (Beaune): 702

Parc de la Tête d'Or (Lyon): 743

Parc de Loisirs des Planards (Chamonix): 678

Parc de Merlet (Coupeau): 678

Parc des Buttes-Chaumont (Paris): 88

Parc des Rochers des Doms (Avignon): 530–531

Parc Monceau (Paris): 88, 94

Paris: 38–165; eating, 134–152; excursion areas, 166–188; helpful hints, 41–44; information, 40–41, 844; layout of, 39–40; nightlife, 105–109; planning tips, 38–39; shopping, 103–105; sights/activities, 56–103, 875–876; sleeping, 109–134; tours, 52–56, 108–109; transportation, 44–52, 152–165; walking tour, 56–65, 108. *See also specific neighborhoods*

*Pariscope:* 40–41, 105, 107

Paris Museum Pass: 42, 68, 70

Paris Plage: 65

Paris Sewers: 83

*Paris Story* (film): 93

Parte Vieja (San Sebastián): 422, 426–427

Passports: 6, 7

Path of Fauvism (Collioure): 493

Pech Merle caves: 392

*Pelota:* 404

Penitents, Chapel of (Les Baux): 552

Père Lachaise Cemetery (Paris): 67, 101

Perfume: 93, 103, 604–605, 630

Pernand Vergelesses: 715

Petit Balcon Sud: 681–682

Petite Venise (Colmar): 771–772

Petit Palais (Avignon): 530

Petit Palais (Paris): 94

Peyrepertuse Château: 486–487

Pfister House (Colmar): 772

Philip the Fair Tower (Villeneuve): 535

Picasso, Pablo: 77, 97, 444, 495, 513, 534; Museum (Antibes), 646, 647; Museum (Paris), 67, 98, 100

Picnics: 25, 27. *See also* Markets

Pigalle (Paris): 102

*Piments d'Espelette:* 395, 398, 415

Place de la Bastille (Paris): 93, 107

Place de la Liberté (Sarlat): 341

Place de la Madeleine (Paris): 104

Place de la République (Arles): 510

Place de la République (Paris): 132

Place de l'Horloge (Avignon): 529

Place des Oies (Sarlat): 341

Place des Terreaux (Lyon): 752–753

Place des Vosges (Paris): 96–97; eating, 140, 142

Place Drouet d'Erlon (Reims): 810

Place du Château (Carcassonne): 479

Place du Château St. Léon (Eguisheim): 789

Place du Forum (Arles): 508, 510, 515, 522

Place du Guesclin (Dinan): 264, 266

Place du Palais (Avignon): 529–530

Place du Palais (Monaco): 637

Place du Peyrou (Sarlat): 338

Place du Tertre (Paris): 102

Place du Vieux Marché (Rouen): 196–198, 207

Place Lamartine (Arles): 514–515

Place Louis XIV (St. Jean-de-Luz): 401

Place Rossetti (Nice): 598

Place St. Michel (Paris): 61–62

Place Ste. Cécile (Albi): 461

Place Vendôme (Paris): 104

Plague Cemetery (Rouen): 203

Plan de l'Aiguille (Alps): 675, 679

Planpraz (Alps): 673, 677, 679, 681

Planquery: sleeping, 227

Playa de La Concha (San Sebastián): 429

Plaza de la Constitución (San Sebastián): 426

Pointe du Grouin: 274

Pointe du Hoc Ranger Monument: 241–242

Politics: 825, 828–829

Pommard: 705, 716

Pompidou Center (Paris): 67, 97

Pont Bonaparte (Lyon): 744–746

Pont de Normandie: 215–216

Pont du Gard: 544–548; map, 546

Pont Neuf (Paris): 65

Pontorson: 248, 260

Pont St. Bénezet (Avignon): 531–532

Pont St. Julien: 583

Pont Valentré: 392

Pont Vieux (Carcassonne): 480

Popes, Palace of the (Avignon): 532–533

Population: xviii

Porte de Mars (Reims): 809

Port Vendres: 494, 495

Port Winston (Arromanches): 237

Post offices: 847–848. *See also specific destinations*

Pouilly-Fuissé: 762

Pray Château: 296

Presqu'île (Lyon): 752–755; eating, 760–761

Prince's Palace (Monaco): 637–638

Promenade des Anglais (Nice): 597, 598–601, 617–618

Promenade Plantée Park (Paris): 100–101

Provence: 499–584; cuisine, 502–503; map, 501; markets, 503; planning tips, 499–500; tours, 500–502; transportation, 500. *See also specific destinations*

Puligny Montrachet: 704, 716; sleeping, 709

Puycelci: 469–470

Puyméras: eating, 567

Puymin: 561

Pyrénées: 1, 486–487

**Q**

Quai Branly Museum (Paris): 83

Quartier Latin (Paris): *See* Latin Quarter

Quéribus Château: 487

**R**

Railpasses: 833, 850–851, 852–853

Rail travel: *See* Train travel

Rance River Valley: 268–269

Réattu Museum (Arles): 513

Reims: 802–814; map, 807

Reims Cathedral: 805–806, 808

Remigny: 732

Renoir, Pierre-Auguste: 77

Rental properties: 22–23

RER (Réseau Express Régionale): 44–45, 46, 48, 154, 849

Reservations: hotels, 23–24; form, 874; trains, 851, 854

Resistance: 663; and Deportation History Center (Lyon), 745, 755–756

Restaurants: *See* Eating; and *specific destinations*

Rhône Valley: 739–762

Ribeauvillé: 787

Richard (the Lionhearted): 201, 317, 327, 355, 727

Riquewihr: 786–787

Rivau Château: 283, 326

Riviera: 585–657; art scene, 589; cuisine, 588–589; map, 588; planning tips, 586; transportation, 586–588

Rocamadour: 380–387

Roc de Chère: 664

Rochepot Château: 716–717

Rodin, Auguste: 753; Museum (Paris), 66, 84–85

Roman Amphithéâtre (Arles): 511–512

Romanèche-Thorins: 762

Roman sites (ancient Romans): Alise Ste. Reine, 725–726; Arles, 504, 507–508, 511–512; La Trophée des Alpes, 631; Lyon, 749–750; Orange, 554, 555–557; Paris, 57, 59, 85–86; Pont du Gard, 544–548; Pont St. Julien, 583; Rouen, 192; Vaison la Romaine, 561, 563

Roman Theater: *See* Théâtre Antique

Rosary Chapel (Vence): 653–654

Rouen: 192–207; eating, 206–207; maps, 195, 199; sights/activities, 196–205; sleeping, 205–206; transportation, 193–194, 207

Rouen Big Clock: 198, 200

Rouen Cathedral: 200–202

Rouen Museum of Fine Arts: 204

Rouffignac caves: 371–372

Roussillon: 576–581; map, 578; market, 503

Route de la Champagne: 812

Route des Anciennes Abbayes: 205

Route des Grands Crus: 703–706

Route du Vin (Alsace): 782–793; map, 785; tours, 783–784

Route of the Bastides: 468–469

Royale de Fontevraud Abbey: 327

Rue Cler (Paris): 105, 110–117, 135–140

Rue de la Poissonnerie (Nice): 596–597

Rue de la République (Sarlat): 342

Rue de la République (St. Jean-de-Luz): 401

Rue de la Salamandre (Sarlat): 340

Rue des Rosiers (Paris): 98, 144–145

Rue des Teinturiers (Avignon): 533–534, 541

Rue Droite (Nice): 598

Rue du Jerzual (Dinan): 267

Rue Gambetta (St. Jean-de-Luz): 403

Rue Montorgueil (Paris): 105

Rue Mouffetard (Paris): 105, 131–132, 149–150

Rue St. Romain (Rouen): 202

Russian Cathedral (Nice): 597, 605–606

Ryes: sleeping, 235

## S

Sacré-Cour (Paris): 67, 101–102

Sade, Marquis de: 583–584

St. Aubin: 703, 709, 716–717

St. Bénezet Bridge (Avignon): 531–532

St. Bernard: 664

St. Catherine's Tower (Dinan): 267

St. Cécile Cathedral (Albi): 461–464

St. Cirq Lapopie: 390–392

St. Croix Church (Kaysersberg): 792

St. Cyprien: market, 335

St. Emilion: 376–380

St. Genies: market, 335

St. Georges de Boscherville Abbey: 205

St. Germain-des-Prés church (Paris): 86, 107

St. Jean-Baptiste church (St. Jean-de-Luz): 403

St. Jean Cathedral (Lyon): 745, 750

St. Jean-de-Luz: 398–408; map, 402

St. Jean-Pied-de-Port (Donibane Garazi): 416–419

St. Julien Bridge: 583

St. Laurent: 239–240

St. Maclou Church (Rouen): 202–203

St. Malo: 274, 275–276

St. Marcellin-lès-Vaison: 564

St. Martin Cathedral (Colmar): 772–773

St. Michael's Chapel (Rocamadour): 384

St. Nazaire Church (Carcassonne): 478–479

St. Ouen flea market (Paris): 104

St. Pierre Chapel (Villefranche): 622, 624

St. Rémy: market, 503

St. Romain: 716; sleeping, 709

St. Sacerdos Cathedral (Sarlat): 340

St. Salvy Church and Cloister (Albi): 466

St. Sauveur Church (Dinan): 267–268

St. Saveur Church (Rocamadour): 384, 385

St. Suliac: 269

St. Sulpice Church (Paris): 86–87, 107

St. Trophime Church (Arles): 510–511

St. Vincent Church (Les Baux): 552

Saint-Antonin-Noble-Val: 458, 469

Ste. Catherine Church (Honfleur): 211–212

Ste. Madeleine Basilica (Vézelay): 726–730

Ste. Marie Cathédrale (Bayonne): 410–411

Ste. Mère Eglise: 242–243

Sainte-Chapelle (Paris): 62–63, 66

Stes-Maries-de-la-Mer: 516–517

Saint-Exupéry Airport (Lyon): 742

St-Paul-de-Vence: 655–656

Sanctuary of Our Lady of Rocamadour: 384

San Sebastián: 419–438; eating, 434–437; maps, 423, 432; sights/ activities, 426–431; sleeping, 431– 434; tours, 425; transportation, 422, 424, 437–438

San Sebastián Port: 422, 427–428

San Telmo Museum (San Sebastián): 426–427

Santiago Cathedral (Bilbao): 452

Santiago de Compostela: 392, 410, 414, 416

Santons Museum (Les Baux): 552

Sare (Sara): 415

Sarlat: 335–347; eating, 346–347; map, 339; markets, 335, 337, 341; sights/activities, 338–342; sleeping, 342–346

Sarlat Cathedral: 340

Sarragan Caves: 552–553

Satie (Erik) House (Honfleur): 214

Sault: market, 503

Sauvigny Gate (Semur-en-Auxois): 721

Savigny-les-Beaune: 715

*Saving Private Ryan* (movie): 240, 837

Savoie: *See* Alpes-Savoie

Schweitzer (Albert) House (Kaysersberg): 792

Seasons: 5–6

Séguret: 570–571; sleeping, 565

Seine River: 39, 208, 215–216; beach (Paris), 65; cruises, 52–54, 152

Semur-en-Auxois: 718, 720–722

Sentier du Littoral: 239

Servoz: 681–682

Sèvres-Babylone (Paris): 104

Sévrier: 664; eating, 668

Sewers of Paris: 83

Shakespeare and Company (Paris): 44

Shopping: budgeting, 4; hours, 8; Paris, 103–105; VAT refunds, 12–13. *See also specific destinations*

Sightseeing: budgeting, 4; general tips, 14–15; priorities, 4. *See also specific sights and destinations*

Sigolsheim: 793

Sleep code: 17

Sleeping: 15–24; budgeting, 3–4; hotel chains, 845–846; reservations, 23–24; form, 874. *See also specific destinations*

Sleeping Beauty castle (Ussé): 326

Sorbonne University (Paris): 60–61

Sorgue River: 574

Souillac: market, 335

Spain: Basque Country, 398, 419– 455; Col de Banyuls, 495

Special events: 867–869

Strasbourg: 793–801; map, 795

Strasbourg Archaeological Museum: 798

Strasbourg Cathedral: 797–798

Strasbourg Museum of Fine Arts: 798

Suzette: 568–570

Switzerland: 683–684

Synagogue (Avignon): 533

**T**

Taittinger: 811–812

Taizé: 736–738

Talloires: 664

Tanners' Quarter (Colmar): 771
Tapisserie de Bayeux: 222–224
Tarascon: 544
Tarn River Gorge: 471
Taxes: VAT refunds, 12–13
Taxis: Paris, 49, 51; tipping, 12. *See also specific destinations*
*Téléphériques,* in Chamonix: 671–675, 677–678
Telephone numbers, useful: 841, 844–845
Telephones: 23, 838–841; calling chart, 842–843
Temperature, average monthly: 870
Théâtre Antique: Arles, 511; Lyon, 745, 749–750; Orange, 555–557
Théâtre des Jacobins (Dinan): 266
Time zones: 7–8
Tipping: 12
Tomb of the Unknown Soldier (Paris): 92
Tonnellerie François Frères (St. Romain): 717
Toulouse-Lautrec, Henri de: 102; Museum (Albi), 464–466
Tour de Madeloc: 494–495
Tour de Solidor (St. Malo): 276
Tour Eiffel (Paris): 66, 80–83, 108
Tourist offices: 831–832. *See also specific destinations*
Tour Montparnasse (Paris): 88–89
Tour Philippe-le-Bel (Villeneuve): 535
Tours: Alsatian wines, 783–784; Avignon, 528–529; Burgundy wines, 697, 706; Chartres Cathedral, 182; Colmar, 769; D-Day beaches, 231–234; Dordogne, 331–332; Loire Valley, 281–283; Lyon, 744; Mont St. Michel, 249; Nice, 594–596; Paris, 52–56, 108–109; Provence, 500–502; Rick Steves', 833; Riviera, 587; San Sebastián, 425; three-week, 850–851, 858–859; Versailles, 171–173
Toy and Doll Museum (Isle-sur-la-Sorgue): 575
*Traboules:* 745, 750, 752
Train travel: 6, 848–856; baggage check, 854–855; *Eurostar,* 158–159; information, 844; map, 855; Paris, 152–159; reservations, 851, 854; terms and abbreviations, 849; whirlwind three-week tour, 850–

851. *See also specific destinations*
Tranchée des Baïonnettes (Verdun): 819
Transportation: 848–867; budgeting, 3; Paris, 44–52, 152–165. *See also* Boat cruises; Bus travel; Car travel; Train travel; and *specific destinations*
Travel advisories: 844
Travel smarts: 7
Treverien: 269
Trianon (Versailles): 175
Trip costs (budgeting): 3–4
Trocadéro (Paris): 108
Truffles: 332–333, 334
Tuileries Garden (Paris): 70, 77, 90
Turckheim: 786
*Txiquiteo:* 435

### U
Unicorn tapestry: 85–86
Unterlinden Museum (Colmar): 773–776
Ussé: 283, 326
Utah Beach: 238–239, 242–243
Uzès: market, 503

### V
Vacqueyras: market, 503
Vaison la Romaine: 559–567; map, 562; market, 503
Valençay Château: 283, 315
Valle d'Aosta (Italy): 684
Valréas: market, 503
Vandenesse-en-Auxois: 719–720
Van der Weyden, Roger: 700–701
Van Gogh, Vincent: 77, 504, 508, 510, 514–515, 534, 552; Fondation Van Gogh (Arles), 512
VAT refunds: 12–13
Velleron: 575
Venary les Laumes: 719, 725
Vence: 652–655
*Ventas:* 416
*Venus de Milo:* 74
Vercingétorix: 725–726, 826
Verdun: 802–803, 814–821; map, 818
Verdun Battlefields: 815–820
Versailles: 166–180; eating, 179–180; map, 170; sights/activities, 167–178; sleeping, 178–179
Versailles Gardens: 174–178
Versailles Palace: 66, 167–176
Ver-sur-Mer: sleeping, 234–235

Veynes: 657
Vézelay: 726–730
Viaduc de Millau: 471
Victory Monument (Verdun): 820
Vieil-Armand WWI Memorial: 788
Vienne River: canoeing, 318
Vierville-sur-Mer: 240–241
Vieux Bassin (Honfleur): 210–211
Vieux Lyon: 750–754; eating,
    759–760
Vieux Nice: 596–598; eating, 614–615
Village des Martyrs (Oradour-sur-
    Glane): 374–375
Villandry: 283, 325–326
Villedieu: eating, 567
Villefranche-sur-Mer: 620–627;
    map, 623
Villefranche-sur-Saône: 762
Villeneuve Château (Vence): 653
Villeneuve-lès-Avignon: 535
Vineyards: *See* Wine and vineyards
Virgin Rock (Biarritz): 413
Vitrac Port: 348, 350
Vougeot: 703
Vouvray: 293; sleeping, 297

**W**
Water, drinking: 32
Way of the Cross (Rocamadour):
    381–385
Weather: 5–6, 870
Wine and vineyards: 30–31, 33;

Amboise, 292; Avignon, 534;
    Beaujolais, 762; Bordeaux, 376,
    377–378; Carcassonne, 480, 489;
    Chinon, 318; Collioure, 493–494;
    Côtes du Rhône, 558, 563, 568–
    570; Dordogne, 329–330, 333;
    Loire Valley, 286, 292–293, 318;
    Provence, 500–502; Vouvray, 293.
    *See also* Alsatian wines; Burgundy
    wine; Champagne
Wine Road (Alsace): 782–793; map,
    785; tours, 783–784
*Winged Victory of Samothrace:* 74
World War I: 92, 174, 304, 721;
    Verdun Battlefields, 815–820;
    Vieil-Armand WWI Memorial,
    788
World War II: 62, 92, 232–233,
    374–375, 418, 793; Battle of
    Normandy Memorial Museum
    (Bayeux), 225; D-Day beaches,
    229–247; Deportation Memorial
    (Paris), 59–60; German Military
    Cemeteries (Normandy), 242,
    256; Holocaust Memorial (Paris),
    98; Museum of the Surrender
    (Reims), 809

**Z**
Zellenberg: 787
Zermatt: 679
ZooParc de Beauval: 293

Thur. April 1 - fly to Paris
Fri    April 2 - arrive Paris
Sat           3 - Paris
Sun           4 - Paris
Mon           5 - Paris
Tue           6 → Versaill
Wed           7
Thur.    >    8 > Bayeau
Fri           9
Sat          10   Mont St
                   Michel

Sun    -     11  >
Mon    -     12  >  Paris
Tue    -     13